AMERICAN

REFERENCE

BOOKS

ANNUAL

1999 VOLUME 30

AMERICAN REFERENCE BOOKS ANNUAL

1999 VOLUME 30

Bohdan S. Wynar EDITOR IN CHIEF
Susan D. Strickland ASSOCIATE EDITOR

ASSISTANT EDITOR
Shannon M. Graff

Comprehensive annual reviewing service for
reference books published in the United States and Canada

1999

LIBRARIES UNLIMITED
ENGLEWOOD, COLORADO

LIBRARIES UNLIMITED, INC.
P.O. Box 6633
Englewood, CO 80155-6633
1-800-237-6124
www.lu.com

_____

Library of Congress Cataloging-in-Publication Data

American reference books annual, 1970-
    Englewood, Colo., Libraries Unlimited.

        v. 19x26 cm.

Indexes:
    1970-74. 1v.
    1975-79. 1v.
    1980-84. 1v.
    1985-89. 1v.
    1990-94. 1v.

        I. Reference books--Bibliography--Periodicals.
I. Wynar, Bohdan S.   II. Strickland, Susan D.   III. Graff, Shannon M.
Z1035.1.A55   011'.02
ISBN 1-56308-765-0(1999 edition)
ISSN 0065-9959

Contents

Introduction xiii

Contributors xv

Journals Cited xxvii

Part I
GENERAL REFERENCE WORKS

1—General Reference Works

Acronyms and Abbreviations. 3
Almanacs. 3
Bibliography 5
  Bibliographic Guides 5
  National and Trade Bibliography 5
    International 5
    United States 6
    Asia. 8
    Canada 8
Biography 9
  International. 9
  United States. 15
  Canada 17
  Great Britain 17
Dictionaries and Encyclopedias 18
Directories 22
Government Publications 26
Handbooks and Yearbooks 27
Indexes 28
Museums 29
Periodicals and Serials. 30
Quotation Books 31

Part II
SOCIAL SCIENCES

2—Social Sciences in General

Social Sciences in General 35

3—Area Studies

General Works 37
United States 38
  General Works 38
  California 39
  Indiana 40

Puerto Rico 40
Africa 41
  General Works. 41
  Burkina Faso. 42
  Maghreb 42
  Mali 43
  Namibia 43
  Sub-Saharan Africa 43
Asia 44
  General Works. 44
  Cambodia 45
  China. 46
  Japan 48
  Vietnam 49
Australia 49
Europe 50
  General Works. 50
  Albania. 51
  Austria 51
  Bosnia 52
  Czech Republic 52
  Former Soviet Republics 52
  France 53
  Germany 54
  Great Britain 55
  Hungary 55
  Ireland 55
  Malta. 56
  Netherlands 56
  Romania 57
Latin America and the Caribbean 57
Middle East. 58

4—Economics and Business

General Works. 59
  Bibliography 59
  Biography 60
  Business History 60
  Dictionaries and Encyclopedias 61
  Directories 62
  Handbooks and Yearbooks 65
Business Services and Investment Guides . . . 67
  Directories 67
  Handbooks and Yearbooks 69
Consumer Guides 72
Finance and Banking 75
Industry and Manufacturing 76

v

4—Economics and Business (*continued*)

International Business 78
  General Works 78
    Dictionaries and Encyclopedias 78
    Directories 79
    Handbooks and Yearbooks 85
  Arab Countries 94
  Asia 94
  Canada 96
  Europe 97
  Latin America and the Caribbean 103
Labor 104
  Bibliography 104
  Directories 104
  Handbooks and Yearbooks 107
Management 109
Marketing and Trade 110
Occupational Health and Safety 111
Office Practices 112
Taxation 113

5—Education

General Works 115
  Bibliography 115
  Biography 116
  Directories 117
  Handbooks and Yearbooks 119
Alternative Education 122
Computer Resources 123
Early Childhood Education 125
Elementary and Secondary Education 125
  Bibliography 125
  Directories 125
Higher Education 127
  Dictionaries and Encyclopedias 127
  Directories 127
  Financial Aid 135
  Handbooks and Yearbooks 138
International Exchange Programs and
  Opportunities 140
Nonprint Materials and Resources 141
Vocational and Continuing Education 142

6—Ethnic Studies and Anthropology

Anthropology and Ethnology 145
Ethnic Studies 146
  General Works 146
  Africans 149
  Asian Americans 150
  Blacks 150
  Gypsies 152

  Indians of North America 152
    Bibliography 152
    Biography 154
    Chronology 155
    Dictionaries and Encyclopedias 155
    Directories 157
    Handbooks and Yearbooks 157
  Jews 158
  Latin Americans 159

7—Genealogy and Heraldry

Genealogy 161
  Directories 161
  Handbooks and Yearbooks 162
  Indexes 163
Heraldry 164
Personal Names 164

8—Geography and Travel Guides

Geography 165
  General Works 165
    Atlases 165
    Canada, 165; *International*, 165
    Biography 168
    Dictionaries and Encyclopedias 169
Place-Names 170
Travel Guides 171
  General Works 171
  United States 172
  Asia 176
  Australia 176
  Europe 177
  International Travel 177

9—History

Archaeology 181
American History 182
  Atlases 182
  Bibliography 183
  Biography 186
  Chronology 186
  Dictionaries and Encyclopedias 186
  Handbooks and Yearbooks 190
African History 195
Asian History 196
  General Works 196
  China 197
  Indic 198
  Japanese 199
  Philippine 199
  Vietnamese 200

Canadian History 200
European History 201
  General Works 201
  Danish 202
  Eastern Europe 202
  French 204
  Greek 205
  Russian 206
  United Kingdom 206
Middle Eastern History 208
World History 210
  Bibliography 210
  Biography 211
  Chronology 212
  Dictionaries and Encyclopedias 214
  Handbooks and Yearbooks 219
  Indexes 221

10—Law

General Works 223
  Bibliography 223
  Biography 224
  Dictionaries and Encyclopedias 225
  Directories 227
  Handbooks and Yearbooks 229
  Indexes 233
  Quotation Books 233
Criminology 234
  Bibliography 234
  Dictionaries and Encyclopedias 235
  Handbooks and Yearbooks 236
Environmental Law 238
Human Rights 240
Intellectual Property 241
Victims of Abuse 241

11—Library and Information Science and Publishing and Bookselling

Library and Information Science 243
  General Works 243
    Biography 243
    Dictionaries and Encyclopedias 244
    Directories 245
    Thesauri 246
  Archives and Manuscripts 246
  Collection Development 247
  Information Technology 247
  Intellectual Freedom and Censorship 248
  Library Automation 250
  Research 250
  Special Libraries and Collections 251

Publishing and Bookselling 253
  Biography 253
  Catalogs and Collections 253
  Directories 254
  Handbooks and Yearbooks 254

12—Military Studies

General Works 257
  Bibliography 257
  Biography 257
  Dictionaries and Encyclopedias 259
  Directories 260
  Handbooks and Yearbooks 262
Air Force 263
Marine Corps 264
Navy 264
Weapons 266

13—Political Science

General Works 269
  Bibliography 269
  Biography 269
  Dictionaries and Encyclopedias 271
  Handbooks and Yearbooks 273
Politics and Government 274
  United States 274
    Bibliography 274
    Biography 274
    Dictionaries and Encyclopedias 277
    Directories 278
    Handbooks and Yearbooks 279
  Canadian 285
  Europe 285
Ideologies 287
International Organizations 287
International Relations 288
Public Policy and Administration 289

14—Psychology and Parapsychology

Psychology 291
  Dictionaries and Encyclopedias 291
  Handbooks and Yearbooks 292
Parapsychology 293

15—Recreation and Sports

General Works 295
  Biography 295
  Dictionaries and Encyclopedias 295
  Directories 296
  Handbooks and Yearbooks 296

15—Recreation and Sports (*continued*)

Baseball 297
Basketball 301
Fishing 302
Football 302
Golf 303
Hockey 303
Olympics 305
Skating 305
Skiing 306
Softball 306

16—Sociology

General Works 307
Aging 308
Community Life 309
Disabled 309
Family, Marriage, and Divorce 311
Gay and Lesbian Studies 313
Philanthropy 314
    Directories 314
    Handbooks and Yearbooks 320
Sex Studies 320
Social Welfare and Social Work 321
Youth and Child Development 321

17—Statistics, Demography, and Urban Studies

Demography 323
Statistics 325
    International 325
    United States 327
Urban Studies 327

18—Women's Studies

Bibliography 329
Biography 330
Catalogs and Collections 332
Chronology 332
Dictionaries and Encyclopedias 333
Handbooks and Yearbooks 334

Part III
Humanities

19—Humanities in General

Humanities in General 339

20—Communication and Mass Media

General Works 343
    Biography 343
    Dictionaries and Encyclopedias 343
    Directories 344
    Handbooks and Yearbooks 345
Authorship 346
    General Works 346
    Style Manuals 348
Radio, Television, Audio, and Video 350

21—Decorative Arts

Collecting 351
    General Works 351
    Antiques 351
    Coins (and Paper Money) 353
    Dolls 354
    Firearms 355
    Knives 355
    Memorabilia 356
    Toys 356
Crafts 357
Interior Design 358
Photography 359

22—Fine Arts

General Works 361
    Bibliography 361
    Biography 362
    Catalogs and Collections 363
    Dictionaries and Encyclopedias 364
    Directories 365
    Handbooks and Yearbooks 366
    Indexes 367
Architecture 367
    Biographies 367
    Dictionaries and Encyclopedias 368
    Handbooks and Yearbooks 369
Drawing 370
Graphic Arts 370
Painting 371

23—Language and Linguistics

General Works 373
    Bibliography 373
    Dictionaries and Encyclopedias 374
    Directories 375

English-Language Dictionaries 376
    General Usage 376
    Etymology 377
    Euphemisms 377
    Foreign Words and Phrases 378
    Idioms, Colloquialisms, Special Usage . . . 378
    Juvenile 379
    Other English-Speaking Countries 379
    Sign Language 380
    Slang 381
    Spelling 381
    Terms and Phrases 382
    Thesauri 383
    Visual 384
Non-English-Language Dictionaries 384
    General Works 384
    Albanian 385
    Andalusi Arabic 385
    Dutch 385
    French 386
    German 387
    Igbo 389
    Japanese 389
    Kyrgyz 390
    Louisiana Creole 390
    Native American 390
    Norwegian 391
    Spanish 391

24—Literature

General Works 395
    Bibliography 395
    Bio-bibliography 396
    Biography 398
    Dictionaries and Encyclopedias 401
    Handbooks and Yearbooks 403
    Indexes 410
Children's and Young Adult Literature . . . 411
    General Works 411
    Children's Literature 412
       Bibliography 412
       Biography 417
       Dictionaries and Encyclopedias 417
       Handbooks and Yearbooks 418
       Indexes 419
    Young Adult Literature 420
       Bibliography 420
       Handbooks and Yearbooks 421
Classical Literature 423
Drama 424
Essays 427

Fiction 427
    General Works 427
    Crime and Mystery 428
    Historical Fiction 429
    Science Fiction, Fantasy, and Horror 430
    Short Stories 431
National Literature 431
    American Literature 431
       General Works 431
         Bibliography, 431; *Bio-bibliography*,
         433; *Biography*, 433; *Dictionaries and*
         Encyclopedias, 435; *Handbooks and*
         Yearbooks, 435
       Drama 436
       Individual Authors 437
         Anne Tyler, 437; *Emily Dickinson*, 437;
         Esther Forbes, 438; *F. Scott Fitzgerald*,
         438; *Hamlin Garland*, 439; *Jessamyn*
         West, 439; *Tennessee Williams*, 439;
         Toni Morrison, 440
       Poetry 440
    British Literature 441
       General Works 441
         Bibliography, 441; *Biography*, 441;
         Handbooks and Yearbooks, 443
       Fiction 444
       Individual Authors 445
         Jane Austen, 445; *C. S. Lewis*, 446;
         Charles Dickens, 446; *George Orwell*,
         447; *Lawrence Sterne*, 448; *Oscar Wilde*,
         448; *William Shakespeare*, 449; *Thomas*
         Hardy, 452; *Thomas More*, 453; *Virginia*
         Woolf, 453
    Canadian Literature 453
    Caribbean Literature 454
    Chinese Literature 454
    East European Literature 455
    French Literature 455
    German Literature 456
    Japanese Literature 457
    Russian Literature 457
    Spanish Literature 458
Poetry 458

25—Music

General Works 463
    Bibliography 463
    Biography 464
    Dictionaries and Encyclopedias 465
    Handbooks and Yearbooks 467
    Indexes 468
Composers 468

25—Music (*continued*)

Instruments 476
  Guitar 476
  Piano 476
  Violin 477
Musical Forms 477
  Blues 477
  Choral 478
  Classical 478
  Operatic 479
  Orchestral 481
  Popular 481
    General Works 481
    Jazz 483
    Musicals 485
    Reggae 485
    Rock 486
    Sacred 488

**26—Mythology, Folklore, and
Popular Culture**

Folklore 491
Mythology 493
Popular Culture 494

27—Performing Arts

General Works 497
  Biography 497
  Directories 498
  Handbooks and Yearbooks 499
Dance 499
Film, Television, and Video 501
  Bibliography 501
  Bio-bibliography 502
  Biography 503
  Dictionaries and Encyclopedias 504
  Directories 507
  Filmography 509
  Handbooks and Yearbooks 514
  Indexes 515
  Videography 516
Theater 517

28—Philosophy and Religion

Philosophy 519
  Bibliography 519
  Dictionaries and Encyclopedias 520
  Handbooks and Yearbooks 521
  Indexes 523

Religion 523
  General Works 523
    Bibliography 523
    Biography 524
    Dictionaries and Encyclopedias 525
    Directories 527
    Handbooks and Yearbooks 527
  Bahá'í Faith 528
  Bible Studies 528
    Bibliography 528
    Dictionaries and Encyclopedias 528
    Handbooks and Yearbooks 529
  Christianity 531
    Biography 531
    Catalogs and Collections 533
    Dictionaries and Encyclopedias 533
    Handbooks and Yearbooks 534
  Hinduism 536
  Judaism 536
  Taoism 537

**Part IV
SCIENCE AND TECHNOLOGY**

**29—Science and Technology
in General**

Atlases 541
Bibliography 541
Bio-bibliography 542
Biography 543
Chronology 545
Dictionaries and Encyclopedias 546
Directories 550
Handbooks and Yearbooks 552
Quotation Books 554

30—Agricultural Sciences

General Works 555
Food Sciences and Technology 555
  Dictionaries and Encyclopedias 555
  Directories 557
  Handbooks and Yearbooks 559
Forestry 560
Horticulture 561
  Dictionaries and Encyclopedias 561
  Handbooks and Yearbooks 561
Veterinary Science 564

31—Biological Sciences

Biology 565
   Dictionaries and Encyclopedias 565
   Handbooks and Yearbooks 566
Botany 566
   General Works 566
     Dictionaries and Encyclopedias 566
     Handbooks and Yearbooks 567
     Indexes 568
   Flowering Plants 568
   Trees and Shrubs 570
   Weeds 570
Natural History 571
Zoology 572
   Birds 572
   Domestic Animals 576
   Fishes 578
   Insects 578
   Mammals 579
   Marine Animals 580
   Reptiles and Amphibians 581

32—Engineering

General Works 583
Chemical Engineering 584
Civil Engineering 584
Electric Engineering and Electronics 586
Environmental Engineering 586
Materials Science 587
Mechanical Engineering 588

33—Health Sciences

General Works 589
   Atlases 589
   Bibliography 590
   Dictionaries and Encyclopedias 590
   Directories 593
   Handbooks and Yearbooks 595
Medicine 598
   General Works 598
     Dictionaries and Encyclopedias 598
     Directories 601
     Electronic Resources 603
     Handbooks and Yearbooks 603
   Alternative Medicine 605
   Ophthalmology 607
   Pediatrics 608
   Psychiatry 609
   Specific Diseases and Conditions 609
     General Works 609
     AIDS 610

     Diabetes 611
     Leprosy 611
     Pain 612
Nursing 612
Pharmacy and Pharmaceutical Sciences . . . 614

34—High Technology

General Works 617
Computing 618
Telecommunications 619
   Dictionaries and Encyclopedias 619
   Directories 621

35—Physical Sciences and Mathematics

Physical Sciences 625
   General Works 625
   Chemistry 626
     Dictionaries and Encyclopedias 626
     Handbooks and Yearbooks 628
   Earth and Planetary Sciences 629
     General Works 629
     Astronomy and Space Sciences 632
     Climatology and Meteorology 634
     Geology 636
     Hydrology 637
     Mineralogy 637
     Oceanography 638
     Paleontology 638
Mathematics 639

36—Resource Sciences

Energy Resources 643
Environmental Science 644
   Atlases 644
   Biography 645
   Dictionaries and Encyclopedias 646
   Handbooks and Yearbooks 647
Natural Resources 652

37—Transportation

General Works 653
Air 653
Ground 655
Water 655

   Author/Title Index 657

   Subject Index 687

Introduction

PURPOSE AND SCOPE

American Reference Books Annual, a far-reaching reviewing service for reference books, is now in its 30th volume. The 1,578 books and CD-ROMs reviewed in this volume cover imprints from 1998 and some from 1997 that were received too late to be reviewed in the previous volume. Titles not reviewed in ARBA 98, have been reviewed in ARBA 99. In the 30 volumes of ARBA published since 1970, a total of 51,776 titles have been reviewed. Five cumulative indexes for ARBA cover the years 1970-1974, 1975-1979, 1980-1984, 1985-1989, and 1990-1994. This year, the sixth cumulative index, covering 1995-1999, will be published. These indexes expedite the use of the annual volumes.

ARBA differs significantly from other reviewing media in its basic purpose, which is to provide comprehensive coverage of English-language reference books published in the United States and Canada during a single year. The categories of reference books reviewed in ARBA and the policy regarding them can be summarized as follows: (1) Dictionaries, encyclopedias, indexes, directories, bibliographies, guides, concordances, atlases, gazetteers, and other types of ready-reference tools are routinely reviewed in each volume of ARBA; coverage of this category of reference materials is nearly complete. (2) General encyclopedias that are updated annually, yearbooks, almanacs, indexing and abstracting services, and other annuals or serials are usually reviewed at intervals of three, four, or five years. The first review of such works generally provides an appropriate historical background. Subsequent reviews of these publications attempt to point out changes in scope, editorial policy, and similar matters. (3) New editions of reference books are ordinarily reviewed with appropriate comparisons to the older editions. (4) Traditionally, foreign reference titles have been reviewed only if they had an exclusive distributor in the United States. In 1987 coverage was expanded to include Canadian publications that do not have U.S. distributors. Prices for such titles are in Canadian dollars unless otherwise indicated. Substantial coverage of Canadian reference publications has been achieved and will continue until it is as complete for Canada as it is for the United States. Other foreign-title coverage is restricted to English-language publications from Great Britain, as well as a few select sources from Australia and other countries. (5) Reprints are reviewed in ARBA on a selective basis as they often are produced in limited quantities. (6) Titles produced for the mass market in the areas of collectibles, travel guides, and genealogy receive selective coverage.

Certain categories of reference books are usually not reviewed in ARBA: those of fewer than 48 pages, those produced by vanity presses or by the author as publisher, and those generated by library staffs for internal use. Highly specialized reference works printed in a limited number of copies and that do not appeal to the general library audience ARBA serves may also be omitted.

Because there has been a significant increase and interest in electronic publishing, ARBA has begun reviewing this medium. More than 40 CD-ROMs receive comprehensive and lengthy evaluations in this edition. Future volumes will continue to include reviews of these state-of-the-art information storage devices in a variety of subject areas.

REVIEWING POLICY

To ensure well-written and erudite reviews, the ARBA staff maintains a roster of more than 400 scholars, practitioners, and library educators in all subject specialties at libraries and universities throughout the United States and Canada. Because ARBA is not a selective reviewing source, such as *Choice* or *Library Journal*, the reviews are generally longer and more critical, to detail the strengths and weaknesses of important reference works. Reviewers are asked to examine books and provide well-documented critical comments, both positive and negative. Coverage usually includes the usefulness of a given work; organization, execution, and pertinence of contents; prose style; format; availability of supplementary materials (e.g., indexes, appendixes); and similarity to other works and previous editions. Reviewers are encouraged to address the intended audience but not necessarily to give specific recommendations for purchase. An adequate description and evaluation of the reference book are sufficient. All reviews in ARBA are signed.

ARRANGEMENT

ARBA 99 consists of 37 chapters, an author/title index, and a subject index. It is divided into four alphabetically arranged parts: "General Reference Works," "Social Sciences," "Humanities," and "Science and Technology." "General Reference Works" is subdivided by form: bibliography, biography, catalogs and collections, dictionaries and encyclopedias, handbooks and yearbooks, indexes, and so on. Within the remaining three parts, chapters are organized by topic. Thus, under "Social Sciences" the reader will find chapters titled "Economics and Business," "Education," "History," "Law," and "Sociology."

Each chapter is subdivided to reflect the arrangement strategy of the entire volume. There is a section on general works followed by a topical breakdown. For example, in the chapter titled "Performing Arts," "General Works" is followed by "Dance" and "Film, Television, and Video." The latter is divided into sections by format, which include "Biography" and "Filmography." Subdivisions are based on the amount of material available on a given topic and vary from year to year.

ACKNOWLEDGMENTS

In closing, we wish to express our gratitude to the many talented contributors without whose support this volume of ARBA could not have been compiled. We would also like to thank the members of our staff who were instrumental in its preparation: Pamela J. Getchell, Kay Minnis, Beth Partin, Judy Gay Matthews, and Jo Anne Ricca. A final thanks goes to Ed Volz, the former Associate Editor of ARBA, and Melissa R. Root, former Assistant Editor, for their contributions to this volume.

Bohdan S. Wynar, Editor in Chief

Editorial Staff

Contributors

Sandra E. Belanger, Reference Librarian, San Jose State Univ. Library, Calif.

Carol Willsey Bell, Head, Local History and Genealogy Dept., Warren-Trumbull County Public Library, Warren, Ohio.

George H. Bell, Assoc. Librarian, Daniel E. Noble Science and Engineering Library, Arizona State Univ., Tempe.

Adrienne Antink Bendel, Medical Group Management Association, Lakewood, Colo.

Kenneth W. Berger, Team Leader, Reference/ILL Home Team, Perkins Library, Duke Univ., Durham, N.C.

Bernice Bergup, Humanities Reference Librarian, Davis Library, Univ. of North Carolina, Chapel Hill.

Teresa U. Berry, Reference Coordinator, Univ. of Tennessee, Knoxville.

John B. Beston, Santa Fe, N.Mex.

Barbara M. Bibel, Reference Librarian, Science/Business/Sociology Dept., Main Library, Oakland Public Library, Calif.

Terry D. Bilhartz, Assoc. Professor of History, Sam Houston State Univ., Huntsville, Tex.

Ron Blazek, Professor, School of Library Science, Florida State Univ., Tallahassee.

Richard Bleiler, Reference Librarian, Univ. of Connecticut, Storrs.

Laura K. Blessing, Personnel Librarian, Univ. of Texas, Arlington.

Marcia Blevins, Reference Supervisor, McMinnville Public Library, Oreg.

Edna M. Boardman, Library Media Specialist, Minot High School, Magic City Campus, N.D.

Mary Pat Boian, Assoc. Editor, *Foster's Botanical & Herb Review*, Beaver, Ark.

Bobray Bordelon, Social Science Reference Center, Firestone Library, Princeton Univ. Libraries, N.J.

Mary L. Bowman, Reference Librarian, Noel Memorial Library, Louisiana State Univ., Shreveport.

James K. Bracken, Head, Second Floor Main Library Information Services, Ohio State Univ., Columbus.

William Bright, Research Associate in Linguistics, Univ. of Colorado, Boulder.

Georgia Briscoe, Assoc. Director and Head of Technical Services, Law Library, Univ. of Colorado, Boulder.

Simon J. Bronner, Distinguished Professor of Folklore and American Studies, Capitol College, Pennsylvania State Univ., Middletown.

Sue Brown, Reference Librarian, Louisiana State Univ., Shreveport.

Patrick J. Brunet, Library Manager, Western Wisconsin Technical College, La Crosse.

Betty Jo Buckingham, (retired) Consultant, Iowa Dept. of Education, Des Moines.

John R. Burch Jr., Technical Services Librarian, Hagan Memorial Library, Cumberland College, Williamsburg, Ky.

Frederic F. Burchsted, Reference Librarian, Widener Library, Harvard Univ., Cambridge, Mass.

Robert H. Burger, Head, Slavic and East European Library, Univ. of Illinois, Urbana-Champaign.

Joanna M. Burkhardt, Head Librarian, College of Continuing Education Library, Univ. of Rhode Island, Providence.

Ingrid Schierling Burnett, Reference Librarian, Univ. of Southern Colorado Library, Pueblo.

Hans E. Bynagle, Library Director and Professor of Philosophy, Whitworth College, Spokane, Wash.

Diane M. Calabrese, Freelance Writer and Consultant, Silver Spring, Md.

John Lewis Campbell, Assistant Head of Reference Department, Univ. of Georgia Libraries, Athens.

Joseph L. Carlson, Library Director, Vandenberg Air Force Base, Calif.

Ruth A. Carr, Chief, U.S. History, Local History, and Genealogy Div., New York Public Library.

Joseph Cataio, Manager, Booklegger's Bookstore, Chicago.

G. A. Cevasco, Assoc. Professor of English, St. John's Univ., Jamaica, N.Y.

Bert Chapman, Government Publications Coordinator, Purdue Univ., West Lafayette, Ind.

Boyd Childress, Reference Librarian, Ralph B. Draughon Library, Auburn Univ., Ala.

Dene L. Clark, (retired) Reference Librarian, Auraria Library, Denver, Colo.

Juleigh Muirhead Clark, Public Services Librarian, John D. Rockefeller, Jr. Library, Colonial Williamsburg Foundation, Va.

Paul F. Clark, Assoc. Professor, Pennsylvania State Univ., University Park.

Richard W. Clement, Assoc. Special Collections Librarian, Univ. of Kansas, Lawrence.

Harriette M. Cluxton, (formerly) Director of Medical Library Services, Illinois Masonic Medical Center, Chicago.

Gary R. Cocozzoli, Director of the Library, Lawrence Technological Univ., Southfield, Mich.

Joshua Cohen, Director for Outreach and Continuing Education, Mid-Hudson Library System, Poughkeepsie, N.Y.

Donald E. Collins, Assoc. Professor, History Dept., East Carolina Univ., Greenville, N.C.

Barbara Conroy, Career Connections, Santa Fe, N.Mex.

Kay O. Cornelius, (formerly) Teacher and Magnet School Lead Teacher, Huntsville City Schools, Ala.

Paul B. Cors, Catalog Librarian, Univ. of Wyoming, Laramie.

Deborah Cottin, Staff, Libraries Unlimited, Inc.

Bob Craigmile, Information Technology Librarian, Jackson County Library System, Medford, Oreg.

Kathleen W. Craver, Head Librarian, National Cathedral School, Washington, D.C.

Mark J. Crawford, Consulting Exploration Geologist/Writer/Editor, Madison, Wis.

Milton H. Crouch, Asst. Director for Reader Services, Bailey/Howe Library, Univ. of Vermont, Burlington.

George M. Cumming Jr., Librarian and Systems Administrator, Center for European Studies, Harvard Univ., Cambridge, Mass.

Gregory Curtis, Director, Northern Maine Technical College, Presque Isle.

William J. Dane, Supervising Librarian, Special Libraries, Newark Public Library, N.J.

Joseph W. Dauben, Professor of History and History of Science, City Univ. of New York.

Peter de Leon, Professor of Public Policy, Univ. of Colorado, Graduate School of Public Affairs, Denver.

Dominique-René de Lerma, Professor, Conservatory of Music, Lawrence Univ., Appleton, Wis.

Gail de Vos, Adjunct Assoc. Professor, School of Library and Information Studies, Univ. of Alberta, Edmonton.

Anthony J. Dedrick, Coordinator, Access Services, Auraria Library, Denver, Colo.

Barbara Delzell, Research and Development Center Manager, Hewlett-Packard, Vancouver, Wash.

Margaret Denman-West, Professor Emeritus, Western Maryland College, Westminster.

Donald C. Dickinson, (retired) Professor, Graduate Library School, Univ. of Arizona, Tucson.

David Dodd, Branch Manager, Aptos Library, Santa Cruz City-County Library System, Calif.

David A. Doman, PAC Instruction Specialist, Pikes Peak Library District, Colorado Springs, Colo.

Margaret F. Dominy, Head, Mathematics-Physics-Astronomy Library, Univ. of Pennsylvania, Philadelphia.

Kristin Doty, Freelance Librarian, Brunswick, Maine.

Lamia Doumato, Head of Reader Services, National Gallery of Art, Washington, D.C.

Karen Markey Drabenstott, Asst. Professor, School of Information and Library Studies, Univ. of Michigan, Ann Arbor.

John A. Drobnicki, Asst. Professor/Reference Librarian, City Univ. of New York—York College.

Joe P. Dunn, Charles A. Dana Professor of History and Politics, Converse College, Spartanburg, S.C.

Lee S. Dutton, Librarian, Hart Southeast Asia Collection, Founders Library, Northern Illinois Univ., De Kalb.

Cheryl Eckl, (formerly) Staff, Libraries Unlimited, Inc.

David Eggenberger, Freelance Writer and Editor, Vienna, Va.

Marianne B. Eimer, Interlibrary Loan/Reference Librarian, SUNY College at Fredonia, Fredonia, N.Y.

Marie Ellis, (retired) English and American Literature Bibliographer, Univ. of Georgia Libraries, Athens.

Marcus P. Elmore, Lafayette, Colo.

Jean Engler, Reference Librarian, Koelbel Public Library, Englewood, Colo.

Edward Erazo, Head of Reference, Florida Atlantic University, Boca Raton, Fla.

Jonathon Erlen, Curator, History of Medicine, Univ. of Pittsburgh, Pa.

Patricia A. Eskoz, (retired) Catalog Librarian, Auraria Library, and Asst. Professor Emeritus, Univ. of Colorado, Denver.

G. Edward Evans, Univ. Librarian, Charles Von der Ahe Library, Loyola Marymount Univ., Los Angeles, Calif.

Elaine Ezell, Library Media Specialist, Bowling Green Jr. High School, Ohio.

Andrew Ezergailis, Professor of History, Ithaca College, N.Y.

Ian Fairclough, Technical Services Manager, Yakima Valley Regional Library, Laramie, Wyo.

Evan Ira Farber, College Librarian Emeritus, Earlham College, Richmond, Ind.

Megan S. Farrell, Collection Development Librarian and Asst. Professor, Dupre Library, Univ. of Southwestern Louisiana, Lafayette.

Eleanor Ferrall, Librarian Emerita, Hayden Library, Arizona State Univ., Tempe.

Judith J. Field, Senior Lecturer, Program for Library and Information Science, Wayne State Univ., Detroit, Mich.

George L. Findlen, Dean, General Education and Educational Services, Western Wisconsin Technical College, La Crosse.

Virginia S. Fischer, Reference/Documents Librarian, Univ. of Maine, Presque Isle.

Jerry D. Flack, Assoc. Professor of Education, Univ. of Colorado, Colorado Springs.

Patricia Fleming, Professor, Faculty of Library and Information Science, Univ. of Toronto.

Michael Florman, Staff, Libraries Unlimited, Inc.

James H. Flynn Jr., (formerly) Operations Research Analyst, Dept. of Defense, Va.

Michael A. Foley, Honors Director, Marywood College, Scranton, Pa.

Harold O. Forshey, Assoc. Dean, Miami Univ., Oxford, Ohio.

Joanna F. Fountain, Adjunct Faculty, Graduate School of Library and Information Science, Univ. of Texas, Austin.

Lynne M. Fox, Information Services and Outreach Librarian, Denison Library, Univ. of Colorado Health Sciences Center, Denver.

A. David Franklin, Professor of Music, Winthrop Univ., Rock Hill, S.C.

David K. Frasier, Asst. Librarian, Reference Dept., Indiana Univ., Bloomington.

Suzanne G. Frayser, Social Science Research Consultant and Faculty, Univ. College, Univ. of Denver, Colo.

Susan J. Freiband, Assoc. Professor, Graduate School of Librarianship, Univ. of Puerto Rico, San Juan.

David O. Friedrichs, Professor, Univ. of Scranton, Pa.

Ronald H. Fritze, Assoc. Professor, Dept. of History, Lamar Univ., Beaumont, Tex.

Paula Frosch, Assoc. Museum Librarian, Thomas J. Watson Library, Metropolitan Museum of Art, New York.

Sandra E. Fuentes, User Services Librarian, Middle Tennessee State Univ., Murfreesboro.

Monica Fusich, Reference and Instruction Librarian, Henry Madden Library, Fresno, Calif.

Ahmad Gamaluddin, Professor, School of Library Science, Clarion State College, Pa.

Vera Gao, Catalog Librarian, Auraria Library, Univ. of Colorado, Denver.

Zev Garber, Professor and Chair, Jewish Studies, Los Angeles Valley College, Calif.

Diane L. Garner, Librarian for the Social Sciences, Harvard College Library, Cambridge, Mass.

Joan Garner, Staff, Libraries Unlimited, Inc.

Pamela J. Getchell, Staff, Libraries Unlimited, Inc.

Gerald L. Gill, Assoc. Professor/Business Reference Librarian, James Madison Univ., Harrisburg, Va.

John T. Gillespie, College Professor and Writer, New York.

Lois Gilmer, Library Director, Univ. of West Florida, Fort Walton Beach.

Elizabeth A. Ginno, Coordinator of Library Computer Information Resources, Univ. Library, California State Univ., Hayward.

Barbara B. Goldstein, Media Specialist, Magothy River Middle School, Arnold, Md.

Anthony Gottlieb, Asst. Clinical Professor, Univ. of Colorado School of Medicine, Denver.

Allie Wise Goudy, Professor, Western Illinois Univ., Macomb.

Shannon M. Graff, Staff, Libraries Unlimited, Inc.

Pamela M. Graham, Latin American and Iberian Studies Librarian, Columbia Univ., New York.

Rachael Green, Reference Librarian, Noel Memorial Library, Louisiana State Univ., Shreveport.

Stephen W. Green, Coordinator, Reference and Instruction Services, Auraria Library, Denver, Colo.

Richard W. Grefrath, Reference Librarian, Univ. of Nevada, Reno.

Arthur Gribben, Professor, Union Institute, Los Angeles, Calif.

Kwabena Gyimah-Brempong, Professor of Economics, College of Business Administration, Univ. of South Florida, Tampa.

Susan B. Hagloch, Director, Tuscarawas County Public Library, New Philadelphia, Ohio.

Blaine H. Hall, English Language and Literature Librarian, Harold B. Lee Library, Brigham Young Univ., Provo, Utah.

L. Hallewell, Visiting Professor, UNESP, Marilia, Brazil.

Deborah Hammer, Head, History, Travel and Biography Div., Queens Borough Public Library, Jamaica, N.Y.

Gary Handman, Head, Media Resources Center, Univ. of California, Berkeley.

Roland C. Hansen, Readers' Services Librarian, the School of the Art Institute of Chicago.

Ralph Hartsock, Senior Music Catalog Librarian, Univ. of North Texas, Denton.

Karen D. Harvey, Assoc. Dean for Academic Affairs, Univ. College, Univ. of Denver, Colo.

Joy Hastings, Manager, Technical Library, Hunt-Wesson, Inc., Fullerton, Calif.

Robert J. Havlik, Librarian Emeritus and Exhibit Coordinator, Univ. of Notre Dame, Ind.

Fred J. Hay, Librarian of the W. L. Eury Appalachian Collection and Assoc. Professor, Center for Appalachian Studies, Appalachian State Univ., Boone, N.C.

Lucy Heckman, Reference Librarian (Business-Economics), St. John's Univ. Library, Jamaica, N.Y.

James S. Heller, Director of the Law Library and Assoc. Professor of Law, Marshall-Wythe Law Library, College of William and Mary, Williamsburg, Va.

David Henige, African Studies Bibliographer, Memorial Library, Univ. of Wisconsin, Madison.

Carol D. Henry, Librarian, Lyons Township High School, LaGrange, Ill.

Diana Tixier Herald, Librarian, Freelance Writer, Grand Junction, Colo.

Mark Y. Herring, Dean of Libraries, Oklahoma Baptist Univ., Shawnee.

Susan Davis Herring, Reference Librarian, Univ. of Alabama Library, Huntsville.

Janet Hilbun, Student, Texas Woman's Univ., Denton.

Marquita Hill, Cooperating Professor of Chemical Engineering, Univ. of Maine, Orono.

V. W. Hill, Social Sciences Bibliographer, Memorial Library, Univ. of Wisconsin, Madison.

Christopher J. Hoeppner, Reference Instruction Librarian, DePaul Univ., Chicago.

Frank Hoffmann, Professor, Library Science, Sam Houston State Univ., Tex.

Susan Tower Hollis, Assoc. Dean and Center Director, Central New York Center of the State Univ. of New York.

Paul L. Holmer, Reference Librarian, Buley Library, Southern Connecticut State Univ., New Haven.

Leslie R. Homzie, Asst. Reference Librarian, Univ. of Delaware, Newark.

Shirley L. Hopkinson, Professor, Div. of Library and Information Science, San Jose State Univ., Calif.

Marilynn Green Hopman, Librarian, NASA Johnson Space Center, Scientific and Technical Information Center, Houston, Tex.

Renee B. Horowitz, Professor, Dept. of Technology, College of Engineering, Arizona State Univ., Tempe.

C. D. Hurt, Director, Graduate Library School, Univ. of Arizona, Tucson.

Jonathan F. Husband, Program Chair of the Library/Reader Services Librarian, Henry Whittemore Library, Framingham State College, Mass.

Ludmila N. Ilyina, (retired) Professor, Natural Resources Institute, Winnipeg, Man.

David Isaacson, Asst. Head of Reference and Humanities Librarian, Waldo Library, Western Michigan Univ., Kalamazoo.

Barbara Ittner, Staff, Libraries Unlimited, Inc.

Eugene B. Jackson, Professor Emeritus, Graduate School of Library and Information Sciences, Univ. of Texas, Austin.

D. Barton Johnson, Professor Emeritus of Russian, Univ. of California, Santa Barbara.

Marjorie H. Jones, Educational Media Specialist, Bryan Senior High School, Omaha, Neb.

Kelly M. Jordan, Engineering Reference Librarian, Pennsylvania State Univ., University Park.

Suzanne Julian, Public Services Librarian, Southern Utah Univ. Library, Cedar City.

Elaine F. Jurries, Coordinator of Serials Services, Auraria Library, Denver, Colo.

Sue Kamm, Head, Audio-Visual and Stack Maintenance Divisions, Inglewood Public Library, Calif.

Thomas A. Karel, Assoc. Director for Public Services, Shadek-Fackenthal Library, Franklin and Marshall College, Lancaster, Pa.

John Laurence Kelland, Reference Bibliographer for Life Sciences, Univ. of Rhode Island Library, Kingston.

Dean H. Keller, Assoc. Dean of Libraries, Kent State Univ., Ohio.

Barbara E. Kemp, Asst. Director, Dewey Graduate Library, State Univ. of New York, Albany.

Caroline M. Kent, Head of Research Services, Widener Library, Harvard Univ., Cambridge, Mass.

Jackson Kesler, Professor of Theatre and Dance, Western Kentucky Univ., Bowling Green.

Robert H. Kieft, Coordinator for Reference Services and Collection Development, Magill Library, Haverford College, Pa.

Vicki J. Killion, Asst. Professor of Library Science and Pharmacy, Nursing and Health Sciences Librarian, Purdue Univ., West Lafayette, Ind.

Sung Ok Kim, Senior Asst. Librarian/Social Sciences Cataloging Librarian, Cornell Univ., Ithaca, N.Y.

Norman L. Kincaide, Citation Editor, Shepard's/McGraw-Hill, Inc., Colorado Springs, Colo.

Christine E. King, Reference—Music Library, State Univ. of New York, Stony Brook.

Janet J. Kosky, Mukwonago Community Library, Wis.

Lori D. Kranz, Freelance Editor; Assoc. Editor, *The Bloomsbury Review*, Denver, Colo.

Betsy J. Kraus, Librarian, Lovelace Respiratory Research Institute, National Environmental Respiratory Center, Albuquerque, N.Mex.

Linda A. Krikos, Head, Women's Studies Library, Ohio State Univ., Columbus.

Carol Krismann, Head, William M. White Business Library, Univ. of Colorado, Boulder.

Marlene M. Kuhl, Library Manager, Baltimore County Public Library, Reisterstown Branch, Md.

Colby H. Kullman, Assoc. Professor and Editor, *Studies in American Drama*, Univ. of Mississippi, University.

Keith Kyker, Educational Media Specialist, Okaloosa County Schools, Valparaiso, Fla.

Robert V. Labaree, Reference/Public Services Librarian, Von KleinSmid Library, Univ. of Southern California, Los Angeles.

Linda L. Lam-Easton, Assoc. Professor, Dept. of Religious Studies, California State Univ., Northridge.

Lizbeth Langston, Reference Librarian, Univ. of California, Riverside.

Mary Larsgaard, Asst. Head, Map and Imagery Laboratory Library, Univ. of California, Santa Barbara.

Binh P. Le, Reference Librarian, Abington College, Pennsylvania State Univ., University Park.

Michael R. Leach, Director, Physics Research Library, Harvard Univ., Cambridge, Mass.

Charles Leck, Professor of Biological Sciences, Rutgers Univ., New Brunswick, N.J.

Hwa-Wei Lee, Dean of Libraries, Ohio Univ., Athens.

Joann H. Lee, (formerly) Head of Reader Services, Lake Forest College, Ill.

R. S. Lehmann, Rocky Mountain BankCard System, Colorado National Bank, Denver.

Polin P. Lei, Assoc. Librarian, Information Services, Arizona Health Sciences Library, Tucson.

Richard A. Leiter, Director, Law Library, Howard Univ., Washington, D.C.

John A. Lent, Drexel Hill, Pa.

Tze-chung Li, Professor, Graduate School of Library and Information Science, Rosary College, River Forest, Ill.

Charlotte Lindgren, Professor Emerita of English, Emerson College, Boston.

Larry Lobel, Virtuoso Keyboard Services, Petaluma, Calif.

Koraljka Lockhart, Publications Editor, San Francisco Opera, Calif.

Jeffrey E. Long, Interlibrary Loan/Photocopy Services Library Assistant, Lamar Soutter Library/Univ. of Massachusetts Medical Center, Worcester.

Jeffrey R. Luttrell, Leader, Humanities Cataloging Team, Princeton Univ. Library, N.J.

Marit S. MacArthur, Reference Librarian, Auraria Libraries, Univ. of Colorado, Denver.

Sara R. Mack, Professor Emerita, Dept. of Library Science, Kutztown Univ., Pa.

Theresa Maggio, Head of Public Services, Southwest Georgia Regional Library, Bainbridge.

Kay Mariea, Staff, Libraries Unlimited, Inc.

Judith A. Matthews, Physics-Astronomy/Science Reference Librarian, Main Library, Michigan State Univ., East Lansing.

George Louis Mayer, (formerly) Senior Principal Librarian, New York Public Library and Part-Time Librarian, Adelphi, Manhattan Center and Brooklyn College.

Peter H. McCracken, Reference Librarian, Joyner Library, East Carolina University, Greenville, N.C.

Dona McDermott, Research Specialist, Center for Business Research, Long Island Univ./C. W. Post Campus, Long Island, N.Y.

James R. McDonald, Professor of Geography, Eastern Michigan Univ., Ypsilanti.

Christopher Michael McDonough, Lecturer, Dept. of Classics, Princeton Univ., N.J.

Dana McDougald, Lead Media Specialist, Learning Resources Center, Cedar Shoals High School, Athens, Ga.

Peter Zachary McKay, Business Librarian, Univ. of Florida Libraries, Gainesville.

Robert B. McKee, Professor, Mechanical Engineering, Univ. of Nevada, Reno.

Jean C. McManus, Interim Head of Serials Department, Hesburgh Library, Univ. of Notre Dame, Ind.

Margo B. Mead, Technology Instruction Librarian, Louis M. Salmon Library, Univ. of Alabama, Huntsville.

Michael G. Messina, Assoc. Professor, Dept. of Forest Science, Texas A & M Univ., College Station.

G. Douglas Meyers, Chair, Dept. of English, Univ. of Texas, El Paso.

George A. Meyers, Chairman, National Labor Commission, Baltimore, Md.

Robert Michaelson, Head Librarian, Seeley G. Mudd Library for Science and Engineering, Northwestern Univ., Evanston, Ill.

Bogdan Mieczkowski, Professor of Economics, Ithaca College, N.Y.

Seiko Mieczkowski, Hobart & William Smith Colleges, Geneva, N.Y.

Ann E. Miller, Federal Documents Librarian, Perkins Library, Duke Univ., Durham, N.C.

Bill Miller, Director of Libraries, Florida Atlantic Univ., Boca Raton.

Elizabeth B. Miller, Instructor, College of Library and Information Science, Univ. of South Carolina, Columbia.

Richard A. Miller, Professor of Economics, Wesleyan Univ., Middletown, Conn.

Carol L. Mitchell, Southeast Asian Bibliographic Services Librarian, General Library System, Univ. of Wisconsin, Madison.

James Moffet, Head, Reference Dept., Baldwin Public Library, Birmingham, Mich.

Paul A. Mogren, Head of Reference, Marriott Library, Univ. of Utah, Salt Lake City.

Terry Ann Mood, Humanities Bibliographer, Univ. of Colorado, Denver.

Anne C. Moore, Electronic Resources Librarian, New Mexico State Univ., Alamogordo.

Gerald D. Moran, Director, McCartney Library, Geneva College, Beaver Falls, Pa.

Betty J. Morris, Staff, Libraries Unlimited, Inc.

K. Mulliner, Asst. to the Director of Libraries, Ohio Univ. Library, Athens.

Craig A. Munsart, Teacher, Jefferson County Public Schools, Golden, Colo.

Deborah D. Nelson, Student, Library and Information Services Dept., Univ. College, Univ. of Denver, Colo.

Kerie L. Nickel, Librarian, St. Mary's College of Maryland, St. Mary's City.

Eric R. Nitschke, Reference Librarian, Robert W. Woodruff Library, Emory Univ., Atlanta, Ga.

Christopher W. Nolan, Head, Reference Services, Maddux Library, Trinity Univ., San Antonio, Tex.

Carol L. Noll, Volunteer Librarian, Schimelpfenig Middle School, Plano, Tex.

O. Gene Norman, Head, Reference Dept., Indiana State Univ. Libraries, Terre Haute.

David G. Nowak, Asst. Professor and Reference Librarian, Mississippi State University Libraries, Mississippi State.

Marshall E. Nunn, Professor, Dept. of History, Glendale Community College, Calif.

Herbert W. Ockerman, Professor, Ohio State Univ., Columbus.

Lawrence Olszewski, Manager, OCLC Information Center, Dublin, Ohio.

Ray Olszewski, Independent Consultant, Palo Alto, Calif.

John Howard Oxley, Halifax, N.S.

Joseph W. Palmer, Assoc. Professor, School of Information and Library Studies, State Univ. of New York, Buffalo.

Robert Palmieri, Professor Emeritus, School of Music, Kent State Univ., Ohio.

Penny Papangelis, Health Sciences Librarian, Western Kentucky Univ., Bowling Green.

J. Carlyle Parker, Librarian and Univ. Archivist Emeritus, Library, California State Univ., Turlock.

Elizabeth Patterson, Head, Reference and Computer Reference Services, Robert W. Woodruff Library, Emory Univ., Atlanta, Ga.

Gari-Anne Patzwald, Freelance Editor and Indexer, Lexington, Ky.

Harry E. Pence, Professor of Chemistry, State Univ. of New York, Oneonta.

Karin Pendle, Professor of Musicology, Univ. of Cincinnati, Ohio.

Julia Perez, Biological Sciences Librarian, Michigan State Univ. Libraries, East Lansing.

Kevin W. Perizzolo, (formerly) Staff, Libraries Unlimited, Inc.

Glenn Petersen, Professor of Anthropology and International Affairs, Graduate Center and Baruch College, City Univ. of New York.

C. Michael Phillips, Asst. Reference Librarian, Robert Scott Small Library, College of Charleston, S.C.

Phillip P. Powell, Asst. Reference Librarian, Robert Scott Small Library, College of Charleston, S.C.

Carl Pracht, Reference Librarian, Southeast Missouri State Univ., Cape Girardeau.

Ann E. Prentice, Dean, College of Library and Information Services, Univ. of Maryland, College Park.

Pete Prunkl, Freelance Writer, Hickory, N.C.

Randall Rafferty, Reference Librarian, Mississippi State Univ. Library, Mississippi State.

Varadaraja V. Raman, Professor of Physics and Humanities, Rochester Institute of Technology, N.Y.

Lisé Rasmussen, Reference Librarian, Dowling College, Oakdale, N.Y.

Jack Ray, Asst. Director, Loyola/Notre Dame Library, Baltimore, Md.

Nancy P. Reed, Information Services Manager, Paducah Public Library, Paducah, Ky.

James Rettig, University Librarian, University of Richmond, Richmond, Va.

Diane B. Rhodes, Life Sciences and Agriculture Librarian, Arizona State Univ., Tempe.

Jo Anne H. Ricca, Staff, Libraries Unlimited, Inc.

Robert B. Marks Ridinger, Head, Electronic Information Resources Management Dept., Univ. Libraries, Northern Illinois Univ., De Kalb.

Constance Rinaldo, Head, Collection Services, Biomedical Libraries, Dartmouth College, Hanover, N.H.

Cari Ringelheim, Staff, Libraries Unlimited, Inc.

Anne F. Roberts, Adjunct Professor, School of Education, State Univ. of New York, Albany.

John M. Robson, Institute Librarian, Rose-Hulman Institute of Technology, Terre Haute, Ind.

Deborah V. Rollins, Reference Librarian, Univ. of Maine, Orono.

John B. Romeiser, Professor of French and Dept. Head, Univ. of Tennessee, Knoxville.

Melissa Rae Root, (formerly) Staff, Libraries Unlimited, Inc.

Samuel Rothstein, Professor Emeritus, School of Librarianship, Univ. of British Columbia, Vancouver.

Michele Russo, Acting Director, Franklin D. Schurz Library, Indiana Univ., South Bend.

Kenneth I. Saichek, President, Saichek/Vail Associates and C.E.O., Kybercom, Wauwatosa, Wis.

Nadine Salmons, Technical Services Librarian, Fort Carson's Grant Library, Colo.

Edmund F. SantaVicca, Librarian, Information Commons, Estrella Mountain Community College Center, Litchfield Park, Ariz.

Steven J. Schmidt, Assoc. Librarian, Indiana Univ./Purdue Univ. at Indianapolis Libraries.

Willa Schmidt, Reference Librarian, Univ. of Wisconsin, Madison.

John P. Schmitt, Regis Univ. Library, Denver, Colo.

Deborah K. Scott, Asst. Librarian, Employer's Reinsurance Corp., Overland Park, Kans.

Ralph Lee Scott, Assoc. Professor, East Carolina Univ. Library, Greenville, N.C.

Scott Seaman, Head, Circulation Services, Norlin Library, Univ. of Colorado, Boulder.

Karen Selden, Catalog Librarian, Univ. of Colorado, Boulder, Colo.

Sheryl Sessa, Librarian, Comsewogue Public Library, Port Jefferson State, N.Y.

Deborah Sharp, Head Librarian, Lexmark Information Center, Univ. of Kentucky, Lexington.

Bruce A. Shuman, Dallas, Tex.

Linda Keir Simons, Head of Client Services, Univ. of Dayton Library, Ohio.

Esther R. Sinofsky, Library Media Teacher, Alexander Hamilton High School, Los Angeles, Calif.

Robert M. Slade, Independent Consultant, North Vancouver, B.C.

Mary Ellen Snodgrass, Freelance Writer, Charlotte, N.C.

Steven W. Sowards, Head, Social Sciences/Humanities Reference, Michigan State Univ. Libraries, East Lansing.

Jerri Spoehel, Freelance Writer and Editor, Las Cruces, N.Mex.

Howard Spring, Asst. Professor, Univ. of Guelph, Ont.

Jan S. Squire, Reference and Instructional Services Librarian, Univ. of Northern Colorado, Greeley.

Beth St. Cyr, (formerly) Staff, Libraries Unlimited, Inc.

Karen Y. Stabler, Head of Information Services, New Mexico State Univ. Library, Las Cruces.

Victor L. Stater, Assoc. Professor of History, Louisiana State Univ., Baton Rouge.

Allen E. Staver, Assoc. Professor, Dept. of Geography, Northern Illinois Univ., De Kalb.

Kay M. Stebbins, Coordinator Librarian, Louisiana State Univ., Shreveport.

Norman D. Stevens, Director Emeritus, Univ. of Connecticut Libraries, Storrs.

John W. Storey, Professor of History, Lamar Univ., Beaumont, Tex.

Patricia C. Strickland, Paralegal, Brenda Keen Schwartz, P.C., Houston, Tex.

Susan D. Strickland, Staff, Libraries Unlimited, Inc.

Ellen R. Strong, Asst. Curator of Manuscripts and Rare Books, College of William and Mary, Williamsburg, Va.

William C. Struning, Professor, Seton Hall Univ., South Orange, N.J.

Bruce Stuart, Professor and Parke-Davis Chair, Univ. of Maryland, Baltimore.

Mila C. Su, Senior Asst. Librarian, Pennsylvania State Univ., Altoona.

Timothy E. Sullivan, Asst. Professor of Economics, Towson State Univ., Md.

Tom Sullivan, Asst. News Editor, Philadelphia, Pa.

Richard H. Swain, Reference Librarian, West Chester Univ., Pa.

James H. Sweetland, Assoc. Professor, School of Library and Information Science, Univ. of Wisconsin, Milwaukee.

Nigel Tappin, (formerly) General Librarian, North York Public Library, Ont.

Glynys R. Thomas, Sawyer Library, Suffolk Univ., Boston.

Katherine Margaret Thomas, (formerly) Biologist, Long Point Bird Observatory, Toronto.

Paul H. Thomas, Head, Catalog Dept., Hoover Institution Library, Stanford Univ., Calif.

Mary Ann Thompson, Asst. Professor of Nursing, Saint Joseph College, West Hartford, Conn.

Peter Thorpe, Professor Emeritus, Univ. of Colorado, Denver.

Linda D. Tietjen, Senior Instructor, Instruction and Reference Services, Auraria Library, Denver, Colo.

Bruce H. Tiffney, Assoc. Professor of Geology and Biological Sciences, Univ. of California, Santa Barbara.

Andrew G. Torok, Assoc. Professor, Northern Illinois Univ., De Kalb.

Gregory M. Toth, Reference Librarian, State Univ. of New York, Brockport.

Mary L. Trenerry, Media Specialist, Millard Public Schools, Omaha, Neb.

Carol Truett, Assoc. Professor, Appalachian State Univ., Boone, N.C.

Felicity Tucker, (formerly) Staff, Libraries Unlimited, Inc.

Dean Tudor, Professor, School of Journalism, Ryerson Polytechnical Institute, Toronto.

Elias H. Tuma, Professor of Economics, Univ. of California, Davis.

Diane J. Turner, Science/Engineering Liaison, Auraria Library, Univ. of Colorado, Denver.

Robert L. Turner Jr., Librarian and Asst. Professor, Radford Univ., Va.

Michele Tyrrell, Media Specialist, Arundel Senior High School, Gambrills, Md.

Arthur R. Upgren, Professor of Astronomy and Director, Van Vleck Observatory, Wesleyan Univ., Middletown, Conn.

Judith A. Valdez, Instructor/Reference Librarian, Auraria Library, Univ. of Colorado, Denver.

Susanna Van Sant, Librarian, Michigan State Univ., East Lansing.

Debra S. Van Tassel, Reference Librarian, Univ. of Colorado, Boulder.

Vandelia L. VanMeter, Professor and Library Director, Spalding Univ., Louisville, Ky.

Jennie Ver Steeg, Education Liaison/Social Science Librarian, Northern Illinois Univ., De Kalb.

Bridget Volz, Freelance Librarian and Weaver, Estes Park, Colo.

Graham R. Walden, Assoc. Professor, Information Services Department, Ohio State University, Columbus.

Jeff Wanser, Coordinator, Reference and Government Documents, Hiram College Library, Ohio.

Richard S. Watts, Coordinator, Technical Processing Dept., San Bernardino County Library, Calif.

J. E. Weaver, Dept. of Economics, Drake Univ., Des Moines, Iowa.

Karen T. Wei, Head, Asian Library, Univ. of Illinois, Urbana.

Michael Weinberg, Reference Librarian, Ronald Williams Library, Northeastern Illinois Library, Chicago.

Lynda Welborn, Director of Libraries, Colorado Academy, Denver.

Emily L. Werrell, Reference/Instructional Services Librarian, Northern Kentucky Univ., Highland Heights.

Andrew B. Wertheimer, Librarian, Woodman Astronomical Library, Univ. of Wisconsin, Madison.

Lee Weston, Reference Services Manager, James A. Michener Library, Univ. of Northern Colorado, Greeley.

Lucille Whalen, Dean of Graduate Programs, Immaculate Heart College Center, Los Angeles, Calif.

Cathy Seitz Whitaker, (formerly) Social Work Librarian, Hillman Library, Univ. of Pittsburgh, Pa.

David L. White, Professor, History Dept., Appalachian State Univ., Boone, N.C.

Robert L. Wick, Asst. Professor and Fine Arts Bibliographer, Auraria Library, Univ. of Colorado, Denver.

Agnes H. Widder, Humanities Bibliographer, Michigan State Univ., East Lansing.

Albert Wilhelm, Professor of English, Tennessee Technological Univ., Cookeville.

Connie Williams, Information Manager, Merrick & Company, Aurora, Colo.

Lynn F. Williams, Professor, Div. of Writing, Literature, and Publishing, Emerson College, Boston.

Robert V. Williams, Assoc. Professor, College of Library and Information Science, Univ. of South Carolina, Columbia.

Frank L. Wilson, Professor and Head, Dept. of Political Science, Purdue Univ., West Lafayette, Ind.

Mark A. Wilson, Professor of Geology, College of Wooster, Ohio.

Glenn R. Wittig, Director of Library Services, Criswell College, Dallas, Tex.

Bohdan S. Wynar, Staff, Libraries Unlimited, Inc.

Eveline L. Yang, Manager, Information Delivery Programs, Auraria Library, Univ. of Colorado, Denver.

Hope Yelich, Reference Librarian, Earl Gregg Swem Library, College of William and Mary, Williamsburg, Va.

Henry E. York, Head, Collection Management, Cleveland State Univ., Ohio.

Arthur P. Young, Director, Northern Illinois Libraries, Northern Illinois Univ., De Kalb.

Louis G. Zelenka, Freelance Librarian, Jacksonville, Fla.

Magda Želinská-Ferl, Professor/Faculty Advisor, Union Institute, Los Angeles, Calif.

Susan Zernial, Staff, Libraries Unlimited, Inc.

L. Zgusta, Professor of Linguistics and the Classics and Member of the Center for Advance Study, Univ. of Illinois, Urbana.

Xiao (Shelley) Yan Zhang, Cataloger, Mississippi State Univ. Library.

Anita Zutis, Adjunct Librarian, Queensborough Community College, Bayside, N.Y.

Journals Cited

FORM OF CITATION	JOURNAL TITLE
BL	*Booklist*
BR	*Book Report*
C&RL	*College & Research Libraries*
C&RL News	*College & Research Libraries News*
Choice	*Choice*
EL	*Emergency Librarian*
JAL	*Journal of Academic Librarianship*
LJ	*Library Journal*
RBB	*Reference Books Bulletin*
RQ	*RQ*
RUSQ	*Reference & User Services Quarterly* (formerly *RQ*)
SLJ	*School Library Journal*
SLMQ	*School Library Media Quarterly*
TL	*TeacherLibrarian* (formerly *Emergency Librarian*)
VOYA	*Voice of Youth Advocates*

Part I
GENERAL
REFERENCE
WORKS

ACRONYMS AND ABBREVIATIONS

1. **Elsevier's Dictionary of Acronyms, Initialisms, Abbreviations, and Symbols.** Fioretta Benedetto Mattia, comp. New York, Elsevier Science, 1997. 646p. $187.00. ISBN 0-444-82589-4.

This reference provides English acronyms as well as French and Italian abbreviations related to science, government, computers, libraries, associations, economics, and medicine. The constant proliferation of acronyms in our society makes it unlikely any publication can be inclusive for so many subjects. The compiler barely scratches the surface for any given category, and the presentations of data are inconsistent. In the introductory notes the reader is promised each entry will identify the acronym's interest area except where self-evident. There are numerous notations for which the appropriate arena is not intuitive. Many of the Italian and French notations are not translated, even though their meanings are not obvious. The appendixes provide abbreviations for universities, banks, airports, North Atlantic Treaty Organization bodies, publishers, and periodicals. Again, we are given only a partial listing of the vast number possible. Rather than trying to provide every acronym known to man, a focus on fewer fields in more depth would be more helpful.—**Adrienne Antink Bendel**

ALMANACS

2. **Canadian Almanac & Directory 1999.** 152d ed. Ann Marie Aldighieri and others, eds. Toronto, Ontario, Micromedia; distr., Farmington Hills, Mich., Gale, 1998. 1v. (various paging). $249.00. ISBN 1-895021-50-2. ISSN 0068-8193.

The *Canadian Almanac & Directory 1999* is a definitive almanac in the 1st section covering astronomy, honors, national and provincial information, customs, and statistics for Canada, Great Britain, and the Commonwealth. Sections 2 through 10 are various directories compiled into a single volume. The directory sections encompass professional organizations, religious denominations, trade unions, foundations, companies, health care facilities, school boards, schools, universities and colleges, and legal firms. Each directory supplies contact names, addresses, and telephone and fax numbers. World Wide Web addresses are provided in the entries. A "Website Directory" is available at the end of each directory. A table of contents outlines each section. A "Topical Table of Contents," an "Alphabetical Fastfinder," and an extensive index help users to find the information. This title is recommended to public, academic, and special libraries that need current information about Canada, its provinces, and the British Commonwealth.—**Kay M. Stebbins**

3. **Canadian Sourcebook, 1998.** 33d ed. Barbara Law and Renee Sgroi, eds. Don Mills, Ont., Southam, 1997. 1v. (various paging). index. $197.00. ISBN 0-919-217-95-8. ISSN 1480-3038.

This appears to be a business-oriented almanac. Sections in the book include the previous two years in review, general information, geography, natural resources, people, religion, education, a section titled "Sources of Information" (libraries and archives, book publishers, periodicals, directories, and associations), transportation, labor, law, banking and finance, business and trade, constitution, federal government, provincial government, intergovernmental agencies, and municipal governments. This reviewer noted that a number of the things first seen in this book are items that are difficult to find, such as the official words to the national anthem and the proper form of address for the lieutenant governor of British Columbia. However, after further research it was noted that one college, four trade magazines, the technical society responsible for the instigation of this review series, a competitor to the Southam-owned newspaper on the North Shore, and one of the top telecommunications consultant companies in the country are missing. In other words, a majority of the items this reviewer was looking for simply were not found in this source. There is a definite "eastern," or "Ontario," bias—one magazine headquartered in Vancouver is not listed, but a satellite publication based in Toronto is. Members of Parliament have their Ottawa telephone and fax numbers listed but not their constituency offices.

Lack of attention to detail seems to be the main problem with this publication. Under agriculture a single table format is adhered to even though it means that the main table, citing total number of farms, is fractured and disjointed. That main table is important because a number of subsequent tables are meaningless without reference to it.

Of course there is a lot of interesting information. For headquarters offices and marketing departments wanting quick, but not necessarily serious, information on a variety of topics, this has a use. For media offices wanting instant contacts it might be better than nothing if one is willing to research thoroughly. For those doing important research it might be a starting point, but definitely should not be used alone.—**Robert M. Slade**

4.   **Chase's Calendar of Events 1998.** Lincolnwood, Ill., National Textbook, 1997. 736p. illus. index. $59.95pa. ISBN 0-8092-3017-8. ISSN 0740-5286.

Now in its 41st edition, the major change for this reference calendar/almanac from the previous review (see ARBA 97, entry 5) is the packaging of both print and CD-ROM versions together. Picking any day, users are able to discover famous birthday anniversaries, significant national events and special celebrations, and birthdays of currently living notable persons. With the majority of the approximately 12,000 entries organized chronologically, this work continues to be a primary resource for ready-reference. Having a comprehensive subject index, a section devoted to milestone anniversaries, and the inclusion of such topics as presidential proclamations, time zones, and major awards from 1997 enhances its functionality as an almanac. Also of note are such themes as the world, the United States, education, people, and scheduled 1998 events found in the spotlight section. The glossary supplies definitions of terms related directly to calendars, such as Gregorian or Julian.

The CD-ROM format provides new ways to access information, allowing keyword searching in a single content area and advanced Boolean searching within the entire database. In comparing entries, the electronic version appears to have the identical information found in the print version. Considered user-friendly by the reviewer, it is easy enough to maneuver within the six primary content areas. Additional boxes are provided that allow the user to explore nine various instructional categories, which range from finding help in refining search strategies to obtaining information about the reference work. One distracting feature is that the text inserted in the menu boxes on the initial page overflows. The links, however, connect properly to the appropriate titles when chosen. Even though the disc is easy to install, the publishers have included a toll-free technical support number on the instruction sheet.—**Marianne B. Eimer**

5.   **Whitaker's Almanack 1999.** 131st ed. London, Stationery Office; distr., Farmington Hills, Mich., Gale, 1998. 1279p. index. $105.00. ISBN 0-11-702240-3.

This essential reference for those in the United Kingdom as well as for Anglophiles the world over is now in its 131st edition, having been published annually since 1868. The coverage is exhaustive for Great Britain, covering such diverse topics as the royal family; various levels of titled nobility; recipients of awards, decorations, and medals; members of Parliament and local governments; election, economic, and population statistics; police and prisons; religion and churches; education; health and environment; transportation; media; sports; and the arts. Government departments are described and their addresses and officers given; society, association, and institution addresses and executives are also listed. Calendars, chronologies, and astronomical charts are provided for each month of 1999. In some sections the focus is wider than the United Kingdom—for example, maps, international organizations, the European Union, and profiles of countries of the world. A 150-page summary of events from September 1997 through August 1998 is found near the conclusion of the work. Every library needing at least one single-volume definitive reference work about Great Britain should have this source on standing order.—**Lee Weston**

6.   **The World Almanac for Kids 1999.** Elaine Israel, ed. Mahwah, N.J., World Almanac Books, 1998. 320p. illus. maps. index. $8.95pa. ISBN 0-88687-826-8.

The *World Almanac for Kids 1999* is an easy-to-follow, comprehensive guide to facts and information about many subject areas. Art, computers, and health and science are just a few of the chapters, which are arranged alphabetically with subdivisions of the major points of interest. There is even a brief description of the approaching millennium that informs the reader the new millennium does not actually begin until January 1, 2001. "Facto the Factosaurus" leads readers to many interesting and eye-catching facts. Photographs, illustrations, graphs, and charts supplement the multitude of information given by the almanac. Color maps also complement the "Countries" and "United States" chapters.

Besides factorial information, the almanac also provides important information on life. It supplies pertinent advice on health, AIDS, and even what to do when offered drugs. The "Money and Business" chapter has a section that discusses budgets. In addition, the almanac addresses environmental issues such as air pollution and recycling.

Overall, the book is a good resource for miscellaneous facts and information. It provides important information while also being fun and entertaining for children. It is not, however, the best source for in-depth research. Even though it is well organized, finding a particular fact can be troublesome. The index is not as complete as one would like. As a research tool, it would be best to supplement the almanac with other, more detailed sources. [R: BL, 15 Oct 98, p. 442-443]—**Cari Ringelheim**

BIBLIOGRAPHY

Bibliographic Guides

7.   **Bibliographic Guide to Conference Publications 1996.** New York, G. K. Hall/Simon & Schuster Macmillan, 1997. 2v. $395.00/set. ISBN 0-7838-1748-7. ISSN 0360-2729.

This 2-volume set, last reviewed in ARBA 92 (see entry 3), is part of G. K. Hall's Bibliographic Guides series of annual subject bibliographies. It contains the holdings of the Research Libraries of the New York Public Library and the Library of Congress in its subject area with the imprint date of 1990 to the present that were cataloged between January 1, 1996, and December 31, 1996. It should be noted that the entries in the 1996 edition contain, when applicable, the Library of Congress call number, the Dewey Decimal Classification number, and the New York Public Library's Classmark. This valuable bibliography is recommended for research institutions.

—**John R. Burch Jr.**

National and Trade Bibliography

International

8.   **CD-ROMs in Print: An International Guide to CD-ROM, CD-K, 3DO, MMCD, CD-32, Multimedia, and Electronic Products.** 12th ed. Amy R. Suchowski and others, eds. Farmington Hills, Mich., Gale, 1998. 1654p. index. $155.00pa. ISBN 0-7876-1445-9. ISSN 0891-8198.

Gale is well known for providing directories to works in print; this 12th edition of *CD-ROMS in Print* provides bibliographic data, hardware specifications, and availability information for more than 15,000 CD-ROM titles. Most of the 1,654-page volume comprises individual titles of CD-ROMs listed in alphabetic order by title. The 2d section provides an international listing of companies producing CD-ROMs. The company listings include address, telephone number, Internet address, contact information, and the titles published. Companies are also indexed by type of activity within the CD-ROM market and by geographic location. Six additional indexes grant access to CD-ROM titles by multimedia features, Macintosh compatibility, electronic books/other platforms, audience level, and subject.

As with any directory, not all information can be counted on to be accurate or up to date. With the increasing number of CD-ROM publishers and the growing number of CD-ROM products, it is impossible to have a complete listing of every CD-ROM producer and every CD-ROM title. Because the information furnished in this directory is based on facts provided by CD-ROM producers and "reliable secondary sources," some entries are more complete than others. As stated in a previous review of this title (see ARBA 97, entries 16 and 17), this guide presents valuable information for both librarians and the general public.—**Susan D. Strickland**

United States

9. **American Book Publishing Record, Cumulative 1997.** New Providence, N.J., R. R. Bowker, 1998. 2v. index. $364.75/set. ISBN 0-8352-3977-2. ISSN 0002-7707.

Last reviewed in ARBA 1995 (see entry 17), this cumulation includes 60,400 entries, an addition of 18,400 entries from the 1994 edition. The format remains the same—volume 1 classifies all titles published or distributed in the United States in 1997 by Dewey Decimal Classification (DDC) 000s through the 600s; volume 2 comprises DDC 700s through the 900s, plus separate sections for adult and juvenile fiction. Each entry includes complete bibliographic information, Library of Congress Classification Number, price, and subject headings. Three indexes provide author, title, and subject access to the classified list. The subject index consists of primary subject terms, personal names, and uniform titles. Government publications, serials, dissertations, and journals are excluded.

A standard reference source, this title documents publishing history of the previous year. Although a great deal of information is available in these volumes, competing resources on the Internet (e.g., Library of Congress) necessitate careful consideration before investing.—**Susan D. Strickland**

10. **Bowker's Directory of Videocassettes for Children 1998.** New Providence, N.J., R. R. Bowker, 1998. 1184p. index. $59.95pa. ISBN 0-8352-4059-2.

Bowker has once again done what it does so well: produce an essential reference tool. This initial annual edition of the *Bowker's Directory of Videocassettes for Children* is a comprehensive, usable directory for all those who select children's videocassettes. The directory lists 30,055 videocassettes in 2 sections—8,818 entertainment videos and 21,237 educational videos chosen for an audience grade level of K-12.

Each entry contains all data about that title available, including running time, producer, age suitability, awards earned, Motion Picture Association of America rating, a brief annotation, and ordering information. The publisher states that "selection of titles . . . was done to encompass a broad spectrum of our audience, not only for children and their parents, but professionals, paraprofessionals, and young adults" (p. viii). The videocassettes in each section may be accessed by several indexes, adding to the flexibility and usefulness of the book. The entertainment index contains 10 individual indexes. In addition to the main title index, listings for awards, cast/director, genre, series, Spanish language, laser videodisc, 8MM, closed captioned, and international standards are provided. The educational listing has 8 indexes: title, subject, series, laser videodisc, 8MM, closed-captioned, international standards, and manufacturers/distributors. Because the main listing for all the videocassettes is alphabetic by title, with no age group listed, an additional index for both sections of recommended age levels would be helpful. It is hoped that future editions of this annual volume will add this needed item. This is an excellent book for any reference collection that contains bibliographies of children's material.—**Nancy P. Reed**

11. **The Complete Directory of Large Print Books and Serials 1998.** New Providence, N.J., R. R. Bowker/Reed Reference Publishing, 1998. 1046p. $175.00pa. ISBN 0-8352-3955-1. ISSN 0000-1120.

Large print publishing is an ever-growing industry. It not only serves the older U.S. population with declining eyesight, but those persons who are visually impaired or children as well. This large, soft cover directory lists all actively available large print books and serials identified in the R. R. Bowker databases. The work is divided into 7 index sections—title, author, general reading subject, textbooks subject, children's subject, newspapers and periodicals, and publishers and distributors—and the format of bibliographic data is consistent with other titles in the *Books in Print* (see ARBA 98, entry 15) family. The unique feature of this directory is that it is presented in its entirety in 14-point type, the base type size for large print books.

The title index serves as the primary index inasmuch as it contains all the available bibliographic information for each entry. However, some helpful data, such as book and type size, is missing for most of the entries. One other complaint pertains to the inclusion in every entry of the expression "large type ed."; such identification certainly seems unnecessary in a directory where all items by definition satisfy that criteria. The other indexes supply only author and title information. The general reading subject index is subdivided into 24 categories, such as biography, cooking, fiction (general), romance, self-help, travel, and westerns. The textbooks subject index contains eight divisions, including business and personal skills, English language arts, and social studies. The children's subject index is divided into seven classes: classics, science fiction, and stories. An eighth class (mystery) appears even though it was not identified as such at the top of the index. The headings used in each of these subject indexes are listed at the beginning of each index. The newspapers and periodicals index is arranged alphabetically; it is not a "Serials—Subject Index" as so identified via the running heads. This work, previously known as *Large Type Books in Print*, is an important reference aid for bookstores and public libraries.—**Glenn R. Wittig**

12.   Justice, Keith L. **Bestseller Index: All Books, by Author, on the Lists of** *Publishers Weekly* **and** *The New York Times* **Through 1990.** Jefferson, N.C., McFarland, 1998. 483p. $115.00. ISBN 0-7864-0422-1.

In alphabetic order by author's name, Justice offers entries for the approximately 9,000 titles that appeared on the *Publishers Weekly* (1919-1990) and *The New York Times* (1935-1990) hard cover and paperback bestseller lists. The two lists offer information on publisher; genre; number of weeks, entry position, and peak position on each list; and total number of weeks. Front matter argues the need for and explains the compilation and editorial conventions of the volume, whereas "A Brief History of the Bestseller Lists" chronicles the development of the *Publishers Weekly* and *The New York Times* lists. A title index concludes the volume. Justice proposes only to trace books' "chart activity" in order to provide raw data to both popular and scholarly audiences. He mentions, however, issues of cultural value, historical change, and the "culture business." Students would have been helped had he adumbrated lines of inquiry and interpretation or at least appended a bibliography of scholarship on best-sellers and reading publics. A project of great patience and potential utility, entries were compiled, as the preface notes, on cards rather than as a database, with the exception of the appendixes' tabulations of "Authors with 10 or More Listed Books," "Books Listed for 100 Weeks or More," "Authors Listed for 100 Weeks or More," and "Complete List of Authors and Their Total Weeks." Justice's data await electronic conversion before they can be integrated into scholarship on publishing, reading, and popular taste or can be useful beyond the needs of the browser, biographer, or fact hunter. [R: Choice, July/Aug 98, p. 1831]—**Robert H. Kieft**

13.   Rinderknecht, Carol, and Scott Bruntjen, comps. **A Checklist of American Imprints for 1846: Items 46-1 Through 46-7783.** Lanham, Md., Scarecrow, 1997. 588p. $69.50. ISBN 0-8108-3212-7. ISSN 0361-7920.

Rinderknecht and Bruntjen's "checklist" series of imprints identify early monographs, state and local documents, pamphlets, broadsides, and other material published in the United States during the period from 1820 to 1875. National Union Catalog (NUC) location codes show where each item may be found. A complete list of NUC symbols is appended to volume 200 of *The National Union Catalog, Pre-1956 Imprints*, published by Mansell in 1972.

Based on the World Press Archive's American Imprints Inventory of the 1930s, the series also draws heavily on more recent bibliographies, including work done at Catholic University, which operates the publication program of the historical records survey. Alphabetically arranged by author, each entry lists the author or sponsoring agency, the complete title, bibliographic information, and the NUC location for extant copies. Beginning with the 1840 volume, the compilers have simplified their entry numbers by adding an identification of the year and volume in which it appears. Citations of multiple titles by the same author or agency now include the full name at each entry. These changes have made the checklist easier for researchers to use. This ongoing series is proving to be of great value to researchers, and this volume maintains the high standards the compilers have set. This work is recommended for research collections.—**Susan B. Hagloch**

14.   **Words on Cassette 1998.** New Providence, N.J., Bowker-Saur/Reed Reference Publishing, 1998. 2v. $155.00/set. ISBN 0-8352-3964-0.

This 13th edition of the *Words on Cassette* lists 61,370 individual titles produced by more than 2,000 audiocassette publishers. With the 12th edition, Bowker included a section on the "Best Audiobooks & Audio Winners," which is again included in the edition under review, this time covering awards presented between 1994 and 1997. A feature new to this edition is the flagging of entries produced by members of the Audio Publisher's Association.

The 1st volume in this 2-volume set lists individual books on tape in alphabetic order by title. A standard entry comprises title, author, read by, running time, number of cassettes, Library of Congress Card Number, audience, grade level, price, ordering information, and a brief narrative description of the work.

The 2d volume consists of the award record, producers/distributors listing, and 3 indexes—authors, readers/performers, and subjects. The author and readers/performers indexes refer to title and page number. The subject index is rather simple; most subject headings have numerous entries. For example, the "Art" heading has well over 200 titles listed. The producers/distributors list provides detailed information about the various companies that produce audiobooks. Entries have address, telephone number, and the name of various imprints. One glaring omission is the absences of e-mail or Internet addresses. This work could benefit from this addition; thus providing library patrons the opportunity to order the audiobooks on the Internet directly from the producer.
—**Susan D. Strickland**

Asia

15.   Shulman, Frank Joseph, comp. **Doctoral Dissertations on China and on Inner Asia, 1976-1990: An Annotated Bibliography of Studies in Western Languages.** Westport, Conn., Greenwood Press, 1998. 1055p. index. (Bibliographies and Indexes in Asian Studies, no.2). $245.00. ISBN 0-313-29111-X.

Painstakingly compiled over a 22-year period, this latest bibliography by Shulman continues his fine earlier works, *Doctoral Dissertations on China: A Bibliography of Studies in Western Languages, 1945-1970* (see ARBA 73, entry 257) and *Doctoral Dissertations on China, 1971-1975: A Bibliography of Studies in Western Languages* (see ARBA 79, entry 369). The current volume contains more than 10,000 dissertations in whole or in part on China, Hong Kong, Macao, Mongolia, Taiwan, Tibet, and overseas Chinese communities completed between 1976 and 1990. Some 1,300 dissertations completed between 1945 and 1975 that were omitted in earlier publications are also included. It is truly a comprehensive and multidisciplinary bibliographic guide covering arts and humanities, social sciences, education, theology, law, medicine, architecture, and natural sciences. About one-half of the dissertations cited were submitted to institutions in the United States and the other half completed in 39 other countries. Slightly more than one-half of the dissertations have never appeared in *Dissertations Abstracts International* (DAI).

The entries are classified by broad topics, with a detailed table of contents that can also serve as a subject index. Each entry provides standard bibliographic information, including author, title, institution, year and type of degree awarded, academic discipline, number of pages, DAI reference (when available), and indication of availability of the titles. Short and descriptive annotations are provided, with the exception of some non-English titles. Two statistical tables with distributions of degrees by country/year of the degree and by awarding institutions are informative. The volume concludes with a guide to the availability of the dissertations and three indexes: author, institution, and subject (limited to personal names found in the titles or annotations). Although most of the citations have appeared in Shulman's bibliographic journal *Doctoral Dissertations on Asia*, a compilation of this magnitude brings together a substantial body of China-related dissertations for researchers, students, and librarians, and is a significant contribution. It is an indispensable reference for any higher institution with Asian studies programs.—**Karen T. Wei**

Canada

16.   **Canadian Book Review Annual 1997.** Joyce M. Wilson and others, eds. Toronto, Canadian Book Review Annual, 1998. 654p. index. $115.00. ISBN 0-9682421-0-3. ISSN 0383-770X.

Begun in 1975, *Canadian Book Review Annual* (CBRA) has become the definitive review source for Canadian-authored, Canadian published, English-language publications. CBRA provides authoritative critical reviews, ranging in length from 100 to 400 words, for the current and the previous year's publications that arrived too late for inclusion. Also included are some English translations of French-Canadian and some foreign-language titles, as well as miscellaneous titles that may have been omitted in the past or published before the inception of CBRA. Full bibliographic data are given.

CBRA is a reflection of Canadian National Bibliography in that it attempts to be a comprehensive guide to all types of publications, including reference works, fiction, and nonfiction, as well as children's books. These include softcover editions of books not reviewed if published in hardcover. Publications are divided into reference, arts and humanities, literature and language, social science, science and technology, and children's literature. These 6 sections are subdivided into a total of 56 subsections. The volume concludes with a directory listing of publishers and a subject/author/title index.

It is noteworthy that reviews of children's books include target audience, age range, and a rating. CBRA provides a convenient single selection tool for librarians and the general public interested in Canadian literature.
—**Andrew G. Torok**

BIOGRAPHY

International

17. **Almanac of Famous People: A Comprehensive Reference Guide to More Than 30,000 Famous and Infamous Newsmakers from Biblical Times to the Present.** 6th ed. Frank V. Castronova, ed. Detroit, Gale, 1998. 2v. index. $99.00/set. ISBN 0-7876-0044-X.

The *Almanac of Famous People* comprises a selection of names and references to collective biographies, mostly from the *Biography and Genealogy Master Index* (see entry 404). Alternative names, date and place of birth and death, nationality, occupation, and a one-sentence description are added to each entry. The 2d volume includes indexes by year, month and day, and place of birth and death, plus occupation. Month and day, place of birth and death, and occupation are not accessible in *Biography and Genealogy Master Index* (BGMI).

The subtitle of this work is misleading—although many entertainers and politicians are included, there are numerous entries for scholars and scientists, among others. A cursory inspection of the occupation index showed significant omissions: William Jones and Ferdinand de Saussure (linguists), E. E. Evans-Pritchard, and A. R. Radcliffe-Brown (anthropologists); Christian Thomsen, Boucher de Perthes, and M. Aurel Stein (archaeologists); and W. V. Quine (philosopher), to name a few. *Almanac of Famous People* cannot be assumed to include all the most significant people in each field.

The new edition has the same features as the last. About 2,500 new names are included. This continues to be a valuable source, especially for individuals and small libraries that cannot afford BGMI, but also for the sake of its indexing.—**Frederic F. Burchsted**

18. **The Cambridge Biographical Encyclopedia.** 2d ed. David Crystal, ed. New York, Cambridge University Press, 1998. 1179p. $54.95. ISBN 0-521-63099-1.

Too many reference books try to be more than they should be. A case in point was the 1st edition of this work (see ARBA 95, entry 25), but those excesses have now been eliminated in this 2d edition. Items that can easily be found in more appropriate reference works, such as maps and illustrations, essays on science and the arts, and a listing of contemporary events, have been deleted. Only the tables listing political leaders, Nobel and Pulitzer prize winners, athletic figures, and so forth have been retained in a "Ready Reference" section. This tightening of focus has allowed an increase in the number of entries to 16,000, a full 1,000 more than the previous edition held, even though this edition contains 100 fewer pages than the 1st edition.

Coverage leans toward twentieth-century personalities from English-speaking countries, with greater attention paid to ethnic and minority groups than in the previous edition and in other biographical reference works. Alphabetic entries averaging 70 words give parts of a person's name not generally used (i.e., middle and original names), year of birth and death (when appropriate); and a phonetic pronunciation of a name when not obvious to a native speaker of English. Biographical information includes achievements that made the person prominent, with names and dates of books, films, or other accomplishments. There are more than 22,000 cross-references to related entries and to the "Ready Reference" section. Full-page entries are accorded to some 40 well-known people, such as Napoleon Bonaparte, Ludwig van Beethoven, and Isaac Newton.

The 150-page "Ready Reference" section claims to be a comprehensive presentation of more than 10,000 prominent people in tabular form, but the tenure of Ignace Jan Paderewski as premier of Poland in 1919 is not shown, though noted in his main entry, and in fact no political leaders of Poland are listed for the entire period of 1795 through 1945. This reviewer believes that this section could also be eliminated, as the information is more appropriately found in other reference books. With its improvements and additions, this remains an indispensable library reference work. [R: Choice, Nov 98, p. 489]—**Larry Lobel**

19.   **The Complete Marquis Who's Who on CD-ROM.** [CD-ROM]. New Providence, N.J., Marquis Who's Who/Reed Reference Publishing, 1998. Minimum system requirements (Windows version): IBM or compatible 386. CD-ROM drive. Windows 3.1. 4MB RAM. Minimum system requirements (Macintosh version): 68020 or faster processor. CD-ROM drive. 6MB RAM. $945.25.

Remarkable in its scope and ease of access, this database includes biographies of more than 700,000 individuals, complete with professional and personal details verified by the entrants, from current and past volumes of 18 separate Marquis directories. These include the regional directories, specialized professional directories, *Who's Who in America*, *Who's Who in the World*, *Who's Who of American Women*, and *Who Was Who in America* (vols. 9 and 10). Due to the large number of entries, listings are divided between two CD-ROMs. The first contains listings that appear in a current Marquis volume. The second CD-ROM includes listings that appeared in a previous volume but do not appear in a current volume. The database covers 1985 to the present.

Through a series of interactive templates, users can easily search any number of fields to retrieve pertinent biographies. These fields include last name, first name, birth place, birth year, occupation, category, full-text search for words or phrases, educational and career information, general information, mailing address information and biographical sketch. One or more of these elements can be combined to customize searching as necessary. Wildcard and focused searches are also possible, as are printing, exporting, creating bookmarks, and creating a "shadow file" that allows users to create their own database—all, of course, within the parameters of the licensing agreements.

Considering the cost of the various print volumes, the cost of this electronic database stands to save thousands of dollars for most libraries needing this information. The database has a variety of uses and potential users, not the least of which are students, researchers, marketers, alumni associations, fund-raising organizations, and reference librarians. This CD-ROM is highly recommended for its value-added qualities.—**Edmund F. SantaVicca**

20.   **Contemporary Heroes and Heroines, Book III.** Terrie M. Rooney and Karen E. Lemerand, eds. Farmington Hills, Mich., Gale, 1998. 699p. illus. index. $63.00. ISBN 0-7876-2215-X.

Contemporary Heroes and Heroines, Book III adds 100 profiles of men and women whose exemplary achievements will interest and inspire young adults to previously published *Book I* and *Book II* (see ARBA 93, entry 45, and ARBA 91, entry 12). Each entry includes a photograph; basic statistics about each hero and heroine; a discussion about motivations, ambitions, and accomplishments; and a mailing address for those still living. Each profile is concluded with a list of sources used.

The entries are alphabetic in the body of the volume. The table of contents is an alphabetic list of the included individuals with a brief description of their claim to fame. The contents pages are followed by the heroes and heroines listed by their field of endeavor. The index of this volume covers all three volumes of the series. This set is a handy source of biographical information in compact form, a useful tool for small or financially challenged libraries. This Gale publication is also available through LEXIS-NEXIS under "Gale Biographies." [R: BL, 15 Nov 98, p. 610]—**Sue Brown**

21.   **Dictionary of International Biography 1998: A Biographical Record of Contemporary Achievement.** 26th ed. Cambridge, England, International Biographical Centre; distr., Bristol, Pa., Taylor & Francis, 1998. 587p. illus. $240.00. ISBN 0-948875-03-8.

After 25 years of reference work this reviewer has found that there is a limit to the number of biographical dictionaries a collection needs, and this may be beyond that limit. The 26th edition of the *Dictionary of International Biography* (DIB) published in Cambridge, England, attempts to reflect "contemporary achievement" in every field of interest and from every country. Few entries are carried from one issue to the next, and the total sums 190,000 entries to date. The publisher lists 20 other titles in its series, but DIB seems to be the flagship.

The entries are usual for such dictionaries—listed alphabetically by name, with birth date, family information, achievements, and the like. The publisher assures us that those included have not paid for inclusion and that the names are chosen by a distinguished panel of experts. There is no cumulative index. One feature that is helpful is the reference to other biographical sources where the person is included. That list includes about 200 sources—all the dictionaries one has ever heard of as well as some one has not. The entries include about one picture per page. A survey of these special inclusions indicates that the majority of these are academics, as are many of the total entries included.

Any library having this series may wish to continue, but if not, there is no need to bother purchasing this volume. A further limitation is that the title is not included in Gale's *Biography and Genealogy Master Index* (see entry 404). When looking for biographies, there are numerous other sources.—**Paul A. Mogren**

22. **Encyclopedia of Biography.** 1996 ed. C. S. Nicholls, ed. New York, St. Martin's Press, 1996. 1046p. illus. index. $80.00. ISBN 0-312-17568-X.
     This encyclopedia is a nice companion to *Webster's Biographical Dictionary*. The *Encyclopedia of Biography* has biographical entries for people that *Webster's* does not, and the reverse is also true. The *Encyclopedia* includes biographies of more than 10,000 people with particular concern for the twentieth century, women, scientists, sports figures, musicians, writers, and artists. Entries for each person are short (one or two paragraphs) but are packed with detail. The entry for Kareem Abdul Jabbar includes his height (which my patron was looking for), his favorite shot (the sky-hook), his original name, his awards, whom he played for, and his winning championships. The entries are made more interesting with portraits, quotations, and suggestions for further reading. The appendix at the end contains many useful tables, including winners of the Booker, Pulitzer, and Nobel Peace Prize; the archbishops of Canterbury; English sovereigns; rulers of France, Scotland and Russia; and other historical facts. The *Encyclopedia of Biography* is highly recommended for quick help with biography questions and is sure to be useful for years in the reference collection.—**Carol D. Henry**

23. **Encyclopedia of World Biography.** 2d ed. Detroit, Gale, 1998. 17v. illus. index. $975.00/set. ISBN 0-7876-2221-4.
     This new edition of the standard work represents a comprehensive source for biographical information on nearly 7,000 internationally known individuals who have made substantial contributions to human culture and society. The 1st edition was published nearly 25 years ago with several supplementary volumes by its former publisher, Jack Heraty and Associates. This 2d edition includes all entries from the 1st edition and its 3 supplements with some updates, along with 530 new entries especially prepared for this edition. Most selections are well justified. For example, entries from the first volume include Hugo Alvar Henrick Aalto (Finnish architect), Abba Arila (Jewish scholar), Abdul-Hamid II (Turkish sultan), Ralph David Abernathy (associate of Martin Luther King, Jr.), Bella Stavisky Abzug (liberal attorney from New York), Dean Acheson (secretary of state), Felix Adler (educator), Alexander Archipenko (sculptor), Ludovico Ariosto (Italian Renaissance poet), and hundreds of others. Most biographical sketches contain reference sources for additional information. A consolidated index enables the user to locate desired data as well as photographs. [R: Choice, Sept 98, pp. 81-82; RUSQ, Summer 98, p. 377-378; SLJ, Aug 98, p. 190; VOYA, Oct 98, p. 306]—**Bohdan S. Wynar**

24. **Heroes and Pioneers.** Judy Culligan, ed. New York, Macmillan Library Reference/Simon & Schuster Macmillan, 1998. 414p. illus. index. (Macmillan Profiles, v.3). $75.00. ISBN 0-02-865059-X.
     Volume 3 of the Macmillan Profiles series *Heroes and Pioneers* provides brief biographies for 137 multicultural figures from ancient times through the present and is written especially for the older elementary or middle school student. Those personages who are included in the volume were chosen based on their relevance to school curriculum, their importance in history, and their representation of a broad cultural range. The people featured in this volume include America's founding fathers; American and foreign national heroes; wartime heroes; reformers, humanitarians, and civil rights activists; crime fighters; peace activists; explorers and astronauts; and pioneers. Helpful page format design includes timelines, notable quotations, pull quotes highlighting essential facts, difficult words defined in sidebars, and additional sidebars amplifying topics. A table of contents, an index, a glossary, and a reading list for additional information about each person are provided. A list of contributors and sources is also given. Length of biographies runs from half a page to several pages depending on the contributions of the person. Although this volume is not useful for in-depth research by students, it provides concise biographies

that give students the essential facts and contributions for each person included. The broad scope of the book makes it a worthwhile purchase for general school and public library use.—**Janet Hilbun**

25. **Index to Marquis Who's Who Publications 1998.** New Providence, N.J., Marquis Who's Who/Reed Reference Publishing, 1998. 520p. $110.00. ISBN 0-8379-1435-3. ISSN 1080-1154.

The *Index to Marquis Who's Who Publications 1998* provides access to entries in 15 Marquis "Who's Who" publications. As stated in the work's preface, this amounts to nearly 309,000 individual's names. The publications indexed include *Who's Who in American Law*, 9th edition; *Who's Who of American Women*, 20th edition; *Who's Who in American Education*, 5th edition; *Who's Who in Entertainment*, 3d edition; *Who's Who in Medicine and Healthcare*, 1st edition; *Who's Who in the Media and Communications*, 1st edition; *Who's Who in the Midwest*, 25th edition; *Who's Who in American Nursing*, 6th edition; *Who's Who in Science and Engineering*, 4th edition; *Who's Who in the South and Southwest*, 25th edition; *Who's Who in America*, 52d edition; *Who's Who in the East*, 26th edition; *Who's Who in Finance and Industry*, 15th edition; and *Who's Who in the West*, 26th edition.

Entries for the index are abbreviated with both time and edition number. For example, *Who's Who in American Law*, 9th edition is abbreviated as "AL09." Most abbreviations are fairly obvious, but it does require a quick flip to the front of the book to remember that WP26 stands for *Who's Who in the West*, 26th edition. Although the font is small, the print quality makes it legible. The paper stock quality is good, hopefully avoiding the page tears that plague some other indexes.

If a library has already invested in obtaining the majority of the 15 print publications included in the index, the extra $110 for this book may seem relatively inexpensive. Considering the less than stellar reviews for Marquis' searchable CD-ROM product, a print index may be well advised (see ARBA 98, entry 28). Often libraries must discontinue print versions to afford the cost of updating electronic products. Keeping the print publications and buying a comprehensive print index may seem a safer, although conservative, course of action.

With no glaring mistakes or problems to be found, the index appears to be a welcome addition to any reference collection that utilizes Marquis Who's Who publications. If the library owns most of the indexed works, this book should be kept in ready-reference as a handy timesaver. This index is highly recommended for large public or academic libraries that use Marquis "Who's Who" products as significant biographical reference resources.

—**Sandra E. Fuentes**

26. **The International Who's Who of Women.** 2d ed. London, Europa; distr., Detroit, Gale, 1997. 628p. index. $390.00. ISBN 1-85743-027-1. ISSN 0965-3775.

Created by the respected publisher of *The Europa World Book* (see entry 66), this biographical reference about women is now in its 2d edition. The book provides essential information about the lives and achievements of more than 5,500 notable women from around the world. Entries are arranged alphabetically, each including name, title, academic degrees, address, telephone number, telex and fax numbers, date and place of birth, nationality, family details, education, profession, career history, present position, honors, awards, prizes, major publications, films, plays, recordings, and leisure interests. A career index helps users locate information about women in specific fields or professions.

The purported goal of the book "to redress the balance [of women's unequal representation in who's who books]" is certainly worthy and the data are useful. However, the publisher does not clearly define the scope of the book or discuss the selection criteria. This leaves one to wonder why, for example, there are entries for U.S. writers Ann Tyler and Louise Erdrich, but not for Barbara Kingsolver or for the award-winning poet Mary Oliver. Also, as might be expected, there is more thorough representation of women from English-speaking countries than those from other areas. Such discrepancies are inevitable in this type of work, but the issue could be clarified to some degree by a brief statement from the publisher.

Of more concern to potential purchasers is the overlap with other publications. Presumably, many or even most of the names in this volume appear in *International Who's Who 1998-99* (Europa, 1998). Because the prices of the two books are comparable, but the coverage is different (*International Who's Who* covers more than 20,000 individuals—including a large percentage of women), potential users of this book should consider which of the two publications will better suit their needs and budgets.—**Barbara Ittner**

27.   Madigan, Carol Orsag, and Ann Elwood. **When They Were Kids: Over 400 Sketches of Famous Child-hoods.** New York, Random House, 1998. 326p. illus. index. $14.95pa. ISBN 0-375-70389-6.

Anecdotal sketches about the childhoods of celebrities, focusing on their home, school, and social life, compose this volume. It covers personalities throughout history and from many disciplines (e.g., art, science, entertainment, politics). Inclusion depends upon the quality of the stories and their suitability to existing subject categories. The aim throughout the work is to display factors important in their development and themes of childhood familiar to us all.

The 8 chapters, with topics such as "Thoughts and Aspirations," "Hard Knocks," and "Being Different," are divided into subsections, including past traumas and inspirations. Interspersed throughout are quotes from the personalities as well as black-and-white portraits. There is an extensive bibliography and an index, enabling access to all stories about a subject or person.

The arrangement of this book highlights common occurrences in childhood, rather than individual celebrities. Although such a slant provides a different perspective on famous figures, it also necessitates looking elsewhere if full biographical information is sought.—**Anita Zutis**

28.   **Men of Achievement 1997.** 17th ed. Nicholas S. Law, ed. Cambridge, England, International Biographical Centre; distr., Bristol, Pa., Taylor & Francis, 1997. 705p. illus. $225.00. ISBN 0-948875-27-5.

The foreword to this work states that it includes some 5,000 men "of remarkable achievement throughout the world and brings the total of those recognized in the series so far to more than 30,000. And there is still a long way to go." According to the publisher, many learned societies, universities, and other national and international institutions (far too numerous to list) have closely cooperated with the International Biographical Centre (IBC) by recommending high-achieving members for inclusion in *Men of Achievement*. The publisher also has in its warehouse *Two Thousand Women of Achievement*, which was later expanded into *The World Who's Who of Women*.

Men of Achievement also contains two long lists: "Deputy Directors General of the IBC" and a shorter list titled "Research Fellows of the IBC." There are several individuals listed with pictures in the "Dedication" section. There are brief biographies and an "Honours List." There is no question that this dictionary contains the names of some important people who are nationally known. It also contains many less important people and, unfortunately, many individuals of interest only to local communities.—**Bohdan S. Wynar**

29.   **Who's Who in Australasia and the Pacific Nations.** 3d ed. Cambridge, England, International Biographical Centre; distr., Bristol, Pa., Taylor & Francis, 1997. 491p. $165.00. ISBN 0-948875-42-9.

Increasingly, Websites provide a wide range of biographical information about people throughout the world. That information is sometimes very brief, and to date, Websites have not replaced biographical dictionaries as the ultimate source for information about, in particular, lesser-known people. The larger the library, and the more extensive access it provides to electronic information, the greater the need for a comprehensive collection of biographical dictionaries.

What was *Who's Who in Australasia and the Far East* in its first 2 editions (see ARBA 91, entry 16) has now become *Who's Who in Australasia and the Pacific Nations*. It is 1 of 19 such publications by the International Biographical Centre. Although the International Biographical Centre charges no fees and includes people by invitation only, it does inundate potential candidates for inclusion with mailings, all of which promote the purchase of the book. One wonders whether or not the primary market for this, like so many other contemporary biographical dictionaries, is not sales to those included rather than to libraries.

This is a standard biographical dictionary. A one-page introduction and a long list of abbreviations are followed by a straightforward alphabetic listing of brief biographical information for about 4,000 people in a wide variety of occupations, professions, and trades in some 32 countries and territories. An appendix lists about 300 organizations, societies, and associations that have contributed—presumably by making mailing lists of their members available for solicitation—to the compilation of this publication. As biographical dictionaries go, this is a reasonable and useful publication but one of considerably greater value in the countries covered than in the United States. In most cases, biographical information about prominent people from Australasia and the Far East, which is what most U.S. library users are apt to be seeking, can be found in other sources. For larger libraries *Who's Who in Australia*, which includes more than 8,000 Australians alone, and other country-by-country biographical dictionaries are likely to be more useful.—**Norman D. Stevens**

30. **Who's Who in the World 1998.** 15th ed. New Providence, N.J., Marquis Who's Who/Reed Reference Publishing, 1997. 1602p. $369.95. ISBN 0-8379-1119-2. ISSN 0083-9825.

It is difficult to review any Marquis "Who's Who" directory because the "Who's Who" books are already accepted as staples in reference collections and most librarians are familiar with them. This acceptance does emphasize the fact that Marquis "Who's Who" publications tend to be consistent in format and quality.

Who's Who in the World is a perfect starting place for students who sometimes lack basic facts when beginning a biographical paper on an internationally notable person. Up to 19 types of biographical information may be included in an entry, from name and occupation to more difficult to obtain items, such as religious affiliation and an office mailing address. Readers can easily interpret any confusing entries by turning to the large-font "Key to Information" and "Table of Abbreviations." A wide variety of professions and concerns are represented, from world political leaders to child psychologists. Writers and researchers for a variety of fields may use it to check for accurate spelling, dates, and background information on individuals.

The obvious drawback of *Who's Who in the World* is that the world is too large a scope for any editorial board to provide complete satisfaction in its final selection of entries. Previous reviews of *Who's Who in the World* have pointedly analyzed the balance of coverage. Criticism is usually directed to an over-abundance of Western names or Western origins in a work of multinational scope (see ARBA 97, entry 29). A Western bias is not unexpected for such a large, U.S.-produced work, and librarians know that some compensation with other material may be required.

Another problem with evaluating the utility of this book is the sheer variety of alternate choices, often in nonprint formats. Patrons, particularly students in academic library environments, frequently ask for data that can be sent to a network printer or saved on a disc. With CD-ROM and online database products on the market, many librarians now reach for their mouse and keyboard first when answering a biographical reference question. However, it should be noted that among the popular electronic products are those that index print biographical resources. Also, Marquis Who's Who does produce a CD-ROM product titled *The Complete Marquis Who's Who on CD-ROM* (see ARBA 98, entry 28).

Patrons doing biographical research may also have higher expectations about information. Many library users ask for something that will contain a picture, provide human interest, or describe rather than list a person's accomplishments. *Who's Who in the World* is not suited to providing information that would suggest the personality behind the name, nor are there pictures.

Despite problems with changing expectations, it is often necessary to consult a work such as *Who's Who in the World*. This book is a comprehensive starting point, providing information that aids more thorough searching. It is often difficult to find information on people of recent international accomplishment. The comprehensiveness of *Who's Who in the World*, relative to biographical dictionaries and subject encyclopedias, makes it an automatic selection for reference collections. In the future, demands of a changing information world may require librarians to reevaluate the preferred status of *Who's Who in the World*. For now, it is a safe bet for biographical reference and is recommended for public and academic libraries.—**Sandra E. Fuentes**

31. **Who's Who 1998: An Annual Biographical Dictionary.** 150th ed. New York, St. Martin's Press, 1998. 2208p. $225.00. ISBN 0-312-17591-4.

Reviewing *Who's Who* is similar to reviewing the U.S. Constitution; it is not a book, it is an institution, a work in progress. This reference work is the original biographical dictionary upon which all the other Who's Who biographies of the world are based. Beginning with the 1st edition in 1849, the annual is an autobiographical reference, listing the most important and influential people of the time. The 30,000 individuals included in this latest edition are from all occupations and all parts of the world. A close examination of the listings, however, uncovers a decidedly British and masculine preponderance of entries.

Entry into *Who's Who* is by invitation only. The anonymous selection board makes its choices by keeping abreast of current events, accepting suggestions, and soliciting advice from experts in various fields. Potential candidates are carefully screened because a listing in *Who's Who* is for a lifetime. In this 150th edition, only 1,000 new names have been added. No "five-day wonders" are included in this reference work. A new entrant is sent questionnaires to fill in should he or she accept inclusion. In a continuing effort to keep the material timely, all subjects of biographies are given the opportunity to update their information annually. The editors claim tens of thousands of amendments made annually. Also included is an obituary.

This classic reference work is an excellent primary reference source for any library. Its rather expensive price might make it more suitable for purchase every three or four years for smaller libraries.—**Nancy P. Reed**

32. **World Biographical Index.** 3d ed. New Providence, N.J., K. G. Saur, 1997. Minimum system requirements: IBM or compatible 386. CD-ROM drive. Windows 3.1. 4MB RAM. 5MB hard disk space. Mouse. DM 1,980.00. ISBN 3-598-40396-8.

The *World Biographical Index* provides access to biographical information on thousands of individuals throughout history. The main use of this comprehensive index is to locate a biography contained within 1 of the 11 indexed biographical archives produced by K. G. Saur. Entries cite the proper archive to locate biographical information on the desired individual.

This multilingual resource provides an additional service—it directs users to general reference books containing biographical data about the individual in question. Although some titles may be esoteric or in a foreign language, others, such as Runes' *Who's Who in Philosophy*, may be available in larger public or academic libraries.

Two types of searches are available: biographical and bibliographic. The biographical screen allows users to search 11 different fields (e.g., name, gender, birth date, death date, occupation). The bibliographic screen provides three access points: source, bibliographic data, and archive. Each field has a separate index so users can click on the index, select the proper term (e.g., Wilson, Woodrow), and conduct the search. The search results screen provides enough information to determine if the person found is the person needed.

Installation is simple, but one should be careful when beginning the start up—the proper language must be selected. Attempting to understand setup directions in German can be problematic for the monolingual librarian.
                                                                                    —**Susan D. Strickland**

United States

33. **Dictionary of American Biography.** [CD-ROM]. New York, Scribner's/Simon & Schuster Macmillan, 1997. Minimum system requirements: Windows 3.1 or higher, 16 MB RAM, and color monitor required. Also available for Macintosh computers. $599.00/single user. ISBN 0-684-80583-9.

Containing the biographies of more than 19,000 notable Americans (all of whom died before January 1981), the CD-ROM version of the venerated *Dictionary of American Biography* is an impressive attempt to make often dry historical information more engaging and possibly more accessible to students. The resource contains hypertext cross-references and the ability to search in numerous modes, such as by occupation, gender, and keywords as well as the usual access by the last name of the subject. Advanced searching techniques are also provided, including Boolean searching, truncation, proximity operators, wildcards, and use of exact phrase.

The program operates in a Windows 3.1 or Window 95 environment and uses Netscape Communicator as its browser. However, users do not need to be online for the program to function. Installation on a PC with Windows 95 was a simple two-step operation; if the PC has Communicator already installed, the process will be shorter. Written comprehensive instruction is provided.

The program includes a help section, called "Research Reminders," which deals basically with the occupations search facility. Use of the latter involves clicking on a picture of a representative of the selected occupation; a list of those indexed under that category then appears. This system works reasonably well (although a later version may want to change the category "Indian Chief"). The list of 700 occupations listed in the "In-Depth Search" section is both general and specific—categories range from the general *inventor* to *apiarist*, from *senator* to *singing evangelist*.

The major problem with this program lies with its hypertext links and would keep this reviewer from utilizing the program. Whatever cross-referencing program Macmillan used found all references to any of the subjects regardless of context. Samuel Clemens's father was John Marshall Clemens. Clicking on the father's name in order to find out more information about him sends the user to the biography of the Supreme Court Justice, John Marshall; which has nothing to do with Samuel Clemens. Both of Ed Sullivan's parents are hypertext links—neither has any connection to Ed Sullivan, nor does the hypertext link to Sir Walter Scott in the same entry deal with the Scottish author. The problem may not occur in each and every entry, but it appears often enough to be confusing to student researchers.

A call to the Macmillan Company revealed that at present, graduate students are working their way through the program looking for errors and that a new version is not scheduled until the year 2000. The representative seemed unaware of the cross-referencing problem. For the time being, the print version, although not glitzy, is a better choice for research. [R: RUSQ, Summer 98, p. 334; BL, 15 May 98, p. 1656]

—**Michele Tyrrell**

34.   **The Last Word:** *The New York Times* **Book of Obituaries and Farewells: A Celebration of Unusual Lives.** Marvin Siegel, ed. New York, William Morrow, 1997. 426p. $25.00. ISBN 0-688-15015-2.

Marvin Siegel has been a newspaperman in New York City for almost 40 years, and during that time he has seen obituaries published in *The Times* ranging from colorful to downright entertaining. In *The Last Word* he has collected 100 of these obituaries by some of *The Times'* most well-known writers, including Charlayne Hunter-Gault, Anna Quindlen, Wendy Wasserstein, and William Styron. For the most part, the people selected to have their obituaries reprinted here are not celebrities but individuals who have made an impact on our modern world and a few who have lived quirky lives.

The Last Word provides fascinating reading. One learns about the man who invented nylon, the first Miss America, the man who perfected popcorn, and the zoot suit. But as a reference work it leaves much to be desired. It is not indexed, which makes it almost unusable as a reference tool. It is necessary to read through each obituary to find out what makes the individual interesting. This is fine, of course, if one is just looking for an interesting read. The items are dated at the end, but the editor does not indicate if that is the date the item appeared in *The New York Times* or if that was when "advance obituary" information was obtained.

The work is most definitely recommended for all library collections large and small, but it should not be considered a reference work or be placed in a reference collection. It should be considered for private collections because it will provide hours of interesting reading.—**Robert L. Wick**

35.   **The Scribner Encyclopedia of American Lives: Volume 1, 1981-1985.** Kenneth T. Jackson, Karen Markoe, and Arnold Markoe, eds. New York, Macmillan Library Reference/Simon & Schuster Macmillan, 1998. 930p. illus. $110.00. ISBN 0-684-80492-1.

The lives of 494 notable individuals who died between 1981 and 1985 are chronicled in this 1st volume of American biographies to be published by Scribner since their legal settlement with the American Council of Learned Societies. Although not every person included was born in the United States, all made their major professional contributions or obtained their notoriety—five crime figures are included—while living here.

Each entry begins with date and place of birth and death, followed by a brief description of the person's accomplishments. Significant details noted for each person include parents' names and professions, spouse's names and dates of marriages, number of offspring, and place of burial. Most entries are about two pages in length and are accompanied by a photograph. Locations of personal papers, titles of autobiographies and biographies, and citations to obituaries are appended to each entry. An occupations index and a directory of contributors complete the volume.

This work is authoritative, well written, and attractively produced. The editors have deftly woven the contributions of many different authors into one seamless and captivating work. The result is a reference work that contains more than simply straightforward facts. After volume 2 is published in December 1998, successive volumes are scheduled for publication every five to eight years. The economical price and the publication schedule should fit this reference tool into the budget of many different types of libraries.—**Deborah Sharp**

36.   **Who's Who in the Midwest 1998-1999.** 26th ed. New Providence, N.J., Marquis Who's Who/Reed Reference Publishing, 1998. 698p. index. $259.95. ISBN 0-8379-0728-4. ISSN 0083-9787.

Another collection of fine-print, abbreviated biographies of persons nominated by peers and others, this volume includes persons living or influential in Illinois, Indiana, Iowa, Kansas, Michigan, Minnesota, Missouri, Nebraska, North Dakota, Ohio, South Dakota, and Wisconsin as well as Manitoba and western Ontario. Although one suspects that quantity may take precedence over a diligent search for the most qualified, surely that is not all bad. Although the biographee is used most often as source, the facts on some prominent people are researched by the staff. The editors appear to make every effort to make each entry as accurate as possible, asking biographees to verify the version that will actually be printed. The introductory material states that the Who's Who series serves the need for general information. Although this volume is not comprehensive for persons of achievement and influence in the population, libraries that serve patrons seeking current biographic data may want to include volumes in the large series by this publisher.—**Edna M. Boardman**

37.   **Who's Who in the South and Southwest 1999-2000.** 26th ed. New Providence, N.J., Marquis Who's Who/Reed Reference Publishing, 1998. 818p. index. $259.95. ISBN 0-8379-0829-9. ISSN 0083-9809.

Who's Who in the South and Southwest is one of four titles in the Marquis Who's Who in America Regional series. Concentrating on people who have had a major influence on the South and Southwest as well as Mexico and Puerto Rico, this volume covers governmental officials, judges and lawyers, educators, administrators, executives in the media, religious leaders, physicians and health care professionals, professional sports figures, union leaders, heads of charities, scientists, and artists in all fields.

There are 19 possible categories of information that make up each biography, including address, occupation, work history, memberships, political affiliations, writings, career highlights, and certifications. The editorial staff and board of advisers gather possible entries from their own recommendations and from people in the public who nominate themselves or others. People can now nominate themselves by e-mailing the Marquis Website. The names are then screened according to their positions of responsibility and their level of achievement. The information in the entries is checked for completeness by the biographees themselves, ensuring accuracy. There is also a professional index that lists biographies by occupation; under each occupational category the names are listed by country, state, and city.

Who's Who in the South and Southwest would be useful in any large public library business collection as well as in smaller public libraries in the region. Anyone trying to find business and social contacts in the southern part of the country will use this resource.—**Carol D. Henry**

Canada

38.   **Canadian Who's Who 1997, Volume XXXII.** Elizabeth Lumley, ed. Buffalo, N.Y., and Toronto, University of Toronto Press, 1997. 1360p. $170.00. ISBN 0-8020-4996-6.

A bulky volume of more than 1,300 pages in 11-by-8½-inch size, bound in red, the annual *Canadian Who's Who* (CWW) is so distinctive that it has been shown as a prop in advertisements for luxury apartments. Firmly established as the basic reference source about Canadians selected for inclusion on the basis of the position they hold or the contribution they have made to Canadian life, CWW 1997 presents 15,000 current autobiographies. The format is three columns per page with entries ranging from six lines (Jean-Luc Brassard, freestyle skier) to two columns for astronaut Roberta Bondar. For this volume more than 5,000 individuals were invited to complete the questionnaire used in new entries, whereas those listed in previous editions were twice requested to update their biographies. Although there is a standard sequence for the structure of entries, biographees are free to tell their stories, with one writer identifying himself as an "exemplary person" and another, the lower-case poet bill bissett, reporting "59 books uv poetree 7 wun person shows." Bearing in mind that participation is voluntary, my sample searches in this volume indicate broad representation of Canadians in business, politics, research and academic life, aboriginal affairs, cultural industries, journalism, belles lettres, classical and popular music, sports, and labor. CWW, now also available on CD-ROM, remains a Canadian standard.—**Patricia Fleming**

Great Britain

39.   Kanner, Barbara Penny, and others. **Women in Context: Two Hundred Years of British Women Autobiographers, a Reference Guide and Reader.** New York, G. K. Hall/Simon & Schuster Macmillan, 1997. 1049p. index. $60.00. ISBN 0-8161-7346-X.

This impressive reference work does an excellent job of filling a sizable gap in women's history by providing in one large volume both an extensive bibliography of previously unrecognized autobiographies by British women and detailed summary abstracts of those autobiographies. Kanner and her contributors have identified 1,040 autobiographies by 812 women. The guide is limited to narratives by British women, born between 1700 and 1920, that meet the current definition of autobiography but are not widely recognized by academic researchers. Although a few of the writers are well known (Hester Thrale Piozzi, Sylvia Pankhurst), most have received little or no attention. Many are from the middle and lower classes, and recount their education, relationships, and careers as working-class women. Overall, the collection provides a detailed, personal view of women's lives that, as stated in the introduction, often "violate[s] our . . . indoctrination concerning . . . gender roles, parental ties, sibling interactions, and sexual mores" (p. xxxi).

Entries are arranged alphabetically by the author's name. As might be expected, the largest number come from the more recent periods, with only 69 of the 1,040 entries prior to 1800, whereas nearly 500 are from 1861 or later. Each entry includes 4 parts—a bibliographical entry for the autobiography; brief biographical data covering family, career, major activities, other publications, and social class of origin; a detailed summary abstract of the autobiography listing key points, observations, and attitudes; and a brief additional statement focusing on the author's major messages.

The introduction provides a thoughtful overview of the social and cultural milieus presented in the autobiographies analyzed as well as a discussion of the stylistic changes in women's autobiographies over time. Three indexes provide useful access points. The first lists authors by 20-year birth date cohorts; the second indexes key biographical facts about each author, such as career, social class, area of activism, and others; and the third is a subject index drawing terms from the complete entries.

Kanner has given us an extremely valuable reference work that will be of special interest to researchers in women's history, women writers, and social history of the eighteenth and nineteenth centuries. It is especially important in its focus on previously unrecognized writers, particularly those from the middle and lower social classes whose lives and experiences provide windows into often-overlooked social and cultural venues. It should be a welcome addition to any collection serving serious researchers in women's studies, history, or literature. [R: RUSQ, Summer 98, p. 309-310]—**Susan Davis Herring**

DICTIONARIES AND ENCYCLOPEDIAS

40.   Auchter, Dorothy. **Dictionary of Historical Allusions and Eponyms.** Santa Barbara, Calif., ABC-CLIO, 1998. 295p. index. $65.00. ISBN 0-87436-950-9.

One indication that a language is growing and developing is the incorporation of words and phrases carrying a history, or alluding to well-known historical persons and events. Such is the case in this work by Dorothy Auchter. In this respect it joins a multitude of comparable collections of allusions and eponyms. However, what distinguishes it from its counterparts are the citations establishing word and phrase origins.

Adrian Room's revision of *Brewer's Dictionary of Phrase and Fable* (15th ed.; HarperCollins, 1995) contains some of the same eponyms and historical allusions—*Gretna Green marriages, hair shirt, martinet, tontine,* to name a few. In fact, Auchter refers more than once to Brewer's 14th edition, as well as other similar sources, to substantiate a term's origin. This emphasis on historical origin is the unique focus of the dictionary. Auchter documents each of the nearly 600 entries with 2 to 6 sources. These references to secondary sources include reference works, articles in journals and magazines, and a wide variety of monographs. In a singular instance the entry for the eponym "crapper" cites an article and notes the URL (uniform resource locator) for finding it full-text on the Internet.

Although there is no cumulative bibliography, the short lists following each entry serve this function, as well as noting additional secondary sources useful for searching similar types of words. For example, the *Dictionary of the Middle Ages* (see ARBA 90, entry 533) and *The Oxford Classical Dictionary* (3d ed.; Oxford, 1996) might also be checked for clues to meanings. The subject index groups the entries into broad categories, such as drugs, politics, and trade and commerce, based on origin.

The entries themselves are both interesting and well written. For readers who love words, the book is a delight. Because of its unique feature, the dictionary should find a niche in academic and public libraries. The latter may also want an additional copy for the circulating collection. [R: BL, 1 Nov 98, p. 532, 534; Choice, Dec 98, p. 657]
—**Bernice Bergup**

41.   **The Canadian Oxford Dictionary.** Katherine Barber, ed. Don Mills, Ont., Oxford University Press Canada, 1998. 1707p. $39.95. ISBN 0-19-541120-X.

The Canadian Oxford Dictionary defines approximately 130,000 English words as they are used in Canada and around the world, but it is more than a dictionary, offering semiencyclopedia information on approximately

6,000 place-names, 6,000 significant people, 300 mythological figures, and more than 400 historical events. Pronunciations are given for most words, all foreign place-names, and people's names, although not for compound phrases when the individual word pronunciations are given elsewhere. The preferred spelling is by Canadian usage ("colour") rather than the American ("color"), and the definitions include variant spellings, alternative forms of names, a part of speech identifier, and the word's inflection. Plurals of nouns are given, as are lists of adjectival and adverbal comparatives and superlatives. Illustrative examples are provided, as are general usages, derivatives, homographs, and cross-references. Brief etymologies are furnished; the approximate date of the word entered Canadian English is not, nor are there any illustrations.

Canadian libraries will certainly welcome this well-made dictionary, as will those American academic libraries in which Canada and its history are a significant part of the curriculum. It must be emphasized, however, that the dictionary's focus is on Canadian English, and those wanting definitions of French Canadian and joual terms will need to rely on such other works as the *Dictionnaire du Français Québécois* (1985).

—**Richard Bleiler**

42.   **Chambers 21st Century Dictionary.** Mairi Robinson and George Davidson, eds. New York, Larousse Kingfisher Chambers, 1996. 1654p. $30.00. ISBN 0-550-10625-1.

The dustwrapper of the *Chambers 21st Century Dictionary* states that "it uses a completely new and innovative approach to the material it presents, bringing the language we use every day alive." However, in most respects it is a perfectly ordinary dictionary, providing definitions for approximately 110,000 words and idiomatic phrases that are in general contemporary usage. Pronunciations are given for most words. Definitions include an idiomatic phrase; alternative headwords, variant spellings, and cross-references are given when necessary, as are the plurals of nouns and an etymological indication of the origin of the word and the approximate date it entered the English language. The dictionary itself contains occasional lists and sidebars giving, for example, common abbreviations, nonprefixed words, and explanations of the differences between *avoid* and *evade* and *farther* and *further*. There are no illustrations, nor are syllabications given.

The *21st Century Dictionary* is intended primarily for a British audience. Its preferred spellings are British (i.e., "colour" and "favour") rather than the contemporary American ("color" and "favor"), and its definitions occasionally reflect a focus that will more likely than not fail to assist contemporary Americans: two of the four definitions of *PC* are "police constable" and "privy councillor." Although *WWW* is among the contemporary acronyms defined, *URL* is not, and users may be bewildered at the list of abbreviations that defines *et cetera* as the abbreviation of "et cetera" and fails to list "etc." Larger academic libraries may find a use for this dictionary, but it need not be an essential purchase.—**Richard Bleiler**

43.   Dalzell, Tom. **The Slang of Sin.** Springfield, Mass., Merriam-Webster, 1998. 385p. index. $20.00; $14.95pa. ISBN 0-87779-356-5; 0-87779-627-0pa.

The author of *Flappers 2 Rappers* (Merriam-Webster, 1996), Berkeley labor lawyer, and noted "slang-meister," author Dalzell offers an entertaining and exhaustive, although uneven, tour of slang having to do with sin. Dalzell defines sin loosely in his introduction, encompassing nearly anything that might make one feel guilty, including drinking coffee, fortune-telling, and pornographic movies. The focus is on the social history of the slang, which is broken down into 8 chapters, each focusing on a general category of vice, such as gambling, drugs, or sex. Each chapter begins with a vivid introduction to the history of and fascination with the vice in question; most of each chapter is devoted to alphabetically organized short entries, each giving a short definition. Occasionally an example sentence or date of origin is given, but most entries are a sentence long. No pronunciation guide or etymology is offered in these short entries, leaving the words of one era or country of origin to mingle with those of another.

The short entries are not the strength of the work, however. Throughout, words are singled out for longer featured sidebar entries, which include etymology and usage. Also, at the end of each chapter, several "word histories" are included, in which Dalzell traces the origin and usage of a word in detail, using an impressive variety of supporting materials, even tracing the word's previous "false etymologies." Each chapter concludes with a bibliography of sources cited, and there are hundreds, if not thousands. One wishes short references to these sources could be included for all the entries for those readers interested in the author's documentation, but with its 85-page entry "sindex," such a change would likely triple the size of an already dense work meant primarily for browsing.

The breadth of words and vices covered makes this work seem less coherent than *Flappers 2 Rappers*. As Dalzell notes in the introduction, slang is the product of an identity group, and as this volume does not focus on such a group as did the author's last title, the function of slang as a sign of group membership is somewhat less apparent. The book's layout is relatively clear, although there are no guide words. Typeface varies enough to keep it browseable, although the matte finish paper and the three-color pen and ink and photograph montages of illustrator Istvan Banyai make the book look a bit dated, rather like a high school social science textbook of 25 years ago. Dalzell's colorful writing deserves more visual punch.

There are interesting exclusions: a lot of drugs and sex, but no rock and roll. Nevertheless, the creative chapter on the seven deadly sins; a rare discussion of the slang of pornographers, which includes the names of individual performers in the etymologies; and a history of the use of "gate" as a suffix for scandal are real gems. This work is an entertaining, well-researched addition to high school, academic, or public library collections.
—**Jennie Ver Steeg**

44. **DK Illustrated Oxford Dictionary.** New York, Oxford University Press and New York, DK Publishing, 1999. 1008p. illus. index. $50.00. ISBN 0-7894-3557-8.

This work is a collaboration between DK Publishing and Oxford University Press. It is compiled from Oxford's U.S. Dictionaries Program and is easy to use. In keeping with the DK tradition, this dictionary is filled with photographs and illustrations.

The front matter consists of a "How to Use the Dictionary" section, which is explicit, along with a "Key to Symbols," "Structure of Entries," a "Pronunciation Guide," and an "Abbreviations" list. The main body of the dictionary is user-friendly, and most pages have at least one photograph or illustration. Under some general terms there are sidebars of accompanying pertinent information. For example, under *flower* there is a sidebar with a close-up photograph of a flower with arrows pointing out various important aspects of the flower as well as photographs of other varieties of flowers.

This work concludes with a reference section that includes political and physical maps of the world and the United States and Canada; countries of the world (which includes the flag and other pertinent information of each country); the constellations of the sky; measurements; lists of symbols, including chemistry and biological symbols; Braille; mathematical symbols; and even laundry codes. There is a map of the time zones, a list of birthday gems, wedding anniversary gifts, and a section on grammar and style. This dictionary belongs in everyone's reference library. [R: LJ, Dec 98, p. 86]—**Pamela J. Getchell**

45. **Encyclopedia Americana.** Danbury, Conn., Grolier, 1997. 30 vols. illus. maps. index. $995.00/set. ISBN 0-7172-0130-9.

The editors of *Encyclopedia Americana* (EA) have developed yet another excellent general use encyclopedia. In this, the 1998 international edition, the editors have included 42 new articles, 22 replacement articles, 95 major revisions, and 1,913 minor revisions; bringing the total number of individual entries to 45,000, the number of illustrations to 23,000, and the number of maps to 1,300.

Since last reviewed in ARBA (see ARBA 95, entry 53), EA has continued to meet its objective of serving "as a bridge between the worlds of the specialists and the general reader." Although the title implies a bias toward the United States, the entries are international in scope. Contributors from around the globe, including the countries of Argentina, Australia, England, and Canada, provide worldwide views of current and historical topics. Scholars from notable institutions, such as Harvard, the University of North Carolina, and the University of Virginia, add authority to the content of this encyclopedia.

The editors provided a detailed report outlining the new features of this 30-volume set. In the area of humanities, new articles on popular topics, such as "Literature" by Professor Ronald Schleifer from the University of Oklahoma, "Slave Narrative" by Professor William L. Andrews from the University of North Carolina at Chapel Hill, and "Literature for Children" by Professor Mitzi Myers from the University of California at Los Angeles, enlighten readers on the latest theories and ideas. New and updated biographies include notable individuals, such as author Jean Toomer, Nobel Prize winner Dario Fo, and historical figure Thomas Jefferson. Although the biographical entry on Jefferson provides an updated bibliography, it does not include any information about Jefferson's relationship, presumed or proven, with his slave Sally Hemings, nor does it address Jefferson's ownership of slaves and his internal dilemma about the peculiar institution. An unfortunate omission in light of the recent DNA proof identifying Jefferson as the father of at least one of Hemings' children.

In the area of social sciences, new biographies of world figures, including U.S. secretary of state Madeleine Albright, secretary-general of the United Nations Kofi Annan, and British prime minister Tony Blair, reflect the changing international political climate.

In the Arts, the articles on "Architecture" and "Rock Music" were expanded and now include additional color photographs. Six new biographies consist of essays on popular individuals in the motion picture industry—actor Milton Berle, actor Clint Eastwood, director George Lucas, director Martin Scorsese, director Steven Spielberg, and actor Mae West. The article for British rock group, the Beatles, is nothing but a short paragraph, while more information and a color photograph is provided under the revised "Rock Music" essay. The encyclopedia does not grant separate entries to individual members of the Beatles, thus neglecting the political and social impact of the music of John Lennon after the dissolution of the band.

No publication is without errors, specially a 30-volume set that attempts to achieve comprehensiveness. Despite the types of errors and omissions listed above, *Encyclopedia Americana* does a good job of serving the general user, specifically high school students, undergraduates, and patrons at a public library. Librarians should consider this set for purchase on an annual or biennial basis. [R: RBB,15 Sept 97, p. 256-258; BL, 15 Sept, p. 252, 254]—**Susan D. Strickland**

46.   Kane, Joseph Nathan, Steven Anzovin, and Janet Podell. **Famous First Facts: A Record of First Happenings, Discoveries, and Inventions in American History.** 5th ed. Bronx, N.Y., H. W. Wilson, 1997. 1122p. index. (Wilson Facts Series). $95.00. ISBN 0-8242-0930-3.

In its 5th edition, Kane's classic is substantially reworked. The 4th edition filed entries in one alphabetic sequence with cross-references and offered four indexes—year, date, personal name, and geography. The 5th edition is changed from this format. First, it consolidates the old information and adds 1,000 new entries, numbering them in the text for a total of 8,155. Second, it organizes entries topically through an "Extended Table of Contents," which sorts entries into 630 easily surveyed categories and subcategories. Third, it arranges entries chronologically within the topical categories. Finally, it adds a 5th index by subject, which affords access by the names of such prominent groups as African Americans, Native Americans, and women and picks out firsts that are mentioned in the body of entries. A comparison of "College," "Computer," and "Satellites" from the 4th edition with "Education—Colleges and Universities," "Computers," and "Space—Satellites" from the 5th edition amply demonstrates the effects of these changes. The vocabulary of library catalogs and topical reference works is always problematic in that users face something of a guessing game as they match their vocabulary with the compiler's; Kane, Anzovin, and Podell's new edition multiplies the ways in which readers can approach its contents and thereby creates more opportunities for guessing right. *First Facts* shares much of the same information as seen in almanacs, chronologies, and books of lists but also provides interesting awards, superlatives, and "bet-you-didn't-know!" facts more associated with the trivia buff, barstool wagerer, journalist, or browser than with the scholar. It will be useful to the student looking for inspiration, details for an argument, or "what happened when" background for a paper. [R: Choice, July/Aug 98, p. 1825; BL, 15 Nov 98, p. 609]—**Robert H. Kieft**

47.   **World Book Multimedia Encyclopedia, 1998.** [CD-ROM]. Chicago, World Book, 1998. 2 discs. Minimum system requirements: IBM or compatible 486DX/66 MHz. Double-speed CD-ROM drive. Windows 3.1. 16MB RAM. 25MB hard disk space. SVGA 256-color monitor. 16-bit sound card. Mouse. $65.00.

The *World Book Multimedia Encyclopedia, 1998* is clearly targeted at the K-12 educational market. It contains all of the 17,000 articles of the print version, plus an additional 1,000 article unique to this 2-CD-ROM version. The "Internet Bonus Kit" includes a third CD-ROM containing access to the Internet via the IBM Global Network, America Online, or CompuServe, and the *World Book Health and Medical Annual* (see ARBA 98, entry 1543). The *World Book Multimedia Encyclopedia* is well integrated with the Internet, including links to more than 3,000 Websites. Articles are updated monthly, and many additional resources are available at the World Book main Website. The extended multimedia items are stored on the second CD-ROM, which requires the user to eject the first CD-ROM and replace it with the second. This can be awkward, particularly for less sophisticated users. Searching is quick and easy, and each article provides ready links to related items on both the CD-ROM and the Internet. Multimedia items are well integrated. A number of features are aimed at K-12 students, including "Homework Wizards" that guide students through the processes of making a chart, writing a report, or constructing a timeline. The editors have attempted to write each article for the anticipated age level that will be using it. This results in a considerable variability of both vocabulary and complexity and sophistication of entries.

This may work well in an educational setting, but for an adult library user this variability can be unsettling and may even be a disservice as some entries are too simplistic and superficial. The *World Book Multimedia Encyclopedia, 1998* is a good choice for a K-12 school library. [R: RUSQ, Summer 98, p. 339; LJ, 15 Feb 98, p. 179]

—**Richard W. Clement**

DIRECTORIES

48.   **By the Numbers: Nonprofit Organizations.** Helen S. Fisher, ed. Detroit, Gale, 1998. 663p. index. $79.00pa. ISBN 0-7876-1861-6. ISSN 1096-4967.

For those who want to know who leaves money to charities, the age of the oldest Peace Corps volunteer, or the leading corporate donors to United Way, that information and more is all in *By the Numbers: Nonprofit Organizations*. It may not read like a novel, but its timelines track events from ancient days to the present. Anyone interested in data about nonprofits will be pleased to find this material collected in one place. Researchers who need to work quickly will be happy that the information is easy to find, especially with the help of the 17-page table of contents and the 64-page index. Corporate planners, strategists, market research professionals, new business developers, and business students are also among those who will use the volume.

The scope of the volume is broad. Its divisions include funding sources, recipients of funding, and performing sectors (organizations and volunteerism) as well as nonprofits profiles. Chapters here deal with political activities, unions, and some international statistics. The information has come from a wide range of newspaper and magazine articles, trade publications, annual reports, newsletters, associations, online services, and Web pages. Largest listings are of assets and grants of foundations made by state. Based on Internal Revenue Service data, the total number of nonprofit entities is 1.2 million. They range from renowned museums to small soup kitchens. The nonprofit sector forms approximately one-sixth of the U.S. economy, making it extremely varied and important.—**Jerri Spoehel**

49.   **Directory of National Helplines, 1998.** Ann Arbor, Mich., Pierian Press, 1997. 140p. index. $15.95pa. ISBN 0-87650-379-2.

This slim directory provides information on health, economic, social, environmental, and travel organizations. This is the book to consult for information on issues ranging from animal welfare, fraud, hospices, and marrow donors to runaways, taxation, and weight loss. Each entry includes the toll-free telephone number, fax information, Website and e-mail addresses, publications available, and a brief description of services provided by the group.

Many, but not all of the organizations in the *Directory of National Helplines* can be found in directories with a broader scope such as *Consumer Sourcebook* (see ARBA 93, entry 235) and *The National Directory of Addresses and Telephone Numbers* (see ARBA 93, entry 69). However, because this work is more narrowly focused on selected areas of consumer interest as noted above, there are numerous groups unique to this publication. Added value is also provided with the inclusion of Website addresses for 80 percent of the entries. An electronic version of the directory is also available. Priced reasonably, this book is a valuable reference work for health, counseling, and social workers and reference librarians in academic, public, and special libraries.

—**Elaine F. Jurries**

50.   **Encyclopedia of Associations: An Associations Unlimited Reference.** 32d ed. Sandra Jaszczak and Tara E. Sheets, eds. Detroit, Gale, 1997. 2v. index. $460.00. ISBN 0-7876-0845-9. ISSN 0071-0202.

51.   **Encyclopedia of Associations: Regional, State, and Local Organizations. A Guide to Over 113,000 United States Nonprofit....** 7th ed. Amy Hall, ed. Detroit, Gale, 1997. 5v. index. $530.00/set. ISBN 0-7876-1074-7.

The *Encyclopedia of Associations* remains a standard reference tool for most libraries; providing an extensive categorized list of 23,000 nonprofit associations. Everything from the American Council of Spotted Assess to the American Bar Association is included. In the 32d edition, the editors have redesigned the page layout of the work. Instead of 2-column entries, 3 columns are used to reduce the amount of paper needed by 600 sheets for each set. This new format does not detract from the readability.

The 7th edition of the *Encyclopedia of Associations: Regional, State, and Local Organizations* also follows this 3-column format. More than 113,000 entries identify associations and nonprofit organizations in the United States and its territories. This 5-volume set is divided into geographic regions; within each volume, entries are arranged first by state, then by city.

Entries continue to provide basic information for each association—address, telephone number, fax number, number of members, date founded, awards, affiliations, services provided, publications, and meetings. Some entries include e-mail or Website addresses; however, this information is often out of date. With a growing number of associations establishing a presence on the Internet, careful consideration should be given before purchasing such a costly set.—**Susan D. Strickland**

52.   Erickson, Judith B. **Directory of American Youth Organizations, 1998-1999: A Guide to 500 Clubs, Groups, Troops, Teams, Societies, Lodges, and More for Young People.** 7th ed. Minneapolis, Minn., Free Spirit, 1998. 207p. index. $21.95pa. ISBN 1-57542-034-1. ISSN 1044-4440.

This unique directory is updated and revised every two years. The 7th edition includes more than 500 adult-sponsored, national youth groups and organizations of all kinds. As in previous editions (see ARBA 96, entry 902; ARBA 91, entry 895; and ARBA 89, entry 785), the directory is arranged by broad interest categories, such as hobbies and special interests, sports, religion, conservation, self-help, peace and understanding, character building, and service groups. Each entry includes a brief description of the group, contact person, address, telephone and fax numbers, e-mail address, and Website address, if available. The book is well indexed and will be easy for young people to use themselves.

In addition to direct use by children and teenagers, this work will be indispensable to parents, teachers, librarians, and others who are interested in connecting young people with groups and activities that interest and stimulate them. It is highly recommended for all school and public libraries.—**Elaine F. Jurries**

53.   Kaufeld, John, and Jennifer Kaufeld. **The Official America Online Yellow Pages.** New York, Osborne/ McGraw-Hill, 1998. 502p. illus. index. $24.99pa. ISBN 0-07-882416-8.

The Official America Online Yellow Pages is a categorized directory of services available online to subscribers of America Online (AOL). About 2,000 entries are classified into 150 major categories. Generally the classification scheme is sensible and helpful, although occasionally a choice (e.g., "Hot") seems vacuous, and a few are less than fully descriptive (e.g., "Special Needs" contains listings for "Deaf and Hard of Hearing," "Disabilities," and "Gifted"). The indexing is weak, which is a serious problem for a book of this sort. The topic index is almost an exact repeat of the table of contents, and the keyword index is limited to the collection of actual words from listings. Neither index, for example, lists "handicap" as a cross-reference to "disability" or "special need."

The descriptions themselves are peppy and enthusiastic, so much so that the book reads more like an extended advertisement for AOL than a guide to what is useful on the service. Interspersed are highlighted messages that read like a mix of public service announcements ("Kids. Keep them safe.") and promotions for various AOL services ("Shop online. With America Online's Certified Merchant program, it's guaranteed.").

Aside from the book's uncritical tone, its biggest potential problem is datedness. Published in 1998, it remains reasonably current at the time this review was written. But by mid-1999, one can expect much of its content to be out of date. Just like its namesake in telephony, this yellow pages needs regular updating to be useful. Whether annual updates are planned is unclear from the book.

This book will be of modest use to libraries that provide access to AOL on-site. If kept current with annual updates, it would serve as a reasonable introduction to AOL for people considering whether to buy the service and looking for a low-key sales pitch to help them decide.—**Ray Olszewski**

54.   Levy, Cynthia J., and Jeffrey D. Schultz. **Global Links: A Guide to Key People and Institutions Worldwide.** Phoenix, Ariz., Oryx Press, 1998. 177p. index. $59.95pa. ISBN 1-57356-224-6.

Suppose a student approached a reference librarian while he or she was working at the library reference desk and asked for help finding the addresses of several important people in the world. That librarian spent some time on the ready-reference materials but still could not find all the addresses that the student wanted. Now, with the newly published *Global Links*, librarians can find out information like this in a split second. Written by Levy and Schultz, two experts in the field of political science, *Global Links* has become a quick reference guide to key people and institutions worldwide. There are 243 nations and their territories included in this guide, from Afghanistan to Zimbabwe, and from William Jefferson Clinton, president of the United States, to Saddam Hussein, president of Iraq. Contact information is listed under each country. Each entry contains the name of the official mailing address, telephone number, fax number, e-mail address, and Website. There are also two indexes in the end of the directory: one index of heads of state, presidents, and prime ministers, and one by country, both with Websites that are available. The users of this guide will be businesspeople, librarians, information managers, teachers, students, researchers, diplomats, and travelers who need to identify and contact government officials and political leaders. One thing that the users should keep in mind is that as the world is changing, so are the leaders. The information in this volume is accurate as of April 1998.—**Xiao (Shelley) Yan Zhang**

55. **National Directory of Nonprofit Organizations 1998.** Ned Burels, ed. Detroit, Taft Group/Gale, 1998. 3v. index. $485.00. ISBN 1-56995-240-X. ISSN 1048-8154.

This 9th edition of the *National Directory of Nonprofit Organizations* (NDNO) is printed in three large, softbound books. Volume 1, parts 1 and 2, is a listing of nonprofit organizations with annual revenues of $100,000 or more. Volume 2 includes organizations with revenues of $25,000 to $99,999. This information is from Internal Revenue Service (IRS) filings.

Each tome begins with an IRS filing status table, an activity groups table, and an activity look-up table. Following the tables, each book contains an alphabetic listing of organizations. Each entry provides the name of the organization, address, telephone number, IRS 501(c) filing status, employer identification number, charitable deduction eligibility, annual income, and activity identifier code. Each book contains an activity index as well as a geographic index by state and zip code.

The stated purpose of the NDNO is to provide useful information to marketers, sales staff, and nonprofit professionals who need contact information about the largest nonprofit organizations in the United States, and it does fulfill this purpose.—**Sue Brown**

56. **National E-mail and Fax Directory 1999.** Susan J. Cindric and Sheila Dow, eds. Farmington Hills, Mich., Gale, 1998. 2015p. $126.00pa. ISBN 0-7876-1256-1. ISSN 1520-040X.

This new directory—an enhancement of the previous *National Fax Directory* (1996 ed.; see ARBA 97, entry 51)—provides basic contact information for more than 160,000 businesses, agencies, and research centers, and includes e-mail, fax, telephone number, and mailing address for all entries. Included are associations, corporations, educational institutions, financial institutions, government agencies, labor unions, manufacturers, media and publishing organizations, medical and health facilities, nonprofit organizations, research centers, and wholesalers and distributors.

The volume is divided into 2 sections. The 1st is a straight alphabetic listing that includes name, address, e-mail address, fax number, and telephone number. As appropriate, the publishers indicate if the fax number has a human intermediary. A 2d section is arranged alphabetically by subject, with indication of the corresponding Standard Industrial Classification code. Entries provide the same basic information as in the 1st section. Prefatory information for the volume includes a list of subject headings, indication of standard time difference, and a listing of U.S. area codes.

Although comprehensive, the work is uneven in its inclusion. Some research centers of colleges and universities are included but not others. Major community college systems are missing. Business coverage is similarly uneven. As a whole, one must approach the work with a "hit or miss" mentality. Major corporations are present, whereas other smaller corporations are merely a possibility. Recommended with reservation for those collections where users have a constant need for this information. It might be easier and less costly to merely search the World Wide Web.—**Edmund F. SantaVicca**

57. **State and Regional Associations of the United States 1998.** 10th ed. Buck Downs, R. Willson Hardy, Nathan L. Cantor, and Nicholas P. Karr, eds. Washington, D.C., Columbia Books, 1998. 587p. index. $79.00pa. ISBN 1-880873-29-X. ISSN 1044-324X.

State and Regional Associations of the United States 1998 is a directory of state and regional trade and business associations, professional societies, and labor organizations. It is well organized and easy to use and provides six cross-referenced indexes.

The main index is arranged alphabetically by state and contains the full listing for all of the organizations within that state. Each entry provides the year the organization was founded, telephone and fax numbers, mailing address, e-mail and Website addresses, executive directory, total membership, total staff, annual budget, historical note, and annual meeting dates and location.

The subject index is an extremely useful cross-reference that groups associations of the same ilk. Another useful index is the alphabetically arranged acronym index. Three other indexes are for budget, executives, and association management companies. This directory is a solid reference tool for business, professional, and academic pursuits as well as general public interests.—**Mary L. Trenerry**

58. **Web Site Source Book 1998: A Guide to Major U.S. Businesses, Organizations, Agencies, Institutions, and Other Information....** 3d ed. Detroit, Omnigraphics, 1998. $85.00pa. ISBN 0-7808-0283-7. ISSN 1089-4861.

This business address book provides convenient access to a new technology using a nonthreatening, old-age technology. It does not mention the criteria for selecting which U.S. businesses to include. However, among the 25,000 listings, this work claims to have all Fortune 500 companies and all U.S. senators and representatives, whether they have a Website or not.

Users can locate a company through the alphabetic section or through the subject category section. In both sections, a company listing contains the full contact information, making flipping between an index and the main section unnecessary. Each listing contains the organization's name; address; telephone, fax, and toll-free numbers; Website address; Website e-mail address; and company e-mail address. There is often a note about which department receives the fax or telephone call (e.g., human resources). A list with page numbers of all subjects and subcategories precedes the subject section. A small sample of subjects includes gelatin, candy stores, wholesale clubs, Billy Graham, Gene Siskel, Roger Ebert, candles, birth and death records, credit unions, zoos, and government.

One weak point in the book is its subject classification. Because this is a business address publication, a business librarian would first look for a Standard Industrial Classification (SIC) index. That information is not included. Nor is there any clear pattern for the subject nomenclature. Both United Parcel Service Inc. and UPS Inc. are easy to locate in the alphabetic section. This reviewer tried a half-dozen words and phrases before finally hitting upon "Shipping Agents (Freight/Cargo) and Freight Forwarders." Generally, *see* and *see also* references in the subject headings redirect readers, but there were no alternative listings under "freight" or "cargo." Nor does a listing in the alphabetic section give the subject heading for a company. If one knows the name of a company and is looking for others with similar products or services, one cannot use the alphabetic listing to find the appropriate subject heading.

Taken simply as a Web address book for established companies and public figures and institutions, this publication would be useful for all libraries, including school and government publication collections.
—**Susan D. Baird-Joshi**

59. **Who's Wealthy in America, 1998: A Prospecting List and Directory of More Than 110,000 Affluent Americans.** Deborah J. Morad and Laurie Fundukian, eds. Detroit, Taft Group/Gale, 1998. 2v. index. $445.00. ISBN 1-56995-245-0.

This updated 8th edition contains information on more than 112,500 individuals with an "inferred net worth of at least $1 million" (see ARBA 94, entry 211 for a review of the 3d edition). The 1st volume is alphabetically arranged by last name and contains the name, address, telephone number, age, education, current market home value, duration of residence, philanthropic interests, and contributions to political action committees. The 2d volume provides details on wealthy individuals who are officers, directors, or 10 percent principal stockholders of publicly held companies registered with the Securities and Exchange Commission or other government regulatory agencies. The 2 volumes contain 4 useful indexes: geographic, political contributions, insider stock/stockowner, and alma mater. Although this work does not purport to be a comprehensive list of wealthy Americans, it is surprising that a random check of a dozen names listed in the latest *Forbes 400* issue of the richest Americans only found one name in this volume. Nevertheless, it is a useful source for institutions and organizations seeking potential donors.—**Donald Altschiller**

GOVERNMENT PUBLICATIONS

60.   Hoffmann, Frank W., and Richard J. Wood. **Guide to Popular U.S. Government Publications 1995/1996.** 5th ed. Englewood, Colo., Libraries Unlimited, 1998. 300p. index. $38.50. ISBN 1-56308-607-7.

    Of the more than 12,000 titles available from the U.S. government, the authors have selected about 1,500 of those published in 1995 and 1996 for this annotated bibliography. "Popular," in this context, refers more to the usefulness of the publication than to the number of copies sold. Directories and other publications that age quickly are not included. However, a listing of publication catalogs is included. A typical listing, "The ACE Plan . . . ," presents data about airport capacities and suggests ways to improve access. The value of the index is reduced because citations are indexed by title rather than subject matter. The most useful part of the book may be its instructions on how to locate and obtain publications on a given subject.—**Robert B. McKee**

61.   Notess, Greg R. **Government Information on the Internet.** Lanham, Md., Bernan Associates, 1997. 778p. illus. index. $45.00; $34.50pa. ISBN 0-89059-081-8; 0-89059-041-9pa.

    Although most books about the Internet are out of date by the time they are published, this one should hold up well over time because government sites tend to be fairly stable and because it is exceptionally well done. Nevertheless, one hopes that the publisher already has a contract for the 2d edition well underway because change is the watchword when describing the Internet.

    The focus of the volume is on U.S. federal government Internet sites (mostly World Wide Web sites with some gopher and FTP sites included) with a smattering of state, local, international, and foreign national government sites included. Complementing these government listings, however, is the inclusion of the most important nongovernment sites that provide access to government information for free or for a fee. The volume is organized alphabetically by large semitopical areas such as agriculture, business, Congress, education, health sciences, military, and state government, with subcategory breakdowns of the topics. Eighteen chapters are included, with an average of about 25 pages per topic.

    Within each of these topical chapters and subtopical areas, each entry has a specific format: entry number, title (sometimes imposed by the author), sponsoring agency, primary access URL, alternative access method, description of the site, subject headings indexed under, and any appropriate Superintendent of Documents (SuDocs) call numbers. The format, layout, and information provided on each entry is easy to use and generally sufficiently informative.

    Although the individual entries are excellent, the indexes are the true jewels in this work. Indexes are provided for each primary and alternative URL, SuDocs call number, publication title, agency name and acronym, and subjects. One could not ask for better access paths to a volume.

    As noted earlier, this is primarily a guide to U.S. government Internet sites, and it should be recognized that only a minimal beginning has been made on state government, foreign national governments, and, especially, international intergovernmental organizations (IGOs). Only a few of the principal United Nations (UN), UN-related, and other major IGO sites have been included here, despite the fact that extensive Websites do exist for many other IGOs. This is simply notification for the reader and not necessarily a criticism of this work. It does an excellent job with what it covers, and to include other levels of government as thoroughly would have made it an even more hefty and expensive tome than it is now.—**Robert V. Williams**

62.   Pearson, Joyce A. McCray, and Pamela M. Tull. **U.S. Government Directories, 1982-1995.** Englewood, Colo., Libraries Unlimited, 1998. 159p. index. $45.00pa. ISBN 1-56308-290-X.

    Anyone searching for information in government publications will appreciate one more finding aid. The arrangement is an improvement over previous directories of directories. Instead of an emphasis on issuing agencies, the subject is the focus of this directory. Within each of the 12 subject chapters, detailed descriptions of publications are listed by agencies. In addition to the agency and authors or editors, within each annotated entry there are monthly catalog, OCLC, shipping list, and item numbers provided as well as publication date and superintendent of documents (SuDoc) numbers to facilitate location.

    There is a list of regional depository libraries in appendix A. These libraries have the responsibility of retaining government documents and providing interlibrary loan services. Appendix B explains the use of Government Printing Office sales publication reference file (PRF), which lists publications and subscriptions currently for sale by the superintendent of documents. Appendix C lists government bookstores throughout the United States.

Author/title and subject indexes complete the publication. This is a helpful government documents tool, especially in libraries that do not have ready access to commercially available online catalogs.—**Sue Brown**

HANDBOOKS AND YEARBOOKS

63.   Ash, Russell. **The Top 10 of Everything 1999.** New York, DK Publishing, 1998. 256p. illus. index. $24.95; $17.95pa. ISBN 0-7894-3524-1; 0-7894-3523-3pa.

For trivia buffs, the merely curious, and those seeking hard statistics or rankings, this book will likely prove to be invaluable. The range of current events, history, science, art, music, and many other areas are explored and tabulated in an easy-to-read volume.

Although this book does not contain any "best" categories or any personal favorites of the author, it does include many items that fit into categories of tallest, fastest, worst, and most. In order to be included, the rankings had to have been quantifiable. In most cases, the author identifies his sources of information, although there are some areas where Ash has used multiple sources and identifies none of them, making himself the sole source of information to be identified in a reference setting.

The work is arranged in broad categories, with subcategories in each section. Most of the data are presented in tabular format, although there are a multitude of "snap facts" that enhance the text and are scattered throughout. Some of the charts have a "then and now" theme, showing comparative change during the past decade. Well illustrated with a fine subject index, the work will serve as an excellent reference tool in most public and school library collections, especially when supplemented by almanacs and other reference annuals.

—**Edmund F. SantaVicca**

64.   **The Associated Press Library of Disasters.** Danbury, Conn., Grolier, 1998. 8v. illus. maps. index. $279.00/set. ISBN 0-7172-9169-3.

Major disasters, especially those that result in a substantial loss of life and property, have always fascinated us. They have been and remain dramatic events that appeal to humans. They invariably attract a great deal of attention from the news media. They are also historical events with a human element that teachers and students find worth examining in the classroom. This new series of eight 112-page volumes on a wide assortment of such disasters constitutes an excellent source of contemporary information for younger readers. Although its primary focus is on twentieth-century disasters, each section begins with a short summary of well-known earlier disasters (e.g., the Lisbon earthquake of 1755) that provides some historical perspective. The main focus of each volume is on the presentation of brief information about 25 to 30 or more disasters as reported, at the time, in news stories from the Associated Press. Each story is accompanied by an introductory summary and contemporary black-and-white photographs. A glossary in each volume defines the terms. There is also a set index in each volume that makes it easy to find information about specific events, places, or subjects.

Many of the disasters, like the sinking of the *Titanic* or the *Challenger* space shuttle explosion, are well known and have received extensive treatment in other readily available sources. An equal if not greater number, like the 1920 Wall Street bombing or the 1935 hurricane in Haiti, are less well-known and information about them is less readily available, especially in school or smaller public libraries. These texts and pictures provide an opportunity for teachers and students to examine and compare different disasters at different times and in different places. They also allow for a comparison of how news coverage of such events varies from time to time and from country to country. This is a relatively expensive set that will be of value mainly in libraries in middle and high schools where the curriculum emphasizes history, social studies, and factual reporting. It will be most useful where teachers and librarians can provide guidance in locating other relevant material, placing these stories in perspective, and examining the human and social impact of disasters. [R: SLJ, Nov 98, p. 151]

—**Norman D. Stevens**

65.   Cohl, H. Aaron. **The Book of Mosts.** New York, St. Martin's Press, 1997. 340p. $22.95. ISBN 0-312-15482-8.

In the introduction, Cohl writes that his goal in this compilation was to present "the most brilliant, the most flamboyant, the most unbelievable facts" (p. ix). The facts are arranged in 22 subject areas including geography, money, crime, sports, air travel, and health. Information is generally presented as lists, with short introductions.

The book includes such facts as the highest mountains, the biggest divorce settlement, hockey play with the most goals, the most romantic cruises, and the most watched television episodes. Brief citations are provided for the facts; the most recent information dates from 1995. As with any such compilation, some facts are already out of date. For example, the section on movies does not include *Titanic*, which would now top several of the lists.

This work is similar in coverage to other books of facts such as *The World Almanac and Book of Facts* (World Almanac, 1997) and *The Guinness Book of Records 1996* (Bantam, 1996) that include many of the same facts and are cited as the source of some of Cohl's facts. There is no clear organization of the material and, surprisingly, no index is provided. This work is really intended for casual browsing rather than ready-reference. *The Book of Mosts* may answer an occasional question, but for those libraries that own the titles mentioned above and the *Statistical Abstract of the United States* (Bernan Press, 1997), this is not a necessary purchase. [R: RBB, 1 Nov 97, pp. 506-508]—**Terry Ann Mood**

66.   **The Europa World Year Book 1998.** 39th ed. London, Europa; distr., Farmington Hills, Mich., Gale, 1998. 2v. index. $760.00/set. ISBN 1-85743-041-7. ISSN 0956-2273.

Now in its 39th edition, the *The Europa World Year Book* remains a classic source for current information about countries and organizations worldwide. Volume 1 provides great details about more than 1,650 international organizations including the United Nations, the European Union, and NATO. Entries for organizations detail the mission and charter of the organization, identify committees and related organizations, outline the functions of the organization, and include specific contact information—address, telephone, Website address, and names of individuals in various offices or positions.

Beginning in volume 1 and continuing in volume 2, each country receives an entry comprised of surveys on recent events, demographics, and economic conditions. Governing documents are included as are classified directory entries—government leaders, religious organizations, the press, numerous business associations, and tourism. Addresses and telephone numbers are contained in many entries; however, few e-mail and Website addresses are offered.—**Susan D. Strickland**

67.   **The FAQs of Life: Over 2,500 of the Most Frequently Asked Questions and Their Answers, on Every Topic Imaginable.** Camille N. Cline, ed. Kansas City, Mo., Andrews McMeel Publishing, 1997. 662p. index. $16.95pa. ISBN 0-8362-3574-6.

The FAQs of Life is like a surf through the Internet, but it is all in one place and is quite reliable. It is like those "odd question" files that librarians have kept behind the desk on cards, slips of paper, or even online—but this book has it collected, authenticated, and indexed in one handy place.

The book contains answers to 2,500 questions that the editor feels are the most commonly asked. Many questions about computers and alternative medicine give it a contemporary flavor, although other popular categories such as food, law, travel, and gardening are also well-covered. The editor has divided the questions and answers into 18 chapters with numerous subheadings under each. There is a good index with useful terminology. Generally, the editor lists the sources and writes in a lively, engaging style. It is a great read—librarians will love it. Each entry is under half a page, making it just right for instant gratification. Even when the question does not have an answer (e.g., the Coca-Cola formula), the surrounding information is useful.

Libraries should definitely select this title. At just $16.95 it is reasonably priced, and it should stand in reference collections along with such classics as *Famous First Facts* (see entry 46), the *New York Public Library Desk Reference* (see ARBA 95, entry 80), and the *World Almanac and Book of Facts* (see ARBA 96, entry 7). [R: LJ, 1 Feb 98, p. 76]—**Paul A. Mogren**

INDEXES

68.   **Book Review Index: 1997 Cumulation.** Beverly Baer, ed. Detroit, Gale, 1998. 952p. $240.00. ISBN 0-7876-1209-X. ISSN 0524-0581.

As a long-standing entry in sources providing access to reviews of books, periodicals, and books on tape, this publication stands out as one of the most comprehensive and reliable. Since 1963, through its several issues a year plus the cumulations, this resource has indexed reviews in hundreds of publications, both of general and scholarly interest. The main entries are arranged by author name, and a title index is also provided. As well as standard bibliographic information, the entries also include codes that indicate whether the item is aimed at children or young adult, and codes for reference or periodical material when applicable. Ranges for word counts of the reviews are also provided. This work is recommended for all libraries that need broader coverage of reviews than those provided by *Book Review Digest* (see ARBA 98, entry 65 for a review).—**Lee Weston**

MUSEUMS

69.   Danilov, Victor J. **Hall of Fame Museums: A Reference Guide.** Westport, Conn., Greenwood Press, 1997. 275p. index. $69.50. ISBN 0-313-30000-3.

This is a resource book that is devoted to a wide variety of halls of fame. These halls are defined as places that present or honor a group of individuals in particular categories who have been selected as especially note-worthy for specific achievements. To be included in this guide, the halls must give evidence of a physical presence and must be open to the public regularly. Some 274 places, such as museums, galleries, exhibit halls, sports arenas, civic centers, and association headquarters, are included.

The first 5 chapters provide a sequential and logical presentation of the historical and recent development of halls in the United States. The historical roots date back to Europe. The first hall of fame in the United States was established by an act of Congress in 1864. The modern era of halls of fame began with the founding of the Hall of Fame for Great Americans in 1990. The major expansion happened in the 1990s when the construction, expansion, and relocation of new facilities increased more than ever before.

Most of the 274 halls listed in this guide are national or international in scope and are nonprofit. Sports and games halls of fame are the most numerous, well known, and visited, occupying half of the listings in the direc-tory. The nonsports halls of fame include other aspects of U.S. culture and society, such as agriculture, aviation, business, and religion. Unusual halls of fame cover such topics as Barbie Dolls, cockroaches, crayons, and sneakers. The last section of this book is devoted to a brief description of the halls of fame in other countries.

Halls of fame are often important elements of a community or field, and many are major tourist attrac-tions. Most important, the halls of fame play an important role in presenting and representing the popular culture in the society. Compared to Doug Gelbert's *Sport's Hall of Fame: A Directory of Over 100 Sports Museums in the United States* (see ARBA 93, entry 820), this directory is significantly broader in scope and richer in its resources. Readers will find useful and interesting information that helps define the heroism and popularity at various times in society. *Hall of Fame Museums* is recommended for both public and college libraries. [R: RUSQ, Summer 98, p. 360]—**Eveline L. Yang**

70.   James, Elizabeth, comp. **The Victoria and Albert Museum: A Bibliography and Exhibition Chronology, 1852-1996.** Chicago, Fitzroy Dearborn, 1998. 804p. index. $95.00. ISBN 1-884964-95-8.

This work is a chronological, indexed list of all the publications and exhibitions of the Victoria and Albert Museum during its first 144 years. Each publication listed "must contain an explicit statement that it was published or co-published by the museum."

An introduction provides a brief history of the Victoria and Albert Museum along with an outline of the organizational subdivisions, satellites, and departments of the museum. Each entry provides a citation number, title, publisher (in-house publication was not always possible), physical description, series title, and notes. There are 4 indexes that provide efficient access to the material in this publication. One can search by name, title, series, or subject. This is a well-organized, specialized index for the serious researcher.—**Sue Brown**

71.   Norris, Joann, ed. **Children's Museums: An American Guidebook.** Jefferson, N.C., McFarland, 1998. 217p. illus. index. $28.50pa. ISBN 0-7864-0443-4.

The need for children's museums has steadily grown during the past 20 years. That need has been met by the growth in the number of museums available to families seeking meaningful educational experiences for their children. *Children's Museums* is a listing of museums claiming to have educational and participatory exhibits or programs of interest to children.

Norris's research included the *Official Museum Directory*'s (1992 ed.; see ARBA 93, entry 79) list of more than 275 children's museums. After contacting them all, she found that some had closed but learned of others that were not included in the *Official Museum Directory*. Her final list provides information on 242 children's museums.

Each entry is arranged by state and includes a brief description, history, an overview of exhibits, the age group for which the museum is appropriate, hours of operation, admission fees, other sites of interest in the area, the museum's address, the telephone number, the fax number, Internet sites, and e-mail addresses, when available. Many entries include only the museum's name, address, and telephone number. Users should call ahead for updated information. This volume is an excellent purchase for all libraries.—**Mary L. Bowman**

PERIODICALS AND SERIALS

72.   **Magazines for Libraries.** 9th ed. By Bill Katz and Linda Sternberg Katz. New Providence, N.J., R. R. Bowker/Reed Reference Publishing, 1997. 1402p. index. $180.00. ISBN 0-8352-3907-1. ISSN 0000-0914.

Published since 1969, *Magazines for Libraries* is the standard source for pertinent information about magazines and serial publications. All Katz's editions are reviewed in ARBA and there is no need to repeat the previous comments. This work is a good source for more than 7,000 periodicals, which were selected from a total of more than 165,000 periodicals published worldwide. Information provided remains the same as in previous editions—title, date founded, frequency of publication, price, editor, publisher, address, Website address, whether or not it is refereed, indexing, and information for ordering. There are occasional errors in the subject index. For example, entry 4940 does not deal exclusively with Ukraine but covers poetry from several countries, including Ukraine. There is only one entry for Ukraine periodicals, omitting such important publications as *Harvard Ukrainian Studies, Journal of Ukrainian Studies, Ukrainian Quarterly,* and others. Similar situations occur with other minorities. This reviewer suggests selecting a different resource for these areas. In general, *Magazines for Libraries* is an excellent publication.—**Bohdan S. Wynar**

73.   **The Standard Periodical Directory 1998.** 21st ed. New York, Oxbridge Communications, 1997. 2272p. index. $795.00. ISBN 0-917460-89-8. ISSN 0163-7010.

There have been several reviews of *The Standard Periodicals Directory* in ARBA (20th ed.; see ARBA 97, entry 65). It has been recommended as "a standard reference source" and the reviewer suggested that "it should be used in coordination with *Ulrich's International Periodicals Directory.*" Indeed, this publication is a cumulative source for some 90,000 publications, but it is somewhat inferior to *Ulrich's International Periodicals Directory* (see entry 74).

The volume is arranged by broad subject categories, including accounting, advertising and marketing, and the like. There is an outline index and title/ISSN index, but no subject index. In other words, it is not easy to find books dealing with a specific topic, such as nationalities. Most entries should be under such headings as "politics" or "international relations," but most are under "ethnic" with the misleading reference "for specific ethnicities, look under the name of the specific ethnic group." This reviewer looked under "Ukrainism" and out of some 50 entries at least one-half are no longer published or not included. *Ukrainskyi istoryk* is not an ethnic publication, but serves as one of 10 historical research journals and is not located in Littleton, Colorado, but is in Kent, Ohio. *Svoboda* is not a daily, but a weekly, and its location is again "dated." This small sample indicates that information is not recent and occasionally simply incorrect. *The Standard Periodical Directory* should be used with a great deal of discretion, providing of course that libraries will be willing to pay a rather substantial subscription price for this publication.—**Bohdan S. Wynar**

74.   **Ulrich's International Periodicals Directory 1998.** 36th ed. New Providence, N.J., R. R. Bowker/Reed Reference Publishing, 1997. 5v. index. $459.95/set. ISBN 0-8352-3967-5. ISSN 0000-0175.

Last reviewed in ARBA 97 (see entry 66), *Ulrich's International Periodicals Directory* remains the standard print resource for finding information on the enormous number of periodicals published each year. This 36th edition arranges more than 156,000 serial titles into 869 subject headings. The numerous indexes offer access to titles by ISSN, publications of organizations, and title change, a feature most helpful for serials librarians. The varied listings consist of refereed journals, titles available on CD-ROM or online, and controlled circulation serials. The section on newspapers is divided into two lists, one for dailies and the second for weeklies. Each is arranged by geographic location and separate indexes provide additional access.

The classified listing of serials comprises 3 volumes of this 5-volume set. The subject headings are adequately descriptive and sufficiently subdivided. *See* references direct users to appropriate entries, thus increasing accessibility. Individual entries vary in length; all provide general bibliographic and ordering information and many include a description of the publication, indexing references, and details of title changes. The e-mail address and the URL for the publisher are often supplied.

With this set, users can locate periodicals on the most esoteric topic—*Scottish Pottery Studies*, *Edward Howell Family Association Newsletter*, and *Pool & Spa Marketing*, just to name a few. As with any directory, it is difficult to keep each entry current. This edition updated 112,000 entries and added nearly 7,000; approximately 80 percent of the information can be considered current.—**Susan D. Strickland**

QUOTATION BOOKS

75.   **American Heritage Dictionary of American Quotations.** By Margaret Miner and Hugh Rawson. New York, Penguin Books, 1997. 638p. index. $29.95. ISBN 0-670-10002-1.

This book does exactly what its title implies: It provides a comprehensive listing of more than 5,000 quotations by U.S. authors since the early seventeenth century. It lists the quotations chronologically in approximately 500 subject categories and also provides a keyword index and an author index.

This reviewer's reaction to the book was to question the need for yet another book of quotations, specifically one limited to American quotations. After spending a half hour reading the various quotes and their contextual annotations (about 30 percent of the quotes are so explicated), one begins to develop a perspective of not only U.S. history, but also U.S. literary, philosophical, political, and educational development. Of course, none of this is encyclopedic, and a good many quotations, particularly pre-nineteenth century, are left out. But what is there is good.

Of particular use to scholars and students in American social studies, history, and literature, this book remains a useful reference work. [R: RBB, 15 Feb 97, p. 1040]—**Kenneth I. Saichek**

76.   **Cassell Companion to Quotations.** By Nigel Rees. London, Cassell; distr., New York, Sterling Publishing, 1998. 640p. index. $29.95. ISBN 0-304-34848-1.

Sometimes, just locating the wording of a given saying is not enough; sometimes, having some information on the saying's source or of similar versions of a saying can add to the understanding of some of our language. For those occasions, this book is an excellent source. Rees, who has been working with sayings for more than 20 years through the BBC program *Quote . . . Unquote*, is particularly well suited to compile a book such as this. He admits that this is not the largest book of quotations available and that he has omitted many sayings for which there is no dispute. Each of the more than 5,000 sayings, however, includes some commentary on its source, the circumstances in which it was first spoken, or other forms it has taken through the years. The group of anonymous sayings is especially interesting. The quotations from the Bible provides interesting commentary on Old and New Testament links as well as information on how these sayings have been quoted through the years. The 578 pages of sayings are arranged alphabetically by author, and a sayings index assists the user in finding particular quotations. This is a useful volume for anyone wanting to know more about many of the sayings that are a basis of much of our language. [R: LJ, Aug 98, p. 79; BL, 15 May 98, pp. 1654-56.]—**Kay Mariea**

77.   **Colombo's Concise Canadian Quotations.** John Robert Colombo, ed. Toronto, Colombo & Company, 1998. 280p. index. $40.00 spiralbound. ISBN 1896308-45-7.

Colombo is an avid and enthusiastic collector of "quotable Canadiana." Since 1974 he has published five collections of quotations by Canadians and about Canada. This title is a reprint of the 1976 edition, which has been out of print since 1978. It is a spin-off of *Colombo's Canadian Quotations* (Hurtig, 1974) and contains quotes by 1,000 authors from 400 B.C.E. to 1976. The parent title included 6,000 quotations. This concise version contains 2,500 quotes, of which 800 were added after 1974.

The entries are organized under 600 alphabetic categories and are cross-referenced to related topics. There is an author index with keywords listed under each name. Each entry cites the source of the quote, the date, and the context in which it was made.

Libraries collecting Canadian literature that do not already own this title will certainly want to add it while they have the opportunity. One caveat applies: In 1991 and 1994 Colombo published the *Dictionary of Canadian Quotations* (see ARBA 93, entry 90) and *Colombo's All-Time Great Canadian Quotations* (Stoddart, 1994). This reviewer was unable to compare these volumes with the reviewed title. Libraries owning either of these should compare content before purchasing.—**Marlene M. Kuhl**

78. **The Concise Oxford Dictionary of Quotations.** 3d ed. Angela Partington, ed. New York, Oxford University Press, 1997. 595p. index. $9.95pa. ISBN 0-19-280070-1.

"Many are called but few are chosen," may well be the byword in any publication of a concise edition of a classic reference work. Such is the case with this book, which, for its size and scope, is a fine example of selection and inclusion. The listing includes the classic and best known quotes (an appendix identifies those most frequent misquoted). The entries are listed alphabetically by author, and uniform titles are listed within this same sequence. The titles of works are italicized and are also alphabetically arranged under the author. Diaries, speeches, and letters are listed in chronological order, and secondary sources are the final entry. The keyword index is useful for identifying those half-remembered quotations as well as a great source for the right quote for a particular occasion or a specific theme. There is, as well, a small appendix of "Sayings of the Nineties," from Diane Abbott to Boris Yeltsin. The final short section includes slogans from the world of advertising and politics and other forms of propaganda. It is, as is the case with most slightly overlarge paperback books, unwieldy to use; the pages do not stay open and are gathered too tightly so that frequent use will produce an easily damaged spine. This work in no way replaces its progenitor, the *Oxford Dictionary of Quotations* (see ARBA 98, entry 83) but is a useful resource for home or office.—**Paula Frosch**

79. MacHale, Des, comp. **Wit: Humorous Quotations from Woody Allen to Oscar Wilde.** Niwot, Colo., Roberts Rinehart Publishers, 1998. 310p. index. $14.95. ISBN 1-57098-213-9.

Wit: Humorous Quotations from Woody Allen to Oscar Wilde is a delightful little book of humorous quotations that cover a wide range of subjects, including art, business, food, literature, love, politics, and religion, to name only a few. The arrangement is alphabetic by subject and includes a vast number of authors, from Woody Allen and Roseanne Barr to Bill Cosby, Malcolm Forbes, Bob Hope, and many others. *Wit* will make an excellent gift and is recommended for public libraries.—**Mary L. Bowman**

80. Newman, Richard. **African American Quotations.** Phoenix, Ariz., Oryx Press, 1998. 504p. index. $49.95. ISBN 1-57356-118-5.

This is a book of quotations by African Americans, with very few exceptions—John Brown being one and Marcus Garvey another. Included are more than 2,500 quotations by approximately 500 persons from the eighteenth century to the present. Entries are arranged alphabetically by subject, and then by author within each subject. After each quote is the name of the speaker, dates, and occupation. The approximately 264 subjects range from achievement to youth. Some of the other subjects included are Afrocentrism, anger, black consciousness, brotherhood, Christianity, the civil rights movement, despair, dreams, evil, Harlem, heroes, individuality, lynching, morality, oral tradition, prejudice, racism, reading, relationships, self-acceptance, slavery, spirituality, success, and victory. The quotations are decidedly and purposely reflections of the African American viewpoint. Emotions demonstrated by the words within this book range from despair to joy, anger to forgiveness, shame to pride. They are words of the black experience in the United States.

Unlike many books of quotations, this one is amazingly easy to use. Bold, large headings introduce each subject; the quotations are numbered from 1 to 2,512; there is double spacing between each entry; and the type is large enough to read without a magnifying glass. Name, subject, and occupation indexes provide convenient access.

All libraries should welcome this reference as a valuable resource in African American literature collections. [R: LJ, 15 Sept 98, p. 65; BL, 1 Oct 98, p. 352, 354; SLJ, Nov 98, p. 156]—**Dana McDougald**

Part II
SOCIAL SCIENCES

2 Social Sciences in General

SOCIAL SCIENCES IN GENERAL

81. **Index to International Public Opinion, 1996-1997.** Elizabeth Hann Hastings and Philip K. Hastings, eds. Westport, Conn., Greenwood Press, 1998. 738p. $325.00. ISBN 0-313-30461-0. ISSN 0193-905X.

This index contains data taken from surveys in 70 countries that ask questions about 101 different countries. The surveys were generally done between the spring of 1996 and the spring of 1997. However, there are many earlier dates included. Data were compiled by 207 research firms.

This work is divided into 4 parts: single nation surveys, multinational surveys, a bibliography, and indexes. The single nation surveys section is divided into 23 major topic categories, each of which is divided into more specific groups. The questions cover a broad spectrum of social, political, and economic interests. The surveys contain items of current as well as historical interest. There are three indexes: by topical categories, by countries and regions in which the surveys were conducted, and by countries and geographic areas referenced in surveys. The indexing is the weakest part of the volume. The entries refer to pages, making the reader search the whole page for the topic of interest rather than to a specific entry on each page. This weakness was noted in a previous review (see ARBA 94, entry 75). Also, the indexing is not always reliable. For example, in the bibliography there is a survey listed called "Man and Ape—a Feeling of Closer Kinship." Trying to find the questions taken from it was impossible. It was not listed under animals, human origins (which referenced pages on sports), or reproduction technology (which also referenced some of the same pages on sports, as did the entry for human origins). There were no entries under ape, man, kinship, or relationships. Also, it would be useful if each question had a reference back to the specific survey from which it came. This is an interesting and important source. It is too bad that the indexing is done so poorly.—**Robert L. Turner Jr.**

82. **The Statesman's Yearbook 1998-1999: The Essential Political and Economic Guide to All the Countries of the World.** 135th ed. Barry Turner, ed. New York, St. Martin's Press, 1998. 1815p. illus. maps. index. $115.00. ISBN 0-312-21588-6.

This 135th edition is an essential political and economic guide to the countries of the world. The 1st section covers international organizations. Part 2 covers the individual countries of the world, and includes such things as territories and population, climate, governing bodies, defense, international relations, economy, energy and natural resources, industry, foreign economic relations, communications, justice, religion, education, and welfare. Interspersed in this information are six essays focusing on topical issues. There is also a fold-out core section that provides a political world map and flag illustrations for 192 countries and an international economic relations section ranking all major partners. The paper printing and binding are of average quality. The type size is small, but appropriate for a reference book of this nature. This one-volume reference is unparalleled in offering economic, political, and social information on conditions of the countries in this ever-changing world. This reviewer has no problem recommending this book because the previous edition is used several times per week. This book should be in all reference libraries around the world.—**Herbert W. Ockerman**

83. **Walford's Guide to Reference Material, Volume 2: Social and Historical Sciences, Philosophy, and Religion.** 7th ed. Alan Day and Michael Walsh, eds. London, Library Association; distr., Lanham, Md., Bernan Associates, 1998. 1144p. index. $269.00. ISBN 1-85604-223-5.

This very well-known work, usually referred to as Walford, now has two new editors, Alan Day and Michael Walsh. *Walford's Guide to Reference Material* covers social and historical sciences, philosophy, and religion. The arrangement is the same as in previous editions, based on the Universal Decimal Classification, and most entries are examined in good Walford tradition. They include full bibliographic descriptions, ISBN, the price if in print, and brief annotations. This edition is substantially enlarged and updated to mid-1997. The section on Eastern Europe, which was an obvious weakness in the previous edition, now looks much better. After looking for entries pertaining to Ukraine, this reviewer found two bibliographies and three encyclopedias, all published abroad. Perhaps the next edition will include several works published in Ukrainian. The sections on USSR, RSFSR, and Russia in Europe have only three entries total. Coverage of area studies needs some improvement in this otherwise excellent reference source with a long tradition. [R: Choice, Sept 98, p. 84]

—**Bohdan S. Wynar**

3 Area Studies

GENERAL WORKS

84. **Cultures of the World: Belarus, Guatemala, Liberia, New Zealand, Papua New Guinea, and Tanzania.** By Patricia Levy and others. Tarrytown, N.Y., Marshall Cavendish, 1998. 6v. illus. maps. index. (Cultures of the World). $136.50/set. ISBN 0-7614-0811-8 (Belarus); 0-7614-0812-6 (Guatemala); 0-7614-0810-X (Liberia); 0-7614-0808-8 (New Zealand); 0-7614-0813-4 (Papua New Guinea); 0-7614-0809-6 (Tanzania).

Cultures of the World is a multivolume set of books covering cultures of 96 countries. The newest set presents Belarus, Guatemala, Liberia, New Zealand, Papua New Guinea, and Tanzania. Each volume opens with a brief introduction to the country and continues with 12 topical chapters covering geography; history; government; the economy; the peoples of the country (for example, Belarusians, Liberians, Tanzanians); lifestyle; religion; language; the arts; leisure; festivals; and food. Immediately preceding the index are a map of the country, quick notes, a glossary, and a bibliography. The age levels for which the texts are targeted are identified as 4th grade and up; however, the simple vocabulary and excellent illustrations will appeal to younger readers as well. Olympic enthusiasts will enjoy reading about countries with whom they may be less familiar whose athletes are represented at the Games.

The entire set is highly recommended for purchase for all libraries serving children. The collection will add depth and quality of information on the 96 countries represented. It is also recommended for families who may want to select individual volumes for countries of special interest.—**Margaret Denman-West**

85. **DISCovering Nations, States, & Cultures.** [CD-ROM]. Detroit, Gale, 1998. Minimum system requirements: IBM or compatible 386. CD-ROM drive. DOS 5.0. Windows 3.1. 4MB RAM. Mouse. $600.00. ISBN 0-7876-0558-1.

This CD-ROM product contains information on about 200 nations, all 50 states, 12 Canadian provinces, and 500 cultural groups. Also included are 1,650 images, including more than 500 photographs and 600 maps. Entries follow a standard format so that comparing two countries or two states is made simple. Entries are thorough and well written, with demographic, economic, historical, and political information included. Hyperlinks are provided so that locating related topics is easy. The main menu allows users to search by culture, place, full-text, or picture gallery. Users searching for a particular culture can type in the search or select from a long list of cultures. In the case of places, individuals can select countries or states by clicking on maps or selecting from an alphabetic list. The full-text searching allows users to locate any word or group of words that appear anywhere on the CD-ROM. The picture gallery allows users to select from the pictures, seals, flags, and maps that are available on the CD-ROM. An electronic dictionary and glossary are also searchable. A teacher's guide and user's manual accompany the disc.

This product will be available online in January 1999 via GaleNet. The CD-ROM product is recommended to any library serving high school through college students and wanting information on geography in a format other than in book format. [R: JAL, Sept. 98, p. 431-432; BL, 1 Nov 98, p. 534]—**Carl Pracht**

86. **The Hutchinson Guide to the World.** 3d ed. Phoenix, Ariz., Oryx Press, 1998. 666p. maps. $65.00. ISBN 1-57356-220-3.

This guide is divided into 3 sections—"Countries of the World," "Gazetteer," and the appendixes. The 1st section, "Countries of the World," offers approximately a page and a half entry for each country. In each entry there is a small map of the country in relation to the surrounding region. This section consists of information about government, economy and resources, population and society, transportation, and a chronology. A box of "practical information" is also provided, which includes such items as embassy contact information and the country's chamber of commerce. The "Gazetteer" section provides brief, albeit thorough, information, as well as several maps. Interestingly, there are a number of frank comments in the entries; for instance, Santa Barbara, California, is better known for its wealthy residents and as a resort." The appendixes include information such as a listing of parts of countries (e.g., provinces in China, regions in France, and states and urban territories in India). A number of maps and charts are provided. However, an oversight of the editors is that the map of the United States is missing the border between Utah and Colorado.

Overall, this is a fine guide, but is not an essential addition to all collections. It is, however, an excellent source for short overviews of the countries of the world. [R: BR, Nov/Dec 98, p. 69-70; LJ, Aug 98, pp. 76-77; Choice, Nov 98, p. 502]—**Leslie R. Homzie**

87.   **The Middle East and North Africa 1998.** 44th ed. London, Europa; distr., Detroit, Gale, 1997. 1136p. (Regional Surveys of the World Series). $370.00. ISBN 1-85743-037-9. ISSN 0076-8502.

Approximately one-third of this handbook provides a general survey of regional issues (religion, terrorism, oil, water resources, Arab-Israeli relations) and entries on regional organizations, such as League of Arab States and OPEC Fund for International Development. This section is followed by detailed surveys of 21 countries. Information provided for each country includes physical and social geography, lengthy entries on economy and history, statistical tables, and a bibliography. Sources for statistical data are standard international sources such as the United Nations' *Statistical Yearbook* (41st ed.; see ARBA 98, entry 816) as well as less readily available regional resources. This title provides the detail, clarity, and authority librarians have come to expect from Europa handbooks.
—**Ahmad Gamaluddin**

88.   **The USA and Canada 1998.** 3d ed. London, Europa Publications Ltd.; distr., Detroit, Gale, 1998. (Regional Surveys of the World). $410.00. ISBN 1-85743-044-1.

This 3d edition of *The USA and Canada* (see ARBA 95, entry 106 for a review of the 2d edition) consists of 3 sections: introductory essays on the United States and Canada; a section on the United States; and a section on Canada. The introductory essays provide updated and in-depth analysis of the implications of the North American Free Trade Agreement on U.S. and Canadian relations. Essays are prepared by 27 authorities on a variety of issues. These include the bureaucracy of government, social groups in the United States, natural resources and manufacturing, and immigration and refugee policies in Canada. Maps, chronologies, and statistical tables are also included. The United States is clearly the more expanded of the sections.

Comprehensive directories are at the end of the specific country sections. They provide contact information to a wide range of associations, commercial organizations, government agencies, and diplomatic representation; e-mail addresses, however, are limited. This is a solid work recommend for large public libraries and research institutions. There are a few minor errors. For example, Michigan is listed in the chronology as being admitted to the Union on two different dates. Unfortunately, some entries are more updated in scope than others. Overall, however, this work is a successful undertaking.—**Leslie R. Homzie**

UNITED STATES

General Works

89.   Carpenter, Allan, and Carl Provorse. **The World Almanac of the U.S.A.** rev. ed. Mahwah, N.J., World Almanac Books; distr., New York, St. Martin's Press, 1998. 411p. maps. index. $10.95pa. ISBN 0-88687-831-4.

This volume is an updated and expanded version of an almanac last reviewed in ARBA 95 (see entry 108). The main body of the almanac is arranged in two parts: portraits of each state and state comparisons. Part 1 has been added to give an overview of the nation as a whole and includes national statistics on the same topics listed under each state's heading and moments in history dating from John Cabot's reaching Massachusetts in 1497 to the 1998 investigation of President Bill Clinton. Tables comparing the United States with the other G-7 economic powers using estimates from the *CIA World Factbook* and a single-page statistical profile of the United States in the next millennium complete part 1.

Part 2, containing statistical and informational data for each state, has been updated and expanded with information as recent as 1997. Three new categories of information—living quarters, communication, and attractions—were added for each state. In keeping with electronic resources, one or two World Wide Web addresses are given for each state. These are often official state homepages. The major improvement to this volume is the expansion of the state comparison section. All 50 states are now compared in the various categories and are ranked from highest to lowest. The tables are presented in an easy-to-read format. The increased entries in the indexes, as well as replacing the index to statistics with a topical index, has improved the usefulness of the book.

—**Elaine Ezell**

90.   Mitchell, Susan. **American Attitudes: Who Thinks What About the Issues That Shape Our Lives.** 2d ed. Ithaca, N.Y., New Strategist, 1998. 446p. index. (American Consumer Series). $89.95. ISBN 1-885070-17-9.

Useful to social scientists and demographers is the 2d edition of the now biennial General Social Surveys (GSS) conducted by the National Opinion Research Center (NORC) of the University of Chicago. NORC is widely known and respected as a leading demographic research organization, and the GSS has been providing insight into the opinions of the U.S. public since 1972. The study is conducted using face-to-face interviews of 1,500 to 3,000 English-speaking persons in the United States who are asked to provide their opinions on a variety of topics. The data in the current report are culled from the 1996 survey, from which 164 topics have been selected. Selection of the questions or topics for this publication are based on their timeliness and broad representative qualities. These topics are arranged in 9 categorical chapters, each of which begin with a brief introduction. The results of each of the topical questions are presented with two-page coverage beginning with a brief narrative and exposition, followed by a table providing statistical comparison of the reactions of men and women, blacks and whites, age categories ranging from 18 to 70 and over, and differing educational levels. Where available, results from previous surveys (1975 and 1986) are provided for the purpose of further comparison in identifying trends and shifts of opinion. A detailed table of contents and brief subject index facilitate access to specific information.

—**Ron Blazek**

California

91.   **Los Angeles A to Z: An Encyclopedia of the City and County.** By Leonard Pitt and Dale Pitt. Berkeley, Calif., University of California Press, 1997. 605p. illus. maps. $34.95. ISBN 0-520-20274-0.

Few cities rival Los Angeles in terms of size, excitement, and audacity. The playground of beautiful people as well as the capital of the casting couch, this contradictory, cataclysmic, convoluted, and captivating city embodies the quests of the American Dream and Manifest Destiny. Leonard and Dale Pitt's A to Z encyclopedia of the city and county of Los Angeles captures the fascination and downright zaniness of the City of Angels in a manner that is appealing to both the serious researcher and the casual browser. Entire encyclopedias devoted to a single city are rare; the fact that such a large one could be compiled on Los Angeles alone signifies the need for such a title.

Entries cover anything one can imagine: neighborhoods, history, movies (of course), scandals, people, beaches, earthquakes (both a general article and specific examples), and the list goes on. The nearly 2,000 entries are broken up by quotations, illustrations, even maps. The main encyclopedia starts with a biographical presentation of Lakers superstar Kareem Abdul-Jabbar and ends with a brief entry on Zuma County Beach, with stops in between for fraternal societies, poet Robinson Jeffers, the Los Angeles City Charter, murder cases, the Rose Bowl, sharks, and the Walk of Fame—a fair indication of the breadth of this encyclopedia. There is even an entry on the perpetual smog and attempts to control it, under "Air Pollution" and "Air Pollution Control," with a cross-reference leading from "Smog." Illustrations range from the Santa Monica Pier (ca.1910 and at present), an avocado packing plant, the gateway to the Bel-Air Estates, Tom Bradley, nine of the Hollywood Ten, the La Brea Tar Pits, Aimee Semple McPherson, and Venice Beach (although a closer shot showing its uniqueness would have been welcome). Famous and infamous quotations abound as well, including such gems as Rodney King's oft-mocked 1992 statement, "People, I just want to say, you know, can we all just get along?" and historian J. S. Holliday's astute observation, "Here you can change your stripes, give up being a Catholic or come out of the closet, whatever."

An exemplary aspect of the encyclopedia is its inclusiveness. When one thinks of L.A., it is usually of its beaches, Hollywood, and the freeway system. Los Angles County is a diverse and expansive geographic region, and it is refreshing to see such entries as the Los Angles County Fair, held annually in Pomona. Entries such as those on the First American Methodist Episcopal (AME) Church, the Japanese American Cultural and Community Center, Koreatown, Olvera Street, and Tongva Indians speak to the immense cultural diversity of the area. The encyclopedia is also up-to-date. O. J. Simpson's entry discusses not only his football and acting careers but also the 1997 civil trial (and resulting settlement) brought about by the Brown and Goldman families for his alleged murder of Nicole Brown Simpson and Ronald Goldman.

The text ends with a series of appendixes, including a chronology, census data from 1990, incorporation and consolidation of cities, the organization of city and county government, and a list of selected readings. This list provides both nonfiction and fiction works, the latter consisting of such titles as Helen Hunt Jackson's *Ramona*, Walter Mosley's *Devil in a Blue Dress*, and Nathanael West's *The Day of the Locust*. Of use would have been an index to quotations or an index in general—but then again, half the fun of this encyclopedia is the browsing factor. Serious researchers will fast find themselves sidetracked into the seemingly inexhaustible details and trivia found in this volume. The only other complaint would be the occasional typographic error. For example, the entry on Occidental College refers to the Mary Norton *Lapp*—not Clapp—Library. However, the authors welcome changes for the next edition, so one hopes any mistakes will be rectified.

Overall, this encyclopedia only leaves one question unanswered. Leonard Pitt's credentials list him as professor emeritus of history at California State University, Northridge, and Dale Pitt is listed as a freelance writer, editor, and indexer, but one must wonder: Are they any relation to Brad?—**Melissa Rae Root**

Indiana

92. **The Indiana Factbook 1998-99.** 5th ed. Terry Creeth, ed. Bloomington, Ind., Indiana University Press, 1998. 381p. maps. $39.95pa. ISBN 0-253-21257-X. ISSN 0886-330X.

The 5th edition of *The Indiana Factbook* is a familiar old friend to librarians and researchers. Little has changed from the previous editions, other than the fact that all of the tables have been updated whenever possible. When there is not any new data, the old tables have been reprinted. The directory section has also been dropped because of the struggle required to keep them current and the growing use of the World Wide Web.

The Indiana Factbook is designed to be a quick reference tool for people looking for facts on population, health, education, housing, income, employment, agriculture, and business (mostly within Indiana). It offers county-by-county comparisons, based upon the latest census projections, including rankings and percentages. The volume is divided into 3 sections. The 1st section puts Indiana in perspective with the rest of the United States. Section 2 compares the way Indiana's 92 counties stack up in everything from agricultural production to vital statistics. The final section presents individual profiles of each county.—**Steven J. Schmidt**

Puerto Rico

93. Fernandez, Ronald, Serafín Méndez Méndez, and Gail Cueto. **Puerto Rico Past and Present: An Ency-clopedia.** Westport, Conn., Greenwood Press, 1998. 375p. illus. index. $59.95. ISBN 0-313-29822-X.

This volume is a thoughtful, wide-ranging guide to contemporary Puerto Rican culture and society. To the degree that it deals in depth with the past (as the subtitle suggests), however, it is for the most part a recent past; the past half-century or so.

For English-speaking readers trying to make sense of social and political references in current Puerto Rican discourse, the volume will be of immense value. It explains the overwhelmingly localized and frequently opaque references that appear in nearly every issue of Puerto Rico's newspapers. To cite but one representative example, the discussion of the *carpetas* (secret dossiers on people and activities the U.S. government deemed subversive) is clear, concise, and illuminating. The volume is also especially helpful with biographies of impor-tant contemporary artists, intellectuals, and politicians on the island.

If, however, one is interested in the history of Puerto Rico before it became a U.S. possession, or in place-names, or in the economy, there is not a great deal of help to be found here. There are, for example, no separate entries for the island's *municipios*, nor entries for the once-vital coffee and sugar industries. Despite these short-comings, the volume deserves a place in any reference collection. [R: VOYA, Oct 98, pp. 306-307; BL, July 98, p. 1908; Choice, Nov 98, p. 489]—**Glenn Petersen**

AFRICA

General Works

94.   **Africa: Africa World Press Guide to Educational Resources from and About Africa.** Trenton, N.J., Africa World Press, 1997. 197p. illus. maps. index. $21.95pa. ISBN 0-86543-588-X.

The work, as stated in the preface, focuses on writers, producers, and organizations that are "not now adequately represented in the mainstream media and in materials used in libraries" outside Africa. Apparently, because of that focus many of the standard reference sources on Africa are not covered. The work does certainly provide extensive coverage of materials produced by individuals from Africa, and consequently is useful as a supplementary guide to the more traditional works currently available. The first 3 chapters cover general resource materials and are followed by 24 subject-oriented chapters. These are followed by chapters covering supplementary materials, African literature, films and videotapes, and curriculum resources. These last 4 chapters are quite brief (e.g., only 69 curriculum resources are listed for a continent comprising 53 nations). The work concludes with an extensive reference and bibliographic list, a directory of organizations, and a comprehensive name index to the volume.

Each of the core 24 chapters contains a brief introduction that is often slanted and overly repetitive in its criticism of mainstream materials and attitudes toward Africa. A consistent theme throughout seems to be that only the compilers present the African or Third World perspective. The reader is constantly barraged with critical labels attached to mainstream resource materials, such as "racist," "sweeping generalities," and "stereotyping." There is a disconcerting and nonproductive pattern in the introductions of minimizing, ignoring, or offering rather obtuse redefinitions of real issues, such as famine and lack of economic development in Africa. Nevertheless, the work does provide information on a collection of useful resources typically not found in the standard bibliographic and historical guides to Africa.—**Anthony J. Dedrick**

95.   **Cultural Atlas of Africa.** rev. ed. Jocelyn Murray, ed. New York, Facts on File, 1998. 240p. illus. maps. index. $50.00. ISBN 0-8160-3813-9.

Africa's rapidly changing social climate requires reexaminations of cultural information, and former International African Institute's researcher Murray's volume should improve most libraries' resources. This update of the 1981 edition (see ARBA 82, entry 325), written by an international team of experts, prominently features 96 specially drawn maps and 284 color and 85 black-and-white illustrations, supplemented by textual commentary. A 12-page overview of Africa's physical background introduces the volume. Part 2, the cultural background, features excellent maps and photographs on languages, religion, history and archaeology, architecture, the arts, and literacy. The book's final half, part 3, covers individual nations, with 2 pages on each country given over to maps, short overview essays, and some statistical data. A gazetteer, index, and flag page conclude the volume.

As handsome as this work is upon first glance, closer examination reveals basic flaws. First, too many maps and photographs are split by the binding, making good photograph reproduction difficult. Second, statistical data are limited; any good almanac will provide more detail on the nations. Finally, some sections (e.g., "early man") do not reflect any research over the past 20 years, at least as is demonstrated by Murray's bibliography—a serious flaw for any volume on cultural studies. However, because this is the only up-to-date atlas focusing on African culture, *Cultural Atlas of Africa* is recommended for all public and academic libraries.

—**Anthony J. Adam**

Burkina Faso

96. McFarland, Daniel Miles, and Lawrence A. Rupley. **Historical Dictionary of Burkina Faso.** 2d ed. Lanham, Md., Scarecrow, 1998. 279p. maps. (African Historical Dictionaries, no.74). $75.00. ISBN 0-8108-3405-7.

Burkina Faso is a landlocked, arid, poor country in West Africa with a 1996 population of 10.6 million. Previously known as Upper Volta, the former French colony shares borders with Ghana, Togo, and Benin to the south, Côte d'Ivoire to the southwest, Mali to the west and northwest, and Niger to the northeast. The 2d edition of *Historical Dictionary of Burkina Faso* is an important source of reference material for both English- and French-speaking readers. Typical of the books in the series, this dictionary is an excellent first source for those doing research on the country. Covering work from precolonial times to the present, the 279-page book contains copious information on Burkina Faso that cannot be found in any one source.

The book is organized into two components: the dictionary and the bibliography. The dictionary covers pages 5 through 157, whereas the bibliography covers pages 158 to 253. Two appendixes—covering provincial capitals and the various national governments—conclude the book. The authors provide a concise introduction to the book that links the two parts perfectly together. The dictionary, like most in the series, is organized in alphabetic order and covers everything from acacia plants to the ninth-century Moro Naba, Zwetembusma. The bibliography section, which is preceded by a short introduction, is organized according to subject matter. Subjects covered range from general references, the country and its people, politics, economics, and business through vegetation and flora. Perhaps the most unique part of this book is the long and detailed historical chronology of events in Burkina Faso from precolonial times to the present. This chronology reveals the academic background and interests of the authors.

This dictionary is a real gem of a book that belongs in every library. It must be owned by anyone who is interested in Burkina Faso.—**Kwabena Gyimah-Brempong**

Maghreb

97. Pazzanita, Anthony G., comp. **The Maghreb.** Santa Barbara, Calif., Clio Press/ABC-CLIO, 1998. 328p. maps. index. (World Biographical Series, v.208). $85.00. ISBN 1-85109-310-9.

The Maghreb region of North Africa extends from southwest Mauritania to the eastern Libyan and western Egyptian deserts, and includes the countries of Algeria, Libya, Mauritania, Morocco, and Tunisia. Because the study of this region was almost entirely the domain of French scholars until the mid-twentieth century, few English-language works about the region appeared before this time. The 531 books, monographs, and articles Pazzanita selected and annotated for this volume are primarily from this relatively new and growing body of English-language literature, although some sources written in French, Spanish, and German are also included. In addition, most of the sources treat the Maghreb as a region rather than present information in a country-specific format. Pazzanita, who also compiled the 1996 World Bibliographical Series volume *Western Sahara* (see ARBA 97, entry 105), provides concise, knowledgeable, and well-written descriptive and analytical annotations of these sources. The volume is also well-organized, arranging the annotations into 20 subject-oriented chapters covering the region's history, geography, economy, politics, and people. Access is further enhanced by logically subdividing larger chapters, providing cross-references to useful annotations found elsewhere in the volume, and providing separate author, title, and subject indexes. The volume also contains an excellent introductory essay describing the region's cultural and political history, a chapter containing annotations of dictionaries and other bibliographies about the region, a glossary, and a map of the region. Pazzanita has created a valuable resource for anyone who desires English-language materials about this region of North Africa, making *The Maghreb* another fine addition to the well-known World Bibliographical Series.—**Karen Selden**

Mali

98. Stamm, Andrea L., Dawn E. Bastian, and Robert A. Myers, comps. **Mali.** Santa Barbara, Calif., Clio Press/ABC-CLIO, 1998. 327p. index. (World Bibliographical Series, v.207). $90.00. ISBN 1-85109-166-1.

The World Bibliographical Series' goal is to compile a bibliography of country information for every country in the world. *Mali* is volume 207 of this series. The 1st chapter is a bibliography of works about Mali and its people. The chapters are bibliographies of print, electronic, and nonprint resources categorized by topics. The topics begins with intriguing chapter titles, such as "Explorers' and Travelers' Accounts (to the Early 20th Century)," and a bibliography of the early historical accounts of the discovery and settling of Mali. The handbook continues with bibliographic chapters about the demographics, languages and dialects, the laws, business and the economy, education, literature, the flora and fauna, oral literature and folklore, and the arts. The end chapters are the bibliographies for statistical works, reference books, newspapers and periodicals, and other general and regional bibliographies pertaining to Mali. There are 3 indexes: an author index, title index, and a subject index. The index entries refer the reader to the entry number for a specific work and not page number.

This series as well as this volume would be helpful for collection development in large academic libraries needing country information or with special collections that need information about various countries. This would be a valuable handbook for the government libraries that focus on international business and U.S. relations with other countries.—**Kay M. Stebbins**

Namibia

99. Schoeman, Stanley, and Elna Schoeman, comps. **Namibia.** rev. ed. Santa Barbara, Calif., Clio Press/ABC-CLIO, 1997. 292p. index. (World Bibliographical Series, v.53). $85.00. ISBN 1-85109-278-1.

This book is part of the world bibliographical series that includes almost 200 publications on countries and states of the United States. It is aimed at a general audience. Giving current, reliable, and accessible information reflecting different points of view, this work is largely confined to reference works, books, journal articles, and news reports. The 843 entries are divided into 39 categories, such as tourism and travel guides, history, language, gender issues, legal matters, and fisheries. There are three indexes to assist the user: author, title, and subject. It is not meant to be a comprehensive compilation. There is also an introductory chapter that contains a brief background on Namibia, including its people, geography, ecological features, history, politics, and potential for socioeconomic development. Like all bibliographies published in book form, it cannot be completely up-to-date. It does include periodicals, such as newsletters, that could be used by the reader to check on the latest material. Entries in languages other than English are included with freely translated titles. The annotations are in English, but it is not clear that the language of the articles, when other than English, is given.—**J. E. Weaver**

Sub-Saharan Africa

100. **Encyclopedia of Africa South of the Sahara.** John Middleton, ed. New York, Scribner's/Simon & Schuster Macmillan, 1997. 4v. illus. maps. index. $475.00/set. ISBN 0-684-80466-2.

It is hard to overstate the importance of this encyclopedia. In 4 thick volumes it has 878 signed articles covering the history, cultures, languages, politics, and ethnic groups of this wondrous region. The coverage is factual and detailed, a welcome change from the patronizing tone and western biases of older sources on Africa. The articles provide the dates and figures one would expect as well as a beautifully written, scholarly analysis of each topic.

The set is arranged like a traditional encyclopedia. Articles have a bibliography and cross-references. They include numerous maps, illustrations, diagrams, and black-and-white photographs. Volume 4 has an excellent 125-page index, and a directory of contributors with their affiliations. An appendix includes a series of essays arranged by region or country and describing centers for African studies in those locales and the history of African studies there. Another appendix is a chronology by region, from the emergence of early humans through 1997. In another appendix, Middleton has produced an 83-page chart of 700 ethnic and identity groups with their locations, linguistic affiliations, and other information.

This single set can service many needs. It has facts and scholarly essays covering centuries of African civilization. It is well laid out with high quality graphics and a strong sewn binding. Its breadth and quality will make it a major reference source for decades. [R: Choice, Sept 98, p. 98; BL, 1 June 98, pp. 1802-1804]

—**Cathy Seitz Whitaker**

ASIA

General Works

101.   Breton, Roland J.-L. **Atlas of the Languages and Ethnic Communities of South Asia.** Newbury Park, Calif., Sage, 1997. 230p. maps. index. $65.00. ISBN 0-8039-9367-6.

This geographical atlas is the first presentation of the characteristics of the distribution of languages in the seven countries of South Asia. It contains an introduction dealing with India as an exemplary field for geolinguistics; sections on ethnic subdivisions; linguistic survey and census; the relation between language and race, tribe, caste, and religion; and a conclusion drawing attention to geolinguistic studies, language preservation, and territorial management in other countries.

The atlas is divided into 2 parts. The 1st part is about the general relationship between language and the complex ethnocultural structure of the subcontinent. The 2d part has 60 plates in the form of maps and graphs along with commentaries. The 2d part graphically analyzes the relationship between ethnic groups and space throughout the Indian subcontinent. The atlas also contains up-to-date graphs and tables, a glossary, an index, and a summary of the whole text. The author, an eminent scholar and professor of geography at the University of Paris, has written nine books on languages, population, civilization, and races, and has 140 main contributions to different standard journals. The 1st edition of this book was published in French in 1976. The present English edition comes after the author's 18 years of scrutiny of the linguistic panorama of the Indian subcontinent, several visits, and various publications in this field. This atlas is a resource tool for any library and is of particular value to all those with special interest in the areas of linguistics, geography, cultural studies, anthropology, ethnology, and political science.—**Vera Gao**

102.   Collinwood, Dean W. **Japan and the Pacific Rim.** 4th ed. New York, Dushkin/McGraw-Hill, 1997. 228p. illus. maps. index. (Global Studies Series). $20.25. ISBN 0-697-37423-8.

The recent Asian financial crises and its impact on the global economy have reinforced the importance of Asia and the Pacific Rim in today's world affairs. Indeed, we can no longer afford to view Asia as an exotic and faraway place, but an integral part of our socioeconomic life. Consequently, the need to understand the social, political, and cultural dynamics of this region is of paramount importance.

The work under review should play a role in helping us to get a general understanding of the countries of this region. What makes this publication useful is that under the "country reports" it provides users with up-to-date essential facts, from demography to education to transportation of all the countries in Asia and the Pacific Rim. In addition to the "country reports," users should also find informative the narrative "regional essays," which focus on the religious, cultural, sociopolitical, and economic differences and similarities of the countries in the region. Equally valuable are the articles covering issues such as human rights, feminism, and democratization, which are selected from well-known periodicals such as the *Far Eastern Economic Review*, *The Economist*, and *Foreign Affairs*. Also included in the text are maps, a glossary of terms and abbreviations, a bibliography, and a subject index.

Although users may find most of the materials included in this volume elsewhere, this work readily provides facts and related articles on these countries, making it a convenient and handy source. It is most useful for high school students taking advanced social studies classes as well as undergraduate students enrolling in introductory comparative politics and international relations courses.—**Binh P. Le**

103.   Kemp, Herman C., comp. **Bibliographies on Southeast Asia.** Leiden, The Netherlands, KITLV Press; distr., Detroit, Cellar Book Shop Press, 1998. 1128p. index. (Bibliographical Series, no.22). $126.50. ISBN 90-6718-121-8.

This is the most comprehensive bibliography of bibliographies on the Southeast Asian mainland ever published. It contains more than 5,000 items that include bibliographies, abstracts, and indexes. For the most part they were gathered from libraries in Europe, North America, and Asia. Many of the items were extracted from scholarly journals and monographs. Materials included in this publication were published in Southeast Asian as well as European languages. Bibliographies published on the Internet were intentionally omitted.

Entries are organized alphabetically by title under 34 broad topic areas, ranging from agriculture to geography to theses and dissertations. Typically, each item includes the title, author, place of publication, publisher, date, pagination, annotation status, number of items contained in each bibliography, holdings, and cross-references. With regard to holdings information, the item provides only the locations where the items were retrieved (e.g., OCLC, KITLV, or RLIN). In other words, holdings status is limited to only a dozen libraries where the materials were located. Also included in the text are an author index, a subject index, and a title index. As usual, the most useful index is the subject index. However, one may find the title index especially helpful because titles are arranged alphabetically under individual country. This should prove handy for those who want to see what is available on a particular country.

This work will be an invaluable research tool. However, what should prove to be particularly beneficial are abstracts and indexes to Asian periodicals and newspapers due to the fact that indexing and abstracting have not been a common practice in Southeast Asia. All in all, this will be valuable for Asian graduate students, scholars, and librarians. Research collections and large public libraries cannot afford to miss this work.—**Binh P. Le**

104.   Norton, James H. K. **India and South Asia.** 3d ed. New York, Dushkin/McGraw-Hill, 1997. 212p. illus. maps. index. (Global Studies Series). $20.25. ISBN 0-697-37424-6.

This is a sophisticated reference about South Asia and the countries that make up the subcontinent, including Afghanistan. After an introduction (part 1), the book begins with a series of 5 "images" of South Asia that successively explain its history and social environment (including languages and religions) as well as Hinduism's "Great Tradition," the success of democracy in South Asia, and Mahatma Gandhi's life. The second part of the book consists of a series of "Country Reports" containing information for all of the states of South Asia—India, Afghanistan, Bangladesh, Bhutan, the Maldives, Nepal, Pakistan, and Sri Lanka. The report on India, for example, includes a short narrative on India's geography, economy, and climate; an elucidation of Indian society; an explanation of recent changes; functioning of India's government and politics; challenges to India's democracy; functioning of the caste system today; and India's diplomatic role and position in the region. Each report includes a map; statistical information on population, communication networks, government, military forces, and the economy; black-and-white photographs; a historical timeline; and indicators of the country's development, freedom, health and welfare, and achievements. The final part of the book contains 35 articles drawn from the world press. These articles assess the regions' or individual country's political scene, cultural developments, and social and environmental changes or technical affairs. The text concludes with a useful, but incomplete, glossary and bibliography. Because the text includes a lot of information and some sophisticated analysis of South Asia, this is a book for the serious questioner, not for children.—**David L. White**

Cambodia

105.   **Cambodia.** Helen Jarvis, comp. Santa Barbara, Calif., ABC-CLIO, 1997. 412p. maps. index. (World Bibliographical Series, v. 200). $84.00. ISBN 1-85109-177-7.

This work is an annotated guide to 993 selected (mainly English-language) publications on Cambodia (Kampuchea), a small, culturally rich, but politically and militarily troubled nation situated in the heart of mainland Southeast Asia. For many years readers interested in bibliographic information on Cambodia have had to rely mainly on library catalogs or various abbreviated listings such as those of Mary Fisher (1967), Charles F. Keyes (1979), or Zaleha Tamby (1982). Jarvis's compilation is the only general guide currently available on information sources on Cambodia. It is intended for use by the "informed general reader" and includes selected popular and scholarly books and articles. The compiler has drawn on catalog records from the Australian Bibliographic

Network in the preparation of this work. Bibliographic entries are mainly for English-language books and a limited number of articles; French-language publications are cited very selectively. The bibliographic entries are organized by subject in 38 sections and are fully annotated. Some 50 annotations previously published in David Marr's *Vietnam* (see ARBA 94, entry 122) have been incorporated in the guide. Substantial attention has been given by the compiler to publications on Cambodian politics, history, and other social sciences or humanities topics. References to the Khmer Rouge, Pol Pot, and the Cambodian holocaust of the 1970s may be found under several subject headings, such as "History," "Politics, Administration, Government, and Defense," and "Human Rights, Genocide, Constitution, and Legal System." A limited number of publications in the natural sciences are cited. Although the annotated bibliography constitutes most of the volume, a historical introduction; a chronology; and a useful author, title, and subject indexes are provided. This work is recommended for academic and other reference collections. [R: Choice, Oct 98, p. 298]—**Lee S. Dutton**

China

106.   Blunden, Caroline, and Mark Elvin. **Cultural Atlas of China.** rev. ed. New York, Checkmark Books/Facts on File, 1998. 240p. illus. maps. index. $50.00. ISBN 0-8160-3814-7.
    This is a well-crafted book that provides a visual and cultural overview of China, through a blend of readable text and vividly presented maps, illustrations, and photographs, most of which are in full color. The attractive maps, used for geographical, demographical, and historical purposes particularly stand out, as do interesting sidebars, such as that on the excavation of the underground army of the First Emperor of Quin, and the full, informative captions of illustrations and figures.
    The book is divided into sections on space, time, and symbols and society. The "Space" section provides geographic and demographic contexts for the history that follows, using maps to trace the regional structure of China—typology, climate, agriculture, settlement patterns, and population density. The section titled "Time" surveys China from the Peking Man era to modern times, bringing in aspects of politics; society; and art of the archaic, imperial, and modern worlds. "Symbols and Society" is even more fascinating, as it uses a thematic approach to look at aspects of Chinese culture, including origins of the Chinese language and writing system; the traditions of poetry; philosophy and religion; architecture; principles of mathematics; the arts of theater, ceramics, and music; agriculture and cuisine; family life; and the interaction of China with the West. Also provided are a chronology, bibliography, gazetteer, and index.
    This updated version of the 1983 volume *Cultural Atlas of China* has been amended to include new textual and visual information and three new features on Taiwan, the Chinese Diaspora, and China's "natural environment." The latter has an emphasis on water and the Three Georges Dam project. Because of the brevity of their treatment and the importance Taiwan and the Diaspora should be accorded, it would have been better to have not included these sections. This work is recommended for making this complex country accessible to the general public.—**John A. Lent**

107.   **China: A Directory and Sourcebook.** 2d ed. Chicago, Euromonitor International; distr., Farmington Hills, Mich., Gale, 1998. 221p. index. $590.00. ISBN 0-86338-800-0.
    This 2d edition sourcebook on major business establishments in China and Hong Kong (new to this edition) and official economic and trade statistics is intended to help foreign companies do business in China and Hong Kong. The 4 sections in the 221-page quick reference book include "Overview of the Socioeconomic Environment," "Major Companies," "Key Sources of Information," and "Statistical Datafile." Two indexes, one by main business sectors and one a general index, serve as quick finding aids.
    Because the Chinese market is both complex and changing rapidly, it is not easy for any sourcebook to cover all of the essential information needed in a single volume. For a busy businessperson, this volume provides useful but hardly definitive information. The market review, for example, offers background information on the operating environment, such as macroeconomic and consumer trends across the country. Section 2 lists more than 500 of China's key companies as well as some 300 companies from Hong Kong. Each entry includes information on a company's operations, key personnel, and up-to-date financial data. Rankings of the top 50 companies, using the Euromonitor company measurements, for both China and Hong Kong also are provided. Section 3 identifies some 500 information sources from official organizations, trade offices, publications, and

libraries to online sources and Websites. Section 4 consists of some 100 statistical tables of marketing parameters. Judging by its high price and limited content, this book may be of value only to newcomers to the China and Hong Kong business markets who need some introductory information to get started.—**Hwa-Wei Lee**

108. **China: Facts & Figures Annual Handbook, Volume 23.** James Mulvenon, ed. Gulf Breeze, Fla., Academic International Press, 1998. 511p. $97.00. ISBN 0-87569-202-8.

China: Facts & Figures Annual Handbook continues to provide an impressive array of information in narrative, document, directory, map, tabular, and chart formats. Following summary information and a chronology for 1997, the topical coverage includes government, economics, foreign affairs and trade, economics, demographics, social issues, science and technology, tourism, and culture. Sources of information (e.g., Chinese government, international agencies, U.S. government, news media, and others) are identified throughout. The data are mostly for 1996 and 1997, although many tables and charts have retrospective data as far back as 1979. Lacking an index, users must rely on the clearly structured table of contents for access. The level of detail is impressive, and users will find valuable the compilation in one source of such important materials as communiqués, speeches, white papers, and other documents; listings of officials down to the provincial level; trade data spanning the needs of both researcher and investor; black-and-white tables and graphs that are easy to read; and "yearender" reviews for Beijing's *Renmin Ribao*. This is one of the more impressive annual reference tools in Chinese studies; there are other yearbooks, including those that come from government sources, but they tend to be erratic in their frequency, publishers, and titles. They also tend to be much more expensive. This series is highly recommended for both academic and public libraries supporting research in Chinese studies.—**Kenneth W. Berger**

109. **Modern China: An Encyclopedia of History, Culture and Nationalism.** Wang Ke-wen, ed. New York, Garland, 1998. 442p. illus. maps. index. $75.00. ISBN 0-8153-0720-9.

This 1-volume encyclopedia provides surprising breadth and depth of information on the history and culture of China since the mid-nineteenth century. The entries vary in length, and cover nearly 1,000 topics. The encyclopedia is arranged with a brief, informative introduction, followed by a listing of entries by subject (probably the least useful section of the book, more so when placed among prefatory sections), a chronology, identification of contributors, maps, 427 pages of entries arranged alphabetically, and an index. Many of the entries are by recognized experts on the topics, and the contributors in general reflect breadth of background and institutional affiliation. A useful feature is the inclusion of references to relevant publications at the end of each entry. A limited number of well-selected illustrations are spread throughout the entry pages. For readers interested in modern (post-Opium War) China, this encyclopedia is a handy scholarly reference tool. The content is comprehensive yet concise. The treatment of many controversial topics is, in general, balanced and objective. The volume should serve as a general reference resource; however, many of the entries may be confusing to a novice because of frequent use of acronyms and romanized Chinese terms (with English translations when initially used in an entry). [R: BL, 1 June 98, pp. 1812-1814; Choice, July/Aug 98, p. 1837]—**Hwa-Wei Lee**

110. Ogden, Suzanne. **China.** 7th ed. New York, Dushkin/McGraw-Hill, 1997. 212p. illus. maps. index. (Global Studies Series). $19.60. ISBN 0-697-37421-1.

This 7th edition of *China* in the Global Studies Series continues to offer current and useful information for understanding contemporary China, Hong Kong, and Taiwan. Background essays focusing on the geographic, cultural, sociopolitical, and economic characteristics of each of the three regions are carefully written and supported by detailed maps, facts, and summaries of statistical information. The author, a political scientist specializing in the study of China, is also responsible for the selection of 30 reprinted articles that follow the essays. Among the 30 articles selected from international journals and newspapers, 24 focus on China, and 3 each are on Hong Kong and Taiwan. The articles were primarily published in 1996, with a few culturally oriented pieces published as early as 1988 and 1989. An annotated table of contents of the articles and a topic guide precede the articles section for ease of use. The volume concludes with an annotated list of selected Websites, a glossary of terms and abbreviations, a bibliography, and an index.

The author has succeeded indeed in providing accurate information to help readers gain a basic knowledge and understanding of the events that are shaping China today. The volume also includes numerous black-and-white maps and illustrations, some of which are in need of updating or replacement. It would also be more attractive if the illustrations were in color. *China* is recommended for high school or lower-level undergraduate students as well as members of the general public wanting information on current events in China, Hong Kong, and Taiwan.

—**Karen T. Wei**

Japan

111.   Bruijn, Ria Koopmans-de. **Area Bibliography of Japan.** Lanham, Md., Scarecrow, 1998. 297p. index. (Scarecrow Area Bibliographies, no.14). $48.00. ISBN 0-8108-3374-3.

This bibliography provides a general overview of recently published writings on subjects relating to the geographic area of Japan and Japanese culture within that area. Most of the 2,676 entries listed are for books in the English language, although there are a few for works in modern European languages. The latter were cited when there was insufficient material on the specific subject in English. The main focus is on works published since 1980. Certain works of classic stature that were deemed necessary for background information or of such historical importance have been included. Many of the classics have been reprinted, bear recent imprint dates, and are readily available in bookstores and libraries. Journal articles, individual essays, dissertations, and most books of less than 100 pages have been purposely excluded. Entries are organized under a wide range of subject headings established by the author. Some, such as history, literature, and religion, are subdivided logically. Some subjects are more heavily represented than others, a fact explained by the lack of publication in some subject areas, at least of materials relating to Japan. Cross-references are provided when necessary to avoid ambiguity, when overlapping subjects occur, or to lead from a secondary to a primary heading. Entries give basic bibliographic data. There are no annotations. An author index allows rapid access to the works of specific authors. A short guide lists additional bibliographic sources for both books and periodical literature on the subject. This compilation appears to have been carefully and thoroughly prepared. It should be of much help to students, teachers, researchers, and the general public who are interested in learning more about Japan. [R: Choice, Sept 98, pp. 99-100]—**Shirley L. Hopkinson**

112.   Schilling, Mark. **The Encyclopedia of Japanese Pop Culture.** Boston, Cheng & Tsui, 1997. 343p. illus. index. $22.95pa. ISBN 0-8348-0380-1.

When Americans think of Japanese culture, they often think of tea ceremonies, karate, or No theater, but for the majority of Japanese this is a very distant past. In about 70 biographical and topical entries, Schilling (a 20-year resident and observer of Japanese culture) samples some of the more common and interesting cultural trends, from the concern with blood types to Juliana's Discotheque, in a readable style resembling a student guidebook. This work combines an eclectic knowledge and a sense of humor. It is obvious from the entries that Schilling has done his homework, although he offers no further sources beyond a three-page bibliography at the book's end. It should be noted that entries are arranged alphabetically with most cross-references in bold. There are also a table of contents and subject guide; however, the index contains no cross-reference from keywords such as *Ramen* to the entry *Instant Ramen*, which decreases its potential as a ready-reference. These essays are considerably longer and more eclectic than similar articles in *Japan: An Illustrated Encyclopedia* (see ARBA 94, entry 115). Schilling's work is also more readable than the more academic *Handbook of Japanese Popular Culture* (Greenwood, 1989), which covers 12 topics from new religions to architecture. Schilling is also more comfortable with topics that Japanese sources are more likely to gloss over for fear of offending more conservative readers. Articles last several pages and frequently are complemented with a black-and-white photograph, making the book easy to peruse. This work will be a popular item in both the circulating and reference collections in public and college libraries.—**Andrew B. Wertheimer**

Vietnam

113. **Who's Who in Vietnam 1998-1999.** international ed. John L. Pellam, ed. Laguna Beach, Calif., Barons Who's Who, 1997. 365p. illus. $210.00. ISBN 1-882292-11-1.

Given the technical, social, political, and economic conditions in Vietnam at the present time, the gathering of the information presented in this work was a monumental task. However, for users who are unfamiliar with Barons' publishing specialization, the title of the publication under review may cause some confusion. For example, there are no biographical sketches provided for many of the present and recent prominent Vietnamese leaders such as Nguyen Van Linh (the former General Secretary of the Vietnamese Communist Party and the main architect of the Vietnamese economic renovation, commonly known as Doi Moi), Le Kha Phieu (the current VCP party boss), and Do Muoi. Thus, despite the publisher's claim, which states that "selections were made from the fields of government, business, commerce and industry, journalism, medicine, science, and education," *Who's Who in Vietnam* does not include many Vietnamese with distinction outside the Vietnamese business world. In addition, it provides more than the title suggests. In fact, the second half of the book contains information on Vietnamese and international companies conducting business in Vietnam.

Who's Who in Vietnam comprises 2 sections. The 1st section contains about 1,100 entries, most of which are Vietnamese people. (It also includes Vietnamese American, American, English, French, Dutch, Australian, Chinese, and Korean businesspeople.) The entries are far from comprehensive. For example, Nguyen Xuan Oanh, one of Vietnam's most prominent politicians, educators, economists, and businessmen, was omitted. Similarly, Ly Quy Chung, another prominent politician and businessman, was also left out. Selection for inclusion was through nomination. Initially, the nomination forms were sent to top executives who were asked to nominate individuals to be included in the directory. The nominations were then evaluated by the editorial staff. No qualifications for the editorial staff are mentioned. In addition, a small number of entries were gathered from Vietnamese periodicals. Each entry consists of name, title, family and educational background, career, achievements, and address. Entries are arranged in alphabetic order, using traditional Vietnamese form (e.g., Do Muoi instead of Muoi Do, or Do, Muoi).

The 2d section of the directory is composed of 2 parts. The 1st, categorical listings, provides information on about 1,000 domestic (both private and state-owned) and international firms conducting business in Vietnam. Business enterprises are organized under broad subject categories, such as accounting and auditing, agriculture, airlines, electric powers, and the like. Each entry consists of name, address, telephone and fax numbers, main employees, and when possible, a brief description of the nature of the business. The 2d part, alphabetic listings, lists the firms included in the previous portion in alphabetic order. Also included in the text is an index that lists individuals under professional categories.

The information present appears to be accurate and is easy to use. Besides, to the reviewer's knowledge, this is the only "Who's Who in Vietnam" of any kind or with this scope in existence. Thus, despite some minor shortcomings, *Who's Who in Vietnam* should prove extremely essential for those who want to do business in Vietnam.—**Binh P. Le**

AUSTRALIA

114. Patterson, Kathryn. **New Zealand.** rev. ed. Brad Patterson, comp. Santa Barbara, Calif., Clio Press/ABC-CLIO, 1998. 337p. maps. index. (World Biographical Series, v.18). $98.00. ISBN 1-85109-279-X.

Kathryn Patterson, the director and chief archivist at the National Archives of New Zealand, and Brad Patterson, a research fellow at the Stout Research Centre at Victoria University of Wellington, have produced an informative volume on New Zealand for ABC-CLIO's World Biographical Series. Each volume in this series includes an introduction and an annotated bibliography of important works that deal with the country's history, geography, economy, political life, culture, religions, and social organizations.

The 59-page introduction to this volume is a highly readable discussion of the changes that have transformed New Zealand during the last two decades, including the consequent changes that have resulted from the movement toward economic deregulation and the subsequent shrinking of the role of the state. Following the introduction is a listing of 972 critical works, most of which have been published since 1980, that deal with New Zealand culture, geography, and history. Included with the bibliographical data for each entry is a 125-word abstract that summarizes and assesses the importance of each work. The entries are conveniently arranged by subject category. The volume concludes with three indexes—author, title, and subject—and two maps. Although the price of the volume will discourage private purchase, area studies specialists as well as students of New Zealand history and life will find this volume useful. *New Zealand* is recommended for research and university libraries.

—**Terry D. Bilhartz**

EUROPE

General Works

115.   **The OMRI Annual Survey of Eastern Europe and the Former Soviet Union 1996: Forging Ahead, Falling Behind.** Armonk, N.Y., M. E. Sharpe, 1997. 428p. maps. index. $85.00. ISBN 1-56324-925-1. ISSN 1088-3304.

This 2d annual survey of the 27 countries of the former Soviet bloc is divided into 9 parts. Each part contains essays, sidebars, profiles of key personalities, and documents relevant to a specific country or topic for 1996. Part 1 is an introduction by J. F. Brown that succinctly summarizes the importance of that year's events. Parts 2 through 6 cover, respectively, Central Europe, Eastern Europe, Southeastern Europe, Russia, and Trancauscasia and Central Asia. Parts 7 through 9 cover broad topical issues, including regional economic developments, democratic institutions, and issues in foreign policy. The more than 40 contributors are either Open Media Research Institute (OMRI) employees or are in academia, government, and the private sector and have knowledge of the area. The maps, summary statistics, and well-written and informative essays provide a comprehensive and authoritative view of developments in Eastern Europe and the former Soviet Union for 1996.—**Robert H. Burger**

116.   Rogel, Carole. **The Breakup of Yugoslavia and the War in Bosnia.** Westport, Conn., Greenwood Press, 1998. 182p. illus. maps. index. (Greenwood Press Guides to Historic Events of the Twentieth Century). $39.95. ISBN 0-313-29918-8.

This volume should be a part of all public libraries, as well as an essential reference source for journalists and members of all media dealing with world events. It deals in facts, a commodity that is often hard to come by in the part of the world herein discussed. The book starts with a brief chronology of events and then offers a historical overview of the breakup of Yugoslavia and the subsequent Bosnian war. A fascinating chapter on myths, propaganda, and Balkan politics is next, followed by a section on the responses of the international community. Next come the biographies of the most important players, ranging from Arkan to Warren Zimmermann. These biographical sketches are detailed and well researched, with the largest amount of space devoted, understandably enough, to the biography of Serbian President Slobodan Milosevic.

Another fascinating part of this book is the section devoted to the most important documents of the war. These include selected United Nations Security Council resolutions, relevant newspaper and magazine articles, President Bill Clinton's speech on the Dayton Accords, an excerpt from a book written by Croatian President Franjo Tudjman, and even excerpts from the celebrated *Zlata's Diary*. A glossary of selected terms is included, as is an annotated bibliography and a short list of films and CD-ROMs. Strange for a book of this nature, not a single Slavic diacritical mark is used, which make some of the names quoted in it look rather peculiar.

—**Koraljka Lockhart**

117.   Warmenhoven, Henri J. **Western Europe.** 5th ed. New York, Dushkin/McGraw-Hill, 1997. 276p. illus. maps. index. (Global Studies Series). $20.25. ISBN 0-07-290285-X.

One of eight volumes in the Global Studies Series, *Western Europe* gives up-to-date information and statistics on 24 countries and the Vatican City-State. Four introductory chapters discuss the history and culture of Western Europe, the labor movement, and the welfare states in the area. For each country, statistics on geography, population, health, religions, education, communication, transportation, armed forces, and the economy and brief information on the system of government are presented, followed by text giving historical background and the current social and political situation. Black-and-white photographs and maps accompany each country's entry.

The information on each country is supplemented by 24 well-written articles selected from periodicals and newspapers published throughout the world on a wide variety of political and social issues from European

Union hopes and fantasies to ethnic groups who seek self-determination and the resurgence of the political right in several countries. Some articles focus on a single country. Others are concerned with the area as a whole.

Supplementary sections include a list of sources for statistical reports, a glossary of terms and abbreviations, a bibliography arranged by country, a list of sources with a general or regional perspective, a list of periodicals that cover the area, and a list of selected World Wide Web sites for Western Europe. An index provides access by names and subjects in one alphabetic list. This compilation can be used as a ready-reference tool or as an introductory textbook on the area or on any of the countries or subjects. It is highly recommended for all reference collections.—**Shirley L. Hopkinson**

Albania

118.   Young, Antonia, with John Hodgson and Nigel Young. **Albania.** rev. ed. Santa Barbara, Calif., Clio Press/ABC-CLIO, 1997. 293p. index. (World Bibliographic Series, v.94). $85.00. ISBN 1-85109-260-9.

Timely in view of the political problems in the Kosovo province of Yugoslavia with its 90 percent Albanian-majority, this volume contains numerous references to that province. The total number of sources listed is 922, divided into 41 categories that start with a section titled "The Country and Its People" and end with "Bibliographies." All entries are carefully annotated, some critically and some with comparisons drawn against other similar sources, which adds to the usefulness of this reference source. Additional features include a brief introduction to Albania, a chronology of events, a table of place-names with their alternative forms as adopted in different languages, short biographies of notable persons in Albania's history, and a useful guide to the pronunciation of Albanian words. The volume ends with an index of authors whose works were mentioned in it, an index of titles, and an index of subjects. A map of localities and rivers of Albania (no roads or railroads are shown) concludes the volume. The final items of information end with late 1997. This reviewer regrets not having had this source at his disposal some years ago when doing research on Albania, as it is a most useful guide to the country. [R: Choice, July/Aug 98, p. 1840]—**Hermina G. B. Anghelescu**

Austria

119.   **Vienna.** C. M. Peniston-Bird, comp. Santa Barbara, Calif., ABC-CLIO, 1997. 159p. maps. index. (World Bibliographical Series, v. 201). $62.00. ISBN 1-85109-275-7.

This annotated bibliography directs readers to a wide range of sources about Austria's political and cultural capital, Vienna. Librarians will be familiar with ABC-CLIO's World Bibliographical Series. Having covered the nations of the world, the set is now looking at smaller regions, including world-class cities. The format is unchanged—citations with summary paragraphs describe publications on geography, history, society, culture, and politics. The compiler, a longtime resident of Vienna with a Ph.D. in Austrian studies, provides a starting point for anyone in search of sources on the Viennese and life in their city, from Wolfgang Amadeus Mozart to coffeehouses to Sigmund Freud. Most cited works are books in English, but maps, theses, articles, and German-language materials cover specific topics as needed.

Almost 500 entries are organized in 2 dozen chapters. Both scholarly and popular works are included—some published as recently as 1995—with selected historical titles from the nineteenth century or even earlier where appropriate. A 20-page introduction identifies major themes in Viennese history. There are a short glossary and a simple map of the 23 city districts, and thorough indexing by author, title and subject.

The only comparable work is Denys Salt's 1986 bibliography on Austria, which appeared in the same series (see ARBA 87, entry 126), but despite some overlapping coverage, this newer volume successfully distinguishes between what is Viennese and what is Austrian. This useful, well-designed book will assist students, travelers, and general readers.—**Steven W. Sowards**

Bosnia

120.   Cuvalo, Ante. **Historical Dictionary of Bosnia and Herzegovina.** Lanham, Md., Scarecrow, 1997. 353p. (European Historical Dictionaries, no.25). $45.00. ISBN 0-8108-3344-1.
   Although this useful handbook is designated as an historical dictionary, it is actually much more. About one-half of the pages in this volume are devoted to entries for historical terms, persons, and events that are centrally relevant to the history of Bosnia and Herzegovina. The other half of the book contains materials that will be of great use to anyone studying these countries. After a brief introduction, the author provides a 50-page chronology of major events in the history of Bosnia and Herzegovina and maps relevant to this chronology. Prior to the entries of historical terms, an overview of the geography, religious orientation, and history of this region is given. Following the entries for the historical terms, Cuvalo has compiled a multilingual bibliography of Bosnia and Herzegovina that also includes regional histories and other works relevant to that history.
   This work delivers much more than the title indicates. It will be of use for anyone doing research on Bosnia and Herzegovina during any time period.—**Robert H. Burger**

Czech Republic

121.   Otfinoski, Steven. **The Czech Republic.** New York, Facts on File, 1997. 122p. illus. maps. index. (Nations in Transition). $17.95. ISBN 0-8160-3080-4.
   Anyone needing introductory information about the Czech Republic will welcome the appearance of Otfinoski's work, which is part of Facts on File's Nations in Transition series. The opening chapter introduces the reader to this "beautiful and enchanting" country, displaying a standard image of the Hradčany castle in Prague. In the following 36 pages the author gives us a historical overview of the Czech Republic from prehistory to present. He then presents the reader with mini-lessons on Czech government, religion, economy, culture, daily life, and information on some of the important cities and towns. In the last chapter the author offers ideas on present problems and future solutions. Otfinoski provides the most current information possible and communicates today's reality of political, economic, and cultural transformations.
   The material is clearly and logically organized, making use of boxes for highlighting important data. Although this is an adequate, cursory lesson on the Czech Republic, it is not a clear and thought-provoking portrait of the Czech people as stated in the objectives of the Nations in Transition series. The material chosen covers events and personages already familiar to Western audiences, including Hus, Kafka, and Dvorlak. Among the missing legends is Bozena Nemcova, who influenced generations of Czech and Slovak writers, including Kafka.
   Although the chronology satisfactorily reflects the contents of this work, the further reading section is minimal. The illustrations and maps are a nice addition to this book, and the index has convenient explanatory notes. This reasonably priced work can function as a resource for travelers wanting a quick introduction to the Czech Republic as well as for younger audiences interested in Slavic countries. *The Czech Republic* is recommended for all libraries with an interest in Eastern Europe.—**Magda Želinská-Ferl**

Former Soviet Republics

122.   **Documents of Soviet-American Relations, Volume 3: Diplomatic Relations, Economic Relations, Propaganda, International Affairs, Neutrality 1933-1941.** Harold J. Goldberg, ed. Gulf Breeze, Fla., Academic International Press, 1998. 371p. index. $95.00. ISBN 0-87569-133-1.

123.   **Documents of Soviet History, Volume 4: Stalin Grasps Power 1926-1928.** Alex G. Cummins, ed. Gulf Breeze, Fla., Academic International Press, 1998. 398p. index. $95.00. ISBN 0-87569-138-2.
   Documents of Soviet-American Relations covers the following: diplomatic relations, economic relations, propaganda, international affairs, and neutrality for the years 1933 to 1941. *Documents of Soviet History* discusses Joseph Stalin's grasp of power from 1926 to 1928. Volume 3 has a chronological list of documents, a selected bibliography, and indexes. Volume 4 has a classified list of documents by main topics, a glossary, and several

indexes (personal names, subjects, institutions, and geographic and place-names). This is a standard work about Soviet documentation that reminds us of Henry Commager and Milton Cantor's *Documents of American History* published in several editions or other similar works.—**Bohdan S. Wynar**

124.   Kort, Michael. **Russia.** rev. ed. New York, Facts on File, 1998. 200p. illus. maps. index. (Nations in Transition). $19.95. ISBN 0-8160-3776-0.

The Nations in Transition series is intended for middle school and high school students and provides a quick, easy-to-read overview of a specific country. History, politics, and personalities are emphasized. Although there is basic background information included, these texts have limited usefulness for undergraduates.

The volume on Russia is an attractive book, filled with photographs and maps and a few biographical profiles. Revised from the 1995 edition, the book resembles a condensed textbook more than a reference source. The chapters survey the history of Russia and its geography, culture, politics, economy, and daily life. There is a brief chronology of Russian history, with an emphasis on the events from 1989 to the present, and a short bibliography. Although this work may provide an adequate introduction for younger students, high school students (and beyond) would greatly benefit from a more substantial work, such as the newly published *Russia: A Country Study*, edited by Glenn E. Curtis (Government Printing Office, 1998). Even the *Europa World Year Book* (see entry 66) is a better place to find recent information and statistical data.—**Thomas A. Karel**

125.   Milner-Gulland, Robin, and Nikolai Dejevsky. **Cultural Atlas of Russia and the Former Soviet Union.** rev. ed. New York, Checkmark Books/Facts on File, 1998. 240p. illus. maps. index. $50.00. ISBN 0-8160-3815-5.

The 1st edition of this atlas was published in 1989, and this revised edition supplements and complements some information covered previously, especially in such areas as religion (e.g., millennium of official conversion to Christianity that took place in 988 C.E.). There is an updated section on Josef Stalin's regime, new information on independent republics, and new entries in the bibliography. Part 3, "Regions and Countries of the Former Soviet Union," briefly covers significant changes. In examining the section on Ukraine, this reviewer found, unfortunately, that the information is too brief to be of substantial assistance to the reader, and occasionally there are some errors. For example, the population of Ukraine is not "over 51 million" but more than 52 million. There are several minorities in Ukraine but not "more than a hundred nationalities," and the information on Ukrainian industry and agriculture is not adequate. There is nothing about Ukrainian history or culture. In general, the atlas has good illustrations, the bibliography is adequate for the uninitiated, and the book, produced by Facts on File in Great Britain, is printed on high-quality paper.—**Bohdan S. Wynar**

126.   **Russia & Eurasia Facts & Figures Annual, Volume 24.** Lawrence R. Robertson, ed. Gulf Breeze, Fla., Academic International Press, 1998. 502p. maps. $77.00 subscription/$97.00 non-subscription. ISBN 0-87569-199-4.

Academic International Press has established a considerable tradition with its many years of producing this annual publication. Volume 24 consists of several parts, covering the individual independent states with an introductory section: Commonwealth of Independent States. Each section includes chapters on basic indicators; chronology; health and welfare; economy, industry, and agriculture; energy and environment; and foreign trade, investment, and aid. The section on Russia is large (pp. 20-181), but other states receive less information. For example, Ukraine, the second largest state after Russia, receives only 31 pages. After examining the information on Ukraine more closely, this reviewer found that most statistical data pertains to 1997, with some sections (e.g., education or food consumption) covering the years 1991 to 1996.—**Bohdan S. Wynar**

France

127.   Chambers, Frances, comp. **Paris.** Santa Barbara, Calif., Clio Press/ABC-CLIO, 1998. 138p. index. (World Bibliographical Series, v.206). $54.00. ISBN 1-85109-271-4.

The World Bibliographical Series from Clio Press covers some 200 countries and cities around the world. Literature on Paris is voluminous. This volume on Paris includes 430 entries of the most important and most accessible readings for English readers drawn from books, journals, and newspapers. Entries are organized by subject matter, including topics such as history, geography, politics and administration, architecture, arts and literature, guidebooks, society, and the economy. Designed primarily for English-speaking readers, it focuses on

English publications but includes French entries for those topics where English-language materials are limited. Each entry includes full bibliographical information and a short (often only one line) summary of contents. An introduction includes a rapid summary of the history of Paris. Entries are organized under broad subject sections. Indexes allow readers to search by authors, titles, and specialized topics from *abattoirs* to *Zurich*. *Paris* is recommended for research libraries. [R: Choice, Nov 98, p. 500]—**Frank L. Wilson**

128. **Encyclopedia of Contemporary French Culture.** Alex Hughes and Keith Reader, eds. New York, Routledge, 1998. 618p. index. $140.00. ISBN 0-415-13186-3.

In an effort to provide an overview of the richness of French culture from the end of World War II to the present day, the editors of the *Encyclopedia of Contemporary French Culture* have gathered together more than 700 articles contributed by some 90 scholars, most of which are from universities in Great Britain, on a wide range of topics from intellectual life to food and drink in France and francophone countries. Although the articles vary in length, the shorter entries contain cross-references either within the text or at the end of the article that lead the reader to the longer, more comprehensive articles. An extensive back-of-the-book index is useful in identifying a variety of articles that treat a particular individual or a specific topic. The target audience for the encyclopedia is not narrowly focused but is aimed at students of European culture in all areas, from political science or economics to dance and drama. The closest counterpart to this encyclopedia is the *Oxford Companion to Literature in French* (see ARBA 96, entry 1252), which expanded its scope from traditional literary genres to include new art forms such as cinema. By contrast, the unique value of this encyclopedia is in its emphasis on the vitality of francophone culture beyond mainland France, especially in the areas of popular culture and the performing arts. It is clear that the nature of contemporary French culture presented in this encyclopedia is defined less exclusively as a "community of cultural or racial heritage" and more inclusively as a "contractual association of individuals (irrespective of race, religion or origin)" (p. 293). *Encyclopedia of Contemporary French Culture* is recommended for academic libraries supporting an interdisciplinary program in the humanities. [R: LJ, 1 Oct 98, pp. 76-78; BL, 15 Sept 98, pp. 260-262]—**David G. Nowak**

Germany

129. **Modern Germany: An Encyclopedia of History, People, and Culture, 1871-1990.** Dieter K. Buse and Juergen C. Doerr, eds. New York, Garland, 1998. 2v. illus. maps. index. (Garland Reference Library of the Humanities, v.1520). $150.00. ISBN 0-8153-0503-6.

Modern Germany is a well-organized, well-edited, and well-written handbook, filling a surprising gap in the reference coverage of modern German history. Signed articles of one to four columns cover biographies of important figures in all fields, including abortion, Gestapo, youth movements, agriculture, and old age. A careful balance is maintained among diverse fields, including science, business and economics, politics, and high culture. The articles are clear, concise, and interesting. Useful and carefully selected bibliographies of 1 to 10 items (including citations to works in German) complete each article.

A subject guide at the beginning of volume 1 offers an overview of coverage by organizing subtopics under more general headings. A detailed index to topics and authors of the articles closes the set. Although the index is useful, it does show confusion on the part of the editors as to whether to emphasize the German or English forms of names and subjects, and sometimes the English renderings vary. Different name forms for the same body or topic often point to different articles (e.g., the entry for "Peoples' Chamber" refers the reader to one article, the one for "Volkskammer" to another).

The editors' claim that it is the "first English language work of such comprehensiveness" seems quite justified; there are encyclopedias covering specific periods in detail, such as *The Encyclopedia of the Third Reich* (Macmillan, 1991), and the *Historical Dictionary of Germany* (see ARBA 96, entry 546) covers the Roman period to the present in one volume. However, there is nothing in English and no recent work in German that offers the same scope. *Modern Germany* is highly recommended for all academic and for large public libraries. [R: Choice, Sept 98, p. 100; BR, Sept/Oct 98, pp. 75-76]—**V. W. Hill**

Great Britain

130.   Gardiner, Vince, comp. **The Channel Islands.** Santa Barbara, Calif., ABC-CLIO, 1998. 179p. illus. index. (World Bibliographical Series, v.209). $61.00. ISBN 1-85109-302-8.

This is the latest in the series of the ABC-CLIO bibliographic references on countries of the world, major cities, and regions. The Channel Islands are a string of islands near the Normandy coast of France, with a population of about 150,000 permanent residents. Although this country is located close to France geographically, the Channel Islands are historically, economically, and politically linked to the United Kingdom. They have a special political association with Great Britain that leaves them out of the European Union and possessing considerable financial autonomy. The compiler provides a short introduction to the history and status of the Channel Islands. There is also a chronology from prehistoric eras to the present.

The entries cover a range of dimensions including history, geography, tourism, folklore, finance and banking, the economy, and so on. Each entry has a two- to three-sentence abstract. Nearly all are in English. Access to the entries is facilitated by separate indexes based on the author, title, and subject. This will be a useful addition to major research libraries.—**Frank L. Wilson**

Hungary

131.   Hill, Raymond. **Hungary.** New York, Facts on File, 1997. 182p. illus. maps. (Nations in Transition). $17.95. ISBN 0-8160-3120-7.

This book is part of a series that covers some Central and Eastern European countries. The volume is a popular introduction to Hungarian history and problems, with half of it devoted to Hungarian history up to 1989 and half to post-communist politics and government, economy and trade, foreign policy and defense as well as some peripheral topics about the arts, media, and contemporary snapshots. There are some vexing, unnecessary explanations of elementary concepts. Unfortunately, the Hungarian alphabet with its 44 characters is not explained, nor is the pronunciation of Hungarian words provided. Some of the most recent statistics are from 1993, and some information comes from 1995, which—in view of the quickly changing Central European situation—renders some of the discussion already obsolete. The difficulties created by the Hungarian geopolitical situation are properly stressed, as is the nationalities issue. The usual problems of transition (inflation, unemployment, privatization, foreign ownership, modernization) are included without many specifics. The Visegrad alliance with Poland, the Czech Republic, and Slovakia is mentioned in several places, and the pact of association with and eventual membership in the European Union is emphasized. Human interest stories and popular themes are given prominence.

The book ends with a chronology of events in Hungarian history. The bibliography is disappointingly brief, but the index is good. This volume can be used as an introduction to contemporary Hungary for foreign tourists and will be useful for a high school project on that country.—**Bogdan Mieczkowski**

Ireland

132.   Boylan, Henry. **A Dictionary of Irish Biography.** 3d ed. Niwot, Colo., Roberts Rinehart Publishers, 1998. 462p. illus. $35.00. ISBN 1-57098-236-8.

Coming some 20 years after its first publication, this 3d edition of *A Dictionary of Irish Biography* offers corrections and additions to the original database. As a general principle, the dictionary includes short and concise biographies only on deceased individuals who were born in Ireland, had an Irish parent or were of Irish descent, lived and worked in Ireland, or made a significant contribution to Irish affairs. It excludes legendary or mythological characters and provides only the salient facts and events of the subjects' careers in chronological order. The dictionary includes, when possible, a short quotation to add a sense of the individual. As a general rule of thumb, the author asked the question, "Is there any reason the reader might want to know about this person, or would he or she be of interest only to a descendant or a narrow specialist in some field?" In short, the aim of the work is to bring to the common reader the stories of many gifted Irish men and women.

With that aim in mind, this book is filled with brief but informative overviews of the lives and contributions of interesting individuals, from politicians to poets, revolutionaries, television personalities, entertainers, and great churchmen.

True to its stated aims, included are individuals from within and without Ireland. Politicians such as Erskin Childers, Brian Faulkner, and Seán MacBride; poets such as Patrick Kavanagh, Seán O'Casey, and W. B. Yeats; revolutionaries such as Michael Collins, Jeremiah O'Donovan Rossa, Robert Emmet, Michael Collins, Eamon de Valera, and Bobby Sands; entertainers such as Tom and Willie Clancy (of Clancy Brothers fame), Eamon Andrews, Milo O'Shea, and Jimmy O'Dea; and churchmen and scholars such as Cardinal Tomás O Fiaich, Friar Luke Wadding, Peadar O Dubhda, and Douglas Hyde are all featured here.

No doubt, some individual of importance has been omitted from this excellent dictionary. Regardless of this, *A Dictionary of Irish Biography* is an interesting and informative contribution to personal and public libraries. [R: LJ, Dec 98, p. 86]—**Arthur Gribben**

133.   **Ireland: A Directory 1998.** 32d ed. Dublin, Institute of Public Administration; distr., Chicago, Euromonitor International, 1997. 480p. illus. index. $150.00. ISBN 1-872002-54-4. ISSN 0073-9596.

Whether one needs statistics on the Irish population or wants to know who is in political office, *Ireland: A Directory 1998* will have the answers. This book, which claims to be a "comprehensive directory of Irish life," certainly lives up to its billing. It contains a lot of information on both the private and public sector of the country, from basic facts on Ireland's population, health, education, and trade to information on radio stations, banking, companies, and volunteer organizations. Photographs of officials, a map of Ireland, and several charts enhance the work. A detailed index in the back of the book directs the reader to areas of interest, and a handy bookmark attached to the spine allows one to mark pages. This work would make a welcome addition to the reference area of any library with an interest in Ireland.—**Kelly M. Jordan**

Malta

134.   Boswell, David M. and Brian W. Beeley, comps. **Malta.** rev. ed. Santa Barbara, Calif., Clio Press/ABC-CLIO, 1998. 274p. index. (World Bibliographical Series, v.64). $79.00. ISBN 1-85109-269-2.

The World Bibliographical Series covers some 200 countries and cities around the world. This is a revision of an earlier volume on Malta. Although Malta is a small island with a population of only 376,000, it has had an important place in world history. This volume includes 980 entries of the most important readings drawn from books and journals. Most citations are from publications between 1983 and 1996. Earlier citations can be found in the 1st edition of this volume compiled by J. R. Thackrah (see ARBA 87, entry 130). Entries are organized by subject matter, including topics such as history, geography, flora and fauna, politics and administration, architecture, arts and literature, guide books, society, and the economy. Although the entries are in English, the compilers admit that access will be a problem because most of the works are by Maltese authors, printed in Malta, and often not available in British or U.S. libraries. The compilers do point to archives in Britain with extensive collections on Malta and discuss access to libraries in Malta. Each entry includes full bibliographic information and a short annotation, often including specific page references for specific content. An introduction includes a rapid summary of the history and socioeconomic status of Malta and a discussion of other bibliographies. The entries are organized under broad subject sections. Indexes allow readers to search by authors, titles, and specialized topics. This work is recommended for research libraries.—**Frank L. Wilson**

Netherlands

135.   van Os, Andre, comp. **Amsterdam.** Santa Barbara, Calif., ABC-CLIO, 1997. 104p. maps. index. (World Bibliographical Series, v.203). $53.50. ISBN 1-85109-277-3.

Readers will find many uses for this annotated bibliography of 326 works in the English language on the city of Amsterdam and its people. Students, scholars, and interested laypeople will find a good selection of books on Amsterdam's history, government, economy, society, arts, architecture, and urban planning. For prospective tourists, there are a large number of general guidebooks, atlases, and a street guide, along with specialized guides directed to a specific audience such as backpackers and cyclists, vegans, and gays and lesbians. Tourists and armchair travelers alike will enjoy any of the 16 pictorial books and photograph collections. Those who are concerned with health matters will find several serious studies of licit and illicit drug use in the city, the evolving HIV epidemic, and AIDS prevention measures. The bibliography also has special sections on such topics as Jewish life in Amsterdam, English-language fiction set in Amsterdam, translated Dutch fiction set in Amsterdam, libraries, galleries, museums, and archives as well as computer games relating to the city. The Internet is not neglected, with 22 items listed. The excellent annotations are descriptive and critically evaluative and will be of help to readers making selections from the titles listed. A short introduction traces the city's history and contemporary status and describes the bibliography and its limitations, which are due mainly to a shortage of English-language publications and translations. Supplementary sections include a list of useful addresses and a black-and-white map. There are separate author, title, and subject indexes. This compilation meets the usual standards of the series and will be of value in subject and general bibliography collections.—**Shirley L. Hopkinson**

Romania

136.   Siani-Davies, Peter and Mary Siani-Davies, comps. **Romania.** rev. ed. Santa Barbara, Calif., Clio Press/ABC-CLIO, 1998. 348p. index. (World Bibliographical Series, v.59). $99.00. ISBN 1-85109-244-7.

The fall of Romania's communist dictatorship in 1989 and the subsequent upheaval in the country's political, social, and cultural institutions necessitated a revision of the 1985 edition of this volume (see ARBA 87, entry 132 for a review). This revised bibliography refers almost entirely to material published since 1985, with only a few duplications of the most important earlier works referenced in the 1st edition. The 21-page introduction gives an excellent overview of Romania's place in the world as well as its history, geography, politics, and people. The 977 entries (increased from 797 in the 1st edition) are categorized into 34 subject areas and cover a broad range—geography and geology, tourism, prehistory and archaeology, minorities, economy, and the arts are a small sampling. Each entry refers to a book, chapter of a book, or article about some aspect of Romanian life, which are summarized in 150- to 200-word paragraphs that provide surprisingly succinct and vivid descriptions. The majority of works referred to are in English. Thorough author, title, and subject indexes follow. The binding, paper, and printing are high quality and easy on the eyes. The book fulfills well its stated goal of giving the reader a good overview of the country.—**Larry Lobel**

LATIN AMERICA AND THE CARIBBEAN

137.   Boultbee, Paul G., and David F. Raine, comps. **Bermuda.** Santa Barbara, Calif., Clio Press/ABC-CLIO, 1998. 165p. (World Bibliographical Series, v.205). $74.50. ISBN 1-85109-170-X.

Although not nearly as comprehensive as A. C. H. Hallett's *Bermuda in Print* (Juniperhill Press, 1995), volume 205 of ABC-CLIO's World Bibliographical Series is an excellent bibliography and makes for a good introduction to this mid-Atlantic, subtropical chain of islands and self-governing territory of the United Kingdom. Librarian (and compiler of three previous volumes in this series) Boultbee and archivist (and author of a number of popular works on Bermuda) Raine have selected 545 citations, organized into 37 major categories. Subject categories and arrangement are typical of the series.

Each of the numbered citations includes an annotation. Collectively, these well-written annotations serve in themselves as a guidebook to Bermuda's history, culture, economy, ecology, and current circumstances. Excluded are foreign-language publications, theses, audiovisual materials, and anything (other than bibliographies) about the Bermuda Triangle. The text contains a map that includes most of the places mentioned in citations and annotations and a comprehensive author/title/subject index.

This bibliography was carefully produced and is accurate in detail, upholding the high standard that this series has achieved in previous volumes. It would, however, have benefited from a longer and more in-depth introduction like those produced for some of the other volumes in this series. For instance, one could read the introduction and each of the annotated citations and still not know that the majority of Bermuda's population is of African descent.—**Fred J. Hay**

138.   **South America, Central America, and the Caribbean 1999.** 7th ed. London, Europa; distr., Farmington Hills, Mich., Gale, 1998. 798p. $370.00. ISBN 1-85743-055-7. ISSN 0258-0661.

A compilation of facts by 37 contributors satisfies deep and detailed curiosity about 48 countries stretching from Mexico to South Georgia, which is south of the Falkland Islands. Each country is microscopically dissected, organized, and explained in precise British detail. This massive undertaking begins with eight introductory essays ranging from trade blocs and integration to the politics of drugs and the environmental impacts of tourism. Current and specific information contained in this volume evaluates basic economic indicators such as rate of inflation, imports and exports, balance of payments, and foreign debt. The spectrum swings from adult literature, energy consumption, cellular phone distribution, and number of daily publications to the effects of Roman Catholic thought on the populace. Each country's history, from its inception to the spring of 1998, provides a full and fair assessment based on scholarly research and detachment. The economy of each country goes beyond coffee and bananas to the impact of tourism-terrorism as opposed to eco-tourism, and from the necessity of petroleum exploration to environmental benevolence.

This book provides an understanding of exactly what is necessary for a country to remain solvent and independent while retaining its culture. Charts are copious and consistent for each country, describing diverse complexities such as forest removal, fishing, finance, and broadcasting as well as their relation to national vitality.

Whether a reader is interested in one or all 48 countries, the thoroughness of research and communication prevail. This is an expensive book, well worth its price in trade for its content.—**Mary Pat Boian**

MIDDLE EAST

139.   Auchterlonie, Paul, comp. **Yemen.** rev. ed. Santa Barbara, Calif., Clio Press/ABC-CLIO, 1998. 349p. maps. index. (World Bibliographical Series, v.50). $91.00. ISBN 1-85109-255-2.

Yemen is volume 50 in the World Bibliographical Series published by Clio Press. (There are 204 volumes published or planned.) Compiled by Auchterlonie, this book is a revision of the 1984 edition (see ARBA 86, entry 156). The publisher reports that it is "much healthier" than the first work but in an unusual statement says, "There are still significant gaps in our knowledge of Yemen," citing 10 examples from archives to sports. The Republic of Yemen lies in the southwest corner of the Arabian Peninsula. About the size of France, it has a population of some 14 million (less than one-fourth of the French population).

Auchterlonie has divided his bibliography into 34 topics ranging from "The Country and Its People" to the "Visual Arts." Each of the 938 citations carries a descriptive note. There are 3 indexes—authors and editors, titles, and subjects. The "gaps" reported by the publisher are not apparent, and until taken care of, this volume is more than adequate. [R: Choice, Oct 98, p. 295]—**David Eggenberger**

4   Economics and Business

GENERAL WORKS

Bibliography

140.   **Harvard Business School Core Collection, 1998: An Author, Title, and Subject Guide.** Sue Marsh, ed. Boston, Harvard Business School Press, 1998. 430p. index. $65.00pa. ISBN 0-87584-774-9.

This work is a bibliographically annotated catalog of essential business-oriented textbooks, handbooks, biographies, company histories, and other pertinent publications collected within the Baker Library at the Harvard Business School. As defined, this collection of roughly 3,500 business books is intended to provide students, faculty, and other interested users with a manageable index of relevant materials that is revised and updated annually. These materials, representing a diverse array of business topics, are listed alphabetically by subject and indexed by title and author. This handy and useful reference work also includes a list of notable business books that have won awards or been named to various best books lists.

Since its inception in 1969, items have been added or removed from the collection to keep the series current and practical. Some 50 items within the core collection are designated as "core classics" and as such provide a meaningful overview of the development and evolution of the business curriculum, at least over the past few decades. Because the materials included within the collection reflect both the teaching and research interests of the faculty at the Harvard Business School, business educators and researchers in other business programs can essentially use this list to more efficiently identify topical materials. Conveniently, this reference work also includes the names and addresses of applicable publishers in an appendix.—**Timothy E. Sullivan**

141.   **International Business and Trade Directories: A Worldwide Directory of Directories.** 2d ed. Richard Gottlieb, ed. Lakeville, Conn., Grey House Publishing, 1998. 1151p. index. $200.00; $185.00pa. ISBN 1-891482-07-6; 0-939300-44-3pa.

As the "global economy" changes from a buzzword to an essential, the emphasis on foreign trade will continue to increase. First published in 1995, this 2d edition of a useful directory has nearly 4,000 new entries and 4,952 updates to existing entries. Within 81 industry groups such as biotechnology, jewelry, toys, video, and water supply, entries are arranged alphabetically. Each industry chapter is broken down into 10 regions of the world, which are again broken down by specific country.

Each entry includes content descriptions with number of pages, prices and ISBN, publisher's name and address, homepage and e-mail addresses, editorial staff information, and telephone and fax numbers. The content descriptions vary from a line or two of general descriptors (e.g., wholesale distributors, importers, manufacturers, liquidators), to six or seven lines with facts and figures. "The Directory of Apparel Specialty Stores" entry states that it "profiles more than 3,400 men's and boys' wear ... in over 39,000 stores" (p. 824) and continues to state that it lists 13,235 individual personnel of these firms. .

Three useful indexes complete the volume: an entry index, a geographic index, and a publisher index. The geographic index is particularly helpful because it is sometimes difficult to find a directory for a specific country and a specific industry. Libraries with an international business focus, especially in the marketing area, will want to purchase this volume.—**Susan C. Awe**

Biography

142.   **Nonprofit Sector Yellow Book: Who's Who in the Management of the Leading Foundations, Universities, Museums, and Other Nonprofit Organizations.** Winter 1999 ed. Michele A. Barile, Karen Y. Chan, and Stacey Bronoel, eds. New York, Leadership Directories, 1998. 1048p. index. $215.00pa. ISSN 1520-9148.

This is the latest title in the Leadership Directories series that now totals 14 directories. This directory will be published semiannually and includes contact information for more than 40,000 nonprofit executives and trustees who are associated with some 1,000 nonprofit institutions. For some individuals one will find a biographical sketch or a picture. The scope of this volume includes charitable service organizations, preparatory schools, library systems, medical institutions, museums, performing art groups and centers, and foundations, and the largest section covers colleges and universities. Each section has attempted to provide information on the administrative staff, including address, telephone number, and e-mail addresses, when available. The sections also provide a list of trustees or outside directors.

As has been true in other titles of this series, new material will be added semiannually. Instead of acquiring this individual title, the purchaser can consider acquiring either the CD-ROM or Internet version that includes all 14 titles. Smaller libraries that have general requests for information regarding nonprofit organizations will find this a useful purchase. Larger libraries may find most of this particular title's contents duplicated in other, more comprehensive directories such as the *Foundation Directory* (19th ed.; see ARBA 98, entry 787).
—**Judith J. Field**

143.   **Tycoons and Entrepreneurs.** Judy Culligan, ed. New York, Macmillan Library Reference/Simon & Schuster Macmillan, 1998. 349p. illus. index. (Macmillan Profiles, v.2). $75.00. ISBN 0-02-864982-6.

This volume comprises some 120 profiles of tycoons and entrepreneurs from the eighteenth century to the present. Some of the articles were adapted from the publisher's other reference titles, whereas others were commissioned specifically for this volume. The profiles are brief (one to three pages) and written in an engaging style. Their subjects represent a broad range of business and cultural backgrounds. The volume concludes with an index, a 10-page glossary of business terms, and a 20-page list of references to additional readings on many of the figures profiled.

The work's preface indicates that a team of high school teachers and librarians was consulted during the book's preparation. This volume would be a good addition to a reference collection serving young adults. Undergraduates might find this a useful quick reference or starting point for research but would likely need to consult additional sources for more in-depth information.—**Christopher J. Hoeppner**

Business History

144.   Walker, Juliet E. K. **The History of Black Business in America: Capitalism, Race, Entrepreneurship.** New York, Macmillan Library Reference/Simon & Schuster Macmillan, 1998. 482p. index. (Twayne's Evolution of Modern Business Series). $45.00. ISBN 0-8057-1650-5.

The History of Black Business in America: Capitalism, Race, Entrepreneurship is a thorough, scholarly, and well-researched text. It is also one of the first comprehensive resources on this subject. Prior works have focused narrowly by time, place, or industry. This work covers the span of U.S. history and includes information on major figures, industries and services, and companies. The arrangement of the work is chronological and includes subthemes within sections, such as the influence of discrimination, government policies, culture, and social life on business. Sections on business before the twentieth century are especially valuable because information is scattered and difficult to access for this period. The post-1945 section draws most heavily from the resource *Black Enterprise*, compiling information that would require consulting hundreds of issues. Some topics, such as black sports enterprises, that have been covered thoroughly in other resources receive less attention in order to emphasize less well known enterprises. The index is a thorough listing of names, businesses, and themes found throughout the work. This is not an essential purchase for most libraries, but will prove a rich resource for those where there is strong interest in business or African American history.—**Lynne M. Fox**

Dictionaries and Encyclopedias

145.   Collin, P. H. **Dictionary of Business.** 2d ed. Middlesex, Great Britain, Peter Collin, 1994; repr., Chicago, Fitzroy Dearborn, 1998. 331p. $45.00. ISBN 1-57958-077-7.

There must be an enormous demand for business dictionaries, judging by the quantity of them published annually (see ARBA 98, entry 153; ARBA 96, entry 178 and 180; and ARBA 95, entry 185, just to name a few). Of course, coverage is not always equivalent, with some focusing on specific areas such as high finance and stock markets, others with an emphasis on economic terminology or management and marketing. Originally a British publication, this entry into the field is targeted toward the general user and intends to provide broad, basic coverage in its 4,500 entries. Definitions are intentionally simple—all but 470 words used in the definitions are themselves defined in the dictionary. Both British and U.S. spelling and vocabulary are included, but the pronunciation guide, which uses International Phonetic Association symbols, favors British form. Illustrative quotations from worldwide newspapers and magazines, translated into simpler language when necessary, are an unusual and useful feature in a dictionary of this type. Supplements offer help with numbers, telephoning, business letters, financial documents, and world currencies. Although inclusion of specialized or technical terminology is limited, this dictionary seems to be comprehensive enough for the average user, with an easy-to-use and attractive design.

—**Larry Lobel**

146.   **Routledge Spanish Dictionary of Business, Commerce, and Finance. Diccionario Ingles de Negocios, Comercio y Finanzas.** By Emilio G. Muniz Castro. New York, Routledge, 1998. 822p. $99.00. ISBN 0-415-09393-7.

This general business and commerce dictionary covers a broad range of terminology from the main fields of business. The editorial team consisted of leading subject experts who verified the accuracy, currency, and translation of the terms. The work attempts to include essential vocabulary; only terms that can be applied in a business context are included. (This is how it differs from a general English-Spanish dictionary.) Terms are also included from both North American and British English; and on the Spanish side, they are included from both Latin America and Spain. Interestingly enough, the English part of the dictionary is more than 10 percent bigger than the Spanish part. English compound terms are especially well represented in this work, as are idiomatic expressions in both languages (e.g., *golden handshake* and *golden parachute* were listed in one entry). Additionally, entries contain one or more subject headings for terms by usage. As with most dictionaries, the parts of speech are provided in the entries, as is gender for the Spanish-language nouns. There is a special section for abbreviations used in the entries for parts of speech as well as geographic codes and level codes. Multiple indexes, letter and resume samples, glossaries of job titles, and other useful information make this dictionary an exceptional single-volume reference. The two-column format is generously spaced; headings and subheadings in the entries are set in bold typeface that is easy on the eyes. This fine reference work is highly recommended.

—**Edward Erazo**

147.   Urrutia, Manuel R. **Dictionary of Business, English-Spanish, Spanish-English: Accounting, Management, Finance, Economics, and Marketing.** [repr. ed.] Balderas, Mexico, Editorial Limusa; distr., Cincinnati, Ohio, AIMS International Books, 1998. 394p. $59.95pa. ISBN 968-18-5482-9.

This paperbound work is the first reprint of the 1995 edition of the same title. Its stated purpose is to provide a bilingual dictionary that pulls together "the terms of most common usage, both in English and in Spanish" from five separate fields of the business world into one convenient volume for business professionals and their support staff. In the preface, the author notes the inclusion of idioms and idiomatic expressions, a feature based on his own work as an editor. Libraries lacking the previous edition should consider adding this relatively inexpensive volume to their business and foreign-language reference holdings.—**Robert B. Marks Ridinger**

Directories

148.   **Brands and Their Companies Supplement: New Consumer Products and Their Manufacturers with Addresses and Phone Numbers.** 17th ed. Christine A. Kesler, ed. Detroit, Gale, 1998. 2v. (A Gale Trade Names Directory). $765.00/set. ISBN 0-7876-2286-9.

Gale's *Brands and Their Companies* continues to be a mainstay of business reference collections. It provides accurate, up-to-date information regarding more than 362,000 brand names and identifies the 80,000 domestic companies that are currently or have previously produced or distributed these products. In format, *Brands and Their Companies* has remained fundamentally unchanged since the previous two reviews in ARBA (see ARBA 93, entry 188 and ARBA 91, entry 259). It is still composed of 2 listings—the 1st is arranged alphabetically by brand and provides a 1- to 3-word product description as well as the name of the manufacturer or distributor. However, the entries no longer contain reference source codes. The 2d section contains an alphabetic company listing, including the addresses and telephone, fax, and toll-free numbers of the companies. This listing is no longer printed on yellow paper, but is indicated by a fore-edge mark. Pertinent company Website and e-mail addresses have been included when available in the new edition. *Brands and Their Companies* remains an invaluable reference source for all academic, public, and pertinent special libraries.—**Mark A. Allan**

149.   **The Corporate Directory of U.S. Public Companies 1998: Company Profiles and Indexes.** San Mateo, Calif., Walker's Western Research, 1998. 2778p. index. $360.00. ISBN 1-879346-33-8.

This 1-volume work is an alphabetic listing of more than 10,000 U.S. public companies and foreign companies offering American Depository Receipts, followed by 8 indexes that provide alternate access to the information. Each entry supplies the usual name (and former name if any), address, and telephone number, along with an Internet address when available. Other basic information includes state of incorporation; number of employees; names of the auditor, stock agent, and legal counsel; and the DUNS number. Stock data provide relevant stock exchange and ticker symbol, outstanding shares, shares held by company personnel, total number of shareholders, and the closing price as of November 1997. The business description is brief, followed by primary and secondary SIC numbers; a list of subsidiaries; names and titles of officers, directors, and owners, along with their ages and salaries when available. Last presented is financial data, including current assets, plant equipment, total assets, current and total liabilities, net worth, P/E ratio, indicated annual dividend, and debt/equity ratio. The latest annual data and the five-year history of sales, net income, and earnings per share may or may not include 1997. The format is concise and user-friendly, and offers multiple access with indexing by company name, officers and directors, owners, SIC numbers, subsidiary/parent companies, geographic location, stock exchange/ticker symbol, and Fortune 1,000 ranking. This directory is also available on CD-ROM.—**Jean Engler**

150.   **Directory of Corporate Affiliations 1998: Master Index.** Christine Kerwin and others, eds. New Providence, N.J., National Register/Reed Elsevier, 1998. 5v. $1,029.95. ISBN 0-87217-217-1.

The *Directory of Corporate Affiliations*, published since 1967, provides business researchers with an invaluable source of basic corporate hierarchy and reportage information for almost 15,000 U.S. and non-U.S. parent companies as well as more than 100,000 subsidiary companies. It is a multifaceted reference tool that can be used to determine either "who owns whom" or to identify a particular companies' affiliates, subsidiaries, divisions, or joint ventures.

Two of the set's five volumes provide a variety of useful indexing. One may search by company name, Standard Industrial Code, or geographical terms. There are also indexes for brand names and personnel. The three other volumes are organized into U.S. public companies, U.S. private companies, and international public and private companies. Companies are arranged in each volume alphabetically. One of the strengths of the set is that each company entry pulls together all its U.S. and non-U.S. subsidiaries into one list.

The criteria for inclusion are described in the front matter as being flexible. Domestic companies need to have revenues greater than $10 million, "substantial" assets or net worth, or more than 300 employees. Foreign companies must have revenues of more than $50 million. Typical directory information one might expect to find includes company address, fax number, e-mail address, ticker symbol and stock exchange, basic financial data, number of employees, description of business, key personnel, board of directors, legal firm, and auditor. The corporate "family tree" information varies with the complexity of the company, but can include listings of affiliates, divisions, joint ventures, and subsidiaries. The entry also indicates the reporting relationships with the company.

Although U.S. public and private companies receive the greatest coverage, more than 2,424 parent companies are non-U.S. in origin. Of the more than 100,000 subsidiaries listed in the volumes, some 54,000 are located outside the United States and, of this latter number, nearly 40,000 are foreign-owned.

Although this is an important reference source, it should be noted here that the print format of the *Directory of Corporate Affiliations* poses some problems for business reference librarians. The set consists of five oversized paperback volumes, each nearly 2,000 pages in length. Users must move back and forth between the indexes and the "Public," "Private," or "International" volumes to view company data. This is possible but awkward if one is researching a long list of companies. The product is also available as a CD-ROM as well as through online service providers like LEXIS-NEXIS and Dialog. Although neither electronic format was examined for this review, readers may wish to consider investigating an electronic alternative. Also, if the set is expected to get heavy use, the volumes should be bound. This adds to the set's considerable cost. The value provided by the *Directory of Corporate Affiliations*, however, far exceeds its cost and awkwardness. This is an essential tool and is recommended for any serious business reference collection.—**Gordon J. Aamot**

151. **FaxUSA, 1998: A Directory of Facsimile Numbers for Businesses and Organizations Nationwide.** 5th ed. Kay Gill and Darren L. Smith, eds. Detroit, Omnigraphics, 1998. 1422p. $110.00pa. ISBN 0-7808-0291-8. ISSN 1075-7112.

This 5th edition of *FaxUSA* includes 110,000 fax numbers. The 1,500-page softbound volume is organized for easy access to needed numbers. There is an alphabetic listing and a geographic section by state and city. Each entry includes the name of the business, complete address, telephone numbers, and classification codes to identify the line of business or type of institution.

Selection of business listings is based on annual sales; however, there are other categories included, such as colleges and universities, associations, chambers of commerce, military facilities, libraries, newspapers, sports and entertainment personalities, corporate executives, and government agencies. This publication would be an asset to any library.—**Sue Brown**

152. Levine, Jeffrey P. **Pittsburgh Business Directory.** Pittsburgh, Pa., Pittsburgh Business Times, 1997. 1041p. index. $49.95. ISBN 0-9650280-1-1. ISSN 1093-457X.

This 2d edition, published by the Pittsburgh Business Times, covers companies located in the greater Pittsburgh area. Businesses must have 35 or more employees to be included. A total of 1,312 companies are listed. Those 1,239 entries for private companies, subsidiaries, or nonprofits provide basic directory information and run about one-half page in length. Entries for the 73 public companies located in the Pittsburgh area contain more informative two-page entries. Of special interest are the 73 executive biographies for selected officers of public companies. Companies are listed alphabetically and the author has provided several useful indexes—county, zip code, officer, executive biography, and SIC code. According to the front matter, the author has also written similar works for other cities, including Boston, Kansas City, New York City, and Chicago.

This is a well-organized and reasonably priced directory that will be of great interest to those business collections in and around Pittsburgh. Business librarians in other parts of the country, however, will find it a less compelling purchase.—**Gordon J. Aamot**

153. **National Consumer Phone Book USA 1998.** Detroit, Omnigraphics, 1997. 1103p. $60.00pa. ISBN 0-7808-0277-2.

This directory claims nearly 55,000 listings for associations, businesses, manufacturers, government agencies, educational institutions, and other entities that provide information and services for consumers. Additionally, it includes people who are prominent in the news as well as the print and broadcast media themselves. Most listings appear once in an alphabetic section (white pages) and at least once in a classified section (yellow pages). Each occurrence of a listing contains the name of the company, organization, or individual, along with the mailing address, main telephone number, fax number, toll-free number, e-mail address, and World Wide Web address. In the white pages, the last item in each listing is a number that corresponds to a classified heading in the yellow pages. This is useful for identifying competitors. Though a listing may occur under more than one heading, the number accompanying it in the white pages refers to the organization's or person's principal activity. Unfortunately, there is no easy way to determine under which other headings a listing may appear.

Compiling a directory is a major undertaking, not only in gathering and editing the material, but also in deciding what to include. One does not expect perfection (at least, not in the 1st edition), but accuracy and attention to detail are part of what makes such a reference tool useful. On these two points the editors have done a reasonably good job. A random check of a few dozen telephone numbers produced 100 percent accurate hits. (There was no answer at one number, but that does not prove that it is inaccurate.) Cross-checking addresses resulted in only a slightly lower percentage. However, a local athletic shoe store was listed as being in Telham, Alabama, rather than Pelham, Alabama. Jerry Springer is listed in the white pages but does not appear under "Television Talk and Interview Programs" in the yellow pages (though he is listed under "People," which some users may question). Other than "U.S. companies, organizations, agencies, and institutions that serve consumers," there are no stated criteria for inclusion. Thus, we are left to guess why Stephen King, Chris Isaak, Pat Buchanan, H. W. Wilson, and Krystal are listed but Garrison Keillor, Garth Brooks, James Carville, EBSCO, and Morrison's are not.

The editors have packed between the covers of this directory a lot of helpful information that would have to be sought in numerous other reference books. It will be particularly useful in libraries whose budgets do not allow the purchase of all those other titles. This work is recommended with hope that it will continue to improve.

—**Craig W. Beard**

154.   **National Directory of Corporate Public Affairs 1998.** Valerie J. Steele and others, eds. Washington, D.C., Columbia Books, 1998. 1v. (various paging). index. $95.00pa. ISBN 1-880873-27-3. ISSN 0749-9736.

This directory supplies information on corporate lobbyists, public relations officials, political action committees, and foundations for 1,900 large- to medium-sized U.S. corporations. It has 2 main sections, 2 indexes, and 2 appendixes. The 1st section (double-columned, 8½-by-11-inches, and 498 pages) is alphabetic by company. Subsidiaries are cross-referenced to parent companies. Entries list Washington, D.C., offices, public affairs officers at headquarters and elsewhere, corporate foundations with contacts, and political action committees. Addresses, titles, and telephone and fax numbers are supplied. E-mail addresses have been included where available as a new feature, although there seem to be few of them.

The 2d section (297 pages) is alphabetical by personal name. It provides directory information, title, and company. For independent lobbyists or consultants, it indicates services offered. Direct corporate employees names are in bold typeface.

An industry index lists companies by sector. The geographic index gives corporations alphabetically by state, city, and name, based on headquarters location. A 145-page appendix gives law and government relations firms that offer lobbying services alphabetically by state and name. Representatives are listed in the state where they maintain an office and cross-referenced from other states where they offer services. Entries give clients among the 1,900 companies and directory information. Another appendix (47 pages) lists lobbyists representing corporations at the state or territory level. It is arranged by jurisdiction and then lobbyist company name. Explanatory materials are clear. A foreword is supplied by the president of the Public Affairs Council, an organization for public relations professionals.

This series should be purchased by research collections covering business government relations and special interests. Large general reference collections might also consider it if funds and client interests warrant.

—**Nigel Tappin**

155.   **National Directory of Minority-Owned Business Firms.** 9th ed. Washington, D.C., Business Research Services; distr., Detroit, Gale, 1998. 1100p. index. $275.00pa. ISBN 0-933527-63-2.

This directory contains a list of about 47,000 minority-owned businesses. Criteria for being listed in the directory include the need for at least one of the principal owners to be a member of a minority group, the minority owners to own at least 51 percent of the business and have dominant control over it, and the business to be a productive venture. Minority groups considered for the directory include U.S. citizens or persons who have permanent residence in the United States who are African American, Hispanic American, Asian American, Native American, Native Hawaiian, or Hasidic Jew. The book is arranged numerically by Standard Industrial Classification (SIC) codes, which are broadly indexed by major category in the table of contents. Within each SIC code, businesses are arranged alphabetically by state, then by city (in bold typeface), and finally by business name. Most entries include name and address of business, telephone and fax numbers, contact name, type of business, minority type, county, and congressional district. A company index is in the back of the volume. Several entries also contain sales figures, number of employees, and date found.

Few e-mail addresses are listed, and geographic access still is problematic as indicated in the last review of this title (see ARBA 95, entry 200). Nevertheless, this directory will be useful for business, large public, academic, and governmental libraries that frequently search for minority businesses. [R: Choice, Dec 98, p. 670]

—O. Gene Norman

156.   **National Directory of Woman-Owned Business Firms.** 9th ed. Washington, D.C., Business Research Services; distr., Detroit, Gale, 1998. 659p. index. $275.00pa. ISBN 0-933527-64-0.

This 9th edition of the *National Directory of Woman-Owned Business Firms* contains more than 28,000 entries and is a must for those endeavoring to comply with federal guidelines. The table of contents lists the SIC codes with a brief description. Once the applicable code is determined, the entries are located using the number at the top of the page. Each business is listed by geographic order within each SIC category. The geographic loca-tion is printed in bold typeface within each entry. There are up to 17 points of information about each firm, such as the company name; address; and full contact information, including fax and telephone numbers, government contracting experience, and number of employees. In addition, the designation of "minority" is given if the owner is black, Hispanic, Asian, Native American, or Native Hawaiian. A company name index is located at the end of the volume. There is no charge for those companies included in this directory, and a toll-free telephone number is provided to request a free listing form.—**Sue Brown**

157.   **National Trade and Professional Associations of the United States 1998.** 33d ed. Buck Downs, R. Willson Hardy, Nathan L. Cantor, and Nicholas P. Karr, eds. Washington, D.C., Columbia Books, 1998. 733p. index. $129.00pa. ISBN 1-880873-28-1. ISSN 0734-354X.

Published since 1966, this reasonably priced directory continues to be a useful reference tool for public, special, and university libraries. Now encompassing approximately 7,600 active trade associations, societies, organizations, and labor unions, exclusions remain as identified in previous editions (see ARBA 94, entry 54, for a review of an earlier edition).

The introduction, without identifiable author, effectively describes the function, types, activities, and historical development of associations. The concise, alphabetic entries contain basic contact, financial, and activities data. In addition, lists of associations can be retrieved by subject, geography, budget (in 14 categories), executive, and acronym indexes. A separate alphabetic arrangement of management firms completes the volume. New with the 33d edition is the addition of key executives and staff besides the chief executive officer.

This smaller, more focused directory has a place in business reference collections. Although the data collec-tion methods are unspecified, its less complicated format makes it easier to use than the more comprehensive *Encyclopedia of Associations* (see entries 50 and 51). This edition's extensive coverage of e-mail addresses and World Wide Web sites is a definite plus.—**Sandra E. Belanger**

Handbooks and Yearbooks

158.   Allen, Larry. **The ABC-CLIO World History Companion to Capitalism.** Santa Barbara, Calif., ABC-CLIO, 1998. 404p. illus. index. $60.00. ISBN 0-87436-944-4.

Using an encyclopedia format, the author shows the evolution of capitalism—from its medieval beginnings through the nineteenth-century's laissez-faire experience to today's current breed and its interaction with socialism, ecological concerns, and social issues. Subjects are presented alphabetically rather than chronologically. A time line provides landmark dates from 1492 with Columbus's discovery of the New World to 1997 and the return of the Labor Party to power in Great Britain.

The selections are concisely written. Key events, laws, policies, and personalities from the United States and major European nations are discussed. Readers see how capitalism has changed over time and across national boundaries. For example, New Zealand initiated minimum wage laws in 1894. It was not until 1911 that Massa-chusetts enacted similar legislation. The U.S. federal government did not address this issue until 1938. Although the author occasionally preaches, especially on the environment, this is a useful reference for the general student of economic history.—**Adrienne Antink Bendel**

159. **Business Statistics of the United States.** 1997 ed. Courtenay M. Slater, ed. Lanham, Md., Bernan Associates, 1998. 398p. index. $65.00pa. ISBN 0-89059-083-4.

In order to satisfy the demand for essential statistical data on the U.S. economy gathered in one convenient volume, the Bureau of Economic Analysis (BEA) of the U.S. Department of Commerce first published *Business Statistics* in 1965. After 27 consecutive years, the BEA was forced to discontinue publication due to budgetary constraints. Fortunately, in 1995 Bernan Press revived the earlier handbook, retaining the same name, *Business Statistics of the United States*. The 1997 edition is expertly edited by Slater, under whose direction more than 2,000 time series were selected from the enormous, often confusing, outpouring of government figures. Significant trends during the past 30 years are captured in a lead article that increases timeliness by providing key data for the first half of 1997. Other articles discuss changes in the sometimes controversial Consumer Price Index as well as an overview of the North American Industry Classification System. Data on various aspects of the U.S. economy are provided in monthly and annual form for 1968 through 1996. Each aspect, such as gross domestic product, is introduced by a graph and concise highlights of major trends. Profiles of major industry groups are then presented, followed by selected historical series composed of annual and quarterly data for 1960 through 1987 and monthly data for 1962 through 1992. Annual data for states and regions, 1971 through 1996, expand the scope of the volume. Extensive notes offer useful descriptions of the included data series, as well as sources of the data for those who require further details. A table of contents and an index aid in locating specific statistical information. The book is a classic reference on the U.S. economy—comprehensive, authoritative, and convenient. It can save time and effort for a broad spectrum of readers, including economists, managers, teachers, students, and general readers.—**William C. Struning**

160. **The Elgar Companion to Classical Economics.** Heinz D. Kurz and Neri Salvadori, eds. Northhampton, Mass., Edward Elgar, 1998. 2v. index. $300.00/set. ISBN 1-85898-282-0.

The editors of this two-volume set are professors of economics at the University of Graz, Austria (Kurz), and the University of Pisa, Italy (Salvadori). The nearly 200 contributors hail from universities in Europe, North America, Asia, and Australia. The volumes are informative, with synoptic entries that end with cross-references and selected bibliographies. The coverage extends to contributions that precede the classical period proper, including references to ancient Greece. Coverage then continues with leading twentieth-century economic theorists, such as Joseph Schumpeter, Piero Sraffa, and Tibor Scitovsky, who have more recently revived the interest in classical economics, as well as those who have interpreted classical thought within the context of twentieth-century economic thought. The books contain diagrams, mathematical formulae, and a broad panorama of criticism, including Marxian.

Several European contributors to these volumes did not seem to want to be bothered with first names of the classical thinkers, such as Frederic Bastiat, who appears somewhat neglected. Authors who were practitioners as well, such as Alexander Hamilton, are not mentioned, although Johann von Thuenen is referred to repeatedly. Interesting areas of classical thought emerge from this work, such as the notion of externalities, the input-output analysis, structural change, and the spread of classical economics to various countries. Contributions of leading individual economic theorists are also included.

This set of two volumes is a valuable reference tool, convenient in its accessibility, its breadth of coverage, and its brevity of treatment. No economics library collection can afford to be without this anthology.
—**Bogdan Mieczkowski**

161. **Handbook of Economic Methodology.** John B. Davis, D. Wade Hands, and Uskali Mäki, eds. Northhampton, Mass., Edward Elgar, 1998. 572p. index. $215.00. ISBN 1-85278-795-3.

The editors, who are also contributors to this volume, are respectively from Marquette University, University of Puget Sound, and Erasmus University in Rotterdam. They, and their more than 100 contributors from the United States, Canada, the United Kingdom, Holland, Italy, Denmark, France, Finland, Ireland, Sweden, Germany, Hungary, Cyprus, Australia, and Japan, provide a multidisciplinary perspective on economic concepts and methodology. An extensive index amplifies the list of contributors and their entries, providing easy access for those interested in particular topics or authors. The separate area of economic methodology is new, and is allied to the philosophy of science and the history of economic thought. It also reveals a tendency to expand in a variety of different directions with a wide range of new perspectives. This evolutionary aspect of the field of methodology receives good coverage in the volume. Each entry, averaging three to four pages, is accompanied by a helpful and satisfying bibliography. The entry on "Experimental Economics" is, however, only one page long, and its bibliography includes just three articles, whereas the entry on the "Economics of Science" runs eight pages, and includes notes and a two-page list of references. The quality of entries is high; they are both succinct and readable.

This source is indispensable to historians of economic thought as well as to experts on methodology, and it is useful to those teaching and doing research on any subject in economics. This reviewer found it useful for explanation of concepts even in principles of economics. Scholars in other social sciences may also find this handbook useful and pertinent. The *Handbook of Economic Methodology* is highly recommended.—**Bogdan Mieczkowski**

162. **North American Industry Classification System: United States, 1997.** Lanham, Md., Bernan Associates, 1998. 1247p. index. $32.50; $28.50pa. ISBN 0-89059-097-4; 0-89059-098-2pa.

In order to analyze and to understand the structure and functioning of an economy, it is necessary to establish a viable industrial classification system. In 1939 the first Standard Industrial Classification (SIC) became available for the United States. Despite periodic revisions, by the 1990s a thorough overhaul was required to accommodate the emergence of new industries; growth in the service sector; and the need to coordinate the systems of Canada, Mexico, and the United States. In 1997, the Economic Classification Policy Committee (ECPC) of the Office of Management and Budget (OMB) completed a new system reported as *North American Industry Classification System: United States, 1997* (known as NAICS), published jointly by Bernan Associates and the National Technical Information Service (NTIS).

NAICS divides the economy into 20 sectors. Industries in each sector are grouped on the basis of similar production processes. NAICS uses a six-digit code to classify establishments: the first two the sector, the third the subsection, the fourth the industry group, the fifth the NAICS industry, and the sixth the national industry. The Census Bureau, the Bureau of Labor Statistics, the Internal Revenue Service, and other U.S. government agencies will convert from SIC to NAICS over the next few years. Despite many similarities between NAICS and the United Nation's International Standard Industrial Classification (ISIC), differences remain that will be enumerated in a proposed concordance.

This volume is an essential text for any library because NAICS will soon become the standard industrial classification system for North America. Fortunately, the book is offered at a modest cost. [R: LJ, Dec 98, p. 94]
—**William C. Struning**

BUSINESS SERVICES AND INVESTMENT GUIDES

Directories

163. **Directory of Companies Offering Dividend Reinvestment Plans.** 14th ed. Sumie Kinoshita, ed. Laurel, Md., Evergreen Enterprises, 1997. 140p. $32.95pa. ISBN 0-933183-23-2.

Dividend reinvestment plans (DRPs) allow investors receiving dividends to acquire additional shares in the dividend-paying company rather than receiving the amounts in cash. This directory, now in its 14th edition (see ARBA 90, entry 203 for a review of an earlier edition), lists more than 900 companies offering such plans. In addition to contact information, each entry lists the ticker symbol and primary exchange where the company's stock is traded. Costs, eligibility requirements, and minimum and maximum limits on cash purchases, along with other operational details, are also noted. A separate section lists companies based outside the United States that offer American Depositary Receipts (ADRs) in the U.S. market and have DRPs.

In order to participate in a DRP, an investor must first purchase stock in the company. Historically, this has required the use of a broker. In recent years, however, a growing number of companies have taken advantage of a change in federal securities law to offer their stock for sale directly to the public. An appendix provides a list of such companies, accompanied by lists of companies offering individual retirement arrangements and companies offering discounts on shares purchased through a DRP. A bibliography is also included.

Since their origins 30 years ago, dividend reinvestment plans have grown in numbers and in popularity among investors as a low cost way to accumulate shares in publicly traded companies. It should be noted that much of the information included in this directory is freely available via the World Wide Web through such sites as Netstock Direct (www.netstockdirect.com) and the DRP Club (www.cris.com/~Drpclub). However, if a printed directory is desired, this volume is a worthwhile addition to collections serving investors.

—**Christopher J. Hoeppner**

164. **Directory of Companies Required to File Annual Reports with the Securities and Exchange Commission, 1997.** Baton Rouge, La., Claitor's Publishing Division, 1998. 572p. $43.00pa. ISBN 1-57980-189-7.

This directory's coverage is apparent in its title. Approximately 13,000 companies are required to provide annual filings to the Securities and Exchange Commission (SEC). The body of the directory lists these companies alphabetically. The only other items of information provided are the SEC's docket number for the company, the month in which the company's fiscal year ends, and an industry code based on the 1987 Standard Industrial Classification Manual. Codes are assigned based on the major product or service activity of the company as determined from its SEC filings, and the directory's introduction acknowledges that it may "appear to be somewhat subjective" in the case of enterprises with various products or services. A separate section of the directory lists all companies under their respective industry classifications.

This inexpensive directory has long been a mainstay in business collections. In today's environment, however, it is a less important holding than in the past. The SEC now promptly makes public company filings accessible via the EDGAR database at its World Wide Web site, so a user can readily ascertain a company's status as public and the nature of its business in this manner. In addition, of course, many directories from commercial publishers provide more information about public companies than is available in this directory.

—**Christopher J. Hoeppner**

165. **The 1998 Franchise Annual: "The Original" Franchise Handbook and Directory.** Ted Dixon, Lori Marsh, and Jo-Anne Rittenhouse, eds. Lewiston, N.Y., Info Franchise News, 1998. 318p. index. $39.95pa. ISBN 0-9692267-6-4. ISSN 0318-8752.

Edited by Dixon for the past 21 years, this handy reference source is now in its 29th year of operation. It continues to distinguish itself as the top resource in the area of franchising and represents the most informative tool for the prospective investor. The initial handbook section provides descriptive information about franchising, including tips and suggestions for investment. The segment called "Investigating the Franchiser" is most helpful in its treatment of the business, the territory, and especially the contract and the identification of Federal Trade Commission regulations. State regulations are treated in a subsequent segment of the handbook section.

The major part of the text is contained in the 2d section, the directory, which provides entries for 3,975 franchise possibilities. These are organized into 3 geographic divisions: "American Listings" contains 2,418 entries, "Canadian Listings" has 1,027 entries, and "Overseas Listings" provides 530 entries. The American and Canadian listings are divided into 47 categories alphabetically arranged from "Accounting and Tax Services" to "Wedding Related Services," with a final category designated "Miscellaneous." The overseas listings have 10 categories. All major franchise operations are treated, with each entry containing the normal directory information (name, address, telephone number) along with a description of the product or service, dates of establishment, fee, royalty, investment required, and whether or not financing is available. The work concludes with an alphabetic index by company name.—**Ron Blazek**

166. Walden, Gene. **The 100 Best Stocks to Own in America.** 5th ed. Chicago, Dearborn Financial Publishing, 1998. 383p. index. $22.95pa. ISBN 0-7931-2574-X.

The author recommends using this list of the best stocks to select 10 to 12 companies to study further by requesting annual reports directly and visiting the public library to look up recent articles about the companies and read the latest *Value Line Investment Survey* and *Standard & Poor's Stock Reports*. Walden suggests monitoring the trading ranges for each stock and selecting the four or five that appear to be the best values. He recommends buying and holding a small number of companies, taking advantage of dividend reinvestment and stock purchase plans. Today, of course, one can also visit one or more of the many Internet sites focusing on investments, such as Hoovers Online at http://www.hoovers.com or Quicken.com at http://www.quicken.com.

To select the list, he screened approximately 2,000 major U.S. companies. The primary criteria for selecting companies was record of growth in earnings per share. He also considered revenue growth, stock price performance, and dividend yield. He rated his selected companies by ranking them using 6 categories: earnings per share growth, stock growth, dividend yield, dividend growth, consistency, and shareholder perks. The author sells a twice-yearly newsletter for $12.95 that follows the stocks. Each company report contains the company's name, address, telephone number, ticker symbol, top officers, a chart showing the ratings for each category, a narrative profile of the company, details regarding the rankings, a table listing key financial and market performance data, and a stock chart. Walden's top five picks are Medtronic, Fannie Mae, Gillette, Norwest, and Schering-Plough.

Waldon's approach to stock market investing concentrates solely on individual large company growth stocks with established records. He completely leaves out value stocks, small stocks, newer companies, and international companies. Mutual funds offer an attractive complementary or alternative approach that reduces the risk of stock market investing through greater diversification. As he points out, only 29 companies made his best 100 lists in each of the five editions of his book.—**Peter Zachary McKay**

167.   **Walker's Manual of Penny Stocks.** Harry K. Eisenberg, ed. Lafayette, Calif., Walker's Manual, 1998. 500p. index. $45.00pa. ISBN 0-9652088-3-4pa.

Eisenberg, editor of this and other resources for investors such as *Walker's Manual of Community Bank Stocks* (see ARBA 98, entry 187) and *Walker's Manual of Unlisted Stocks* (3d ed.; see ARBA 98, entry 172), has set out to dispel some of the myths of penny stock investments, such as their high-risk speculative nature and their potential to swindle investors who purchase stocks. Eisenberg's intent is to focus attention on companies that are not well known or that are not followed by institutional investors. In his introduction he notes that he obtained his information from company reports and documents, and that in most cases the information has been audited and filed with governmental agencies. A brief discussion of recent SEC rulings on how stocks are defined and where they are listed helps the reader understand the history and potential investment capabilities of penny stocks. Factors he considered in selecting companies for this manual include profitability, number of employees, longevity and history, financial solvency, and existing revenue stream. Eisenberg also warns the beginning investor to be conservative and to do the research necessary to evaluate potential investment possibilities. A glossary aids the new investor by explaining the terminology of investing and how figures are derived.

There are 500 company profiles, arranged alphabetically, following the introduction. The information is presented in an easy-to-follow chart, and contains information organized into 2 sections. "Per Share Information" includes stock price, earnings and dividends per share, and price/earnings ratio; "Annual Financial Data" includes operating results, balance sheet and performance, and financial condition. A brief one-paragraph company description introduces the data, and a paragraph of comments explains the data. For example, a comment will explain why a stock has behaved in a certain way, what the market situation is for that company's product, advances or setbacks in research and development, refinancing, or incipient bankruptcies. A list of officers and ownership information, along with pertinent information such as the SIC codes, number of employees, auditor and market maker, and contact information, follows.

This manual is intended for the private investor who may be interested in penny stocks (defined by the SEC as stocks that sell for under $5 per share) but is concerned about possible risk and worried about scams. Aside from the company data (always very useful when investing), Eisenberg's guidelines will assist the beginning investor in understanding financial information and analyzing other companies using similar criteria. This manual is recommended for public libraries with business collections and large reference collections.—**Kerie L. Nickel**

Handbooks and Yearbooks

168.   **Handbook of North American Stock Exchanges.** 1997 ed. Austin, Tex., Meridian Securities Markets, 1997. 149p. $95.00pa. ISBN 0-9648930-9-6.

The *Handbook of North American Stock Exchanges* provides valuable directory and statistical information for the American Stock Exchange, Mexican Stock Exchange, Montreal Stock Exchange, NASDAQ Stock Exchange, New York Stock Exchange, and Toronto Stock Exchange. Each entry includes name, address, telephone and fax numbers, listing requirements, regulatory agency (e.g., Securities and Exchange Commission), foreign investors, commissions and fees, disclosure requirements, and investor protection information. Directory information, however, does not include Website information for the exchanges; only URLs for regulatory agencies are provided. The publisher should consider listing of Website information in future editions.

Among statistics provided are number of listed companies, market capitalization, share trading, Dow Jones Industrial Average, and top stocks by trading volume. In most cases, statistics presented cover the years

1975 through 1996. Stocks are also ranked by such indicators as trading value, trading volume, price-earnings ratio, dividend yield, and market capitalization. The appendix provides a guide to the calculation of indexes and other performance measures as well as formulas. Data were obtained from the exchanges represented.

The *Handbook of North American Stock Exchanges* is a useful guide that provides a starting point for researching the various exchanges and stock performance. The publisher should consider adding a brief bibliography of additional resources, including citations, for the various publications by each exchange as well as the annual handbooks and other publications. This source is recommended to academic and public library business collections.

—**Lucy Heckman**

169.   **Hoover's Handbook of American Business 1998.** 8th ed. Austin, Tex., Hoover's, 1998. 2v. index. $119.95/set. ISBN 1-57311-037-X. ISSN 1055-7202.

Hoover's Handbook of American Business 1998 provides comprehensive, readable, readily accessible profiles of 750 major U.S. companies. Each profile includes timely facts relative to addresses, telephone, and fax numbers; key executives; products and services offered; essential financial and sales data; primary competitors; and, in most cases, a chart depicting stock prices during the past decade. Although other handbooks offer similar data, *Hoover's* is unique in providing historical perspective and insights into strategic operations that underlie and explain bare facts and figures. Included in the handbook are 56 lists, drawn from various sources that rank the largest and most influential U.S. companies over a broad spectrum of criteria. Although entries are presented in alphabetic order, an alphabetic index aids in locating profiles of individual companies quickly. In addition, profiles are indexed by industry, and a further index locates brands, companies, and people named in the profiles. The 2-volume set contains an immense amount of pertinent and reliable information on U.S. businesses conveniently housed in a single volume. The handbook represents a one-stop source of information for researchers, investors, job-hunters, executives, brokers, educators, and students, as well as a point of departure for those requiring further details.—**William C. Struning**

170.   **Hoover's Handbook of Emerging Companies 1998.** 5th ed. Austin, Tex., Hoover's, 1998. 318p. index. $64.95. ISBN 1-57311-034-5. ISSN 1069-7519.

For those libraries unable to afford expensive, more comprehensive directories, the Hoover's series titles are bargains. With the focus being exclusively on U.S.-based firms, the inclusion of the word "emerging" in the title can be misleading; the companies are not from emerging economies. This annual work, now in its 5th edition, can be viewed as a companion piece to *Hoover's Handbook of American Business* (see entry 169) and *Hoover's Handbook of Private Companies* (see entry 171). The majority of the 250 companies profiled are public. The emphasis is on companies with revenues between $20 million and $1 billion that have had sales growth of at least 25 percent annually in the past 5 years and positive net income for the last year. Exceptions were made for key players in important industries. Because 107 of the companies profiled are new, one should keep the older edition. Some companies were dropped because they were unable to keep up with competitors, were acquired, or are no longer considered emerging.

Each profile provides an overview, brief history, founding date, officers, directory information, product or services listing, brand names, divisions, subsidiaries, joint ventures and key competitors, and six years of financial and employment data. The format is consistent and easy to read. Website addresses are given for the company when available. Rankings by growth in sales, net income, and employment are provided. In addition, rankings by stock appreciation, market value, profit margin, return on equity, and price earnings are given. Other lists are compiled from top business publications. Finally, excellent indexing allows access by industry, headquarters location, brand name, company cross-reference, and people. This title is an inexpensive way to acquire basic information on U.S. companies and makes a useful supplement to Hoover's other major titles.—**Bobray Bordelon**

171.   **Hoover's Handbook of Private Companies 1998.** 3d ed. Austin, Tex., Hoover's, 1998. 736p. index. $129.95. ISBN 1-57311-038-8. ISSN 1073-6433.

This edition of the handbook covers 713 companies, of which 503 are brief "capsules" containing contact information (including Website address), a paragraph-length company description, and the names of key officers and competitors. The remaining 210 organizations are covered in greater depth, each receiving a 2-page entry that includes a history of the company and an overview of its current operations, along with expanded directory data and limited financial information—typically, sales and net income figures—for the past 10 years. The front of the volume offers lists ranking the companies by sales and number of employees and reprinting *Inc.*'s most recent list of the 500 fastest-growing private companies in the United States. The companies are indexed by industry and headquarters location, and a third index has entries for people, brands, and companies names in the profiles.

Hoover's handbooks and other publications have been well regarded for providing a great deal of information in affordable packages. Gathering information about privately held businesses is a challenge to the researcher and reference librarian, and since its introduction four years ago (see ARBA 98, entry 164, and ARBA 95, entry 192), this handbook has quickly become a highly valued source. Especially useful is its inclusion of charitable and not-for-profit organizations and government-owned enterprises, all of which get minimal coverage in other sources of this kind. Since the prior edition the editors have increased the number of organizations included by almost 20 percent and, of course, updated the content. This is a title that continues to merit a place in any business collection.—**Christopher J. Hoeppner**

172. **Hoover's Handbooks Index 1998.** Austin, Tex., Hoover's, 1998. 257p. $34.95. ISBN 1-57311-039-6.

Hoover's Handbooks Index, now in its second year, provides a collective index to four of Hoover's most popular works—*Hoover's Handbook of American Business* (see entry 169), *Hoover's Handbook of Private Companies* (see entry 171), *Hoover's Handbook of Emerging Companies* (see entry 170), and *Hoover's Handbook of World Business* (see entry 222). The index is included free for those purchasing the four titles as a set. Although each of the individual works contains its own index, this collective index eliminates the need to see in which volume a company is contained and whether or not a company is public or private, domestic or international. Given that only 1,500 companies are profiled in the four volumes, consulting the individual volumes is not a Herculean task. The main index combines the indexes of the four volumes and offers the standard access by the name of the brand, company, or person. Additional indexes by industry group and headquarters location provide additional access points. Although well indexed, this work will be of little value to those libraries only purchasing part of the set. This index is recommended only for those libraries getting the index free as part of their purchase of the entire set.—**Bobray Bordelon**

173. **Morningstar Mutual Fund 500.** 1997-98 ed. Betsy Grace and others, eds. Chicago, Morningstar; distr., Burr Ridge, Ill., Irwin Professional Publishing, 1998. 606p. index. $35.00pa. ISBN 0-7863-1090-1.

Since 1984, Morningstar has established itself as one of the most trusted and quoted sources on the mutual funds industry. Today, most business publications regularly feature lists of the top performing or the largest mutual funds. Morningstar has taken a different approach by profiling a wide range of investment choices intended to allow the investor to assemble a portfolio. The principles of successful investing, assembly of a portfolio, and an explanation of its famed ratings system are detailed. An annual industry review, performance summaries by broad type, benchmark averages, various rankings, and a summary of manager and mutual fund name changes are also provided. Most of the work consists of full-page profiles of 450 open-end funds and 50 closed-end funds. Each profile features 12 years of annual and 8 years of quarterly data as well as basic risk analysis, operations information, expenses and fees, and composition. The information presented is a combination of narrative, statistical, and evaluative. One of the most useful features is the detailed user's guide. In addition to standard definitions and methodology, warnings are often given about misuses of data and evaluative items.

Even though only a fraction of the mutual funds in existence are included, the most closely followed funds are presented here. Although sources such as *Investment Company Yearbook* (CDA-Wiesenberger, annual) come close to being comprehensive with basic data, few services offer great detail on any but the largest funds. This source is useful and inexpensive for libraries needing coverage of major mutual funds. Like any investment source, one should consult a variety of sources and always have access to the latest data.—**Bobray Bordelon**

174. **Standard & Poor's Stock and Bond Guide.** 1998 ed. Frank LoVaglio, ed. New York, McGraw-Hill, 1998. 461p. $22.95pa. ISBN 0-07-052678-8.

This reference provides financial performance indicators for 14,000 stocks, bonds, mutual funds, and annuities using 1997 year-end data. Previous to this publication, detailed Standard & Poor's information was available only on a subscription basis. The book gives 19 key measures for stocks, such as historic and current price ranges, trading volumes, price to earnings ratios, dividend payments, annual earnings, and the Standard &

Poor's rankings. The bond guide provides 18 major data elements, such as long-term debt, capitalizations, debt ratings, yields to maturity, and the like.

The introduction effectively shows the reader how to use the statistics to evaluate a security. The Standard & Poor rating system is also explained. Each section of the guide has detailed definitions for all table headings, abbreviations, and footnote terms. It would be helpful if the publisher had included a table of contents. Without it, the user may not realize the full extent of the resource. For example, tucked in between the sections on U.S. stocks and bonds are notations for foreign bonds and a listing of major underwriters with contact telephone numbers. This reference gives the individual investor pragmatic tools to make informed decisions.

—**Adrienne Antink Bendel**

CONSUMER GUIDES

175.   **The Directory of Mail Order Catalogs '98: The Most Comprehensive Guide to Consumer....** 12th ed. Gottlieb, Richard, ed. Lakeville, Conn., Grey House Publishing, 1998. 953p. index. $150.00pa. ISBN 0-939300-91-5.

This annual update follows previous editions by listing mail order catalog companies in 44 chapters covering product types ranging from clothing and home to sporting goods and tools, subdivided by specific products within each group. In addition to name, address, and telephone number (including a toll-free number), e-mail and Website addresses are included when available. Another characteristic of this directory is the listing of officers, credit cards accepted, cost and frequency of catalogs, circulation statistics, size of catalog, mailing list information, number of years in business, and amount of sales when provided by the company.

The table of contents and two indexes, one by company name and the other by product, offer easy access to the appropriate numbered entry. There are 8,930 entries, with a few duplications for some large companies with diverse products. According to the introduction, 400 catalogs were deleted from the previous edition, and about 1,500 new ones were added along with corrections for many entries. Users are encouraged to submit information for additional listings. The publisher also offers labels, magnetic tape, and diskette formats of the directory.

This title is helpful to the consumer but unique in its industry focus. Libraries needing only a consumer resource may be served by *The Catalog of Catalogs* (see ARBA 95, entry 226, and ARBA 91, entry 195), but libraries with a business clientele will need to consider this title. A list of industry contacts and the reporting of sales and other data qualify this work as a source for industry information for an area of consumer sales that is continuing to increase. Although Internet resources continue to expand availability to catalog information and online marketing for the consumer, the organization, scope, and continuous updating and revision of this work ensures its place as a standard reference.—**Margo B. Mead**

176.   **Encyclopedia of the Consumer Movement.** Stephen Brobeck, Robert N. Mayer, and Robert O. Herrmann, eds. Santa Barbara, Calif., ABC-CLIO, 1997. 659p. index. $99.50. ISBN 0-87436-987-8.

Most people today take for granted the assumption that consumers are protected by a safety net of federal laws and regulations. The changes in public awareness and public policies that brought about these protections were, in large part, the result of "the consumer movement," ably chronicled in this important new reference work.

The 198 alphabetically arranged entries cover a broad range of consumer-related topics and represent the editors' attempt to summarize what is known about the consumer movement. Each encyclopedia entry is between 1,000 and 5,000 words and written by an expert with either academic or professional experience in the subject matter. The essays fall into 7 subject categories. There are 9 general essays that discuss topics such as "Consumer Problems in Market Economics" and "U.S. Consumer Movement: History and Dynamics." A selection of 7 entries, such as "Children as a Vulnerable Market" and "Immigrants as Consumers" addresses issues of consumer populations. "Consumer Movement Activities" consists of 20 entries and includes essays on "Boycotts, Consumer" and "Whistleblowers." The largest group, with 66 entries, covers government agencies and consumer organizations. Here one finds long articles on such entities as the Food and Drug Administration and Better Business Bureaus. Four entries are devoted to leaders of the consumer movement, including Ralph Nader. The second-largest amount of coverage, with 51 entries, is devoted to consumer protection. These essays fall into the categories of "Health and Safety," "Economic and Financial," and "Marketing" issues. Lastly, there are 41 essays devoted to international consumer movements, though the emphasis is on Europe.

The editors have done a commendable job in planning the content, recruiting the contributors, and organizing the work itself. Readers will appreciate the subject index, listing by broad subject categories, and the alphabetic list of essays. The editors have also added *see also* references that direct readers to related essays and compiled short bibliographies of supplemental readings for each entry. Its relatively modest price of $99.50 makes it even more appealing. This is a useful, affordable reference work that belongs in both academic and public library reference collections and any special library serving an institution with an interest in consumer issues. [R: BL, 1 April 98, pp. 1344-45]—**Gordon J. Aamot**

177.   **Orion Blue Book: Audio 1997.** 1997 ed. Scottsdale, Ariz., Orion Research, 1997. 869p. $179.00. ISBN 0-932089-72-0. ISSN 0883-8437.

This annual publication has been published since 1973 and is a standard reference tool for used audio equipment dealers. Covering more than 1,400 manufacturers and 61,000 products dating back to the 1950s, it is also used by insurance companies, freight adjusters, law enforcement agencies, attorneys, the Internal Revenue Service, and pawnbrokers in addition to libraries. Anyone who seeks an accurate value of used equipment needs this title.

Each volume lists retail price, used price, the year the model was introduced, and the year it was discontinued as well as manufacturer, model, and type. Used prices are determined by national dealer surveys and have proven to be an accurate reflection of the marketplace. Orion produces a list of other blue books; all produced in print, on diskettes, and on CD-ROM. Other information includes type code explanations, definition of terms, board of advisers, questions most frequently asked about Orion, directory of manufacturers, and a survey form for dealers. This resource should be bought where demand warrants.—**Susan C. Awe**

178.   **Orion Blue Book: Camera.** 1998 ed. Scottsdale, Ariz., Orion Research, 1998. 423p. $144.00. ISBN 0-932089-42-9. ISSN 1046-3861.

In 1973, California stereo store owner Roger Rohrs compiled a list of stereo equipment and its trade-in value. It seems that Rohrs's salespeople were allowing too much trade-in value on used stereo equipment. Twenty-five years later, Rohrs's simple list has evolved into a 13-volume Orion Blue Book series listing values of everything from guitars to computers. *Camera* is the 16th edition of the work, and has been updated yearly since 1983.

Thousands of photographic equipment items manufactured by more than 100 companies are listed in this hefty volume. Each entry includes the year(s) of manufacture, the model number, product name, the "new" list price, the recommended retail used price, and the wholesale average, in both mint and average conditions. Manufacturers are listed in alphabetic order. A directory of manufacturer addresses and telephone numbers is also included.

As with any pricing guide, two questions arise. Those questions involve the determination of the values, and the geographic variables involved. The editors determine the values listed in *Camera* based on responses from dealer surveys. (A blank survey is included in the back of the book.) Such a self-report method is far from scientific. One surmises that a single reported sale of a rare item could profoundly affect its value in the book. However, a scientific survey of each item is probably unrealistic for a work of such a large scope. The geography question is a bit trickier. A board of advisers consisting of seven camera dealers has reviewed the values in the book. However, the Deep South and northeastern parts of the United States are not represented on the board. Certainly, different regions, states, and cities can offer different trade-in values. Do the surveys received represent a cross-section of the United States? The answer is neither stated nor implied.

A local pawnbroker said that *Camera* would be a useful tool in his business. He commented that the wholesale prices seemed a bit low, but the book could provide a good starting place. He also noted that the "average" and "mint" classifications provided only general benchmarks, and no criteria for evaluating cameras was offered. Other pricing guides use a percentile scale (60 percent, 70 percent, and so on) to describe a used item's condition. Still, the scope and completeness of *Camera* impressed the pawnbroker.

Library patrons are often interested in the market value of their possessions, although these prices are often surprisingly low. *Camera* meets this need.—**Keith Kyker**

179. **Orion Blue Book: Copier.** 1998 ed. Scottsdale, Ariz., Orion Research, 1998. 85p. $39.00. ISBN 0-932089-91-7.

Orion Research has been publishing directories of used equipment prices for 25 years. Among the 13 titles, each of which is available in book or diskette format, are guides for tools, musical instruments, guns, and computers. These guides serve as reference sources for marketplace values for a wide variety of users and are also used by dealers as training manuals. Prices were obtained from dealer surveys throughout the country.

The "Guidelines" section offers tips on buying and using the equipment; a "Definition of Terms" section clarifies abbreviations; a "Directory of Manufacturers" section includes address, telephone numbers and fax numbers; and a "Copier Equivalency Chart" section is arranged by manufacturer (about 50), and includes unit type, year introduced and discontinued, model, and retail and used prices.

Inconsistencies in terms used in the main text versus terms defined detract from the volume's facility. Future books should resolve such problems and continue to provide guidance through the ever-complex and ever-expanding field of used copier equipment.—**Anita Zutis**

180. **Orion Blue Book: Professional Sound 1998.** 1998 ed. By Roger Rohrs. Scottsdale, Ariz., Orion Research, 1998. 560p. $144.00. ISBN 0-932089-88-7. ISSN 1044-4793.

Rohrs has developed numerous "blue books" that provide price and source information for new and used items, from power tools to vintage guitars. This volume on "pro sound" is for locating professional-level sound equipment. Most of the volume is arranged alphabetically by manufacturer or supplier with a list of what sound equipment each sells. Entries include name of equipment, year made, prices for new and used equipment, condition information for used (e.g., mint or average), and the prices for each. The Orion Research Website at www.bluebook.com shows examples of each available book along with publisher order information. This title may be useful to large public libraries ad music schools with a technical curriculum.—**Glynys R. Thomas**

181. **Orion Blue Book: Video & Television 1998.** 1998 ed. Scottsdale, Ariz., Orion Research, 1998. 523p. $144.00. ISBN 0-932089-89-5.

This is one of a series of Orion Blue Books that provides a listing with prices for video and television equipment. Other Blue Books cover audio, guitars and musical instruments, cameras, piano prototypes, computer equipment, copiers, guns, power tools, and car stereos. The publisher surveys dealers to gather data in determining prices, and an experienced board of advisers reviews the data and help provide an accurate pricing. Categories for each individual listing include type of unit, year released for sale and year discontinued (if a second year is listed), manufacturer, power in wattage, model new list retail price, retail used price, wholesale mint price (excellent working order and appearance), and wholesale average price to a customer for an item. Generally, the book is arranged alphabetically by name of corporation followed by type of equipment. Then the arrangement is sub-grouped by model, alphabetically and numerically by model number. Helpful introductory material includes guidelines for pricing, explanation codes for type of equipment, a definition of the brief terms used in each entry, and a directory of manufacturers.

This book has been used by retail dealers, insurance companies, manufacturers, libraries, pawnbrokers, freight adjusters, law enforcement personnel, divorce and probate attorneys, and the Internal Revenue Service. Few publications appear to be available that provide this type of information. Libraries that can afford it and that serve clientele who require used television equipment price information should consider adding this useful tool.
—**O. Gene Norman**

182. **Orion Blue Book: Vintage Guitars & Collectibles 1998.** summer ed. Scottsdale, Ariz., Orion Research, 1998. 236p. $180.00. ISBN 0-932089-21-6. ISSN 1056-8581.

Listed alphabetically by brand name in this book are nearly 10,000 vintage guitars and associated equipment—"vintage" being defined here as made from the mid-1920s to 1969 and thus collectible. The information, in an easy-to-read table format, includes year of manufacture, model name/number, and four prices: two for selling and two for buying from a customer (one for excellent condition, one for average condition). Considering its interest primarily to dealers in vintage guitars and secondarily to collectors, along with its high cost and frequency of publication, this *Orion Blue Book* will not be a practical purchase for most public libraries.—**Lori D. Kranz**

183.   Rudman, Theo. **Rudman's Cigar Buying Guide: Selecting & Savoring the Perfect Cigar for Any Occasion.** Chicago, Triumph Books, 1997. 394p. index. $14.95pa. ISBN 1-57243-233-0.

184.   Rudman, Theo. **Rudman's Complete Guide to Cigars: How to Find, Select, & Smoke Them.** 4th ed. Chicago, Triumph Books, 1997. 376p. index. $14.95pa. ISBN 1-57243-245-4.

These two guides overlap, but are not identical. The *Complete Guide* contains more than 100 pages introducing readers to the history, production, selection, and smoking of cigars. The remaining two-thirds of the work contain a country-by-country list of the major cigar brands. The list uses a 5-star system to evaluate more than 900 of the 4,500 cigars included. This 4th edition has been updated by 47 pages of new brands. This new information is not integrated into the main list. Rather, the new brands are listed on colored pages at the beginning of the work.

The *Cigar Buying Guide* includes a 16-page section, "Smoking for Pleasure," giving guidance on how to select, keep, and smoke cigars. The vast majority of the work comprises lists—a quality rating index, a cigar-sized index, and a "world directory" of cigars. The rating index evaluates more than 500 cigars using the "the author's subjective" 5-star rating system. The price index rates more than 2,000 cigars into 6 categories (below $1 to more than $20). The size index lists more than 3,700 cigars in 16 size categories. The directory lists more than 3,700 cigars by country and brand and includes the quality and price ratings, a brief overview of cigar making in each country, and brief descriptions of most brands listed, with an index identifying cigar brands by country.

The author is a South African cigar connoisseur and, hence, has much more access to Cuba and Cuban cigars than any U.S. citizen. Both works include extensive coverage of Cuban cigars, considered by most experts to be the best in the world, and the *Complete Guide* includes a short summary of the laws pertaining to Cuban cigar imports into the U.S. (an officially licensed traveler to Cuba may bring back less than $100 worth, but Cuban cigars may not be brought into the U.S. from any other country, and anyone illegally trading or dealing in Cuban cigars is liable for a $50,000 fine or imprisonment or both).

Although each work contains lists called "directories," they cannot be considered true directories because the lists do not contain addresses, telephone numbers, fax numbers, or e-mail address. The works are both relatively inexpensive paperbacks and are not made to stand up to heavy reference use. This should not be considered a fatal defect because they also contain a large amount of quality and price information that is sure to be rapidly outdated. Both of these guides are suitable for libraries needing to provide reference works to meet the needs of the currently increasing number of cigar smokers. Of the two, the *Complete Guide* is the work of choice for most libraries because it contains the most general information on cigars and cigar smoking and includes the quality ratings; it lacks only the price and size ratings of the *Cigar Buying Guide.*—**Richard H. Swain**

FINANCE AND BANKING

185.   **Elsevier's Dictionary of Financial Terms in English, German, Spanish, French, Italian, and Dutch.** rev. ed. Diana Phillips and Marie-Claude Bignaud, comps. New York, Elsevier Science, 1997. 644p. $230.00. ISBN 0-444-89950-2.

This dictionary is comprehensive and easy to use. It includes terms from various areas of economics and finance as well as allied ones from accounting, law, and insurance. It has a "Basic Table" in which terms in English, their synonyms, and related expressions are translated into the five other languages of the dictionary in alphabetic order. This extensive section is followed by a six-part list of terms in each of the six languages, with reference to the page(s) in the "Basic Table." The pages of the latter contain two columns, and those in the six-languages part contain three columns, indicative of the large volume of material covered in this book. Abbreviations include grammatical categories and gender. A spot check revealed an impressive collection of synonyms and alternative translations that will be of great service to the user of this volume. In view of the increasing globalization of economic relations and existence of the European Union and other preferential trading blocks, this book is of great value to translators and business practitioners as well as to academics. This dictionary is highly recommended.

—**Bogdan Mieczkowski**

186.   Fitch, Thomas P. **Dictionary of Banking Terms.** 3d ed. Hauppauge, N.Y., Barron's Educational Series, 1997. 527p. (Barron's Business Guides). $16.95pa. ISBN 0-8120-9659-2.

More than 3,000 terms related to the banking and financial services industry are defined and described in the latest edition of the *Dictionary of Banking Terms.* Included, in addition to definitions of such terms as *bank credit* and *common stock,* are entries for organizations (e.g., New York Stock Exchange) and key legislation (e.g., Glass-Steagall Act). Provided with some of the definitions are illustrations, charts, and graphs. Cross-references are also included.

The dictionary has been updated to reflect changes since the 1993 edition, notably developments in global banking, electronic banking, and legislation. Additionally, several obsolete terms have been deleted, and the list of abbreviations and acronyms has been expanded since the last edition. *Dictionary of Banking Terms* is highly recommended to business reference collections in academic, special, and public libraries. This reference source is comprehensive and contains clear explanations of terms.—**Lucy Heckman**

INDUSTRY AND MANUFACTURING

187.   **Agriculture, Mining, and Construction USA: Industry Analyses, Statistics, and Leading Companies.** Arsen J. Darnay, ed. Farmington Hills, Mich., Gale, 1998. 1133p. maps. index. $205.00. ISBN 0-7876-2827-1.

Gale continues its USA series by adding the three sectors of the economy in *Agriculture, Mining, and Construction USA.* The work includes 77 industries as defined by the 1987 Standard Industrial Classification (SIC) code. Primary data from the *Economic Census of the United States* (1977, 1982, 1987, 1992) are supplemented by establishment, employment, and compensation data for 1993-1995 from *County Business Patterns* (Gordon Press, 1995). Projections are made through 1998. Statistics on 127 agricultural commodities are derived primarily from *Agricultural Statistics.* Individual company information comes from *Ward's Business Directory* (Gale, 1998). Finally, data on 100 occupational groups as defined by the Bureau of Labor Statistics *Industry-Occupation Matrix* are included. With the exception of *Ward's Business Directory,* all of the sources are governmentally produced and available in depository libraries. The value of this book comes from its combining of sources and footnotes, allowing the researcher to easily discern the original sources. The first part of this work presents national and state data organized by sector and SIC code. The second part presents state and county data.

When combined with the other volumes in the series, a detailed portrait of U.S. industry can be obtained. With the 1997 *Economic Census* (construction, mining) and the *Census of Agriculture* (the 1997 edition being conducted by the U.S. Department of Agriculture and not the Census Bureau) scheduled to debut in the spring of 1999, this volume will soon be useful for historical purposes only. As Gale begins to provide updates to the series using the 1997 censuses, it should include both the North American Industry Classification System (NAICS) as well as the SIC codes along with a concordance. This work will be useful for ready-reference purposes in business library collections. [R: BL, 1 Dec 98, p. 698]—**Bobray Bordelon**

188.   **By the Numbers: Emerging Industries.** Lazich, Robert S., ed. Detroit, Gale, 1998. 534p. index. $79.00pa. ISBN 0-7876-1859-4. ISSN 1096-4967.

By the Numbers is a series of four volumes of statistical data about various industries. This volume, *Emerging Industries,* mainly covers computers (hardware and software), other electronics, and biotech.

Market research is a valuable commodity, so it comes as little surprise that the good information is generally not cheap, and the cheap information generally not good. This is the case with this volume. Aside from some tables drawn from U.S. government sources (and readily available elsewhere), this collection is a haphazard mishmash of tables and summaries drawn from various publications. Usually the ultimate source of the data is a well-known research firm such as IDG or Dataquest, but the actual data can come from anywhere, including trade publications, daily newspapers, and financial newspapers and magazines.

Little care is taken with even the basic requirements of documentation for the tables. For example, what products do the terms *hand-held computer, electronic organizer,* and *PDA* cover? Separate market share reports for these three categories appear as tables but provide no explanation of how the definitions differ.

Even more egregiously, the tables do not distinguish historical data from estimates of the future, requiring a careful look at the source citation to give one guidance in this area. Table 39, for example, lists market shares for the "global multimedia market" (another undefined term) for 1994, 1997, and 2000. Although one can assume the year 2000 data are estimates, one needs to note that the cited source has a June 1997 date to infer that the 1997 data are at least partly projected. Not clearly marking estimates as such violates a basic rule of data presentation.

Researchers with a professional need for market research in these areas should not rely on the odd assembly of tables provided here; for them, more systematic (and costly) reports are available. This collection may suffice to assuage casual curiosity, but not more than that. [R: Choice, Nov 98, p. 499]—**Ray Olszewski**

189.   **How Products Are Made: An Illustrated Guide to Product Manufacturing. Volume 3.** Kristine M. Krapp and Jacqueline L. Longe, eds. Detroit, Gale, 1998. 500p. illus. index. $80.00. ISBN 0-7876-1547-1. ISSN 1072-5091.

How is an acrylic fingernail made? What is the history of the Stetson hat? What is the future of champagne? This 3d volume (for a review of the 1st volume, see ARBA 95, entry 237) answers the preceding questions and more. Four- to six-page signed essays give the background, history, and future of 100 consumer and producer goods. Each entry also details raw materials used, product design, the manufacturing or extraction process, quality control, and by-products or waste for each product. Short bibliographies consisting of books, periodicals, and Websites follow each essay. Illustrations provide step-by-step instruction on the manufacturing process. This ongoing series contains a cumulative index. Cross-references are provided, and main entries are in bold typeface. Whether a junior high school student, an undergraduate, or a layperson, one will find informative and easy-to-read essays. This work is recommended for most reference collections.—**Bobray Bordelon**

190.   Lazich, Robert S. **Market Share Reporter, 1998: An Annual Compilation of Reported Market Share Data on Companies, Products, and Services.** 8th ed. Detroit, Gale, 1997. 588p. index. $220.00. ISBN 0-7876-1460-2. ISSN 1052-9578.

This annual compilation is now in its 8th edition. Since last reviewed by ARBA (see ARBA 94, entry 193), geographic coverage has changed. Although the focus has remained on the United States, the 5th edition marked the shift from international to North American coverage. *World Market Share Reporter* (see ARBA 96, entry 240) now covers the rest of the international market. Arrangement continues to be by Standard Industrial Classification (SIC) code. No mention is made of the new North American Industry Classification System (NAICS). Because coverage varies somewhat in each edition, one should retain older editions. Each edition updates or provides new tables. Therefore, older editions are also needed for historical comparisons.

This tool conveniently assembles market shares from 1,133 sources. Although the data may not always be the latest, the listing of sources enables the researcher to find newer or historical information. Most SIC codes are included, but variations in coverage reflect current interests of the business press. Special emphasis is given to those industries that are large, on the cutting edge, competitive, or in the news. Even though market shares are generally given for 1997, historical or projected market shares are occasionally provided. More than 2,000 entries representing 511 SIC codes detail corporate, brand, product, service, and commodity market shares. Appendixes outline the SIC codes and provide an annotated source list. Excellent indexing by source; geographic area; product; service; and issue, company, and brand name is provided. *Market Share Reporter* is also available electronically as part of the integrated Gale Business Resources. This title is highly recommended for all business collections.—**Bobray Bordelon**

191.   **U.S. Industry and Trade Outlook '98.** New York, McGraw-Hill, 1998. 1v. (various paging). index. $69.95pa. ISBN 0-07-032931-1.

From 1959 through 1994, the U.S. Department of Commerce published annual editions of a much respected and consulted reference, *U.S. Industrial Outlook* (see ARBA 94, entry 218 for a review). Recent developments and trends in major segments of U.S. industry were captured in a single, convenient volume, providing authoritative insights and guidance for business practitioners, researchers, students, and the general public. Following a hiatus of several years, in 1998 the Commerce Department and McGraw-Hill combined their considerable talents and resources to revive the former series under the title of *U.S. Industry and Trade Outlook '98*. The resulting volume breaks total U.S. industry into 50 broad categories, each containing historical data from 1989 and prospects for the future. Each category is supported by references for further investigation and, where helpful, a glossary. Significant trends of each industrial segment are highlighted by charts and tables. An overall prospective of U.S. industry is presented in preliminary chapters as well as a world economic outlook that underlines a pervasive theme of the book, the increasing dependence of U.S. industry on exports. The table of contents and a detailed index ease efforts to locate specific information of interest to a particular reader. This work provides a great deal of information in one place and will also be useful as a point of departure for further research. [R: Choice, Sept 98, p. 102-104]—**William C. Struning**

192. **USA Oil Industry Directory 1998.** 37th ed. Margaret Acevedo, ed. Tulsa, Okla., PennWell Publishing, 1998. 344p. index. $165.00pa. ISSN 0082-8599.

This directory lists more than 3,000 oil and gas companies involved in various activities, such as drilling, exploration/production, pipeline gathering, and refining/petrochemicals. In addition to production company information, this directory includes the names of brokers and dealers, marketing companies, and national associations affiliated with the petroleum industry. The purpose of this directory is to provide a complete listing of contacts for decision-makers in the petroleum industry who depend on them.

The directory is divided into industry segments with listings organized alphabetically by company name. Each entry includes company address, telephone and fax numbers, e-mail addresses (when applicable), names of key executives, plant information, and pertinent descriptions. Each main company name is designated with a black box (bullet) and is in all capital letters. Subsidiary companies are listed under their corporate parent but are referenced in the company index. Companies that are new to this year's edition, such as ROC Gases, are listed with an asterisk. The 2d section, entitled "Index/Surveys," is arranged alphabetically by state and then by plant name. In addition to the geographic index, there are company and personnel indexes. Also included is a survey, entitled "OGJ200," that is reprinted from the *Oil & Gas Journal*.

This edition incorporates industry changes, mergers, and acquisitions as provided by the companies at the time of printing. Hence, Burlington Resources Inc. appears on this year's list as the parent company instead of Meridian Oil Inc. Amoco's merger with British Petroleum is not listed, however. The publisher promises that the directory will be continuously updated. This useful, comprehensive reference source is recommended for engineering students and employees of the petroleum industries.—**Marilynn Green Hopman**

INTERNATIONAL BUSINESS

General Works

Dictionaries and Encyclopedias

193. **NTC's Dictionary of Japan's Business Code Words.** By Boye Lafayette De Mente. Lincolnwood, Ill., National Textbook, 1997. 425p. $25.95. ISBN 0-8442-8344-4.

This book will be an aid to businesspeople and others who are conducting business with the Japanese. This is not a standard dictionary of terms and brief definitions but rather a dictionary of 229 terms or keywords in which the author attempts to provide a cultural frame of reference for the term. These explanations are from one and a half to two pages in length. This contextual way of defining business practices will lead one to a great understanding on how business is to be conducted with the Japanese. This text will prove to be useful for those collections where the clientele is focused on trade with Japan. The author has published extensively in this area, including similar books for China and Mexico (see ARBA 97, entries 107 and 134, respectively).—**Judith J. Field**

194. Shim, Jae K., Joel G. Siegel, and Marc H. Levine. **The Dictionary of International Business Terms.** Chicago, Glenlake and Chicago, Fitzroy Dearborn, 1998. 317p. $45.00. ISBN 1-57958-001-7.

This dictionary contains a variety of words and terms from business and economics. Although the basis for inclusion is not explained, the terms include those related to business, such as *bearer bond* and *matrix structure*; to economics, such as *near money* and *imperfect market*; to international activities, such as *currency basket* or *most favored nation*. The definitions are generally short. Of particular value are the listings of acronyms both as an acronym referenced to the full wording and with the entry for the full term. There are six appendixes, the first on export periodicals with address, telephone number, and cost. Other information sources are listed in another appendix along with hotline numbers. There is also an appendix on very general sources of statistical information. The appendix on Internet sites for international business and trade is slightly annotated. Although the dictionary contains names of the currencies for some countries, a more complete list of countries, territories, and islands with the currency name and symbol is in a separate appendix. The last appendix gives 12 organizations that could be contacted for sources for assistance in conducting business.—**J. E. Weaver**

Directories

195.   **Asia-Pacific Petroleum Directory, 1998.** 14th ed. Margaret Acevedo, ed. Tulsa, Okla., PennWell Publishing, 1998. 160p. index. $165.00pa. ISSN 1096-1348.

196.   **Latin America Petroleum Directory, 1998.** 17th ed. Bob Williams, ed. Tulsa, Okla., PennWell Publishing, 1998. 288p. index. $165.00pa. ISSN 0193-8738.
    The content for both publications is compiled yearly from information gathered by a questionnaire that the publishers have developed. Company listings in these directories are free and reflect the information that the companies provided in their responses to the questionnaires. Thus, for some companies only a name and address are found, and others have only a condensed corporate history. In cases where there are subsidiaries, the parent company is designated by a black box and the subsidiaries follow. The indexes do include individual listings for subsidiaries. Any new company listings are indicated with a star. Both volumes include a statistical section that is arranged country-by-country and then by company on such topics as pipelines and oil production. The Latin American volume includes a brief chapter discussing the future outlook for the petroleum industry in Latin America. PennWell Publishing is known for its publications in the field of oil and gas, and these publications reflect this expertise.—**Judith J. Field**

197.   **Directory of Multinationals: The World's Top 500 Companies.** 5th ed. Martin C. Timbrell and Diana L. Tweedie, eds. London, Waterlow Specialist Information; distr., Detroit, Gale, 1998. 2v. $595.00/set. ISBN 0-333-674642.
    The 5th edition of this book is the only published work on the world's largest (sales in excess of U.S. $1 billion and overseas sales in excess of $500 million) international firms. The manuscript now includes for the first time service, retail, and construction companies to reflect the nature of today's high technology and service-oriented companies. The 500 profiles combine 5-year financial results and detailed analysis. Each company's entry provides contact details, including address, telephone and fax numbers, and Website information; name of directors and principal shareholders; products; structural organization; background discussion; commentary on the company's current situation; a list of subsidiary and affiliates broken down by countries; principal brand names; sales figures; geographic analysis; and product analysis. The five-year financial summary includes debt, capital expenditures, research and development and engineering expenses, earnings per share, total employees, and financial information on the current year. This two-volume set would be of interest to people who want to interact with multinational companies and organizations. The paper, printing, and binding are above average quality. This book should be in all major libraries.—**Herbert W. Ockerman**

198.   **Fitzroy Dearborn International Directory of Venture Capital Funds 1998-99.** Jennifer Schellinger, Patrick Heenan, and Monique Lamontagne, eds. Chicago, Fitzroy Dearborn, 1998. 1886p. index. $175.00. ISBN 1-884964-87-7.
    This monumental directory is prefaced by a review authored by specialists in the field of entrepreneurial finance. Immediately following are authoritative essays that examine the ways in which entrepreneurs ought to target and attract the financing they need. A final essay provides information on venture capital funds in Europe, Asia, and the Pacific Rim. Most of this work is a directory for entrepreneurs electing to seek out the venture capital market. Firms are listed within one of five sections, each in alphabetic order. The first four sections include funds in the U.S. and Canada and are broken down as follows: "General Companies"; "High Tech/Medical Funds"; "Minority and Socially-Useful Funds"; and "Strategic Partners." These are followed by a section that lists venture capital funds outside the United States and Canada. Four indexes round out the directory. They include an alphabetic list of all companies, an index of fund executives and their company affiliation, a geographic index, and a category index that lists funds according to their investment preference.

Each listing includes standard directory information, such as name, address, telephone and fax, other office locations, mission, fund size, year of founding, average investment, minimum investment, investment criteria, industry group preference, and companies in portfolio. An interesting feature is names of officers, executives and principals, occasionally including the universities they attend and the degrees they attained.

The only directory as comprehensive as the *International Directory of Venture Capital Funds* is *Pratt's Guide to Venture Capital Sources* (see ARBA 93, entry 197). With minor differences, both works provide comparable information, along with multiple indexes. Pratt's arrangement is different in that it lists U.S. companies in alphabetic order under state. Foreign firms appear in a separate alphabetic list. Library patrons should find each directory's arrangement to be equally useful with a little practice on their part. Business collections in mid-sized academic and public libraries need to carry one directory or the other; business collections in large academic and public libraries should carry both directories. Likewise, economic development agencies should carry both directories.—**Dene L. Clark**

199.   **Galante's Venture Capital & Private Equity Directory.** 1998 ed. Steven P. Galante, ed. Wellesley, Mass., Asset Alternatives, 1998. 1142p. index. $395.00pa. ISBN 0-9652137-5-7.

200.   **Galante's Venture Capital & Private Equity Directory.** 1997 ed. [CD-ROM]. Wellesley, Mass., Asset Alternatives, 1997. Minimum system requirements: IBM or compatible 486/66MHz. CD-ROM drive. Windows 3.1. 8MB RAM. 20MB hard disk space. SVGA monitor capable of supporting 800 x 600 resolution. Mouse. $395.00. ISBN 0-9652137-2-2.

This annual, international directory, first published in 1996, contains profiles of approximately 1,800 companies supplying venture capital. The publisher focuses on the venture capital industry, and produces four newsletters and organizes conferences.

The print directory has an introductory section containing brief essays on venture capital, a glossary of terms used in the directory, and ranked lists of the largest companies. The company profiles are the core of the directory. All sizes of companies are represented, with a range from $1.5 million to $7.5 billion in capital managed. Nearly four-fifths of the total are U.S.-based, with more than one-half concentrated in four states: New York, California, Massachusetts, and Texas. The foreign-based companies, almost one-half of which are British or Canadian, represent 34 countries. The U.S. section is arranged alphabetically by company name; the foreign section by country, and then alphabetically.

To determine which types of information were typically provided, 100 entries were randomly sampled. Beyond the standard contact information, more than one-half of the entries contained background (e.g., chief personnel, founding date, capital under management, number of staff); investment pace and policies (e.g., average new investments, current activity level, compensation method, syndication policies); investment criteria (e.g., minimum/maximum/preferred size, type of capital provided, funding stage/industry/geographical preferences); and description of the company's focus.

There are 6 indexes: company name; location (state/city, country/city); contact personnel; 18 funding stage preferences (e.g., seed, startup, acquisition); 31 industry preferences; and 23 geographic preferences. The latter three are set up as matrices, with company names listed on the left of the page and the preference at the top, with bullets in the cells indicating the companies with those preferences.

The print directory was compared with two other substantial directories: the 1997 edition of the annually published *Pratt's Guide to Venture Capital Sources* (21st ed.; see ARBA 93, entry 197); and the 1996 edition of the biennially published *Fitzroy Dearborn International Directory of Venture Capital Funds* (2d ed.; see ARBA 97, entry 181). *Galante* has almost 50 percent more entries than *Pratt* and more than 75 percent more than *Fitzroy*. There are 50 entries common to the three that were analyzed for variations in the types of information supplied. Although the three contain many of the same types of information, there are variations in the frequency with which they appear. *Galante* and *Pratt* more routinely than *Fitzroy* supplied the type of organization, date of founding, capital under management, current activity, and geographic preferences. Quite often the two supplied compensation methods and syndication policies, entirely lacking in *Fitzroy*. *Galante* significantly surpassed *Pratt* in frequency of reporting data on the number and dollar amounts of investments. *Galante* uniquely contains the following: type of capital provided, number of staff worldwide, description of company focus, and brief data on venture funds managed. *Galante* should consider adding some of the unique types of information in *Pratt* (e.g., minimum operating data required from applicants, portfolio composition by industry) and *Fitzroy* (names of portfolio companies and officer background). All three have an industry preference index. *Galante's* is the most useful because of its matrix arrangement. *Galante* and *Pratt* have funding stage indexes, with *Galante*'s the more useful, again because of its matrix arrangement. Neither has *Galante*'s geographic preference index. *Pratt* and *Fitzroy* have more extensive introductory essays about venture capital.

The electronic version comes in 2 formats, on 1 CD-ROM and 10 diskettes. The reviewer examined the CD-ROM only. In terms of content, the CD-ROM is almost a mirror of the print. However, it allows quick construction of lists of companies that meet specific criteria. Searching is performed from the initial screen, by clicking one of four tabs: Firm (by company name, state, country, city); Background (by type of organization, capital managed, number of staff); Investments (by funding stage preference, investment size); and Geography and Industry (by preferences). Searching by multiple criteria from more than one tab is possible (e.g., searching for companies providing start-up funds for biotechnology companies in the Midwest or Southeast and managing more than $100 million in capital).—**John Lewis Campbell**

201.   **Hoover's Masterlist of Major International Companies 1998-1999.** Gordon T. Anderson and others, eds. Austin, Tex., Hoover's, 1998. 313p. index. $89.95. ISBN 1-57311-043-4.

This new directory and handbook in Hoover's series of corporate information tools builds on and expands earlier Hoover titles, including *Hoover's MasterList of Major Latin American Companies* (see ARBA 98, entry 211) and *Hoover's MasterList of Major European Companies* (Hoovers, 1996). It will interest business selectors looking at print reference tools on major non-U.S. companies.

The directory lists and profiles 1,658 corporations. The editors try to include all non-U.S. companies with sales above $5 billion and all companies making up major foreign stock indexes (e.g., FTSE, DAX, MIB, Hang Seng, Strait Times, Nikkei, SBF, TSE, Swiss Market, Amsterdam Exchange, Mexican Bolsa IPC). This is supplemented with the highest-ranking companies by sales in 22 smaller but significant economies on 5 continents ranging from Australia and Austria to Israel, China, and South Africa. All foreign corporations trading on major U.S. exchanges and having sales over $120 million are also included. There are two rankings: a top 500 list by sales and a top 500 companies by employee totals. Access features include indexes by industry, headquarters location, and short names. The last index is inaccurately labeled as one by "Stock Exchange Symbol" in the contents.

The lists themselves are arranged alphabetically by formal corporate name, although some words like *Grupo* seem to be ignored in ordering. Listings include headquarters address, telephone and fax numbers, and Website address, if available; chief executive and financial officers; ownership type; stock exchange listings; sales, net income, and employment for 1993 to 1997; and annual growth if available. Entries also include a narrative paragraph characterizing business activities. This is a handy, well-produced reference. It will be useful in business print collections with the appropriate client interests.—**Nigel Tappin**

202.   **Information Sources 1998.** Lewon, Paul, ed. Detroit, Gale, 1998. 266p. index. $125.00pa. ISBN 0-7876-1959-0. ISSN 0734-9637.

Information Sources 1998 lists information about those companies who are members of the Information Industry Association (IIA). More than 550 companies are members, including AT&T, Dow Jones & Co., The Dun & Bradstreet Corporation, several divisions of McGraw-Hill, and the Washington Post Company. The Information Industry Association represents companies that are involved in creating, distributing, and facilitating the use of information in print and digital formats. Entries for each company vary. In addition to a company address, telephone number, fax number, e-mail and Website address, most include the name of the IIA representative, key personnel, company description, key products or services, foreign operations, Internet site profile (if applicable), and how their products or services fit into the consumer market.

An index of key executives lists in alphabetic order by surname both the IIA representative and a key executive for each member company. The key executive's name in this index does not necessarily correspond to the key personnel listed for each company's main entry. This makes locating the name, title, and contact information of key executives by company name extremely difficult. One would have to know the name of the key executive, or scan through all the names, searching for the name of a specific company. Two geographic indexes categorize member companies by state in the United States and by country outside the United States. A foreign operations index lists by country all IIA companies that have international business operations. A product and service index is useful to find lists of IIA companies grouped by categories as to primary functions or types of services rendered. Additional information is provided about IIA, the 1998 IIA board of directors, past chairs, and award programs.

This directory will be most useful to those who are members of the Information Industry Association, and those who need to find more information about its 1998 membership.—**Elizabeth B. Miller**

203.   **International Directory of Company Histories. Volume 16.** Tina Grant, ed. Detroit, St. James Press, 1997. 705p. index. $161.00. ISBN 1-55862-219-5.

204.   **International Directory of Company Histories. Volume 17.** Tina Grant, ed. Detroit, St. James Press, 1997. 713p. index. $161.00. ISBN 1-55862-351-5.

205.   **International Directory of Company Histories. Volume 18.** Jay P. Pederson, ed. Detroit, St. James Press, 1997. 723p. index. $161.00. ISBN 1-55862-352-3.

206.   **International Directory of Company Histories. Volume 19.** Tina Grant, ed. Detroit, St. James Press, 1998. 673p. index. $161.00. ISBN 1-55862-353-1.

207.   **International Directory of Company Histories. Volume 20.** Jay P. Pederson, ed. Detroit, St. James Press, 1998. 695p. index. $161.00. ISBN 1-55862-361-2.

208.   **International Directory of Company Histories. Volume 21.** Tina Grant and Jay P. Pederson, eds. Detroit, St. James Press, 1998. 709p. index. $161.00. ISBN 1-55862-362-0.

Since the first volumes of *International Directory of Company Histories* (IDCH) were published in 1988, librarians, students, and business researchers have found the set to be an invaluable tool for quick reference on company backgrounds. The addition of volumes 16 through 21 brings the total number of companies covered in IDCH to more than 3,000 and includes some significant enhancements.

To be included in the directory, a company must have annual sales greater than 100 million U.S. dollars and be regarded by the editors as "influential" in its geographic region or industry. Although most are public companies, nonprofit organizations and private firms account for about 10 percent of the entries. Subsidiaries and divisions may also be included if they meet the general inclusion criteria. The companies covered are mostly from the United States. A quick tally of the non-U.S. firms in these six volumes indicates that approximately 15 percent are international in origin.

As with the earlier volumes, each company entry is two to four pages in length and has a standard format. The authors of the essays are primarily freelance journalists. The reader first finds a box with basic directory information, including address, year incorporated, number of employees, annual sales, stock exchange, and SIC code. The following narrative history is based on publicly available sources, such as articles, books, corporate annual reports, and company press releases. These short essays are informative and can include a wide range of information. Typically one can expect to find a description of the business, how the company started, growth strategies over time, acquisition information, impact of new technologies, labor conflicts (if applicable), and important personnel changes. Each entry also includes lists of principal subsidiaries or divisions and a reading list of sources for further reference.

Each volume of IDCH contains cumulative company and industry indexes for the entire set. So, one need only consult the latest volume to locate company information appearing anywhere in the set. Index entries for companies with full histories are indicated in bold typeface. Companies mentioned but not specifically covered are indicated by light typeface. Company entries that are updated from previous volumes are indicated by the letters "upd" in bold typeface. Approximately 35 of the entries in each volume are updates of earlier entries. This means that roughly 20 percent of the total number of entries are updates of earlier histories.

Several additional pieces of useful information were added to these latest IDCH volumes. Beginning with volume 16, one usually finds a "company perspective" box that includes a short summary of the company's mission, goals, and ideals. Because so many students and other business researchers are interested in company mission statements, the addition of "company perspective" information is welcome as well. However, because many researchers—especially students—need to cite specific sources, it would be more useful if this information were documented so one could tell if it came from the annual report, a press release, or a company's Website. Also, beginning with volume 17, one may find a company's URL (if available) and, according to the preface, "citations to on-line research." A significant number of the entries examined included a company URL, but there were very few citations to "on-line research" in the reading lists at the end of each entry unless one includes citations to newswire services.

Despite these minor annoyances, the *International Directory of Company Histories* remains a vital reference tool for any business collection and is highly recommended for all academic and public libraries serving business information needs.—**Gordon J. Aamot**

209.   Liu, Lewis-Guodo. **Internet Resources and Services for International Business: A Global Guide.** Phoenix, Ariz., Oryx Press, 1998. 389p. index. $49.95pa. ISBN 1-57356-119-3.

This is a well-organized guide to international information on the Internet. There are 2,500 entries for Internet sites covering 175 countries. Each entry includes a title, Website address, and an annotation. International business is the stated focus of this reference work; however, the economy, culture, religion, language and social, political, and legal systems are covered as well. The included sites were developed, organized, and maintained by government agencies, businesses, or higher education.

An introductory chapter on global economics and the impact of the Internet on international business is followed by a chapter on resources such as the International Chamber of Commerce, Organization for Economic Cooperation and Development, and the World Trade Organization, among others. The following 6 chapters are sites by countries listed alphabetically within continent groupings.

Following the site listings are generous indexes. There is a 24-page Website title index, a 25-page country index, and a 103-page subject index. *Internet Resources and Services for International Business* provides an excellent shortcut to international information. [R: BL, 15 Oct 98, p. 442; LJ, 15 Nov 98, p. 61]—**Sue Brown**

210.   **Trade Shows Worldwide 1998: An International Directory of Events, Facilities, and Suppliers.** 12th ed. Deborah J. Untener and Kimberly N. Hunt, eds. Detroit, Gale, 1997. 1444p. index. $265.00pa. ISBN 0-7876-1120-4. ISSN 1046-4395.

Trade Shows Worldwide (TSWW) offers an extensive array of U.S. and foreign resources useful to the trade show researcher. First published in 1985, this annual directory's 18,609 total entries represent a 38 percent expansion since the review of the 1993 edition (see ARBA 94, entry 298). There are 5 major sections: "Tradeshows and Exhibitions"; "Sponsors and Organizers of Tradeshows"; "Facilities, Services, and Information Sources"; "Rankings"; and indexes. Data in the entries are based upon questionnaire responses from trade show organizers and sponsors, telephone calls, and other Gale publications.

Entries for trade show and exhibitions vary in length, but may contain up to 26 elements; among them entry numbers, trade show name, exhibition management company, sponsor, frequency, founding year, audience, number of visitors, space requirements, type of products displayed, number of exhibitors, meeting room requirements, fees involved, publications containing information about the show, and the date of the show. Entries for sponsors and organizers of the trade shows provide contact information (including e-mail and Web addresses in some cases) and cross-references to the shows that they are associated with in part 1. Arrangement is by name.

There are 4 indexes. The indexing for 25 entries was checked and found to be quite thorough, except for subject and keyword. For example, the National Association of Wheat Growers Convention is under the heading "Agriculture," but not "Grain Industry," and is not keyword indexed under "Wheat."

TSWW was compared with a smaller, less expensive directory, *Tradeshow and Convention Guide* (TCG). TSWW has almost five times as many trade show entries as TCG and almost four times as many management organizations, but slightly fewer facilities. Its foreign coverage is proportionally greater. Comparison of 25 entries common to the directories found that they usually agreed on the information that they supplied, but that TSWW had more details about the audience, booth size, and costs.

Gale could enhance TSWW through more thorough subject and keyword indexing of trade shows, provision of greater physical description of facilities, and the addition of a trade show entry element indicating whether space requirements and the number of exhibitors and visitors has been audited. This standard directory is a highly recommended purchase for libraries serving a business clientele. It is also available on magnetic tape and CD-ROM.—**John Lewis Campbell**

211.   **World Directory of Marketing Information Sources.** 2d ed. Chicago, Ill., Euromonitor International; distr., Detroit, Gale, 1998. 561p. index. $595.00. ISBN 0-86338-765-9.

The goal of this hefty 2d edition of the *World Directory of Marketing Information Sources* is to serve as a comprehensive source leading to worldwide key business research organizations and their publications and services. The introduction states that all entries have been revised, with many of the entries expanded in this edition. A new section, listing country and industry directories of companies, has been added as well as available Website and e-mail addresses throughout the volume. Focusing on consumer market information, the volume was compiled by Euromonitor's in-house team of researchers who contacted each organization.

Organized in 9 sections, the book covers official government sources and publications, trade development bodies, trade and business associations, market research publishers and companies, major business libraries, trade and business journals, company directories, and online databases. Each section subdivides into international, pan-regional, and country-by-country entities. Coverage includes 75 countries, from Afghanistan to Zimbabwe. The information varies by section but includes mailing address; telephone and fax numbers; e-mail and Website addresses; availability of the information source; frequency of updating; year established; contents; and specialties, services, and language. The top of each right-hand page indicates the section and country on that page, promoting ease of use for this massive volume.

This is a comprehensive listing of a variety of marketing sources throughout the world. It is nicely organized, although the print is small. Each country is listed in white type on a black band, and each source under that is in larger bold typeface. The information headers are in smaller bold typeface, and each publication is marked with a bullet. It is possible to find one's way once one has understood the organization. Ease of use has obviously been well considered. There are some omissions (i.e., *Fortune* is not listed in the journals); however, given the size and scope of the volume, this is to be expected. The work is an invaluable business reference source from a known quality publisher; it is recommended for all business reference collections.—**Carol Krismann**

212.   **World Retail Directory 1997-98.** 3d ed. London, Euromonitor; distr., Detroit, Gale, 1997. 482p. index. $990.00. ISBN 0-86338-752-7.

The 3d edition of this directory is arranged alphabetically by country and covers 2,700 retailers of consumer goods in 85 countries. Major retailers are ranked by millions in U.S. dollars. Individual company entries provide financial data in national currencies. In addition to basic directory information, each entry includes major subsidiaries, key personnel (which is sketchy at best), and number of outlets. Many individual countries include a listing of top retailers indexed alphabetically, both by type of retailer (e.g., department store operator, mail order company) and by sector (e.g., clothing and textiles, food, home furnishings).

A criticism of the previous edition was that it did not list "new technologies (e.g., listservs, World Wide Web homepages)" (see ARBA 97, entry 222). The 3d edition claims to have corrected this oversight by including e-mail addresses and Websites in a typical company entry. However, an examination of the book turns up few such inclusions. For example, the top 20 U.S. companies all have Web pages and not one of them is listed in this book. The next edition should include Web pages for every company that has them.

These omissions notwithstanding, this work does fill a niche. It is recommended for large public and academic libraries and specific special libraries.—**Deborah Sharp**

213.   **Worldwide Offshore Petroleum Directory 1998.** 30th ed. Margaret Acevedo and Elizabeth Arceneaux, eds. Tulsa, Okla., PennWell Publishing, 1998. 528p. index. $165.00pa. ISSN 1096-1356.

Formerly known as the *Worldwide Offshore Contractors & Equipment Directory*, this volume is in its 30th edition. PennWell Publishing proudly points out that this is not a directory of advertisers—companies do not pay to be listed. Companies are listed because they answered an annual questionnaire that updates and verifies each entry for changes caused by mergers, acquisitions, or personnel changes.

The directory is divided into industry segments with listings arranged alphabetically. Segment examples include exploration and production, services companies, and suppliers and manufacturers. The entries are arranged by parent company. Parenthood is designated by a black box above the all-capital-letter entry. Under each parent, in smaller typeface, is a list of the relevant subsidiaries. New companies or those with significant changes are marked with a star.

The directory has two major indexes, alphabetic and geographic. The alphabetic index lists all entries from parent to subsidiary in one listing. This arrangement makes it possible to find a subsidiary without knowing the parent company's name—a useful feature. Access is also possible by state or country using the geographical index. This directory is "the" directory in this field and as such is useful for any library serving users interested in the petroleum industry.—**Susan B. Ardis**

214. **Worldwide Petrochemical Directory 1998.** 36th ed. Anne K. Rhodes and Margaret Acevedo, eds. Tulsa, Okla., PennWell Publishing, 1998. 295p. index. $165.00pa. ISSN 0084-2583.

This volume is the 36th edition in a series of petroleum industry directories published by PennWell Publishing. As usual, the issue is divided into regions (continents and countries) with listings arranged in alphabetic order by company. Each main company is designated with a black box and is in all capital letters. Subsidiary companies are listed under their corporate parent but are referenced in the company index. Companies that are new to this year's edition or have had significant changes have been designated with a star. The contents of the directory are as follows: geographic regions—United States, Canada, Latin America, Europe, Asia-Pacific, Middle East, and Africa; supplementary information on engineering and construction; a company index; a geographic reference; and statistical surveys.

This issue is entirely new, having been updated by questionnaire research in return for a free company listing. Included information has been verified and incorporates all industry changes, mergers, and acquisitions as provided by participating companies at the time of printing. The directory is the standard reference guide to the petroleum industry; it contains the most reliable and compatible information from one of the world's leading providers. Therefore, this edition can be recommended as a book of ready-reference for all decision-makers involved in the petroleum business.—**Ludmila N. Ilyina**

Handbooks and Yearbooks

215. **Consumer Asia 1998.** Chicago, Ill., Euromonitor International; distr., Detroit, Gale, 1998. 607p. maps. $850.00pa. ISBN 0-86338-761-6.

216. **Consumer China 1998.** Chicago, Ill., Euromonitor International; distr., Detroit, Gale, 1997. 187p. $830.00pa. ISBN 0-86338-755-1.

217. **Consumer Middle East 1998.** Chicago, Ill., Euromonitor International; distr., Detroit, Gale, 1998. 223p. $830.00. ISBN 0-86338-757-8.

These three volumes continue Euromonitor's Consumer publications, four of which were reviewed a year ago (see ARBA 97, entries 268-271) and included Canada, Mexico, South Africa, and the United States. Their purpose is to analyze markets and present a wide range of market statistics.

The organization is the same as those covered in last year's review and includes 3 sections: overview of the market and economy; marketing parameters, such as demographics and consumer expenditures; and market size for various consumer product categories. The *Middle East* and the *Asia* volumes also include a section on consumer markets with comparative country data and a section covering each country's consumer goods market. Aside from the narrative overview, the content is entirely statistical, usually in tabular form with historical time series ranging from 1990 to 1997, including some with single-year data. These volumes do not contain forecasts as the ones previously reviewed did.

The *China* volume includes many tables that display individual cities and provinces. The *Asia* volume provides an outline map of each country included. The map of China shows all of its provinces, but there is no such map in the *China* volume where it is needed. There are also no maps in the *Middle East* book.

As with the country volumes reviewed in 1997, these volumes retain the same faults. Foremost among those is the fact that there is no index, only a table of contents listing every table. Such an omission is remarkable given the high price of these books and makes locating specific data unnecessarily cumbersome. Page headings indicate sections only, so that scanning for individual data is slowed considerably. Information sources for tables are given only in the most general way, such as "State Statistical Bureau," "National Statistics," or "Euromonitor" rather than a documentary source, thus making follow-up and verification difficult.

Even with these flaws, these Euromonitor publications are an important source of information difficult or impossible to find anywhere else. Data on these emerging markets are almost nonexistent for the general public, so these volumes represent a significant contribution. These sources would be useful to libraries serving the needs of international business students or businesses contemplating going international.—**Gerald L. Gill**

218.   **Consumer International 1997/98.** 4th ed. Chicago, Euromonitor International; distr., Detroit, Gale, 1997. 509p. index. $1,050.00. ISBN 0-86338-740-3.

Consumer International, a companion volume to the publisher's *Consumer Europe* (see ARBA 95, entry 278) and *Consumer Eastern Europe* (see ARBA 96, entry 251), is a compendium of consumer market information on 27 major non-European markets. These include the United States, Mexico, Canada, Australia, and New Zealand in addition to China, India, Israel, Japan, and South Africa. The remainder of the nations come from Central and South America as well as Southeast Asia. The 27 nations range from the world's most highly developed economies to countries whose market economies are in their infancy. In spite of this diversity, the volume presents available market information on consumer trends for more than 200 narrowly defined consumer product categories. These consumer product categories are the major retail items purchased for household use. The publisher uses the same product classification system for all titles. This allows the user to make easy comparison between retail consumption in European nations and those market economies that appear in *Consumer International*.

In most cases, there are three tables for each retail category: volume data, covering a six-year time series; value series, in national currency, for the same time frame; and statistical calculations, such as growth rate from 1991 to 1996 and per capita spending in 1996. The comparative data in this reference work are not available elsewhere, making this title an extremely valuable resource for corporations engaged in international trade and researchers who are studying foreign economic systems. Special libraries serving these clienteles should acquire this title. Because of the cost of this title, only those academic and large public libraries that have endowments covering international trade or foreign economic systems will have the funds to purchase this work.—**Dene L. Clark**

219.   Dori, John T., and Richard D. Fisher Jr., comps. **U.S. and Asia Statistical Handbook.** 1997-98 ed. Washington, D.C., Heritage Foundation, 1997. 95p. maps. $9.50pa. ISBN 0-89195-243-8.

Although this handy statistical reference is intended as a convenient aid to U.S. legislators, congressional staff, and other influential people, it is of potential use to a broader audience. The main text is a collection of economic, political, and social information (mainly statistics) on about 35 countries, including the United States. The title is a bit of a misnomer in that a number of Pacific countries outside Asia, including Australia, New Zealand, and some larger island states, are included. Material is drawn from major statistical handbooks. The information for each nation is arranged under 5 headings—land, population, politics, economy, and military. Included are statistics such as literacy rates, gross domestic product (GDP), imports and exports, and trade and investment balances with the United States. Under the "Politics" heading such items as indexes of "economic freedom," political and civil liberties, and how often the country voted with the United States at the United Nations are included. Statistics mainly date from 1995 and 1996.

Many other features are of potential interest, especially to those favoring deregulation, economic liberalization, free trade, and minimal government. There are 9 charts covering topics such as U.S. bilateral trade deficits, foreign direct investment, and defense spending for selected countries or regions. There are political maps to locate the countries. Notes on "Barriers to U.S. Asian Trade" highlight issues under 15 countries, including the United States, from the foundation's pro-globalization perspective.

This is an inexpensive, user-friendly publication with an avowedly right-of-center perspective. Large libraries with many statistical yearbooks will own many of the sources from which it is drawn. Smaller collections with the relevant clientele may find it worth considering.—**Nigel Tappin**

220.   **Handbook of North American Industry: NAFTA and the Economies of Its Member Nations.** John E. Cremeans, ed. Lanham, Md., Bernan Associates, 1997. 1998. illus. $89.00. ISBN 0-89059-173-7.

This book is written for economists, businesspeople, and the general reader with an interest in the implications of the North American Free Trade Agreement (NAFTA). Part 1 contains both articles on NAFTA and those issues that have impacted the North American economy as a whole, such as the peso crisis and the implications of an independent Quebec.

Nearly 85 percent of the book is arranged in standardized chapters covering industries in agriculture, mining, construction, trade, manufacturing, and service-oriented industries. Most chapters contain 11 standard tables covering specific topics and 4 standard figures. The material for this section has been gleaned from U.S., Canadian, and Mexican government agencies. The first 6 tables for each industry refer to the U.S. economy, while tables 7 and 8 refer to Canada and tables 9 and 10 to Mexico. Table 11 provides information on international trade and attempts to show how each country has fared in this new bilateral trade environment. The preface includes a detailed explanation of each table with examples and a discussion of how the industry classification codes for each country differ. A new North American Industry Classification System (NAICS) has been adopted and is in the process of being implemented by the three countries. In the appendixes the reader will find a brief outline of NAICS, the executive summary by the president of the United States on the impact of NAFTA, a synopsis of the NAFTA accord, and information on the governmental structure of the three countries.

Some of the statistical information included is as current as of 1996, but a lot of the U.S. material is cited from the 1993 economic census. This is a good work to consult to get general economic and trade information and will serve as a reference point for reviewing the impact of NAFTA in years to come. This book will be most useful in large business collections where this type of economic data is regularly requested. [R: Choice, Oct 98, pp. 296-298]—**Judith J. Field**

221.   **Handbook of World Stock Indices.** 1997 ed. Austin, Tex., Meridian Securities Markets, 1997. 434p. $125.00pa. ISBN 0-9648930-5-3.

During the past few years, several directories listing international stock exchanges have appeared. *The Handbook of World Stock and Commodity Exchanges* (see ARBA 93, entry 222) is the most useful for a comprehensive listing of exchanges along with their histories. *The International Guide to Securities Market Indices* (see ARBA 98, entry 175) offers the most extensive computational methodology as well as information on a wide range of security instruments.

Handbook of World Stock Indices covers 47 stock exchanges in 42 countries. Arrangement is alphabetic by the name of the exchange; a country index is not provided. Generally 20 years of data chronicles the exchange's monthly high, low, close, and averages. All data were obtained from the stock exchange itself unless otherwise noted. A useful feature is the methodology used to calculate each index along with the number of companies and stocks listed on each exchange. A further breakdown by domestic versus foreign is provided along with number of shares outstanding. A market capitalization profile of each market by industry is also given. Constituent lists are selectively listed.

This work is a subset of another publication, *World Stock Exchange Factbook* (see ARBA 97, entry 186). The fuller version is arranged alphabetically by country and contains additional information on disclosure requirements, restrictions to foreign investors, investor protection, and mergers and acquisitions. The "subset" does provide more data on the number of listed companies—20 years versus 5 years. The most substantial difference is in price: $295 for the *World Stock Exchange Factbook* as opposed to $125 for this work. Given that most regulatory information can be found on the stock exchange's homepages, this work is clearly the better buy. One will not obtain the comprehensive data available in online services such as Datastream International. The World Wide Web can be hit or miss for data and is typically not archived. This work is an inexpensive means of obtaining summary data in one permanent place.—**Bobray Bordelon**

222.   **Hoover's Handbook of World Business 1998.** 5th ed. Austin, Tex., Hoover's, 1998. 607p. index. $79.95. ISBN 1-57311-035-3. ISSN 1055-7199.

Hoover's 5th edition of the *Handbook of World Business* profiles 250 of the "most influential" public, private, and government-owned companies based outside the United States. Profiles are alphabetic, with information organized into 7 sections: a brief overview of current operations; a company history; names of executives with ages and salaries when available; location, telephone and fax numbers, and Website information; a list of the company's major products, services, subsidiaries, and joint ventures; key competitors; and up to 10 years of various financial data. Three indexes provide access by industry type; by headquarters location; and by brands, companies, and people named in the profiles. A highly useful feature of this directory is its "List-Lover's Compendium," a smorgasbord of lists ranking companies by size, wealth, industry, U.S. trade connections, and so forth. Hoover's publishes three other equally valuable yet affordable directories (on American business, private companies, and emerging companies), and all four are available individually or as a set with a combined index. Hoover's is also available online.—**Jean Engler**

223.   **Industrial Commodity Statistics Yearbook, 1995. Annuaire de Statistiques Industrieles Par Produit.**
29th ed. New York, United Nations, 1997. 901p. $115.00. ISBN 92-0-061171-3. ISSN 0257-7208. S/N
E/F.97.XVII.9.

The 29th annual volume in its series, this edition provides information about the production of various industrial commodities. Statistics are presented in tabular form with extensive notes in both English and French. The
work is organized by commodity under three major headings: mining and quarrying, manufacturing, and electricity and gas.

Most of the commodities are grouped in the manufacturing section, which includes beverages, tobacco,
textiles, wearing apparel, and 15 further subheadings. To make the information easily accessible for researchers,
the tables organize each item alphabetically by country or geographic area. For example, under the manufacturing
subhead of wearing apparel, one finds a table for women's and girl's raincoats. This table gives 10 years worth
of production figures, which show that worldwide production in 1995 was less than half that of 1986. At the
same time, U.S. production ceased after 1992.

The book also contains a comprehensive index in English and French of the tabulated commodities,
followed by a table that provides the correspondences among several coding systems used to describe commodities.
These coding systems include the Standard International Trade Classification and its various revisions.

Prepared by the Statistical Division of the United Nations, this work also contains information from additional government agencies and publications, such as the Food and Agriculture Organization of the United Nations
and the World Bureau of Metal Statistics. Thus, the value of this work for researchers stems from the availability
of these statistics, gathered from many international sources, in one volume.—**Renee B. Horowitz**

224.   **International Marketing Data and Statistics 1998.** 22d ed. Chicago, Euromonitor International; distr.,
Detroit, Gale, 1998. 611p. index. $375.00. ISBN 0-86338-762-4. ISSN 0308-2938.

Now in its 22d edition, this source provides a lot of statistical information for the inquiring business researcher.
Touching every area of the globe except Europe, which is covered in the publisher's *European Marketing Data
and Statistics* (31st ed.; see ARBA 97, entry 273), this volume presents the user with a wide array of data on
demographics, economics, business, trade, commodity, consumer services, and products.

This compendium opens with a short guide to how to use it followed by a listing of the important sources
of information for each country. The section on marketing geography includes some basic statistics and current
overview for all countries covered. The next 23 sections provide in-depth statistical analyses in a broad spectrum
of subjects, such as demographic trends and forecasts, economic indicators, environment, culture and education,
travel, and many other business topics. The last section gives regional comparisons in selected areas. A 4-page
index provides access to the 230 tables.

The tables are well organized and present the data in an easy-to-follow format. They are divided into major
regions, such as South America, ASEAN/NICs, and Caribbean. Much of the data start with 1977, 1980, and then
1990 to 1996, with a percent change from 1977 to 1996. Symbol explanations (if any) are at the end of the table,
usually three pages from the beginning. This can be a problem for first-time users because there is no footnote or
asterisk to alert one to this. Numbered footnotes are gathered at the end of each section.

This is an important source for those libraries that can afford it. For those libraries that find Euromonitor's
Consumer series too expensive, this is a good substitute, covering similar statistics for even more countries. Any
medium to large public or academic library would find this volume as useful as the *Europa World Year Book*
(see entry 66) and an excellent supplement to it.—**Gerald L. Gill**

225.   **International Marketing Forecasts.** Chicago, Ill., Euromonitor International; distr., Detroit, Gale,
1997. 403p. index. $790.00. ISBN 0-86338-729-2.

Once again Euromonitor brings its considerable expertise and knowledge to bear upon an area of international business information—this time into the choppy waters of marketing predictions. This title represents the
1st edition of an annual study. The methodology used is fully explained in the introductory pages. The forecasted
figures are based on Euromonitor's own database and analyses.

Coverage consists of 27 countries. Not all countries are represented in every table. Some specific products,
such as housewares, may include only a few countries because of limited availability of data for smaller economies.
The benchmark year is 1995, with 1996 and 1997 serving as baseline comparisons. The forecasts run through
1998, 1999, 2000, 2005, and 2010. There are 239 markets, including food and drinks, health care products,

cosmetics and toiletries, housewares, clothing, appliances, consumer electronics, automobiles, and personal goods, among others.

The presentation generally consists of two tables per page. An index of products covered is included. Each major section begins with a list of tables followed by the sources of data. Care should be exercised in relying on the forecasts in this volume. Predictions and even baseline figures can vary not only from other sources but also from other Euromonitor publications as well. For example, inflation rates as represented in *International Marketing Forecasts* vary significantly from those in *Consumer Canada 1996* (see ARBA 97, entry 268), issued just one year earlier. There is a significant difference for congruent years; for example, for 1999, 3.4 percent is given in this volume, whereas 1.9 percent is presented in *Consumer Canada 1996*. In both cases the source is Euromonitor. Users should be made aware of these differences when referring to these or any other forecasts. With the caveat noted above, this book can serve as an excellent source for international marketing data and trends for both business and academic users.—**Gerald L. Gill**

226.   **International Tax Summaries, 1998: A Guide for Planning and Decisions.** By Coopers & Lybrand Global Tax Network. New York, John Wiley, 1998. 1v. (various paging). $135.00 (with disc). ISBN 0-471-18234-6.

Coopers & Lybrand Global Tax Network, a leading international accounting and consulting firm, has published *International Tax Summaries* annually since 1982. This edition presents an overview of the tax systems of 125 countries. Each country's entry is divided into as many as 37 topical areas, including details of income taxes on corporations and individuals, sales and value-added taxes, inheritance and gift taxes, payroll, and other types of taxes. There are several sections of particular interest to nonresidents who are contemplating living or doing business in another country, such as incentives and grants to business, exchange controls, investment restrictions, and personal income taxes on nonresidents. The book includes a CD-ROM that allows keyword searching of the complete text using the Folio Views search engine.

This volume has been a standard reference for practitioners in the international tax arena since it first appeared. However, the writing style is concise and nontechnical, making the book useful to business managers and others who are not tax specialists. Although the book, of course, should not be relied upon as a substitute for professional consultation, it will greatly assist the reader in identifying and understanding key issues and in discussing these with a practitioner. This title is highly recommended for international business collections.

—**Christopher J. Hoeppner**

227.   **North American Labor Markets: A Comparative Profile.** Lanham, Md., Bernan Associates and Dallas, Tex., Commission for Labor Cooperation, 1997. 137p. $35.00pa. ISBN 0-89059-070-2.

This comparative profile of labor markets in North America is the first report issued by the Secretariat of the Commission for Labor Cooperation, a body established through a supplementary accord to the North American Free Trade Agreement (NAFTA). Spanning the 11-year period from 1984 to 1995, the report presents charts and graphs comparing labor market trends in Canada, Mexico, and the United States. The charts and graphs portray similarities and differences in such basic concepts as employment, unemployment, earnings, labor productivity, income distribution, and employment benefits. The charts and graphs covering employment issues go into extensive detail by industry, occupation, gender, firm size, hours of work, nonstandard employment, part-time employment, occupational skill level, and unionization. The charts and graphs are naturally based on data furnished by agencies within the three countries that are signatories of NAFTA. Two outstanding features of the work are discussions of the data and their sources and the interpretation of the data.

Many of the data on the U.S. workforce are readily available to libraries within the United States. Aside from selected large research and academic libraries, this fact is not true for comparable data from Canada or Mexico. *North American Labor Markets* is therefore a particularly valuable tool to libraries within the United States. It should be equally valuable in Canadian and Mexican libraries. At the low retail price, all but the smallest public libraries should acquire this work as well as all academic libraries with business or social science collections.

—**Dene L. Clark**

228.   Pagell, Ruth A., and Michael Halperin. **International Business Information: How to Find It, How to Use It.** 2d ed. Phoenix, Ariz., Oryx Press, 1997. 445p. index. $84.50. ISBN 1-57356-050-2.

As any experienced researcher will say, locating international business information is often a difficult and frustrating job. This volume makes the job much easier. It contains excellent information resources, thoughtful analysis, and expert advice. The selection criteria for the 2d edition are the same as for the 1st edition (see ARBA 95, entry 255). The focus is on core materials that are authoritative, available, and affordable. Occasionally some works are mentioned with the recommendation not to buy them. Each chapter covers a different subtopic of international business. The book contains exhibits, tables, appendixes, citations to significant texts on the subject, and a selected bibliography with each chapter. Websites are also included where relevant.

Librarians will find this resource useful for collection development and research assistance. It is an excellent resource for academic, corporate, and public libraries.—**Deborah Sharp**

229.   **Ranking of World Stock Markets.** 1997 ed. Austin, Tex., Meridian Securities Markets, 1997. 195p. $75.00pa. ISBN 0-9648930-3-7. ISSN 1096-648X.

This quick reference guide ranks 47 stock exchanges from around the world in terms of size, growth, profitability, liquidity, and volatility as well as other performance measures. Five years of data are presented for 19 of the 21 market measures. The tables give monetary amounts in inflation adjusted dollars (1996), and some also give the corresponding foreign currency equivalents in unadjusted (nominal) amounts. The display varies slightly depending on the ranking. For instance, in the "Per Share Traded" table the numbered ranks are followed by the exchange, then the average price per share traded in U.S. 1996 dollars, and finally the notes (e.g., "includes unit trusts" or "includes equity derivatives").

Each table has a corresponding bar chart on the facing page presenting the same statistical information in graphic form. The 47 markets covered include American, New York, and NASDAQ from the United States along with a good representation of exchanges in Europe (19), Asia/Pacific (11), and Latin America (7). The rankings include number of listed companies, number of listed stocks, capitalization, company size, trades, dividend yield, and year change.

This is an easy, quick, and efficient tool that adds dimension to directories of exchanges. It provides a more complete and comparative picture of the world's most active and influential stock markets. These rankings are straightforward, uncluttered, easy to read, and dramatize the importance of emerging markets. This source is recommended for any library where there is an interest in investing, especially global investing.—**Gerald L. Gill**

230.   **Retail Trade International.** 1998 ed. Chicago, Ill., Euromonitor International; distr., Detroit, Gale, 1998. 5v. $1,950.00/set. ISBN 0-86338-747-0.

Retail Trade International, now in its 9th edition, is published every 3 years. Euromonitor's newest edition reviews and analyzes retail trade globally and for each of 50 countries around the world in 3,070 pages of text and more than 2,500 statistical tables. An 88-page overview summarizes the data from the 50 country profiles and examines it at the regional and national level. A glossary of terms, methodology, sources, and exchange rates are included in the introduction. The glossary does not include all terms. The word "turnover" (meaning sales), which is used in many tables, is the most glaring omission. There is no index, but a detailed table of contents and list of the hundreds of tables are included.

An in-depth portrait of the retail conditions existing in the market is provided for each county. These country chapters begin with a bulleted section of key findings, followed by an analysis of the general economy and retail business, infrastructure, issues, and sales. Also covered are food and nonfood distribution. There is a section that details the major retailers, along with rankings and market shares and a description of each of these companies. In some cases, a financial, business, and competitive analysis is given. The final part presents the retail outlook, which forecasts until the year 2005. Each country chapter is structured so that narratives precede the data and place it in context. Historical data in these tables cover the years 1992 to 1997.

The amount of information presented is quite extensive. The chapter on Belgium is 60 pages long; the one on France 114 pages. Food and nonfood retailing is further broken down into 25 smaller categories, such as supermarkets, discounters, bakers, variety stores, mail order firms, footwear stores, and other. Figures are given in the national currency.

Once again Euromonitor has provided an excellent source for international business by providing information not available elsewhere or available only with great expense and difficulty. This set is simply a gold mine of data and perspectives. It would be improved by the addition of an index, especially for the retail companies covered. It is an invaluable tool for business students and researchers interested in global retail markets. Because of its cost, this source will most likely find its way into large academic libraries and corporate information centers.

—**Gerald L. Gill**

231. **Statistics on Occupational Wages and Hours of Work and on Food Prices 1997. Statistiques des Salaires et de la Durée du Travail par Profession et des Prix de Produits Alimentaires. Estadisticas Sobre Salarios y Horas de Trabajo por Ocupacion y Precios.** Washington, D.C., International Labour Office, 1997. 309p. $31.50pa. ISBN 92-2-007353-6. ISSN 1020-0134.

Statistics on Occupational Wages and Hours of Work and on Food Prices, published in English, French, and Spanish, is a compilation of a worldwide study made each October by the International Labour Organization (ILO) on the subjects indicated in the title. This latest issue covers the years 1995 and 1996.

The 159 occupations and 49 industry groups covered are selected for their importance in relation to the number of workers employed, those that fall within the scope of the ILO Industrial Committees, and those seen as important in relation to certain terms of employment of workers, such as women and salaried employees, among others. The 93 food items covered represent, as much as possible, the dietary habits in countries throughout the world. This detailed study, produced by the ILO's Bureau of Labor Statistics, also carries a list of articles published by the bureau between 1990 and 1993.

Although the ILO advises care in the use of this publication, in view of the rapid expansion of globalization in manufacturing, finances, and communications, this publication is an invaluable reference source for industry, statisticians, researchers, and others interested in changing developments both at home and abroad.

—**George A. Meyers**

232. **Structural and Ownership Changes in the Chemical Industry of Countries in Transition.** New York, United Nations, 1997. 164p. $75.00pa. ISBN 92-1-116675-6. S/N E.97.II.E.17.

Designed for private sector investors, this report presents the status of the chemical industry in 17 Central and Eastern European countries. Based on questionnaires completed by the government and information published in the technical press, the economic and industrial development in the region is compared through primarily statistical data. The volume consists of an introduction and 17 chapters, one for each country, with the introduction assessing conversions, privatization, restructuring, and other developments in the industry during a five-year period ending in 1996. With eight tables on gross domestic product, or GDP (e.g., share of the industry GDP) and other comparative data (e.g., growth of output), this introduction emphasizes the chemical industry's importance as a backbone of all industry, illustrates beginning opportunities for foreign investment, and assesses progress in privatization efforts.

The individual country chapters, which vary in content and length depending on the extent of information received, follow a similar format in reporting production data, recent laws and regulations, ownership changes, structural changes (e.g., infrastructure, outlook), and statistical data. Private ownership information ranges from the number of companies in the industry to detailed descriptions of products and company partnerships. This work is recommended for libraries serving the chemical industry and an international business clientele.

—**Sandra E. Belanger**

233. **The World Economic Factbook 1997/98.** 5th ed. Chicago, Euromonitor International; distr., Detroit, Gale, 1997. 457p. maps. $390.00. ISBN 0-86338-758-6.

The World Economic Factbook is a compilation of political and economic information and statistics for more than 207 countries. Data are compiled from national sources, including national statistical agencies. Additional data are drawn from agencies such as the International Monetary Fund and the United Nations and from national press and specialist publications. Each country entry includes currency, location, head of state, head of government, ruling party, political structure, political risk, economy, past elections, main industries, inflation rate, GDP, birth rate, total exports and imports, life expectancy, and population. There is also an additional section of maps representing Europe, the Middle East and Africa, Oceania, North and Central America, and South America.

There is an especially informative country rankings section. The countries are ranked by area (in kilometer), mid-year population, population density, child population, elderly population, birth rate, average household size, urban population, GDP growth rate, per capita GDP, inflation rate, total imports, total exports, and tourism receipts. *The World Economic Factbook* is highly recommended to academic research libraries.—**Lucy Heckman**

234.   **World Investment Report 1998: Trends and Determinants.** New York, United Nations, 1998. 428p. $45.00pa. ISBN 92-1-112426-3. S/N E.98.II.D.5.

The 8th annual *World Investment Report* indicates that countries are continuing to forge stronger economic links with each other. This report looks at the implications of the Asian financial crises, analyzes current trends in foreign direct investment and international production, and examines the key aspects of the world's largest transnational corporations, noting major regulatory changes at the national and international levels. This report tends to improve the understanding of the role of foreign direct investment (FDI) in the world economy. The book is divided into chapters that look at global trends, including international production; mergers and acquisitions; the world's largest transnational corporations; the largest transnational corporations from developing countries; investment policy issues, such as trends and double taxation treaties; host country determinants of foreign direct investment; developed country's, such as the United States, western Europe, and Japan's, role in foreign investment; Africa's trends and recent country successes; Asian Pacific trends and the financial crisis in Asia; Latin American and Caribbean areas trends and FDI exports and the balance of payments; and Central and Eastern Europe trends. This is followed by a rather extensive reference section and annexes.

The printing, paper, and binding are average for the softcover publication, and the print is large enough for its intended use. The book is liberally sprinkled with boxes, tables, and figures to make the information easier to visualize and understand. Like all United Nations books, the information is of excellent quality and the only place this type of information is available. It should be in all major research libraries.—**Herbert W. Ockerman**

235.   **World Labour Report 1997-98: Industrial Relations, Democracy, and Social Stability.** Washington, D.C., International Labour Office, 1997. 283p. $39.95pa. ISBN 92-2-110331-5.

Industrial relations among employees and their employers, associations, trade unions and the public, and the intertwined complexity of economics and social issues that impact them comprise the *World Labour Report 1997-98*. The work is published by the International Labour Organization (ILO), a specialized United Nations agency established in 1919 as an agency of the League of Nations. The 9 chapters in the work cover trade unions, industrial relations, and social dialogue as well as a discussion of the future. The enormous changes that have already taken place around the world are reflected in detailed chapter discussions. The work contains an excellent statistical appendix with dozens of tables; this appendix is accompanied by a separate section of technical notes on selected tables. Also of note are the numerous figures and boxes containing articles and background notes on various related topics throughout the work.

As we move into the twenty-first century, industrial relations are of particular interest due to issues such as privatization, communication, competition, marginalization, isolationism, and globalization—the ability to move funds as well as blue- and white-collar jobs from one country to another with relative ease. This report deals with a number of serious issues, such as unions and social partnerships, and discusses them in depth. Labor, management, and government, the tripartite relationship that is the theory on which the ILO was founded, is the basis of a social contract or a social democratic structure. However, it is difficult to find a discussion of the antilabor offensive as a factor in the decline of union membership in the report. Written at an academic level, this report is best suited for the research-level library.—**George A. Meyers**

236.   **World Marketing Data and Statistics on CD-ROM.** [CD-ROM]. 4th ed. Chicago, Ill., Euromonitor International; distr., Detroit, Gale, 1998. Minimum system requirements: IBM or compatible 486 DX2 66. Double-speed CD-ROM drive. Windows 3.1 or Windows 95. 8MB RAM (16MB RAM for Windows 95). 10MB hard disk space (20MB for Windows 95). $1,490.00. ISBN 0-86338-751-9.

This compact disc, originally reviewed in ARBA 97, entry 281, contains many business statistics pertaining to countries worldwide. The information included in this product is also available in two annual Euromonitor print publications, *European Marketing Data and Statistics 1998* (see ARBA 97, entry 273) and *International Marketing Data and Statistics 1998* (see ARBA 95, entry 252).

Data for 209 countries are included in the product, with information for some data types extending back to 1977. The information is divided into 23 subject categories, including advertising and media, consumer market sizes, demographic trends, economic indicators, external trade, and retailing and retail distribution. These 23 classifications are further broken down into 1,055 data types. Representative data types from the preceding categories include: "Home Ownership of TV's—Latest Year"; "Per Capita Sales of Baby Care Products 1996"; "Urban Population 1980-1996"; "GDP from Manufacturing—Latest Year"; "Imports (cif) of Basic Manufacturers,

SITC Classification 6—Latest Year"; and "Retail Sales through General Food Outlets—Latest Year." As might be expected, not all data types are available for all countries, and the information reported is often dated.

A strength of this electronic product is the capability of the user to manipulate retrieved data sets, creating customized reports comparing information of different data types and countries in a variety of different formats. *World Marketing Data and Statistics on CD-ROM* is recommended for information centers requiring extensive international business data in an electronic medium.—**Mark A. Allan**

237. **World Trade Organization Dispute Settlement Decisions: Bernan's Annotated Reporter. Volume 1.** Lanham, Md., Bernan Associates, 1998. 535p. index. $75.00. ISBN 0-89059-105-9.

This book is an important reference source for a fairly small set of the population. It is produced by the exclusive publisher of the World Trade Organization (WTO). The book includes all WTO panel reports and appellate decisions for cases from January 29, 1996, through February 25, 1997. Other volumes will cover later cases. Most of the book gives detailed information on nine cases. After a two-page summary of the complainant, respondent, third parties, decision date, procedural history, conclusion, and annotations, the report of the panel is given. The specific reports vary but generally include factual aspects of the case, the main arguments, submissions by interested parties, interim review findings, conclusions, issues raised in appeal, treaty interpretation, and article interpretation, among other items. The language is very technical and detailed. There are four tables that contain an overview of dispute settlement activity, countries involved in disputes, treaty provisions interpreted, and Basic Instruments and Selected Documents (BISD) and dispute references (by case). An index is provided. The resolution of disputes by the WTO has far-reaching implications, both political and economic. Numerous businesses and industries will be affected by the outcomes. It is also important information for scholars. Although the work of the WTO will affect everyone, this level of detail on the work of the organization will not be desired by many.—**J. E. Weaver**

238. **Yearbook of Labor Statistics, 1997. Annuair des Statistiques du Travail. Anuario de Estadisticas del Trabajo.** 56th ed. Washington, D.C., International Labour Office, 1998. 1269p. index. $189.00. ISBN 92-2-007354-4.

This annual compendium from the specialized United Nations agency is a well-known source in its field. It contains comparative statistics by country on employment and labor-related concepts. In this edition, the compilers at the Bureau of Statistics, International Labour Office seek to provide data series from 1987 to 1996 for all the countries of the world. However, not all states supply or keep measures for all statistics included for the period. Hence, some numbers are unavailable. Notes indicate numbers may not be fully comparable, as all national statistical offices do not use the recommended standards. The international standard classifications for industrial activities, occupations, education, and employment status are included in appendixes, along with a key to the arrangement of countries in the tables. Reading the tables is complicated because different countries use different versions of classification standards.

The main body of the work is arranged in 9 chapters containing thematically grouped tables. Data are provided for working population, employment and unemployment, wages, prices, costs, occupational injuries, and strikes and lockouts. Most chapters break down the numbers by a variety of characteristics. For example, unemployment is broken down by age, education, and previous occupation and sector. Price indexes include food, clothing, fuel, and general measures. Countries are grouped geographically and then alphabetically.

The preface, chapter introductions, table headings, and other explanatory materials are rendered in English, French, and Spanish. Access is provided through a detailed table of contents and through an index listing by countries with page references to tables where they appear.

This series should be in all research collections with a remit covering international business and economic statistics. Larger general reference collections should also consider it where funds and client interests warrant.

—**Nigel Tappin**

Arab Countries

239.   **Major Companies of the Arab World 1998.** 21st ed. J. Wassall and Y. McLelland, eds. London, Graham and Whiteside; distr., Detroit, Gale, 1997. 1221p. index. $830.00. ISBN 1-86099-074-6.

This unique, well-produced, and very expensive directory lists an estimated 7,500 companies from 20 Arab countries or areas: Algeria, Bahrain, Egypt, Gaza/West Bank, Iraq, Jordan, Kuwait, Lebanon, Libya, Mauritania, Morocco, Oman, Qatar, Saudi Arabia, Somalia, Sudan, Syria, Tunisia, United Arab Emirates, and Yemen. Non-Arab Muslim countries such as Pakistan are excluded, as are non-Arab Middle Eastern countries like Israel. Data for each entry can include company name; address; local and international telephone, telex, and fax numbers; e-mail address; board of directors; management; principal business activities; trade names; major branch offices; principal banks and auditors; limited financials, such as sales, profits before and after taxes, returned profit, and earnings per share; shareholder capital; principal shareholders; date of establishment; private or public status; and number of employees.

Data are submitted without charge by companies who meet one of seven criteria, which include sales, national importance, prominence of directors or shareholders, new market players, major importers and exporters, or large branches of multinational corporations. There is a blue section in which SIC/activity and alphabetic-by-country indexes are provided. These are in a more easy-to-read format than indexes in most business directories of this size. No print equivalent exists. A CD-ROM version is available, which costs £690, or about $1,100. There are many valuable data here, although one wonders how this would compare to some of the online services available from Dun & Bradstreet or Kompass. Gale is selling this English product for $830, whereas Graham and Whiteside advertise the price as 460 pounds (about $750). This work is highly recommended for the quality of the data for all libraries serving business interests in Arab countries. Libraries with DIALOG or other computerized services and limited interest may find that on-demand searching will be more cost effective than purchasing the directory, no matter what the quality of the contents.—**Patrick J. Brunet**

Asia

240.   **Asia: A Directory and Sourcebook.** 2d ed. Chicago, Euromonitor International; distr., Detroit, Gale, 1997. 394p. index. $430.00. ISBN 0-86338-696-2.

Asia: A Directory and Sourcebook, published by Euromonitor, is a good example of the risk business publishers take when creating expensive reference works. The spectacular decline of emerging Asian markets during 1998 renders the introductory statement, "Asia's position as the fastest-growing region in the world economy will not be challenged in the foreseeable future," somewhat regrettable. The concentration of capital in a few, powerful oligarchies and the hidden costs of garnering government support for business ventures are not mentioned. However, these problems, although perhaps a bit embarrassing to the publisher, do not make the volume useless. On the contrary, the vicissitudes of the Asian economies make this reference resource valuable to those who wish to do business while the dollar is strong and costs have dropped for Asian produced goods. Directory information includes major employers in Asian countries, contact information, product line information, and data through 1995 on employment and productivity. The section listing trade associations and publications, and information resources in Asian countries is a godsend to those who must do even more homework to make the most of Asia's economic conditions. This text is especially useful for specialized libraries emphasizing Asian business development in their collections. Its cost may deter some libraries with less interest in the region.
—**Lynne M. Fox**

241.   **The China Handbook.** Christopher Hudson, ed. Chicago, Fitzroy Dearborn, 1997. 334p. index. (Regional Handbooks of Economic Development: Prospects onto the 21st Century). $55.00. ISBN 1-884964-88-5.

This is the 1st volume in a series of development handbooks intended for college-level students. It could be used as a text or readings in courses in comparative economics, development studies, political economy, or area studies as well as a basic reference book.

The text aims to place Chinese economic development in broad political, sociological, and post-1949 historical contexts. It is a series of essays by academics from North America, Hong Kong, and Europe. Each chapter includes further readings and full bibliographic citations. Chapters end with paragraph-length characterizations of contributor's qualifications and affiliations. Extensive charts and tables with statistical information accompany the many essays. Two advisers from Oberlin College and the University of Illinois assisted the editor in selecting topics.

The 21 chapters are divided among 4 subject sections. History leads off with chapters on Maoist and Deng periods. Regional context offers scholarly essays on relations with Taiwan, Hong Kong, Japan and Korea, and Southeast Asia. There are 10 chapters that deal with various aspects of the economy, including industry, agriculture, finance, and private enterprise. The 5 chapters on social issues include information on population, minorities, and education. The essays average about 13 pages in double-columned format. The academic style is accessible to both scholars and laypeople.

A number of attractive features are in appendixes—a chronology from 1949 through July 1997, a glossary of political and economic terms, a list of holders of the highest offices with thumbnail biographies, and an annotated bibliography of major reference and specialist works. The index is short but adequate.

This quality reference will be useful to academic and large public libraries with the relevant subject mandates. It would make a useful course reading or text for college courses as well.—**Nigel Tappin**

242.   **China Marketing Data and Statistics.** By the China State Statistical Bureau. Chicago, Ill., Euromonitor International; distr., Detroit, Gale, 1997. 643p. maps. $390.00. ISBN 0-86338-780-2.

Chinese economic policies have evolved from the closed door policy of the Cultural Revolution to the reign of Deng Xiaoping's policy of economic reconstruction. A highlight of the economic reconstruction was the return of Hong Kong to China in 1997. This event helped to focus the world's attention on China and its evolving economic policies. This directory is the result of China's government departments cooperating with the publisher, Euromonitor, to compile a thorough survey about China's economic resources and its physical characteristics for the information needs of individuals and businesses wanting to do business in China.

The 1st chapter is an overview of China's geographic and natural resources and China's place in the world today. Following are individual chapters on each of the major cities, provinces, and regions. Each of these chapters describes the location within China; the geography; natural resources; population; administrative areas; the economy; industry, markets, and retail sales; infrastructure, foreign trade, and economic cooperation; education, science, and culture; scenic spots and historical sites; and the standard of living. The latter section of the book is a section of statistical tables covering industry, education, the economy, employment, and family income. The text and the labels for the maps and tables are in English and Chinese.

It is a thorough collection of information about China substantiated by marketing data and statistics. This directory is recommended to large academic and special business libraries who require information about doing business in China. [R: BL, 15 Oct 98, p. 437; Choice, Nov 98, p. 500]—**Kay M. Stebbins**

243.   **The India Handbook.** C. Steven LaRue, Lloyd I. Rudolph, Susanne Hoeber Rudolph, and Philip Oldenburg, eds. Chicago, Fitzroy Dearborn, 1997. 335p. index. (Regional Handbooks of Economic Development: Prospects onto the 21st Century). $55.00. ISBN 1-884964-89-3.

This volume is the 2d in a series of economic development handbooks intended for an audience of college-level students. It is designed to be used as a text or book of readings in courses on comparative economics, development, political economy, or area studies, as well as a basic reference book. It covers the Indian Union, but not the entire subcontinent.

The editor was assisted in selecting topics by a panel of three advisers affiliated with Columbia University. Chapters are contributed by academics with affiliations in North America, Europe, and India. Each ends with a list of further readings and a paragraph-length author note, and many have statistical charts and graphs.

The work is divided into 5 sections that deal with historical context since independence (1947), economic policy, social and cultural aspects of growth, the international context, and outlook for the future. These are similar, but not identical, to those in *The China Handbook* (see entry 241), suggesting suitable tailoring of the standard format to the scholarship on each country or region. The 19 chapters cover a diverse range of issues, including agriculture, planning globalization, regional organizations, population, and multiculturalism. The work has a number of features that make it useful as a ready-reference work, including a detailed chronology from 1947 through April 1997, a glossary of relevant terms, notes on several major political and economic figures, and a 10-page bibliography with paragraph-length annotations. The index is a bit short, but adequate.

This reference book will be useful for academic and large public libraries with the relevant subject mandates. It would make a useful course reading or text for a college course.—**Nigel Tappin**

244. **Japan Trade Directory 1997-98.** Tokyo, Japan, Japanese External Trade Organization; distr., Detroit, Gale, 1997. 1v. (various paging). illus. maps. index. $335.00. ISBN 4-8224-0779-9.

An importer or exporter will find a wide variety of materials available in this comprehensive reference source on more than 22,000 Japanese products and services and 2,800 companies. Part 1 includes an alphabetic list of products and services for import and export. Part 2 lists, in separate alphabets, company information, trade and industrial associations, and trade names. The prefectural guide is found in part 3 with tourist attractions; business and tourist information; and their main products, crafts, and industries. Part 4 contains advertising of products and services, including numerous illustrations. The detailed alphabetic list of companies in part 2, B provides the English and Japanese names of companies, address, telephone number, telex and fax numbers, e-mail address, name of president, type of business, year established, capital available, annual sales, number of employees, bank references, office hours, major overseas offices, trade name, and availability of a catalog.

Compared with the 1993-1994 edition that was last reviewed (see ARBA 94, entry 244) this 1997-1998 edition lists approximately 1,500 fewer products and services and some 200 fewer companies. A CD-ROM version of the directory also is enclosed in the book with accompanying operating instructions. This updated, specialized directory is quite useful and will fill a gap in business collections that need information on Japanese companies engaging in import and export activities.—**O. Gene Norman**

245. **Major Companies of the Far East and Australasia 1998.** J. L. Murphy and D. Walsh, eds. London, Graham and Whiteside; distr., Detroit, Gale, 1997. 3v. index. $1,395.00/set. ISBN 1-86099-072-X.

This 3-volume set is the 14th edition of this annual publication. The 1st volume covers Brunei, Cambodia, Indonesia, Malaysia, the Philippines, Singapore, Laos, and Thailand. China, Hong Kong, Japan, North Korea, South Korea, Mongolia, Myanmar, Taiwan, and Vietnam are featured in the 2d volume. The 3d volume includes Australia, New Zealand, and Papua New Guinea. Data on about 12,000 of the largest companies in the region, selected on the basis of the size of their sales volume, premium income, or total assets as appropriate, are given. As available, the set includes name of the company, address, telephone number, telex number, fax number, e-mail address, and Website; names of the chairman, president, board members, and senior management; principal activities of the company; principal brand names and trademarks; principal agencies and branch offices; parent company; principal subsidiaries and associates, bankers; auditors; principal law firm; financial information for the past two years; public/private status; principal shareholders; date of establishment; and number of employees.

Company entries are arranged alphabetically within each country section. There are 3 indexes. The 1st is an alphabetic index of all companies in each volume irrespective of their main country of operation; the 2d is an alphabetic index to companies within each country; and the 3d starts with the Standard Industrial Classification (SIC) index categories and then lists the companies by their various business activities within their main country of operation within the SIC code.—**J. E. Weaver**

Canada

246. **Canadian Insurance Claims Directory 1997.** 65th ed. Gwen Peroni, ed. Buffalo, N.Y., University of Toronto Press, 1997. 404p. index. $40.00pa. ISBN 0-8020-4901-X. ISSN 0318-0352.

This standard directory provides insurance professionals with addresses, telephone numbers, and fax information on claims adjusters and related services in Canada and the United States. It also provides material on insurance organizations and companies.

The main part of this work is organized geographically by country, followed by province, territory, or state, and then by locality. Under each locality, entries are subdivided by service type. Most of the entries are adjusters and to a lesser extent counsel, with other categories occurring principally in the sections for larger communities. Canadian listings occupy 212 pages, and U.S. entries cover 152 pages. U.S. communities have fewer numbers of listings, even for large centers. There are no significant prefatory materials, leaving no indication of selection criteria or of whether the list is comprehensive for Canada. The one-page section titled "International" contains a boxed advertisement for a service network covering South and Central America and the Caribbean.

There are maps for 10 Canadian provinces and 4 U.S. states (Florida, New York, Pennsylvania, and Washington) with major communities marked. There are few listings for the Canadian territories, probably explaining the absence of maps for them. At the back, Canadian directory information is provided for four national and regional adjusters and claims managers associations, insurance crime prevention bureau offices, fire marshals and commissioners, superintendents of insurance, five insurance associations, and insurance companies (a 15-page list). Access features include a general index (mainly consisting of organization names), an index of advertisers by class of insurance-related services, very brief indexes of insurance-related services (other than the main categories of "adjusters" and "counsel") and associations, and a contents. This established work belongs in large business reference collections and special libraries with the relevant client interests.—**Nigel Tappin**

247.   **Researching Canadian Markets, Industries, & Business Opportunities.** Rockville, Md., Washington Researchers, 1997. 263p. index. $275.00pa. ISBN 1-56365-085-1.

Canada is the world's seventh largest economy and the United States' primary trade partner. Washington Researchers's purpose for this guide is to provide the researcher with current and accurate information about the Canadian markets and industries, and spotlight and identify other Canadian business opportunities.

The 1st chapter begins the research with a guide titled "How to Research the Directory." The editors believed that it is important to aid the researcher in retrieving information quickly and easily. This chapter helps to simplify one's research strategy. The guide is divided into 4 parts. The 1st addresses U.S government sources that would be helpful in tracking Canadian business interests. It is a complete list of federal and state agencies and departments that have information about Canada. Each entry has an explanation of the benefits of requesting information (e.g., newsletters, key people, statistics) from the particular government office agency or department. The 2d part lists Canadian government sources, both federal and provincial. The 3d section presents publications, databases, CD-ROMs, and Internet sources for researching Canadian markets, and the 4th part describes international and private sector organizations, security analysts, and banks of Canada.

This guide to Canadian business and investments will be helpful for the researcher in special libraries concerned with banking and investments. It would also be helpful in academic libraries with international business programs as well as large public libraries with business information sections.—**Kay M. Stebbins**

Europe

248.   **Consumer Eastern Europe 1998/9.** 6th ed. Chicago, Euromonitor International; distr., Farmington Hills, Mich., Gale, 1998. 521p. $950.00. ISBN 0-86338-815-9.

One of the greatest challenges for marketers and business researchers interested in Russia and Eastern Europe is the lack of reliable market information for this region. Although the emerging markets in this part of the world are still not nearly as well documented as those of developed markets in the West and Asia, the situation is improving, and this 5th edition of *Consumer Eastern Europe* makes an important contribution toward that end.

The 10 countries covered in *Consumer Eastern Europe 1998/9* include Bulgaria, the Czech Republic, Estonia, Hungary, Latvia, Lithuania, Poland, Romania, Russia, and Slovakia. The data, covering 1991 to 1996, are nearly all numeric, with very little narrative analysis. The data are derived primarily from national statistical sources and are presented as they appear in the original publication. Some figures are also included from international organizations like the United Nations.

The work is organized in 13 sections. Section 1 provides a 31-page narrative overview of the regional economy and discussion of the relative strengths of each individual country's economy. Section 2 provides easily comparable marketing parameters for the countries covered. The standard headings in this section include "Demographics," "Economic Indicators," "Standard of Living," "Household Characteristics," "Retail Distribution," "Consumer Expenditures," "Service Industries," and "Consumer Markets." The data in this section and the following sections are presented in either a tabular or chart format. Section 3 pulls together consumer market data from the 10 countries for a comparative view of the whole region. The data are presented in comparable volume units or in U.S. dollars. Sections 4 through 13 provide country data arranged alphabetically by country. Each country's section provides background socioeconomic data, marketing parameters, and consumer market data for a wide range of consumer products. Consisting of 410 pages, these last 10 sections make up the bulk of the work.

The publisher offers a word of caution about the reliability of the data. Since 1989, governments have attempted to restructure and improve their data collection systems, but there are still some instances of false or misleading information being published. For example, data on national spending for alcohol seems improbably low given the steep price increases that have been imposed to combat alcoholism. In some cases, shortfalls may also result from structural inconsistency. For example, consumption figures may refer to the official sector only and omit market stalls. Lastly, many consumer transactions take place on the black market, and it is very difficult to account for these unofficial sales.

There are several things one should consider when debating whether or not to purchase this relatively expensive title. First, although the content is strong and the publisher reputable, one has to wonder why Euromonitor chose to market this $850 volume as a paperback. Any library that purchases it should plan on paying for binding, too. Second, the scope of the volume excludes Albania, Slovenia, Croatia, and Serbia. There is some general information on these countries included in section 1, but there are no individual country chapters. One assumes that there were no comparable data series available for these countries, but the inconsistency is not explained in the front matter. Also, a general map of the region would have been a useful addition. A final factor to consider is the timeliness of the data and the need to continually update it. Because current information is so critical in market research, the value of the data in any source like this has a relatively short shelf life. The 1997/8 volume is the 5th edition published since its first appearance in 1992, and a new edition is planned for late 1998. If one is serious about meeting the information needs of one's academic or professional clientele, this book really needs to be considered more as a subscription with ongoing financial commitments than a one-time purchase.

All in all, *Consumer Eastern Europe* provides a valuable service by pulling together scattered national statistics into one well-organized and easily comparable format. Given the price, most librarians considering purchasing this source will need to carefully balance the needs of their users and the other demands on their purchasing budget. If, however, one's library supports an international business program with a strong interest in Eastern Europe and can afford it, this work will be an extremely useful addition to the reference collection.

—**Gordon J. Aamot**

249.   **Consumer Europe 1998/9.** 14th ed. Chicago, Euromonitor International; distr., Farmington Hills, Mich., Gale, 1998. 622p. index. $1,090.00. ISBN 0-86338-803-5.

Market information on European consumer trends is available from industry or government sources but is often difficult or time-consuming to find. *Consumer Europe 1998/9* provides a valuable service by pulling together in 1 volume standardized consumer data for 240 product categories.

The geographical scope of this work is limited to the major countries of Western Europe. The 16 countries covered include France, Germany, Italy, United Kingdom, Belgium, the Netherlands, Denmark, Finland, Norway, Sweden, Portugal, Spain, Austria, Greece, Ireland, and Switzerland. The majority of the volume, more than 500 pages, is devoted to product data. The product data are organized into 16 broad categories. These begin with an overview of basic socioeconomic parameters and then continue with foods, drinks, tobacco, household cleaning products, over-the-counter health care, disposable paper products, cosmetics and toiletries, housewares, home furnishings, clothing and footwear, domestic electrical appliances, consumer electronics, personal goods, leisure goods, and automotives. The tables are organized by product and include data for each of the 16 countries.

The data provided vary with the product, but can include volume of sales and value of sales for each country. The most recent data for each product are from 1997. The tables also provide five to six years of historical annual data. Also included for each product is a table with a series of calculations based on the raw data contained in the main tables. These calculations include market share percentage, growth rates, market size, and per capita data. The work also contains brief listings of key information sources. These include official international, pan-regional, and national organizations and statistical offices. One also finds a short directory of major European trade associations. Finally, a product index allows the user to quickly locate data on specific products.

This volume is compiled from hundreds of different sources but draws largely upon Euromonitor's "Market Direction" database of market reports. These reports cover some but not all of the product categories included in *Consumer Europe*. Euromonitor also contacted major manufacturers, trade associations, organizations, and trade journals to request market data. Each product section begins with a page that discusses, in general terms, the kinds of data sources that were consulted and what national or industry factors might affect the validity of the data. For example, under "Fish" the editors state that the data has been gathered "from national fish marketing organizations and/or from national statistical sources." Although a list of organizations consulted for data is included at the end of the volume, it would have been most helpful if the editors had footnoted their sources in some or all of the product tables. If a researcher wants to consult the original source, he or she must rely on guesswork to identify the producing organization and then try to track down the specific publication.

All in all, however, *Consumer Europe 1998/9* is an extremely useful compilation of consumer market data for Western Europe. The price of the work is not insignificant. This source is recommended for reference collections supporting strong international business programs and with equally strong acquisition budgets.

—**Gordon J. Aamot**

250.   **Directory of Consumer Brands and Their Owners 1998: Eastern Europe.** Chicago, Euromonitor International; distr., Farmington Hills, Mich., Gale, 1998. 310p. index. $990.00. ISBN 0-86338-784-5.

This volume in the Euromonitor series aims to be the most comprehensive guide to Eastern European product brands, owners, marketing areas, and competitors in that region. Companion volumes in this series cover Asia Pacific, Europe, and Latin America, and are available in a CD-ROM version entitled *The World Database of Consumer Brands* (see entry 259), which also covers North America.

An introduction explains the scope, organization, definitions, criteria, and research methods used to compile a vast amount of information. A table of contents breaks down the level of categories so the reader can go directly to the product area of interest. The data are presented in two sections: the first lists brands by product sector, together with the owner's name and the country where it is headquartered; and the second section profiles brand-owning companies, sorted by country and arranged alphabetically by the brand-owner's name within each country. Profiles consist of the owner's name, corporate affiliations, Eastern European headquarters address and contact information (including Internet addresses where available), main activities, shareholding information, number of employees, and a brief financial snapshot. Some entries include notes that give additional information such as plans for expansion, mergers, trade and market share disputes, and exports. Euromonitor has tried to include not only all of the major companies, including multinationals with headquarters in the region, but also the smaller companies that own well-known or established brands.

Brands are classified into three levels of categories. Nineteen broad categories are broken down into smaller sections, some of which are further refined. The "Food" category, for example, has 34 subcategories into which are sorted 136 types of foodstuffs—making the "Food" category the largest section of the volume, followed by "Cosmetics and Toiletries" with 13 subcategories, and "Drinks" with 5 subcategories and 49 third-level categories. A sample search through the "Food" category led to some surprising classifications. "Hot Beverages" is included with "Food" and not with "Drinks," and pasta has become a "Bakery Product." "Delicatessen Foods" becomes its own subcategory, without an explanation of the types of foods that it covers. Unless the reader is already familiar with the brands, the information will not be helpful. Two indexes, one of consumer brands and one of brand-owning companies, allow the reader to look up proprietary names quickly, and also to see where U.S. parent companies are headquartered in Eastern Europe.

This volume in the Euromonitor series will be invaluable to businesspersons who are considering expansion into Eastern European markets and thinking of identifying possible partnerships as well as monitoring competition. This work is recommended for business and corporate libraries as well as large reference collections.

—**Kerie L. Nickel**

251.   **Directory of Consumer Brands and Their Owners 1998: Europe.** 3d ed. Chicago, Ill., Euromonitor International; distr., Detroit, Gale, 1998. 2v. index. $1,190.00/set. ISBN 0-86338-750-0.

This 2-volume directory is part of a larger series that also includes volumes on Eastern Europe, Asia Pacific, and Latin America as well as Western Europe and Turkey. The 1st volume deals with brands by 20 broad product categories, divided into subcategories and within those into finer classifications. It provides brand names, their corporate owners, and the country of the owner. More than 54,000 brands are included, owned by almost 6,000 companies. An index of consumer brands, not shown in the table of contents but occupying 114 triple-column pages, closes that volume.

The 2d volume shows the brand-owning companies by country—18 Western European countries in all. The information on companies provides address, telephone and fax numbers, e-mail address, main activities, parent company, name(s) of key personnel, number of employees, a list of brands owned, and financial information for one to four years. The volume is completed with an index of brand-owning companies, taking up 29 pages with triple columns. The two volumes together make for easy study of individual brands, of competing brands internationally or within national markets, and for the basic assessment of the firms in question. The information provided is voluminous but compact, and it is impeccably presented.—**Bogdan Mieczkowski**

252.   **Eastern Europe: A Directory and Sourcebook.** 2d ed. Chicago, Euromonitor International; distr., Farmington Hills, Mich., Gale, 1998. 252p. index. $590.00. ISBN 0-86338-804-3.

This pricey directory lists major companies in the old Warsaw Pact countries of Bulgaria, the Czech Republic, Estonia, Latvia, Lithuania, Poland, Romania, Russia, Slovakia, and the Ukraine. It is divided into 4 sections: 1-page textual overviews of the socioeconomic environment of each country; an alphabetic list of major companies by country; an information directory listing trade development bodies, trade and business associations, market research companies, major business libraries, major business and trade journals, business directories, online resources, and databases; and a 13-page datafile of statistics. There are two broad indexes: a product and service index and an alphabetic list of companies by company name. In section 2 the type of data that may be provided for each company include name; address; telephone, fax, and telex numbers; e-mail and Website addresses; year established; main activity; major subsidiaries; chief executives; number of employees; details of products, operations, and brands (such as market share); and notes and limited financials. Data are mostly from 1996 and 1997, although textual remarks describe changes as recent as September 1998.

The book is substantially changed from its 1st edition. No comparable title is published in the United States, but Gale distributes *Major Companies of Central & Eastern Europe and the Commonwealth of Independent States, 1999* (see entry 257), which is jointly published by Dun & Bradstreet and Graham & Whiteside. Data elements are essentially the same for both titles, although *Major Companies* has an extensive list of directors and managers and some financials as recent as mid-1998. Both have alphabetic indexes by company name and product and subject or SIC. *Major Companies* includes approximately 9,000 companies from 27 countries (from Albania to Kazakhstan), whereas *Eastern Europe* lists approximately 1,500 companies from the 10 countries noted above. A comparison of the number of entries found only 8 of Euromonitor's 34 Bulgarian companies duplicated in the Dun & Bradstreet title. A second comparison found 62 of Euromonitor's 133 Polish companies duplicated in the Dun & Bradstreet title. About 40 percent of the addresses of the duplicated titles were different. They complement, not compete with each other. Both are expensive, but Eastern European data is hard to come by. Both can be recommended for academic, large public, and corporate libraries serving clients with a strong interest in Eastern European business. Libraries that can afford only one East European business directory will find Euromonitor's *Eastern Europe: A Directory and Sourcebook* a more useful tool and the first choice for purchase for its relative affordability, geographic focus, and the many leads it can provide in the highly volatile Eastern European business environment.—**Patrick J. Brunet**

253.   **European Directory of Retailers and Wholesalers.** 2d ed. Chicago, Euromonitor International; distr., Detroit, Gale, 1997. 618p. index. $990.00. ISBN 0-86338-577-X.

This title is more than just a directory of more than 4,800 Western European retailers and wholesalers of consumer goods, it also ranks the largest retailers of these items on the basis of product turnover. The work begins with a list of the top 100 retailers in Europe, ranked by their turnover computed in U.S. dollars. Each of the following 17 chapters addresses the retailers and wholesalers of an individual Western European nation, and each chapter starts with a ranking of the top 25 to 50 retailers in the country. Subsequent chapter entries are arranged in alphabetic order by company name, and provide additional data such as contact information, retail or wholesale sector (e.g., consumer electronics, food), type of retailer (e.g., mail order company, supermarket operator), number of outlets, number of employees, private labels, and brief financial information. Four indexes follow—a company name index, an index of retailers by sector, an index of wholesalers by sector, and an index of both retailers and wholesalers by type. Each index entry includes the country in which the business is based. The additional information allows an individual to easily determine which companies located in a particular country transact in a given retail or wholesale sector, or to recognize retailers with a particular type of business operation. This expensive work will find use in libraries whose patrons demand ready-reference information on the Western European retail and wholesale industry.—**Mark A. Allan**

254.   **European Marketing Data and Statistics 1998.** 33d ed. Chicago, Euromonitor International; distr., Detroit, Gale, 1998. 471p. index. $375.00. ISBN 0-86338-763-2. ISSN 0071-2930.

European Marketing Data and Statistics 1998 is another in the respected Euromonitor International series of business data resources. When one needs to know which European country spends the most on computers, digestive remedies, or bath and shower products, the information can be found here. Data are arranged in table form and reported for 1990 through 1996. Tables showing long-term trends also include data from 1977, 1980, and

1985. Unfortunately, this resource does not provide current information that is useful for tracking the impact of the Asian economic downturn on the European economy. Contact addresses for the European agencies that collect and provide business data are listed for consultation. Access to specific data is through a table of contents and a brief but helpful index. Libraries with a heavy demand for data related to international studies, international business development, and entrepreneurship will want to invest in this reference.—**Lynne M. Fox**

255.   **Europe's Major Companies Directory 1997.** 2d ed. Chicago, Ill., Euromonitor International; distr., Detroit, Gale, 1997. 777p. index. $550.00. ISBN 0-86338-725-X.

Anyone what has tried to find detailed information about businesses located in foreign countries knows the frustration that comes with not having a comprehensive listing of such companies worldwide or within a particular region. The publication of the 2d edition of *Europe's Major Companies Directory* partly ends this frustration. The 777-page directory covers 5,600 companies in 16 European countries—Austria, Belgium, Denmark, Finland, France, Germany, Greece, Ireland, Italy, the Netherlands, Norway, Portugal, Spain, Sweden, Switzerland, and the United Kingdom. It covers major companies with a 1994 turnover of at least $100 million from all the sectors of the economies covered.

The directory is divided into two main sections. The main directory covers the first 752 pages, and a comprehensive index covers the last 25 pages. The directory section is arranged by alphabetic order for each country, making it easy to locate a company. The listing for each company begins with a rank listing of the top 50 companies in that country. Each company listing includes company name; address; telephone, fax, and telex numbers; company ownership; major subsidiaries; key personnel; number of employees; turnover for the last four years; analysis of turnover; profit; end of financial year; and notes covering company news and recent developments. The details with which the directory is presented make it a unique product in business directories in that it gives one enough information to conduct a quick analysis of the business and financial position of a company one wants to contact. A comprehensive A to Z listing of all major companies in the directory, not ordered by country, is presented in the index.

This much expanded edition of the directory will be much more useful than the 1st edition. *Europe's Major Companies Directory* is highly recommended to any organization interested in doing business in Europe, all business schools, and all libraries.—**Kwabena Gyimah-Brempong**

256.   **Europe's Medium-Sized Companies Directory.** 2d ed. Chicago, Ill., Euromonitor International; distr., Detroit, Gale, 1997. 661p. index. $590.00. ISBN 0-86338-724-1.

The 2d edition of this directory (see ARBA 97, entry 242) profiles 6,500 companies that represent main sectors of the western European economy, including manufacturing, mining, trading, banks and insurance companies, service companies, and utilities. Other criteria involve ranking by turnover, which varies from between $100 million and $10 million for smaller countries and between $299 million and $50 million for larger countries. Entries are alphabetic first by country and then by company and typically provide address, telephone, fax, and telex numbers; year established; business activity; ownership; major subsidiaries; key personnel; main products or brands; number of employees; turnover for three years; profit figures that are somewhat dated; analysis of turnover; financial year-end date; and occasional notes about business developments. There is a general index of company names, but no index for the user who wants to search by industry type.—**Jean Engler**

257.   **Major Companies of Central & Eastern Europe and the Commonwealth of Independent States 1998.** 7th ed. C. Tapster and A. Ford, eds. London, Graham and Whiteside and Bucks, UK, D&B Europe; distr., Detroit, Gale, 1997. 1323p. index. $935.00. ISBN 1-86099-076-2.

The 7th edition of this publication has been completely revised by a joint publishing venture of Graham & Whiteside and Dun & Bradstreet. It includes 8,000 of the most prominent businesses in the central, the eastern, and the former Soviet republics. The kinds of businesses include trade organizations, privatized companies, manufacturers, financial institutions, and key government organizations relating to business.

The most helpful section of the directory is the "Country Summaries." It contains overviews of individual countries and an assessment of their business environment. Dun & Bradstreet has assigned an indicator number of the risk of doing business with these countries. The information provided gives insight into the demographic, political, and economic factors of the countries.

Each country's entry lists the capital city, major cities, land area, population, languages and dialects, heads of state, gross national product, currency and exchange rates, and membership in political and economic groups. The key information in this section is economic indicators for the years 1992 to 1996. The business environment includes the investment policy, banking system, company framework, and import and exchange controls. The "Country Particularities" is a helpful section because it provides information to alert one to the cultural and practical variations that will facilitate successful business in the particular country. A list of 108 companies that were founded from 1397 to 1846 are listed. It is an interesting list because the year 1848 is "Europe's Year of Revolutions," and these companies have survived for more than 150 years of political struggle.

The index is printed on blue pages for easy access. There are three indexes: alphabetic company index, alphabetic country with companies index, and a U.S. SIC number and business activities index. This 7th edition is recommended to the large academic and public library that requires international business information.

—**Kay M. Stebbins**

258.   **Major Companies of Europe 1998.** J. Bradley and others, eds. Detroit, Gale, 1997. 4v. index. $1,645.00/set; $515.00/vol. ISBN 1-86099-067-3.

This is an extensive 4-volume series providing current and comprehensive information concerning approximately 22,000 of Europe's largest public and private companies in more than 20 Western European countries. Volume 1 includes Austria, Belgium, Denmark, Ireland, Finland, and France, for a total of 1,265 pages. Volume 2 covers Germany, Greece, Italy, Liechtenstein, and Luxembourg and contains 1,118 pages. Volume 3 includes the Netherlands, Norway, Portugal, Spain, Sweden, and Switzerland and consists of 1,087 pages. And volume 4 cover the United Kingdom and requires 778 pages, for a total of 4,248 pages. Each entry contains the company name, contact information, senior executives (more than 164,000 total), principal activities, subsidiary companies or parent companies, banking information, law firm utilized, financial information, shareholders, and number of employees. Each volume includes an alphabetic index, index by country, SIC code listing, and business activities index. This is an extensive library resource and would be valuable to anyone doing business in the European area. The fact that the information is current makes it even more valuable. If only a portion is needed, individual volumes are available. The printing, paper, and binding are acceptable for library use.—**Herbert W. Ockerman**

259.   **The World Database of Consumer Brands and Their Owners 1998 on CD-ROM.** 2d ed. Issue 1 (Western Europe). [CD-ROM]. Chicago, Ill., Euromonitor International; distr., Detroit, Gale, 1998. Minimum system requirements: IBM or compatible 486 DX2 66. Double-speed CD-ROM drive. Windows 3.1 or Windows 95. 8MB RAM (16MB RAM for Windows 95). 10MB hard disk space (10MB for Windows 95). $1,990.00. ISBN 0-86338-748-9.

Aimed at the market researcher or businessperson, this database offers online access to information drawn from the print version of *Directory of Consumer Brands and Their Owners 1998: Europe World Retail Directory* (see entry 251). Coverage includes extensive information on more than 6,200 consumer good manufacturers and the 55,600 brands they market across 815 consumer product sectors in 12 Western European countries. The product sectors cover the gamut, from adhesives to home furnishings, from pipe tobacco to writing instruments. A typical company record includes contact information, subsidiaries, key personnel, an employee census, financial information, market share data, major products and brands, and general notes. The publisher emphasizes that every effort was made to include accurate and current information.

It is unfortunate that the user interface of this product somewhat hinders access to the remarkable amount of brand, company, and market information provided. This reviewer found navigating the database confusing without the aid of a user guide, and even with instructions, found searching initially cumbersome. Users are presented with a main screen sectioned into quadrants of region/country, market sector, brand name, and company name information, and may combine those elements in searches. However, one may find the search and viewing options outlined in the user guide complicated and must also become familiar with 15 tiny search tool icons. The nature of the information contained in this database clearly calls for flexibility of access points in searching, but the particular search design presented here might be refined to make it more intuitive. A positive feature to note includes the ability to print mailing labels of company addresses.

Despite the patience required to become adept at using this comprehensive database, this CD-ROM product is a rich source of consumer brand information. It is recommended for corporate or academic business libraries.

—**Judith A. Matthews**

Latin America and the Caribbean

260. **Directory of Consumer Brands and Their Owners 1998: Latin America.** Chicago, Euromonitor International; distr., Farmington Hills, Mich., Gale, 1998. 282p. index. $990.00. ISBN 0-86338-786-1.

The aim of this directory is to provide a complete list of Latin American consumer brands and their owners in South America. The editors of the directory have listed 7,000 leading brand products and more than 1,000 major companies.

The directory is easy to read. The first half of the book is a classified list of the products. Each entry is arranged in broad categories ranging from "automobiles" to "writing instruments." Each product entry names the product by brandname and the company that owns the brand. The second half of the book describes the companies that own the products. The company entry contains the name of the company, address, e-mail address, telephone number, corporate information, subsidiaries, number of employees, and a summary of financial information and notes of interest about the company. An index of consumer brands and an index of brand-owning companies are available at the back of the volume.

Euromonitor has attempted to provide a complete guide to worldwide consumer brands and the companies that own them. This Latin American directory joins the other three publications: *Directory of Consumer Brands and Their Owners: Europe* (see entry 251), *Directory of Consumer Brands and Their Owners: Eastern Europe* (see entry 250), and *Directory of Consumer Brands and Their Owners: Asia Pacific* (Euromonitor, 1998).

This reviewer recommends this volume for large public, academic, and special libraries' business collections. Many of the brands are familiar to the American public and it is interesting to see the Spanish brand names in the same U.S. products.—**Kay M. Stebbins**

261. **Latin America: A Directory and Sourcebook.** 2d ed. Chicago, Euromonitor International; distr., Farmington Hills, Mich., Gale, 1998. 272p. index. $590.00. ISBN 0-86338-805-1.

The publisher's intention in this 2d edition of *Latin America: A Directory and Sourcebook* is not to provide exhaustive coverage of the Latin American market, its leading companies, and principal business information resources. Rather, the goal is to provide, in a single volume, a balanced mix of these three categories that researchers will find useful and valuable. The volume covers the major economies of Latin America. The countries included are Argentina, Brazil, Chile, Colombia, Ecuador, Mexico, Peru, and Venezuela.

The work begins with an 18-page "Overview of the Socio-Economic Environment." This relatively brief market overview provides background information on key issues that affect foreign businesses operating in the Latin American environment. These include macroeconomic information as well as demographic and consumer trends. Nearly half of the volume is devoted to the 2d section, "Major Companies." This listing provides basic directory information for almost 1,000 companies. The arrangement is by country and then by company. Entries are brief, but can include e-mail and Website addresses, brand names, and market share information. Turnover information (sales) is provided for the latest three or four years available. A few companies have 1997 sales data listed, but the most recent information for the majority of entries is 1996 or 1995. An especially nice addition to the 2d edition is the list of companies ranked by sales that appears at the beginning of each country section.

Approximately one-quarter of the work is devoted to the 3d section, "Key Sources of Information." This section lists more than 1,000 sources a researcher might consult for further information on the Latin American markets. Arranged by category, it includes "Official Organizations and Publications," "Trade Development Bodies," "Major Trade and Business Associations," "Leading Research Companies," "Major Business Information Libraries," "Major Trade and Business Journals," "Business Directories," and "Major Business Information Web Sites." Each entry provides a short description of the resource and contact information. The last section consists of 36 tables that provide comparative market information for the 8 countries covered in the volume. The data are derived from national statistical office sources, inter-governmental agencies, and Euromonitor reports. The volume concludes with 2 indexes—a general index and one arranged by industry sector.

This work is well organized and as current as most print sources can be, and it contains a lot of information. The publisher has achieved its goal of packaging a wide range of information useful for researching the Latin American market into one volume. At $590, however, it is not inexpensive, and prospective purchasers will want to consider whether or not this source might duplicate some of the information they already have in their collections. For example, one might find some overlap between the contents found here and that found in other directories, bibliographies, international business services, and government publications that cover Latin

American markets and companies. However, the real value of *Latin America: A Directory and Sourcebook* is not so much in the extent of the information provided in each category as in the convenience of having it all pulled together in one easy-to-use volume. With that in mind, it is recommended for reference collections supporting international or Latin American business programs.—**Gordon J. Aamot**

262.   **Major Companies of Latin America and the Caribbean 1998.** David Shave, ed. London, Graham and Whiteside; distr., Detroit, Gale, 1998. 1330p. index. $730.00. ISBN 1-86099-103-3. ISSN 1369-5428.

The 3d edition of this directory has been expanded to cover 9,000 companies. Data provided include the director and senior executives, description of business activities, brand names and trademarks, branches and subsidiaries, number of employees, financial information for the past two years, principal shareholders, and date of the company's establishment. The 8½-by-12-inch format is composed of 1,330 pages. Companies are organized under countries, and this is followed by an index that alphabetically lists all companies, an alphabetic index to companies within each country, and business activity index, including CIS code listing. The paper and binding are above average, and the print size is adequate for a directory. The book will be useful for anyone doing business in this part of the world and should be an excellent reference for most major libraries.—**Herbert W. Ockerman**

LABOR

Bibliography

263.   **Vocational Careers Sourcebook: Where to Find Help Planning Careers....** 3d ed. Maki, Kathleen E. and Kathleen M. Savage, eds. Detroit, Gale, 1997. 701p. index. $79.00. ISBN 0-8103-6470-0. ISSN 1060-5630.

This publication continues to provide crucial information to individuals seeking employment or a career change (see ARBA 93, entry 412 for a review of the 1st edition). It complements the federal government's *Occupational Outlook Handbook* (1996-97 ed.; see ARBA 98, entry 238) by providing citations to numerous career and test guides, periodicals, associations, and other resources that supply additional data about the 134 vocational occupations listed in the *Occupational Outlook Handbook*.

Bibliographic information for the print titles is supplied and, in most cases, a brief description of the work is included. The publisher's or association's address, telephone, and fax numbers are provided, as well as the organization's e-mail address and Website address when available. Three appendixes round out the *Vocational Careers Sourcebook*, including a listing of resources about careers and job-hunting on the Internet; a directory of state occupational licensing agencies; and a Bureau of Labor Statistics ranking of occupational growth. This work is highly recommended for all libraries, although some academic institutions may chose to forgo the title due to its focus on careers that do not require higher education.—**Mark A. Allan**

Directories

264.   **Adams Electronic Job Search Almanac 1998.** Steven Graber and Andy Richardson, eds. Holbrook, Mass., Adams Publishing, 1998. 306p. index. $9.95pa. ISBN 1-55850-753-1.

This handy one-volume paperback gives all the essentials for starting a job search in the electronic age. The introduction includes information on purchasing the necessary hardware and software (including an advertisement for software produced by Adams). Later chapters cover how to create an electronic résumé and the appropriate use of video and multimedia résumés. The 2d part of the volume explains commercial online services, Usenet newsgroups, the World Wide Web, gopher, TELNET, and bulletin board systems. Each of these sections is accompanied by a listing of job search sites with annotations that give the frequency of updates, location of jobs, key features, and insider tips, which details the uniqueness of each Website. These Websites are listed alphabetically and there is no subject access.

It is impossible for one source to list all electronic Websites on any given subject. Although *Adams Electronic Job Search Almanac* lists several hundred Websites, there are many not included. Because this title was designed primarily for the mass market, no criteria for inclusion are given. Also, as with any title about electronic resources, this is constantly in need of updating.

The last section includes information on computer-assisted job interviews, computerized assessment tests, and a review of job-hunting and career management software. There also are a brief glossary of terms and an index.

Although not the definitive source on electronic job-hunting, *Adams* does provide the essential information to get started. With its poor quality paper and binding, however, it probably will not hold up in a typical reference collection. But with its reasonable price, small libraries may want to purchase it to assist the novice electronic job-hunter.—**Michele Russo**

265.   **Adams Jobs Almanac 1998.** Steven Graber and Jennifer J. Pfalzgraf, eds. Holbrook, Mass., Adams Publishing, 1997. 919p. index. $15.95pa. ISBN 1-55850-752-3.

Thoroughly and intelligently researched, this job seeker's directory contains everything most job hunters need in their job search. Part 1, in 2 chapters, describes the job outlook for 1998 and the long-range job outlook. Part 2, in 4 chapters, details the job search, resumé, cover letter, and job offer. Part 3, in 28 chapters, is the heart of the directory. Here, 7,000 U.S. employers appear in alphabetic order by industry under headings such as "Accounting and Management Consulting," "Banking/Savings and Loans," "Computer Hardware, Software, and Services," and "Retail." Each company's profile lists common positions, educational requirements, and benefits, along with addresses, telephone and fax numbers, jobline numbers, e-mail and Web addresses, and hiring managers. The profiles also describe the firms' operations, note the number of employees, and cite the geographic locations where employees may work. The industry chapters are prefaced by an honest assessment portraying the economics of the industry in the 1990s. Part 4 guides the reader through the intricacies of applying for positions with the federal government. Part 5 rounds out the directory with a geographical index and an alphabetic index.

Libraries may furnish employment sources with company directories such as *Standard and Poor's Register of Corporations, Directors, and Executives* (see ARBA 92, entry 135 for a review), or they may acquire true employment directories such as *Career Guide: Dun's Employment Opportunities Directory* (Dun & Bradstreet, 1995). The book under review is also a true employment directory. The reviewer could not locate entries for United Airlines or the Adams Mark Hotel chain in *Adams Jobs Almanac*, but oversights can be found in most directories. At a modest $15.95, the directory should be found in almost every public and academic library. The paperback binding is the only feature that this reviewer could criticize.—**Dene L. Clark**

266.   **Almanac of American Employers 1998-99.** Jack W. Plunkett and others, eds. Galveston, Tex., Plunkett Research, 1998. 695p. index. $149.99pa. ISBN 0-9638268-9-1.

The heart of *The Almanac of American Employers 1998-99*, edited and published by Plunkett, consists of individual profiles of the 500 U.S. companies selected by the publisher as offering the most attractive job opportunities among U.S. corporations. Each profile contains a broad spectrum of information of interest to a prospective employee, including access data, names of key contacts, types of business conducted, fields of career opportunities, sales/profit data, outlook for growth, prospects for women and minorities, payments to top executives, compensation benefits, number of employees, research and development expenditures, divisions/affiliations, and competitive advantages. However, the almanac is more than simply a collection of profiles. Also included are practical hints and guidelines for job-seekers, trends in the U.S. economy that are likely to affect employment, an extensive list of Websites related to job-seeking, and aggregate employment of specific industries and occupations, as well as outlooks for each.

Employers are indexed alphabetically, by industry and by geographic location. Other indexes rank companies by sales, sales growth, research and development expenditures, and advancement potential for women and minorities. A further index enables job-hunters to search for companies that offer employment in their particular field. For cross-referencing, an index of subsidiaries, brand names, and selected affiliations is included. This is an accessible and useful guide for corporate job-seekers. Purchasers of the hard copy almanac may send for a diskette version at no cost to enable further analysis via spreadsheet and to aid the printing of mailing labels.

—**William C. Struning**

267.   Crispin, Gerry, and Mark Mehler. **Career Xroads: The 1998 Directory to the 500 Best Job, Resume, and Career Management Sites on the World Wide Web.** 3d ed. Kendall Park, N.Y., MMC Group, 1998. 373p. index. $22.95pa. ISBN 0-9652239-4-9. ISSN 1088-4629.

This is an annual annotated directory of more than 500 job, résumé, and career management sites on the World Wide Web. The authors excluded bulletin boards and gopher sites, most international job sites, and company and search firm sites. Its intended audience is both the recruiter and job-seeker who is knowledgeable in using the Internet. *Career Xroads* includes a detailed table of contents; authors' notes; 10 articles on a variety of Internet job-related topics, such as how to use chat rooms, newsgroups, and listservs, and how to prepare your resume for e-mail; an illustrated page on how to read the directory; 293 pages of alphabetic listings and reviews; and cross-reference sites indexed 11 different ways.

This is a "virtual book" because it has both its own Website and e-mail address where the authors keep readers abreast of any changes or additions to the current edition. One only needs to register their e-mail address with them for the quarterly updates. This professionally written directory consequently has a good shelf life. Its paper copy is published each November with approximately 25 percent new material. The authors claim that approximately 5 percent of the published Websites change or stop existing during the current edition. The only small annoyance is the repetitive advertising for the authors' Website and courses.—**Nadine Salmons**

268.   Dikel, Margaret Riley, Frances Roehm, and Steve Oserman. **The Guide to Internet Job Searching.** 1998-99 ed. Lincolnwood, Ill., VGM Career Horizons/National Textbook, 1998. 278p. index. $14.95pa. ISBN 0-8442-8199-9.

This guide is issued under Public Library Association auspices. It is well designed, user-friendly, and compares well with similar guides. The authors, lead by Dikel, formerly of Worcester Polytechnic Library, are experts in their fields.

Chapters conceptually divide into 2 main parts. The first 3 chapters cover the main issues in using the Internet as an aid to job searching. This 33-page section serves as a concise, accessible overview from which to access the Internet free or for low cost, to e-mail résumés, to do employer research, and to network. It is amazing how much is packed into relatively little space. The format of these chapters, with headings, subheadings, and tips in bold typeface, makes it easy to skim for what the reader may want. Six related titles are recommended for further reading. The book is an ideal starting point for reference librarians as well as users.

The remaining 11 chapters provide annotated listings of Internet job search sites by field of employment. In addition to various business categories these include health care, sciences, humanities and social sciences, government, and general resources. Readers outside the United States will note a 22-page international resources chapter. It includes eight pages on Canada subdivided by province, as well as sections for Latin America, Europe, New Zealand and Australia, and elsewhere. Listings include site titles, Internet address, and a sentence- or paragraph-length description. These chapters are subdivided by industry or relevant topical divisions.

Appendixes cover job search services and online networking. Access points include contents, general index, and index of cited resources. The absence of any reference to remote employment and contract opportunities is notably missing from this work. All public, research, and specialty libraries with the relevant mandates should buy this key reference tool.—**Nigel Tappin**

269.   **Employment Opportunities, USA—A Career News Service and Internet Guide.** Denver, Colo., Washington Research Associates, 1998. 1v. (various paging). $184.00 spiralbound. ISBN 0-937801-10-0. ISSN 1076-4798.

Employment Opportunities, USA is a looseleaf service with quarterly updates, which covers 14 industries, including telecommunications, teaching, banking, health care, computers, law, art, music, dance, and social work. There is no prefatory section that might explain the rationale for selecting some industries and not others. The section for each industry begins with an overview describing the general opportunities and major issues. These overviews are well researched, often quoting from leading publications in the field. Information in these sections includes the general work environment; career trends in the industry; potential problems, such as the high rate of burnout in the teaching field; the effects of technology within a field; and average salaries. The 2d section for each industry is a listing and brief description of print and Internet sources to locate potential jobs in the industry. For some industries there is also a listing of job information services with their addresses and telephone numbers. There is no index. Although it is virtually impossible to have a comprehensive listing of available jobs, *Employment Opportunities, USA* is an excellent source for learning about the primary resources for the industries covered.—**Michele Russo**

270.   Oldman, Mark, and Samer Hamadeh. **The Internship Bible.** 1998 ed. New York, Princeton Review/ Random House, 1997. 664p. illus. $25.00pa. ISBN 0-679-78395-4.

Oldman and Hamadeh wrote this book as a follow-up to their first book, *America's Top 100 Internships*, in response to requests from readers for information on more internship opportunities. The stated goal of this work is to educate and inspire readers. In the introduction the authors state their qualifications and their research methodology.

The information in this book was collected from numerous sources—surveys and interviews with internship coordinators and former interns and visitors to colleges and business sites. They gathered information using both traditional and electronic formats. Included in this work are any internship programs, regardless of what name they are given. The two criteria for inclusion are that the position must be temporary (i.e., must have an end date) and something must distinguish the position from entry level or staff positions. The listings cover more than 100,000 internship opportunities in more than 100 general fields of work.

Listings are international in scope and are listed alphabetically by organization name. Entries include the name of the company, locations, vocational discipline(s) at the organization (sales, marketing, finance), duration of the internship, deadlines for submission of applications, a description of the work, any perks offered, general information that might be useful to a potential applicant, required qualifications, and where and how to apply. In addition, the listing includes a selectivity rating (number of applicants and number of interns accepted are specified) and a compensation rating (including a specific dollar amount).

Also interspersed throughout the book are brief quotes, bits of advice, and lengthier profiles from "famous" former inters. For example, George Plimpton comments on his experience as a "copy boy" at *Time Magazine*, and astronaut Richard Hieb discusses his NASA internship. The authors offer advice about how to dress for success, how to write a résumé, and how best to apply for selective programs.

The company listings are followed by several other lists: top 10 internships in the United States, highest compensation, most selective, deadlines, required academic level, perks (e.g., free housing, free meals, vehicles, travel), interest or subject, and location. The tone of this work is informal and sometimes irreverent. The work will be useful to students seeking internships in both general and specific fields. *The Internship Bible* is recommended for all career-related collections.—**Joanna M. Burkhardt**

271.   **Profiles of American Labor Unions.** Donna Craft and Terrance W. Peck, eds. Farmington Hills, Mich., Gale, 1998. 1700p. index. $275.00. ISBN 0-8103-9059-0. ISSN 1099-5358.

Formerly titled the *American Directory of Organized Labor*, this new edition is reorganized and updated to include information on more than 280 parent unions, 33,000 locals, and 1,200 independent unions. Also included are nearly 800 current bargaining agreements and biographical profiles of more than 170 U.S. labor leaders from past and present.

Information about each parent union includes contact information, organizational data, key officials' names, union finances, a general description, a brief history, and present activities. A list of local, state, and regional branches linked to the parent union follows. The "Independent Unions" section includes contact and financial information and, when available, selected bargaining contracts linked to the union. There are 4 indexes: industry, geographic, key officials, and the master index. The foreword is written by United Auto Workers (UAW) president Stephen P. Yokich, who addresses the topic of labor unions at the dawn of the new millennium. This is followed by the preface, which discusses the developments in organized labor in the late 1990s, the decline in union membership, notable mergers and absorptions, a few labor disputes, and the future of labor unions. This easy-to-use source will be valuable to labor researchers, labor-law attorneys, sociologists, historians, and union personnel, and belongs in reference collections of most public and academic libraries. [R: BL, 15 Dec 98, p. 765]—**Michele Russo**

Handbooks and Yearbooks

272.   **Civil Service Career Starter.** New York, LearningExpress, 1997. 1v. (various paging). index. $14.00pa. ISBN 1-57685-120-6.

It is well known that the government is a big employer, so big, in fact, that it is intimidating. This publication endeavors to make information about government jobs more accessible. It does so in this attractively formatted paperback volume. The paper is bright ivory instead of grayish newsprint, and the large print and the space between the lines and in the margins invite the weary job-hunter to spend the evening at home studying.

The opening chapters describe what types of positions are typically available, the federal and state classification systems, and how to find out what jobs are available and what is needed for an application. Information on job duties, responsibilities, salaries, and application procedures for 4 of the "top 40" federal job titles—postal worker, law enforcement officer, administrative assistant, and firefighter—follows. Two practice examinations are interspersed with helpful advice for improvement, including methods of practice and useful books for more help. This guide concentrates on skills for understanding, communicating, and reasoning and has sections on reading comprehension, grammar, vocabulary, spelling, and mathematics. It provides 20 math questions and 20 vocabulary and spelling questions. The list of contributors includes adult educators and test skills specialists and their skills are evident in the arrangement and content of the test questions. Future civil servants will use this book.—**Juleigh Muirhead Clark**

273.   Lauber, Daniel. **Professional's Job Finder 1997-2000.** River Forest, Ill., Planning/Communications, 1997. 518p. illus. index. $36.95; $18.95pa. ISBN 1-884587-07-0; 1-884587-04-6pa.

Beginning with the premise that only 7 percent to 20 percent of job vacancies make it into the local newspaper, Lauber lists and describes other avenues for job hunting. Instead of listing companies topically or geographically as many job-hunting books do, the author takes a different strategy. He concludes that if they are not advertising in the newspaper, organizations are likely locating their candidates in professional journals and job services.

Professional's Job Finder is arranged by topics and these include "Animals," "The Arts," "Entertainment," "Financial Industry," and "Pest Control." The coverage varies. "Education" has only two entries, and the reader is referred to another book in the series. "Theater" has 3 pages with 10 sources for job advertisements, 4 job services (3 on the Internet), and 5 theater directories. Each entry is annotated with contact information, cost, and abstracts that vary in length from one line to two paragraphs and generally describe how this source can be useful to the job hunter. For instance, after reading this section, a job seeker would far rather subscribe to *ArtSearch*, which comes out semimonthly and features 200 to 400 positions, than to *TCI*, which publishes only 10 issues per year with 4 or 5 job advertisements in each issue.

The last part of the book is a list of job sources by state. These typically list state employment agencies and regional publications by this publisher and others. The publisher also supports a Website at http://jobfindersonline.com, where updated information will be available. An index concludes the book. Job-seekers will use the information and ask librarians to supply the periodicals described.—**Juleigh Muirhead Clark**

274.   **Professional & Technical Careers: A Guide from World Book.** Chicago, World Book, 1998. 496p. illus. index. $35.00. ISBN 0-7166-3311-6.

Professional and Technical Careers contains more than 600 careers described in terms appropriate for an international adolescent audience. Colorful, friendly, cartoon-like pictures illustrate the introductory section on career planning. In the chapter entitled "What Is Work?" the differences between paid employment, self-employment, volunteer work, and unemployment are described, as well as practical information to help the student understand the implications for mental and physical health, gender, age, personality, and appearance.

The main body of text is an alphabetic guide to specific careers. It begins with a guide to using the book, which is followed by a general subject index. The student can review the list of careers arranged topically, with headings such as "Outdoor/Active," "Artistic/Creative," or "Service and Sales." The articles are usually one page in length, but sometimes as long as seven. The longer articles have profiles of individuals who do a particular job—for example, an Indian broadcaster, a Malaysian teacher, an Irish international aid worker, a Canadian writer. Usually, the educational requirements for the United States and the United Kingdom are listed. Highlighting the articles are color-coded boxes listing skills and personal qualities needed, school subjects a student should enjoy, and general advice to contact a relevant professional organization. To find out what this organization would be, the student must consult another source.

The final chapter of the book tells the reader where to go for further information in the reader's specific country. The U.S. section relies heavily on *The Occupational Outlook Handbook* (1996-1997 ed.; see ARBA 98, entry 238), but also includes a list of state employment agencies. The most unique feature is how to get information on finding a job in a foreign country, such as the topic "Working in New Zealand for Foreign Nationals." An index concludes the book and will send the fledgling toy maker to the article on "Craftwork."

The articles are informative, and the international flavor is refreshing. Not only are adolescents learning about the world of work, they are also learning about work in the world. Pair this volume with *The Occupational Outlook Handbook* for specifics on work in the United States. [R: SLJ, Nov 98, p. 158; BL, July 98, p. 1908]
—**Juleigh Muirhead Clark**

275.   **State Occupational Outlook Handbook.** David Bianco, ed. Detroit, Gale, 1998. 759p. index. $95.00. ISBN 0-7876-1705-9. ISSN 1096-2859.

This reference work is a useful compilation of state-level market information. It includes information on an average of 600 occupations for each state. Entries provide data on three important aspects of the labor market— outlook, wages, and employment. The outlook section for each occupation includes projected employment through the year 2005, the wages section lists the most recent wage and salary levels, and the employment section provides the number of individuals currently employed in that occupation. A useful index of occupations by states makes the handbook easy to use. This handbook will be a valuable resource for virtually any library. It is highly recommended. [R: Choice, Sept 98, p. 102]—**Paul F. Clark**

276.   **The Top 100: The Fastest Growing Careers for the 21st Century.** rev. ed. Chicago, Ferguson, 1998. 415p. index. $19.95pa. ISBN 0-89434-265-7.

The information found in *The Top 100* is based on the projections of the Labor Department of the United States and its division, the Bureau of Labor Statistics. Among the top growth fields for jobs in the near future are health care, computers, and education. Health care should expand because of the increase in the number of older people. Everyone has seen the growth in the computer field, but this book provides the caveat that layoffs and downsizing are not unknown in an industry in which constant change is the order of the day. Career subfields, often mentioned in the text (in italics for easy recognition) and included in an overall index, bring the number of occupations discussed to more than 500. Not all of the 100 careers projected to be the fastest growing up to the year 2006 will require a college education. High school completion and job training are all that is required for 33 percent of these jobs. A bachelor's degree claims 28 percent, whereas 8 percent must have a master's degree or higher.

The book is arranged by career so that using it is easy and fast. Entries are roughly three pages in length and follow this sequence: definition, nature of the work, requirements, opportunities for experience and exploration, methods of entering, advancement, employment outlook, earnings, conditions of work, and sources of additional information (with particulars for relevant associations, unions, and government agencies). Shaded bars at the bottom of each page show the classification codes for the occupation, school subjects that fit in with the job, minimum education level, salary ranges, and personal interests. In the text, aspects of each career are covered practically and candidly, with little attempt to gloss over the drawbacks or unpleasant parts of a job.

The idea behind this book is almost the same as that of the competing Macmillan title, *100 Best Careers for the 21st Century* (Arco/Macmillan, 1996). Although the purposes, scope, and treatments are much alike, the arrangements differ, with the title under discussion here using an A to Z format and the other title grouping careers by nature of the work. The sound profiles offered by *The Top 100* make it a necessity for any setting that attracts young people. [R: RBB, 1 Jan 98, p. 868; VOYA, April 98, p. 77]—**Randall Rafferty**

MANAGEMENT

277.   **Encyclopedia of Small Business.** Kevin Hillstrom and Laurie Collier Hillstrom, eds. Farmington Hills, Mich., Gale, 1998. 2v. index. $395.00/set. ISBN 0-7876-1864-0.

The *Encyclopedia of Small Business* provides information on the various issues and topics related to entrepreneurship from franchising to tax planning to home-based businesses. This reference work includes 505 essays arranged alphabetically by topic with a master index at the end of volume 2. Entries include various small business-related topics as well as names of key organizations and agencies, among which are the Internal Revenue Service and the International Franchise Association. Cross-references are provided where applicable, and each entry includes a selection of books and articles for further reading. Each entry's essays are thorough in definitions and explanations. For example, the entry for *accounting* defines the term, describes related agencies and rulings, and discusses how to choose an accountant. The entry for the *International Franchise Association* describes the history and purpose of the organization in addition to its address. The editors started their own editorial services business, Northern Lights Writers Group.

The *Encyclopedia of Small Business* is recommended to entrepreneurs interested in starting a business, and to those studying entrepreneurship. It serves as an excellent starting point for researching various topics and issues as well as a point of reference for entrepreneurs to locate information. This reference source is recommended to both university and public library collections. [R: LJ, Dec 98, p. 88; BL, 15 Dec 98, p. 763]—**Lucy Heckman**

278.   **The Portable MBA Desk Reference: An Essential Business Companion.** 2d ed. Nitin Nohria, ed. New York, John Wiley, 1998. 680p. index. (The Portable MBA Series). $35.00. ISBN 0-471-24530-5.

The 2d edition of *The Portable MBA Desk Reference* (see ARBA 95, entry 203) was prepared under the editorial direction of Nohria, a professor at Harvard Business School. It is one of 11 titles in the Wiley Portable MBA Series. Roughly one-half of the reference work consists of an alphabetically ordered encyclopedia of a wide spectrum of current business terms and topics. Each entry is concisely defined in nontechnical language, followed by a discussion of its application in the business world and, in many cases, one or more practical examples. Extensive cross-references to other entries enable the reader to appreciate relationships among concepts. Approximately one-third of the book is devoted to sources of business information, arranged by 48 subject areas. Much more than simply a list, each entry for a printed reference contains title, author(s), frequency of publication, publisher or source, and a brief but pertinent description of the information offered. Electronic entries are also accompanied by descriptions as well as access information. A directory of publishers, vendors, and providers gives contact information, such as addresses, telephone, and fax numbers. A 3d section of the volume contains appendixes that offer a wide variety of interesting and useful facts in list or tabular form. The table of contents, list of entries by topic, list of references, and an index enable readers to quickly locate desired information. The book provides authoritative and readable data in user-friendly format at a relatively modest cost.

—**William C. Struning**

MARKETING AND TRADE

279.   **Americans 55 & Older: A Changing Market.** Sharon Yntema, ed. Ithaca, N.Y., New Strategist, 1997. 345p. index. $69.95. ISBN 1-885070-10-1.

The segment of the American population age 55 and older represents a significant force in the consumer market. By the year 2005 it is projected that there will be 66 million in this age group as the baby boom generation (born 1946 through 1964) becomes part of this population segment. *Americans 55 & Older* is a statistical study of various factors of this population and is divided into 9 chapters: "Attitudes," "Education," "Health," "Income," "Labor Force," "Living Arrangements," "Population," "Spending," and "Wealth." Statistical tables in this source are based on data compiled by federal government agencies, including the Census Bureau, the Bureau of Labor Statistics, the National Center for Health Statistics, and the National Center for Education Statistics. If government statistics were not available, the editor located data from other surveys and studies, notabley, the General Social Survey (GSS) of the University of Chicago's National Opinion Research Center. Each section includes analysis of statistics presented as well as statistical tables. For example, the section "Smoking and Drinking Are Less Common Among Older Americans" contains a narrative that analyzes the statistics and provides a statistical table that includes a citation for the source of the data. Also included are a glossary and an index.

Yntema has compiled a much-needed study of this important segment of the population. It should prove helpful to researchers in business administration, sociology, and psychology. This source is especially recommended to academic library collections. [R: Choice, July/Aug 98, p. 1835]—**Lucy Heckman**

OCCUPATIONAL HEALTH
AND SAFETY

280.   **Encyclopaedia of Occupational Health and Safety.** [CD-ROM]. 4th ed. Jeanne Mager Stellman, ed. Washington, D.C., International Labour Office, 1998. Minimum system requirements: IBM or compatible 486. CD-ROM drive. Windows 3.1 or Windows 95. 8MB RAM. 4MB hard disk space. SVGA monitor (640 x 480 resolution and 256 colors). $495.00.

This product contains information indispensable to those individuals interested in workplace hazards. The software encompasses the contributions of more than 2,000 specialists from more than 65 countries and is alternatively available in a print format consisting of 4 volumes. This vast quantity of information lends itself to a CD-ROM format. The electronic product utilizes the Enigma information retrieval system, Version 3.6, which the reviewer found to be an attractive and intuitive interface. Locating information in the work is made simple by allowing the user to search by either a general or an advanced query; use of an online table of contents for either tables, figures, or all material (including article text); or the use of authors, subjects, and chemical indexes. Unfortunately, the use of the electronic indexes may lead to some material with little or no relevance to the indexed entry. For example, in using the subject index to locate material on *hantavirus*, the subentry prevalence of "antibody to" was selected. A "Windows Find" command was executed to purview the located text (dealing with respiratory cancer) for variations of the terms *hantavirus* and *antibodies*. No matches for these words were located in the indexed article. Although some indexing terms did contain desired material upon searching the text via the find command, others did not. This deficiency adds to patron frustration and lessens the functionality of the product. The enclosed software license also limits the use of the software to a nonnetworked environment. Ultimately, this product is for those libraries willing to overlook the product's indexing shortcomings and that will make it available at a stand-alone workstation. [R: LJ, 1 Nov 98, p. 132]—**Mark A. Allan**

281.   Stuart, Ralph B., III, and Chris Moore. **Safety & Health on the Internet.** 2d ed. Rockville, Md., Government Institutes, 1998. 351p. index. (Government Institutes Internet Series). $49.00pa. ISBN 0-86587-613-4.

This work extensively expands the 1st edition (see ARBA 98, entry 239) by providing brief descriptions of Websites and discussion groups concerning all aspects of occupational health and safety. More than a directory, however, the guide also includes chapters devoted to examining the Internet as a research tool and the different formats of information available through the Internet. Both of these chapters are sufficiently detailed to provide a basic understanding of how information is arranged and disseminated on the Internet and the ways in which the World Wide Web can serve as a resource for safety and health information. The introductory chapter is overly simplistic for even the casual user, but it gives practical information on topics such as Netiquette for new users.

The chapter devoted to searching the Internet is useful and includes a number of sample pages from the top 50 safety Websites. Other chapters also give general overviews about networking and marketing occupational health and safety information on the Internet. The list of safety and health Websites (including FTP and Gopher sites) are arranged under general categories, such as professional organizations, and by subject, such as construction safety. Entries include the site name, its URL, and a brief description of purpose. Descriptions of a site's content are rarely mentioned. The directory of discussion groups is also arranged alphabetically by subject and includes the group name, a brief discussion of its purpose, and subscription and contact e-mail addresses. The information resources listed were active as of October 1998.

An appendix of administrative notes from the SAFETY mailing list and hs-canada listserv (the purpose for inclusion is not specifically articulated) and a basic glossary of Internet terms are included with a subject index. Although this work appears to be intended for new users, its thorough coverage of the subject matter and accompanying attempt to place the Internet as a research instrument into proper context makes it a highly recommended research guide for occupational health and safety professionals and those in related disciplines.

—**Robert V. Labaree**

OFFICE PRACTICES

282.   **The New York Public Library Business Desk Reference.** New York, John Wiley, 1998. 494p. index. $34.95. ISBN 0-471-14442-8.

Increasing complexity of the business world requires those who work in offices to have access to a rapidly growing, constantly changing body of information. Unfortunately, needed information must frequently be sought in numerous, diverse sources, many of which may well be unknown to an employee or a manager. Thus, many of those who seek information turn to libraries for help. The New York Public Library gathered often requested, essential business information in a single volume, *The New York Public Library Business Desk Reference*. The contents cover a wide range of topics, such as office design and equipment, business communications, office systems, managing people, finance, legalities, public relations, marketing, travel, and the basics of research. Wherever possible, topics are treated with respect to the interests of both employers and managers. Each chapter contains suggestions for locating further details via relevant organizations, books, and other publications as well as on-line references. Despite its broad scope, the text provides quick and ready access to many common office procedures. Moreover, it can serve as a point of departure for more detailed investigations. Clear presentation and skilled editing bring a sense of unity to diverse business activities. Cross-referencing, a table of contents, a glossary, and an index facilitate searches for specific information. [R: BL, 1 June 98, p. 1814]

—**William C. Struning**

283.   **The SOHO Desk Reference.** Peter H. Engel, ed. New York, HarperCollins, 1997. 540p. $35.00. ISBN 0-06-270144-4.

The target market for this book is the business entrepreneur. Arranged in a dictionary-style, this 540-page book is actually more encyclopedic in scope and depth of topic coverage. The work ambitiously purports to be "your one-stop guide to running your small business."

This reference includes a table of contents, a section on editorial contributors, and a brief introduction stating scope and purpose. The remainder of the book is dedicated to approximately 500 alphabetically arranged entries that are more substantial than the 7,500 entries in, for example, Jerry M. Rosenberg's *Dictionary of Business and Management* (see ARBA 95, entry 187). A typical entry ends with a useful section, "Next Action Steps," that may include standard print as well as online references and addresses of potentially helpful organizations.

Engel, the author of 10 books and an associate professor in the entrepreneurial program at the University of Southern California, edited this first-of-its-kind work. He was ably assisted by an editorial board, an advisory board, seven editorial contributors, and a variety of research support associates. The expertise of these professionals is weighted toward the practical rather than the strictly theoretical, which helps to slant the book toward what entrepreneurs in the "real world" will really need to know.

The SOHO Desk Reference is seriously flawed in its lack of an index to steer readers to the correct entry. An example of how information tends to get buried in the entries without an index is the topic "organizational charts." The information, which could have been easily located with an index, may not be discovered where it appears in "Administration and Organization (A & O)." Other topics that are not evident from the table of contents and that one would expect to find in such a work include time management, records management, succession plans, business structure, systems or systems analysis, Internet, and desktop publishing and computers. If these topics are covered, an index or a more detailed table of contents would make them accessible.

Although this book, despite its flaws, can be recommended for serious business collections in public, academic, and special libraries as well as for the private collections of practicing and prospective entrepreneurs, it should not be the sole source for entrepreneurial information. A recommended supplement is William A. Cohen's *The Entrepreneur and Small Business Problem Solver: An Encyclopedia Reference and Guide* (2d ed.; see ARBA 91, entry 152), which covers the topics in a more detailed, textbook fashion and includes a back-of-the-book index.—**Linda D. Tietjen**

TAXATION

284. Zelio, Judy. **State Tax Actions 1997.** Denver, Colo., National Conference of State Legislatures, 1998. 57p. $35.00pa. ISBN 1-55516-560-5.

Written for members of state legislatures and related professionals (e.g., public policymakers) this succinct, informative report presents tax highlights and changes with eight statistical appendixes. A cooperative effort of two organizations, the National Association of Legislative Fiscal Officers (NALFO) and the National Conference of State Legislatures (NCSL), this book features state tax law changes, revenue impacts, and tax policy implications. Touted as offering facts with objective analysis and perspective, the methods employed in data collection have not been specified.

Taxation is one of those issues of interest to everyone. The concise state-by-state comparisons and summary meet the intended goal of informing legislators in a timely and efficient manner and will attract students with papers to write. However, tax practitioners have more authoritative information available through existing subscriptions and new electronic databases. If future editions identify the research methodologies used and the location and availability of source documents, this series should prove useful, particularly to public and undergraduate libraries.

—**Sandra E. Belanger**

5 Education

GENERAL WORKS

Bibliography

285. **Educator's Guide to Free Multicultural Materials 1998.** Kathleen Suttles Nehmer, ed. Randolph, Wis., Educators Progress Service, 1998. 165p. index. $32.95pa. ISBN 0-87708-311-8.

This new publication from the Educators Guide to Free Materials series, well-known and highly respected during the past 64 years for useful guides to both print and nonprint media, adds yet another subject to the list. Some educators think of multicultural education as teaching children about diverse cultures, traditions, and beliefs in populations around the world. Others define it as providing teaching materials to help teachers work with students from varying backgrounds, belief systems, and cultures. This guide has been developed to respond to both of these approaches to multicultural education.

The "How to Use" guide is easy to follow, and the organization of entries is appropriate. Section titles include "Countries," "Diversity," "Holidays and Ceremonies," "Languages," "Nationalities in the United States," "Prejudice and Discrimination," and "Teacher Reference." Entries are provided for print and nonprint media and for Websites available for downloading. In addition to information on free materials, items available for loan are also cited. Loaned items may require the borrower to pay for return postage. Entries are annotated, and ordering information is provided. The three color-coded indexes are by title, subject, and source. This should be a top priority for public and school libraries.—**Margaret Denman-West**

286. **Educator's Guide to Free Science Materials 1998-1999.** 39th ed. Randolph, Wis., Educators Progress Service, 1998. 248p. index. $32.95pa. ISBN 0-87708-312-6.

A familiar axiom from the business world advises that there is no such thing as a free lunch. The axiom can be adapted to free science materials for classrooms, which promotes a variety of viewpoints, such as coal can be clean, geology is fun, uranium is useful, and waterways get help from beavers. Even so, it is reasonable to say, "Thank goodness for promotional materials!" They give teachers the opportunity to enrich classes with technological and hands-on materials, and as this catalog illustrates, the range is great: Sign up for a free loan of the video of Dr. Seuss's story "The Lorax" or request a packet of free oleander seeds.

Entries, which include postal address, telephone and fax numbers, and often URL or e-mail addresses of the source, are grouped by category—from aerospace to physics. The indexes to materials are excellent, arranged by title, subject, and source. One nonscience category, "Teacher-Reference," includes primers on contemporary topics (e.g., sexual harassment, outcome-based education, and school discipline).

There are a few glitches—sexual harassment pops up under "Foreign Languages" in the subject index. And although most of the materials are genuinely free, a few are used as bait (e.g., first one is free; then pay for other copies). But the hundreds of free offerings predominate, making this a superb resource.

—**Diane M. Calabrese**

287.   **Educator's Guide to Free Social Studies Materials 1998-1999.** 38th ed. Randolph, Wis., Educators Progress Service, 1998. 312p. index. $33.95pa. ISBN 0-87708-313-4.

This excellent guide, intended for use during the 1998-1999 academic year, provides social studies educators with information about free materials that are available to them. More than 1,500 items—films, filmstrips, slides, audiotapes, videotapes, and printed matter—are provided for 10 categories. These include citizenship, communications and transportation, famous people, U.S. geography, world geography, government, history, maps, social problems, and world affairs. Each item is concisely described, and the name and address (and sometimes the telephone and fax numbers, Website address, and e-mail address) of the source providing it are given. Three indexes—title, subject, and source—make information easy to access, and a "What's New" list identifies more than 800 titles new to this edition. A sample request letter is also included. Any education collection used by social studies teachers or teacher educators will benefit from having this fine book.—**G. Douglas Meyers**

288.   **Guide to Free Computer Materials 1998-1999.** 16th ed. Kathleen Suttles Nehmer, ed. Randolph, Wis., Educators Progress Service, 1998. 335p. index. $38.95pa. ISBN 0-87708-306-1.

Guide to Free Computer Materials 1998-1999 lists 1,271 free materials grouped under the headings of business, communications, education, graphics, magazines, maintenance, peripherals, programming, software, and systems, and stressing education. Education is further divided into 16 topics, such as computer education, dictionaries, early learning, general, guidance, health, home economics, languages, mathematics, music, science, social studies, and teacher reference. Contents of the entries vary. Each entry includes, in general, title, brief description, availability, platform, format, special notes, sources, and Website and e-mail addresses. Many free materials are demos. In the business section alone, there are 72 demos out of some 116 items.

According to the editor, "The World Wide Web allows you to find virtually any information you are look-ing for." AskERIC is free but not listed in this book. Also missing are numerous Websites from government agencies, the commercial community, and educational institutions free for use and downloading. It is not clear what criteria are used in this book for inclusion and exclusion of free materials.

The book also provides tips for acquiring free materials, such as "Your Letters to Request" for free materials and "How to Cooperate with the Sponsors" in requesting their materials. There are 3 indexes: title, subject, and source. The work concludes with "What's New," a listing of the 807 new materials included in this edition. The book is of reference value to schools.—**Tze-chung Li**

Biography

289.   Gordon, Peter, and Richard Aldrich. **Biographical Dictionary of North American and European Edu-cationists.** London, Woburn Press; distr., Portland, Oreg., International Specialized Book Services, 1997. 528p. illus. (The Woburn Education Series). $67.50. ISBN 0-7130-0205-0.

Some 500 biographies are included in this companion to the authors' *Dictionary of British Educationists.* There are two criteria for inclusion: "entries were almost entirely restricted to those whose main careers were from 1800 onwards," and "none of the subjects is still alive" (introduction). Each biography is about one page long and includes in most cases a select bibliography.

The book contains educationists in some 20 countries. However, more than one-half of biographees are Americans, followed by educationists in Germany, Canada, France, Switzerland, Russia, Belgium, and other countries. A quick check showed countries represented by less than two biographies each include Bulgaria, the Czech Republic, Finland, and Greece. Coverage thus appears to be unbalanced.

Most of the biographies can be found in other reference sources, such as the *Encyclopaedia Britannica* (Encyclopaedia Britannica, 1998) and the *Columbia Encyclopedia* (see ARBA 98, entry 42, for a review of the CD-ROM version). Although biographies were well selected, this reviewer would like to see the inclusion of such educationists as Edwin Robert Anderson Seligman in economics, Roscoe Pound in law, Harold Dwight Lasswell in political science, and Albion Woodbury Small in sociology. The book would enhance its reference value if the format of the *Dictionary of American Biography* (see entry 33) were followed by supplying a number of indexes on subject fields, colleges attended, and birth places. The book is well written and features in one place a collection of prominent educationists in North America and Europe. It is a valuable reference source.

—**Tze-chung Li**

Directories

290. **Funding Sources for K-12 Schools and Adult Basic Education 1998.** Phoenix, Ariz., Oryx Press, 1998. 665p. index. $34.50pa. ISBN 1-57356-143-6.

As greater and greater demands are placed upon federal and state budgets, the need for auxiliary funding to help maintain special or discretionary school programs becomes even more critical. Funding for such programs is often available from a wide variety of outside sources; this book lists more than 1,500 sources in the United States and Canada and explains the procedures for obtaining funding. Funding programs listed are available for K-12 education in such areas as curriculum development and teacher training as well as adult educational programs, such as K-12 equivalency/GED, adult and family literacy, and English as a second language. Information is current as of December 1997.

Most of the text is devoted to an alphabetic listing of grant programs. Each entry includes general background, restrictions, requirements, sample awards, amounts of grants, application dates, names, Websites, telephone and fax numbers, and address of contact.

There are comprehensive indexes by subject, sponsoring organizations, program type, and geography. An alphabetic listing of Internet Websites by sponsoring organizations and a guide to proposal planning and writing are included in the front matter and should be helpful to both experienced and first-time grant writers.

This book is an outgrowth and expansion of a long-term database maintained by the publisher and will be useful as a basic resource in every school and administrator's library. [R: BL, July 98, p. 1906]—**Craig A. Munsart**

291. **Peterson's Internships 1998: More than 40,000 Opportunities to Get an Edge in Today's Competitive Job Market.** 18th ed. Princeton, N.J., Peterson's Guides, 1997. 647p. index. $24.95pa. ISBN 1-56079-835-1. ISSN 1082-2577.

This directory lists paid and unpaid internship opportunities for students enrolled in high school through graduate school, with listings of internships within the United States and those in other countries. It is much expanded from the last reviewed 1996 edition (see ARBA 97, entry 256). More than 5,000 more internships are listed, and the broad subject categories and indexes have been expanded in number. Peterson's is known for the introductory essays at the beginning of its books, and this is true for this work as well. Helpful essays at the beginning of the directory provide a general and focused view of internships. Various topics are covered, such as how to apply for an internship, which includes a sample cover letter and résumé; a very good essay on international internships; and a profile of an internship at a specific institution, the Smithsonian. There is also information provided on how to go about finding an internship in a particular area of interest, and there are several profiles of successful interns included.

The main part of the directory is the organization listings. They are arranged alphabetically by several broad subject categories—business and technology; communications; creative, performing, and fine arts; environmental organizations and parks; human services; international relations; internship referral and placement; public affairs; and research organizations. Within each of these categories there are subcategories; for instance, human services contains education, health services, and social services. The entries within each subject breakdown are arranged alphabetically under the organization's name. Entries include general information about the institution, including what they do, when they were established, and the number of employees. This is followed by a list of what internships are available and what qualifications the position requires, and the benefits provided by the organization to the intern. Numbers on how many applications were last received and information on how to contact the institution round out the entries.

What makes the directory very useful are the eight indexes at the end of the book. There is a field of interest index arranged alphabetically by the broad subject categories and subcategories. The other alphabetically arranged indexes include geographic by state, employer by organization name, academic level required from high school through graduate school, international applicants accepted, paid internships, unpaid internships, and a possibility of permanent employment index. What might have helped some of the lengthier indexes, such as the academic level required index, is a running title of the subcategories. This is an extremely useful book for students to have access to as they look for real world experiences. It is highly recommended for academic, public, and school libraries.

—**Jan S. Squire**

292.   Schlachter, Gail Ann and David R. Weber, eds. **Financial Aid for African Americans 1997-1999.** San Carlos, Calif., Reference Service Press, 1997. 510p. index. $35.00. ISBN 0-918276-56-X.

Nearly 1,500 funding opportunities available to African Americans (high school through postdoctoral) for education, research, travel, training, career development, or innovative effort in all areas of the sciences, social sciences, and humanities are described in detail in this informative and well-organized reference work. Entries of funding organizations are grouped into six categories: scholarships, fellowships, loans, grants, awards, and internships. For each entry, information is provided about the funding program's title; the sponsoring organization's name, address, and telephone number; and data about purpose, eligibility, financial matters, duration, special features, limitations, number of awards, and application deadline. Aside from descriptions of these financial aid programs open to African Americans, information about financial aid sources in general is provided in a fine annotated bibliography with approximately 60 publications listed. Six indexes—by program title, sponsoring organization, residency, tenability, subject, and calendar—aid readers in finding information efficiently and effectively. A gold mine of funding information, *Financial Aid for African Americans* belongs in every library serving African Americans, particularly those housed in high schools and institutions of higher education. [R: RUSQ, Summer 98, p. 356; BL, July 98, p. 1903]—**G. Douglas Meyers**

293.   Schlachter, Gail Ann, and R. David Weber. **Financial Aid for Asian Americans 1997-1999.** San Carlos, Calif., Reference Service Press, 1997. 380p. index. $30.00. ISBN 0-918276-57-8.

For people of the United States of Chinese, Japanese, Korean, Vietnamese, Filipino, or other Asian ancestry who are looking for financial support for education, this is the right directory. The premier edition of *Financial Aid for Asian Americans* describes funding opportunities open to Asian Americans to support study, research, creative activities, past accomplishments, future projects, professional development, and work experience. More than 500 sponsors, private and public agencies, and organizations are listed in this directory. The funds are available to Asian Americans in every major subject area and at any level—from high school through postdoctorate and professional.

The directory is divided into 3 sections. The 1st section describes 1,084 funding opportunities. Entries in this section are grouped into scholarships, fellowships, loans, grants, awards, and internships. Each entry has information on program title, sponsoring organization, purpose, eligibility, financial data, duration, special features, limitations, number awarded, and deadline. The 2d section provides an annotated bibliography of general financial aid directories. The sources in this section are open equally to all segments of American society. The 3d section contains 5 indexes that aid the search for appropriate financial aid opportunities. The indexes consist of the program title index, the sponsoring organization index, the residency index, the subject index, and the calendar index.

The authors of this directory have been working together for years and have published a number of financial aid titles. Their works have been given awards by different publishers. [R: BL, July 98, p. 1903]
—**Xiao (Shelley) Yan Zhang**

294.   Schlachter, Gail Ann, and R. David Weber. **Financial Aid for the Disabled and Their Families 1998-2000.** San Carlos, Calif., Reference Service Press, 1998. 450p. index. $40.00. ISBN 0-918276-65-9. ISSN 0898-9222.

For more than 10 years *Financial Aid for the Disabled and Their Families* has provided a valuable resource for locating and applying for financial assistance. Funding opportunity listings are arranged by disabilities as specified in Public Law 94-142, the Education for All Handicapped Children Act. Subdivisions within each section include scholarships, fellowships or grants, loans, grants-in-aid, awards, and internships. Funding is available for everything from specific needs, such as music lessons, to full-ride college scholarships. Indexes provide access across sections by program titles, sponsoring organization, residency requirements, geographic area for funding, and by subject areas. A calendar index helps users with time constraints locate funding sources with deadlines that match the user's needs. Entries are kept up-to-date in Reference Service Press's online database. There are about 49 million persons with disabilities, who make up the United States' largest minority population. These significant numbers indicate that this well-researched, comprehensive, and organized volume is an essential purchase for most public, high school, and academic libraries. Other libraries whose institutions train professionals or who serve persons with disabilities should also acquire this valuable directory.—**Lynne M. Fox**

295.   **The World of Learning 1999.** 49th ed. London, Europa Publications; distr., Farmington Hills, Mich., Gale, 1998. 2080p. index. $495.00. ISBN 1-85743-049-2. ISSN 0084-2117.

In its 49th edition, *The World of Learning* remains a standard reference source (43d ed.; see ARBA 94, entry 308). Divided geographically, each country has a list of learned societies, research institutes, libraries and archives, museums, universities, and other educational institutions. Each entry provides address, telephone number, fax number, and the names of key personnel. Entries for universities include the date founded, number of students and faculty, and lists department heads; some list the faculty for each division within the university and others provide the number of volumes held by the university library. As with any directory, currency is always a problem. This directory appears to be current. The entry for Texas Woman's University lists the current administrators accurately, even though a great deal of change has occurred in the past years. The editors neglected to include e-mail addresses or Website information for the institutions identified in this work.

The most helpful aspect of this work is the information provided on foreign institutions. Many of the institutions outside of the United States include a list of faculty members organized by department—a useful feature for individuals trying to locate international scholars.—**Susan D. Strickland**

Handbooks and Yearbooks

296.   **Education Sourcebook: Basic Information About National Education Expectations and Goals....** Jeanne Gough, ed. Detroit, Omnigraphics, 1997. 1123p. index. (Personal Concerns Series). $72.00. ISBN 0-7808-0179-2.

In today's competitive world, education becomes the gateway toward success. For the sake of their children's future, parents may be wondering when to send their kids to school or how to prepare them for school life. Students may wonder about choices regarding postsecondary education. Adult learners want to know what is out there for them to update their knowledge and learn new technologies. For all of these questions and many more, you can find out the answers in one single resource: *Education Sourcebook*. The book is divided into 4 parts. Part 1, "Educational Expectations," covers standards, national educational goals, and expectations kindergarten teachers have for children. Helping children prepare for school, including preschool activities, using the library, and helping children learn specific subjects such as math and science is the focus of part 2. Part 3, "Issues and Concerns in Education," addresses questions that parents and students may face as children advance from grade to grade. Topics include students at risk, preparing children for college, and learning disabilities. Part 4, "Adult Education and Literacy," contains 4 chapters on adults returning to education—the GED tests, adults as learners, adult literacy, and new technologies and the literacy system. There are also two appendixes at the end of the book that contain references for achieving readiness goals and for educational reforms and students at risk. A keyword index is also available for easily locating information. Both well edited and well bound, this informative sourcebook will be a good reference for parents, students, adult learners, educators, and general readers.

—**Xiao (Shelley) Yan Zhang**

297.   **Educational Rankings Annual 1998: 3,500 Rankings and Lists on Education, Compiled from Educational and General Interest Published Sources.** Lynn C. Hattendorf, ed. Detroit, Gale, 1997. 733p. index. $180.00. ISBN 0-7876-1161-1. ISSN 0077-4472.

This annual is arranged in alphabetic order by subject—about 400 subjects plus many *see* references—for a total of 3,500 rankings and lists on education, compiled from educational and general interest published sources. Each item contains the ranking title, ranking basis or background, number lists, ranking, and source. Some items provide remarks for additional details relating to the list from the source material, whereas others include only remarks. It has a detailed dictionary index, which provides a listing of rankings under each subject and institution—a good feature. The book would have been even more useful had a listing of cited sources been given.

As its title page indicates, the book provides rankings on reputation, faculty publications, tuition rates, library facilities, test scores, alumni achievement, faculty salaries, and admissions selectivity. The book gives numerous data on educational rankings. The introduction begins with 19 questions of interest, such as rankings in chemistry and mathematics departments, journals in various subject fields, most doctoral degrees to foreign students, the average of SAT scores, and highest enrollment in kindergarten.

The book has an international coverage, including Australia, Canada, China, England, Taiwan, and other countries. The term "educational" in the title is broadly used to include books, publishing, journals, dictionaries, encyclopedias, hospitals, libraries, museums, employment, and many others. However, some rankings are missing, such as the tallest library building and the largest dictionary.

Rankings in education can be found in a number of places. The present book gathers numerous data on rankings in education from various sources. It is an invaluable reference work.—**Tze-chung Li**

298.   Fitzpatrick, Kathleen A. **Indicators of Schools of Quality. Volume 1: Schoolwide Indicators of Quality.** Schaumburg, Ill., National Study of School Evaluation, 1997. 231p. $40.00.

This timely book serves as a research-based resource designed to improve student learning and performance. It brings together the collaborative thinking of educators in all curriculum areas as well as those connected to the accreditation process in schools. This publication promotes thoughtful reflection on the research on student learning and focuses attention on the attributes of schools of quality as a guide to designing plans for school improvement.

In this publication, the National Study of School Evaluation serves as a vehicle through which schools can look at research-based principles and their indicators of quality as an impetus for school improvement and student performance at a time where school reform and change are necessary as schools move into the twenty-first century. Although there is a strong emphasis in the book to avoid prescriptions or formulas considered to be the "best way" to apply the research-based indicators to improve student learning, school personnel are urged to rely on their professional judgment and artistry in realizing the full benefits of the principles and practices making a difference in student learning.

The book is composed of two parts. Part 1 targets the desired results for student learning based on consensus of what students should "know and be able to do." Derived from the collaborations of professional associations and their work on voluntary national standards, the book looks at the common goals across all professional education standards. Part 2 shows how schools can be reassured "that their instructional and assessment efforts contribute to a coherent curriculum and how the organizational conditions of their school contribute to high quality teaching and learning."

This book is an excellent guide that provides a catalyst for change for school administrators and teachers as they move toward their goals for school improvement. Use of the *Indicators of Schools of Quality* can serve as the impetus for education communities across the country to commit to the goal of continuous school improvement as the twenty-first century approaches.—**Betty J. Morris**

299.   Gerald, Debra E., and William J. Hussar. **Projections of Education Statistics to 2008.** Washington, D.C., National Center for Education Statistics; distr., Lanham, Md., Bernan Associates, 1998. 192p. $25.00pa. ISBN 0-16-049597-0.

This report, the 27th in a series from the National Center for Education Statistics in the U.S. Department of Education, includes statistics at the national level for elementary and secondary schools as well as institutes of higher education. Among these statistics are numbers for enrollment, graduates, classroom teachers, and expenditures beginning in 1983, along with projected numbers to the year 2008. From this report readers can learn, for example, that elementary and secondary enrollment is expected to increase 6 percent from 1996 to 2008 and that higher education enrollment is projected to increase 12 percent during that same time period. Readers will also note that high school graduates are expected to increase by 20 percent, that the number of bachelor's degrees is expected to increase by 9 percent, and that the number of doctor's degrees awarded to women is expected to increase by 34 percent. As enrollment increases, readers will note that the number of classroom teachers is expected to increase by 14 percent from the 1994-1995 school year to the 2007-2008 year, that their salaries are projected to increase 3 percent during that time period, and that per pupil expenditures are expected in increase about 24 percent. Some information is also available for nonpublic schools.

Coverage of state-level statistics is not as comprehensive, being limited to projections of public elementary and secondary enrollment and high school graduates. The largest increases in enrollment, according to this report, are expected in Arizona, California, Hawaii, and New Mexico. The largest decreases are expected in the District of Columbia, Iowa, Maine, and West Virginia.

Information is easy to access, being available in both narrative and tabular form and aided through a comprehensive table of contents. Appendixes explain methodologies used to develop projections. Although the review copy was secured from Bernan Associates at a list price of $25.00, libraries can also purchase a copy from their local or regional U.S. Government Printing Office, Superintendent of Documents. Full text of this document is also available on the National Center of Education Statistics Website at http://www.nces.ed.gov.—**Jan Bakker**

300.　Jurinski, James John. **Religion in the Schools: A Reference Handbook.** Santa Barbara, Calif., ABC-CLIO, 1998. 209p. index. (Contemporary World Issues). $39.50. ISBN 0-87436-868-5.

Jurinski's *Religion in the Schools: A Reference Handbook*, a volume of ABC-CLIO's Contemporary World Issues series, examines "how the issue of religion in the schools has had a polarizing effect on communities, and how the courts and legislatures have shaped the nature of the debate." The author explores six current controversial issues: school prayer and other in-school religious activities, release time programs, access to schools for religious groups, flag salutes and compulsory attendance, religion and public school curriculum, and support for church-affiliated schools. Content and organization include an introduction of the issues with their pertinent court cases and legislation, a chronology of events, biographical sketches of influential people, excerpts from relevant documents and court cases, and quotes from individuals who have influenced the laws. The volume concludes with a directory of organizations and associations attempting to influence all aspects of religious legislation; listings of print, nonprint and Internet resources; a glossary; and an index.

This comprehensive work is suitable for middle and high school libraries as well as for adult use. The overview of religion in the schools includes enough information to make it an adequate research tool, although the volume is not without faults. In one instance, the author states that the Texas state board selects one approved text for each subject. Later in the book, he states correctly that the board selects several texts, and local school districts choose from these texts. The chapter that includes documents and court rulings is difficult to use; the format does not distinguish between explanatory material and actual quotations or excerpts. Despite these problems, the book provides useful information in a well-organized, interesting manner. [R: BL, 1 Nov 98, p. 532]
—**Janet Hilbun**

301.　Raffel, Jeffrey A. **Historical Dictionary of School Segregation and Desegregation: The American Experience.** Westport, Conn., Greenwood Press, 1998. 345p. $75.00. ISBN 0-313-29502-6.

As director of the School of Urban Affairs and Public Policy at the University of Delaware, Raffel is well equipped to compile a significant guide to this area of "the American experience." His 50- to 500-word entries describe more than 270 key court decisions, people, school desegregation plans, legislation, organizations, concepts (e.g., contact theory), and publications related to school segregation at the elementary through postsecondary levels. Each of these well-written entries concludes with a brief bibliography, and the volume itself features excellent general and geographic secondary bibliographies in addition to a useful introductory essay and chronology from 1787 through late 1996.

Although Raffel of necessity limits the depth of coverage, all the key players are here, and the coverage of significant decisions alone makes this a valuable tool for anyone interested in U.S. law, education, or sociology. Cross-references abound, and researchers can easily trace subjects. One addition that would have increased the utility of this work is referencing of Web-based full-text court cases, but that is a minor point for an otherwise exceptional resource. Currently, only Faustine Jones-Wilson's *Encyclopedia of African-American Education* (see ARBA 97, entry 285) covers school desegregation in such detail and complements Raffel admirably, although there are numerous nonreference books that relate the history of school segregation. This reference is highly recommended for all academic and public libraries. [R: LJ, 1 Nov 98, p. 72; BL, 15 Dec 98, p. 764-765]
—**Anthony J. Adam**

ALTERNATIVE EDUCATION

302.   **College Degrees by Mail and Modem 1998: 100 Accredited Schools....** Berkeley, Calif., Ten Speed Press, 1997. 204p. illus. index. $12.95pa. ISBN 0-89815-934-2.

Revised for the 1998 edition, this annual guide to 100 accredited colleges and universities offering distance education degrees is a more select listing than *Bear's Guide to Earning College Degrees Nontraditionally* (12th ed.; Ten Speed Press, 1995). Of the 20 top cyber-universities listed in *Forbes* (June 16, 1997), only 9 are listed in this 1998 guide. No selection criteria are given for the 100 selected institutions of higher learning, and *Bear's* states that because there are so many degree-granting colleges and universities, "a whole lot of schools had to be left out." Notably missing are Duke University's Fuqua School of Business Global Executive MBA program and Carnegie Mellon University's MBA and MS programs. Also missing is mention of the California Virtual University (http://www.california.edu), a catalog of online and distance education offerings by California's accredited colleges and universities, sorted by subject, type of degree, and type of college or university.

The 100 accredited colleges and universities selected for inclusion in the 1998 guide are listed alphabetically, and a full page of information is devoted to each institution, identifying the degree(s) offered, field(s) of study, tuition (from a key indicating a broad range of cost categories, including free or very low and very expensive), residency requirements, and contact information along with the Website address to the home page of the degree-granting institution. These homepage URLs, however, do not necessarily lead directly to Web-based information about distance learning programs. For example, the homepage to George Washington University (GWU) is given for the master of arts in education technology and the master of science in electrical engineering/computer science distance education programs. After using GWU's Website search feature and a bit of searching savvy, only the educational technology leadership program was located at http://www.gwu.edu/~etl/. An introductory chapter on important issues addresses types of degrees and accreditation. Information in the appendixes identifies some schools as diploma mills and frauds. Other helpful information in the appendixes includes an index to subject area studies offered by the colleges and universities listed in the 1998 guide, a glossary of terms, and advice for people in prison.

An inexpensive and popular guide for a number of years for those seeking information on home study, this book now faces serious competition from other recently published, albeit more costly, resources such as *External Degrees in the Information Age* by Henry A. Spille (Oryx, 1997), *College Online: How to Take College Courses Without Leaving Home* by James P. Duffy (John Wiley, 1997), and *Peterson's Distance Learning* (Peterson's Guides, 1997).—**Elizabeth B. Miller**

303.   **The Complete Learning Disabilities Directory, 1998.** Lakeville, Conn., Grey House Publishing, 1997. 649p. index. $115.00pa. ISBN 0-939300-88-5.

The title page identifies this compendium of resources for those working with the learning disabled as "a one-stop sourcebook," and so it is. The directory is divided into 20 topic sections that provide quick access to a wide range of agencies, associations, programs, publications, products, and services associated with learning disabilities. New to this edition are chapters covering information on adult literacy, attention deficit disorder, and school and learning centers. Every effort is made to keep the directory current; readers are encouraged to update or add listings and to suggest new topics.

The Complete Learning Disabilities Directory is an exceptionally practical and worthwhile resource. It is organized so that parents, students, teachers, and other professionals can use it with ease. The more than 6,100 entries are indexed by entry number, and the subject index is organized for quick subject access. Continuous updating and revising on the part of the publisher guarantees that the most current information is available to the users.
—**Margaret Denman-West**

304.   Phillips, Vicky, and Cindy Yager. **The Best Distance Learning Graduate Schools: Earning Your Degree Without Leaving Home.** New York, Princeton Review/Random House, 1998. 322p. index. $20.00pa. ISBN 0-679-76930-7.

Ten short chapters of this book introduce distance learning and offer advice concerning admissions, method of delivery, accreditation, financial aid, and corporate sponsorship, among other things. About one-half of the chapters also contain testimonials from individuals who have used or are using distance education to obtain their degrees. In this reviewer's opinion, however, the testimonials detract from the overall work.

The major portion of the book is devoted to profiles of what the authors consider the top 195 institutions offering graduate programs through distance learning. The type of information provided is uniform and is presented in one or two pages per institution. Institutional addresses (including e-mail and URL addresses) and telephone numbers are followed by text divided into sections: campus visits, admission, programs, tuition and fees, and notes. The "Notes" section describes the way individual institutions deliver instruction. Some "Notes" sections discuss accreditation and other issues.

End materials include information about the authors, bibliography and references, and several indexes—alphabetic list of school profiles index; area of study index; and major area of study index, including names of institutions and types of degrees offered. The alphabetic list of school profiles index and the area of study index are duplicated and enlarged by the text and the major area of study index.

Despite some distractions, this work deserves a place among the literature of distance education or distance learning. It provides enough solid information about the selected institutions for informed choices to be made.

—**Lois Gilmer**

305.   Williams, Jane. **The Authentic Jane Williams' Home School Market Guide.** 1998 ed. Placerville, Calif., Bluestocking Press, 1998. 456p. index. $150.00 spiralbound. ISBN 0-942617-29-0. ISSN 1080-4730.

At first glance *The Authentic Jane Williams' Home School Market Guide* appears to serve a narrow audience, being an information source for marketers of materials for home schooling. However, the opening section states that 1.2 million school-age children in the United States are taught at home, with a projected 15 percent growth rate. This being the case, an alphabetic listing of 550 individuals, businesses, and organizations that target home school families could be a valuable resource not only for the specialized marketers for which it is written but also for the home schooling families themselves as they research text materials and services.

The information provided for each entry includes full address, telephone, fax, e-mail, and Website listings as well as other product descriptions. Following the main alphabetic listing of home schooling businesses and organizations is a series of useful specialty indexes, including advertising opportunities, book clubs, businesses for sale, catalogs, conferences, consultants, speakers, support groups, and Websites (another useful resource for library patrons). An index to the complete volume serves to tie together the *Home School Market Guide*.

In areas where there is a strong home school component, this admirable collection of home school data would be a useful addition to the public library. Considering the book as it is intended, as a business marketing source, any business library could justify its purchase.—**Marcia Blevins**

COMPUTER RESOURCES

306.   **Educational Software Preview Guide, 1998.** By the Educational Software Preview Guide Consortium. Eugene, Oreg., International Society for Technology in Education, 1998. 131p. $14.95 spiralbound. ISBN 1-56484-129-4.

In order to provide K-12 students with the best possible instructional programs, teachers and educational technologists need a means of identifying the latest, high quality educational software. This guide is intended to meet that need. It provides brief descriptions of more than 1,300 instructional software programs in most major subject areas and grade levels. All of the programs have been favorably and widely reviewed and have been selected for inclusion by the Educational Software Preview Guide Consortium.

The educational software descriptions are arranged alphabetically by title within 37 subject categories. Included among these subjects are the arts, mathematics, science, social studies, health and physical education, and language arts. There are additional categories for such areas as computer science, the Internet and World Wide Web, multimedia production, the school to work transition, and reference library materials, among others. For each title listed, there is information identifying the publisher, hardware compatibility, appropriate grade levels, and price. A brief annotation describes the software, and an instructional mode category includes such identifying labels as drill and practice, problem solving, simulation, tutorial, authoring system, creative activity, demonstration/presentation, guided practice, Limited English Proficiency, and more. Once a potentially interesting program has been identified, the user can contact the publisher for a catalog or a preview copy of the software (if available). Complete addresses, telephone numbers, and World Wide Web addresses for publishers can be found in an appendix. Additional appendixes include an alphabetic list of titles, a directory of national educational software distributors, and an educational technology resource evaluation form.

Educational technologists and school library media specialists may already be on mailing lists for many of the publishers identified here, or they may routinely acquire some of their catalogs at professional conferences. However, for identifying somewhat more obscure publishers and software programs, or for informing educators who are not technology specialists, this guide can be an inexpensive and useful current awareness service. It is recommended for public libraries, school libraries, and academic libraries supporting teacher education programs.
—**Stephen H. Aby**

307.   Miller, Elizabeth B. **The Internet Resource Directory for K-12 Teachers and Librarians.** 98/99 ed. Englewood, Colo., Libraries Unlimited, 1998. 403p. index. $25.00pa. ISBN 1-56308-718-9.

Once again Elizabeth Miller has produced a wonderful resource directory for both teachers and librarians. Using highly refined selection criteria, Miller has increased the number of entries by 400, bringing the grand total up to 1,442. Of these new entries several include the Internet address for organizations and agencies that develop national and state education standards; for example, see entry 371 for the Standards for the English Language Arts.

One of the distinguishing features of this book is the online updates. Every month the author verifies the Internet address for each entry; when one changes, it is posted on a Web page provided by the publisher. Therefore, this title does not suffer from the problem of becoming quickly outdated as is the problem for a good number of print Internet directories.

Teachers, librarians, and even students will find detailed annotations for remarkable Internet resources in 11 different subject categories, each significantly subdivided. Everything from the Maya Angelou home page to the Anne Frank home page are included in this edition. [R: BR, Nov/Dec 98, p. 68]—**Susan D. Strickland**

308.   Sharp, Vicki F., Martin G. Levine, and Richard M. Sharp. **The Best Web Sites for Teachers.** 2d ed. Eugene, Oreg., International Society for Technology in Education, 1998. 352p. index. $22.95 spiralbound. ISBN 1-56484-136-7.

More than 700 Websites have been selected for this guide for "busy teachers who may not have time to carry out lengthy searches." The authors used standard evaluation criteria (e.g., appropriateness, authority, reliability, organization) in the selection process. The introduction includes hints on using a Web browser, such as how to delete directory segments from a URL that may have changed. Entries are organized into chapters that cover the K-12 subject areas of art, bilingual education, drama, English as a second language (ESL), foreign language, health/physical education, journalism, language arts, math, multicultural, music, science, social studies, special education, and vocational/technical education. A "Multisubjects" chapter lists sites that link to lesson plans and teacher information on a wide variety of curriculum areas (e.g., the AskERIC Virtual Library and Teachers Helping Teachers). Many of the chapters are divided into sections on lesson plans, other resources, and exhibits and museums. Although most of the sites are written specifically for teachers or aimed at the general public, some are fun for students. Examples of the latter include Pi-search, where one can enter any number and find its location in pi, and "The Yuckiest Site on the Internet." Commercial, educational, government, and personal Websites are all included.

Each entry provides the title of the Website, its URL, a description, and a screenshot of the homepage, which is so small that it does not add much useful information. Descriptions of site content are very brief (generally one or two sentences), and some do not convey either the utility or breadth of material available for classroom use. For instance, the entry for the Library of Congress does not note that there is a section specifically for educators called "The Learning Page," where there are plans for using reproductions of primary source materials available at the Library of Congress Website. With this book in hand, however, most educators will take the time to explore listed sites on their own. The index lists sites alphabetically by title and by title under chapter headings but not by type. For instance, it might be helpful to have categories such as "dictionaries," "online activities," or "museums." Appendixes that list newsgroups, mailing lists, and search tools could be expanded to include basics like Yahoo! and AltaVista (although these and other search engines can be found by using the "All-in-One Search Page," one of three search tools listed). Nonetheless, the number and quality of sites covered and the book's low price will accommodate most school and public libraries as well as those academic libraries with curriculum resource centers for pre-service teachers.—**Deborah V. Rollins**

EARLY CHILDHOOD EDUCATION

309.   Peltzman, Barbara Ruth. **Pioneers of Early Childhood Education: A Bio-Bibliographical Guide.** Westport, Conn., Greenwood Press, 1998. 140p. index. $65.00. ISBN 0-313-30404-1.

This is a bio-bibliography that seems much more bibliographical than biographic. The author has included 34 men and women ranging from early philosophers such as Johann Amos Comenius and John Locke through pioneer practitioners, including Maria Montessori and Jean Piaget. The list includes both European and U.S. educators with special mention of African-American early childhood educators.

Each entry within the alphabetic arrangement begins with three paragraphs of biography. The biographical portion covers the educator's professional contributions with little acknowledgment of a personal life. Lists of primary and secondary sources immediately follow this portion. Each bibliographical entry is annotated, and the annotations are often critical in nature.

After the bibliography of primary and secondary sources, there follows a chronological list of the educators, a bibliography of general sources, and an index. The chronological list helps give the user a better historical sequence. The selected bibliography lists what appear to be classic works in the field. They range in publication date from the early part of the twentieth century to the present. The index, which directs the reader to entry numbers, is basic without much conceptual detail.

For researchers in the history and philosophy of early childhood education, this is an essential source. It appears to be unique in the field.—**Phillip P. Powell**

ELEMENTARY AND SECONDARY EDUCATION

Bibliography

310.   Speck, Bruce W. **Grading Student Writing: An Annotated Bibliography.** Westport, Conn., Greenwood Press, 1998. 323p. index. (Bibliographies and Indexes in Education, no.18). $75.00. ISBN 0-313-29932-3.

This extensive resource includes annotated entries for more than 1,300 books and articles on the grading of student writing. The author acknowledges the challenges faced by writing teachers who find the assignment of grades a necessary act. The sheer scope of the variety of entries included underscores the range of topics that relate to the grading of writing. Indeed, perhaps limiting the publication years of the entries to 1980 to 1996 instead of 1970 to 1996 would provide a more tightly focused resource.

The broad categories include "Methods of Classroom Assessment of Writing," "Classroom Assessment Issues," and "Standardized/Large-Scale Testing of Writing." Each category includes a wide variety of subtopics, allowing the user to zero in on topics of interest. An author index and subject index provide further flexibility.

This will be a useful resource for professors of writing, researchers, and teachers who are searching for ways to improve or evaluate their grading methods. Thanks to its exhaustive number of entries, it should prove particularly useful for doctoral students in search of a related research project. [R: Choice, Sept 98, p. 90]
—**Suzanne I. Barchers**

Directories

311.   **The Comparative Guide to American Elementary & Secondary Schools.** Milpitas, Calif., Toucan Valley, 1998. 774p. index. (Toucan Comparative Guide Series). $85.00pa. ISBN 1-884925-63-4.

Toucan Valley, a prolific publisher of regional demographic guides, offers a compilation of short profiles of every U.S. public school district serving 2,500 or more students, noting that this encompasses about 80 percent of all U.S. school districts. Information is arranged alphabetically, first by state, then within each state by county, and finally within county by city. The city index will prove invaluable to users unfamiliar with the county in which a city is located. Demographics and contact information are provided (although total population of the communities themselves are not given), as well as a national socioeconomic status indicator score based on level of participation in the National Free School Lunch Program. Student/teacher ratio, ethnic makeup of the student population, district expenditure per student, and numbers of librarians and guidance counselors are also included. Although informative, the raw numbers given do not serve as good indicators of district quality, as the standards one might use to compare districts are not given.

The sources of data used are noted in the introduction, primarily NCES and census data. This straightforward guide is an easy way to find general information about the districts without going directly to the sources of data; however, due to the lack of statistics that could be used for real indicators of school success, it cannot be recommended to parents relocating and wondering about ACT scores or the percentage of students going on to higher education. It also cannot be used by teacher candidates wondering about average salaries, nor can it be used with any authority by businesspeople wanting to boost their communities. As usual, those looking for basic information on individual schools will likely opt for Patterson's, and those looking for more explicitly evaluative, although more subjective, information may still wish to use the now somewhat outdated *Public Schools USA* (2d ed.; see ARBA 93, entry 350), although it does cover fewer districts. This work will be valuable for academic and large public library collections. [R: BL, 1 Oct 98, p. 356-358]—**Jennie Ver Steeg**

312.   **Educational Opportunity Guide, 1998: A Directory of Programs for the Gifted.** 1998 ed. Durham, N.C., Duke University Talent Identification Program, 1998. 328p. $15.00pa. ISBN 0-9639756-4-1.

The Talent Identification Program at Duke University is best known for its talent searches in 16 southern and midwestern states. The program is designed to identify academically talented seventh-grade students using standardized test measures such as the College Board's Scholastic Assessment Test (SAT). Once identified, talented youth have many options from which to choose. *Educational Opportunity Guide* is a directory of more than 400 programs for talented youth conducted on college campuses, in schools, and at other sites across the United States and abroad. Among the types of programs highlighted are summer programs, internships in science and math, fine arts experiences, wilderness camps, and international travel opportunities. Each entry provides the name, location, duration, expenses, audience age, and description of the specified program. Criteria for admittance and scholarship information are furnished along with contact people, addresses, e-mail addresses, and Website information, where applicable. This guide is a fine preview of existing resources for parents, teachers, and gifted students.—**Jerry D. Flack**

313.   Leana, Frank C. **The Best Private High Schools and How to Get In: The A-Z Guide to the Private School Admission Process.** 2d ed. New York, Princeton Review/Random House, 1998. 222p. $20.00pa. ISBN 0-375-75208-0. ISSN 1093-9989.

"A private, four-year boarding school education may well cost over $80,000. This is a high price. Even higher is the emotional cost of making the wrong choice." This quote from the introduction of this useful resource underscores the critical decision-making involved when choosing a private high school. Nearly one-fourth of the book discusses topics such as why one chooses a private school, the application process, and obtaining financial assistance.

The balance of the book provides profiles of 145 private high schools. Each profile includes location, programs, demographics, enrollment, endowment admission requirements, attendance costs, financial aid information, curriculum, faculty, and a narrative. Several indexes at the end of the source make this easy to use and sample. Parents in search of a school or counselors seeking alternatives for students with specific needs will find this no-frills book an invaluable resource.—**Suzanne I. Barchers**

314.   **Peterson's Private Secondary Schools 1998-99.** 19th ed. Princeton, N.J., Peterson's Guides, 1998. 1431p. illus. index. $29.95pa. ISBN 1-56079-972-2. ISSN 1066-5366.

With many parents choosing to send their children to private rather than public schools, this reference work provides guidelines to aid parents through every step of the school selection and admissions procedures. Comprehensive, up-to-date listings for 1,500 private secondary institutions are provided, including day, boarding, religious, military, junior boarding, and special needs schools. Participating institutions provide all information published in the guide. Beginning with a "Family Guide" section, the handbook gives parents step-by-step instructions for using the guide, as well as hints on planning, finding the "perfect match," testing, and financing. A quick-reference chart lists data for those schools deemed suitable for inclusion in the guide. These schools are listed alphabetically by state, and information regarding the number of students accepted, grade levels, student and faculty ratios, and school academic offerings is given.

Profiles of each institution provide general information, such as type of school, religious affiliation, grade levels, founding date, number of buildings, accreditation, and enrollment. Other information includes student and faculty profiles, subjects offered, graduation requirements, special academic programs, college placement, student life (e.g., dress code, discipline standards, religious service attendance, community service requirements), summer programs, tuition and financial aid, admissions, athletics, computers, and contact persons. Announcements about the schools written by school administrators present information designed to complement data appearing in the profiles. Some schools also choose to submit full descriptions. These descriptions are cross-referenced in the profile section. A separate section profiles schools for students with special educational needs, those institutions that consider special needs education to be their primary focus.

Specialized directories listing types of schools, special academic curricula, financial data information, English as a second language (ESL) programs, and special needs programs follow. Many of the schools listed in the directories are not profiled in the guide. An alphabetic index is also provided. This comprehensive volume is impressive in both its scope and its organization.—**Janet Hilbun**

HIGHER EDUCATION

Dictionaries and Encyclopedias

315. **International Dictionary of University Histories.** Carol Summerfield and Mary Elizabeth Devine, eds. Chicago, Fitzroy Dearborn, 1998. 780p. illus. index. $125.00. ISBN 1-884964-10-9.

This heavy, weighty tome of 780 pages is filled with descriptions and brief histories of more than 200 institutions from around the world. The editors have chosen the entries for educational reasons. Thus, one has Stanford University, the University of Chicago, and Yale University and other Ivy League schools, but also those institutions that were begun for a specific reason, such as Brandeis, Mount Holyoke, Gallaudet, and Atlanta University. The essays give the chronology of each institution, plus some history and descriptive information. Readers will find much to excite their interest as they discover that the Egyptian university Al-Azhar in Cairo was founded in 972 C.E.

Of interest as well is an introductory essay on the origin of the university movement, stressing the early Italian institutions at Bologna, Vercelli, and other early universities in Paris, Oxford, Cologne, and Heidelberg. The essay traces the development of universities in Ireland, highlighting Cardinal John Newman, and in the United States where Thomas Jefferson's model in the University of Virginia is stressed, followed by the main universities and then the second wave of the land grant colleges. The essay delineates the balance sought for all universities—current higher education administrators would do well to read this essay today. With its focus on international universities, this reference work reminds us once again of our Western tradition and roots and does much to counter the insularity of many U.S. academic institutions of higher learning. Impressive black-and-white photographs accompany each entry. [R: Choice, Oct 98, p. 298]—**Anne F. Roberts**

Directories

316. **Accredited Institutions of Postsecondary Education, 1997-98: Program Candidates.** Alison Anaya, ed. Phoenix, Ariz., Oryx Press, 1998. 751p. index. $54.95pa. ISBN 1-57356-085-5. ISSN 0270-1715.

This comprehensive reference work covers degree-granting institutions, including branch campuses and non-degree-granting institutions, such as career centers, training centers, job corps centers, and others. Information provided about the institutions include name, address, telephone and fax numbers, brief description, dates of first and most recent accreditation, and name of accrediting body. Additional information, such as type of academic calendar used, level of degrees offered, name and title of the chief executive officer, and latest enrollment figures, makes it a valuable source for students and education professionals.

This reviewer learned of some postsecondary institutions in her own state through this work. It is hard to imagine any serious omissions because the book includes information about institutions with enrollments of less than 100. The subject key to professional accrediting bodies provides details on the subject areas covered by the different professional accrediting bodies.

There are several special sections in the book. One section reports major changes in institutions (e.g., name changes, closings). The section on candidates for accreditation includes degree-granting institutions both within and outside the United States. Other sections are on public and private systems of higher education.

Appendixes describe the accrediting process; present a joint statement on transfer and award of academic credits; and give names, addresses, and telephone numbers of special accrediting groups, regional accrediting bodies and professional accrediting bodies. The index, arranged by institution name, completes this highly recommended work.—**Lois Gilmer**

317. **Barron's Best Buys in College Education.** 5th ed. By Lucia Solórzano. Hauppauge, N.Y., Barron's Educational Series, 1998. 716p. index. $14.95pa. ISBN 0-7641-0430-6.

Like the many other Barron's publications, this is a source filled with information for the prospective college freshman. *Barron's Best Buys in College Education* is almost solid text, but it is not overwhelming in its presentation.

There is a relatively brief introduction prior to the main section where the reader will find the descriptions and discussions of the nearly 300 schools included. A brief discussion of the selection process is presented, with two common qualities pervading—good value and high, but not necessarily unattainable, academic standards These are colleges that are not always well-known nationally, but often have solid regional reputations. Most information is gathered either from other Barron's publications or by the use of questionnaires. Besides statistical information, student opinions are weighed heavily. Finally, the introduction concludes with an explanation of each segment within a given entry.

The arrangement is alphabetic by state then by institution. The colleges included are public and private large and small. Following the heading of the college name and its address is a box containing standard statistical information, including enrollment, average SAT scores, student/faculty ratio, and tuition. What follows is a much lengthier, more anecdotal, description of the college. Having some knowledge of at least a couple of the colleges listed, the reviewer found that these portions were both entertaining and accurate on most accounts. Although most narratives were positive, they did not fail to include some of the downsides of these colleges when appropriate This offering from Barron's Educational is recommended for high school and public library collections.
—**Phillip P. Powell**

318. **Barron's Guide to Graduate Business Schools.** 10th ed. By Eugene Miller. Hauppauge, N.Y., Barron's Educational Series, 1997. 725p. index. $14.95pa. ISBN 0-8120-9559-6. ISSN 1043-190X.

The latest edition of this standard guide has a slightly different arrangement than previous editions (see ARBA 94, entry 168 for a review of the 8th edition). After an introductory section titled "Getting into Graduate Business School," Barron's provides an extensive chart that allows for quick comparisons among the 650 U.S programs covered in this book. The chart lists data for requirements, concentrations available, enrollment, characteristics of the student body, faculty, admissions, calendars, and tuition. The remainder of the book is filled with full-page (or slightly shorter) profiles for each school's program. The information in this section expands on the data in the comparative chart and gives additional details on financial aid, computer facilities, library and research facilities, placement services, and international students. Appended to the profiles are similar descriptions for 29 Canadian schools. This book will continue to be extremely useful for academic libraries; most libraries will want both Barron's and its chief competitor, *Peterson's Guide to MBA Programs* (see ARBA 96, entry 355).
—**Thomas A. Karel**

319. **European Directory of South-East Asian Studies.** Kees Van Dijk and Jolanda Leemburg-Den Hollander, comps. and eds. Leiden, The Netherlands, KITLV Press; Detroit, Cellar Book Shop Press, 1998. 618p. index. $30.00pa. ISBN 90-6718-135-8.

This directory is a revised, updated, and enlarged version of the 1987 *Directory of West European Indonesianists* compiled by the Koninklijk Instituut voor Tall-, Land-, and Volkenkunde (KITLV). Coverage has been expanded to include all of Southeast Asia and scholars from Eastern Europe, Europeans temporarily residing in Southeast Asia, and non-European scholars who are attached to a university in Europe. Southeast

Asia is defined as the region encompassing Brunei, Burma, Cambodia, Indonesia, Laos, Malaysia, Papua New Guinea, the Philippines, Singapore, Thailand, and Vietnam.

More than 1,250 scholars are listed alphabetically by surname. Entries give a large amount of information in a relatively small space. Titles, office and home addresses with telephone number and fax numbers, and present position or function are all provided. Also included are the person's university with year of graduation, date the doctorate was awarded, title of the doctoral thesis, field of main interest and special research interests, countries and regional specializations, other Southeast Asian countries of interest, recent experience in consulting, and a list of the person's publications. An index of main countries of interest, subdivided by disciplines, and an index by country of residence together with main country of interest provide rapid access for those who wish to locate specialists in specific places or by field of interest.

This guide will be of primary interest to subject specialists seeking to locate colleagues in Europe or in Southeast Asia. It will also be of interest to teachers and students of Southeast Asian studies and to nonspecialists who seek sources of information on the area. Collection development specialists and reference librarians will find the lists of publications useful. [R: Choice, Dec 98, p. 657-658]—**Shirley L. Hopkinson**

320.   Gilbert, Nedda. **The Best 75 Business Schools.** 1999 ed. New York, Princeton Review/Random House, 1998. 296p. index. $20.00pa. ISBN 0-375-75200-5. ISSN 1067-2141.

Although this, the 6th annual guide, does indeed describe the top 75 business school programs, equal space is devoted to guidance issues. This initial section generalizes what can be expected in terms of academic focus, experience, and outcomes from attending such a school. Perspectives from recruiters, students, and alumni are quoted. Becoming a successful applicant, testing preparation, college financing, and admissions strategies are described in a brisk, easy-to-read style appealing to aspiring students. An extensive chapter gives examples of successful applications and essays from specific universities, providing a sense of what is sought through that critical process.

Schools are rated on the basis of collective opinions of 18,000 students in terms of social life, academic emphasis and results, facilities, and recruiting. Each school is profiled on two pages with a straightforward overview (on finances, employment, admissions, and student life), descriptions of the student body, and academics. Quotes from students survey the "hits and misses" of these areas.

This guide presents objective and subjective information and distinguishes them from one another. Its comprehensive nature is a great advantage for a potential student who would be well advised to look extensively at this potential $50,000 investment carefully before making the final decision. This directory is invaluable for guidance counselors and career advisers and will be useful for libraries and personal reference.—**Barbara Conroy**

321.   Gourman, Jack. **The Gourman Report of Undergraduate Programs.** 10th ed. New York, Random House—Princeton Review, 1997. 398p. $21.95pa. ISBN 0-679-77780-6.

The claims of this publication—providing "the most authoritative and accurate assessments of higher education" or "the only qualitative guide to institutions of higher education"—have long been deplored by recognized authorities. Such claims would be laughable except that the appearance of reliability, and now publication under the auspices of *The Princeton Review* and Random House, make them dangerous. Gourman's methods for obtaining the information are never clearly stated, and the results—the ostensibly precise rankings over a variety of subject areas—are at first glance questionable and on further examination contrived and outlandish. How, for example, can one believe a ranking of chemistry programs in which the top five institutions vary by five one-hundredths of a point? Or that, although this is presumably a guide to undergraduate programs, almost no primarily undergraduate institutions are included? A library making this publication available to patrons, and certainly without serious warning, is doing a disservice to them.—**Evan Ira Farber**

322.   **Graduate Group's New Internships for 1997-1998.** West Hartford, Conn., Graduate Group, 1997. 172p. $27.50 spiralbound.

323.   **7th Annual Graduate Group's Internships in Federal Government.** 7th ed. West Hartford, Conn., Graduate Group, 1997. 242p. $27.50 spiralbound.

324.   **6th Annual Graduate Group's Internships in State Government.** 6th ed. West Hartford, Conn., Graduate Group, 1997. 156p. $27.50 spiralbound.

There is nothing fancy about these books—no slick pages, no spiffy desktop publishing. Yet, these volumes do provide valuable information not easily found elsewhere. *Graduate Group's New Internships* (NI) acts as a supplement to the above listed subject-specific internship guides. The contents of NI will be added to the subject guides later. More than 100 new internships are spelled out in enough detail to inform the enterprising student how to land a summer internship and quite possibly how to build a career.

Company name, contacts, address, telephone, eligibility, compensation (if any), and the application procedures are listed in all three guides. Either a photostat or brief distillation of same provides the needed data. Armed with this tool, any student can apply for an internship working as few as one day a week to as many as five. These books will never win any appearance awards, but they will reward readers time and again.

—**Mark Y. Herring**

325.   **Guide to the Most Competitive Colleges.** Hauppauge, N.Y., Barron's Educational Series, 1998. 764p. illus. index. $14.95pa. ISBN 0-7641-0029-7.

This new work from Barron's Educational is even more selective than most of its genre, covering only about 50 of the most competitive schools in the country. Many of the colleges chosen for inclusion are undoubtedly the "best," but some of the exclusions are surprising, particularly big state schools such as Berkeley, and the Universities of Michigan, Illinois, and North Carolina, which many would rate higher than some of the private schools included here. Most of these schools are also in the northeastern United States.

Each school's profile is based on essays written by graduates. The profiles vary a great deal in length, although all of them are glowing in their praise of these institutions. They all include some basic information on admission requirements, academic life, social life, financial aid, and graduates. Closing essays provide tips on applying, essay writing, financing college, and study strategies. There are also summaries of each school, and comparative tables on admission rates, SAT scores, and costs.

This directory will be useful to high-achieving high school students, their parents, and guidance counselors looking for information about these particular schools. Its title is misleading, however, as there are many other competitive and academically rigorous schools, especially outside the northeast, that have been excluded.

—**Christine E. King**

326.   **Index of Majors and Graduate Degrees 1998.** 20th ed. New York, College Entrance Examination Board, 1997. 695p. index. $18.95pa. ISBN 0-87447-563-5.

This 20th annual edition of the *Index of Majors and Graduate Degrees* offers the prospective first-year or transfer student valuable information that may help to determine which college or university to attend. This year's edition lists more than 600 undergraduate and graduate programs at nearly 3,000 U.S. institutions. The stated purpose of the guide is to help students, counselors, and educators seeking to identify higher education institutions in suitable locations offering particular fields of study from the associate degree through postdoctoral and professional levels. The guide lists majors according to the 1990 Classification of Instructional Programs as well as data collected during the College Board's Annual Survey of Colleges. This edition is based on information provided by participating colleges, universities, and graduate institutions in the winter and spring of 1997. Updated information is also available from the College Board's Website at www.collegeboard.org.

Index of Majors and Graduate Degrees is both well planned and presented. The user can locate information about how major fields of study are defined, brief descriptions of each of these fields, and which colleges and universities offer them. Italicized abbreviations indicate whether the program offers degrees at the associate, bachelor's, or graduate levels.

One of the few areas for improvement in the guide can be found in the special academic programs section, where nonstandard educational opportunities such as distance learning, internships, and semester-at-sea programs are listed. It would seem that novel and persuasive interdisciplinary groupings cutting across college and departmental boundaries could also be included in the liberal arts and career combination section. For instance, some universities are now offering majors in which a student can combine a major in a foreign language with advanced business training. There is no provision for such programs in the current guide.

In conclusion, *Index of Majors and Graduate Degrees* serves as an essential reference guide for college-and graduate school-bound students, as well as their counselors, who are interested in knowing where various majors and degree programs can be found. It does not list the quality of the programs. Many such guides rating the quality of individual programs now exist, and the reader should be aware of this aspect of this index before consulting it.—**John B. Romeiser**

327.   **The International Student Handbook of U.S. Colleges 1998.** 11th ed. New York, College Entrance Examination Board, 1997. 325p. $18.95pa. ISBN 0-87447-564-3.

Planning for and applying to college can be a lengthy and involved process that is made all the more difficult for international students. Distance, language differences, lack of knowledge of U.S. educational institutions, and many other obstacles can make applying to a U.S. college or university a daunting task. This handbook attempts to explain this process to foreign students in great detail. It raises questions, provides key information, and supplies worksheets that will help students identify their needs and find the appropriate college.

The handbook is divided into 2 major sections. The 1st section, "Applying to College in the United States," has subsections on U.S. higher education, choosing colleges, college costs, comparing colleges, college requirements, test information, college decisions, planning by calendar, and a glossary of terms. These small chapters provide background information on their topics and, in some cases, student worksheets for self-evaluation purposes. The 2d section, "Information on United States Colleges and Universities," is primarily devoted to detailed information on both undergraduate and graduate study in the United States. For each level of study, entries are arranged alphabetically by state, then by institution. Categories of data provided include public or private control, degrees offered, student enrollment (including foreign students), tests required (including TOEFL minimum), application deadline and fees, student services (including the presence of an ESL program), academic costs, maximum credits and charges, and financial aid. There is an accompanying directory of college admissions addresses (including many Websites) as well as a list of sources of information in other countries.

This is an essential volume for foreign students, although it does require the user to know some English. Also, to determine if a college has a particular degree program, the student would have to acquire a book like *The College Handbook* (see entry 350) or, if possible, access a college Website. Overall, this handbook has vital information for foreign students and should greatly aid their planning for study in the United States.—**Stephen H. Aby**

328.   **National Faculty Directory 1999.** 29th ed. Farmington Hills, Mich., Gale, 1998. 3v. $755.00/set. ISBN 0-7876-1461-0. ISSN 0077-4472.

Last reviewed in ARBA 94 (see entry 339), this work remains the primary source for locating teaching faculty at junior colleges, colleges, and universities in the United States, with some in Canada. A roster of colleges and universities classifies each institution by geographic location. Each institutional entry provides address and telephone numbers; Website addresses are not present. Most of this 3-volume work comprises an alphabetic list of teaching faculty members at the listed institutions. For each faculty member an institutional address is given, unfortunately direct telephone numbers and e-mail address are absent. After a cursory check, the information appears to be current. This work will not be useful in locating nonteaching, research, or emeritus faculty members; only individuals active in the classroom can be found in this work.—**Susan D. Strickland**

329.   **Peterson's Colleges with Programs for Students with Learning Disabilities or Attention Deficit Disorders.** 5th ed. Princeton, N.J., Peterson's Guides, 1997. 663p. index. $32.95pa. ISBN 1-56079-853-X.

This directory includes information from more than 1,000 accredited 2-year and 4-year colleges that provide comprehensive and special services for those students having learning disabilities (LD) and attention deficit disorders (ADD). This edition reflects a name change from the previous edition, which was entitled *Peterson's Colleges with Programs for Students with Learning Disabilities* (see ARBA 96, entry 341) and the inclusion of more than 200 more programs. There are sections in the directory that include sample letters of inquiry, a "Personal Summary Chart" to assist the student in listing features of a school's services, and an "Information Resources" list of organizations that are related to LD and ADD. A "Quick-Reference Chart" is provided to aid in identifying whether a school provides comprehensive or special services, is a two- or four-year college, or charges a special fee. The arrangement is alphabetic by state, then college, with the page number provided to the college's entry.

Each comprehensive and special services college entry has two main sections: "Learning Disabilities Program or Services Information" and "General College Information." The comprehensive sections provide an additional checklist summary chart. Under the LD section there is a summary of the history of the LD program or services offered, the number of students served, the number of staff members, the amount of special fees charged, application and admission requirements, and what specific services are provided. Specific services include information on what is provided at the school; diagnostic testing, tutoring, remediation, advising, special courses, counseling, and auxiliary aids (taped textbooks, tape recorders, calculators, notetakers). The general college information summary provides an enrollment profile, graduation requirements, number of computers on campus, expenses and financial aid information, and the name of a contact person. The directory includes an alphabetic index listing of all colleges and universities, with those having comprehensive programs listed in bold typeface.

A compact disk is included that provides several useful academic options. Useful features include the ability to customize college selection based on several categories (majors, region and state, LD services, costs, entrance difficulty, and type of institution). Also, there is the ability to create a comparison chart for up to four institutions at a time, the ability to print checklists of needed items for each college, and the ability to customize letters of inquiry.

This is a useful directory for those persons considering colleges that will provide services or programs that are sensitive to the needs of students with LD or ADD. It is an important source for all libraries.—**Jan S. Squire**

330. **Peterson's Guide to Four-Year Colleges 1999 (with CD-ROM).** 29th ed. Princeton, N.J., Peterson's Guides, 1998. 3258p. illus. index. $24.95pa. Minimum system requirements (Windows version): IBM or compatible 486. Double-speed CD-ROM drive. 8MB RAM. Color monitor. Minimum system requirements (Macintosh version): 68030 processor with System 7.1. Double-speed CD-ROM drive. 8MB RAM. Color monitor. ISBN 1-56079-987-0. ISSN 0894-9336.

Peterson's Guide to Four-Year Colleges 1999 continues as a pace-setting access tool for information on predominantly undergraduate colleges. The prefatory material is extremely helpful. This section contains such concisely written sections as "Considering College Quality," "How to Make a List of Appropriate Colleges," "Surviving Standardized Tests," "Preparing to Get Admitted," "Financial Aid," and "Using the Internet in Your College Search." There are 4 quick-reference college search indexes that will facilitate the process: a state-by-state summary table index, an entrance difficulty index, a cost ranges index, and a majors index. There is a separate section on the military and higher education.

The main section comprises college profiles of approximately 2,000 institutions. Each profile covers such information as indicators of quality, profile of undergraduates, academic programs, majors, library resources, computing, college life, housing, athletics, career planning, expenses, financial aid, and application procedures. This section is followed by a collection of more extensive profiles of 1,000 universities that elected to furnish such information. The print guide is accompanied by a CD-ROM, which enables users to link to the Peterson's homepage, where they may explore such topics as colleges and universities, graduate programs, study abroad, summer camp, private schools, 5,000 company profiles, and executive education programs (Bricker's database). Meticulously edited and imaginatively formatted, this volume is an exemplary reference resource. This CD-ROM is recommended with great enthusiasm for all types of libraries.—**Arthur P. Young**

331. **Peterson's Honors Programs: The Only Guide to Honors Programs at More Than 350 Colleges and Universities Across the Country.** By Joan Digby. Princeton, N.J., Peterson's Guides, 1997. 436p. index. $21.95pa. ISBN 1-56079-851-3.

Students seeking a directory of honors programs at colleges and universities in the United States will find this to be the only one currently available. Checking the catalogs shows that the last one compiled by the same organization, the National Collegiate Honors Council, was in 1967.

Formatted like other Peterson's guides, this book has a major difference. Because of the comparative brevity of the book, the print is substantially larger than in most other Peterson guides. This guide contains a large amount of introductory material with the most important portion being the introduction. The reader is given explanations for the compilation of the book followed by sections that define honors programs. The final section includes an explanation of symbols used within each entry. The symbols are simple, but the explanation is helpful. Following the introduction are segments whose purpose and benefits this reviewer finds questionable. Included are profiles of honors program alumni and essays discussing honors from several points of view. Although providing additional detail and a new spin for the reader, the essays have a repetitious quality. Many of the same ideas have been put forth previously in the introduction. Finally, the "Honors Snapshots" serve little purpose.

Each entry, arranged alphabetically by institution name, contains all or some of the following information: program descriptions, participation requirements, admission information, scholarship availability, living expenses, tuition, the campus, and who to contact. Much of it is standard information designed for a specific audience. Examination of several college Websites shows that text was often lifted directly from what a college itself had written about its honors program. This directory will be particularly suited for secondary school libraries and public libraries. [R: BL, 1 Feb 98, p. 940]—**Phillip P. Powell**

332.   **Profiles of American Colleges.** 22d ed. Hauppauge, N.Y., Barron's Educational Series, 1997. 1615p. index. $23.95pa. ISBN 0-7641-7000-7. ISSN 1065-5026.

If number of editions is an indicator of a book's success, then this would appear to be the reference to have in every high school counselor's office and in each college-bound student's home. In all honesty, it has the appeal of a city telephone book with small typeface, no pictures, many pages, and an overwhelming amount of information. It is difficult to imagine that many seniors would actually make use of the assessment tools provided (a college planning values assessment, a self-knowledge questionnaire, and a checklist of questions for evaluating colleges and universities), but dedicated parents may, and counselors surely would use them.

One of the most practical components of this resource, a step-by-step guide to college acceptance, is provided on the inside covers. The guide is well-organized and easy to understand; needed information is quickly located. The 3 parts are printed on blue paper for convenience and include a basic introduction to college, colleges facts and finances in chart form for comparison, and an index of college majors. Part 4 groups the colleges from most competitive, highly competitive, very competitive, competitive, and noncompetitive in terms of selectivity of admissions. This section further explains how to read and understand the college profiles and provides an example as an aid. Finally, more than 1,650, 4-year, accredited colleges and universities are profiled. Separate sections include religious colleges, ROTC, study in Canada and Mexico, study abroad, a section for international students, and a key to abbreviations. A list of publications to assist in the preparation for application and an index are included.

Two computer disks (Macintosh and PC) are included. The review disk did not work. However, the disks, which are undoubtedly interactive, may make the book more attractive to seniors graduating in the age of computers.
—**Karen D. Harvey**

333.   **Research Centers Directory 1999.** 24th ed. Donna Wood, ed. Detroit, Taft Group/Gale, 1998. 2v. index. $530.00/set. ISBN 0-7876-2195-1. ISSN 0278-2731.

Research Centers Directory is a comprehensive guide to the programs, staffing, publications, and services of some 14,100 centers, laboratories, institutes, experiment stations, farms, research support facilities, and the like. The organizations featured in this guide are distinctive in that they can be formally identified by a specific name and they are established for carrying out continuing research programs. The programs cover such areas as agriculture, environment, medicine, engineering, business and economics, religion, government, education, humanities, and labor and industrial relations.

The 1st volume of this 2-volume set provides information for the research centers featured. Information for each organization include: research center name and acronym, address, telephone and fax number, e-mail address, head of organization, description, research budget, staff, financial support, publications, scholarships, library holdings, and services, among other pertinent information. The 2d volume contains 4 indexes: a master index, personal name index, geographic index, and subject index. This set is a valuable and reliable resource tool that will be used often in libraries of all kinds.—**Shannon M. Graff**

334.   **Rugg's Recommendations on the Colleges.** 15th ed. Philadelphia, Running Press, 1998. 164p. $19.95pa. ISBN 1-883062-22-5.

Rugg's guide can be viewed as a college guide by opinion poll. It identifies, from among a universe of 780 colleges judged to be the country's best, those that excel in specific majors. The majority of those polled for this edition have been students at the schools, hardly the most objective judges of comparative academic rigor. Student polling accounts for 70 percent of the sample; high school counselors and academics for another 20 percent; and the remainder from "unsolicited 'tips' from many individuals," many who are parents of college students. The core of the 780 colleges is formed by those 260 that are home to a chapter of Phi Beta Kappa, a fairly objective and easily defensible criterion. The others were selected by Rugg's staff, who "felt [they] are as good (or better) as several of the Phi Beta Kappa colleges or have excellent specialized programs." The qualifications of Rugg's staff are not explained. The lack of a fuller explanation of the book's inputs—how data were provided and the qualifications and experience of the staff—cast a cloud of doubt over the entire book's credibility.

Most of the book is a listing of recommended schools for various majors. The majors are listed in two major alphabetic sequences. The first lists "traditional" majors, such as architecture, classics, English, geology, music, and psychology, and the second lists "miscellaneous majors," including, criminal justice, equestrian studies, jazz, naval architecture, and sports medicine. Under each traditional major, schools are listed in three categories, each based on its selectivity in admissions. The "miscellaneous majors" section lists them alphabetically under each major. An appendix lists all of the schools, their average SAT-1 and ACT scores, and the majors for which they are recommended.

Because the credentials and qualifications of those whose collective opinions have produced the recommendations are unknown, the recommendations themselves are at best questionable and at worst suspicious. That said, the most useful part of the book is probably the appendix in which Rugg, an experienced high school guidance counselor, lays out a recommended timeline for students to follow in the college selection application process. Even this is imperfect, using the fall of a high school student's senior year as its belated starting point for gathering information about colleges.

Librarians who believe demand for books on a topic outweighs other selection criteria will want to add this to their collections with even less useful guides, such as the notoriously undocumented recommendations in Gourman reports (see entry 321). Those who apply more qualitative criteria will steer clear.—**James Rettig**

335.   Spaihts, Jonathan. **The Best Graduate Programs: Humanities and Social Sciences.** 2d ed. New York, Princeton Review/Random House, 1998. 578p. index. $25.00pa. ISBN 0-375-75203-X. ISSN 1099-7504.

In this numbers-conscious age of information, an advice industry lavishes tips, strategies, and "straight talk" on students, and this Princeton Review guide is a typical product. Introductory chapters coach the decision to attend; discuss choosing, applying to, paying for, and "surviving" graduate school; and offer an annotated directory of professional associations. There are 56 profiles of "top" schools that follow, which rank schools based on uncited National Research Council and Council of Graduate Schools findings. In addition to such data, this work bases its best profiles on questionnaires returned by students and on interviews with administrators and faculty. Each profile includes a short narrative about the school's history and character, admission practices, academic and campus life, and the local area's quality of life, followed by inconsistently supplied statistics for individual academic departments. An appendix tabulates survey data for 18 fields, and indexes schools listed, schools by state, programs, and departments.

The advice given is fine, but the writing's tone and the self-laudatory foreword sound sophomoric. Lingua Franca's *Real Guide to Grad School* (Lingua Franca, 1997) offers a more sophisticated journalistic introduction to the graduate experience, and *Peterson's Guide to Graduate and Professional Programs* (25th ed.; see ARBA 92, entry 309) offers wider coverage of schools.—**Robert H. Kieft**

336.   Spaihts, Jonathan. **The Best Graduate Programs: Physical & Biological Sciences.** 2d ed. New York, Princeton Review/Random House, 1998. 523p. index. $25.00pa. ISBN 0-375-75204-8. ISSN 1099-7512.

This book lists 63 best graduate schools for the physical and biological sciences, according to research by the National Research Council and the Council of Graduate Schools. There is a two-page summary for each of the universities that includes information regarding admissions, academics, campus life, and the area. Following the university summary, individual departments for the top 40 programs are highlighted, and important comparative statistics are provided. The appendixes include the National Research Council rankings and indexes for locating programs by state, program, or department. In addition, there are chapters on topics such as choosing a school, applying and getting in, and paying for school. This resource is recommended to libraries wanting to expand college guides beyond tools such as the Peterson's guides or the *Gourman Report* (see entry 321).

—**Carl Pracht**

337.   **World List of Universities and Other Institutions of Higher Education.** 21st ed. New York, Stockton Press; distr., New York, Macmillan General Reference/Simon & Schuster Macmillan, 1997. 1149p. index. $170.00. ISBN 0-333-61624-3. ISSN 0084-1889.

The 21st and largest edition of the biennial directory compiled by the International Association of Universities (IAU), this volume presents information from 179 countries and territories. An introductory note emphasizes that the classification of organizations as "universities" or as being involved in higher education follows accepted usage in each country. The 11,700 entries contain the formal name of each body (in both English and the national language, where appropriate); communication addresses including e-mail and Websites; names of the chief academic and administrative officers and the directors of international relations; the major divisions of study offered; and founding dates. Data on the purpose, current officers, and publications of the IAU are also included. Indexing is alphabetical by country. Libraries of all types that can afford only one directory of global higher education should acquire this work despite its rather expensive price.—**Robert B. Marks Ridinger**

Financial Aid

338.   **The B* Student's (or Lower) Complete Scholarship Book.** By Student Services, L. L. C. Naperville, Ill., Sourcebooks, 1997. 290p. index. $18.95pa. ISBN 1-57071-144-5.

The B* Student's (or Lower) Complete Scholarship Book consists of more than 2,200 separate entries, each giving cursory information on scholarships or other financial aid for higher education that have an emphasis other than academic achievement. The entries are brief, providing contact information, deadline, and the fields of study for which the scholarship is intended. Icons indicate the field of study and special criteria (e.g., athletics, disability, ethnic). The introduction provides advice on identifying potential sources of financial aid for college, and general advice on financing one's higher education. The entries are cross-referenced in indexes by major and by special criteria. The strength of this volume is its collection of a variety of information that would not be readily available otherwise. Errors in the entries—for instance, Indiana University is misidentified as the University of Indiana—may indicate larger problems of reliability.—**Marcus P. Elmore**

339.   **The Big Book of Minority Opportunities: The Directory of Special Programs for Minority Group Members.** 7th ed. Elizabeth Oakes, ed. Chicago, Ferguson, 1997. 636p. index. $39.95pa. ISBN 0-89434-204-5. ISSN 0093-9501.

With 3,516 entries and other valuable data in 636 pages, this book truly is big. It focuses on awards for African Americans, Asian Americans, Hispanic Americans, and Native Americans. The book also lists some programs for women and people with disabilities. Types of awards are scholarships, fellowships, internships, career guidance and job training programs, summer study and employment opportunities, and vita or skill banks. The reader must carefully study the book's organization before using it. Rather than listing awards or organizations in alphabetic order, it uses various indexes and alphabetizes programs within 3 areas: "Programs for Majors in Specific Fields" (from agriculture to social sciences), "Programs for Majors in Any Field," and "Programs for Specific Minority Groups" (except Asian Americans).

The entries provide organizations' names, addresses, telephone and fax numbers, and e-mail and Web page addresses, along with descriptive program notes and application and filing deadlines. A short unannotated bibliography, a page on Internet resources, and a glossary of terms follow. There are 3 important indexes in the back of the books: state index, general index, and index of organizations (e.g., colleges, funds, commissions, associations, and tribal councils). *The Big Book of Minority Opportunities* will be enormously helpful to high school and college minority students, counselors, job-seekers, employers, and program directors as they investigate the wide range of minority opportunities.—**Marshall E. Nunn**

340.   **College Costs & Financial Aid Handbook 1998.** 18th ed. By the College Scholarship Service New York, College Entrance Examination Board, 1997. 334p. $17.95pa. ISBN 0-87447-562-7.

The 1998 edition of *College Costs & Financial Aid Handbook* is designed for parents and students who seek information on college costs and financial aid. It is useful not only for high school seniors and juniors, but also for parents. Because of the increasing cost of higher education in the United States, students and their parents need a guide that explains how, when, and where to apply for meeting college costs. The book provides step-by-step advice on applying for financial aid and gives strategies for planning to pay for college. Question and answer sections for each step are helpful features that the book provides. In addition, there are tables for student expenses and parent's contributions, sample cases and worksheets of three students, and a glossary section that lists important terms. If the book included a checklist for the financial aid process and a calendar, it would be more helpful for users.

After readers become familiar with financial aid plans, the book guides them to lists of individual college costs. There are 18 categories of up-to-date costs and financial aid information provided here for 3,100 colleges. Other useful features that set this book apart from similar ones are indexes for colleges that offer academic, music or drama, or art scholarships; colleges that offer athletic scholarships; colleges that offer tuition and fee waivers and special tuition payment plans; and an alphabetic list of colleges. The handbook is a useful guide that every high school and college library should keep in its reference room.—**Sung Ok Kim**

341.   **College Financial Aid: The Best Resources to Help You Find the Money.** Issaquah, Wash., Resource Pathways; distr., Ashland, Ohio, Bookmasters, 1997. 266p. index. (College Information Series). $24.95pa. ISBN 0-9653424-5-X.

In this information age, with so much information on college financial aid available in libraries, in bookstores, and on Internet Websites, it is hard to determine which information sources are most useful. This book lists and reviews about 150 resources in various media. The reviews are arranged by the type of media, including print resources, Internet Websites, software resources, videotape resources, and commercial online services. The editors attempt to cover up-to-date materials and to provide current information on availability. An overall star rating system (1 to 4 stars) within each media section ranks the resources, and the best resources are listed first.

Each review provides detailed information on where to buy or how to access each resource, including ISBN numbers for obscure print media, direct order numbers for publishers, and URL addresses for sites on the Internet. Appendixes at the end of the guidebook address frequently asked questions and define special terms and acronyms. Indexes to all resources reviewed are provided, either by title, by author, or by publisher. No comprehensive or broad subject index is provided, but "Index for Steps in the Financial Aid Process" and "Index for Privately Funded Scholarships," which are intended for browsing, substitute fairly well for this omission. The book is recommended for high school libraries, college libraries, and public libraries. It is also recommended for home purchase.—**Vera Gao**

342.   Dennis, Marguerite J. **Complete College Financing Guide.** 4th ed. Hauppauge, N.Y., Barron's Educational Series, 1997. 244p. index. $14.95pa. ISBN 0-8120-9523-5. ISSN 1092-5554.

College costs are increasing, so books to help parents and others who pay the bill are increasing in number and quality. Like most of these books, Barron's has articles on the key players, how to apply, how financial aid decisions are made, tips on how to improve chances of getting funds, how to plan for college costs in advance, and what some alternative sources of funds are. It lists all federal and state programs by college along with separate lists of colleges that have employment and funding opportunities for military personnel, veterans, women, minorities, and the handicapped.

Competitor publications include *College Costs and Financial Aid Handbook* (see ARBA 94, entry 353), *Peterson's College Money Handbook* (see ARBA 98, entry 303), *The Financial Aid Book* (Perpetual Press, 1994), and Daniel J. Cassidy's *The Scholarship Book* (see ARBA 94, entry 333). All have the same aim—helping parents and student applicants. All have the same general content—procedural advice and lists. The most unique is Cassidy's book, which is a general resource for the financial aid professional more than for parents and student applicants. It includes 105 helpful publications on a multiplicity of topics. *The Financial Aid Book*, sponsored by the Student Financial Services corporation, is the hardest to use because it forces users to wander through complicated indexes to locate the college listings that have what they want. Peterson's is possibly the best with its realistic section on commonly asked questions, special information boxes in the text, lucid overview of federal programs, and table of after-aid costs by college by state. What is missing in all these books is specialized information on scholarship aid; readers must turn to specialty publications for that. Any of these books will help those needing information. This reviewer's preference is Peterson's.—**George L. Findlen**

343. **The Graduate Student's Complete Scholarship Book.** By Student Services, L. L. C. Naperville, Ill., Sourcebooks, 1998. 177p. index. $18.95pa. ISBN 1-57071-195-X. [R: Choice, Sept 98, p. 98]

344. **The Minority and Women's Complete Scholarship Book.** By Student Services, L. L. C. Naperville, Ill., Sourcebooks, 1998. 176p. index. $18.95pa. ISBN 1-57071-193-3.

Two specialized scholarship finders from Student Services join the crowded college reference shelf. *The Minority and Women's Complete Scholarship Book*, which also covers religious affiliations and disabilities, contains a mix of graduate and undergraduate awards in its more than 1,200 entries. *The Graduate Student's Complete Scholarship Book* has more than 1,100 entries, including all of the graduate listings in the other book (based on a sampling). Entries, which are arranged alphabetically by name of the program or award, note dollar amount, deadline, fields or majors (e.g., medical, education, all areas), and mailing address. A brief paragraph describes each award, including special requirements such as in-state residency, grade point average (GPA) minimums, previous educational experiences, ethnic background, sex, and other criteria. Types of awards range from scholarships issued by individual high schools and colleges to those from foundations and associations. Both need- and merit-based monies are covered. The font used for title entries and the graphic elements, including icons for majors and special criteria, detract from rather than add to interpretation of the text. Patrons should use the indexes, which list the numbered entries by majors, school name, and special criteria (e.g., athletics, ethnic background, and GPA, all of which are further subdivided). A geographic requirements index would be a welcome addition. The books might be easier to use if all the indexes were combined, and if subdivisions (e.g., paralegal) were broken out in the alphabetic list in addition to falling under broad headings (e.g., vocational).

Although similar in coverage, the series of specialized scholarship titles from Reference Service Press by Gail Schlachter appear to cover more awards (see entries 292, 293, 294, 772, and 773). However, these new books will certainly be used in any reference collection. Librarians in schools and colleges may want to advise counselors and financial aid officers that free institutional access to the Student Services database (375,000 awards at the time of this review) is available from fastWEB at www.fastweb.com. Patrons can also create their own profile at the site and search for free. [R: Choice, Sept 98, p. 100]—**Deborah V. Rollins**

345. **Peterson's Scholarships for Study in the USA & Canada 1999.** 2d ed. Princeton, N.J., Peterson's Guides, 1998. 429p. $21.95pa. ISBN 0-76890-142-1.

Peterson's Scholarships for Study in the USA & Canada was briefly mentioned in ARBA 98 (see entry 294). This work describes some 900 programs for graduate students and more than 200,000 for undergraduate programs. More than $2.5 billion in aid is spent each year for some 800,000 awards. The 3d edition of this standard directory, along with *Peterson's College Money Handbook* (15th ed.; see ARBA 98, entry 303) and *Peterson's Scholarships, Grants, & Prizes*, makes up an important void to students seeking financial assistance. All of these volumes are excellent and reliable sources. A detailed introduction in each of Peterson's guides is a useful tool for the uninitiated.—**Bohdan S. Wynar**

346. **Peterson's Sports Scholarships & College Athletic Programs.** 3d ed. Princeton, N.J., Peterson's Guides, 1998. 865p. index. $24.95pa. ISBN 1-56079-830-0. ISSN 1069-1383.

This guide to scholarships and financial aid for athletes at 1,700 higher education institutions in the United States is a must for college-bound high school athletes. The primary entries are organized alphabetically by college name, rather than by state. Listings include contact information (including e-mail address and fax number) of the athletic department, facilities, administrators, scholarships, and the names and telephone numbers of coaches for each sport for that year. One-quarter of the entries reflect four-year schools that do not award scholarships, but do offer aid packages. Users must follow a complex series of steps in the two indexes—men's sports and women's sports—to determine which schools actually offer scholarships. Under a particular sport, users select the association or division affiliation of the school, followed by the state, and finally arrive at the schools that award scholarships in that sport. In this way the directory provides two primary access points to scholarship information: alphabetic by college name and by male or female sport.

The introductory material includes several concise and helpful articles. The most informative, "Financing Your College Education," by Stephen and Howard Figler, summarizes the pros, cons, and how-tos of athletic scholarships in five pages. Other topics include motivational words by popular college coaches, advice to international athletes, and "Keeping Your Balance" by Derrick Harmon, former Cornell University football player and San Francisco 49er. This directory is highly recommended for high school, public, and academic libraries in areas with active high school athletic programs.—**Anne C. Moore**

347.   Sponholz, Joseph. **Winning Athletic Scholarships: Guaranteeing Your Academic Eligibility for College Sports Scholarships.** 1998 ed. New York, Princeton Review/Random House, 1997. 177p. $18.00pa. ISBN 0-679-77879-9.

This book is a helpful guide for young people who are talented enough to be considering athletic scholarships to college. During the last few years, controversy about the place of student athletes at colleges and universities has erupted around the country. Athletes are often ill-prepared for the life of a student athlete, both emotionally and academically. This book will go a long way toward rectifying that.

Chapters in the work define the major organization that oversees college athletics (the National Collegiate Athletic Association [NCAA]), eligibility requirements, and recruiting. Chapters on "The Real Story" give advice from top NCAA coaches about how they view recruits and recruiting. A chapter on the SAT tests includes not only advice but a practice test as well. Appendixes consist of 45 pages, listing various athletic scholarships around the nation. A list of team names rounds out a useful reference work that is appropriate for school and public libraries. As the author makes clear, there is very much at stake in NCAA athletics for both the schools and their prospective student-athletes. This book will help both immensely.—**Bob Craigmile**

Handbooks and Yearbooks

348.   **American Universities and Colleges.** 15th ed. New York, Walter de Gruyter, 1997. 1841p. index. $199.95. ISBN 3-11-014689-4.

Information on more than 1,900 schools of education fills the 15th edition of this industry standard. The first of the 5 parts of this compendium is devoted to essays that contain factual data on higher education in the United States. Following this is a section on professional education that details various degree programs available, listing the states and then the institutions where they are offered. The 3d section of this work is the largest. This is composed of an alphabetic listing by state and then by school that profiles each institution. Included are such data as characteristics, accreditation, a brief history, institutional structure, calendar, degree requirements, distinctive educational programs, degrees conferred, fees and other expenses, financial aid, departments and teaching staff, enrollment, characteristics of student body, student life, and so on. Appendixes, which have information on academic costume code and ceremonies, the number of doctorates and master's degrees conferred since 1869, available ROTC programs, summary data on institutions, and the American Council on Education, are followed by both institutional and general indexes.

Libraries where patrons need such comprehensive information on higher education will want to have this reference work on their shelves. However, because the volume has a 1997 copyright, users will need to further research any data that may change from year to year (e.g., tuition, degree requirements) to have accurate information. [R: Choice, Sept 98, p. 96]—**Jo Anne H. Ricca**

349.   Andersen, Charles J., comp. **Fact Book on Higher Education.** 1997 ed. Phoenix, Ariz., Oryx Press, 1998. 254p. index. $49.95. ISBN 0-89774-820-4. ISSN 0363-6720.

Although many of the statistics about higher education displayed in this recommended reference source can be found at Internet sites such as FedStats, it is their compilation and organization in one volume that justifies its purchase. Schools of education, college admissions offices, development offices, and academic libraries will find this 1st edition since 1945 a welcome resource.

The book is divided into four readily accessible parts: demographic and economic data; enrollment data; institutions and finance, faculty, staff, and students; and earned degrees. Each of these sections contains a one- to two-page summary of statistics that highlights important trends regarding, for example, the statistics of women in higher education or the status of minorities in higher education.

There are a total of 188 footnoted statistical tables. Each one features a graph or other visual depiction of the accompanying data to enable users to quickly discern major trends or changes. All data are tabulated and displayed in thousands, making it less likely that users will err in interpreting and reporting their findings.

Although no new data collection has occurred since the 1985 edition, data for the years 1985 through 1996 from sources such as the U.S. Department of Education, Bureau of the Census, Department of Commerce, Bureau of Labor Statistics, and the National Science Foundation are cited. The volume concludes with a bibliographic guide to sources cited (including nongovernmental sources) and an index. [R: Choice, July/Aug 98, p. 1836]

—**Kathleen W. Craver**

350. **The College Handbook 1998.** 35th ed. New York, College Entrance Examination Board, 1997. 1754p. index. $23.95pa. ISBN 0-87447-561-9.

This is the granddaddy of reference tools designed to help high school students and their parents find the perfect college. Because it is not the only option on the market, it has to work to stay competitive; it remains the publication to beat. The core of the 1,754-page book is its statistic-laden descriptions, which are given alphabetically by state. In addition to providing admissions criteria, costs, and admissions office address and telephone number, each entry lists majors available and general facts about the college. What makes the book worth having are the articles and lists provided in the front of the book. The articles explain how admissions offices go about selecting students, teach applicants how to approach the ubiquitous application essay, and provide a checklist to follow during the application process. Lists identify colleges by size (small, medium, large, and extra large) and type of location (rural, suburban, or urban); provide dates of colleges having early decision and early action dates; list colleges having a special mission (Bible, education, or military); and list colleges by NCI division and sport. Another strength is that this book is updated annually.

It is different from one of its competitors, *Peterson's Guide to Two-Year Colleges, 1998* (see ARBA 98, entry 293) and *Peterson's Guide to Four-Year Colleges* (see entry 330), which publishes separate lists of colleges by level. Both Peterson's Guides and the College Entrance Examination Board publish nearly the same information. The College Entrance Examination Board's typeface and yellow newsprint are more difficult to read than the typeface and white paper of Peterson's Guides. A second competitor, Charles T. Straughn and Barbarasue Lovejoy Straughn's *Lovejoy's College Guide* (see entry 351), carries both 2-year and 4-year institutions, as does the College Entrance Examination Board publication. Libraries will want to carry one of the three publications. *The College Handbook* remains the strongest of the three.—**George L. Findlen**

351. **Lovejoy's College Guide.** 24th ed. Charles T. Straughn II and Barbarasue Lovejoy Straughn, eds. New York, Macmillan General Reference/Simon & Schuster Macmillan, 1997. 1557p. illus. index. $29.95pa. ISBN 0-02-861689-8. ISSN 0076-132X.

This classic guide to higher education belongs in every library patronized by prospective college students and their parents, guardians, and counselors. This edition comes with a CD-ROM from which information can by accessed with a variety of search strategies, and the book itself, although mammoth, is formatted so that it is easy to use. There are 2 prefatory sections, a 12-page section on financial aid and admissions issues, and a 250-page section that is mostly an alphabetic list of different academic majors and the schools where they may be studied, along with any germane program accreditation information. There is a section at the end of the book on athletic and nonathletic (e.g., band) programs, as well as one showcasing approximately 100 schools with "extended profiles" that include color photographs. There is also a bit of material on foreign institutions.

The heart of the book is section 3, a 1,000-page list of some 4,200, 2-year, 4-year, and graduate schools. Numerous details are provided about the undergraduate programs at the 4-year institutions: selectivity, cost, enrollment data, student-faculty ratio, academic programs, facilities, special programs, admissions and graduation rate statistics, and student life. The many Website addresses and names and addresses of directors of admission enhance the value of this important reference work.—**G. Douglas Meyers**

INTERNATIONAL EXCHANGE PROGRAMS
AND OPPORTUNITIES

352.   **Open Doors 1996/97: Report on International Educational Exchange.** Todd M. Davis, ed. New York, Institute of International Education, 1997. 208p. maps. $42.95pa. ISBN 087206-243-0. ISSN 0078-5172.

This unique and comprehensive statistical source profiles international students studying in the United States and U.S. students studying abroad. More than 125 tables and figures bring together data on the widely varied aspects of international study, including student demographics, enrollment trends, field of study, host institutions, and foreign student funding and expenditures. The annual is further enhanced by brief articles (sidebars) by experts in international education dealing with topics such as marketing, education exchange, and issues for the twenty-first century. Although there is no index, a detailed table of contents and lists of figures, tables, and sidebars make access to required information relatively easy.—**Ahmad Gamaluddin**

353.   **Peterson's Study Abroad 1998: Over 1,600 Semester & Year Abroad Academic Programs.** 5th ed. Princeton, N.J., Peterson's Guides, 1998. 1064p. illus. index. $29.95pa. ISBN 1-56079-861-0. ISSN 1069-6504.

Peterson's is the largest educational information and communications company in the United States, providing users with books, software, and online services in support of education. The current edition of *Peterson's Study Abroad* is one such resource. It is the complete guide to more than 1,600 semester and year abroad academic programs, including academic courses, language programs, internships, voluntary service, and country-to-country study programs. For students wishing to study abroad, no matter what major, this is the first source that should be consulted because it guides the user through the whole process, from selecting a program to preparing for it. The book is divided into 3 parts. Part 1 provides articles of guidance, which help in planning the trip, budgeting money, and discusses health issues. Multicountry and single-country program descriptions, including country-to-country programs and program descriptions, are discussed in part 2. Under each program, the detailed information is provided, such as the host; academic focus; program information; dates; eligibility requirements; student profile; program details; living arrangements; schedule; costs; and contact person, address, telephone and fax numbers, and e-mail and Website addresses if available. Part 3 provides indexes, including field of study, program sponsors, host institution, and internship programs. Many pictures are displayed in the book that illustrate students' life and their study environment abroad. Besides the students, librarians and educators are also targeted audiences of this guide.—**Xiao (Shelley) Yan Zhang**

354.   **Study Abroad 1998-1999. Etudes a l'Etranger. Estudios en el Extranjero.** 30th ed. Paris, United Nations Educational, Scientific, and Cultural Organization; distr., Lanham, Md., Bernan Press, 1997. 1221p. index. $29.95pa. ISBN 92-3-003401-0.

This directory, last reviewed in ARBA 90 (see entry 348), contains 2,908 entries valid for 1998 and 1999 on post-secondary education in both academic and professional fields. There are 120 countries and territories listed. In addition, it contains information on scholarships, student employment, and financial assistance from institutions offering both continuing education courses and university-level courses. The work is organized into 2 sections: international organizations scholarships and courses and national scholarships and courses by country. Entries are in one or more languages—English (E), Spanish (S) and French (F)—and include information on addresses, fees and duration of courses, and applications (if available). Some entries are especially long, such as the ones for the United Kingdom and the United States. The international organizations index, national institutions index, and subjects of study index are especially useful for locating entry numbers by institution and subject area. The third index was used as an example to locate courses in English, Spanish, and French. United Nations Educational, Scientific, and Cultural Organization (UNESCO) publishes the paperback reference. This 30th edition is also improved because it suppressed countries and institutions that did not reply by the deadline, instead of including them with notations that read "no reply" as in previous editions. The work is also available on CD-ROM. With the new interest in life-long learning around the world, this work makes a fine reference for any library.—**Edward Erazo**

355. **Vacation Study Abroad.** 48th ed. Sara J. Steen, ed. New York, Institute of International Education, 1998. 480p. index. $39.95. ISBN 087206-242-2. ISSN 1046-2104.

The Institute of International Education (IIE) has published *Vacation Study Abroad* and its companion volume *Academic Year Abroad* (Institute of International Education, 1998) for 48 years. Together they are the most comprehensive annual directories in international study available. IIE, a nonprofit organization, which has 650 college and university members in the United States and abroad, has been providing information on educational exchange for more than 75 years. *Vacation Study Abroad* provides information on more than 2,000 programs in 70 countries. These include summer programs of any length from one week to several months, and short courses of varying lengths in the fall, winter, and spring. About 60 percent of the programs are sponsored by U.S. colleges, and the rest are offerings from foreign universities, language schools, and other organizations. Many programs combine study with travel.

The arrangement is by region of the world, then alphabetically by country, city, and sponsoring institution. Indexed data provided for each entry include costs and fares, academic credit, eligibility and academic levels, fields of study, availability of scholarships and work-study, dates and duration of stay, languages of instruction, housing, contact, e-mail and Website addresses, and telephone and fax numbers. The preface provides helpful practical tips and additional resources to consult. *Vacation Study Abroad* still has a place in all library collections, as its audience includes all adult learners, and not just students.—**Christine E. King**

NONPRINT MATERIALS
AND RESOURCES

356. **Educational Media and Technology Yearbook, Volume 23.** 1998 ed. Robert Maribe Branch and Mary Ann Fitzgerald, eds. Englewood, Colo., Libraries Unlimited, 1998. 296p. index. $65.00. ISBN 1-56308-591-7. ISSN 8755-2094.

Designed to help media professionals and educators practice their craft in a changing, expanding field, this volume regards technology as a way of organizing thought, science, art, and human values through a wide variety of media. Twelve essays depict trends, issues, and recent developments. Supplementary sections include a 50-page annotated list of North American organizations interested in education media and instructional technology; descriptions of 141 graduate programs in instructional technology, educational media and communication, and school library media; and a 50-page annotated bibliography and mediagraphy.

The first essay, "Trends in Media and Technology in Education and Training," reviews key issues including the incorporation of traditional audiovisual media (e.g., videotapes, transparencies, print materials); computer-based media; telecommunication-based media; and advanced interactive technologies (e.g., multimedia, hypermedia, virtual reality), into the mainstream. "Quest for Knowing" explores the need for teachers and students to ask critical and reflective questions concerning school experiences. "The State of Programs of Instructional Technologies in the United States and Canada" reveals varied content among such programs. "Instructional Design and Teacher Planning" discusses an apparent inability of the field of instructional design to influence teachers and students in public schools. Two articles on interactive multimedia in college teaching report that multimedia technology can help teachers achieve modest yet valuable gains in student learning and identifies characteristics of technology that hold the greatest promise for college teachers. "Reading and Writing Across the Media" summarizes how current scholarship is redefining and extending literacy understanding, materials, and instruction to encompass far more than reading and writing print text; demonstrates how by using diverse technologies and literacy processes, educators may extend their instructional beliefs and frameworks; and offers lesson plans reflecting new literacy conceptions. "The Bread and Butter of the Internet" proposes a 4-level model to assist teachers in their understanding of the Internet and its use: Engineering Level (infrastructure); Application Level (software allowing gathering and sharing of information); Information Service Level (combination of information with hardware and software that allows users to meet their information needs); and Use Level (how educators apply information including security, acceptable use, and intellectual property issues).

The scholarly approach, yet friendly writing style, of this work will make it attractive to patrons of school libraries, academic libraries, and others. It is a key resource for those who are trying to sort out the impact that technology may have on the learning process of students of all ages.—**Jan Bakker**

357. **Educator's Guide to Free Videotapes 1998.** 45th ed. James L. Berger, ed. Randolph, Wis., Educators Progress Service, 1998. 338p. index. $32.95pa. ISBN 0-87708-307-X.

The videotape is now a universal teaching resource in public and private schools. Thus, it is hard to imagine a library that would have no use for this standard work now in its 45th edition. The book's cost, although not cheap, is still reasonable for a reference selection tool, and the videotapes secured as a result of its use should more than pay for itself.

The editor claims that 196 new titles have been added to the work, bringing the total included to 1,746 titles. Additionally, many older titles no longer available have been eliminated. It should be noted that this edition is intended for use during the 1998-1999 school year. Major subject areas included are business and economics, career education, fine arts, guidance, health, home economics (e.g., cooking, family living, nutrition), mathematics, physical education and recreation, religion and philosophy, science (e.g., aerospace education, environmental education, general science), social studies (e.g., citizenship, geography, history, and world affairs), special education, teacher reference, and technology education. All videos are subarranged alphabetically by title.

A noteworthy new feature is that complete order information is included with each entry, eliminating the need for cumbersome cross-references. Additional timesavers are telephone numbers, fax numbers, e-mail addresses, and URLs for Websites, when available. There is also a "What's New" index in addition to the title, subject, source, and NASA source index. New titles are clearly marked with a "new" symbol throughout the main list.

One final feature worth mentioning is the three-page evaluation sheet for industry-sponsored educational materials, which could easily be adapted for evaluating almost any instructional resources. In summary, this work is highly recommended for all school library media centers and school professional collections, whether at the district or building level, and should be of special value to those schools facing extremely tight budgets.

—**Carol Truett**

VOCATIONAL AND CONTINUING EDUCATION

358. **Bricker's International Directory 1998: University-Based Executive Development Programs.** 29th ed. Princeton, N.J., Peterson's Guides, 1998. 1031p. index. $395.00. ISBN 1-56079-863-7. ISSN 1078-2257.

This new edition of *Bricker's International Directory* retains many of the features of the last edition (see ARBA 94, entry 225) but has returned to a single-volume format. The number of programs included has grown during the years and now stands at 810 at 89 institutions in 28 countries, compared with "over 600" in the last reviewed edition. Criteria for inclusion remain as they have been: university sponsored English-language management training programs, open to the public and intended for relatively high level executives seeking appropriately advanced presentation of subject matter.

The largest section of this work contains the program descriptions, grouped by 11 broad subjects such as "General Management," "Business Strategy," "Marketing and Sales," and "Technology Management." Programs are described in a uniform, one-page format that includes each one's objectives, intended audience, topical focus, composition of faculty, contact information, 1998 schedule, costs, and a detailed profile of 1996 participant characteristics.

Smaller sections, as noted in the last ARBA review, present information on industry-specific programs, custom programs and services, and executive MBA programs. The volume is provided with indexes by sponsoring institution name, geographic location, and more than 130 specific topics.

With its focus on university-based programs, *Bricker's* complements the listing of companies in the *Training and Development Organizations Directory* (6th ed.; Gale, 1994) and continues to be a convenient, logically laid out, and well-indexed reference work. It will be of great value to corporate human resource departments and staff developers as well as others with interests in business education.—**Gregory M. Toth**

359.   **Ferguson's Guide to Apprenticeship Programs.** 2d ed. Elizabeth H. Oakes, ed. Chicago, Ferguson, 1998. 2v. illus. index. $89.95/set. ISBN 0-89434-243-6.

This 2-volume set, now in its 2d edition, will be invaluable to students looking for career options that will let them earn money while learning marketable skills from experts in their field. This expanded and revised resource provides information on more than 7,500 programs in 52 job categories. It will be useful for those high school graduates who do not go on to college. It will also be handy for adults facing layoffs or looking for alternative career paths. A helpful introduction explains apprenticeship programs and how to use this reference source to locate fields ranging from agricultural workers to midwives and writers.

Although this book is not a listing of every available apprenticeship and on-the-job training program, it is an excellent place to start, and it also provides many different ways to find further information. The set is divided into four parts. Section 1 lists programs in 52 job categories. Section 2 provides programs for individuals who meet certain eligibility requirements. Section 3 lists job centers and vocational schools with on-the-job training or apprenticeship programs; preparatory programs; and the offices for local, state, and federal job training programs. Section 4 includes a glossary, career resources on the Internet, a selected list of occupational titles taken from the *Dictionary of Occupational Titles* (DOT), a job index, and a state index. This guide is highly recommended for high school, public, community college, academic, and special libraries serving young adults looking for careers. [R: BL, 15 Nov 98, p. 610]—**Diane J. Turner**

360.   **Peterson's Vocational and Technical Schools and Programs, West.** 3d ed. Princeton, N.J., Peterson's Guides, 1998. 632p. index. $34.95pa. ISBN 1-56079-865-3. ISSN 1069-1375.

Peterson's Vocational and Technical Schools and Programs, West profiles 5,000 western U.S. postsecondary educational institutions offering academic awards, certificates, or diplomas for less than 2 years of study. Each of these vocational and technical schools is profiled with full contact information, including Websites. Entries include student body demographics, numbers of faculty members, costs, and the availability of home study. Program descriptions indicate the number of class hours required, program length, tuition and fees, placement rates, and the availability of financial aid.

Direct access to the data is through the career program index, with listings from accounting and business administration to welding and woodworking. Each of these career listings is arranged by state. An additional index leads to the entries by name of institution. Typical of Peterson's Guides titles, this volume is designed for quick access and current information.

In addition to the directory aspect of this volume, four articles detail how technical and vocational training programs benefit those who use them. These are written for the individual seeking these opportunities, yet they are also invaluable to librarians, career counselors, and academic advisers. They quote statistical information on the returns of training and offer guidance to students on financial aid and the use of apprenticeships.

—**Barbara Conroy**

361.   **Professional Careers Sourcebook: Where to Find Help Planning Careers That Require College or Technical Degrees.** 5th ed. Kathleen E. Maki and Kathleen M. Savage, eds. Detroit, Gale, 1997. 984p. index. $95.00. ISBN 0-8103-6469-7.

Questions about careers are frequent at the reference desk, and most reference books on the topic will receive heavy use. The latest edition of *Professional Careers Sourcebook* (PCS) is no exception. It suggests beginning research on a career with the *Occupational Outlook Handbook* (1996-97 ed.; see ARBA 98, entry 238), followed by this title or its companion, *Vocational Careers Sourcebook* (see entry 263) for more detailed information. PCS is essentially an index to additional resources on 122 careers, which are arranged in broad subject groupings; for example, the profiles for chemists, geologists, meteorologists, and physicists and astronomers are found under the heading "Physical Scientists." A master list makes it easy to find profiled careers without identifying each category.

Each profile consists of a page with a brief job description, salary ranges, and employment outlook to the year 2005, followed by a number of categories of career information, including career guides, professional associations, standards or certification agencies, test guides and exams, educational directories, grants and scholarships, reference guides, professional or trade periodicals, and conferences. Entries in these categories include complete contact information (address, telephone and fax number, e-mail address and Website) as well as a brief annotation of the book, periodical, association, or award. For example, among the 49 career guide listings for "Librarians" are citations to entries in *Jobs Rated Almanac*, *American Almanac of Jobs & Salaries*, and *Guide to Federal Jobs*. Because many such publications will also be in the library, PCS is a good first stop for patrons and librarians before rummaging through other career guides. Entries for awards refer to the granting body, rather than to their citations in other reference sources. Inclusion and omissions in each category are still odd, and are not always those an individual working in each profession would recommend. Appendixes cover electronic resources (e.g., CareerWeb, the Riley Guide), state government licensing agencies, and Bureau of Labor Statistics data on occupational growth rankings. A detailed index to all profiles, publication titles, award names, and corporate bodies concludes PCS. Most libraries will want to add this title to their careers collection, along with Gale's enormously helpful *Job Hunter's Sourcebook* (3d ed.; see ARBA 98, entry 233), which lists sources of help-wanted ads and other resources essential for actually finding a job.—**Deborah V. Rollins**

6 Ethnic Studies and Anthropology

ANTHROPOLOGY AND ETHNOLOGY

362. **Anthropology Bibliography on Disc.** [CD-ROM]. New York, Macmillan Library Reference/Simon & Schuster Macmillan, 1997. Minimum system requirements: IBM or compatible. CD-ROM drive with MSCDEX 2.0. 512K RAM. $995.00. ISBN 0-7838-0076-2.

This CD-ROM is a cumulative catalog of the Tozzer Library of Harvard University. The library collects in all areas of anthropology, with a strong emphasis on Mesoamerican and Mayan studies. The catalog records contained in this product are for books, journals, series, maps, and audiovisual materials. Most of the works included are in English, Germanic, Romance, Scandinavian, and Slavic languages. This product does not contain information on articles and edited collections, but that is available on another CD-ROM product from G. K. Hall titled *Anthropological Literature on Disc* (see ARBA 98, entry 317).

The CD-ROM is easy to install. Users can read directly from the disc, or it can be installed and used on a network. By installing it on a network, the library can customize various screens within the program. The only documentation with the CD-ROM is an installation guide that includes instructions on customizing screens. Although no other paper documentation is included, the online help is excellent.

Navigating the system is done through function keys and keyboard commands. The screen displays are functional with no attempt at making them attractive. The records are typical catalog records, which include basic bibliographic information and subjects, notes, and content fields. The default search is a keyword search. Traditional online searching operators are used, such as *and*, *or*, *truncation*, and *nested* searches. A browse function allows the user to search by title, author, or other fields. The only problem this reviewer had with searching was in trying to move from a list of tagged records back to the full list of titles. The search had to be completely retyped. This is a minor problem and should not impact the ability of the user to find research material.

The display of a brief record shows material type, language, date, title, and description. The full record shows those fields as well as all others. The brief display can be customized to the user's needs. Bibliographic entries can be printed or downloaded immediately, or they can be tagged and printed or downloaded later.

The audience best suited to this CD-ROM product is students or scholars of anthropology, especially those interested in Mayan and Mesoamerican cultures.—**Suzanne Julian**

363. Inhaber, Herbert. **Masks from Antiquity to the Modern Era: An Annotated Bibliography.** Lanham, Md., Scarecrow, 1997. 313p. illus. index. $45.00. ISBN 0-8108-3360-3.

Inhaber, a scientist at a defense facility in South Carolina, claims to have included more than 1,200 citations in this bibliography. The unnumbered citations are arranged by format, divided by geographic and subject headings, and are arranged alphabetically by author. Each entry includes author, title, publisher, date, keywords, and annotation. In the "Books and Catalogs" section, some entries include ISBN, but none include pagination. Annotations for monographs and dissertations are much more substantial than the very brief annotations included for periodical articles and nonprint media. Annotations include the author's assessment of reader level (e.g., "general article," "for specialists") and availability (although the "rare" designation is applied to materials he obtained through interlibrary loan at the Nancy Carson Branch of the Aiken County, South Carolina, public library).

The index is confined to the keywords assigned by Inhaber to each entry. Also included are a brief list of museums from around the world that have mask collections and, although not listed in table of contents or discussed in preface, 16 plates of masks the author has collected in his travels to Asia, Oceania, and the Americas.

This bibliography is in many ways an amateurish production, but it is also a labor of love by a longtime collector and student of masks. As the publisher notes, before this book there was no major bibliography on the topic. This volume is a most welcome addition to the reference collection.—**Fred J. Hay**

364.   **Worldmark Encyclopedia of Cultures and Daily Life.** Timothy L. Gall, ed. Detroit, Gale, 1997. 4v. illus. maps. index. $299.00/set. ISBN 0-7876-0552-2.
    This set covers more than 500 cultural groups in 4 volumes: Africa; Americas; Asia and Oceania; and Europe. The overall format is attractive, logical, and easy to use and parallels organization of its companion set, *The Worldmark Encyclopedia of the Nations* (8th ed.; see ARBA 96, entry 105). Articles begin with a primary location map and a photograph of the people. Although all maps and photographs are black and white and lack appeal, they provide good information about the culture. Each article follows a standard 20-heading outline, with a focus on traditions, living conditions, and personalities of cultural groups today. The consistency in format adds to the ease of use of the set. Topics in the outlines include a general introduction, with historical information about the culture, language, folklore, religion, food, clothing, education, and other subjects about everyday life in today's world. A bibliography lists benchmark publications about the culture. A glossary of terms and a comprehensive index appear at the end of each volume. The breadth of coverage and the affordable cost (under $300) make this set a recommended purchase for school and public libraries. [R: SLJ, Aug 98, p. 190]—**Lynda Welborn**

ETHNIC STUDIES

General Works

365.   **American Immigrant Cultures: Builders of a Nation.** David Levinson and Melvin Ember, eds. New York, Macmillan Library Reference/Simon & Schuster Macmillan, 1997. 2v. illus. index. $195.00. ISBN 0-02-897208-2.
    Italian Americans, African Americans, Germans from Russia, Korean Americans, Amish, Polish Americans . . . the list is almost endless. The trend in the United States to define ourselves by ethnic background and place our heritage in front of our nationality has led to a repudiation of the "melting pot" concept of the United States and has increased the study and acceptance of diversity in this country.
    American Immigrant Cultures: Builders of a Nation is an extensive 2-volume reference work profiling 161 ethnic groups who came to America, either forcibly (enslavement or exile) or voluntarily. The editors took a broad approach, defining "ethnicity" as "if members of the group or members of other groups consider it to be a distinct cultural entity. The basis of that distinctiveness is most commonly place of birth, place of ancestor's birth, physical features (race), religion and language, as well as various combinations of these factors." Indigenous peoples—Native Americans and Hawaiians—are not discussed.
    Each article (ranging from 3 to 10 pages) includes the name of the group (and alternatives), defining features, patterns of cultural variation, immigration and settlement history (including reasons for immigration), demographic data, language(s) spoken on arrival and changes thereof, cultural characteristics, and extent of assimilation or determination not to. Often included is information on trends in discrimination toward an ethnic group. Conclusions at the end of most articles offer good starting points for further study. References and bibliographic information is included at the end of each. A detailed index follows in volume 2.
    Social historians, history students, and anyone interested in the complex society of the United States will find this a valuable reference work. It is recommended for all libraries. [R: Choice, July/Aug 98, pp. 1834-1835]—**Kevin W. Perizzolo**

366.   Cashmore, Ellis, with others. **Dictionary of Race and Ethnic Relations.** 4th ed. New York, Routledge, 1996. 412p. index. $100.00; $27.99pa. ISBN 0-415-15167-8; 0-415-13822-1pa.
    Quality research and an authoritative list of contributors are assets of the *Dictionary of Race and Ethnic Relations*, but the dictionary is best suited to an academic audience and will not meet every library's needs. Written by the author, the scholarly 10-page introduction—primarily an essay on four key episodes in race relations in the 1990s—is different from introductions usually found in reference books. Librarians may wish for a better description of the scope, structure, and best utilization of the resource; however, Cashmore's introduction seems to illustrate

how a concept or name is determined to be significant. Cashmore mentions significance as a criteria for the inclusion of new terms, such as "causes célèbres."

Concerns about the lack of clear criteria were noted in previous reviews (see ARBA 95, entry 394). Although the criteria issue has been somewhat addressed, readers may still disagree with the selection, coverage, or accessibility of entries. Despite the rationale, readers may dislike the O. J. Simpson and Rodney King trials being grouped into one entry as part of the "causes célèbres" phenomenon. *Womanist*, an important term in U.S. feminism among women of color, is not indexed, although it is described in the entry on "Black Feminism."

The contributors represent several countries, but the work emphasizes Great Britain and the United States. Most contributors use an academic writing style that shrinks from definition, instead providing background, discussion, and insight. This writing style works against the resource being a true dictionary. The book seems more like a compact subject encyclopedia. Entries even contain short reading lists, as do many encyclopedias. These lists are excellent starting points for further investigation.

It can sometimes be difficult to evaluate the currency of a new edition. This is a problem with this volume. Although several new terms have been added, existing entries have not been updated in a consistent manner. For example, the entry on South Africa seems to end by vaguely describing "the early nineties." The entry for Nelson Mandela stops with his election in 1994, whereas the entry on apartheid mentions an important court case of 1996. Despite some criticisms of its consistency, the *Dictionary of Race and Ethic Relations* is a useful resource for scholarly research. This book is recommended for academic libraries that support graduate-level programs in sociology, race relations, and related cross-disciplinary areas. It is also recommended for large public libraries that support public research.—**Sandra E. Fuentes**

367. Lassiter, Sybil M. **Cultures of Color in America: A Guide to Family, Religion, and Health.** Westport, Conn., Greenwood Press, 1998. 207p. index. $65.00. ISBN 0-313-30070-4.

Greenwood states in its press release that this book "should be of interest to academics, health care professionals, sociologists, clergy, and laypersons." It should be of interest but, unfortunately, it is not likely that it will be. Lassiter, a retired nurse and nursing school professor, has compiled 9 chapters, each focusing on one non-Euro-American ethnic group: Africans, African Americans, Alaskan Americans, Hawaiian Americans, Haitian Americans, Native Americans, Puerto Rican Americans, and West Indian Americans. No consideration is given Hispanic Americans (other than Puerto Ricans) or to the country's fastest-growing ethnic minority, Mexican Americans, much less the sizable communities of Cubans and other Spanish-speaking peoples from the Caribbean and Latin America.

The chapters are inadequately researched and poorly written. The book suffers from many of the same problems as many freshmen term papers: overgeneralization (e.g., treating African cultures as a single entity), insufficient bibliography with too much reliance on popular sources, controversial and speculative theories stated as fact (e.g., pre-Columbian Africans in the Americas), a plenitude of errors, and serious omissions (e.g., the prevalence of gallstones among certain Native American populations). Each chapter is a presentation of disparate fragments about a people, their culture, their history, and their health. The same information, when accurate, can be found in most general encyclopedias. The reviewer is left wondering why a respected academic press would publish a book of so little practical utility and of such low scholarly standards.—**Fred J. Hay**

368. Levinson, David. **Ethnic Groups Worldwide: A Ready Reference Handbook.** Phoenix, Ariz., Oryx Press, 1998. 436p. illus. index. $65.00. ISBN 1-57356-019-7.

Levinson, former vice president for the Human Relations Area Files at Yale University and editor-in-chief of *The Encyclopedia of World Cultures* (see ARBA 92, entries 334 and 335), has written a handbook that provides an up-to-date synopsis on the state of ethnic relations all over the world. The organization of this title differs significantly from *The Encyclopedia of World Cultures* in that instead of being organized by culture groups, it is organized by country. This organization allows the examination of ethnic relations within countries such as Bosnia-Herzegovina and Croatia. This perspective also enables one to study how the same ethnic group is treaded in different countries, such as the Kurds in Iraq and Turkey.

The author notes in the preface that there are no definite criteria as to what constitutes a minority group. A broad definition is applied that takes into account such factors as identification by themselves or others, religion, language, history, and regional localization. The handbook is divided into four parts: Europe, Africa, Asia and the Pacific, and the Americas. Each part contains maps, an introduction, a bibliography, and country-by-country profiles. The profiles contain information categorized in three ways: general overview, ethnic composition, and ethnic relations. The ethnic relations portion, rather than being comprehensive, is used to highlight the ethnic relations that have the greatest impact on national issues. The index, by Virgil Diodato, is extremely comprehensive.

This handbook synthesizes a great deal of information that, although available, can be difficult to find and organize. It serves as an excellent complement to *The Encyclopedia of World Cultures* and is an alternative for those libraries that did not purchase the expensive multivolume set. [R: SLJ, Aug 98, p. 194; BL, July 98, p. 1905; Choice, Dec 98, p. 670]—**John R. Burch Jr.**

369.   **Multiculturalism.** Robert Emmet Long, ed. Bronx, N.Y., H. W. Wilson, 1997. 179p. index. (The Reference Shelf, v.69, no.5). $20.00pa. ISBN 0-8242-0918-4.

This collection of previously published essays and articles covers the "ism" of multiculturalism; that is, ongoing political debates concerning the intrinsic worth and utility of contemporary movements to promote multicultural perspectives. The volume's greatest asset, however, also contributes to one of its few drawbacks. The contents are drawn from a wide variety of sources, ranging from newspapers and periodicals through journals of opinion to scholarly publications, and they speak for all sides of the controversy. The editor's brief commentaries introducing the four sections do not, unfortunately, discuss or evaluate the venues from which these works have been drawn nor attempt to limn the backgrounds, qualifications, or outlooks of their authors. Readers who are not already steeped in this literature, then, may have difficulty gauging the respective credibility, for example, of pieces by the distinguished academic philosopher Richard Rorty and the weekly news magazine pundit John Leo. This flaw notwithstanding, the collection does provide a coherent account of the debates, conveniently marshaled in one volume.—**Glenn Petersen**

370.   Olson, James S. **An Ethnohistorical Dictionary of China.** Westport, Conn., Greenwood Press, 1998. 434p. index. $89.50. ISBN 0-313-28853-4.

With more than 1.2 billion people divided into hundreds of ethnic groups, all dominated by the Han people, China's politics and its foreign policy are bound to be affected by ethnicity and ethnic rivalry. China's ethnic issues and definitions are, therefore, of interest to the rest of the world. The author chooses to define ethnicity broadly, thereby being as inclusive as possible. This book contains more than 600 main entries for Chinese ethnic groups, plus a significant cross-referencing structure. Many entries are of essay length, covering the history, the culture, and the significant events of modern times that happened to that ethnic group. Olson, the author of more than 25 books on U.S. and world history, is a distinguished professor of history and the chair of the Department of History at Sam Houston State University. The appendixes include useful information, including 1990 populations of officially recognized nationalities in the People's Republic of China, a chronology of Chinese history, and a list of autonomous ethnic political units in the People's Republic of China. There is also a general index in addition to the cross-references, and a selected bibliography of English titles. The weakness of the dictionary is the lack of each ethnic group name in the original language with each main entry. This would be useful because the author has used different transliteration systems for the western spelling of the ethnic group names.

This book gives librarians, students, scholars, and educated readers a ready-reference for background information to understand ethnic groups in China, and to interpret events in the light of the country's strong level of ethnicity.—**Vera Gao**

371.   **Peoples of the World: Customs and Cultures.** Amiram Gonen and Barbara P. Sutnick, eds. Danbury, Conn., Grolier, 1998. 10v. illus. maps. index. $289.00/set. ISBN 0-7172-9236-3.

The stated goal of this set is to promote understanding of "how our global neighbors live and think," particularly among students in middle and high school. With this noble purpose and the current dearth of information on the subject for young people, the set is, at first glance, promising. However, potential buyers and users should be cautioned about its shortcomings before they make a purchase.

The text covers some 1,200 cultures (i.e., ethnic groups and nations) currently in existence around the world. Each group is described in terms of who they are, where they live, and where they come from. Information is also given about the size of the population, its history, role as a minority or majority, political and economic status, religion, language, and culture. Color photographs, drawings, and 280 maps accompany many of the articles. In addition, there is a brief glossary and index. All this is fine, but a closer look at the work's content reveals significant problems.

The most disturbing problem with this set is its misrepresentation of peoples through photographs. A student using this set might come away with the impression that Dutch women walk about the streets of Holland wearing wooden shoes, ankle-length dresses, shawls, and pointed caps. Although for some countries or groups (e.g., England, Russia) contemporary images are provided, for others (e.g., Germany, Mexico, Japan) the images are decidedly dated. And photograph captions and text do not always clarify this issue. For example, the article on Mongolia depicts the traditional nomadic way of life and animal husbandry practices of the people, but fails to mention that most Mongolians today are urban dwellers and that there are industries in the country apart from livestock. Other generalities and a lack of detail in the text can also mislead readers. The famine in Ukraine during the 1930s that was artificially induced by the Soviet regime is described simply as "a hunger" that occurred in that country. Coverage of other groups is too brief to inform (e.g., for the Laz of Turkey we are given only a two-line entry).

Some 20 pages of glossary and index are repeated in each of the 10 volumes, which seems a waste, especially when one considers the content of these features. For instance, "yurt" (the traditional home of Mongolian nomads) does not appear in the glossary or index, although a drawing of a yurt does appear with the entry on Mongolia and in its caption. A more detailed glossary and index could have easily been included with only one of the volumes at the expense of repetition. If the editors had made the effort to develop these features, they would have used their pages more effectively.

With these rather serious flaws, this set should never be used as a single, authoritative reference. However, if used in conjunction with other more accurate or detailed sources, it could provide a good starting point. [R: BL, 1 Oct 98, p. 366]—**Barbara Ittner**

372. Russell, Cheryl. **Racial and Ethnic Diversity: Asians, Blacks, Hispanics, Native Americans, and Whites.** 2d ed. Ithaca, N.Y., New Strategist, 1998. 706p. index. (American Consumer Series). $89.95. ISBN 1-885070-15-2.

There are 7 major chapters in this compendium, supplemented with lists of unnumbered tables and charts, an introduction, a glossary, a bibliography, and an index. Each of the initial 5 chapters deals with one ethnic group: Asians, blacks, Hispanics, Native Americans, and whites. Chapter 6 addresses the total population, focusing on highlights, education, health, household, housing, income, labor force, population, spending, and wealth as they relate to the ethnic group. Chapter 7 deals with attitudes and addresses highlights, U.S. unity, black progress, integration, freedom of expression, group stereotypes, and immigration based on the 1996 General Social Survey conducted by the National Opinion Research Center at the University of Chicago.

An interesting, although not very enlightening finding is that "Americans are more tolerant than ever towards people of other races and ethnicities" (pp. 2-3), but who these Americans are is not clear. The data are mainly census data, rearranged to display the diversity of the population. Issues of definition are treated in a pragmatic way but not always clearly: People from the Middle East are classified as white from an Asian world region. The rearranged data should be useful for quick, simplistic answers but not for serious research. Scholars usually rearrange the data according to their hypotheses and methodology. The data are short on showing trends because often data from only one census year are reported. Whether this volume is planned as the first in an annual series is not stated.

—**Elias H. Tuma**

Africans

373. **African Biography.** Virginia Curtin Knight, ed. Detroit, U*X*L/Gale, 1998. 3v. illus. maps. index. $84.00/set. ISBN 0-7876-2823-9.

Aimed at middle school students and older, this 3-volume work contains biographical entries on 75 notable Africans who lived from 1182 to modern times. Alphabetically arranged by biographical subject, the volumes include essays on individuals ranging from South African President Nelson Mandela to Nobel Laureate in literature Nadine Gordimer to the late Ethiopian Emperor Haile Selassie. Other entries describe lesser-known people who have achieved distinction as labor leaders, musicians, or religious figures, to name only a few fields. The entries contain more than 150 illustrations and maps, sidebar information related to the individual, and a bibliography. In addition, the volumes include a glossary, a timeline of significant events in African history, and name and subject indexes. *African Biography* is an excellent reference source: well written, nicely designed, and usefully organized. The editor deserves particular praise for resisting the pressures of politically correct publishing: the work does not omit critical material on some frequently praised individuals, includes notable white Africans, and covers the underreported topic of Arab slave trading. One note of criticism: The authors of these fine essays should have been included in each entry.—**Donald Altschiller**

Asian Americans

374.   Hurh, Won Moo. **The Korean Americans.** Westport, Conn., Greenwood Press, 1998. 190p. illus. maps. index. (The New Americans). $39.95. ISBN 0-313-29741-X.

This is not a reference book in the strictest sense of the word, rather it is a sociological and cultural survey of Korean Americans. Although the Library of Congress classifies it as history, only part 2 is concerned with the historical overview of Korean immigration to the United States.

This title is part of the publisher's The New Americans series and is "designed for high school and general readers who want to learn more about their new neighbors" (p. xiv). It is also suitable for undergraduate college students. The author is a professor of sociology at Western Illinois University who has written extensively on Korean Americans, ethnic and race relations, and comparative sociology. In 1984 he published *Korean Immigrants in America.* Hurh is a well-established and respected researcher and author in Korean American studies.

Part 1 introduces the reader to the Korean cultural heritage. Part 2 is a historical overview of Korean immigration to the United States. Part 3 is the longest section, examining Korean American adaptation and adjustment to American society. Part 4 emphasizes "Unique Characteristics of Korean Americans and Their Impact on American Society." The appendix lists "Notable Korean Americans" in 3½ pages. Sections containing references and further reading, both unannotated, follow. There are 11 black-and-white photographs and one map as well as statistical tables and figures. Some of the statistics are rather dated, and many of the photographs and statistics emphasize the Korean American experience in Chicago. Special features include an emphasis on the uniqueness of Korean Americans in comparison with other Asian Americans and other minority groups, plus the effective use of personal narratives throughout the text.

Hurh's book successfully summarizes important historical, socioeconomic, and cultural information about Korean Americans in an authoritative manner and in an easy-to-read style. Thus it is a valuable and needed addition to current Korean American studies.—**Marshall E. Nunn**

Blacks

375.   Bute, E. L., and H. J. P. Harmer. **The Black Handbook: The People, History, and Politics of Africa and the African Diaspora.** Herndon, Va., Mansell/Cassell, 1997. 392p. index. $24.95pa. ISBN 0-304-33543-6.

Attempting to assemble in a single volume a dictionary and a handbook that describes "the key events, personalities, ideas, facts and figures of historical and contemporary Africa and the African Diaspora," Bute and Harmer create a somewhat satisfactory bridgework between basic references on African and African American history and politics. Patrons should note, however, that "Africa" here means Africa south of the Sahara (thus, no entries on Egypt, Nubia, or Somalia). The "Diaspora" is limited to the United States, United Kingdom, and the Caribbean, with no mention of South America or Canada. This factor is especially disheartening in light of such recent works as Junius Rodriguez's *Historical Encyclopedia of World Slavery* (see entry 531) and Ronald Segal's *Black Diaspora* (Farrar, Straus & Giroux, 1995). Entries often seem haphazardly chosen—12 hurricanes are included, but Wole Soyinka and Chiekh Diop are absent.

The arrangement also proves problematic. Brief entries (15 to 100 words) fall into 1 of 3 chapters: "People"; "Places and Events"; and "Terms, Movements, and Ideas." However, additional chapters include "Colonialism," "Countries," and "Political Parties and Leaders," with a final chronology. With overlapping categories, one must use the index to locate what is needed. The authors also do not provide any bibliographic information or illustrative material. Despite its flaws, however, *The Black Handbook* is an inexpensive source of non-U.S. historical and political information that most public and academic libraries will find useful. [R: Choice, Feb 98, p. 976]—**Anthony J. Adam**

376.   **Contemporary Black Biography, Volume 16: Profiles from the International Black Community.**
Shirelle Phelps, ed. Detroit, Gale, 1998. 297p. illus. index. $55.00. ISBN 0-7876-1225-1.

The latest volume in this excellent series follows the same guidelines as earlier numbers: 60 alphabetically arranged 4-page biographical profiles of important and influential people of African heritage in a wide variety of fields, including the arts, sports, business, politics, and education. Patrons should be aware that "contemporary" does not necessarily mean "living" in this series; one entrant died in 1954. Each essay includes a photograph of the subject, a section titled "At a Glance" for basic data, a signed essay, and a brief primary and secondary bibliography. Many of the essays also list Websites for additional information. This series is designed for general users, much like H. W. Wilson's Current Biography series and as such is suitable for inclusion in public, high school, and academic libraries. As with earlier volumes, the volume at hand concludes with separate indexes for nationalities, occupations, cumulative names, and subjects. Volume 16 will be a welcome addition to libraries for its subjects, which include Muhammad Ali, dancer George Faison, Air Force Major General Marcelite Jordan Harris, and Tanzanian President Benjamin Mkapa. Most libraries will want to purchase the entire series to provide comprehensive access to patrons.—**Anthony J. Adam**

377.   **Index to Black Periodicals 1997.** Thorndike, Maine, G. K. Hall/Macmillan, 1998. 474p. $295.00. ISBN 0-7838-0079-7. ISSN 0899-6253.

The *Index to Black Periodicals* (IBP), under various titles since 1950, was often the only indexing source for articles from black periodicals and thus a vital resource especially for black college libraries. However, other major publishers (e.g., H. W. Wilson and UMI) now feature these titles in their products. For example, of the 34 periodicals listed in the 1997 IBP, 21 (62 percent) are also indexed in *UMI's Periodical Abstracts*, which includes more than 600 periodicals. These 21 titles are commonly found in most libraries: *Jet, Ebony*, and *Black Scholar*. IBP does include more obscure titles, such as *Headway, Black Renaissance*, and *Muslim Journal*, but the hefty price of this index must be weighed against the need for other resources. Additionally, IBP 1997 surprisingly does not index MELUS, NBA Bulletin, NMA Journal, *Black American Literature Forum, Black Elegance, Black Collegian*, or the *Black Music Research Journal*, to name a few. Subject headings are also problematic. Articles on historically black colleges, for example, are under "Universities and Colleges, Black." It is much simpler to locate articles on most topics through electronic services than through IBP. The paper index is disappearing as a modern research tool, and perhaps IBP would do best to move to an electronic format or rethink its scope for research institutions. This index is recommended only for comprehensive collections.—**Anthony J. Adam**

378.   Rodgers, Marie E. **The Harlem Renaissance: An Annotated Reference Guide for Student Research.**
Englewood, Colo., Libraries Unlimited, 1998. 139p. illus. index. $28.00. ISBN 1-56308-580-1.

Rodgers's work, designed for students in grades 7 through 12 as a general introduction to the period 1920 to 1933, is the first annotated bibliography to cover all fields—music, sports, film, dance—rather than literature alone (e.g., Margaret Perry's *Harlem Renaissance* [Garland, 1982]). That being the case, even college librarians and teachers will find this work useful to a degree.

Each section features brief biographies of significant contributors to the field (e.g., Aaron Douglas in "art"), followed by a 10- to 20-item annotated bibliography of books, articles, and videos theoretically understandable at the given age level. Whether a 12th grade student will understand or be willing to read some of these sources is debatable, but Rodgers has, overall, chosen essential secondary materials that elucidate the period. However, the general format is confusing. For example, Jessie Fauset is covered under "Women," "Major Influences," and "Literature," and Rodgers repeats the Sylvander citation on her in the first two categories but not the third. Indeed, it is fairly easy to find duplicate citations under different categories for the same individual; a different general arrangement, or perhaps cross-references, would have helped.

Although no other work designed for grades 7 through 12 covers this same period, teachers and librarians should consult the excellent *African-American Encyclopedia* (see ARBA 94, entry 402), now in eight volumes, for general and specific information. Of additional interest, but difficult to find, is the National Alliance of Black School Educators' *Blueprints for Teaching and Learning about the Harlem Renaissance* (NABSE, 1994), a collection of essays on aspects of the period. *The Harlem Renaissance* is recommended for all high school and college libraries. [R: BL, 1 Sept 98, pp. 159-160; Choice, Nov 98, p. 492, 494]—**Anthony J. Adam**

379. **Who's Who Among African Americans 1998/99.** 10th ed. Shirelle Phelps, ed. Detroit, Gale, 1997. 1839p. index. $140.00. ISBN 0-7876-0109-8. ISSN 1081-1400.

Published by Gale Research since the 6th edition, this race-based series in its present edition covers more than 20,000 African Americans eligible for inclusion by virtue of election or appointment to office, notable career achievements, or outstanding community service. Some African Americans who are not U.S. citizens but contribute substantially to American life are also included. However, although data have obviously been updated, the overall number of entries has not changed since the 8th edition (see ARBA 95, entry 415). As with many biographical publications, nominees provide data for inclusion to the editors; for nonrespondents, the editors cull secondary sources for entries. This resource uses the standard format of most "Who's Who" publications (e.g., personal data, career highlights, address), but the current edition unfortunately drops the lengthy abbreviations table found in earlier editions. The editors at Marquis, however, should take note of the excellent geographic (subdivided by city) and occupational indexes that conclude the Gale editions. A separate, brief section of obituaries is also included after the main entry section. As many of these individuals may not be found in Marquis's and other publications, all libraries will benefit from investing in the current volume. *Who's Who Among African Americans* is also available online through LEXIS-NEXIS as part of the Gale Biographies file.—**Anthony J. Adam**

Gypsies

380. Kenrick, Donald, with Gillian Taylor. **Historical Dictionary of the Gypsies (Romanies).** Lanham, Md., Scarecrow, 1998. 231p. (European Historical Dictionaries, no.27). $55.00. ISBN 0-8108-3444-8.

The title of this work is a bit misleading because this book includes information on all the clans and language groups of this region, not just the Romany speakers, and is limited only to Europe. However, this is unquestionably the only such source currently available.

Topics covered include languages and dialects, organizations, technical terms, laws, and people. In addition to items specific to the Gypsies, there are also many entries for related items, such as celebrities with some Gypsy ancestry. The typical entry is about 50 to 150 words long, except for the national entries, which tend to be several pages. Although there is no documentation with the individual articles, there is an extensive bibliography.

The main arrangement is alphabetic, with terms, places, and names interfiled. Although there is no index, an extensive cross-referencing system nearly makes up for the lack. Additional features include a detailed chronology, current estimates of Gypsy and traveler populations, and a brief summary of recent international resolutions concerning Gypsies.

Because there is considerable confusion about both Gypsies and travelers, along with continuing interest in the subject, this work may find use in nearly any sort of library. Given the lack of readily accessible information, however, it is most unfortunate that the entries are not better documented and provided with suggestions for further reading. Fortunately, Diane Tong's *Gypsies: A Multidisciplinary Annotated Bibliography* (see ARBA 96, entry 405) does provide such suggestions.—**James H. Sweetland**

Indians of North America

Bibliography

381. Holmes, Marie S., and John R. Johnson, comps. **The Chumash and Their Predecessors: An Annotated Bibliography.** Santa Barbara, Calif., Santa Barbara Museum of Natural History, 1998. 228p. index. (Santa Barbara Museum of Natural History Contributions in Anthropology, no.1). $32.50pa. ISBN 0-936494-28-X.

Unless one has Eugene N. Anderson's 1964 and 1978 annotated bibliographies on the Chumash (see ARBA 79, entry 773, for a review), there is no more comprehensive bibliography on the topic than this publication. This volume contains 1,177 annotated entries covering traditional publications and to a surprising degree includes environmental impact and cultural resources conservation reports (classic examples of "gray literature"). A random sample from Anderson's 1964 bibliography indicates all of his entries appear in this volume. The compilers state that 95 percent of the items cited are available either at the Santa Barbara Natural History Library; the Anthropology Department at the University of California, Santa Barbara; or the Institute of Archaeology at

UCLA. Entries are arranged in seven broad topics—ethnology and ethnohistory; rock art; linguistics; archaeology; physical anthropology; first contacts: 1542-1780; and education and juvenile. The two shortest sections are linguistics (60 entries) and educational and juvenile (25 entries). The latter section is unusual in a bibliography of this type, and there is an informative paragraph about possible classroom uses in the introduction. Entry annotations are generally short (1 or 2 sentences) descriptions; none are more than 300 words long. The compilers provide an 11-page bibliographic history of Chumash studies as well as a section listing reviews of many of the post-1960 publications included in the bibliography. Because there are no cross-references or *see* references in the bibliography itself, the author and subject indexes are very useful. This work is an excellent value for the price. [R: Choice, Nov 98, pp. 501-502]—**G. Edward Evans**

382.   Magnaghi, Russell M. **Indian Slavery, Labor, Evangelization, and Captivity in the Americas: An Annotated Bibliography.** Lanham, Md., Scarecrow, 1998. 557p. index. (Native American Bibliography Series, no.22). $110.00. ISBN 0-8108-3355-7.

In the introduction, the compiler of this extensive bibliography states, "The domination of the Indians of the Americas began in 1492 and continues in varying degrees of intensity down to the present. This bibliography focuses on the imposition of policies upon one people by an external government or another people, an imposition that shows itself in a number of forms." This statement succinctly presents the focus and content of this extraordinarily useful resource. The topics addressed in the book—slavery, Indian labor, religious acculturation, and captivity—are increasingly interesting to the general public as well as the scholar. Recently, the dark side of the Colombian encounter, westward expansion, and U.S. history have begun to surface, and this bibliography provides access to information, from multiple perspectives, that will add considerably to a more complete and objective understanding of our own history and of contemporary Native American issues.

The bibliography provides access to resources about these topics as they were implemented throughout the Americas, allowing the reader an opportunity to compare European attitudes and policies toward Indians through a variety of Eurocentric experiences and to study Indian responses to these impositions on their cultures. Because of the compiler's familiarity with many languages, English, French, Italian, Portuguese, and Spanish books and articles have been included. The annotations are generally one-sentence descriptions; however, when appropriate, further explanation is given. On occasion, an evaluative comment is made, leading the reader to resources that are important or critical in a particular area.

The book contains 8 major sections: "General Sources" (entries 1-90); "Native Experience" (entries 91-107); "Origins: Europe, Spain, Canary Islands" (entries 408-437); "Theory and Legal Aspects" (entries 438-579); "Latin America" (entries 580-2155); "United States and Canada" (entries 2156-3132); "Captivity" (entries 3133-3625); and "South Pacific Region" (entries 3626-3639). The 1st section, "General Sources," is particularly helpful as an introduction to these topics and includes bibliographies, indexes, manuscript guides, reference works, and texts. The 2d section, "Native Experience," deals with captivity and slavery prior to the European encounter and its intended to provide important background.

It is reasonable to conclude that this book provides a sorely needed reference for scholars and should be in the collections of academic libraries. However, there are resources cited that are written for a more general audience, and others who are interested in these particular topics will find accessible materials. The section on captivity, which seems quite exhaustive, is especially interesting; many are diaries or first-person accounts that have reached print. [R: Choice, Oct 98, p. 298]—**Karen D. Harvey**

383.   White, Phillip M., and Stephen D. Fitt. **Bibliography of the Indians of San Diego County.** Lanham, Md., Scarecrow, 1998. 313p. maps. (Native American Bibliography Series). $58.00. ISBN 0-8108-3325-5.

Similar in format to the other books in this publisher's Native American Bibliography Series, this work focuses on several indigenous peoples of southernmost California—the Diegueno, Luiseno, and Cupeno—known more commonly as Mission Indians. The 695 entries are largely organized around 34 subjects, including arts and crafts, biography, culture, folklore, and linguistics, with a separate section for archival and government materials. Archaeology, however, is deliberately not covered extensively. Books, theses and dissertations, journal articles, and conference papers are among the entries listed, and each is accompanied by an annotation, usually descriptive, running from one sentence to a paragraph. Citations are current through 1995. Author, title, and subject indexes are included. An added feature is a series of articles providing an overview of each of the Native American groups, and one on federal reservations in San Diego county. Both the entries and the articles are well written and informative. This bibliography is recommended for collections in anthropology, Native American studies, and western U.S. history.—**Jeff Wanser**

384.   White, Phillip M., comp. **The Native American Sun Dance Religion and Ceremony: An Annotated Bibliography.** Westport, Conn., Greenwood Press, 1998. 115p. index. (Bibliographies and Indexes in American History, no.37). $55.00. ISBN 0-313-30628-1.

White has published two previous bibliographies on Native Americans, one of which, *American Indian Studies: A Bibliographic Guide*, was reviewed in ARBA 96 (see entry 421). All many people know about the Sun Dance is what they saw in the series of movies *A Man Called Horse*. If those individuals did nothing more than read the introductory essay, they would begin to understand the significance of the Sun Dance as well as how different it was and is from the film portrayal. The 335 annotated entries are arranged by nation, using the names common among the general public rather than the Native American preferred name. Annotations are descriptive, with some quotations taken from the book or article. The length of the annotations range from two to three sentences in length to almost a full page. An average length is between 250 and 300 words, which is long enough to provide readers with sufficient information to decide if they want to secure the item. Scope of coverage is almost any printed material in English. Excluded are audiovisual materials, unpublished manuscripts, diaries, letters and personal papers, and novels.

One may think that 335 entries would exhaust English-language print material on the Sun Dance, and in fact, White states the bibliography is comprehensive. However, as anyone who has compiled a bibliography knows, one is never complete. In this case, there are several items that are not in the book; for example, Peter Bolz's article "Ethnic Identity and Cultural Resistance" and Raymond DeMellie's *Sioux Indian Religion* (University of Oklahoma Press, 1989) are missing. However, without question, this is the most complete single source for references on Sun Dance, making it a worthwhile addition to any collection serving Native Americans or those who have an interest in Native American studies. [R: Choice, Dec 98, p. 666]—**G. Edward Evans**

385.   Wolf, Carolyn. **Indians of North and South America, Second Supplement: A Bibliography Based on the Collection at the Willard E. Yager Library....** Lanham, Md., Scarecrow, 1997. 492p. index. $59.50. ISBN 0-8108-3301-8.

In 1977, Scarecrow Press published Wolf's *Indians of North and South America* (see ARBA 78, entry 682), a bibliography of library resources at Hartwick College, Oneonta, New York. In 1988 the first supplement (see ARBA 89, entry 365) documented the growth of the collection. The present volume covers new acquisitions from 1987 to 1995.

The main listing contains 3,495 items, including books, periodical articles, doctoral dissertations and master's theses, and major collections in microform—including pamphlets and archival materials. The listing is, in general, by Library of Congress' "main entries" (i.e., it is alphabetic by author, but collections of essays are listed by titles rather than by editors and the names of editors of collections are given in cross-references). There are indexes for titles, series, subjects, and tribes cited as well as for names of caves, mounds, reservations, and archaeological sites.

In spite of the book's title, it appears that Hartwick College's recent acquisitions include relatively little on Indians of Latin America. The usefulness of the volume will be primarily for on-site research and interlibrary loans on the native peoples of the United States and Canada.—**William Bright**

Biography

386.   Sonneborn, Liz. **A to Z of Native American Women.** New York, Facts on File, 1998. 228p. illus. index. (Encyclopedia of Women). $27.95. ISBN 0-8160-3580-6.

There is substantial overlap between this volume and Gretchen Bataille's *Native American Women: A Biographical Dictionary* (see ARBA 94, entry 956). This volume contains 101 biographies, whereas Bataille's volume contains 231. Anyone making a quick comparison might think that there were at least 25 entries in this volume that do not exist in the Bataille guide. However, if one is familiar with the variations in Native American names and how one might organize them, the list of "unique" biographies drops to 12. A comparison of individuals that appear in both titles—for example, Jeanine Pease-Windy Boy—shows the similarities and differences between the two books. In this volume the entry is under "Pretty-on-Top, Janine Pease" rather than the more frequently seen "Pease-Windy Boy." Both entries are roughly the same length; however, there is more recent information in this volume—in this case her being awarded a 1994 MacArthur Fellowship. Sonneborn's selections are primarily a mix of nineteenth- and twentieth-century women, and roughly one-third of those are living today. There are 11 entries for women born before 1800. Her introductory essay, which is a concise discussion of the role of Native American women, does not indicate what her basis for selection was. One cannot quarrel with the list she has, but one does wonder how she decided who to include and why just 101 individuals. There is an index for a person's primary activity (e.g., poet, lawyer), another by tribal affiliation, a year of birth index, as well as a general index. (This is also similar to the Bataille volume.) There are a number of *see* references that are essential in addressing the issue of variant names mentioned above. Given the relatively modest price, medium- and large-sized Native American collections should have this title, if nothing more than for the most current information on those who are still alive. [R: LJ, Aug 98, p. 80; Choice, Dec 98, p. 670]—**G. Edward Evans**

Chronology

387.   Swisher, Karen Gayton, and AnCita Benally. **Native North American Firsts.** Detroit, Gale, 1998. 263p. illus. index. $44.95. ISBN 0-7876-0518-2.

As a new entry among the now numerous reference volumes that discuss North American Indians, this book offers a view of Native North American history in a novel format. The main text is organized alphabetically by topic, including "Arts, Crafts, and Design," "Business and Economics," "Sports and Games," among others. Under each topic, the 1,500 entries are chronologically arranged; for example, under "Sports," the first entry is 1897, the date when Louis Sockalexis (a Penobscot from Maine) became the first American Indian to sign with a major league baseball team. Most of the entries are, in fact, mini-biographies of individuals who contributed to Native American history in their respective fields; the information given is based on earlier reference volumes. Coverage is good, including Native Alaskans and Native Canadians; a smaller number of entries refer to Indians of Mexico, Central America, and South America.

The volume provides cross-references, a bibliography, a "Calendar of Firsts" organized by month and date, and an index by year. A general index also provides easy access to the names of individuals whose achievements are chronicled. The book is attractively designed and is illustrated with numerous photographs.

Unfortunately, the work shows signs of haste in preparation, including a fair number of editorial and typographical errors. A few entries have drawn uncritically on their sources. Nevertheless, the book is enjoyable for browsing and will be a useful reference, especially for students of Native American background in secondary schools and colleges.—**William Bright**

Dictionaries and Encyclopedias

388.   **The Encyclopedia of Native American Legal Tradition.** Bruce Elliott Johansen, ed. Westport, Conn., Greenwood Press, 1998. 410p. index. $95.00. ISBN 0-313-30167-0.

Edited by Bruce Elliot Johansen with contributions by members of academia, a Native American judge, and a leader of a Native American tribe, the book is a smattering of many Native American nation's legal and political systems; major Native American law cases, treaties, and congressional acts; profiles of key players; and issues of related interest. Within these pages one can find a diverse collection of information—the history of the Native American Bar Association; details of major treaties; a description of the *Worcester vs. Georgia* decision; a comprehensive outline of Micmaq constitutional law; a definition of natural man and woman; and a profile of Andrew Jackson.

The book itself is arranged alphabetically with highlighted words cross-referencing other related entries. At the end of most of the entries, there are books listed for further reading. If that does not whet the appetite, additional readings are also found in a selected bibliography in the back of the book, along with the index. Although the work does not have many illustrations, this reviewer found it really did not matter. The interesting entries do more to keep one entertained than do most pictures.

The Encyclopedia of Native American Legal Tradition is an excellent addition to Native American studies, law, and U.S. history collections. Anyone studying law, U.S. history, and Native American studies will find it of interest. This work is highly recommended. [R: Choice, July/Aug 98, p. 1837]—**Kelly M. Jordan**

389.   **The Gale Encyclopedia of Native American Tribes.** Sharon Malinowski, Anna Sheets, Jeffrey Lehman, and Melissa Walsh Doig, eds. Detroit, Gale, 1998. 4v. illus. maps. index. $349.00/set. ISBN 0-7876-1085-2.

Celebrate this new resource; it is exceptionally convenient, comprehensive, appropriately respectful of the common as well as the diverse attributes of Native American people and cultures, and is a treasure for those interested in the cultures of our indigenous people. For an encyclopedia of this type, it is especially important to understand both its organization (convenience and usefulness) and the values (respect and accuracy) that guide its development.

Organized into 4 volumes, the encyclopedia includes essays about approximately 400 Native American tribal groups. Written for public, high school, and academic libraries, the organization follows the common and important structure of geographic or cultural regions: Northeast, Southeast, Caribbean, Great Basin, Southwest, Middle America, Arctic, Subarctic, Great Plains, Plateau, California, Pacific Northwest, and Pacific Islands. For 10 of the major areas (Caribbean, Middle America, and Pacific Islands are excluded) a regional overview is provided. The following various sections in each essay are uniformly set apart for easy reference and comparison: introduction (tribal name, pronunciation of the name, location, and language family); history; religion; language; buildings; subsistence; clothing and adornment; healing practices; customs; oral literature; current tribal issues; and bibliography and further reading. There are more than 200 biographical profiles, 650 illustrations, and detailed maps included in the 4 volumes. Basic information and a brief timeline of important events in tribal history, in boxed formats, are included in each essay. The oral literature section, which generally provides an excerpt of a tribal story, is particularly appealing and gives a sense of wholeness to these tribal overviews. The biographies are also important for they highlight not only historical figures, but contemporary Native American leaders in a variety of fields. In addition, each of the 4 volumes contains a cumulative general index of tribes, Native people, pertinent non-Native people, wars and battles, treaties and important legislation, reservations, Native groups and associations, religious groups, lists of federally recognized tribes in the United States and Canada, volume-specific tables of contents, and a cumulative table of contents for the entire series.

The dedication to authenticity and respect for Native American people and their cultures is to be admired. The series was directed by a multicultural board with extensive involvement of Native American scholars and leaders, and the editors have attempted to ensure that the material is "objective yet sensitive to tribal communities, and not solely representative of the perspective of the dominant society." Native authors and scholars have written and reviewed these essays, and some were submitted to scholars in the field who were asked to review them. Other essays were sent to tribal councils for review. The tribal affiliation is noted when the author of an essay is Native American. It is noted that photographs that captured sacred or secret practices were not used. This resource is accessible and well structured for high school students seeking information for class assignments and is an excellent starting point for more sophisticated general research into Native American history and cultures. [R: BL, 1 Sept 98, pp. 158-159; Choice, Oct 98, p. 296]—**Karen D. Harvey**

390.   Pritzker, Barry M. **Native Americans: An Encyclopedia of History, Culture, and Peoples.** Santa Barbara, Calif., ABC-CLIO, 1998. 2v. illus. index. $150.00/set. ISBN 0-87436-836-7.

These large-format volumes constitute a new addition to the many reference works already available on North American Native people. They aim to present information on the native people of the United States and Canada—American Indian, Eskimo, and Aleut—including notes on traditional cultures, on history with white people, and on present-day legal and social status. Organization is in terms of 10 geographic and cultural areas; within each of these tribes are listed geographically. However, the work illustrates the dangers that lie in wait when a large reference work is prepared by a single person with less than encyclopedic knowledge of the topic. The result here is that factual errors are found on virtually every page.

At the end of volume 2, there are several supplementary sections. One is a glossary of a mere four pages, with some strikingly inept definitions. The three-page bibliography includes only books of general coverage, but nothing on individual tribes. Three appendixes list native communities in Canada and Alaska.

Positive features that can be noted about the work include handsome design and typography, well-chosen photographs, and a good index. However, one should not go to these volumes in the hope of finding reliable information. [R: LJ, Dec 98, p. 94; BL, 1 Dec 98, p. 700]—**William Bright**

Directories

391.   **Native American Information Directory.** 2d ed. Kenneth Estell, ed. Farmington Hills, Mich., Gale, 1998. 372p. index. $95.00. ISBN 0-8103-9116-3. ISSN 1063-9632.

The updated 2d edition of this useful directory lists more than 4,400 resources pertaining to the indigenous peoples of the United States and Canada. The 5 main sections of the book deal with Native American Indians in the contiguous 48 states of the United States; Alaska natives (e.g., Indians, Eskimos, and Aleuts); native Hawaiians; aboriginal Canadians (e.g., Indians, Inuits, and Métis); and "General Resources." Within each of these, subsections are devoted to categories that include tribal communities and associations, cultural organizations, government agencies and programs, library collections and research centers, education programs and services, publishing outlets, video outlets, and online databases. Individual entries give mailing addresses, telephone and fax numbers, and descriptive information.

In some subsections, entries are ordered alphabetically, but in others the arrangement is either not alphabetic or information is not represented at all. However, all entries are numbered and can be accessed through the accurate and complete index at the end of the book. For researchers in current Native American affairs, this directory should be an indispensable tool.—**William Bright**

Handbooks and Yearbooks

392.   **The Cambridge History of the Native Peoples of the Americas. Volume 1: North America, Part 1.** Bruce G. Trigger and Wilcomb E. Washburn, eds. New York, Cambridge University Press, 1996. 564p. index. $40.00. ISBN 0-521-34440-9.

This book is part 1 (of 2 parts) in volume 1 (of 3 volumes), which is intended to "synthesize existing knowledge" (p. xiii) in order to provide "the first comprehensive history of the Native peoples of North America from earliest times to the present" (p. xix). The editors are a Canadian anthropologist and a U.S. historian, respectively.

Part 1 begins with chapters on native views of history and native peoples in Euro-American historiography, followed by 3 archaeological chapters that deal in turn with hunter-gatherer cultures, native farmers, and "agricultural chiefdoms of the Eastern Woodlands." Chapter 6 discusses the early encounter of Native North Americans with Europeans in the sixteenth century. The last two chapters in part 1 begin a sequence, to be continued in part 2, that presents ethno-historical findings on different geographical areas, beginning with the east coast of North America and with the Mississippi Valley. Each chapter ends with a useful "bibliographic essay." There is a general index, but no unified bibliographical listing.

All the chapters are written by acknowledged experts, and each is packed with authoritative information. However, a possible criticism is that the authors do little more than mention the relevance of research on Native American languages. To be sure, one archaeologist acknowledges that "glottochronology," a technique that was supposed to permit dating of prehistoric languages, is now largely discredited. But he goes on to posit early linguistic connections that are at best controversial among specialists. Still later, the same writer seems to accept glottochronology uncritically, and takes for granted several dubious linguistic groupings in his discussion of prehistoric peoples. Other contributors to the book barely mention the Native languages. An extra chapter, giving a balanced treatment of the linguistic prehistory of North America, would have made a valuable addition to this book. [R: LJ, 1 May 97, p. 94]—**William Bright**

393.   Heard, J. Norman. **Handbook of the American Frontier: Four Centuries of Indian-White Relationships. Volume V: Chronology, Bibliography, Index.** Lanham, Md., Scarecrow, 1998. 233p. index. (Native American Resources Series, no.1). $59.50. ISBN 0-8108-3283-6.

For those libraries that have purchased the first 4 volumes of this set, this index volume is now available. It has been a long wait—volume 1 appeared in 1987 (see ARBA 89, entry 354). Reviews of the intervening volumes appeared in ARBA 92 (see entry 367), ARBA 95 (see entry 440), and ARBA 98 (see entry 357). Heard's entries in the first 4 volumes are filled with useful information, and now that the index is available one can see the true reference value of the set. Volume 5 consists of a 65-page chronology of white-Native people relations, a 20-page bibliography, and a 165-page index. The chronology begins with the year 1513 and Ponce de Leon's landing near the mouth of the St. James River in Florida and ends with the 1918 defeat of the Yaqui by U.S. Cavalry near Nogales, Arizona. The bibliography is the list of books Heard consulted in the process of preparing the entire set. The most important aspect is, of course, the detailed index. Here one finds references as well as *see* references to several thousand personal, place, and tribal names (assuming an average of 50 terms per page, there are well over 8,000 entries). Given the wealth of material contained in the 4 volumes, one might wish for greater topical indexing—there are some entries but not many. However, had the author provided the same level of detail as he did for names, there might have been a much longer wait for the index. This is an essential purchase for any library with the earlier volumes.—**G. Edward Evans**

Jews

394.   **Jewish Women in America: An Historical Encyclopedia.** Paula E. Hyman and Deborah Dash Moore, eds. New York, Routledge, 1997. 2v. illus. index. $250.00/set. ISBN 0-415-91936-3.

Studies of Jewish women in America gain a necessary reference with the publication of these two volumes. Subtitled "An Historical Encyclopedia," the work is mainly composed of biographical entries of figures both living and dead (800 in all) and 110 topical entries. Each biographical entry extends for at least two columns, and several, such as the one for Betty Friedan, extend for several pages. The entries include a separate heading for works by the figures and a bibliography of works about the figure. Many of the biographies are accompanied by impressive photographs of the figures. The kinds of women found in the encyclopedia are mainly drawn from national politics, popular letters, music, and film. One can find many entries in the volumes for notables not included in reference works such as *Dictionary of Jewish Biography* (see ARBA 92, entry 381) and *Jewish-American History and Culture: An Encyclopedia* (see ARBA 93, entry 442).

More than serving as a Jewish women's "who's who," however, these volumes hold special significance for the topical entries. Although it may appear that the scales between the topical entries and biographies could have been tipped even more toward the topical entries, as they were, for example, in *Jewish-American History and Culture*, the attention to women's roles and perspectives make important contributions to Jewish studies, American studies, and women's studies. In penetrating entries such as "Advertising and Consumer Culture" (by Andrew R. Heinze), "Leisure and Recreation" (by Jenna Weissman Joselit), and "Peace Movement" (by Sherry Gorelick), users gain an accessible set of interpretations to place the biographical entries in historical and socio-logical contexts. The volumes have indexing features that users will find welcome. An alphabetic list of entries precedes the 1st volume, and the 2d volume contains an annotated bibliography and guide to archival resources. The editors include biographical notes on the contributors in a separate section. They help users tremendously with inclusion of a classified list of biographical entries in addition to a general index. [R: RBB, 15 Jan 98, p. 862]
—**Simon J. Bronner**

395.   Scheindlin, Raymond P. **A Short History of the Jewish People: From Legendary Times to Modern Statehood.** New York, Macmillan General Reference/Simon & Schuster Macmillan, 1998. 274p. illus. maps. index. $22.95. ISBN 0-02-862586-2.

With more than 3,000 years of existence, writing a short history of the Jews would appear to be an impossible task. Rabbi Scheindlin has succeeded in providing an excellent overview by discussing the dominant communities of each historical period. He reads the Bible and historical sources critically to create an objective view of the major events and personalities that have shaped the Jewish people.

Taking a chronological approach, the chapters begin with the Israelite origins before 1220 B.C.E. and continue to the present. Each chapter begins with a timeline showing events in Jewish history along with those in general history. There are maps to explain the locations and movements of the various Jewish communities. Black-and-white photographs of places and artifacts bring the text to life. Sidebars contain supplemental infor-mation on topics such as the city of Safed; Jewish businesswomen; and Talmud, Midrash, and Piyyut. The author discusses the importance and contributions of the often neglected Sephardic and Middle Eastern

(Mizrahi) communities. He explains that Jews interact with the cultures of the nations in which they live. They manage to retain their unique identity while adapting to new homes.

This small volume is a fine introduction to Jewish history. A bibliography provides sources for further study. Although the book is best suited to circulating collections, small public, school, and synagogue libraries may use it as a reference source.—**Barbara M. Bibel**

396.   **Two Jews, Three Opinions: A Collection of 20th-Century American Jewish Quotations.** Sandee Brawarsky and Deborah Mark, eds. New York, Perigee Books/Putnam, 1998. 575p. index. $24.95. ISBN 0-399-52449-5.

With 18,000 entries, Joseph Baron's *A Treasury of Jewish Quotations* has had the fitting reputation as the main household and library reference tool on Jewish quotations, but American Jewry has greatly changed since its 1956 publication. This twentieth-century niche is nicely filled by Brawarsky and Mark's *Two Jews, Three Opinions*. Ranging from quotes from Goldie Hawn's lines in *Private Benjamin* to comments of Henry Kissinger on Israeli-Palestinian relations, the editors have assembled a wonderful collection of wit and intelligence from contemporary North American Jews, along with quotes by a few Israelis, European Jews, and President Bill Clinton. Their definition of who is a Jew is wide enough to include the late Allen Ginsberg and others who identify with a cultural Jewish identity. The more than 2,000 quotations represent the contrast of American Jewry and include Hasidic and secular Jewish voices on issues from sex to Israel, although the topics and quotes tend to reflect more of a cultural identification than theological issues. This topicality is welcome on major issues, such as the Pollard case and black-Jewish relations, but the two pages on the O. J. Simpson trial seemed a bit extravagant from a historical perspective. Still, these twentieth-century additions are often fun to read and help one ponder how much has changed since Baron's treasury. In this sense, *Two Jews, Three Opinions* will be an excellent companion to its predecessors.

As a reference book, however, one should note that the index only lists references to contributors. Also, in addition to the lack of an index to subjects, cross-references are only provided between related existing subject groupings. Citations also range in detail but usually include two or more works of biographical detail.

—**Andrew B. Wertheimer**

Latin Americans

397.   Gonzalez-Pando, Miguel. **The Cuban Americans.** Westport, Conn., Greenwood Press, 1998. 185p. illus. index. (The New Americans). $39.95. ISBN 0-313-29824-6.

The New Americans series from Greenwood Press seeks to introduce new, post-1965 immigrants to a general readership, examining the migration and settlement processes of different national groups. Gonzalez-Pando's volume, *The Cuban Americans*, provides a readable and rich narrative of the experience of immigrants from this Caribbean nation. Although the author's own political leanings inevitably surface throughout the text, the book offers a good basic introduction to the study of Cuban immigrants in the United States.

Following the general format designed by the series editor, the author provides an overview of the genesis of Cuban immigration; a period account of the development of the Cuban American community in South Florida; and thematic chapters on economic achievements, cultural and national identity politics, and the development of involvement in more formal political participation. The book's appendix contains an annotated listing of notable Cuban Americans, a chronology of Cuban immigration, a brief set of statistics, and a short bibliography.

The greatest strength of this work is the frequent integration of oral histories into the narrative, allowing the voices of Cuban immigrants to speak for themselves. However, the author has drawn primarily from interviews with prominent and powerful Cuban Americans, and seems to offer little material from ordinary Cubans whose experiences may be more representative of this group's experience. The chapters on cultural and national identity and on politics are impressively balanced and provide original insight into the complex experience of Cuban Americans, countering prevailing simplistic stereotypes of this group's conservative politics.

Although the author notes that the Cuban American community has become increasingly diverse in its racial and class composition, it would have been useful to develop this theme more fully. The statistical information provided is minimal, especially when compared to other volumes in the New Americans series. More data on the educational, economic, and racial profile of the Cuban American community would enhance this book's usefulness as a general reference and facilitate comparison with the experiences of other national immigrant groups. The author also focuses almost exclusively on Miami. Although this is clearly the heart of Cuban American settlement in the United States, other major centers of residence such as Union City, New Jersey, warrant more coverage.

Despite these shortcomings, *The Cuban Americans* fills a gap in the extensive scholarship on Cubans in the United States by providing an informative text appropriate for secondary school and general audiences. This volume should go far in fulfilling the series' goals of introducing and increasing understanding of the United States' newest immigrant groups. [R: BR, Nov/Dec 98, p. 80; SLJ, Oct 98, p. 154; VOYA, Dec 98, p. 380]

—**Pamela M. Graham**

398.   **Handbook of Latin American Studies: Social Sciences, Number 55.** Dolores Moyano Martin and P. Sue Mundell, eds. Austin, Tex., University of Texas Press, 1997. 928p. index. $85.00. ISBN 0-292-75211-3. ISSN 0072-9833.

The *Handbook of Latin American Studies* (HLAS) is devoted to the social sciences (anthropology, economics, geography, government and politics, international relations, and sociology), with alternating volumes devoted to the humanities. The closing date for works annotated in this volume was early 1995. Publications received and cataloged at the Library of Congress after that date will be annotated in the next social sciences volume, HLAS 57. Although this is an excellent source for Latin American studies, there is still a concern for its timeliness with such a lengthy time between the compilation of the data and its publication. However, as of December 1996 all bibliographic records corresponding to HLAS volumes 1-58 are available at no charge to those with a graphical browser such as Netscape and WebExplorer, as well as those using the nongraphical browser LYNX. The URL for HLAS Online is http://lcweb2.loc.gov/hlas/. With the implementation of electronic access to the HLAS, one would expect that the issue of the currency of the information would be resolved.

As for improvements to the print volume itself, a new chapter, "Electronic Resources," inaugurated in HLAS 54, will now be included in each volume. This constantly changing and rapidly advancing field calls for a separate chapter written by a specialist in this area. As stated by the author of this chapter, the electronic sector will continue the promising and exciting transformations examined in HLAS 54, with new resources from and about Latin America posting especially dramatic gains. Fortunately, due to numerous major products newly available on compact disc or via the Internet, social science offerings are unquestionably stronger than they were two years ago, despite the demise of one premier Latin Americanist database. Recent additions of note to this chapter include the *International Bibliography of Social Sciences*, with coverage of worldwide journal literature dating back to 1981, and *International Political Science Abstracts* (IPSA). IPSA fills a long-standing need for a comprehensive political science electronic resource, providing global coverage of articles drawn from more than 2,000 journals, many of which are not treated by other databases. With additions such as these, one would expect this particular chapter to expand greatly as time goes on.

As in previous volumes, the excellent subject and author indexes, title list of indexed journals, and list of abbreviations and acronyms make for easy use. This reviewer found the abbreviations lists of indexed journals to be extremely useful. With the inclusion of more than 5,000 entries, this volume of the *Handbook of Latin American Studies* continues to be a premier source of retrospective bibliographic information for anyone with an interest in Latin America.—**Judith A. Valdez**

7 Genealogy and Heraldry

GENEALOGY

Directories

399.   Dollarhide, William, and Ronald A. Bremer. **America's Best Genealogy Resource Centers.** Bountiful, Utah, Heritage Quest, 1998. 139p. maps. $15.95pa. ISBN 1-877677-90-6.

Because genealogists are among the most avid information seekers, reference volumes such as this one that locate new materials or facilitate access to known materials are always welcome. As the title implies, the work covers the best locations for genealogical materials in the United States. The "best," of course, are the opinions of the two authors and might be disputed by other genealogists, but both seem well qualified for making the selections. They are recognized genealogists who have written and lectured extensively, but perhaps more importantly, they have personally visited and surveyed more than 3,000 collections in their travels throughout the country. From these they made their selection of some 600 resource centers they considered the best.

The main text of this slim volume presents the top 10 resources in the country, described in some detail, followed by 1-page descriptions of resources in each state. A few states are divided, with separate pages for different areas, as for northern and southern California or New York City and outside the city. Facing the resource page is a full-page outline map of the state, with locations of the resources designated. These include federal, state, regional, and local collections that may be found in libraries, archives, historical societies, or museums. Included also are a section describing the National Archives Regional Facilities and State Vital Statistics Offices, the latter specifying costs of birth, marriage, and death records. There is no index to the volume, but the table of contents and simple arrangement seems to make one unnecessary.

Although there are other works that describe genealogical collections, this one is unique in that it lists only those resources that are considered the most useful and points out the importance of the collections. It might have been helpful to list fax numbers and Website addresses when available, in addition to the regular directorial information. The volume is a worthwhile source for any libraries serving genealogists and would be particularly useful to those planning to visit various genealogical collections.—**Lucille Whalen**

400.   Weiner, Miriam. **Jewish Roots in Poland: Pages from the Past and Archival Inventories.** New York, YIVO Institute for Jewish Research and Secaucus, N.J., Miriam Weiner Routes to Roots Foundation, 1997. 446p. illus. maps. (Jewish Genealogy Series, v.1). $50.00. ISBN 0-96565-080-4.

One of the many changes coming from the end of the Cold War was the opening up of Polish archives. This opening is important to the many Jews whose ancestors once lived in Poland, and who have been trying to discover their history since the disruptions of mass migrations, pogroms, and the devastation of the Holocaust. Much of this historical search is done by individuals and groups of amateur genealogists. Until recently, this research was confined to Yizkor (community memorial) books and holdings of major Judaica archives, such as YIVO in New York and Yad Vashem in Jerusalem—and the microfilms collected at the Family History Library in Salt Lake City. Arthur Kuzweil's *From Generation to Generation: How to Trace Your Jewish Genealogy and Family* (HarperCollins, 1996) is still the best introduction to this first step in research. Until recently the serious researcher had no complete guide to plan a trip to Poland to see remaining archival records. Professional Jewish genealogist Weiner, co-editor of *The Encyclopedia of Jewish Genealogy* (Aronson, 1997), spent almost a decade working with the Polish State Archives and more than 500 other archives in Poland, Belarus, Lithuania, and Ukraine to discover some 6,000 Jewish and civic records for communities within Poland's current borders. These records are listed in order of community and again by depository. Archival holdings of concentration camp archives are also detailed.

Beyond this important key function, the work is also a handbook to conducting archival research and contains a descriptive bibliography and resource guide to Internet sources. It also is extremely well illustrated with more than 500 black-and-white and color photographs of synagogues, cemeteries, and maps, along with reproductions of sample official documents of Jewish life in Poland. Weiner has included a number of brief descriptions of activities by archives that will be of interest to readers, but somewhat less useful as a ready-reference tool because there is no index. The author also admitted that some of the archival information is not complete. These comments should be taken as suggestions for a 2d edition rather than as rationale for libraries not to purchase this important guide, which will be received with much interest in many communities. One can only hope that this series will be joined by guides to records of other Jewish communities.—**Andrew B. Wertheimer**

Handbooks and Yearbooks

401.   Herber, Mark D. **Ancestral Trails: The Complete Guide to British Genealogy and Family History.** Baltimore, Md., Genealogical Publishing, 1997. 674p. illus. index. $34.95. ISBN 0-8063-1541-5.

This impressive book is one that truly attempts to live up to its subtitle—complete guide. Herber is an attorney by profession who traces his own family and obviously knows how to lead the neophyte in the use of British records.

A beginner will find this work extremely useful, with its coverage of how to get started, including in-depth explanations of what to expect. More experienced researchers will be equally delighted with record descriptions, examples of documents, and up-to-date material about newly opened records and the movement of some records to new locations. Many British records are similar to their U.S. counterparts, but the terminology may be somewhat strange at the beginning. An exceptionally detailed index will guide the user to explanations and solutions. Chapter by chapter, the author does an admirable job of guiding any genealogist through the labyrinth of sometimes unfamiliar records.

Ancestral Trails is highly recommended to any person wishing to tackle research in British records and most certainly should become a part of any library's genealogical collection. [R: Choice, Sept 98, p. 82]

—**Carol Willsey Bell**

402.   Newman, John J. **American Naturalization Records 1790-1990: What They Are and How to Use Them.** 2d ed. Bountiful, Utah, Heritage Quest, 1998. 127p. $12.95pa. ISBN 1-877677-91-4.

This interesting guide to American naturalization records was originally published in 1985, and was updated in 1998. The author leads the user through the maze of available records, with numerous samples of types of documents. Among the useful topics covered are the naturalization laws from 1790 to 1906, and from 1906 to 1990. The record types created during these two time periods are quite different, and the laws determine what may be found. Other sections address the special records created when aliens served in the military or purchased land before becoming a citizen. An appendix defining selected terms is most useful, as is a more modern discussion on Internet sites.

This work is definitely a must for anyone needing to research naturalization records and for library genealogical collections. It would have been greatly enhanced if an index had been included.—**Carol Willsey Bell**

403.   **Printed Sources: A Guide to Published Genealogical Records.** Kory L. Meyerink, ed. Orem, Utah, Ancestry, 1998. 840p. index. $49.95. ISBN 0-916489-70-1.

This work begins with a useful how-to chapter, which is followed by 19 chapters devoted to subjects like family-local histories, journals, printed source records, bibliographies, censuses/tax lists, cemetery records, probate records, military sources, immigration records, and court and legal records. A final chapter on "medieval genealogy" focuses on the United Kingdom and is addressed to those sanguine enough to attempt to trace their family history back to, and then within, the Old World. Finally there are appendixes on CD-ROMs for family historians, major U.S. genealogical libraries, and genealogical publishers and booksellers. Each chapter opens with an overview orienting users to the riches that follow.

It can readily be seen that this is a remarkably comprehensive and up-to-date compilation. Even the OCLC database and the Internet are given substantial attention. Although there is a chapter on "ethnic sources," major attention is devoted to northern and western European backgrounds, with sources of African and Asian American genealogy mentioned largely in passing. Clearly this merely reflects the state of play in these fields, and highlighting the disparity might result in efforts to eliminate it. There is a 40-page index of considerable details, although titles in it are left unitalicized.

One cannot help but be impressed by the breadth and scope of this work. Not only will it benefit seasoned ancestor hunters but will allow those with newly acquired enthusiasm to make rapid progress—if its sheer magnitude leaves them undaunted. In this respect, the chapter on journals, especially the imposing list of "query magazines," is certain to facilitate the first steps in genealogical research as well the plethora of specific information such as addresses, telephone numbers, and Websites.

Printed Sources lives up to the description of *sine qua non*. Moreover, it shows that the recent trend in reference publishing in which word processing capabilities often substitute for informed human intervention, usually with depressing results, can be reversed. Happily, its price means that those who will need it will be able to acquire it with alacrity in the certainty that their investment will quickly be amortized in time saved and opportunities multiplied. More reference books should be like this. [R: LJ, Aug 98, p. 78]—**David Henige**

Indexes

404.   Biography and Genealogy Master Index 1999: A Consolidated Index to More Than 460,000 Biographical Sketches.... Geri Speace, ed. Farmington Hills, Mich., Gale, 1998. 1288p. (The Gale Biographical Index Series). $348.00. ISBN 0-7876-1272-3.

The *Biography and Genealogy Master Index 1999* includes more than 460,000 sketches in more than 100 biographical dictionaries. The sources used are both current and retrospective of many well-known titles containing sketches about people. Among some of the topics covered are literature, mathematics, playwrights, African Americans, and media and communications. Many of the biographical publications indexed are volumes regularly published by Gale Research, which announces that data are available from them in various formats: GALE NET, diskette/tape, CD-ROM, or online. This greatly facilitates the retrieval of information cited in the *Master Index*. This important volume in Gale's continuing series is a necessity in major library collections, and a welcome addition to the field of significant finding aids.—**Carol Willsey Bell**

405.   Index to U.S. Marriage Record, 1691-1850. [CD-ROM]. Bountiful, Utah, Heritage Quest, 1997. Minimum system requirements: IBM or compatible 486. Double-speed CD-ROM drive. Windows 95 or Windows 98. 16MB RAM. 15MB hard disk space. $39.95.

This CD-ROM contains the records of more than 500,000 marriages from 17 states and the District of Columbia that took place before 1850. The names of grooms and maiden names of brides are listed for a total of more than 1,000,000 names. Each entry includes groom, bride, marriage date, and county and state in which they were married. Every name is indexed so one can search for one name or two names that are linked. The CD-ROM comes with its own search engine, Word Cruncher, which allows for multiple searches of up to four words at a time. Boolean type modifiers permit complex search instructions. For each state there is a lengthy introductory text giving some history of the state's settlement and an explanation of its requirements for recording marriages, and the years covered for that state in this index.

The 12-page printed manual gives quick-start instructions for installing the software and running the program. More detailed directions are supposed to be available from the help menu once the program is installed on a computer, but this reviewer was unable to access this feature. Installation of the software was not difficult, although instructions in the manual often did not coincide with what appeared on the screen. For example, the manual tells the user to locate the table of contents in the search pull-down menu, but this is actually found in the view pull-down menu. This high concentration of vital records in one location is an invaluable resource for genealogists, who will undoubtedly make great use of it once the bugs are worked out and it is made more user-friendly.

—**Larry Lobel**

HERALDRY

406.   **Flags of the World.** Danbury, Conn., Grolier, 1998. 9v. illus. maps. index. $239.00/set. ISBN 0-7172-9159-6.

In nine 64-page volumes, Grolier presents 2-page spreads that include a full-page color map of a state, province, or nation and, facing it, information about the flags' color, shapes, symbols, and history. In addition, there is boxed information on key facts about the region's economy, currency, government, religion, language, customs, geography, main features, and people. The alphabetic arrangement is supported by a full index to the set at the conclusion of each sturdily bound volume.

The editors envision this set being used by young students who need to trace state and national emblems. Much of this information is available, in a smaller version, in encyclopedias intended for children, but the brief information on the origin of the flag seems to be in *World Book Encyclopedia* only (see ARBA 97, entry 48).

Elementary school libraries may find that the multivolume format is convenient if the curriculum calls for many students to obtain this information at one time, but this reviewer wonders whether a one- or two-volume work would not have made this same information more affordable.—**Vandelia L. VanMeter**

PERSONAL NAMES

407.   Norman, Teresa. **The African-American Baby Name Book.** New York, Berkley, 1998. 176p. $12.00pa. ISBN 0-425-15939-6.

The author of *A World of Baby Names* (Berkeley, 1996) has created another source of names, this one specifically for the African American community. The book lists more than 10,000 names, along with general advice on how to select one. Alphabetic entries (separate sections for male and female) include the country of origin and root language for each name, a brief definition, variant spellings, and frequently an example of a noted African American bearing the name. The book reflects the diversity of popular and contemporary names as well as the ethnic and religious names that celebrate black history and culture. The main competition may come from *The Complete Guide to African-American Baby Names* by Linda Wolfe Keister (Signet, 1998), which contains about 4,000 entries but has random commentary that is somewhat more extensive and interesting.

—**Jean Engler**

408.   Room, Adrian. **Dictionary of Pseudonyms.** 3d ed. Jefferson, N.C., McFarland, 1998. 404p. $55.00. ISBN 0-7864-0423-X.

The 1st edition of this fine reference work was published in 1981 under the title *Naming Names*. This is a revised and expanded version of that publication. The number of entries has doubled from the earlier edition to 8,000, and the stories behind many names have been updated through 1997. There are pseudonym dictionaries that list more entries, but they generally do not contain the engrossing and well-written comments describing the evolution of the names.

The entries are international in scope. In the preface, the author describes some of the latest additions— more magicians and mystics; a wider inclusion of Welsh bards; East European writers; cartoonists; and Italian singers, particularly the castrati who adopted the names of their patrons. Entries within the dictionary vary from a few lines, such as the entry for the Israeli archaeologist Yigael Yadin, to more than half a page, as in the entry for Greta Garbo. The entries include the real name, birth and death dates, country of origin, and the profession of the owner, in addition to the source of the pseudonym when known. Introductory chapters describe the selection of a pseudonym, names for a living, and how to make a name for yourself. The appendixes contain sections on pseudonyms used by Voltaire and Daniel Defoe, writers with multiple pen names, French official name changes, and real names that are sometimes confused as pseudonyms. The volume concludes with a bibliography of works on name changes.

The *Dictionary of Pseudonyms* is both scholarly and entertaining. The author of more than 40 reference books, Room has carefully researched sources and includes interesting stories from the lives of the people. Published with a library binding on alkaline paper, this dictionary is recommended for any reference collection. [R: LJ, 1 Oct 98, p. 78; Choice, July/Aug 98, p. 1826]—**Ingrid Schierling Burnett**

8 Geography and Travel Guides

GEOGRAPHY

General Works

Atlases

Canada

409. **Concise Historical Atlas of Canada.** William G. Dean, Conrad E. Heidenreich, Thomas F. McIlwraith, and John Warkentin, eds. Buffalo, N.Y., University of Toronto Press, 1998. 180p. maps. $85.00. ISBN 0-8020-4203-1.

This concise atlas is based on the 3-volume *Historical Atlas of Canada* (see ARBA 94, entry 458; ARBA 91, entry 516; and ARBA 88, entry 529). However, it is more of a simple edition, rather than a concise edition. No maps or graphs were reduced, nor the text abridged. Plates were copied verbatim, a number of which received a 5 percent cut in size. Also, many of the plate titles have been changed. The colors in the 3-volume edition are brighter than those in the concise edition. No new plates have been added to extend the coverage of the 3-volume edition beyond 1961.

The concise edition is arranged in three parts: "National Perspectives," "Defining Episodes," and "Regional Patterns," with additional topical subdivisions. Each part has an introductory essay. The text is in English. All notes and sources used appear at the end of the atlas. There is no index, a major flaw of both editions.

It is a better investment for libraries to acquire the excellent 3-volume edition for $285 rather than economize for the $85 concise edition. However, because most libraries may restrict the circulation of the 3-volume edition, the concise edition, if permitted to circulate, may be more useful for many library patrons.—**J. Carlyle Parker**

International

410. **Cartographic Satellite Atlas of the World.** Los Angeles, Calif., Warwick; distr. Willowdale, Ont., Firefly Books, 1997. 152p. illus. maps. index. $35.00. ISBN 1-895629-99-3.

This atlas of the world uses aerial photography and satellite imagery. The maps are composites of these images showing Earth in actuality. Elevation data are matched to space imagery and shaded relief applied to generate a three-dimensional look, and relief data of the ocean floor have been utilized in creating an effect of peering through the water to see the variations of terrain (or elevation) that exist under the vast seas that cover two-thirds of the planet. Helpful traditional cartography elements delineating the nonvisible components of the world, such as political boundaries and names of places and cities, have been placed over the photographs.

This fascinating account of our physical world is priceless because it is 100 percent accurate. The "what you see is what you get" photography shows the world in all its beauty and flaws. A few aerial maps of major metropolitan areas (i.e., Hong Kong, Chicago, and Istanbul) are included along with an infrared image of New York. But the main purpose of this atlas is to give a "space view" of the planet.

In reviewing these maps, one's preconceived perception of continents and islands will undoubtedly change. During this reviewer's excursions over the maps, it was noticed that the state of Nevada is more rugged than figured, South America is almost completely covered with vegetation, and the upper one-third of Africa is nearly all desert.

The wonderful thing about studying these maps is knowing they are absolute. They also effect an awareness of how humankind has always and continues to abuse and scar this miracle called Earth. Whether one's belief in the creation of our planet is based on faith or science, these images emphasize how small and fleeting one human life is in comparison.

Cartographic Satellite Atlas of the World is highly recommended for all libraries in all lands of all the world that is shown within. It is an amazing compilation and valuable geography resource. [R: Choice, July/Aug 98, p. 1828]—**Joan Garner**

411.   **DK Student Atlas.** New York, DK Publishing, 1998. 160p. illus. maps. index. $19.95. ISBN 0-7894-2399-5.

An excellent atlas for adults as well as students, this volume opens with an outstanding 24 pages that would be most helpful to anyone who is not familiar with atlases. Divided into 2 sections, "Learning Map Skills" and "The World," the book covers such topics as how maps are made, how to read them, how to use this particular atlas, the earth's structure, climates and life zones, and borders and boundaries. After this introductory material, the actual atlas opens with an excellent flat map of the world with all the nations, seas, and oceans clearly delineated. Each area of the world is then covered in separate sections, with larger continents broken down further into specific geographic areas. Each area covered contains a map of that area and various other thematic maps that represent such data as population concentrations, climate, food production, or other subjects deemed pertinent. Along with the maps are various bits of factual information, photographs, and charts. The front inside cover provides a key to regional maps and a map of the continents; those at the back display flags of the various nations.

Although necessity demands rather small print in many instances, the labeling of the maps and the layout of the pages is clear and user-friendly. A brief examination of the index found it to be accurate. Students should find most anything they need from an atlas in this well-thought-out resource, and educators will find the front matter to be an excellent guide for teaching students how to use atlases in general. This resource is recommended for all school and public libraries. [R: SLJ, Nov 98, p. 159; BL, 1 Sept 98, p. 153]—**Jo Anne H. Ricca**

412.   **Facts on File Children's Atlas.** rev. ed. By David Wright and Jill Wright. New York, Facts on File, 1997. 96p. illus. maps. index. $18.95. ISBN 0-8160-3713-2.

Beginning with the array of flags on the end pages, this atlas is filled with color and captivating tidbits about the world and its people. Originally published in 1987, this volume has been updated substantially and is filled with succinct but creative examples and brief text to accompany the maps and photographs. Each topic or area is accorded one double-page spread that also includes postage stamps; flags; and appropriate questions, with indicators of where to find the answers. There are 9 major sections beginning with "Our Planet Earth," which contains basic information about climates, reading postage stamps, and understanding maps and ends with quiz questions and an index. The remaining 7 sections follow the same format—the first double-page spread is an overview of the area under consideration, and the following double-page spreads in each section offer a closer look at specific countries. For example, the first pages on Europe include a map of the area with population facts, a puzzle, a quiz involving license plate symbols, and three photographs illustrating the diversity of the climate in the region. The following eight double-page spreads include facts and figures that are particularly appealing to the intended audience—photographs and information about LegoLand in Scandinavia, most popular makes of cars in France and Germany, the Greek alphabet, and reborn countries in Eastern Europe. The other generalized sections are Asia, Africa, the Pacific, North America (with the United States having three double-page spreads), South America, and the Arctic and Antarctica. This is an enjoyable, if brief, look at our world and its history, people, and accomplishments.—**Gail de Vos**

413.   **Hammond Atlas of the World.** 2d ed. Maplewood, N.J., Hammond, 1998. 312p. maps. index. $85.00. ISBN 0-8437-1172-8.

This atlas is 11-by-14⅝-inches in size, with nearly all maps being double-paged, 11⅝-by-20-inch in size. The inside margins between facing pages are in most cases tolerable, but not perfect. Most of the map scales range from 1:12,000,000 to 1:500,000. Some readers will require the use of a magnifying glass in order to read the font size of many of the smaller communities on all maps.

The majority of the maps are political maps, along with a few thematic, physical, and satellite maps. The publisher reports that the 85-page index contains 110,000 entries. Based on the reviewer's study of Nevada, the index includes 93 percent of the names of Nevada communities printed on the atlas's maps. The 7 percent lacking may simply be indexing errors.

A comparison with the 1st edition of this title (see ARBA 94, entry 448) indicates that there are many revisions. A sampling of cities that have been renamed in recent years found that Sri Jayawardanapura (Kotte) in Sri Lanka, and Chennai (Madras) in India, along with numerous others in India and Myanmar (Burma), are listed under their new name, with their previous name in small type in parentheses either under or following the new name. Another revision and improvement is the front endsheet, which contains a key to the atlas's maps. All political map colors have been changed and improved to represent elevations of both land and water; however, national forest and grassland boundaries have been dropped. Some insert maps have been enlarged; however, others have been deleted. Country populations have been added to the "Population of Major Cities." This work is recommended as a necessary acquisition for all libraries because of the major revisions stated above. It is also recommended that the 1st edition not be withdrawn.—**J. Carlyle Parker**

414.   **Maps on File.** 1998 ed. New York, Facts on File, 1998. 2v. maps. index. $195.00/set looseleaf w/binder. ISBN 0-8160-3816-3. ISSN 0275-8083.

The two volumes in *Maps on File* follow the standard "on file" format of a large looseleaf three-ring binder, heavy stock paper, and sectional dividers. The more than 500 maps are printed in black and white for easy duplication, for which permission is given for nonprofit educational use. The notebooks are divided into 14 sections plus an extensive index. The table of contents provides a helpful list of the maps in each section, with corresponding section and map numbers. Type style and symbols indicate major physical and political features. Country maps indicate the major cities, bordering states or countries, major rivers, roads and railways, a directional symbol for north, and a scale in miles and kilometers. The scales are not consistent among the maps, which makes comparisons difficult. The amount of detail in the maps also varies greatly. A historical section of only 3 maps and an outline of 19 maps are also included. The copyright dates of the maps range from the early 1980s to 1998. The older maps are primarily economic and statistical, with sources of the economic information often being indicated on the maps. This title has been published since 1981 with yearly updates available. This work is designed primarily for educational photocopying and not as a reference atlas.—**Elaine Ezell**

415.   **Oxford Atlas of Exploration.** New York, Oxford University Press, 1997. 248p. illus. maps. index. $40.00. ISBN 0-19-521353-X.

Although humans have always been explorers, as documented by this superb atlas, their motives for exploration have varied widely over time. In pursuit of game, for example, prehistoric hunters ventured from Africa to Europe, arriving eventually in Australia some 50,000 years ago. And by way of the Ice Age land bridge, they crossed from Siberia to Alaska about 14,000 years ago and within a scant millennium stood at the tip of South America. More recent explorers have been prompted by both material and noble impulses. Whereas financial gain, for instance, drove those fifteenth- and sixteenth-century conquistadors such as Cortés in Mexico and Pizarro in Peru and all those gold-crazed pursuers of El Dorado, the love of knowledge was a more compelling force for the nineteenth-century explorations of Charles Darwin aboard the *Beagle* and Baron Von Humboldt in South America. The earliest written accounts of explorations dates from the fourth millennium B.C.E., and so this atlas begins with the ancient Egyptians, Phoenicians, and Greeks and moves swiftly across Asia, Africa, the Americas, the distant Pacific, and the polar icecaps. In the process, attention is drawn to figures such as Ptolemy, James Cook, and Carl Linné.

Replete with an abundance of colorful maps, drawings, and photographs as well as a biographical section highlighting the careers of explorers from Erik "The Red" to Marco Polo to Henry Stanley, a time chart of explorations around the globe, and a thorough index, this would be a worthwhile addition to high school and college reference collections. Although the cartography is not quite as sharp as that of *The Times Atlas of World Exploration* (see ARBA 92, entry 408), the narrative is as clear and precise. This work will appeal to students and interested patrons.

—**John W. Storey**

416. **Reader's Digest Illustrated Great World Atlas.** New York, Reader's Digest/Random House, 1997. 288p. illus. maps. index. $40.00. ISBN 0-89577-988-9.

The introductory and instructional "The Story of the Earth" consists of 48 well-written and elaborately illustrated pages. The 33-page section "Nations of the World," located just before the index, contains brief but useful information concerning 198 of the world's nations. Both of these sections were prepared for the atlas by Duncan Baird Publishers of London, with statistical data from *The Europa World Year Book*, courtesy of Europa Publications, London.

The overall size of this atlas is 10¾-by-15 inches, and nearly all maps are double-paged, measuring 12½-by-18¾ inches. In general, map scales range from 1:1,000,000 to 1:80,000,000. Maps are primarily political, with topographic detail, and a few are physical maps. There are only 13 maps for the United States. The majority of the maps and the index to the maps were created especially for the atlas by Rand McNally.

The index contains more than 40,000 entries. However, a sample study of the entries for Nevada indicates that only 34 (54 percent) of the 63 cities, towns, and junctions on the 4 maps that include all or parts of Nevada are indexed. Only four of those index entries refer to the map where Nevada is shown in one piece. All of the other index entries for Nevada, including all of the state's largest cities, are keyed to maps of adjacent states that contain parts of Nevada.

Nearly all names of places and physical features are readable without the use of a magnifying glass. However, place-names in dark-colored areas used for elevation designations are difficult to read because of the limited differentiation of the dark colors and the black ink. Regardless of its good features, because of the indexing issues and because its elevations are given in meters, this atlas would not benefit U.S. libraries. [R: BL, 1 Feb 98, pp. 940-941]—**J. Carlyle Parker**

Biography

417. **Explorers.** Englewood Cliffs, N.J., Salem Press, 1998. 2v. illus. maps. index. (Magill's Choice). $95.00. ISBN 0-89356-970-4.

This attractive, 2-volume set of 78 biographical essays on prominent explorers will serve as a first resource for students of exploration history. The explorers profiled range widely in time and accomplishments, from the mysterious Carthaginian seafarer Hanno (ca.520 B.C.E.) to American astronaut Sally Ride.

The short biographies were written by 65 academics. Despite this extraordinary authorial diversity, the essays follow strict rules and read consistently well, showing the strong hand of the editors (who are curiously left anonymous). Each biography starts with a brief abstract of the explorer's identity and history, followed by the main text divided into "early life," "life's work," and "impact." A short annotated bibliography is included after each profile, providing immediate reference to the primary historical sources. There are occasional portraits and photographs included in the essays, along with a few maps (of which the reader could use more).

The biographies are for the most part very well written. They do not follow any particular political or cultural formula. Asian explorers such as Cheng Ho and Hsüan-tsang are included with the traditional western Europeans, such as James Cook and Henry Hudson. Some pioneers not often thought of as explorers made the cut, including John Winthrop of Massachusetts and Stephen Austin of Texas. The editors were thoughtful enough to include Sacagawea as well as Meriwether Lewis and William Clark. For some reason, three pioneering aviators (Amelia Earhart, Charles Lindbergh, and Jacqueline Cochran) are considered explorers. They were heroes of course, but they do not fit the prevailing model of participants in geographically based exploration. Their inclusion brings up the nagging and inevitable questions about who was *not* profiled. The aviators could have been replaced with, for example, Giovanni da Verrazano, Alexander von Humboldt, and Jim Bridger. The intrepid Antarctic explorers Robert Scott and Ernest Shackleton also deserved space. This set is recommended for all libraries, particularly those used by high school and undergraduate students.—**Mark A. Wilson**

418. **Explorers and Discoverers, Volume 5: From Alexander the Great to Sally Ride.** Nancy Pear and Daniel B. Baker, eds. Detroit, U*X*L/Gale, 1997. 237p. illus. maps. index. $34.00. ISBN 0-7876-1990-6.

This volume is a supplement to the publisher's 4-volume original set (see ARBA 94, entry 463); reviews of this set commented on its focus on women and non-European explorers, who are frequently slighted in other works. The supplement features 30 biographies of men and women who have expanded the horizons of our world and universe. The people range chronologically from Fa-Hsien (ca.374-462), a Buddhist monk who made an epic 15-year journey to India, to Pedro de Alvarado (1485-1541), a Spanish conquistador, to Steve Fossett (1945-), a contemporary adventurer who has broken sailing and aviation records. Also included are two historic machines, the *Mir* space station and H.M.S. *Titanic*, as well as the National Geographic Society, the largest non-profit scientific and educational institution in the world.

The alphabetically arranged, illustrated biographies average from five to seven pages in length. Maps provide geographic details of specific journeys. Additionally, 16 maps of major regions of the world lead off the volume, and a chronology of exploration by region, a list of explorers by date of birth, and an extensive cumulative index conclude the volume. The index is well designed. For example, one of the entries concerns Barry Clifford, a treasure hunter who discovered and salvaged a pirate vessel. A check of the index found an entry under *pirate* as well as *Clifford*, a valuable addition because a user of the volume might be interested in information about pirates but not know Clifford's name.

In telling of the exploits of a person, the editors include the reasons why the person chose to make a particular expedition and also give credit to those who accompanied him or her and contributed to the survival of the group. Entries are readable for the middle grades and up. The set and its supplement will greatly enrich the reference collection but will also be of interest to browsers.

Another good 1-volume work that examines the life and work of 12 explorers is William Scheller's *The World's Greatest Explorers* (Oliver Press, 1992). A volume to consider to support the use of this Gale set is *The Times Atlas of World Exploration: 300 Years of Exploring, Explorers, and Mapmaking* (HarperCollins, 1991). [R: BL, 15 Dec 98, p. 765]—**Vandelia L. VanMeter**

Dictionaries and Encyclopedias

419.   **The Grolier Student Library of Explorers and Exploration.** Danbury, Conn., Grolier, 1998. 10v. illus. maps. index. $299.00/set. ISBN 0-7172-9135-9.

This 10-volume set, geared toward young adults, tells about global exploration through narrative and historical accounts. The stories and biographies cover both well- and lesser-known explorers of land, sea, air, and outer space. They attempt to answer such questions as "Why did this person explore? What was the impact on the native population? On the natural environment?" Instruments and technology created to enhance and expand exploration are also discussed. Of particular note is the set's international focus. It provides information about the exploration of Asia, Africa, and the Middle East that truly supplements traditional history textbooks and general encyclopedia articles. The discussion of North America includes Canada, especially the search for the fabled Northwest Passage.

The first 4 volumes progress chronologically from prehistoric times to the Victorian Era. Volume 1 highlights the earliest explorers, for example, early humans, the ancient Egyptians, Greeks, Romans, and Persians, up to medieval Europe. Volume 2 continues with the "Golden Age" of Christopher Columbus, the Elizabethans, the Spanish, and the Portuguese. Volume 3 follows "Europe's Imperial Adventures" with tales of James Cook, North America, India and the Far East, and Russia's explorers. Volume 4 closes the chronology with coverage of Charles Darwin, the Northwest Passage, the hunt for Franklin, Australia, Tasmania, Antarctica, and the Russians. The next 5 volumes focus on specific geographic areas: Latin America, North America, Australasia and Asia, Africa and Arabia, and the polar regions. The topics range from the conquistadors, Jewish settlers, and quinine to the Great Plains, the Nile, West Africa, and both poles. Volume 10 looks at space and the ocean, including early flights with people on board, the Soyuz Program, *Apollo 13*, the *Challenger* disaster, and even the *Titanic*.

Each volume runs roughly 80 pages with a plethora of sidebars, maps, color illustrations, and a set index. The maps will be particularly helpful to students working on assignments to trace exploration routes. However, the blue used to indicate some routes sometimes is indistinguishable from the map background. The page layouts, typeface size, and abundant use of color will attract browsers as well as report writers. The set would probably be best for grades 5-10. [R: SLJ, Nov 98, p. 152]—**Esther R. Sinofsky**

PLACE-NAMES

420.   Bright, William. **1500 California Place Names: Their Origin and Meaning.** Berkeley, Calif., University of California Press, 1998. 170p. $12.95pa. ISBN 0-520-21271-1.

How can the origin of a name be both obscure and obvious at the same time? In the case of the town with the melodious moniker of Coalinga, California (koh uh LING guh), few would suspect it is merely a Hispanic version of a place originally called Coaling Station by the Southern Pacific Railway. Another surprising derivation is that of Cashlapooda Creek (kash luh POO duh), believed to be a rough version of *cache la poudre*, French for "hide the (gun) powder."

The author, a professor of linguistics who specializes in Native American languages, has written and edited several books on place-names such as *Colorado Place-Names* (see ARBA 94, entry 470). This handy pocket guide is the abridged version of a larger book on California place-names. The "small book" has been expanded from its original 1,000 names to 1,500. Each place is located by county, and a frontispiece state map shows all California counties. The phonetic pronunciations given for each word, as seen in the above examples, are simple and effective. Most entries are only a sentence or two long, but give an adequate explanation of the origin and meaning of each place-name. A space-saving feature is the inclusion of all names derived from the same term under the heading of the common term. For example, under *Palo*, a Spanish word for "tree," are found the names of Palo Alto, Palos Verdes, and Palo Escrito Peak. This is an inexpensive and excellent alternative to the unabridged version, and will fulfill the needs of most readers.—**Larry Lobel**

421.   Gallant, Frank K. **A Place Called Peculiar: Stories About Unusual American Place-Names.** Springfield, Mass., Merriam-Webster, 1998. 276p. illus. index. $14.95pa. ISBN 0-87779-619-X.

Author and poet Stephen Vincent Benét once wrote, "I have fallen in love with American names," about the charming and unusual place-names of many U.S. towns. The literature on U.S. place-names is vast; *The Bibliography of Place-Name Literature: United States and Canada* (see ARBA 83, entry 541) has been revised twice since 1948. In addition to this literature written by professional historians, folklorists, and geographers, the topic interests many nonspecialists. In the past few decades, general bookstores have stocked titles such as *Scratch Ankle, U.S.A.: American Place-Names and Their Derivation* (A. S. Barnes, 1969) and *All Over the Map Again: Another Extraordinary Atlas of the United States Featuring Towns That Actually Exist* (Ten Speed Press, 1996).

Published by the venerable dictionary publisher Merriam-Webster *A Place Called Peculiar* exemplifies the best qualities of a popular reference work—a prodigiously researched work that is both well written and graphically pleasing. Gallant spent two and a half years researching and writing this volume, finally narrowing down 75,000 village, town, and city names to 517 entries. Confessing that his choices are "folkloric, homespun and colloquial," the author also loves "patently funny names" (e.g., Monkeys Eyebrow, Kentucky; Tightsqueeze, Virginia; and Smut Eye, Alabama, to name only a few). The result of his research is a fascinating and entertaining work. Particularly commendable is the author's diligent research, which involved contacting librarians and historical societies throughout the country. This work truly justifies the publisher's blurb: "a delightful combination of serious fun and serious reference."—**Donald Altschiller**

422.   Mills, A. D. **A Dictionary of English Place-Names.** 2d ed. New York, Oxford University Press, 1998. 411p. $12.95pa. ISBN 0-19-280074-4.

This affordable, concise dictionary, revised to incorporate the 1996 changes in England's counties and boundaries, is a must for all public and academic libraries, as it will appeal to both the historian and the traveler. The author, a member of the Council of the English Place-Name Society and of the Society for Name Studies in Britain and Ireland, provides more than 12,000 alphabetized place-names. Each entry contains its location by county, at least one early spelling of the name and its first recorded date, the meaning of the name, and its language-origin (e.g., Old English, Old Scandinavian). The historical introduction includes two county maps of England. At the back of the book are a glossary of common elements in English place-names and a bibliography.
—**Lori D. Kranz**

423.   Rayburn, Alan. **Dictionary of Canadian Place Names.** New York, Oxford University Press, 1997. 461p. index. $37.50. ISBN 0-19-541086-6.

Canada is a large country with a diverse heritage. The nation's culture and heritage are significantly reflected by its place-names. Many names were derived from different languages, including Cree, Mi'kmaq, Inuktitut, French, German, and Spanish. Also, a large number of cultural and physical features were named after foreign battles and military leaders. Names were also given after celebrated heroes and persons who played a major role in local development. As a matter of fact, there are very few place-name books written about the country, considering the richness and variety of Canada's toponymic tapestry. *Dictionary of Canadian Place Names* is the most current and authorized place-name book of Canada. A total of 6,225 names are included in this book. Place-names include cities, towns, villages, regions, districts, county municipalities, national and provincial parks, lakes and islands, rivers, and mountains as well as better-known names of capes, points, straits, channels, bays, and inlets. Most entries for populated places include the date of naming, establishment of postal services, and changes in municipal status. Heights of mountains, areas of lakes and islands, and lengths of rivers are noted. A list of reference sources is provided for further consultation. The author is an expert on Canadian place-names; this is his seventh book on place-names. This work is a great asset to the reference collection in all kinds of libraries. It will also provide hours of leisure browsing for people who are interested in Canadian places, culture, and history.—**Xiao (Shelley) Yan Zhang**

TRAVEL GUIDES

General Works

424.   Arden, Andrea. **On the Road with Your Pet: More Than 4,000 Mobil-Rated Lodgings in North America for Travelers with Dogs, Cats, and Other Pets.** New York, Fodor's Travel Publications/Random House, 1998. 624p. index. $12.00pa. ISBN 0-679-03548-6.

Travelers with pets often have to decide what to do with them when away from home. Mobil Travel Guides have made the decision easier with this guide. The lodging entries are recompiled from its existing travel guidebooks and include only those establishments that accept pets (dogs and cats presumed). Instead of many books with regional groupings of states, all of the United States and Canada appears in one book, divided first by state or province, then by city. Except in the largest cities, there are typically about one to three entries per city. Mobil guides use *see also* references for towns nearby, which is a great help for trip planners. The entry is just the same as in the regular books, and includes a quality rating of one to five stars as well as price ranges, check-in time, amenities, and recreation, among other items. Telephone numbers and e-mail addresses are provided, and travelers are encouraged to check first to assure that policies have not changed before leaving home.

The front section deals with pets and how to travel with them successfully, and there are appendixes for pet first aid and pet resources, including a listing of a few tourists' attractions that admit pets too.

Mobil Travel Guides are useful in general, but typically do not list as many lodgings per location as American Automobile Association (AAA) tour books, so those who have definite destinations in mind should check those and other hotel books as well.

Useful in any public library, the Mobil guide is suitable for the reference desk because most users will only need to jot down a few locations and then can take home the standard Mobil regional books. However, Mobil could save a lot of trouble by just adding a "pets accepted index" to future volumes of their standard guides.

—**Gary R. Cocozzoli**

425.   Dervaes, Claudine. **The Travel Dictionary.** new ed. Tampa, Fla., Solitaire Publishing, 1998. 372p. maps. $19.95pa. ISBN 0-933143-58-3.

This dictionary lists and defines many terms that people working in the travel industry may find useful. Some terms of questionable value are included as well, such as "affluent," "ivory tower," and "subsoil." Also included are lists of selected states and provinces, travel industry organizations, travel agency co-ops, airport codes, and airline codes. There is a brief bibliography of travel industry reference books, travel video companies, and travel magazines and newsletters. Communication codes, a 24-hour clock and time zone chart, a metric conversion table, a table of currencies, and a size conversion table for the United States, England, and Europe also appear. Capitals of the world, code listings for hotel, car rental, fare and reservation systems, related Websites, world trivia, geographical terms, and maps of the continents round out this book's offerings.

There is no indication in the book as to how or why terms were chosen. Lists are heavily oriented toward the United States and are not exhaustive. For example, abbreviations for states and provinces include the United States, Canada, Australia, and Brazil only. This dictionary will be of interest to beginning students in the travel industry.—**Joanna M. Burkhardt**

426.   **The Traveler's Handbook.** 7th ed. Miranda Haines and Sarah Thorowgood, eds. Old Saybrook, Conn., Globe Pequot Press, 1997. 959p. maps. index. $21.95. ISBN 0-7627-0145-5.

The abundance of information contained in this compact book makes reading it almost as exciting as actually going on a trip. Chapters are written by well-qualified people from diverse professions and cover everything from the basics of traveling to fine details, such as telephone numbers and addresses of agents who will buy or sell one's car abroad. Every aspect of travel—culture, finance, medical issues, and then some—is considered in articles that range from philosophical discussions to essential facts and practical advice. Although probably less in demand than the typical guide to a certain country or region, this volume is meant to fortify those who would describe themselves as world travelers as opposed to tourists who visit foreign locales on a more superficial level.

The book is divided into 2 sections, the 1st being a collection of essays that address the what, when, where, how, and why of travel in more generic terms, whereas the 2d part is a directory complementing each previous section with statistics, contacts, and telephone numbers. There is advice for every kind of traveler: student, solitary, aged, pregnant, gay, vegetarian, and disabled as well as pertinent information about specific countries' immunization and driver's license requirements, telecommunications, holidays, electric voltage, and map suppliers. Both kinds of information are enlightening for planning a successful trip overseas. The credentials of the writers lend authority to the conclusions drawn.

The one disadvantage for American readers is the largely British authorship and perspective; some of the more technical material is specific to the United Kingdom. However, because many overseas trips begin in Europe, this is not a serious drawback, and the tremendous amount and diversity of relevant information presented make this a highly recommended addition to the travel section. Perhaps someday the editors will consider an American version of the same work, but until then this book will provide everything needed to inspire and prepare the enterprising traveler.—**Janet J. Kosky**

United States

427.   Barnes, Judy, Jolane Edwards, Carolyn Lee Goodloe, and Laurel Wilson. **Coasting: An Expanded Guide to the Northern Gulf Coast.** 3d ed. Gretna, La., Pelican Publishing, 1998. 367p. illus. maps. index. $13.95pa. ISBN 1-56554-343-2.

This guide to the coastal areas of Alabama, Mississippi, and the Florida panhandle has been expanded and updated for the 1994 edition. Key areas between Waveland, Mississippi, and Carabelle, Florida (near Apalachicola), are covered. Each city or town is detailed with places of historical interest, restaurants with their specialties, unique shopping areas, and some hotels or bed and breakfast facilities. Also included are major convention centers, golf courses, museums, gambling centers, indoor and outdoor entertainment, and nature areas. Almost one-half of the book details Alabama, home of the authors.

Interesting facts are also interspersed within the text, including local recipes; folklore; historical tidbits; festivals and events; and general information, such as what to do in case of a hurricane. Maps, addresses, telephone numbers, and hours of operation will help visitors find their way. Numerous illustrations are used throughout the book, many depicting local scenery or logos of restaurants.

The index is an alphabetic arrangement of the establishments mentioned in the text and lists twice as many places as the index of the 2d edition. A composite list of local tourist information centers would be helpful for those wanting more information. This extensive guide to a lesser-known coast will be helpful in any travel collection and should be available in southeast libraries. An armchair traveler will find this an interesting read.
—**Margo B. Mead**

428.   Clotworthy, William G. **Presidential Sites: A Directory of Places Associated with Presidents of the United States.** Granville, Ohio, McDonald & Woodward, 1998. 357p. illus. index. $18.95pa. ISBN 0-939923-64-5.

Presidential Sites: A Directory of Places Associated with Presidents of the United States is a compilation of various sites, primarily in the United States (five foreign sites are mentioned), that have some reference to the 41 presidents of the United States. The sites include birthplaces, workplaces, monuments, memorials, battlefields, churches, libraries, institutions, and burial places. The entries are arranged by president, in chronological order. President George Washington has the longest entry, with more than 60 pages, followed by Abraham Lincoln with 17 pages. Each site is briefly described, with its location and significance noted. Data such as the president's military career (if served), historical background, details on specific homes and memorials, and colorful annotations that accompany site descriptions make this intriguing volume interesting reading and at the same time make one aware of the United States' rich historical heritage. Appendixes include a section on museums, churches, and other sites associated with presidents; colleges attended by the presidents; presidential sites by state and country; and a bibliography that deals with the presidential sites. There is a name/site index.

This work will be of special value to library reference divisions, U.S. historical scholars, archivists, park rangers, and docents, but even the average reader will find it fascinating. *Presidential Sites* is an engaging volume and comes highly recommended. It will entice one to visit some of these locations as well as reexamine one's memory to see if one has ever been there.—**Robert Palmieri**

429.   **The Complete Guide to America's National Parks.** 10th ed. New York, Fodor's Travel Publications/ Random House, 1998. 448p. index. $18.00pa. ISBN 0-679-03515-X.

Published in cooperation with the National Park Foundation, this book includes information on all 376 "units" of the National Park Service as well as Affiliated Areas and National Heritage Areas that merely draw on the expertise of the National Park Service. The foundation is the nonprofit partner of the National Park Service and was created to raise support from corporations, foundations, and individuals to enhance the national parks.

This book is truly valuable in its scope and coverage. The 376 units include national parks, national preserves and reserves, national memorials, monuments, historic sites, and historical parks, parks associated with American military history, and several categories of national recreation areas. The book is arranged by state and includes four territories. Although 376 National Park Service units are covered in 407 pages, the information about each is useful. Coverage for most units includes a brief history of the unit; what to see and do there; information on camping, lodging, and food supplies; tips and hints; fees, permits, and limitations; directions for getting to the unit; and address, Websites, and telephone numbers for more information. At the end of each state's coverage is a *see also* reference to coverage of related areas.

There are 20 pages of maps to introduce the reader to what is available in the country. There are separate lists of trails in the National Trails System and rivers in the Wild and Scenic Rivers System. A search for the new national park in Utah turned up no information, but this may be understandable for this edition.

The text is readable, although not all the errors were corrected in proofreading. The sheer volume of information more than compensates for any grammatical faults. This book is strictly text with only a few pictures. Its only drawback is that due to the easily accessible information it contains, it may not be on the reference shelf very long.—**Bev Cummings Agnew**

430.   **Cruising Guide to New York Waterways and Lake Champlain.** By Chris W. Brown III. Claiborne S. Young, ed. Gretna, La., Pelican Publishing, 1998. 464p. illus. maps. index. $28.95pa. ISBN 1-56554-250-9.

Enriched with illustrations, charts, and tables, this addition to Pelican's cruising guide series brims with both nautical and customs information essential for navigating New York's waterways, and with cultural and historical background on the many ports of call that line these routes. Drawing upon almost 40 years of boating experience and lore, as well as the fruits of research born of 4 years of on-site cruising in the writing of this book, Brown provides facts and insights that range from the hours during which a given low-clearance bridge is raised to allow passage of river traffic to telephone numbers for accessing emergency services by a canal to assessments of restaurants along a lakeshore.

Appropriately arranged in travel sequence through its 16 chapters, this reference introduces its readers to the natural conditions (e.g., river turbulence, floating debris) and manmade contrivances (e.g., locks, tie-ups) that hinder or assist one's cruise north on the Hudson River to Lake Champlain and Montreal, thereupon to the Great Lakes Ontario and Erie, finally returning eastward through the Finger Lakes region of the Empire State.

Especially helpful throughout this volume are the more than 120 boxed "Skipper Tips," which, for example, translate archaic chart lingo (p. 90); advise of rules peculiar to specific locks (p. 170); and discourse upon the use of range markers (p. 66). The chatty text is supplemented by some 200 black-and-white maps and photographs, displaying the shorelines, depths, and other salient features of these lakes, rivers, channels, marinas, and waterway-fronting communities. Ancillary resources listed in this handbook's back matter include United States and Canadian purveyors of both nautical supplies (e.g., charts, books) and local organizations that dispense tourist and community information. Also found here are metric conversion charts, defined compass heading terms and symbols, and useful essays on "Marina Etiquette" and "Boat Builders of New York."

Several minor defects mar this otherwise superb work. The 8-part appendix lacks a glossary for such terms as *gunk hole* and *reach*. Also regrettable is the absence of a listing in the table of contents for this volume's invaluable 14-page index. This said, Brown's guide book stands up well against such rival publications as *Cruising Guide to the Northeast's Inland Waterways* (2d ed.; International Marine Publishing, 1995) and the *Cruising Guide to Lake Champlain, the Waterway from New York City to Montreal* (5th ed.; Lake Champlain Publishing Company, 1997).—**Jeffrey E. Long**

431. Halper, Evan, and Paul Karr. **Hostels U.S.A.: The Only Comprehensive, Unofficial, Opinionated Guide.** Old Saybrook, Conn., Globe Pequot Press, 1998. 395p. illus. $14.95pa. ISBN 0-7627-0118-8.

A fun source for adventure sums up this work. Hosteling can be an inexpensive way to see parts of the country, meet new individuals, and experience life. This work is one of the few guides available on the topic. Another title worth mentioning (in fact the authors mentions it) is *Hosteling U.S.A.* (Globe Pequot, 1997). Written in an inviting and relaxed manner, the work covers hostels in North America north of the Mexican border. The work is divided into regional sections and Canada for ease of use by the individual. Within the regional break-down, states are listed alphabetically, as are the towns and cities within the state. The reader is forewarned; not all states have a listing. In the section on New England, for example, Rhode Island does not make it into print.

Each entry consists of a ranking of the hostel's strengths and weaknesses, the quality of the experience, its environmental friendliness, its accessibility to families, and a rating. The rating system is explained in the introduction to the volume. The authors provide a short history and background to hosteling in the introduction as well. Several topical lists make up the end of the book, with listings for most green friendly, top hostel, best deals, and most children friendly, among others.

With the growing interest in alternative vacations that are both an entertaining experience and are inexpensive, this work will find a useful place on any library shelf supporting questions on travel or the leisure industry, but will be especially useful in public library settings where a varied clientele will be grateful for an additional title in this field.—**Gregory Curtis**

432. **Interstate Exit Authority.** Norcross, Ga., Interstate America, 1998. 655p. maps. $21.95pa. ISBN 1-880477-14-9.

Highway maps may show major streets and attractions within cities and towns, but they do not show all of the typical restaurants, service stations, and other businesses along the roads. This guidebook endeavors to list every business located within one-quarter mile of every interstate highway exit in the United States (excluding Alaska). Fast-food and standard restaurants, places of lodging, automobile and truck service stations, automated teller machines, and medical facilities are some of the entries included. Although the businesses have nothing more than their names listed (except for those that purchased small advertisements), travelers will no doubt be glad to know that a favorite fast-food joint or a preferred gas station is located at an upcoming exit.

Entries are listed by consecutive exit numbers for each U.S. interstate road, starting at one end of the highway and following it all the way to its southern or eastern terminus. Each stretch of highway is shown on a simple map that shows major crossing highways and exits but little else. Clear use of typefaces and layout for the business names makes the large amount of data readable.

Travel information is typically useful either as a planning guide or a quick resource. This guide falls into the second category. Although drivers would enjoy having it with them on interstate trips, its value as a reference book is limited. Patrons are unlikely to need most of these listings before trips, and they will need more complete information from other guidebooks for overnight accommodations.—**Christopher W. Nolan**

433.   McAlester, Virginia, and Lee McAlester. **A Field Guide to America's Historic Neighborhoods and Museum Houses: The Western States.** New York, Alfred A. Knopf/Random House, 1998. 735p. illus. maps. index. $29.95pa. ISBN 0-375-70172-9.

The most appealing aspect of this field guide is the sheer amount of information that the authors are able to place in just one volume. The detail found in virtually every entry is amazing, particularly considering the breadth of the coverage the authors provide. The field guide describes historic neighborhoods and museum houses in all of the mainland states west of the Mississippi River. Hence, from Texas to Washington state and from southern California to North Dakota, historic homes and neighborhoods are profiled. The authors provide an extensive and very useful introduction that provides a brief history of the American West, including excellent discussions of historic benchmarks, such as the founding of the California missions, to better help readers understand the historic structures that remain. Cogent discussions explain the evolution of domestic architecture found in the West, and influential building styles such as those found in Victorian- and Romantic-era neighborhoods. The book chapters are divided and alphabetized by states, and the cities and unique neighborhoods and museums within each state are also listed alphabetically. Black-and-white contemporary and archival photographs illustrate the homes, neighborhoods, and museums highlighted, and city grid maps help readers easily locate the featured structures. Telephone numbers are provided for museums and museum houses open to the public. Excellent context is provided for the best possible understanding of individual buildings. For example, readers not only learn much about the Molly Brown House in Denver, Colorado, but the authors also provide detailed information about the "Millionaire's Row" of which the Brown House is but one site. The Molly Brown House entry provides a detailed account of the lives of Molly and J. J. Brown and information about the architect of the Brown House, William Lang.

Side panels amplify understanding at appropriate places throughout the text. For example, the Italianate style of architecture is illustrated and further described in sidebar information accompanying the Eureka, California, entries because of the prominence of that style in northern California. In profiles of the unique historic neighborhoods to be found in Santa Fe, New Mexico, an informative side panel discusses "earth-wall" construction.

The book contains an extensive index and an appendix that explains land surveys and the division of land in the American West. Additional recommended reading about the architecture and history of the Western states is provided. *A Field Guide to America's Historic Neighborhoods and Museum Houses: The Western States* is an invaluable reading resource for both armchair travelers and those who want to make their own pilgrimages to the historic domestic structures of fully one-half of the nation.—**Jerry D. Flack**

434.   *Vegetarian Journal*'s **Guide to Natural Foods Restaurants in the U.S. & Canada.** 3d ed. Garden City Park, N.Y., Avery Publishing, 1998. 370p. $12.95pa. ISBN 0-89529-837-6.

Presently there are more than 14 million vegetarians and vegans, and their numbers are growing as more people are becoming increasingly health conscious or deciding to follow this path for moral or personal reasons. It has not been easy for vegetarians to locate a place to have true vegetarian food, not just lettuce and a cucumber sandwich. Even if not a truly natural foods restaurant, many establishments now offer a vegetarian menu in addition to their regular fare. Although many ethnic cuisines (e.g., Chinese, Indian, Thai) are thought to be mainly vegetarian, they often use animal products in sauces in their cooking or have meat, poultry, or fish dishes. This book attempts to seek out establishments offering purely vegetarian dishes or those having 10 or more vegetarian options.

In a succinct style, information on more than 2,000 restaurants is noted alphabetically by state, then city and province. Descriptions note the variety of cuisine—Chinese, Italian, Mexican, Vietnamese, vegan, vegetarian— followed by data on types of dishes, house specialties, days open, type of service catering or take-out options, availability of vegan or macrobiotic, beverage assortment, credit cards accepted, and price range. An added bonus is the "vegetarian vacation guide" listing camps, resorts, spas, bed and breakfasts, and tour services (domestic as well as international), all with a vegetarian flair. Completing the volume are local vegetarian group contacts.

Even if one is not following a vegetarian food style, this guide can help one stay on a healthy diet when traveling or eating out. Unique and refreshing dining and lodging possibilities await those who want to experience healthier eating and traveling. This directory is a nice complement to a dining reference collection.—**Joy Hastings**

Asia

435.   **Thailand.** New York, DK Publishing, 1997. 504p. illus. maps. index. (Eyewitness Travel Guides). $24.95 flexibinding. ISBN 0-7894-1949-1.

Finding a single appropriate travel guide to Thailand can be a challenge when local bookstores often offer more than 20 titles. The increasing number of specialized guides, targeting everyone from business travelers to trekkers and scuba divers, makes it even more difficult to find a comprehensive guide that balances the need for practical advice about hotels and dining with the need for in-depth information about the country's history, people, and places. Eyewitness Travel Guides' *Thailand* admirably achieves this balance in a profusion of color photographs, maps, and drawings. This visually pleasing guide provides practical travel information on places to visit, stay, eat, and shop within the context of Thailand's history and culture.

The 1st chapter, "Portrait of Thailand," provides the first-time visitor with an introduction to Thai history, climate, and culture through the effective use of a timeline, architectural drawings, maps, lush photographs, and a brief narrative. The remaining chapters are organized by region—"Bangkok," "The Central Plains," "Northern Thailand," "Northeast Thailand," "Gulf of Thailand," and "Southern Thailand." Each chapter comprises detailed information about cities, archaeological sites, beaches, and parks, intermingled with the region's history and culture. The final sections, devoted to "Travelers' Needs" and a "Survival Guide," offer up-to-date information on the food and restaurants, a wide range of lodging facilities, entertainment opportunities, tips on shopping, a useful guide to the Thai language, and tips on traveling safely in Thailand. This guide will serve a traveler well, even if the traveler never leaves the armchair.—**Carol L. Mitchell**

Australia

436.   **Australia.** New York, DK Publishing, 1998. 576p. illus. maps. index. (Eyewitness Travel Guide). $29.95 flexibinding. ISBN 0-7894-3531-4.

This title is 1 of 13 guides to cities, countries, or language phrasebooks in DK Publishing's Eyewitness Travel Guide series. The highly visual three-dimensional approach of these guides sets them apart from most contemporary travel guides. They provide tourists with the ability to visualize what buildings looks like, how streets are laid out, where places are located in relationship to one another, and the like. That approach, along with a focus on brief descriptions about places, buildings, and many other aspects of a country's features, history, and customs, make these the most valuable contemporary travel guides. Both their layout and their content give these guides wider appeal for libraries as an excellent source of general information about a country.

The guide to Australia, which is typical of the series, consists of 576 fact-filled pages. A 50-page introduction provides excellent general information about the country and its history. The next 400 pages are broken down into 16 regions within the 7 states in Australia. Each contains an area map; street-by-street maps; sights at a glance; detailed information about specific sights; story boxes with historical information; cut-away views of historic buildings; and color photographs of locations, buildings, artwork, and people. A compact 60 pages covers traveler's needs that includes listings of a selected number of hotels and restaurants, and some brief practical information about day-to-day necessities (e.g., how pay phones work). Those listings are linked back to the main guide by the use of the same color thumb codings as well as by an arrangement that ties specific hotels and restaurants to particular locations within an area. A detailed index makes any particular piece of information easy to find. This is a fun guide for the armchair traveler and a practical guide for the real traveler.

Increasingly, Websites provide a wide range of biographical information about people throughout the world. That information is sometimes very brief, and to date, Websites have not replaced biographical dictionaries as the ultimate source for information about, in particular, lesser-known people. The larger the library, and the more extensive access it provides to electronic information, the greater the need for a comprehensive collection of biographical dictionaries.—**Norman D. Stevens**

Europe

437.   Fodor's Upclose Europe: The Complete Guide, Thoroughly Up-to-Date Savvy Traveling.... New York, Fodor's Travel Publications/Random House, 1998. 922p. maps. index. $20.00pa. ISBN 0-679-03395-5.

Previously published under the title *Berkeley Guide to Europe*, the current volume continues to provide information that travelers will need when visiting most European countries. One country that is conspicuously missing from this guide is Russia. Some countries are grouped regionally; for example, Estonia, Latvia, and Lithuania are considered together under the heading "Baltic Republics." The chapter for each country includes a brief history, basics of money, how to get to the country, getting around once there, where to eat and sleep, festivals and holidays, visitor information, what to do in case of an emergency, language, and customs of the country. Other information particular to the country or region is given if unique to that location. In addition to general information about the country, larger cities are defined with information similar to that for the country listed under each city listing. Maps of both the country and of the cities listed with important reference points are included. This information is certainly helpful to users of the volume in determining what to view and when to visit the attraction.

This work will be useful in academic, public, and special libraries for the amount of information it provides to potential travelers anticipating a journey to Europe. As with any travel guide, frequent updates will be essential to maintaining the currency and accuracy of the work. At its affordable price, buying new editions will not be a problem for most libraries choosing its purchase.—**Gregory Curtis**

438.   Lopez, Billie Ann, and Peter Hirsch. Traveler's Guide to Jewish Germany. Gretna, La., Pelican Publishing, 1998. 314p. illus. maps. index. $22.50pa. ISBN 1-56554-254-1.

Considering the objective of the Third Reich to eradicate the Jews, one would not expect there to be enough left of the German Jewish culture to fill a book on this topic. The startling truth is that, aside from Israel, there are more sites associated with Jewish history and religion in Germany than anywhere else. Because of a weak central government until the late 1800s, Jews were not as vulnerable to organized expulsion in Germany as they were in other European countries. This illustrated guide to the past 1,000 years of German history describes synagogues, cemeteries, ritual baths (*mikveh*), concentration camps, memorials, documentation centers, museums, schools, archaeological sites, and homes of famous Jews. The city-by-city directory gives technical information, such as visiting hours, reference points and street directions for locating the site, and a brief history of significant facts for each point of interest.

Other features include a glossary of Hebrew or Yiddish as well as German words associated with the sites, map sketches showing relative distances and locations of towns reviewed, and a chronology of events that shaped the German Jewish culture. As an explanation of traditions and a summary of the persecution of Jews throughout Europe, the timeline is valuable in itself and would have been potentially useful for other topics of study, had a bibliography of sources been included.

Both authors currently reside in Austria and have visited most of the sites discussed in this book, which was first published in Europe. Their travel tips, including proper etiquette and helpful German phrases, add a practical dimension to a fascinating documentation of sacred and historical legacies of German Jewry. The empirical approach of cataloging tangible evidence complements the growing number of theological best-sellers and new releases involving the Jewish religion.—**Janet J. Kosky**

International Travel

439.   Alternative Travel Directory 1998: The Complete Guide to Work, Study, & Travel Overseas. 4th ed. Clayton A. Hubbs and others, eds. Amherst, Mass., Transitions Abroad Publishing, 1998. 375p. index. $19.95pa. ISBN 1-886732-05-1.

For the "been there, done that" crowd comes a resource for the person who is seeking something different and wants more than prepackaged tours, crowded tour buses, and mad dashes from one city to another. The editors of *Transitions Abroad*, a magazine for the independent-minded traveler, have published a tool for the adventurous globetrotter who wants to experience and feel a place, its culture, and people. This volume directs travelers toward programs and resources that encourage independent travel, study, and work abroad. There are 3 sections with chapters giving a region or country-by-country overview of available opportunities and programs. Some topics featured include archaeology, cooking, ecology, hiking, internships, volunteerism, and walking, among others. Extensive resources (e.g., books, CD-ROMs, magazines, newsletters), Internet sites, and organizations guide those researching their travel choices. Also noted are programs for the disabled, families, and seniors. The intrepid traveler and even the "casual" tourist will find this directory an outstanding compilation. This directory is published annually with updated information available on a Website at www.transabroad.com. Well organized, this book is a great starting point for unique foreign travel. This directory is a useful addition to any library, public or private. [R: LJ, 15 April 98, p. 66]—**Joy Hastings**

440.   Man, John, Chris Schüler, Geoffrey Roy, and Nigel Rodgers. **The Traveler's Atlas: A Global Guide to the Places You Must See in a Lifetime.** Hauppauge, N.Y., Barron's Educational Series, 1998. 224p. illus. maps. index. $29.95. ISBN 0-7641-5121-5.

Never has travel been more convenient or accessible than our current day. The authors begin this book by stressing this point as well as their opinion that traveling is a life-changing experience that brings both wonder and understanding of other cultures to its participants.

This beautifully illustrated book is divided into specific areas of the world and then further divided into "must see" locations within that area. Just about every area of the globe is represented here—North America, Central and South America, Africa, the Mediterranean and the Near East, northern Europe, northern Asia, central Asia, India and Southeast Asia, Australia, and the Pacific. The "must see" locations are generally three to five pages long and feature a map, a detailed description of the area, and a sidebar titled "Fact File." The information provided for each site varies, but facts about currency, climate, best time to visit, nearest airport, city accommodations and population, and a suggested list of what to take are examples of what is included.

The book is ideal for beginning world travelers looking for ideas for their next designation. It is not, however, thorough enough in any one specific area to be comprehensive. Travelers will most likely want to consult other resources on their destination while preparing for their trip. With its magnificent photographs and engaging text, *The Traveler's Atlas* will be thoroughly enjoyed by both experienced as well as armchair travelers.

—**Shannon M. Graff**

441.   Seldon, Philip. **The Business Traveler's World Guide.** New York, McGraw-Hill, 1998. 668p. $19.95pa. ISBN 0-07-061997-2.

Because foreign trade opportunities continue to develop, there is an increasing need for international travel information for business professionals. This compact guide proposes to provide relevant facts about 150 cities in 80 countries throughout the business-oriented world. In the approximately three pages devoted to each country, some of the most useful information covered for planning a trip is that country's time zones; business hours; holidays; currency data; tipping norms; and most valuable, local customs and business etiquette. For each city outlined, two or three pages contain technical items such as travel distances and times between airport and city centers and minimum connecting times for transfers to other cities.

However, pertinent details have been sacrificed for the sake of comprehensiveness. Lists of hotels, restaurants, entertainment, and shops give addresses and telephone numbers only with no attempt at descriptions or ratings. Only names of places of interest are given, and there are no maps in this work. Most travelers will want to consult a more thorough source, such as the Passport to the World series from World Trade Press, for specifics in both confirming travel plans and preparing for a successful business trip. Therefore, this brief guide is perhaps most useful in a business library as an introduction to business representatives who travel to many different cities on several continents.—**Janet J. Kosky**

442.   **World Mountaineering: The World's Great Mountains by the World's Great Mountaineers.** Audrey Salkeld, ed. London, Mitchell Beazley/Reed Consumer Books; distr., New York, Bulfinch Press/Little, Brown, 1998. 304p. illus. maps. index. $50.00. ISBN 0-8212-2502-2.

World Mountaineering features more than 50 of the world's most challenging mountains that experienced climbers strive to conquer, including Mount Everest in Asia, Mount McKinley and Grand Teton in North America, and Kilimanjaro in Africa. The work is organized into geographic regions, with each mountain given a narrative description as well as breathtaking photographs and maps. The descriptions include a timeline of the mountains climbing history, the various ways in which the peak can be climbed, facilities surrounding the area, when to go, gear needed, recommended guidebooks, rescue and insurance information, and any information specific to the mountain. Each location's narrative is authored by an expert climber who has had first-hand experience on the mountain featured. A glossary and an index aid in the guide's accessibility.

This book serves as both a travel guide as well as handbook for those interested in mountaineering. Its vivid photographs and engaging text will capture the interest of many readers. *World Mountaineering* will be a welcome addition in the reference and circulating collections of public libraries.—**Shannon M. Graff**

9   History

ARCHAEOLOGY

443.   Archaeology of Prehistoric Native America: An Encyclopedia. Guy Gibbon and others, eds. New York, Garland, 1998. 941p. illus. maps. index. (Garland Reference Library of the Humanities, v.1537). $165.00. ISBN 0-8153-0725-X.

The 1990s have witnessed the development of a substantial number of encyclopedic reference works in archaeology centered on either a branch of the discipline or a specific geographic region; for example, the *Encyclopedia of Underwater and Maritime Archaeology* (1992) and the *Oxford Encyclopedia of the Archaeology of the Near East* (see ARBA 98, entry 429). This expensive, illustrated volume treats the known prehistory of North America from Paleo-Indian times to European contact. More than 750 articles, with accompanying readings, are introduced by a "Reader's Guide," which defines North America's natural and cultural areas, continental prehistory as currently known, the history of local archaeological practice, and dating conventions. A detailed outline groups all entries by physiographic regions (e.g., the Arctic and Subarctic, California, Great Basin, Eastern Woodlands, Northwest Coast, Plains, Plateau, Southwest) and two subject areas, the Pre-Clovis/Paleo-Indian and a "general" category. This last contains more than 140 essays on climate and environment, types of stone tools, special topics ranging from archaeoastronomy to petroglyphs and ridged-field agriculture, and exploited natural resources. Indexing covers persons, subjects (with a heavy emphasis on individual site names), and publication titles. This work will be most useful for large public libraries and university libraries supporting degree programs in anthropology and field archaeology.—**Robert B. Marks Ridinger**

444.   Aston, Mick, and Tim Taylor. The Atlas of Archaeology. New York, DK Publishing, 1998. 208p. illus. maps. index. $29.95. ISBN 0-7894-3189-0.

The most recent example of an expanding genre of atlases on world archaeology and prehistory, this lavishly illustrated volume covers more than 1,200 sites and is divided into 2 sections. The 1st section covers 10 major eras of human civilization, including Paleolithic hunter-gatherers, the Neolithic, the time of the first cities, the Iron and Classical Ages, medieval cultures, and industrial settlements. Each chapter begins by presenting in detail an example of a place seen as illustrating the major features of the time under study, followed by comparative data on similarly dated sites. The 2d section opens with a 20-page section of maps marking all significant archaeological sites worldwide, followed by short detailed entries on the local and regional importance of each. A glossary of terms used and a short bibliography complete the work. Indexing provides access by subject, site name, and individual names. *The Atlas of Archaeology* would be a useful update to reference collections in all types of libraries that have older, similar works, such as the *World Atlas of Archaeology* (see ARBA 86, entry 486), and *Past Worlds: The Times Atlas of Archaeology* (1988).—**Robert B. Marks Ridinger**

445.   Brier, Bob. Encyclopedia of Mummies. New York, Facts on File, 1998. 248p. illus. index. $35.00. ISBN 0-8160-3108-8.

From the lighthearted to the gruesome, *The Encyclopedia of Mummies* documents the fascination people have had with the dead since the beginning of civilization. The alphabetic listings begin with *Abbott and Costello Meet the Mummy* and go to Gaetano Zumbo, an Italian wax sculptor who often used human corpses as a base for his wax work. Entries run from a few sentences to many pages. Included are numerous photographs and drawings.

Brier has managed to collect more information into one slim volume than could be found elsewhere. Covering the ancient embalmer's art of Egypt to natural mummification in various parts of the world to a modern resurgence in the practice in the western United States, the author gives basic scientific information on the various processes. Ethical considerations are discussed as well. Detailing fact, fancy, and myth, Brier has included entries on such famous ancient mummies as Ramses II, III, V, and the Marquise of Tai as well as such famous modern ones as Napoleon, Lenin, and Eva Perón (Evita). Not just a "who was who," the book goes on to include information on how mummies have helped solve mysteries such as the ill-fated Franklin expedition of 1845 (the entire crew probably died of lead poisoning).

A whimsical appendix listing the mummy films is included. Another appendix details museum collections from around the world. An extensive bibliography of other sources and a detailed index follow. Although not recommended as a complete scholarly source, *The Encyclopedia of Mummies* is recommended as a fun, quick starting point for most middle and high school libraries. [R: Choice, July/Aug 98, p. 1825]—**Kevin W. Perizzolo**

446.   **Encyclopedia of Underwater and Maritime Archaeology.** James P. Delgado, ed. London, British Museum Press and New Haven, Conn., Yale University Press, 1997. 493p. illus. maps. index. $55.00. ISBN 0-300-07427-1.

Delgado, executive director of the Vancouver Maritime Museum, has produced an impressive encyclopedia of underwater and maritime archaeology. This volume was initially published as *British Museum Encyclopedia of Underwater and Maritime Archaeology* by the British Museum Press in 1997. Many of the individual essays are written by such experts as George F. Bass, who excavated at the sites discussed. The editor acknowledges some imbalance in the attention given to North American sites while inviting suggestions for entries for future editions, especially Asian sites and sites formerly behind the Iron Curtain.

A subject list by topic provides helpful guidance for the reader as well as an indication of the breadth of subjects covered in this volume, ranging from sites arranged both chronologically and by location to general articles on such topics as legislation, legal issues, organizations, institutions, approaches, and essays on particular regions and nations. There are inevitably some overlap and some awkwardness in the treatment of such a broad range of subjects, but the reader is helped immensely by a system of cross-referencing using bold typeface in a given entry to refer to other articles. A particularly useful feature is a short list of suggested additional reading at the end of each article. Numerous illustrations of generally high quality, many of which are in color, enhance the volume.

The editor and his staff have provided a useful and much-needed encyclopedia that fills a significant gap in the archaeological literature. This encyclopedia will be useful to specialists and nonspecialists and deserves a place in any library with an interest in archaeology.—**Harold O. Forshey**

AMERICAN HISTORY

Atlases

447.   **Atlas of Historical County Boundaries: Iowa.** John H. Long, comp. Gordon DenBoer, ed. New York, Macmillan Library Reference/Simon & Schuster Macmillan, 1998. 248p. maps. index. $130.00. ISBN 0-13-366386-8.

The ambitious goal for the series to which this volume belongs is to detail all the changes in the boundaries and areas of the more than 3,000 U.S. counties, from colonial times to 1990. Earlier works in the series have received high praise for their sound scholarship. This volume also merits such accolades.

The atlas opens with a 6,000-word introduction that details the purposes, sources, and methods used in the production of the volume, as well as a brief history of the constitutional provisions within the state of Iowa that are pertinent to the creation of its counties. The heart of the work consists of 171 pages of maps and county chronologies, alphabetically arranged for each of Iowa's present 99 counties as well as the former counties now extinct. The work also contains 18 census outline maps for Iowa, beginning with the 1836 Territorial Census of the Wisconsin Territory and concluding with a map entitled "Iowa at State and Federal Censuses 1873-1990," the current Iowa county map that has remained unchanged since 1873. The final pages before the bibliography and index provide nine maps that depict the jurisdictional divisions in the region from the purchase of the Louisiana Territory in 1803 to the creation of the state of Iowa in 1846.

This reference work succeeds in its goal of providing a frame of reference for understanding boundary changes within Iowa. The volume, however, makes no attempt to explain why or how these changes occurred. This highly specialized volume with hard-to-find information about county changes in Iowa will be welcomed by genealogists, geographers, and historians conducting local and state research.—**Terry D. Bilhartz**

448.   **Atlas of Historical County Boundaries: North Carolina.** Gordon DenBoer, comp. John H. Long, ed. New York, Macmillan Library Reference/Simon & Schuster Macmillan, 1998. 434p. maps. index. $130.00. ISBN 0-13-366469-4.

The county system was transplanted by early colonists from England to North America and became an important center of justice and local administration. With the exception of Alaska, which has never had counties, and Connecticut, which abolished counties as operational institutions in 1960, the rest of the nation relies heavily today upon the more than 3,000 counties that serve varied functions within the individual states. As the repository of legal documents, judicial proceedings, census reports, and other data, the county courthouse has been an essential source for historical records; indeed, state and local history is often told in terms of counties. However, few counties have retained their original boundaries, and indeed shifting of borders has been normative.

A five-volume *Historical Atlas and Chronology of County Boundaries, 1788-1980* and the *Historical U.S. County Outline Map Collection, 1840-1980*, both published in 1984, were important sources, but both were limited in scope. This volume, part of a 40-volume reference project, attempts a complete geographic history of counties in North Carolina from its founding to the present. The volume contains large, detailed maps and a chronology of all changes in the boundaries of every country that has ever existed in the state. A separate chronology lists geographic changes by date. Other useful features include the county map of the state at the time of every state and federal census, an index of places in their contemporary county, and an extensive bibliography. Long, historian and cartographer at the Newberry Library since 1971, is the editor for all the volumes in this series.

This volume and indeed the whole project are first-rate pieces of scholarship. Genealogists, family and local historians, and attorneys, among others, may find such a reference work useful at various times. Nevertheless, only large libraries will probably wish to include such a source in their acquisition budgets.—**Joe P. Dunn**

Bibliography

449.   Adamson, Lynda G. **Literature Connections to American History, K-6: Resources to Enhance and Entice.** Englewood, Colo., Libraries Unlimited, 1998. 542p. index. $33.50pa. ISBN 1-56308-502-X.

Current educational methods involve more than textbook reading. This useful bibliographic tool links the study of American history with supplementary sources, both historical fiction and nonfiction, found in books and other multimedia material. These resources offer wide appeal to young readers and enhance the learning experience.

The work is divided into 2 major parts. The 1st is a series of chapters arranged by chronological periods or, in several cases, broad issues, such as "Immigrants and Multicultural Heritage." Each chapter has sections broken down by age categories and further subarranged by type of work (historical fiction, biography, nonfiction). Recommended works are listed briefly by author and title. The 2d major part contains annotated bibliographies (books, CD-ROMs, and videotapes listed separately) of all listings included in the 1st section. Each bibliography is arranged alphabetically by author and gives full bibliographical details as well as suitable grade levels for use. This section is followed by author and illustrator, title, and subject indexes that refer back to entry numbers in the annotated bibliographies.

This is an excellent tool for teachers and for librarians attempting to build an age-appropriate collection beyond simple children's fiction. The annotations are brief but well written. However, one must deduce from them whether the work is fiction or nonfiction, because there is no reference back to the listings in the first chapters—a minor inconvenience. Recommendations emphasize new titles, most with copyright dates of 1990 or later. Although this is welcome, users may also wish to be aware of older publications that may still be of value.

—**Patricia A. Eskoz**

450.   Adamson, Lynda G. **Literature Connections to American History, 7-12: Resources to Enhance and Entice.** Englewood, Colo., Libraries Unlimited, 1998. 624p. index. $34.50pa. ISBN 1-56308-503-8.

Educators will welcome this new bibliographic resource when planning courses in literature, history, and social studies. Many teachers find it difficult to identify nontextbook (books and multimedia) works of historical fiction, biography, and nonfiction history. The titles presented here are suitable for teacher background reading, but most are aimed at the students. An extensive listing of titles by historical period and grade is augmented by a bibliography with 2- to 5-sentence annotations, publisher, format, and price. Appended indexes speed location of materials by title, author, and subject.

District libraries should make this available to curriculum committees who may like to include fresh materials in their courses of study but continue to assign the titles they have used forever because they have had no professionally developed alternative lists to choose from. Large history and literature departments will find it to be some of the best money they spend this year. [R: BR, Sept/Oct 98, p. 78; VOYA, Oct 98, p. 310]

—**Edna M. Boardman**

451.   Brown, Lynda W., Donald B. Dodd, Lloyd H. Cornett Jr., and Alma D. Steading, comps. **Alabama History: An Annotated Bibliography.** Westport, Conn., Greenwood Press, 1998. 438p. index. (Bibliographies of the States of the United States, no.7). $79.50. ISBN 0-313-28223-4.

This is the 7th volume in the excellent series of Bibliographies of the States of the United States. The four authors, all retired academics and scholars, have produced a valuable piece of work, the first comprehensive annotated bibliography on Alabama since 1898. The 3,321 entries are arranged in 9 chronologically divided units preceded by a unit on the environment of Alabama and followed by 2 concluding units on general reference sources and on historical sites. Each time period is divided into several topical subdivisions. The scope is interdisciplinary and encyclopedic, with coverage of topics such as agriculture, literature, art, education, religion, folklore, and many other areas of interest. Other valuable features include a map of waterways and major cities, a chronology, and author and subject indexes. The one- or two-sentence annotations are extremely useful.

It would be impossible to overemphasize the value of the entire series. Every volume in it that this reviewer has seen is excellent. This particular addition is certainly no exception. It is the beginning point for investigation of almost any aspect of Alabama's past. One regret was that considering that football has been the second religion of the state, one would have expected a topical subdivision devoted to the subject. Indeed, very little is found on this important part of the state's past in the volume. [R: Choice, Oct 98, p. 295]—**Joe P. Dunn**

452.   Clark, Suzanne M. **New England in U.S. Government Publications, 1789-1849: An Annotated Bibliography.** Westport, Conn., Greenwood Press, 1998. 598p. index. (Bibliographies and Indexes in American History, no.36). $125.00. ISBN 0-313-28128-9.

Students wishing to review expressed concerns of New England's congressional delegations, review federal publications by state, or discover documents of interest are well served by this bibliography. The author examined published sets of federal documents as well as printed and electronic bibliographies to congressional and executive publications. Unless there is reason to believe that a certain committee print or executive document has not been included here, users no longer need to use B. P. Poore (covering 1774-1881), the commonly called "Tables and Index" (covering 1817-1893), or a number of different titles produced by the Congressional Information Service. Complete citations and helpful annotations expedite identification and location of titles within the various U.S. serial publications, including the American State Papers, Congressional edition or set, Congressional Globe, and others.

Coverage of speeches delivered in the House of Representatives or Senate are usually limited to those running to 1,000 words or more. References to maps are excluded "unless they are part of larger New England reports of documents." Subject indexing is carefully done. Arrangement of publications in chronological order by Congress and session within each state encourages discovery via browsing or careful reading of entries. A separate author index includes the complete name of all congresspeople cited as well as organizations and place-names. Users will want to check both author and subject indexes for major organizations and place-names; for example, the Bank of the United States, Boston harbor, and California territory are found in the subject index.

The author's careful review of this literature often provides two or more title citations, increasing the chances for users to locate titles in libraries with incomplete collections of federal publications. The bibliography complements an important series of state bibliographies sponsored by the Committee on New England Bibliography—an important set of bibliographies that includes a few federal documents. An annotated, formal bibliography listing all sources included or checked for references would serve to help laypersons better understand historical periods covered by important congressional sets, years covered by retrospective bibliographies consulted by the author, and something of the huge task involved in producing this helpful bibliography. This is a required purchase for academic libraries in New England and New York. All depository libraries will want to own this volume. [R: Choice, Nov 98, p. 500]—**Milton H. Crouch**

453.   Stephens, Elaine C., and Jean E. Brown. **Learning About . . . The Civil War: Literature and Other Resources for Young People.** North Haven, Conn., Linnet Professional Publications/Shoe String Press, 1998. 259p. index. (Learning About). $32.00; $22.50pa. ISBN 0-208-02449-2; 0-208-02464-6pa.
    Written by two education professors, this volume combines teaching strategies with annotated bibliographies of the Civil War. The book is the second title in Linnet Professional Publications' Learning About series, which is described as "annotated teaching resources for use by educators, librarians, and parents in selecting and using literature and other resources for school-age youth in selected areas of the curriculum." Strongly based on the educational philosophy of integrated teaching units as an approach to teaching history, the book begins with a very general introduction to the Civil War. An explanation of the role of literature in context area teaching, the role of teachers, and ways to use literature to teach about the Civil War follows. A lengthy section explaining "literature involvement" strategies, which gives detailed instructions and examples for each strategy, and a list of guidelines for using fiction and nonfiction in the classroom concludes the section.
    Most of the book divides the Civil War into 6 separate teaching areas ranging from background events leading to the war through its battles and individual experiences and the rebuilding of the nation. Each chapter introduces an aspect of the war; gives prior reading "Think About" questions; and includes at least 10 focus books with complete bibliographies, quotes, brief summaries, teaching considerations, and three or four suggested student activities. A further annotated bibliography ends each chapter. Age level recommendations are given for each suggested book. The last chapter of the volume lists additional resources: audio recordings; films, laser-discs, and videos; simulations and computer software; Websites; selected museums and historical sites; and lesson plans, posters, and other teaching aids. An appendix includes the National Standards for U.S. history that the book addresses, and charts show which standards for each focus book addresses. An index of authors and titles is included, but the book has no topical index for easy reference.
    Fiction, nonfiction, and reference books are all included in the bibliographies. Teaching strategies include well-accepted procedures and a wide variety of activities for several age levels. The comprehensiveness in covering the subject, especially for the middle and high school classroom, makes this a useful volume to use both as a guide for library purchases and as a teaching resource.—**Janet Hilbun**

454.   Tischauser, Leslie V. **Black/White Relations in American History: An Annotated Bibliography.** Pasadena, Calif., Salem Press and Lanham, Md., Scarecrow, 1998. 189p. (Magill Bibliographies). $32.00. ISBN 0-8108-3389-1.
    Tischauser, a professor of history at Prairie State Community College, annotates more than 700 significant monographs published from 1944 to 1996 focusing on the historical, sociological, and psychological functions of race in U.S. history. Divided into 10 chapters covering major aspects of this issue (e.g., local studies, Recon-struction), this work provides students with an introduction to basic works published primarily by university and major house presses, with a smattering of small press titles. Besides the single-volume monographs expected here, Tischauser includes many essential large collections available from Carlson and other publishers, although important books by Thomas Sowell and Taylor Branch are absent. In addition, including books comparing the styles of such leaders as Martin Luther King Jr. and Malcolm X would have been helpful for novices to the civil rights era. Overall, however, the author adequately includes what he can within a few pages. The brief (25 to 100 words) annotations are usually more descriptive than critical and occasionally should be more detailed. As with other titles in this series, this volume is meant neither to be comprehensive nor in-depth, but rather to introduce those unfamiliar with U.S. racial studies to this area. *Black/White Relations in American History* is recommended for undergraduate and public library collections as a complement to *Black-White Racial Attitudes* (see ARBA 77, entry 427) and *Racism in the United States* (see ARBA 91, entry 384). [R: Choice, Nov 98, p. 504]
                                                                        —**Anthony J. Adam**

Biography

455.   Durham, Jennifer L. **Benjamin Franklin: A Biographical Companion.** Santa Barbara, Calif., ABC-CLIO, 1997. 322p. illus. index. $45.00. ISBN 0-87436-931-2.

In this excellent tool, Benjamin Franklin's life is arranged by subject matter rather than chronologically. There are approximately 250 entries, covering topics one would expect to find, such as the Declaration of Independence and his relations with the Pitt family in Pennsylvania, as well as other diverse subjects such as Franklin's thoughts on astronomy, electricity, fire, and medicine. Articles are arranged alphabetically, and each contains both a list of related entries and suggestions for further reading, which usually refer the reader to primary sources (e.g., letters) in one of the published sets of Franklin's papers. Although the biographical articles (e.g., Thomas Jefferson) do give details of the person's life, they concentrate on the person's relationship or interaction with Franklin. Other features include a chronology of Franklin's life, black-and-white illustrations and portraits, *see* references, an appendix of selected writings, and both a bibliography and index. Written in an accessible manner, this reference source is highly recommended for all libraries and all levels. [R: BR, Sept/Oct 98, p. 58]

—**John A. Drobnicki**

Chronology

456.   **Events That Changed America in the Eighteenth Century.** John E. Findling and Frank W. Thackeray, eds. Westport, Conn., Greenwood Press, 1998. 209p. illus. index. (Greenwood Press "Events That Changed America" Series). $39.95. ISBN 0-313-29082-2.

The editors of this work have selected 10 events that they believe had the most impact on the United States in the eighteenth century—the Great Awakening, the Era of Salutary Neglect, the French and Indian War, the Stamp Act, the Boston Tea Party, the Declaration of Independence, the American Revolution, the Constitutional Convention, the XYZ Affair, and the Revolution of 1800. Each chapter is divided into 2 parts, the 1st being a concise, factual presentation prepared by the editors, and the 2d containing a longer, interpretive essay written by a specialist as well as a brief annotated bibliography. The articles are well written and balanced, and the authors do not limit themselves exclusively to the 10 topics at hand. For example, the chapter on the Stamp Act also discusses the Royal Proclamation of 1763 and the Sugar Act. Other features include a glossary, chronology, index, and 10 black-and-white illustrations. Although the articles are longer than those in *Great Events from History: North American Series* (rev. ed.; see ARBA 98, entry 497), the documentation is inconsistent, with only a few quotations having parenthetical references to sources. Several authors that one would expect to find in the bibliographies—for example, Lawrence Henry Gipson, Charles M. Andrews, Max Farrand—are not included. Also, more explicit discussions of the historiographical debates regarding the 10 events would have made the volume even more valuable, particularly for graduate students. Libraries that already have the aforementioned 4-volume Magill set can pass on this one, but this source should prove valuable for U.S. history circulating collections.

—**John A. Drobnicki**

Dictionaries and Encyclopedias

457.   **American Decades on CD.** [CD-ROM]. Detroit, Gale, 1998. Minimum system requirements: IBM or compatible 486. Double-speed CD-ROM drive. MS DOS 5.0. Windows 3.1. 8MB RAM. 5MB hard disk space. SVGA graphics card and monitor (256 color). 8-bit Sound Blaster-compatible sound card. Mouse. $129.00. ISBN 0-7876-1916-7.

Developed to meet curricular needs in high school learning environments, this resource includes information pertinent to many research projects and personal interests of secondary students. Using curriculum lists as well as insights from teachers, librarians, and media specialists, the producers have assembled more than 1,000 biographical entries of the most studied people in the curriculum, with in-depth treatments for 250 individuals.

In addition, the database includes approximately 1,500 subject-specific and overview essays; a navigable timeline featuring world and national events; more than 100 primary documents; a variety of lists and tables for each year, including such information as award winners, wage and price information, popular songs, film, and literature; and more than 1,300 images and 35 minutes of audio and video clips. All of this is easily accessible through a main screen that provides user options, depending on desired focus. From the main menu, the user can perform a free-text search, or navigate in one of seven major areas: browse a specific decade, perform a subject search, search topics in the news, examine primary documents, navigate the timelines, search biographies, or perform an advanced search. Other options include retrieving help screens, choosing options for saving or printing, and scanning the multimedia gallery provided. Information is arranged and accessed in a pleasant and logical manner, providing ease of access for students. A teacher's guide is also provided for those instructors who wish to "test drive" the product through various topics common to the secondary curriculum. This CD-ROM is recommended as a learning tool and as a supplement to high school library collections needing resources in cultural history. [R: BR, Nov/Dec 98, p. 86; BL, 15 May 98, pp. 1650-1651]—**Edmund F. SantaVicca**

458.   **The American Heritage Encyclopedia of American History.** John Mack Faragher, ed. New York, Henry Holt, 1998. 1106p. illus. index. $45.00. ISBN 0-8050-4438-8.
        This one-volume encyclopedia, edited by Yale University professor of American history Faragher, is easy to use and packed with historical facts pertaining to American history—from the pre-Columbian period to the present day. Historians from colleges and universities around the United States are among the more than 125 contributors. It is an excellent resource for students and curious researchers.
        The nearly 3,000 alphabetically arranged entries cover important people, issues, genres, places, and events in government, science, arts, religion, and many other areas that contributed to the ever-changing culture of the United States. Summaries range in length from a short paragraph to a full page. Black-and-white pictures with corresponding captions illustrate the pages. A complete index is included, and cross-references and bibliographic information add to many of the entries for further research. The appendix includes the texts of the Declaration of Independence and the U.S. Constitution; lists of presidents, vice presidents, chief justices, and associate justices of the Supreme Court; a list of states; and a timetable of important historical events from 1699 through 1998. [R: BL, 15 Nov 98, p. 605]—**Felicity Tucker**

459.   Craig, Robert D. **Historical Dictionary of Honolulu and Hawai'i.** Lanham, Md., Scarecrow, 1998. 297p. illus. maps. (Historical Dictionaries of Cities, no.5). $55.00. ISBN 0-8108-3513-4.
        Because there was no written language before the end of the eighteenth century, there is little known about the Hawaiian Islands before that time. Since then, however, the island chain has had an impressive past, involving power struggles among island rulers, consolidation of the island chain under Kamehameha I (1810), formation of the Republic of Hawaii (1894-1898), annexation by the United States (1898-1959), and eventually statehood (since 1959). Hawaii's primary industries have evolved from sandalwood (1810 to 1830) to whaling (1830-1840) to sugar and pineapple (1840-1980s) to tourism (1990s); all have had a significant impact on American and Pacific Rim cultures.
        Craig's volume provides informative and insightful entries on all of these aspects of Hawaiian history as well as entries on many individuals important to past and present Hawaiian culture. The 250-plus entries range from the 5 King Kamehamehas to a current push for sovereignty, from eastern and western religions prevalent in the islands to the Kodak Hula Show and *Hawaii Five-O* television series. Every major island has a long entry. Entries are clear and contain many cross-references. Although the volume is intended as a reference source, it could also provide a good general background on Hawaiian culture and history as well. The volume starts with maps and a helpful chronology and introduction. Several photographs are included, which are better than the charts that can be misleading or inaccurately developed. A long bibliography, organized topically by subject, plus a variety of appendixes ranging from population to Hawaiian holidays concludes the volume.—**Peter H. McCracken**

460.   **Encyclopedia of American Indian Wars, 1492-1890.** Keenan, Jerry. Santa Barbara, Calif., ABC-CLIO, 1997. 278p. illus. index. $60.00. ISBN 0-87436-796-4.
        Native American wars have long been a topic of interest. Many books have been written on the subject, analyzing everything from cultural differences to war tactics. It seems that everything one could possibly know about Native American wars has been rehashed again and again in countless books published over the years. Yet the public has an insatiable appetite for Native American war lore.
        A somewhat different approach to this well-trod subject has been offered by Keenan in his *Encyclopedia of American Indian Wars, 1492-1890.* The work presents well-known and little-known details of Indian warfare.

It consists of descriptions of the subjects, and most feature a useful list of books for further reading. For those interested in reading more, there is an additional list of general readings in the back of the book.

It does not take long for the reader to be consumed by the work. Although some of the entries could use more details, Keenan's work in an interesting, easy read of the leaders, battles, treaties, and lore that make up this nearly 400-year time period. [R: SLJ, Nov 98, p. 154]—**Kelly M. Jordan**

461.   **Encyclopedia USA: The Encyclopedia of the United States of America, Volume 25.** Donald W. Whisenhunt, ed. Gulf Breeze, Fla., Academic International Press, 1998. 247p. $256.00. ISBN 0-87569-076-9.

Begun in 1983, *Encyclopedia USA* continues to plod. Seeking to be both exhaustive (literally anything having to do with the United States is likely to be included) and substantive (the entries are often quite lengthy), this work, 15 years and several editors later, has not even completed the 5th letter of the alphabet. The 25th volume covers only "Ear to Edu." At such a pace, this opus will still be in progress well into the next millennium and could easily surpass 100 volumes.

Criticism of this encyclopedia's trudging and laborious manner is offset by the quality of its content. Clearly written entries by qualified authorities treat everything from the New Madrid, Missouri, and San Francisco earthquakes, Eastern religions in America, and agricultural education to Thomas Edison, economic determinism, and the movie *Easy Rider*. Awaiting readers on almost every page is a treasure trove of information, as in the four-page piece on "Ecosystem" or the five-page account of "Eating in America." The bibliography accompanying each entry will point students and scholars to additional sources. Unless glaring, one is inclined to overlook omissions, for no encyclopedia can include everything. But this encyclopedia's attempt to be all-inclusive prompts the question: Where are the features on Clement Eaton, Sarah Edmonds, Earthspirit Community, and EarthSave? Shortcomings notwithstanding, students and scholars will find this work useful.—**John W. Storey**

462.   Moseley, Edward H., and Paul C. Clark Jr. **Historical Dictionary of the United States-Mexican War.** Lanham, Md., Scarecrow, 1997. 345p. illus. index. (Historical Dictionaries of Wars, Revolution, and Civil Unrest, v.2). $59.00. ISBN 0-8108-3334-4.

In this work, two Latin American history scholars provide a good review of this historical conflict between Mexico and the United States. An introductory essay lists the United States' justifications for war, reviews reasons why many U.S. citizens questioned these justifications, and helps explain the war from Mexico's perspective—an unjustified invasion, occupation, and annexation of territory. An excellent chronology increases the reference value of the work. Most of the entries are devoted to giving biographical information on military leaders, although more U.S. leaders than Mexican leaders are represented. The descriptions of major battles help users understand complex military maneuvers and objectives. Fourteen line-drawn maps complement these discussions.

The subject dictionary is well produced, with quality paper, an attractive format, clear typeface, and a sturdy binding. Black-and-white illustrations are printed on coated paper and grouped together in one signature.

For many students and librarians the biographical entries will be the dictionary's most useful feature. In the bibliographic essay, both Mexican and U.S. primary sources and archival collections are identified but not fully described. Citations of 95 participant accounts provide an excellent selected subject bibliography that will prove useful to anyone needing additional information.—**Milton H. Crouch**

463.   **The New Encyclopedia of the American West.** Howard R. Lamar, ed. New Haven, Conn., Yale University Press, 1998. 1324p. illus. index. $60.00. ISBN 0-300-07088-8.

This massive tome is a limited revision of Lamar's favorably reviewed *Reader's Encyclopedia of the American West* (2d ed.; HarperCollins), first published in 1977. Like its predecessor, it consists of approximately 2,400 articles of varying lengths on the West and westering experience. Articles cover the expected topics of battles, forts, and tribes as well as notable cowboys, ranchers, military personnel, explorers, and trappers, among others. Its biographies are a particular strength, although Dan Thrapps's 4-volume *Encyclopedia of Frontier Biography* (University of Nebraska Press, 1991) remains the unsurpassed biographical reference of the West. Less well-known but equally important topics are also covered, such as territorial governments, environment, mining, transportation, legislation, and notable western historians. Other articles cover cultural aspects such as films; literature; photography, myths; and artists and writers, such as Louis L'Amour and Zane Grey.

Lamar, a former Yale president and prominent historian of the American West, states in the preface that more than 300 notable historians contributed to this work and, indeed, looking at the list of contributors, most names are familiar. Unfortunately, so are most of the articles. A comparison of approximately 100 articles found more than half with unchanged text from the 1st edition. About 20 percent of the reviewed articles had additional paragraphs added to the end of the article, and the remainder are either rewrites or new articles. Most of the new articles cover the hot topics of the past 20 years—ethnic groups, environment, and twentieth-century and cultural issues. The articles show little political correctness among the new western historians, although Patricia Limerick and other practitioners are contributors. Few entries from the 1977 edition were dropped, and a few, such as Walter Prescott Webb's entry, were actually shortened. This edition is substantially more illustrated than the 1st edition, but most of the illustrations are filler. Very few maps were added to a tool that already needed more maps. A personal name index is included, but his does not cover any concept or fact other than names. The lack of a proper index will continue to reduce the utility of this work. The writing level is accessible to high school students, with enough detail to serve as an overview for graduate students. One notable improvement is that the bibliographies are updated for all articles (including those where text was not changed), and citations are as recent as 1997. There is considerable cross-referencing by capitalizing terms in the text.

The field of western U.S. history reference has grown since 1977. This remains the best of the many good 1-volume works, such as Richard Slatta's *Cowboy Encyclopedia* (see ARBA 96, entry 510) and *Cowboys and the Wild West* (see ARBA 95, entry 541). The 4-volume *Encyclopedia of the American West* is as scholarly, has a vastly superior index, and larger, more legible type, yet it has approximately the same amount of articles and costs $395. It complements rather than supercedes Lamar's work. Still a browser's delight, at $60 it is reasonably priced for a 1-volume encyclopedia of this size and is recommended for high school, public, and academic libraries. The high percentage of unchanged material from the 1977 edition make this an optional purchase for those libraries that already own the earlier edition. [R: LJ, 1 Sept 98, pp. 174-175; BL, 15 Nov 98, p. 613]—**Patrick J. Brunet**

464.   **North America in Colonial Times: An Encyclopedia for Students.** Jacob Ernest Cooke and Milton M. Klein, eds. New York, Scribner's/Simon & Schuster Macmillan, 1998. 4v. illus. index. $375.00/set. ISBN 0-684-80538-3.

This 4-volume set is an adaptation for young adults of the 3-volume *Encyclopedia of the North American Colonies* (see ARBA 95, entry 540), of which Cooke was the editor in chief. Unlike the earlier set, which contained long, scholarly articles arranged topically, this set's articles are arranged alphabetically and have been drastically shortened. For example, the former contains an 83-page section on education with articles on specific topics, whereas the latter's entry for education is only 2½ pages. There are 475 unsigned articles covering a wide range of topics, including people, individual colonies, cities, organizations, events, and social issues (e.g., "Childhood and Adolescence"; "Women, Roles of"). Aside from the British colonies in North America, the authors also cover the French, Dutch, Russian, and Swedish colonies, in addition to the Caribbean and the many Native American groups. The language has also been revised for a younger audience, and the set's layout has been changed to make it more appealing; for example, definitions of unfamiliar words conveniently appear in the left panel, adjacent to the text. The set contains 200 black-and-white illustrations, 16 maps, 16 color plates, and an overall index. Readers are referred to related articles and illustrations by *see* and *see also* references and cross-references. Although each article in the parent set contained a bibliography, this new source contains only an overall list of "Suggested Sources," which does include primary, secondary, and online sources. Materials for young readers are helpfully denoted by asterisks. As with any source of this size, there will be omissions and criticisms that some topics are covered too briefly; one example is that, although the set contains many articles about slavery, the entry on the Declaration of Independence does not mention how Thomas Jefferson's early draft contained a condemnation of the slave trade. This set is recommended for public library young adult reference collections, and for academic libraries that serve young people.—**John A. Drobnicki**

465.   **Scribner's American History and Culture.** [CD-ROM]. New York, Macmillan Library Reference/Simon & Schuster Macmillan, 1998. Minimum system requirements (Windows version): IBM or compatible 486. CD-ROM drive. Windows 3.0 or higher. 16MB RAM. 30MB hard disk space. SVGA monitor. $650.00. ISBN Windows version: 0-684-80584-7. ISBM Macintosh version: 0-684-80614-2.

Easily installed and clearly organized, this CD-ROM continues the tradition of issuing standard reference titles in electronic format, providing the full texts of more than 7,200 articles from the *Dictionary of American*

History and its 1996 supplement *The Presidents: A Reference History* (1996) and *The Encyclopedia of American Social History* (1993, with 1998 updates). There are 1,100 biographies from supplements 9 and 10 to the *Dictionary of American Biography* that complete the text, which is augmented by 12 suggested research topics and more than 600 photographs and a timeline. Of particular value are the 75 "Selected Historical Documents," which range from the Mayflower Compact of 1620 to the 1965 decision of *Griswold v. Connecticut* dealing with the right to privacy. Free-text searching allows access by keywords and phrases, subject area, and time period. This CD-ROM will be valuable as a networked resource for school, large public, and undergraduate collections whose paper equivalents of the component titles have seen heavy use.—**Robert B. Marks Ridinger**

Handbooks and Yearbooks

466.   **The American Dream: The 50s.** Alexandria, Va., Time-Life Books, 1998. 192p. illus. maps. index. (Our American Century). $19.95. ISBN 0-7835-5500-8.

Time-Life Books has produced another attractive volume for general consumption. Not meant to be an in-depth look at the decade of the 1950s, this volume touches on the cultural, political, and historical icons of a complicated 10-year span in U.S. history. For the baby boomer generation, this volume holds many memories. The short narrative format, liberally interrupted with beautiful half-tones and four-color prints, presents the period in an attractive, nostalgic manner. Baby boomers can now see themselves as part of history, along with television and the cultural icons that medium spawned. From black-and-white to living color, from tail fins to sports cars, from James Dean to Marilyn Monroe, the Kennedys to Martin Luther King Jr., this volume has them all. The beautiful book is a welcome addition to any personal, middle school, high school, and public library reference collection.—**Norman L. Kincaide**

467.   **American Eras: Development of a Nation 1783-1815.** Robert J. Allison, ed. Detroit, Gale, 1997. 423p. illus. index. $85.00. ISBN 0-7876-1484-X.

American Eras: Development of a Nation 1783-1815 is the first volume in Gale's new history series. It is identical in format and content to Gale's American Decades series, which covers the twentieth century. Aside from slight differences in chapter composition (e.g., lifestyle, social trends and fashion, and medicine and science are combined in the "Eras" volume), the subjects covered and the detail offered are the same (depending, of course, on the availability of pertinent information). Each subject chapter, for example, "Religion," begins with a chronology of events, continues with a general essay or overview of religion in the new nation, and then delves into more specific areas such as African American religion, women in religion, and the rise of evangelicalism. Each of these sections has a brief bibliography. The "Headline Makers" section contains short biographies of notable people, again with bibliographies for each. The chapter ends with an annotated bibliography. Illustrations are attractively and intelligently utilized throughout the text, as are excerpts from contemporary writings. The volume concludes with a detailed index and a list of general references.

The American Decades volumes have proved useful for students needing topical information on subjects such as education, recreation, and the arts that are not often covered in standard histories. The bibliographies provide excellent jumping-off points for further research. The American Eras books should be equally appreciated by those studying earlier periods of U.S. history.—**Deborah Hammer**

468.   **American Eras: The Reform Era and Eastern U.S. Development 1815-1850.** Gerald J. Prokopowicz, ed. Detroit, Gale, 1998. 379p. illus. maps. index. $85.00. ISBN 0-7876-1482-3.

This is the 5th of the projected 8 volumes in the American Eras series. (See ARBA 98, entry 444 for a review of *American Eras: Civil War and Reconstruction, 1850-1877.*) Covering pre-twentieth-century U.S. history, these volumes rely less on political than social history to create a sense of what life was like. This volume surveys the efforts of the young country to establish its own identity.

In addition to a short but highly useful introduction to the period as a whole, there are 11 chapters: "World Events"; "The Arts"; "Business and the Economy"; "Communications"; "Education"; "Government and Politics"; "Law and Justice"; "Lifestyles, Social Trends, and Fashion"; "Religion"; "Science and Medicine"; and "Sports and Recreation." Within each chapter, there is a chronology, a general overview, descriptions of newsworthy events, and short biographies of key players. This reviewer was pleased to see a list of contemporary publications at the end of each chapter, but would have preferred even more titles. Because the books in this series are geared to high school students and undergraduates, introducing primary sources here is commendable. There are also a general index, an index of photographs, and a short bibliography. The black-and-white illustrations used throughout are interesting and pertinent.

Like the American Decades volumes that cover the twentieth century, this series is a wonderful resource for putting an era in perspective. The lively format is designed to pique the interest of even the most history-phobic student. This work and the series as a whole are recommended for high school, undergraduate, and public library collections.—**Hope Yelich**

469.   **American Eras: The Revolutionary Era 1754-1783.** Robert J. Allison, ed. Farmington Hills, Mich., Gale, 1998. 394p. illus. index. $85.00. ISBN 0-7876-1480-7.

American Eras: The Revolutionary Era 1754-1783 is the 6th volume in the series American Eras from Gale. Each volume in the series treats a specific time period, such as the Civil War and Reconstruction, the westward expansion, and the colonial era. Two more volumes are scheduled for publication in 1999.

This volume on the revolution begins with an overview of the period and a chronology of world events. The world chronology serves to put into context the U.S. events that are the volume's focus. Eleven chapters follow the chronology, each with a separate theme, such as religion, government and politics, education, or society. Like the volume itself, each chapter begins with a chronology. Following the chronology are a series of essays, each illuminating the theme of the chapter. For example, in the chapter on the arts, there are essays on the poetry, the theater, and the printing trade of the period. In the chapter on government and politics, there are essays on several of the laws that contributed so heavily to the beginning of the revolution—the Stamp Act, the Sugar Act, and the Tea Act; essays on particular events such as the Continental Congress; and essays on the forms of government in both Massachusetts and Pennsylvania.

Each chapter also contains a series of short biographies of people of the period, both well known and anonymous. Thomas Jefferson, Benedict Arnold, George Washington, and John Adams are all there as well as accounts of inventors, ministers, and college presidents, collected in each chapter under the heading "Headline Makers." Three characteristics of the volume are particularly noteworthy. First, the volume is heavily illustrated. Pages of historical documents, contemporary illustrations of both historical events and typical everyday activities, portraits, and illustrations of artifacts are all included. Second, each chapter contains a "Bibliography of Publications," a list of documents of the period that represent the theme of the chapter. In the chapter on religion, for example, this bibliography contains the writings of both Jonathan Edwards and John Woolman. Finally, there are in each chapter several brief articles or excerpts of articles written by people of the period. Some of these are by well-known people—an essay by Benjamin Franklin on education, for example, in the education chapter. There are also intriguing glimpses from anonymous sources: a piece about recreation on board ship in the sport and recreation chapter, and a piece by an anonymous immigrant on the immigrant experience, in the chapter on lifestyles, social trends, and fashion. All these details serve to make the book more real, immediate, and personal.

This is a book for the high school or beginning undergraduate student, not for the scholar. Beginning students of the period might find enough here of interest to encourage more study, and libraries that serve this clientele will probably want to purchase all in the series.—**Terry Ann Mood**

470.   **Executive Order 9066: The Incarceration of Japanese Americans During World War II.** [CD-ROM]. Danbury, Conn., Grolier, 1997. Minimum system requirements: 486/66 MHz processor & quad-speed CD-ROM drive, Windows 3.1 or higher. $125.00 stand-alone; $249 network. ISBN 0-7172-3409-6 stand-alone; 0-7172-3410-X network.

Approximately 120,000 people, one-third by law not allowed to become naturalized citizens and two-thirds of them native-born Americans, were forcibly removed from their homes on the West Coast. Charged with no crimes and imprisoned without trial, they were forced to sell businesses and personal goods at a fraction of their value. "Military necessity" caused them to be relocated into what were called euphemistically "internment camps" or "relocation centers" complete with barbed wire, guard towers, and machine guns pointing at loyal American citizens. *Executive Order 9066* documents with honesty and balance the violation of Japanese Americans in the United States. Narrated by Pat Morita of *The Karate Kid* and *Happy Days* (and himself interned as a boy), the program is easily navigated through four areas: "Chronology," "Profiles," "Topics," and "Places."

The chronology section begins with the Chinese Exclusion Act of 1882, the Alien Land Laws of 1913 and 1920, the U.S. Supreme Court ruling in 1922 prohibiting Issei (Japanese-born resident aliens) from becoming naturalized citizens, through the war and the steps that led to camp creation. Stories of those in the military and the government who objected to the plan and the many who resigned because of it are included. Each segment is documented with newsreel and home movie footage, historical commentary, personal photographs, and further narration by Morita. The profiles section includes the stories of six famous Japanese Americans, including George Takei (Sulu from *Star Trek*), all of whom were interned and how the experience changed their lives.

The topics section runs through 10 separate areas of interest, from "Before the War" to "The Struggle for Redress." As with the chronology portion, each section is filled with movie clips, photographs, commentary, narration, and historical facts. Included are not-so-subtle ironies, such as the Japanese American 442d (the most highly decorated military unit in history) helping liberate the Nazi concentration camp Dachau at the same time that their families remained in camps in the United States. The places section takes the reader to the more than two dozen internment camps, relocation centers, and isolation camps. Extensive maps and photographs document the areas, which were chosen for their remoteness and isolation. Included is the little-known fact that Canada and countries in South America also pursued internment policies of their own.

Discussing in depth a subject not taught or even mentioned in high schools 20 years ago, *Executive Order 9066* is a must for every middle and high school librarian, history teacher, and homeschooler. A short, printed study guide is included with study questions and research projects. The CD-ROM is highly recommended.
—**Kevin W. Perizzolo**

471. **Facts About the American Wars.** John S. Bowman, ed. Bronx, N.Y., H. W. Wilson, 1998. 750p. illus. maps. index. (Wilson Facts Series). $60.00. ISBN 0-8242-0929-X.

Since the revolution, the United States has engaged in at least 10 major wars and more than 150 smaller wars and foreign interventions. Some 30 percent of the total U.S. experience has been during a time of war. Thus, the task that the editor undertook was an ambitious project. Bowman has a qualified background, as he has written or edited several previous almanacs, including ones on the Civil War, the American West, the Vietnam War, and the twentieth century, and he has served as general editor of the *Cambridge Dictionary of American Biography* (see ARBA 96, entry 35). This volume is the latest addition to the Wilson Facts Series, a collection of fine reference tools.

The treatment of each war follows a common 21-part format, which includes such issues as causes of the war, battles and campaigns, the home front, results, casualties, military innovations, negotiations, legends and trivia, songs, notable phrases, civilian and military biographies, and further readings. At the heart of each entry is a detailed chronology of events, which despite all the other elements of the volume is the most important contribution. The book is well laid out, easy to employ, and full of useful information. The basic text is augmented by a strong preface and introduction, good illustrations and maps, a glossary of military terms, cross-references throughout, a general bibliography on the subject of war, and an index. In sum, this is an extremely valuable reference source. One minor quibble is that although the names of the compilers of each section are listed in the table of contents, nowhere do we learn who these individuals are. Because this one volume serves the scope of U.S. history, it is a good investment for all libraries and is highly recommended.—**Joe P. Dunn**

472. Gelbert, Doug. **American Revolutionary War Sites, Memorials, Museums, and Library Collections: A State-by-State Guidebook to Places Open to the Public.** Jefferson, N.C., McFarland, 1998. 255p. index. $39.95. ISBN 0-7864-0494-9.

Arranged alphabetically by state and subdivided by city, Gelbert's book provides locations and descriptions of sites and collections related to the Revolutionary War, defined in its broadest sense (the mid-1760s to 1787). Most of the entries contain hours of operation and telephone numbers as well as addresses and whether or not admission fees are charged, along with annotations of the site's significance. Canada is treated as a colony and thus interfiled between Arkansas and Connecticut. Although the author portends to include important library collections, there is no mention of the New York Public Library, the New York Historical Society, or the Northeast Region branch of the National Archives in New York City. There is a proper name index that does not include names of museums/libraries—thus, one must browse if the city/state name is not known.

Although this new source is better organized, *Landmarks of the American Revolution* by Mark Boatner (see ARBA 76, entry 326) contains more sites and longer descriptions and covers areas that Gelbert does not include (for example, in Alabama, Louisiana, and Mississippi), but Boatner does not include museums or libraries. The source under review should prove useful, especially for travel reference collections; however, libraries that already own the aforementioned source by Boatner can skip this one, unless they could use it for the circulating collection.—**John A. Drobnicki**

473. Levy, Peter B. **The Civil Rights Movement.** Westport, Conn., Greenwood Press, 1998. 226p. illus. (Greenwood Press Guides to Historic Events of the Twentieth Century). $39.95. ISBN 0-313-29854-8.

This volume is intended for use in secondary schools and college libraries. Levy's clear, well-written, and historically balanced prose is well suited for this purpose. Levy's six essays concern overview and origins of the civil rights movement, in-depth examination of activism and resistance in Mississippi, civil rights and the legal process (including a good discussion of affirmative action), the legacy of the movement, and an especially welcome chapter on the underreported leadership role of women in the movement. Also included are a chronology (1857-1996), biographies of 20 key movement leaders, extracts from 15 primary documents (from Truman's Committee on Civil Rights, 1947, to Arthur Fletcher's "Remarks on the Philadelphia Plan," 1969), a glossary, an annotated bibliography, and an index.

As a historical overview and summary of the civil rights movement, this work is excellent. Not that there are not omissions—only passing mention of Memphis and St. Augustine and nothing on Wilmington (or Ben Chavis, the future director of the National Association for the Advancement of Colored People [NAACP]), or NAACP insider and politician, Grace Towns Hamilton. And brilliant novelist William Faulkner was hardly a "sage," especially on racial matters.

As a reference book, it is less useful. The chronology is insufficiently detailed, too few extracts from primary documents are included, and there is not a separate list of acronyms and initialisms. The annotated bibliography has too few entries, the annotations are too brief to be useful, no sound recordings (e.g., speeches of Martin Luther King Jr., Malcolm X, freedom songs, etc.) or journal articles are included, and the author does not attempt to ameliorate its egregious brevity by listing any of the many bibliographies and reference works on the movement.
—**Fred J. Hay**

474. McDermott, John D. **A Guide to the Indian Wars of the West.** Lincoln, Nebr., University of Nebraska Press, 1998. 205p. $16.95pa. ISBN 0-8032-8246-X.

There is no question that the U.S. Army serving in the trans-Mississippi West during the last half of the nineteenth century faced difficult physical and psychological challenges. In addition, the army was caught between two segments of society—one calling for the extinction of the region's native peoples and the other demanding the groups be saved for civilization and Christianity. This slim volume provides a concise and excellent summary of the challenges as well as a guide to major historic western war sites. Slightly more than 50 percent (110 pages) of the text describes the problem faced by both the army and the native peoples as they fought one another for more than 50 years. McDermott's coverage of the army is generic, and although he mentions all the native people of the region, the author focuses on the "horse culture" groups in the northern plains. At times the author generalizes too much for complete accuracy. For example, he states plains groups had a carelessness with land. That phrasing conveys a rather negative image of the actual native concept, which was that no one owned the land. Further, groups did have territorial boundaries that they defended against intrusions by other groups. Nevertheless, the encyclopedic part 1 provides a sound overview of the challenges and conditions both sides faced. Topics covered in part 1 include material culture; life ways; approaches to warfare; background issues; and the portrayal of the events in art, literature, and film. The historic sites section is organized by state and contains typical tour guide information, location, hours, fees, and one- or two-paragraph descriptions of the site. Types of sites covered are forts, battlefields, and Native American heritage locations.

Although Norman Heard's 5-volume set titled *Handbook of the American Frontier* (see entry 393) provides greater depth of information, this volume is a smoother, more integrated treatment of the material. Because there is no index, one must depend on the table of contents to locate information. This is a worthwhile addition to a western history reference collection.—**G. Edward Evans**

475. **Supplement to the Official Records of the Union and Confederate Armies.** Janet B. Hewett, Noah Andre Trudeau, and Bryce A. Suderow, eds. Wilmington, N.C., Broadfoot Publishing, 1998. 12v. maps. index. $900.00/set. ISBN 1-56837-275-2.

Without exception, the most important compilation of primary source documents on the American Civil War is the 128-volume *The War of the Rebellion: The Official Records of the Union and Confederate Armies*, popularly referred to as the "Official Records." Any scholarly publication on the subject that does not cite this title is immediately suspect. Therefore, when a supplement to this monumental work is published, it deserves special attention. Broadfoot deserves major credit for adding significantly to this important collection with thousands of records omitted from the original work as well as other supplementary material that relates to, but is not part of, the original *Official Records*. A team of historians, librarians, archivists, and others spent years searching period newspapers, libraries, archives, other repositories, and microfilm collections for documents that were missed in the original compilation. Historians, genealogists, and Civil War buffs will appreciate the task of the publisher's team reading documents often faded with age and written in difficult script, weeding out duplicates and false reports, and organizing and indexing these materials.

The *Supplement to the Official Records of the Union and Confederate Armies*, which when completed will total approximately 100 volumes, is in essence four different but related works compiled under one title. Subtitles indicate the varying contents—part 1, reports; part 2, records of events and itineraries; part 3, correspondence; and part 4, files of the (U.S.) secret service. Because of these differences and the fact that each part may be purchased separately, this work will be reviewed in segments as they appear.

Part 1, with which this review is concerned, consists of 10 volumes plus a 2-volume index. Volumes 1 through 7 closely resemble the original *Official Records* in every respect, matching corresponding volumes in number and format and supplementing their subject matter. These contain reports on military engagements, battles, and maneuvers written by Confederate and Union officers during the war, as well as postwar accounts reconstructed by participants. Although remaining true to the original in all respects, the supplement improves on the earlier publication in several respects. Full names and ranks have been added in brackets for individuals only partially identified in the original documents. Geographic and other terms helpful in understanding particular documents are similarly included. The text has also been clarified by the addition of words (in brackets) inadvertently or otherwise omitted by the original writer. As in the original *Official Records*, volumes 1 through 7 each begins with a summary of principal events, and a listing of documents followed by the documents themselves. The source for each item is identified as well as its present location. Volumes 8 through 10 differ in format from the original *Official Records*. By providing the complete text of a military court martial and court of inquiry, these relate in great detail battles of Five Forks, Virginia, and Palmetto Ranch, Texas. Volume 10 also includes a 400 page history of the U.S. Signal Corps during the period 1860-1865.

Access to the battles, persons, and subjects covered in the *Supplement* are generally excellent through the two index volumes. However, this reviewer found one serious flaw in the index. Regiments listed under state entries fail in some cases to identify the unit as white, colored (in Civil War terminology), Union, or Confederate. A user searching for the First North Carolina (white) Union regiment, for example, may be led instead to the First North Carolina Confederate or the First North Carolina Colored. Although this error is intended for correction in a cumulative index to the entire 100-volume set, this needs to be corrected through errata slips or the provision of corrected pages for insertion at appropriate places.

As noted, this is a work of great importance. Libraries that already possess the original *Official Records* should purchase the *Supplement*. Other libraries with an interest in the Civil War should purchase, depending on budgets, the entire or pertinent portions of the *Supplement to the Official Records*.—**Donald E. Collins**

476. **The Tree of Liberty: A Documentary History of Rebellion and Political Crime in America.** rev. ed. Nicholas N. Kittrie and Eldon D. Wedlock Jr., eds. Baltimore, Md., Johns Hopkins University Press, 1998. 392p. illus. index. $24.95pa. ISBN 0-8018-5643-4 (v.1); 0-8018-5811-9 (v.2).

The editors of this work broadly interpret political crime to include dissent, protest, disobedience, violence, and rebellion against governmental authority. More than 400 documents have been culled from statutes, legal decisions, pamphlets, broadsides, diaries, and speeches. The major events and participants in political crime in the United States, whether in purely political or in social, economic, religious, or gender struggles, are included. Among the earliest documents are the *Mayflower Compact* (1620) and the more recent document, *The Unabomber Manifesto* (1995).

The 2 volumes, "Colonial Era to World War II" and "Cold War to New World Order," organize the sources chronologically and thematically. Chapter titles include "Consolidation and Schism: Suffrage, Citizenship, and the Right of Secession, 1821-1861," "World War I and the Rise of Totalitarianism, 1917-1940," and "The Cold War and the Battle Against Subversion, 1947-1967." Each document is preceded by an introductory paragraph that offers context. Documents are sometimes abridged, with material extraneous to political dissent deleted. A cited source, either a monographic reprint or an original court reporter, permits easy access to the full document. The editors include several documents from the Internet while noting their ephemeral nature.

A useful bibliography is included as well as a proper name index and table of cases. The concordance and user's guide is an index to topical subjects (e.g., conscription, habeas corpus, Native Americans, and picketing). Selective illustrations capture the flavor of the texts. This is an extremely valuable compilation that will be a useful addition to any academic library or historical reference collection.—**Ruth A. Carr**

AFRICAN HISTORY

477. Grotpeter, John J., Brian V. Siegel, and James R. Pletcher. **Historical Dictionary of Zambia.** 2d ed. Lanham, Md., Scarecrow, 1998. 571p. (African Historical Dictionaries, no.19). $95.00. ISBN 0-8108-3345-X.

Nineteen years after John Grotpeter wrote the 1st edition of the *Historical Dictionary of Zambia*, Brian V. Siegel, an anthropologist, and James R. Pletcher, a political scientist, published the 2d edition. The dictionary follows the same format: a chronology, the dictionary, and a selected bibliography. Significant early dates have been changed in the chronology. For example, in the 1st edition the estimated time of early man in Zambia was 30,000 B.C.E.; in the 2d edition the date has been changed to 123,000 B.C.E. Also, the chronology now includes events between 1979 and 1996. The original dictionary included approximately 1,160 entries; the new edition has only a few more entries. These entries cover such topics as place names, biographies of significant people, information on ethnic groups and languages, significant events, and information on economic and social issue. Compared to the earlier edition, some entries have been dropped, others added, and others have been rewritten and updated. Some entries are only a sentence long, whereas others are more extensive, such as the entry on the "United National Independence Party," which is approximately five pages long. The selected bibliography is arranged by broad topics. Again, many of the bibliographic citations remain the same; however, the authors have added some new citations since 1978. This book is recommended for libraries with an interest in African studies. [R: Choice, Oct 98, p. 296]—**Karen Y. Stabler**

478. Jenkins, Everett, Jr. **Pan-African Chronology II: A Comprehensive Reference to the Black Quest for Freedom in Africa, the Americas, Europe and Asia, 1865-1915.** Jefferson, N.C., McFarland, 1998. 572p. index. $65.00. ISBN 0-7864-0385-3.

This volume follows an earlier one with the same title, devoted to the years 1400 to 1865 and published in 1996 (see ARBA 97, entry 426). It consists of a chronological list of events and people, with a light preponderance toward African American history. Throughout the work sidebars provide extended information about a person or event in some way commemorated in one of the years covered by the volume. Thus, for example, the Seminole wars (pp. 110-115), the Australian boxer Peter Jackson (pp. 203-205), or St. Peter Claver (pp. 223-226) are treated at some length. These are usually interesting—interesting enough that they may stimulate readers to pursue matters further. Unfortunately, it will be difficult for them to do so because there are no tie-ins between entries and sources, and the bibliography of approximately 75 items seems too short to have sufficed for the author's task. The events for each year are covered in six regional sections (United States, Americas, Europe, Australia, Asia, and Africa), each of these subdivided in turn into a large number of topics. The inevitable fragmentation that results is mitigated by good cross-referencing and a comprehensive index—which need not have included dates as well as page numbers. Accent marks are missing throughout.

The rate of factual error seems quite small, despite the breadth of the coverage; however, important events are often not distinguished from those that had little contemporaneous or subsequent impact. The arrangement the author has adopted means that there are three ways of finding information: trolling through the volume (not without its benefits but hardly efficient), knowing the year in which an event occurred, and consulting the index. In short, there is almost no way to attack this work frontally. Although this is a handicap, it is admittedly hard to find an alternative organization to the volume that would improve matters. As this work demonstrates, serendipity does have its attractions, and its comprehensiveness and cross-referencing—once a hit is made—render it an interesting and informative introduction to the African experience throughout the world. All the more reason why users will probably wish for a better citation system. [R: Choice, Sept 98, p. 99]—**David Henige**

479.   Killion, Tom. **Historical Dictionary of Eritrea.** Lanham, Md., Scarecrow, 1998. 535p. (African Historical Dictionaries, no.75). $65.00. ISBN 0-8108-3437-5.

Eritrea is the newest African country, having achieved independence from Ethiopia in 1991. As a result, this is only the 1st edition of this dictionary, whereas those of other African countries are undergoing their 3d incarnation. In length, the volume more closely parallels these later editions and is able as well to benefit from some of the improvements that these have gradually incorporated over the past 20 years. For instance, it includes extensive cross-referencing in the form of capitalized words within entries, a decided improvement over earlier editions in this series. An index would have helped even more. The entries are longer than is traditionally the case, but the preponderant attention to modern times is all too much in keeping with the longstanding practice of these historical dictionaries. Stronger points are the 80-page bibliography divided on chronological and topical lines and a 20-page chronology that carries events almost until the end of 1997. There is also the usual list of acronyms and four hand-drawn maps that ought to have been computer-produced.

Given Eritrea's short independent life and small size, this volume is able more thoroughly to cover the country, both past and present, than other volumes in this series. As a result it supersedes the *History Dictionary of Ethiopia and Eritrea* published in 1994. It would have been helpful, however, to have consolidated lists of officials. Having entries for some individuals and not others wrenches too much information from its historical setting and virtually interdicts opportunities for users of achieve any kind of continuity. This is presumably one effect of having so many of these volumes written by nonhistorians.—**David Henige**

480.   St. John, Ronald Bruce. **Historical Dictionary of Libya.** 3d ed. Lanham, Md., Scarecrow, 1998. 452p. maps. (African Historical Dictionaries, no.33). $75.00. ISBN 0-8108-3495-2.

This volume departs from the African Historical Dictionaries series' norm by having fewer but longer entries, but in terms of its focus and technique it is much the same as other volumes in the series. The dictionary includes a table of abbreviations and acronyms; a detailed chronology for the period since 1969; a brief introduction; 13 appendixes (chronological tables of rulers, a few export statistics, and 7 maps); and a bibliography that runs to 110 pages. The work is likely to be useful for the last feature, and those interested in affairs in Libya since the establishment of the republic may find some entry-level information in the entries, the majority of which deal with this limited period.

In short, this volume is not really "historical," with few entries dealing with Libya's 25 centuries of recorded history before 1969. An effect of this is greatly decontextualized data. For instance, the Hafsid Dynasty and the Hilalian invasions are mentioned in passing in certain entries but are never adequately identified for readers, nor given an entry of their own. Other historical actors—the Almohads and Almoravids, for instance—who played a marginal role in Libyan history are accorded greater attention. There is strangely little on the Sanusiyya, who dominated Libyan religious and secular affairs for more than a century before 1969.

The bibliography at the end of the volume could have been published separately, for it is of value, and it could even have been combined with the post-1969 chronology and with a prosopography of modern Libyan leadership. Beyond these tools, however, it is difficult to know what audience would be served with the remainder of the dictionary.—**David Henige**

ASIAN HISTORY

General Works

481.   Klooster, H. A. J. **Bibliography of the Indonesian Revolution: Publications from 1942 to 1994.** Leiden, The Netherlands, KITLV Press; distr., Detroit, Cellar Book Shop Press, 1997. 666p. index. (Bibliographical Series, v.21). $65.00. ISBN 90-6718-089-0.

Indonesia's revolutionary struggle for independence from the Netherlands during the period 1945 to 1949, was a seminal experience in the development of national identity and the emergence of a Third World outside the bifurcated categories of the Cold War. For most Indonesians, it is receding into mythology because less than 4 percent of the present population were adults during the revolution. Yet this volume demonstrates, by drawing primarily on the holdings of Dutch libraries, that there is an enormous written record (both contemporary and reflective) on the revolution.

The author contends that many people writing on the revolution are unfamiliar with earlier publications. The 7,014 entries here should eliminate any excuse for such omissions. Moreover, Klooster provides an 84-page introductory bibliographic essay highlighting major works and approaches that should be required reading for anyone considering research on the nation or era. The 480 pages of entries are divided among general works, the Japanese occupation, publications from 1945 to 1950, later writings, and the Moluccan questions remaining after the revolution. Each of these sections is subdivided for Indonesian, Dutch, and other authors, the divisions reflecting the predominant languages of the entries: Indonesian, Dutch, and English.

Access is simplified by indexes to authors, personal names, geographic names, and subjects. Eight pages of abbreviations are an essential addition for a nation that has made acronyms commonplace linguistic elements. Although the revolution had dramatic political and economic consequences for Indonesia and internationally, the transformation of the population intellectually and philosophically has been even more dramatic. This is best reflected in the literary output of the era and up to the present, and Klooster wisely includes *belles lettres*. Although one may quibble with elements of the treatment, the magnitude and comprehensiveness of the volume commend it to any research or other library supporting research on Indonesia. [R: Choice, Sept 98, p. 99]—**K. Mulliner**

482.　Singh, D. Ranjit, and Jatswan S. Sidhu. **Historical Dictionary of Brunei Darussalam.** Lanham, Md., Scarecrow, 1997. 178p. illus. maps. (Asian/Oceanian Historical Dictionaries, no.25). $64.00. ISBN 0-8180-3276-3.

This volume, by two of the few scholars researching Brunei Darussalam, provides a valuable introduction to the oil-rich, smallest (population 305,000) nation in Southeast Asia. Its wealth (and that of its ruler, Sultan Hassanal Bolkiah, who has been called the richest man in the world) has given it influence well beyond its size. The sultan, for example, has been identified as financing the purchase of Harrod's by Mohamed Al-Fayed (father of Princess Diana's companion, Dodi Al-Fayed), owning major hotels in the United States and Great Britain, and funding the contras in Nicaragua in the 1980s.

The dictionary departs from the style of earlier titles in the series by including a number of photographs. Other added materials include a lengthy bibliography, appendixes of rulers, British residents, cabinet officers and functions, statistical tables, and a glossary. Because Brunei is neglected or omitted in many treatments of Southeast Asia, this volume offers background information that will be needed by anyone wishing to research the nation and its royal family (especially given the personal rather than institutional nature of Brunei government). The likelihood of such interest has increased in 1998 as allegations of financial mismanagement and sexual shenanigans by the sultan's brother and former finance minister, Prince Jefri, have attracted international media attention. [R: Choice, Sept 98, p. 101]—**K. Mulliner**

China

483.　Sullivan, Lawrence R, with Nancy R. Hearst. **Historical Dictionary of the People's Republic of China: 1949-1997.** Lanham, Md., Scarecrow, 1997. 279p. (Asian/Oceanian Historical Dictionaries, no.28). $56.00. ISBN 0-8108-3349-2.

Sullivan and Hearst's *Historical Dictionary* complements and updates Edwin Pak-wah Leung's *Historical Dictionary of Revolutionary China, 1839-1976* (see ARBA 93, entry 523). Unfortunately, it suffers from many of the same problems. As a dictionary, rather than an encyclopedia, it would be more useful with many short definitions of terms, events, concepts, places, and people, but too many important concepts lie buried in other articles. For example, there is no specific article on the June 1989 student protest and crackdown in Beijing (although it is referred to in many articles using a wide variety of terms); the length of the Long March is not given in its article (although it does appear elsewhere); and nonspecialists will have trouble finding references to Quemoy and Matsu, and to the Ussuri River clashes with the Soviet Union. Even more disturbing are the various spins on the death of Lin Biao in 1971, depending upon where it is noted. With no index, important individuals who did not merit their own articles are not accessible. Other problems speak to the lack of proper editing—casual, derogatory phrasing not appropriate to a reference work; a predilection for placing some terms in quotations; inclusion of information of either no apparent relevance or trivial interest; and the frequent appearance of current matters on issues in a manner not at home in a historical dictionary.

Subject experts will be able to figure out where to look for what they want, but may not find much they do not already know; nonexperts will have more difficulty using this as a reference tool. The lack of a compact alternate source makes this a necessary item for most academic and research collections with appropriate subject interest. [R: Choice, Sept 98, p. 102]—**Kenneth W. Berger**

Indic

484.   de A. Samarsinghe, S. W. R., and Vidyamali Samarsinghe. **Historical Dictionary of Sri Lanka.** Lanham, Md., Scarecrow, 1998. 214p. maps. (Asian/Oceanian Historical Dictionaries, no.10). $38.50. ISBN 0-8108-3280-1.

This volume provides concise reference information on the island state known prior to 1972 as Ceylon. Sri Lanka has long-standing cultural and geographic connections with neighboring India as well as a distinctive linguistic and historical identity of its own. After 150 years of British colonial rule, Ceylon first became independent in 1948. The main features of the *Historical Dictionary of Sri Lanka* are a concise chronology, an introductory survey of Sri Lankan culture and history, the dictionary, and a bibliography. The authors give primary attention to twentieth-century and contemporary topics, although earlier historical periods are also represented. Entries in the dictionary section briefly describe selected Sri Lankan institutions, events, persons, or places. Entries on caste, land reform, language policy, Tamil homeland, and other subjects are also included. Significant attention is given to the ethnic conflicts between Sri Lankan Tamils and Sinhalese that, since the late 1970s, have troubled this predominantly agricultural country. The selected bibliography, which is arranged by topic, cites mainly English-language books and some articles. The authors of this work are a husband and wife team of Sri Lankan origin who now reside in the United States. The *Historical Dictionary of Sri Lanka* will be a welcome addition for academic or other libraries with South Asian collections.—**Lee S. Dutton**

485.   Riddick, John F. **Who Was Who in British India.** Westport, Conn., Greenwood Press, 1998. 445p. index. $115.00. ISBN 0-313-29232-9.

This is the first attempt to compile a biographical reference on Britons who served, resided in, or traveled in India during the Raj period since the 1906 publication of Charles E. Buckland's *Dictionary of Indian Biography*. The current publication covers approximately 350 years, from the late sixteenth century to Indian independence in 1947. It contains entries for almost 3,500 men and women, most from the British Isles but some from other countries in the Empire or the continent of Europe. As would be expected, a large number of biographees were military officers, government officials, civil service employees, and members of parliament. However, the scope is wide: archaeologists, religious leaders and clergy, businesspeople, missionaries, scientists, explorers, literary figures, orientalists, medical workers, and travelers are represented. The number of women is small (31 are listed), but this reflects the status of women during the time. Most were educators, novelists, missionaries, or medical workers, although two vicereines and one historian are included. Each entry gives basic information and lists positions held in India or in other countries, major contributions, and titles of their publications, if any. A bibliography of sources and a list of abbreviations are provided. A personal name index is arranged under occupational categories, allowing the researcher to locate persons in a particular field. Many of the biographees would be known only to subject specialists, but some are well known for other contributions of general interest, such as novelist Rumer Godden, the Mountbattens, and Elihu Yale, whose generous contributions to the fledgling American University caused it to bear his name. This work is highly recommended for all subject and for large reference collections.—**Shirley L. Hopkinson**

Japanese

486.   Modern Japan: An Encyclopedia of History, Culture, and Nationalism. James L. Huffman, ed. New York, Garland, 1998. 316p. illus. maps. index. (Garland Reference Library of the Humanities, v.2031). $95.00. ISBN 0-8153-2525-8.

Entries from 103 contributors cover a wide variety of topics relating to the political, cultural, and economic history of Japan from the early 1850s to the present time. Each entry is signed and includes one or more bibliographical references in the English language. Emphasis is placed on the development of the intense Japanese nationalism, from its beginnings as a fear-driven response to the opening of the country by the western world, to the nation building of the Meiji Era and the empire-building period from 1900 to 1945, to the market building since 1945. However, many entries relating to the arts, religion, literature, and education are also included. Entries for persons give biographical data and evaluate the person's influence upon the political or economic climate of his or her time. Organizations are described in terms of membership, ideology, and influence. The effect of journals and other publications is assessed. Although the development of nationalism is stressed, there is a good balance, with entries for persons or groups who opposed the belligerent nationalistic trends. Supplementary materials include a chronology of events from 1853 to 1996, two black-and-white maps that show Japan in relation to contemporary Asia, and an introduction by the editor that sketches the history of Japanese nationalism and discusses important scholarly works on the subject. A subject list gathers the entry topics under 30 broad headings and shows the scope of the encyclopedia. Included are subjects such as concepts, cultural nationalism, the emperor system, women, eras, the military, and philosophy and the world of ideas. A detailed index provides access to specific topics and names found in the broader entries. This encyclopedia will be essential in all subject and area studies collections, as well as in general reference collections. [R: BL, 1 June 98, pp. 1812-1814; Choice, July/Aug 98, p. 1837]—**Shirley L. Hopkinson**

Philippine

487.   Guillermo, Artemio R., and May Kyi Win. Historical Dictionary of the Philippines. Lanham, Md., Scarecrow, 1997. 363p. (Asian/Oceanian Historical Dictionaries, no.24). $62.00. ISBN 0-8108-3243-7.

Reference works are essential to the cultivation of Southeast Asian studies. The best of these specialized works—bibliographies, dictionaries, catalogs, and statistical compendiums—provide both the novice and the experienced scholar with effective guides to the field and its resources. Although as demanding to write, reference books receive far less regard than the scholarly monograph. This is unfortunate, for it may lead to the production of reference tools by unqualified authors that hinder, rather than promote, the study of a discipline. Given the importance of well-written reference texts to the development of a field like Southeast Asian studies, there is a glaring dearth of dictionaries, indexes, bibliographies, and other resources essential to the study of the region. One attempt to meet the need for an introductory reference book is the Asian/Oceanian Historical Dictionaries series by Scarecrow Press. Applying a standard format, each book starts with a chronology and brief introduction that is followed by the main dictionary section, consisting of entries covering persons, places, events, and institutions. The dictionary ends with a bibliography intended to guide beginning scholars to additional information.

The series as a whole may be seen as useful, although the quality of individual titles varies greatly. *Historical Dictionary of the Philippines* calls the entire series into question with numerous factual errors, uneven contents, a noncurrent bibliography, and ideological overtones. This dictionary fails to guide a reader through the complex history of the Philippines even when it attempts to explain more recent events associated with Ramos. It omits major historical events and people, including the Treaty of Paris and writers like Lope Santos and Carlos Bulosan, whose pens supported social and political movements. Factual errors abound, with the editors asserting that the Propaganda Movement was "carried on by Filipinos living in Spain and France" and that the Thomasite teachers were "predecessors of the Peace Corps." A strong anticommunist and pro-American bias further misleads readers with claims that the most notable American contribution to the Philippines was the "introduction of the democratic form of government" and that all leftist political organizations were eventually "crushed" or "nipped in the bud" by the government. It is evident that the authors of the volume have little background in Philippine history. The need for an elementary guide to Philippine history and historical research is needed more than ever. It is the editors of the series who must justify the publication of a reference work that cannot be recommended for public or academic library reference shelves.—**Carol L. Mitchell**

Vietnamese

488.   Duiker, William J. **Historical Dictionary of Vietnam.** 2d ed. Lanham, Md., Scarecrow, 1997. 353p. (Asian/Oceanian Historical Dictionaries, no. 27). $68.00. ISBN 0-8108-3351-4.

The 1st edition of this important book was published in 1989 (see ARBA 90, entry 526). Recent changes inside Vietnam and its relations with other nations have increased the need for a new and expanded edition. Duiker, professor emeritus of East Asian Studies at Pennsylvania State University and the respected author of several seminal studies of Indochina and Vietnam, prepared both editions.

This new edition has been thoroughly revised and expanded. It has many new entries and also has a change in focus, with greater attention devoted to economics and business issues. There is more emphasis on recent events and individuals. There are a number of new entries on science and technology; the legal system; and filmmaking. A final change is the use of diacritical marks in the Vietnamese-language entries in the dictionary section. As in the 1st edition, there is a liberal and effective use of cross-references.

After a nine-page incisive introduction that surveys Vietnamese history from ancient to modern times comes the dictionary. Its 271 pages remain the heart of the work, and its entries expertly cover the entire sweep of Vietnamese history and culture. Although entries on the Vietnam War figure prominently in this source, readers should consult *Dictionary of the Vietnam War* (see ARBA 89, entry 457). The bibliography is quite extensive and impressive, consisting of an introductory essay as well as listings of sources by chronological and subject divisions. It is followed by two appendixes, one on a brief chronology of events in Vietnamese history and the second on demographic and economic statistics. There are also four maps, as in the first edition.

The 2d edition of the *Historical Dictionary of Vietnam* is a scholarly and valuable reference book prepared with great care by an established authority in this field. As such, it should find a place in every library. [R: Choice, July/Aug 98, p. 1836]—**Marshall E. Nunn**

CANADIAN HISTORY

489.   Gobbett, Brian, and Robert Irwin. **Introducing Canada: An Annotated Bibliography of Canadian History in English.** Pasadena, Calif., Salem Press and Lanham, Md., Scarecrow, 1998. 373p. index. (Magill Bibliographies). $45.00. ISBN 0-8108-3383-2.

More than just a well-organized, annotated bibliography of recent publications on numerous aspects of Canadian history published in English, this volume also contains brief attributes of research trends, both past and present. The pragmatic annotations provide the reader with information about the work discussed, a brief glimpse of the background of the event or issue being discussed, and both the strengths and weaknesses of the work. Often the annotations include *see also* and *see instead* references to other works and the rationale behind these references. The bibliography is divided into 10 sections, each beginning with general works on that topic with the exception of one section. The exception is "Intellectual, Cultural, Educational, and Science History," which looks at a sense of place; moral reform, religion, and secularization; education and the university; science, technology, and medicine; sports history; and media and communication in Canada. The other 9 sections include general texts and reference materials; native aspects of history; political history; economic and business history; working-class and labor history; women's and family history; ethnic and immigration history; regional and urban history; and external relations and military history.

The scope of the included works is broad, with a few titles published in the 1970s but the majority of titles more recent. This reviewer is confused, however, by the omission of *The Beaver: Exploring Canada's History* magazine, when more marginal history periodicals are included.—**Gail de Vos**

EUROPEAN HISTORY

General Works

490. **Ancient Civilizations of the Mediterranean.** [CD-ROM]. Princeton, N.J., Films for the Humanities & Sciences, 1997. Minimum system requirements: IBM compatible 386. CD-ROM drive. Windows 3.1 or higher. 3MB hard disk space. SVGA display. Mouse. $149.00.

One of the more broadly scoped electronic products relating to the classical world and its archaeology, this colorful and easy-to-navigate CD-ROM focuses on six ancient cultures—Egypt, the Etruscans, Greece, Rome, Carthage, and Phoenicia. Distinctive directional icons are drawn from the unique history of each individual culture; for example, a bust of Queen Nefertiti for Egypt and the mythical chimera for the Etruscans are presented. Each section summarizes available data on the religious life, economy, arts, and social structure for the civilization under study. The map icon of "Places" presents a selection of representative sites illustrated by slides (a feature present in the Egyptian section, although the icon itself is lacking), whereas the "History" icon gives access to chronologies of important events. Two limited glossaries are provided, the first of which gives biographical information on selected notable individuals from each culture, chiefly political leaders, artists, writers, and scientists. The "Terminology" glossary is longer and emphasizes the technical language of art and architecture. A flaw in these sections is that not all letters contain either names or terms, and some major figures, such as the Ptolemies of Egypt, are not mentioned at all. This product is most useful for school and large public libraries serving secondary school clientele. [R: VOYA, June 98, p. 155]—**Robert B. Marks Ridinger**

491. **Ancient Greece and Rome: An Encyclopedia for Students.** Carroll Moulton, ed. New York, Scribner's/ Simon & Schuster Macmillan, 1998. 4v. illus. maps. index. $350.00/set. ISBN 0-684-80507-3.

This 4-volume set is designed to provide a single reference source students can go to for information regarding classical Greece and Rome. Some features incorporated into this work include text that is broken down into easy-to-follow subheadings; more than 200 illustrations, maps, diagrams, and drawings; graphic timelines that clarify the chronology of events; sidebars that highlight interesting stories; notations that remind students to refer to the index; difficult words that are marked by an asterisk and defined in the margins; and a complete bibliography that is included for further reading.

Perhaps one of the best designed reference works to come along in a long time, these 4 volumes are beautifully laid out and formatted. Great care and consideration can be seen with the turning of each page, and the extensive coverage of subject matter is remarkable. History, government, culture, the arts, architecture, agriculture, religion, mythology, and famous figures of nonfiction and fiction are all there. The expected subjects are listed as well as some nice surprises. "Euclid" is expected, but "shellfish" is a surprise. The sidebars and margins are so full of fascinating tidbits and pieces of information it is easy to become engrossed in these peripheral data alone. The plethora of maps and illustrations help to break up the text, making research more entertaining, and 4 sections of color plates (1 in each volume) show artifacts of "Daily Life," "Art and Architecture," "People," and "Culture."

The tone of this reference source for middle and high school students is just right. The narrative is easy to follow and understand, although the younger students may find the long (often Latin-based) names of ancient people and places hard to digest, and the older students may find the descriptions blunt and all too brief.

The all-inclusive cross-referencing is to be praised as much as it is to be cursed. By plodding from cross-reference to cross-reference, a fairly decent and complete definition may be obtained on any specific subject. But be forewarned—the majority of descriptions cross-reference an item from volume to volume to volume. If all 4 volumes are not at the student's disposal, he or she might become discouraged and seek out other reference materials. Because of this, the set may be better suited for a small school library over a large public library where books are often off their shelves. However, a public library will probably be in a better position to purchase the set than a small school library because the books are rather pricey.

Often in reviewing reference and research sources such as this, it is the bona fide mission of the reviewer to find that which is missing or not sufficiently detailed. However, this reviewer opted not to spend the many hours and effort to find and therefore criticize the work for the lack thereof, but to thoroughly enjoy all that is there (which is staggering). *Ancient Greece and Rome* is highly recommended to all who can afford it, and it is suggested that the rest save up to get it. This 4-volume set is guaranteed to get a good workout wherever it is. [R: BL, 1 Oct 98, p. 354; SLJ, Nov 98, p. 156; VOYA, Dec 98, pp. 387-388]—**Joan Garner**

492.   Heyn, Udo. **Peacemaking in Medieval Europe: A Historical and Bibliographical Guide.** Claremont, Calif., Regina Books, 1997. 194p. index. (Regina Guides to Historical Issues, v.7). $34.95. ISBN 0-941690-71-7; 0-941690-72-5pa.

Volume 7 in the Regina Guides to Historical Issues series, this title contains an extended essay (some 75 pages divided into 8 chapters) on the history and process of peacemaking in Europe from the tenth to sixteenth centuries; a reader's guide to the literature, with excerpts from primary documents; annotated lists of more than 1,000 selected sources and studies; and author and subject indexes. Heyn has published scholarly articles on the subject of medieval peacemaking in works such as the *Encyclopedia of Arms Control & Disarmament* (see ARBA 94, entry 797) and journals such as *War & Society*. As with many European studies, Heyn's essay and bibliography is heavily slanted toward western Europe and sources and studies are primarily in German, English, or French with a few sources in Latin and other languages (e.g., Spanish) included.

The essay and the study guides will be of primary interest to medievalists. This work is recommended for academic and research libraries with large, graduate-level collections in the history of medieval Europe and the history of political science.—**Jonathan F. Husband**

Danish

493.   Thomas, Alastair H., and Stewart P. Oakley. **Historical Dictionary of Denmark.** Lanham, Md., Scarecrow, 1998. 533p. maps. (European Historical Dictionaries Series, no.33). $65.00. ISBN 0-8108-3544-4.

This compilation covers the entirety of Danish history from prehistoric times, the Viking era, through the age of exploration and colonization when Denmark was a world force, up to the present period of peace and prosperity. There are entries for people from all fields of endeavor; events in history; political parties; organizations; terms relevant to the government of Denmark; places of importance, such as the Tivoli Pleasure Gardens; and such broad, general subjects as agriculture, theater, music, religion, unemployment, and welfare. An introduction summarizes Denmark's geography, people, history, relations with other countries, the World War II occupation, and Denmark's modern constitution.

There are several appendixes. Charts list monarchs with dates, official names, nicknames, and prime ministers and cabinets. Statistical tables give political and economic data. There is also a population growth graph. A lengthy bibliography, primarily of English-language titles, most published since 1965, suggests sources for further study. Its entries are arranged under eight categories: general, culture, economics, history, law, politics, science, and society. A list of abbreviations and acronyms is also provided, as is a chronology of Danish history from ca.14,000 B.C.E. to 1998.

The compilation was begun by noted Scandinavian studies scholar Oakley. After his death in 1995, the project was continued by Thomas, a professor of Nordic studies at the University of East Anglia. This dictionary will be an essential addition to subject collections and a useful reference aid in general reference collections.
—**Shirley L. Hopkinson**

Eastern Europe

494.   Detrez, Raymond. **Historical Dictionary of Bulgaria.** Lanham, Md., Scarecrow, 1997. 466p. (European Historical Dictionaries, no.16). $82.00. ISBN 0-8108-3177-5.

Beginning with a chronology of Bulgarian history (500 B.C.E. through February 1997), the author provides information on people, political parties, historical events, institutions, and cultural topics relating to Bulgaria. There are more than 500 entries arranged alphabetically, with *see* references and cross-references, but there are no maps, and the volume does not have an index. Articles range in length from one sentence to several pages, and a transliteration table and a list of political parties and organizations are included. A few articles, such as "Anti-Semitism" and "Jews," could have been consolidated, and the author uses "Moldavia" instead of the preferred "Moldova." At least one error was noticed: Dimitar Blagoev died in 1924, not 1923. The 100-page bibliography contains mostly English-language sources, with a few Bulgarian, French, and German items (titles are translated into English). Items are not annotated and are arranged by broad subject ("Cultural") and subdivided further by topics ("Folklore," "Music"), and full bibliographic information is provided. Most of the items are scholarly, but journalistic items are included where appropriate. The bibliography is more up-to-date, particularly on the post-communist period, than the volume titled *Bulgaria* compiled by Richard J. Crampton in the World Bibliographic Series (ABC-CLIO, 1989). This source fills a gap in the reference literature and should be considered by academic and large public libraries.—**John A. Drobnicki**

495.   Georgieva, Valentina, and Sasha Konechni. **Historical Dictionary of the Republic of Macedonia.** Lanham, Md., Scarecrow, 1998. 359p. (European Historical Dictionaries, no.22). $49.50. ISBN 0-8180-3336-0.

The authors begin this volume with a chronology of Macedonian history from 600 B.C.E. to November 1995 before providing an introductory overview of the country's history and economy. The dictionary itself contains nearly 400 alphabetically arranged articles, ranging in length from one sentence to several pages, and topics covered include historical figures, politicians, relations with particular countries, and institutions.

There are numerous omissions, however: There are no articles on the press/media, the Holocaust, Jews, or even the United Nations (although the UN is mentioned elsewhere). Although certain topics are highly controversial, the authors do not always mention both sides—thus, their brief discussion of the grievances of the substantial Albanian minority neglects to mention that 99 percent of them voted for autonomy in a 1992 referendum, nor is there mention of the government's attempts to shut down the controversial Albanian-language University of Tetova. Macedonia's highly strained relationship with Greece is not always portrayed from a detached, objective point of view. The authors speak of the Greek name game and blame the United States' initial reluctance to recognize Macedonia on the powerful Greek-American lobby.

Users may find the authors' system of cross-referencing to be annoying or intrusive because they use "(q.v.)" rather than bold or italic typefaces to refer readers elsewhere. There is one black-and-white map (which was printed in two different places), and a few articles should have been consolidated (e.g., "Ethnic Minorities" and "Minorities") The bibliography contains primarily scholarly English-language books and articles, as well as a few Websites, Usenet newsgroups, and listservs. The most serious drawback, however, is that although the book was published in late 1998, it includes nothing after November 1995, omitting three years of current events, such as the July 1997 violence in Gostivar. Because information on Macedonia is not always readily available in one handy reference source, this book is recommended with the above reservations.

—**John A. Drobnicki**

496.   Hochman, Jiří. **Historical Dictionary of the Czech State.** Lanham, Md., Scarecrow, 1998. 203p. (European Historical Dictionaries, no.23). $46.00. ISBN 0-8108-3338-7.

Following the standard format in this series, the author begins with a chronology of Czech history (700 B.C.E.-June 1997), before giving a general introductory overview of topics such as geography, history, and the economy. The dictionary itself contains more than 200 alphabetically arranged entries, providing information on events, political parties, people, institutions, and cultural topics, along with *see* and cross-references. Articles range in length from two sentences to several pages, but there are several omissions—the dictionary lacks entries on composer Bedřich Smetana (although there is a cross-reference for him) and on Czech foreign relations, as well as articles on its bordering neighbors, such as Poland. There is no entry on Czech-Soviet relations, and a few biographical articles lack birth and death dates, such as Jan Kubis, one of Reinhard Keydrich's assassins. One of the book's two maps mistakenly labels Moravia as "Monrovia." The highly selective bibliography is primarily limited to scholarly materials published in the past 20 years, and includes books and journal articles in English and Czech (English translations are helpfully provided), as well as a few in French and German arranged by broad subject. It is not nearly as comprehensive as *Czech and Slovak History: An American Bibliography* (Library of Congress, 1996), which was limited to English-language sources. Hochman also provides a list of principal Czech academic journals as well as a list of 31 leading libraries and information centers, with addresses and e-mail addresses. This work should be considered by all academic and large public libraries.

—**John A. Drobnicki**

French

497.   Fierro, Alfred. **Historical Dictionary of Paris.** Lanham, Md., Scarecrow, 1998. 245p. maps. (Historical Dictionaries of Cities, no.4). $68.00. ISBN 0-8108-3318-2.

This dictionary covers the breadth of Paris history and cultural development. The entries address traditional subjects as well as popular culture, from Clovis I to the origin of the Samartine department store's name. The author's goal is to give a total compendium of the city's major events, people, places, and monuments, including Americans associated with Paris. Given the brevity of the book, omissions are inevitable. A few that jump to mind are General Leclerc and Poilane bread.

Fierro adds broad topics, such as trees, theaters, and public assistance. Although he relates these terms back to the Parisian experience, unless one reads the volume from cover to cover, these will not be found. This reference also provides a brief history of the city, an extensive bibliography, and statistical appendixes with population data, among other things. Even with its flaws, the French aficionado will find this work useful. [R: C&RL, Oct 98, p. 712]—**Adrienne Antink Bendel**

498.   **Historical Dictionary of World War II France: Occupation, Vichy, and the Resistance, 1938-1946.** Bertram M. Gordon, ed. Westport, Conn., Greenwood Press, 1998. 432p. index. $95.00. ISBN 0-313-29421-6.

This is the last of a series of reference books from Greenwood Press intended to provide a convenient single source of information on a given historical period in France. Entries are arranged in a dictionary format, and include not only military, political, and biographical information but also entries devoted to economic, social, and cultural topics. Details of the daily life in occupied and Vichy France are also provided. Articles are relatively short; the one on Charles de Gaulle, for instance, is less than two pages long. This book can also be used as a bibliographical resource because each article gives references for further reading. A new feature not present in other volumes in the series is a general bibliography under broad topics at the end of the volume. A chronology provides dates not only within the period but related events up until 1998. Two-fifths of the mostly academic contributors reside outside the United States, with one-third being French. Although this book is not a substitute for comprehensive histories of the period, it should prove useful to anyone wanting a convenient reference source on all aspects of France during the period, as well as an excellent, up-to-date guide to bibliographic references on the period. This work is recommended for all libraries collecting in history.—**Marit S. MacArthur**

499.   Ross, Steven T. **Historical Dictionary of the Wars of the French Revolution.** Lanham, Md., Scarecrow, 1998. 267p. (Historical Dictionaries of War, Revolution, and Civil Unrest, no.6). $72.00. ISBN 0-8108-3409-X.

This work is divided into 2 parts: the dictionary, covering 184 pages (including maps and a chronology) and a bibliographic essay and bibliography, covering 80 pages. The dictionary includes articles on battles, alliances, treaties, statesmen, soldiers, weapons, and tactics as well as changes and innovation in warfare. The subjects are well selected and the articles informative and suitable for interested researchers who cannot read French.

The bibliographic essay and bibliography seem to have been tacked on to the dictionary and written for an entirely different audience. Whereas the dictionary will be helpful to the undergraduate or nonspecialist, the bibliography is mostly composed of French-language materials. Some of these, such as guides to French archives, will be of use only to the most advanced of researchers and will be available only in the largest libraries. The bibliography is organized into sections for guides, bibliographies, works on European and French history, histories of the revolution, campaigns, warfare, armies, weapons, and bibliographies and memoirs. Dates of publication range from the early nineteenth century to the mid-1980s. These citations as well as the remarks in the bibliographic essay have been taken from Ross's 1984 publication *French Military History, 1661-1799: A Guide to the Literature* (see ARBA 85, entry 461). With the exception of perhaps a half-dozen titles, the work reviewed has not been updated and includes the misspellings, incorrect citations, and superseded editions of the 1984 work. The bibliographic essay, which in the earlier work had alphanumeric links to the bibliography, has no such links here and no index. Because the essay discusses works only by the author's name, readers must hunt through the subject sections to find titles and publication data. In at least five instances a work mentioned in the essay is not listed anywhere in the bibliography.

Were this title more sure of its intended audience and its bibliography more up-to-date and more accurate, it might be recommended. Libraries serving readers who are interested in the military of this period will do well with David G. Chandler's *Dictionary of the Napoleonic Wars* (see ARBA 94, entry 521) or Philip J. Haythornthwaite's *The Napoleonic Source Book* (see ARBA 92, entry 492), both still in print and both covering the wars of the revolution.—**Eric R. Nitschke**

Greek

500.   Adkins, Lesley, and Roy A. Adkins. **Handbook to Life in Ancient Greece.** New York, Facts on File, 1997. 472p. illus. maps. index. $45.00. ISBN 0-8160-3111-8.

The authors of this work, both professional classical archaeologists associated with the Museum of London, have written more than 80 pieces on various aspects of ancient civilization, including *Handbook to Life in Ancient Rome* (see ARBA 95, entry 586) and *Dictionary of Roman Religion* (Facts on File, 1996). Their latest offering continues in this tradition of providing readable information about Greco-Roman culture in an accessible format.

The book is organized thematically, with sections on "City-States and Empires," "Rulers and Leaders," "Military Affairs," "Geography," "Economy and Trade," "Towns and Countryside," "Written Evidence," "Mythology and Religion," "Science and Art," and "Everyday Life." The volume features many illustrations, most of which are quite useful; this is a good place to find, for instance, a chart of various pottery shapes. There is also a 32-page, closely printed alphabetic index for easy reference, although users should be careful to take into account spelling variants (e.g., one finds under *khoe* a specific sort of liquid libation, but under *Choes* the name of the holiday on which such libations were made). The bibliography runs to 12 pages, and appears to be fairly up-to-date. The glory of ancient Greece cannot be encapsulated in a single volume by even the best informed and pithiest of scholars, and naturally various details have been omitted. This reviewer was particularly sorry not to find an entry for *kottabos*, the drinking game in which wine dregs were flung at targets from empty cups. All in all, however, the concentration on the daily life of nonelites is useful.

The Adkins's book, nonetheless, has some serious conceptual blindspots; it is shocking that they include only a single page of information about women, and only one-half page about homosexuality, both as subsections under "The Family." We live in the 1990s, not the 1890s, but users would never know it reading the Victorian truisms on gender and sexuality included here. But it is not a trendy book, of course, so perhaps it should not be faulted for being what it is—a solid though not exhaustive guide to ancient Greek life. [R: RBB, Aug 97, p. 1926]
—**Christopher Michael McDonough**

501.   Garland, Robert. **Daily Life of the Ancient Greeks.** Westport, Conn., Greenwood Press, 1998. 234p. illus. maps. index. (The Greenwood Press "Daily Life Through History" Series). $45.00. ISBN 0-313-30383-5.

Garland's *Daily Life of the Ancient Greeks* is the newest offering from Greenwood Press's "Daily Life Through History" Series, which also includes titles on Mesopotamia (see entry 511), the Incas, the Mayas, England in various periods, and present-day United States. Of the numerous handbooks to the study of classical Greek civilization now available, this is among the best. It will probably be of most use to middle and high school students. Following a brief historical outline, the book treats these areas: space and time, language (including alphabet and literacy), the people, private life, the public sphere, pleasure and leisure, and the impact of Ancient Greece and modern culture. Garland summarizes usefully what is known about a wide variety of issues in classical antiquity, refraining from the arch tone of older handbooks that only dealt with the lives of the aristocracy. Here one can find out about the daily doings of women, slaves, and children in addition to the generals and politicians. It is also interesting to note in the final discussion dealing with classical impact not only the usual discussion of etymology and democracy but also a half-page summary of the "Black Athena" debate.

Overgeneralization and omission are of course problems in the making of handbooks, and this is no exception; the section on sexual mores, for example, is far too abbreviated. Furthermore, the maps, because they are line-drawn, are not terribly helpful. It is difficult to figure out what is land and what is water. The quality of illustration is otherwise fairly good; the reproduction of a drawing of a monster from the lead curse tablet (p. 129) is striking and informative. But, as with so many handbooks of this variety, the pictures are far too few. Finally, the further reading section includes suggested translations, anthologies, reference works, novels, magazines, videos, and CD-ROMs. It is worth noting that, although several sophisticated scholarly books have been included, there are unfortunately no articles listed in the bibliography. However, with these problems noted, *Daily Life of the Ancient Greeks* is still a well-designed and useful resource. [R: BL, 1 Nov 98, p. 532]

—**Christopher Michael McDonough**

Russian

502.   Raymond, Boris, and Paul Duffy. **Historical Dictionary of Russia.** Lanham, Md., Scarecrow, 1998. 411p. (European Historical Dictionaries, no.26). $72.00. ISBN 0-8108-3357-3.

According to the publisher, Scarecrow Press has produced 33 European historical dictionaries, some already in their 2d edition. Number 26 in this series focuses on Russia, and is written by Boris Raymond (Russian name Boris Romanov), a Russian bibliographer and a professor of library science. In the task of writing this dictionary Raymond was assisted by Paul Duffy, who works at Dalhousie University's library, as well as a few individuals residing in Russia.

In format and execution, the Russian dictionary is quite similar to other volumes in this series. It is obviously not a scholarly work, but will be of some assistance to the uninitiated. There is a longer introduction about the history of Russia (written with some Russian bias), and most entries in the dictionary are brief and to the point. The reader will find here biographies of some individuals, geographical names, and important events. The authors indicate that they cover only the history of Russia and of the Russian Federated Republic since 1991.

As one can expect, there are some errors and misinterpretations. For example, Petr Grigorenko was a well-known Ukrainian dissident and participant in the Moscow and Kyiv Helsinki Monitoring Group. The Variangian Theory concerning the establishment of Kievan Rus (Kyivan Rus') is open for discussion in scholarly circles, and this fact should have been mentioned. There are a number of "blind" references; for example, under "Lavra" there is a reference to "Pochevskaia Lavra in Volhynia," but no entry under "Pochevskaia'" or its correct spelling "Pochaiva'ka." Speaking about "Polteva, Battle of," one should mention that this was a battle between Peter the Great and his opponents, Charles XII of Sweden and Ukrainian Hetman Mazepa. Ukraine lost its independence after Polteva.

Most "longer" articles are simply too short to tell the user more about a subject than he or she will find in a general encyclopedia. But, all in all, this is a useful dictionary, albeit one that should not be consulted for Ukrainian, Belarussian, or other non-Russian topics. [R: BL, 15 Dec 98, p. 765]—**Bohdan S. Wynar**

United Kingdom

503.   **The Oxford Companion to British History.** John Cannon, ed. New York, Oxford University Press, 1997. 1044p. maps. index. $60.00. ISBN 0-19-866176-2.

British history is a subject of perennial interest to academics, students, and the general public. All of these groups will welcome this attractive new reference work from Oxford University Press. Edited by the respected historian John Cannon, it consists of more than 4,000 signed entries written by 121 recognized scholars. Individual entries range in length from 50 words to several thousand words and deal with people, laws, battles, cities, counties, and institutions, along with such broad topics as sports, population, and feudalism. Cross-references are supplied in the body of individual entries, and *see* references are scattered throughout the work. There are 12 black-and-white maps and 6 genealogical charts included.

The publication of this new *Oxford Companion to British History* invites comparison with the recent *Columbia Companion to British History* (see ARBA 98, entry 465). Both books contain more than 4,000 entries, although the *Columbia Companion*'s entries tend to be shorter. A survey of the entries under the letter "K" in both volumes reveals that the *Oxford Companion* included 64 entries compared to the *Columbia Companion*'s 62 entries. Only 35 entries appeared in both volumes, whereas 29 were unique to the *Oxford Companion* and 27 were found only in the *Columbia Companion*. The *Oxford Companion* includes more entries about places, which is consistent with statements in the preface, and the *Columbia Companion* includes more political topics. Furthermore, the Oxford volume is more oriented to U.S. interests. Although both volumes have an entry on the Boston Tea Party, only the *Oxford Companion* has one for the Boston Massacre. It also has an entry for King

William's War. No core topics, however, are omitted by either work. Given such significant differences in their coverage, most libraries will want to buy both reasonably priced volumes.—**Ronald H. Fritze**

504.   Panton, Kenneth J., and Keith A. Cowlard. **Historical Dictionary of the United Kingdom. Volume 2: Scotland, Wales, and Northern Ireland.** Lanham, Md., Scarecrow, 1998. 465p. maps. (European Historical Dictionaries, no.17). $60.00. ISBN 0-8108-3441-3.

Since his rise to power in 1997, British prime minister Tony Blair has begun a process of devolving some political power to Scotland and Wales. This devolution, coupled with ongoing peace initiatives in Northern Ireland, makes it useful to examine the histories of these regions. This second volume of Panton and Cowlard's *Historical Dictionary of the United Kingdom* serves as an introductory reference to the individuals and events shaping the history of Scotland, Wales, and Northern Ireland (see ARBA 98, entry 467, for a review of the 1st volume).

This work opens with key historical events, Scottish monarchs, British secretaries of state for these regions, local government maps, and a contextual introduction. The main section of this compilation includes an alphabetic list of important individuals and events in historical and contemporary Scotland, Wales, and Northern Ireland. These entries feature cross-references in bold typeface to entries on related subjects. A concluding bibliography refers to important historical books on these regions, key scholarly journals, selected government documents, and a reference to a Website of Edinburgh University's School of Scottish Studies. Entries profiled in the dictionary include the Society of United Irishmen, recent British Secretary of State for Scotland Malcolm Rifkind, kilt, former British Labour Party leader Neil Kinnock, current British Conservative Party leader and former Secretary of State for Wales William Hague, Irish Republican Army, golf, Scots Gaelic, Edinburgh International Festival, medieval scholar John Duns Scotus, Church of Scotland, Battle of Bannockburn, and Aberdeen.

This 2d volume of the *Historical Dictionary of the United Kingdom* is a helpful introduction to Scottish, Welsh, and Northern Irish history. The entries are objective and succinct, and the authors provide ample bibliographic citations for users desiring more substantive study and analysis of chronicled individuals and personalities. An additional project the authors and publishers may want to consider would be an annotated compilation of credible scholarly Websites dealing with the history of these regions. This work is a worthwhile addition to any library desirous of maintaining a high-quality British history collection.—**Bert Chapman**

505.   Rasor, Eugene L. **Earl Mountbatten of Burma, 1900-1979: Historiography and Annotated Bibliography.** Westport, Conn., Greenwood Press, 1998. 139p. index. (Bibliographies of British Statesmen, no.21). $65.00. ISBN 0-313-28876-3.

This work is a fine subject bibliography. It offers a clearly defined topic handled by a compiler possessing an extraordinary familiarity with the sources, a bibliographic essay that not only evaluates the source material but situates it in the larger realm of the subject's life, world events and other scholarship, a judiciously selected bibliography enhanced by succinct yet informative annotations, and a simple linking apparatus to tie together the essay and the list of sources.

In chapters on archival and manuscript material, biographical works, and works on Mountbatten's ties with the royal family, naval career, World War II commands and experiences, postwar military career, and assassination, the author notes and describes the sources documenting this full, privileged, and often controversial life. What a help to the researcher to have the literature, with its various sides, opinions, proponents, and opponents, so well delineated. Still, this work does not claim to list everything written about Mountbatten. Absent are newspaper articles and articles from popular magazines. The author concentrates on book-length studies and selected articles from scholarly journals published from 1937 to 1996, with most titles published from the late 1950s to the mid-1990s. The bibliographic portion is supplemented by a chronology and author and subject indexes.

This is a most suitable purchase for academic and public libraries serving readers with an interest in British history, World War II, or the independence of India, not to mention Mountbatten himself.—**Eric R. Nitschke**

506.   **Who's Who in British History: Beginnings to 1901.** Geoffrey Treasure, ed. Chicago, Fitzroy Dearborn, 1998. 2v. index. $250.00/set. ISBN 1-884964-90-7.

Originally published between 1988 and 1997 as a chronologically arranged set of 8 volumes, this edition of *Who's Who in British History: Beginnings to 1901* has been condensed into 2 large volumes, in which the articles are arranged alphabetically. The smaller format and rearrangement of the articles make the book easier to use, especially for readers unsure of the dates of their subject. The editor has, however, included a chronological list of all of the subjects of each volume before the main text. Although the scope of the book makes it impossible to include the truly obscure, the book's coverage is impressive, and the articles themselves are informative and well written. The authors have taken recent historiographical developments into consideration, and although never tendentious, they do not shy away from offering judgment: "Sir Isaac Newton's scientific career had a strangeness all its own," for example (p. 912), or describing George Jeffreys as "the most brutal of James II's agents" (p. 719). British monarchs and major political and literary figures receive broad coverage, but scientists, artists, and engineers all claim their places. Many of the articles direct the reader to further sources of information, although in some cases there are more recent sources than those cited.

Although neither as detailed nor as wide-ranging as the forthcoming *New Dictionary of National Biography* (DNB), *Who's Who* is a valuable reference for a reader in search of quick information or clues for further reading. Unlike the DNB, it will occupy a minimum of shelf space and still provide basic information about important figures in British history. Students, casual readers, and scholars in need of historical detail will all find these volumes to be extremely valuable. [R: BL, 1 Sept 98, p. 165]—**Victor L. Stater**

MIDDLE EASTERN HISTORY

507.   AbuKhalil, As'ad. **Historical Dictionary of Lebanon.** Lanham, Md., Scarecrow, 1998. 269p. (Asian Historical Dictionaries, no.30). $65.00. ISBN 0-8108-3395-6.

Lebanon (from the Semitic root l-b-n, meaning "whiteness," in reference to the snow-covered peaks of Mt. Lebanon) in the 1950s and 1960s may have indeed, as the foreword suggests, been an oasis of peace and prosperity in an area of the Middle East dominated by a series of tumultuous events between Israel and the Arab world. In the 1970s and the 1980s, the Lebanese Civil War shattered this image and exposed a community life dominated by competitive fragmentary groups engaged in shortsighted promises and broken alliances. Sketching five stages of a historical profile—ancient and medieval, Ottoman rule, the French Mandate, independence period, and post-Civil War—AbuKhalil portrays a harsh account of Lebanese culture and society not as progress but as despair and locates it not only in the past but in the present, thereby making it easier to assess the future. The how and why, who are the major players (individuals and groups), and what events over the decades make the difference are the focus of this indispensable guide. For the most part, the listings are properly researched and fairly presented. A 33-page bibliography with items in Arabic, English, French, and German complements the volume. As collator and commentator, AbuKhalil has done an admirable job.—**Zev Garber**

508.   Bidwell, Robin. **Dictionary of Modern Arab History: An A to Z of Over 2,000 Entries from 1798 to the Present Day.** New York, Kegan Paul International; distr., New York, Columbia University Press, 1998. 456p. $225.00. ISBN 0-7103-0505-2.

G. Rex Smith's posthumous publication of Bidwell's *Dictionary of Modern Arab History* is a welcome addition to the literature on the modern Arab world. Bidwell had spent 14 years working on this dictionary prior to his sudden death in June 1994. The period covered by the more than 2,000 entries extends from 1798, the date of Napoleon's invasion of Egypt, to the time of Bidwell's death. His extensive knowledge of the modern Middle East and its leaders, including personal contacts with many of those leaders, makes this a lively although idiosyncratic work. There are some surprising omissions. For example, there is no article on King Hussein of Jordan, even though there are entries for Crown Prince Hassan as well as their father Talal. This gap is in striking contrast to the extensive articles on both Anwar Sadat and Hosni Mubarak. Despite omissions of this kind—which are to be expected in a dictionary produced by a single author rather than a committee—this volume will be a valuable reference source and belongs in any library with an interest in modern Arab history.—**Harold O. Forshey**

509.   Blumberg, Arnold. **The History of Israel.** Westport, Conn., Greenwood Press, 1998. 218p. index. (The Greenwood Histories of the Modern Nations). $35.00. ISBN 0-313-30224-3.

The book is organized as a chronological narrative on the importance of the land of Israel to the people of Israel, with three major emphases: a road map on the Zionist idea from biblical times to the creation of the state of Israel (May 14, 1948), equipped with timelines, short biographical sketches, and a annotated bibliography; 50 years of the state of Israel, with a focus on governmental, military, political, religious, and social issues; and a heady examination with a tilt to the right on the turbulent road to recognition and peace between Israel and the

Arab world. This is not comprehensive history so much as it is an illustrative analysis of key moments in a story against all odds: how a tribe of wandering desert nomads conquer a land, lose it, and after 2,000 years, reclaim it. The author treats the history to the Six-Day War (1967) gingerly, as a concession to the series objective to treat up-to-date material, but the last 30 years are filled with rich detail and insight not well known to the general public. For example, the biblical name Judea and Samaria was the term of record during the Turkish and British Mandate periods to describe the West Bank, and thus it was not superimposed on the map of Palestine for political advantage by the Israelis. However, there are factual errors, such as the Hebrew language is primarily transcribed in the Aramaic script (adopted ca.700 B.C.E.); Theodore Herzl, father of political Zionism, proposed the conversion of the Jews of Vienna to Christianity in a diary entry ("Began in Paris around Pentecost 1895"), not in an essay; the title of Chaim Nachman Bialik's gripping poem on the Kishinev pogrom (begun on April 6, 1903) is properly translated, "In the City of Slaughter," not "A Tale of Slaughter." Nonetheless, these mistakes pale in light of the book's strength. This is a reader-friendly history primer to the making and makeup of the state of Israel.

—**Zev Garber**

510. David, Rosalie. **Handbook to Life in Ancient Egypt.** New York, Facts on File, 1998. 382p. illus. maps. index. $45.00. ISBN 0-8160-3312-9.

This handbook presents ancient Egyptian life through an interdisciplinary approach, using the three main sources available to investigators: monuments such as temples and tombs, objects and artifacts from archaeological sites, and written materials available from different times of history. The author, a notable Egyptologist, works with the material through 11 chapters of varying lengths, each with many subsections. She includes discussions of historical background, geography, society and government, religion of the living, funerary beliefs and customs, architecture and building, written evidence, the army and navy, foreign trade and transport, economy and industry, and everyday life. Where appropriate, photographs, line drawings, and maps are included to support the text.

Each chapter includes references to other readings by topic, thus encouraging the reader to explore further. Unfortunately, a number of revised and recent works do not appear in the bibliography. For example, *The Third Intermediate Period in Egypt (1100-650)* (Aris & Phillips, 1973) published a revised edition in 1996, and *The Origins of Osiris* (Hessling, 1966) published a significantly revised edition as *The Origins of Osiris and His Cult* in 1980 (E. J. Brill). *Ancient Egyptian Kingship*, edited by David O'Connor and David Silverman (E. J. Brill, 1995); *Religion in Ancient Egypt*, edited by Byron Shafer (Cornell University Press, 1993); and A. J. Spencer's *Early Egypt* (Oklahoma University Press, 1993), to note a few, do not appear at all. In addition, some outright errors appear. For example, Tuthmosis III is not the son of Tuthmosis I, King Hor-Aha is now commonly accepted as the first dynastic ruler, and sister marriages are generally seen as rare.

Despite these concerns, this volume belongs on the shelves of the public and school library. The breadth and thoroughness of its coverage will serve the beginning student well, and there is nothing else known to this reviewer quite like it. [R: BL, 1 Oct 98, pp. 363-364]—**Susan Tower Hollis**

511. Nemet-Nejat, Karen Rhea. **Daily Life in Ancient Mesopotamia.** Westport, Conn., Greenwood Press, 1998. 346p. illus. index. (Greenwood Press "Daily Life Through History" Series). $45.00. ISBN 0-313-29497-6.

Nemet-Nejat's lively account of daily life in ancient Mesopotamia fills an important gap in the literature. The other treatments of this subject, such as the classic work by H. W. F. Saggs, *Everyday Life in Ancient Meso-potamia* (Dorset Press, 1965), are now well out of date. Writing for both students and educated laypeople, Nemet-Nejat begins her book with a useful timeline and then a brief discussion of the rediscovery of ancient Mesopotamia and the decipherment of the ancient texts. This is followed by a description of the geographical setting of Mesopotamia and its peoples and languages in chapter 2 and then a historical overview in chapter 3. Chapters 4 through 11 are arranged topically, treating such subjects as writing, education, city life, private life, science, and religion. She concludes with a brief assessment of the legacy of ancient Mesopotamia. A glossary and selective bibliography provide additional help for the reader. This is a fascinating and authoritative synthesis of an extensive body of material pertaining to life in ancient Mesopotamia, and it will be a frequently consulted reference by those with an interest in this subject. This work is highly recommended.—**Harold O. Forshey**

WORLD HISTORY

Bibliography

512.   Adamson, Lynda G. **Literature Connections to World History, K-6: Resources to Enhance and Entice.** Englewood, Colo., Libraries Unlimited, 1998. 326p. index. $30.00pa. ISBN 1-56308-504-6.

513.   Adamson, Lynda G. **Literature Connections to World History, 7-12: Resources to Enhance and Entice.** Englewood, Colo., Libraries Unlimited, 1998. 511p. index. $32.50pa. ISBN 1-56308-505-4.

Adamson's *Literature Connections to World History*, published in two volumes (one covering grades K-6 and one 7-12) features two main sections. The first part of each volume lists authors and book titles in categories of historical fiction, biography, CD-ROM, and videotape within specific geographic regions and time periods according to grade level. Chapter divisions in the first section are by chronological time periods. The second part of each volume contains annotated bibliographies of the titles listed in the first section. Individual works are easily accessible using the author/illustrator, title, and subject indexes. Not all titles included are now in print, but the author explains that the older entries should still be available in libraries.

Teachers will appreciate the ease of making lesson plans using Adamson's grade level-matched bibliographies for their history study units; and, the video and CD-ROM titles will help them to bring historical events to life in the classroom. Librarians, however, will find these two volumes to be excellent book selection tools; reviewing the grade level and time period categories and the book annotations, they will be able to enrich their collections as well as fill any holes with precision. These works are highly recommended for school and public libraries and for individual teachers who might wish to own personal copies.—**Marcia Blevins**

514.   Edwards, Paul M., comp. **The Korean War: An Annotated Bibliography.** Westport, Conn., Greenwood Press, 1998. 345p. index. (Bibliographies and Indexes in Military Studies, n.10). $79.50. ISBN 0-313-30317-7.

The first major commitment of armed forces under the auspices of the United Nations, the Korean War was also the United States' first limited was as opposed to a punitive expedition. As one of the few small "hot" was of the Cold War, Korea helped define U.S. foreign policy not only in Asia, but also in the world as a whole. As the Cold War mindset fades from memory, the war that helped to define containment will be viewed in a context completely foreign to those who lived through the Korean War and the 40-odd years of the Cold War.

This work advances the understanding of the conflict by cataloging the sources for research on the Korean War. This is more than an assembly of source material on military operations. Edwards includes the causes, involvement of various nations, special topics, prisoners of war, propaganda, responses to the war on the home front, the result of the war, and its consequences. This work is well organized, annotated, and is highly recommended for government, public, college, and university reference collections. [R: Choice, July/Aug 98, p. 1836]—**Norman L. Kincaide**

515.   **The Eighteenth Century: A Current Bibliography n.s. 16—for 1990.** Jim Springer Borck, ed. New York, AMS Press, 1998. 533p. index. $123.50. ISBN 0-404-62221-6. ISSN 0161-0996.

516.   **The Eighteenth Century: A Current Bibliography n.s. 17—for 1991.** Jim Springer Borck, ed. New York, AMS Press, 1998. 500p. index. $139.50. ISBN 0-404-62222-4. ISSN 0161-0996.

Well-organized and annotated, these works lists significant books, articles, and reviews published on eighteenth-century subjects during 1990 and 1991. The 1990 volume includes six sections that deal with printing and bibliographic studies; historical, social, and economic studies; philosophy, science, and religion; and fine arts, literary studies, and individual authors from the eighteenth century. Some publications from years prior to 1990 are also represented. Although not all entries are annotated, those that are have extensive information. The problem with bibliographies such as these is the lag time between the publication of the works cited in the bibliography and the publication of the bibliography. Considering the time it takes scholars to research and write an article or a monograph, plus the lag time between submission and publication of their work, some of the scholarly work cited in this bibliography must be older than 10 years. With database upgrades continually providing for better means of collecting and collating data, there must be a more efficient means of compiling bibliographies that are not already eight years out of date. Despite this shortcoming, these bibliographies are a valuable addition to any college and university library reference collection.—**Norman L. Kincaide**

517.   Rasor, Eugene L. **The China-Burma-India Campaign, 1931-1945: Historiography and Annotated Bibliography.** Westport, Conn., Greenwood Press, 1998. 282p. index. (Bibliographies of Battles and Leaders, no.22). $75.00. ISBN 0-313-28872-0.

This is the author's fourth of five projected volumes on the Asian/Pacific theater of World War II and the seventh of nine that he plans to complete on the war. All of his contributions follow a common format. The first 40 percent of the book is a historiographical narrative that treats such reference sources as bibliographies; guides; encyclopedias; dictionaries; atlases; archives; histories; and specialized topics, such as each of the individual countries involved, operations, organizations, personalities, fiction, movies, and many other things. The 2d part of the book is an alphabetic listing of 1,613 annotated citations. The book also includes a chronology and an extensive author and subject index. As are all of the author's previous volumes, this is another thorough, complete, and outstanding contribution that will be valuable for all research libraries. [R: Choice, Oct 98, pp. 298-299]

—**Joe P. Dunn**

Biography

518.   Baker, Rosalie F., and Charles F. Baker III. **Ancient Romans: Expanding the Classical Tradition.** New York, Oxford University Press, 1998. 267p. illus. maps. index. (Oxford Profiles Series). $35.00. ISBN 0-19-510884-1.

Ancient Romans chronicles the lives and accomplishments of 40 historically important Roman personalities, including some that are frequently overlooked in works intended for this audience. In addition to providing the basic information of a traditional reference work, *Ancient Romans* also offers glimpses into personal lives and little known customs. The biographies are arranged within five chronological categories. Each division begins with a brief overview of the times, an arrangement that clarifies relationships among personalities and events.

All names are first given in the version familiar to today's readers, followed by the Roman equivalent. Numerous maps and abundant illustrations of the persons featured add to the usefulness of this sturdily bound work.

The work concludes with information on legendary heroes and heroines; a chronology of the emperors; a family tree that traces the Julian and Claudian families; a timeline of major events; a helpful glossary of literary, political, religious, and social terms; a bibliography of materials suitable for both adults and younger readers (with levels indicated); a listing of major personalities by profession; and finally, a thorough index.

The biographies are exceptionally readable, making each subject memorable. An equally valuable title is the companion volume entitled *Ancient Greeks: Creating the Classical Tradition* (see ARBA 98, entry 472).

—**Vandelia L. VanMeter**

519.   **Dictionary of World Biography, Volume 1: The Ancient World.** Frank N. Magill, ed. Chicago, Fitzroy Dearborn and Englewood Cliffs, N.J., Salem Press, 1998. 997p. illus. index. $125.00. ISBN 0-89356-303-7. [R: SLJ, Nov 98, p. 156; BL, 15 Sept 98, pp. 258-260; Choice, Dec 98, p. 657]

520.   **Dictionary of World Biography, Volume 2: The Middle Ages.** Frank N. Magill, ed. Chicago, Fitzroy Dearborn and Englewood Cliffs, N.J., Salem Press, 1998. 1049p. illus. index. $125.00. ISBN 0-89356-314-5.

The *Dictionary of World Biography, Volume 1: The Ancient World* and the *Dictionary of World Biography, Volume 2: The Middle Ages* are the first two volumes of a projected 10-volume series that is a revision and reordering of Salem Press's 30-volume *Great Lives from History*. The dictionary, which is arranged chronologically (whereas *Great Lives* was arranged geographically), includes new entries, updated bibliographies, a new page design, and new illustrations. Volume 1, for example, includes 218 essays from *Great Lives* and adds 43 new biographies; volume 2 gathers 259 essays from *Great Lives* and adds 19 new biographies, for a total of 278 essays. In all cases, biographies spanning two eras were moved into the period that best encompassed the subject's life work or major accomplishments. Following these 2 volumes are volumes on the Renaissance (Salem Press, 1999), the seventeenth and eighteenth centuries, the nineteenth century (2 volumes), the twentieth century (3 volumes), and an index.

The articles in this series range from 2,000 to 3,000 words, and follow a standard format—ready-reference information, a brief statement of the subject's contributions, early life, and life work, in addition to a summary that provides an overview of the individual's place in history. Each essay is supplemented by an annotated, evaluative bibliography.

Major world leaders are included from such areas as government, politics, religion, philosophy, science, exploration, art, military affairs, and scholarship. The articles combine breadth of coverage with quick access via indexes to area of achievement, geographic location, and name (with cross-references for varied spellings).

The clear writing style of both sets will appeal to secondary students and adults. Typical is this quote from the summary to the essay on Ptolemy: "It would be unreasonable to expect great scientific breakthroughs during the second century A.D., and they did not happen. What did occur was the gradual advancement of knowledge to which Ptolemy contributed." The essay continues with a summary of the scientific legacy that was made possible by Ptolemy's "clear and careful prose." The text is identical to the *Great Lives* essay; the bibliography includes all the entries found in *Great Lives* and is enriched by the addition of five recent publications. The dictionary uses whiter paper that provides better contrast between page and print. The addition of illustrations and the updated bibliography, with helpful annotations, make this an appealing reference tool, although the larger size and greater weight of each volume may be of concern to some users.

Libraries that own the complete Great Lives series will wish to consider carefully whether they should assume the expense of a new 10-volume set. Those who have only a portion of the 30-volume Great Lives set may wish to opt for the addition of the attractive new *Dictionary of World Biography.*—**Vandelia L. VanMeter**

521.   Schmittroth, Linda, and Mary Kay Rosteck. **People of the Holocaust.** Detroit, U*X*L/Gale, 1998. 2v. illus. index. $49.00/set. ISBN 0-7876-1743-1.

In 2 volumes, Schmittroth and Rosteck present biographies of persons associated, in a variety of ways, with the Holocaust. Averaging about eight pages each, the biographies cover those who perpetrated the Holocaust or who played a role in encouraging the Nazis, those who were its victims, and others who worked to help the victims and end the Third Reich. Those covered include Adolf Hitler and his officials, world leaders and policy makers, and other notables, such as the religious leader Dietrich Bonhoffer; American priest Charles E. Coughlin; accused concentration camp officer John Demjanjuk; the young Anne Frank; and Simon Wiesenthal, a survivor involved in the effort to find war criminals.

Each biography begins with a photograph and a brief statement of the individual's role in the Holocaust; it concludes with a sidebar that provides added information about the person or related events and a bibliography. Each volume opens with a timeline and a glossary and concludes with an index to both volumes. The thorough index provides access to many persons who did not receive a full biography as well as information on events and places.

This reference work is intended for students ages 10 and older. The biographies are much more readable than typical entries in encyclopedias, the other primary source for this information in a school library. In addition to the glossary, any term that is used in the biographies that may not be familiar to a reader is defined within the text. Young readers will find this helpful, but older readers would prefer a footnote format and less repetition of explanations that interrupts the flow of the narrative. These sturdily bound volumes will withstand heavy use and will provide strong support for a variety of curricular units in grades 4 through 8.

Other recent publications that provide accounts of the Holocaust suitable for students include *We Remember the Holocaust* by David A. Adler (Henry Holt, 1989), based upon interviews with people who were children or teenagers when the events they described occurred; *We Are Witnesses: Five Diaries of Teenagers Who Died in the Holocaust* by Jacob Boas (Henry Holt, 1995); *Passage to Freedom: The Sugihara Story* by Ken Mochizuki (Lee & Low Books, 1997); and *Tell Them We Remember: The Story of the Holocaust* by Susan D. Bachrach (Little, Brown, 1994). [R: BL, 15 Sept 98, p. 268; VOYA, Dec 98, pp. 388-389]—**Vandelia L. VanMeter**

Chronology

522.   **Great Misadventures: Bad Ideas That Led to Big Disasters.** By Peggy Saari. Betz Des Chenes, ed. Detroit, U*X*L/Gale, 1998. 4v. illus. maps. index. $99.00/set. ISBN 0-7876-2798-4.

Great Misadventures brings to light examples of human error, greed, incompetence, and poor judgment from ancient to modern times, showing that the qualities that can lead to success can also cause failure and that human beings are inspired by self-interest as often as they are motivated by selflessness. Each entry (generally ranging from five to nine pages in length) offers historical background and a clear description of the event, with a discussion about why the misadventure is significant.

The essays are arranged chronologically within 4 subject volumes: "Exploration and Adventure," "Science and Technology," "Military," and "Society." The table of contents and timeline that open each volume are identical, encouraging an understanding of the relationships among the various events. Cross-references direct users to related entries throughout the set, and sources for further reference at the end of each entry offer direction to more information on each topic. The text is supported by illustrations and photographs, maps, and call-out boxes that highlight related persons or facts to enhance understanding; terms that may be unfamiliar to the target audience are explained within the essays. Each volume closes with a comprehensive index to all four volumes.

Suitable for readers in grades five and up, this unique set will find a wide audience of fascinated readers. No similar publication is known for this audience.—**Vandelia L. VanMeter**

523.   Matz, David. **An Ancient Rome Chronology, 264-27 B.C.** Jefferson, N.C., McFarland, 1997. 228p. index. $34.50. ISBN 0-7864-0161-3.

Matz's *An Ancient Rome Chronology, 264-27 B.C.* fills out the various timelines of Roman Republican political and cultural history that are sometimes found in standard reference works and brings them all together in a single volume. As a compilation of various lists of dates, it is a useful compendium. The work is divided into 6 sections, dealing with politics, laws and speeches, military events, literary milestones, art, and architectures, with appendixes covering various other chronologies. As the subtitle suggests, the book handles the period between 264 and 27 B.C.E. This latter date is a good terminus for political matters (in 27 Octavian took the title Augustus, thus irrevocably ushering in the Roman Empire); for literature, however, it makes far less sense. Virgil has only begun the *Aeneid* by this time and, as for Ovid, all one finds under "Literary Milestones" is this: "31 [B.C.:] At the age of 12, Ovid left his hometown of Sulmone to journey to Rome to complete his education." That he went on to write some of the most magnificent poetry of the Augustan age goes without mention because it happened after the arbitrary date of 27. Among the appendixes is a catalog of omens, well worth reading all by itself. No list can be all bad that begins, "218-217 [B.C.:] A baby, only six months old, exclaimed 'Victory!' in a public market place. An ox ascended a staircase in an apartment building, and then hurled itself out a window." All in all, it is a book that will be of some value as a quick reference; the bibliography is sparing, however, and readers who want to know more will have to go to the *Oxford Classical Dictionary* (Oxford University Press, 1996).

—**Christopher Michael McDonough**

524.   **Timelines of World History.** New York, Quadrillion, 1998. 160p. illus. index. $17.99. ISBN 1-85833-854-9.

More than 300 illustrations and text written by an international team of historians provide a chronology of the political and cultural history of five main regions of the world: the Americas, Africa, East Asia, West Asia, and Europe. The political timeline discusses the major historical events in the lives of cities and nations. The cultural timeline charts simultaneous global developments—from art and religion to music, literature, and architecture. Interspersed with the timelines are 14 "Window on Time" essays, which provide comparisons of topics of significance for two or more regions.

For example, the 6-page section covering the period 1000-500 B.C.E. has 11 illustrations, a half-page timeline of political events, essays entitled "Carthage," "Early Mound Builders," "Assyrians and Persians," "Early Japan" (2), "The Emergence of Greece," "Redating Chavin de Huantar," "The Greeks," "From Old to New Babylon," "Connections with the Middle East," and finally an essay on the "Age of Alexander" that is over one full page. Tiny views of the globe placed by each essay are intended to help the user locate the geographic region under discussion. The work is indexed and concludes with a concise bibliography.

The brevity of the essays makes this attractive volume most suitable for use in a home library or to provide an overview that will lead students to seek more complete information elsewhere. Its value lies in the way in which it quickly provides the cultural and political framework for greater understanding of specific events within a colorful and readable format.

Worthwhile titles that provide much more depth and detail of coverage (suitable for middle, junior, and senior high students) include *The Chronicle of the World* (see ARBA 97, entry 464) and *The Chronology of World History* (ABC-CLIO, 1995).—**Vandelia L. VanMeter**

525.   **The Wilson Chronology of Ideas.** By George Ochoa and Melinda Corey. Bronx, N.Y., H. W. Wilson, 1998. 431p. index. (Wilson Chronology Series). $55.00. ISBN 0-8242-0935-4.

This reference, organized chronologically beginning in 48,000 B.C.E. and ending in 1997 C.E., is a list of "milestones" in human thought, categorized under 13 areas such as religion, education, linguistics, and the social sciences—in short, those ideas that relate to "the meaning and purpose of existence." Ideas in art and science/ technology are covered in two other books in the Wilson Chronology Series: *The Wilson Chronology of the Arts* (see entry 818) and *The Wilson Chronology of Science and Technology* (see entry 1307).

Each entry is one to six lines in length; birth and death dates are listed in an appendix. The index is admirably detailed, making access by subject and proper name simple. The authors claim their book is global in scope, but the vast majority of the entries lean toward Euro-American concepts. *The Wilson Chronology of Ideas*, by virtue of its brevity, would probably be more useful to the browser than to the researcher.—**Lori D. Kranz**

Dictionaries and Encyclopedias

526.   Cotterell, Arthur. **From Aristotle to Zoroaster: An A to Z Companion to the Classical World.** New York, Free Press/Simon & Schuster Macmillan, 1998. 483p. illus. maps. index. $30.00. ISBN 0-684-85596-8.

This dictionary attempts to broaden the term "classical world" to include not only Greece and Rome but also Persia, India, and China. The nearly 300 entries range in length from several paragraphs to several pages and cover the period from ca.600 B.C.E. to A.D. 600. Cross-references appear at the end of the entries along with recommended, relevant titles. Appendixes include maps of empires, a chronology, and an index of names and subjects that are not main entries.

Greek and Roman topics are included along with political and cultural coverage of major Asian empires of the classical period. There are entries on Chinese and Indian dynasties, eastern religions, and significant personalities. Overview articles discuss music, art, and literature in each civilization. Any dictionary covering classical civilization cannot avoid being compared to the *Oxford Classical Dictionary* (Oxford University Press, 1996) and the review title suffers in comparison. Although the focus of the Oxford title is the Greco-Roman world, it covers eastern civilizations from the perspective of their contact with Greece and Rome and therefore covers much of the same material more comprehensively.

Dictionary entries, by their nature, require that definitions be focused and succinct. Failure to adhere to this principle is evidenced in the review title by entries that are not always logically organized and sometimes digress from the topic being defined. For example, *Agrippa* rates a one-paragraph entry, of which half discusses his wife, *Julia*. *Porus* is given short shrift in his entry, with most of the text relating what happened to Alexander after he returned the Indian ruler to his throne. Readers with little or no knowledge of the classical world would not discover the location of *Parthia* until well into the article. Nor is there any explanation of why Alcibiades was charged with sacrilege. There are no main entries for India or China. These omissions are complicated by the fact that neither empire appears in the list of references to topics that are not main entries. A student looking for a discussion of the Greek city-state would be hard pressed to find it because it does not appear as a main or secondary entry. Even the term *polis* is not included.

Perhaps the author would have done better to concentrate on producing a well-organized, in-depth dictionary of the eastern classical world. There are things included that do not appear in other titles focusing on Greece and Rome, but this title does not begin to approach the scholarship of the Oxford in such basic things as citing of sources. None are cited in this title. This dictionary is a browsing volume and is by no means a reference source.
—**Marlene M. Kuhl**

527.   **Encyclopedia of the Vietnam War: A Political, Social, and Military History.** Spencer C. Tucker, ed. Santa Barbara, Calif., ABC-CLIO, 1998. 3v. illus. maps. index. $275.00/set. ISBN 0-87436-983-5.

To many who lived through the Vietnam War, the sense of what was happening overall may not have been as clear in the day-by-day reporting of military operations and political events. Thus, Tucker's *Encyclopedia of the Vietnam War* provides a detailed, coherent, and straightforward review of the French and U.S. involvement not only in Vietnam but also in Laos and Cambodia. For a particularly cogent account users might consult the six articles outlining the U.S. role in Indochina and Vietnam pre-1954 to 1997, when the United States established full diplomatic relations with the Socialist Republic of Vietnam.

Relying on some 130 contributors, Tucker sketches the history of Indochina, forming the context for what was to become a defining period in twentieth-century U.S. history. Of particular note is the wide, objective coverage given to the communist role in the war.

More than 900 articles and 22 maps provide military, ethnographic, political, and geophysical information, prefaced by an overview of Vietnamese history written by Tucker himself. These articles constitute most of the first 2 volumes. In addition, volume 2 concludes with a selected bibliography of nonfiction works, one on literature and film, a chronology of events in Vietnam through April 1975, and a glossary that includes numerous abbreviations and slang terms. Volume 3 is comprised solely of documents, including memos, letters, interviews, speeches, and statements, among others. The source where these can be found is noted, including some Websites where documents are available on the Internet.

A recent spate of titles on the Vietnam War includes another encyclopedia edited by Stanley I. Kutler and titled *Encyclopedia of the Vietnam War* (see ARBA 97, entry 433). Although there is some overlap between the two, Tucker is more comprehensive; there are more detailed articles and the bibliographies are more substantial. Only two contributors to Kutler's work also contributed to Tucker's work. The volume in hand has the advantages of both size and depth, including more maps as well as documents.

If they have to choose, academic libraries will want to add this set to their collection. Depending on their size and resources, public libraries may opt for one or both titles. [R: LJ, Dec 98, pp. 88, 90; BL, 15 Nov 98, pp. 611-112]—**Bernice Bergup**

528.   Epstein, Eric Joseph, and Philip Rosen. **Dictionary of the Holocaust: Biography, Geography, and Terminology.** Westport, Conn., Greenwood Press, 1997. 416p. index. $49.95. ISBN 0-313-30355-X.

The Holocaust is one of the most horrible events in human history because it was a planned, calculated genocide. Trying to understand it is difficult. As the survivors die, firsthand knowledge disappears. This dictionary provides access to a great deal of material in a format that is easy to use.

The alphabetic entries range in length from one sentence to half a page. They include biographies of people such as Joseph Kramer, Mordechai Chaim Rumkovski, and Levi Primo; geographic locations, including Bukovina, Germany, and Rudninkai Forest; organizations, such as the Hebrew Immigrant Aid Society, Polish Government in Exile, and Red Cross; and events, including Kristallnacht, Operation Harvest Festival, and Wansee Conference. Abbreviations and slang terms are included. Words within entries that have their own entries appear in bold typeface. *See* references facilitate access to information when necessary. Most entries have a source listed for suggested reading on the subject. A detailed bibliography and index complete the text.

With its 2,000 brief entries, *The Dictionary of the Holocaust* provides a great deal of information in a compact form. Entries for cities, such as Sarajevo, include the pre- and postwar Jewish population and dates of occupation and deportation of Jews. The entry for zyklon-b explains that using the gas costs five cents per victim, and it could kill people in anywhere from 30 seconds to 20 minutes, depending on the technology used. This information has a great deal of impact. It brings the events to life for readers and helps them understand what happened. This work is a welcome addition for public, school, and academic libraries.—**Barbara M. Bibel**

529.   **A Global Encyclopedia of Historical Writing.** D. R. Woolf and others, eds. New York, Garland, 1998. 2v. index. (Garland Reference Library of the Humanities, v.1809). $175.00/set. ISBN 0-8153-1514-7.

This 2-volume set must have been an enormous undertaking. And the efforts of the editorial staff and the contributors have paid off in a work that is well organized, well written, and informative. This reviewer would have doubted the viability of a short biographical and long subject narrative style, but these 2 volumes carry off the task wonderfully. This encyclopedia examines the men and women who have written the histories of human endeavor and chronicles the historiography of the various regions of the world. This work brings historians and historiography together alphabetically in one set. Short biographies of historians are gracefully interspersed with long articles on various national and regional historiographies.

History is made by those who are remembered, and it is written by those who remember. In this respect the work also discusses the purpose behind historical writing and the origins of historiography. Historians have written for their contemporaries and for future readers. To a certain extent part of history is winning the battle of history. Whoever gets the story out first has the advantage until revision overtakes an initial account. This 2-volume set is a must for college and university libraries and history department reference collections. It is also highly recommended for those historians who teach historiography. [R: LJ, Dec 98, p. 90; BL, 15 Dec 98, p. 764]—**Norman L. Kincaide**

530. Harding, Les. **Dead Countries of the Nineteenth and Twentieth Centuries: Aden to Zululand.** Lanham, Md., Scarecrow, 1998. 393p. illus. maps. index. $45.00. ISBN 0-8108-3445-6.

Originally inspired by stamp collecting and the realization that many countries no longer exist, Harding attempts to list and describe all such countries that existed in the nineteenth and twentieth centuries. He uses the philatelic definition of a dead country: a location that issued postage stamps at some point. The place did not have to be an actual sovereign country. The places Harding discusses no longer issue postage stamps, mainly because they no longer exist. Countries, colonies, protectorates, and princely states that have existed since 1800 are listed, with basic statistics and a short almanac-style entry included. The almanac-style entry explains how the country came into existence, what happened to it during its existence, and why it no longer exists. Most entries are accompanied by a picture of the country's stamp and a travelogue-style quotation. The book is divided into chapters by geographic areas. Each chapter includes a map locating the countries mentioned. The volume includes a bibliography and an index listing each individual country.

The book is full of information and provides not easily obtainable facts in a coherent and concise manner. Illustrations and maps, however, are of poor quality, and the travelogue quotations detract rather than add to the book's appeal. The line maps are greatly out of proportion. Countries are numbered and keyed to the map by geographic area, whereas chapter entries are alphabetic, making the maps difficult to use for easy reference. The stamps included as illustrations are often poorly reproduced. Although the country's area, capital, and population are included as introductory material for each entry, trying to find the dates of the country's actual existence means reading the entire entry. Nonetheless, the book is informative and could serve the historian or author well, although, of course, it is not completely up-to-date because of recent changes in more volatile parts of the world.

—**Janet Hilbun**

531. **The Historical Encyclopedia of World Slavery.** By Junius P. Rodriguez. Santa Barbara, Calif., ABC-CLIO, 1997. 2v. illus. index. $95.00/set. ISBN 0-87436-885-5.

This set is a superb example of what an excellent reference book should be. It is authoritative, unique, informative, and well written. It is a pleasure to bury one's nose into these nicely illustrated pages. Most of the contributors are academics drawn from around the world, and the work reflects a high level of scholarship. Slavery is examined from every angle around the globe and through the passage of the history of human civilization. The African slave trade, slaves in ancient Greece and Rome, the Peruvian slave trade, and others are all discussed in their proper social, historical, and even religious contexts. Abolitionists, pro-slavery advocates, and political leaders who took a strong pro- or antislavery stand are highlighted as well. Each entry concludes with a short list of titles for additional reading. A 60-page bibliography includes works in numerous languages and is a welcome addition. Although not nearly as in-depth on the coverage of U.S. slavery as is Randall Miller's and John David Smith's monumental *Dictionary of Afro-American Slavery* (see ARBA 98, entry 438), it fills a major void in the reference literature. This set is highly recommended for all libraries. [R: SLJ, Aug 98, p. 195; LJ, 15 Feb 98, pp. 133-134; VOYA, Dec 98, p. 388]—**Stephen W. Green**

532. Hogg, Ian V. **Historical Dictionary of World War I.** Lanham, Md., Scarecrow, 1998. 267p. illus. maps. (Historical Dictionaries of War, Revolution, and Civil Unrest, no.3). $50.00. ISBN 0-8108-3372-7.

With more than 400 entries, this dictionary is not intended as a comprehensive guide but rather as an introductory work for students with little or no knowledge of the events leading up to and taking place during World War I. Brief battle summaries, biographical sketches, and entries on related topics are included as well as a lengthy introductory essay on the conflict. A chronology of events, a topically arranged bibliography of further readings, a list of battles, and general maps of the theaters of war also are included.

This title provides a greater focus on some of the lesser known figures of the war as well as other areas of international conflict outside the Western Front, a helpful addition to scholarship but not necessarily what one would expect to find in such an introductory work. Compared to Stephen Pope and Elizabeth-Anne Wheal's *The Dictionary of the First World War* (see ARBA 97, entry 474), this work provides less general information and more specialized coverage of some of the smaller episodes and figures of the war. Particularly strong in its coverage of battles and biographies, this work provides less focus on the broad themes and issues that students are likely to seek. For example, detailed entries are provided for such engagements as the Battle of Katshanik (fought between Serbian and Bulgarian forces in 1915), but no entry is provided for the cavalry, the principal form of military offense that was made completely redundant by the use of trench warfare and resulted in one of the greatest shifts in military science in generations. Novice scholars may get a somewhat slanted introduction to the subject if they rely solely on this work, but as a supplement to other excellent general works such as that by Pope and Wheal, this will be a useful addition.—**Elizabeth Patterson**

533.   **Holocaust Series.** William L. Shulman, ed. Woodbridge, Conn., Blackbirch Press, 1998. 8v. illus. maps. index. $18.95/vol. ISBN 1-56711-200-5 (v.1); 1-56711-201-3 (v.2); 1-56711-202-1 (v.3); 1-56711-204-8 (v.4); 1-56711-205-6 (v.5); 1-56711-206-4 (v.6); 1-56711-207-2 (v.7); 1-56711-208-0 (v.8).

The chronology presented in this 8-volume series on the Holocaust begins in ancient times. Volume 1 is an overview of the history of the Jewish people to August 1935 and provides an explanation of this, and other, anti-Semitic movements. The next 5 volumes cover events from 1935 to after World War II. The 7th volume is a collection of primary sources, and the 8th is a resource guide of media for further study.

Each readable 80-page volume is filled with photographs and illustrations. The text blends historical narrative and moving accounts written by survivors as each volume explores the unique aspects and events that shaped the period. Terms unfamiliar to the intended audience are explained in context. Sidebars, insets, maps, and other special features provide further explanation. Each volume has its own index, appendixes, and glossary. The sturdy binding and thoughtful layout add appeal to the series.

This topic is a disturbing one for the intended audience—students grades 4 through 8—but the editorial board made a decision "not to shock or horrify." "Learning about the Holocaust should be disturbing—but there is a delicate line between informative realism and sensationalism. The most brutal accounts and documentation of the Holocaust can be found in many other sources; we believe that in our series, much of this story will be revealed through the powerful and moving images we have selected." This series could have been presented in fewer volumes, but the price for each is reasonable and the 8-volume format does allow access by several students at once. This matter-of-fact account will support curriculum units.

Other coverage of the Holocaust suitable for this same audience is found in a 4-volume alphabetically arranged set entitled *The Holocaust* (see ARBA 97, entry 502), and a 1-volume work entitled *The Holocaust: Understanding and Remembering* by Helen Strahinich, from the Issues in Focus series of Enslow Publishers (1996). [R: SLJ, Feb 98, p. 134]—**Vandelia L. VanMeter**

534.   **The Hutchinson Dictionary of Ancient & Medieval Warfare.** Chicago, Fitzroy Dearborn, 1998. 365p. $75.00. ISBN 1-57958-116-1.

As a compact handbook to recorded military history and practice, *The Hutchinson Dictionary* defines terms and describes warfare from its earliest instances to about 1500, when gunpowder came into use. Contributors are specialists in military history.

Coverage centers on the ancient and medieval eras in western Europe, Greece, China, Japan, South and central Asia, and Persia. Thus, there are entries for the Battle of Kadesh in ancient Syria between the Hittites and Egyptians in 1275 B.C.E.; the Battle of Zanhuang in which the Mongols defeated the Song Chinese in 1225; and the Battle of Ashingdon in 1016 between the Danes and the Saxons.

In addition to battles and wars, the more than 2,500 entries identify rulers, commanders, heroes, and ordinary soldiers as well as describe ancient and medieval military weapons and armor. Users can identify an *armt*, a type of close helmet prevalent in fifteenth-century Italy; a German hatchet (*francisca*) employed from the third to seventh centuries; or a *koshigatana*, a small Japanese dagger used from the eighth to twelfth centuries. Featured entries appear against a gray background; for example, military order; Tan Taizong, a Chinese emperor; and a Near Eastern chariot.

Although a clearly defined scope and selection criteria are lacking, some inferences can be made by examining the selective bibliography. This includes recent titles reflecting current scholarship in the field as well as older works, such as the *Cambridge History of India* (1928), volume 3 on Turks and Afghans in the section on central, South, and Southeast Asian warfare. Most titles in the bibliography carry a one-line description such as that for P. Connolly's *Greece and Rome at War* (1981), identified as "excellent on armour and weapons." Even though descriptions are especially lucid, the work would be greatly enhanced by illustrations.

What distinguishes this dictionary is the combination of battles and armaments. It is a scholarly work minus the trappings. Its usefulness, however, is not limited to scholars. With its broad geographic and chronological coverage it will serve general readers as well.—**Bernice Bergup**

535.   **Macmillan Encyclopedia of World Slavery.** Paul Finkelman and Joseph C. Miller, eds. New York, Macmillan General Reference/Simon & Schuster Macmillan, 1998. 2v. illus. maps. index. $195.00/set. ISBN 0-02-864607-X.

This comprehensive, 2-volume encyclopedia of world slavery summarizes current knowledge about all forms of human bondage throughout the world. Although many Americans think of slavery as manifested in the bringing of African slaves to the continent, slavery has existed since ancient times and has not always been based upon racial lines. The entries cover slavery in ancient Israel, Greece, Rome, southern Europe during the Middle Ages, the Americas during the seventeenth and eighteenth centuries, more recent slave labor camps in Germany and Russia, and slavery today in some parts of the world. Other forms of forced labor, including serfdom, peonage, coolie status, and conscription under government corvée, are represented, as are antislavery and abolition movements that emerged in Europe and the Americas. An alphabetic list of 417 subjects covers a wide range of topics and includes names of persons, places, events, laws, organizations, and general subjects such as freedom, labor systems, and emancipation. Some headings have a number of subtopics listed. A directory of contributors gives the specialist's university affiliation and the titles of their articles. An introductory section contains 25 black-and-white maps portraying geographic entities, major slave revolts in North America, the cotton kingdom, and other relevant subjects. The volumes are illustrated with photographs and facsimiles. The articles are well written by authorities on their subjects, and contain short, selected bibliographies of sources. This work will be an essential addition not only to subject collections, but to general reference collections.—**Shirley L. Hopkinson**

536.   McElroy, Lorie Jenkins. **Voices of the Holocaust.** Detroit, U*X*L/Gale, 1998. 2v. illus. index. $49.00/set. ISBN 0-7876-1746-6.

The Holocaust is one of the most horrible events in world history. It is also one of the most difficult to present to young students. With the recurrence of genocide in Bosnia and Rwanda and the increase in hate crimes in the United States, teaching young people about this event is extremely important. *Voices of the Holocaust*, an anthology of excerpts from 34 documents written by people affected by this event, is an excellent tool because it provides primary sources and places them in historical context.

The 2-volume set is divided into 6 chapters that cover broad topics: anti-Semitism, escalation, Holocaust, resisters, liberation, and understanding. Each chapter begins with a historical overview. Each excerpt in the anthology has an introduction to place the document and its author within a historical context and a "Things to Remember" section that provides background information. Difficult words are defined within the text in parentheses. The excerpts themselves appear in their original format, with difficult words in bold typeface. These words are defined in glossaries that appear as sidebars. A "What Happened Next" section follows the text and explains its impact on both the author of the document and the audience. "Did You Know?" provides facts about the document and its author. Each entry has a brief bibliography. Many also have boxed author biographies and related historical information. Black-and-white photographs illustrate the text. Each volume contains a timeline that starts in 1899 and ends with the first disbursement from the Swiss fund for Holocaust survivors in 1997.

The documents excerpted here cover a broad range of subjects that will be of interest to students from middle school through high school: sections of seminal works such as *The Protocols of the Elders of Zion* and *Mein Kampf*; a newspaper account of *Kristallnacht*; sections from memoirs and diaries by Anne Frank, Primo Levi, and Hannah Senesh; Edward R. Murrow's account of the liberation of Buchenwald; and writings by Elie Wiesel and Art Spiegelman. These bring history to life and document both the inhumanity and the courage of those involved. They also demonstrate the importance of remembering the Holocaust and working to prevent a repetition of such atrocities. Two companion sets, *People of the Holocaust* and *Understanding the Holocaust*, provide further background for students and teachers. These sets are excellent resources for school, public, and synagogue libraries. [R: BL, 15 Sept 98, p. 268; VOYA, Dec 98, pp. 388-389]—**Barbara M. Bibel**

537.   Minahan, James. **Miniature Empires: A Historical Dictionary of the Newly Independent States.** Westport, Conn., Greenwood Press, 1998. 340p. maps. index. $75.00. ISBN 0-313-30610-9.

The editor of this publication is the author of *Nations Without States: A Historical Dictionary of Contemporary National Movements* (see ARBA 97, entry 583), a book that probably was more successful than this current volume will be. It seems that the title is a misnomer. What is meant by "miniature" empire? Some 25 states are covered, including not only states created after the collapse of the Soviet Union, but also non-Soviet states such as Ethiopia and Namibia. It is not understood what is "miniature" about Russia or Ukraine, and if one is including Ethiopia, a dozen other African countries could also be included. In other words, the criteria for inclusion are not clear and the introduction by Minahan explains very little. In general, the information on individual countries is hardly adequate. For example, the information on Ukraine (pp. 273-285) contains a brief bibliography (5 books) of rather uneven quality. It provides information on the population (including national minorities, with rather unreliable statistics) and a little on history and geography, but nothing on economy, national resources, or government.

—**Bohdan S. Wynar**

Handbooks and Yearbooks

538.   Axelrod, Alan, and Charles Phillips. **What Everyone Should Know About the 20th Century: 200 Events that Shaped the World.** Holbrook, Mass., Adams Publishing, 1998. 337p. index. $12.00pa. ISBN 1-58062-066-3.

In 1- to 3-page essays, this small volume describes 200 events of the twentieth century, beginning with the Spanish-American War (1898) and ending with the 1995 bombing of the Oklahoma City Federal Building. The authors make no claim to comprehensiveness in subject or theme, but consider their selections "jumping-off points"—events that "shaped our lives and told us something about the century in which we live" (p. xiv). Although concise, the essays are well written, interesting, and straightforward in tone. Each entry is titled headline-style and includes a date, such as "Sun Yat-sen Stages a Chinese Revolution (1911)" (p. 47) and "Rockefeller Proposes a System of Fallout Shelters (1959)" (p. 214). A reading list and a general index complete the book. It is recommended for students choosing research topics as well as for browsers. Because of its reasonable cost, libraries may wish to keep copies in both their reference and circulating collections.—**Lori D. Kranz**

539.   Feldman, George. **Understanding the Holocaust.** Detroit, U*X*L/Gale, 1998. 2v. illus. maps. index. $49.00/set. ISBN 0-7876-1740-7.

Explaining the Holocaust to young students is difficult. The horror of this period is almost beyond comprehension. The U*X*L division of Gale has produced a 6-volume set that brings the events and people of this era to life. The first 4 volumes, *People of the Holocaust* and *Voices of the Holocaust*, cover individuals and primary sources. *Understanding the Holocaust* provides the historical background for the earlier titles.

The 2 volumes, with consecutive paging, are divided into 14 chapters. Each volume contains a complete table of contents and index for the set, a reader's guide, a timeline, a glossary, a bibliography of fiction and non-fiction works, and a list of organizations. They also have an author's note explaining the difficulties involved in determining the exact number of Holocaust victims and their countries of origin.

The chapters cover subjects such as "Germany and the Jewish People Before the Holocaust," "The Rise of the Nazi Party," "The Warsaw Ghetto," "Life and Death in Nazi-Dominated Europe," "Judgments," and "Remembering the Holocaust." Each one explains the historical events clearly and objectively. Illustrations, maps, and charts supplement the text. Sidebars provide explanations of difficult concepts and additional material, such as an account of the Dreyfus Affair, a selection from Yevgeny Yevtushenko's poem *Babi Yar*, and a profile of Hermann Goring. The information is accessible to readers over the age of 10.

Understanding the Holocaust provides an excellent introductory overview of a difficult subject. It is a reasonably priced set that can stand alone. Adding the companion volumes will offer greater depth by bringing firsthand accounts of these events to the students who read them. These books belong in all public and school libraries. [R: BL, 15 Sept 98, p. 268]—**Barbara M. Bibel**

540.   Fischel, Jack R. **The Holocaust.** Westport, Conn., Greenwood Press, 1998. 196p. illus. index. (Greenwood Press Guides to Historic Events of the Twentieth Century). $39.95. ISBN 0-313-29879-3.

Attempting to reach both interested students and general readers, Fischel has produced a readable synthesis of current Holocaust scholarship based on secondary sources. Most of the book consists of a historical and interpretive overview, covering the background of Adolf Hitler and Nazism, life in the Third Reich, the Final Solution itself, and resistance to the Holocaust. The biographical section does not contain sources or suggestions for further reading and is highly selective, covering only 20 major participants; thus, Rudolf Hoess is included, but not Rudolf Hess, Alfred Rosenberg, or Albert Speer. The book has an annotated bibliography of 66 sources, which cites Thomas Keneally's 1982 novel *Schindler's Ark* (later translated into film director Steven Spielberg's *Schindler's*

List) as an "excellent study," failing to mention that it is a fictionalized dramatization of Oskar Schindler's activities rather than a scholarly historical study.

The volume also contains a chronology, glossary of 96 terms and phrases, 13 black-and-white photographs, and excerpts from 10 original documents. *Dictionary of the Holocaust* by Eric Joseph Epstein and Philip Rosen (see entry 528) contains many more definitions and biographical entries, although it lacks the narrative and historical aspects. Libraries that already own Yisrael Gutman's *Encyclopedia of the Holocaust* (see ARBA 91, entry 520) or Abraham J. and Hershel Edelheit's *History of the Holocaust* (see ARBA 95, entry 588) will not need this volume for their reference collections, but it is well written and can be used by students in circulating collections as a general overview of the Holocaust.—**John A. Drobnicki**

541.   Heyman, Neil M. **World War I.** Westport, Conn., Greenwood Press, 1997. 257p. illus. maps. index. (Greenwood Press Guides to Historic Events of the Twentieth Century). $39.95. ISBN 0-313-29880-7.

As the century races to a conclusion, the events that have shaped world society for the past 100 years will be reexamined to determine their importance and influences. Certainly one of the most far-reaching forces that affected the twentieth century was World War I.

This volume is designed as a one-volume ready-reference to the conflict. Each section provides an overview of different aspects of the war, including such essential topics as a chronology of events, capsule biographies of the primary personalities, a glossary of terms, and essays explaining major issues of the conflict. An annotated bibliography of 25 pages will assist the student or researcher requiring additional information. Many will require other sources, for this treatment of World War I is more an almanac than an encyclopedia. Incredibly, nowhere are Wilson's Fourteen Points enumerated, not even in the "Primary Documents" section or the "War" section. The disgraceful political rejection of the Treaty of Versailles by the U.S. Senate receives one paragraph. The photographs are well-chosen, and the index is useful if not exhaustive.

Despite some omissions that will leave researchers new to World War I groping in the dark, this is a handy single-volume source. Monumental events and complex personalities are distilled to concise descriptions, and many peripheral issues of the war caused by the disruption of society—women's rights, public morals, and the arts—are handled well. This book would be an excellent start for any library to bolster its underrepresented collection of reference materials on World War I.—**James Moffet**

542.   **A Historical Guide to World Slavery.** Seymour Drescher and Stanley L. Engerman, eds. New York, Oxford University Press, 1998. 429p. illus. index. $65.00. ISBN 0-19-512091-4.

The literature of world slavery has grown immensely during the past few decades. Well-done general surveys, such as *The Slave Trade* (Simon & Schuster, 1997) are still rare, however. The present volume, containing approximately 70 articles of varying lengths written by a distinguished body of international scholars, focuses on regional approaches to and perspectives on world slavery, including structures, institutions, concepts, and processes of contemporary historiographic significance. Because of this broad-based perspective, the articles are relatively generalized (e.g., "Economics," "South America"), although occasionally a more specific topic (e.g., "Pawnship") is singled out. Scholars will appreciate the historiographic attention not normally found in guides to world slavery, although general readers might find the lack of details a problem. All articles conclude with brief secondary bibliographies for further study and include numerous cross-references. Additionally, the editors include "nontraditional" topics, such as contemporary and wage slavery, underlining the fact that the institution is not always race-related. *A Historical Guide to World Slavery* will be particularly useful in conjunction with *The Historical Encyclopedia of World Slavery* (see entry 531), which examines the same territory from a more specific approach. This work is recommended for all academic libraries. [R: Choice, Sept 98, p. 99; LJ, 1 April 98, p. 80]—**Anthony J. Adam**

543.   Kort, Michael. **The Columbia Guide to the Cold War.** New York, Columbia University Press, 1998. 366p. index. (Columbia Guides to American History and Cultures). $40.00. ISBN 0-231-10772-2.

Many history students believe Walter Lippman coined the term *Cold War*, but Don Juan Manuel, a fourteenth-century Spanish political commentator, was the first to use this term when he said, "cold war neither brings peace nor gives honor to the one who makes it." The book's four key sections are a narrative describing the causes of the Cold War; an encyclopedic listing of key events, policies, and people; a chronology of major developments annually from 1945 to 1991; and an annotated resource guide with books, journals, Websites,

archival collections, and even novels and movies indicative of each phase of the Cold War. The author gives an objective, readable account of the key moments, personalities, and policy initiatives as well as the cultural impact of this time in history. This book is unique in its balance. The author describes the three schools of historiography for the period—the traditionalists who saw the Soviets as the prime instigators of the Cold War, the revisionists who disagreed about the magnitude of the Russian threat, and the postrevisionists who felt the pendulum had swung too far and found themselves closer to the traditionalists. This book is unique in that the author not only includes references from each orientation, but in addition identifies each work as to its school of thought. This gives a well-rounded account of an otherwise emotionally laden era and enables the reader to make reasoned interpretations of events and historical figures that many will still remember. To take the pivotal event of the second half of the twentieth century and to produce such a fair, concise, and readable study guide is a compliment to the author.
—**Adrienne Antink Bendel**

544.   Sibley, Katherine A. S. **The Cold War.** Westport, Conn., Greenwood Press, 1998. 212p. illus. index. (Greenwood Press Guides to Historic Events of the Twentieth Century). $39.95. ISBN 0-313-29857-2.

This handy volume is not to be compared to the *Cold War Reference Guide* (see ARBA 98, entry 508). Sibley's work is concise and not meant to be encyclopedic. The intent of the work is to introduce the subject of the Cold War to the secondary school and community college audience. There is a chronology of events, a historical narrative, a biographical section, a glossary of terms, and an annotated bibliography. For any historical period, events must be understood in context. One must understand the difference between the Yalta Conference and the Marshall Plan and how these shaped the post-World War II world. The passing of the Cold War is still a recent memory, although its inception is as old as the memory of World War II. This small volume sets a tone for further inquiry into this long and complex historical event and is highly recommended for middle school, high school, and community college reference collections, as well as for young adult collections.—**Norman L. Kincaide**

Indexes

545.   **Historical Abstracts on Disc.** [CD-ROM]. expanded ed. Santa Barbara, Calif., ABC-CLIO, 1998. Minimum system requirements: IBM or compatible. CD-ROM drive. DOS 3.0. 512KB memory. 20MB hard disk space. $5,250.00.

This mainstay of historical research is available in either a basic subscription covering the years 1982 to the present or in an expanded subscription covering 1972 to the present. Similar to its print counterpart, it includes access to citations or abstracts of more than 420,000 journal articles, more than 24,000 dissertations, and more than 51,000 book citations. Source materials come from more than 50 languages, with subject scope being 1450 to the present.

Researchers are able to do simple searching combining any number of nine search fields: subject, descriptors, author/editor, title, date, journal name, time period, document type, and language. Records retrieved present the following information for each entry: document type, descriptors, author, title, citation, abstract (usually 50 to 100 words), language, time period, and a print/entry number. Original title, if in a foreign language, is also provided. With relative ease, users can manipulate and control searches, tag entries, and print or download desired items, with a clear advantage of being able to optimize searching to retrieve appropriate documents.

Technical aspects and concerns are addressed in a separate text file, with appropriate directions for installation, networking, technical support, and more. Although compatible with Windows 93 and NT platforms, the product is presented in a DOS format. A variety of help screens enhance problem solving.

As an annotated bibliography of historical literature, this work will long remain a key reference tool in the research and university library setting. Selection librarians will need to weigh usefulness against cost-simultaneous user pricing is slightly higher—and perhaps urge the publisher to move to a Web-based access format.
—**Edmund F. SantaVicca**

10 Law

GENERAL WORKS

Bibliography

546. Baum, Harald, and Luke R. Nottage. **Japanese Business Law in Western Languages: An Annotated Selective Bibliography.** Littleton, Colo., Fred B. Rothman, 1998. 223p. $67.50. ISBN 0-8377-0366-2.

This volume seeks to provide guidance on print and Internet resources that discuss Japanese business law in European languages. Most material cited is in English and German, with some in French and other languages. The Meiji Reformers, founders of the modern Japanese state, chose the Imperial German system as model for the legal system. Thus, German scholarship provides unique insights. English material dominates.

The work is divided into 3 parts. The 1st part is an introduction to the literature. The two remaining sections are the core. The 2d part covers general works, is extensively annotated, and is divided into 9 topical sections covering periodicals, bibliographies, primary and secondary legislation in translation, introductory works on Japanese law (general and business), and more. It has a substantial list of Internet sites of government bodies, universities, associations, and law firms. Inevitably the latter will date quickly given the rapid change on the World Wide Web. However, most of the sites look to remain useful in the long term. The 3d part is a selective bibliography of materials, primarily published between 1970 and 1997. It is not annotated. The 15 topics run from legal philosophy and history through services to tax law. Each section has further subdivision.

This work will prove useful to scholars, practitioners, and students exploring its topic. It should also be of interest to law librarians seeking to collect in the field. Large academic law libraries and smaller legal collections with appropriate client interests should acquire it.—**Nigel Tappin**

547. Benamati, Dennis C., Phyllis A. Schultze, Adam C. Bouloukos, and Graeme R. Newman. **Criminal Justice Information: How to Find It, How to Use It.** Phoenix, Ariz., Oryx Press, 1998. 237p. index. $59.95. ISBN 0-89774-957-X.

As might be expected from the title, this book does not give criminal justice information but tells where to find various kinds of data and knowledge. On a given topic, one may find sources for locating experts, statistics, literature, government, and legal documents. One chapter is devoted to international criminal justice information.

The intended audience is broad—from high school researchers to professors and from police officers to public policy makers. The media covered includes print, Internet, and electronic sources. One objective of the book is to include, for distance researchers, all the information one would have traditionally sought from a reference librarian.

The index is useful and comprehensive. An extensive list of Websites related to criminal justice that are arranged in helpful categories is appended to the work. Once category is for militias, cults, bombers, arsonists, and federal responses. Another is prostitution, pornography, and satanic crime. The preface includes summaries and objectives of each chapter in the hope that the book will be accessed from many different points rather than read cover-to-cover.

The book definitely meets its objective. The effectiveness of this book makes it a valuable reference tool. The combined expertise of the four authors provides a broad base of criminal justice academic knowledge and information management knowledge, in contrast to "on the street" experience. The book is well researched and covers many sources. It is well written, nicely organized, and interesting.—**Bev Cummings Agnew**

548.   Bryson, William Hamilton. **Bibliography of Virginia Legal History Before 1900.** 2d ed. Buffalo, N.Y., William S. Hein, 1997. 281p. index. $50.00. ISBN 1-57588-407-0.

This 2d edition of an important reference source on Virginia legal history prior to 1900 is important, as the author notes in his introduction, precisely because it comprises one of the most formidable and documented state legal histories of the United States. In addition to explaining the importance of Virginal legal history within our own national development, Bryson has written an introduction that not only justifies this type of historical investigation but also challenges the widely accepted view that legal history in general constitutes little more than an attempt to justify the status quo. The bibliography itself is an alphabetic list of entries by names and, if no author is identifiable, by title. Thus it is not unusual to find an 1895 source alongside a 1962 source. There are 1,452 entries. An extended appendix comprises "Virginia Codes Before 1900," "Virginia Acts of Assembly Before 1900," "Virginia Legislative Journals Before 1900," and the "Virginia Reports Before 1900." There is as well a "Table of Cases," a "Table of Statutes," and a useful and indispensable index. Therefore, if one knows the author or the issue, one can track down the references rather easily. For anyone doing research on Virginia legal history, this resource will prove extremely useful. But anyone doing any research on any state history would profit from examining the structure of this bibliography.—**Michael A. Foley**

549.   **The Lawyer's Research Companion: A Concise Guide to Sources.** Joanne Zich and Gary McCann, eds. Buffalo, N.Y., William S. Hein, 1998. 218p. index. (AALL Legal Research Series, no.4). $39.50; $26.95pa. ISBN 1-57588-418-6; 1-57588-442-9pa.

This handy paperback with its introduction and 8 chapters provides an overview to legal research, and will be as valuable to law students as it will be to seasoned practicing attorneys. It does not instruct in the techniques of legal research but provides, as its title indicates, "a concise guide to sources." The nine articles, written by different authors, are well organized with frequent short headings and are similar in style with no "legalese." Each article references diverse sources for information with appropriate emphasis on Internet sites. The topics include foreign and international law, federal tax law, legislative history, and online legal research tools, among others.

The chapter on nonlegal research is particularly valuable for lawyers and nonlawyers alike because it provides an outline of information sources that even specialists will appreciate being directed to. For example, the section on statistical information includes tools to locate statistical data. The data cannot be found in this work, but the information to find them is.

The most attractive features of this book are its user-friendly organization and concise, well-written, and practical information. This book will be useful for any law student or for anyone who occasionally needs to locate information beyond his or her area of expertise.—**Patricia C. Strickland**

Biography

550.   **Who's Who in American Law 1998-1999.** 10th ed. New Providence, N.J., Marquis Who's Who/Reed Reference Publishing, 1998. 981p. index. $285.00. ISBN 0-8379-3513-X. ISSN 0162-7880.

This tome accomplishes its purpose of presenting a compilation of biographical information on approximately 22,000 lawyers and professionals in law-related areas arranged alphabetically by name in columnar format. According to the editor's standards of admission, the two criteria for inclusion are "(1) incumbency in a defined position of responsibility or (2) attainment of significant level of achievement." The Marquis researchers compile information on their own and additionally "invite" professionals deemed outstanding by their board of advisers to submit biographical information and practicing attorneys to indicate practice areas. Seemingly, an individual who fails to respond will not be included. Although undoubtedly each individual entry is worthy, the book is by no means comprehensive, nor does it purport to be.

Entries are concise (approximately 20 to 30 per page), and the key to information and table of abbreviations conveniently explain abbreviated information. The book includes a fields of practice index arranged by state within numerous areas of practice, such as aviation, bankruptcy, family and matrimonial, patent, personal injury, and trademark and copyright, among others. Practicing lawyers are listed alphabetically by city within each state, making it easy to locate a lawyer with an area of expertise in a particular geographical area. The book also includes a professional index for other professionals, which is similarly arranged. One will find information on Ruth Bader Ginsburg in the main biographies section and her name indexed only under District of Columbia in "Judicial Administration" in the professional index. The professional index is of little use. The value of the book lies simply in the ease in locating short biographical information on some individuals in the law profession. The value to any library is marginal. This is a well-presented book that is not essential to anyone.

—**Patricia C. Strickland**

Dictionaries and Encyclopedias

551. Arnest, Lauren Krohn. **Children, Young Adults, and the Law: A Dictionary.** Santa Barbara, Calif., ABC-CLIO, 1998. 346p. index. (Contemporary Legal Issues). $45.00. ISBN 0-87436-879-0.

Arnest has written a concise guide to legal issues affecting or relating to children and young adults. The book could not be easier to use, and the information provided is clearly, concisely, and coherently presented. As the subtitle notes, this is a dictionary. The table of contents is a six-page alphabetic list of all entries. For example, the range includes adoption issues, curfew, equal protection, grandparent visitation statutes, medical treatment, parental rights, school prayer, and visitation rights. Within the separate entries, other dictionary entries are cross-referenced in bold typeface. For example, under "Medical Treatment," the entries on "Abortion Rights" and "Necessaries" are boldfaced. In addition, major Supreme Court decisions (e.g., *Ginsberg v. New York*, *Goss v. Lopez*, *In re Gault*) are explained briefly but concisely and usefully. Arnest begins, however, with a broad but informative 23-page overview of the history (beginning in 1650) of legal perspectives on children.

For those interested in additional information, a reading guide is included at the end of the dictionary. In addition, a "Table of Cases" identifies court decisions referenced or discussed in the dictionary. The dictionary includes, as noted, explanations of major court cases (most of which are Supreme Court decisions) affecting children. The book concludes with a "Table of Statutes" and an excellent index. Anyone working with children and young adults will find this one-volume dictionary extremely useful. It is highly recommended for all libraries.

—**Michael A. Foley**

552. Bailey, Joseph A. **The Concise Dictionary of Medical-Legal Terms: A General Guide to Interpretation and Usage.** Pearl River, N.Y., Parthenon, 1998. 148p. $29.95. ISBN 1-85070-680-8.

It is difficult to discern who the audience for this book is. An endorsement by a workers compensation judge suggests that the legal profession will find it of value, but in fact the medical terms defined are far outnumbered by standard legal terms that any attorney will be familiar with. In addition, there are numerous terms that are general in nature, and whose definitions are primarily etymological or historical (e.g., anxiety, curriculum vitae, desire). Some of the terms and their definitions seem almost laughable, such as *childish adult* being described as those individuals having "childish traits." The definitions that would seem to be most helpful are those for technical terms encountered in workers compensation law (e.g., *Claim for Reoccurrence*, *Retroactive Prophylactic Restriction*); these, however, are relatively few in number. In short, it is difficult to recommend this book for any library. Medical professionals would be better served by Black's Law Dictionary (6th ed.; see ARBA 94, entry 529), and lawyers would do better with one of the standard medical dictionaries or a source that focuses specifically on forensic medicine.—**Jack Ray**

553. Braun, Marina, and Galina Clothier. **English-Russian Dictionary of American Criminal Law.** Westport, Conn., Greenwood Press, 1998. 327p. $89.50. ISBN 0-313-30455-6.

This criminal law dictionary is the first part of a larger project that will cover other areas of the law. The need for such a dictionary has been acutely felt, especially since the end of the Cold War, by court interpreters, instructors and students of legal translation, and compilers of certification materials as well as attorneys and law enforcement personnel who deal with Russian-speaking clients.

The dictionary does not contain all words pertaining to criminal law, but is limited to the most frequently used words (specific legal terms as well as jargon and slang used in legal, court, and law enforcement settings). In addition to definitions, each entry also supplies examples of the term. The appendix contains 17 examples of court-related documents with their Russian translations. These documents include such things as Miranda rights, petition to wave jury trial, a summons notice, and others. This dictionary and its planned counterparts should prove especially useful for those working with Russian emigrant communities in the United States.

—**Robert H. Burger**

554.   Burgess, Heidi, and Guy M. Burgess. **Encyclopedia of Conflict Resolution.** Santa Barbara, Calif., ABC-CLIO, 1997. 356p. index. $55.00. ISBN 0-87436-839-1.

This reference work provides statistics for the 50 states and Washington, D.C., in 26 geographic, economic, demographic, and cultural categories. More than 400 data elements are provided on a broad range of variables. Most of the information is presented in tables by specific topic. For example, the table on average expenditures per pupil in public elementary and secondary schools shows as the first entry the national average of $5,574. This is followed by the average for each New Jersey student, which ranks first among the states with $9,712, on down to Utah, which is ranked 51st with an average of $3,218 spent per student. Each table is preceded by introductory material that defines the statistic, gives the source, provides the date collected, and interprets trends.

The 2d section of the book provides one-half-page summaries that indicate how each state compares nationally on 42 key data points from the more detailed tables. For example, Colorado is profiled as number 31 in expenditures per elementary and secondary pupil and number 19 on total college enrollment. The detailed index coupled with the table of contents makes it easy to determine quickly if the statistics needed are in this volume.
—**Gerald D. Moran**

555.   Chandler, Ralph C., Richard A. Enslen, and Peter G. Renstrom. **The Constitutional Law Dictionary. Volume 2: Governmental Powers, Supplement 1.** Santa Barbara, Calif., ABC-CLIO, 1998. 285p. index. $60.00. ISBN 0-87436-925-8.

When is a dictionary not a dictionary? When it is published as part of the ABC-CLIO series of case digests. *The Constitutional Law Dictionary* includes 2 volumes—*Individual Rights* and *Governmental Powers*. Volume 1 was published first in 1985, and has been updated three times since, most recently in 1995 (see ARBA 96, entry 606). The *Governmental Powers* volume was published in 1987 and is supplemented here. In each volume, the authors provide abstracts—typically 1,000 to 2,000 words in length—on significant decisions of the U.S. Supreme Court.

In this supplement to the *Governmental Powers* volume, the authors selected and abstracted 138 cases from the Supreme Court's 1986-1987 through 1996-1997 terms under the broad headings of "Judicial Power," "Executive Power," "Legislative Power," "Federalism," "Federal Commerce Power," and "Taxing, Spending, and State Economic Regulation." Each abstract has two parts: The case synopsis includes the issue and holding of the case; the case's significance provides an analysis of the decision in the context of the larger legal issues, including relevant legislation, constitutional provisions, and earlier court decisions. The final chapter in the dictionary furnishes 1,000- to 1,500-word essays on each of the justices that have served on the Supreme Court during the terms covered in the supplement. These clearly written essays provide insight into the judicial philosophy of each justice.

The Constitutional Law Dictionary will be most valuable to those who have some familiarity with the issues discussed; it is not for the uninitiated novice. College and university students should find it valuable, as will law students and others conducting research and scholarship on constitutional issues.—**James S. Heller**

556.   **Courtroom Drama: 120 of the World's Most Notable Trials.** Elizabeth Frost-Knappman, Edward W. Knappman, and Lisa Paddock, eds. Detroit, U*X*L/Gale, 1998. 3v. illus. index. $79.95/set. ISBN 0-7876-1735-0.

Courtroom Drama: 120 of the World's Most Notable Trials presents 25 centuries of intriguing and influential trials that have helped shape the course of world history. Falling into 13 categories, the cases cover assassinations, murders, war crimes, courts-martial, religious crimes, espionage, treason, negligence, political corruption, freedom of speech, family law, human rights, and constitutional cases.

The earliest courtroom drama dates from 399 B.C.E.; for refusing to worship the gods of the city of Athens, the philosopher Socrates was sentenced. The Timothy McVeigh trial, which deals with the worst act of terrorism in U.S. history—the bombing of the Oklahoma City Federal Building in 1995—is among the most recent trials. Others are the *Jones v. Clinton and Ferguson* lawsuit brought by Paula Jones against President Bill Clinton for sexual harassment that allegedly occurred when he was governor of Arkansas. *Vacco v. Quill* and *Washington v. Glucksberg* together make up the right to die cases heard by the Supreme Court.

Volume 1 contains cases on the Constitution, family law and reproductive rights, freedom of speech, human rights, and negligence. Volume 2 contains cases on assassinations, espionage, murder, and political corruption. Volume 3 features cases on military trials and courts-martial, religion and heresy, treason, and war crimes. Each volume begins with an alphabetic listing and a chronological listing. Each entry covers who was involved in the trial, where it took place, when it occurred, what the outcome was, and what the significance is. Most of the cases in this book resulted in true trials, meaning that a court—usually a judge or a panel of judges—followed established rules and procedures and impartially examined disputes between parties over fact or law. Others are jury trials in which lawyers presented evidence to a jury that delivered a verdict. Others are not real trials at all. The Salem witchcraft persecutions, for example, were not true trials because no attorney was present to represent the accused. Still, they were among the great social upheavals in colonial New England. Communist dictator Joseph Stalin's "show trials" made a mockery of justice because their verdicts were foregone conclusions.

The trials are arranged chronologically by category. There is an alphabetic listing as well. For easy reference, a "Words to Know" section at the beginning of each volume defines key terms. More than 120 sidebars provide related information, whereas 172 photographs add to the text. A cumulative index concludes each volume.

Each trial begins with a bold box in which the principals of the trial are listed. The claims of either the plaintiff or defendant are listed. The lawyers' names are included as well as the place and date of the trial. The verdict is listed and, most important, the significance of the trial. Following is a profile of the trial in a two- to five-page entry. An in-depth essay follows, describing the events leading up to the trial, key moments of the trial, and the aftermath of the decision. This 3-volume set will be a welcome addition to a middle school, high school, or public library. Once again, Gale has produced a book of high quality. [R: BR, Sept/Oct 98, p. 68; SLJ, Aug 98, pp. 188-190]—**Barbara B. Goldstein**

557.   **West's Encyclopedia of American Law.** St. Paul, Minn., West Group; distr., Farmington Hills, Mich., Gale, 1998. 12v. illus. index. $995.00/set. ISBN 0-314-05538-X.

In 12 volumes, with entries ranging from "Abandonment" to "Zoning," *West's Encyclopedia of American Law*, dedicated by the West Group "to librarians and library patrons throughout the United States and beyond," is *the* legal encyclopedia for public, college, and university libraries. The new 1998 encyclopedia supersedes West's 1983 *Guide to American Law: Everyone's Legal Encyclopedia* (see ARBA 85, entry 505), and does so marvelously.

With more than 4,000 entries, color illustrations, citations to important court decisions, references to pertinent statutes, and "in focus" pieces that provide added information on some of the more interesting and controversial issues, this encyclopedia offers the layperson a solid introduction to American law. However, this encyclopedia will not replace a treatise or scholarly article on a topic, of course; the entries are informative, although not extensive.

With a table of cases cited and name and subject indexes, this reference work is easy to use. Appendixes abound; the Magna Carta, Treaty of Paris, Articles of Confederation, Emancipation Proclamation, and the National Organization of Women Statement of Purpose are examples of the diverse documents reprinted. Presidential speeches, from George Washington, Abraham Lincoln, Woodrow Wilson, Franklin Roosevelt, John F. Kennedy, and Ronald Reagan, are presented here as well.

Librarians need this set on their shelves. Especially because the publisher acknowledge George Wythe—the founder of this reviewer's law school, William and Mary—as the United States' first law school professor and teacher of eventual Chief Justice John Marshall. As of January 1999 this encyclopedia is not available in electronic format. Both librarians and patrons will wear out the pages of this significant reference set.

—**James S. Heller**

Directories

558.   **ABA Official American Bar Association Guide to Approved Law Schools.** 1999 ed. Rick L. Morgan and Kurt Snyder, eds. New York, Macmillan General Reference/Simon & Schuster Macmillan, 1998. 480p. $21.95pa. ISBN 0-02-862192-1.

This annual publication contains information on law schools approved by the American Bar Association (ABA) as of October 1, 1997. The information is compiled by the ABA from questionnaires completed annually by law schools. Unlike some similar publications, it does not contain information from law students.

Introductory chapters are essays on subjects such as finance and debt management and career outlook. Comparison charts cover career placement, bar passage, expenses, faculty and students, and admissions. The majority of the book is detailed information on each of the 178 approved law schools. The ABA does not rate the schools against each other. Deans of 164 law schools have signed a letter titled "Law School Rankings May Be

Hazardous to Your Health!" which denounces rating systems. The letter emphasized that students should make personal choices based on their own criteria.

California libraries may prefer something like *The Best Law Schools* (see entry 560) by Hollander and Tallia, because it includes information on schools accredited by both the American Bar Association and the California Bar Association. According to the 1998 edition of the Princeton guide, only 16 of California's 57 law schools were accredited by the ABA as of 1997; 17 of the 41 not accredited by the ABA were accredited by the CBA. Another title, *The Barron's Guide to Law Schools* (11th ed.; see ARBA 96, entry 581), includes minimal information on schools in Massachusetts, Alabama, Virginia, and California not approved by the ABA. The ABA book merely lists names and addresses of 32 unapproved law schools.

This 1999 edition differs from the *ABA Approved Law Schools: Statistical Information on American Bar Association Approved Law Schools 1998 Edition* in only a few respects. The new edition lists but does not contain information on schools of law at Chapman University and at the University of the District of Columbia, which were both provisionally accredited in early 1998. The 1998 edition information was collected from questionnaires completed during the fall of 1996, whereas the 1999 edition is from 1997. The 1999 edition includes the deans' letter regarding school rankings. Two chapters were combined, and one chapter, "ABA's Role in the Accreditation Process," was added.—**Bev Cummings Agnew**

559.   Buckley, John F. **Multistate Guide to Benefits Law.** Frederick, Md., Panel Publishers/Aspen, 1998. 1v. (various paging). index. $145.00pa. ISBN 1-56706-378-0.

This comprehensive, comparative guide to employment benefits will be extremely useful for benefits administrators because it succinctly summarizes in tabular form the ways in which the states treat various aspects of this intricate area of law. An opening chapter discusses some current issues in benefits (domestic partners, flexible spending accounts, and independent contracts). The following chapters deal in turn with health benefits; disability and leave benefits; retirement, life insurance, and legal expanses insurance benefits; unemployment compensation; state taxation of benefits; overtime and compensatory time, severance, and holidays; health and safety obligations; and workers' compensation laws. This last chapter includes sections on who and what is covered by the states' laws, what benefits are provided, and how the laws are administered. A subject index allows for access to specific topics. This guide is not a looseleaf product and obviously will become dated, but the publisher provides a subscription to an update service. It is recommended for law libraries and human resource specialists.

—**Jack Ray**

560.   Hollander, David Adam, and Rob Tallia. **The Best Law Schools.** 1998 ed. New York, Princeton Review/Random House, 1997. 516p. illus. index. $20.00pa. ISBN 0-679-77781-4.

If, as the wisecrack has it, 100 lawyers on the ocean floor is "a start," then opening this tome is a hilarious beginning. Chapters on law school education and law school admissions are not only informative but wonderfully beguiling. At one point the authors write, "The process of applying to law school, while simple enough in theory, is viewed by many to be as painful as a root canal." Such comments help to speed the assimilation process of a vast amount of helpful nuts, and bolts, advice. If ever there was a book that lived up to its self-proclaimed intent, this book is it.

Prospective law school enrollees are taken on a no-holds barred explanation of how to apply to a law school, one's odds of getting in, and what parts of the application process must be impeccably presented. If users of this book follow its advice to the letter and still do not get in, it was never meant to be. Other chapters proffer the same useful advice on career choices within law, financing, women and the law, diversity and the law, and more. Even the interview with Lawrence Velvel, a "maverick" law school dean, is filled with pragmatic advice and Solomonic hints.

The last section of the book, the entries on law schools themselves, is brimful of statistics, library assessments, and more. After a brief survey of the school, there are sections on admissions, employment profiles, "hits" and "misses," and student demographics. This title is a must selection.—**Mark Y. Herring**

Handbooks and Yearbooks

561. American Indian Law Deskbook: Conference of Western Attorneys General. 2d ed. Joseph P. Mazurek, Julie Wrend, and Clay Smith, eds. Niwot, Colo., University Press of Colorado, 1998. 501p. index. $65.00. ISBN 0-87081-471-0.

The intricacy of law is such that even the word "is" can have variegated meanings. Applying those arabesque meanings to a kind of law not widely known or understood will make for a real muddle. That is why such great thanks is owed to North Dakota Attorney General Nicholas Spaeth, who wrote the foreword to the 1st edition of the volume in hand. The objective of the Conference of Western Attorneys General has always been "to present a comprehensive and objective treatise in a difficult and controversial area." The current volume is an update to the original 1993 edition.

This update provides a significant discussion of tribal sovereign immunity, including tribal common law immunity from suit. Controversial hunting and fishing issues are also treated with little hope of unraveling the statutory and factual contexts into an agreed-upon theme of judicial decision-making. Other chapters follow their original appearance but with added adjudications from the past five years. The 14 chapters that fill out this formidable tome include other issues, such as the Indian Child Welfare Act, cooperative acts between Indian country and states, taxation, bingo, environmental regulations, and more. Tables of cases, statutes, and codes make finding cited sources easy and quick. The ample bibliography culls the best and brightest writing on Native American law today. The final pages consist of an index for the nonlawyerly at heart.

It goes without saying that midwestern and western libraries of nearly all sizes will want to have this volume and its predecessor on hand for patron reference. Large libraries supporting either law schools or legal courses will also want to consider its purchase.—**Mark Y. Herring**

562. The Citizen's Companion to U.S. Supreme Court Opinions, 1996-97 Term. James F. May, ed. Milpitas, Calif., Toucan Valley, 1998. 822p. index. $79.00pa. ISBN 1-884925-62-6.

This book covers all the U.S. Supreme Court majority opinions from the 1996-1997 term. Each opinion is preceded by a summary that explains, in simplistic terms, the key issues in the case as well as the dissenting and concurring opinions. The summary is followed by the majority opinion, which has been edited by an attorney to exclude most of the legal references and all dissenting and concurring opinions. Only the Supreme Court Reporter volume number and an Internet site are given for further study. The opinions are arranged in topical order.

This book may have a niche in some libraries that have no access to U.S. Supreme Court opinions, and the summaries alone may be useful for unsophisticated readers. The opinions, however, have been edited so much that they are not useful if any other source is available. Omitted are case citations, statute citations, and parenthetical explanations, when those explanations occur within a list of case citations. The parenthetical explanations are often helpful to illustrate a point. This omission results in large sections of the opinion being deleted, relevant or not, ostensibly because they contain too many case citations. Not all references to case names are omitted, but without the citations to those cases, a method of finding them has been eliminated. A serious lay researcher would appreciate having access to all the cases on a subject, not just those from a particular term. An index does refer to other opinions in the volume with similar issues, which compensates for the lack of references to other cases on related subjects decided during the term. [R: BL, 15 May 98, p. 1656]—**Bev Cummings Agnew**

563. Eisaguirre, Lynne. Sexual Harassment. 2d ed. Santa Barbara, Calif., ABC-CLIO, 1997. 285p. index. (Contemporary World Issues). $39.50. ISBN 0-87436-971-1.

The 2d edition of this reference work is both qualitatively and quantitatively improved from the 1st edition. There is a great deal of material included from the first, which one would expect given that this book offers a comprehensive survey on the issue of sexual harassment. Those familiar with the 1st edition will recognize Eisaguirre's work here, and they should be eager to peruse it. The chapter headings are identical to those of the 1st edition. Chapter 1 offers an additional 13 pages, including the current status of various controversies, such as the Clarence Thomas/Anita Hill, courtroom, military, and corporate controversies. The references, which appear at the end of the chapter, have increased from 8 to 20. Chapter 2, "Chronology," begins with 1934 as did the 1st edition but ends in February 1997, with the beginning of the McKinney case (which has since been resolved with controversies of its own). The references at the end of this chapter, unfortunately, remain the same 8 references cited in the 1st edition. Chapter 3, "Biographical Sketches," adds just five new sketches, most notably Robert Packwood and

Paula Corbin Jones. There are 6 references in the new edition, an increase of 1 from the 1st. Chapter 4, "Facts and Statistics," remains very similar to the 1st edition. Five new cases have been added (through 1994), and there are now four pages of references rather than two. Chapter 5, "Organizations," has added 7 new organizations to the listing and dropped 8. Chapter 6, "Selected Print Resources," has added some 13 new annotated entries. This is a most useful chapter for those who want to read more specifically on sexual harassment. Chapter 7, "Selected Nonprint Resources," now includes almost 4 pages of Internet resources. The glossary and index remain quite helpful. For anyone doing research on sexual harassment, this reference book cannot help but point the researcher in the right direction.—**Michael A. Foley**

564.   **International Labor and Employment Laws, Volume 1.** William L. Keller, ed. Washington, D.C., BNA Books, 1997. 1v. (various paging). $295.00. ISBN 1-57018-025-3.

International Labor and Employment Laws is a tremendous accomplishment in and of itself, and a useful one as well. There has long been a need for surveys of laws on many topics, as research of this sort is among the most tedious of all to accomplish working from scratch. In particular, any reference tool that assists in cross-jurisdictional research on subjects affecting businesses is particularly useful as companies expand into wider and wider markets across the country and around the world.

As businesses in the United States expand across international borders, one of the first things that they need to confront are employment laws of the other country, which often vary greatly from those of the United States. Conducting any kind of foreign law research is difficult in the best of times, but finding convenient sources of information that provide comparisons of the laws of each jurisdiction has been, until now, next to impossible.

This book sets out to "provide concise, up-to-date information on the relevant labor and employment law requirements of the world's major economies . . . [including] the European Union, the International Labor Organization, and NAFTA/NAALC." The book generally meets this goal. It is organized into 3 major divisions: "European Union and Selected Countries," "NAFTA and Selected Countries," and "Other Countries." The EU section treats the laws of the United Kingdom, Belgium, Germany, France, Spain, and Italy. The NAFTA section treats the laws of the United States, Mexico, and Canada. The "Other Countries" section covers Japan, South Africa, and Brazil. There are also 8 appendixes that contain the full text of many important documents from various countries and international organizations. The final section of the book is an 85-page bibliography of sources of primary and secondary legal research materials for each state or international entity.

The treatments of laws of each country are necessarily brief and concise. Given the identities of the authors of each section, the reliability of the information is expected to be accurate. In general, the organization of the material follows a distinct pattern. In each country section, for example, Roman numeral one is the section on "Individual Employment." Unfortunately, subsections do not follow the same pattern. This lack of internal organization can be a little confusing and renders the book less useful than it otherwise might be.

If the book has any flaws in its coverage, it is that the treatment of the laws of the United States is unnecessarily long compared with those of other countries. However, it is debatable whether this is actually a flaw. The book is recommended for any library that serves patrons who give legal advice to businesses that may have some form of presence in foreign markets.—**Richard A. Leiter**

565.   **National Survey of State Laws.** 2d ed. Richard A. Leiter, ed. Detroit, Gale, 1997. 605p. $68.00. ISBN 0-8103-9052-3.

This updated edition follows the same format as the 1993 volume (see ARBA 94, entry 569). The 43 sequentially arranged tables are grouped into 8 areas of law: business, criminal, education, employment, family, general civil laws, real estate, and tax laws. The laws are current as of March 1, 1996, which may pose problems for libraries lacking access to LEXIS-NEXIS or other online legal databases. Each table lists federal laws first, if applicable, followed by state laws. There are four to five columns per table. Each table includes citations to federal and state codes followed by major topics related to the eight legal areas. Among the 43 topics included are deceptive trade practices, illegal drugs, prayer in public schools, minimum wage, child custody, right to die, and personal income tax. The topic cross-reference table shows where additional references may be found in the volume. For example, laws related to homosexuality will be found in two topic areas: family law (adoption, annulment, and prohibited marriages), and criminal law (capital punishment and prohibited consensual sex). An appendix, "Statutory Compilations Used in This Book," provides citations to each state's legal code. This handy compilation of state laws will be useful to law schools as well as most academic and large public libraries.

—**Gary D. Barber**

566.　**Occupational Safety and Health Law, 1997 Cumulative Supplement Covering 1987-1995.** Victoria L. Bor and John C. Artz, eds. Washington, D.C., BNA Books, 1997. 614p. $85.00pa. ISBN 1-57018-091-1.

The American Bar Association's Section of Labor and Employment Law studies and reports on developments in the law affecting labor relations. In 1988 the Section's Occupational Safety and Health Law Committee published (through the Bureau of National Affairs) *Occupational Safety and Health Law.* That important treatise covered legal developments under the federal Occupational Safety and Health Act (OSHA) from its enactment in 1970 through 1986. This is the committee's second update to the original publication, and it covers legal developments through 1995.

The treatise—and, of course, this update—addresses the history, administration, enforcement, and interpretation of OSHA, including legislation, administrative rules and regulations, and interpretative administrative and judicial decisions. Although oriented primarily at practitioners, the editors intend this publication to be of value to the academic community and to the "sophisticated nonlawyer." The treatise covers virtually every aspect of OSHA (at least as much as one can cover in one volume) and does so objectively and clearly. The editors did a good job presenting the updates in as consistent a manner as was possible, considering that more than two dozen different authors contributed to the 1997 update.

However, when you have a 600-page update to a 900-page book, and when it has been a decade since the publication of the original work, it is time for a new edition. One hopes the next offering from BNA Books and the American Bar Association is a new edition of *Occupational Safety and Health Law,* rather than another update. In any event, the original work and this update are essential for all large law libraries and, of course, for lawyers who practice in the field of labor law or workplace issues. What else is out there? For one-volume works, consider *Occupational Safety and Health Law* by Mark A. Rothstein (West Publishing, 1998) or *Practical Guide to the Occupational Safety and Health Act* by Walter B. Connolly Jr. and Donald R. Crowell (Law Journal Seminar Press, updated through 1997).—**James S. Heller**

567.　Sitarz, Daniel. **Divorce Yourself: The National No-Fault Divorce Kit.** 4th ed. Carbondale, Ill., Nova Publishing, 1998. 333p. index. (Legal Self-Help Series). $34.95pa. (with disk). ISBN 0-935755-64-0.

This handbook with disk, although deeply critical of the national family law bar, provides a clearly written, well-organized primer on the divorce process that is aimed at those who would seek to obtain a no-fault divorce by agreement. The introduction and early chapters provide valuable practical advice on how to begin the process of physically separating, dividing bills and obligations, closing accounts, doing an inventory of property, and understanding the difference in marital and separate property. Frequent caveats advise the reader to seek the advice of an attorney or other expert if he or she at any time feels intimidated by the other spouse or needs help with valuation issues. Included are worksheets; generic forms; a glossary of legal terms; and, in the appendix, a compilation of each state's divorce laws (ranging in length from two to three pages per state) with references to the applicable statutes.

This book is a wonderful guide for a reasonably intelligent married couple with no children and virtually no property. For parties with children, however, its simplistic approach and generic forms are dangerous. It is one thing to agree to a certain amount of child support—it is another to try to enforce a decree several years later and find that the generic language is not specific enough for enforcement. Texas, for example, requires clear command language for enforcement, especially by contempt. Perhaps some states may not be so specific, but who would want to take that kind of chance? As for calculating child support, the author includes a generic worksheet and chart that were adapted from guidelines used in many states and dutifully advises the reader to refer to the appendix and check with the clerk of the court for local child support guidelines or rules in effect. Under Texas in the appendix, the author references child support guidelines set out in statute and provides the applicable rate. Unless he or she actually looks up the statute, however, the reader would not have the appropriate frame of reference for what a Texas judge would order under Texas statute absent an agreement of the parties.

The author is to be commended for his explanations of divorce procedures and the differences from state to state, his practical advice, and his emphasis on spouses dealing fairly with each other in navigating through the divorce process.—**Patricia C. Strickland**

568.   Stark, Jack. **The Iowa State Constitution: A Reference Guide.** Westport, Conn., Greenwood Press, 1998. 181p. index. (Reference Guides to the State Constitutions of the United States, no.29). $75.00. ISBN 0-313-30624-9.

The casual or sleepy-eyed librarian will glance over this title and soporifically move on to the next. To do so would be a mistake, for state constitutions are the heart and soul of this republic. Such books as these strengthen the understanding of the United States. Studying state constitutions accentuates the umbilical connection between the U.S. Constitution and the individual agreements drafted by the states for their own governance. Apart from the similarities, there is also the richness in uncovering what rights states allowed that never made their way into the U.S. Constitution.

Iowa's relatively new document, drafted more than a half-decade after the founding of this country, offers interesting insights into rights that continue to baffle legal minds. Stark provides a rich history of Iowa's constitutional history that is replete with extenuations to the federal one. The subsequent commentary on Iowa's Constitution enlarges the reader's understanding of Iowa specifically and the United States generally. Careful readers will come to understand the federal government as it now operates.—**Mark Y. Herring**

569.   Stern, Robert L., Eugene Gressman, Stephen M. Shapiro, and Kenneth S. Geller. **Supreme Court Rules: The 1997 Revisions.** Washington, D.C., BNA Books, 1997. 106p. $65.00pa. ISBN 1-57018-095-4.

In 1997 the U.S. Supreme Court made 1 major and 11 relatively minor revisions of its 1995 rules for practice. In so doing, however, the Court actually rescinded the 1995 rules and replaced them with this 1997 revision. Hence, this volume contains not merely the "1997 revision" but the 1997 revised rules in their entirety. The rules, as revised, are a supplement to BNA's *Supreme Court Practice* (7th ed., 1993). The most important rule change is the requirement that authorship by a party before the court of any amicus curiae ("friend of the court") brief filed by a private party must be disclosed; further, that outside financial contributions to the preparation and submission of amicus briefs must be revealed. Evidently, the Court suspected that parties before them were ghostwriting (and possibly paying for) some of the amicus briefs that were ostensibly coming from outside parties.

In addition to the rules, this volume contains several revised documents from the Clerk of the Court—guides for counsel arguing before the Court, for those preparing writs for the Court, and for prospective indigent petitioners; instructions and a form for admission to the bar of the Court; and a guide to oral arguments for visitors. A clearly written analysis of the 1997 revisions precedes the rules. Although the new rules are available elsewhere, this compilation is highly recommended for libraries concerned with Supreme Court practice.—**Jack Ray**

570.   Svengalis, Kendall F. **Legal Information Buyer's Guide & Reference Manual 1997-98.** Barrington, R.I., Rhode Island LawPress, 1997. 587p. index. $79.95pa. ISBN 0-9651032-1-8.

With a 20-year background in the field, Svengalis has produced a guide for the purpose of aiding in the cost-effective acquisition of legal materials. The volume is directed primarily at solo practitioners and lawyers in small- or medium-sized law firms without the benefit of a law librarian, as well as other libraries such as academic and public settings. The 1st edition appeared in 1996, with this 2d edition continuing the aim of increasing consumer awareness through a discussion and presentation of thorough pricing information on the vast body of the legal publishing world. Svengalis notes that publishers market directly to lawyers rather than focusing on law librarians. The numbers make the stark reality of the situation quite clear: There are some 2,500 law librarians versus more than one million lawyers. Interestingly, of the some $4 billion spent annually on legal materials, 60 percent plus or minus is spent by law librarians. The average lawyer spends about $4,000 per year on information, and according to Svengalis, many volumes are seldom used, are wrong for the practitioner's specialty, or are simply overpriced. By providing options and comparisons, the author seeks to suggest the most cost-effective purchasing approaches, with representative used law book prices provided.

One-half of the book covers reviews of legal treatises in 48 subject areas, such as constitutional law, insurance law, and trial practice. The rest of the volume considers the primary law sources for each state as well as the District of Columbia. The appendixes are particularly useful, with topics such as leading legal publishers' histories, legal publishers' contact information, and used law book dealers and prices. Other topics covered include looseleaf services, treatise costs, and the text of the Code of Federal Regulations entry on the guidelines for the law book industry.

The scope of the work is extensive, and the arrangement is clear and easy to use. The format is paperback, with full letter-size pages (8½ by 11 inches). The indexing is adequate, given the outline nature of the text. Individual annotations are concise and carefully written. Svengalis has produced a guide and manual that should be part of all law libraries and libraries with law-related disciplines as well as other academic and public libraries. This work is highly recommended.—**Graham R. Walden**

Indexes

571.   **Index to the House of Commons Parliamentary Papers on CD-ROM.** [CD-ROM]. Alexandria, Va., Chadwyck-Healey, 1995-1997. Minimum system requirements: IBM or compatible 386. CD-ROM drive and controller card with Microsoft CD-ROM Extensions 2.10. MS-DOS 3.3. Windows 3.1. 4MB RAM. 5MB hard disk space. VGA color monitor and card. $2,250.00. ISSN 1363-3597.

This index represents an important development in the field of British parliamentary papers research. Virtually every document of parliament produced in the past 200 years is neatly indexed in this well-thought-out and executed CD-ROM product. The index comes with software that must be installed on a computer in order to use the CD-ROM. The software is extremely easy to install on a Windows 95 computer and, once installed, access to the material on the CD-ROM was convenient. From a technological perspective, the materials are designed in a way that takes maximum advantage of the virtues of the latest advances in computing software.

Once the appropriate material is installed, searching on the CD-ROM is easy and intuitive. With virtually no training one can easily deduce how to use the indexes. This is assuming at least a basic understanding of how computerized database searching works. Even still, one would expect that a person with little or no exposure to computer-based research systems would be able to quickly learn the basics of searching with these materials.

The search window is clear and straightforward. There is a separate line in which to put search terms of each type. For example, there is a line for keyword searching, a separate line for subject searching, title, and so on. Additional search terms can easily be added to each line by clicking on a box to the right of the search-term box, or additional search segments can be added by clicking in the appropriate segment box.

As with any index, the one complaint that may be anticipated from patrons is that it does not include full text. Therefore, this title, for all its technological virtue, is only recommended for libraries with a collection of parliamentary papers. The reverse is also true; it is hard to imagine a library with such a collection that could justify *not* having this useful tool.—**Richard A. Leiter**

Quotation Books

572.   Frost-Knappman, Elizabeth, and David S. Shrager, with Scarlet Riley. **The Quotable Lawyer.** rev. ed. New York, Checkmark Books/Facts on File, 1998. 1998. index. $34.95; $18.95pa. ISBN 0-8160-3753-1; 0-8160-3778-7.

This revised edition of *The Quotable Lawyer* certainly belongs in any public or university library. There are more than 3,000 quotations, as noted in the editors' introduction, "made not only by jurists and lawyers, but also by priests, poets, playwrights, prophets, politicians, humorists, actors and activists" (p. ix). Of those quotes, several hundred are by women, voices that have not been included to this extent in other collections. The book's organization is alphabetic by category. There are 157 categories, including such diverse divisions as "affirmative action," "bribery," "common law," "dissent," "education," "guilt," "juries," "murder," "poverty," "sin," and "war," to name just a few. The entries are arranged chronologically in each section, and the quotations ranged from the humorous to the profound. All sources are cited, thereby enabling the reader to pursue the idea more fully if interested. There is a selected bibliography, a substantive subject index, and an author index. If someone is looking for a legal quote on almost any topic related directly or indirectly to the law, that quote more than likely can be found here. Even if no quote is need, the book is a delight to peruse in any order that one is inclined. The range of topics and writers included here makes this collection an exceptional addition. The work is highly recommended.—**Michael A. Foley**

CRIMINOLOGY

Bibliography

573.   Bennett, John M. **Sendero Luminoso in Context: An Annotated Bibliography.** Lanham, Md., Scarecrow, 1998. 229p. index. $60.00. ISBN 0-8108-3559-2.

This work contains 1,456 entries for publications relating to Sendero Luminoso (Shining Path), the violent Peruvian revolutionary movement. The bibliography is arranged by subject. Entries contain complete bibliographic information, and most have annotations, many of which are unfortunately too brief to be meaningful. Some items are included even though they were not seen by the author.

In many ways the content of *Sendero Luminoso in Context* duplicates Peter Stern's *Sendero Luminoso: An Annotated Bibliography of the Shining Path Guerrilla Movement, 1980-1993* (see ARBA 97, entry 502), a work that Bennett indicates is "an *essential* work for Sendero Luminoso studies." However, it also supplements Stern's work with some more recent works and with more materials that deal with the social, cultural, and economic contexts in which Sendero Luminoso arose and flourished. Of particular note is a section that includes general works with brief accounts of Sendero Luminoso, and chapters on statistical sources, other leftist groups, and literary works that feature Sendero Luminoso. The subject arrangement, as opposed to Stern's chronological arrangement, will also be helpful to some users.

Although the Sendero Luminoso movement appears to be virtually extinct, its remnants are still active, and it has had a lasting impact on Peru. Consequently, interest in it will persist. Public and college libraries and libraries where there is particular interest in Latin American affairs will probably want to own both books.
                                                                        —Gari-Anne Patzwald

574.   McConnell, Elizabeth Huffmaster, and J. Laura Moriarty, comps. **American Prisons: An Annotated Bibliography.** Westport, Conn., Greenwood Press, 1998. 321p. index. (Bibliographies of the History of Crime and Criminal Justice, no.1). $75.00. ISBN 0-313-30616-8.

This inauspicious start to a new bibliographic series contains annotated entries for selected references cited in the *Encyclopedia of American Prisons* (see ARBA 97, entry 505), chosen because they are "recognized as the classic or substantive sources," "readily available," and "sources which the authors were able [to] access." The 1,073 entries for monographs, periodical articles, and court cases are arranged according to the headings under which they are cited in the encyclopedia; however, the number of entries is misleading because many items appear under more than one heading (e.g., the landmark prisoner's rights case *Wolff v. McDonnell* accounts for seven entries) with appropriately modified annotations. Many entries relate to subjects in addition to those under which they appear, and the attempts to compensate for this through the index are not always successful (e.g., *The Hate Factory* by W. G. Stone, a work on a New Mexico prison riot, appears under "homicide," but does not appear under "riots" either in the body of the book or in the index). The compilers have included most of the major monographs on U.S. prisons. The periodical articles are representative, although many are from professional journals (e.g., *Corrections Today*), and there may be too few from scholarly journals to satisfy serious researchers. Adequate bibliographic information is provided, and annotations are concise and generally sufficient.

The rationale behind this work is questionable because the encyclopedia articles should serve as adequate annotations for the works that they cite. Most topics are covered only superficially, and the items cited are often older works, making the guide primarily of use to those seeking a general overview or historical background on topics relating to U.S. prisons. Because of the dearth of bibliographies on prisons, many specialized collections will probably purchase this book, but users should be made aware of limitations imposed by the compilers' somewhat idiosyncratic selection criteria and of the need to search other sources for more recent materials on current topics.—**Gari-Anne Patzwald**

575.   Ross, Lee E. **African American Criminologists, 1970-1996: An Annotated Bibliography.** Westport, Conn., Greenwood Press, 1998. 108p. index. (Bibliographies and Indexes in Afro-American and African Studies, no.36). $59.95. ISBN 0-313-30150-6.

The premises for this volume, in the author's opinion, is that the contributions of African American criminologists have been generally neglected by other criminologists and policy-makers, and in light of the vastly disproportionate representation of African Americans among those processed by the criminal justice system, the findings and insights of African American criminologists are especially important. In fact, only a small proportion of criminologists (of any race) produce work that measurably influences other scholars and policy-makers. It is possible that the work of African American criminologists is proportionately more neglected relative to that of most white criminologists, but this is not demonstrated. The author of this volume concedes that African American criminologists do not necessarily share an Afrocentric perspective. If this is so, it would be necessary to differentiate work with such a perspective from that no different in assumptions and methodology from white criminologists' work, but this is not done here.

Following a brief introduction by Ross, the balance of this volume is devoted to a compilation of abstracts (3 to 4 per person) of African American criminologists who responded to the author's solicitation. A listing of these works and of doctoral dissertations completed by African American criminologists, along with an index, rounds out the volume. Although the fact that African American criminologists have published scholarship on a range of significant topics is certainly documented here, the overall reference value of the volume is somewhat more questionable. [R: Choice, Nov 98, pp. 502-503]—**David O. Friedrichs**

Dictionaries and Encyclopedias

576. Champion, Dean J. **Dictionary of American Criminal Justice: Key Terms and Major Supreme Court Cases.** Los Angeles, Roxbury and Chicago, Fitzroy Dearborn, 1998. 349p. index. $45.00. ISBN 1-57958-073-4.

Anyone who seeks a quick, clear, and coherent definition of a criminal justice term or a leading Supreme Court criminal justice case should turn here to begin that search. As Champion notes in the preface, this text is not designed to replace more comprehensive legal dictionaries such as *Black's Law Dictionary* (6th ed.; see ARBA 92, entry 529). The definition portion of the text, 133 pages, covers not only terms but also brief descriptions of key figures in the history of criminology and key theories about antisocial behavior. For example, one finds here a brief description of attention deficit disorder, jury nullification, Marxian ideology of punishment, Richard Quinney, and XXY syndrome. Thus, the range of terms, theories, and personalities is great. The disadvantage of such range is that these terms, theories, and figures receive short attention. However, for those needing a quick and reliable definition or description, this reference work will prove helpful.

The strength of the book rests in the 290 pages devoted to leading Supreme Court cases. In addition, the book concludes with an excellent 20-page index of the cases, divided into more than 60 categories, including "aggravating and mitigating circumstances," "correction," "death penalty," "exclusionary rule," "inmate rights," "plea bargaining," and "stop and frisk," to mention just a few. The case of descriptions offer sufficient information to determine if the case is relevant to the researcher's needs. The material is clearly and coherently written. The title is highly recommended for public and university and college libraries.—**Michael A. Foley**

577. Grossman, Mark. **Encyclopedia of Capital Punishment.** Santa Barbara, Calif., ABC-CLIO, 1998. 330p. illus. index. $65.00. ISBN 0-87436-871-5.

The revival of capital punishment in the United States in the final quarter of the twentieth century, when it has been firmly abolished in most western nations, is something of a historical anomaly. Although public polls indicate that the substantial majority of Americans support capital punishment, it remains a continuous and hotly debated issue. Whether steady declines in the homicide rate and increasing numbers of executions in the final years of the twentieth century will have an impact on public and political support for capital punishment remains to be seen.

This encyclopedia provides a large number of entries (ranging in length from a paragraph or two to several pages) on many different topics related to capital punishment. The entries include names of people, (from individuals in high profile cases convicted of capital crimes and executed to judges, crusaders, and commentators prominent in the capital punishment controversy), organizations promoting abolition (e.g., Amnesty International), prominent death penalty cases resulting in important rulings (e.g., *Gregg v. Georgia*), and methods of execution (e.g., drawing and quartering, electric chair, gas chamber, guillotine). This reference work also includes a substantial bibliography of relevant books, a timeline, and an index.

The author of this volume, a professional writer, has obviously engaged in a substantial amount of research. The entries are clearly written and informative and often based upon a range of references listed at the conclusion of the entry. If the volume is biased toward the contemporary U.S. experience (especially in the selection of appellate court cases) it also includes many historical and foreign entries. The volume is attractively produced and includes a selection of dramatic illustrations from the history of capital punishment. Interested members of the public and students are the principal audience of this encyclopedia; for serious scholars it provides some basic information as opposed to an in-depth examination of concepts and issues. Although much of the information included here is quite readily available through other reference sources, this encyclopedia is certainly a handy source on an issue of enduring interest. [R: LJ, 15 Oct 98, p. 62]—**David O. Friedrichs**

578.   **Outlaws, Mobsters, & Crooks: From the Old West to the Internet.** By Marie J. MacNee. Jane Hoehner, ed. Detroit, U*X*L/Gale, 1998. 3v. illus. index. $84.00/set. ISBN 0-7876-2803-4.

Outlaws, Mobsters, & Crooks is a collection of short biographies (on average 8-10 pages in length) of a wide range of North American outlaws. Written for a middle/high school audience, the 3 volumes present familiar figures such as Jesse James or Al Capone as well as the more obscure (Roger Touhy or JoAnne Chesimard). The 75 outlaws (the editor's introduction, called the "Readers Guide," indicates 73 but counts pairs as one) are grouped into 10 categories. Volume 1 includes mobsters, racketeers and gamblers, and robbers; volume 2 includes computer criminals, spies, swindlers, and terrorists. Volume 3 covers bandits and gunslingers, bootleggers, and pirates. The set contains such contemporary figures as Timothy McVeigh and Aldrich Ames. Each article contains basic biographical information as well as interesting sidebars—for example, the Bonnie and Clyde article contains a poem written about them; the Carlo Gambino section contains a family tree.

Each volume is organized in the same fashion. There is an overall table of contents that lists the contents of all three volumes, followed by the reader's guide, a list of the outlaws alphabetically, and a timeline. In addition, all volumes are indexed. There should be no reason not to find an individual, even if the reader is unsure of the figure's category. Numerous black-and-white photographs, charts, and small graphics add to the appeal of the information. Chapter headings look as if done on an old, manual typewriter, the typeface found in newspaper offices.

This work will be appealing both for research needs and for browsing. Students looking for blood and gore, however, may be disappointed—the editor has chosen not to include serial killers and mass murderers. [R: BL, 1 Nov 98, p. 540]—**Michele Tyrrell**

Handbooks and Yearbooks

579.   **Crime in America's Top-Rated Cities: A Statistical Profile 1997-1998.** 2d ed. Rhoda Garoogian and Andrew Garoogian, eds. Boca Raton, Fla., Universal Reference, 1997. 757p. $85.00pa. ISBN 1-881220-37-0.

Identical in format to the 1st edition, which appeared in 1995 and covered the years 1995 through 1996, the 2d edition of this massive paperback compendium provides statistics for the past 20 years (1977 to 1996) in all major crime categories (murder, rape, robbery, and others) for some 75 cities with populations of more than 100,000. The editors have done a skillful job in repackaging information culled from numerous government sources (especially the *FBI Uniform Crime Reports*) to present multiyear graphs and tabular data under uniform subject headings.

Entries for each city contain statistical data and graphs prefaced by a brief profile of the city's crime problem between 1977 and 1996, its anticrime programs, and the statistical risk an individual there has of becoming a crime victim. This source also includes city-by-city statistics on hate crimes, law enforcement personnel, correctional facilities, inmates and HIV/AIDS, capital punishment, and gun laws. Although information on most aspects of crime is obtainable through a variety of government sources, this statistical profile of several cities (judged in various magazine surveys to be among the best places for business and living) represents a clear and concise presentation of this important and high demand data. In 1996, *Choice* identified the 1st edition of this source as an "outstanding academic book of the year." This edition is highly recommended for large public, college, and university libraries.—**David K. Frasier**

580.   Helmer, William, and Rick Mattix. **Public Enemies: America's Criminal Past, 1919-1940.** New York, Facts on File, 1998. 368p. illus. index. $35.00; $17.95pa. ISBN 0-8160-3160-6; 0-8160-3161-4pa.

The period between 1919 and 1940 has been described as a "golden age" of U.S. crime. Many colorful criminals—including Al Capone, Clyde Barrow, John Dillinger, Baby Face Nelson, and Pretty Boy Floyd—were active during this time (coinciding with Prohibition and the Depression). Much has been published during the years on these criminals and their era. The principal author of the present volume has made some noteworthy contributions to this literature. This volume provides readers with an engagingly written, systematically organized guide to the "public enemies" and their associates who dominated the crime scene during the two decades in question. Many of the stories recounted, and much of the information, will be quite familiar to dedicated students of this era; however, the authors make a reasonably credible case that they present a more reliable account than can be found in the many competing publications of Jay Robert Nash (e.g., *Bloodletters and Badmen*, 1973).

More specifically, this volume includes brief biographical sketches of all the better-known, and many of the lesser-known, public enemies of the Jazz Age and Desperate Years eras. Accounts of the major events (e.g., the Noble Experiment, the St. Valentine's Day Massacre) are also provided. Readers are also given descriptive accounts of principal gangs or mobs, such as the Black Hand; investigative enterprises, such as the Wickersham Commission; and crime-fighting technological breakthroughs, such as bulletproofing cars. A detailed chronology may prove especially useful to serious students of crime and crime control during these years. The more casual reader will surely find the many featured boxes on a variety of topics—for example, the man responsible for giving Scarface Al Capone his scars—entertaining and informative. The volume concludes with an extensive, annotated bibliography. Altogether, this volume is an attractive and well-informed work that will both entertain and enlighten those who wish to know more about a colorful and noteworthy era in the history of U.S. crime and its control.
—**David O. Friedrichs**

581.   Nelson, Bonnie R. **Criminal Justice Research in Libraries and on the Internet.** Westport, Conn., Greenwood Press, 1997. 276p. index. $75.00. ISBN 0-313-30048-8.

This is a revision of the 1st edition published in 1986 (see ARBA 87, entry 631). Anyone doing research in criminal justice can gain useful insights from this revised edition. The book is divided into 4 parts. Part 1, comprising of 4 chapters, provides substantive background information on research in general, including, but not limited to, information regarding primary and secondary resources; differences between popular, scholarly, and professional literature; the information flow in criminal justice; direction on how to become an efficient researcher; how to do a bibliographic search; and how to use the Internet. Part 2, comprising 7 chapters, discusses the actual research. Most people, regardless of research experience, can find something useful here. Part 2 begins, as one might expect, with the library catalog. Here, the researcher will find information on Internet searches of libraries. Another chapter offers a guide to encyclopedias, dictionaries, and annual reviews. The researcher will find as well substantive search information on the following: indexes and abstracts; newsletters, newspapers, and news broadcasts; documents, reports, and conference proceedings; statistics; and printed bibliographies. Part 3 examines special problems in research such as in legal resources, research in forensic science, historical research with primary sources, and resources for the study of criminal justice in other countries. The chapter on forensic science is a completely new and welcome addition to the book. Appendixes, a glossary, and indexes conclude the book. Here, the researcher will find a list of many subject headings for criminal justice in the Library of Congress; useful criminal justice directories; a guide to some select criminal justice commission reports; a glossary; and an author and title index, an Internet resources index, and a subject index. The book does indeed offer a lot of information on criminal justice research and is highly recommended.—**Michael A. Foley**

582.   **Villains and Outlaws.** Judy Culligan, ed. New York, Macmillan Library Reference/Simon & Schuster Macmillan, 1998. 361p. illus. index. (Macmillan Profiles, v.4). $75.00. ISBN 0-02-865058-1.

As part of the Macmillan Profiles series, this volume draws from other works in the series to present an introduction to the lives and times of world and American figures who are perceived to be villains and outlaws. Because this would be a lengthy list, the editors have based their criteria for selection on three factors: importance in history, relevance to standard curricula, and representation of a broad cultural range. Within these criteria biographees are selected from seven groups, including gangsters, assassins, old west outlaws, and corrupt political leaders. Although most of the material is taken from other Macmillan reference works, the biographies have been rewritten by scholars to appeal to a younger audience, and approximately 30 have been written specifically for this volume. Within the 113 biographical articles, a few are for more than one person—for example, the infamous Bonnie and Clyde and the Rosenbergs, a husband and wife spy couple.

The table of contents indicates the pages for each biographee although access is quick by going straight to the alphabetic list. Additional material includes a list of sources—the specific Macmillan works used and the authors of the original articles, along with the authors of the new articles; suggested readings for each person included; and a glossary and an index. Several features accompanying the biographical texts make the volume especially useful, such as photographs and illustrations, timelines and relevant quotations, frequent "pull quotes" highlighting essential facts from the text, and definitions of some uncommon terms. Occasionally, there are half-page insets of explanatory material as, for example, information on the Salem witch hunt accompanies the article on Lizzie Borden. The use of this added material is enhanced by the excellent typography and page layout. A slightly larger text print with bold black headings, wide margins, the use of shaded violet coloring for the timelines and insets, and violet ink for the other margin material not only enhance the attractiveness of the volume but make it easier to find pertinent information quickly.

As a reference tool, this work provides convenient access to well-written biographical material that is not always easily available elsewhere. It should be in all school and public libraries and would be useful in community colleges and undergraduate libraries also. For pleasurable reading, especially for students, this should have a wide audience.—**Lucille Whalen**

583.   **Violence in American Society.** Frank McGuckin, ed. Bronx, N.Y., H. W. Wilson, 1998. 183p. index. (The Reference Shelf, v.70, no.1). $70.00pa. ISBN 0-8242-0941-9.

Given the recent trend of well-publicized violence in the United States (especially those incidents committed by children and adolescent students in schools), this issue in the well-regarded H. W. Wilson serial, The Reference Shelf, is particularly timely. Like other numbers in the series—for example, *Terrorism in the United States* (see ARBA 98, entry 557)—this sourcebook groups reprints of articles and book excerpts under subject headings designed to intelligently explore complex social issues. Brief editorial comments introduce sections on the theories and causes of violence, a review or analysis of violent crime in the United States, the behavioral effects of violent media images, and individual and national efforts to prevent violence. The material is targeted at the undergraduate student preparing a term paper or speech.

In the volume under consideration, 19 articles are reprinted from popular sources, including *American Heritage*, *The New Republic*, *Atlantic Monthly*, and *Redbook*. A select bibliography cites an additional 50-plus sources (many with abstracts). An appendix lists useful organizations and help hotlines focusing on domestic violence and abused, missing, runaway, or exploited children. An index is included.

Although material on violence in the United States is readily available in various print and computer indexes, this well-edited volume presents an overview of the problem in a useful and coherent manner. It is recommended for college and university libraries.—**David K. Frasier**

ENVIRONMENTAL LAW

584.   Donahue, Debra L. **Conservation and the Law: A Dictionary.** Santa Barbara, Calif., ABC-CLIO, 1998. 380p. index. (Contemporary Legal Issues). $45.00. ISBN 0-87436-771-9.

In the words of the author: "This book is designed to help the reader understand what the law of conservation encompasses and how it works." To do this, the book opens with a very brief chapter explaining the scope, history, principle themes, major players, and contemporary issues in resource conservation and the law. It assumes the reader has little experience with the law, making the book useful for high school to postgraduate students.

The body of the book consists of an alphabetic list of about 240 individual entries that the author considers significant to the subject. Entries may be 1 to 10 paragraphs long and cover such topics as statutes, regulations, court decisions, administrative decisions, organizations, major personalities, and terms. The author, a law professor at the University of Wyoming, admits to a "western states bias" in the entries and claims the entries are "extensive rather than intensive." Despite this claim, there are no entries for David Brower or Supreme Court Justice William O. Douglas—two famous conservationists involved with the law.

Entries emphasize the conservation of federal public lands and their natural resources. Neither international nor tribal law is included. And more importantly, the book does not treat air or water pollution laws or hazardous waste management. Readers are advised to consult *Environment and the Law: A Dictionary* (see ARBA 97, entry 514), a companion text in the Contemporary Legal Issues series. (A few duplicate entries occur in both titles.) Several similarly titled books have been published that cover similar information to a greater or lesser extent. *Environmental Law Handbook* (14th ed.; see ARBA 98, entry 559) is an example.

This book is a valuable special reference tool. It will also be useful to gain a basic understanding of a popular area of law by reading all the entries from cover to cover or just those dealing with a given area of conservation law, such as mining law. A bibliography, tables of cases, statutes, regulations, acronyms and directory of organizations, and an index enhance the value of the book. [R: LJ, Aug 98, p. 74]—**Georgia Briscoe**

585.   **Environment, Property, and the Law: Federal and State Case Decisions & Journal Articles.** Ronald H. Rosenberg, ed. New York, Garland, 1997. 3v. (Controversies in Constitutional Law). $225.00/set. ISBN 0-8153-2696-3.

This 3-volume compilation of judicial decisions and readings on private property and the environment is designed to give scholars and students a comprehensive introduction to the topic in one location. To do this, the editor selected 17 U.S. Supreme Court cases, 3 federal appellate cases, and 9 state cases as well as 13 articles from major law reviews, 8 state code sections, 2 U.S. House of Representative reports, and 1 executive order. The editor is a professor of environmental law at the College of William and Mary. He believes the result of his selections "is a collection of representative materials intended to provide the reader with a strong foundation in the area of American constitutional law and property." These volumes would be of much greater value if the editor at least explained the reason for the selection, or if he gave even a minor analysis or digest of each selection. A table of cases is standard in any legal work, yet it is absent from this title.

Certainly this is a topic that belongs in a series titled "Controversies in Constitutional Law." However, the only original material in all 3 volumes is a 7-page, broad introduction to the subject in the front of volume 1. The introduction mentions five cases important to this controversial area of law, yet only two of them are reprinted in the compilation. Every selection in this compilation could easily be found in any small- to medium-sized law library or on the Internet. And a good-sized public library would have the Supreme Court cases. The editor states in his introduction that the "evolution of the Fifth Amendment takings doctrine has generally been considered primarily the province of the Supreme Court." Almost any scholar or student should be able to select and locate important Supreme Court cases on his or her own or with the help of a librarian. These three volumes are a high price to pay for very little convenience.—**Georgia Briscoe**

586.   Lewis, Cynthia A., and James M. Thunder. **Federal Chemical Regulation: TSCA, EPCRA, and the Pollution Prevention Act.** Washington, D.C., BNA Books, 1997. 551p. index. $145.00. ISBN 1-57018-042-3.

This reference will be invaluable to attorneys, researchers, engineers, city managers, and environmentalists who need to decipher the Toxic Substance Control Act (TSCA), the Emergency Planning and Community Right-to-Know Act (EPCRA), and the Pollution Prevention Act (PPA). Environmental law has so many rules and regulations at the federal and state level that it is impossible to learn them all. This book attempts to guide readers through the maze of federal regulations so they can better understand and comply with the reporting requirements for the aforementioned acts. Five hypothetical case studies are provided that will enhance understanding of how compliance issues could be addressed under certain circumstances. The table of contents and the alphabetic index make it easy to find topics. The authors also provide a useful "table of cases" section for further research into specific areas of chemical law.

This valuable reference source, which briefly covers the evolution of environmental law, will be useful in special libraries that deal with environmental issues and academic libraries that support chemical engineering and environmental programs. Public libraries will also find it a useful tool for citizens interested in how environmental law could be used to eliminate chemical pollution in their hometown.—**Diane J. Turner**

587.   Musgrave, Ruth S., and others. **Federal Wildlife Laws Handbook with Related Laws.** Rockville, Md., Government Institutes, 1998. 679p. index. $95.00. ISBN 0-86587-557-X.

The authors state that "this handbook is designed to serve as a single, comprehensive source of information on the many federal laws and other federal legal authority that influence fish and wildlife management." The majority of the book consists of summaries of more than 280 laws, treaties, and other documents written in clear and understandable lay language, as opposed to the legalese in which Congress promulgates the statutes. "Wildlife" for the purposes of the book means nondomesticated animals and fish. The summaries are current through the 104th Congress, ending December 31, 1996, with some laws from 1997.

The book is divided into 2 parts. Part 1 is an overview of wildlife law and is presented in 3 chapters. Fully cited, these thorough chapters untangle the political, legislative, and judicial trends that have shaped wildlife laws from the 1900s. They also explain how various government entities use their authority to help shape wild-life policy in the United States. Part 2 is the summaries of statutes, cooperative agreements, executive orders, memoranda, and treaties. Excellent judgment has been used to determine which laws to include in the handbook that will most benefit wildlife managers. From the "African Elephant Conservation Act" to the "Tuna Conventions Act," the alphabetic summaries are divided into useful sections—overview, findings and policy, selected definitions, main body of the summary, administration and enforcement, appropriations authorized, and editor's notes. Citations and dates of enactment and amendment are listed. A bibliography, glossary, and index close the large volume.

Environmental legislation is one of the most confusing and fastest-growing areas of law. This book goes a long way toward making sense of them and will benefit not only wildlife managers but also anyone trying to make sense of the maze. It will make a good addition to a reference collection that needs to simplify the legal world for common people.—**Georgia Briscoe**

HUMAN RIGHTS

588.   **The Encyclopedia of Civil Rights in America.** David Bradley and Shelley Fisher Fishkin, eds. Armonk, N.Y., M. E. Sharpe, 1998. 3v. illus. index. $299.00/set. ISBN 0-7656-8000-9.

The editors of this 3-volume encyclopedia consider the term "civil rights" in its broadest interpretation, that is, the concept as it applies to all rights that people have in relation to government, and not as it is frequently used by scholars or jurists, who draw a sharp distinction between civil rights and civil liberties. The nearly 700 articles, arranged alphabetically throughout the 3 volumes, generally cover broad topics such as historical events and issues, but there are many shorter articles as well. These include brief accounts of court cases, biographical information on lesser-known persons involved in civil rights, and rights organizations. Many of the articles are illustrated with black-and-white photographs or other graphics.

Although the work is intended for adults, the editors point out that articles were written with the needs of students in mind. The straightforward text is presented in an easy-to-read format, made more readily accessible through the use of simple titles in bold typeface, followed by a concise definition or identification. Subheadings in bold typeface are used in longer articles. Interspersed throughout the well-written articles are numerous cross-references designated by small capitals. Every entry is signed by an author whose identification may be found in the beginning of the 1st volume. Longer articles are followed by suggested readings, which are briefly annotated. These are in addition to works listed in the lengthy bibliography, which is arranged by broad topics found in the appendix.

Other material found in the appendix, which adds to the usefulness of the set, are copies of the Declaration of Independence and the Constitution, both of which are referred to frequently; a table of court cases; a chronology of events from 1619 to 1997; an annotated list of rights organizations; an annotated list of films relating to civil rights; both a general index and a court case index; and a list of entries under 25 broad categories. This list is included at the end of each volume and there is also a list of articles included in each volume, at the beginning of that volume. Although these are helpful, it might have been more useful to include the general index in each volume. For example, if one goes to volume 2 looking for information on homosexuals or lesbians, neither term is found. It is necessary to go to the list by categories at the end of the volume, select the proper category ("Age, Sex, and Family Subjects"), and skim down the entries for that category to find an article on gay rights. Or one could go to the general index in the 3d volume and find a reference to the article from the term "homosexuality," although there is no entry for lesbians or lesbianism.

There are other problems with access. In spite of the frequent cross-referencing, some articles can still be missed if references are relied on for finding other information on a topic. The comprehensive article on dis-crimination, for example, contains a section on the elderly with two cross-references, but neither refers the reader to the excellent article on age discrimination.

In spite of occasional lapses in indexing and cross-referencing, however, this encyclopedia provides in one set extensive information on civil rights in thoroughly researched, readable articles by experts. Because so many of the topics are in constant demand and would seem to be for some time to come, it is highly recommended for both academic and public libraries.—**Lucille Whalen**

INTELLECTUAL PROPERTY

589.   **Trade Secrets: A State-by-State Survey.** Pedowitz, Arnold H. and Robert W. Sikkel, eds. Washington, D.C., BNA Books, 1997. 1189p. $165.00. ISBN 1-57018-084-9.

This survey is by members of the subcommittee Labor and Employment Law Section of the American Bar Association. It is in a series of sourcebooks under the aegis of this section for practitioners. The other two titles in the series are *Convenants Not to Compete* and *Employee Duty of Loyalty*.

The book is admirably organized. Prefatory materials present standardized questions answered for each state. A finding aid provides page references to where answers for these questions are found for each state. In chapters for each state, the main body identifies and summarizes the principal statutory and case authorities dealing with trade secrets, issue by issue. Practitioners can determine relevant criminal civil legislation governing these issues for each jurisdiction together with relevant precedents. The book lists indicate which states have enacted a form of the Uniform Trade Secrets Act (UTSA). These state chapters also provide reference to pertinent review articles in the literature. Topics covered include definition; bases for trade secret protection; judicial interpretations of the UTSA, state statutes, and common law; relevant evidence; protected information classes; injunctive relief, damages, and costs; and any related proprietary information protection under the state's law. Appendixes contain many useful features, such as the text of the UTSA and state-by-state red line text comparisons of the state law with the model for 42 jurisdictions that had implemented it prior to the copy deadline.

This sourcebook will be an excellent place to start for practitioners, legal researchers, and law librarians. Law libraries serving relevant specialties should strongly consider adding it to their print collection.—**Nigel Tappin**

VICTIMS OF ABUSE

590.   Glenn, Leigh. **Victims' Rights.** Santa Barbara, Calif., ABC-CLIO, 1997. 231p. index. (Contemporary World Issues). $39.50. ISBN 0-87436-870-7.

The timely subject of victims' rights is now included in ABC-CLIO's Contemporary World Issues series, following the standard format for the series: introduction, chronology, biographical sketches, directory of organizations, and resources. A definition of victims' rights and how they are related to constitutional amendments, legislation, court cases, the role of politics, and social activism are included in the comprehensive introduction. This is followed by a chronology, dating from 2370 B.C.E. to 1997, which constitutes a substantial part of the volume, including court cases, commission reports, and events that are not clearly related to victims' rights, such as the notation for 1932 that Mississippi is the first state to adopt a constitutional provision for popular election of local district attorneys. The 11 biographical sketches following make interesting reading, but with the exception of Ronald Reagan, the people included are generally unknown. It is unlikely that users will be seeking information on the people included.

Inserted in the usual series outline is a chapter on policy, legislation, and court cases, which brings together much of the material related to victims' rights that is not always easy to track down. Most useful in this section are the descriptions of the legislation that has been passed and the court cases, which are arranged by the different amendments to the constitution. The directory section that follows lists and describes not only the main victims' rights organizations, but also larger general organizations that may have committees devoted to the subject or that can direct people to other groups that might answer their needs. The slim chapter on resources provides a number of useful works on the subject, but many in both print and nonprint media are only peripherally related to victims' rights, for example, the *Uniform Crime Reports of the United States*. An index appended to the volume facilitates quick access to the materials in each section.

Although this handbook does provide valuable material on the subject of victims' rights, most notably in the information on court cases, much of the volume seems superfluous. It would have been more helpful to have additional information on the resources and less on the chronology and biographical aspects of the subject. Nevertheless, this work should be useful for those libraries serving students and other special groups who have an interest in the topic. [R: BR, Sept/Oct 98, p. 74]—**Lucille Whalen**

11 Library and Information Science and Publishing and Bookselling

LIBRARY AND INFORMATION SCIENCE

General Works

Biography

591.   **American Book Collectors and Bibliographers. Second Series.** Joseph Rosenblum, ed. Detroit, Gale, 1997. 431p. illus. index. (Dictionary of Literary Biography, v.187). $146.00. ISBN 0-7876-1842-X.

Pendant volume to *Dictionary of Literary Biography Volume 140: American Book Collectors and Bibliographers, First Series* (see ARBA 95, entry 971), this anthology of critical essays surveys the book collecting activities and bibliographic scholarship of 47 male and 3 female Americans. At the time of publication, all were deceased, except for C. E. Frazer-Clark Jr., Donald Gallup, and Mary Hyde. Numbering among this book's 39 contributing writers are 10 who submitted articles to the *First Series*. Editor Rosenblum has returned to oversee this subsequent effort, and is credited herein with having composed five essays as well as having had a hand in a sixth.

Articles average about 7 pages each, ranging from 4-page entries on William B. Greenlee and Paul Lemperly to a 12-page piece on Paul Louis Feiss and a 14-page piece on John Quinn. Bibliographies list principal publications by each biographee as well as useful secondary sources and major repositories of each subject's papers. Such diverse bibliophiles are profiled as songwriter Jerome Kern (who accumulated a nonpareil collection of rara avises); Newbery Librarian Pierce Butler; institutional acquisitor Harry Ransom; and colonial printer Isaiah Thomas.

Black-and-white renderings of these book aficionados and representative manuscripts and title pages of their writings and collectibles are scattered throughout the text. The judicious use of anecdotes further expands one's sense of familiarity with such figures as John S. Van E. Kohn, a bibliographer and bookstore proprietor who directed clerks to blow dust onto tomes in order that they be more salable to those with antiquarian leanings.

In its treatment of those for whom the amassing of books was anything from a cool business venture to a love affair to an unbridled obsession, this reference work shares with readers a similarly wide sampling of subject matter covered by these persons' collections. Hoarders have seized books on everything from the provincial (e.g., North Caroliniana and Marylandiana) to the widely coveted (e.g., Johnsoniana and Whitmaniana). Some of the staggering buying coups of Hans Peter Kraus are highlighted, as are some of his notorious gaffes, such as his failure to purchase some scuffed-up items whose provenance later revealed them to be the Dead Sea Scrolls.

Occasionally, however, the critical essays stray into aspects of biographees' personal lives that are, at best, of marginal concern to the scholar. For example, Ruth Rosenberg's article on librarian Bella da Costa Greene lapses into an expatiation upon Greene's sexual proclivities. Also, it remains unclear as to why booksellers Nicholas Gouin Dufief, Charles Sessler, and Frances Steloff should be dealt with in this DLB volume, rather than in a counterpart to DLB volume 154 (see ARBA 97, entry 553). The space accorded these individuals would have been better awarded to such deserving subjects as John Carter Brown, Edward Everett Ayer, and Charles Frederick Gunther.

Finally, although the editor has added seven titles to the work's suggested reading list, he has unaccountably deleted the citations for Starrett and Wroth that had graced the bibliography contained in the previous volume. Notwithstanding these flaws, this work will serve well those who need or wish to pursue information on precursors to today's collectors and bibliographers. [R: Choice, Oct 98, p. 283]—**Jeffrey E. Long**

592.   **Nineteenth-Century British Book-Collectors and Bibliographers.** William Baker and Kenneth Womack eds. Detroit, Gale, 1997. 531p. illus. index. (Dictionary of Literary Biography, v.184). $146.00. ISBN 0-7876-1073-9.

   Baker and Womack have gathered extended profiles of 53 consummate bibliophiles, arranged alphabetically by subject surname. In usual *Dictionary of Literary Biography* fashion, articles are signed by reputable scholars whose affiliations are supplied in the volume's back matter. The editors' introduction identifies factors that influenced the activities of nineteenth-century British book collectors and bibliographers. Whereas the people encompassed by this volume are dissimilar in many respects, they remain united in their devotion—and, in some cases, obsession—regarding the amassing of tomes or the cataloguing of same in bibliographies.

   This survey's wide array of entrants includes explorers (Richard Francis Burton) industrialists (Lord Brotherton), printers (William Blades), forgers (Harry Buxton Forman), librarians (Henry Bradshaw), physicians (William Osler), statespeople (William Ewart Gladstone), polymaths (Andrew Lang), and families (the Rothschilds). Most of these bookish minds flourished during the latter half of the nineteenth century; only eight of those profiled were to live beyond World War I.

   The articles contain half-tone portraits and other illustrations, as well as bibliographic references. The essays typically run to several thousand words apiece, although those on Thomas Phillips, Thomas James Wise, and Anthony Panizzi each extend to nearly 10,000 words. The analyses are consistently informed by sound critical judgments, and they incisively trace formative influences upon the biographees' lives and writings. Those entrants whose academic legacies interweave pure scholarship with stained fabrication are expertly unraveled and examined as well.

   Shortcomings within this work, though rare, do exist. Sadly, no pictures appear of Edward Edwards, Alexander Balloch Grosart, Charles Edward Sayle, or Rowland Williams. Ironically, the entry on Victorian book illustrator Myles Birket Foster provides three likenesses of the artist himself and one of his residence but none of his artistry, save the depiction of two bookplates that he designed for his personal library. Moreover, some users of this reference work may question whether high principles of scholarship have been upheld because the essay on Bertram Dobell was provided by the head of the bookselling firm founded by Dobell himself.

   These comments aside, the defects discovered in this reference are easily eclipsed by its virtues. With this volume, the continuing DLB series has maintained its exemplary standards of scholarly integrity that for fully two decades have distinguished it from other literary research tools.—**Jeffrey E. Long**

Dictionaries and Encyclopedias

593.   **Encyclopedia of Library and Information Science. Volume 60, Supplement 23.** Allen Kent and Carolyn M. Hall, eds. New York, Marcel Dekker, 1997. 384p. $99.75. ISBN 0-8247-2060-1.

594.   **Encyclopedia of Library and Information Science. Volume 61, Supplement 24.** Allen Kent and Carolyn M. Hall, eds. New York, Marcel Dekker, 1998. 368p. $99.75. ISBN 0-8247-2061-X.

   Encyclopedia of Library and Information Science is a well-known work to most librarians. In volume 6 of *Library and Information Science Annual*, volumes 52 through 59 were reviewed, indicating that this encyclopedia will be of interest to large library collections, especially to library schools and other libraries that offer library science courses. Volume 60 contains 18 articles and volume 61 offers 21 articles. Both volumes contain a number of interesting and well-documented articles. For example, Gordon Hogg, University of Kentucky Libraries, Lexington, writes a long article titled "Bolshaia Sovetskaia Entsiklopeiia" and Richard Pearse from Andersen Consulting in Etobicoke, Ontario, writes about library open-distribution systems and copyright infringement in Canada and the United States. Both articles are in volume 61. Interesting articles are also in volume 60; for example, "Faculty Evaluation in Schools of Library and Information Science," written by Barbara Moran, Dean of the School of Information and Library Science at the University of North Carolina at Chapel Hill and "Education for Health Sciences Librarians" by Lucretia McClure of the University of Rochester Medical Center, Rochester, New York.—**Bohdan S. Wynar**

Directories

595.   The Burwell World Directory of Information Brokers. 13th ed. Helen P. Burwell, ed. Houston, Tex., Burwell Enterprises, 1998. 354p. index. $59.50pa. ISBN 0-938519-14-X.

As the value of information has grown, the demand for professional information brokers has likewise increased. This directory lists professional research and document retrieval services. The entries include the basic contact information and specific information about the types of searches and databases searched. The entries are listed alphabetically by state. Each entry is assigned a number, which is used as an identifier in the index. There are 11 indexes, the most useful of which are services, subject, and databases searched. Other indexes include a foreign languages index, a countries and databases index, and a U.S. city index, a company and contacts index. This new edition has changed in the type of entries. There are two types—the abbreviated or the full. The abbreviated is free and includes only organization name, address, telephone number, and e-mail address. The full listing adds subjects, services, fee structure, expertise, and an annotation. This two-tiered approach diminishes the effectiveness of the directory. For the abbreviated listings, the subject, services, and databases searched information is unavailable and is not included in the appropriate indexes. The directory is a helpful tool for those wishing to find an information broker, but without the full listing for all entries it is not as functional as it should be.—**Joshua Cohen**

596.   The Internet-Plus Directory of Express Library Services: Research and Document Delivery for Hire. Steve Coffman, Cynthia A. Kehoe, and Pat Wiedensohler, eds. Chicago, American Library Association, 1998. 200p. index. $55.00; $49.50 (ALA members). ISBN 0-8389-0688-5.

This title is the successor to the *FISCAL (Fee-based Information Service Centers in Academic Libraries) Directory of Fee-Based Research and Document Supply Services* (4th ed.; see ARBA 94, entry 639). The biggest change in this new edition is that it no longer limits entries to fee-based services, but includes libraries and archives that offer research or document delivery services directly to the general public either free or for a charge. The Internet coverage has also been greatly expanded and includes e-mail, TELNET addresses, and URLs to library profiles as well as a list of all libraries with an Internet Website.

The first section lists more than 5,000 libraries and their URLs on the Internet by country. Many of the world's largest research libraries as well as thousands of academic, public, and special libraries are included. The next section consists of five indexes: subject specialties index, services offered index, geographic index, service name index, and a bibliographic holdings code index (OCLC symbols). The last section, titled "Service Profiles," provides general contact information, a brief narrative description, detailed information on services offered (e.g., book loans, article copies, research services), subject specialties, price, delivery, and payment information for nearly 400 libraries.

Because this directory is international in scope, it is nearly impossible to have 100 percent accuracy and inclusion. However, only a few minor errors were noted. A very useful section is the introduction, which includes information on doing library research on one's own or having someone else do it. The editors suggest that it is best to begin with one's local libraries because they may own what is needed or can obtain it faster and cheaper than using one of the fee-based services listed in the directory. The directory is quite useful for those who need extended or specialized research but because charges vary from free to $10 to $150 per hour for research, it does pay to shop around. *The Internet Plus Directory of Express Library Services* provides one-stop shopping.—**Michele Russo**

597.   The Sourcebook of Local Court and County Record Retrievers 1998: The Definitive Guide to Searching for Public Record Information at the State Level. Carl R. Ernst and Michael L. Sankey, eds. Tempe, Ariz., BRB, 1998. 602p. $45.00pa. ISBN 1-879792-43-5.

This sourcebook is an invaluable guide to finding people throughout the country who will retrieve documents from federal, state, and local courts and from county agencies. Even if one knows nothing about this process, the sections in the beginning of the book can be of great help. The section "How to Use This Sourcebook" is clear and easy to understand. "Obtaining Public Record Information" is informative and helpful in explaining the process.

There are two basic sections to this guide: a list of record retrievers by county within each state and profiles of each organization. The state and county list gives the name and telephone number of the organization as well as a checklist showing which types of records they will retrieve. The individual profile for each retriever provides the retriever's name, address, telephone number (including toll-free numbers if available), fax number, Website address, local retrieval and service of process area, summary of types of retrieval, billing and payment terms, project turnaround times, other geographic areas serviced through correspondents, and special expertise. The information is supplied by the vendors themselves in response to a survey; therefore, the information contained in this directory is as accurate as the suppliers have provided.

Several features of this sourcebook make it more than just another directory. One chart helps the user decide whether they require a retriever or a full-service provider for the records they need as well as explaining the difference between the two. Another chart provides useful questions to ask a retriever that can help to decide if the person called is the right one for the project. For anyone needing to obtain local court records in a timely manner, this book can be an asset.—**Dona McDermott**

Thesauri

598.   **ASIS Thesaurus of Information Science and Librarianship.** 2d ed. Jessica L. Milstead, ed. Medford, N.J., Information Today and Silver Spring, Md., American Society for Information Science, 1998. 169p. (ASIS Monograph Series). $39.95pa. ISBN 1-57387-050-1.

First published in 1994 (see ARBA 95, entry 636), this thesaurus provides a framework for individuals indexing and assigning subject headings in information science. Following the National Information Standards Organization *Guidelines for Construction, Format, and Maintenance of Monolingual Thesauri*, the editors have compiled a useful thesaurus. The scope notes are clear enough to be useful and brief enough to limit confusion. In this edition, 136 new descriptors were added and 33 were deleted; increasing the total number of descriptors to 1,353. Broad Terms (BT), Narrow Terms (NT), and Related Terms (RT) are identified in each thesaurus entry and the relationship between broad terms and narrow terms are demonstrated in the Hierarchical Display. The Rotated Display or Key Word in Context (KWIC) "shows each descriptor arranged in alphabetical order by every word appearing in the term." Librarians with large collection in librarianship or information science will find this thesaurus useful.—**Susan D. Strickland**

599.   Rapkin, Lenore. **A Civil Law Lexicon for Library Classification: A French-English Civilian Passport to Library of Congress Subject Headings.** Buffalo, N.Y., William S. Hein, 1998. 269p. $78.00. ISBN 1-57588-399-6.

The avowed purpose of this lexicon is to assist researchers investigating civil law and librarians assigning civil law subject headings. Because the scope is restricted to Quebecois private law, however, its usage may in reality be rather limited.

The preeminence of the French-Canadian orientation is immediately obvious in that the main body of the text is arranged alphabetically according to the French term, followed by the English-language equivalent and appropriate Library of Congress Subject Heading (LCSH), although it is unclear which "latest" edition of LCSH is being used. The one and only index makes cross-references from the English term to the French one. There is no cross-reference index from LCSH to the main body. Furthermore, if an official English equivalent for a French term does not exist, the author fabricates one, as is the case for "exception as to gaming" derived from the French "exception de jeu." The English neologisms do not appear in the English-language index and because the terms are not "official" anyway, one may be hard pressed to justify their inclusion in the glossary in the first place. For the narrow audience to whom this unique lexicon is directed, it serves a worthwhile purpose, but that audience is narrow indeed.—**Lawrence Olszewski**

Archives and Manuscripts

600.   Randall, Lilian M. C., Judith H. Oliver, Christopher Clarkson, and Claudia Mark. **Medieval and Renaissance Manuscripts in the Walters Art Gallery: Volume III, Belgium, 1250-1530.** Baltimore, Md., Walters Art Gallery and Baltimore, Md., Johns Hopkins University Press, 1997. 2v. illus. maps. index. $149.95. ISBN 0-8018-5317-9.

This is the 3d volume of a projected 4-volume catalog of manuscript collection of the Walters Art Gallery. The 1st volume covered French manuscripts from 875 to 1420, whereas the 2d (see ARBA 94, entry 29) covered French manuscripts through 1540. The 4th volume will provide information on the Italian and Spanish manuscripts in the collection.

The focus of the collection, which was compiled from 1895 to 1931 by Henry Walters, a former railroad magnate, was devotional illuminated texts. The 3d volume provides information on 84 codices and 82 unbound texts of south Netherlandish origin. Each catalog entry contains a detailed description of the text, decoration, textblock, binding, history, and provenance, and includes a bibliography. A general index is supplemented by indexes of iconography and incipits. The catalog is compiled by Lilian M. C. Randall, curator of manuscripts and rare books, at the Walters Art Gallery from 1974 to 1995.

The only drawback to this set is the illustrations. As in the earlier volumes, the illustrations are published separately in volume 2 rather than located near the descriptive entry. Moreover, only 22 out of 78 pages of illustrations are in color. This set would be enhanced by more color illustrations, which are more appropriate to the subject matter.

This specialized and well-researched catalog is an excellent complement to the collection it represents. This volume is recommended for all academic and specialized libraries with a focus on medieval and Renaissance manuscript studies.—**Monica Fusich**

Collection Development

501.   Gillespie, John T., and Ralph J. Folcarelli. **Guides to Collection Development for Children and Young Adults.** Englewood, Colo., Libraries Unlimited, 1998. 191p. index. $23.00pa. ISBN 1-56308-532-1.

Based on the authors' earlier work, *Guides to Library Collection Development* (see ARBA 95, entry 653), this resource supplies information on both recent and classic bibliographic sources for use in the selection and acquisition of materials for libraries serving children and young adults.

The annotated guide is divided into 5 main sections: periodicals, sources for both children and young adults, sources for children (preschool through grade 6), sources for young adults (grades 7 through 12), and sources for professionals. Within the children's and young adult sections are several subdivisions by content. Included are guides to audiovisual materials, software, and online services. Complete bibliographic information and the price are provided for each title as well as indication of audience and type of library level. Author/title and subject indexes complete the up-to-date and easy-to-use guide. [R: BL, 15 Sept 98, pp. 256-258]

—**Dana McDougald**

Information Technology

502.   **Information Industry Directory 1998: An International Guide to Organizations....** 18th ed. Joseph C. Tardiff and Mary Alampi, eds. Detroit, Gale, 1997. 2v. index. $580.00/set. ISBN 0-7876-0812-9. ISSN 1051-6239.

Information Industry Directory (IID) has been tracking the growth and development of the international electronic information and publishing industries for nearly two decades. The most recent edition includes close to 350 new entries, making the total of companies covered 8,835 and giving this work the distinction of being the leading reference source on the information industry.

This work presents profiles of organizations and systems that provide databases, CD-ROM products, Internet service, information storage retrieval software, and other information sources. Entries are arranged alphabetically by name and then by the products or services provided. Because companies submit their own information, the entries vary in length, and, as the introduction points out, longer entries are not indicative of the importance or size of the firm. The entries tend to be comprehensive and cover such details as the company's contact information (mailing address, telephone and fax numbers, and e-mail address); staff size; a description of services and products; publications issued by the company; intended market; how to receive price information; and a section for additional information. In this 2-volume set, the 1st volume and half of the 2d volume contain the 8,835 entries provided. The other half of volume 2 consists of 33 indexes, 26 of which list entries by function or by service. The remaining indexes are arranged by company name, database name, publications, software, personal names, geography, and subject. Although having 34 indexes is overwhelming at first, it makes it possible to find the entry being searched for regardless of how little information there is to go on, as well as to find new and unknown companies in the industry and compare their services and rates.

Along with including 350 new entries, the companies listed in the previous edition were given the opportunity to update their information in this edition to reflect mergers, new locations, and new services. IID also offers an interedition supplement that reflects newly formed or newly identified information organizations as well as supplies the directory on diskette or magnetic tape in a fielded format. Given the ever-changing nature of the electronic information field, it is essential for academic libraries and information science-related institutions to purchase the updated editions of this work so they can provide the most current information to library patrons.

—**Shannon M. Graff**

Intellectual Freedom and Censorship

603.   **Banned Books: Literature Suppressed on Political Grounds.** By Nicholas J. Karolides. New York, Facts on File, 1998. 584p. index. (Banned Books). $35.00. ISBN 0-8160-3304-8. [R: VOYA, Dec 98, p. 393; Choice, Nov 98, pp. 489-490]

604.   **Banned Books: Literature Suppressed on Religious Grounds.** By Margaret Bald. New York, Facts on File, 1998. 362p. index. (Banned Books). $35.00. ISBN 0-8160-3306-4. [R: Choice, Nov 98, pp. 489-490]

605.   **Banned Books: Literature Suppressed on Sexual Grounds.** By Dawn B. Sova. New York, Facts on File, 1998. 282p. index. (Banned Books). $35.00. ISBN 0-8160-3305-6. [R: VOYA, Dec 98, pp. 394-395; Choice, Nov 98, pp. 489-490]

606.   **Banned Books: Literature Suppressed on Social Grounds.** By Dawn B. Sova. New York, Facts on File, 1998. 321p. index. (Banned Books). $35.00. ISBN 0-8160-3303-X.

Banned Books, a 4-volume series edited by Ken Wachsberger, focuses on more than 400 works known to have been widely suppressed for their "political, social, religious or erotic content, in the United States and around the world, from biblical times to the present day." Wachsberger defines censored literature as works "legally 'banned'—or prohibited 'as by official order' . . . or censored in a broader sense: targeted for removal from school curricula or library shelves, condemned in churches and forbidden to the faithful, rejected or expurgated by the publishers, challenged in court, even voluntarily rewritten by their authors . . . [it also includes cases in which] authors have been verbally abused, physically attacked, shunned by their families and communities, excommunicated from their religious congregations and shot, hanged or burned at the stake by their enemies. . . ."

These works—including novels, histories, biographies, children's books, religious and philosophical treatises, dictionaries, poems, polemics, and other forms of written expression—are arranged alphabetically by title. The choices for inclusion reflect works most frequently covered in school curricula and mass media presentations. Each entry, ranging from three to six pages in length, includes the following information: author, original date and place of publication, original publisher, type of work (genre), summary of plot or contents, censorship history, and a selective bibliography of further readings.

In addition to the lucidly written and factually accurate entries, each volume includes exhaustive appendixes comprised of biographical profiles of the authors whose works are covered in the main text, a bibliography devoted to books that survey censorship as well as suppressed writers and works, and a complete listing of works discussed in the other volumes of this series. The indexes to each volume—an integrated listing of authors, works, and related subject matter—provide a thorough access point to the contents of the text. The titles *Literature Suppressed on Social Grounds* and *Literature Suppressed on Religious Grounds* are particularly noteworthy for their faceted subheadings. They enable the user to precisely pinpoint needed information; for example differentiating between works by Ray Bradbury, Geoffrey Chaucer, Benjamin Franklin, Ernest Hemingway Hugh John Lofting, Mark Twain, and Walt Whitman with respect to expurgated and bowdlerized literary treatments.

Overall, the series represents a well-researched addition to the literature of censorship. Whether purchased individually by title or as a complete series, *Banned Books* will prove indispensable to libraries and classrooms in high schools and institutions of higher learning. [R: VOYA, Dec 98, pp. 394-395; Choice, Nov 98, pp 489-490]—**Frank Hoffmann**

607.   **Censorship.** Lawrence Amey and others, eds. Pasadena, Calif., Salem Press, 1997. 3v. illus. index. (Ready Reference). $280.00/set. ISBN 0-89356-444-3.

Censorship, issued as part of Salem Press's Ready Reference series, provides a broad-based survey of censoring activities worldwide spanning all periods of recorded history. The encyclopedic entries—997 in all, contributed by 353 scholars—cover key creative works and media, writers and artists, historical events, concepts, places, laws and court cases, organizations, statespeople and government entities, and other institutions relating in some manner to intellectual freedom. For example, a typical creative work entry includes subheadings for type of work (i.e., media format); publication/release date; key creative personnel (author, director, and the like); subject matter; and significance; followed by an incisively worded essay, generally ranging from one-half to three pages in length. The contributions are often supplemented by a black-and-white picture, a bibliography, and the liberal use of *see also* references.

Although the work effectively imparts a relatively balanced, albeit superficial, overview of the censoring phenomenon, gaps are perhaps inevitable given the overall breadth and diversity of the subject. Omissions are particularly evident within the popular culture field. As a case in point, references to popular music artists are token at best; no mention is made of the Greenwich Village avant-garde folkies, the Fugs, rhythm and blues pioneer Hank Ballard, seminal rock 'n' roller Gene Vincent, and countless controversial rap/hip-hop performers.

Supplementary resources represent a major strength of the tool. Volume 3 is appended by a list of federal court cases; a directory of pro- and anticensorship groups; a glossary of terms; a general bibliography (limited to books as opposed to journal articles, dissertations, and other media); an index of court cases; an index of books, films, and other artistic works; and a subject index. The indexes and a comprehensive list of entries by category—which, inexplicably, is duplicated in all three volumes—are paged by roman numerals rather than as part of the pagination of the main text.

Censorship should prove useful to students, educators, and laypeople requiring a general introduction to various components of this field. However, anyone in need of a more detailed, scholarly approach is advised to consult other sources.—**Frank Hoffmann**

608.   Riley, Gail Blasser. **Censorship.** New York, Facts on File, 1998. 202p. index. (Library in a Book). $26.95. ISBN 0-8160-3373-0.

This source, on its front cover, claims to have "all the essential tools . . . in one volume" relating to censorship. Indeed, its coverage of the topic is international in scope and spans all historical periods. Riley, a writer and practicing attorney, possesses impressive credentials for a work of this nature. While serving as an assistant district attorney for Harris County (Houston, Texas), her duties included determining when charges should be filed on obscenity issues and arguing these issues to the judge and jury. One of her works, *Miranda v. Arizona: Rights of the Accused*, was cited by the Children's Book Council as a Notable Children's Trade Book in Social Studies for 1995.

The book is divided into three major sections. Part 1—"Overview of the Topic"—includes chapters on the history of censorship, the law of censorship, a chronology of key events, and a biographical listing of a wide array of individuals who have played a role in the evolution of censorship. Part 2—"Guide to Further Research"—includes an essay entitled "How to Research Censorship"; an annotated bibliography subdivided into bibliographies, books, encyclopedia entries, periodicals, articles, government documents, films, and transcripts of broadcasts that provides a representative sampling of resources on censorship; and a list of organizations and associations—various national, state, and local groups committed to fighting censorship in its myriad forms (but none committed to censoring behavior). The appendixes include acronyms and initialisms of groups or entities involved with censorship, a glossary of notable intellectual freedom terms/concepts, the First Amendment to the U.S. Constitution, the flag desecration statutes and bills, the Communication, Decency Act, and the Electronic Freedom of Information Act Amendments of 1996.

The work's overall effectiveness, however, is marred by superficial treatment of the topic and a lack of balance in presentation. The bibliography's annotations—generally consisting of one truncated sentence—do not provide a clear picture of the work being described. The acronyms section simply provides the full name of the organization alongside the listed initialism. Many of these organizations (e.g., ABA/American Bar Association) are not cited anywhere else in the text. The utility of the tool is further undercut by the author's failure to maintain consistency in the use of headings throughout the text. For example, the introductory paragraph to chapter 6 lists headings such as "films" and "transcripts of broadcasts" as part of the annotated bibliography; however, the text proper employs the following headings in their place: "audiovisual materials," "videos" and "transcripts available through Journal Graphics." Journal Graphics is not cited or explained anywhere else in the book; if it indeed provides transcripts to radio and television program, then how does one employ its services?

In short, it is hard to visualize an appropriate audience for the book. On the one hand, coverage is far too terse and generalized for the serious researcher; on the other hand students looking for a concise overview of the topic will find existing reference tools (e.g., encyclopedias) adequately suited to their needs.—**Frank Hoffmann**

Library Automation

609.   Cibbarelli, Pamela R., and Shawn E. Cibbarelli, comps. **Directory of Library Automation Software, Systems, and Services.** 1998 ed. Medford, N.J., Information Today, 1998. 430p. index. $89.00pa. ISBN 1-57387-044-7.

The purpose of the *Directory of Library Automation Software, Systems, and Services* is to provide a survey of commercially available library automation software, systems, and services that are targeted to the library marketplace and marketed in North America. The *Directory* is a continuation of the *Directory of Information Management Software for Libraries, Information Centers, Record Centers*, and Pamela Cibbarelli continues as compiler.

The "Directory Software" section takes up three-fifths of the directory and arranges descriptions of software alphabetically by the name of the software system. Descriptions always include the following set of descriptive information: name of software system; name of company distributing software including street, World Wide Web and e-mail addresses; hardware; system requirements; programming language; system components and applications; system features; details on MARC compatibility; markets that the supplier is targeting; installations; published reviews and articles about the system; price; and supplier's comments. Especially helpful are the supplier's comments that enlist the supplier's language to tell what the software system does. Descriptions should also include headings under which software systems are indexed so readers can consult these headings in the index to find software systems like the ones they have found of interest. The remainder of the work consists of nine sections on related library automation information, such as a list of conferences and meetings in chronological order, list of library automation consultants in alphabetic order, and selected bibliographies of library automation publications in alphabetic order. An index to the directory's 10 sections concludes the book. Regardless of the extent to which libraries have invested in library automation, this directory will be an indispensable assistant to librarians contemplating or steeped in automation.—**Karen Markey Drabenstott**

Research

610.   Quaratiello, Arlene Rodda. **The College Student's Research Companion.** New York, Neal-Schuman, 1997. 151p. illus. index. $35.00pa. ISBN 1-55570-275-9.

Quaratiello, a library instruction and reference librarian, wrote this book after becoming frustrated at trying to teach the basics of library research to undergraduates in just an hour. She succeeds well in guiding students through the research process, discussing in a breezy, conversational style such areas as topic selection, classification systems, periodical and CD-ROM indexes, online databases, and the pros and cons of resources on the Internet. (She does not mention government documents.) Her clever comparisons between research work and taking a car journey aid in giving the book's chapters some consistency and commonality. She is detailed and thorough, using well-known "hot" topics to illustrate her various points and procedures. For example, although mentioning that most electronic indexes do not go back much more beyond a decade, she uses the 1959 Woodstock Festival to show how the print *Readers' Guide to Periodical Literature* works.

It is unfortunate, however, that Quaratiello's publisher did not urge her to make effective use of bullets, check marks, white space, blocked text, broken text, hands-on examples, and boldfaced highlights. Readers would find, for example, a step-by-step illustration of how a question can be answered using an Internet search engine much more interesting than a lengthy explanation of pure text, accompanied by muddy screen-captures that are difficult—if not impossible—to read. Admittedly, content is more important than format (as Quaratiello stresses), but undergraduates would find the book much more inviting to read and study if a bit more attention had been paid to style. Compare these pages, for instance, with those in Robert I. Berkman's *Find It Fast: How to Uncover Expert Information on Any Subject* (4th ed.; see ARBA 98, entry 575).

That said, both instruction librarians as well as undergraduates will find much of use here. The title is recommended for that audience.—**Jack Bales**

Special Libraries and Collections

611.   Forrester, William H., comp. **Directory of Medical Health Care Libraries in the United Kingdom and Republic of Ireland 1997-8.** 10th ed. London, Library Association Publishing; distr., Lanham, Md., Bernan Associates, 1997. 273p. index. $70.00pa. ISBN 1-85604-219-7.

Compiled by Forrester and other staff members of the British Medical Association Library from submitted questionnaires, this edition of the well-known directory has undergone a change in arrangement. It is now arranged alphabetically by library or organization, with entry numbers. Town, professional staff, and hospital indexes refer to these entry numbers. Medical, hospital, nursing, and allied health libraries are included.

Information includes address, telephone numbers, and librarians' names; type, hours, and some policy statements; holdings and classification system; library management systems and computerized systems; publications; and network connections. A list of abbreviations and acronyms is in the preface. There are 851 entries, mostly complete, with a copy of the questionnaire to solicit additional listings. There is also a list of the Regional Librarians Group members. Mailing labels are available from the publisher. This directory will be useful for library organizations, for schools and suppliers, and for librarians and others professionally interested in the fast-changing health care picture and its information systems in the United Kingdom and the Republic of Ireland.

—**Harriette M. Cluxton**

612.   Kelly, W. A. **The Library of Lord George Douglas (ca.1667/8?-1693?).** Binghamton, N.Y., Medieval & Renaissance Texts & Studies, State University of New York, 1997. 166p. index. $20.00pa. ISBN 0-86698-221-3.

Lord George Douglas was born in 1667 or 1668 and lived for about 25 years. He was a pupil at Glasgow University, had a lawyer and classical scholar for a tutor, and studied on the Continent at Holland, Germany, Italy, Belgium, and elsewhere. This bibliography and introductory matter began as the author's master's thesis in the Department of Librarianship, University of Strathclyde. A record in manuscript of Douglas's book collection had lain at the National Library of Scotland for some centuries until the author, while browsing the stacks at the National Library's Department of Printed Books, noticed that the name George Douglas as well as the coat of arms of the Queensberry branch of the Douglas family appeared with some frequency.

Douglas collected books from 1686 on when, under the tutelage of his tutor Alexander Cunningham, Douglas toured the Continent. Douglas had money but was under some constraints from his father not to be extravagant. So he seems to have spent wisely, often being able to buy important books of the time in secondhand shops at a bargain price. In this manner Douglas amassed a library of some 800 titles.

Kelly points to two types of books: the legal books and the nonlegal books. He remarks that, although extensive, the legal group is by no means a complete collection. The works comprising the greater part of the nonlegal library given by Douglas were in philosophy, mathematics, classical literature and antiquities, and Italian literature. He was especially interested in numismatics, and so his collection in that area is of high quality. Among the illustrious authors represented in the collection are Hippocrates, Thomas Hobbes, Homer, François La Rochefoucauld, François-Félix Faure, and Euclid.

The largest part of this book is an alphabetic list of the collection by author, usually followed by title of work, place of publication, publisher, date and size (quarto). There are two appendixes: books bought for Douglas and previous owners of certain books. Aside from an overall index, there are indexes of editors, commentators, and translators; of printers, publishers, and booksellers; and of places of publication. This book fills a niche in Scottish library history.—**Randall Rafferty**

613.   **Smithsonian on Disc: Catalog of the Smithsonian Institution on CD-ROM.** 4th ed. [CD-ROM]. New York, G. K. Hall/Simon & Schuster Macmillan, 1997. Minimum system requirements: IBM or compatible. CD-ROM drive with Microsoft CD-ROM Extensions 2.0. 512K RAM. $995.00. ISBN 0-7838-1809-2.

G. K. Hall's catalogs of specialized research collections are an important tool for public and technical service librarians as well as advanced level patrons. *Smithsonian on Disc* is a CD-ROM catalog that contains about 500,000 bibliographic records from 17 branch libraries of the Smithsonian Institution, with interests ranging from air and space to zoology, with substantial holdings on history, sciences, and the arts. Bibliographic records of archival holdings are included in the book.

An instruction manual on the program is included, but there is minimal additional supporting documentation provided. One important question that remains unanswered is what percentage of the Smithsonian's impressive collections have been automated and are, thus, available on this product.

The CD-ROM is relatively easy to load and operate, and is certainly less cumbersome than the several volumes of printed copies of cards. However, before purchasing the volume librarians may wish to consider how unique this collection is and decide if they may not be better served by connecting to the Web version of the Smithsonian Online Public Access Catalog (OPAC) at the homepage of the Smithsonian Institution Libraries. The speed of the Web version is somewhat slower than the CD-ROM, but it is more current, significantly cheaper, and easier to operate than the CD-ROM, which operates from a DOS command system rather than the ease of Windows and hypertext. Although few libraries will likely want to purchase this database catalog because of its redundancy, price, and lack of specificity, G. K. Hall should be commended for making it commercially available to libraries that wish to offer proprietary access to this impressive collection of collections.—**Andrew B. Wertheimer**

614.   Walsh, James E. **A Catalogue of the Fifteenth-Century Printed Books in the Harvard University Library, Volume 5.** Binghamton, N.Y., Medieval & Renaissance Texts & Studies, State University of New York, 1997. 477p. illus. index. (Medieval & Renaissance Texts & Studies, v.171). $45.00. ISBN 0-86698-212-4.

This volume brings to a conclusion the publication of the catalog of fifteenth-century printed books in the Harvard University Library (see ARBA 97, entry 547; ARBA 96, entry 42; ARBA 94, entry 31; and ARBA 92, entry 36), providing a brief history of the collection and cumulative indexes to the previous 4 volumes. The brief history is 72 pages long and presents sketches of 33 named collections that contributed incunabula to the library, roughly in the order of their reception, and descriptions of 18 funds available for the purchase of books from this period. There is a special index to this important, brief history.

Seven indexes follow: author/anonymous title index; editors and translators and secondary works, identified and anonymous index; printers and places index; provenance index; index of incunabula containing manuscripts; index of incunabula with identified bindings; and points of bibliographical interest index. There are concordances for the volumes at Harvard and Hain, Proctor, the Gesamtkatalog, and Goff; a list of works cited throughout the catalogue; errata and addenda to volumes 1-3; and eight plates.

This essential volume caps the publication of one of the most important catalogs of incunabula produced in the United States.—**Dean H. Keller**

615.   **World Directory of Business Information Libraries.** 3d ed. Chicago, Euromonitor International; distr., Detroit, Gale, 1998. 355p. index. $590.00. ISBN 0-86338-799-3.

In alphabetic order, the table of contents lists 166 countries for which library information is given. Directory information includes address, telephone and fax numbers, e-mail address, Website address, year established, chief officers with titles, the person to direct inquires to, number of staff, and type of library (e.g., academic, public, business, or company). Library information includes operating hours, whether or not it is open to the public, and stock—meaning type of materials and services. Stock may include collection size with description of books, periodicals, CD-ROMs, indexes, and online access. Materials could be corporate reports; directories; technical and trade journals; and subject area of expertise, such as accounting, banking, information technology, market research, and policy analysis. Services include the type of activities provided, such as library loan, photocopying, Internet access, and reference.

There are two indexes, a general index, and an index of libraries by sector. The general index is an alphabetic listing of each library. The index by sector is an index by subject or area of expertise, of which representative examples were given above. There are 84 of these, with the largest sections being economics, statistics, and company information.

A quick check of a recently published list ranking U.S. business schools revealed that libraries for 2 of the top 10 and 6 of the top 20 were not included. This simply illustrates the difficulties of compiling a worldwide directory. A regional, language, or cultural bias is difficult to avoid. Of the G-7 economic powers, there were 27 pages for the United Kingdom, 17 pages for the United States, 15 pages for Canada, 4 pages for Italy and France, and 3 for Japan. For those who need to know the address and the operating office of Uttar Pradesh Institute of Administration Library in India, this becomes invaluable if there is no other source. This directory is one of a series of business information source titles published by Euromonitor that are available on CD-ROM and on Euromonitor's Website. The *World Directory of Business Information Libraries* may be supplemented with other Euromonitor directories and directories from the U.S. distributor Gale Publications when needed.—**Robert M. Ballard**

PUBLISHING AND BOOKSELLING

Biography

516.   Dickinson, Donald C. **Dictionary of American Antiquarian Bookdealers.** Westport, Conn., Greenwood Press, 1998. 272p. index. $75.00. ISBN 0-313-26675-1.

As a segment of the entire book trade, antiquarian booksellers are a small part; yet, the men and women who labor in what is often anonymity are unique and frequently fascinating individuals. In a concise 1-volume reference work, Dickinson portrays 205 notable book dealers, all of whom died before August 1, 1997. Nearly one-half operated in the New York City metropolitan area, and the cities of Philadelphia, Boston, San Francisco, and Los Angeles account for another 59. There are 20 foreign book dealers represented here, which does not make for very diverse geographical representation. Only three were located in the southern United States. Despite this seeming imbalance and its rather expensive price tag, this is a useful book.

Entries are alphabetic; average about a page in length; and include a biographical summary (necrology and location of business), a narrative sketch of each book dealer, and a brief source list. The sketches attempt to identify the collector's area of specialization, notes on sales catalogs, the disposition of their stock, and any influence the individual had on institutional or private collections. Recognizable names include Hubert Howe Bancroft, George S. MacManus, and Joseph Sabin, among others. Entries are well written, although a more careful proofreading would benefit the publisher and reader. Although many of the individual antiquarians are covered in standard biographical sources, such a compilation still makes a useful, yet highly specialized, reference work. [R: Choice, Nov 98, p. 489]—**Boyd Childress**

Catalogs and Collections

517.   Brodersen, Martha, Beth Luey, Audrey Brichetto Morris, and Rosanne Trujillo. **A Guide to Book Publishers' Archives.** New York, Book Industry Study Group, 1996. 140p. index. $28.00pa. ISBN 0-940016-63-X.

The increasing utility that scholars in the fields of textual editing, the history of printing and publishing, and literary history find in publishers' archives makes this guide especially useful and timely. The authors of the guide are persuasive in their suggestion that these archives might also serve the needs of researchers interested in the history of higher education, the sociology of knowledge, and the evolution of academic disciplines. The number of archives of religious and immigrant presses along with presses that reflect the gamut of political opinion would indicate that scholars in these fields might consider these resources as well.

The guide identifies more than 900 collections representing about 600 publishers and includes individuals such as founders of presses, editors, and designers. There are extensive cross-references and an index. Entries are arranged alphabetically by publishers' names and contain the size of the collection, years covered, nature of the material in the archive, the existence of finding aids, and restrictions on access and use. Finally, the location of the archive is given.

Addresses of publishers that maintain their own archives are provided, but addresses of libraries are not given on the theory that these addresses are readily available in many reference sources. If a publisher reports that no archive is maintained, that information is recorded. The authors anticipate a 2d edition of their guide, which they hope will include significant additional entries. [R: C&RL, Sept 97, p. 466]—**Dean H. Keller**

Directories

618.   **Directory of Publishing 1999: United Kingdom, Commonwealth, and Overseas.** 24th ed. New York, Cassell, 1998. 525p. index. $99.00. ISBN 0-304-70412-1.

Directory of Publishing is a resource welcome to writers and their agents, editors, and distributors who seek to publish or market printed material in English-language markets outside the United States. It will enable the user to contact or take a rough measure of publishers and distributors and their interests. This work contains information such as imprint, areas of publishing interest, number of titles published each year, names of editors, number of employees, ISBN number range, fax number, postal codes, e-mail addresses, and postal addresses. Not all items appear for all sources. This annual source updates its information with questionnaires filled out by agencies or persons listed; no old material is presented here. It lists 1,500 publishers, 21 countries, and 121 authors' agents from 7 countries. Latest revision takes needs of electronic media into account. It can be used to trace the names of whom to contact and ownership of UK publishers. Indexes of personal names, companies, imprints, and publishers' overseas representatives are featured. This is a highly specialized source but should be of great use to writers and distributors.—**Edna M. Boardman**

619.   Farry, Mike, comp. **The Directory of Publishers in Religion.** Atlanta, Ga., Scholars Press, 1998. 186p. index. (Scholars Press Handbook Series, v.10). $19.95pa. ISBN 0-7885-0410-X.

This directory includes a selection of U.S. publishers in the field of religion. A variety of types of publishers are included, such as university presses, institutes, small and ethnic presses, large commercial presses, and religious denominational presses. Although all of the world's major faiths are represented, Christian presses predominate.

The directory is designed primarily for prospective authors. Therefore, it includes information on the editorial mission, acquisitions needs, and submission guidelines. In addition, each entry includes an address, telephone and fax numbers, World Wide Web homepage, corporate staff, faith/denominational/cultural focus, subject areas, types of publications, number of titles, and recent and forthcoming titles. The information comes from participants in a survey of U.S. publishers that "devote a significant portion of their book publishing program to religion-related topics" (p. vii).

The work is organized alphabetically by name of publisher. There are three types of indexes, which are an important, useful feature of the book. The faith/denominational/cultural focus index lists publishers by specific faith. The subject area index lists publishers under six broad subject areas: religious life/practice, religious thought/theology, religious studies, religion and society, sacred literature, and religious education. The types of publications index lists publishers by audiences, formats, and genres.

A preface includes a section on how to use the directory and a description of the indexes. Plans are underway to update and expand the directory every two years. Although the directory is not comprehensive, because of the amount and type of information included for each publisher and the extensive indexing it is a useful, important resource for academic libraries supporting religious studies programs, as well as for religious and theological libraries of all types.—**Susan J. Freiband**

Handbooks and Yearbooks

620.   **By the Numbers: Publishing.** Robert S. Lazich, ed. Detroit, Gale, 1998. 510p. index. $79.00pa. ISBN 0-7876-1860-8. ISSN 1096-4967.

This compendium of statistical information on publishing in the United States contains 566 tables grouped into 14 chapters. (There is a detailed keyword index.) *Publishing* is broadly defined so that not only are there chapters on book, magazine, and newspaper publishing but also chapters on the catalog and greeting cards industries and on music publishing. Additional chapters cover the printing and supplier industries, employment and compensation, crime (pirating), censorship, and awards and best-sellers. Most of the data pertain to the 1990 to 1997 period, and a fair amount of them come from readily available sources such as *Publishers Weekly*, *The New York Times*, *The Wall Street Journal*, *U.S.A. Today*, and the economic census of 1992.

This is a handy one-volume source of data on the U.S. publishing industry of the 1990s, and it will certainly save the reference librarian or market researcher in search of such information much time. There is some slight overlap with The Bowker Annual (see ARBA 98, entry 576), but otherwise there are no competing reference works. For its price, this work should have been hardbound. [R: Choice, Oct 98, p. 283]—**Joseph Cataio**

621.   Perle, E. Gabriel, and John Taylor Williams. **The Publishing Law Handbook.** 2d ed. Gaithersville, Md., Aspen, 1998. 2v. index. $285.00 looseleaf w/binder. ISBN 0-13-035601-8.

First published in 1988, *The Publishing Law Handbook* has evolved into an authoritative reference source for all segments of the publishing industry. The authors have filled their 2-volume resource with "model agreements, checklists, and helpful guides to provide a thorough understanding of various matters relating to intellectual property and publishing law." Publishing practices and procedures comprise volume 1, with the 2d volume concentrating on copyright practices and procedures. The material in each volume is expanded, revised, and updated annually in an effort to keep publishing professionals up to date of the latest changes in the law and aware of any specific developments that may influence decision making.

This publication has a revised chapter on electronic publishing due to the burgeoning expansion in this area that covers among other things, Website liability, intellectual property rights, and new federal regulations. Other chapters include a review of the rights of the press concerning closed proceedings and appendixes of state access laws and open meeting laws; the latest information on the issues surrounding for-profit photocopying for educational purposes and fair use; an overview of case law concerning work for hire; copyright infringements of photographs and ways to avoid them; a revision of information concerning trademark law in regard to intellectual property ownership as regards the Internet; and a discussion of the impact of U.S. law on the growing power of moral rights claimed by European creators, the Berne Convention, and the Treaty of Rome. Fourteen chapters in all have been updated or revised to make them current, and there is a new appendix that covers The Conference on Fair Use (CONFU) Interim Report. The index and table of cases have been updated to accommodate all changes in the text.

This 2-volume set is a must purchase for anyone who needs to stay current concerning case law and the legal ramifications that surround publishing.—**Jo Anne H. Ricca**

12 Military Studies

GENERAL WORKS

Bibliography

622. **A Guide to the Sources of United States Military History: Supplement IV.** Robin Higham and Donald J. Mrozek, eds. North Haven, Conn., Archon/Shoe String Press, 1998. 580p. $69.50. ISBN 0-208-02422-0.

The 4th supplement to *A Guide to the Sources of United States Military History* is an essential resource for scholars, students, and military professionals researching U.S. military history. Although the nature of research is changing with the advent and growing use of the Internet, there is still a place for the more traditional forms of bibliographic presentation. The original guide was published in 1975, and this supplement indicates the evolution of the succeeding volumes. Some chapters from previous supplements have been deferred to future volumes; among those are nuclear war and disarmament, science and technology in the twentieth century, and the U.S. Army Corps of Engineers. Other chapters have returned with this volume, namely "Military Law" and "Museums." Other chapters trace the European background to U.S. military affairs, the American Revolution, the Mexican War, and the Civil War. Each branch of the service has its own chapter for the period from 1945 to 1991. There is no specific chapter on the Cold War yet—a topic that may need its own chapter in a future supplement.

Among the contributors are Robin Higham, founder of the guide; Dennis Showalter of Colorado College; Frederick Harrod from the United States Naval Academy; and Roger Launius, chief historian of the National Aeronautics and Space Administration. Each chapter engages in a lengthy discussion of the topics and issues facing historians for a particular period or topic, followed by an extensive unannotated bibliography. For anyone wanting to engage in research on U.S. military institutions, combat operations, or the culture of the military in the United States, this volume is highly recommended. College, university, government, and individual reference collections will do well to own a copy of this resourceful volume.—**Norman L. Kincaide**

Biography

623. Baron, Scott. **They Also Served: Military Biographies of Uncommon Americans.** Spartanburg, S.C., MIE Publishing, 1998. 333p. illus. index. $18.95pa. ISBN 1-877639-37-0.

What president of the United States served as his regiment's lieutenant colonel during the Spanish-American War and in 1898 lead his troops on foot to charge Kettle Hill in Cuba? Theodore Roosevelt. Who was the gourmet cook and author who served with the Office of Strategic Services in Ceylon and China during World War II? Julia Child. Name the author of children's books who shortly after the attack on Pearl Harbor drew a cartoon of a battered Uncle Sam Cat rising from a rocking chair with the caption, "End of the Nap?" Theodor Seuss Geisel, "Dr. Seuss." Who was the officer who signed Clark Gable's honorable discharge in 1945? Ronald Reagan. Name the talk show host who became the first black enlisted marine to complete and graduate from both the Naval Academy Preparatory School and the U.S. Naval Academy at Annapolis? Montel Williams.

Answers to questions like these are to be found by the thousands in *They Also Served*, a collection of more than 500 condensed military biographies of some of America's most famous people. Baron enlists his celebrities in military uniform under 11 curious headings: politics, government, and the law; women in the military; entertainment; poets, authors, and journalists; science and medicine; adventurers and explorers; sports and athletes; business and industry; academics, clergy, and idealists; notorious; and interesting and unusual. The fascinating stories, facts, and trivia told about these extraordinary Americans are of such broad appeal that *They Also Served* makes an excellent coffee-table book or bedside companion as well as a valuable reference guide and research tool.

—**Colby H. Kullman**

624.   **The Great Admirals: Command at Sea, 1587-1945.** Jack Sweetman, ed. Annapolis, Md., Naval Institute Press, 1997. 535p. illus. maps. index. $49.95. ISBN 0-87021-299-X.

Collected thumbnail biographies of "the great admirals" appear with some regularity, and often include a familiar roster of individuals—Sir Francis Drake, Horatio Nelson, David Farragut, Heihachiro Togo, Sir John Jellicoe, and William Halsey Jr. The present volume includes these standards, plus others of less general recognition—Niels Juel, Pierre-André de Suffren, and Andrew Cunningham. The editor's criteria for selection included that the individuals commanded in battle at sea and had distinctive personal ability and that their actions had historical importance. Sometimes these criteria play off each other; as noted in the introduction, Tegetthoff's victory over the Italians had little historical importance, although it was a brilliant action. The chapters are grouped in 6 units, from the first age of European fighting sail in the late 1500s through the lines of battle of the eighteenth century to the dreadnought period and the subsequent age of the use of aircraft in naval battles. Missing is any consideration of the great admirals of antiquity. The chapters are authored by individual experts, and vary in style. All are readable, and some quite enjoyable. In general they tend to focus more on the person than the action, but battles are succinctly summarized and generally accompanied by maps of explanation. Further references are given in each chapter, although they vary in degree of detail. This reviewer would not regard any chapter as a primary reference, but several are good secondary summations.—**Bruce H. Tiffney**

625.   Wooster, Robert. **The Civil War 100: A Ranking of the Most Influential People in the War Between the States.** Secaucus, N.J., Citadel Press/Carol Publishing Group, 1998. 272p. illus. maps. index. $27.50. ISBN 0-8065-1955-X.

This book presents one historian's view of people he regards as the 113 most influential men and women of the Civil War. Wooster, a professor of history at Texas A&M University in Corpus Christi, goes beyond the typical list of political and military leaders to include authors, artists, reformers, business people, diplomats, and, as he refers to them, "villains." Arranged in order from most to least influential, each entry includes a portrait, an occasional additional illustration, and a brief biography approximately two to three pages in length. Wooster supplements his list with a brief history of the period written in the form of an introduction to the volume, a five-page chronology, two maps showing the location of major battles, and six pages of appendixes relative to the war. An index provides access to topics mentioned within entries.

This reviewer, also a Civil War historian and former reference librarian, finds much to criticize in this book. Although the author's purpose was to include individuals based on their influence on the war, he often neglects to discuss the influence of that person within their entries. Thus, the book often fails in its main purpose and becomes simply biographical. The selections themselves are the opinions of one man and are therefore open to question. Similar lists by other historians would doubtless vary greatly. In regard to the validity of certain selections, a few examples will suffice. President Andrew Johnson, who merely followed Abraham Lincoln's Reconstruction plans and had no lasting impact on the war or its aftermath, is rated sixth most influential. Mary Chesnut, whose only contribution was keeping a diary, is rated number 53. The choice of Varina Davis as the 101st most influential person solely because of the importance of her husband Jefferson Davis leaves the selection criteria open to serious question.

There is little in this book that cannot be found easily in standard biographical reference works. It is therefore recommended only for individuals with an interest in the Civil War. [R: LJ, 1 May 98, p. 95]

—**Donald E. Collins**

Dictionaries and Encyclopedias

526.   Berner, Brad K. **The Spanish-American War: A Historical Dictionary.** Lanham, Md., Scarecrow, 1998. 443p. (Historical Dictionaries of War, Revolution, and Civil Unrest, no.8). $85.00. ISBN 0-8108-3490-1.

Berner's *The Spanish-American War: A Historical Dictionary* coincides with the centennial commemoration of that event in Spain and the United States. Ironically, the country that won what then Secretary of State, John Hay, called a "splendid little war," has seemed less interested in remembering the conflict than Spain, where the government mounted numerous exhibitions and scholarly debates. Even Cuban scholars have expressed surprise at the lack of U.S interest in the war that led to Cuba's independence.

The brief, three-month war had enormous consequences in that it divested Spain of its remaining colonial possessions in the Caribbean and the Pacific and, for the first time, propelled the United States into a global leadership role. The role of the press emerged forcefully as well thanks to the yellow journalism of the Hearst and other chains of newspapers that helped voice popular sentiment.

The Spanish-American War: A Historical Dictionary covers the war in all its major arenas, including Cuba, Guam, the Philippines, Puerto Rico, and Spain. Its primary focus is on the major battles, correspondents, military leaders, newspapers, politicians, weaponry, and writers as well as on the Spanish and U.S. navies. Each entry is succinct and cross-referenced by means of bold typeface text to other entries in the dictionary. The volume concludes with an extensive selected bibliography. This work will be an important addition to college and university libraries as well to the collections of historians and others interested in U.S. military and diplomatic history.

—**John B. Romeiser**

527.   Dunnigan, James F., and Albert A. Nofi. **The Pacific War Encyclopedia.** New York, Facts on File, 1998. 2v. illus. maps. index. $125.00/set. ISBN 0-8160-3439-7.

The Pacific theater during World War II was the greatest naval campaign in military history. Two distinguished and prolific military historians, Dunnigan and Nofi, provide the most complete encyclopedia (2 volumes) of this theater. The reference work treats major military leaders and heroes; battlefields; all land, air, and sea campaigns and battles; order of battle; weapons; strategy and politics; economics, politics, and logistics; and much more. The A to Z entries are quite detailed, often lengthy, and are well written. They also include numerous pictures and tables. Many of the essays are followed with references. A separate section provides an extensive chronology with lengthy month-by-month essays, an extremely valuable feature that is possibly the volume's best contribution. Appendixes include a listing of present names for names known at the time and several pages of code words and code names employed during the war. The annotated bibliography is very useful.

Although this is a good reference tool for students, veterans of the campaigns, and interested laypeople, it is a bit expensive. Many librarians may decide that more general World War II reference sources will have to suffice. [R: BL, 1 Oct 98, pp. 365-366]—**Joe P. Dunn**

528.   Jessup, John E. **An Encyclopedic Dictionary of Conflict and Conflict Resolution, 1945-1996.** Westport, Conn., Greenwood Press, 1998. 887p. index. $175.00. ISBN 0-313-28112-2.

This encyclopedia greatly expands Jessup's *The Chronology of Conflict and Resolution: 1945-1985* (see ARBA 90, entry 650). Articles cover events, concepts, people, places, treaties, and so forth; longer articles include suggested readings, but there is no other bibliography.

Appropriate for an encyclopedia, access is primarily through alphabetic headings and a subject index. There is extensive use of cross-referencing that is mostly helpful, but there are some serious errors. The heading for "Congo—Brazzaville" refers to the heading "Republic of Congo," which in turn refers to "Congo (Brazzaville)," for which there is no heading. Similarly, "Russia" points to "Union of Soviet Socialist Republics," which points to the introduction—which has no mention of the USSR. Print quality is also poor, a problem exacerbated by the lack of paragraph breaks within long entries that often cover several issues (such as those for Ireland and Japan).

The detailed coverage offered by Jessup makes this an appropriate purchase for more comprehensive collections, keeping in mind the work's flaws. As an alternative, many collections will want to consider Jacob Bercovitch and Richard Jackson's *International Conflict* (see ARBA 98, entry 696). At less than half the price of Jessup's encyclopedia, it includes basic articles on nearly 300 specific conflicts and an extensive bibliography on general materials and resources focused on regions. [R: BL, 15 Nov 98, p. 611]—**Kenneth W. Berger**

629.   Marley, David F. **Wars of the Americas: A Chronology of Armed Conflict in the New World, 1492 to the Present.** Santa Barbara, Calif., ABC-CLIO, 1998. 722p. illus. maps. index. $99.00. ISBN 0-87436-837-5

The author has taken on the ambitious task of providing a complete chronology of every war and armed conflict, whether larger or small, fought in North, South, and Central America and the Caribbean from the entry of Europeans into the hemisphere in 1492 to the present. With minor exceptions, he has succeeded in this through the use of numerous brief but easy-to-read narratives that he presents in a logical chronology arranged by period and geographic area. Numerous maps and illustrations add to an understanding of many of the conflicts described. Significant events are placed in bold typeface at the beginning of many entries, and a 28-page index helps users locate events covered within the text. A bibliography of suggested further reading, organized to match the main contents, is also provided.

There are a number of shortcomings that must be mentioned. Even a cursory examination found errors. Confederate President Jefferson Davis was not captured near Abbeville, Georgia, but in Irwinville (p. 552). The Tuscarora Indians joined the Iroquois Confederacy, not the Seneca as stated on page 237. The narrative of the Battle of Moore's Creek Bridge, North Carolina, contains sufficient errors or misuse of language to make users wary of other entries. The battle was fought by Highland Scots, not "Anglo-loyalists," who were marching, not "retreating," to join British forces in Wilmington and who found the bridge not "destroyed" but only the flooring purposely removed by the patriots to prevent easy crossing (p. 307).

Having expressed those misgivings, however, this reviewer likes the book and believes readers will find it useful. Although the language is informal, using such words as "fetch," "youngsters," and "make off with" (for removing), this very fact, and the easy reading style, will appeal to readers from all educational and a wide range of age levels. Given the growth in the Hispanic population of the United States, this book's coverage of Latin American military history should prove useful. This book is recommended for public, school, and college libraries with an interest in all American history.—**Donald E. Collins**

630.   Newell, Clayton R. **Historical Dictionary of the Persian Gulf War 1990-1991.** Lanham, Md., Scarecrow, 1998. 363p. maps. (Historical Dictionaries of War, Revolution, and Civil Unrest, no.9). $65.00. ISBN 0-8108-3511-8.

The *Historical Dictionary of the Persian Gulf War 1990-1991* begins with a lengthy list of abbreviations and acronyms; a small selection of area and military maps; and detailed chronology that begins in 1710, and ends with continuing disputes over sanctions and weapons inspections in April 1998. In between are hundreds of entries providing brief contextual definitions and descriptions of places, people, military units and equipment, national players, and events. There is no index, but there is extensive, effective use of cross-referencing.

Among the supplementary materials, the bibliography of books and articles is the most interesting section. It is divided into 35 categories, with a preceding outline, ranging from background to politics to economics to military issues (e.g., logistics; ground, air, and maritime activities; weapons; friendly fire) to personal accounts to more specialized and unusual aspects, such as "women and the war," environment, reporting, and fiction. There are also sections on reference materials, book reviews, biographies, and bibliographies. Three documentary appendixes include the full text of 40 relevant United Nations resolutions; Chapter VII of the UN Charter; and General Schwarzkopf's February 27, 1991, briefing on the commencement of the ground campaign.

The historical dictionary is a good companion to the chronological approach of Harry G. Summer's *Persian Gulf Almanac* (Facts on File, 1995). Although lacking illustrations, this book is superior in content to Mark Grossman's *Encyclopedia of the Persian Gulf War* (ABC-CLIO, 1995). Libraries seeking a slightly less expensive alternatives should consider Richard A. Schwartz's *Encyclopedia of the Persian Gulf War* (McFarland, 1998). [R: LJ, 15 Nov 98, p. 61]—**Kenneth W. Berger**

Directories

631.   **Directory of U.S. Military Bases Worldwide.** 3d ed. William R. Evinger, ed. Phoenix, Ariz., Oryx Press, 1998. 441p. index. $125.00. ISBN 1-57356-049-9.

The 3d edition of this directory includes information on almost 1,200 military installations in the United States and overseas. Entries are arranged under sites (cities, towns, and the like) within states and similarly under countries for overseas facilities. Each entry includes, as available, the name; address; telephone number(s);

Website URL; e-mail address; "profile" (branch, size and location, major units, brief history, visitor attractions, plans for closing, if any); key contacts (e.g., commanding, public affairs, and procurement officers); personnel counts (military and civilian) and expenditures; and special services, such as libraries, housing, medical and recreational facilities, and base exchanges. Two appendixes identify 1995 and 1997 planned and complete base closures and reassignments. There are three indexes: an alphabetic list of bases by official name, a branch of service listing, and an alphabetic list of units.

The named personnel are most likely to be of limited use because they may already be out-of-date, but the volume continues to be of tremendous value to those researching military issues. Potential users will range from serious scholars of military affairs to military personnel and civilians considering moving to a military base location to military buffs of all ages with basic information needs (who will especially appreciate the e-mail addresses and URLs). The directory is highly recommended for public and academic library reference collections. However, as an alternative, libraries may consider *Carroll's Military Facilities Directory* (see ARBA 96, entry 686), which is also available online and on CD-ROM. It contains similar directory information, although the profiles are not as detailed. It is comparably priced but has less than half as many entries.—**Kenneth W. Berger**

632.   **Military Contracts/Procurement Locator.** [CD-ROM]. Washington, D.C., Congressional Quarterly, 1997. Minimum system requirements: IBM or compatible 486. CD-ROM drive. MS DOS 3.0. 512KB real memory. 20MB hard disk space. $695.00.

This CD-ROM is a valuable resource to anyone who works in some capacity with military contracts, contractors, and subcontractors. Military contracts, military dictionary of terms, small business and subcontracting, SIC codes, and contractors currently barred from Department of Defense contracts are the five databases featured on this CD-ROM. All provide a good overview of the military contract activities of the latest 12-month period.

The "Military Contracts Locator" database contains information on more than 255,000 awarded Department of Defense contracts within the last 12-month period. Here you can find contracts by subject, agency, and contractor name to the money amount of the contract agreement. The "Military Dictionary of Terms/Acronyms" database features definitions of some 105,000 words used in military-speak, from acronyms to weapons systems. The "Small Business and Subcontracting Locator" database lists information on subcontracting opportunities at military installations and with Department of Defense contractors. This database can be searched many ways, from area of specialization to base/Department of Defense contractor zip code. The "SIC (Standard Industrial Code)" database provides information on federal economic statistics and can be searched by industry group number, name, and description. The "Contractors Barred from the Department of Defense Contracts" database provides the names of the contractors and nature and terms of the disbar action.

Searching the databases is relatively easy through the use of menus and command keys. Searches can be done by individual field (e.g., by contractor name), the use of Boolean terms, truncation, and browsing through the subject fields. Help with search strategies, installation, and detailed information on each database can be found in the extensive manual that accompanies the CD-ROM.—**Kelly M. Jordan**

633.   **Military Personnel/Installations Locator CD-ROM.** [CD-ROM]. Washington, D.C., Congressional Quarterly, 1997. Minimum system requirements: IBM or compatible 486. CD-ROM drive. MS DOS 3.0. 512KB real memory. 20MB hard disk space. $495.00.

CQ Staff Directories—not to be mistaken for Congressional Quarterly—is widely recognized for its congressional, federal, and judicial directories, which are also on disc. CQ also produces two other discs covering military contracts and federal grants. This CD-ROM, however, is a break from the traditional government information CQ usually provides. The *Military Personnel/Installations Locator* (MP/IL) is a multifaceted approach to military personnel and base information as well as a dictionary of terms and acronyms. Briefly described, the CD-ROM includes more than 100,000 terms and acronyms, 128,000 Department of Defense personnel, and 1,000 installations. Designed for a specific client in the defense contract industry, the MP/IL has been canceled by CQ and will no longer be issued. As it is, the MP/IL is a unique reference tool for a limited but important audience.

Installation is rather simple—it took about eight minutes using a floppy disk—and experienced CD-ROM users will be able to comprehend use just as easily. The presentation is in a DOS format, which is surprising considering today's Windows environment. The three components—terms and acronyms, personnel, and installations—generally use the same commands. Each has a browse search mode as well as a search feature. Once selected, the information can be displayed, sorted, printed, or downloaded. Help screens are available throughout the database.

The User's Manual is excellent and includes installation instructions; search commands and features, such as truncation, wild cards, and positional operators; and item descriptions. There is no index to the manual, but the table of contents is very detailed.

The terms and acronyms include definitions, a category (e.g., acronym, building, rank, weapons system, and agency), and in which branch the term or acronym is used. The personnel file includes title or rank, agency or organization, location, telephone number, and a brief biography when available from a CQ biographical source. There are only a small number of such biographies. The most comprehensive of the three files is the installations database, where one can find base information ranging from congressional district in which the base is located to the status of the base (operational or closed).

Other information includes base housing, school, and medical facilities; commands located at the specific base; base populations (civilian and military); brief driving directions to the base; and local attractions and points of interest. Installation personnel, including commander, procurement or contract officer, and public affairs officer, are provided. Information varies from base to base, but surprisingly, when a base has been closed, detailed information regarding closure is extensive. An example is Fort McClellan (Alabama), which includes 16 screens of closure documentation and justification.

The MP/IL is a unique tool, but given the technology available and rapidly changing personnel information, would be more suitable as a Website. With CQ canceling the project, MP/IL may be rejuvenated in the future. As it is now, MP/IL is a highly specialized source with an audience limited to corporations and organizations with an economic interest in the industrial-military complex.—**Boyd Childress**

Handbooks and Yearbooks

634.   Heller, Mark A., and Yiftah Shapir. **The Middle East Military Balance, 1996.** New York, Columbia University Press, 1998. 452p. maps. $50.00. ISBN 0-231-10892-3.

This thorough review of military strength in the Middle East provides highly specific country-by-country data on weapons, military personnel, training, and defense expenditures. An extensive introduction detailing regional military and political developments; a chronology of 1996 events; summary tables of comparative data on various aspects of military strength and the involvement of Russia, China, France, Great Britain, and the United States; and a glossary of weapons systems enhance the primary text. Although the 1996 date in the title may concern those looking for the most current information, it must be remembered that collection and collation of international statistical data, particularly on sensitive subjects, is a long process. This is an important resource that pulls together significant information for those with an interest in the Middle East. Libraries with an interest in this field will find this book of particular interest.—**Ahmad Gamaluddin**

635.   Schaefer, Christina K. **The Great War: A Guide to the Service Records of All the World's Fighting Men and Volunteers.** Baltimore, Md., Genealogical Publishing, 1998. 189p. illus. maps. index. $22.50. ISBN 0-8063-1554-7.

World War I was truly a world conflict with millions of participants from more than 25 different countries around the globe. Schaefer, a certified genealogical specialist and author of two previous genealogical guidebooks, attempts to provide a comprehensive guide to the service records of all these participants. The 1st part of the book provides background on the organization of the military, the order of battle, a time line of the war, and types of records that can be employed. Part 2 takes a country-by-country approach, discussing the military of each participant, the records depositories of each country, archival guides, and suggested readings. These brief bibliographies are one of the volume's more useful features. Part 3 provides information on the aftermath of the war, including casualties in each country, prisoners of war, and the major political changes wrought by the war. Part 4, the appendix, provides Internet sources, a glossary, and a general reading list.

Although this volume contains a tremendous amount of information, it will be of interest to only a small number of specialized researchers. Only the largest research libraries will find it particularly useful. However, at its inexpensive price, other libraries can consider making it available. [R: LJ, 15 Nov 98, p. 62]—**Joe P. Dunn**

AIR FORCE

636.   Cochrane, John, and Stuart Elliott. **Military Aircraft Insignia of the World.** Annapolis, Md., Naval Institute Press, 1998. 137p. illus. $29.95pa. ISBN 1-55750-542-X.

Authors Cochrane and Elliott have produced a splendid reference item that will be of value to aviation buffs and hobbyists alike. Their coverage of insignia on aircraft from around the world is the only up-to-date reference of its kind, and is something that virtually all public, military, and aviation libraries will want to acquire. Presenting the countries in alphabetic order, insignia is then listed chronologically. The authors indicate that 1910 was the first time aircraft markings were used, but it was not until aircraft proved themselves to be valuable military commodities that countries took markings seriously. France was the first country to mandate particular markings and was soon followed by most of the large countries, such as England and the United States. It is interesting to note that many of the early markings resembled bulls-eyes and were resented by pilots who felt that this gave the enemy something to aim for in a dogfight. There is also a nice bit of aviation history for each country, and the colors used in the illustrations are vivid and contrast very nicely with the gray outlines of parts of the airplane that carry insignia. *Military Aircraft Insignia of the World* is highly recommended for definitive coverage of a specialized subject.—**Joseph L. Carlson**

637.   Francillon, Rene J., and Carol A. McKenzie. **The Naval Institute Guide to World Military Aviation 1997-1998.** Annapolis, Md., Naval Institute Press, 1997. 884p. illus. $150.00. ISBN 1-55750-265-X.

This work is an illustrated survey of the world's air forces and the aircraft they fly. In addition to the designated air forces, it includes other services, such as armies, navies, coastal patrols, and paramilitary organizations that operate military aircraft. It does not include either civilian agencies or civilian aircraft. In an introductory essay, the author summarizes the current state of major air forces, those of smaller but regionally active nations, and conditions in the world military aircraft marketplace.

The work is presented in 2 parts, the 1st giving statistics and information about the air force of each nation and the 2d part that presenting data and descriptions of current military aircraft. In the 1st section are basic statistics concerning population, gross domestic product, defense budget, and total armed forces manpower. This is followed by a list of major airbases and an organizational breakdown (order of battle) of the air force that lists the various services, commands, divisions, squadrons, among others, and the principal aircraft flown by each. A final list provides the number, type, and name of each aircraft in each country's arsenal. Representative aircraft are illustrated for each country.

In the 2d section, military aircraft are inventoried by name of manufacturer. For each aircraft, one is given technical and performance data, variant models, names of countries operating the aircraft, and a brief history. Numerous photographs accompany each description, and many line drawings are provided as well.

This is the 2d edition of a work first published in 1995 (see ARBA 96, entry 697). A 3d edition is promised. Although a comparison of this work with *Jane's All the World's Aircraft* (87th ed.; see ARBA 97, entry 1440) would seem natural, *Jane's* is an annual and includes civilian as well as military aircraft and does not include the "order of battle" data on each air force. *Jane's* in many cases offers more descriptive and technical data than this work and is equally if not better illustrated. It also costs twice as much as this work. Jane's Information Group also publishes a looseleaf (or CD-ROM) annual, *Jane's World Air Forces, Order of Battle and Inventories*, that provides information on those topics at $750 a year. Although not seen by this reviewer beyond the sample provided at Jane's Information Group's Website, it would seem that Jane's version covers much the same territory as that in the first section of this work, but updated thrice yearly.

The Naval Institute Guide to World Military Aviation 1997-1998 is eminently suitable for the library that does not have users who need the very latest information on either military aircraft or on air forces. Well illustrated and comparatively inexpensive, it is suitable for public, academic, and special libraries that serve a clientele interested in the state of contemporary air power and aircraft.—**Eric R. Nitschke**

MARINE CORPS

638.   Gailey, Harry A. **Historical Dictionary of the United States Marine Corps.** Lanham, Md., Scarecrow, 1998. 253p. maps. (Historical Dictionaries of Wars, Revolution, and Civil Unrest, no.5). $50.00. ISBN 0-8108-3401-4.

Gailey, professor of history at San Jose State University, has written a useful reference that begins with the Continental Marines, the predecessor of the modern corps during the American Revolution, and follows the history of the U.S. Marine Corps through the Gulf War. The dictionary itself includes entries on weaponry, conflicts and interventions, and notable individuals. The coverage of some of the conflicts differs in the amount of detail presented. For example, the Gulf War is covered in five different entries: "Desert Storm," "Desert Shield," "Desert Calm," "Gulf War," and "Iraq." The entry for "Desert Calm" seems trivial because it basically details how the Marine Corps withdrew from the theater of operations. This level of coverage seems like overkill compared to "Operation Just Cause," which is detailed completely in the entry "Panama." The Gulf War entries also expose the limited use of cross-references in this title. "Iraq" has a cross-reference to "Gulf War." "Desert Storm" and "Desert Shield" cross-reference each other.

Sections entitled "Chronology" and "Abbreviations and Acronyms" supplement the information. There are also six black-and-white maps: "The Western Front, 1918"; "Haiti and the Dominican Republic"; "Nicaragua"; "World War II Pacific Theater"; "North and South Korea"; and "Vietnam." The maps are useful, but there should have been many more to supplement data on operations such as the Gulf War. Despite these caveats, this book is recommended for libraries collecting in the area of military science.—**John R. Burch Jr.**

NAVY

639.   Bruce, Anthony, and William Cogar. **An Encyclopedia of Naval History.** New York, Facts on File, 1998. 440p. illus. index. $50.00. ISBN 0-8160-2697-1.

This work is a useful compendium of naval history from 1571 (the Battle of Lepanto) to today. Information is provided on ships, sailors, events, and places. There are more than 1,000 entries, ranging from 150 words to several pages, with the average article about 250 to 300 words long. There are generally 3 to 4 articles per 2-column page of this 8½-by-11-inch volume. The arrangement is alphabetic with numerous cross-references. The black-and-white illustrations include portraits of naval personages. Information is included on the navies of all nations, but the emphasis is on U.S. and British naval history. There is no bibliography, but sourcebooks are appended to many articles. The layout and design are good, with highly legible typography and a sturdy binding. There is a synoptic index and a comprehensive index provided. A few minor errors were noted, such as the fact that David Bushnell went to Yale, not Harvard (p. 55), and the USS *Nautilus* (SSN 571) is preserved at the U.S. navy submarine base at Groton, Connecticut, not at Annapolis (p. 261). The authors are respected academics, authors, and bibliographers. Anthony Bruce works for the Committee of Vice Chancellors—the association of British universities—and William Cogar is director of the U.S. naval academy museum and a professor of naval history at Annapolis. [R: BL, July 98, p. 1904]—**Frank J. Anderson**

640.   **Jane's Major Warships 1997.** David Miller, ed. Alexandria, Va., Jane's Information Group, 1997. 2v. illus. index. $1,050.00/set. ISBN 0-7106-1417-9.

This work provides information on major naval combatant vessels from around the world. It excludes auxiliaries, coast guard and army vessels, harbor craft, and training ships. The 1st volume of this work has sections for aircraft carriers and their affiliated aircraft, submarines, cruisers, and destroyers. The 2d volume, not available for review, is to cover frigates, corvettes, amphibious warfare vessels, and mine countermeasure ships.

The arrangement of this volume is by ship type. Under each type, ships are arranged by class according to country of origin (where they were built) and then by country of current ownership. This is a departure from the arrangement of *Jane's Fighting Ships* (see ARBA 97, entry 573; ARBA 95, entry 698; and ARBA 91, entry 694) in which the ships are listed by country of ownership, ship type, and then ship class. Each vessel is described in terms of history, design characteristics, general specifications, weapons systems, command and control systems, and electronic warfare systems. Modernization programs are described, as are current programs for ship types presently building. The amount of information concerning weapons, C+C and electronic warfare systems is more extensive than that given in *Jane's Fighting Ships* and is in a narrative rather than sidebar style. The somewhat confusing arrangement by country of origin seems intended to group ships of the same class together for the purpose of attaching these extended technical remarks to individual ships in the class. There are several indexes, including one for hull (pennant) numbers and for ship and class names. Photographs are in black and white (*Jane's Fighting Ships* uses more color photographs each year), and they and the ship schematics are clear and informative.

The title page lists this as "First Edition 1997," and the publisher indicates that there is a 1999/2000 edition in the works. The question for libraries is whether *Jane's Major Warships* will fill needs that *Jane's Fighting Ships* does not. The former contains more information on each ship and class than does the latter. However, the latter contains many more illustrations than the former, includes the noncombatants and smaller combatants that the former does not, is updated annually, and costs only $410. Libraries serving academic and general publics will be fine with *Jane's Fighting Ships*. Those serving more specialized clienteles may find this volume worthwhile.

—**Eric R. Nitschke**

641.   Morris, James M., and Patricia M. Kearns. **Historical Dictionary of the United States Navy.** Lanham, Md., Scarecrow, 1998. 405p. (Historical Dictionaries of War, Revolution, and Civil Unrest, no.4). $85.00. ISBN 0-8108-3406-5.

This dictionary comprises numerous brief entries, along with some encyclopedia entries dealing with wars and significant battles. There are entires for every secretary of the navy from Benjamin Stoddert to the present day. The preface discusses the information included and how it is treated. Front matter includes lists of acronyms and abbreviations, ship type designations, and a chronology from 1775 to 1997. The dictionary itself takes up 363 pages, and is followed by a bibliography of 39 pages. The dictionary is somewhat inconsistent; for instance, there is an entry about the Simon Lake-designed 0-11 to 0-14 submarines, but nothing about the 0-1 to 0-10 boats in the same class. The entry for *capstan* is misleading because it seems to indicate that capstans were used only on sailing ships rather than their being common devices currently used on ships large and small. There is no cross-reference from *capstan* to *windlass*, but there is a "Windlass, *see* Capstan" entry. There is an entry for *Bolo Line* but no entry for or cross-reference to the more familiar *Heaving Line*. There is a 7-page section, with 14 photographs of ships and aircraft that do not contribute much to this volume. The dictionary entries do not refer to the photographs. The bibliography of 10 divisions begins with categories of reference and histories, and then it is arranged by time periods. No bibliography of submarine literature is listed, although several exist. Roscoe's *U.S. Destroyer Operations in W.W. II* is cited, but not his similar book on submarine operations. Books listed in the bibliography indicate imprint and date, but not collation; thus it is impossible to distinguish between pamphlet literature, such as Butt's 28-page *Brief History of Norfolk Naval Shipyard* and more substantial documented histories. Annotations would have been useful. The authors are credentialed academics; Morris is a professor of history and Kearns is a librarian. Typography, layout, and design contribute to the ease of use of this volume.

—**Frank J. Anderson**

642.   **The Nelson Almanac: A Book of Days Recording Nelson's Life and the Events That Shaped His Era.** David Harris, ed. Annapolis, Md., Naval Institute Press, 1998. 192p. illus. index. $38.95. ISBN 1-55750-647-7.

October 21, 2005, will be a significant date in British history. The bicentennial of the Battle of Trafalgar will mark the British Navy's defeat of the combined French and Spanish navies and the end of Napoleon's plans to conquer England. That victory had a sour note, however; it included the death of Admiral Horatio Nelson, the nation's greatest naval hero. The National Maritime Museum in Greenwich and the *HMS Victory*, Nelson's flagship now at Portsmouth, have both begun decade-long countdowns to the day, and interest in Nelson and his achievements will continue to grow.

One example of this interest is *The Nelson Almanac*, "a glorious jumble of facts & events" reflecting Nelson's life and achievements. Each day of the year has a quote from Nelson's letters and a comment on an event in his life on that date. A dozen brief articles by noted maritime historians cover aspects of Nelson's life, ranging from his early experiences at sea to his continued legacy in Britain, and shorter entries describe famous and infamous individuals and events contemporary to Nelson. Although not a biography, the text scrutinizes its subject and goes beyond a basic overview of Nelson's life. The layout is appealing, and the volume contains numerous excellent reproductions and images.

The upcoming bicentennial will prompt expanded interest in Nelson's life and death, making this source timely and relevant. Although more useful in circulating collections than in reference collections, it is appropriate for public and academic libraries.—**Peter H. McCracken**

643.   Polmar, Norman, Eric Wertheim, Andrew Bahjat, and Bruce Watson. **Chronology of the Cold War at Sea 1945-1991.** Annapolis, Md., Naval Institute Press, 1998. 241p. index. $39.95. ISBN 1-55750-685-X.

The Cold War began on September 2, 1945, the day the Japanese surrendered to Allied Forces on board the *USS Missouri.* It ended on December 30, 1991, when the Soviet Union disbanded and President Mikhail Gorbachev resigned. Three months later, *Missouri* was decommissioned. Polmar, author of numerous works on modern U.S. and Soviet submarines, naval warfare, and the Cold War, shows that naval power played a critical role in this ongoing conflict. "Fighting" in the war was sporadic; although some months may have just one or two entries, entries during the Vietnam War occur almost daily.

The preface stresses the international roles of military buildup, research and development, the need for military intelligence, and U.S. and Soviet intervention throughout the world. Many entries, however, focus on U.S. firsts, such as the first vessels in a class to be commissioned, the first demonstrations or use of a weapons system, or the first woman to hold a given command. Apart from Soviet space successes, nearly all research and development successes are from the United States, reflecting the book's intended audience.

The day-by-day approach may limit the utility of the volume because one cannot follow a specific event's developments over weeks or months or more. However, it illustrates the complicated order in which events occurred. The book contains useful ship and personality indexes, but no subject index. It is more extensive than *Cold War Chronology* (see ARBA 94, entry 795) and *Chronology of Conflict and Resolution, 1945-1985* (see ARBA 90, entry 650), which is not limited to naval events. This work is a useful addition to any academic library and is vital for collections in diplomacy or military and naval history.—**Peter H. McCracken**

WEAPONS

644.   Ali, Javed, Rodrigues Leslie, and Michael Moodie. **U.S. Chemical-Biological Defense Guidebook.** Alexandria, Va., Jane's Information Group, 1997. 468p. index. $895.00pa. ISBN 0-710-61646-5.

More and more one reads about the threat of chemical and biological weapons (CBWs) in the hands of terrorists and the adequacy of timely and effective responses to potential attacks by these weapons. This up-to-date guide provides information to military officials and to community "first responders" about the nature of these CBWs; their munitions and delivery systems; means of detection, analysis, decontamination, and medical response; protective gear; threat assessments (the CBW programs of the countries who produce and may use the weapons); and the domestic preparedness for a CBW contingency. The concluding chapter discusses the need for CBW education, an integrated strategy for intelligence, an appropriate defense, military options, export and arms controls, and the international cooperation necessary for countering CBW terrorism. Among the nine appendixes are a list of CBW acronyms, an FBI "incident contingency" plan, and various congressional reports on preparedness and response. More and varied photographs and illustrations would have been helpful.

Because of the extremely high cost of this guide, the most likely purchasers will be the libraries of research laboratories, military posts, and governmental agencies. Although the high-quality paper is a definite asset, there is some doubt that the binding will hold up to repeated use. For this price, a sturdy hardbound book should have been offered.—**Charles R. Andrews**

645.   **Jane's Infantry Weapons 1998-99.** Terry J. Gander and Charles C. Cutshaw, eds. Alexandria, Va., Jane's Information Group, 1998. 791p. illus. index. $350.00. ISBN 0-7106-1797-6.

Jane's publications fill a unique reference need, and this annual should be useful for libraries with larger collections or a military focus. Main sections of the book include personal weapons, crew-served weapons, ammunition, sighting equipment, and suppressors. Each section is further subdivided into sections such as pistols, rifles, and machine guns, and then lists newest models first for each country named. For each model, the text provides information about its development, a technical description, specifications, manufacturer, and production status. Photographs provide excellent support for the data. The book ends with a section titled "National Inventories," which is a concise summary of weapons known to be used by military forces in various countries, and an index of manufacturers as well as an alphabetic index.—**Jean Engler**

646.   **Jane's Land-Based Air Defense 1998-99.** 11th ed. Tony Cullen and Christopher F. Foss, eds. Alexandria, Va., Jane's Information Group, 1998. 375p. illus. index. $350.00. ISBN 0-7106-1799-2.

Listing almost every conceivable type of anti-aircraft weapon—missiles, missile systems, guns, gun sights, and control systems—this profusely illustrated, oversized ($8\frac{1}{2}$-by-$12\frac{1}{2}$-inch) volume consists of 9 sections on weaponry. In each section the country of manufacturer is alphabetically listed. Within each country, the latest equipment is usually detailed first and the oldest last, enabling the reader to plot the development of systems. Every weapon is specifically detailed, and its variants are included.

The volume is sturdily bound and printed on heavyweight glossy paper. In order to accommodate the vast amount of material, the print size is quite small, perhaps posing difficulty for some readers, but the satisfactorily sized black-and-white photographs and diagrams have excellent clarity. Illustrations new to this edition are dated with the year of publication. Users will welcome the inventory appendix, alphabetically listing each country and its armed forces' air defenses. A manufacturers' index and a general alphabetic index conclude the volume. Because of its steep price, this outstanding Jane's publication will most likely appeal to highly specialized and large research libraries.—**Charles R. Andrews**

647.   Marchington, James. **Knives: Military Edged Tools & Weapons.** Herndon, Va., Brassey's (U.S.), 1997. 153p. illus. $32.95. ISBN 1-85753-187-6.

This interesting, copiously illustrated handbook makes clear from the start that, although its emphasis is upon military knives and their deadly purpose in hostile environments, the knives can also be used to prepare food, build and tend a fire, cook with, build a shelter or a raft, and serve as a signaling device. As the author states, to an outdoors person or a soldier knives are a necessity, not a luxury. The book is divided into six sections, each treating different categories of knives—fighting knives and daggers, bayonets, combat and survival knives, multitools, folding knives, and utility and special purpose blades. In addition to a photograph of each knife, there is an accompanying text about the quality, design, and primary purpose. A sidebar lists the manufacturer, dimensions, blade material, edge, grip, construction, and sheath. Military personnel past and present and readers of military novels will recognize the Fairbairn Sykes commando knife, the World War I trench knife, and the Ka-Bar Marine combat knife, widely used in World War II. Among the multitools, the sportsperson will learn all there is to know about the ubiquitous Swiss army knife.

Attractively formatted, well bound, and with durable paper, this compact handbook should find a place in many public, academic, military, and newspaper libraries.—**Charles R. Andrews**

13 Political Science

GENERAL WORKS

Bibliography

648. **Handbook of Political Science Research on the Middle East and North Africa.** Bernard Reich, ed. Westport, Conn., Greenwood Press, 1998. 392p. index. $89.50. ISBN 0-313-27372-3.

One would be hard-pressed to name a more potentially explosive region than the Middle East, made all the more combustible by failed U.S. foreign policy. Indeed, most of the concerns shared in foreign regions are the result of our own inept foreign policies. Consider the woes in Bosnia as the direct result of President Woodrow Wilson's misunderstanding of the region and his disinterest in consulting beyond what he already knew.

The countries in this volume include Algeria, Egypt, the Gulf Arab States, Iran, Iraq, Israel, and more than a dozen others. Each chapter covers the field of study, provides an analysis of the study in the area so far, and sketches an agenda for future study. Detailed, annotated bibliographies make it easier for the scholar or the student to locate the best works in the region. Those using this volume need never fear making an error of Wilson's magnitude.

Written by experts, each chapter reads like a bibliographic essay. But there is often much more information than the merely bibliographical. History, politics, demographics, and more are often treated in detail and fully explained.

Nearly every library will want to own a copy of this volume, if for no other reason than to provide students with an excellent starting point for research in areas that may be geographically obscure and politically inscrutable. [R: Choice, Nov 98, p. 501]—**Mark Y. Herring**

Biography

649. **Profiles of Worldwide Government Leaders 1998.** 4th ed. Alan J. Day, ed. Washington, D.C., Keesing's Worldwide; distr., Farmington Hills, Mich., Gale, 1998. 850p. index. $297.00. ISBN 1-886994-12-8. ISSN 0894-1521.

This 4th edition is current to May 1998, and it lists some 3,000 ministers and heads of state for 199 countries. It maintains the integrity of respected Keesing's Worldwide, which also publishes *Worldwide Government Directory* (1992 ed.; see ARBA 93, entry 724) and *Worldwide Directory of Defense Authorities*. The arrangement is alphabetic by country, with basic defining almanac data as well as biographical directory-style listings containing information such as birthdate, education, private and political career, and addresses. There is a name index at the back.

This is all straightforward, but the information is derived from official requests, embassies, and the press, and all are not necessarily verified. Although all names are listed, many do not have details or profiles—this only occurs when the editor had the information. Every page has an annoying blurb at the bottom stating copyright protection by Keesing's.

The book is useful, but in an ever-changing political world this work can be dated rather quickly. One still needs to check on the Internet for the latest position holder, and then use this book's name index to see a biography or see if there has been a cabinet shuffle. In general, official Internet homepages should be more useful than this work if only currency and addresses are required.—**Dean Tudor**

650. **Whitaker's Almanack World Heads of Government 1998.** Roger East and Catherine Ashment, eds. London, The Stationery Office; distr., Detroit, Gale, 1998. 295p. illus. index. $95.00. ISBN 0-11-702205-5.

Prime ministers, military commanders, presidents, religious leaders, and revolutionaries are profiled, with official photographs included. There is about a 40 percent overlap with *Whitacker's Almanack World Heads of State* (see entry 651) because in those cases the head of state is also the head of government, in many instances as "executive president." The justification for the two volumes, according to the editors, is for purposes of clarity. The entries are current as of January 1, 1998. Each capsule presentation includes biographical information as well as the political significance in the context of current and past circumstances.

In the world of politics, knowing something about the financial circumstances of the players can be useful for an understanding of the total picture. For example, if the leader has considerable personal wealth, knowing the origins of the assets as well as the area(s) in which they are held can help explain some political choices. It would have been useful to explore this avenue because a number of the current entries are influenced by issues related to personal finances. Additionally, campaign contributions can also provide some key insights, and when these are known to be from a single individual, corporation, or sector of the country, this information should be noted. The depth of these additions could be in keeping with the scope of the rest of the work, thus, not substantially adding to the page count but significantly boosting the overall usefulness of the two parallel titles.

All sovereign states are included, as well as "entries which make claim to statehood," including locations that have governments but lack independent sovereign status. In four cases no head of government was in place at the end of 1997.

The biographical sketches cover education and political careers for each entry. The closest the volume approaches to personal consideration is a one-line entry on the marital status along with a note on the number of children. The black-and-white photographs are for the most part acceptable (with a few notable exceptions, including the one for Hashimoto of Japan, which looks as if something went wrong with the digitizing, along with several others where the quality is suspect).

Overall, the volume is a good contribution. Many other works provide access to various parts of the contents, but this is a handy single-volume approach to be used in conjunction with the parallel title. With some modest adjustments these titles will take their places as highly useful and frequently used ready-reference tools.
—**Graham R. Walden**

651. **Whitaker's Almanack World Heads of State 1998.** Roger East and Catherine Ashment, eds. London, The Stationery Office; distr., Detroit, Gale, 1998. 287p. illus. index. $95.00. ISBN 0-11-702204-7.

Every head of state as of January 1, 1998, receives an entry in this work, including an "official" photograph, a factual biography, and a presentation of the individual's political significance. A review of the entries for such leaders as Fidel Castro, Saddam Hussein, and Boris Yeltsin demonstrates the effort that has been exerted to carefully synopsize the political record of each. The biographical sketches outline the progression of offices and positions held, whereas the discussion of the circumstances surrounding the political realities of each head of state is designed to provide a thumbnail sketch of the individual's career. Entries are included for elected presidents, hereditary royals, civilian politicians, and military commanders.

The book is arranged alphabetically by country name. Where more than one head of state is claimed, perceived, or otherwise held in doubt, East and Ashment have chosen to be inclusive and have produced entries for each, such as in the case for Somalia—with pages for Ali Mahdi Mohammed and Hussein Aydid. The purpose of the work is to be informative, not critical. Therefore, evaluative text is absent. Similarly, the editors note the exercise of "political judgement" in some of the entries with respect to inclusion or lack thereof.

There are a number of current titles available that present some of the information found in this work; notably the *Who's Who in International Affairs* (see entry 652) and the *Current Leaders of Nations* (see ARBA 92, entry 671). However, the one- to two-page summaries found in the new *Whitaker's Almanack World Heads of State* will address many reference questions quickly and effectively in a single resource. This work is highly recommended.—**Graham R. Walden**

652.   **Who's Who in International Affairs 1998.** 2d ed. London, Europa; distr., Detroit, Gale, 1997. 543p. index. $425.00. ISBN 1-85743-045-X. ISSN 0956-7984.

This updated directory has more than 7,000 biographical entries of international dignitaries. These include political figures, academics, and scientific and cultural leaders. Academic degrees, educational institutions, nationality, current employment status, career summary, and publications are supplied in the entries. The inclusion of leisure interests is new to this edition. Various contact information is also provided—address, fax number, telephone number, and occasionally an e-mail address. Some entries are more extensive than others. There are a number of abbreviations in the entries; however, an exhaustive listing of abbreviations is provided in the beginning of the book. A comprehensive list of international telephone codes is also included in the beginning of the book. The index is excellent. For example, it is divided into two sections, by organization or country and by nationality. One unclear part in the entries is the educational element. For instance, the degrees received and schools attended are listed, but in some cases they do not necessarily seem to correspond. In general, this is a solid reference tool that will enhance a college or university library's collection.—**Leslie R. Homzie**

Dictionaries and Encyclopedias

653.   Burg, David F. **Encyclopedia of Student and Youth Movements.** New York, Facts on File, 1998. 254p. illus. index. $50.00. ISBN 0-8160-3375-7.

Throughout history young people have gathered for companionship, enlightenment, prayer, secrecy, and social exclusiveness and to change the world. The first general reference work on the subject, the *Encyclopedia of Student and Youth Movements*, covers youth groups of all kinds and their purposes throughout history.

The groups covered in *Encyclopedia of Student and Youth Movements* represent the wide variety of such endeavors. There are groups of youths formed by youth, groups formed by adults for youths, students banding together to express their political views, students wanting to change the world, and students striving to preserve it. This volume covers an often neglected subject from a historical standpoint, exploring the effects such movements have had on society and how they have shaped our perception of who has the ability and determination to change the world.

It should be noted that there is far more left out of this encyclopedia than is included. Obviously, numerous organizations, movements, demonstrations, and other events involving students or youths are missing. Their absence is based on the fact that there are simply too many to include. For example, in the year 1900 when there was a total of 237,000 college and university students throughout the United States, known student organizations numbered 611—and both of these totals had increased by 1990. During the academic year 1969-1970, more than 9,000 student demonstrations involving nearly two-thirds of all the colleges and universities occurred in the United States alone.

This encyclopedia has included subjects for entries based upon certain criteria. Overall, Burg has focused on including those events, organizations, and people that had either a large impact at the time of their appearance or a large influence on subsequent events. Many youth movements—for example, the Young Men's Christian Association (YMCA) and the Girl Scouts—have a lengthy and continuing history that readily justifies inclusion. Others, such as the Hitler Jugend, had a relatively brief existence but a profound political or social influence of historic consequence.

The author has tried to make clear why the event, person, movement, organization, or cause has historic merit. He has also included some entries whose reason for being or historic context strongly argued in favor of their receiving attention. For example, although apparently neither the International Union of Students (IUS) nor the International Student Conference (ISC) had any measurable or endurable political or other influence on students, these organizations' histories clearly evidence the impact of the Cold War. Organizations and groups include but are not limited to those that are political, social, and academic; protest movements; fraternities and sororities; dueling societies; drinking and eating clubs; and religious societies and movements, including independent, state, state-church, or party-sponsored groups. Some individual organizations and groups included are Children's Crusade, the Boys Scouts, the Japanese Red Army, Youth for Christ, the Hitler Youth, the Camelots de Roi, the Bosnian Black Hand, the South Korean National Unification League, the Catholic Boys' Brigade, skinheads and provos, the American Youth Hostels, the Black Panthers, the Junior Optimists, and hundreds of others. Significant persons and events included are Abbie Hoffman; Tiananmen Square (1989); Berlin Uprising of 1848; Bobbie Seale; and the events of 1968 in France, the United States, and Czechoslovakia.

The fact is that student and youth movements attracted only slight interest among historians and sociologists until the student eruptions of the 1960s garnered massive public and media attention. Consequently, writings that trace the history and significance of student and youth movements are relatively scarce. But those movements do merit study, not only by historians and sociologists, by also by educators, political scientists, psychologists, economists, and even the public as a whole. This book will prove to be a beginning point for long-term or ongoing effort to provide a more comprehensive reference work. [R: BL, 15 Oct 98, p. 438]—**Barbara B. Goldstein**

654. **Dictionary of Government and Politics.** 2d ed. P. H. Collin, ed. Middlesex, Great Britain, Peter Collin, 1997; repr., Chicago, Fitzroy Dearborn, 1998. 302p. $45.00. ISBN 1-57958-072-6.
    Containing approximately 5,000 words and phrases, this dictionary primarily covers the vocabulary of government in Great Britain and the United States. Throughout the text, "comment" sidebars expand the basic definitions, which occasionally provide historical information. The final section includes a chronological listing of presidents of the United States, prime ministers of Great Britain, and the titles of cabinet posts in these respective countries. The selection of terms is quirky, including such commonplace words as "qualify," "foe," "dwelling," "decade," and "civilization," to list only a few. Why would a reader consult a dictionary of government to find such definitions? More problematic are the sparse definitions of government terms, which frequently are only a sentence. The *Dorsey Dictionary of American Government and Politics* (see ARBA 89, entry 640) is a more authoritative and useful reference source.—**Donald Altschiller**

655. **The Routledge Dictionary of Twentieth-Century Political Thinkers.** 2d ed. Robert Benewick and Philip Green, eds. New York, Routledge, 1998. 277p. index. $75.00; $24.99pa. ISBN 0-415-15881-8; 0-415-09623-5pa.
    This is the 2d edition of a short, but useful, dictionary of twentieth-century political thinkers. Students needing a quick introduction to major ideas and representative influences and works of twentieth-century political thinkers will find these biographical entries helpful. Although more than 100 scholars throughout the world pen the entries, there is a uniformity and continuity among the entries. For example, a list of representative works by the thinker and a select list of works about the thinker conclude each biographical entry where possible. In addition, the entries clearly and coherently explain the major ideas advanced by the thinkers; the entries are, for the most part, free from technical jargon. The range of political thinkers is wide and representative of the gamut of political thinking. There are, according to the compilers, 174 biographies. Some of these entries, however, are justifiably short. In addition, there is an excellent index, which lists thinkers according to different categories. More than 100 categories direct the reader to pursue a concept through the perspectives of several writers. For individuals in search of a brief sketch of some twentieth-century thinker, one cannot go wrong beginning here.
                                                                                —**Michael A. Foley**

656. **The World Encyclopedia of Parliaments and Legislatures.** George Kurian, ed. Washington, D.C., Congressional Quarterly, 1998. 2v. maps. index. $289.00/set. ISBN 0-87187-987-5.
    Under the sponsorship of the Commonwealth Parliamentary Association and the International Political Science Association's Research Committee of Legislative Specialists, Kurian has provided a valuable new reference. This encyclopedia provides information on each country's legislative bodies. It also includes brief essays on countries without current legislative bodies. In addition, there are entries for the European Parliament of the European Union and the United Nations General Assembly. The encyclopedia includes a series of a dozen comparative essays on various aspects of legislative politics, such as executive-legislative relations, lobbying, committees, second chambers, and an excellent introductory essay by Gary W. Copeland and Samuel C. Patterson. Finally, there is a short glossary of legislative terms.
    The various contributors are outstanding legislative scholars and historians. The country entries are comprehensive and provide key information. Space limitations and the need to include material on such items as parliamentary buildings, procedures, and rights of membership make the entries more descriptive than analytic in nature. In many cases, this makes it difficult to assess the importance of the legislative bodies in the overall political system. Each entry also includes a bibliography, focusing on English-language sources. Among the useful information in the introduction to each country's entry are addresses and telephone and fax numbers. It would have been useful to include e-mail addresses and Website addresses as well because most legislative bodies now offer

such means of access. This is an important new reference and should be included in all college and university libraries. Other major libraries should include this in their reference collections.—**Frank L. Wilson**

Handbooks and Yearbooks

657.   **The Annual Register 1997: A Record of World Events.** Alan J. Day, ed. Bethesda, Md., Keesing's Worldwide; distr., Farmington Hills, Mich., Gale, 1998. 624p. index. $175.00. ISBN 1-886994-13-7.

Any source that has been published annually since 1758 has to have something going for it, and the *Annual Register* is no exception. A review of world events, this book summarizes the world's news for the year 1997. Its features include overviews of events by topic and by country. It is both exhaustive and thorough. The country sections include a commentary for the year on the whole region, then the country. It is a good source of information about countries or regions that are not regularly covered in the media. Given its British origin, the book is heavy on U.K. news (there are 48 pages on the United Kingdom and 15 on the United States), but that is an advantage because American readers often do not get that perspective. Also included are key statistical data on countries; texts of important documents of the year, such as the Kyoto Climate Change Protocol; obituaries of prominent persons; and topical articles on issues such as the arts, science, and defense. There is also a good index.

Like *Europa World Yearbook* (see entry 66), *The Annual Register* offers good information on countries, but in the *Register*, unlike *Europa*, the news analyses are focused on the specific year of publication. The writing is good, and the authors are identified and are clearly experts, although almost exclusively British.

There are things here not readily found elsewhere, like the full text of international documents. Readers in all types of libraries will appreciate this complete summary, and librarians will appreciate the ease with which this item can be referred to readers with questions about current events.

Libraries that have the earlier volumes of this work will certainly want this volume, but this is a well-researched, attractive volume that even libraries that do have back runs may wish to consider buying. The annual $175 price tag is, sadly these days, not considered too expensive.—**Paul A. Mogren**

658.   **Countries of the World and Their Leaders Yearbook 1999.** Brian Rajewski, ed. Farmington Hills, Mich., Gale, 1998. 2v. illus. maps. index. $225.00/set. ISBN 0-7876-1508-0.

This title has been frequently reviewed by ARBA (see ARBA 96, entry 710, and ARBA 94, entry 723). Many observations of previous reviewers continue to be appropriate. The contents of the two-volume set are reprints from Department of State and other U.S. government units. These materials are available via the depository program free of charge. Earlier reviews noted that the *Europa World Year Book* (see entry 66) "provides the user with far more detail" and that the *Stateman's Yearbook* (see ARBA 92, entry 77) is less expensive. These observations are still pertinent. One major criticism has been that the entries have not been kept current. In a sample of 50 countries entries, about 14 percent were dated prior to 1990 (these were all from the late 1980s).

The positive factors that Gale Research has provided and that have made this title a standard in many reference collections are the attractive format and the useful combination of various resources, including U.S. embassies, consulates, and foreign service posts; chiefs of state and cabinet members of foreign countries; foreign travel; travel warnings; international treaty organizations; the current status of the world's nations with new nations noted; and the background notes from the Department of State, which are the core of the publication. Students in their first couple of years of college rely on this set for the preparation of a variety of papers. Upper-level students are likely to appreciate the added scope, depth, and analysis provided by the Europa titles. Reference staff will find answers to many of their questions in this conveniently assembled set.—**Graham R. Walden**

POLITICS AND GOVERNMENT

United States

Bibliography

659.   Stevens, Kenneth R., comp. **William Henry Harrison: A Bibliography.** Westport, Conn., Greenwood Press, 1998. 266p. index. (Bibliographies of the Presidents of the United States, no.9). $75.00. ISBN 0-313-28167-X.

William Henry Harrison's one-month term as president hides the fact that he led a substantial and multi-faceted life as a national political leader, for example, serving in local Ohio politics, in Congress, and as U.S. minister to Colombia. He was also an accomplished general during the War of 1812 and was responsible for negotiating significant land cessions from Native American tribes.

This bibliography is a comprehensive guide to the literature by and about the ninth president of the United States. Similar to other volumes in this series, the book begins with a chronology of Harrison's personal and political life. Part 1 follows, with citations to archived collections of personal and administrative papers, manu-scripts, and other primary documents of the president, his family, and key members of his administration. Also included is a list of popular and campaign newspapers in support of or opposition to his election to the presi-dency. Parts 2 and 3 cite Harrison's writings and biographical sources. Parts 4 through 12 are arranged in general chronological order and cite materials that cover personal developments as well as his military, Ohio legislative, congressional, and presidential careers up until his death, which is reflected in a chapter devoted to funeral sermons, eulogies, and orations. The remaining chapters cover the literature about political associates, his private life, historiographical materials, iconography, and visual media.

The overall quality of this work is enhanced by its broad consideration of key individuals with whom Harrison interacted during his political career. This consideration is especially critical given his very brief term as president. Most entries include a one-sentence description. The volume concludes with comprehensive author and subject indexes. This bibliography is another well-researched and highly recommended work from the Bibliographies of the Presidents of the United States series.—**Robert V. Labaree**

Biography

660.   Brown, David S. **Thomas Jefferson: A Biographical Companion.** Santa Barbara, Calif., ABC-CLIO, 1998. 266p. illus. maps. index. (ABC-CLIO Biographical Companion). $45.00. ISBN 0-87436-949-5.

ABC-CLIO Biographical Companions are handy one-volume compendiums of famous individuals in Western civilization. This example covers topics in the life of Thomas Jefferson. Through 180 short essay entries (within average length of five paragraphs), important events and people associated with Jefferson are described. Topics are varied and cover areas such as the Non-Intercourse Act, slavery, economic nationalism, Society of the Cincinnati, election of 1800, and XYZ Affair. In addition to the essays, there are three useful survey chapters. The first covers primary source documents in the life of Jefferson (including the *Declaration of Independence*); the second is a chronology of Jefferson's life, followed by an eight-page bibliography (no annotations). The volume concludes with an index.

This companion is an attractive, well-designed volume. The covers of the hardback are reproduction marble paper with insets of Jefferson and the *Declaration of Independence*. There are 44 well-selected illustrations that convey effectively the breadth and scope of this great man. One of these illustrations, "Pierre L'Enfant's Map of the City of Washington," is so small as to be almost useless, if not perhaps even unreadable. Generally speaking, however, the quality of this work is excellent. The essays are concise and well done and convey a feeling of Jef-ferson and his time. The book is recommended for all types of libraries. It describes effectively a true giant of the U.S. landscape. [R: BL, 15 Oct 98, p. 445; LJ, 1 Sept 98, p. 168]—**Ralph Lee Scott**

661.   Rayhawk, Peggie, and Jeanne Pettenati. **The New Members of Congress Almanac: 106th U.S. Congress.** Lanham, Md., Bernan Associates, 1998. 63p. illus. index. $40.00pa. ISBN 1-886222-14-2. ISSN 1091-2126.

This work gives detailed profiles of the 40 new members of the House of Representatives and 8 new members of the Senate that were swept into office as a result of the November 1998 elections. Also included are profiles of eight members of the House who won special elections since *The New Members of Congress Almanac, 105th U.S. Congress* was published in 1996 (see ARBA 98, entry 654), but who subsequently won full-term elections in November 1998. The almanac alphabetically lists new senators first, followed by profiles of representatives. Those elected mid-term in the 105th Congress are identified with asterisks in the table of contents. Each profile provides a black-and-white picture of the individual; personal data, including birth date and place; education; professional achievements; and primary, runoff (if necessary), and general election results in percentages. The remainder of the profile consists of a descriptive analysis of the individual's political background; an outline of the political campaign; highlights of previous work in elected office; and position on key social, economic, political issues facing the nation. Profiles of representatives also mention the political and geographic composition of their congressional district. Entries conclude with additional information about the congressperson's spouse and family activities.

In general, the profiles are concise and succeed in giving the reader a broad understanding of the individual's personal background and political goals and aspirations. Although libraries could wait until the new almanac is published to obtain a complete profile of the 106th Congress, how many new members of Congress does one remember from six, four, or even two years ago? For those libraries that can afford the expense, this work, archived over time, can become a useful ready-reference source that supplements the comprehensive almanacs.
—**Robert V. Labaree**

662.   Southwick, Leslie H., comp. **Presidential Also-Rans and Running Mates, 1788 Through 1996.** 2d ed. Jefferson, N.C., McFarland, 1998. 830p. illus. index. $99.50. ISBN 0-7864-0310-1.

This 2d edition provides biographical sketches of 136 persons nominated for president or vice president who did not win the election. There are 95 major party candidates and significant third-party ones given substantial space, whereas 41 lesser-knowns are covered to some extent. Third-party candidates are included if they received 10 percent of the vote; others are here if they received 2 percent of the popular vote or 5 percent of the Electoral College vote. The arrangement follows that of the earlier edition (see ARBA 85, entry 649). There are 55 chapters that cover elections from 1788 to 1996. In addition, the two confederate states of the United States' elections are summarized, as well as the vice-presidential confirmations of 1973 and 1974 (Gerald Ford and Nelson Rockefeller, respectively).

Each entry provides a brief description of the nominating convention, tallies the popular and electoral votes, and lists the winners and losers. The biographical essays are replete with personal data and commentary about the candidates' political history. An "Analysis of Qualifications" section is part of each sketch, an especially interesting feature where "what if" scenarios are played out. A brief bibliography of journal and book sources is appended to each entry, with a general bibliography at the back of the volume. Other added features include a table of "Prospects for Success" and portraits of all losing candidates (usually a campaign poster from 1856 on). New to this edition are lists of historical sites that may be visited and motion pictures about the candidates or their candidacy. A comprehensive index completes the volume.

This book about political also-rans continues to fill an important gap in U.S. political history and is recommended for academic and large public libraries. [R: BL, 1 May 98, pp. 1552-1554; Choice, July/Aug 98, p. 1838]
—**Gary D. Barber**

663.   **U.S. Government Leaders.** Frank N. Magill, ed. Pasadena, Calif., Salem Press, 1997. 3v. illus. index. (Magill's Choice). $175.00/set. ISBN 0-89356-954-2.

U.S. Government Leaders surveys 124 important government and political leaders. The profiles are updated versions of entries in two of Magill's *Great Lives from History* sets—the *American Series* (see ARBA 88, entry 513) and the *American Women Series* (see ARBA 96, entry 942). Eleven entirely new essays were added. The leaders selected are those individuals "most asked for" by secondary and undergraduate college students in the view of the publishers. All U.S. presidents are included as well as various leaders during the colonial and early republic periods. More recent profiles focus on prominent members of Congress, politicians, and members of presidential cabinets, especially secretaries of defense and state. There are also various selections that do not fit these obvious categories: Jesse Jackson, H. Ross Perot, Colin Powell, and Alan Greenspan, for example.

Each essay begins with the leader's name; birth date and place; death date and place, when appropriate; and a summary of their life divided into three sections: "Early Life," the formative influences; "Life's Work," major achievements; and "Summary," an overview of the leader's significance and impact on U.S. history. Each of the signed profiles also includes a bibliography of no more than a dozen major monographs published in the 1980s or 1990s. These entries usually have short annotations that identify the content and approach of the works. There are three reference tools at the end of the third volume. The timeline lists each of the leaders included in the set chronologically by birth. There are also a list of U.S. presidents in order of service and a name index of all leaders covered.

The value of this 3-volume set is not for its use for scholarly research or even for its basic information that is for the most part readily available in such sets as the *Dictionary of American Biography* or *Current Biography*, not to mention standard encyclopedias. Its value lies in its presentation that is designed for secondary and under-graduate college students who seek a convenient package of information about major political figures. In this regard, the set is especially useful because it goes beyond the standard biographical information to provide basic analysis on such points as early influences, personal motivations, political orientation, and lasting significance of the leaders. All this is done in a succinct, easy-to-use format. In this regard, *U.S. Government Leaders* is a useful addition to reference collections. [R: BL, 1 Mar 98, pp. 1172-1173]—**Henry E. York**

664. **The Vice Presidents: A Biographical Dictionary.** L. Edward Purcell, ed. New York, Facts on File, 1998. 474p. illus. index. $50.00. ISBN 0-8160-3109-6.

Vice presidents have been the butt of jokes, leaders in their own right, and scoundrels. The office is rarely taken seriously until its ultimate function, that of replacing the president, is required. Not surprisingly, there are few reference sources that focus on the vice presidency and those who have been vice president.

Organized chronologically, this unique biographical dictionary provides an introduction to the develop-ment of the vice presidency through the personalities and political history of the men who have served in this office. Each entry details the individual's life, service as vice president, his effect on the office, and concludes with a short bibliography. Contributors to the volume include historians, political scientists, and independent scholars. Unfortunately, this variety affects the quality of the entries; a number of entries could use tighter focus and editing, whereas others provide excellent concise biographies. The bibliographies focus mainly on books and disserta-tions, with only a few journal citations. The section titled "Chronology of Events" provides historical context. Although this is a biographical dictionary, an essay on the history and analysis of the office of vice president would have been a useful addition to the volume.

A biographical dictionary can provide only short entries for each individual. Therefore, for notable figures, such as John C. Calhoun, Theodore Roosevelt, or Harry Truman, the volume provides a factual sketch that focuses on a part of a larger career. For others, such as Charles Warren Fairbanks, it provides a much needed brief biography of a lesser known individual. School, public, and academic libraries should purchase this volume. [R: BL, 15 Mar 98, p. 1270; Choice, July/Aug 98, p. 1840]—**Ann E. Miller**

665. **Washington Representatives 1998.** 22d ed. J. Valerie Steele, Neil E. Hochman, Tiffany M. Jones, and Shanea L. Smith, eds. Washington, D.C., Columbia Books, 1998. 1242p. index. $95.00pa. ISBN 1-880873-30-3. ISSN 0192-060X.

This volume focuses on the 17,000 people in Washington, D.C. who attempt to influence government policy on behalf of private, public, public interest, and foreign interests. The volume lists alphabetically those registered as lobbyists as well as others who identify themselves or are identified by others as involved in representing interests. Each entry provides information on the individual's addresses (including e-mail and fax numbers), major clients, and type of registration (e.g., lobbyist or foreign agent). In many cases the entries also provide information on the representative's background and prior government jobs. A 2d section is an alphabetic list of organizations with Washington representation, including legal firms, advocacy groups, industry associations, trade unions, and so on. The organization listings often include background on the history and causes of the group as well as the names of its Washington representatives. Separate indexes identify organizations by their subject matter, PACs based on their industry ties, and foreign agents by country.

In an era when interest group politics is crucial to understanding policy-making and campaign finances, this directory is very important. The annual volume means that the information is up-to-date and usually accurate. It is vital for those interested in identifying groups and organizations involved in supporting specific causes. It is useful also for researchers interested in interest group politics and campaign finance. This work is recommended for large municipal libraries and research libraries.—**Frank L. Wilson**

666.   **Who's Who in American Politics 1997-1998.** 16th ed. New Providence, N.J., Marquis Who's Who/Reed Reference Publishing, 1997. 2v. index. $259.95/set. ISBN 0-8379-6900-X. ISSN 0000-0205.

Formerly published by R. R. Bowker, this title remains substantively unchanged since this work was last reviewed in ARBA 95 (entry 519). It contains brief biographical sketches, categorized alphabetically by state, of approximately 29,000 individuals who are influential in local, state, and federal politics. A name index references the pertinent geographic area in the text where information about a particular political figure can be found. Organization remains a problem in this resource, with entries for federal officials being included under the District of Columbia or their place of legal residence. Entries for some individuals are not indicative of their current political position, and some entries that meet the requirements for inclusion have been omitted. For example, Ruben Smith's entry has not been updated to reflect his current status as mayor of Las Cruces, New Mexico, and the mayor of Santa Fe, New Mexico, is not included in this work. Overall, however, most libraries will want to purchase this title for ready information about politicos across the nation.—**Mark A. Allan**

Dictionaries and Encyclopedias

667.   **Encyclopedia of American Government.** Joseph M. Bessette and R. Kent Rasmussen, eds. Englewood Cliffs, N.J., Salem Press, 1998. 4v. illus. maps. index. $210.00/set. ISBN 0-89356-117-7.

The *Encyclopedia of American Government* (EAG) is a reference work developed around current curricular design for students in middle and secondary school social studies and civics units of study. The 200 alphabetically arranged articles are supposed to be written in a jargon free language, stressing essentials and defining terms as they are introduced; however, the definition of *conservatism* is regarded as modern and *liberalism* is defined as welfare liberalism. The definitions are not jargon free; the bibliographies include contemporary works, but most listings are university press volumes and do not appear to be suitable for middle school and ninth-grade level civics units.

The format is awkward; it has continuous paging for the four volumes, yet lacks a complete four-volume table of contents in each volume. It also places the U.S. Constitution in the back of a volume as an appendix instead of making it an article on its own with an essay analyzing it, which would be more appropriate. The primary resource should be in the text, not an appendix to a reference source on U.S. government. From this set, students would not know that freedom of speech, press, assembly, and petition are in the Bill of Rights. An essay should be included on each of these basic U.S. freedoms. There is an essay on religion that deals with the basic facts from the First Amendment. The EAG is adequate and can be recommended for middle school libraries with some hesitation.

—**Gerald D. Moran**

668.   **A Historical Guide to the U.S. Government.** George Thomas Kurian and others, eds. New York, Oxford University Press, 1998. 741p. illus. index. $95.00. ISBN 0-19-510230-4.

The great English statesman, Edmund Burke, saw what U.S. government strived to become: what the people think it is. He also understood that bad government had in the groves of its academy vistas viewing gallows only. The United States has had both its pellucid moments and its gallows humor. Apart from being among the largest nations of the world, it is also, public opinion notwithstanding, the least governed. Doubters should turn to *A Historical Guide to the U.S. Government* for substantiation. No, this is not some flag-waving paean to patriotism. Rather it is a candid, measured examination of what makes these purple mountains and these fruited plains so utterly and unashamedly beautiful.

In an alphabetic arrangement, various experts write expansively on presidential advisement, the Federal Aviation Administration, Department of the Navy, Public Health Service, and the White House Office. Gone from these pages are the sullen, sordid stories that disgrace our national headlines on a daily basis. Here instead are those contrivances of human wisdom that have been honed into agencies that manage more than 260 million people from, literally, the four corners of the globe.

Entries range from 500 words to more than 1,000. The appendix includes more than 2 dozen documents that have helped shape our government during the past 220 years. Included are excerpts from the act establishing the Executive Department (1789) to Executive Order 12866 (Regulatory Planning and Review 1993). There is even humor here, as in the Paperwork Reduction Act (1980). This is a must purchase for many libraries. [R: BL, 1 June 98, pp. 1808-1812]—**Mark Y. Herring**

Directories

669. **Congressional Directory: 105th Congress.** Washington, D.C., Heritage Foundation, 1997. 287p. illus. maps. $13.95pa.

This compact, 7½-by-4 ¼-inch directory published by the Heritage Foundation is everything that the title of the work states and more. The U.S. Senate listings are published on blue paper, and contain pertinent information such as the individual senator's district; address, telephone, fax, e-mail, and World Wide Web information; educational and professional background; Senate committee service; staff; and expiration of term. Senate committees and subcommittees also receive individual entries, including membership, telephone and fax numbers, and addresses. U.S. House of Representative entries, although published on white pages, receive the same attention. Each senator's and representative's entry is illustrated with a photograph of the individual, most often in color.

The final third of the book contains other color-coded sections with additional information. Gray pages contain an introduction to the legislative process, pointers for communicating with members of Congress, and a valuable glossary of legislative terms. Yellow pages contain maps of congressional districts, identification of the pertinent senators and representatives, and the percentage of the vote each received in the last election. Closing out the volume is another section of white pages, this time providing contact information pertaining to state governors; members, departments, and agencies of the federal executive branch; and seemingly out-of-place information regarding the jurisdictions of the previously listed federal Senate and House committees.

This title is a valuable, yet compact work, in which the color-coding scheme provides readily accessible directory information about the federal government. The work contains additional information relevant to all U.S. citizens. As such, it is an ideal candidate for every library's ready-reference collection.—**Mark A. Allan**

670. **Encyclopedia of Governmental Advisory Organizations 1997.** 11th ed. Donna Batten, ed. Detroit, Gale, 1997. 1562p. index. $550.00. ISBN 0-7876-1154-9. ISSN 0092-8380.

This latest edition of *Encyclopedia of Governmental Advisory Organizations* continues the comprehensive and well-organized information on advisory organizations in the United States. The groups included are permanent, continuing, and ad hoc advisory committees that report to the president, Congress, and various government departments and agencies as well as important regional and interstate commissions. Historically significant defunct organizations are also included with their ending dates.

The descriptive entries are listed within 10 general subject chapters ranging from agriculture to transportation, subarranged by similar keywords. Information is from a variety of primary sources, such as public laws and the Federal Register. Mail and telephone questionnaires are used to update information. Each entry contains data for the committee, including acronyms; contact information, with e-mail and home page when provided; history and authority; activities; members and staff; publications or reports; and meetings. An introduction and user's guide explain the scope of the work.

There are five indexes for access. The main index is an alphabetic and keyword index to the name of the committee, including any name change. There are a personal name index, a publications and reports index, an index listing committees formed by presidential term, and another listing federal department or agency. Three appendixes give the names and contact information for committee management officers; a list by state of regional government depository libraries; and the full text of the Federal Advisory Committee Act, P.L. 92-463.

The new edition comes one year after the previous edition and notes 100 additional entries, although there are only 56 more numbered entries than in the 11th edition. The encyclopedia is also available on diskette or magnetic tape. Depending on the need for the most current information, the expense of the new edition may be justified. Academic, special, and large public libraries without this title should consider adding this reference for its current and historical information.—**Margo B. Mead**

671.   **The Heritage Foundation Congressional Directory: 105th Congress.** Washington, D.C., Heritage Foundation, 1997. 287p. illus. maps. $13.95. ISBN 9-996-31764-1.

A compact volume designed for lobbyists, the *Heritage Foundation Congressional Directory* brings little additional information to libraries that already hold standard congressional directories. The directory provides address, telephone numbers, and basic personal information for members of the House of Representatives and Senate. Color photographs of members enhance the usual listings. The Heritage Foundation has taken the extra step of adding Web addresses to the entries of individual members when available. The committee pages contain only the most basic membership and staff information, plus Web addresses. Unfortunately, the listing of committee jurisdictions is located at the back of the volume, separate from the listing of the committees themselves. Overall, librarians will find more complete information on congressional committees and committee staff in other directories.

The maps of congressional districts are small and difficult to read. Only California has breakout maps with additional detail. Additional maps of densely populated urban areas, such as New York, Chicago, or the southeastern coast of Florida, would be useful. Information thrown in for good measure includes a list of state governors, executive branch agencies and senior staff, and the senior staff at the Heritage Foundation.

The volume does provide helpful and nonpartisan advice to individuals seeking to become more involved. Sections on the legislative process, or writing or calling your senator or representative are helpful information in any library. The maps of the Mall and downtown Washington guide onsite lobbyists. Sections on what a congressional office can and cannot do and rules on gift giving for both the House and the Senate have been added.

Libraries would be better served by purchasing a larger, more complete congressional directory. *The Heritage Foundation Congressional Directory*, although useful for lobbyists, provides only the most basic information for libraries.—**Ann E. Miller**

672.   **Staff Directories on CD-ROM.** [CD-ROM]. Washington, D.C., Congressional Quarterly, 1997. Minimum system requirements: IBM or compatible 486. CD-ROM drive. MS DOS 3.0. 640KB real memory. 20MB hard disk space. $495.00.

This CD-ROM version of *Staff Directories* was first reviewed in ARBA 94 (see entry 737). The copy under review is version number 11, October 1997. The central purpose of this product remains the same: to provide the names, federal address, and telephone and fax numbers of key officials in the executive branch derived from the *Federal Staff Directory*; judges, court officials, U.S. marshalls, U.S. attorneys, and law clerks derived from the *Judicial Staff Directory*; and members of Congress and their staff covered by the *Congressional Staff Directory*. The CD-ROM version comes with a well-organized and nontechnical User's Manual that comprehensively describes the installation process and the hardware required to run the system and the contents of the disc, including a detailed overview of searching techniques, examples of searches for each field of each directory, and a troubleshooting section. The system installs easily but continues to allow searching only one directory at a time. A menu bar listing function key commands is located at the top of each screen, allowing for easy maneuverability within a directory and quick access to help screens. The system allows Boolean searching, adjacency, and word truncations. Entries may include brief biographical information and "tokens" (hyperlinks) to portraits and other images. Also included is a data field of agency Internet addresses and bulletin board telephone numbers, a full-text search option, and cross-references.

A note in the User's Manual mentions that future versions should include links to the staff of officials and organizational charts. In addition, it is hoped that the newly published *Municipal Staff Directory* will also be included in the CD-ROM version. This system is recommended for libraries with concerns about shelf space or that emphasize electronic media and its inherent searching capabilities, but this version merely parallels the print editions in terms of content and scope.—**Robert V. Labaree**

Handbooks and Yearbooks

673.   Bagby, Meredith. **Annual Report of the United States of America, 1998: What Every Citizen Should Know About the REAL State of the Nation.** 1998 ed. New York, McGraw-Hill, 1998. 112p. $15.95pa. ISBN 0-07-006708-2.

This is the 4th edition of *The Annual Report of the United States of America*. The intent remains the same: to explain in plain, unambiguous language the ways in which federal tax dollars have been collected, distributed, and used during the past several years. The financial review in chapter 9 provides charts and tables on a variety of receipts and outlays of the federal government synthesized from the "United States Government Annual Report, Fiscal Year 1996." Among the information given are government outlays by function, fund activity by agency or department, and a statement of federal agency operations in fiscal years 1995 and 1996.

The other chapters offer a descriptive analysis of topics related to government operations and the political, economic, and social landscape of the United States for approximately the past three years. Chapter 5, for example, offers an overview of federal social programs and initiatives with particular emphasis on how they work and attempts at legislative reform. Imbedded throughout the text are charts, tables, and histograms that provide a visual representation of data mentioned in the text or are used to highlight a particular point. The text is readable, and the charts and tables are clearly presented. The report concludes with a list of the names, addresses, and titles of key personnel in the Clinton administration as of January 1, 1998, and the names, mailing address, telephone and fax number, and e-mail of the 105th Congress. Also included is a brief outline of major actions by Congress and the Supreme Court.

The lack of references to factual statements made in the text compromises the scholarly integrity of the work, and the fact that the author expresses appreciation to Ross Perot for inspiration in seeking accountability from government hints at an underlying purpose. Nevertheless, the author appears to present a balanced account of current government fiscal policy and programmatic initiatives, and as such, the book is recommended for nonscholars seeking basic information on U.S. fiscal policy and expenditures.—**Robert V. Labaree**

674.   Barone, Michael, William Lilley, and Laurence J. DeFranco. **State Legislative Elections: Voting Patterns and Demographics.** Washington, D.C., Congressional Quarterly, 1998. 403p. maps. $135.00. ISBN 1-56802-200-X.

State Legislative Elections is another Congressional Quarterly publication similar to *U.S. Primary Elections, 1995-96* (see ARBA 98, entry 673), in that it compiles and interprets election and demographic statistics from the 50 states during the 1990s. In this instance, the electoral statistics are for state legislative elections. They are presented by district, along with census data on average household income; college education; percentage of households receiving Social Security; and the percentages of African Americans, Hispanic Americans, and Asian Americans residing in the district. Political analyst Barone provides a one-page essay on each state that explains how the local demographics, especially the urban, suburban, and rural mix, influence which party wins local elections and how this further influences national politics. A longer introductory essay discusses the above from a national perspective. The book is arranged alphabetically by state and then numerically by district. Maps help to define the urban, rural, and suburban boundaries. This book contains much information, clearly presented. It will be useful for colleges and large public libraries. [R: Choice, Sept 98, p. 96; BL, July 98, p. 1910]

—**Deborah Hammer**

675.   **Congress and the Nation: A Review of Government and Politics, 1993-1996. Volume 9.** Washington, D.C., Congressional Quarterly, 1998. 1275p. index. $225.00. ISBN 1-56802-240-9. ISSN 1047-1324.

Congressional Quarterly's newest volume of *Congress and the Nation* continues to provide the concise and well-researched information that this title is known for. Not only does the work consolidate in 947 pages the federal political events that occurred during the 103d and 104th Congresses, it contains appendixes that provide significant political data. These appendixes include information such as congressional voting statistics on major issues, the texts of prominent presidential speeches, and a listing of presidential vetoes. The work is equally helpful for either a retrospective look at broad governmental and public policy topics or for vital information on narrower political issues. The organization of the volume as described in ARBA 95 (see entry 731) lends itself to the former approach. The comprehensive index provides access to narrower issues by scholars and laypeople alike. For example, direction to material on the White House travel office scandal can be found in the index under either "White House staff" or "Congressional Investigations." All libraries that require materials in the subject areas of political science and public policy should add this volume to their core reference materials.—**Mark A. Allan**

676.   **Congressional Elections 1946-1996.** Washington, D.C., Congressional Quarterly, 1998. 375p. index. $34.95pa. ISBN 1-56802-248-4.

This resource is valuable to researchers for two primary reasons. First, the book provides a compilation of both general and special congressional election results covering the 50-year period from 1946 to 1996. Election returns are presented in separate sections covering the House and Senate. Explanatory footnotes are included

where appropriate. Although the information can be obtained elsewhere, Congressional Quarterly has again succeeded in compiling data from a variety of sources into a presentation that accentuates access and a variety of research endeavors. Second, the statistical tables are supported by a comprehensive introductory essay that examines the political landscape of Congress as viewed through the lens of election returns. Additional essays cover the historical significance of southern primaries, House elections, and reapportionment and redistricting. The book also includes briefer, one-page "boxes" that examine a specific issue, such as Senate appointments and special elections. Each descriptive analysis examines key issues and places the post-World War II Congress in proper historical, social, and political context. Congressional Quarterly has done a splendid job of complementing data with detailed analysis. Essays are unsigned, but most cite additional sources. The volume includes a list of political party abbreviations, a bibliography, name indexes to congressional members, and a general index.
—**Robert V. Labaree**

677.   Cook, Rhodes, Richard M. Scammon, and Alice V. McGillivray. **America Votes 22: A Handbook of Contemporary American Election Statistics.** 1996 ed. Washington, D.C., Congressional Quarterly, 1998. 542p. $147.00. ISBN 0-87187-918-2.

The 22d volume of *America Votes* adheres to the same general format as previous editions. The 1st section provides historical data on presidential elections from 1920 through 1996 and presidential primaries from 1968 to 1996. Also included are contemporary statistics regarding special elections held between 1994 and 1996, congressional election results through the 1sst session of the 105th Congress, and current national voter turnout information. The remaining chapters contain detailed statistical profiles of elections in each state and the District of Columbia. The profiles include postwar (1942 or 1946) voting results for president, governor, and senator; county-level results of the 1995-1996 election cycle for president, governor, and senator; and votes cast for House of Representative candidates by congressional district. Results are split between the Republican and Democratic political parties with a notes section outlining votes for third-party or independent candidates. A map of congressional districts is also included with each state profile. Throughout its publication history, this one-stop research tool has consistently provided easily accessible, clearly presented data on federal elections in the United States. It is particularly useful in providing a detailed breakdown of presidential election results. However, most of the data are not cumulative from one volume to the next, rendering comparative analysis over time cumbersome. Although this is an essential resource for almost any collection, a compact disk version that facilitates cross-tabulation of detailed data from earlier editions would be a welcome enhancement.—**Robert V. Labaree**

678.   Eckl, Corina, and Arturo Pérez. **State Budget Actions 1997.** Denver, Colo., National Conference of State Legislatures, 1997. 48p. $35.00pa. ISBN 1-55516-561-3.

Presenting findings from the National Conference of State Legislatures's annual survey of legislative fiscal officers, this report summarizes state budget activities for 1997 with projections for 1998 for state legislators, legislative staffs, and related professionals (such as public policy professionals). Following the introduction, the state finances overview focuses on general fund budgets and selected spending categories. Two chapters cover state finances for 1997 and 1998, and four chapters consider specific funding areas, such as education, corrections, and Medicaid. Twelve tables and three figures illustrate these data, whereas eight appendixes present budget expenditures and estimates. For example, appendix C indicates how budget surpluses were used.

This well-written report informs its intended audience; however, further research has been stymied by the lack of a topical index and the failure to specify the survey questions and the location of the complete results. With the public clamoring for budgetary information, public libraries should consider purchasing this report despite the limitations noted.—**Sandra E. Belanger**

679.   **Historic Documents of 1997.** Washington, D.C., Congressional Quarterly, 1998. 962p. index. $135.00. ISBN 1-56802-385-5. ISSN 0892-080X.

Published since 1972, each annual edition of this work reproduces the full text or a significant portion of official statements, speeches, legal materials, special studies, and reports that, in the judgment of the editors, will be of lasting interest to scholars, librarians, and students. No other qualifiers are used to help the reader determine how documents are selected for inclusion in each volume. Ellipsis points are inserted within the document when the text is not reproduced in full. Each document is introduced by a well-written but brief essay that provides background information relating to the item's overall relationship to current events; the document's political, historical, or social significance; and, in many cases, the ways in which the document or speech speaks to broader issues of public policy. The introductory essays are written in italics to distinguish them from the document text. Accessing a particular document is relatively easy if the user knows the approximate date of the speech, report, or other item because documents are arranged chronologically. The user can also browse the table of contents to find materials. The edition under review contains a cumulative five-year index that builds on a separate volume, *Historic Documents Index, 1972-1995* (see ARBA 98, entry 682). These cumulative indexes should be consulted when it is unclear which volume may contain a particular document. Each edition is a useful guide to important speeches or documents that have been produced as a result of contemporary issues or events. This is an excellent resource series, but the quality could be further enhanced if the selection process is clearly stated and supplementary readings are provided to help to place the materials in greater context.—**Robert V. Labaree**

680.   **The Municipal Year Book 1998.** Washington, D.C., International City/County Management Association, 1998. 348p. index. $79.95. ISBN 0-87326-973-X. ISSN 0077-2186.

People are led to believe, in part because of the media focus on national news, that the federal government governs everyone's life. The reality, however, is that people's lives are as affected, if not more affected, by state and local government. Indeed, that reality has become more complex as the federal government shifts responsibility to state governments, which in turn pass on those responsibilities to local governments. This reference guide offers a substantive guide to local government. Anyone who wants to understand local government more clearly and fully will benefit from the availability of the information provided here.

The book is divided into five sections: management issues and trends, intergovernmental relations, staffing and compensation, directories, and references. In the 1st section, the researcher will find useful articles on workplace violence policies, performance measurements, women as chief administrative officers, the New England town meeting, and issues and trends in municipal government. One of the 3 essays in the 2d edition explains recent Supreme Court cases that affect local government. Section 3 details salaries of municipal and county officials and police and fire personnel for 1997. In section 4 one finds, among other things, a list of municipal officials in U.S. cities with populations greater than 2,500. This list includes, whenever possible, the chief elected official, the appointed administrator, the clerk to the governing board, the chief financial officer, the fire chief, the police chief, and the public works director. The last section details sources of information people in local government will find useful.

For issues relating to local governance, this reference work provides an excellent overview of issues and information more people should know. It is highly recommended.—**Michael A. Foley**

681.   **National Party Conventions 1831-1996.** Washington, D.C., Congressional Quarterly, 1997. 312p. illus. index. $34.95pa. ISBN 1-56802-280-8.

This volume is another in an important series of Congressional Quarterly publications on U.S. national politics. Although there are monographs describing the evolution of party conventions in the United States, this volume provides the basic facts and statistics on this peculiar feature of our political system. The key feature of the volume is the "Convention Chronology," which provides short summaries of the major party conventions by election year. The summaries cover political maneuvering before and during the conventions. Included in the summaries are brief extracts from the parties' platforms. Statistical information includes key votes on rules, issues, and nominations broken down by state. *National Party Conventions 1831-1996* is highly recommended for public libraries and school libraries. It is a valuable source of information for beginners and scholars on U.S. party politics.
—**Frank L. Wilson**

682.   **Presidential Elections 1789-1996.** Washington, D.C., Congressional Quarterly, 1997. 280p. maps. index. $34.95pa. ISBN 1-56802-065-1.

Congressional Quarterly, perhaps the most authoritative source on Washington, D.C., affairs, provides a valuable resource on U.S. presidential elections in this volume. There are brief narrative essays on issues, such as the Electoral College, the expansion of the popular vote for the presidency, primary elections, and national conventions. The real value of this volume, however, is the compilation of historical statistics on every election since the foundation of the republic. Tables, maps, and figures present these data in readily understandable format. The range of information is extensive, including the votes for minor candidates by state since 1824. There are brief biographical notes on major presidential and vice presidential candidates. I can think of few facts pertaining to presidential elections that cannot be found in this volume. Convenient, readable, and affordable, this volume should be included in all public libraries and all levels of school libraries. It is easily accessible and valuable for both the political scientist working on a scholarly project and an elementary school student preparing a sixth-grade paper.—**Frank L. Wilson**

683.   Stanley, Harold W., and Richard G. Niemi. **Vital Statistics on American Politics 1997-1998.** 6th ed. Washington, D.C., Congressional Quarterly, 1997. 440p. index. $44.95. ISBN 1-56802-374-X.

   In the 10 years since publication of the 1st edition of *Vital Statistics on American Politics*, tremendous changes in access to information have taken place. Although the overall format and size of this 6th edition has remained relatively constant, the information contained within this comprehensive volume has been substantially revised and reorganized to provide a more useful reference. Initially a convenient collection of data on a wide range of topics affecting U.S. politics culled from reference volumes, government publications, journals, and other monographs, it was organized by chapters similar to U.S. government textbooks, with brief introductions to chapter tables followed by questions, with a teacher's manual available. In the last edition, these questions were eliminated. However, in the introduction, the authors note some of the difficulties inherent in utilizing electronically available data, theoretically easier to access but not always provided in the same format as previously, if at all. Therefore, while covering the same basic topics (e.g., government branches, policy, elections, media, federalism, and others), the current 11 chapters reflect not only data availability but also format accessibility. A new feature in this edition is a brief listing corresponding to chapters of relevant URL addresses for Internet and Web access that prefaces substantive references. An index concludes the volume. Although the information contained is available from other sources, this single volume provides a convenient and useful reference.
                                                                              —**Virginia S. Fischer**

684.   Tomaselli-Moschovitis, Valerie. **Government on File.** New York, Facts on File, 1998. 1v. (various paging). illus. maps. index. $165.00 looseleaf w/binder. ISBN 0-8160-3560-1.

   This title is an excellent resource for educators and students who require pictures, diagrams, and charts that portray the workings of government, in particular the U.S. government. These illustrations and the accompanying text depict such concepts as the foundations of government, governmental structure and functions, policy-making, and other governmental processes. A chapter is devoted to state and local government, and another to international and economic topics. The illustrations are clear, concise, and comprehensive. For example, a chart illustrating the impeachment process depicts the governmental process, its constitutional foundation, and the number of officials who were impeached between 1789 and 1996, and also includes an illustration of Andrew Johnson—the only president impeached during this time frame. Dividers are provided in this spiralbound volume, making the task of identifying a relevant illustration a relatively simple matter. This format also allows for the easy removal of the various illustrations for reproduction. The publisher grants explicit permission to photocopy material in this work for nonprofit, educational, and authorization purposes, which makes this a valuable source for classroom handouts. Unfortunately, but understandably, permission is not granted for the electronic reproduction of these materials. The work is recommended for libraries serving students and educators in junior high through undergraduate school settings. [R: BL, 15 Sept 98, pp. 262-264]—**Mark A. Allan**

685.   Vile, John R. **A Companion to the United States Constitution and Its Amendments.** 2d ed. Westport, Conn., Praeger/Greenwood Press, 1997. 288p. index. $24.95pa. ISBN 0-275-95785-3.

   The irony of getting a book like this *this* year is too exquisite for words. President Clinton will be the proud recipient of my review copy as it strikes me that he needs the companion more than I; indeed, more than most. It will be a faithful companion and one that will not lead to future trouble. The Clinton scandal that has led to the drawing up of the articles of impeachment has shown so many Americans ignorant of their own Constitution as to be alarming. But this book, whether in reference or in the general collection, will go a long way to palliate their stultifying offenses.

   For example, Vile's book would have informed pundits and most Americans that voting out the articles of impeachment in the House of Representatives does not mean the president loses his job; it means the Senate will hold a trial to see if the president loses his job. If President Clinton had had this book for bedside reading, he might not only have ascertained the certain meaning of the verb "is," but he would have understood that "high crimes and misdemeanors" refers not only to federal offenses, but also to personal conduct.

Vile's book is a veritable American history lesson, filled with information on the colonial setting of the Constitution, the Declaration of Independence, the idea of equality of human rights, the Articles of Confederation, the various plans offered (e.g., Virginia, New Jersey), and more. Then Vile tackles the document itself with special attention focused on its various parts: executive, judicial, and congressional. The remainder of the book, beginning with chapter 6, focuses on the amendments. Important court cases are cited and various interpretations exposed.

This is a remarkable book coming at an extraordinary time. Such books coming at such times remind us not only how permanent our government is, but also how astonishingly stable it can be during the most difficult of crises.—**Mark Y. Herring**

686.   Vile, John R. **The United States Constitution: Questions and Answers.** Westport, Conn., Greenwood Press, 1998. 316p. illus. index. $39.95. ISBN 0-313-30643-5.

Intended to help high school students understand the constitutional dimensions of U.S. government, this guide uses a question-and-answer format to present detailed information about the U.S. Constitution (i.e., can a president be sued for actions he took before assuming the office of the presidency?). Each chapter covers a specific issue or set of amendments. The final chapter focuses on key dates and events in U.S. constitutional history. The answers given vary in length from a simple sentence to a short paragraph. Following the question-and-answer chapters are eight appendixes that contain the text of the U.S. Constitution, the Declaration of Independence, and the Articles of Confederation; "100 Questions and Answers Used By the Immigration and Naturalization Service"; and lists of the speakers of the House, the U.S. presidents, the U.S. Supreme Court justices, and the 50 states with their dates of admission to the union and the number of representatives based on the 1990 census. The work concludes with a comprehensive subject/name index.

Given its intended audience, this is a somewhat useful supplement to general encyclopedias and specialized guides and handbooks. However, the guide is of little value to anyone other than secondary school students because the questions and answers are not placed in any historical, political, or social context; the bibliographies concluding each chapter cite only general survey texts; and the legal cases accompanying the bibliographies are not referenced back to the question or answer in which they were mentioned.—**Robert V. Labaree**

687.   Wetterau, Bruce. **Desk Reference on the Federal Budget.** Washington, D.C., Congressional Quarterly, 1998. 344p. index. $49.95. ISBN 1-56802-378-2.

Individuals requiring nontechnical insight into the U.S. government's revenues and expenditures will find Congressional Quarterly's *Desk Reference on the Federal Budget* an excellent source of information. Organized in a question-and-answer format, the book resolves the most common inquiries about the budget. Definitions of a wide range of budgetary terms such as *recession*, *corporate welfare*, and *backdoor spending* are given. Statistical information in the form of more than 35 charts and graphs details historical data, including the size of the economy, the consumer price index, and the budget deficit. Additionally, the impact of each of the last 11 presidential administrations upon the federal budget is considered. Perhaps most important, the amounts of money currently spent by major federal departments and agencies on their respective activities are scrutinized, along with the possible impact of budget cuts on these governmental entities.

The text is broadly arranged by chapter, and narrowly organized by 516 frequently asked questions (e.g., "How have federal farm subsidies changed over the years?"). This dichotomy may be confusing to some readers because chapters are listed in the table of contents by page number, whereas the index identifies topics by question number. Nevertheless, this nonpartisan information resource is an excellent book for answering a single budgetary question, or for a more extensive education regarding the federal budget. As such, it is a useful tool for both the reference and the circulating collections. This work is recommended for all libraries.—**Mark A. Allan**

688.   White, Jean Bickmore. **The Utah State Constitution: A Reference Guide.** Westport, Conn., Greenwood Press, 1998. 231p. index. (Reference Guides to the State Constitutions of the United States, no.30). $75.00. ISBN 0-313-29351-1.

Constitutions are not static documents, subject as they are to reform because of changes in the societies they serve. The text of any state's constitution is readily available to its citizenry. The series of which this reference guide is a part goes a step further, however, by combining the constitution text with explanatory comments.

Part 1 is a historical introduction to the state's constitution, from its earliest draft to the most recent amendments. Part 2 spells out each section, immediately followed by an essay that explains its provisions and any pertinent court decisions and legislative actions. A bibliographic essay and a table of cases provide additional sources. The detailed table of contents lists each constitutional article and section. From a random check, the subject index at the end of the book appears to be fairly thorough.

Obviously, the title under review will appeal most to libraries in Utah and to libraries holding other volumes in the series. It is also recommended to any library with a solid political science or state history collection.

—**Lori D. Kranz**

Canadian

689.   McNenly, Jennifer, with Andrew McGregor, comps. **A Bibliography of Works on Canadian Foreign Relations 1991-1995.** Toronto, Canadian Institute of International Affairs, 1998. 1v. (various paging). index. $75.00pa. ISBN 0-919084-65-6.

This volume is the most recent issue in the series published by the John Holmes Library of the Canadian Institute of International Affairs. It covers materials on Canada's external affairs, economic development, and defense relations since 1945 that were written between 1991 and 1995. Previous volumes covering back to 1971 are still in print. The current volume contains more than 8,000 records for Canadian and foreign materials, in English and French, including books, journal articles, treaties, government documents, theses, and conference papers. Coverage is not claimed to be exhaustive; all items included have been examined.

The subject index constitutes the main body of this bibliography. The unannotated entries use a subject list provided in the preface. Items are cross-listed as appropriate, with full records under each heading. There are also an author index and a list of journals reviewed. This is an essential work for any library or researcher with a serious interest in Canada, especially Canada's foreign relations and international affairs. It is encouraging to note that the John Holmes Library has plans to release future editions of the bibliography on CD-ROM. Its Website (http://www.ciia.org) currently provides an extensive set of links to sites relating to international relations. These resources are not included in the printed bibliography.—**Henry E. York**

Europe

690.   Cook, Chris, and John Paxton. **European Political Facts, 1900-1996.** 4th ed. New York, St. Martin's Press, 1998. 434p. index. $65.00. ISBN 0-312-21231-3.

The twentieth century has seen Europe's political scene witness enormous upheaval as evidenced by two world wars, the collapse of the Soviet Union, the rise of international organizations such as the European Union, and ongoing political instability in the Russian Federation. This edition of *European Political Facts* strives to provide a concise reference source to the individuals, nations, and organizations affecting twentieth-century European political development and evolution.

A preface profiles changes in European politics since the 1973 publication of the *European Political Facts* inaugural edition. The heart of this reference contains listings and descriptions of international organizations, heads of states, parliaments, principal government ministers, elections, political parties, judicial institutions, national security and treaties, colonial dependencies, population, and new countries. A glossary concludes this compendium.

Individuals, countries, and organizations covered include the International Court of Justice, Organization for Economic Cooperation and Development (OECD); Iceland's Althing (parliament); recent Irish president Mary Robinson; national election returns for countries as diverse as Bosnia-Herzegovina, France, and Norway; and political parties such as France's National Front, the British Conservative Party, and Latvia's Farmers Union. Coverage of judicial institutions include descriptions of the Finnish, Italian, and Swiss court systems along with military conflicts such as the Russo-Polish war of 1919-1920, the Warsaw Pact treaty, colonial dependencies such as the Belgian Congo and Denmark's Faroe Islands, country population and population density data, and concise descriptions of countries created or reformed following the collapse of the Soviet Union such as Belarus, Moldova, and Slovenia.

European Political Facts belongs in the reference collection of any library maintaining a quality European political and historical collection. One improvement would be to explain the source of the country population data contained in chapter 10. Do these data originate from national censuses or from the *United Nations Demographic*

Yearbook? Users are left to guess. Inclusion of Websites for the countries, institutions, and international organizations profiled would also be an enhancement. These shortcomings aside, this is still an essential addition to academic and most public library reference collections. [R: Choice, Nov 98, p. 500]—**Bert Chapman**

691.   **Encyclopedia of the European Union.** Desmond Dinan, ed. Boulder, Colo., Lynne Rienner, 1998. 565p. index. $110.00. ISBN 1-55587-634-X.

Dinan has edited this useful reference tool covering a myriad of aspects of the European Union—from its origins in 1950 to the present. In treating terms (sometimes arcane), major figures, countries, policy issues, and other organizations, the contributors offer entries ranging from a brief paragraph to several pages. Most of the longer signed pieces include brief bibliographies. Following the alphabetically arranged entries, Dinan has provided a chronology, a list of abbreviations and acronyms, and 12 appendixes, with tables covering treaty issues, summits, and so on. The indexing and cross-references are excellent. This resource is recommended without qualification to those needing information about the European Union, which undoubtedly will increasingly change the world balance of power, both economically and politically.—**Lee Weston**

692.   **The EU Institutions' Register: Répertoire des Institutions Européennes.** 3d ed. Belgium, Euroconfidentiel S. A.; distr., Concord, Mass., Paul & Company Publishers, 1998. 1v. (various paging). $120.00pa. ISBN 2-930066-43-1.

"A direct line to the EU's key decision-makers" is promised in the preface to this directory of personnel in each of the European Union's major institutions. The work begins with a useful overview of the major institutions or agencies of the EU, with brief explanations of principal responsibilities, functions, and activities. The directory itself is subdivided into corresponding sections based on these institutions. The directory systematically works through the labyrinth of the bureaucracy, listing names, titles, major responsibilities, and telephone numbers for each official. Although the coverage of the EU structure is comprehensive, the amount of information on each individual is limited. At the end of each section are a name index and a keyword index, which provides access to the structure by topic. There are some unique features in each section. For example, in the section on the European Parliament, there are lists of members by committee and by political party group. A general index gives consolidated access to all individuals by name and by keyword. This publication is bilingual, in English and French.

This directory will be useful for anyone with a significant interest in identifying or contacting offices or officials. For others, a more general source, such as the *Europa World Year Book* (see entry 66), would probably suffice. This directory would be more useful as an Internet product for reasons identified in the preface: "personnel and responsibilities change constantly, especially with the European Commission."—**Henry E. York**

693.   Watson, William E. **The Collapse of Communism in the Soviet Union.** Westport, Conn., Greenwood Press, 1998. 175p. illus. index. (Greenwood Press Guides to Historic Events of the Twentieth Century). $39.95. ISBN 0-313-30162-X.

This book contains interesting facts about the collapse of Soviet communism, the important historic event of the twentieth century. The author combines narrative description, analysis, biographical profiles, and the text of key documents. The contents of the volume include a foreword by R. M. Miller, a preface, a chronology of events, and a section on the collapse of communism in the Soviet Union. Five essays examine how costly internal and external imperial policies, a poorly functioning economy, and the anti-Mikhail Gorbachev movement among people hastened the end, and how the August 1991 coup attempt sealed the fate of Soviet communism. The documents illustrate the reform attempts by Gorbachev, party opposition to any reforms of the system, the subsequent collapse of the party and the USSR, and the creation of the Commonwealth of Independent States (CIS). Fifteen biographies explain the careers of individuals involved in the decline and fall of Soviet communism; the principal opponents of the reform; the president of Russia, Boris Yeltsin; and the post-Soviet Communist Party leader, Gennady Zyuganov. The primary documents chapter contains the text of 22 documents, including writings by Gorbachev and Yeltsin, the establishment of the Emergency Committee, the Minsk Agreement, and the Statement on Economic Policy of the CIS. This book is important for student research as well as for all journalists and writers who would like to understand the political situation in Russia.—**Ludmila N. Ilyina**

IDEOLOGIES

694.   Blum, George P. **The Rise of Fascism in Europe.** Westport, Conn., Greenwood Press, 1998. 196p. illus. index. (Greenwood Press Guides to Historic Events of the Twentieth Century). $39.95. ISBN 0-313-29934-X.

This volume in Greenwood Press's Guides to Historic Events of the Twentieth Century series examines in a cursory manner the phenomenon of European fascism as it arose between the two world wars. Designed primarily as an introductory source for high school and undergraduate students, it is actually part monograph, part reference work. The monographic section is an 80-page essay attempting to explain the rise of fascism in Europe by examining in outline such topics as the seizure of power in Germany and Italy, economy and society under fascism, the ideology's relationship to the origins of World War II, and domestic resistance movements. Although the author deals briefly with anti-Semitism, Jews, and the "final solution," an extended treatment of fascism and the Holocaust clearly lies outside the scope of his short essay. The reference portion of the volume includes 80 pages of biographies, 45 pages of primary documents, a short glossary of selected terms, a brief chronology, and, possibly the most valuable section, a bibliographical essay. Although certainly a useful beginning point for high school students and possibly college freshmen, the volume serves mainly to invite further study on the part of the reader.

—**Lee Weston**

695.   Docherty, James C. **Historical Dictionary of Socialism.** Lanham, Md., Scarecrow, 1997. (Historical Dictionaries of Religions, Philosophies, and Movements Series). $48.00. ISBN 0-8108-3358-1.

Docherty has produced a useful introductory source that provides information about leading concepts, movements, and figures associated with socialism. As pointed out in the preface, the emphasis is on the political wing of labor and the social democratic movement in Europe, India, Africa, the Middle East, Latin America, Japan, and the United States. Consequently, one will find limited information about communism, as another title devoted to this subject is in preparation for this series. Exceptions are made for such figures as Vladimir Lenin and Karl Marx, but not for Leon Trotsky or Joseph Stalin. The entries are most useful in the case of obscure personalities or documents, such as Jens Krag or the Frankfurt Declaration. Less useful perhaps are the entries on prominent figures, as they are generally much briefer than encyclopedia entries; yet, they do have the virtue of relating their subjects to the broader topic of social democracy.

Cross-references are quite good except in limited cases; for instance, no entry for Werner Sombart appears referring to the entry that appears under the title of his work *Why Is There No Socialism in the United States?* The dictionary also contains a useful introduction providing a conceptual and historical overview, a section on statistics, a bibliography, a chronology, and a glossary of terms. Overall, this is a useful reference tool, placing the key elements of democratic socialism into clear ideological and historical perspective. [R: Choice, Sept 98, p. 96]—**Lee Weston**

INTERNATIONAL ORGANIZATIONS

696.   **International Instruments of the United Nations: A Compilation of Agreements, Charters, Conventions....** Irving Sarnoff, comp. New York, United Nations, 1997. 459p. $30.00pa. ISBN 92-1-100612-0. S/N E.96.I.15.

This compendium contains major instruments adopted by the United Nations General Assembly from its inception in 1945 through 1995. Part 2 is the main body of the work, containing treaties, proclamations, and so on. It occupies 380 double-columned pages in small type, arranged in 9 thematic sections from disarmament to space, mercenaries, and international law. They are not in alphabetic order. There is a lot of history and substance here, including the treaty governing the use of extraterrestrial bodies, the Nuclear Non-Proliferation Treaty, the Universal Declaration of Human Rights, and the Declaration on the Rights of the Child. Texts of more than 100 documents appear.

The introduction; appendixes; and parts 1, 3, and 4 contain materials enhancing the book's potential as a reference. Included are a 5-page discussion of definitions of treaties and agreements in international law, with bibliographic references; an overview (part 1) of the General Assembly, including officers, committee structure, and authority under the charter; the text of the United Nations Charter; the Statute of the International Court of

Justice (ICJ); major United Nations agencies' addresses; listings of major United Nations-sponsored conferences; and diagrammatic outlines of United Nations structure.

This is undoubtedly a useful document for government publications collections. A reservation that should be noted is that a good deal of the material may be duplicated in larger collections. For example, the United Nations yearbook contains the texts of the United Nations Charter and the Statute of the ICJ as well as a wealth of material on United Nations structure. Many large- to medium-sized libraries may own it. Assessing what this work adds to a collection is key. Larger collections that do not contain materials with major overlap for this work should certainly purchase it, funds permitting. [R: Choice, Mar 98, pp. 1172-1173]—**Nigel Tappin**

INTERNATIONAL RELATIONS

697. Bahamonde, Ramón, comp. **International Policy Institutions Around the Pacific Rim: A Directory of Resources in East Asia, Australasia, and the Americas.** Boulder, Colo., Lynne Rienner, 1998. 317p. index. $35.00pa. ISBN 1-55587-795-8.

This book was compiled for the Pacific Council on International Policy, a nonprofit organization founded in cooperation with the Council on Foreign Relations in 1995 for the purpose of helping "leaders from many sectors in the U.S. West . . . to improve their own understanding of key global trends, network more effectively with counterpart institutions, and contribute to illuminating and resolving shared policy concerns" (preface). Some 289 institutions around the Pacific Rim are included in the directory, organized by region and countries into Asia, Australia and New Zealand, Canada, Latin America, and the Western United States. Asia consists of China, Hong Kong, Indonesia, Japan, Malaysia, the Philippines, Singapore, South Korea, Taiwan, Thailand, and Vietnam. The countries of Argentina, Brazil, Chile, Colombia, Ecuador, Mexico, Peru, and Venezuela are included for Latin America. Obvious omissions are North Korea and Panama.

The directory offers concise profiles of institutions. Background and objectives; programs; publications; funding sources, the head of the institutions; the contact officer; and the institution's address, telephone and fax numbers, and e-mail addresses and URLs are given for each institution. The introduction claims that the directory lists nongovernmental organizational resources. In fact, many institutions are governmental as evidenced by their funding sources. The book ends with two indexes: an index by institutions and an index by head of institution. By random check, information in the directory is current and accurate. The compiler has done a remarkable job.

—**Tze-chung Li**

698. Elfstrom, Gerard. **International Ethics: A Reference Handbook.** Santa Barbara, Calif., ABC-CLIO, 1998. 240p. index. (Contemporary Ethical Issues). $40.00. ISBN 0-87436-864-2.

International ethics as a field deals with how people *ought* to treat one another on a global plane stretching across international boundaries. The author, a professor of philosophy at Auburn University, provides in the introduction of *International Ethics* an overview of the historical development of the field and of contemporary issues. There is a basic division among those who feel that international ethics is futile and others who feel that globalization has made all people increasing aware of and interdependent on others they will never know face to face.

With this perspective established, the author examines international ethics with chapters devoted to chronology, biographical sketches, significant documents, a directory of organizations, and a glossary. There is a 30-page bibliography of selected print resources that is annotated but lacking any subject breakdown. There is also a bibliography of nonprint resources, including CD-ROMs and Internet sites. The main body of this book consists of essays of four or five pages dealing with the key issues in international ethics. These issues include questions of global problems (pollution, crime, disease), national sovereignty (immigration, international intervention), trade (free trade, multinationals, exploitation of resources), and the development of international governing bodies. Each essay ends with a bibliography for additional reading.

The most useful parts of this handbook are the opening sections and essays on key topics that provide an introductory framework for anyone approaching international ethics as a novice. Both students and others interested in this topic will find this work a convenient, informative overview of the field. As a reference work, as a directory of biographical or organizational information, or as a bibliography of resources, it is less useful as electronic databases and Web search engines can now offer a wider array of materials that may well be more current and more related to specific research interests. [R: LJ, Aug 98, p. 74; VOYA, Dec 98, p. 388]—**Henry E. York**

699.   Lesch, Ann M., and Dan Tschirgi. **Origins and Development of the Arab-Israeli Conflict.** Westport, Conn., Greenwood Press, 1998. 191p. illus. maps. index. (Greenwood Press Guides to Historic Events of the Twentieth-Century). $39.95. ISBN 0-313-29970-6.

    As part of a series, this book follows a specified format—foreword, preface, chronology, text, biographies, primary documents, glossary of terms, bibliography, and an index. The chronology and the glossary are the most valuable for students. The text, although well organized and written, is too brief—one paragraph covers the seventh century to World War II. The text chapters include a good overview of the Arab-Israeli conflict, a survey of Jewish and Palestinian (Arab) nationalist movements, Zionism and the creation of Israel, the place of the Palestinians in the conflict, the role of the United States, and a concluding chapter. The biographies are those of a few figures central to the drama of the conflict; this list is skimpy on Palestinian names. A more critical gap is evident in the documents section—no documents are mentioned from the period 1937 to 1964, such as the United Nations Partition Plan that calls for a two-state solution, United Nations Resolution 194 relating to the refugees' right to return or receive compensation, and the resolution regarding the status of Jerusalem. Other omissions include United Nations Resolution 338, which reaffirms Resolution 242, and Resolution 425 calling for Israeli withdrawal from Lebanon. The bibliography is divided into categories: Palestinians, Israel and Zionism, Arab states, and the United States and the conflict, as if one could write about any of these topics without touching on the others. Strangely, there seems to be no references to early peace efforts or to joint Palestinian-Israeli publications. Given the well-known expertise of the authors, these omissions can hardly be ignored.—**Elias H. Tuma**

700.   Smith, Dan, with Kristin Ingstad Sandberg, Pavel Baev, and Wenche Hauge. **The State of War and Peace Atlas.** 3d ed. New York, Penguin Books, 1997. 128p. illus. maps. index. $16.95pa. ISBN 0-14-051373-6.

    The State of War and Peace Atlas is a nicely executed graphic guide to the various causes of local, regional, and international armed conflict, including civil wars, terrorism, ethnic violence, and militant faiths. Clear and visually arresting color maps demonstrate the correlations among such factors as poverty, security networks, economic disparities, and refugee populations in understanding where the global flashpoints are or are likely to flare up in the near future. This book is better for depicting relative categories than in presenting hard statistical data or figures in a tabular format. The United Nations and other peacekeeping initiatives are also chronicled with color maps and graphic devices. A "Table of Wars 1990-1995" delineates the type of war, site of conflict, combatants, when the war began, and its current status. Some of the information in *The State of War and Peace Atlas* may be found in the most recent *SIPRI Yearbook* (Taylor & Francis, annual) and the *Military Balance* (International Institute for Strategic Studies, annual), albeit in a generally less bipolar framework of analysis than these two standard reference publications. This is a good and inexpensive work for all public, high school, and academic libraries.—**Stephen W. Green**

PUBLIC POLICY AND ADMINISTRATION

701.   **The Guide to Public Policy Experts, 1997-1998.** Thomas C. Atwood and Thomas Mead, eds. Washington, D.C., Heritage Foundation, 1997. 695p. illus. $16.95pa. ISBN 0-89195-068-0.

    The 1980s and 1990s have seen the growth of numerous conservative and libertarian public policy experts due to the influence of the Reagan and Bush administrations and Republican congressional control since 1995. These experts have served in policy-making positions during the Reagan and Bush eras, congressional offices, and in conservative or libertarian think-tanks such as the Heritage Foundation, the Cato Institute, and the American Enterprise Institute.

    This directory provides listings of conservative/libertarian public policy experts from throughout the United States and selected foreign countries. Specific contents of this guide include alphabetic and subject indexes of these experts, breakdowns of these individuals by state, listings of conservative/libertarian public policy organizations in the United States and Canada, compilations of ideologically allied organizations in foreign countries, and conservative periodicals.

    Entries for individual experts include name, address, institutional affiliation, telephone and fax numbers, e-mail (if available), and areas of expertise. Organizational entries include this same information and Website URL if available. Subject index breakdowns of experts include national security, foreign policy, taxation and budget, environment, education, crime, culture, and others. Specific individuals listed include Jeane Kirkpatrick, Ed Meese, Angelo Codevilla, Grover Norquist, Richard Perle, Milton Friedman, Ralph Reed, Linda Chavez, and Lynne Cheney.

This guide should prove to be a useful reference source for individuals and organizations, such as television stations, wishing to include the views of conservation or libertarian representatives in their activities or programs. It is logically arranged and user-friendly. A future addition the publisher may wish to make in a periodically issued companion volume would be inclusion of biographical information and publications produced by these individuals in print or electronic format. *The Guide to Public Policy Experts* also belongs in the reference collections of academic or other libraries with significant public policy or political science collections.—**Bert Chapman**

702.   **International Encyclopedia of Public Policy and Administration.** Jay M. Shafritz, ed. Boulder, Colo., Westview Press, 1998. 4v. index. $495.00/set. ISBN 0-8133-9973-4 (v.1); 0-8133-9974-2 (v.2); 0-8133-9975-0 (v.3); 0-8133-9976-9 (v.4).

Shafritz has taken on the heroic task of pulling together two fields—public policy and public administration—that generally describe themselves as lacking distinct boundaries. In addition, he and his colleagues have attempted to present an international perspective. To do this, Shafritz and the associate editors and board of editors have asked a large number of authors for contributions, many of which are quite good and some quite illuminating (e.g., essays on Chinese, Indonesian, Latin American, Indian, and Persian administrative traditions). Most topics and issues in U.S. public administration are addressed, with somewhat less coverage in terms of public policy. In short, the volumes generally serve as a useful introduction to most topics, issues, and major events in the field.

Of course in works of this nature, certain shortcomings are inevitable. Most of these have to do with exclusions. Why some public policy or administrative persons are chosen and others excluded is hard to fathom. To include Yehezkel Dror and exclude Harold Lasswell (who is consensually considered to be the "father of the policy sciences") is simply inexcusable. Similarly, why would one have an essay on positivism and none on postpositivism, or include no entry for "democracy"? Many of the essays are more descriptive than critical in nature, thus downplaying some important debates. And, lastly, some of the essays on specific personalities are simply unctuous in tone and fatuous in content.—**Peter de Leon**

703.   **United Nations Directory of Agencies and Institutions in Public Administration and Finance.** New York, United Nations, 1997. 169p. $25.00pa. ISBN 92-1-023066-3. S/N E/F/S.97.II.H.2.

This is a long overdue updated version of a directory last published in 1981. There are brief profiles for administrative agencies in 43 countries. The agencies are assigned to 13 "primary function" categories, such as "National Policy Formation," "Budget and Financial Administration," "Regulatory Administration," and "Institutional Education." For each agency the name, address, telephone number, and fax number are given, along with a short description of the agency's activities. Personal names and e-mail addresses are not included. A detailed outline of the primary function categories is helpful for comparative purposes because similar functions are handled by different agencies in different countries. This directory will be of most use for specialists in international public administration and, therefore, is recommended for university library collections.—**Thomas A. Karel**

Psychology and Parapsychology

PSYCHOLOGY

Dictionaries and Encyclopedias

704. **Encyclopedia of Mental Health.** Howard S. Friedman, ed. San Diego, Calif., Academic Press, 1998. 3v. illus. index. $500.00/set. ISBN 0-12-226675-7.

The concept of mental health has changed a great deal. Current research demonstrates the intricate relationship of the mind and body. Biochemical imbalances play significant roles in schizophrenia and various mood disorders. Ordinary activities such as commuting and using a computer affect behavior. This new encyclopedia examines mental health using an interdisciplinary approach. It emphasizes health by looking at ways to promote wellness and prevent mental illness.

The encyclopedia editor and contributors are academics who are acknowledged experts in their fields. Their names and affiliations appear at the beginning of each article. Most of the material here is new, but some entries are reprinted from the *Encyclopedia of Human Behavior* (see ARBA 95, entry 778). This is noted at the end of the article. The 3 volumes contain alphabetically arranged articles that are 10 to 20 pages long. Each article begins with an outline and a glossary defining terms as they are used specifically within the context of that article. All articles have bibliographies. Each volume contains the table of contents for the entire set and instructions for using the encyclopedia. There is a detailed index in volume 3. Using the index ensures finding all relevant material on a given subject area because the articles cover broad topics. Cross-references also direct users to related material.

The articles cover a wide range of subjects: adolescence, commuting and mental health, human-computer interaction, mental hospitals and deinstitutionalization, brain scanning and neuroimaging, and psychopharmacology. Specific conditions and therapies are covered as well, including Alzheimer's disease, mood disorders, behavior therapy, and family therapy. A search for information about recovered memory turned up nothing in the table of contents. There is no specific index entry either. Bits and pieces show up under dissociative disorders, hypnosis, and child sexual abuse, but there is no article on this controversial topic.

This is, however, a fine encyclopedia with a great deal of excellent information on subjects of interest to both professional and educated lay readers. Academic, health science, and large public libraries will find it useful. [R: Choice, Sept 98, p. 92]—**Barbara M. Bibel**

705. Kahn, Ada P. **Stress A-Z: A Sourcebook for Facing Everyday Challenges.** New York, Facts on File, 1998. 390p. index. $40.00. ISBN 0-8160-3295-5.

Kahn has assembled what she considers to be the 500 most common stress producers in today's society. The listings range from life-changing events (e.g., death, chronic disease) to societal conditions (e.g., crowding, crime) to annoyances (e.g., telemarketers). Also included are terms related to the relief of stress, names of people in the field, and field-related terminology. Entries on the causes of stress detail how they affect health and methods that can be employed in coping with or relieving their impact. Many include one or more references to other sources or to related organizations, and there is an abundance of cross-references. The length of the entries ranges from a few sentences to several pages. A 14-page bibliography of sources, arranged by subject, concludes the volume.

As a selective list of topics and terms related to stress, this dictionary does a good job of providing a basic overview of each and of giving sources for further study and information. The addition of Websites would add to its value. It should prove to be a useful addition to many libraries. [R: LJ, 15 Oct 98, p. 62; BL, 15 Dec 98, p. 766]

—Jo Anne H. Ricca

706.   **Psychology Basics.** Frank N. Magill, ed. Pasadena, Calif., Salem Press, 1998. 2v. index. $118.75. ISBN 0-89356-963-1.

This 2-volume set of *Psychology Basics* breaks all the rules for an introductory text. It has no color photographs, self-tests, graphs, exercises, or questions for discussion. With all these exceptions to the norm, one might wonder if these books are something that all college libraries need. The answer is a definite yes. *Psychology Basics* contains the information undergraduates need for their term papers or to delve deeper into a favorite subject. The editor came up with the right format for each article and kept a tight rein on the 90 contributors. Each 6-page article contains sections that review, apply, and show the larger context of 101 important psychological topics and 9 theorists. A short annotated bibliography follows each article, and every confusing term is defined at the outset and in the glossary. There are, however, some problems. The contributors, who are excellent teachers giving their favorite lectures, cite classic studies and leading theorists, but, with annoying regularity, do not cite any of the original works. Contributors also have a variety of interpretations as to applications or the larger context. Some nail the distinctions; others think they are being asked for an advanced overview. Writing styles vary, but most articles are clearly written and interesting. Some names like Robert Zajonc and terms like *dementia praecox* cry out for a pronunciation guide. This 2-volume set is highly recommended. [R: BL, 1 June 98, p. 1816]

—Pete Prunkl

Handbooks and Yearbooks

707.   **The Handbook of Child Psychology.** 5th ed. William Damon, ed. New York, John Wiley, 1998. 4v. index. $150.00/vol. ISBN 0-471-17893-4.

Now in its 5th edition, this handbook should still be considered a standard reference work in the field of developmental psychology. It reflects previously established scholarly traditions of utilizing editors who are renowned in their areas of expertise. It has evolved into a useful tool for undergraduates, graduates, practitioners, and researchers, and provides authoritative coverage and in-depth analysis of both theoretical and practical topics. Significantly expanded from the 4th edition, there are now contributions from 112 authors, most of whom are professors at institutions of higher education around the world. The scope of the work continues to be comprehensive, with concepts and practices having significance for students and practitioners also in such areas as education, psychiatry, sociology, pediatrics, history, medicine, and anthropology.

Comprising 4 volumes, the handbook documents the current status and future trends in the understanding of developmental psychology. Volume 1 is devoted to "Theoretical Models of Human Development," documenting the growth of developmental psychology into an interdisciplinary science; volume 2 details the current understanding of cognitive development, its history, and predictions of future directions in cognition, perception, and language; volume 3 provides state-of-the-art reviews of ongoing work dealing with social, emotional, and personality development issues; and volume 4 covers "Child Psychology in Practice," providing concrete examples for analysis.

A detailed table of contents at the beginning of each volume and an additional breakdown of subject matter in the beginning of each chapter provides an excellent topical approach. Chapters conclude with extensive scholarly references, supplying additional avenues for research. All volumes have both author and subject indexes listed in the back, providing easy access to data. This set is suitable for all academic libraries and special libraries with an interest in this area.—**Marianne B. Eimer**

PARAPSYCHOLOGY

708.   Bjorling, Joel. **Consulting Spirits: A Bibliography.** Westport, Conn., Greenwood Press, 1998. 213p. index. (Bibliographies and Indexes in Religious Studies, no.46). $65.00. ISBN 0-313-30284-7.

Can a book that discusses spirit contact through Ouija boards, angels, and psychics earn a place in an academic library? Because the author approaches the subject as an interested observer who has sifted through the academic, scientific, and phenomenological literature on the role of spirits in culture and society without trying to prove or disprove anything, the answer is yes. This book contains information on topics, issues, and controversies few studied in high school and none in Sunday school. Be warned, however, that curious students will find this a treasure chest of fascinating topics and will pester librarians for some of its more obscure source material.

Each of Bjorling's 8 chapters contains an average of 5 pages of text, footnotes concerning references used in the text, and a guide to references. The recommended reading and brief annotations of selected works and a list of references organized by topic are taken from material published between 1856 and 1995.

Among the book's few disadvantages is the lack of a subject index. A 17-page author index does not make up for this omission. There is a subject index of sorts, using Bjorling's major topics and the number of references devoted to each of them.

The longest list of references (359 pages) concerns psychical research, with spiritualism in America coming in a distant second (149). Other subjects with more than 100 references are beliefs (125), voodoo (136), spiritualism in England and Europe (110), and Christian critiques (115). References to the Ouija board are the book's fewest. Other relatively short-listed topics are psychic detectives (20), spiritualism in Latin America (20), Santeria (15), and electronic voice phenomena (19). Other topics include oracles, poltergeists, spirit contact in China, philosophical and skeptical critiques, channeling, angels, and a listing of popular works on spirits.

Nothing is made known of the occupation or academic background of the author. This book and sites on the Internet give only a listing of his other books and this brief description: "Joel Bjorling is a specialist in the field of new and alternative religions." [R: Choice, Oct 98, p. 288]—**Pete Prunkl**

709.   Devereux, Paul, and Peter Brookesmith. **UFOs and Ufology: The First 50 Years.** New York, Facts on File, 1997. 192p. illus. index. $29.95. ISBN 0-8160-3800-7.

The authors of this work are British UFO researchers who define their chosen field of study as "an encounter with ourselves." They have written an entirely unusual, insightful, and refreshing book.

UFOs and Ufology explores all the famous UFO events and discoveries of the past 50 years—abductions, crop circles, Marfa lights, and others. After a well-written, engaging report of the event, the authors provide their interpretation. Often using a psychosocial methodology more common in Europe than here, they first analyze those who report or experience UFO sightings, abductions, or alien encounters. Devereux and Brookesmith argue convincingly that UFO truths are more often "in here" than "out there." Environmental, cultural, and religious factors are then added to the mix. Their analyses reduce breathless, emotional, and challenging accounts to projections, lucid dreams, reenactments of religious myths, atmospheric conditions, drugs, hoaxes, or some other logical or psychological explanation.

Devereux and Brookesmith are ufologists. This broad group includes enthusiasts, believers, skeptics, researchers, and those who accept or reject the hypothesis that sightings and abductions are evidence for extraterrestrials.

This slim book is produced in an appealing 9-by-11-inch format with color photographs and fascinating sidebars. It belongs in every public and high school library in the country. Students who use *UFOs and Ufology* for their term papers and reports will come to college ready to appreciate the value of studying psychology, theology, and sociology. This source is highly recommended. [R: SLJ, Dec 98, p. 148]—**Pete Prunkl**

15 Recreation and Sports

GENERAL WORKS

Biography

710.   Woolum, Janet. **Outstanding Women Athletes: Who They Are and How They Influenced Sports in America.** 2d ed. Phoenix, Ariz., Oryx Press, 1998. 412p. illus. index. $49.95. ISBN 1-57356-120-7.

    In this 2d edition, Woolum has revised and expanded several sections, including the chapter that provides an overview of the history and development of women's sports. Unfortunately, there is no discussion of issues concerning minorities other than African American and disabled athletes in this section. The largest section of the book is the biographical section. More than 20 additional entries, including a boxer and a bullfighter, have been included in this edition. There are bibliographies for some of the individuals, but all titles listed are books. A new chapter concentrates on selected teams in selected sports that have received national recognition. Each entry has information on the history of the team, a list of achievements, and a brief biography of members of the team. It is puzzling why other teams were excluded that deserve mentioning, such as the 1984 women's volleyball team and the 1998 women's ice hockey team. There is no discussion on issues in women's team sports, including the changes in the training venues for the national teams or the advent of professional teams. The selected bibliography contains book titles and is sport-specific.

    One problem that could have been discussed is the issue of locating information on women athletes and women's sports and additional resources that could be checked because identifying information on outstanding athletes is not always an easy task. The national organizations only include addresses; many have Websites that could have been included. At a time when several reference sources on women athletes and their sports are prevalent, *Outstanding Women Athletes* updates the previous edition and complements *Encyclopedia of Women and Sports* (see ARBA 97, entry 644) and *Encyclopedia of Women and Sports in America* (Oryx Press, 1998). The title at hand is recommended for libraries with the earlier edition and public, school, and academic libraries. [R: SLJ, Nov 98, p. 159]—**Mila C. Su**

Dictionaries and Encyclopedias

711.   **Sports in North America: A Documentary History. Volume 1, Parts 1 and 2.** Thomas L. Altherr, ed. Gulf Breeze, Fla., Academic International Press, 1997. 2v. index. $97.00/set. ISBN 0-87569-188-9.

    Academic International Press is a well-established publisher of reference works and collections of historical documents. In the most recently published volume (2 volumes bound as 1) on sports in North America, the colonial period, the American Revolution, and new republic are covered in more than 1,700 documents. Following a brief introduction, documents range from a few lines to several pages and include coverage of a broad range of sports. Not to be confused with the modern era of sports, the sporting events from the eighteenth century through 1820 include shooting, cock fighting, gouging, fencing, fishing and hunting, and even a few Native American sports. The documents themselves are from newspapers, magazines, travel accounts, children's books, published diaries, ordinances, legal compendiums, memoirs, and other relevant sources. Many documents are interesting and represent a unique reflection on sports and competitive events from U.S. history. Indexes by subject, names, and place-names, as well as a brief bibliography, conclude each volume.

"SportsDocs," as the series of 6 volumes is called, spans the years to 1920 (see ARBA 97, entry 642, and ARBA 94, entry 826 for reviews of previous volumes). Two more volumes covering the 1930s and 1940s are planned, and the entire set will include 10 to 12 volumes when complete. Once completed, the publisher should seriously consider a comprehensive guide and index. Despite several minor typographical errors characteristic of Academic International Press reference series, SportsDocs holds significant potential to fill a void in documenting the history of sports and its relationship to U.S. society. [R: Choice, July/Aug 98, p. 1890]—**Boyd Childress**

Directories

712.   **Sports Phone Book USA, 1998: A National Directory of Professional, Intercollegiate, and Amateur Sports.** Darren L. Smith, ed. Detroit, Omnigraphics, 1998. 535p. index. $65.00pa. ISBN 0-7808-0191-1.

This resource serves multiple purposes as a directory for professional, intercollegiate, amateur, and recreational sports. The focus is predominantly on U.S. organizations, but some Canadian organizations are included. The directory is divided into 2 sections, alphabetic and classified. Each entry includes the name of the organization, institution, team, or league; mailing address, telephone number, fax number, and when available the e-mail address and toll-free telephone number. No additional information such as descriptions of the organization or a list of key personnel are included. Information is noted on various sport facilities, including museums and halls of fame, publications, sports media (e.g., television, cable, radio), and sporting goods' services. College information includes institutions in all three divisions of the NCAA, NAIA, NJCAA, and a selection of conferences. The amount of coverage for the groupings of high school and community associations; Olympic organizations; sport governing bodies; women, youth, and the disabled; and list of disabled organizations ranges from good to fairly extensive. The senior category (a new avenue of sport for the "older" generation) is very short and could be expanded by including the growing number of "masters" sports. Perhaps someday the gay games and related organizations can be included. The index refers only to the listing in the classified section. This resource is similar but not as detailed as Gale's *Sport Fan Connection* (see ARBA 93, entry 822) and *Sports Marketplace* (see ARBA 88, entry 794) and complements much of the information found on SPORTquest's Website at http://www.sportsquest.com. For a resource that will provide quick access to most queries, this directory serves its purpose and is recommended for academic and public libraries. [R: Choice, Nov 98, p. 503]—**Mila C. Su**

Handbooks and Yearbooks

713.   **The Book of Rules: A Visual Guide to the Laws of Every Commonly Played Sport and Game.** New York, Checkmark Books/Facts on File, 1998. 224p. illus. index. $24.95. ISBN 0-8160-3919-4.

To borrow an old quote, if you want to play the game, you have to know the rules. In this reasonably priced, highly illustrated volume covering 30 individual games (or sports), playing rules are outlined and, in some instances, detailed. Subjects range from common sports, such as baseball, basketball, and football, to more specialized games like rounders and petanque. Generally, the rules are clearly written, and the diagrams and illustrations provided are useful. For several of the games, basic skills and tactics are listed as well as "gray areas," or controversial rules often left open to interpretation by officials. Coverage runs from 3 to 4 pages (e.g., lacrosse, netball) to 12 to 15 pages (e.g., football, track and field). Overall, the book includes reference to most of the basic rules, but for the advanced student of the game(s), there are concerns. The rules cited are for professional sports, such as basketball and football. An example is the rule for the held ball (or simultaneous possession) in basketball—the book cites the professional rule. Yet, the closely guarded rule (5 second count) is for the college game. For football, there is no distinction between the college and professional rules regarding hash marks and the placement of the ball. These trouble spots detract from the volume, and book selectors should be warned. Ironically, the book's cover includes a picture of Dennis Rodman, one of sport's greatest examples of why there is a need for rules.

—**Boyd Childress**

714.   Thompson, William N. **Legalized Gambling: A Reference Handbook.** 2d ed. Santa Barbara, Calif., ABC-CLIO, 1997. 298p. index. (Contemporary World Issues). $39.50. ISBN 0-87436-947-9.

Like other books in the Contemporary World Issues series, this book addresses the contemporary societal issues in an authoritative and objective manner. The 1st edition of this book was published 3 years earlier (see ARBA 95, entry 803). Most of the materials presented in this 2d edition build upon the 1st edition. Many additions reflect the dynamic gambling industry and dynamic political issues. Because the political boundaries do not stop the impact of gambling, the author added the study on legalized gambling in Canada in this edition. The format of the 1st edition is continued in the 2d edition. The book begins with a chapter that gives a historical perspective on the gambling industry. Great emphasis is placed on the political issues and governmental controls. The first chapter also attempts to address the questions of why people gamble and what the pros and cons are for legalized gambling.

The chronology in the 2d chapter covers gambling events in North America since 1612. It is noteworthy that in 1776, Thomas Jefferson gambled as he composed the Declaration of Independence. The Gambling Hall of Fame includes some colorful personalities, such as Donald Trump and Rudolph W. Wanderone, also known as Minnesota Fats. It is also interesting to read that the 1871 Chicago fire was started by a dice-throwing hand that accidentally upset a lantern.

The legislation and statistics give reference to much valuable information about the gambling industry. The author selected numerous representative statutes and cases to illustrate the major policy developments in the gaming field. The section titled "Points of View" records the statements and opinions expressed by legislators, politicians, and gamblers such as Pete Rose.

The last two chapters are graced with rich and relevant resources. Chapter 6 provides selected print resources that include books, periodicals, Websites, and online newspapers. The nonprint resources listed in chapter 7 include information about the video recordings and their distributors. All resources are annotated.

Readers interested in studying the gambling industry and its impact on society will be richly awarded by the information in this book. This resource is highly recommended for academic and public libraries.

—**Eveline L. Yang**

BASEBALL

715.   **Bill James Presents . . . STATS All-Time Major League Handbook.** Bill James, John Dewan, Neil Munro, and Don Zminda, eds. Skokie, Ill., STATS Publishing, 1998. 2696p. $54.95. ISBN 1-884064-52-3.

One's attitude toward this volume may hinge on the reader's opinion of Bill James. To some, his compilation in recent years of a whole new set of baseball data is long overdue and nothing less than magisterial; to others, he is seen as an over zealous number cruncher constantly adding to a sport's statistics that already border on mad excess. This hefty new entry from the James organization weighs in at about 7 pounds, and totals nearly 2,700 pages. On one hand, it presents more individual player regular season statistics from the earliest era to the present (1876-1997) than any previous source. On the other hand, many will see some of the statistics as of dubious value, whereas other information included in one or both of the leading related sources, such as year-by-year team rosters and lineups, post-season play statistics and scores, and lists of season and all-time leaders in various categories, are not to be found in this volume. Moreover, as James himself admits in his introduction, many will find they need a magnifying glass as standard equipment when using it. Given what is omitted, the reason for the large book and small print can largely be attributed to statistics James wants to include that have previously been neglected. For instance, the entry for Moe Drabowsky, a journeyman hurler whose career spanned 17 seasons in the bigs, covers one-fifth of a page in *Total Baseball* (see ARBA 98, entry 737) and one-fourth of a page in *The Baseball Encyclopedia* (9th ed.; see ARBA 94, entry 830), while it takes up two-thirds of a page in this source. This enables James to show a pitcher's complete batting statistics. We may then learn that Moe hit 3 doubles in 1963 and 10 over his entire career. This is also done for fielding averages for all the positions played by a player for any given year. Thus we discover that Mickey Mantle committed two errors in the one game he played at third base in 1952.

James also introduces newly created statistics that are explained at some length in a preface and a statistical methods appendix. One of the new measures is runs created by hitters per season. This figure is then used to determine the number of runs per game a team would score if all their hitters were as productive as the player in question. A league average is shown in the next column. Curiously, these runs-created statistics are also compiled for pitchers where the numbers are often so small that they most likely do not produce statistically significant results. Another new statistic provided is "Component ERA," which factors in more data than the ERAs which, of course, are also included in the pitcher entries. Lists of season and all-time leaders in these unique categories would have proved interesting. Instead the reader is forced to discover the league leader through a bold typeface entry, as is the case for all other categories. For many fans this source will prove fascinating and indispensable, but libraries will have to judge for themselves their particular need for this exhaustively researched yet overindulgent work.

—**Lee Weston**

716.   McNeil, William F. **The Dodgers Encyclopedia.** Champaign, Ill., Sagamore, 1997. 464p. illus. $39.95. ISBN 1-57167-154-4.

This work is more a narrative history of the Dodgers than an encyclopedia. It begins with an overview of Dodger history, followed by a chapter of selected player biographies that are heavy on superlatives and relatively light on facts. A chapter on famous Dodger managers includes only 4 of the 22 men who have managed the Dodgers—among the missing is Chuck Dressen, who won pennants in two of his three seasons as Dodger manager. Other chapters contain narrative descriptions of World Series, pennant races and playoffs, and no-hitters—all, unfortunately, lacking in statistics. Appended statistics and records are in a difficult-to-follow format and are decidedly minor league when compared to *The Baseball Encyclopedia* (see ARBA 96, entry 803), which is still the best source of factual information on Major League Baseball. There are also chapters on executives, sportscasters, and ballparks. A bibliography is included.

The Dodger Encyclopedia is too selective to serve as a reference book, and with its often ill-chosen and poorly reproduced black-and-white photographs, it will not even be useful as a coffee-table book. Die-hard Dodger fans, however, will enjoy the lengthy anecdotal chapter of "memories through the years."—**Gari-Anne Patzwald**

717.   Smith, Myron J., Jr., comp. **Baseball: A Comprehensive Bibliography. Supplement 2 (1992 Through 1997).** Jefferson, N.C., McFarland, 1998. 310p. index. $59.50. ISBN 0-7864-0531-7.

The second supplement to *Baseball: A Comprehensive Bibliography* is meticulous and thorough. After an impressive list of journals consulted (not just the expected sports magazines), each self-explanatory chapter title is followed by more detailed information of what can be found in that section, as well as cross-referencing suggestions. Also included are Websites, with the caveat that such information can move or change quickly. Not all sites are listed, but the compiler makes a point of including those of general interest that can be used to access more specific information. Website names are boldfaced in the text for easy identification.

This bibliography is devoted strictly to nonfiction. As the compiler points out, there are many bibliographies on baseball in fiction, and the enormous number of subjects included in this book make the exclusion of fiction understandable: labor strikes and player statistics, Websites, collectibles, mascots, trivia, legend and lore, baseball as business, and baseball as history—almost all compiled without help from Major League Baseball or the Hall of Fame in Cooperstown. There is one small complaint: The biography section really needs birth dates (and death dates, if the subject has died) for each entry to prevent confusion. Otherwise, this is a wonderful cross-referencing tool that is recommended for any baseball collection.—**R. S. Lehmann**

718.   *The Sporting News* **Complete Baseball Record Book.** 1997 ed. Craig Carter, ed. St. Louis, Mo., Sporting News Publishing, 1997. 542p. index. $17.95pa. ISBN 0-89204-573-6.

Just as yesterday's sports records have yielded over time to even greater athletic feats, so it is that the latest volume of this annual series has demonstrably outpaced its predecessors' efforts (see ARBA 94, entry 838). Capably edited again by Carter, this compendium brims with Major League Baseball superlatives that range from hitting and pitching accomplishments, to player longevity with one team, to team winning streaks, to highwater attendance marks. As in previous editions, records are included for the National League, American League, American Association, Union Association, and Players League.

Several statistical categories have been introduced with this year's compilation. Under the "General Reference" part of this work's "Regular Season" section, the solitary table listing players who through their careers have garnered at least 800 extra-base ("long") hits has been supplemented by a table that provides data on players who have had at least 100 such hits within one season. Also gracing this handbook for the first time is a table detailing each occasion when a player has hit for the cycle. New with this edition as well are lists of all teams that have won or lost the first eight games of a season.

Enhanced ease of use of this volume has been achieved by the increased and judicious use of bold typeface and gray header bars. With its price holding firm to the price of the previous year's edition, this remains an indispensable trove of baseball facts that belongs in most collections.—**Jeffrey E. Long**

719.   *The Sporting News* **Selects Baseball's Greatest Players: A Celebration of the 20th Century's Best.** By Ron Smith. St. Louis, Mo., Sporting News Publishing, 1998. 224p. illus. $29.95. ISBN 0-89204-608-2.

This work appears to be more of a coffee-table book than a true reference work. Because *The Sporting News* was once *the* only baseball authority and has been in publication for more than 100 years, the photographs accompanying the 100 short biographic sketches are wonderful.

However, the depth of information here is shallow indeed. A reader longs for more information on Babe Ruth's excesses (Ruth was voted number 1) and Ty Cobb's many demons (voted number 3), or the appalling racism and threats that accompanied Hank Aaron's (voted number 5) breaking of Babe Ruth's home run record. A trivia quiz and top 10 lists by current and former baseball people accompany the text. What the book does very well is create discussion. In their top 100, *The Sporting News* has included Negro League players, but also Shoeless Joe Jackson and Pete Rose. Eyebrows will rise because neither Mickey Mantle nor Joe DiMaggio is in the top 10 (Mantle is number 17 and DiMaggio is number 11).

This book will be wonderful for a large library or one with younger readers, such as a junior high school library. Otherwise, a more in-depth reference work is recommended.—**R. S. Lehmann**

720.   **STATS Minor League Handbook 1998.** Skokie, Ill., STATS Publishing, 1997. 382p. $19.95pa. ISBN 1-884064-43-4.

The largest part of this companion to the *STATS Major League Handbook* (STATS Publishing, 1997) is the listing of career statistics for every player at the AA or AAA level in 1997 (except for those who also played in the majors in 1997). Pre-1997 major league statistics, if any, are also provided. The statistics for pitchers are broken down into "How Much He Pitched," "What He Gave Up," and "The Results." For other players, batting and baserunning numbers are included. Class A and rookie league players are listed separately, and only their 1997 statistics are provided in a single line. Other features of this handbook are team statistics by league, combined AA and AAA batting and pitching leaders (highest batting average by 24 points was Mike Kinkade's .385 for AA El Paso), 1997 park data (how well the home team versus the visitors performed at each park), "Triple-A Splits" (comparisons of batters' and pitchers' statistics versus left-handed and right-handed opponents, as well as at home and on the road), and "1997 Major League Equivalencies" (in which, through an elaborate series of calculations, a AA or AAA hitter's numbers are translated into major league numbers). Although this last section seems a trifle fanciful, this book clearly goes well beyond the presentation of basic facts and should appeal to serious minor league, as well as major league, baseball fans and researchers.—**Jack Ray**

721.   **STATS Player Profiles 1998.** Skokie, Ill., STATS Publishing, 1997. 557p. $19.95pa. ISBN 1-884064-44-2.

Most good reference collections will offer interested researchers at least two sources in which to learn the names of pitchers that Tony Gwynn, for instance, hits best and is least successful against. *STATS Player Profiles 1998* goes much further into the statistical details of each major leaguer's performance than that. Those interested in baseball statistics are used to hearing how a given hitter performed against right-handed pitchers versus left-handed pitchers, and some sources list the difference in performances on grass versus artificial turf, or in day games versus night games. *STATS Player Profiles 1998* includes these categories and many, many more.

The 1997 pitching and hitting performance statistics are broken down into at least 30 different categories for most players. In addition, for players with sufficient longevity in the major leagues, this volume lists the same information for the past five years. Finally, tables listing the top 10 performers in 1997 in each of the many categories are included, along with tables for 5-year batting and pitching leaders. This is a complete, valuable addition to the baseball reference shelf.—**David A. Doman**

722.   Sullivan, Dean A., comp. **Middle Innings: A Documentary History of Baseball, 1900-1948.** Lincoln, Nebr., University of Nebraska Press, 1998. 238p. illus. index. $45.00. ISBN 0-8032-4258-1.

Middle Innings: A Documentary History of Baseball, 1900-1948 uses periodical articles to give a flavor of the era. And what an era it was. Its greatest influences were the two world wars, Babe Ruth, and the ongoing battle between players and management over wages and working conditions (specifically the reserve clause), which led to the Federal League and baseball's antitrust exemption, the Black Sox scandal, the installation of a commissioner, and eventually to the current labor-management standoff.

The greatest names in sports writing, such as Grantland Rice and Ring Lardner, wrote in this era, but Sullivan does not quote just from them. One wishes he prefaced every article with the writer's name, no matter how obscure, especially article number 58, which contains language that today is considered deeply racist. Reading this, in the florid prose of the early twentieth century, makes the reader realize how far baseball and people have come. It is fitting that the book ends with Jackie Robinson's debut in the majors. It was truly the end of an era.

Robinson's entry into baseball was paved by World War II, when blacks and whites shared the trenches and broke down racial barriers. If the book has any weakness, it is a lack of articles on baseball in wartime, for both world wars, and not having at least one view of Lou Gehrig's famous retirement speech at Yankee Stadium. The book succeeds as a quick overview of a remarkable time and is recommended as an introduction or supplement to the books listed in its bibliography.—**R. S. Lehmann**

723.   *USA Today* **Baseball Weekly Almanac, 1997.** Paul White, ed. New York, Henry Holt, 1997. 400p. illus. $12.95pa. ISBN 0-8050-5147-3. ISSN 1091-7071.

USA Today launched *Baseball Weekly* in 1991 to compete with the highly successful baseball coverage of *The Sporting News*. Following on the success of *Baseball Weekly* (with a circulation of 280,000), the *Baseball Weekly Almanac* was first published in 1992, once again rivaling *The Sporting News Almanac* (ARBA 98, entry 736). Both are pages of team and individual player statistics as well as attractive compilations for the fan, broadcaster, sportswriter, and library requiring coverage for America's national pastime. *Baseball Weekly Almanac* is more than 400 pages, with the majority of the publication focusing on the major leagues. The arrangement includes a summary of the 1996 season (the 1997 almanac was provided for review), team-by-team (American, then National Leagues) season reviews and statistics, and all-time team pitching and batting records (no fielding records are provided). Individual player records for the past season conclude major league coverage. A minor league section follows with excellent Class AAA and AA player statistics. Class A and rookie league coverage is limited to a brief season review and league directory. Another all-too-brief section on college, high school, Olympic, and youth league baseball is disappointing. As with most sports record books, there is no index.

Devoted fans will stay with *The Sporting News* annual, but *Baseball Weekly* and the almanac are reliable, accurate sources of information. Libraries will find it more difficult to decide between the two. For even more comprehensive coverage (at a considerably more expensive price), try *The Baseball Encyclopedia* (see ARBA 94, entry 830) and *The Baseball Encyclopedia Update* (see ARBA 96, entry 803).—**Boyd Childress**

724.   Wright, Marshall D. **The International League: Year-by-Year Statistics, 1884-1953.** Jefferson, N.C., McFarland, 1997. 494p. $45.00. ISBN 0-7864-0458-2.

The International League, one of baseball's top minor leagues, has been going strong since its beginnings as the Eastern League in 1884. Wright chooses to end this chronicle with the 1953 season, since in 1954 a league franchise (the Baltimore Orioles) was for the first time completely displaced to make way for a major league franchise (the St. Louis Browns). Nevertheless, there is no logical reason for ending the league's history at that point, and it is hoped that a volume covering the 45 seasons that have elapsed since 1953 will some day appear. The organization of this book is identical to that of Wright's history of the American Association (see ARBA 98, entry 738). The one-page season overviews focus on a salient feature of the year: outstanding players, such as Rip Collins (1930), Lefty Grove (1923), and Urban Shocker (1916); dominating teams, such as the Rochester Red Wings (1931) and Newark Bears (1937); and noteworthy events or performances, such as Jackie Robinson's breaking the color line with the 1946 Montreal Royals, and Alfred Todd, age 43, catching 104 games for the war-torn 1945 Royals.

The backbone of this book, however, is the annual player and team statistics, which Wright has painstakingly compiled with the assistance of a number of other intrepid baseball researchers. This is not an easy task, because minor league records are scattered among numerous primary sources and in some cases are missing altogether.

International League cities will have a particular interest in acquiring this book, but all libraries with serious coverage of baseball history will want it as well.—**Jack Ray**

BASKETBALL

725. Official Rules of the National Basketball Association 1997-98. 1997-98 ed. St. Louis, Mo., Sporting News Publishing, 1997. 57p. illus. $6.95pa. ISBN 0-89204-586-8.

Understanding the complications of something as arcane as the National Basketball Association's official rules, including, in particular, the one describing an illegal defense, is not always simple. Unfortunately, even the most seasoned announcers do not explain the ins-and-outs of those rules, and even the most experienced television fan does not always fully understand them. Having a printed copy of those rules in a compact and inexpensive format is essential to a full understanding of the game. Having the current annual official rules is important because there are typically important changes each year. This small paperback edition of the rules published by the *Sporting News* is the best ready source of information on those rules. It provides just the rules—no commentary or explanation—along with a detailed index. Although this is an essential tool for announcers, commentators, sportswriters, and ardent fans, most libraries are likely to find this an extraneous purchase. The number of users who will turn to their local library for an understanding of this year's change in the rules governing a time-out when a player is going out of bounds is likely to be minuscule. In any case, although it is inexpensive, the size and format of this pamphlet make it an easy target for illegal removal from the library. There is nothing in the NBA's official rules governing that circumstance.—**Norman D. Stevens**

726. Sachare, Alex. The Chicago Bulls Encyclopedia. Chicago, Contemporary Books, 1998. 308p. illus. index. $39.95. ISBN 0-8092-2804-1.

There used to be a time when the Chicago Bulls were synonymous with mediocrity and early playoff losses. The rise of the new National Basketball Association (thanks in part to Larry Bird, Magic Johnson, and especially Michael Jordan) brought this to an end. The Bulls are the dominant professional basketball team of the 1990s, and perhaps the greatest ever. No athlete is more well known than Jordan. His continued success has, until the recent lockout by the owners, assured the NBA and Chicago Bull's fans of continued good times.

This book chronicles this success well. The pre-Jordan era, 1966 to 1984, is covered in a scant 32 pages. Lacking a championship or player of legendary caliber, the team in that period was a series of lost prospects (Robert Parish was drafted by the Bulls) and dashed hopes.

The rest of the book's chapters cover the various rivalries, coaches, owners, and other players who have been part of the Bull's story. The final chapter asks the inevitable question about their place in history among the great teams. It is an interesting debate, but ultimately comes down to opinions about what factors are most important in assessing greatness. An appendix containing a player register and team records round out what will surely be a must-have for Bulls fans.

The many pictures of Jordan will guarantee this book's popularity. This book is appropriate for public as well as school libraries.—**Bob Craigmile**

727. Standard Catalog of Basketball Cards, 1998. By Editors of Sports Collectors Digest. Iola, Wis., Krause Publications, 1997. 286p. illus. $19.95pa. ISBN 0-87341-551-5.

Sports card collecting is one of the most popular hobbies of the 1980s and 1990s. Although catalogs of baseball and football cards have been published for several years, the *Standard Catalog of Basketball Cards, 1998* is the initial offering for that sport.

As the editors note, "the most important feature in identifying, and pricing, a sports card is its set of origin." Entries in the book are alphabetic by the name of the set, then put in chronological order by year. Within each set players are identified by number and alphabetically by last name in unnumbered sets.

A black-and-white picture of a representative card from most sets appears in the listings to help users identify the cards. Entries for each set include a generic description of the cards, the number of cards in the set (not the quantity printed), and whether the cards were distributed as inserts or a series. The book provides prices for mint condition complete sets and for each player's card.

Helpful elements in the front matter include how cards are graded and information on errors and variations and counterfeits and reprints. A description of card producers offers a brief history of the hobby. There are entries for international sets, other professional leagues (notably the Continental Basketball Association and early women's leagues), high school, and college teams.

As with any catalog, the *Standard Catalog of Basketball Cards* should be supplemented by one of the periodicals devoted to the hobby for current price information. The editors intend to update the publication annually. At its modest price the book will be useful in public and school libraries.—**Sue Kamm**

728.   **STATS Pro Basketball Handbook 1997-1998.** Skokie, Ill., STATS Publishing, 1997. 424p. $19.95pa. ISBN 1-884064-39-6.

For years, *The Sporting News* has provided the most comprehensive register of National Basketball Association (NBA) team and player statistics (see ARBA 98, entries 741-742; see ARBA 95, entries 809-810). These have been considered the standard source for more than 15 years. STATS Publishing is now considered a significant competitor with greater potential for player and team information. The volume has three major sections—a player register, player profiles, and team statistics. The register includes players career numbers and vital statistics (position, college, height, weight, and others) for all 1996-1997 active players. The profile section provides detailed 1996-1997 season statistics, including a month-by-month statistical breakdown; home and road averages; performances in wins and losses; and a player's numbers with one, two, or three days' rest between games. The team section provides a game-by-game summary for each team. Another section lists 1996 and 1997 leaders in 96 categories and NBA career leaders in 36 separate categories. These categories include the basic scoring, rebounding, and assists leaders as well as lists such as assists-to-turnover ratio, minutes played per game, and triple doubles. Regular NBA fans will recognize how radio and television announcers use these statistics in broadcasts. Endorsed by numerous media personnel, the STATS volume is a reasonably priced alternative for professional basketball by the numbers, with even more information than *The Sporting News* publications and the NBA's Website http://www.nba.com.—**Boyd Childress**

FISHING

729.   **Fishing Tackle Source Directory.** By William A. Mussen Jr. Jefferson, N.C., McFarland, 1998. 220p. index. $25.00pa. ISBN 0-7864-0537-6.

If an angler or fly fisherman is fishing across North America, this book should be a part of the equipment. More than 600 fishing tackle manufacturers and suppliers are listed in this handy volume. Entries provide addresses, descriptive contents of catalogs, telephone numbers, and e-mail addresses for the entire spectrum of tackle manufacturers, foreign as well as domestic, fresh as well as saltwater tackle. Indexes divide these tackle sources by tackle type, by location in state and country, and a short list of e-mail addresses. The information was gathered by means of manufacturer and supplier surveys. With the growth of the Internet, a more efficient means to update this information would be through a Website for this book. The e-mail address list, no doubt, will grow rapidly and need electronic updating. This handy book is a must for serious anglers and fly fishermen and is recommended for public library reference collections.—**Norman L. Kincaide**

FOOTBALL

730.   **NCAA Football: The Official 1997 College Football Records Book.** Chicago, Triumph Books, 1997. 552p. illus. $16.95pa. ISBN 1-57243-202-0. ISSN 0735-5475.

NCAA Football: The Official College Football Records Book is a must for anyone intrigued by intercollegiate football records. This annual publication of the National Collegiate Athletic Association (NCAA) provides comprehensive statistical coverage of the year's football results and schedules for the upcoming year. Schools may be elected to join the 1,200 members of the NCAA if they are accredited by the appropriate regional agency, offer a minimum of 4 sports each for both men and women, and comply with NCAA rules. The football records book covers all three divisions and includes individual, team, and division statistics. Black-and-white action photographs round out the presentation. Although the volume lacks an index, page tabs clearly identify the categories

covered. A table of contents precedes each section. This book is a treasure trove of information for college football aficionados. Each page reveals several gems of history or trivia. Bowl games, coaches, awards, cliffhangers,
stadiums, crowd size, standings, and rule changes are just a few of the statistics provided. Players themselves
will enjoy remembering what they did on a given day in a given year. As a supplement to this volume, highlights
of current statistics are available from the NCAA Website at http://www.ncaa.org. The reader can request statistics
on an individual or team within a division or conference via e-mail. This volume will be popular in public libraries
and academic libraries at schools with football teams.—**Anne C. Moore**

GOLF

731.   **Official Rules of Golf.** Chicago, Triumph Books, 1997. 190p. index. $9.95pa. ISBN 1-57243-221-7.
     Official Rules of Golf is the official source of the international regulations as approved by the United
States Golf Association and the Royal and Ancient Golf Club of St. Andrews, Scotland. Any game, match, or
tournament worldwide is conducted according to this book.
     The main body of the book is revised every four years, but appendix 1, "Local Rules," is revised every two
years. The first topic covered in the *Official Rules* is the etiquette of the game, which covers treatment of other
players as well as care of the fairways and greens. The rules themselves are extremely detailed, dealing with
what seems to be every possible contingency. For example, rule 19 covers 4 pages and discusses every possible
circumstance by which the ball could possibly be deflected or stopped and what happens next.
     Appendix 1 discusses local rules that pertain to abnormal conditions for an individual golf course. Each
local course may add such rules "if they are consistent with the policy of the Governing Authority for the country
concerned as set forth in Appendix 1 to these Rules." Also included in the manual are regulations about equipment and the amateur status of golfers.
     Physically, the paperback book is sized to fit comfortably in a pocket or golf bag. This official rulebook
for golf is designed to be carried by golfers and officials on the golf course. In the opinion of this reviewer, it
would be of limited value in a reference collection.—**Nancy P. Reed**

HOCKEY

732.   Cerutti, Steve. **The Official Fantasy Hockey Guide: The Definitive Hockey Pool Reference.** Chicago,
Triumph Books, 1997. 276p. illus. $14.95pa. ISBN 1-57243-207-1.
     Fantasy hockey is a game for those fans, now numerous, who dream that they could do a great job of
coaching or managing a National Hockey League (NHL) team. Using the information provided by this guide,
those fans can easily set up and participate in fantasy hockey leagues.
     The *Guide* is divided into 4 sections that deal with the methods and rules for organizing and operating the
fantasy league; strategies for planning and managing a team, especially drafting and trading players; statistical
and evaluative data for each team and each player in the NHL; and a miscellany of appendixes covering such
matters as Internet resources and results of the 1997 draft.
     This is primarily a "how-to" book for the participants in a fantasy hockey league. However, the material in
part 3, "Team and Player Evaluations," would be of considerable value to almost everyone who watches or reads
about the NHL. Cerutti's analyses are not only factually informative but also perceptive and refreshingly critical—
he pulls no punches. Despite the limited scope and audience suggested by the title, this book would in fact be
worth having by any library catering to hockey fans.—**Samuel Rothstein**

733.   **The National Hockey League Official Guide & Record Book 1997-98.** Chicago, Triumph Books,
1997. 464p. illus. $18.95pa.
     As the official guide of the National Hockey League (NHL) for the past 66 editions, this resource fulfills
its purpose of providing information on all aspects of the NHL. Unique to this volume is a tribute to Mario Lemieux,
information on the Olympics, a comparison of International Hockey rules to NHL rules, and the results of the
first World Cup of Hockey. The resource is divided into eight sections, and there is no index.

The first section contains information about the administrative structure of the NHL and an abbreviated history of the NHL. The information about the on-ice officials no longer includes biographical descriptions; a list with their numbers and career statistics is provided. The club section includes team information, such as the franchise date; conference; which players' numbers have been retired; biographical information on the coach and general manager; and many other statistics, records, and information. When available, the World Wide Web address is included in the details of the club directory. There are overall statistical summaries of players, their minor league affiliations, retired players and goalies, and player transactions. The remainder of the sections include statistics of the Stanley Cup and other records in the NHL. A limited number of photographs include the team facility and players of the past and present. This work will be useful in collections where interest in hockey or sports statistics prevails.—**Mila C. Su**

734.   **The National Hockey League Stanley Cup Playoffs Fact Guide 1998.** Chicago, Triumph Books, 1997. 208p. illus. $12.95pa. ISBN 1-57243-227-6.
        Chock full of statistics and records, this resource documents the history of the Stanley Cup playoffs. This is not a coffee-table book title as there are no photographs or an index. There is a description of the National Hockey League's playoff format, its history and changes, and a reverse chronological list of the Stanley Cup champions and finalists. There are 5 sections in the book that begin with the team playoff histories. Arranged in alphabetic order, each team's playoff experiences are listed. The next section is a chronological description of playoff final scores and highlights. Starting with the year 1927, entry, quarter and semifinal information are added. The last 3 sections focus on playoff records, Stanley Cup finals, and Stanley Cup finals with information on the final series game summaries from 1980 to 1997. The data included in these sections include statistical summaries of all-time players; team and individual, leading playoff scorers, and overtime scorers; coaching records; and a multitude of final series results. A nice inclusion is "This Date in Stanley Cup History," an overview snapshot of important days in the long history of the oldest challenge series in North America. This book is recommended for hockey fans as well as public and academic libraries.—**Mila C. Su**

735.   **Official Rules of Ice Hockey.** Chicago, Triumph Books, 1997. 192p. index. $9.95pa. ISBN 1-57243-248-9.
        There are now more than 29,000 registered teams playing ice hockey in the United States. Every one of those teams' coaches and managers, all of the referees, and most of the players should, ideally at least, have a copy of the *Official Rules of Ice Hockey*.
        In addition to the rules themselves, this publication offers a well-printed text, clear illustrations (for referee signals and rink layouts), and at a reasonable price. Its handy size means that a copy can fit neatly into one's pocket. Add in a good glossary and useful index, and the *Official Rules* constitutes a publication that is highly recommended for all hockey participants and many libraries.—**Samuel Rothstein**

736.   **STATS Hockey Handbook 1997-1998.** Skokie, Ill., STATS Publishing, 1997. 536p. $19.95pa. ISBN 1-884064-40-X.
        For sports fans and scholars, especially those with a passion for baseball, handbooks that provide detailed statistical information about players and teams are a lifeline to their favorite sport. Following the trend set by baseball, every major and most minor professional sports in the United States now have one or more statistical handbooks. Although hockey draws far less attention than baseball, basketball, or football in many parts of the United States, it is no exception. Given its more limited appeal, many public libraries may not need any handbook, and most will probably require only one and, even then, may not require a new edition each year. Many Canadian public libraries and U.S. public libraries in cities with a strong hockey fan base may want more than one handbook.
        The *STATS Hockey Handbook* is, unfortunately, in almost direct competition with the older and more established *Sporting News Hockey Register* (ARBA 97, entry 658). There is little difference between the two, and, therefore, most libraries are likely to stay with the more established handbook if they already have earlier editions. That is a reasonable choice. Both of those tools provide basic information about each player currently on the roster of a National Hockey League team. The *STATS Handbook* includes information on career statistics; skater profiles; goalie profiles; team statistics on a game-by-game basis; standings; leader boards; game stars; and debuts, first goals, and first wins. It provides more information of potential interest to many fans in its 120 more pages, but it also costs $5 more than *The Sporting News Hockey Register*. In reference book publishing, as

in sports, competition is always welcome. On that basis alone *STATs Hockey Handbook* deserves to be purchased and used.—**Norman D. Stevens**

737.   Townsend, Murray. **The 1997-98 Hockey Annual.** Los Angeles, Calif., Warwick; distr., Willowdale, Ont., Firefly Books, 1997. 288p. $16.95pa. ISBN 1-895629-90-X.

Townsend, the author of "Townsend's Hockey Pool Tips," a column in *The Hockey News*, compiles and presents information on National Hockey League teams and their players. What is different in this source, compared to other statistical resources, is the detail in the recap of the previous season and the team preview. The book is separated into 3 parts: team information, the ultimate pool picks, and the statistic grab bag. The teams are arranged by conference and then by alphabetic order. Within the team ranking, Townsend includes information on the goaltenders, defense, forward, coach, management, and special teams. The team description highlights the overall high and low points, statistics, team preview, and first round draft. Townsend's annual rating method also includes the special teams, statistics, searching and management, overview, draft selection, and prognosis and prediction of the final team standings. Along with the typical statistics and team rankings, comparisons of home versus away and conference and nonconference play are also included. The section on the player pool arranges the information in point order. Townsend's reliability index (formula) includes age, power play effectiveness, career points, season, injuries, streaks, and club dependability. The grab bag is a mix of conference, division, and individual statistics, rankings, and standings. Predictions are usually amusing in retrospect, especially with the number of upsets that have occurred. Hockey pool information is usually published in magazine format, and Telemedia's *Sportsforecaster Hockey 1997-98* is cheaper and covers much of the information. This book is recommended for pool and statistic enthusiasts.—**Mila C. Su**

OLYMPICS

738.   **Chronicle of the Olympics, 1896-2000.** New York, DK Publishing, 1998. 330p. illus. index. $29.95. ISBN 0-7894-2312-X.

This volume updates the previous edition (see ARBA 97, entry 660) with complete results for the Olympic Games in Atlanta, Georgia. The chronology provides an overview for each of the Olympic Games, with highlights of the opening ceremony and various events. This section is the major focus of this title, along with a variety of photographs that capture different moments of competition. The snippets of drama, tension, and competition that highlight each of the Olympic Games and attempt to capture the spirit experienced at that time is the main difference between this and other titles on the Olympics. A total of 26 new entries have been added. An overview of expectations and the new events at the 1998 Winter Games and the 2000 Summer Games in Sydney, Australia, is presented. The next section contains statistics on all of the Olympic Games by each game, the total number of participants (further broken down by gender and country), and the medallists for each event. Other tables and charts include the top five medal-earning countries and the top five "outstanding athletes." *Chronicle of the Olympics, 1896-2000* is recommended for public and school libraries. Individuals and academic libraries may want to consider its purchase as a supplemental resource. [R: SLJ, July 98, p. 114]—**Mila C. Su**

SKATING

739.   Malone, John. **The Encyclopedia of Figure Skating.** New York, Facts on File, 1998. 264p. illus. index. $35.00. ISBN 0-8160-3226-2.

This attempt to fill the need for a comprehensive reference book about figure skating contains alphabetically arranged articles, most of which are about figure skating champions. The articles are inconsistent in content, and most do little more than list years of birth and medals won by skaters. Few of the articles give any information about the skaters' backgrounds or their careers following competition, and many articles are padded with the author's opinions and with references to skaters against whom the subjects competed. There are many inaccuracies: the last name of world champion Petra Burka is spelled "Burke"; German champion Heinrich Burger's last name is spelled two different ways in the same article; and skater Toller Cranston's birth date is listed as 1952, when it is actually 1949. Diacritics are also excluded from proper names (e.g., Anna Hubler should be Anna Hübler). Jumps and other moves that comprise figure skating are described but not illustrated. Cross-references are either missing or inadequate. For example, there is an entry for Alena Vrzanova, but no cross-reference to "Aja Zanova," the name by which the skater is better known as a result of a successful professional career. In some areas coverage is inadequate. There are few articles about coaches who were not themselves skating champions, and the world of professional show skating receives little attention.

The writing of this work is pedestrian, and illustrations are primarily photographs of skaters, many of which are badly reproduced. There is no indication that the author is aware of or has used any of the many figure skating books or periodicals that have been previously published. This is a disappointing work and, given its inaccuracies, cannot be recommended. [R: Choice, July/Aug 98, p. 1825]—**Gari-Anne Patzwald**

SKIING

740. **The Good Skiing and Snowboarding Guide 1998.** Hardy, Peter, and Felice Eyston, eds. Woodstock, N.Y., Overlook Press, 1997. 591p. maps. index. $24.95pa. ISBN 0-87951-810-3.

Those planning ski vacations will appreciate this guide to more than 500 resorts around the world. The 1998 edition has expanded snowboarding coverage and includes ski Websites as well as updated maps (about 74) and fact summaries.

The section titled "Resort Verdicts" provides a summary, in chart form, of the advantages and disadvantages of resorts covered in detail in later sections. Here, resorts can be listed by either country, continent, or category (e.g., "The Best of Europe"). This is where the usefulness of the resort index becomes apparent. Resort location maps follow, locating particular resorts, and detailed reports on ski areas supply information on mountain activities. Full-color ski maps are included, as are ski fact boxes with tourist, slope, lesson, lift pass, transportation, and accommodation information. Other chapters discuss choice of a resort, the Internet, purchase of equipment, transportation to the resort, and slope safety, and they list tour operators and national tourist offices.

This guide is a complete sourcebook for skiers and snowboarders alike, compiling a lot of information into one volume. All that is needed now are good snow conditions.—**Anita Zutis**

SOFTBALL

741. **The Official Rules of Softball.** Chicago, Triumph Books, 1998. 203p. $9.95pa. ISBN 1-57243-274-8.

This book is a valuable source for ascertaining the rules of softball as approved by the American Softball Association for fast, slow, and 16-inch pitch. The information is grouped into 2 sections: "Official Playing Rules" and "Points of Emphasis." In the 1st section, information is broken into 12 rules: definitions, playing field, equipment, players and substitutes, the game, pitching regulations, batting, batter-runner and runner, protests, umpires, scoring, and use of playing rules. In "Points of Emphasis," one can find information on situations involving such issues as appeals, dugout conduct, media coverage, and tiebreakers. These tips are encouraged for use in interpreting various situations. A good index is included.—**Mila C. Su**

16 Sociology

GENERAL WORKS

742. Kronenwetter, Michael. **Encyclopedia of Modern American Social Issues.** Santa Barbara, Calif., ABC-CLIO, 1997. 328p. index. $65.00. ISBN 0-87436-779-4.

In this work the author, a prolific writer of books on political and social issues for both young people and adults, explains the key issues that face Americans today and that are likely to remain key issues in the future. These include old standbys (welfare, anti-Semitism, the death penalty, and child abuse) as well as new subjects (ebonics, charter schools, secondhand smoke, the V-chip). Acknowledging that each topic could easily lend itself to a book-length analysis, Kronenwetter instead concentrates on stripping the complexities of an issue to its most easily understood essence and, when appropriate, putting it in historical context. The volume can be compared to the newspaper *USA Today*; the entries are short (for the most part), simply written, free of jargon, and informative.

The nearly 200 topics are arranged alphabetically by subject, with a bibliography and good index at the end of the volume. The information is current, including such instances as the appointment of Madeleine Albright as secretary of state in January 1997. The index helps to locate entries whose headings are not always obvious. The discussion on the constitution of families is not under *families* but under *household makeup*. However, an entry under *families* in the index points to the relevant pages. Kronenwetter does not explain the criteria used for choosing the titles for the bibliography, and although many are current studies, some seem dated (e.g., a book edited by Kenneth M. Davidson on sex discrimination from 1974).

The reading level is aimed at those in middle school, but the simple and clear language makes this a valuable resource for anyone familiar with the issues discussed.—**Hope Yelich**

743. Schwandt, Thomas A. **Qualitative Inquiry: A Dictionary of Terms.** Newbury Park, Calif., Sage, 1997. 183p. $46.00pa. ISBN 0-7619-0254-6.

In the area of qualitative research, Sage Publications is well known. They have published the works of prominent methodologists—Yvonna Lincoln, Egon Guba, Anselm Strauss, Norman Denzin, and others. With this book, Schwandt offers in-depth explanations of terms used by these notable qualitative researchers. Individuals who are unfamiliar with the terminology of qualitative research will gain understanding by using this handy dictionary. The definitions vary from one paragraph for relatively simple topics to several paragraphs for more complex terms. Many of the entries include appropriate references to seminal works and cross-references to applicable concepts.

Those unfamiliar with the field often combine all qualitative methodologies into one domain; however, disagreement and dissension occurs within the field. With this dictionary readers can differentiate between grounded theory and naturalistic inquiry, pragmatism and symbolic interactionism, among other topics and concepts. The entries also include terms traditionally used in quantitative research with explanations as to how they apply to qualitative methodologies. This resource is recommended for academic libraries supporting research faculty and graduate programs.—**Susan D. Strickland**

AGING

744.   **Aging Sourcebook: Basic Information on Issues Affecting Older Americans....** Dan R. Harris, ed. Detroit, Omnigraphics, 1998. 889p. index. (Personal Concerns Series, v.3). $72.00. ISBN 0-7808-0175-X.

Aging Sourcebook is volume 3 in Omnigraphic's Personal Concerns Series, which aims at comprehensive, authoritative articles for the layperson chosen and edited from the archives of federal agencies, research institutions, and professional associations. This work is divided into 7 parts: "An Introduction to the Major Issues of Aging," "Social Security and Medicare," "Legal and Financial Issues," "Health and Safety," "Elder Care," "Lifestyle and Leisure," and "End of Life." Most of the articles are reprints of pamphlets published by various federal agencies, the American Bar Association, Lions Club International, and others.

The articles tend to be brief, uncontroversial, and probably most useful to someone with little prior knowledge of the topic. For example, when reading the chapter, "Viatical Settlements," this reviewer was unfamiliar with this term and quickly learned that if one has a terminal illness, one's life insurance policy can be sold to a viatical settlement company for a percentage of the policy's face value (the company pays the remaining premiums and collects the death benefit).

This book is attractive, with large typeface and many references to helpful agencies and organizations (usually with postal mail addresses only). Timeliness is a problem with this work; for example, the following sentence is noted, "Already, according to the latest available Health Care Financing Administration survey (1982). ...." And, quite irritatingly, in several articles readers are told to see charts and graphs "below" that were nowhere to be found in the *Aging Sourcebook* copy received. This should be a useful book for libraries with a large number of senior patrons. [R: RUSQ, Summer 98, pp. 340-341]—**Anthony Gottlieb**

745.   **Directory of Population Ageing Research in Europe.** New York, United Nations, 1998. 611p. index. $55.00pa. ISBN 92-1-100766-6. ISSN 1014-4994. S/N GV.E.98.0.2.

This directory describes approximately 300 projects sponsored by 150 institutions that are conducting research on a wide range of issues dealing with the aging population in Europe. A survey was administered in 1995 and 1996 to all European nations by the Population Activities Unit of the United Nations Economic Commission for Europe in collaboration with the United States National Institute on Aging. Responses from this survey form the core of this publication, providing a useful tool for those seeking to understand current conditions or to undertake future studies. Arranged alphabetically by country, there are listings for 26 areas, plus a general category labeled "International." Subject searches are possible with the help of an item index and a keyword index, both of which are located at the back of the volume.

Entries offer the general description of the research project, such as its official title, beginning and ending dates, main purpose, descriptive keywords, and an abstract of the activities already undertaken or those needing to be completed to fulfill requirements. The project manager's personal information, including his or her name, telephone numbers, and address along with affiliation, follows the general description. Depending upon the country consulted, one may find research on such topics as housing issues, care provision of the elderly, health conditions, and living standards. In trying to identify ongoing research and perhaps determine future areas to be addressed, this is a valuable tool to consult and should be considered useful for those researchers approaching the topic of population aging and its regional effects.—**Marianne B. Eimer**

746.   **Source Book on Ageing: Information Materials for the International Year of Older Persons.** By the Economic and Social Commission for Asia and the Pacific. New York, United Nations, 1997. 2v. index. $15.00/set. ISBN 92-1-119776-7. ISSN E.98.II.F.

This 2-volume sourcebook stems from a 1996 United Nations project sponsored by the Economic and Social Commission for Asia and the Pacific (ESCAP) that was devoted to developing cooperative programs and policies by governments, nongovernmental organizations (NGOs), communities, and families to address conditions of poverty afflicting the elderly. United Nations officials considered this project an essential step leading up to the celebration of the International Year of Older Persons, 1999, which brought about the information found in this useful reference tool. Entry information was generated from survey responses by agencies and organizations in the ESCAP region whose primary focus was aging and related issues. The 1st volume presents profiles of organizations, and the 2d volume provides actual text from mandates adopted by governments that address these issues and promote specific activities to improve quality of life for the aged.

Part 1 of volume 1 is made up of profiles of governmental agencies, alphabetically arranged by country. Length of entry varies, but it is possible to find official names, telephone numbers, fax numbers, addresses, e-mail accounts, publications, functions, major activities undertaken by the agency on behalf of older persons, and the contact person responsible for coordinating the International Year of Older Persons activities. Part 2 includes profiles of NGOs arranged alphabetically and is divided according to national/local, regional, or international scope. Goals/objectives, publications, main function, and brief histories can be found.

Volume 2 contains excerpts of international mandates adopted at major world conferences from 1982 up to the present, those adopted by the United Nations General Assembly, and ESCAP regional mandates. Each volume has an alphabetically arranged table of contents, with an index to NGOs arranged by country/territory included in volume 1. This work should be considered a standard reference work for its subject matter, helpful where there is a need for international materials on aging.—**Marianne B. Eimer**

COMMUNITY LIFE

747.   Stockwell, Foster. **Encyclopedia of American Communes, 1663-1963.** Jefferson, N.C., McFarland, 1998. 262p. illus. index. $55.00. ISBN 0-7864-0455-8.

Most of the world's communes have been established in the United States. The opening of the New World made the United States the ideal location for many experimental communities, and its unspoiled and inexpensive land encouraged social experimentation. This encyclopedia, arranged alphabetically by commune name, covers the more than 500 communes established in the United States from Swanendael, the first communal experiment in the United States in 1663, through Tolstoy Farm, founded in 1963. Entries include the name of the commune, the years it operated, the community's leaders, a brief history, and a discussion of extant buildings or artifacts. For further study, many entries have bibliographical references to point an interested reader toward a more extensive source of information. The full citation for each of these references can be found in the bibliography at the end of the book. There is also a list of all the communes by date order in appendix 1. The book is a useful, quick reference source on U.S. communes. It is recommended for any college and public libraries.—**Vera Gao**

DISABLED

748.   **AFB Directory of Services for Blind and Visually Impaired Persons in the United States and Canada.** 25th ed. New York, AFB Press, 1997. 575p. index. $149.95. ISBN 0-89128-301-3. ISSN 1067-5833.

749.   **AFB Directory of Services for Blind and Visually Impaired Persons in the United States and Canada.** 25th ed. [CD-ROM]. New York, AFB Press, 1998. Minimum system requirements (Windows version): IBM or compatible 386. CD-ROM drive. DOS 3.1. Windows 3.1. 4MB RAM. VGA or EGA monitor. Minimum system requirements (Macintosh version): Macintosh 68020. CD-ROM drive. System 7. 6MB RAM. $149.95. ISBN 0-89128-243-2.

This directory contains a lot of useful information and resources, but the presentation of this information is somewhat hindered by the arrangement of the material. The categories and subcategories used are not in a standard alphabetic arrangement. The use of the subject index that is included at the front of the book greatly assists in sorting out the arrangement of categories and subcategories.

The main part of the directory consists of 2 main geographic sections—the United States and Canada. Within these 2 main geographic headings the entries are arranged in alphabetic order by state or by province. Within each state or province section there are 5 main categories entitled "Educational Services," "Information Services," "Rehabilitation Services," "Low Vision Services," and "Aging Services." Included within the "Education tion Services" category are subcategories of state services, early intervention coordination, schools, infant and preschool, statewide outreach services, instructional materials centers, and university training programs. Included within "Information Services" are libraries, talking book machine distributors, media production services, radio reading, telephone-in newspapers, and information and referral. Included within "Rehabilitation Services" are state services, rehabilitation, computer training centers, and dog guide schools. Within "Low Vision Services" are eye care societies and low vision centers. Within "Aging Services" are state units on aging and independent living programs.

Organizations are cross-listed under different categories. Among the information included in an entry are address and contact information, agency mission, history, funding, staffing, requirements for eligibility of services, types of services provided, and hours of operation. Also included in the directory is a helpful resource section on U.S. and Canadian national programs and legislature related to individuals with disabilities. There are U.S. and Canadian sections on federal agencies, national organizations, and consumer and professional membership organizations. There is also a useful section on producers of alternate media, which lists publishers and producers of print and audio. The "Source of Products" section contains contact information for mail order catalogs and distributors, household, personal and independent living products; low vision products; computer hardware and software; Braille and other literacy materials; medical products; products of the deaf and blind and other multiply disabled persons; and audible and tactile signs. The directory concludes with two alphabetically arranged indexes by organization name for both the United States and Canada. This is a valuable resource tool for all public and academic libraries.—**Jan S. Squire**

750.   **Resources for People with Disabilities: A National Directory.** Elizabeth H. Oakes and John Bradford, eds. Chicago, Ferguson, 1998. 2v. index. $89.95/set. ISBN 0-89434-242-8.

Demand for access to current information on disabilities will increase in importance as the number of persons with disabilities grows. Currently, about 19 percent of the population fits into this group, representing widely divergent needs and issues. *Resources for People with Disabilities: A National Directory* meets the demand for up-to-date information from this population. Four sections cover assistive technology, funding sources, organizations and associations, and publications and conferences. The listings are not exhaustive, but do provide good access to national offices of many organizations or funding sources and a wide variety of publishers and vendors. Some regional chapter listings are included for organizations. Listings include contact information, a description, and the target population or disability type served. When available, e-mail and World Wide Web addresses are included. The directory also provides information for legal or health professionals, case workers, educators, or others who partner with this population. Readable, useful essays describe main sections of the directory. Geographic, disability type, state and city, and organization name indexes allow quick access to specific listings. This directory is recommended for academic or public libraries serving persons with disabilities or the professionals who work with them. [R: Choice, Oct 98, p. 299]—**Lynne M. Fox**

751.   Sweeney, Wilma K. **The Special-Needs Reading List: An Annotated Guide to the Best Publications for Parents and Professionals.** Bethesda, Md., Woodbine House, 1998. 314p. index. $18.95pa. ISBN 0-933149-74-3.

This guide's precedent was *A Reader's Guide for Parents of Children with Mental, Physical, or Emotional Disabilities* by Cory Moore (see ARBA 91, entry 857). The present guide updates that work and is designed primarily for parents or families that have special needs children. Professionals will probably find the list of organizations useful for the fact that it provides places to refer persons who are interested in materials on special needs. The guide includes materials that are current as well as older titles. More than 700 authors and 200 organizations are listed. Because professional information is only included if there are not more easily understood books or the information is useful to parents, it is not comprehensive. It does serve its purpose as an excellent beginning reading list. Entries include a complete bibliographic citation and an annotation. Entries for organizations include their street and e-mail addresses; a URL for their Website; and an annotation that includes the organization's purpose, services, and publications. The guide provides four useful indexes by organization, author, title, and subject, as well as an appendix of publisher's addresses.

There are 2 main sections to the guide. Section 1 provides a list of disabilities and includes several broad topic areas, including disability awareness, infants and toddlers, family life, discipline and behavioral concerns, education, health care, advocacy and legal rights, sign language and alternative communication, technology, community integration, recreation, sexuality, and death. Within these topics are 3 major divisions: books, periodicals, and organizations. Sometimes further delineation is provided. Section 2 lists specific disabilities. This includes specific disorders such as attention deficit disorder, cerebral palsy, Down syndrome, fetal alcohol syndrome, muscular dystrophy, and Tourette's syndrome. There are also listings for several categories of disorders, including prenatal substance exposure, learning disabilities, mental retardation, emotional and behavioral disorders, neuromuscular diseases, physical disabilities, rare disorders, sensory integration disorders, speech and language disorders, and visual impairment and blindness.

This guide provides a useful starting place for identifying print, electronic resources, and organizations for those with special needs. Public and school libraries will benefit most from having the guide in their collection, but it will be of use in academic library collections as well. [R: BL, July 98, p. 1908]—**Jan S. Squire**

FAMILY, MARRIAGE, AND DIVORCE

752. Dabbagh, Maureen. **The Recovery of Internationally Abducted Children: A Comprehensive Guide.** Jefferson, N.C., McFarland, 1997. 226p. index. $42.50pa. ISBN 0-7864-0289-X.

Written for the novice, this research guide grew out of the author's actual experiences and as such reflects her opinions. Filled with legal issues, practical actions to take, and agencies to contact, the guide provides avenues to follow for parents who either may be facing the possibility of international abduction of their children or the actual circumstance. Introductory chapters have been organized to follow the sequence of events that may be encountered by parents trying to recover an abducted child. Case studies are used to illustrate successful attempts at recovery and ways to cope with the aftermath of recovery. The book concludes with a convenient list of the texts of pertinent laws, along with a directory of embassy offices, state clearinghouses for missing children, and passport offices. Appendixes cover such areas as resource guides, supporting agencies, and profiles of Hague member countries. The entire *State Department Publication on International Parental Child Abduction Publication 10053* has been reprinted as appendix A. An alphabetic subject index is included. Appropriate for all public libraries and those academic libraries that support legal and psychological studies, this research guide conveniently provides one source for many useful references necessary for those who find themselves in this particular situation. The volume's value would increase if it were to be updated annually.—**Marianne B. Eimer**

753. **Having Children: The Best Resources to Help You Prepare.** Rich Wemhoff and Molly Pessl, eds. Issaquah, Wash., Resource Pathways; distr., Ashland, Ohio, Bookmasters, 1997. 233p. index. (Lyfecycles Series). $24.95pa. ISBN 0-9653424-3-3.

Geared toward those who are choosing to become parents, this resource guide serves as an excellent starting point in locating highly rated print and multimedia resources dedicated to such topics as pregnancy, adoption, infertility, childbirth, breast-feeding, and the child's first year. Descriptions of nearly 130 resources include many specific details, such as author, title, publisher, the resource's content and focus, and an evaluation of its quality, including an "ease-of-use" category, purchasing information, and author biographies. The editors, a child psychologist and a registered nurse, carefully document the scope of the volume's six sections in the introduction, then clearly identify the best resources for each topic as well as supplemental sources to be consulted. A useful section is that devoted to resource reviews that have been grouped by format starting with the most highly rated sources; it includes the rationale for the concise ratings. Separate indexes have been arranged by author, title, subject, and publisher. The appendixes offer listings of support groups, associations, and other organizations that parents might wish to consult.

This appears to be an extremely useful tool: It is written in a concise, information fashion and offers a wide variety of options for parents to pursue. Although not as comprehensive as *The Parent's Resource Almanac* (see ARBA 96, entry 901), this volume provides in-depth coverage of the topics it includes, ranging from print sources to Internet Websites, videos, and audiotapes. This work should be added to public library collections on parenting and those academic libraries supporting counseling programs.—**Marianne B. Eimer**

754. Martin, Deborah L. **An Annotated Guide to Adoption Research 1986-1997.** Annapolis Junction, Md., Child Welfare League of America, 1998. 358p. index. $24.95pa. ISBN 0-87868-708-4.

Martin has complied an unequaled classified bibliography on adoption research published between 1986 and 1997. This work does not address popular articles; it identifies both quantitative and qualitative research on adoptees, birth parents, and adoptive parents. The classification recognizes the adoptee as the most important person in the adoption triad, while providing sufficient information for both the adoptive and birth parents. Subject headings are timely, germane, and fairly comprehensive—nurture versus nature, special needs adoptions, single parent adoptions—but annotations regarding studies of gay and lesbian adoptive parents are missing. There is no separate subject index. Annotations to works regarding various regional adoption studies are included—Colorado, Denmark, Finland, France, Iowa, Minnesota, Sweden, and Texas.

Each annotation provides complete bibliographic information, plus a brief narrative describing the methodology employed and a brief statement of findings. Some annotations provide additional references to related publications. The volume is indexed by author, providing easy access to an individual author's works. One of the 4 appendixes presents information on each researcher included in the bibliography. The researcher entry comprises complete contact information—name, institutional affiliation, address, and e-mail address. The remaining appendixes consist of classified annotations of literature reviews, a general list of related readings, and a list of theses and dissertations not included in the main body of the book.—**Susan D. Strickland**

755.   Moe, Barbara. **Adoption: A Reference Handbook.** Santa Barbara, Calif., ABC-CLIO, 1998. 303p. index. (Contemporary World Issues). $39.50. ISBN 0-87436-898-7.

Part of ABC-CLIO's Contemporary World Issues series, this volume follows the standard format. Designed as an elementary handbook, this volume provides a general overview of the adoption process for both adoptive parents and birth parents. In rather simplistic terms, Moe describes the different issues involved in adopting an infant or child, with a heavy emphasis on legal topics. The strength of this work lies in the interpretation of the relevant case law and federal legislation; specifically a good explanation of the Interstate Compact is included along with an accurate explanation of the Indian Child Welfare Act of 1978 and timely information from the DeBoer's case.

Chronological and biographical sections briefly outline the history of adoption in the United States and a statistical section reports the number of children adopted in the United States, from within the country and from other nations. A bibliography is divided by age appropriateness; however, subdivisions are not included. Under the listing of books for adults the titles are arranged by author, but not separated for adoptive parents, birth parents, and adult adoptees, thus confusing the user. The lists of relevant video and audiocassettes consist of price, ordering information, and brief descriptions. The author also offers a comprehensive list of organizations involved in adoption, including individual state agencies that regulate adoptions.

The author provides a beginning for individuals and couples interested in adoption; it should not, however, be a library's sole work on the subject. This volume merely explains various aspects of adoption; it does not provide enough information regarding the emotional facets of adoption.—**Susan D. Strickland**

756.   Pardeck, John T., and Jean A. Pardeck. **Children in Foster Care and Adoption: A Guide to Bibliotherapy.** Westport, Conn., Greenwood Press, 1998. 103p. index. $55.00. ISBN 0-313-30775-X.

This work begins by defining bibliotherapy and explaining how it is used with adopted and foster care children. In the 1st chapter, a discussion of how different types of books (e.g., fiction, biographies, fairy tales) can be used to help children is included. Many bibliotherapy strategies and follow-up techniques are discussed in the 2d chapter. Some examples include creative writing, role-playing, and writing a "Dear Abby" letter from the point of view of a main character of a book.

The 3d chapter begins with a discussion of the history of foster care and adoption in the United States. It also explains how children react to foster care and adoption placement and lists the stages children go through in foster care and adoption. The 4th and 5th chapters are annotated bibliographies on faster care and adoption. Approximately 150 titles are listed. Each chapter's works are organized by school level of the child for which the book is appropriate.

Other works, such as *Bibliotherapy with Young People: Librarians and Mental Health Professionals Working Together* (Libraries Unlimited, 1997) and *Books to Help Children Cope with Separation and Loss* (see ARBA 91, entry 363) also cover how to use bibliotherapy with children. *Books to Help Children Cope with Separation and Loss* even includes a short bibliography of books to use with children going through foster placement and adoption. However, *Children in Foster Care and Adoption* includes bibliographies that are more current, and it concentrates only on foster care and adoption issues. Practitioners working with children in this area will appreciate having this type of work devoted solely to foster care and adoption.—**Laura K. Blessing**

GAY AND LESBIAN STUDIES

757. Hogan, Steve, and Lee Hudson. **Completely Queer: The Gay and Lesbian Encyclopedia.** New York, Henry Holt, 1998. 704p. illus. index. $50.00. ISBN 0-8050-3629-6.

The rapid growth in monographs in the field of gay and lesbian studies has presented a challenge to collection managers in all types of libraries, due mainly to the relative scarcity of general reference works on this newly defined subject. *Completely Queer* claims to be "the first authoritative encyclopedia for the gay and lesbian communities," a statement born of the controversy surrounding the 1990 *Encyclopedia of Homosexuality* (see ARBA 91, entry 870). It contains more than 500 articles covering individuals, organizations, countries, periodicals, and creative genres whose aim was to present the contemporary multinational gay and lesbian world and its antecedents within western culture and, where possible, outside it. Each entry concludes with readings selected both for content and the inclusion of substantial bibliography. Useful features include listings of all recipients of book awards granted within the gay and lesbian community and more than 250 photographs, paintings, posters, and cartoons offering a valuable expansion on the text. The work concludes with a 73-page chronology back to 12,000 B.C.E. Indexed by personal names, organization names, and subject, this work is suitable for all reference collections in school and public libraries. Academic libraries holding the older encyclopedia will wish to acquire this volume to use as a beginning reference tool due to its concise format, accessible style, and inexpensive cost. [R: Choice, Sept 98, p. 82; BL, 1 June 98, pp. 1800-1802]—**Robert B. Marks Ridinger**

758. Nordquist, Joan, comp. **Queer Theory: A Bibliography.** Santa Cruz, Calif., Reference and Research Services, 1997. 64p. (Social Theory: A Bibliographic Series, no.48). $15.00pa. ISBN 0-937855-95-2.

Most of the titles in the highly respected Social Theory series of bibliographies are devoted to works about individual theorists such as Michel Paul Foucault and Claude Levi-Strauss, but a few deal with a specific topic. In this case the topic is queer theory, a concept that eschews the customary gay/straight labeling of sexual identification in favor of a broader, less confining, and more liberal definition of gender and sexual orientation.

The 685 books, parts of books, and articles listed in this unannotated, paperback bibliography have been culled from 6 indexes and related sources, some of which are well known like ERIC and *Essay and General Literature Index*, others more obscure such as *Eureka* and *Philosophers Index*. The works are arranged under 6 broad topics with many subsections. For example, the introductory overview section is subdivided into such topics as lesbianism, bisexuality, and race issues, and the section titled "Queer Theory and the Academic Disciples" contains segments on sociology, language, art, and film, among others. Although a few of the works cited date from 1989 and the very early 1990s, more than 70 percent are from 1993 through early 1998. Adequate bibliographic material is supplied for each citation. In the case of periodical articles this includes author, title, name of periodical, volume number, pages, and date. Unfortunately, there are no overall author, title, or specific subject indexes. However, this is a thorough, carefully edited bibliography that is unique in the breadth of its coverage. It will be of use in colleges and universities as well as large public libraries.—**John T. Gillespie**

759. **St. James Press Gay & Lesbian Almanac.** Neil Schlager, ed. Detroit, St. James Press, 1998. 680p. illus. index. $100.00. ISBN 1-55862-358-2.

Although there have been a plethora of published materials on gays and lesbians, particularly in the past 20 years, they include few reference works that present an in-depth overview of all aspects of gay and lesbian culture, as the present volume purports to do. In fact, the scope and depth of this work would seem to make it much more an encyclopedia than an almanac, and there is no clue as to why the editors chose the latter term. Its main focus is on the gay and lesbian experience in the United States, with emphasis on the twentieth century, but also includes some information on bisexual and transgender issues and non-U.S. events.

The almanac is divided into 23 broad categories or chapters, such as health, military, literature, and politics, and these are further subdivided into narrower fields. Most of the chapters deal with some particular aspect of gay and lesbian life, but three useful chapters cut across all aspects of the life: the chronology, which gives an excellent overall history from the 1940s to the mid-1990s; organizations, which presents detailed descriptions of gay and lesbian organizations, including not only regular directory information but Websites and e-mail addresses as well; and significant documents, which contains descriptions and texts of documents from a 1911 Chicago Vice Commission investigation to the Employment Non-Discrimination Act of 1996, which failed to pass Congress by one vote.

Each chapter is preceded by a list of the sections contained in it—such as science and performing arts, with only 4 sections, and others, such as politics, with as many as 16. This example of variation seems to reflect the editorial policy of allowing the collaborative writers for each chapter to follow whatever style they felt most appropriate. Each chapter is followed by a lengthy bibliography of books, articles, and chapters in books, some including other media and Websites. Most chapters include a section on prominent people with short biographical sketches and some photographs. At the end of the volume is a general bibliography, biographical sketches of the authors, and an index. Because of the arrangement of the almanac, it is necessary to use the index frequently for specific information.

Generally, the index is thorough and accurate, but there are a few omissions that raise questions. For example, there is a half-page on the Roman Catholic Church and its stance on homosexuality, but no reference is found to it in the index under Roman or Catholic or churches. Again, there is a section on mental health in the chapter on health, but there is nothing in the index under mental health or mental disease.

In spite of these and other relatively minor problems, the almanac is a scholarly, accurate, well-written compendium that is useful for both those needing in-depth information on gay and lesbian life and for quick reference. It brings together in one large but manageable volume material that previously had to be found in many different works. It is highly recommended for both public and academic libraries.—**Lucille Whalen**

PHILANTHROPY

Directories

760.   **America's New Foundations 1998: The Sourcebook on Recently Created Philanthropies.** 12th ed. Katherine E. Jankowski, ed. Detroit, Taft Group/Gale, 1998. 1429p. index. $180.00pa. ISBN 1-56995-262-0.

Development officers and others interested in discovering new sources of funding should find this 12th edition of *America's New Foundations* (ANF) an invaluable source of information. It identifies and profiles 3,070 private, corporate, and community foundations created since 1988, including approximately 300 foundations new to this edition.

The combined assets of the foundations totaled approximately $11.6 billion; contributions disbursed by the foundations were about $858.2 million. Although many of the foundations profiled are small, some have assets exceeding $1 million. Contributions also range widely, up to a high of $121.4 million. These newly established foundations offer fresh funding opportunities for creative grant-seekers. Many are unknown and, consequently, overlooked by major nonprofit organizations. Many may not have established firm funding criteria or giving patterns. Most give regionally, rather than nationally, so smaller nonprofit organizations with local constituencies are quite eligible.

The six indexes are very useful and include funders by their headquarters state, by grant type, by recipient type, by officers and directors, by grant recipients by location, and a master index. The 198 recipient types are divided into arts and humanities, civic and public affairs, education, environment, health, international, religion, and social services.

Profiles of the foundations contain name, contact, financial and contributions summary, officers and directors, grants analysis, and recent grants. Application information is especially valuable, providing requirements, initial request procedures, best time to submit a request, and programs that are ineligible.—**Jerri Spoehel**

761.   **Corporate Giving Directory 1999.** 20th ed. Lori Schoenenberger and Deborah Morad, eds. Detroit, Taft Group/Gale, 1997. 1811p. $440.00. ISBN 1-56995-260-4. ISSN 1055-0623.

This handy reference book concerns itself with the pool of corporate support in the United States. It leaves to other publications the vast sea of individual philanthropy that accounts for over 80 percent of the money donated annually to the nation's nonprofits. The publishers estimate the size of corporate giving at approximately $3.4 billion annually. Added to that figure are nonmonetary donations such as equipment, products, in-kind services, marketing, promotion, and loaned employees. Sources for both the monetary and nonmonetary corporate giving are included in the *Corporate Giving Directory 1999*.

Detailed corporate profiles of more than 1,000 of the largest corporate giving programs in the United States take up two-thirds of the book's 1,800 pages. After information on sales, profits, *Fortune* rank, employees, headquarters, and major products, the editors explain who runs the company and foundation, their philosophy of giving, how to approach them, and how they decided on grant requests. Priorities and restrictions are also included as well as recent grant recipients and amounts.

The editors devote one-third of the book to rearranging the corporate profiles into 14 useful indexes. Because most corporations say they award grants in locales where their employees work and live, the three location directories may be the book's most important asset. Here corporations are listed by the location of their head-quarters, operating plants, and grant recipients. The three most intriguing indexes sort executive biographical data by birth place, alma mater, and clubs—yacht, country, civic, racquet, city, even literary. By comparing various indexes, business-savvy development directors will discover fascinating connections and associations.

This directory is highly recommended for national nonprofits and community groups willing to do the hard work of matching nonprofit needs with self-serving corporate goals. Recent financial data, in some cases, are from the early to mid-1990s; names and titles of corporate leaders are assumed to be more up-to-date.

—**Pete Prunkl**

762. **Corporate Giving Yellow Pages 1998.** 13th ed. Laura Wisner-Broyles, ed. Detroit, Taft Group/Gale, 1997. 315p. index. $99.00. ISBN 1-56995-263-9. ISSN 1055-4998.

It looks like a telephone book; it reads like a telephone book. *Corporate Giving Yellow Pages 1998* lives up to its title very well. This completely revised 13th edition, which includes nearly 3,700 entries, is a one-stop guide to identifying corporate grant-makers. The cost seems high for a paperback volume of slightly more than 300 pages, but the preface claims the inclusion of companies that operate difficult-to-research direct giving programs, which may prove its value.

The main section, labeled "Directory of Contacts," lists corporate contributions programs arranged alphabetically by the sponsoring company name, the contact person and title, address, telephone number, fax number, and employer identification number. Three indexes help users to identify potential donors: corporations listed by state headquarters, corporations listed by state operating locations, and corporations listed by their major product or by the industry in which they function. Such headings range from coal mining to commodity brokers. A Standard Industrial Classification code is provided for each category. A quick perusal can easily determine whether the grant-writer or donation-seeker will find the pages useful.—**Jerri Spoehel**

763. **The Directory of Corporate and Foundation Givers 1998.** Katherine E. Jankowski, ed. Detroit, Taft Group/Gale, 1997. 2v. index. $250.00. ISBN 1-56995-256-6. ISSN 1054-108X.

This directory is another Taft Group information database book for nonprofit organizations and institutions that presents the most recent data available on the 8,000 major corporate and foundation funding sources for nonprofits. More than $15.1 billion in cash contributions and estimated value of nonmonetary support to non-profit organizations were given in the reporting period, and these givers have assets of more than $183 billion. Nearly 350 new profiles are listed since the last edition (see ARBA 97, entry 686). Of course, the *Foundation Directory* (see ARBA 94, entry 890) is the first source when used with grants indexes, but the title at hand is exceptionally efficient for nonprofit grant-seekers.

The directory details prospective funders with biographical data on foundation officers, directors, trustees, and corporate officers; recent grants lists of the top 10 grants disbursed by all foundations; historical data including profiled list assets and giving figures for 3 years of giving; and contributions received in 1996 and 1997 of almost $3.9 billion. There are nine indexes of the data: funders by headquarters state, funders by operating location, funders by grant type, funders by nonmonetary support type, funders by recipient type, funders by major products/industry, officers and directors by name, grant recipients by state, and master index to funders. Each entry includes the profile name of the corporation or foundation; sponsoring company and information including SIC classifications (however, there are no SIC codes); contact person for inquiries; financial summary, which gives the user access to the financial status and potential for giving; contribution summary, a real asset; corporate officers/giving officers directory with biographies; application information; "other things to know," which reports incidental policies or procedures that could affect funding; grants analysis; and recent grants.

The comprehensive scope of all these data in one sequence in two volumes makes this a real asset for the quick reference service of academic, public, and special libraries, and also for the busy grant-seekers in non-profit organizations. The directory is highly recommended for all academic and public libraries and especially for nonprofit organizations' grant-seekers.—**Gerald D. Moran**

764.   **Directory of International Corporate Giving in America and Abroad 1998.** Katherine E. Jankowski, ed. Detroit, Taft Group/Gale, 1997. 844p. index. $199.00pa. ISBN 1-56995-264-7. ISSN 1046-4263.

The 1998 edition of the *Directory of International Corporate Giving in America and Abroad* is a helpful tool for grant-seekers everywhere. Its two sections contain a total of 650 profiles of companies with an international focus. Section 1 profiles more than 460 foreign-owned companies operating in the United States, and section 2 profiles more than 190 U.S. multinational companies. Companies are arranged alphabetically within these sections by company name. Each listing gives biographical data, the employee identification number (EIN), a giving summary for the past three years, typical recipients of grants, and application information. Additionally, section 2 provides information on the expansion plans of the leading U.S. multinationals for two years and restrictions that the company has on giving activities. A new category in section 2, "About the Company," describes the company's major lines of business and other background information on the company indicating its international outlook and scope. Both sections have multiple indexes to serve as access points, including companies by head-quarters state, grant recipients by location, companies by major products/industry, and companies by grant type indexes. A list of abbreviations and a glossary in the beginning of this work are helpful as well.

This work is well-organized and gives in-depth information for all entries. Much of the information listed in this work is not readily available elsewhere. This work is recommended for libraries with extensive collections in philanthropy and grants.—**Laura K. Blessing**

765.   **Directory of Social Service Grants.** 2d ed. Richard M. Eckstein, ed. Loxahatchee, Fla., Research Grant Guides, 1998. 196p. index. $59.50. ISBN 0-945078-18-8.

More than 1,100 foundations that award grants in social service areas are included in this 2d edition of *Directory of Social Service Grants*. Entries are listed alphabetically within each state and include information such as address, telephone number, types of grants awarded, and typical grant range for each foundation.

The work begins with a discussion entitled "Top 10 Tips for More Competitive Grant Proposals," by Luke A. Cermola. Cermola's helpful hints include "Maintain a 'Consumer' Orientation," "Be Clear in Your Communi-cation," "Summarize for Busy Readers," and "Benefit from Positive Rejection." Social service grant-seekers will appreciate having this information available in the directory. Information about *The Foundation Center* and its directory of reference collections and cooperating collections is included as an appendix. The second appendix is a description of *The Grantsmanship Center* and its resources. Indexes listed include an alphabetic listing of foundations and a subject index to entries. Subjects include child welfare, the disabled, the elderly, family services, food banks/meal programs, the homeless, housing, minorities, miscellaneous, religious welfare, shelters, substance abuse, and women. This work will be a helpful starting place for organizations that are looking specifically for grant money in social services areas. However, resources such as *The Foundation Directory* (19th ed.; see ARBA 98, entry 787) give more information, including financial data of the foundation, types of support offered, publications, and the foundation's purpose.—**Laura K. Blessing**

766.   **Federal Grants and Funding Locator.** [CD-ROM]. Washington, D.C., Congressional Quarterly, 1997. Minimum system requirements: IBM or compatible 486. CD-ROM drive. MS DOS 3.0. 512KB real memory. 20MB hard disk space. $295.00.

Mastering this detailed compilation requires an understanding of proximity operators, truncation symbols, DOS commands, and the wherewithal to study a wordy 77-page user's manual. Rewards for one's diligence include the eligibility criteria, funding considerations, postfunding rules, financial information, past accom-plishments, regulations, guidelines, literature, related programs, selection criteria, and special functions for 1,400 federal grant programs. Two levels of search expertise are included in the package—novice and expert. A broad search is possible at both levels. Expert searches are used for finding estimated funding for programs in fiscal years 1996, 1997, and 1998; related programs; examples of funded programs; and criteria used by the federal grantor agency to evaluate proposals. Although a separate section in the user's manual on search strategies is supplied, one can locate grants by jumping in, typing variables of interest, pressing "enter," and navigating with the F-keys. If intuition, onscreen labels, and the user's manual do not help one succeed, a help line (staffed from 10:00 a.m. to 5:00 p.m. weekdays) is available. The intended audiences are individuals, schools, nonprofit organizations, hospitals, libraries, cities, and colleges and universities. Although exceedingly thorough, the *Federal Grants and Funding Locator* fails in its aim to "make it easy for even the novice computer user to locate, research and evaluate federal grants and funding." From installing to fully employing the benefits of this CD-ROM, little about it is easy.—**Pete Prunkl**

767.   **Foundation Reporter 1999.** 30th ed. Laura A. Wisner-Broyles, ed. Detroit, Taft Group/Gale, 1998. 1919p. index. $415.00. ISBN 1-56995-250-7. ISSN 1055-4998.

The *Foundation Reporter* is a one-volume listing of nonprofit granting foundations in the United States. The criterion for inclusion is $10 million in assets per $500,000 in charitable giving. It is the only source that provides biographical data on the people who make foundation grant decisions.

The editors have made the research efficient by providing 13 separate indexes. Seven foundation indexes (by state, grant recipient locator, types of grants, field of interest, donor, list of foundations, and application deadlines) and six biographical indexes of foundations' officers, trustees, and staff (by name, place of birth, alma mater, corporate affiliation, nonprofit affiliation, and club affiliation). This kind of information will enable the members of a development team to quickly identify foundations were they may make successful applications.

This directory provides more in-depth information than the *Annual Register of Grant Support* (26th ed.; see ARBA 94, entry 888). The *Foundation Reporter* provides contact name, officers, and directors; outlines the application and review process; states the instructions; and lists the past grant analysis. Under broad categories (e.g., arts and humanities, the environment), the analysis lists the name of the recipient, the amount, and the purpose of the grant.

The grant directory is a must purchase for academic and public libraries grant collections. It provides the essential information about the foundations that other directories do not provide. [R: BL, July 98, p. 1902]
—**Kay M. Stebbins**

768.   **Foundations of the 1990s: A Directory of Newly Established Foundations.** Margaret Mary Feczko, ed. New York, Foundation Center, 1998. 1345p. index. $150.00pa. ISBN 0-87954-766-9.

Foundations of the 1990s features foundations created after 1989. Its goal is to give grant-seekers an overview of new foundations so that they may find new funding sources. It lists 9,158 descriptive entries of foundations created after 1989. The introduction includes a definition of a foundation and gives the restrictions that are used in excluding foundations from the main section.

The types of foundations that are included in the main section include independent, company-sponsored, operating, and community foundations. Entries are arranged alphabetically by state and within state by name. Each entry contains directory information, foundation type, establishment data, employee identification number, contact person, donors or principal contributors, asset information, information on expenditures and on grants paid per year, purpose and activities of foundation, fields of interest, types of support, stated limitations, publications, application information, and officers and principal administrators.

Indexes include an index to donors, officers, and trustees; a geographical index; an international giving index; a types of support index; a subject index; and a foundation name index. The 1st appendix is a list of 58 foundations that were not included in the main section of this work because there was not enough information available. The 2d appendix lists 1,984 foundations that were established in the 1990s but were excluded from the descriptive directory because they have since terminated, they have ceased grant-making, or they limit their giving. Each entry explains the reason the foundation was eliminated.

Because of its currentness, other works, such as *The Foundation Directory* (19th ed.; see ARBA 98, entry 787), will not necessarily duplicate the information found in this directory. Libraries collecting heavily in the foundations area will want to purchase this work.—**Laura K. Blessing**

769.   **The International Foundation Directory 1998.** 8th ed. London, Europa; distr., Farmington Hills, Mich., Gale, 1998. 875p. index. $210.00. ISBN 1-85743-054-9.

This single-volume directory of international foundations, trusts, and other similar nonprofits contains information concerning more than 1,500 new and continuing groups. The introduction covers the history of foundations, ranging from the charities organized in medieval times through the 100,000 foundations in Germany before

1914 to the 1990s and the requirements of payouts based on finances. Of particular interest is the discussion of "What Is a Foundation?" because there is no common definition throughout the world. Also presented is a look at foundations in the next century.

Of course, the bulk of the volume is the list of worldwide foundations. Each entry, when possible, contains the institution's name; address; telephone and fax numbers; e-mail and Internet addresses; date and purpose of establishment; and its primary aims, activities, finances, publications, and key executives. Activities range widely. Among them are the arts, the environment, economic affairs, education, human rights, and science. Listings of some countries, such as Croatia or Peru, may include only a single foundation, or the number may be quite long, such as 151 pages for the United States. Two large indexes list the foundations by name and by their main activities. Also included is a list of currency exchange rates and international telephone codes.

The slick purple book jacket protects a handsome dark blue hardcover with gold lettering. Anyone wanting more knowledge on foundations throughout the world would find this 8th edition helpful.—**Jerri Spoehel**

770.   Miner, Jeremy T., and Lynn E. Miner. **Funding Sources for Community and Economic Development 1998: A Guide to Current Sources for Local Programs and Projects.** Phoenix, Ariz., Oryx Press, 1998. 571p. index. $64.95. ISBN 1-57356-086-3. ISSN 1080-6318.

Oryx Press has published the GRANTS database for more than 20 years. The *Funding Sources for Community and Economic Development 1998* is designed to encourage more applicants for grants and to make the grant information readily available by publishing print and online directories for grants. The aim of this publication is to provide up-to-date information about grants for community development projects, health care and humanities research, and performing arts programs. The scope of the foundations include national, state, and community levels. The directory provides 4 indexes: subject index, sponsoring organization index, grants by program types, and a geographic index. A directory for the sponsor's World Wide Web address is also provided.

Grant-seekers can use this directory to match their needs to the particular programs described in the sponsors' entries. Each entry describes the program, amount of grant, requirements for application, dates of renewal, contacts, and Website and street address. This directory is a must for the grants collections of public, academic, and special libraries of private organizations. [R: BL, July 98, p. 1902]—**Kay M. Stebbins**

771.   **The PRI Index: 500 Recent Foundation Charitable Loans and Investments.** Crystal Mandler, Loren Renz, and Rikard Treiber, eds. New York, Foundation Center, 1997. 70p. $75.00pa. ISBN 0-87954-758-8.

The topic of program-related investments (PRIs) may come as a surprise to some grant researchers. PRIs are not common in the world of foundations. Often foundations make PRIs as a supplement to their existing grant programs.

This index describes a PRI as an investment by a foundation to support a charitable project involving the potential return of capital—rather similar to a recoverable grant. The Internal Revenue Service defines a PRI as any investment by a foundation that meets these criteria: Its primary purpose is to further the exempt objectives of the foundation; the production of income is not a significant purpose; and it may not be used to support lobbying.

The PRI Index lists 509 program-related investments of at least $10,000 with a total value of $229,386,288 made by 126 foundations. The following information is included for each PRI listing: funder name and state; recipient name, city, and state; PRI amount; and year of authorization. Section 1 makes listings by foundation name and section 2, by major subject categories (e.g., arts, education, and so on). In section 3 are 4 indexes: PRI-makers by foundation location; PRIs by subject and type of support; PRIs by recipient name; and PRIs by recipient location. Section 4 lists foundations with addresses and limitations.

Although PRIs have been used most extensively to support affordable housing and community development, they have also funded capital projects ranging from preserving historic buildings and repairing churches to preserving open space and wildlife habitats. The index also issues advice on when to seek a PRI, requirements from the funder, plus information on negotiating terms and managing the repayment. The slim paperback with its dark red print on a light gray cover aims at being informative, not glitzy.—**Jerri Spoehel**

772.   Schlachter, Gail Ann, and R. David Weber. **Financial Aid for Native Americans 1997-1999.** San Carlos, Calif., Reference Service Press, 1997. 616p. index. $35.00. ISBN 0-918276-59-4.

Most Native Americans struggle to find the financial support necessary to pursue their dreams for the education that is not only essential for individual growth and development but also for the self-determination and perhaps even survival of their nation and cultures. For many, in both reservation and urban schools, the bureaucracy required to obtain loans, grants, scholarships, and awards appears formidable, and the many opportunities for financial aid are either unknown or seem inaccessible. This reference book provides urgently needed and practical help in a convenient and sensible format. This 1st edition is designed to help American Indians, Native Alaskans (including Eskimos and Aleuts), and Native Pacific Islanders (including Native Hawaiians and Samoans) access the financial aid opportunities available to them for study, research, creative activities, past accomplishments, future projects, and professional development. (Note that the term *Native American* is defined here appropriately to include three separate groups.)

Divided into 3 sections—descriptions of nearly 1,800 funding opportunities open to Native Americans, an annotated bibliography of directories listing general financial aid programs, and a set of 6 indexes—this hefty and comprehensive resource is user friendly. The financial aid section is grouped into the following categories: scholarships, fellowships, loans, grants, awards, and internships. The annotated bibliography of general financial aid directories provides a list of other publications that describe the multitude of resources available equally to all Americans. The indexes section includes a program title index, a sponsoring organization index, a residency index, a tenability index, a subject index, and a calendar index (application due dates). Given these many routes to information, the persistent student or school counselor is likely to find a source to explore further.

Although a financial aid reference is not a book that is usually read cover-to-cover, this one would be extraordinarily useful to browse extensively in order to understand the variety and scope of opportunities available. For example, there are scholarships for emergency use; for specialized training, such as financial assistance to members of the Oneida Tribe who are enrolled in an accredited hospitality management program; for disabled residents of certain counties in southeastern New Mexico who are interested in becoming teachers in that area; for space-related activities in South Dakota; for jazz musicians; for undergraduate faculty for science and engineering research; and for attendance at the American Press Institute. Clear directions are given as to how to use the directory, and a sample entry is provided for further clarification. Finally, an online source is given to provide updates and augmentation to the listings in this edition.

This resource is absolutely essential for high schools, colleges, and universities that serve significant population of Native American students. In fact, it should be visible and easily accessible in the offices of all tribal governments and urban Native American centers. All high school guidance counselors and financial aid offices should, at least minimally, know of its existence. [R: C&RL, Oct 97, p. 653; BL, July 98, p. 1903]

—**Karen D. Harvey**

773.   Schlachter, Gail Ann. **Directory of Financial Aids for Women 1997-1999.** San Carlos, Calif., Reference Service Press, 1997. 578p. index. $45.00. ISBN 0-918276-52-7. ISSN 0732-5215.

The volume at hand is a directory that provides current and comprehensive information in a single source about the special resources set aside for women. Last reviewed in ARBA 96 (see entry 879), it includes scholarships, fellowships, loans, grants, awards, and internships for women only. The directory is an excellent resource for education and career information funding for applicants of any age or level—high school through postdoctoral and professional. This book is a survey-based resource, and if an organization did not respond to the survey, it is not included; therefore, the directory may not be as comprehensive as the author wanted it to be.

This biennial editions revises 75 percent of the previous profiles and adds 250 new entries for a total of 1,844 profiles. The programs discussed are sponsored by government agencies, professional organizations, corporations, sororities, foundations, religious groups, educational associations, and military/veteran organizations. The financial aids for women cover study, research, travel, training, career development, personal needs, or creative activities. Each profile includes name of the organization, purpose of the aid, eligibility of applicants, financial data, duration, special features, limitations, number awarded, and deadline.

This directory is an excellent guide for women, and the price is very reasonable. It should be in the reference collections of all kinds of libraries as well as in the offices of high school counselors, adult career counselors, and academic advisers. The title is a must-purchase guide. [R: BL, July 98, p. 1902]—**Gerald D. Moran**

Handbooks and Yearbooks

774.   **Fund Raiser's Guide to Human Service Funding 1997.** 9th ed. Kenneth Estell and Laura A. Wisner-Broyles, eds. Detroit, Taft Group/Gale, 1998. 1383p. $130.00. ISBN 1-56995-261-2.

Assisting development officers and fund-raisers to find support for their organizations is the purpose of *Fund Raiser's Guide to Human Service Funding*. It offers information on types of support available, application procedures, restrictions on giving, contact information, and biographical information about those who make the grant decisions.

The 9th edition is updated to include information on more than 1,820 private and corporate foundations and corporate giving programs. All have reported at least $10 million in assets or $200,000 in giving. The indexes are excellent, including funders by state headquarters, types of grants, nonmonetary support, recipients by human service activities in 33 categories from animals to youth organizations, geographical preferences of funding activities by state and city, officers and directors, and a master index of all organizations profiled. Individual profiles include name, contact information, financial information, geographical distribution, grant types, nonmonetary support, recipient types, officers, application procedures (initial contact, grant proposal, deadlines, review process), restrictions on giving, other things to know, publications, and recent grants.

The categories of recipients are especially complete. Among the 33 listed are child abuse, community centers, crime prevention, day care, family planning, people with disabilities, refugee assistance, senior services, and veterans organizations. Readers will find all the information both easy to find and use. Black tabs on the edge of pages help to find index locations in each section. The 1,383 pages offer tremendous help for those seeking human service funding. [R: BL, July 98, p. 1902]—**Jerri Spoehel**

SEX STUDIES

775.   **Sexual Behavior in Modern China: Report on the Nationwide Survey of 20,000 Men and Women.** English-language ed. By Man Lun Ng and Erwin J. Haeberle. New York, Continuum Publishing, 1997. 568p. $95.00. ISBN 0-8264-0886-9.

Sexual Behavior in Modern China has been touted as a "Chinese Kinsey Report." Chinese researchers received data from 20,000 men and women of all ages in all geographic regions of the nation. An introduction and methodology chapter answer questions about the conduct of the research project and analysis of data. The survey is extremely detailed, and tables and text convey extensive information. The relationship of sexual behavior to other demographic variables such as education, income, residential setting (village or city), and domestic arrangements provides interesting insight into the everyday lives of the Chinese. This work is recommended for libraries with collection development interest in sociology and demography.—**Lynne M. Fox**

776.   **Sexuality and Gender in the English Renaissance: An Annotated Edition of Contemporary Documents.** Lloyd Davis, ed. New York, Garland, 1998. 416p. index. (Garland Reference Library of the Humanities, v.201; Garland Studies in the Renaissance, v.10). $85.00. ISBN 0-8153-2452-9.

The contemporary literature on matters pertaining to sexuality and gender has grown exponentially in the recent era. There has been much reinterpretation of traditional constructs on these topics. The present volume brings together some resources that shed light on attitudes toward sexuality and gender during the English Renaissance. More specifically, the book is a compilation of religious sermons, moral treatises, ballads, and other documents from this period addressing questions of morality and proper roles of husbands and wives, parents, and children. The editor has produced a general introduction to the volume that provides an understanding of the historical context of these documents as well as makes a case for their relevance for understanding contemporary issues. Brief introductions are provided for the different sections of the volume as well. These sections include the following: sermons and homilies, moral and religious tracts, marriage and household manuals, midwifery, ballads and chapbooks, witchcraft, and law.

Altogether, this is certainly a competently compiled resource. It seems likely, however, that only a small class of scholars with a special interest in the topics addressed, or the period covered, are likely to work their way through these documents with their unfamiliar idioms and often alien sentiments. For such scholars, this volume, which includes a list of works cited and an index, will certainly be welcome.—**David O. Friedrichs**

SOCIAL WELFARE AND SOCIAL WORK

777.   Greve, Bent. **Historical Dictionary of the Welfare State.** Lanham, Md., Scarecrow, 1998. 159p. (Historical Dictionaries of Religions, Philosophies, and Movements, no.15). $44.00. ISBN 0-8108-3332-8.

The familiar layout of the historical dictionary series makes for a user-friendly reference book. This volume is no exception and contains the standard chronology, bibliography, and lengthy dictionary section. The book's limitations lie in its scope, which is enormous and very general. It aims to cover "the core concepts which are fundamental to an analysis of the welfare state or welfare society." It is not by any means a source on contemporary welfare policy. For instance, although there are entries on "family," "church," and "prevention," there are no entries for "food stamps" or "New Deal." Although unstated, it focuses almost exclusively on the United States and Europe. So, although there are entries for most European countries, there is no mention of any African country or the continent. Besides covering individual countries, some important thinkers such as Adam Smith are included. Yet, most of the book covers concepts that most people already understand or that can be easily found in dozens of other reference books.—**Cathy Seitz Whitaker**

YOUTH AND CHILD DEVELOPMENT

778.   **The Gale Encyclopedia of Childhood and Adolescence.** Jerome Kagan, ed. Detroit, Gale, 1998. 752p. illus. index. $99.00. ISBN 0-8103-9884-2.

Gale has added another work to its extensive collection of reference materials. This latest tome is designed for audiences interested in human development, from birth through adolescence, including students of child development, parents, librarians, teachers, health care providers, child psychologists, and other social service professionals. The 800 terms selected for inclusion reflect the range of subfields encompassed by the field of child development—from profiles of notable individuals (Maria Montessori, Fred Rogers, T. Berry Brazelton) and organizations, to essays on childhood illnesses and diseases, to key concepts and theories.

Terms are introduced with one-sentence definitions, followed by discussions ranging in length from 1 paragraph to 5,000 words. Descriptions of individuals, organizations, and specific medical or psychological tests tend to be relatively brief, whereas discussions of instructional or treatment techniques tend to be lengthier. Entries for medical conditions are extensive and deal with causes, treatment, and effect on the child and family. In most instances, the approach to the content topics is balanced and practical. For example, the entries for "whole language" and for "retention in school"—issues that tend to be controversial—present both sides of the issues and cite relevant research. In many cases, both professional journals and popular magazines are included in the "For Further Study" section that follows each entry. For example, the entry for "retention in school" lists articles from the *Journal of Research in Childhood Education* as well as *Better Homes and Gardens*. Adding to the practicality of this volume is the fact that many of the entries conclude with a list of organizations from which readers can request additional information.

A subject index at the back of the volume enables the reader to locate topics as diverse as athletics; cognitive development; dwarfism; father-child relationship; Freud, Sigmund (which has no entry of its own but is referenced in other entries); head lice; intelligence quotient; Iowa test of basic skills; pacifier; poliomyelitis; running away; sleep; special education; and suicidal behavior.

The only drawback appears to be the limitations imposed by size. For this single-volume encyclopedia, the editor selected 800 terms from a beginning list of 1,500. Users may be disappointed by the lack of coverage of some topics. For example, there is no entry for the topic of "school to work," nor is it listed in the index. The treatment of this topic under "vocational education" is somewhat inadequate. Regardless, this encyclopedia is recommended for libraries serving the intended audiences who need to update their reference collections on issues affecting American youth.—**Jan Bakker**

779.   Geddes, Joan Bel. **Childhood and Children: A Compendium of Customs, Superstitions, Theories, Profiles, and Facts.** Phoenix, Ariz., Oryx Press, 1997. 668p. index. $69.95. ISBN 0-89774-880-8.

Devoted entirely to thoughts and attitudes toward children and ideas and facts about children that have been documented through history up to the current year, this volume can be used as a reference tool, but is also something delightful to browse. Its purpose is to attract parents, grandparents, teachers, friends, sociologists, psychologists, anthropologists, and those generally interested in the research of children's impact on society, be it in a microcosmic setting or society as a whole. The narrative is skillfully interwoven with newspaper excerpts, diary entries, and quotations that clearly reflect the subject matter.

Composed of such topics as folklore, child development, art, music, child rearing, sports, and games, it is easy to recognize the value this volume has to offer. Starting with the "History of Childhood," readers will find chapters devoted to the social and psychological characteristics of childhood including children in folklore, mythology, and religion; children and family life; child rearing and education; children with art and music; children and the entertainment arts; and children and literature. Other chapters include those that deal with the physical well-being of children, such as "Childbirth and Newborns," "Health Care and Children with Disabilities," "Child Development," "Child's Play and Toys," and "Children's Games and Sports." The final chapters touch upon sociological issues of children's lives, including poverty, racism, gangs, violence against children, the effects on children of national and world wars, and peace efforts by children and others. A chapter titled "Advocates for Children" completes the volume, listing various benefactors who exhibited an extraordinary amount of time spent on helping children and children's causes. An extensive bibliography organized by chapter has been provided, along with a section devoted to those sources used in more than one chapter that is titled "General Bibliography." An alphabetized subject index allows the user that much more flexibility in locating specific items. This work will be useful as a ready-reference source for both public libraries and academic libraries that offer courses in the social sciences.—**Marianne B. Eimer**

17 Statistics, Demography, and Urban Studies

DEMOGRAPHY

780. Flanders, Stephen A. **Atlas of American Migration.** New York, Facts on File, 1998. 214p. illus. maps. index. $85.00. ISBN 0-8160-3158-4.

This beautifully crafted work addresses migration from prehistory to the present, placing it both in historical perspective and in light of today's pressing issues (e.g., illegal immigration). The 150 maps, charts, and other graphics illustrate the various movements and groups described in the text. Special features include brief biographies, first-person accounts, chronologies, and narratives of major events. Organized chronologically, eight chapters follow the movement of immigrants trying to better their lives, while the remaining two chapters investigate involuntary migration through enslavement (African Americans) and removal (Native Americans). A bibliography of selected sources and a topical index complete the volume.

Taken as a whole, the atlas is a wonderful collaborative effort combining reams of data with attractive visuals suitable for public and undergraduate libraries, although the small amount of information provided on newer migrations (e.g., Vietnamese) should be noted. Its usefulness for graduate and research libraries is limited due to two problems. First, the source of the data presented is not adequately identified; sources are cited obliquely, through agency names, only in tables and the selected bibliography, with no explanation of how data were gathered. Second, the index does not indicate any of the special features (e.g., biographies, chronologies), leaving the researcher in doubt as to whether a search will retrieve a short biography or a mention within a broader topic.—**Sandra E. Belanger**

781. **Moving & Relocation Sourcebook and Directory 1998.** 2d ed. Nancy V. Kniskern, ed. Detroit, Omnigraphics, 1998. 898p. maps. index. $185.00. ISBN 0-7808-0025-7.

This revised edition of *Moving & Relocation Sourcebook* (see ARBA 93, entry 917 for a review of the 1st edition) includes a wealth of information about 100 cities, which are listed alphabetically. In the introduction, the criteria for inclusion are outlined by stating "*Moving & Relocation Sourcebook and Directory* provides important contact information, demographics, and other details for 100 U.S. cities, including major population centers as well as smaller cities that are popular relocation destinations." There are 30,000 total listings, of which more than 21,000 provide contact data; a number of Website addresses are listed. Sections include the city's history (a short synopsis), government offices, major employers, transportation services, and annual events. The current population is included (based on the 1990 census), as well as the projected population for the year 2000. Quality of living indications is also included; for example, crime index, cost of living index, and median home price. This is a very thorough volume, with an interesting mix of cities; however, curiously, three New England states are excluded from this volume (Vermont, New Hampshire, and Maine). This is an excellent source for people who are considering relocating to a new community (a mileage chart is provided), job hunting, and even planning a vacation. [R: LJ, 15 Sept 98, p. 65; Choice, Oct 98, p. 298]—**Leslie R. Homzie**

782.   **Places, Towns, and Townships 1998.** 2d ed. Deirdre A. Gaquin and Richard W. Dodge, eds. Lanham, Md., Bernan Associates, 1998. 924p. $82.50. ISBN 0-89059-072-9.

The 2d edition of *Places, Towns, and Townships* updates and expands the demographic and economic data in the 1993 1st edition (see ARBA 94, entry 937). There is some overlap between the two editions, particularly in population characteristics, housing, and employment data. Both editions draw data from the 1990 U.S. Census of Population and Housing, but the 2d edition supplements these data with Census Bureau 1996 population estimates and data on building permits, FBI uniform crime reports, the 1992 Economic Censuses, and the 1992 Census of Governments.

For those accustomed to the *County and City Data Book* (Claitor's Publishing, 1997), the layout of the tables is standard and easy to follow with subjects across the top and geographic entities on the vertical. The tables in the 2d edition are different from those of the 1st edition. In the 1993 edition there were 63 data elements for places 10,000 and over (table A) and 14 data elements for places under 10,000 (table B). In the 1998 edition there are 72 data elements for places 10,000 and over (tables A, B, and C); 42 data elements for places 2,500 and over (tables B and C); and 16 data elements for places under 2,500 (table C). In the last category, more than 32,000 places are included—all the places that existed at the time of the 1990 census as well as those that came into being between 1990 and 1994.

Data elements on income, education, unemployment, and disability are omitted from the 2d edition. New data elements are added, including more economic coverage for the 2,500 and over class and, for the 10,000 and over class, data on local government finances, residential construction, and crime.

This work remains a unique and valuable reference for its attention to small places. Once can find more recent data on Websites or by going to the source data, but that requires a lot of research. Bringing these data together in one convenient format, *Places, Towns, and Townships* provides a real service. This work is recommended for all libraries that answer statistical questions. [R: Choice, Sept 98, p. 101]—**Diane L. Garner**

783.   Russell, Cheryl. **Americans and Their Homes: Demographics of Homeownership.** Ithaca, N.Y., New Strategist, 1998. 313p. index. (American Consumer Series). $79.95. ISBN 1-885070-16-0.

This book by the former editor in chief of *American Demographics* is divided into eight easy to read and clearly laid out chapters. Chapter headings include "Demographics of Homeownership," "Owners Who Have Moved," and "Affluent Homeowners." The introduction of each chapter provides two pages of bulleted facts; the rest of the chapter comprises charts and graphs. The charts are easy to read with plenty of white space. On the top of each chart a short explanation of the topic is provided. Topics include the spending of homeowners on residential improvements and repairs by region, equipment failures in new homes, number of women living alone who are homeowners, and the source of down payments and mortgages for homes owned by recent movers. The sources of the data are listed at the bottom of each chart; most of them are taken from the Census Bureau's American Housing Survey. A glossary and an index are also included in this book.

In the introduction Russell writes, "By cutting through the statistical clutter with clear tables and explanatory text, it reveals the story behind the American Dream." The book holds firmly to the author's words. This resource is highly recommended for undergraduate and research libraries. [R: Choice, Nov 98, p. 503]—**Leslie R. Homzie**

784.   **The Sex and Age Distribution of the World Populations: The 1996 Revision.** By Department of Economic and Social Affairs, Population Division. New York, United Nations, 1997. 884p. $60.00pa. ISBN 92-1-151313-8. S/N E.98.XIII.2.

One of the tasks of the United Nations is the making and keeping of records and estimates of the population of the world and all of its member nations. This volume is a 1996 revision in a series of similar volumes, and supersedes the previous edition of 1994 (see ARBA 96, entry 912). It summarizes distributions by age and sex for each country and for selected groups of countries, over each fifth year beginning in 1950 and continuing through 1995. It also includes projected figures in a similar fashion from 1995 through 2050. Because the latter are estimates of future populations, they are made for three possible conditions: low, medium, and high fertility outcomes.

Aside from a brief introduction, the book consists of only the tabular data. Thus, it is by its very nature a reference volume—a compendium of the population distribution by age and sex during the century from 1950 to 2050. Updated as it is, it comprises the best data and future projections available. This is a must for any reference library meant to be inclusive in demographics. The assumptions used in the future estimates are to be published in a companion volume soon, also by the United Nations.—**Arthur R. Upgren**

785.   **The Sourcebook of County Demographics.** 11th ed. Arlington, Va., CACI Marketing Systems; distr., Farmington Hills, Mich., Gale, 1998. 253p. maps. $395.00pa. ISBN 0-918417-72-4.

786.   **The Sourcebook of ZIP Code Demographics.** 13th ed. Arlington, Va., CACI Marketing Systems; distr., Farmington Hills, Mich., Gale, 1998. 744p. $495.00pa. ISBN 0-918417-71-6.

These two volumes constitute a portion of a compendium of demographic data for the United States. Data are provided for each state, county, and metropolitan area of the United States in one of the volumes, and for every zip code of the United States in the other. Specifically, population, its change and composition, and data relating to households and income are included in easily accessed tables. The material is up-to-date, and projections are made for the year 2003. Both of the books are convenient sources for many purposes, with the first having wider application of the two, for which these data may apply or be of interest, and for libraries that serve the purposes of demographic study.—**Arthur R. Upgren**

STATISTICS

International

787.   **Compendium of Social Statistics and Indicators, Fourth Issue.** By the Economic and Social Commission for Western Asia. New York, United Nations, 1997. 184p. $45.00pa. ISBN 92-1-128186-5. ISSN 1012-7801. S/N 97.II.L.11.

This report gives social and economic statistics for Bahrain, Egypt, Iraq, Saudi Arabia, Syria, the United Arab Emirates, Yemen, Kuwait, Lebanon, Oman, the Palestinian Authority, Qatar, and Jordan. Data are not included for Israel. The table headings and text are in English and Arabic. An electronic version is also available. Indicators cover population, mortality, and fertility as well as literacy, gross domestic product (GDP), urban versus rural distribution, educational attainment, crime, health care, major categories of household expenditures, and more.

The years for which data are reported vary from measure to measure and country to country, but the data appear to be the most recent available. Generally, three observation periods are provided for trend analysis.

There are major flaws to this publication. Many of the tables do not state if the data displayed are actual numbers or represents hundreds or thousands or millions. For example, under prevalence of disability, 176 blind Egyptians (both male and female and all age groups) are reported for 1976. It is unlikely that this is an actual number. Definitions are often missing. For example, charts are provided for a gender-related development index and a human development index, but there is no explanation as to what these numbers mean and how they are derived. One wonders about the objectivity of the reporting governmental agencies. For example, the notations for Kuwait and Syria show 100 percent of one-year-olds in both countries as immunized for polio and DPT. As this is a perfect score that the United States has not matched, one wonders about biased data. Even with these failings, given the scarcity of sources for this region, this reference is a good place to start when studying western Asian economic and social development.—**Adrienne Antink Bendel**

788.   **Statistical Indicators for Asia and the Pacific. Volume 27, Number 2, June 1997.** By the Economic and Social Commission for Asia and the Pacific. New York, United Nations, 1997. 85p. $17.50pa. ISBN 92-1-119748-1. ISSN 0252-4457. S/N E.97.II.F.12.

There is always a need for reliable, up-to-date statistics for the countries of Asia and the Pacific. In addition to their monthly, quarterly, and annual statistical surveys, many national statistical offices are mounting useful Websites that provide a lot of socioeconomic and trade data. Although these are important and useful compilations, such individual country data make regional analysis difficult. *Statistical Indicators for Asia and the Pacific* solves this problem by presenting social scientists, economists, and planners with extensive monthly data at the regional and country level. Using data taken from "special statements provided by countries or areas, official national publications, the United Nations *Monthly Bulletin of Statistics, International Financial Statistics* of the International Monetary Fund," this quarterly publication succeeds at presenting comparable data for analysis.

Each issue begins with valuable regional demographic data organized into the regions of East Asia, Southeast Asia, South Asia, Central Asia, and the Pacific. Individual country statistics cover banking and finance, important industries, foreign and internal trade by commodity, consumer and wholesale prices, and population for the past three years with an approximate reporting lag of six to eight months. In addition to the numerical data, graphical representations of selected statistical figures highlight and illustrate trends. Those seeking timely statistical data for Asia and the Pacific will find this a useful supplement to the annual publications *Statistical Yearbook for Asia and the Pacific* (see ARBA 98, entry 815) and *Key Indicators of Developing Asian and Pacific Countries* (Asian Development Bank Staff, 1996).—**Carol L. Mitchell**

789.   **World Directory of Non-Official Statistical Sources.** 2d ed. Chicago, Euromonitor International; distr., Farmington Hills, Mich., Gale, 1998. 348p. index. $590.00. ISBN 0-86338-816-7.

This directory lists statistical sources for consumer goods production, industrial and agricultural industries, and national business trends. The reporting bodies are not government agencies, but instead trade associations, market research firms, banks, and trade presses.

Annotations are organized first by international and regional references and then alphabetically by country. Entries are included for 67 nations with extensive coverage of the United Kingdom, Canada, and the United States. Under each country, items are listed alphabetically by the name of the publication, with the publisher's address, telephone and fax number, and e-mail address when available. In addition, the reader is given the frequency of publication, language, price, and a brief description of areas covered. Unfortunately, the language is not always identified for sources published in non-English-speaking countries.

Examples of the wide range of narrowly focused citations are the *Baltic Media Book, European Sandwich, Snack News Review*, an annual report on the German film industry, *Lifestyle Characteristics of Sporting Goods Consumers*, and *Business Expectations*. The publishers are listed separately with contact information cross-referenced to the page numbers of the directory items. Selections are indexed by the source's name, publisher's name, country, and topic (e.g., automobiles, construction, food, insurance, labor). This volume is a useful tool for locating statistical data on a wide variety of industries and fields of interest for which resources may be difficult to find.—**Adrienne Antink Bendel**

790.   **World Population Prospects: The 1996 Revision.** By the Department of Economic and Social Affairs Population Division. New York, United Nations, 1998. 839p. $95.00. ISBN 92-1-151316-2. S/N E.98.XIII.5.

As with the previous volumes of this publication, the statistics presented here are based on the latest round of global demographic estimates and projections (in the case of the book under review, for 1996) by the Population Division of the Department of Economic and Social Affairs of the United Nations Secretariat. For those unfamiliar with this publication, it lists population estimates and projections for the world as a whole, for the more developed and the less developed areas of the world, for 6 major areas, 20 regions, and then for individual countries and areas (228 in this revision). For each country, estimates of the total population are given at 5-year intervals beginning with 1950. They, in turn, are broken down by sex, age distribution, population density, and by demographic indicators (e.g., birth rate, crude death rate, life expectancy). Population projections are also given at 5-year intervals beginning with 1995 and extending to 2025 and then by 10-year intervals beginning with 2030 and extending to 2050. They are also broken down by the same categories found in the population estimates and repeated in 4 variant groupings: medium, high, low, and constant-variant projections. In addition to the statistical tables, there is also included a preliminary section that discusses both the methodology used to arrive at the figures presented and the meaning of the statistics and the significance of the demographic changes for selected topics and geographic areas under consideration.

There are some changes to this revision from previous editions. The base year for the population projections was changed from 1990 to 1995; that is, one set of population estimates was prepared for the 1950 to 1995 period, and the 4 variants of projections now begin with 1995. Detailed estimates are presented for the first time for the Gaza Strip, Macao, and the Western Sahara. The number of countries for which the demographic impact of AIDS is listed has increased from 16 to 28, primarily in Africa, but also including India, Thailand, Brazil, and Haiti. Estimates and projections of international migration were heavily revised in light of recent world upheavals and consequent changes in migratory patterns.

The information presented in this publication is also available on tape and diskettes, but whether a library has it available in print or via computer, the information in this publication is invaluable, convenient, and as reliable as is possible. It should be considered a basic reference tool for all libraries wanting to provide users with current demographic statistics and trends.—**Paul H. Thomas**

United States

791.   **A Statistical Portrait of the United States: Social Conditions and Trends.** Mark S. Littman, ed. Lanham, Md., Bernan Associates, 1998. 404p. $79.00. ISBN 0-89059-076-1.

Although the U.S. government is the primary hunter and gatherer of statistical information, rarely has the government prepared this information in formats that the public finds palatable. Its efforts to compile social indicators have been sporadic, to say the least. *Social Indicators*, published jointly by the Office of Management and Budget and the Bureau of the Census, went to press three times—in 1974, 1977, and 1980. The long-awaited *National Economic, Social, & Environmental Data Bank* (NESE) on CD-ROM, although not particularly easy to use, was well received in 1993. It ceased publication, however, in August 1995. Once again, the public was forced to pick and choose statistics from a smorgasbord of social agencies.

The contributors to *A Statistical Portrait of the United States*, alumni of the U.S. Bureau of the Census, the Bureau of Labor Statistics, and the Bureau of Justice Statistics, have come to the rescue. In this 1st edition, they have compiled statistical data from a wide array of government and private sources and organized them into an easy-to-understand portrait of life in the United States. Focusing on the major changes in the past 25 years, there is a strong emphasis on the 1990s. Few comparisons predate 1970, and, as is typical for statistical compendiums, few statistics are more current than 1996.

The contents are organized into 12 topical chapters, including population; living arrangements; education; health; labor; income; housing; crime; voting; environment; government; and an especially interesting section on leisure, volunteerism, and religion. Each chapter is 5 to 15 pages long, and contains a summary of statistics presented in a concise and cogent narrative that is augmented and enhanced by visual representations of the key data. These summaries highlight trends, point out significant changes, and underscore interesting findings. The figures and tables present relevant data in visual formats that display comparisons over time, by individual characteristics, or with other countries of the world. Both the narrative and the graphics are well-documented, with definitions, explanatory notes, and source references. Each chapter ends with bibliographic references, including Websites, that document the summaries and lead the user to additional information. An appendix provides detailed tabulations of data for each of the 12 topics. As with the body of the text, these tables are well organized, comparative in nature, and compiled to provide a more in-depth picture of U.S. society. The expanded table of contents also serves as an index to the information.

Although the price may deter some smaller libraries, this volume will be of interest to public, academic, and school libraries alike. Because the information is dated, one can only hope that, unlike governmental efforts, this 1st edition will not be the last. [R: BL, 15 Dec 98, p. 766]—**Debra S. Van Tassel**

URBAN STUDIES

792.   **The Encyclopedia of Housing.** Willem van Vliet, ed. Newbury Park, Calif., Sage, 1998. 712p. illus. index. $149.95. ISBN 0-7619-1332-7.

This encyclopedia is the most comprehensive source of information covering the multidisciplinary field of housing research currently available, and, as such, is an important reference tool that belongs in any substantial collection. Entries are arranged alphabetically and vary in length depending on the topic. Short entries primarily focus on organizations or peripheral issues, whereas lengthier essays are written about conceptual topics or issues, such as the savings and loan industry, that are more germane to the study of housing. A majority of the entries include a list of suggested readings intended to direct readers to more in-depth information. Many are supplemented with clearly presented tables, charts, or other illustrations. *See also* cross-referencing is used throughout the volume. A system of nodal cross-referencing is used to assist the user in identifying related terms under broad conceptual categories, thereby enhancing the multidisciplinary utility of the work. The nodal cross-referencing terms are highlighted in bold and listed in the first appendix. Other appendixes include a directory of housing organizations cited in the volume, a list of housing-related publications also cited in the work, and a chronology of major U.S. housing legislation. Three indexes list the contributors, the authors cited in the bibliographies, and keywords appearing in the text of entries. Excluded from this volume are biographical profiles and a comprehensive history of housing. In addition, only selected acts of housing legislation are described. The work primarily limits its coverage to North America, leading this reviewer to hope that an international companion encyclopedia is forthcoming. [R: LJ, 1 Oct 98, p. 78; BL, 1 Sept 98, p. 154; Choice, Oct 98, p. 296]—**Robert V. Labaree**

793.   **Encyclopedia of Urban America: The Cities and Suburbs.** Neil Larry Shumsky, ed. Santa Barbara, Calif., ABC-CLIO, 1998. 2v. illus. index. $175.00/set. ISBN 0-87436-846-4.

Complementing the 1997 *Encyclopedia of Rural America* (see ARBA 98, entry 98) from the same publisher, the purpose of the 547 entries in the 2-volume *Encyclopedia of Urban Life* is to describe and analyze the United States' built environment and its impact on public policy, the economy, religion, education, politics, history, and culture. Coverage primarily focuses on the twentieth century, paralleling the most robust period of urban growth in the United States, although historical references are included when appropriate.

Among the strengths of this work is the fact that the alphabetically arranged entries cover a broad spectrum of well-chosen topics by the editor. For example, the work contains profiles of key political, architectural, and artistic figures associated with the birth and development of urban United States, such as entries on Charles Bulfinch, whose architectural designed heavily influenced the urban landscape of Boston, and Tom Bradley, the charismatic former mayor of Los Angeles. Another category of entries are historical descriptions of major cities, suburbs, and neighborhoods. The encyclopedia is also useful for its descriptions of social and cultural issues closely identified with urban life. A typical example is the detailed essay examining social welfare. Descriptions of city infrastructures, such as subways, and their impact on city planning represent another type of entry. A final identifiable category of topics covered in this work analyzes economic and political issues. Examples under this category include entries about water pollution, the urban policy of the New Deal, and property taxes.

Taken together, these categories of entries, as well as miscellaneous short entries on peripheral subjects, contribute to an overall understanding of urbanization in the United States for the reader. Each entry is written by one of 374 scholars; all are signed and include a bibliography. Cross-references to related entries are provided when needed. A smattering of photographs and reproductions are placed throughout the encyclopedia but they do not necessarily contribute to one's understanding of the text. Volume 2 concludes with a selected bibliography arranged under broad categories, a list of entries by subject, and an index. [R: BL, 1 Dec 98, pp. 690-694]
—**Robert V. Labaree**

794.   **World Urbanization Prospects: Estimates and Projections of Urban and Rural Populations and of Urban Agglomerations.** By the Department of Economic and Social Affairs Population Division. New York, United Nations, 1998. 191p. $37.50pa. ISBN 92-1-151317-0. S/N E.98.XIII.6.

This publication is linked to the United Nation's forthcoming 1996 revision of the *World Population Prospects*. The focus here is on urban agglomerations for major areas, regions, and individual countries. The urban-rural dichotomy is also addressed in the text and tables provided. There are 80 pages of text, with charts and graphs, supplemented by 110 pages of statistical tables for countries and urban areas. The text is divided into 3 major sections: prospects of urbanization and city growth (which includes an assessment of the 15 largest urban agglomerates and other "mega-cities"); methodology for estimation and projections; and sources of data (arranged by country). The appended tables cover the following categories of data: the distribution of population among urban and rural areas, from 1950 to 2030; the growth rates of the population, also from 1950 to 2030; the rate of urbanization and ruralization, 1950 to 2030; and data on urban agglomerations, 1950 to 2015. Anyone watching the growth of the developing nations will be fascinated by many of these tables. Cities in India, China, and Pakistan are on the rise, and by 2015 Lagos, Nigeria, is projected to be the third-largest urban area in the world (after Tokyo and Bombay). By 2015, New York City will have slipped to number 9 on the list and Los Angeles to number 15. This work will be useful for most academic libraries, especially those supporting programs in developing areas and demographics. The data is also available on diskettes, which can be ordered from the United Nation's Population Division ($200 for the urban and rural areas data, and $150 for the urban agglomerations).
—**Thomas A. Karel**

18 Women's Studies

BIBLIOGRAPHY

795. Nordquist, Joan, comp. **The Asian American Woman: Social, Economic, and Political Conditions, a Bibliography.** Santa Cruz, Calif., Reference and Research Services, 1997. 72p. (Contemporary Social Issues: A Bibliographic Series, no.48). $15.00pa. ISBN 0-937855-94-4.

This latest addition to Contemporary Social Issues: A Bibliographic Series published by Reference and Research Services covers, the social, economic, and political conditions of Asian American women. Its main purpose is to provide the most up-to-date and accurate information for quick access to the current literature. Like its earlier companion, *Asian Americans: Social, Economic, and Political Aspects* (see ARBA 97, entry 327), this bibliography of 724 entries covers books, pamphlets, government documents, dissertations, articles in books, and periodical articles. It is divided into 20 main subject areas. The first 7 sections are for each major Asian American group, followed by 13 broad topics such as education, economic conditions, employment, health, family, violence against women, sex roles, images and stereotypes, feminism, political activity lesbians, elders, and testimonials. Entries within each category are subdivided by books and articles. Only English-language publications of the past few years are included. There are no annotations or indexes, although an author index and a title index would enhance the value of the volume. Many of the works are by Asian American women; activist organizations; or alternative, small, feminist, and radical presses. The "Resources" section includes hard-to-find bibliographies and directories as well as relevant Websites.

This volume, to a certain degree, overlaps with the *Asian Americans* volume mentioned above. However, it is a useful compilation not only for quick reference but also for selection purposes. In addition, it is a reasonably priced reference work and a welcome addition to the growing field of Asian American literature. This source is recommended for Asian American studies, women's studies, social studies, and general reference collections for academic libraries.—**Karen T. Wei**

796. **Reader's Guide to Women's Studies.** Eleanor B. Amico, ed. Chicago, Fitzroy Dearborn, 1998. 732p. index. $125.00. ISBN 1-884964-77-X.

Women's studies is a relatively new discipline and it is encouraging to see a comprehensive guide to works in the field. Books covering more than 500 topics and significant individuals have been selected by an international group of contributors. The titles are published, interdisciplinary works on women and gender. All titles are available in English and are completely or mostly about the specific topic or person.

Entries are alphabetic and begin with a list of the books on the topic or individual. Complete bibliographic information is given for each title. The bibliography is followed by an essay discussion that compares and contrasts the works and identifies each title's main points and perspective as well as its relevance to the body of work. Essays are scholarly in tone and succinctly describe the author's contribution to the literature. All articles are signed, and the contributor's credentials are provided.

There is an alphabetic list of entries and a thematic list that organizes them into 42 categories covering such topics as politics and government, music, ancient history, and sexuality. The thematic list is designed to lead the user to all the entries in an area of interest, and names of individuals appear under all appropriate categories. This list also supplements the cross-references. There is also a list of the titles discussed and a general index. The number of titles per topic or individual varies. Some entries have as many as 14 and others, where few books are available, as few as 3. The most extensive categories are religion, politics and government, and writers. Law, life cycles, organizations, and sports have the least. Many notable women have been excluded because not enough book-length material has been written about them.

The guide will be useful to graduate and undergraduate students. It offers them a wide selection, yet enables them to focus on the most outstanding works in an area. Teachers preparing courses and the sophisticated reader with an interest in women's studies will also find the book a valuable resource. It is highly recommended for college and university libraries, especially those with a women's studies program. [R: Choice, Sept 98, pp. 82-84; LJ, Aug 98, pp. 78-79]—**Marlene M. Kuhl**

BIOGRAPHY

797.   Adamson, Lynda G. **Notable Women in World History: A Guide to Recommended Biographies and Autobiographies.** Westport, Conn., Greenwood Press, 1998. 401p. index. $49.50. ISBN 0-313-29818-1.

Aimed at both the general public and students in high school or college, this guide covers international (excluding the United States) women who made noteworthy contributions outside the home and who have had at least one full-length book about their lives published in English (including translations) since 1970 that is listed in the Library of Congress. The 500 alphabetically arranged entries provide short biographical information that focuses on family background, education, occupation, and accomplishments, followed by briefly annotated lists of up to five autobiographies, biographies, diaries, or letters. Entries also note the dates of birth and death, country of origin, and occupation(s). This information is repeated in three useful appendixes that list the women by date of birth (from Egyptian pharaoh Hatshepsut, born in 1503 B.C.E. to Guatemalan activist Rigoberta Menchu, born in 1959), country, title, occupation(s), or area(s) of interest, such as queen, mystic, scientist, sculptor, and writer. The book contains a name index, which seems superfluous because it lists the women in the same order as the guide. However, the index does include cross-references and notes page numbers for mentions of the person in other entries. A subject index would have been much more useful.

This guide is most appropriate for school, public, and small academic libraries, where it could update *The Continuum Dictionary of Women's Biography* (Continuum, 1989). Larger academic libraries might consider it as a supplement to *Women's Diaries, Journals, and Letters: An Annotated Bibliography* (see ARBA 90, entry 853) that compiles nearly 3,000 personal writings of women from around the world, *Index to Women of the World from Ancient to Modern Times: A Supplement* (see ARBA 90, entry 878), and the *Subject Guide to Women of the World* (see ARBA 97, entry 741). [R: BR, Nov/Dec 98, p. 83; Choice, July/Aug 98, p. 1825]
—**Linda A. Krikos**

798.   **Biographical Dictionary of Chinese Women: The Qing Period, 1644-1911.** Lily Xiao Hong Lee and A. D. Stefanowska, eds. Armonk, N.Y., M. E. Sharpe, 1998. 387p. index. $87.95. ISBN 0-7656-0043-9.

This biographical dictionary is a solid contribution to women's studies and Chinese studies. The introduction notes that although there are several important English-language biographical dictionaries covering eminent Chinese, these and other resources largely ignore the contributions of women to Chinese society. The *Biographical Dictionary of Chinese Women* succeeds in providing "more complete biographical data on individual Chinese women" and on "representative Chinese women."

With the exception of 2 fictional women, all of the nearly 200 women represented in this volume have made contributions to arts, literature, politics, and scholarship within and beyond the borders of China. A useful introductory finding list arranges the entries by fields of endeavor, and an index at the end aids finding entries for different versions of names. The main part of the dictionary consists of brief signed entries of one to three pages arranged in alphabetic order. All entries include dates of birth and death, variant spellings of the name, a narrative, and a brief bibliography. Some women were excluded if they were more active during another period of Chinese history; other women are excluded because a dearth of information prohibited enlightening entries.

Given the status of women in historical China, it is clear that these are truly remarkable women who deserve the attention of English-language readers. *Biographical Dictionary of Chinese Women* is a welcome contribution for libraries interested in serving Asian communities, women's studies, and Chinese studies.—**Carol L. Mitchell**

799.   **The Grolier Library of Women's Biographies.** Danbury, Conn., Grolier, 1998. 10v. illus. index. $319.00/set. ISBN 0-7172-9124-3.

The Grolier Library of Women's Biographies surpasses the usual list of notable women to find the unusual contributors to medicine, the arts, teaching, activism, and government. A well-conceived, beautifully executed series, this work entices young researchers as well as teachers, librarians, and parents from cover to index. Each volume opens with a table of contents that lists the entry, a brief description, and page number. In bold typeface are the titles of 20 essay articles, such as "Women's Employment Issues," "Suffrage," and "Women and Islam." A delightfully readable preface discusses the issues of patriarchy and marginalization without rancor through thoughtful commentary and passages from the Bible, Koran, Aeschylus's *Eumenides*, and Elizabeth Cady Stanton's *History of Woman Suffrage*. Equally forthright are 1,750 succinct, informative entries, 1,300 of which are accompanied by photographs or drawings. Concluding each volume is a master index. General headings list entries under groupings such as law, Swiss women, espionage, and performing arts. A puzzling omission is the absence of subheadings for African American women. The final volume appends a 36-page list of works cited and their authors.

The overall plan and coverage of the Grolier biography set is remarkably balanced and useful. Diction and composition set a good example of clear, objective writing and wise selection of data. A worthy adjunct to the work's success is the selection of appealing typefaces, layout, and pagination. A dismaying fault is the near absence of Native American women. The obligatory Pocahontas and Sacagawea receive mention, but editors have omitted them from the subheading "Heroism." Passed over are the best known Native American leaders and role models—Wilma Mankiller, Milly Hayo Francis, Datsolali, Sarah Winnemucca, Martha Brae, Molly Brant, Kateri Tekakwitha, Nancy Ward, Maria Tallchief, Marjorie Tallchief, Gayle Ross, Maconagua, Maria Chona, Buffy Sainte Marie, and Suzette La Flesche Picotte (Bright Eyes). The glaring slight of American Indian women is a serious drawback to a set that otherwise demonstrates sensitivity and appreciation for women's struggles to excel. [R: SLJ, Nov 98, p. 152]—**Mary Ellen Snodgrass**

800.   Harper, Judith E. **Susan B. Anthony: A Biographical Companion.** Santa Barbara, Calif., ABC-CLIO, 1998. 335p. illus. index. (ABC-CLIO Biographical Companion). $45.00. ISBN 0-87436-948-7.

The 123 entries that comprise this volume are well written, well researched, and well organized to offer a comprehensive picture of the life and times of Susan B. Anthony. The intent of this biography is to put into perspective the elements, the personalities, and the events not only as they affected Anthony during her 58-year career as an activist but as they shaped her earlier years and U.S. society as a whole. It is this perspective that makes this volume a valuable addition to any library collection. As the author points out in her succinct introduction, society has greatly changed since Anthony's compelling fight for suffrage, abolition of slavery, and other civil rights. In the 1996 national U.S. election, for example, less than one-half of the eligible voters even went to the polls. Harper also points out that the imperative moment in history for the suffrage movement was the 1848 Seneca Falls, New York, convention that first advocated equality and justice for women; a convention that Anthony neither attended nor was interested in at that moment in time.

It is through the author's highly accessible writing style, cross-references, and inclusion of interrelated subjects that the reader comes to understand the force behind not only Anthony herself but American culture and history during this time. The entries are interspersed with photographs, lithographs, political cartoons, newspaper headlines and posters, and the odd footnote to clarify terms. At the conclusion of each entry is a list of related entries and references for further reading. At the conclusion of the alphabetic entries are supplementary material, including speeches such as the March 1849 Daughters of Temperance Speech, letters such as Anthony's April 1854 dispatch confronting slavery, and excerpts from her 1873 trial as well as an annotated chronology, an extensive bibliography, and a comprehensive subject index. This work is recommended for young adult and adult collections. [R: LJ, 15 Nov 98, p. 61]—**Gail de Vos**

CATALOGS AND COLLECTIONS

801.　Catanese, Lynn Ann. **Women's History: A Guide to Sources at Hagley Museum and Library.** Westport, Conn., Greenwood Press, 1997. 338p. illus. index. (Bibliographies and Indexes in Women's Studies). $75.00. ISBN 0-313-30270-7.

　　　The Hagley Museum and Library, originally established as a private collection of Pierre S. du Pont (a former chairman of du Pont de Nemours and General Motors), holds more than historical materials concerning business and technology. Submerged in accounts of corporate development are letters, diaries, and account books of wives and daughters of company executives that relate to women's domestic and public lives; personnel records that document women's changing roles in labor; and advertising images that relate to women as consumers. Catanese, an archivist and specialist in women's history at the Hagley, developed this guide to provide a context for interpreting the collection within the framework of women's history, thus broadening its historical significance and fostering its use in research by a new group of scholars.

　　　Catanese succeeds in developing a guide that reframes previously ignored materials by providing a meaningful, coherent narrative as well as extensive annotations relating the significance of the collection to gender. The guide groups almost 300 manuscript, archival, and pictorial collections (dating mainly from 1800 to 1962) relevant to women's history into 6 subject-oriented chapters: "French Women and America," "Nineteenth Century Domesticity," "The Leisure Class," "Employment and Entrepreneurship," "Culture of Consumption," and "Benevolence, Reform, Religion, and Politics." Each chapter situates the materials in historical context by an informative narrative introduction and lengthy annotations. Extensive cross-references, a name and subject index, and chapter notes enhance access to these materials. Catanese's contribution will benefit laypeople and scholars alike who have an interest in women's history.—**Suzanne G. Frayser**

CHRONOLOGY

802.　**The Wilson Chronology of Women's Achievements: A Record of Women's History from Ancient Time to the Present.** By Irene M. Franck and David M. Brownstone. Bronx, N.Y., H. W. Wilson, 1998. 507p. index. (Wilson Chronology Series). $55.00. ISBN 0-8242-0936-2.

　　　Although the first of nearly 10,000 factual statements presented in the most recent volume in the Wilson Chronology Series is placed under the date 35,000 B.C.E., the work does not attempt to provide a balanced coverage of women's achievements across time. The first 35,000 years are treated in about 6 pages, and the next 1,000 years of women's history are covered in the ensuing 10 pages. The period from 1000 to 1830 C.E. is covered in another 60 pages of text. More than one-half of the 433 pages of entries discuss people and events in women's history since 1920.

　　　The factual statements contained in the volume are presented in chronological order. The early entries are grouped into long time segments of varying lengths, such as "2500 B.C.-2001 B.C." and "950-999." For people and events between 1500 and 1829, the entries are grouped by decade. Beginning in 1830, there is a separate listing for each year. For each period, the entries are arranged into 4 general categories: "Politics/Law/War," "Religion/Education/Everyday Life," "Science/Technology/Medicine," and "Arts/Literature." Each entry, which is between about 8 and 80 words in length, contains nuggets of factual information about significant women and events in history. Sidebars that include quotations, excerpts from significant documents, and fuller explanations of selected topics also punctuate the text. The volume concludes with a select bibliography and a comprehensive index.

　　　Despite its lack of pre-nineteenth-century material, the volume is a useful source for finding such basic facts as the birth and death years of notable, yet often historically overlooked, women of achievement. It will make a welcome addition to the reference collection of any library that services the needs of high school or collegiate students. [R: BR, Nov/Dec 98, p. 83]—**Terry D. Bilhartz**

DICTIONARIES AND ENCYCLOPEDIAS

803.   **Historical Dictionary of Women's Education in the United States.** Linda Eisenmann, ed. Westport, Conn., Greenwood Press, 1998. 534p. index. $95.00. ISBN 0-313-29323-6.

This reference tool presents information on the history of women's education in the United States from the colonial period to the present. It includes 245 original, signed entries written by 104 scholars from the United States and abroad. Ethnic and religious minorities are covered. The entries are arranged alphabetically and include a short bibliography. Most are at least two pages in length. They include numerous cross-references, boldfaced with an asterisk, an important and useful feature.

The book is aimed at a broad audience: researchers, scholars, teachers, students, and laypeople interested in "examining significant events, ideas, movements, institutions and people concerned with the history of women's education in the United States" (p. vii). The topics were selected by taking into account a representation of geographic, racial, and socioeconomic diversity of schooling for girls and women and both formal and informal educational settings. Issues, events, and themes rather than biographies are emphasized. Coverage varies, based on the availability of solid scholarship. There is a selected bibliography at the end of the volume, including reference books and general secondary sources on women's educational history.

Two particularly useful features are the introduction, which presents a historical overview of women's educational history, and the appendix, a timeline of women's educational history in the United States from 1675 to 1996. The book includes an index with main entry page numbers in bold typeface, simplifying access to desired topics. The list of contributors includes mostly academic scholars. The editor is assistant professor of education at the University of Massachusetts, Boston, and has a record of publications in this area. The book is a valuable contribution to scholarship in women's studies and will be an important addition to reference collections in academic, special, and public libraries. [R: BL, 15 Nov 98, pp. 612-613]—**Susan J. Freiband**

804.   **The Reader's Companion to U.S. Women's History.** Wilma Mankiller and others, eds. New York, Houghton Mifflin, 1998. 696p. illus. index. $45.00. ISBN 0-395-67173-6.

Whether women are brimming with self-esteem or bowing with reticence, their significance as half the energy, half the parents, half the responsible parties of this planet is the focus of this wonderful and thorough assessment of women in U.S. history.

The Reader's Companion to U.S. Women's History explores and explains complex moral codes such as marriage, breeding, and divorce; cruel and unusual punishments over such issues as chattel, privacy, and spirituality; and the verve and ingenuity of women who creatively and persistently overcame rigid expectations throughout U.S. history. Accounts and accomplishments of Hawaiian, republican, lesbian, black, Chicana, Jewish, disabled, farming, feminist, religious, athletic, and Confederate women are a sample of the scope and profundity this work investigates. Much of women's history that has been suppressed or altered comes alive due to five editors urging 323 experts to research specific topics and write concise appraisals of the contributions of women in the history of this country. The attitude is positive, the writing glows, and the information is deep. Eating disorders, music, immigration, violence, and quilting are part of the essence of women's role in U.S. history, proving that the thrust of this book is not to whitewash, but to inform.

The 657 pages of encyclopedic entries in this work enlighten and entertain as good scholarship should. It is an ambitious book, and its culmination leaves the reader wanting more legends, more stories, and more information. [R: SLJ, Nov 98, p. 156; LJ, Jan 98, p. 93; BL, 15 May 98, p. 1660]—**Mary Pat Boian**

805.   **Women in the Third World: An Encyclopedia of Contemporary Issues.** Nelly P. Stromquist and Karen Monkman, eds. New York, Garland, 1998. 683p. index. (Garland Reference Library of Social Sciences, v.760). $135.00. ISBN 0-8153-0150-2.

Women in the Third World goes far beyond an encyclopedia in its breadth and depth of coverage. This excellent compilation of essays provides timely information and insight into the many complex issues facing women living in the economically, culturally, and politically diverse Third World. An important first chapter addresses emerging questions being raised about the theory and research methods appropriate for understanding Third World women. The majority of the book is devoted to an in-depth look at women in relation to broader global and development issues. Each of the sections—"Political and Legal Concerns," "Sex-Role Ideologies," "Demographics and Health," "Marriage and the Family," "Women and Production," and "Women and the

Environment"—includes lengthy contributions by women from differing regions, bringing to the book a comparative perspective. Two examples from this section highlight the "contemporary" nature of this volume. One article examines the impact of mandated economic structural adjustment programs on women's lives; the other proposes positive roles for women in natural resources management.

The following two chapters address the changing lives of women in the Third World and organized movements that promote women's issues. The book concludes with situational reports covering women in different regions of the world. Coverage of the issues is enhanced by contributors who are experts not only in feminist studies but also are feminist advocates living and working in the Third World. Current statistics and up-to-date bibliographies add to the usefulness of this volume. This excellent resource deserves a space in college and large public libraries with an interest in women's studies or Third World issues. [R: Choice, Dec 98, p. 671]

—**Carol L. Mitchell**

806. **Women's Firsts: Milestones in Women's History.** Peggy Saari, Tim Gall, and Susan Gall, eds. Detroit, U*X*L/Gale, 1998. 2v. illus. index. $55.00. ISBN 0-7876-0653-7.

Why would one want one's children to read *Women's Firsts*? It is one of those curious books about which praise is due because it is fun and full. Its scope is enthusiastic, covering women who were the first in the fields of activism, the arts, business, education, government, media, the professions (e.g., architecture, law, medicine, and the military), religion, science, and sports. Women from ancient to modern times and from all over this planet are listed first by domain, then by the year(s) of their most notable accomplishment. The women's birth and death dates, formal education, special awards, photographs, and anecdotes are published, and sources are credited.

Why would one not want one's children to read this book? Because "children" is spelled "childran." Because "Renaissance" and "consumption" and "naval" and "Colombian" are misspelled, and "principle" is used as an adjective. Mother Teresa is said to have joined the Sisters of Loretto (American-founded) when she actually joined the Sisters of Loreto (Italian-founded). Katharine Graham manages to be both Katharine and Katherine in the same paragraph. Whether it is sloppy cut-and-paste or simple disregard of the facts, the accuracy of this book suffers.

The book mentions many obscure, although consequential, women and is a wonderful place to start if you have the Internet or an encyclopedia next to you. Nonetheless, a reader deserves and expects a book that has been proofread. [R: VOYA, Oct 98, pp. 308-309]—**Mary Pat Boian**

HANDBOOKS AND YEARBOOKS

807. Kerschen, Lois. **American Proverbs About Women: A Reference Guide.** Westport, Conn., Greenwood Press, 1998. 200p. index. $59.95. ISBN 0-313-30442-4.

The proverbs included in this volume are culled from a number of previously published sources and are arranged into 16 categories (plus a miscellaneous one) based on women's roles (e.g., wife, bride, mother, old maid) and behavior (e.g., talkativeness, flightiness). Additional chapters include "A Woman's Looks," "Bad Women versus Virtuous Women," and "The Law Under Women." The proverbs in each chapter are listed alphabetically and sometimes include origin (e.g., state, region, country, ethnic group) and date of first recorded use. An alphabetic index to all the proverbs in the volume includes a reference to the publication from which Kerschen selected it. The introduction defines proverbs and their function in society, and the author explains her methodology, defines her terms, and places this publication in the context of other proverb collections. The volume is certainly a unique presentation of proverbs, and its bibliography of secondary sources regarding proverbs, their history and function as well as gender and linguistics, makes the volume useful to many academic library collections. However, it should be noted that this is a reference book with an agenda, Kerschen's belief is that "a disturbing number of American proverbs about women are derogatory . . . [and] these proverbs are detrimental to the progress of women's fulfillment" (p. 124). [R: Choice, Dec 98, p. 658]—**Susanna Van Sant**

808.   **Women in China: A Country Profile.** By the Economic and Social Commission for Asia and the Pacific. New York, United Nations, 1997. 92p. (Statistical Profiles, no.10). $19.95pa. ISBN 92-1-119754-6. S/N E.97.II.F.17.

Finding statistics and other social and economic indicators that address the situation of women in China has been made easier with the publication of *Women in China: A Country Profile*. The descriptive analysis found in the first part is followed by an array of tables and brief bibliography. The book begins by highlighting government efforts to enhance women's lives and provides a general introduction to the social and economic conditions of the People's Republic of China. This is followed by 3 sections, the first offering an overview of population, health, and education. The section on women in the family includes information on the changing nature of Chinese families, highlighting marriage and reproductive patterns. The section covering economic life of women in China reveals a changing workforce, with growing numbers of women working in diverse industrial occupations. Unfortunately, there is a dearth of information about the wages or conditions of women. The final section presents women in public life, detailing women's political participation in the various parties, including the Central Committee of the Chinese Communist Party. Statistics nicely complement the text while presenting information at the provincial level or contrasting urban-rural conditions as well.

Women in China is part of the Statistical Profiles series produced by the Economic and Social Commission for Asia and the Pacific of the United Nations. The 13 volumes published thus far enhance an understanding of the situation of women in this vast region by providing a foundation for comparative research. *Women in China* and other titles in this excellent series fill a gap for libraries needing demographic, social, and economic information on the region.—**Carol L. Mitchell**

809.   **World Population Monitoring 1996: Selected Aspects of Reproductive Rights and Reproductive Health.** By the Population Division of the United Nations Secretariat. New York, United Nations, 1998. 282p. $29.95pa. ISBN 92-1-151319-7. S/N E.97.XIII.5.

Reproductive rights and reproductive health are important factors in the overall well-being of countries. A healthy population will produce healthy children who will not overburden the health care system. This report from the Population Division of the United Nations Secretariat tracks several important indicators worldwide, allowing researchers to analyze the effectiveness of health and educational programs and to implement necessary changes.

An introduction explains the sources and methods used to collect data. It also contains a list of symbols and abbreviations used in the report. Eight chapters discuss major issues in this field: entry into reproductive life; reproductive behavior; contraception; abortion; maternal mortality and morbidity; sexually transmitted diseases (including HIV/AIDS); reproductive rights; and population information, education, and communication. By studying these topics in detail, one can compare different parts of the world and see how the least developed countries in the world compare to developing and developed nations. Tables and graphs within the text show statistics such as female adolescent marriage in Africa, Asia, and Latin America and median age at first marriage by level of women's education. Boxes and sidebars provide brief reports on relevant subjects, such as the use of television soap operas for sex education in Africa and reproductive health services in the private sector. An annex with extensive statistical tables contains detailed demographic information on fertility, life expectancy, infant mortality, and contraceptive use. It also has a table of world abortion policies.

Anyone concerned with public health policy, demography, or women's and children's health will find a great deal of current information here. The table of trends in urban and rural population with projections to 2015 is one of many features that make this a highly recommended source for academic, health sciences, and large public libraries.—**Barbara M. Bibel**

Part III
HUMANITIES

19 Humanities in General

HUMANITIES IN GENERAL

810. Friedman, John B., and Jessica M. Wegmann. **Medieval Iconography: A Research Guide.** New York, Garland, 1998. 437p. index. (Garland Medieval Bibliographies, v.20 and Garland Reference Library of the Humanities, v.1870). $95.00. ISBN 0-8153-1753-0.

Medieval Iconography: A Research Guide, volume 20 of the Garland Medieval Bibliographies series, is a rare reference work, which, while impeccably well-researched, is yet an eminently fascinating read. It is also an important scholarly work in that it goes beyond the seminal Robert Kaske work, *Medieval Christian Literary Imagery: A Guide to Interpretation* (1988) and expands the previous boundaries of the topic of medieval iconography.

The work's introduction provides the authors' working definition of iconography as "visual motifs, whether in medieval art or literature." This interpretation goes well beyond Kaske's strict definition of limiting the topic to sacred or religious images. A whole new terrain for medieval inquiry is opened by the authors' more liberal definition.

Medieval Iconography is divided into 2 sections. Part 1 contains "Art," a general overview of medieval art and a listing of catalogs and locations of illuminated manuscript collections; and "Other Tools," which treats encyclopedias, exempla, and sermon collections that medieval artists may have consulted. Part 2 contains "Learned Imagery," which treats concepts that would have been of interest to a medieval audience, including alchemy, astrology, and mythology; "The Christian Tradition," probably the most self-explanatory chapter title; "The Natural World," which includes topics such as animals, plants, and geography; and "Medieval Daily Life," which includes such topics as baths, beauty, costumes, fools, and magic.

A wide spectrum of knowledge is covered in this work, and the understandable trade-off is less lengthy annotations. Sources are works written about or during the medieval period of what is now known as western Europe. Titles are written in a variety of European, mostly Romance, languages, although English, French, and Latin titles seem to predominate.

This work's one small weakness is its indexing. The back-of-the-book index is a combination author and subject dictionary-style arrangement with an emphasis upon author access. Compounding the shallowness of the subject index, arrangement of entries in the body of the work can be somewhat idiosyncratic. Vocabulary control or a greater depth of subject indexing would greatly enhance the book's ease of use.

Medieval Iconography: A Research Guide is recommended for academic libraries as well as special collections dealing with medieval art, music, literature, and intellectual history. It will especially appeal to researchers interested in "Le Moyen Age" in Europe vis-à-vis its visual, literary, and theological conceits. Its great value is in providing much more than a catalog of visual images, and going the extra step of providing references, which, if used imaginatively, can give a glimpse into the medieval mind as it existed in a time long ago. [R: Choice, Oct 98, p. 290]—**Linda D. Tietjen**

811. **International Directory of Arts.** New Providence, N.J., K. G. Saur, 1997. 3v. illus. index. DM448.00. ISBN 3-598-23075-3.

Art librarians have long relied on the *International Directory of Arts* as the standard reference source for basic information on museums and galleries since its first publication in 1952. The 1997 edition is the most exhaustive set yet published, consisting of three, rather than the usual two volumes. As an international directory supplying factual information, it is the most comprehensive source of its kind, listing museums and public galleries; universities, academies, and colleges; associations; art and antique dealers and numismatics; art galleries; auctioneers; restorers; art publishers; antiquarians; and art booksellers. Each of the sections is arranged by country and broken down further by city. This arrangement does have some limitations because it presupposes a geographical knowledge of every institution in the world. Access to the titles, addresses, telephone numbers, and personnel provided in the more than 100,000 entries in these volumes are dependent on determining the city; no other access was provided. With the addition of the 3d volume in the present edition, the problem of limited access no longer exists. Volume 3 consists of 2 indexes—a name index and a title index provide easy access to individuals and institutions. The *International Directory of Arts* remains the most reliable source for information on the arts and is now even easier to use.—**Lamia Doumato**

812. Miner, Jeremy T., and Lynn E. Miner. **Directory of Grants in the Humanities 1998/99.** 12th ed. Phoenix, Ariz., Oryx Press, 1998. 720p. index. $84.50pa. ISBN 1-57356-087-1. ISSN 0887-0551.

The latest edition of the *Directory of Grants in the Humanities* contains 3,578 current funding programs that support research in literature, language, linguistics, history, anthropology, philosophy, ethics, religion, and the fine and performing arts. As in the other editions (see ARBA 95, entry 931; ARBA 93, entry 946; ARBA 90, entry 883; and ARBA 87, entry 348), the main section lists programs alphabetically by sponsoring organization. The entries include program description, grant title, sponsor's name and address, and contact information. Restrictions and special requirements, deadlines and renewal dates, and geographic restrictions are also listed when available or applicable. Indexes provide easy access by subject, geographic restriction, sponsoring organization, and grants by program type.

This directory also contains a 12-page guide to proposal planning and writing. It is a condensed version of information presented in *Proposal Planning and Writing* by Lynn Miner and Jeremy Griffith (Oryx Press, 1993). The directory information can also be found in the Grants database, available through the Dialog Corporation, and on CD-ROM with bimonthly updates. For libraries that cannot afford these resources, this work is a good alternative. [R: BL, July 98, p. 1903]—**Laura K. Blessing**

813. Russell, Terence M. **The Encyclopaedic Dictionary in the Eighteenth Century: Architecture, Arts, and Crafts. Volume 1: John Harris Lexicon Technician: Incorporating Worlds of Sir Francis Bacon and Sir Henry Wotton.** Brookfield, Vt., Ashgate Publishing, 1997. 226p. index. $67.95. ISBN 1-85928-062-5.

814. Russell, Terence M. **The Encyclopaedic Dictionary in the Eighteenth Century: Architecture, Arts, and Crafts. Volume 2: Ephraim Chambers Cyclopaedia.** Brookfield, Vt., Ashgate Publishing, 1997. 414p. index. $67.95. ISBN 1-85928-063-3.

815. Russell, Terence M. **The Encyclopaedic Dictionary in the Eighteenth Century: Architecture, Arts, and Crafts. Volume 3: The Builder's Dictionary.** Brookfield, Vt., Ashgate Publishing, 1997. 268p. index. $68.95. ISBN 1-85928-409-4.

816. Russell, Terence M. **The Encyclopaedic Dictionary in the Eighteenth Century: Architecture, Arts, and Crafts. Volume 4: Samuel Johnson: A Dictionary of the English Language.** Brookfield, Vt., Ashgate Publishing, 1997. 229p. $68.95. ISBN 1-85928-064-1.

817. Russell, Terence M. **The Encyclopaedic Dictionary in the Eighteenth Century: Architecture, Arts, and Crafts. Volume 5: A Society of Gentlemen: Encyclopaedia Britannica.** Brookfield, Vt., Ashgate Publishing, 1997. 239p. index. $68.95. ISBN 1-85928-065-X.

This series presents a look at the themes of architecture and its allied arts and crafts in eighteenth-century encyclopedic dictionaries. The intellectual thrust of the period was to make the achievements of humankind available to a wider audience by the ordering of knowledge. Each of these five works is linked by architectural themes, from building construction, materials, carpentry, and the classical orders to decorative arts and design, furnishings, and gardens. The letterpress articles include the original prefaces that reveal the philosophical intent and aesthetic aims of the various authors. The introduction to each of the works includes background information, an interweaving of all the volumes of the series, and a short biography of the compiler. The final bibliographic references are complete for the entire series and are repeated in each work.

The Lexicon, volume 1, was one of the first English-language works to offer a systematic compilation of writings on applied arts and crafts, and it offers illustrative material, one of the rare publications of the time to do so. The writings of Francis Bacon—"Of Buildings" and "Of Gardens"—serve as an excellent introduction and offer an insight into the speculation and theorizing of this period. The major section is devoted to the architectural subjects, introduced by a list of headwords.

Chambers's work, with its schematization of knowledge (reproduced here), was a vast compendium of ordered concepts and observations, well illustrated and elaborately cross-referenced. Once again, this offering includes those articles that deal with architectural and related themes.

The 3d volume, one of the earliest encyclopedias of the building trades, provides an insight into the technology of the time as well as a dictionary of the terminology. It was designed for the profession and thus presents an accurate image of architectural theories as well as practical procedures. The original title page offers the work as being of use "not only to Artificers, but likewise to Gentlemen, and others, concerned in Building, etc." The volume is a remarkable combination of resource and inspiration.

Samuel Johnson's *Dictionary* is perhaps the best known of all the five titles in the series. He was the first to use passages from the great English writers to clarify the meaning of words and the different nuances in their meanings. This work includes an extensive examination of Johnson himself as well as an overview of the actual means by which the work was amassed. There is also a section on his particular treatment of the architectural themes in his work, a lexicography rather than an encyclopedia. Readers thus have a source of usage rather than a descriptive treatment of the subject.

Volume 5, the *Encyclopaedia Britannica*, deals with what may well be the most famous book of its kind, still in existence today although the electronic form it has taken is a far cry from the original 3-volume offering in the late eighteenth century. The use of articles written by a wide variety of authors and the inclusion of crafts with science and the arts were major innovations and set the standard for similar future works. The combination of short ready-reference material with long detailed information was a major departure from past compendiums and offered a resource for a more varied audience. No discussion of the *Britannica* would be complete without an evaluation of the influence of Denis Diderot's *Encyclopédie* and the principles of enlightenment and reason being embraced by a "Society of Gentlemen in Scotland. The books in this series are part of an ongoing publishing venture dealing with historical writings in the field of architecture and its allied arts and crafts. The series serves as a fine resource for scholar or practitioner, historian or artisan.—**Paula Frosch**

818. **The Wilson Chronology of the Arts.** By George Ochoa and Melinda Corey. Bronx, N.Y., H. W. Wilson, 1998. 476p. index. (Wilson Chronology Series). $55.00. ISBN 0-8242-0934-6.

In this volume for H. W. Wilson's new Wilson Chronology Series, the authors provide a timeline detailing human creativity that progresses from ca.43,000 B.C.E. to 1997, with 4,000 entries spread over 13 categories of artistic endeavor. The intention is to distinguish what artists do by using the details of hundreds of individual accomplishments to build an overall picture of art in its many forms. In this way, the authors "hope readers will find that larger truths about art emerge from this timeline." The chronology is global in scope and comprehensive in coverage, emphasizing well-established art forms without neglecting the oral traditions and decorative art forms of nonliterate societies and currently emerging art forms.

The work has a simple organization, with years in the left margin and corresponding entries to the right of the year of their occurrence. The category of each entry is noted in the right margin at the end of the entry, and cross-references connect related entries. Categories include architecture, dance, drama, film, graphic arts, music, television, and radio as well as literature and mainstream art forms. As noted above, entries are mostly brief but informative, and frequent sidebars offer somewhat more depth to their subjects. An 87-page index that includes artists' names, titles of works, and subjects enhances the research value of the timeline, providing an entry point for the reader who does not know in what time period to seek a subject. A four-page bibliography points the researcher to fuller treatments of the topics in the chronology, and an appendix listing birth and death dates for many of the artists mentioned supplements the usefulness of the index.

The straightforward organization of this work makes it suitable for many different uses. It can be read straight through for a wide view of human creativity; browsed by the general reader looking for a brief diversion; or researched for an artist, a movement, or an era. The authors demonstrate an understanding of the scope of creativity and cast a wide net, being inclusive rather than exclusive. This volume is suitable for both academic and public libraries.—**Kristin Doty**

20 Communication and Mass Media

GENERAL WORKS

Biography

819. **Who's Who in the Media and Communications 1998-1999.** New Providence, N.J., Marquis Who's Who/Reed Reference Publishing, 1997. 669p. $259.95. ISBN 0-8379-3950-X. ISSN 1094-6985.

This 1st edition of *Who's Who in the Media and Communications* provides current information on 18,500 executives and entrepreneurs driving the fields of telecommunication, journalism, publishing, advertising, marketing, and broadcasting. It includes the biographies of professionals who work in traditional media fields, such as print journalism, radio, television, cable broadcasting, and telecommunications, as well as biographies of those in new media fields, such as the Internet, online information services, and interactive multimedia.

The editors have based the selection of biographees for the book on the "reference value" of each person, which is defined by either the level of responsibility held or the level of achievement attained by the individual. The application of these criteria is necessarily subjective, and most libraries will find themselves in some disagreement with the choices. For example, is Garrison Keillor not a worthy example of creative talent in the film and broadcasting industries? Is Bill Daniels not a significant person in cable TV?

The majority of the biographical entries were composed from information supplied by those being featured. The sketches compiled by the Marquis staff through independent research are denoted by an asterisk. The editors claim this provides "highly accurate and current sketches."

Individuals are in alphabetic order by surnames. Depending upon availability of information, sketches for the biographees include occupation, birth date and place, family members, education, career, published works, civic and political activities, awards and fellowships, memberships, political affiliation, religion, and home and office addresses. No indexes are provided. A useful feature would be an index by field of professional endeavor.

Useful, but overpriced, this book will be appreciated by public or academic libraries without collection strength in media studies. Larger libraries may want it for rapid identification of media- and communication-related figures.—**Vera Gao**

Dictionaries and Encyclopedias

820. **History of the Mass Media in the United States: An Encyclopedia.** Margaret A. Blanchard, ed. Chicago, Fitzroy Dearborn, 1998. 752p. illus. index. $125.00. ISBN 1-57958-012-2.

From its humble beginnings in 1690, when the first colonial newspaper was issued in Boston, U.S. journalism has evolved beyond the printed word into an institution of remarkably diverse media forms. Covering the development of the mass media in the United States during the course of three centuries, this weighty compendium offers a unique historical perspective on this prominent and influential force in U.S. society. Although it encompasses many aspects of media, including advertising, book publishing, broadcasting, magazines, motion pictures, newspapers, photojournalism, public relations, radio, and television, its primary emphasis is on the media as a disseminator of information and a communicator of ideas rather than as an entertainment source.

In compiling this encyclopedia, Blanchard, a professor of journalism and mass communication at the University of North Carolina at Chapel Hill, drew on the expertise of 262 contributors, many of whom are noted scholars in the field of journalism history. Arranged alphabetically letter by letter, the 498 signed entries range in length from 200 to 3,200 words. Most conclude with cross-references to related articles and bibliographic citations to further sources of information. Although it devotes some articles to individual publications, personalities, organizations, or other entities (e.g., *Chicago Tribune*, Huntley-Brinkley Report, Edward R. Murrow, National Press Club), the encyclopedia's major focus is on broader topics or issues. Many entries treat a particular aspect of a single medium (e.g., "Magazine Illustrations," "Motion Picture Propaganda," "Television Advertising"), whereas others deal with the role of the media in relation to major events, movements, political figures, issues, and concepts such as the Vietnam War, the civil rights movement, Ronald Reagan, and libel. In most cases, coverage ends in 1990, but exceptions were made for articles where more currency was particularly appropriate; for example, "Internet," "Mass Media and Tobacco Products," and "Newspaper Technology." A variety of black-and-white photographs and other illustrations complement the text, and the detailed index contains references to these as well as to the content of the articles. Providing additional access is a topical list of entries, which groups articles under 22 categories, such as "Alternative Media, "Legislation," and "News Agencies." Other features include a brief glossary of frequently used acronyms and phrases, a basic bibliography, and a section that notes the professional background of each contributor.

Well conceived and well written, this impressive compilation makes a significant contribution to the study of journalism history. Although it is highly readable, its approach is more scholarly than Daniel W. Hollis's *The ABC-CLIO Companion to the Media in America* (see ARBA 96, entry 964), and it provides greater depth and breadth of coverage on topical issues related to the history of mass media in the United States. A valuable resource for any academic or public library, this excellent encyclopedia belongs in all collections that support programs in journalism and mass communication.—**Marie Ellis**

Directories

821. **Bacon's Business Media Directory 1998: Directory of Print and Broadcast Business Media.** 17th ed. Ruth McFarland, ed. Chicago, Bacon's Information, 1997. 1070p. index. $275.00pa. ISSN 1058-9716.

Bacon's Information, headquartered in Chicago, is best known for its reliable media directories. This annual directory, introduced in 1992, is geared to business use. Magazines, newspapers, networks, syndicates, and personnel are covered and accessed through media, personnel, and subject indexes. A useful section lists freelance journalists according to business specialty.

At $275 this resource is costly; however, most libraries could probably purchase it every other year or with alternative titles, such as *Gale Directory of Publications and Broadcast Media* (see entry 822), or *Burrelle's Media Directory* (see entry 837). Comprehensive business collections will want to own this resource.

—Glynys R. Thomas

822. **Gale Directory of Publications and Broadcast Media: An Annual Guide to Publications and Broadcasting Stations.** 131st ed. Carolyn A. Fischer, ed. Detroit, Gale, 1998. 3v. index. $440.00/set. ISBN 0-7876-1310-X.

This newest edition of a standard reference work provides the same kind of detailed information about U.S. and Canadian publications (excluding newsletters and directories) and broadcast media offered in earlier editions (see ARBA 94, entry 988; ARBA 91, entry 61). There are 350 new entries, which emphasize publications that are also available online. A typical entry for a publication gives the title, publisher, street and e-mail addresses, telephone and fax numbers, frequency, print-method column size, subscription and advertising rates, circulation, key personnel, feature editors, and alternate formats. A broadcast media entry provides, among other information, the call letters, frequency, channel or cable company name, street and e-mail addresses, telephone and fax numbers, formats, owner, operating hours, network affiliation, area of dominant influence, cities and postal areas served, key personnel, local programs, and advertisement rates.

In addition to this information provided by the entrants, there are several key sections that increase the value of the set. Industry statistics, indexes of broadcast and cable networks and publishers, a list of newspaper feature editors, and a variety of subject indexes provide convenient access to often elusive information. Filling a wide variety of information needs, this directory remains one of the essential tools for medium to large academic, public, and special libraries.—**Barbara E. Kemp**

823.   **Hudson's Washington News Media Contacts Directory 1998.** Rhinebeck, N.Y., Hudson's, 1998. 484p. index. $219.00. ISBN 1-891489-00-3. ISSN 0441-389X.

First published in 1968, this useful directory now lists 4,646 news outlets and 5,161 correspondents and editors. The publishers have categorized 25 types of media, including wire services, newspapers, television, radio, magazines, freelancers, and photoservices. Names, addresses, and fax and telephone numbers as well as e-mail addresses are provided, and each entry ends with specialties of subject coverage.

There is also a rough index to subject areas, but the user must go to several different pages to retrieve names. Not everyone is listed in one place, of course, because the main entries are by media categories and not by subject. The specialist magazines, however, are the largest category with one-quarter of the total pages: They are arranged by subject areas. The book concludes with an index to organizations and people.

This listing is obviously meant for public relations firms and lobbyists in order to locate journalists and news media useful for putting out a story about a product or service. Thus, there are thrice-yearly updates and a hefty price—and still there is advertising inside. For $295 one can purchase the list on diskette. Yet, there is no indication of online availability or an Internet Website. In fact, the company does not even have an e-mail address. At the price, this is a marginal purchase for libraries in the nonprofit sector.—**Dean Tudor**

824.   **Willings Press Guide 1998.** 124th ed. Middlesex, United Kingdom, Hollis Directories; distr., Detroit, Gale, 1998. 2v. index. $325.00/set. ISBN 0-900967-625. ISSN 0000-0213.

Published annually for the past 124 years, this series provides an extensive listing of international newspapers and periodicals. Volume 1 focuses on the United Kingdom. Titles are presented in alphabetic order with the publisher's address, telephone and fax numbers, and e-mail address as well as frequency of publication, circulation, names of key contacts, summary of content, and a description of the target audience. The material is indexed by classification (e.g., entertainment, commerce, and others). New titles and publications that are no longer available are noted. A master index and a guide to UK vendors serving the publishing industry are also provided.

Volume 2 contains similar listings and indexes for newspapers and periodicals for the rest of the world. The index by category is divided alphabetically by country. The 2d volume includes advertising representatives (primarily those based in the United Kingdom) and European television stations. This set provides a lot of much-needed information on the world's media.—**Adrienne Antink Bendel**

Handbooks and Yearbooks

825.   Foerstel, Herbert N. **Banned in the Media: A Reference Guide to Censorship in the Press, Motion Pictures, Broadcasting, and the Internet.** Westport, Conn., Greenwood Press, 1998. 252p. index. $49.95. ISBN 0-313-30245-6.

Despite its title, this book is not so much a reference guide as an account of the more notable legal cases regarding attempts to censor the media (but *not* including books) in the United States. The emphasis is on cases of the past 25 years, although a useful but brief history is offered by way of background.

The main text consists of accounts of prominent examples of media censorship that are 5 to 10 pages in length; much briefer accounts (usually not more than 2 pages in length) of media censorship cases form 1812 to 1997; and reports, mostly consisting of quotations, of interviews that Foerstel conducted with 6 media professionals. These "voices from the media" represent experience in newspapers, motion pictures, magazines, broadcasting, and the Internet, and all six people take positions strongly opposed to censorship.

The reference value of this book is limited, especially because the index is brief and pretty much confined to proper name entries. It is clear, also, that the anticensorship views are so strongly favored as to preclude any claim to objectivity. Still, as an interesting, readable, and up-to-date portrayal of a problem that is of major and continuing concern, this book will be wanted by most libraries. [R: SLJ, Nov 98, p. 152; VOYA, Dec 98, p. 388]
—**Samuel Rothstein**

826. **Journalism Ethics: A Reference Handbook.** Elliot D. Cohen and Deni Elliott, eds. Santa Barbara, Calif., ABC-CLIO, 1997. 196p. index. (Contemporary Ethical Issues Series). $39.50. ISBN 0-87436-873-1.

In a world where *morals* and *values* are the buzzwords of the day, this well-researched discussion of the ethics of news reporting is timely and important. The 17 contributors to this volume have impressive credentials in journalism, ethics, philosophy, law, and politics. The chapters in this book focus on several important issues that shape the discussion of journalism ethics today: the control of new organizations by media sources, the increased diversity of news media outlets, morality, objectivity, professionalism, privacy, and accountability. Each chapter is well written and well documented, listing other sources the reader can access for further information on that particular topic. Along with a chronology of key events that have shaped today's perception of journalism ethics, this book also contains biographical sketches of numerous personalities who have shaped the issues, information of important court cases in various journalism areas, and the ethical codes of the various journalism organizations. A directory of pertinent journalism organizations and research centers, a glossary, and an index also assist users of this book. This is an excellent sourcebook on this timely and important topic.—**Kay Mariea**

827. **Plunkett's Entertainment & Media Industry Almanac.** Jack W. Plunkett and others, eds. Galveston, Tex., Plunkett Research, 1998. 626p. index. $149.99pa. ISBN 0-9638268-6-7.

Intended as a general source for researchers of all types, the almanac presents an overview of the entertainment and media industry and analyzes the 445 companies that comprise the Entertainment and Media 400. Although the introduction indicates that information was gathered from a wide variety of sources, neither the research methodology nor the specific resources have been identified. Divided into two sections, a definite highlight of part 1 is the 2 chapters describing, with statistical comparisons, industry trends and the industry's 15 major components. These easy-to-understand comparisons are of value to students and beginning researchers. Chapters 3-7 list important associations and World Wide Web sites, summarize new technologies (e.g., HDTV), show budget examples, and describe career opportunities.

Entries for the Entertainment and Media 400, those corporations that meet 4 criteria—U.S.-based, publicly held, prominent, financial data available—form part 2. Along with basic data, entries offer rankings, financials, and salary/benefits information. Unfortunately, the criteria for inclusion have not been explained adequately, and the financials reflect 1996 performance. Several Internet-based resources, such as Dow Jones Interactive, LEXIS-NEXIS, Disclosure, and Zacks, present more current, reliable financial data, often with industry comparisons and links to corporate and industry Websites.

Five indexes complete the volume: company names with industry codes; headquarters located by state; regions of the United States; firms with international locations; and subsidiaries, brands, and affiliations. These indexes limit rather than enhance access. Indexing all resources alphabetically and by industry group would prompt searches for an entity regardless of industry subgroup, whereas the use of page or entry numbers would assist those for whom English is not a primary language. The list of companies with international operations is useless because neither the list nor the entries identify the countries involved.

This volume has the beginnings of a fine reference work because investors, job-seekers, and the like need to consult competing sources to make informed decisions. To fill that need, this almanac needs to correct deficiencies and reconsider the importance of currentness for a business directory. The price is attractive, but acquisition of an out-of-date resource is likely to entice but not satisfy library users. [R: BL, 15 Oct 98, pp. 443-444; LJ, Aug 98, p. 78; Choice, Nov 98, p. 502]—**Sandra E. Belanger**

AUTHORSHIP

General Works

828. **Children's Writer's and Illustrator's Market, 1998: 850 Places to Sell Your Work.** Alice P. Buening, ed. Cincinnati, Ohio, Writer's Digest Books/F & W Publications, 1998. 389p. illus. index. $19.99pa. ISBN 0-89879-819-1. ISSN 0897-9790.

With this guide writers and illustrators who specialize in works for children (preschool to young adult) can find out where and how to sell their fiction, nonfiction, illustrations, photographs, and plays. Organized in 3 sections—"Tips and Guidelines," "Markets," and "Resources—the book offers general advice on the business of writing (e.g., contracts, copyright, record keeping, legal issues) in addition to a list of 850 markets. Publishers are categorized by type (e.g., books, magazines, electronic publishing), then listed alphabetically. In each entry a complete address is given, along with names of editors and art directors, types of work published, directions on how to contact (specific to writers, illustrators, and photographers), terms, and tips. In addition, entries are coded for listings new to this edition, educational and Canadian publishers, publishing opportunities for students, and book packagers and producers. Age level, subject, photography, and general indexes facilitate access to the listings, and a glossary explains terminology. A final section lists clubs and organizations, conferences and workshops, awards, and other resources pertinent to children's writers and illustrators.

Published by Writer's Digest, this practical annual is highly recommended for all public libraries. Academic libraries with extensive holdings in children's literature or creative writing may also want to consider the purchase, as will school district collections that support student publishing programs.—**Barbara Ittner**

829. **Companion to Historiography.** Michael Bentley, ed. New York, Routledge, 1997. 997p. index. $165.00. ISBN 0-415-03084-6.

Historiography is an elusive term to define because it focuses on the set of assumptions historians make when they study the past. The task of the historiographer may be multiform. One may see the task as expository in explicating the texts of writers who form the canon of works in history. Or, the mission may be seen as critical or corrective by pointing out how the bias of past historians has compromised the objective truth of their histories. Contemporary historiographers have concentrated on the theoretical aspects of historiography by emphasizing epistemological models. In his general introduction, Bentley, professor of modern history at the University of St. Andrews, recognizes that historiography has followed a complex path of development over time. As editor of the *Companion to Historiography*, his intention is to provide a field guide to the territory of historiography for history teachers who need to orient students to the discipline of history before they attempt to write history.

Organized as a collection of essays with contributions mostly by noted British historians, the breadth and scope of areas covered is impressive, ranging from the beginnings of historical writing in the East and West (part 1) to the chronicles of the medieval period (part 2) and concluding with early modern and contemporary theorists of history (parts 3 and 4). The depth of scholarship is also noteworthy. Essay topics encompass ancient Greek self-definition, sexuality in the Middle Ages, popular culture in the early modern West, and a critique of the western concept of orientalism. For the general reader, introductory essays in each part provide an overview of the development of writing on history for the period under discussion. The essays in part 5 are among the most stimulating and provocative. In this concluding section, scholarly efforts are concentrated on ascertaining the value of diverse methodological or ideological approaches to historical writing (literary narrative, or the Marxist, feminist, and *Annales* schools). Another theme elucidated in part 5 is the interplay and overlap between the territory of academic history and related disciplines, such as philosophy, anthropology, and archaeology.

Bentley clearly stated in his introduction that he wished to produce a work that is a true companion—a volume that will be read and not merely consulted like an encyclopedic compilation of factual information. For this reason, it is recommended that academic libraries purchase the *Companion to Historiography* for the circulating collection rather than for the reference collection.—**David G. Nowak**

830. **Grants and Awards Available to American Writers.** 30th ed. John Morrone, ed. New York, PEN American Center, 1998. 274p. index. $18.00pa. ISBN 0-934638-15-2.

Now in its 30th year of publication, PEN American Center's biennial directory of grants and awards for U.S. writers continues to provide accurate and helpful information to its audience. More than 1,000 grants and awards (including foundation support, academic fellowships, writer's residencies, travel grants, and production opportunities for playwrights) are listed alphabetically under sponsoring organizations. Along with the sponsor's name, each entry has a complete mailing address, often including fax, e-mail, and Website address. Brief descriptions give general guidelines on how to apply or obtain more information about the awards. Who the awards are available to, submission deadlines (if any), and the individual to contact are noted. In addition, the entries are coded for fiction, poetry, drama, journalism, general nonfiction, children's literature, and translations. An appendix of state arts councils and indexes of awards, organizations, and categories concludes the book.

Features new to this edition are the numerous inclusions of fax numbers, e-mail addresses, and Websites. The number of scholarships for journalists has increased, and there are 248 new awards listed this year. Some 30 programs that have been discontinued were dropped as well as those programs exclusive to Canadian writers. This edition purports to remain current until mid-1999, when a new edition will be released.

A worthy purchase for public and academic libraries, this guide is also a modest and wise investment for poets, journalists, playwrights, novelists, and other writers seeking funding opportunities.—**Barbara Ittner**

831.   **Theorizing Composition: A Critical Sourcebook of Theory and Scholarship in Contemporary Composition Studies.** Mary Lynch Kennedy, ed. Westport, Conn., Greenwood Press, 1998. 405p. index. $95.00. ISBN 0-313-29927-7.

The growing minutiae of academic specialization continues its constrictions with each new bibliography. It is not that these tools are poorly done; merely that the endless stream confirms the saw that information doubles while knowledge halves and wisdom quarters.

What is called "composition studies" began nearly a quarter of a century ago with a focus on the practical aspects of the writing process. However, like many things in academia, it continued to move away from practicality and toward theory until finally it became a specialization so narrow that only 66 entries are required to fill out a slender volume. Today, composition studies embraces almost no writing at all while focusing on things such as genre, gender, and social construction.

This volume is a list of such terms with bibliographies on the primary and secondary texts related to the terms explained. The entries are all signed. Thus, one will find defined here theories on audience and discourse community, cognitive development, deconstruction, postmodernism, and much more. Entries average about 500 words, but some exceed 1,000. Only the largest of libraries supporting enormous graduate populations in English will find use for this highly specialized tool.—**Mark Y. Herring**

832.   **The Writer's Handbook.** 1998 ed. Sylvia K. Burack, ed. Boston, Writer, 1997. 902p. index. $29.95. ISBN 0-87116-183-4.

This comprehensive guide for freelance writers differs from *Writer's Market* (published by Writer's Digest) in that the articles (110 of them, written by professional writers) make up nearly two-thirds of the 871 manuscript pages. Presumably, many of these are reprints from the publisher's journal, *The Writer*, as well as from other sources. Enlightening and informative, these articles are arranged by topic (e.g., genre fiction, poetry, playwriting, marketing). In addition, the book lists 3,200 potential markets for writers, broadly categorized by type (e.g., article, book, greeting card) and further defined by subject (education, sports and recreation, literary). Entries contain complete address information, a brief summary of what kind of material is appropriate for publication, approximate payment, and how to approach. In addition, the book lists pertinent awards, agents, writer's colonies, conferences, state arts councils, and a glossary of terms. An index to the markets completes the work.

The real value of this book lies in the articles, which will remain current for a number of years. Because they are not updated annually, the market listings may go out of date after the first few years. Finally, the book (market listings in particular) could benefit from subject indexing; for example, indicating specific age levels or such formats as short stories. In spite of these deficiencies, the book will appeal to freelance writers seeking guidance in their careers, and it is priced affordably enough for individual as well as institutional purchase. *The Writer's Handbook* is recommended for public libraries. [R: Choice, Mar 98, p. 1164]—**Barbara Ittner**

Style Manuals

833.   **Merriam-Webster's Concise Handbook for Writers.** 2d ed. Springfield, Mass., Merriam-Webster, 1998. 275p. index. $9.95pa. ISBN 0-87779-625-4.

This is a useful, inexpensive paperback resource for writing students needing basic guidance. It deals with the usual topics of interest: punctuation, capitals, plurals, abbreviations, numbers, quotations, bibliographic notes, proofreading, and copyediting.

This 2d edition has been adapted from *Merriam-Webster's Manual for Writers and Editors* (which itself is the retitled 2d edition of *Merriam-Webster's Standard American Style Manual* [1994]). It is more of a how-to on writing than a style guide, with new material from the larger work on standard parts of a book, copyright issues, and word-usage problems (e.g., confusibles). Thus, the chapter on composition and grammar has been replaced by a glossary of grammatical terms. To my mind, this is actually a step backward—nobody knows how to parse anymore, or even what parsing means. An extensive index completes the work.—**Dean Tudor**

834.   **Merriam-Webster's Manual for Writers and Editors.** Springfield, Mass., Merriam-Webster, 1998. 424p. index. $17.95pa. ISBN 0-87779-622-X.

Even if a writer has a good understanding of English grammar, there are still numerous questions that affect writing, especially when one is writing for publication. Do commas and semicolons go inside or outside quotation marks? Should one use numerals or spell out a number? How should footnotes and bibliography entries be styled? The editors at Merriam-Webster have answered these sorts of questions in the 424-page book. The first 7 chapters discuss various style questions, including information on punctuation; capitalization and italics; plurals, possessives, and compounds; abbreviations; numbers; mathematics and science; and quotations. The chapter on foreign languages is especially interesting, providing information on punctuation, capitalization, word division, and diacritics for 18 languages. Other chapters discuss tables and illustrations, notes and bibliographies, indexes, copyediting, and production questions. The chapter on indexing should be helpful to anyone unfamiliar with the indexing process. The editing chapter should assist many authors to understand what to expect from editing, but it includes little information on electronic editing, which is being done more and more. Although this manual may be helpful to many writers, it tends to provide options for ways to handle various questions rather than straightforward answers. Many writers might be better off asking a publisher which style form or manual the publisher prefers, and then following that form.—**Kay Mariea**

835.   Shields, Nancy E., and Mary E. Uhle. **Where Credit Is Due: A Guide to Proper Citing of Sources—Print and Nonprint.** 2d ed. Lanham, Md., Scarecrow, 1997. 187p. index. $32.50. ISBN 0-8108-3211-9.

Where Credit Is Due: A Guide to Proper Citing of Sources—Print and Nonprint is the 2d edition of a volume addressed to high school or college students faced with the daunting task of writing a research or term paper that must include footnotes and a bibliography and may utilize a variety of sources. In addition to print media, for which many style guides already exist, correct crediting of many electronic and other relatively new information sources that are available to students today are also included.

The book is set up as a series of questions about researching, writing, laying out, and presenting a research or term paper. Appendixes include information about mechanical aspects of writing, such as use of quotation marks, italics, and abbreviations. Sample pages show the correct form for a bibliography and footnotes. The authors have also assembled a glossary containing more than 200 entries. Terms defined in this glossary are preceded by an asterisk in the text. In addition, the work also contains an alphabetically arranged index.

Although the beginning researcher will likely find *Where Credit Is Due* an indispensable guide through the maze of writing a properly credited academic paper, more advanced students will be able to utilize the means of crediting nonprint and electronic information that similar, older works might not contain.—**Kay O. Cornelius**

836.   Thatcher, Virginia S. **English Usage and Style for Editors.** Lanham, Md., Scarecrow Press, 1997. 163p. index. $28.50. ISBN 0-8108-3259-3.

This manual, unlike many style and usage guides, is a basic reference, addressing fundamental editorial situations and providing answers for the most common problems. This makes it fairly easy for students and beginner editors to consult. Each chapter provides "Readings," a list of sources for any further study that may be necessary. Subjects such as punctuation, word usage, spelling, and use of hyphens are discussed and followed by examples.

The book is divided into 2 parts: "Substantive Editing," which helps the reader make decisions in composition, and "Mechanical Editing," which focuses on the finer details and style. The introduction to part 1 defines grammar and analyzes its importance. It describes the origins and evolution of the English language, inflection, and syntax, and although it is an interesting topic, it provides this in more detail than the intended audience might actually desire to read. The difference between the process of substantive editing and that of mechanical editing is more thoroughly covered in the introduction to part 2. A helpful glossary, a bibliography, and an index are included.
—**Felicity Tucker**

RADIO, TELEVISION, AUDIO, AND VIDEO

837.   **Burrelle's Media Directory: Broadcast Media. Radio.** 1998 ed. James L. Hayes, ed. Livingston, N.J., Burrelle's Information Services, 1997. 1728p. index. $250.00. ISBN 1-885601-64-6. ISSN 1074-9446.

These 5 volumes represent the most comprehensive set of media directories available for the United States, Canada, and Mexico. Altogether, they include vital data on more than 48,000 media outlets, broken down by 2,100 daily newspapers, 10,000 nondaily newspapers, 12,400 magazines, 11,000 radio stations, and 1,600 television channels, plus numerous cable outlets and broadcast programming services, among others. More than 200,000 names of people associated with mass media are included as well.

The books are easy to use because of their arrangement and comprehensiveness of information, without the hard-to-decipher abbreviations commonly found in directories. Four of the directories are organized by state and city, whereas the magazine volume is by topic. Each book starts with general information on how to use the data and sample entries and ends with useful appendixes and indexes. Appendixes contain information by ownership group and, in some cases, list media no longer in existence; those of the daily newspaper volume are particularly valuable because they list newspaper-distributed magazines, news services and syndicates, and special interest daily and nondaily newspapers (ethnic, military, religious, senior citizens). Entries consist of demographics of place of publication, full address, market coverage, circulation and audience figures, advertising rates, key personnel by title, and other information.

The editor has taken great pains to ensure completeness and accuracy, gathering data by questionnaires, telephone interviews, and other research means, including the use of monitoring electronic media. They even include in each volume a postcard seeking corrections and amendments. This set is a must for all research libraries; advertising, public relations, and marketing agencies; and major government branches—in short, anyone attempting to reach a media market or outlet. [Also reviewed: Burrelle's *Daily Newspapers*; *Non-Daily Newspapers*; *Magazines*; and *Broadcast Media Television*.] —**John A. Lent**

838.   Moshkovitz, Moshe. **Dictionary of Television and Audiovisual Terminology.** Jefferson, N.C., McFarland, 1998. 175p. $39.95. ISBN 0-7864-0440-X.

Begun as an attempt to collect a list of common televisions terms and their explanations for a college-level technology course, Moshkovitz has compiled an extensive and comprehensive dictionary of terms "used by professionals in everyday work and professional publications of the television and telecommunications industry worldwide." The more than 1,500 entries cover both audio and video terms as well as words from related fields. This dictionary defines the terms only as they relate to television or audiovisual terminology. Definitions vary in length from just a few words to several paragraphs depending on both the term's complexity and importance. In-depth physical or mathematical analysis is not included, and definitions emphasize the practical usage. *See* and *see also* references will aid readers. The extensiveness of the listings should serve both the student and the professional well. [R: BL, 15 Sept 98, p. 258; Choice, Nov 98, pp. 496, 498]—**Janet Hilbun**

21 Decorative Arts

COLLECTING

General Works

839. **Warman's Americana & Collectibles.** 8th ed. Ellen T. Schroy, ed. Iola, Wis., Krause Publications, 1997. 400p. illus. index. $17.95pa. ISBN 0-87069-752-8.

Beginning collectors and librarians are well served by this popular guide, which contains the advice of 44 specialists and is edited by Schroy, a recognized expert in the field. An excellent introduction helps explain the motives behind collecting and retailing collectibles (this is a guide for collectors, not sellers). Collectible is defined broadly here as anything made before 1945. The post-1945 era is broken down into three collecting periods: 1945-1965, 1965-1980, and post-1980. Entries provide a brief history of all collectibles included, pricing information on selected items, and citations to reference sources and current journals as well as addresses and names of clubs, auction houses, and museums. Black-and-white illustrations add to the guide's reference value. Users will appreciate the first section of every entry, "Collecting Hints," which identifies the valuable items and the routine items and helps beginners identify reproductions. An excellent index completes the work.

This guide is recommended for beginning collectors. Librarians will appreciate the listing of published information sources and clubs. Future editions of the work will need to include practical information on using the Internet to the collector's advantage.—**Milton H. Crouch**

Antiques

840. **Antique Trader Books Antiques & Collectibles Price Guide.** 1999 ed. Kyle Husfloen, ed. Dubuque, Iowa, Antique Trader Books, 1998. 906p. illus. index. $15.95pa. ISBN 0-930625-14-5. ISSN 1083-8430.

Now in its 15th edition, the *Antiques & Collectibles Price Guide* is one of many publications from Antique Trader Books, the publisher of *Antique Trader Weekly*. The price guide has a good reputation for its handling of the collectibles market. Collectors from across the United States with expertise in particular areas contributed to the volume.

With more than 900 pages, this lengthy price guide is an annotated list with numerous black-and-white illustrations of collectible items arranged in alphabetic order by category or company name. Coverage is of collectibles from all periods, antique to contemporary. New to this edition is a section on Beanie Babies, in addition to expanded sections on kitchen collectibles, compacts and vanity cases, sporting collectibles, postcards, and radios, among others. Brief introductory paragraphs give useful descriptive and historical facts and include sources for additional information.

Modestly priced, this volume also includes a free online subscription to Antique Trader's Online Price Guide, and is recommended for libraries with an interest in materials covering antiques and collectibles.

—**Ingrid Schierling Burnett**

841.   Maloney, David J., Jr. **Maloney's Antiques & Collectibles Resource Directory.** 4th ed. Dubuque, Iowa, Antique Trader Books, 1997. 651p. index. $28.95pa. ISBN 0-930625-87-0. ISSN 1083-8449.

This is the book to turn to when one is wondering how to contact fellow collectors who might want to buy their collectibles. It also tells you where to get parts or repairs done, what special books or magazines are available, who the experts are, how to join a collectors club, where to go to match a pattern, or who to contact for appraisal or auction. This book had its debut six years ago, and *Library Journal* listed it as the "Best Reference Book" that year. This book is a unique and comprehensive resource for hard-to-find information about the personal property one owns.

Specialized resources contained within *Maloney's* include buyers, collectors, dealers, experts, appraisers, periodicals, suppliers of parts, reproduction sources, reference book sellers, manufacturers/distributors/producers, clubs, societies and associations, museums and libraries, centers for specialized research, matching services, repair/ restoration/conservation specialists, vendors to the trade, Internet resources, and mail-bid and gallery auctions. Many other miscellaneous services ranging from freelance writers and antique buying trips to collector computer software and bottle cleaning kits are also included.

In this 4th edition, there is a greatly expanded cross-referencing system. Readers are directed to other rele- vant categories that may contain information of interest. There are four important appendixes: Educated and Tested ISA Appraisers; Auction Services; General Interest Periodicals; and Repair Firms. A redesigned and highly detailed index is an important part of this edition. There are nearly 2,000 listings with Internet Websites and 3,000 with e-mail addresses.

The goal of this book is to place as much information as possible at the user's fingertips to allow him or her to make decisions based on the facts. Veteran dealers and collectors are well aware that knowledge and information are the keys to success in the world of antiques and collectibles.

The main section of this book, "General Listings," contains more than 15,000 entries in more than 2,900 categories arranged alphabetically by primary classification in capital letters. Subclassifications appear where there are recognized subcategories in upper and lower case letters. Of particular importance is the extensive and comprehensive cross-referencing system that directs the user to related subject matter and that is unique to this publication. Whether buying, selling, trading, or collecting the traditional or most unusual items, *Maloney's Antiques & Collectibles Resource Directory* will be a useful reference to have.—**Barbara B. Goldstein**

842.   **Miller's International Antiques Price Guide 1999.** Elizabeth Norfolk, ed. London, Miller's/Mitchell Beazley; distr., Wappingers Falls, N.Y., Antique Collectors' Club, 1998. 808p. illus. index. $35.00. ISBN 1-84000-060-0.

Designed for the amateur or the professional, a lot of information about antiques and collectibles world- wide can be found in *Miller's International Antiques Price Guide.* In addition to the breadth of coverage, this guide is extremely well organized, with directories, indexes, table of contents, and numerous aids for use by the consumer.

This price guide gives detailed coverage of antiques and their value based on actual prices paid, with hundreds of entries containing illustrations (mostly black-and-white), but also including lengthy sections of color plates. The guide covers major collecting areas: furniture, ceramics, glass, silver, clocks, and art nouveau and art deco. In this 20th edition, additional emphasis is given to French Provincial furniture, Irish antiques, Poole pottery, majolica, carousel animals, and Oriental works of art and ceramics.

Some of the useful tools within the volume include a glossary of terms used in the antiques market, a chart of periods and styles, directories of specialists and auctioneers, and preliminary pages with a key to illustrations. The index guides the user to a particular factory, designer, or craftsman. The pages of entries include explanatory information boxes, recommended further reading, and the unique "Miller's Compares" section that describes why two almost identical items carry different prices.

The volume contains many advertisements, mostly British, which may be distracting but may provide further use for the buyer and presumably hold down the cost of the volume. Published in London, the prices listed are given in dollars. An international bestseller, this may be the one collectibles guide that many libraries will want to own. *Miller's International Antiques Price Guide* is highly recommended.—**Ingrid Schierling Burnett**

Coins (and Paper Money)

843. **The Charlton Standard Catalogue of Canadian Government Paper Money.** 11th ed. Robert J. Graham and Davina Rowan, eds. Toronto, Charlton Press, 1998. 303p. illus. $17.95pa. ISBN 0-88968-187-2. ISSN 0835-3573.

For more than a century banks and governments engaged in a struggle for the lucrative right to issue paper currency. Bank notes were redeemable in gold or silver, whereas governments backed their notes only with securities based on land, of which there was an inexhaustible supply, or by anticipated tax revenues. In Canada the competition ended in 1945 when the government made it illegal for banks to issue any more notes. This paraphrase from the introduction graphically demonstrates how paper money collectors are lured into the hobby by the fascinating history of people and countries that is embodied in the designs found on currency.

All Canadian government paper money during a 300-year period is cataloged, from the French Colonial issues of 1685 to the current Bank of Canada notes. Army bills, provincial issues, municipal notes, Province of Canada bills, Dominion of Canada issues, special serial numbers, and error notes are included. Each note is illustrated in black-and-white, and current values are given in six grades of condition. The introduction includes a brief history of paper money in Canada, an explanation of the numbering system used, a description of printing and engraving processes, a description of the grading system, a glossary, and other useful and interesting information for collectors. This will make an excellent addition to any collection catering to the numismatic field.

—**Larry Lobel**

844. **Collecting World Coins: A Century of Circulating Issues, 1901-Present.** 7th ed. Colin R. Bruce II, ed. Iola, Wis., Krause Publications, 1998. 715p. illus. maps. $28.95pa. ISBN 0-87341-422-5.

As the world becomes a "global village," interest in world coinage has increased manifold. This work targets the novice collector. Here we find countries listed in a "historic-geographical" sequence, meaning that a geographical area that has undergone political or name changes is kept together in one listing (e.g., Belgian Congo will be found under Zaire). This century has certainly seen its share of political changes, and the editor has provided a comprehensive index at the front of the book. Each listing includes a small map locating the country, a brief description, and the history of the country, followed by the coinage from smallest to largest denomination. Each issue is illustrated, both obverse and reverse, with date, mintage, and graded valuation.

Additional appendixes appear in the front of the book. The editor provides helpful explanations on identification, dating traditions, numbering systems, denominations, mintages, and more. A chart of Standard International Numeral Systems displays 25 non-Western numbers typically found on coins. This reviewer found particularly helpful the "Instant Identifier" and "Monograms" pages. Here, the collector compares an unknown coin with the enlarged details from a sample of coins that might cause problems in identification. Bullion charts, coin sizes, and a table of grading terminology round out the explanatory material. This book is a high-caliber resource from a well-known, established numismatic publisher. This work is an excellent resource for public or general academic collections.—**Margaret F. Dominy**

845. **North American Coins & Prices, 1998: A Guide to U.S., Canadian, and Mexican Coins.** 7th ed. David C. Harper, ed. Iola, Wis., Krause Publications, 1997. 528p. illus. $16.95pa. ISBN 0-87341-530-2.

This guide is a handy reference tool to U.S., Canadian, and Mexican coins. Now in a 7th edition, the work has become a standard introduction to coin collecting for new and old collectors alike. In addition to a coin value section, the guide begins with a number of topical essays on coin collecting. The opening essay, "A Small Beginning," is perhaps the best short history of U.S. coin minting available. Other essays cover hunting for coins; grading; coin care, coin clubs, and collection organization; investment value; promoting coin collecting; silver investments; the 1997 Jackie Robinson coin; and "Eight Greats in '98." These essays provide valuable insight into current coin collection trends and offer collectors some basic guidelines for their consideration.

The "Pricing Section" of the guide lists each U.S., Canadian, and Mexican coin and provides for each quality grade the editor's estimate of the coin's current value. The prices given are just a guide to the specific value of a coin, but in general the values for coins that this reviewer checked are about right based on observations at local coins shows. In many ways the value is a starting point for negotiation, rather than a fixed price. These are, of course, the value you would pay to buy the coin, not what a dealer would pay you for the same item. This is an important point for collectors and investors to consider.

Overall, this is an ideal guide. It is compiled by recognized experts in the field, is modest in price, and is efficiently organized for use. If you purchase only one "coin" reference book, this is the one you want. This guide is highly recommended for all libraries.—**Ralph Lee Scott**

846.   **Standard Catalog of United States Paper Money.** 16th ed. By Chester L. Krause and Robert F. Lemke. Robert E. Wilhite, ed. Iola, Wis., Krause Publications, 1997. 212p. illus. $24.95. ISBN 0-87341-536-1.

Now in its 16th edition, this is the "standard guide" to U.S. paper money. As do most "collector" books, this volume has a number of essays that offer readers advice on the hobby. This edition of the *Standard Catalog* contains essays on currency grading; a history of large- and small-size paper notes; a history of national (and state issue) bank notes; fractional paper currency; paper money substitutes; paper currency errors and misprints; a "Guide to Authentication"; and military payment certificates and Philippine currency, 1903-1944. More than one-half of the book is devoted to the valuation of U.S. paper money. The rest of the work consists of the afore-mentioned essays and valuation of the other types of paper monies described in these essays.

All major U.S. paper bills are illustrated with a black-and-white photograph of the front and obverse of the issue. Values are given, mostly for perfect crisp uncirculated (CU) specimens that are consistent with what a collector would pay a dealer for the note. This volume is the "Bible" for U.S. paper money collectors and has a history of being the "standard" now for more than four decades. The volume is hardbound, with more than 600 illustrations. The page layout of this volume is not as attractive as the companion volume *North American Coins & Prices* (see entry 845). In several instances the page becomes so busy that the text becomes hard to focus on. Interestingly, this is not the case with the "coin" volume cited above. There is no index, only a table of contents referred to as the "Index," in the front of the volume.

Most reference collections will want to have this volume in their collection. This edition has the new $100 1996 U.S. Federal Reserve Note, but not the new $50 U.S. Federal Reserve Note. This brings up the question of the need for the latest edition of this work in most working reference collections. Because U.S. currency is under-going current change, and the 16th edition of this "standard" work does not include all the new bills, librarians might want to consider waiting for the 17th edition instead of a current purchase.—**Ralph Lee Scott**

Dolls

847.   Sarasohn-Kahn, Jane. **Contemporary Barbie® Dolls: 1980 and Beyond.** 1998 ed. Dubuque, Iowa, Antique Trader Books, 1997. 262p. illus. index. $26.95pa. ISBN 0-930625-84-6.

The best feature of this 2d edition (the 1st was published in 1995) is the use of hundreds of color photo-graphs displaying Barbie doll models manufactured between 1980 and 1997. The author focuses on contemporary Barbie dolls manufactured for the domestic mass market and distributed nationally. After a brief overview of Barbie's history, three chapters cover Barbie releases from 1980 (when the first African American Barbie was issued) to 1997. However, not every release is pictured. Rather, the author has chosen a representative sample to demonstrate how Barbie has changed over the years. Further chapters deal with dolls based on themes (e.g., international Barbies, holiday Barbies, shopping Barbies); custom Barbies manufactured for specific retailers; couture Barbies conceived by leading fashion designers; ethnic variations of Barbie; and Ken dolls. Final chapters look at the production, marketing, and distribution of the dolls, including sales and promotion through the Internet. The most useful reference feature is the listing of Barbies issued by year from 1980 to 1997. Arranged by year, the list includes the name and number of each model and any variations that were issued. This list could be improved with the addition of references to appropriate photographs in the body of the book. A bibliography and an index complete the work. The bibliography lists mostly newspaper and periodical articles from the 1980s and 1990s. The index would be more useful if it were amplified with names of individual models of the doll. As the book is designed to be a history, no prices are given. In summary, this amalgam of coffee-table book and reference work is a fascinating read for doll collectors, but it has some drawbacks as a library reference work. Adding cross-references and indexing would allow collectors to find photographs and descriptions of individual models more easily.—**Linda Keir Simons**

Firearms

848. Ball, Robert W. D. **Springfield Armory: Shoulder Weapons 1795-1968.** Dubuque, Iowa, Antique Trader Books, 1997. 264p. illus. $34.95. ISBN 0-930625-74-9.

Springfield Armory has been associated with supplying weapons to the military since the Revolutionary War. Its long association with the U.S. military ended in 1968 with the closing of the armory. This work serves to both chronicle the development of rifles produced by the armory as well as function as a collectors' guide. Richly illustrated with color photographs of the models produced as well as detailed photographs for many models, this work will be extremely valuable to military historians studying the development of military rifles over the long history of the armory. The work is arranged chronologically by the date of the model. Each entry includes, in addition to the photographs, detailed information on the size, caliber, furniture, fastenings, and distinguishing markings on the model used in identification. Additional information is provided in a two- to three-paragraph historical development of the model.

The volume begins with a historical introduction to the armory's development. The history continues throughout the volume with additional photographs from the armory's interior, exterior, and some of its weapons in use in the field. Each illustration is captioned, some running two to three sentences.

Considering the importance of the Springfield Armory in supplying weapons to the U.S. military over a significant portion of this country's history, this volume will find use in many libraries. The volume will best serve those libraries supporting an interest in military history, general history, guns, and collecting.
—**Gregory Curtis**

849. **Orion Blue Book: Gun 1998.** 1998 ed. Scottsdale, Ariz., Orion Research, 1998. 272p. $39.00pa. ISBN 0-932089-92-5. ISSN 0883-4881.

Most gun books are designed for the consumer, and include descriptive and historical information about buying, using, and collecting firearms. Comprehensive guides such as *Gun Digest* (see ARBA 98, entry 920) and *Standard Catalog of Firearms* (see ARBA 96, entry 1009) include illustrations and feature articles as well as pricing information. The *Orion Blue Book: Gun 1998*, however, is strictly a price guide, intended for use by professionals—retail dealers, insurance companies, manufacturers, libraries, pawnbrokers, freight adjusters, law enforcement personnel, divorce and probate attorneys, and the Internal Revenue Service. More than 10,000 firearms products manufactured by more than 300 firms from the 1800s to the present are listed. These include blackpowder, drillings, handguns, rifles, and shotguns. Guns are listed alphabetically by manufacturer's name, along with year manufactured and type of action. Seven prices are given for each gun listed—the new retail price and the wholesale and resale prices for used items in excellent, average, or fair condition. Although hobbyists and collectors will not find this book much fun to peruse, with its tabular arrangement and lack of photographs or articles, it is undoubtedly an indispensable reference for people in the business of buying, selling, and putting valuations on firearms.—**Larry Lobel**

Knives

850. Ritchie, Roy, and Ron Stewart. **The Standard Knife Collector's Guide.** 3d ed. Paducah, Ky., Collector Books, 1997. 688p. illus. $12.95pa. ISBN 0-89145-737-2.

At first glance this valuable guide to collecting knives appears to be just another amateur oddity. The table of contents and the first 4 chapters—especially "The Knife Shield's Mystical Relation to Value"—do not begin to suggest the true strength of this guide. Nor does the heavy use of colloquial language ("sure as heck") and self-praise ("most valuable resource") inspire confidence in the work.

Most of the book, beginning with chapter 5 on pocketknife patterns and ending with 7 appendixes that provide detailed information about the products of the major U.S. knife manufacturers, is truly outstanding. Based on their personal experience as collectors and appraisers, Ritchie and Stewart offer a detailed approach to evaluating and appraising individual knives that is unsurpassed in the field of antiques and collectibles. They also help explain how to use their rating process by applying it, and showing the results, to a substantial number of individual knives. Helped along by a large number of photographs and illustrations that aid in the identification of different kinds of pocketknives and pocketknife blades, this is clearly the definitive guide for these highly collected items.

The information on related topics such as kitchen cutlery and straight razors is too brief to be of any real value and, in the case of straight razors, seems largely to be a promotion for their book on that subject. There is some brief, and generally accurate and useful, information on caring for a knife collection, knife sharpening, and other resources. The lack of a detailed index is a drawback, but, for the most part, the information is easy to find, especially for somebody who is, as they say, into knives.

Public libraries in areas with a hunting and sporting community will find this guide of particular value, but as with many kinds of collectibles, the audience of knife collectors is broad and diverse, so this guide deserves wider consideration by all public libraries.—**Norman D. Stevens**

Memorabilia

851.   Baker, Mark Allen **Goldmine Price Guide to Rock 'n' Roll Memorabilia.** Iola, Wis., Krause Publications, 1997. 766p. illus. $24.95pa. ISBN 0-87341-490-X.

This book can open the door to a would-be collector showing how to begin a collection, and most importantly what items are and are not considered worthy collectibles using the industry standards. It is also a valuable price guide and overall reference guide for the experienced collector to base the value of his or her ongoing collection. Many keys to collecting are given to assist the reader in building both a treasured collection and also keeping the collector from falling into the many schemes of fakes and counterfeit items. This is best described in the 2d chapter entitled "Reproductions and Counterfeits." Following this section is the chapter covering the collection of personally owned items such as clothing and jewelry. Many examples of items from Elvis Presley to the Bay City Rollers are offered, along with their current market value. Next are chapters on autograph collecting, presentation discs and awards, and rock and roll posters. Hints, in the form of "Collector's Notes," are presented throughout the book, giving insight into specific titles and topics. The main section of this collector's guide is more than 600 pages of rock and roll items listed alphabetically by celebrity name or group. Each entry has a brief history of the act followed by items of focus and their values in the form of autographs, press kits, tour books, and often overlooked memorabilia not common in many collections. This makes research a breeze when determining the value of items by a particular group or artist. Rounding it all off is a brief photograph gallery, a bibliography, and a "Recommended Reading" chapter.

Overall, this guide is both informational and entertaining. Much like browsing on the Internet, this guide can hold one's attention until one looks at the clock and realizes one has been rummaging through it for hours. It is truly a resource for collectors searching collectibles.—**Michael Florman**

Toys

852.   **America's Standard Gauge Electric Trains: Their History and Operation, Including a Collector's Guide to Current Values.** By Peter H. Riddle. Allan W. Miller and Gay Riddle, eds. Dubuque, Iowa, Antique Trader Books, 1998. 207p. illus. index. $26.95pa. ISBN 0-930625-22-6.

America's Standard Gauge Electric Trains is an illustrated history and guide for collectors. The guide is published by Antique Trader Books, a division of the company that publishes a popular trade weekly for the antiques professional. Standard gauge trains are desired by collectors due to the durability and nostalgic character of sets that reached their height of popularity around World War I and ceased manufacture by World War II. Beautiful color illustrations accompany the text. The guide includes the history of standard gauge manufacturers, descriptions of standard gauge trains and accessories, tips for building sets for trains and accessories, and an evaluation of condition and fair values for purchasing. Information about repair, restoration, and maintenance of the trains is not included in this guide. A price guide for popular items, a glossary, an appendix of train clubs and equipment suppliers, and an index add to the usefulness of the guide. This book is recommended for libraries that serve antique dealers or train enthusiasts.—**Lynne M. Fox**

853.   Brecka, Shawn. **The Beanie Family Album and Collector's Guide.** Dubuque, Iowa, Antique Trader Books, 1998. 158p. illus. index. $19.95pa. ISBN 0-930625-95-1.

The Beanie Family Album and Collector's Guide is a fairly thorough collector's guide with some fine aspects. The introduction has discussions on the future of Beanie Babies, purchasing Beanies as an investment, and values. The main portion of the guide lists all Beanie Babies and other collectible stuffed animals. Each Beanie Baby listed is accompanied by a photograph and description. Most also have a chart depicting the rate of value. The back of the guide consists of a price guide for all the stuffed animals in the guide and a helpful index.

Although the information is fairly complete, the photographs are often out of focus, backgrounds are common, and the lighting creates shadows around the animals. An alternative guide with creative and clear pictures is *Rosie's Price Guide for Ty's Beanie Babies* (Rosie Wells Enterprises, 1998). Another consideration are the various Beanie Baby monthly magazines. This guide can be useful and is recommended on a limited basis.

—**Pamela J. Getchell**

CRAFTS

854.   Crawford, Tad. **Business and Legal Forms for Crafts.** New York, Allworth Press, 1998. 176p. index. $19.95pa. ISBN 1-880559-87-0.

Designed to help artists market their crafts legally and profitably, Crawford's book presents 32 business and legal forms in three formats. In the 1st section Crawford introduces each form with instructions for its use. He discusses what each part of the form means, how to complete the blanks, and what is important to negotiate when using the form. Second, the book presents all the forms in perforated format for the artist's use. Although librarians will not appreciate the easy tear-out feature of this section, the third format, that of a CD-ROM, compensates by providing a permanent record of each form. The CD-ROM is compatible with both Windows and Macintosh operating systems. Crawford provides Adobe Acrobat, WordPerfect, Word, and ASCII versions for each document. The CD-ROM is easy to use and offers professional-looking forms to anyone with a decent printer. The author covers a wide variety of business contracts, including those for basic sales, consignment contracts, commissions, distribution contracts, rentals of art work, exhibition loans, lectures, and licenses of artwork. Also covered are release forms from models and property owners and permission forms from owners of copyrighted materials featured in art work. U.S. government copyright and trademark application forms round out this useful volume. Crawford's explanations are clear and concise. Although not a substitute for actual legal advice, the book can help artists to understand the language of business and to protect their creative work.

—**Linda Keir Simons**

855.   Greenfield, Jane. **ABC of Bookbinding: A Unique Glossary with over 700 Illustrations for Collectors & Librarians.** New Castle, Del., Oak Knoll Press, 1998. 183p. illus. index. $35.00. ISBN 1-884718-41-8.

This heavily illustrated glossary of more than 1,000 bookbinding words is admirably suited to meet the needs of collectors and librarians. The definitions are concise and easy to understand, and the more than 700 black-and-white line drawings give the book a clarity and precision—a visual explicitness that its only real competitor, *Bookbinding and the Conservation of Books* (see ARBA 84, entry 84), lacks. This work is strong in its definitions and illustrations pertaining to the history of the book and of bookbinding in different cultures and centuries. A valuable index of binder's identification marks is included. Greenfield, long associated with Yale University's world-famous Beinecke Rare Book and Manuscript Library and the founder of Yale's Conservation Studio, is one of the pioneers in the development of book conservation techniques, and her knowledge and experience is apparent on every page of this useful and admirably executed work.—**Joseph Cataio**

856.   **Multicultural Projects Index: Things to Make and Do to Celebrate Festivals, Cultures, and Holidays Around the World.** 2d ed. By Mary Anne Pilger. Englewood, Colo., Libraries Unlimited, 1998. 358p. $38.50. ISBN 1-56308-524-0.

In this global society it is essential that people young and old have an understanding of the various cultures of the world so that likenesses and differences can be appreciated. According to the introduction of this book, "the rewards of learning about the culture of one's heritage as well as that of others can only result in a world family of peace."

To further this understanding of various cultures, Pilger has devised this index to things to make and do to celebrate festivals, cultures, and holidays around the world. There are 1,736 books published between the 1940s and the 1990s indexed here, each according to specific topics so that the user will have little difficulty pinpointing a narrow subject. For example, there are nine subdivisions of the topic "Trinidad" with a total of 27 references to books that contain information on cookery, dolls, festivals, games, and more. The volume concludes with a list of books indexed by number and is followed by a list of books indexed by author.

This volume will be valuable to teachers, librarians, school library media specialists, and anyone interested in the various cultures of the world.—**Sara R. Mack**

INTERIOR DESIGN

857.   **Contemporary Designers.** 3d ed. Sara Pendergast, ed. Detroit, St. James Press, 1996. illus. $160.00. ISBN 1-55862-184-9.

The 3d edition of this core reference tool for biographical, bibliographic, and critical material on modern international designers is significantly updated and expanded to cover nearly 690 individual designers and firms. Each entry is distinctive and includes one or more of the following: an autobiographical essay or quotation, a critical review of the designer's impact on the field, a black-and-white photograph of a representative work, and a bibliography of works on and by the designer. The most intriguing selections feature a philosophical piece by the designer. For example, Vico Magistretti eloquently explains the future of design in his theory that we "will want objects that look strong and simple, that need no maintenance and that will never be quickly or economically replaced." Dates and sources for the artists' capsule statements would be extremely helpful for scholars.

Nationality and design field indexes provide convenient access to the entries. Despite the popularity and productivity of computer- and technology-based design during the 1990s, this volume lists only one artist each in the fields of special effects and multimedia and none at all under computer-aided design. Film and stage design notables of the 1990s are also not included. Its strengths are the coverage of industrial, graphic, fashion, and interior design during the twentieth century through 1980. A sprinkling of color plates would enrich the visual appeal and power of the important creations displayed here. In spite of its weaknesses, *Contemporary Designers* is full of fascinating information and holds an important place in both academic libraries and public libraries that include a strong design collection.—**Anne C. Moore**

858.   Lewis, Susan A. **Interior Design Sourcebook: A Guide to Resources on the History and Practice of Interior Design.** Detroit, Omnigraphics, 1998. 307p. illus. index. (Design Reference Series, v.3). $45.00. ISBN 0-7808-0198-9.

Interior Design Sourcebook is the third in the publisher's design reference series; the others are sourcebooks for landscape architecture and architecture. Intended for both an academic and professional audience, in 15 chapters the *Interior Design* volume provides an annotated list of the core works in this widely diverse, complex, and new field. It is an essential volume for design schools. Working professionals may delight in finding references they missed in school on lighting, color, and project types but be disappointed in the book's computer and marketing applications. In this latter area, references are dated foundation documents.

The annotations are well written by those who love interior design; they are also frank, clever, and helpful. The book departs from its annotated format only once for 24 pages of definitions in computer-assisted design. It is an exception that leaves the reader wondering if there can be any essential books in this rapidly changing field. The indexes provided for names, organizations, and subjects are helpful. The *Interior Design Sourcebook* was not meant to replace keeping up with trends and developments, but is a great foundation for students in architecture and interior design.—**Pete Prunkl**

PHOTOGRAPHY

859.   Crawford, Tad. **Business and Legal Forms for Photographers.** rev. ed. New York, Allworth Press, 1997. 224p. index. $24.95pa. ISBN 1-880559-82-X.

The title of this book does not give itself enough credit—it consists of much more than just the forms around which the book is structured. The author and publisher have provided several books designed to help professionals in the arts—photographers, artists, and writers—cope with issues related to their professions. The author is an attorney who specializes in creative copyright and tax law and is a faculty member of the School of Visual Arts in New York City.

The introductory section, titled the "Success Kit," briefly explains contracts and negotiation and lists lawyers' and photographers' organizations that can aid photographers in the role of business operator. Each of the business and legal forms is then presented, with explanations of fine points and tips on how to negotiate each item in the contract. The 26 contracts included are intended to cover all bases for a professional photographer and include modeling agreements; wedding, portrait, and stock agency contracts; book publishing and video rights; and much more. After this explanatory section, each of the forms is reproduced on tear-out sheets that can be photocopied for reuse. Also included with this revised edition is a CD-ROM containing all the forms, which allows them to be customized for individual needs.

The information in this volume does not seem to be available anywhere else except in a limited form in *Photographer's Market* (see ARBA 95, entry 989). With its reasonable price, this book should be acquired by any organization that wants to help professional photographers save a lot of time and money.—**Larry Lobel**

860.   Frost, Lee. **The A-Z of Creative Photography: Over 70 Techniques Explained in Full.** New York, Watson-Guptill, 1998. 160p. illus. index. $24.95pa. ISBN 0-8174-3313-9.

Written for both the creative amateur and the professional, this handbook covers 55 techniques and ideas for more interesting photography, beginning with abstract art and ending with zooming. Entries range from two to six pages in length, and are divided into sections on "what you need" (e.g., equipment, film), "how it's done," and "top tips" on perfecting the technique. The more than 200 outstanding color photographs illustrating the principles under discussion have lengthy captions that analyze the work and note equipment, film type, and exposure details. There are many options here for the person armed with only a compact or automatic camera; examples include framing a scene, shooting a theme, the rule of thirds, line-out, environmental portraits, and black-and-white for beginners. The majority of entries describe methods that call for a manual single-lens reflex camera or specialized equipment (e.g., large-format duping), and many require special film; lighting; lenses; or processing, such as color infrared, grain, cross-processing, slow-sync flash, and polarizing filters.

There is something here for everyone. Vacationers will appreciate sunsets and stained glass windows. Experimental types may want to try image transfer or pinhole photography. The writing is straightforward, although a photography handbook will help the novice because basic terms (e.g., SLR, ISO ratings, softbox, focal length) are undefined. This is sure to be a popular title for anyone who owns a camera, so libraries should buy a second copy for the stacks if one is made available in reference.—**Deborah V. Rollins**

861.   Mautz, Carl. **Biographies of Western Photographers: A Reference Guide to Photographers Working in the 19th Century American West.** Nevada City, Calif., Carl Mautz, 1997. 601p. illus. index. $85.00. ISBN 0-9621940-7-7.

This is a much-improved version of the *Checklist of Western Photographers* whose last edition dates back more than 10 years to 1986. It has been worth the wait. That booklet has been expanded to include the names of more than 15,000 nineteenth-century photographers working in 27 states and Canadian provinces. Most entries are just a line or two, but others run to several paragraphs and often include birth and death dates, working addresses, names of partners, alternative trade names, and bibliographic notes. The treatment varies by state, the result of research having been taken up by different individuals or institutions. Peter Palmquist's contribution for California is particularly informative. Two articles on early photographs are also included. The first, written by William C. Darrah, concerns photographers' imprints and what can be learned from them. The second, by Jeremy Rowe, explains how format and size can be used to date specimens. Both are exceptionally well done and will please novice and expert alike. There is also a photographers' index and a bibliography. This volume is a must for any photographic reference collection or for libraries with an interest in western history. For California libraries in particular, this will be a required acquisition.—**Paul L. Holmer**

22 Fine Arts

GENERAL WORKS

Bibliography

862.   Weisberg, Gabriel P., and Elizabeth K. Menon. **Art Nouveau: A Research Guide for Design Reform in France, Belgium, England, and the United States.** New York, Garland, 1998. 387p. illus. index. (Garland Reference Library of the Humanities, v.1115). $83.00. ISBN 0-8240-6628-6.

This annotated bibliography of 836 items focuses on design reform issues in architecture and the decorative arts from a range of resources that were available from 1885 to 1910. The authors particularly stress interchanges between proponents of "art nouveau" in France and Belgium and the "arts and crafts" movement in England and the United States. The contents of the entries underscore the existence of a set of shared assumptions and beliefs that link the two movements, with an emphasis on the rejection of traditionalism in architecture, the refusal to distinguish between the fine and applied arts, and the celebration of sinuous organic forms as inspiration for the design of everyday objects. The arrangement of the entries is in chronological order by categories (e.g., books, journal articles), which allows the reader to follow the evolution of ideas concerning design reform at the turn of the century as it was reported by the very reformers who were influential in shaping the movement. Because the literature of this defining period of design reform is preoccupied with the impact of forceful personalities, the authors have added entries beyond the original time frame that provide a critical perspective to "art nouveau" by situating this movement within the broader history of decorative arts.

The decision of the authors to be selective rather than exhaustive in the titles chosen to be examined for bibliographic entries in the journal category is most fortunate. By judiciously excluding peripheral publication, they have created a list of about 90 journals that constitute a core collection of primary resources for scholars to consult that are directly relevant to the history of design reform. Conveniently, the subject index is arranged to include entry points by journal name to group together entries taken from a particular publication that was influential during the 1885 to 1910 time period. In addition, both the author and subject indexes provide entry points to articles by and about a wide range of significant individuals, from the noteworthy William Morris to the little known Clement Heaton, in order to furnish a comprehensive overview of the artistic energy that created the design reform movement. This annotated bibliography is an authentic research guide that cannot be ignored by academic scholars who concentrate on the history of the "art nouveau" or the "arts and crafts" movement. It is recommended for purchase by university libraries that support a strong graduate program in art history.

—**David G. Nowak**

Biography

863.   Cummings, Robert. **Great Artists: The Lives of 50 Painters Explored Through Their Work.** New York, DK Publishing, 1998. 112p. illus. index. (DK Annotated Guides). $24.95. ISBN 0-7894-2391-X.

This oversized book gives two facing pages to each artist. One painting is selected to represent the artist's body of work. A few are fortunate enough to have another piece printed, but the focus is on the one painting, where captions and enlargements of particular portions of the piece explore the where and why of color, texture, composition, symbolism, purpose, and so forth. Other captions give insight into the artist's life, chronicle important events during the artist's most productive period, and list other notable works of the painter. Two primary paragraphs begin each section, reviewing the artist and giving an overview of the painting highlighted.

The key to this book is that it is part of the series DK Annotated Guides. Curiously, there is no foreword or introduction. In looking to the subtitle, "The Lives of 50 Painters Explored Through Their Work," a hint of purpose is presumed. If the purpose of this book is to encourage the reader to seek out more in-depth sources on the artist, then it succeeds well. The brevity of the text and visuals will certainly compel most to find out more about each of these 50 artists.

When a specific number is drawn from an established group, personal preference (and admitted bias) always makes one question why this one was chosen but the other not. Of course, Leonardo da Vinci, Michelangelo, and Titian are included, but why not El Greco? Peter Paul Rubens, Rembrandt, and Jean-Honoré Fragonard are there, but not Thomas Gainsborough. The first artists in this compilation are the Limbourg brothers (mid-1440s), and the last mentioned is Jackson Pollock (1912-1956). Are readers to believe the contributors felt there were not any great artists before 1400 or after 1950? Of the 50 artists selected, only 2 are women, and only 3 are from the United States. No Latin American artists are represented. In fact, 45 of the 50 artists here are European. This complaint is not meant to dismiss the artists that are here. Each is a master deserving recognition. However, a more international selection would have been nice to see.

Another curiosity is the formatting of the book. As stated, each artist is given two facing pages. Some of the facing pages read horizontally, and some read vertically. Because the two formats are intermixed, turning the page often requires flipping the book up on its end. At its vertical format, the book is awkward to hold, text is difficult to read, and visuals are arduous to view.

On the plus side, the reproductions are of high resolution and vibrant color, and the captions placed around the paintings are of essential and important information. Also, the book is reasonably priced. This book is marginally recommended to scholastic libraries because students may be able to complete a sketchy one-page essay on an artist from the data supplied here. Otherwise, *Great Artists* is purely a quick coffee-table browsing book. [R: SLJ, July 98, p. 115]—**Joan Garner**

864.   McCracken, Penny. **Women Artists and Designers in Europe Since 1800: An Annotated Bibliography.** New York, G. K. Hall/Simon & Schuster Macmillan, 1998. 2v. index. $200.00/set. ISBN 0-7838-0091-6.

This 2-volume bibliography is a guide to material on 2,000 women artists and designers in Europe during the past two centuries, with brief annotations in English about each. The general section lists 39 reference books and 176 nonreference sources (primarily exhibition catalogs) that mention or focus on women artists and designers arranged alphabetically by author or title. The rest of the bibliography lists reference books, other publications, and individual artists and designers under 13 specialties—book binding, ceramics, fashion, garden design, glass, stained glass, interior design, textiles, graphic arts, painting, performance art/video/mixed media, photography, and sculpture. Women working in ceramics, glass, and textiles are referred to as designers rather than artists as a reflection of actual practice. However, the author missed a golden opportunity to influence tradition by referring to all of these women as artists. The bibliography excludes women artists working in the fields of architecture, landscape design, and nondomestic interior design. McCracken arranges women under her determination of their primary specialty. Under each woman, entries include an overly abbreviated identification of the artist, her works, main publications (in-depth information), exhibitions, and other sources that briefly mention her. The typography of the entries is poorly designed as it emphasizes the repetitive section headings rather than the artist's name.

Indexes in volume 2 provide access by country and artist or designer name. Although a tremendous undertaking, this is just a first attempt at unearthing the hidden history of female artists all over the world. Much research remains in uncovering Greek and Spanish women artists and artists who worked in fields such as ceramics, in which only the studio name is known. This source is recommended for academic libraries at schools with art history programs. The price is prohibitive for most libraries. [R: Choice, Oct 98, p. 292]—**Anne C. Moore**

865.   **St. James Guide to Native North American Artists.** Matuz, Roger, ed. Detroit, St. James Press, 1998. 691p. illus. index. $155.00. ISBN 1-55862-221-7.

This compilation of art historians' reviews of 20 Native American artists' careers and work is an essential reference book for all students of Native American studies, art historians, critics, and collectors as well as lay people following art. The challenge of being a minority population has brought out new fine art, appreciative development of traditional art, and synthesis of these two modes. Sometimes the artists are deliberately confrontational (e.g., Douglas Cardinal). Occasionally an artists' style is prescribed by Euro-Americans (e.g., Dorothy Dunn in 1930s Santa Fe). All the entrants have been accepted at juried exhibits and published before. Identification with the trial of the indigenous populations since Europeans arrived is a motivation for interest, but their exotic work or, contrarily, their work comparable to Euro-Americans' styles is also compelling. Because all humans have reason for anxiety and fear, are fascinated with linear and geometric form, and have ethnic stories worth recalling, finally the universality of the art beckons. This study will send readers out to galleries, museums, and libraries to find art and publication of artworks to deepen this broad and tempting beginning of exposure to Native American work. In itself the book's wisdom will inspire and satisfy.—**Elizabeth L. Anderson**

866.   **Who's Who in American Art 1997-1998.** 22d ed. New Providence, N.J., Marquis Who's Who/Reed Reference Publishing, 1998. 1515p. index. $210.00. ISBN 0-8379-6300-1. ISSN 0000-0191.

Data on North American artists may be in *Who's Who in American Art* if they are alive, if Marquis Who's Who sent them a questionnaire, and if the artists returned a response. More artists commonly found in an art history textbook appear here than renowned local or Native American artists. Formerly included but deceased artists are listed without any information in the last index in the book, so they could be pursued in the earlier publications. The radically abbreviated language makes reading about random people less intriguing than finding familiar ones or those under an interesting index item.

The text, if the artists will tell, includes birth date and place, schooling, works in public collections, exhibits, a bibliography, medium used, and address. Particularly intriguing is Christo's entry because he gave the dimensions and materials of several of his public artworks; most entries do not mention the works, just the site that has one or more pieces. *Artist* is defined broadly here, and educators, historians, administrators, restorers, publishers, architects, and video artists are included; an index of these vocations with adherents is interesting. The index of artists by where they live is also meaningful. Every library with an art school nearby needs this book for researchers.
—**Elizabeth L. Anderson**

Catalogs and Collections

867.   Axsom, Richard H., and David Platzker. **Printed Stuff: Prints, Posters, and Ephemera by Claes Oldenburg.** New York, with Madison, Wis., Madison Arts Center, Hudson Hills Press, 1997. 453p. illus. index. $125.00. ISBN 1-55595-123-6.

For more than three decades Claes Oldenburg has been a popular and innovative U.S. artist, working both in the media of sculpture and print and receiving recognition for his etchings, lithographs, woodcuts, and screenprints. He has worked on a variety of papers, Plexiglas, cardboard, silk, and canvas, and as of the end of 1996, his oeuvre of prints, posters, and ephemera contains more than 250 items. This catalogue raisonné documents these materials, though it is substantially more than a series of lists: Axsom provides a lengthy introductory essay, "Beyond a Laugh and a Pretty Line," that offers a comprehensive appraisal of Oldenburg's printed materials and their relationships to his other works, and the volume also includes selected lists of Oldenburg's exhibitions, a bibliography, and "concordances" (i.e., specialized indexes providing access to the catalogue by literature reference number, by workshop number, and by publishers' catalog number). There is an index that is, unfortunately, not quite perfect.

The catalogue is arranged chronologically, though strict chronology has occasionally been altered to maintain a thematic coherence. Entries provide the artist's intended title of the work; its publication date; the portfolio in which the work belongs; the medium, colors, and support; the measurements of the work (in inches and centimeters); the nature of Oldenburg's signature and inscriptions; the number of prints in a published edition; descriptions of proofs; lists of the printers and other collaborators who worked with Oldenburg; the publisher; and the printing sequence. In addition, when relevant, entries provide a bibliography of the literature discussing the work, an exhibition history, and citations to the comments of other artists. Furthermore, all works that involve color are reproduced in full color, and the catalog includes 381 breathtaking color plates, 52 duotones, and 55 black-and-white illustrations. All libraries supporting studies of twentieth-century artists and printmakers will want this beautifully produced volume.—**Richard Bleiler**

868.   **Record of the Carnegie Institute's International Exhibitions 1896-1996.** Peter Hastings Falk, ed. Madison, Conn., Sound View Press, 1998. 378p. index. $89.00. ISBN 0-932087-55-8.

The Carnegie Institute's International Exhibitions have greatly influenced American artists and been a boon to the Carnegie Museum of Art. Both established and emerging artists from America and Europe have been featured. This volume is part of a series that has documented art exhibits in 10 other prestigious institutions, including the Art Institute of Chicago, the Whitney Museum, and the Pennsylvania Academy of the Fine Arts. It is arranged alphabetically by author with the year of the exhibition and the title of the entry. Entries note if an award was received. Other information might be included, such as lender, purchase, and, for earlier years, if work was submitted but rejected. The series editor notes that each of the indexes in this series begins with a historical chapter that includes pertinent statistics, but in this volume he refers the reader to Vicky A. Clark's *International Encounters: The Carnegie International and Contemporary Art, 1896-1996* as a companion volume. The volume is a valuable addition to libraries with an art section and can be useful in finding information about lesser-known artists. A sorting of exhibits by years would have been a useful addition to this volume.—**Joshua Cohen**

Dictionaries and Encyclopedias

869.   Kovinick, Phil, and Marian Yoshiki-Kovinick. **An Encyclopedia of Women Artists of the American West.** Austin, Tex., University of Texas Press, 1998. 405p. illus. $100.00. ISBN 0-292-79063-5.

A more appropriate title for this work would be *Women Artists Depicting the American West*, for that is what it covers. Describing the life and work of some 1,000 women, this biographical dictionary uses selection criteria based on subject matter of the work rather than residency in the West. Therefore, it does not include Agnes Martin, a prominent abstract artist who lives in New Mexico. Nor does it cover San Francisco's Joan Brown and her whimsical portraits, or any of the folk artists that figure so prominently in the West. Photographers are also excluded.

What it does cover is painters, graphic artists, and sculptors (many of them obscure) whose styles range from realism to early modernism and who have received acclaim for their depictions of the American West—that is, mountain and desert landscapes; portraits of Native Americans, cowboys, or pioneers; wildlife; prairie homes and missions; and so forth.

After a brief history of women in the western art movement, the authors describe individual artists, with biographical sketches that focus on each woman's career as an artist and her work with western subject matter. The biographies are competently written and informative. Selected lists of exhibitions, current locations of work in public collections, references, and rather small black-and-white photos of their work (more than 250) occasionally accompany the descriptions.

It is always a pity when an art book does not contain color reproductions, but black-and-white photographs are better than none at all. However, the work would have more appeal if the authors had limited the number of artists covered and included color reproductions of their work. Because of its focus and rather high price, this book will primarily appeal to libraries at commercial art schools and academic libraries in the western United States that support art or art history programs. It will also be of interest to collectors specializing in this type of art. [R: LJ, Dec 98, p. 92]—**Barbara Ittner**

870.   Lahti, N. E. **The Language of Art from A to Z (writ in plain English).** rev. ed. Brooklyn, N.Y., York Books, 1997. 182p. $11.00pa. ISBN 0-9620147-3-7.

The Language of Art from A to Z (writ in plain English) is absolutely delightful. It portrays a fresh approach to understanding art that results in concise, succinct definitions of standard art terms, pleasing descriptions of art movements, interpretations of the many special techniques used by named artists, and background explanations of world art presented in short essays. Lahti has produced an outstanding book that will appeal to anyone seeking rudimentary but wide-ranging knowledge about the world of art.

The book is trim and has a soft cover, which make it comfortable to carry when touring a museum or an art exhibit. Arranged in a dictionary format, The Language of Art from A to Z is an excellent resource for all ages and a must have for all libraries.—**Mary L. Trenerry**

Directories

871.   **American Art Directory 1997-1998.** 56th ed. Pete R. Palac and others, eds. New Providence, N.J., R. R. Bowker/Reed Reference Publishing, 1997. 906p. index. $210.00. ISBN 0-8352-3819-9. ISSN 0065-6968.

The American Art Directory was first published as The American Art Annual in 1898. This present volume is the 56th edition and has long since become the standard in the field. The information in the directory is obtained through a questionnaire sent directly to the institutions in most cases. In the cases where the information has been obtained from other sources, an asterisk is placed to the right of the institution's name. The work is divided into 4 sections: an alphabetic and geographic index; art schools; art museums; and indexes of organizations, personnel, and subjects.

The "National and Regional Organization" list includes the name of the institution, address, telephone and fax numbers, the name of the executive director, opening times and days, admission charges, the average annual attendance, and membership. More than 140 organizations are listed in this section. They include museums, libraries, associations, and other institutions. The majority of the listings are for museums—more than 2,000. In addition, there are 289 libraries listed, 614 area associations, and 10 corporations with art holdings listed. More than 1,800 art schools, college and university departments of art, art history departments, and architecture schools are listed. Each entry is designated by an "A" (association), "C" (corporate art), "L" (library collection), "M" (museum), or "O" (organization).

The American Art Directory is well known for its accuracy and ease of use. This present edition carries on that reputation. This work is highly recommended for all academic and public libraries with art reference collections. In addition, it is recommended for museums, art schools, corporations, and all other institutions that are involved with art collecting or art education. Due to its price, it is probably not a logical purchase for individuals.

—**Robert L. Wick**

872.   Smith, Constance. **Art Marketing Sourcebook for the Fine Artist: Where to Sell Your Artwork.** 3d ed. Penn Valley, Calif., ArtNetwork, 1998. 245p. index. $23.95pa. ISBN 0-940899-25-3.

The 3d edition of this invaluable reference book contains 2,000 new listings of marketing sources for fine artists. The publisher, ArtNetwork, was founded in 1986 to teach artists how to earn a living from their creations.

The entries are organized by broad categories such as representatives, consultants, and dealers; art galleries, shows, and fairs; and ethnic markets. The new categories in this edition are greeting card publishers and representatives, licensing companies, art print distributors, and museum shows. The listings were solicited from responses to questionnaires. According to the author, only those sources indicating that they are looking for new talent are included. Some of the listings include the following information: geographic limitations, source of artwork, clients, styles, media, best time of year to submit one's portfolio, and how to contact the source.

An alphabetic index listing all of the sources is given at the end of the volume. This volume will be useful for libraries whose clientele includes fine artists.—**Ingrid Schierling Burnett**

873.   **Traveler's Guide to Art Museum Exhibitions, 1998.** 10th ed. Susan S. Rappaport, Jennifer A. Smith, and Susan Coll, eds. Washington, DC, Museum Guide Publications; distr., Bergenfield, N.J., Harry N. Abrams, 1997. 336p. illus. $12.95pa. ISBN 0-8109-6345-0.

This small paperback provides 20 pages listing the major traveling art exhibitions to be shown in 300 major art museums during 1998; 240 pages of information on U.S. art museums and their 1998 exhibits generally; and 69 pages of information on the major art museums in European countries, Israel, Australia, Canada, and Puerto Rico and their 1998 exhibits. The book is indexed by name of institution. The U.S. pages are arranged by state.

The guide's purpose is to provide exhibit information for art lovers who travel and for travelers who love art. Entries provide name, address, telephone number (including country code for non-U.S. places), Website addresses, dates, and brief descriptions of the different exhibits on view during 1998 at each institution. Also included are a paragraph about each facility that illustrates the highlights of the significant artworks held, the collection's size, its architecture, services for the disabled, admission fees, hours, programming for children, tour availability and how to arrange for tours, availability of food and drink on the premises, and details about the museum shop's hours and offerings. The list of traveling exhibits is arranged by exhibit name, which is not very handy, and provides only the institutional locations and dates of the shows. There is a (T) mark beside each entry in the main portion of the book to indicate which are the traveling exhibits; there are also annotations there describing the exhibits. Some entries have one small illustration, usually of a piece held, reflecting the scope and contents of the institution.

According to a review in *Library Journal* (19 April 97, p. 84), this book is not as extensive a source as *Museum Premieres, Exhibitions, and Special Events* (see ARBA 98, entry 72), an annual that began in 1994. This reviewer has not seen that title. Museum exhibit information is available from travel agents, from local newspapers, from magazines such as *The New Yorker*, from museum-specific Websites, from journals in the field such as *Apollo* or the *Burlington Magazine*, and from general art Websites. This guide is a handy little book that brings much information together, albeit only for major U.S. and primarily Western European museums, but at a price that is almost unbelievably low.—**Agnes H. Widder**

Handbooks and Yearbooks

874.   **Art: A World History.** New York, DK Publishing, 1997. 720p. illus. index. $59.95. ISBN 0-7894-2382-0.

As quoted on the book's jacket, "Encyclopedic in Scope—Conceived as a journey through a huge museum, *Art: A World History* looks at the development of art from its earliest beginnings to the contemporary innovations of the late 20th century. From the art of the great preclassical civilizations to the treasures of five continents, all the major movements in the history of world art are chronicled. Developments in art, architecture, and design are set in their social and historical context." This resource combines text, pictures, and special "aside" boxes to highlight relevant historical events and cultures that contributed to the art of that time. It reflects the setting and mood of world societies from the beginning of human expression to the present, showing what happened to shape the art of the time, and it goes on to speculate what art will be in the future. Selected pieces of art are examined, defining what makes them masterpieces (i.e., composition, light and shadow, mastery of drawing technique, symbolism, and the like).

There is an incredible amount of information here. Readers can see the careful thought process put into each page layout and the formatting of data, and the text is concise and intelligent. For example, in defining Egyptian art, one line of the narrative nails it: "Objects are presented as they are conceived, not as they are seen." A simple sentence that explains an entire culture. This exceptional text is worth the acquisition of the book alone, and the numerous masterpiece dissections are invaluable to anyone wishing to gain a better understanding of art. Overall, this art book is a remarkable endeavor.

But the book is not without a few problems. As in this reviewer's look at another DK art book, *Great Artists* (see entry 863), this art source—although greatly improved over the above—still concentrates too heavily on European art. Credibly, Asian and South American art is explored, but not much beyond antiquity. The art of North America is more often than not given an "honorable mention" treatment, and the review of the latter part of the twentieth century is rushed through and too sketchy. For example, the Hudson River School movement of nineteenth-century America gets a 2-by-4-inch box footnote. The more well-known artists of this movement do not have a single painting displayed in this book. And the expansion of the art through the wide variety of new media developed and improved upon in the last 60 years, such as photography, film, and computer art, only receive one-quarter to one-half page.

Art: A World History may be used as a textbook for upper high school and collegiate settings as long as one recognizes that certain areas and eras will need to be augmented independently. And if looked upon this way, it can be recommended to schools and public libraries. [R: LJ, 15 Nov 98, p. 63]—**Joan Garner**

875. **Artist's & Graphic Designer's Market, 1998: 2,500 Places to Sell Your Art & Design.** Mary Cox and Megan Lane, eds. Cincinnati, Ohio, F & W Publications, 1997. 712p. illus. index. $24.99pa. ISBN 0-89879-794-2. ISSN 1075-0894.

This thorough compilation of addresses and advice for fine and commercial artists should assist job searchers. The market described, mostly in the United States, is a contrary and withdrawn suitor. Future employers may want to see original work (a portfolio) or photocopies; they may want novices or those more experienced. Thus, the need for this book. Artists should certainly be professional, economical, and informed. They may be hired to work alone at a studio or work on a team in a studio. Although some art directors encourage artists to find their own talent and preferences, nearly all of them have a limited parameter for hirings. It may be abstract or realistic, but rarely both. Most want the style to be consistent, but a few expect changes in art form. To buy this book is to have 600 reliable pages of who needs varying types of skills: cartoon syndicates, advertisers, galleries, and magazines, among others. Computer art is a fast-growing field. Also, clients who are looking for companies that do art could find them in these listings. People wanting to sense more about the art that goes by them in mail and media might stop to read this.—**Elizabeth L. Anderson**

Indexes

876. **Illustration Index VIII, 1992-1996.** By Marsha C. Appel. Lanham, Md., Scarecrow, 1998. 464p. $65.00. ISBN 0-8108-3484-7.

The 8th volume of *Illustration Index* (see ARBA 90, entry 964 for a review of volume 6) continues the excellent tradition of providing easy access to visual material. The current edition indexes illustrations from 10 mainstream publications from the years 1992 to 1996. The arrangement follows that of previous editions, with 19,000 subject headings encompassing 28,000 entries. Numerous cross-references are provided to guide the user through the volume. Each entry includes the journal citation as well as the format of the illustration (e.g., photography, lithograph, or drawing), whether it is color or black-and-white, and the size. The journal indexes are those located in most libraries such as *Life*, *National Geographic*, *Gourmet*, and *Travel and Leisure*. The author also includes contact information for those who wish to obtain reproduction rights for the illustrations.

Illustration Index has always been a valuable reference source and the current volume is no exception. This volume is enthusiastically recommended for all library collections that need to provide access to visual information.—**Monica Fusich**

ARCHITECTURE

Biographies

877. **Icons of Architecture: The 20th Century.** Sabine Thiel-Siling, ed. New York, Prestel USA; distr., New York, Neues, 1998. 190p. illus. index. $29.95. ISBN 3-7913-1949-3.

For those whose only exposure to architects is the name Frank Lloyd Wright, this work creates whole new vistas to explore. Concerned with important architectural works of the twentieth century, this work identifies and exhibits more than 225 of the best architects and architectural firms throughout the world. This work will serve both as a reference work and as a visual experience for those wishing to expand their visual sense.

Liberally illustrated with both color and black-and-white photographs, plans, and elevations, the work treats the subject matter in rough chronological time sequence beginning with Antoni Gaudi's Sagada Familia and ending with Kisho Kurokawa's International Airport and Frank O. Gehry's Guggenheim Museum project. The works illustrated are grouped by decade and by architect. Each building entry includes three to four photographs, plans, working sketches, a portrait of the architect, his or her important biographical outline notes, and a discussion of the importance of the building within the architect's oeuvre and its importance to the history of architecture.

A selected bibliography of most of the architects featured in the work and architect and place indexes complete the volume. The bibliography includes primarily monographic works; however, some article-length pieces are also listed. Many of the references in the bibliography are to non-English works.

This work will be found useful in collections supporting programs of architecture, art, art history, architectural history, urban planning, or any of the related fields. It will also find a useful place on the shelf of most libraries supporting an overview of world culture and the built environment, in other words, in most libraries except perhaps the more specialized libraries. This work is recommended for its visual appeal and as a brief yet thorough overview of twentieth-century architecture and architects.—**Gregory Curtis**

878.   Sparke, Penny. **A Century of Design: Design Pioneers of the 20th Century.** Hauppauge, N.Y., Barron's Educational Series, 1998. 272p. illus. index. $39.95. ISBN 0-7641-5122-3.

Design is often considered an extravagance and the word "designer" an elitist adjective, applied to "designer jeans" or "designer fragrance." In *A Century of Design* the reader is introduced to the realities of design and the influence design has on our lives through a variety of everyday items, such as furniture, mechanical pencils, dinnerware, or the vehicles that transport us to work. Design is as much a part of our world as the engineering that allows an object to work. Design reflects function, the use of materials, and the society of the time. A building is noteworthy not so much because it stands but because of how well it works and looks; it is no accident that many designers are better known as architects (e.g., Frank Lloyd Wright, Walter Gropius).

The book places 82 twentieth-century designers within the historical context of 6 design movements: the new century, conservative modernism, progressive modernism, new modernism, action and reaction, and toward the millennium. Most of each chapter is devoted to discussions of the individual designers and their work. The book is well illustrated, with both color and classic black-and-white photographs. The accompanying text describes the accomplishments of the designer and details about the use of materials, such as plastics, tubular steel, or bent wood. End matter includes a bibliography, a directory of manufacturers, a listing of museums and design collections, a glossary, and an index. *A Century of Design* will serve equally well as a coffee-table book or as a reference for designers, artists, or students of the arts.—**Craig A. Munsart**

Dictionaries and Encyclopedias

879.   **Architecture and Ornament: An Illustrated Dictionary.** Jefferson, N.C., McFarland, 1998. 198p. illus. $35.00. ISBN 0-7864-0383-7.

This is a highly practical architectural dictionary compiled using an unusual method that involves photographs and drawings to illustrate major as well as minor architectural details—both historical and contemporary—in the beginning sections of the book. These carefully selected illustrations via numbering and words lead to an enormous variety of details that make up the extensive professional vocabulary of those who are involved with architecture from its beginnings through today. After the reader notes the right word for an illustrated detail, he or she may then consult the dictionary section of this easy-to-use reference work. Adding to practicality is a division of elements that are found in most buildings, such as windows and doors, walls, roofs, columns, stairs, and the complexities of ornamentation and moldings. The definitions themselves are crisply written in terms that are readily understandable, and the dictionary section is, of course, highly useful by itself. The book will be of value to those in the building profession, both students and licensed architects, and also to preservationists, new home owners, and the growing number of urban realtors. As a bonus, there is an appendix with a well-conceived outline on how best to prepare written descriptions of a variety of structures, including two- and three-story homes, a church, a Richardsonian style library, an industrial building, and a modern office tower, among others. The book presents accurate information in a most practical way and succeeds admirably in a presenting a refreshingly new dictionary for the architectural field in its broadest definition.—**William J. Dane**

880.   Burden, Ernest. **Illustrated Dictionary of Architecture.** New York, McGraw-Hill, 1998. 261p. illus. index. $49.95; $29.95pa. ISBN 0-07-008988-4; 0-07-008987-6pa.

In architecture first impressions are made from the visual impact of the combination of styles, materials, building elements, and architectural forms of the structure. The next reaction is to classify and define these details to obtain an aesthetic and functional evaluation according to acceptable criteria. It is the purpose of this book to present an illustrated design resource to aid in this process. There is a collection of nearly 5,000 images illustrating more than 3,000 architectural definitions and subdefinitions. More than half of these are design-related, and for many there is more than one illustration per design. The definitions and subdefinitions are listed alphabetically, but there is a world index containing 2,200 entries to further cross-referencing. The photographs and drawings are excellent, and a unique page layout makes clear reference to the definitions. Regrettably, there are no sources for the location of the illustrations. Many photographs are recognizable to a working architect or student. However, others may be left wanting more information about where to find the buildings themselves or, at least, enlargements. [R: BL, 1 Sept 98, p. 160; Choice, Oct 98, p. 288]—**Robert J. Havlik**

Handbooks and Yearbooks

881.   Butler, Robert Brown. **Standard Handbook of Architectural Engineering: A Practical Manual for Architects, Engineers, Contractors & Related Professions & Occupations.** New York, McGraw-Hill, 1998. 1071p. illus. index. $125.00. ISBN 0-07-913692-3.

This comprehensive collection of formulas and tables provides the calculation tools that architects, builders, and environmental and construction engineers need, but it will benefit anyone challenged to do technical calculations. Each chapter provides informational overviews that explain key concepts required to use the formulas. Plumbing, lighting, structures (walls, loads, columns), acoustics (sound transmission), and design (staircases, "The Golden Section") are some of the many topics covered.

A formula is not just listed but is accompanied by examples of practical use, identification of each element of the formula, and the step-by-step process used to solve the problem. The text explains everything in terminology many nontechnical readers will be able to follow, and the illustrated drawings and tables throughout also clarify concepts.

The formula derivation section explains the standardized streamlining of notation used to illustrate each formula in the book. The extensive index is exceptionally legible and pinpoints formulas and tables via a unique typeface in addition to the page reference. An optional software diskette is included with no instruction as to how to get it to work. This format can be a problem for libraries attempting to keep it intact and undamaged; it may require separate handling and may present copyright problems.

This work has no comprehensive equal and will be welcome in all architecture and civil, construction, and environmental engineering collections. The handbook should be considered for most medium- to large-sized public and municipal libraries as well.—**Gary R. Cocozzoli**

882.   **Time-Saver Standards for Architectural Design Data.** 7th ed. Donald Watson, Michael J. Crosbie, and John Hancock Callendar, eds. New York, McGraw-Hill, 1997. 1v. (various paging). index. $150.00. ISBN 0-07-068506-1.

"The aspiration of the architect or master builder then, by definition, is to gain mastery of the knowledge of construction technology." These words, from the introduction to the 7th edition of this standard reference, encapsulate its ambitious purpose. Part 1 presents principles of architectural discussion according to the classification set down in Uniformat II, the professional classification system currently most widely used. It defines and discusses categories of the elements of building according to their place in the construction sequence. Part 2 is compatible with the MasterFormat section of Uniformat, which is used in construction specifications.

Part 1 contains several articles, including "Indoor Air Quality," "Acoustics," "Building Economics," and "Estimating and Monitoring," in addition to other topics. Part 2 includes the subjects of concrete, metal, wood and plastics, furnishings, and conveying systems.

Thorough and well done, this is a book that architects will keep on hand in their offices. Special libraries or those serving architectural students will want to purchase a copy, but it is too specialized for most public libraries.
—**Susan B. Hagloch**

883.   **Time-Saver Standards for Landscape Architecture: Design and Construction Data.** 2d ed. Charles W. Harris, Nicholas T. Dines, and Kyle D. Brown, eds. New York, McGraw-Hill, 1998. 1v. (various paging). illus. index. $125.00. ISBN 0-07-017027-4.

The prime objective of the 2d edition of *Time-Saver Standards for Landscape Architecture* is to be a handbook of data promoting resource-conserving design and construction practices. It is an excellent handbook for any student, practicing architect, planner, engineer, conservationist, land developer, landscape contractor, or others who are concerned with our natural environment and how it is modified.

This landscaping resource includes prefaces from both the 1st and 2d edition, a detailed table of contents, a foreword from the 1st edition, and a list of contributors and reviewers who are "experts or experienced professional practitioners with regard to a specific topic." Each of the 9 divisions has several sections. Each section includes an introduction; concise tables; checklists; "key point" text summaries; and illustrations, references, and sources of technical information and assistance. Also included are an appendix of metric conversion guidelines, a detailed index, and illustration source notes. Dimensions and quantities have been converted to metric value with U.S. units in parentheses when possible. The 2d edition has eliminated several sections, renamed others, and expanded still other sections. It has been redesigned, making for a less cluttered appearance. Drawings are frequently re-inked with more than 2,000 new or revised schematics, photographs, charts, and maps. Although charts are frequently smaller than in the 1st edition, they are also easier to read. Disclaimers stating that the data are to be used only for preliminary planning and design are found both in the preface and scattered throughout the book.—**Nadine Salmons**

DRAWING

884.   **American Book and Magazine Illustrators to 1920, Volume 188.** Steven E. Smith, Catherine A. Hastedt, and Donald H. Dyal, eds. Detroit, Gale, 1998. 450p. illus. (Dictionary of Literary Biography, v.188). $146.00. ISBN 0-7876-1843-8.

Most of the libraries that will acquire this volume for their reference collection already have a standing order for the Dictionary of Literary Biography (DLB) series. Nonetheless, this is a valuable addition to any collection, particularly academic libraries that support curricula in education, children's literature, American literature, U.S. history, art history, or library science. There are 32 contributors from libraries and museums across the country who have written outstanding essays on the work of 42 book and magazine illustrators, mainly from the so-called Golden Age of Illustration from the 1890s to the 1920s. A few of the illustrators date back to the late eighteenth to mid-nineteenth centuries.

The editors' introduction describes the evolution of illustration printing techniques, the role of the illustrator as artist, and illustration as a profession. Each biographical entry is lengthy, from 4 to 20 pages with numerous black-and-white illustrations. Most include a portrait and samples from the works of the illustrators. The entries contain a bibliography of books and magazines illustrated, a biography with a summary of the life and career of the artist, and a list of references.

The volume includes a cumulative index to all of the authors in the DLB series. The titles in the series are listed in chronological order in the front of the volume. The paper meets the American National Standards Institute minimum requirements for permanence of printed library materials. The volume is not inexpensive, but will be a fine addition, particularly for academic library reference collections. [R: Choice, Sept 98, p. 84]

—**Ingrid Schierling Burnett**

GRAPHIC ARTS

885.   Friedl, Friedrich, Nicolaus Ott, and Bernard Stein. **Typography: An Encyclopedic Survey of Type Design and Techniques Throughout History.** New York, Black Dog & Leventhal; distr., New York, Workman Publishing, 1998. 592p. illus. index. $39.98. ISBN 1-57912-023-7.

Take a backward trip through typography land from present-day styles to the beginnings ca.3000 B.C.E. in Mesopotamia and Sumer, from current computerized typography back to cuneiform script design and techniques in a section called "When," which discusses people, places, and significant events in typographic development. The text of the volume is trilingual—English, French, and German. The current graphics period is dubbed

"Multistylistic Typography," and its treatment examines design periods such as psychedelia, art deco, Dada, art nouveau, the Arts and Crafts movement, the Renaissance, Gothic, the Middle Ages, and so on. Each of these chronological eras is illustrated with cogent examples, many in color.

The major portion of the encyclopedia is called "Who," and it lists and elaborates on people, workshops, studios, and corporations of importance to the history of typographic design. Biographies range from Friedrich Achleitner (Viennese author, architect, and teacher) through Piet Zwart (Dutch graphic designer and teacher). In between are such prominent names as John Baskerville, Giambattista Bodoni, William Caslon, and Johannes Gutenberg. This section, profusely illustrated in color, consists of 485 pages. The "how" section discusses the tools of typography from the hand-ax to the computer. There is an index of fonts, illustrated and mentioned, and a selected bibliography. Because the book is arranged in alphabetic order, there is no need for an index.

The authors are professionals in the field. Friedl is a professor of typography at the College of Design in Offenbach am Main. Ott and Stein are partners in a graphic design studio in Berlin. The book has been beautifully printed in Italy. The typographic world will welcome this tour de force and will await an encore from the authors.—**Frank J. Anderson**

886. Tressider, Jack. **Dictionary of Symbols: An Illustrated Guide to Traditional Images, Icons, and Emblems.** San Francisco, Calif., Chronicle Books, 1998. 240p. index. $24.95pa. ISBN 0-8118-1470-X.

Most libraries probably never have enough dictionaries of symbols to satisfy demand, and to a certain extent this newest offering may help supply that demand. Its covers mythology, literature, and art and is nothing if not comprehensive. This broad scope resembles that of Hans Biedermann's *Dictionary of Symbolism* (see ARBA 94, entry 979) and Udo Becker's *Continuum Encyclopedia of Symbols* (see ARBA 95, entry 1441). Tressider's ecumenical and multicultural focus is closer to Biedermann's than it is to Becker's Eurocentric provenance. Yet, in sheer numbers, Tressider has one-half as many entries as Biedermann and one-third those of Becker. Where Tressider differs, however, is in three distinguishing features. First, a series of "panels," modeled to a lesser degree on a similar device in Becker, provide more in-depth coverage of 32 selective topics; some of them (e.g., afterworlds, cardinal points) are almost mini-essays, yet others (e.g., peace, vanity) are shorter than individual entries. A second feature is the placement of cross-references in the margins. This novelty facilitates access to related references, although at times it borders on overkill. Finally, an additional index of supplemental words provides links to important terms that are embedded within other definitions but do not merit an entry of their own. In practice, however, this feature is disappointing because of its inconsistent, selective application. Furthermore, although the definitions are concise and seem reliable, one must accept the information at face value because, unlike the two sources mentioned above, Tressider neither cites his sources nor includes a bibliography. Likewise, the quality of the illustrations pales by comparison with its cohorts. When all is said and done, however, this user-friendly multidisciplinary compilation of symbols helps fill a void. [R: LJ, 15 Mar 98, p. 59]—**Lawrence Olszewski**

PAINTING

887. **American Paintings in the Detroit Institute of Arts, Volume II: Works by Artists Born 1816-1847.** New York, Hudson Hills Press, 1997. 303p. illus. index. $85.00. ISBN 1-55595-142-2.

The Detroit Institute of Art, the fifth largest museum in the United States, owns one of the most comprehensive collections of paintings of U.S. artists. This is the 2d of a 3-volume catalog and reproduces paintings of U.S. artists born between 1816 and 1847. The earlier volume focused on artists born before 1816, and the 3d will cover artists born by 1875. This catalog includes more than 100 paintings by artists such as Mary Cassatt, James McNeill Whistler, Martin Johnson Heade, and many other less-known artists. Each signed entry includes a biographical essay and comprehensive information about the painting, including provenance, exhibitions, and references. This volume includes an introduction by Nancy Rivard Shaw, Curator of American Art, who provides an overview of the collection's history. Fifteen scholars in the field of U.S. art history contributed to this volume. Fully illustrated with 96 color plates and 8 black-and-white photographs, this work also includes a general index and an index of paintings by accession number. *American Paintings in the Detroit Institute of Arts* is highly recommended for all academic and large public libraries.—**Monica Fusich**

888.   Barnhart, Richard M., and others. **Three Thousand Years of Chinese Painting.** New Haven, Conn., Yale University Press, 1997. 402p. illus. index. (The Culture and Civilization of China). $75.00. ISBN 0-300-07013-6.

This splendid volume of Chinese painting combines all the essential elements of an excellent overview. The scope and choice of works to reproduce and discuss are decisive in the history of the subject. The quality of the printing is exceptional and attractively presented. Yet, most important of all, the scholars' essays on the subject are first-rate. To attempt to gather the seminal works for "three thousand years" of Chinese painting is a formidable task. This Yale University Press publication is worthy of its subject. From Neolithic petroglyphs to contemporary communist works, the immense range of Chinese painting is represented by a well-chosen selection. The team of Chinese scholars who assembled the volume are recognized as the top of the field. There are 300 color reproductions included. This book is delightful as an introduction to the general reader as well as indispensable to the scholar. It is the first in a series of publications that readers can look forward to.—**Linda L. Lam-Easton**

889.   Makowski, Colleen Lahan. **Charles Burchfield: An Annotated Bibliography.** Lanham, Md., Scarecrow Press, 1996. 210p. index. $47.50. ISBN 0-8108-3131-7.

This bibliography is intended for anyone studying Charles Burchfield's art. It begins with an extensive exhibition history, followed by sections organized by format (including nonprint media), for a total of 1,450 entries. As might be expected by anyone familiar with research on a twentieth-century artist, half of the entries are for exhibition catalogs and periodical articles, each appropriately annotated. The introduction provides a brief biographical and artistic summary that is supplemented by information in some of the annotations.

The exhibition history with which the book begins is well researched and apparently exhaustive—most entries have catalogs listed and annotated in the following exhibition catalog section. Annotations in the catalog and article sections are the most extensive and descriptive, and usually contain titles of works shown and illustrated. Many annotations of articles are lengthy, providing a useful summary of the content. For the many listed books that cover more than one artist, the author has noted how Burchfield is seen in relation to other artists and to various art movements. In the museum collection section, each entry includes the titles of works held by the institution, with the exception of two institutions whose holdings are too large to enumerate.

Makowski has included an excellent index that contains titles of works, gallery, collection and institution names, and exhibition and book titles. Wallpaper is the only artistic medium that an entry is provided for; this may have been included because of the rather unusual nature of the medium, but it is unfortunate that other media are not similarly represented. Overall, this is a work of solid scholarship, and is both well organized and well executed. [R: RQ, Summer 97, p. 613]—**Kristin Doty**

23 Language and Linguistics

GENERAL WORKS

Bibliography

890. Dalby, Andrew. **A Guide to World Language Dictionaries.** London, Library Association and Chicago, Fitzroy Dearborn, 1998. 470p. index. $95.00. ISBN 1-57958-069-6.

There are a large number of dictionaries to choose from for many of the better-known languages. This book is very selective. Most of the dictionaries listed retain some value, whatever else is published in their field. Sources of information are cited and often quoted at length to show how a word is or was used. They suggest word origins or discuss them at length with references to earlier scholarly work. Special registers in which a word is used are identified, the date of its first or last recorded occurrence is presented, and the evidence to back up the dating is supplied. This makes these dictionaries among the most compelling of reference books. Among the listed dictionaries, there are the oldest, the newest, and multilanguage dictionaries. The author tried to include all the major and historical dictionaries for all the major languages, excepting only those works by those who are not already familiar with the languages.

This guide arranges languages in alphabetic order. There is a short introduction to each language heading that tells where the language is spoken and in what alphabet it is written. Under each language, about a dozen dictionaries are listed under the topics of "Historical Dictionaries," "The Modern Standard," "Older Periods," "Regional Forms or Dialects," "Slang and Special Vocabularies," and "Etymological Dictionaries." Entries for "Other Works of Interest" are listed at the end.

There are tables of non-Latin scripts that assist users who need to consult dictionaries in the relevant languages and need help with the alphabetic order. Some transliterations are added for convenience. There is also an index of personal names and of the titles of dictionaries. This guide is helpful to dictionary users around the world. It will also assist linguists and librarians who need to know the strengths of their own reference shelves and what more is available elsewhere.—**Vera Gao**

891. MacGregor, Alexander P. **Ten Years of Classicists: Dissertations & Outcomes 1988-1997.** Wauconda, Ill., Bolchazy-Carducci, 1998. 105p. $20.00pa. ISBN 0-86516-405-3.

Despite many doubters, advanced studies in the classics are still alive and well in U.S. universities. The proof is this compilation that, by electronically massaging the data appearing in the *Newsletter of the American Philological Association* has produced the following lists: names of graduate students in the classics for the decade 1988 to 1997, with date of degree and gender; field of specialty and dissertation title (if determined); and date and institution of first academic appointment. These lists are followed by 11 tables that analyze the data by a number of attributes, such as subject.

As MacGregor admits and warns, the raw data submitted by the universities were inconsistent and incomplete, and hence somewhat unreliable. Statistically speaking, this compilation represents a large sample rather than a census. Another drawback results from the computer's compression of information. Dissertation titles, which often depend on a subtitle for clarification, are reduced to one line that may be meaningless. Thus, one encounters such titles as "Ghost Story" and "Ports and Imperial Image." No doubt such difficulties will not prove much of a hindrance for classicists themselves. MacGregor's book is indeed an "in-group" production, intended primarily for classics students and their professors. For them it will be of interest and value; for others, only marginally.
—**Samuel Rothstein**

892.   Wolf, Kirsten. **An Annotated Bibliography of North American Doctoral Dissertations on Old Norse-Icelandic.** Ithaca, N.Y., Cornell University Press, 1998. 368p. index. (Islandica, v.50). $80.00. ISBN 0-8014-3493-9.

Wolf, a scholar of Icelandic and Scandinavian oral and written traditions, compiled this bibliography to enable doctoral students to look in once place to determine whether or not their work is unique. Students will still need to research sources for more recent work, but the bibliography is a useful resource for large research libraries. The bibliography can also be studied to uncover trends in Old Norse-Icelandic scholarship in North America. Entries are arranged in 2 parts, the 2d of which broadens the scope of the bibliography considerably by incorporating a section titled "Interdisciplinary and Related Studies." Each section is divided into general, historical, and literary subsections. Citations list the author, title, institution, year, number of pages, and adviser. Enhancements include the DA or DAI entry number and the UMI order number (if available) as well as a citation to published versions of the dissertation. The nonevaluative annotations, which vary in length from a quarter page to a full page and often include quotations, presumably from the introductions of the dissertations themselves, include the names of chapters and parts and a list of the works studied. The volume has author, institution, and adviser indexes as well as a subject index that includes titles of works and proper names in addition to topics.—**Susanna Van Sant**

Dictionaries and Encyclopedias

893.   **The Concise Oxford Dictionary of Linguistics.** By P. H. Matthews. New York, Oxford University Press, 1997. 410p. $13.95pa. ISBN 0-19-280008-6.

The purpose of any concise dictionary is to cover the greatest number of topics in the fewest possible words. In a work that deals with words themselves, this can present a large task. However, this publication, with a single author (and perhaps, therefore, a single opinion of what to include) seems a comprehensive and up-to-date approach to the subject. It includes coverage of language and usage and grammar and technical terms, and although the emphasis is on the English language, grammatical categories of other languages are covered.

In our present-day world of immediate communication, where new words are being coined moment by moment and language is being examined for deeper meanings and implications, this is a most useful reference work. The symbols used are standard in all the Oxford dictionaries, and the citations abound with asterisked cross-references. The work has highly technical phrases that may seem esoteric to the casual reader, many growing out of computer language as well as alterations in the field of linguistics itself. Thus, although it may define the Catalan language in three sentences, "NP (Noun Phrase) accessibility hierarchy" requires numerous cross-references and abbreviations, as well as diagrams. This is another work in the fine line of similar Oxford paperback publications, which are inexpensive, well-produced, and clearly printed. This will be an asset to any large general literary collection and a useful resource for anyone with a passion for the study of language.—**Paula Frosch**

894.   Findlay, Michael Shaw. **Language and Communication: A Cross-Cultural Encyclopedia.** Santa Barbara, Calif., ABC-CLIO, 1998. 229p. illus. maps. index. (Encyclopedias of the Human Experience). $55.00. ISBN 0-87436-946-0.

For those who have ever wondered how the human language originated or why there so many different languages, this volume will be of use. It introduces readers to the questions that linguists, anthropologists, and intercultural communication specialists have raised when trying to describe and understand languages and communication from a cross-cultural perspective. The author explores how western and non-western traditions influence one another, and how sociocultural rules govern the use of language. The entries in this volume examine how people from different cultural backgrounds rely on traditional and emerging cultural rules for social interaction. The examinations lead readers to a greater sensitivity to many of the communication barriers that exist in the world today. The maps at the beginning of the volume show approximate locations of the cultures mentioned in the text. Most of the entries in this illustrated A-to-Z volume are complete with cross-references and bibliographic citations. It also contains a bibliography and an index. Findlay, a professor of anthropology and social science at California State University in Chico, has produced a valuable reference and resource tool for any library. The volume is one volume in ABC-CLIO's Encyclopedias of the Human Experience series, which is written and designed for maximum accessibility. [R: SLJ, Nov 98, p. 151; BL, 15 Sept 98, p. 264; LJ, Dec 98, p. 90; Choice, Nov 98, p. 501]—**Vera Gao**

895.   Maggio, Rosalie. **Talking About People: A Guide to Fair and Accurate Language.** Phoenix, Ariz., Oryx Press, 1997. 436p. $27.50. ISBN 1-57356-069-3.

The latest work by the compiler of *The Nonsexist Word Finder: A Dictionary of Gender Free Usage* (see ARBA 88, entry 1078) and *The Dictionary of Bias-Free Usage: A Guide to Non-Discriminatory Language* (see ARBA 92, entry 1030), *Talking About People* covers 8,000 terms and phrases that may be seen as problematic with regard to fairness and accuracy of human portrayal due to various biases, not all solely gender-related. Each entry provides (often at surprising length) sufficient data about the history, origins, and uses of the term to allow readers a range of informed options of meaning, followed by a list of applicable alternatives. Perhaps the most provocative section of this volume is the opening chapter, "The Writer's Guidelines," which sets forth issues surrounding the recent evolution of awareness of bias-based language and its diverse impacts, challenging all uses to raise their consciousness of this dimension of communication. Among the subjects viewed as worthy of attention are inclusive language, sexist terms and quotations, terms viewed as offensive, exclusive language, unconventional spellings, and the question of when and how to use "feminine" word endings or forms. Given the breadth of coverage and its highly accessible style, this reference should be added to all high school, collegiate, and public library collections.—**Robert B. Marks Ridinger**

896.   **Routledge Encyclopedia of Translation Studies.** Mona Baker and Kirsten Malmkjer, eds. New York, Routledge, 1998. 654p. index. $165.00. ISBN 0-415-09380-5.

Although translation has long been a part of all literary heritages, the discipline and training of the professional translator is a relatively new phenomenon. Indeed, between 1960 and 1994, the number of university-level institutions offering degrees in translation increased from 60 to more than 250. It is this increase in practitioners that makes this work such a valuable reference tool. The book consists of 2 major alphabetic sections, one dealing with the concepts, topics, and practices of the field and the other with the historical view of translation in a variety of cultural and linguistic communities. Thus, the first section treats such subjects as gender metaphorics and psycholinguistics, along with publishing strategies and criticism, and the second examines the traditions of Western Europe, Latin America, China, and Russia, among others.

Extensive and varied experiences by the contributors provide scholarly and wide-ranging views of the topics defined and offer a broad spectrum of theories and techniques. The cross-references and index are accurate and to the point. The topical further reading suggestions, along with the extensive bibliography, are a valuable resource. The six years spent in preparation have resulted in a careful, balanced reference tool that should prove useful for the increasing numbers of scholars interested in translation interpretation and literary theory and analysis. [R: LJ, 1 Nov 98, p. 74; Choice, Dec 98, p. 666]—**Paula Frosch**

Directories

897.   Harris, Brian, comp. **Translation and Interpreting Schools.** Glenside, Pa., John Benjamins Publishing, 1997. 235p. (Language International World Directory, v.2). $95.00. ISBN 1-55619-741-1.

Although this publication is priced beyond many library budgets, it is unique and would be useful in large libraries or in those collections supporting translation programs or substantial language curricula. Its intended audience is students, translators, and translation teachers. Comparable titles are more than 10 years out of date and cover only the United States and Canada. International in scope and containing data collected in 1995, this directory is arranged alphabetically by country with alphabetized entries within each country. Although the compiler identified the programs to be included, he was dependent upon them to complete and return his forms. As a result, there is some variation in the level of detail in each entry. Most include the name and mailing address of the program, telephone and fax number, foundation date, director's name, tuition as of the 1996-1997 school year, number of staff and students, types of degrees (or diplomas or certificates) awarded, language combinations, and specializations offered. Fax numbers, e-mail or Website addresses, and names of the program's publications, if any, are included. The volume is not indexed and might have benefited from a language and school name index. A form for revisions and new submissions is included for a proposed 1998-1999 edition.—**Susanna Van Sant**

ENGLISH-LANGUAGE DICTIONARIES

General Usage

898.   **The Basic Newbury House Dictionary of American English.** Philip M. Rideout, ed. Boston, Heinle & Heinle, 1998. 562p. illus. maps. $20.95. ISBN 0-8384-6015-1.

This dictionary is intended to help beginning to intermediate students of English learn basic meanings, pronunciation, spelling, and other information about approximately 15,000 words common to American English. Definitions are concise and limited to comprehensible basic vocabulary of 2,500 frequently used words. Most entries include brief sample sentences to provide a context of actual use. The International Phonetic Alphabet is the system of pronunciation. Common idioms, current slang, business, and technology terms are included. Both synonyms and antonyms accompany many of the entries. Some culture and usage notes are available also to help users from other countries to understand contexts. After the various labeling conventions are described, the front matter of this book includes 12 short lessons intended as teaching activities that ask students to find dictionary words having to do with subjects such as clothing, school, food, work, greetings, sports, and names. Illustrations are fairly numerous, well drawn, and include some color charts in the middle of the book.

It is a distinct challenge to simplify definitions of abstract words, and some of the definitions are consequently problematic. For instance, one of the words chosen as a sample entry, "judge, noun 1. a person in charge of a court of law who decides how guilty people must be punished," defines this word in a most injudicious manner: it does not take the U.S. presumption that a defendant is innocent until proven guilty into account. Some of the slang terms chosen may not be common or prevalent enough to warrant inclusion in a dictionary of 15,000 very basic words; is *fanny pack* so prevalent among beginning users of English as to warrant both an entry and an illustration in a dictionary such as this? However, this dictionary takes considerable care to distinguish between easily confused words and phrases, such as *iron* as a common metal, as distinguished from a "household machine used to smooth wrinkles," which, in turn, is separated from the idioms, "to strike while the iron is hot," and "to iron something out."

This dictionary will be useful as a personal reference tool for people learning English rather than as an addition to a library's reference collection.—**David Isaacson**

899.   **Larousse English Dictionary.** New York, Larousse Kingfisher Chambers, 1997. 1232p. $15.95pa. ISBN 2-03-420290-2.

This dictionary is unique in its attempt to include British, Australian, and U.S. English to be used by businesspeople, world travelers, or immigrants to these English-speaking countries. It would be particularly useful for it brevity and objectivity in defining terms from business, employment advertisements, American literature, and politics. The definitions are brief and sometimes terse, but the inclusion of British and Australian terms, even those that are vulgar (and noted as such), make its brevity an asset rather than a flaw. Because it focuses on more formal speech, the exclusion of some slang phrases is understandable, although maybe a weakness; "Bloomsbury group" is defined, whereas to "blow off" is not. Most remarkable are the sections listing irregular verbs, and the three sections on living in the United States, United Kingdom, and Australia, which cover such topics as schooling, holidays, how one pays for health care, and when banks tend to be open. It would be fascinating and informative for natives as well and would be a fine introduction to the countries for public or even corporate libraries.—**Jennie Ver Steeg**

900.   **Pronouncing Dictionary of Proper Names: Pronunciations for More Than 28,000 Proper Names....** 2d ed. John K. Bollard, Frank R. Abate, Katherine M. Isaacs, and Rima McKinzey, eds. Detroit, Omnigraphics, 1998. 1097p. $88.00. ISBN 0-7808-0098-2.

Five years after the 1st edition of *Prounouncing Dictionary of Proper Names* (ARBA 94, entry 1084) was published, this 2d edition boasts 5,000 more entries than the earlier one, now totaling 28,000. New entries consist mainly of names that have become prominent during the past five years; an example is *Srebrenica*, which this reviewer did not realize he'd heard until he read the dictionary's phonetic pronunciation of it—Sreb-ruh-NEET-suh—a Bosnian city whose name is often heard on news broadcasts. Also added have been place-names with unpredictable pronunciations, like *Mexia* (muh-HAY-uh), a city in Texas whose residents choose to mispronounce its name.

The new edition was compiled using speech synthesis technology—claimed as a first in dictionary publishing—for greater accuracy of pronunciation, which is the purpose of this large reference work designed for use by broadcasters, journalists, public speakers, and others with a need to know how to properly pronounce frequently occurring or hard-to-pronounce names. These could be important people and places currently in the news, celebrities, political and historical figures, company and product names, biblical names, literary references, and other proper names in current events, popular culture, and sports.

The three-column format displays pronunciations both in a simplified respelling and in the phonetic symbols of the International Phonetic Alphabet (IPA), the standard used by linguists worldwide. The scholarly introduction explains both systems and covers much material of linguistic interest, but there are also simplified pronunciation keys at the bottom of every page. Though a useful and interesting book, its size and price may limit acquisitions. [R: RBB, 15 Oct. 97, p. 426]—**Larry Lobel**

Etymology

901.   Crutchfield, Roger S. **English Vocabulary Quick Reference: A Comprehensive Dictionary Arranged by Word Roots.** Leesburg, Va., LexaDyne, 1997. 364p. index. $39.95. ISBN 0-9659138-0-5.

This one-of-a-kind dictionary begins with a primary root index that lists 260 root words. Following this is the dictionary section where each root is followed by a comprehensive list of words that contain that root, along with the etymology, a definition, and pronunciation for each word. Keywords in a definition, considered to be the most important part of the definition, are highlighted in blue and are compiled into another section called the "Vocabulary Quick Reference." A main entry index lists all of the main entries and the page numbers they appear on in the dictionary section for quick access. A secondary root index includes a list of more than 500 additional roots for which no lists were made.

This reference will be useful for students studying for college entrance exams or for people who want to improve their vocabulary. A basic knowledge of root words and their meanings will greatly enable a person to figure out the meaning of unfamiliar words. [R: Choice, Nov 98, p. 489]—**Dana McDougald**

Euphemisms

902.   **NTC's Dictionary of Euphemisms.** By Anne Bertram. Lincolnwood, Ill., National Textbook, 1998. 314p. index. $16.95. ISBN 0-8442-0842-6.

The American Heritage Dictionary (3d ed.; see ARBA 93, entry 1056) defines *euphemism* as "the act or an example of substituting a mild, indirect, or vague term for one considered harsh, blunt, or offensive . . ." (p. 632). Bertram, preferring to call them "verbal avoidances," collects taboo terms, politically correct terminology, and expressions with cultural connotations. But aside from these rather loose categories, she does not distinguish further among them.

Bertram defines each entry in a single word or short description, followed by two sentences illustrating its use. Some words with multicultural overtones may have a brief explanation to that effect; for example, *juice harp* as a replacement for *Jew's harp*, which may be offensive to Jews, and *rancher* for a person who raises cattle, rather than *cowman*, which does not include women. Occasionally Bertram cautions against use of a word; *minority* may be "offensive to people who are not white." Less frequently Bertram hints at the origin of a euphemism, sometimes alluding to terms as "old-fashioned" or "cute," or describing them as formal or slang. A thematic index assigns entries to broad categories, such as body parts, gender, and mock swearing.

With its emphasis on short definitions, this work will be helpful to high school students and to those learning English. Libraries wanting a more detailed work should consult other collections, such as *Kind Words: A Thesaurus of Euphemisms* by Judith S. Neaman and Carole G. Silver (see ARBA 91, entry 1058).—**Bernice Bergup**

Foreign Words and Phrases

903. **The Oxford Dictionary of Foreign Words and Phrases.** Jennifer Speake, ed. New York, Oxford University Press, 1997. 512p. $30.00. ISBN 0-19-863159-6; 0-19-860236-7pa.

From *aa*, a Hawaiian term for "rough, clinkery lava," to *Zwischenzug*, a German chess term for "a move interposed in a sequence of play in such a way as to alter the outcome," the 8,000 foreign words and phrases in this latest member of the Oxford University Press family of respected dictionaries provide users with a culturally eclectic selection of expressions infused into both American and British English. The bias in selection favors words first introduced in the twentieth century, a time when English has been more open to new words worldwide. The dictionary still includes many expressions from earlier centuries, however, particularly from French and Latin, but examples of their use are chosen from the 1990s. Particular words with exclusively scientific senses are excluded, although any scientific meanings are included if the term has been selected for its nonspecialist applications. Expressions introduced as terms of art in particular sports or other fields of activity that have not moved beyond their narrow area—terms for judo throws and the like—are also excluded.

Each entry includes International Phonetic Alphabet pronunciation symbols, part of speech, the original language, the date the expression came into English, the definition, and sometimes a further explanation of its use and application. Select terms also include illustrative quotations from a current publication. A useful appendix lists the words and phrases by century under the original language from which they entered English. This dictionary is highly recommended for all reference collections.—**Blaine H. Hall**

Idioms, Colloquialisms, Special Usage

904. Hendrickson, Robert. **New Yawk Tawk: A Dictionary of New York City Expressions.** New York, Facts on File, 1998. 181p. (Facts on File Dictionary of American Regional Expressions, v.5). $14.95pa. ISBN 0-8160-3869-4.

Providing nuggets of cultural history, the compiler of the 5th volume in the Facts on File's Dictionary of American Regional Expressions series (see ARBA 98, entry 1007; see ARBA 97, entry 835; see ARBA 95, entry 1043; see ARBA 94, entry 1089 for reviews of previous volumes) once again has created a volume containing expressions, phrases, and terms uniquely found in or emanating from a geographic area, this time targeting New York City. Professing to not only be a dictionary but a collection of little-known stories, this volume begins with a lot of information in the 24-page introduction that the casual user in search of a dictionary format may overlook. Historical and political happenings, social customs, and speech patterns are reported in order to provide background for the diversity of the language, greatly increasing the value of the book.

Similar to all dictionaries, the approximately 2,000 expressions are listed in bold typeface in alphabetic order. Unfortunately, the definitions of the expressions vary widely in their coverage. There may or may not be an explanation included on the history of the usage of a term, where and how it originate, where it is commonly used, and even if it is still in use. Hendrickson has drawn heavily from literary sources and popular movies in an attempt to illustrate the connotations of a phrase or term, but not for every entry. It can also be frustrating if the reader is not familiar with the work cited. In addition, one will find that some entries incorporate the pronunciation of the term into the body of the definition using a "like" word, but this has not been included for all. And one may find example sentences that use the word or phrase to demonstrate its full meaning, but again, not everywhere. The ease of use for the volume would have been improved with the addition of an alphabetic subject/keyword index for beginners searching for that elusive word that is part of a phrase.

For an accurate, in-depth etymological treatment of a phrase or term, one would need to consult additional sources that provide a more uniform listing of terms, such as the *Dictionary of American Regional English* (see ARBA 97, entry 833). More useful for browsing than reference, *New Yawk Tawk* will appeal primarily to those who have a personal interest in New York City. It should not be considered for purchase as a library's only American slang reference work. Libraries may want to acquire this volume for circulating collections or acquire all volumes in the series.—**Marianne B. Eimer**

905.   Spears, Richard A. **NTC's Thematic Dictionary of American Idioms.** Lincolnwood, Ill., National Textbook, 1998. 419p. index. $18.95. ISBN 0-8442-0830-2.

The introduction suggests that this dictionary will be useful both to students learning American English and to native speakers seeking alternative expressions for their ideas. The book's topical arrangement (with 900 themes) makes it more convenient for the latter group, but an index of all the idioms included also permits alphabetic searches. Using this index is somewhat awkward, however, because it locates entries by thematic headings rather than by page numbers. Each entry provides a definition and at least two straightforward sentences to illustrate meaning. Entries for some idioms also offer usage labels and brief comments about derivations, but the inclusion of this information is not consistent. For example, "(as) regular as clockwork" bears the informal label, but "(straight) from the horse's mouth" has none. We learn that "blow-by-blow account" derives from boxing, but we get no clue that "draw a bead on someone" derives from aiming a gun. One specific usage hint, "not necessarily literal," is especially puzzling because this quality characterizes all idioms. On occasion, Spears defines an idiom (e.g., "bank on something") by using another one explained elsewhere in his dictionary. Such definitions may reduce the book's accessibility for language learners.

Although Spears includes about 5,500 idioms, native speakers will find his coverage of some categories sparse (e.g., only three idioms dealing with "cleverness," three with "kinship," and two with "dislike"). At the same time, he provides entries for a number of phrases (e.g., "go astray," "form an opinion," "in great demand") whose meanings could probably be understood from literal definitions. This dictionary of essential idioms should be helpful to those learning American English; its value for others is limited.—**Albert Wilhelm**

Juvenile

906.   **The Kingfisher Illustrated Junior Dictionary.** Heather Crossley, ed. New York, Larousse Kingfisher Chambers, 1997. 192p. illus. $18.95. ISBN 0-7534-5096-8.

Designed for children age seven and up, the *Kingfisher Illustrated Junior Dictionary* lives up to its name—illustrated. There are 2-5 colored illustrations per page, with a number of half-page and nearly 20 full-page illustrations in the 192-page dictionary. The illustrations are appealing and useful, although sometimes items are not carefully tied to definitions on that page; for example, a nilgar and an eland are pictured near a definition of antelope with no connection other than proximity.

There is a guide at the beginning of the dictionary that explains three shapes used for homophones, pronunciation and rhyming words, and opposites. It does not seem likely that the average user will remember what the symbols mean, although the context may be clear enough. However, the fact that pronunciation is provided for less than 13 percent of the words, according to the reviewer's sample, indicates that this dictionary will not provide the kind of support needed by children just learning to read and pronounce words.

Some of the appendixes are helpful, especially those about states and countries. The alphabet on the pages could also be useful, but it tends to make the page too busy.

This is a colorful dictionary that may supplement but will not replace the need for more traditional dictionaries for children, such as *The American Heritage Children's Dictionary* (see ARBA 96, entry 1086).
                                                                                  —**Betty Jo Buckingham**

Other English-Speaking Countries

907.   Fee, Margery, and Janice McAlpine. **Guide to Canadian English Usage.** New York, Oxford University Press, 1997. 549p. index. $45.00. ISBN 0-19-540841-1.

Joining the distinguished series of Oxford University Press guides, this volume will be an essential reference for Canadian English-language usage. Written from the Canadian perspective, usage is defined as all the ways in which English is used in Canada—sometimes much like American or British usage but sometimes not. The strong influence of both cultures is evident in Canada, making the retention of dual spelling, punctuation, and diction problematic for even the language experts. A further complication to the dichotomy is the very real difficulty of determining what writing is Canadian: that published in Canada by Canadians certainly, but what of the influence that education, regionalism, or even editorship may have? It is just these types of vagaries that instigated the project, substantially funded by the Strathy Language Unit.

With the compilation of a database of published writing, the Strathy Corpus of Canadian English (containing 12 million words of complete texts as of publication) supplemented by CD-ROMs of Canadian newspaper and magazine texts, the authors analyzed usage distinctions and derived a comprehensive list of 1,750 entries that comprise this guide. Each entry defines the problem, provides the range of usage alternatives, and, most importantly, illustrates with quotations from the database. Arranged alphabetically with extensive cross-referencing, the guide includes an index of items that do not appear in the text, two short appendixes, and a glossary of specialized terms used in the entries. For those engaged in writing in Canada, this reference will be most welcome.

—**Virginia S. Fischer**

908.   **NTC's Dictionary of British Slang and Colloquial Expressions.** By Ewart James. Lincolnwood, Ill., National Textbook, 1998. 573p. index. $14.95pa. ISBN 0-8442-0839-6.

This dictionary is addressed to people in Britain; many of the expressions here are uniquely British, unfamiliar even to other Commonwealth nationals. Although one may recognize hundreds of expressions imported from the United States, it is noted how few of the British expressions are known here. The dictionary offers striking evidence of the dominance achieved by American English and attests to the increasing marginalization of Britain within the English-speaking world. Many of the terms are as foreign to us as French argot. For example, how many know what a *bluefoot*, a *lag*, or a *hock* is?

Although it is certainly useful, this is not a thoroughly scholarly work. It is essentially the work, but not the lifework, of one man. It is by no means exhaustive, nor does it attempt to ascertain the date of the first usage or area of origin. (Entries seem to be weighted toward the Northeast Midlands and Cockney usage.) Etymologies are not consistently indicated; we are told that *shicer* comes from the German word *Scheisser* but are not told that *in drag* comes from the German phrase *in Tracht*. The book is a labor of love for its author and can be read with the same zest that one sees in his preface. It is scholarly enough to pass muster.—**John B. Beston**

Sign Language

909.   **Random House Webster's American Sign Language Dictionary.** rev. ed. By Elaine Costello. New York, Random House, 1998. 539p. illus. $20.00pa. ISBN 0-679-78011-4.

This is a revised and updated edition of the *Random House American Sign Language Dictionary* and makes claims to be the "only complete signing dictionary with full definitions and different signs for different meanings of the same word." There are more than 4,500 illustrated entries provided in this source, whose author is a founder of the Gallaudet University Press. The dictionary is intended for both the novice and the experienced user of American Sign Language (ASL). At the beginning there are sections that address the deaf community, and the history, nature, and structure of ASL. Information on how signs are put together grammatically and used as parts of speech is discussed. The nine basic hand shapes that are used in ASL are provided. Individual words and phrases are alphabetically arranged in the dictionary. The entries include the definition, an illustration of the sign, a written description of how to make the sign, and *see also* references. Cross-references are provided to related terms or signs. There are several sections at the end of the book on the most common types of signs: the manual alphabet and fingerspelling, numbers (cardinal and ordinal), days of the week, colors, pronouns, and geographic references. This is an improvement from the previous edition, which included some of this information on the inside front and back covers. This is a useful dictionary for any library that serves a population interested in American Sign Language.—**Jan S. Squire**

910.   Sternberg, Martin L. A. **American Sign Language.** unabridged ed. New York, HarperCollins, 1998. 983p. illus. $22.00. ISBN 0-06-271608-5.

This standard dictionary of American Sign Language (ASL) is a valuable resource for anyone using ASL, and used in conjunction with its electronic version it is a practical learning tool for beginners. The strengths of this work lie not only in its breadth of coverage—it contains more than 7,000 signs and 12,000 illustrations—but also in the "sign rationale" and "verbal description" given for each term. These explanations help the reader remember the sign and its meaning. With the word *dear*, for example, the explanation of the meaning behind the sign reads "Stroking a person or the head of a pet," which helps to emphasize the physical sign for the term is petting. For those who learn via visuals rather than text, the illustrations provided are simple outlines of the hand gestures and help with the physical execution of each sign. Another useful feature for the novice are the synonyms given after each word indicating that the sign has multiple meanings.

The dictionary would be a more helpful tool if it had included a section on the history of the ASL, such as that in the *Random House Webster's American Sign Language Dictionary* (see entry 909). For novices, such information as the importance of space while signing and the relationship between the hands and body is important. Another critical omission is common slang and new words, such as *software* and *glasnost*.

Using the print and the CD-ROM version of this dictionary in combination would greatly facilitate the acquisition of American Sign Language. On its own, this print dictionary will be useful for all libraries.

—**Elizabeth A. Ginno**

Slang

911.   Spears, Richard A. **NTC's Thematic Dictionary of American Slang.** Lincolnwood, Ill., National Textbook, 1997. 541p. index. $18.95. ISBN 0-8442-0832-9.

In *NTC's Thematic Dictionary of American Slang* the editors have produced a subject (thematic) index to their *Dictionary of American Slang* (2d ed.; National Textbook, 1995). Why should a library be asked to buy two volumes when one, including the alphabetic listing and the thematic index, would have worked more efficiently? The earlier volume includes a helpful introduction titled "About the Dictionary" and pronunciation guidance, whereas the thematic volume lacks both features. Unfortunately, the user of this dictionary is given little in return for the purchase price. Definitions are elementary in the extreme. We learn, for example, that a *scorcher* is "a very hot day," and that *falling-down drunk* means "a drunk who falls down." Illustrations of usage are just as banal, as in "wow, what a scorcher," and "Jed is turning into a falling-down drunk." Historical information, cross-referencing, and other useful dictionary elements are omitted. Although the other works of this kind are somewhat older, *Dictionary of American Slang* (see ARBA 76, entry 1129), *New Dictionary of American Slang* (see ARBA 88, entry 1076), and the in-progress *Random House Historical Dictionary of American Slang* (see ARBA 98, entry 1015) are more authoritative and better buys. Finally, the binding and paper used in *NTC's Thematic Dictionary of American Slang* do not appear to be of lasting quality.—**Donald C. Dickinson**

Spelling

912.   **The Scholastic Dictionary of Spelling.** By Marvin Terban. New York, Scholastic, 1998. 223p. illus. $15.95. ISBN 0-590-30697-9.

This very simplistic approach to spelling offers the beginner many ways to search the spelling of words, and also different tricks to help the reader memorize these spellings. In the section entitled "How to Look Up a Word," some useful tricks of the spelling trade are offered, such as guide words, syllables, words that have confusing sounds, blends, silent letters, and compounds. Follow this with the section titled, "A Dozen and One Spelling Rules," and the reader will have all the information needed to begin using the remainder of the book, which is packed with more than 600,000 commonly used words in the English language. "The Dictionary of Spelling" section is set up in alphabetic order, and parts of the word that help the search by means offered in the earlier sections are set in bold typeface. The words are broken up into syllables, and many also have "sounds like" hints to assist the reader in finding the right word.

The back of the book offers a few hundred common misspellings for words, such as those which begin with "ph" in place of an "f," or use the letter "g" instead of "j." This section may help to ease the frustration that can occur when one is searching for words simply by sounding them out. In all, this reviewer found this guide to be a complete introductory tool for children learning to spell and a worthwhile addition to school libraries. [R: BR, Sept/Oct 98, p. 72]—**Michael Florman**

Terms and Phrases

913.   Benson, Morton, Evelyn Benson, and Robert Ilson. **The BBI Dictionary of English Word Combinations.** rev. ed. Glenside, Pa., John Benjamins Publishing, 1997. 386p. $38.00; $19.95pa. ISBN 1-55619-520-6; 1-55619-521-4pa.

Mastering words is fundamental to learning the English language. Moreover, using combinations of words correctly is the key for the learners to express themselves fluently and accurately. It is not easy for learners of English to remember the various combinations for different usage. Therefore, a ready-reference tool becomes important for them.

The BBI Dictionary of English Word Combinations is a useful reference book for assisting learners in coping with combining words into phrases, sentences, and texts. This newly revised edition includes 18,000 entries and 90,000 collections. Not only does it include items that were missed in the 1st edition, but a special effort has also been made to identify and incorporate expressions that have entered into the English language in recent years, such as "to browse the web," "to create a home page," "to go online," "to send e-mail," and the like. Each entry provides a definition, examples, and sometimes a usage note. Attention is consistently paid to the difference between American English and British English. A detailed introduction, 26 pages in length, is placed in front of the entries. It discusses the two major groups of word combinations, grammatical collections and lexical collections.

This dictionary is a must-have for learners of English as a foreign language. It also will be a plus for the library reference collection in order to serve a diversified user group. The authors have been working together for many years and have published English dictionaries of many kinds.—**Xiao (Shelley) Yan Zhang**

914.   Bertram, Anne. **Life Is Just a Bowl of Cherries and Other Delicious Sayings.** Lincolnwood, Ill., National Textbook, 1997. 321p. index. $12.95pa. ISBN 0-8442-0900-7.

The title of this book is somewhat misleading. Rather than being a quotation dictionary about food with "delicious" sayings, such as *Never Eat More Than You Can Lift* (see ARBA 98, entry 1429), this is a dictionary of proverbial and clichéd sayings. *Life Is Just a Bowl of Cherries* also differs from a traditional quotation book because of its subject matter, covering sayings that have become a part of the language rather than the famous quotations of individuals. The nearly 1,000 expressions provide a definition, which often is much different and deeper than the saying may indicate; literary sources are provided if available; and sample sentences or brief dialogues exemplify the meaning. The inclusion of literary sources is rare, and most often the source is biblical. The alphabetic entries appear in bold typeface, the definitions are in roman typeface, clichés growing out of the proverb and alternate meanings are in parentheses, and sample sentences are in italics and are separated by boxes.

The arrangement by expression rather than by the person expressing marks this dictionary's distinction from other quotation books but also causes a slight problem. Expressions beginning with the word "A," such as "A fine kettle of fish," are alphabetized under the letter "A." "The" accounts for many entries as well. Quite a few proverbs are alphabetized under "As" in parentheses: "(As) stiff as a poker" and "(As) strong as a horse," for example. However, cross-references and the index guarantee that users will be able to find the sayings for which they are looking. The 80-page phrase-finder index at the end of the volume provides access to the work at large. The index supplies keywords, both nouns and verbs, with a list of expressions containing the word following, so that users can look up the proverb under the correct form in the main dictionary. This dictionary is interesting and certainly reasonably priced, but libraries may want to weigh the need for it before purchasing.

—**Melissa Rae Root**

915.   **NTC's Dictionary of Commonplace Words in Real-Life Contexts.** By Anne Bertram. Lincolnwood, Ill., National Textbook, 1998. 383p. index. $14.95pa. ISBN 0-8442-0846-9.

Bertram, compiler for other specialized NTC dictionaries, offers a collection of 2,800 entries, with 300 illustrations, for objects and products that constitute the quotidian materiality of home, office, work, transportation, personal care, appearance, sports, and many others. A few adjectives and verbs are given, but "real-life" in this dictionary focuses on nouns, which a topical index groups by almost 50 sites, activities, or aspects of life with which they are associated. The intended audience are those new to the English language or those who are "new to domestic matters or . . . home maintenance." Most people in both groups, however, probably already have an inexpensive desk dictionary that does the work of this dictionary. Nonnative speakers, if children, absorb this stuff with the air they breathe, whereas adults, who do not learn a new language as easily or may want the privacy of a book, will learn the vocabulary more conveniently from a much less expensive ESL series such as the Oxford Picture Dictionary's Bilingual Series. Too many definitions repeat the word in order to define it or leave enough unsaid as not really to clarify matters; for example, failing to mention the short sleeves of a polo shirt or defining a sweater as a "thick knitted shirt," an afghan as "a crocheted or knitted blanket," or grits as "coarsely ground corn." No pronunciation guidance is offered, and such eponyms as *Xerox* and *Kleenex* are treated only as proper nouns. This is a slight work that will enhance neither library nor home collections.—**Robert H. Kieft**

Thesauri

916.   McCutcheon, Mark. **Roget's Superthesaurus.** 2d ed. Cincinnati, Ohio, Writer's Digest Books/F & W Publications, 1998. 663p. $19.99pa. ISBN 0-89879-775-6.

This excellent thesaurus contains in one volume a host of reference tools, including a reverse dictionary, built-in vocabulary builders with sample sentences, notable quotations, and more than 400,000 synonyms and antonyms. More than 2,000 new and expanded entries have been added to this updated edition. The alphabetic dictionary-style entries allow ease of use in going directly to the word needed. Informal synonyms or slang are highlighted by an asterisk.

This impressive volume deserves the title of *Superthesaurus* because it offers all the timesaving tools of the trade in a single, comprehensive resource. There is no index to waste time in finding a word; the writer just consults the alphabetic listing. Because many minor words are included as entries, only one reference stop is needed in many cases.

The major features of this volume that make it a one-of-a-kind volume are (1) an array of synonyms to improve word accuracy and avoid repetitiveness; (2) a reverse dictionary or word finder that allows exact descriptive words to be found for a known term; (3) a build-in vocabulary feature that capitalizes vocabulary words, pronounces them, and provides a sample sentence using the word; (4) quotations that double as synonyms and are provided immediately following the normal list of synonyms; (5) antonyms provided at the end of an entry for those words opposite to a synonym; and (6) the use of minor words as head entries, thus avoiding cross-referencing.

The *Superthesaurus* is a must for the student who wants to sharpen writing skills, increase vocabulary, locate a quotation, or to find that specific word for a crossword puzzle. The seasoned writer will find this volume to be a timesaving and convenient tool to use.—**Betty J. Morris**

917.   **Random House Webster's Concise Thesaurus.** New York, Random House, 1998. 687p. $11.95. ISBN 0-375-40197-0.

Based on *Random House Webster's School & Office Thesaurus* (Random House, 1998), the present title is intended for quick reference by students and businesspeople. Approximately 11,000 entries comprise more than 200,000 synonyms and antonyms, and function as a three-in-one reference: a thesaurus combined with a dictionary and usage guide in an alphabetic arrangement. Other features are a brief section on new words and a short essay on avoiding insensitive and offensive language.

Entries list synonyms by part of speech such as noun, verb, and adjective, and by their multiple meanings. Although there are no definitions, synonyms may be categorized as informal, slang, archaic, or regional. Shades of meaning are differentiated through cross-references to some 400 special entries called synonym studies. Here, examples of sentence usage illustrate the particular meanings and connotations.

Individuals needing a quick reference with little detail will appreciate this compact edition. Its binding, however, will not stand up to heavy usage in a reference collection.—**Bernice Bergup**

918.   **Random House Webster's Large Print Thesaurus.** New York, Random House, 1998. 672p. $40.00; $26.00pa. ISBN 0-375-40220-9; 0-375-70211-3pa.

This work is a simple, unadorned book that provides easy access to a basic dictionary of words, their synonyms, and where applicable their antonyms. It differs from the standard thesauri in that it is based purely on a dictionary format rather than the usual conceptual procedure, which often requires extensive use of an index. When there are words with a wide range of synonyms, a short study paragraph follows that explicates the distinctions between closely related but not interchangeable words. There is a section on "New Words," with examples of the analysis of a short list of words, including *bodice ripper* and *finger-pointing*, showing where they belong in the main section, and the guidelines for their use. The needs of the large-print typeface clearly make it necessary to omit many longer lists and indeed many words themselves. The Roget treatment of *redundance* includes verbs, adjectives, and adverbs totaling more than 80 listings. The book lists only *redundant* and then refers the reader to *wordy*, which is only one aspect of the term. This does not mean that the work is not useful. It should be quite handy for students beginning to write creatively, for quick and easy reference in everyday correspondence, and for simple definitions and uses.—**Paula Frosch**

Visual

919.   **Ultimate Visual Dictionary.** Luisa Caruso, Peter Jones, Jane Mason, and Geoffrey Stalker, eds. New York, DK Publishing, 1998. 640p. illus. index. $14.95pa. ISBN 0-7894-2874-1.

Readers familiar with other DK books already know a great deal about the one under review. Like others published by this company, the *Ultimate Visual Dictionary* features brightly colored, detailed illustrations. Because the intent of a pictorial dictionary is to show an object or concept visually rather than to describe it at length, the volume is both informative and beautiful. Several pictures fill each page, many examining the physical structure of plants, animals, and objects. The dictionary is divided into 14 broad subject chapters, half exploring scientific topics. The rest cover transportation; the arts; music; sports; and "everyday things," such as shoes, toasters, and books. Every chapter begins with its own table of contents, followed by 20 to 30 entries. A paragraph introduces each topic before giving way to the illustrations and short annotations. Because each entry takes up only two pages, the reader sees something new with each turn of the page. There is a detailed index and a two-page appendix of "useful data"—units of measurement, scientific and mathematical symbols—that is too short and selective to be very useful.

This is a browsing book, ideal for car trips or doctor's offices. The amount of information, compact size, and attractive price make it ideal for personal collections. Librarians should be aware that most of the pictures are too small to photocopy, and the binding will not stand up to heavy use. Fortunately, the much larger hardback edition, which was published in 1994, is still in print for $39.95. This dictionary belongs in public, academic, and school libraries from middle school on up.—**Hope Yelich**

NON-ENGLISH-LANGUAGE DICTIONARIES

General Works

920.   Sansfaçon, Roland. **Chinese-English-French Kuaisu Dictionary.** Les Presses de l'Université Laval, Sante-Foy; distr., Vancouver, B.C., University of British Columbia Press, 1997. 905p. $49.00pa. ISBN 2-7937-7396-6.

This Chinese dictionary with English and French definitions presents a new approach to arranging and finding Chinese characters. The main body of the dictionary consists of 11,311 characters, both classical and simplified; 8,278 of the most common compound characters; 2,574 etymological components (radicals and phonetic parts of characters); and 772 graphic elements. The author's new approach is based on graphic elements in the writing of Chinese characters. The author developed a classification system by which all Chinese characters can be grouped into 1 of the 11 classes whose variants yield 43 subclasses and 118 series. The author claims that his system offers a quick (kuaisu) way to find Chinese characters. Mastering this system requires one to become familiar with the 11 graphic elements and their subclasses—a more difficult task than the author claims. Perhaps for this reason, the author also provides a number of indexes using traditional methods, such as the Kangxi dictionary radical index, the stroke count radical table, and the Hanzi Pinyin index, among others. Once a character is found, the information given for each entry is concise, yet rich and useful. The dictionary is a useful addition to existing dictionaries in the Chinese language. It presents an alternative approach for the classification and finding of Chinese characters.—**Hwa-Wei Lee**

Albanian

921.   Orel, Vladimir. **Albanian Etymological Dictionary.** Boston, Brill Academic, 1998. 670p. index. $186.50. ISBN 90-04-11024-0.

The present etymological dictionary proposed by Vladimir Orel, professor of historical linguistics at Bar-Ilan University in Israel, is based on several previous works as well as substantial experience as an author and frequent contributor of a series of articles on Balkan etymologies. This dictionary deals with three main stages in the development of the Albanian lexicon: Indo-European, Proto-Albanian, and Albanian (contemporary). The book also includes a short sketch of Albanian historical phonetics and a comprehensive bibliography. Well documented, Orel's work should be on shelves of all major university libraries.—**Bohdan S. Wynar**

Andalusi Arabic

922.   Corriente, F. **A Dictionary of Andalusi Arabic.** Boston, Brill Academic, 1998. 623p. index. (Handbook of Oriental Studies, no.29). $227.50. ISBN 90-04-09846-1. ISSN 0169-9423.

Given the duration of Arab rule over Andalusia (in the historically broader understanding of the term) and the cultural flourishing of the area under that rule, it is no wonder that the relevant archives contain quite a number of texts of varying character, written not only in the classical Arabic idiom but also in the vernacular, local variety of the language. However, Arabic scholarship has devoted most of its efforts to the study of the classical idiom, and in the Arab states, the methods of applied linguistics are largely directed toward the task of preserving the acrolect of the usual diglossia (that is, the classical idiom) through use in the schools and as a unifying common denominator among all the Arab states. Western scholarship, however, has been mostly involved in the study of Arabic influences on the Romance languages in general, and on Hispanic Romance in particular. These circumstances explain why the Andalusi Arabic material had to await the fruitful research of Corriente to be studied on its own merit to a larger extent and to be published for further study.

The present dictionary is a rich collection of the Andalusi Arabic lexical material. It is presented entirely in Roman script, which made the printing easier and the book better accessible to more linguists in the Romance field. However, the entries are constructed on the principle of the (usually triliteral) roots as headwords. The entries themselves contain the lexical material, both as isolated words and within well-selected contexts. The derivation of each lexical item is indicated, and a translation of each context is provided. The entries are not divided into tiers in terms of polysemy of the entryword, but in the majority of cases this is not really necessary. An interesting and important feature of the dictionary is that the source of a word borrowed into Andalusi Arabic is indicated. Accordingly, there is an index listing words quoted within the entries, and the words in this index are classified separately by their origins in Berber, Greek, Latin, and so forth.

Naturally, this is a dictionary not for practical but for scholarly purposes, particularly for Arabic and Romance studies. It was published as a volume in the distinguished series Handbook of Oriental Studies and measures up to the caliber expected of that fine series.—**L. Zgusta**

Dutch

923.   **Hippocrene Standard Dictionary. Dutch-English, English-Dutch.** By Arseen Rijckaert. New York, Hippocrene Books, 1997. 578p. $16.95pa. ISBN 0-7818-0541-4.

This dictionary is a publication and translation of a generic bilingual dictionary of English and Dutch that was originally issued in 1979 from a Belgian publisher, with coverage of more than 35,000 selected words. Features include a table of pronunciation for the Dutch language, a list of abbreviations used in the Netherlands, and a listing of English irregular verbs and their equivalents in Dutch. No indication is given of the criteria by which words were chosen for inclusion or the relationship of this work to other existing dictionaries. The typeface is hard on the eyes, and no data are provided to indicate whether this work is an American issue of the 1993 update. The absence of this type of data will make it difficult for reference librarians who do not possess either of the other editions to evaluate the work. This is a marginal purchase for academic and public libraries.—**Robert B. Marks Ridinger**

French

924.   Burke, David. **Street French Slang Dictionary & Thesaurus.** New York, John Wiley, 1997. 323p. $16.95pa. ISBN 0-471-16806-8.

This is a well conceived and well organized dictionary, which is lively as well as informative. The author's own enjoyment of his work is infectious; his open, unconstrained attitude toward the material is sensible and engaging. When he uses labels, he rejects judgmental terms like "vulgar" or "obscene" in favor of objective assessments like "popular."*Burnes* and *roustons* for the term *testicles*, for instance, are listed as "extremely popular," more commonly used than *couilles*, which is merely "very popular."

The dictionary is more balanced and more useful by not being confined to an alphabetic list of entries (though these do take up the bulk of the book): It also has two street slang thesauruses (arranged by subject)—a longish one of general slang terms, sexual slang and offensive language, and a shorter one, prefaced and highlighted by a "danger" symbol, of slang terms that would give offense in a polite milieu. The author's frequent indications of how a phrase is spoken (rather than written) provide helpful instruction in the slurring patterns of French speech: *j'suis* and *j'crois*, for instance, *y* for *il* and *è* for *elle*, *c't'une* for *c'est une*, and so on.

For those concerned with experiencing French life beyond formal situations—or even with understanding French slang in movies—the dictionary is essential. To familiarize oneself with the slang in this book is not a scholarly chore; it is an enjoyable undertaking.—**John B. Beston**

925.   **The Cambridge French-English Thesaurus.** By Marie-Nöelle Lamy. New York, Cambridge University Press, 1998. 326p. index. $69.95. ISBN 0-521-56348-8.

This reviewer finds it impossible to improve on the language of the excellent preface in describing the purpose of this book: "Many learners of French understand more vocabulary and phrases than they are able to summon when called upon to speak or write in French. Words may be on the tips of their tongues (*ils ont les mots sur le bout de la langue*) or their pens but may not materialize when needed. The aim of [this work] is to fill this need by providing those who wish to add variety and authenticity to their spoken or written French with a reference tool for quick and easy consultation." Somebody should have thought of this before—a bilingual thesaurus, allowing the user who is getting pretty good at French to convey thoughts and ideas with just the right intensity in just the right circumstances.

If the users are speaking to *francophones* (native speakers of French) in their language and want to convey just how incredibly, totally *bored* they were at a movie last night, it would be useful to have a choice of ways to express the boredom, fatigue, and *ennui* felt. It is now possible because this book, the first bilingual thesaurus of its kind, groups numerous different ways to convey emotions, all conveniently found together in category 10.2. Additionally, unlike a standard thesaurus, this book offers a translation for every word, dual French and English dictionary sections, and plenty of current examples.

The Cambridge people, as one might expect, take a veddy British view of the English language, and U.S. users occasionally may need to interpolate more familiar expressions for the ones provided. Also, this is not an introductory text and therefore not recommended for those who have not studied the language before—the user will need prior familiarity with the cantankerous ways of French pronunciation. With those minor caveats, this exciting new work is strongly recommended for all reference collections. It is not just a list of words but a rich network of interconnected ideas in both languages. [R: BL, 1 Oct 98, pp. 354-356]—**Bruce A. Shuman**

926.   **Larousse Concise French/English, English/French Dictionary.** rev. ed. New York, Larousse Kingfisher Chambers, 1997. 629p. $18.95; $10.95pa. ISBN 2-03401644-0; 2003-420501-4pa.

Modestly, this dictionary defines itself as directed beyond beginners but not to those intending to pursue French at an academic level. In reality, it is suitable at quite advanced levels.

In this golden age of foreign language dictionaries, French dictionaries have attained a special eminence. Best among the portable French dictionaries are the *Compact Oxford Hachette French Dictionary* (Oxford University Press, 1995) and this *Larousse Concise French/English, English/French Dictionary*. Each has its special areas of excellence, areas that do not overlap. The *Larousse* is the more assured work. It faces problems of contemporary colloquialisms, technological innovations, and the flood of neologisms with confidence, rendering well words like *wimp*, *hype*, *gross*, *sleazy*, *laptop*, and *VCR* and expressions like "to make a pass at" and "to pick up."

The *Larousse* renderings for the difficult English modal auxiliaries and two- or three-part verbs are intelligent and well selected. It also has useful short explanatory entries for terms familiar only to native speakers, such as *Matignon* and *Marianne* in French, *PC* (politically correct) and *Poppy Day* in English. This is one of the essential French dictionaries and is a good choice for a reference collection.—**John B. Beston**

927.   Ritchie, Adrian C. **Media French: A Guide to Contemporary French Idiom, with English Translations.** Concord, Mass., Paul & Company Publishers, 1997. 268p. $39.95. ISBN 0-7083-1399-X.

Based on the author's earlier *Newspaper French* (University of Wales Press, 1990), *Media French* is billed as including "the most useful terms and some of the more common idioms which the reader of contemporary French will regularly encounter" in the fields of administration, economics, politics, and social affairs. However, these claims require some interpretation because entries often overstate the obvious; *pétition* is defined as "petition," a fairly recognizable cognate; the English equivalents of *lock-out* and *drainage* are, not unsurprisingly, identical to the French. The dictionary includes words like *actuel*, the sole meaning of which will be defined as such in any standard bilingual dictionary. Furthermore, the dictionary must be used to supplement or complement other general bilingual sources otherwise the user would assume the exclusivity of the three meanings of *pierre* as used here (cornerstone, obstacle, and building grant) and miss the most well-known meaning of all, *rock*. Vocabulary is chosen selectively and inconsistently, avoiding words with additional meanings in nonmedia contexts. For example, the various applications of the word *gestion* in computer science are a case in point.

The words are presented with illustrations in British context, apparently fabricated expressly for this publication. Because the author patently assumes that users are reading French texts when they need to consult this lexicon, the illustrative examples are redundant because users will have already established the appropriate frame of reference from the readings. This same assumption of purpose also explains the unilateral French-to-English translations; the failure to provide English-to-French equivalents, either in the dictionary itself or in the index, reduces the book's usage to a rather limited audience. [R: Choice, Feb 98, p. 969]—**Lawrence Olszewski**

German

928.   **Collins German-English, English-German Dictionary.** unabridged ed. By Peter Terrell and Veronika Schnorr. Wendy V. A. Morris and Roland Breitsprecher, eds. New York, HarperCollins, 1997. 1769p. $55.00. ISBN 0-06-270199-1.

This is a new edition of the unabridged *HarperCollins German Dictionary*, which includes 280,000 entries with 460,000 translations. As the editors say, a dictionary is like a map, and this HarperCollins dictionary is a map of the German and English languages, including the language of everyday communication (e.g., newspapers, radio, television), of business, politics, science, technology, literature, and the arts. The previous edition of this dictionary (1990) was published before the demise of the Deutsche Demokratische Republik and the unification of Germany in 1990. However, vocabulary specific to the former East Germany, words like Stasi (Staatssicherheitsdienst), for example, are marked with DDR to indicate their former significance. Moreover, words whose orthography has changed due to the German Spelling Reform of 1996 are clearly noted with a special symbol. The new spelling forms are listed in a supplement that also gives the old spelling as well as a detailed explanation of the grammatical and linguistic rationale behind the reform.

As for the entries themselves, the dictionary is consistently careful to provide straightforward, concise definitions, including idioms and commonly used expressions, along with illustrative phrases showing standard usage of given words. Explicit distinctions to be drawn between different meanings of the same word are clearly indicated, as are informal usages. Special labels indicate whether a word is formal, informal, literary, vulgar, dated, or euphemistic. As for grammatical information, phrasal verbs are clearly identified and genders of German words are clearly shown, as are all relevant grammatical labels. There is even a "Language in Use" section intended to aid users in their own writing of either English or German. Models given include different ways of expressing comparisons, opinions, preferences, and apologies. Examples of job applications, commercial correspondence, and general correspondence; ways to express best wishes, issue invitations or announcements, or construct a Lebenslauf or Curriculum Vitae; and even suggestions for basic phrases to use on the telephone are all provided.

If there is any shortcoming in this dictionary, it is the lack of any indication of how to break words into their correct syllables, a feature that would be of considerable use to editors and anyone writing in English and German and having to know how to break a word at the end of a line when necessary. Apart from this one exception, the *HarperCollins German Dictionary* will offer users a complete guide to both languages, and should be a basic reference work in any school or public library.—**Joseph W. Dauben**

929.   **Klett's Modern German and English Dictionary.** 3d ed. Erich Weis, ed. Lincolnwood, Ill., National Textbook, 1998. 648p. $29.95. ISBN 0-8442-2870-2.

As two-way German-English, English-German desk dictionaries go, the one under review is a short one, but it contains all the elements that one expects of a dictionary. In addition to picking up the latest developments in the two languages, the volume contains numerous aids for orienting the reader. There are a summary of rules of German grammar; a list of the most important irregular verbs; an explanation of the old and new German spelling rules; a key to pronunciation; and lists of abbreviations, of weights and measures, and of numerals. The international system of phonetic signs is used to orient the user into the mystery of pronunciation. Although this system may not be an impediment to linguists and Europeans, U.S. users, because of unfamiliarity with the phonetic signs in that country, may be resistant to it. The dictionary may be best suited for the occasional user. Although it is too hefty for the traveler, it may be too slight for the student and the professional as a main desktop reference.

—**Andrew Ezergailis**

930.   **The Pocket Oxford-Duden German Dictionary.** rev. ed. Dudenredaktion and the German Section of the Oxford University Press Dictionary Department, eds. New York, Oxford University Press, 1997. 856p. $11.95pa. ISBN 0-19-860131-X.

Except for changes on the title page and in the front matter, this book is a paperback reprinting of *The Oxford-Duden German Desk Dictionary* (see ARBA 98, entry 1030), and retains that work's strengths. These include a 56-page glossary of words affected by the new German spelling regulations, unavailable in other bilingual dictionaries of comparable size and price. The text of *Webster's New World German Dictionary* (Macmillan, 1992), for example, precedes the reforms, and the *Random House German-English, English-German Dictionary* (see entry 931) limits discussion to one page.

The market for this book is unclear. For a few dollars more, libraries and readers can have the same text in hardcover. The word "pocket" in the title suggests "students [and] tourists" as an audience, but this volume needs a generous pocket—at 20 centimeters, it hefts like the desk edition. If size is crucial, travelers might prefer the *Collins Gem German Dictionary* (HarperCollins, 1997) or the *Langenscheidt Universal German Dictionary* (Langenscheidt, 1993); either is better suited to slip into a jacket or backpack. Students balancing scope, price, and date of publication can consider mid-size paperbacks like the *Langenscheidt Pocket German Dictionary* (Langenscheidt, 1993), which boasts a flexible plastic cover tough enough to survive school or travel. *The Pocket Oxford-Duden German Dictionary* offers solid content at a fair price, but buyers have alternatives.

—**Steven W. Sowards**

931.   **Random House German-English, English-German Dictionary.** Anne Dahl, ed. New York, Random House, 1997. 546p. $20.00; $12.95pa. ISBN 0-679-44808-X.

This dictionary is a compact reference work designed with the needs of students, business professionals, translators, and even tourists in mind. With more than 60,000 entries, it follows American English spelling. Although it claims to have incorporated "the latest spelling regulations in German issued by the cultural ministers of the German Länder," it does not incorporate changes brought about by the German Spelling Reform of 1996; words still listed in the Random House edition like *Abfluß, Alptraum, dabeisein, Greuel, numerieren, plazieren, rauh, Schlegel,* and *überschwenglich,* for example, should have been given in their new forms, or at least the new forms should have been indicated (e.g., *Abfluss, Albtraum, dabei sein, Gräuel, nummerieren, platzieren, rau, Schlägel,* and *überschwänglich*). It would also have been helpful, especially for students, translators, and editors, had word divisions been indicated so that it would be clear where to divide a word when necessary at the end of a line.

Apart from these shortcomings, the dictionary does provide notes on pronunciation and lists of irregular verbs, geographical names, and common abbreviations in both languages. Recent additions to both English and German due to political, social, and scientific changes of the past few decades are included—words such as *Byte, CD-player/CD-Spieler, Europaparlament, Informatik,* and the like. It would also have been useful to indicate words that were current in the days of the former Deutsche Demokratische Republik (DDR), which are still part of everyday German vocabulary; words like *Stasi* (*Staatssicherheitsdienst*), for example, which refers to the secret police of the DDR (an abbreviation that is also missing from the section of abbreviations, although BRD, Bundesrepublik Deutschland, is included).

The dictionary also provides separate sections devoted to useful words and phrases, basic food terms, days of the week, months of the year, and commonly displayed signs (e.g., *Caution, Road Closed, No Smoking*). The definitions given in this dictionary are succinct; usually only one, sometimes two synonyms for a given word are to be found, with no attempt to indicate subtleties or actual usages of the words defined. Although its conciseness may be a virtue for travelers who do not want a heavy reference work to carry with them, students, translators and libraries will be much better served by the unabridged *HarperCollins German Dictionary* (HarperCollins, 1998).

—**Joseph W. Dauben**

Igbo

932.   Echeruo, Michael J. C. **Igbo-English Dictionary: A Comprehensive Dictionary of the Igbo Language, with an English-Igbo Index.** New Haven, Conn., Yale University Press, 1998. 283p. index. (Yale Language Series). $40.00. ISBN 0-300-07307-0.

This is a unique reference work covering the only one of the three national languages of Nigeria for which no major dictionary exists. The history of lexicography and grammatical compilations produced for Igbo since 1852 is reviewed at length in the introduction, providing a valuable critical context for collection evaluation in this area. Echeruo's work originated as part of a project attempting to use the highly structured nature of Igbo to define rules by which all two- and three-syllable words might be generated. The main body of 4,000 entries provides 9 fields of information for each term: a free-form word (or longer noun or verb phrase), grammatical class, tonal pronunciation, dialect zones where the term occurs, meanings, examples, variants, etymology, and related words. Although the index provides a list of English terms with equivalents in Igbo, the author stresses that it must not be seen as a key to translation. This dictionary will be most useful for reference collections supporting programs in African studies, linguistics, and anthropology, although libraries whose clientele include members of the U.S. Nigerian community may wish to acquire it as well.—**Robert B. Marks Ridinger**

Japanese

933.   Haig, John H., and the Department of East Asian Languages and Literatures. **The New Nelson Japanese-English Character Dictionary.** rev. ed. Boston, Charles E. Tuttle, 1997. 1600p. $59.95. ISBN 0-8048-2036-8.

Nearly three centuries ago, the Chinese derived a system of classifying kanji according to 214 basic elements or radicals, and both the Chinese and the Japanese have been following the system. In addition to this system, the Japanese have *on* (Chinese-Japanese readings) and *kun* (native Japanese readings) systems to find kanji or consult meanings. The present volume is the new edition of *The Modern Reader's Japanese-English Character Dictionary* of 1961, which was critically acclaimed as an authoritative guide to the study of Japanese language. One of the features of the new edition is that it has adopted the universal radical index. Under this system the user is able to find any kanji by using any radical or radical-like element that is a part of kanji. The dictionary contains more than 200 radicals with their formal Japanese names, English translations, and nicknames in English. Because the new edition is aimed also at novice users, this is a thoughtful innovation. Each kanji entry is provided with *on* and *kun* readings and core meanings. But the presentation of these points is not clear, and novice readers are likely to be perplexed. The author should have indicated with sample kanji the distinctions between *on* and *kun* reading as well as the core meanings. Most entries contain compound words for each kanji. Although the entry kanji is not repeated as the first member of every compound, it would be helpful for the user to see that same kanji in each compound word, especially when its pronunciation changes in different compounds. There are 15 appendixes that include information on how to find characters and compounds and how to determine if the radicals will be helpful and useful. The rich content of compound words makes this dictionary a desirable addition to Japanese reference sources.—**Seiko Mieczkowski**

Kyrgyz

934.   **Kyrgyz-English/English-Kyrgyz Glossary of Terms.** By Karl A. Krippes. New York, Hippocrene Books, 1998. 404p. $12.95pa. ISBN 0-7818-0641-0.

This is an abridgment of Yudakhin's *Kyrgyzsko-Russkij Slovar'* containing approximately 6,000 entries. This paperback is intended primarily for beginning students and tourists who speak American English. It should also be mentioned that more advanced users should consult *Tol'kovyj Slovar' Kyrgyzskoho Jazyka* (Explanatory Dictionary of Kyrgyz), also published by Yudakhin. Kyrgyz is a Turkish language related to Kazakh, Turkmen, and Uzbek. A brief introduction to this dictionary discusses the Cyrillic Kyrgyz alphabet, pronunciation, and the arrangement of vocabulary.—**Bohdan S. Wynar**

Louisiana Creole

935.   Valdman, Albert, Thomas A. Klingler, Margaret M. Marshall, and Kevin J. Rottet. **Dictionary of Louisiana Creole.** Bloomington, Ind., Indiana University Press, 1998. 656p. index. $75.00. ISBN 0-253-33451-9.

Louisiana Creole is an endangered language spoken today as a second language in just a few parish locations in Louisiana. Although related to French, it is distinct from Cajun French and colonial French as well as standard French. There is no official spelling, and there are no written rules to the language. It is a spoken language. Even though a few words and phrases may have come into occasional use in the broad geographic area of Acadiana (a general region west and southwest of New Orleans stretching to the Texas border), the authors have identified four specific areas where descendants of African slaves traditionally spoke the language known as Louisiana Creole. The dictionary includes details on orthography and variations of spelling and pronunciation with the meanings in both French and English. Following the dictionary portion are two indexes: by French-Creole and by English-Creole. Surviving speakers of the language were interviewed by the field workers late in this century, and written sources dating as far back as 1850 were consulted. The dictionary portion provides extensive examples of words in context by means of phrases and entire sentences that provide insight into Louisiana's unique cultural heritage.

The introduction, entitled "Observations on Louisiana Creole," is noteworthy. It gives a brief background into the settlement of southern Louisiana by whites, blacks, and persons of mixed race and the origins and changing use of such terms as Creole and Cajun. Although the Louisiana legislature and other governmental entities have encouraged the revitalization of Cajun French, Louisiana Creole has been officially neglected. This significant work and reference tool should encourage its preservation and study by Louisiana scholars.—**Louis G. Zelenka**

Native American

936.   **Western Apache-English Dictionary: A Community-Generated Bilingual Dictionary.** Dorothy Bray, ed., with the White Mountain Apache Tribe. Tempe, Ariz., Bilingual Press, 1998. 485p. $20.00pa. ISBN 0-927534-79-7.

One of the features that makes this dictionary special, if not unique, is that it involved the White Mountain Apache people in its development. Although any bilingual dictionary of native languages requires participation of some native informants (in the anthropological meaning), this project drew on the entire community in order to develop a community resource. Essentially this dictionary's purpose is to assist the White Mountain Apache children in learning and writing their own language. Like many native peoples in North America, the Apache are trying to save their language. This dictionary should help to standardize the written form of their language and to perhaps improve bilingual communication. The current title drew on the *Western Apache Dictionary* compiled by Edgar Perry, which the White Mountain Apache tribe published in 1972. This edition contains 10,500 Apache words (with 4,400 dialect variations) and 2,200 entries, indicating alternative expressions and forms. The Apache/English section is 280 pages long, whereas the English/Apache portion is 204 pages. A 25-page introduction provides a pronunciation guide, writing conventions, verb construction, verb complexes, affixes, pronouns, and particles. Clearly this is a title of limited interest to most libraries, but a useful addition to academic libraries where course work is offered in North American native languages.—**G. Edward Evans**

Norwegian

937.   **English-Norwegian, Norwegian-English Dictionary.** 3d ed. Revised by Egill Daae Gabrielsen. New York, Hippocrene Books, 1997. 599p. $14.95pa. ISBN 0-7818-0199-0.

For almost 20 years this has been an inexpensive dictionary for tourists or anyone needing the basics necessary to gain the general meaning of a word. Its large font makes it easy to read, and the definitions are short. These traits allow for quick consultation. As in earlier editions, the English-Norwegian section is longer by more than 30 pages. There is little change from the 2d edition except that there are more pages, which suggest new terms. However, a random check of 10 pages in each section did not identify any new words. Although this is not the dictionary for serious students or scholars, it is handy to have in the desk to use for a quick reference.
—**G. Edward Evans**

Spanish

938.   Butt, John. **Spanish Verbs.** New York, Oxford University Press, 1997. 276p. (Oxford Minireference). $6.95pa. ISBN 0-19-860036-4.

This 12-centimeter pocket reference serves as a guide to the Spanish verb system, designed for individual student use. It shows 92 common verbs, both regular and irregular, fully conjugated in their most frequently used tenses and moods, as patterns for all Spanish verbs. An overview of what one needs to know about the verb system generally is followed by explanations of the patterns found in regular verbs, radical changing verbs, irregular verbs, spelling changes, transitive and intransitive verbs, and reflexive (pronominal) verbs. The verb directory includes 4,000 Spanish verbs with their American English equivalents, in alphabetic order, each with a reference to its pattern verb in the table of 75 "model verbs."—**Joanna F. Fountain**

939.   **Collins Spanish-English, English-Spanish Dictionary.** unabridged 5th ed. By Colin Smith. New York, HarperCollins, 1997. 1679p. $55.00. ISBN 0-06-270207-6.

The current edition incorporates several thousand new entries in fields of technology, science, business, and entertainment as well as linguistic notes explaining the problems and subtleties of Spanish. Entries occasionally include notes on life and institutions in Spanish-speaking countries, and there is an emphasis on everyday spoken and written language in context-based examples. Distinctions are made between U.S. and British usage of English-language vocabulary, as suggested in an earlier review (see ARBA 94, entry 1133). Detailed entries, including those for phrasal verbs, include grammatical labels for each meaning listed, the subject field(s) in which the term or meaning is used, a mark indicating terms or meanings that are informal, and an indication of gender, as well as the translation or definition. The two thumb-indexed sections are separated by a new 72-page edition of a grammatical section titled "Language in Use/Lengua y uso," which is organized into situational themes. A supplemental appendix provides the user with lists of Spanish and English verbs; aspects of word formation in Spanish; and numbers, including weights and measures in both traditional and metric systems. This work is recommended for any size library and for individual use.—**Joanna F. Fountain**

940.   **Larousse Concise Spanish-English, English-Spanish Dictionary.** rev. ed. Catherine E. Love, ed. New York, Larousse Kingfisher Chambers, 1998. 642p. $18.95. ISBN 2-03-420403-4.

The latest volume in the Larousse family of bilingual Spanish-English dictionaries, this revised concise edition contains more than 90,000 references and more than 120,000 translations—roughly half the coverage provided by the standard version (see ARBA 97, entry 873). Like most foreign language dictionaries, this work helps users avoid embarrassing errors by listing the various options in cases where words have more than one translation. For example, those searching for the Spanish equivalent for *delivery* will find the following choices: distribution (*reparto*), handing over (*entrega*), goods delivered (*partida*), way of speaking (*estilo de discurso*), and birth (*parto*). As seen in this illustration, the entries clarify meanings, which enables users to locate the specific word or phrase needed quickly and with confidence. In addition to the usual preliminary material (abbreviations, pronunciation guides, and so on), and an appendix on Spanish and English verb conjugations, the volume also contains a 32-page cultural supplement on life in the Hispanic world. This supplement covers geography, banking and business, health, transportation, communications, shopping, and other topics of interest to students and travelers.

As with the other Larousse editions currently available, this work is a reliable, easy-to-use, and up-to-date source that is appropriate for home, school, or office. Among dictionaries in the medium price range, the Larousse Concise is an excellent value and will be a popular item with beginning and intermediate students.

—**Melvin S. Arrington Jr.**

941.   **The Oxford Spanish Desk Dictionary: Spanish-English/English-Spanish.** Carol Styles Carvajal and Jane Horwood, eds. New York, Oxford University Press, 1997. 959p. $14.95. ISBN 0-19-521352-1.

Those familiar with the new international edition of *Oxford Spanish Dictionary* will find this compact version an equally reliable and practical resource. *The Oxford Spanish Desk Dictionary* incorporates most of the general features of the larger dictionary in an abbreviated format. Containing more than 80,000 words and phrases and in excess of 115,000 translations, it is designed with portability and quick reference in mind. Markers within entires clearly identify usage and regional variants. For example, for the word *potato* one will find *papa* (Latin American) and *patata* (Spanish). Likewise, under *papas* (or *patatas*) *fritas* users will see a choice between *de paquete* (*potato chips* [American] or *crisps* [British]), and *de cocina* (*french fries* [American] or *chips* [British]).

Also included are specialized terms from a variety of fields, such as computing, finance, music, communications, and sports. Usage boxes interspersed throughout the volume highlight important grammatical points, key vocabulary, and such essential matters as measurements, greetings and introductions, and forms of address. The latter consists of a useful discussion of ways to express "you," among them the Latin American *vos*. With regard to currency, this dictionary contains many relatively new items, such as *AIDS*, but it has not yet recognized NAFTA. In comparison to other compact, relatively lightweight, hardcover, bilingual Spanish-English dictionaries, this is one of the best available. It has easy-to-read type and is modestly priced. Students, travelers, and others seeking Spanish-English equivalents can use it with confidence.—**Melvin S. Arrington Jr.**

942.   **Random House Latin-American Spanish Dictionary: Spanish-English, English-Spanish.** By David L. Gold. New York, Random House, 1997. 626p. $22.00; $14.00pa. ISBN 0-679-45294-X; 0-375-70084-6pa.

Somewhat comparable in size and scope to the *Oxford Spanish Desk Dictionary* (see entry 941) and the *Larousse Concise Spanish-English, English-Spanish Dictionary* (see entry 940), this compact volume containing more than 60,000 entries claims one distinguishing feature—its focus on the Spanish of Mexico, Central and South America, and the Caribbean. In its pages one can find such examples of Latin American usage as *metate* (Mexico and Central America: flat stone for grinding and pounding); *chompa* (Latin America: jumper, pullover); and *vos*, the widely used second person pronoun. In the case of *chompa*, however, the all-encompassing geographic designation given should be replaced by the more narrowly defined marker "Andean." Numerous items in the Oxford dictionary cited above are absent in the Random House; for example, *zopilote* (the Mexican and Central American term for "buzzard"), *tapat'o* (the Mexican name for the native of Guadalajara), *frutilla* (the word used for "strawberry" in Bolivia and the Southern Cone), and *de repente* (meaning "maybe" or "perhaps" in Peru, Bolivia, and the River Plate region). The word *guagua* offers another telling comparison: the Random House dictionary notes that it is the term for "bus" in the Caribbean; the Oxford dictionary provides the Caribbean reference and also indicates that it means "baby" in the Andean countries. Despite its omissions, the Random House dictionary does prove superior to its competition in its thorough, well-written discussion of the basic characteristics of Spanish pronunciation. This one outstanding aspect notwithstanding, it will probably not be the first choice of those seeking a compact, hardcover Spanish-English dictionary.—**Melvin S. Arrington Jr.**

943.   Truscott, Sandra, and María J. García. **A Dictionary of Contemporary Spain.** Chicago, Fitzroy Dearborn, 1998. 301p. $55.00. ISBN 1-57958-113-7.

This handy little guide provides brief but pertinent and up-to-date information on 2,000 institutions, terms, and events relevant to recent and contemporary Spanish life, including government, politics, trade, industry, education, health care, the media, art, music, crime, and society. The entries include 425 personalities and the explanations of 260 acronyms.

There is, unfortunately, no introduction to explain the authors' rationale, and the reader who presumes capitalization indicative of a related entry risks searching for *Exposición Universal de Sevilla* under *Expo 92*. The anglophone user will be further frustrated by the almost exclusive preference for entry under the Spanish, Catalan, Basque, or Galician forms, the only exceptions being (curiously) *Abortion, Adoption, 15-J, Spain-Morocco Tunnel,* and the rather unlikely-to-be-sought *Spanish gun laws.* Even *All Saints' Day, capital punishment, February 23rd, forest fires, money laundering, national flag,* and *Tagus River* have to be looked up under their Spanish equivalents, and there are no cross-references from the corresponding English forms. Although "Basque" is used in the text, information on the language occurs only under separate (but factually similar) entries for *Euskera* (the Basque term) and *Vasco* (the Castilian word). Spanish membership in the European Union is mentioned only under *Eurodiputados* and *Tratado de Adhesión.* There are also other infelicities and inconsistencies in the choice of headings. King Juan Carlos goes under *Borbón* (with cross-reference from *Carlos*) as do his children, but his wife is under *Sofía.* At least three entries are under the definite article. Twelve political scandals are rather unhelpfully grouped under *Caso* (affair), but the Caso Galaxia is under "G" and the Caso Lasa y Zabalabut is referred to entries for the two individuals involved.

However, readers and researchers coming across terms and names in their original form in the Spanish media will find this an excellent (and physically convenient) quick reference book.—**L. Hallewell**

24 Literature

GENERAL WORKS

Bibliography

944. Bibliography of the Myth of Don Juan in Literary History. José Manuel Losada, ed. Lewiston, N.Y., Edwin Mellen Press, 1997. 216p. index. $89.95. ISBN 0-7734-8450-7.

This unannotated bibliography is an impressive piece of scholarship that will be extremely useful to scholars of the Don Juan canon. The book includes 2,817 annotations divided into 7 separate bibliographies based on the original language of the publications: English, French, German, Italian, Portuguese, and Spanish. Each of these bibliographies is divided into three sections: "Versions," "Translations," and "Critical Studies." In the appendix, there are an additional 67 annotations covering versions of the Don Juan myth in Slavonic languages.

The majority of the entries focus on literary works, although important musical and cinematic versions of the myth are included. Classification of the entries is alphabetic by author, except in the case of uniform headings, which are classified chronologically. The entries for musical compositions are primarily classified according to the composer's name. All bibliographic data within the entries are given in the language of origin.

Although this title is a gold mine of information for scholars, one must have a firm grasp on the literature of the subject to use this title because it is poorly indexed. The indexing done on the book is limited to the critical studies section of the bibliographies and only includes major authors that have used the Don Juan motif in their literature. Serendipity is the order of the day for the rest of the text. Fortunately, this title is a work in progress, and the editor will have an opportunity to address this major shortcoming in the next edition.—**John R. Burch Jr.**

945. Law in Literature: An Annotated Bibliography of Law-Related Works. Elizabeth Villiers Gemmette, ed. Troy, N.Y., Whitston Publishing, 1998. 331p. $35.00. ISBN 0-87875-498-9.

Novels featuring lawyers as protagonists and law-related plots are all the rage among readers of popular fiction. A debate over the relationship of literature and law is taking place among scholars as well. Both general readers and literary scholars may find this bibliography of interest.

There are 250 signed annotations of novellas, novels, and plays with law-related themes. This volume is intended to be a companion piece to the editor's three earlier works, which are anthologies of short stories, plays, and novellas in which some aspect of law is featured. The specific legal topics and subtopics identified within each of the works are listed at the end of each annotation. It is not clear whether the annotator or the editor has assigned these.

Works included run the gamut from Aeschylus's *Oresteia* to John Grisham's contemporary legal thrillers. In many of the works, the law-literature relationship is obvious and primary to the plot. Herman Melville's *Billy Budd* and Norman Mailer's *Executioner's Song* are such works. In others, the point is not so clear, and one questions their inclusion because the working of the law in the denouncement of the plot is not the focal point. For example, the theme in *Dr. Faustus* is identified as being "the legality of any contract made with the devil and the problem of the soul as a piece of property." Grisham's *The Firm* is described by the annotator as being not really about the law but rather an adventure story. There is also the issue of the usefulness of applying twentieth-century legal language such as discrimination, minority issues, and aiding and abetting to sixteenth- and seventeenth-century works, such as Shakespeare's *Othello*.

In addition to these content weaknesses, there are practical problems as well. The only index is of the legal topics and subtopics. There is no list of authors or titles. Readers who have forgotten an author or title have no recourse but to page through the book to locate what they need. Despite these criticisms, the bibliography may be of interest to teachers designing a law in literature course, but careful and judicious selection of titles is advised.—**Marlene M. Kuhl**

946.   Lawson, Alan, Leigh Dale, Helen Tiffin, and Shane Rowlands. **Post-Colonial Literatures in English: General, Theoretical, and Comparative 1970-1993.** New York, G. K. Hall/Simon & Schuster Macmillan, 1997. 374p. index. (A Reference Publication in Literature). $65.00. ISBN 0-8161-7358-3.

Part of a continuing series of bibliographies on postcolonial literatures, this book focuses on "the appearance and institutionalization of the study of post-colonial literatures and literary theory within English-speaking academies throughout the world" (p. ix). Rather than focusing on a specific region, as did earlier volumes in the series, this one addresses general works from all over the world, although the subject matter is limited to countries affected by European (primarily British) colonialism.

The book is divided into 2 sections—"Reference Aids" and "Books, Dissertations, Chapters, and Essays." One has to wonder what distinguishes the sections; indeed, the first consists of only 17 titles. Could they not have been combined? The book is arranged alphabetically by author and chronologically if an author has more than one title listed. Entries provide author and title of the work and publication information. Brief annotations are also given and generally relate to what the title offers without giving critical commentary. Cross-references are provided. The volume ends with a general index to authors (about whom articles are written, not authors of the actual annotated entries), topics, geographic areas, and people. The index is keyed to entry rather than page numbers.

As postcolonial theory and study continue to flourish, works such as this one will hold their place in libraries. Academic libraries at universities with strong English departments, and particularly those with earlier volumes in this series, will want this title.—**Melissa Rae Root**

Bio-bibliography

947.   **Contemporary Authors New Revision Series, Volume 59: A Bio-bibliographical Guide to Current Writers....** Daniel Jones and John D. Jorgenson, eds. Detroit, Gale, 1998. 446p. $134.00. ISBN 0-7876-1201-4.

948.   **Contemporary Authors New Revision Series, Volume 60: A Bio-bibliographical Guide to Current Writers....** Daniel Jones and John D. Jorgenson, eds. Detroit, Gale, 1998. 455p. $134.00. ISBN 0-7876-1202-2.

These volumes continue the professional *New Revision Series*, which updates entries in previous volumes of the ongoing *Contemporary Authors* (CA) series and other Gale publications. CA itself continues to be published and contains entries for authors not previously covered in the series. The *New Revision Series* includes "sketches" (Gale's own word) from any previous volume of CA, including from the *New Revision Series* itself, which has needed to be changed.

To examine the kinds of changes that the *New Revision Series* introduces, this reviewer examined all Gale publication entries for the trendy modern novelist David Foster Wallace. The cumulated CA index, printed as a separate paperback volume with alternating volumes of CA, provides access to the volume information for these entries. Wallace was first covered in *Contemporary Literary Criticism, Volume 50* (1987), which includes no biographical material and reproduces snippets of critical comment. At that time, Wallace had published only his first novel, *The Broom of the System*. In 1991, he was first covered in volume 132 of CA. By this time, he had published one additional book, *Girl with Curious Hair*. The entry includes "Sidelights," a column of plot summary and critical comment. It summarizes the plots and critical commentary about the two books based on seven newspaper and magazine articles and also contains sections on personal information, memberships, an address, career information, awards and honors, and a bibliography of the two books.

The entry in the *New Revision Series, Volume 59*, published in 1998, differs significantly from its 1991 predecessor. The "membership" section has been dropped because the author apparently dropped all of his memberships; the personal information has changed slightly; and the awards and honors have expanded significantly, as has the bibliography of his work, quite naturally, because the volume of work has increased considerably. The "Sidelights" section has been expanded by more than 300 percent and has been completely rewritten, based on a greatly expanded list of 16 newspaper and magazine articles. The critical comment is summarized, both the positive and the negative, in a highly objective manner, with ample quotations.

Many of the entries (although not Wallace's) include e-mail and other address information that does not exist in earlier volumes, mention of work in progress, and, occasionally, personal comment by the authors themselves (usually in the case of lesser-known writers about whom not much has been written). Most of the entries are 1 or 2 pages in length, although major figures receive lengthier treatment (Margaret Atwood merits 10 pages; Ian Fleming, 5). Everything about this series, from the quality of the physical volumes to the currentness and professionalism of the entries, suggests that it is a must for any serious library's reference collection, despite the price.

—**Bill Miller**

949.   **Contemporary Authors, Volume 158: A Bio-Bibliographical Guide to Current Writers....** Scot Peacock, ed. Detroit, Gale, 1998. 457p. $140.00. ISBN 0-7876-1185-9.

950.   **Contemporary Authors, Volume 159: A Bio-bibliographical Guide to Current Writers....** Scot Peacock, ed. Detroit, Gale, 1998. 451p. $140.00. ISBN 0-7876-1862-4.

Some days at the reference desk it seems that only two or three sources are necessary to successfully answer all of the day's questions. One of these few sources is always *Contemporary Authors* (CA), now in its 158th and 159th volumes. With more than 100,000 writers listed, CA has been the source for quick information on authors since 1962.

The information provided on each author includes the author's personal information, address, career summary, memberships, awards, writings, works in progress, sidelights, and biographical and critical sources. CA's definition of authors is broad and includes fiction and poetry writers, nonfiction authors, journalists, screenwriters and others in media, authors who write in languages other than English, and literary "greats" of the early twentieth century whose works are popular in schools and colleges. With this broad definition students and patrons can usually find whom they are looking for in CA. CA's usefulness for general quick information on the literati is especially helpful for those students writing book reports that require a blurb about the author.

CA has come out in several series and revisions. The cumulative index, published separately at frequent intervals, does include references to all the series and revisions—a blessing because keeping up with the series order is difficult. With the publication of volume 159, only 146 volumes actually exist. It always takes even an experienced reference librarian a couple of passes before finding the exact volume where an entry appears. The index references in CA to the entire family of Gale literary sources is excellent, although sorting out this family tree is sometimes a challenge.

It is essential for libraries to have the Contemporary Authors series. If one wonders if the whole issue with series and revisions and indexing can be solved by buying the whole series electronically, the answer is absolutely. The GaleNet version is fabulous, with sophisticated indexing and complete coverage. It is not less expensive, however, and libraries, as they do with all electronic products, will have to weigh the options.—**Paul A. Mogren**

951.   **Fools and Jesters in Literature, Art, and History: A Bio-bibliographical Sourcebook.** Vicki K. Janik, ed. Westport, Conn., Greenwood Press, 1998. 552p. index. $95.00. ISBN 0-313-29785-1.

Throughout history every culture and society in the world has been enriched and enlightened by the literary and dramatic presence of fools, jesters, buffoons, schlemiels, and others who amuse audiences with their antics and words. Definitions and characteristics of "fools" vary widely, but most have in common (1) bizarre appearance, costume, speech, voice, or movements; (2) childlike behavior or paradoxical ideas; and (3) the ability to make other people laugh.

After a thought-provoking introduction by the editor, this anthology of more than 60 arbitrarily selected, lively, well-researched essays covers a generous array of the world's fools, with some chapters devoted to specific individuals or groups (e.g., Woody Allen, Jack Benny, Charlie Chaplin, the Marx Brothers, the Three Stooges), whereas others tackle genres (e.g., Pierrot, circus clowns, *Commedia dell'Arte*, Coyote [the trickster], drag queens). Still other chapters treat fictional characters (e.g., Gimpel, Forrest Gump, *King Lear*'s Fool, Puck), and there are even a few surprises (e.g., Paul the Apostle, Socrates, Hamlet). To avoid ethnocentrism, there are entries on Norse, Greek, Japanese, Balinese, and various Native American fools, and, although few female clowns are covered (Gracie Allen, Lucille Ball, Mae West, Martha Raye), the reasons for this are stated.

Curiously, arrangement is alphabetic (rather than chronological or geographical). For each entry brief vital statistics, some background on performers or characters, a description and analysis, some idea of critical reception, and a selected bibliography are provided. Although the subjects vary greatly, the whole is tied together by common threads—all selected fools, jesters, and clowns teach us (if we are paying attention) much about human nature and permit us to look inward at our own behaviors and natures. This work is highly recommended for its extensive coverage and a scholarly, yet readable analysis of who or what makes us laugh—and why. [R: C&RL, Sept 98, p. 614]—**Bruce A. Shuman**

952.   **Literary Lifelines.** Danbury, Conn., Grolier, 1998. 10v. illus. index. $319.00/set. ISBN 0-7172-9211-8.
Literary Lifelines is a disappointing set that gives cursory information about 1,000 alphabetically arranged authors of the past and present (100 per volume). The writers range from the well known (Charles Dickens, Honoré de Balzac) to the relatively obscure (Marina Tsvetaeva, Andrei Bely, Earl Birney) and cover all fields of literature.

Each author is given a double-page spread. On the first page a small, muddy, 2-by-2-inch portrait appears, followed by 4 or 5 brief paragraphs that cover basic biographical information and supply a few critical comments. A small reproduction of a dust jacket, again poorly reproduced, is provided, as is a list of important works by the author (with a maximum of 10). No secondary of critical sources are listed. On the opposite page, there is a list of more than a dozen authors related to the main one either by nationality, period, or genre. Lastly, a timeline is given that lists, by decade, approximately 15 important world events that occurred while the author was alive. Each decade has a small, unattractive drawing illustrating one of the events. For authors with approximately the same birth and death dates, these timelines are virtually the same, including the drawings. No attempt is made to correlate the world events with incidents or influences in the author's life.

Each volume ends with the same glossary of literary terms and an index to the entire set. Author and title entries are listed alphabetically; writers are arranged by century, nationality, and genre. The index is confusing, and a random check showed many omissions, particularly of titles.

It is difficult to suggest an audience for this set; it is too superficial and lacking in substantial information for adults, and many of the entries would be of no value to middle school students. Only a handful of contemporary children's and young adult writers are included, and the information given on appropriate authors is so slight that youngsters would be better served by using a general encyclopedia or a biographical dictionary of children's authors. [R: BR, Nov/Dec 98, pp. 76-77; SLJ, Nov 98, p. 154; BL, 15 Sept 98, pp. 264-266]—**John T. Gillespie**

Biography

953.   **Contemporary Authors Autobiography Series, Volume 28.** Linda R. Andres and Marilyn O'Connell Allen, eds. Detroit, Gale, 1998. 426p. illus. index. $140.00. ISBN 0-7876-1143-3.
The nature and scope of the Contemporary Authors Autobiography Series (CAAS) has not changed since the 6th and 7th volumes were reviewed here 10 years ago (see ARBA 89, entries 986-987). The series remains a vehicle for autobiographical essays by contemporary authors in all genres from around the world, although Americans known primarily for their poetry predominate in this latest volume. As in previous volumes, the authors themselves have chosen the manner and extent of their presentations, so the 13 essays included here—and illustrated with personal photographs supplied by the authors—vary widely in style, approach, and tone. They reflect each writer's personal and subjective viewpoint. In this viewpoint lie both the limitation and the value of this series: It cannot serve as the sole source for complete information on an author's life and works, but it does offer insights of great interest and usefulness to teachers, advanced students, and other serious readers of contemporary literature. The fact, noted by the previous ARBA reviewer, that CAAS is indexed by other Gale literature series but itself provides a cumulative author and subject index only to its own volumes implies the secondary place this series should properly occupy in the research process and in library reference collections.
—**Gregory M. Toth**

954.   **Dictionary of Literary Biography Documentary Series, Volume 16: The House of Scribner, 1905-1930.** John Delaney, ed. Detroit, Gale, 1997. 398p. illus. index. $140.00. ISBN 0-7876-1931-0.
Extended profiles of 53 consummate bibliophiles, arranged alphabetically by subject surname, have been herein gathered by editors Baker and Womack. In usual Dictionary of Literary Biography (DLB) fashion, articles

are signed by reputable scholars whose collegiate or library affiliations are supplied in the volume's back matter. In this work, 9 of this work's 34 contributors have each submitted a pair of articles; Sidney E. Burger and K.A. Manley have each furnished 3 essays.

The editors' introduction identifies factors that catalyzed and otherwise impinged upon the activities of nineteenth-century British book collectors and bibliographers. Although the men of letters encompassed by this volume were dissimilar in many respects, they remained united in their devotion—and, in some cases, obsession— regarding the amassing of tomes or the cataloguing of same in bibliographies. This survey's wide array of entrants includes explorers (Sir Richard Francis Burton), industrialists (Lord Brotherton), printers (William Blades), forgers (Harry Buxton Forman), librarians (Henry Bradshaw), physicians (Sir William Osler), statesmen (William Ewart Gladstone), polymaths (Andrew Lang), and families (the Rothschilds). Most of these bookish minds flourished during the latter half of the nineteenth century; only eight of these men were to live beyond World War I.

The articles contain portraits and other illustrations as well as bibliographic references. The essays typically run to several thousand words apiece, although the essays on Sir Thomas Phillips, Thomas James Wise, and Sir Anthony Panizzi each extend to nearly 10,000 words. The analyses are consistently informed by sound critical judgments and incisively trace formative influences upon the biographees' lives and writings.

Shortcomings within this work, although rare, do exist. Sadly, no picture appears of Edward Edwards, "England's first professional public librarian" (p. 94); neither are there renderings of Alexander Balloch Grosart, Charles Edward Sayle, or Rowland Williams. Ironically, the entry on Victorian book illustrator Myles Birket Foster provides three likenesses of the artist himself, one of his residence, but none of his artistry, except the depiction of two bookplates that Foster designed for his personal library. Moreover, some users of this reference work may question whether high principles of scholarship have been upheld. For example, the essay on Bertram Dobell was provided by the head of the bookselling firm founded by Dobell himself.

These querulous comments aside, the several defects discovered in this reference are easily eclipsed by its numerous virtues. With this volume, the continuing DLB series has maintained its exemplary standards of scholarly integrity that for fully two decades have distinguished it from other literary research tools.

—**Jeffrey E. Long**

955.   **Dictionary of Literary Biography Documentary Series, Volume 17: The House of Scribner, 1931-1984.** John Delaney, ed. Detroit, Gale, 1998. 497p. illus. index. $151.00/vol. ISBN 0-7876-1932-9.

Editor Delaney has completed the 3-volume chronicle of the Scribner publishing house with the publication of this volume covering the years 1931 to 1984. (See Dictionary of Literary Biography Documentary Series 13 and 16 for the previous volumes.) Following the same format used in the other volumes, Delaney has relied mainly on the correspondence files of authors represented by Scribner during this period. The House of Scribner lasted 150 years. That the publishing house flourished for such a length of time is an accomplishment in the annals of U.S. history, and that it remained within one family for such a time is also noteworthy.

However, this volume is not a "history" of the publishing firm of Charles Scribner's Sons or the Scribner Book Companies, Inc. Rather, it is a chronology of some of the experiences of the company, particularly the relationship of the editors and the authors as shown through their correspondence. Thus, it may be of interest to writers and students of the 20 authors selected to represent this period. The correspondence includes letters of editorial guidance and publishing advice on the part of the editors and concerns about payments, contracts, and book content on the part of the writers. There is some value in the biographical information about the writers given through their letters, although some is mundane concerns about their accounts.

Although an interesting volume, particularly as a description of a publishing house of great stature, this is not a necessary acquisition for most libraries, and certainly not for the reference collection. It will probably be limited to those libraries with the funding to have standing orders for the series. [R: LJ, 15 Nov 98, p. 60]

—**Ingrid Schierling Burnett**

956.   **International Authors and Writers Who's Who.** 15th ed. David Cummings and Dennis K. McIntire, eds. Cambridge, England, International Biographical Centre; distr., Bristol, Pa., Taylor & Francis, 1997. 753p. $180.00. ISBN 0-948875-72-0.

According to the foreword, the 1st edition of this biographical dictionary was published in 1934. The publisher notes that "with this Fifteenth Edition, the Consultant Editors have overseen the most extensive revision in history. Several thousand new and/or completely revised entries have been included in this edition, making it the most accurate and up-to-date one-volume biographical source of its kind in the world." As in most other biographical volumes by this publisher, no criteria for inclusion or exclusion are given. In addition to the biographical section, there are several appendixes—literary agents, literary organizations, literary awards and prizes, and American Academy of Arts and Letters.

Any user of ARBA will testify that there are many dictionaries and encyclopedias of writers, poets, and literary agents. There are simply too many to mention here. Indeed, this dictionary lists many people of many nationalities—some important, some less important. Most people interested in Polish affairs know about Leszek Kolakowski, a Polish philosopher. But who is Jouri Klimov, a Russian musician? And why is Lina Kostenko, probably the most important Ukrainian poet, not listed?

In 1998, Gale published a 2d edition of *Encyclopedia of World Biography*, also reviewed in this volume of ARBA (see entry 23). It is a highly respected and standard work on this subject. It contains a list of internationally known poets—Jean Cocteau, Saint-John Perse, or Francis Picabia—none of whom are listed in this volume. Under "German Literature," *Encyclopedia of World Biography* lists several dozen internationally known writers. How many are in this dictionary? There are two entries—one for John Schultz (teacher) and one for Max Schulz (professor of English and writer from Cleveland). And how about Charles Schulz, American cartoonist and creator of "Peanuts"? He certainly is listed in Gale's encyclopedia, but not in *International Authors and Writers Who's Who*. This reviewer recommends this dictionary be used with caution.—**Bohdan S. Wynar**

957. **Nineteenth-Century American Western Writers.** Robert L. Gale, ed. Detroit, Gale, 1997. 469p. illus. index. (Dictionary of Literary Biography, v.186). $146.00. ISBN 0-7876-1682-6.

Like other volumes in the Dictionary of Literary Biography series (DLB), this one focuses on biography as it relates to the work of particular authors. The 38 essays in this book discuss a variety of writers who write about the western United States. Each essay includes an assessment of the author's work as it relates to the actual and imagined western United States, illustrations (including photographs or portraits of the author), a list of major works separated by genre, a selected bibliography, and the location of the author's papers. The West is understood to mean all the land west of the Mississippi River, thus encompassing a great variety of distinctly different regions. The authors are also quite varied in terms of reputation, genre, interests, and style. Mark Twain is the most famous writer in this volume. A number of other writers included, such as Timothy Flint or Lewis H. Garrard, are not well known by general readers. Four women are included—Gertrude Atherton, Ina Coolbirth, Mary Hallock Foote, and Helen Hunt Jackson. Theodore Roosevelt, obviously best remembered as president of the United States, is here because he was also an influential writer. George Catlin is best known as a graphic artist, but his writings about the Native Americans he lived with are significant historical and literary documents. Historians include Frederick Jackson Turner and Francis Parkman as well as the lesser-known Timothy Flint. No dramatists are included; however, a poet, Edwin Markham, is represented. One essay combines a review of two authors, Meriwether Lewis and William Clark, who are best known as explorers. Naturalist John Muir is represented here as well as the darkly satirical Ambrose Bierce.

Gale's brief introductory essay is a fine summary of major themes woven throughout the works of these diverse authors. The style of most of the essays sampled, in keeping with other volumes in the series, makes this volume accessible to a general reader but still useful to a scholarly audience. Some essays, however, could have been edited with more attention for a nonspecialist audience not likely to understand jargon like "intertextuality" or "deconstructionist." This book is a necessary purchase for collections holding other volumes in the DLB series, but it would also be a useful source on its own. As is true of other volumes in this series, a cumulative index to all the previous volumes is at the end of this book.—**David Isaacson**

958. **The Writer's Directory 1998-2000.** 13th ed. Miranda H. Ferrara, ed. Detroit, St. James Press, 1997. 1847p. index. $150.00. ISBN 1-55862-360-4. ISSN 0084-2699.

Published biennially since 1971, *The Writer's Directory* provides brief biographical and directory information for writers from any country who have published at least one work in English. This most recent edition lists 17,875 names, including more than 2,600 new entries. A separate section titled "Obituaries" reproduces the entries for recently deceased writers who were listed in a previous edition and adds the year of death.

Entries are arranged alphabetically and include the writer's full name, pseudonym (if any), nationality, year of birth, categories in which the writer publishes, past and current job title(s) and place(s) of employment, the titles and years of published monographs, writing prizes won (if any), and the writer's mailing address. Pseudonyms and obituary entries are cross-referenced.

The volume is indexed by the writing categories included in each entry. The list of terms is provided as a table of contents to the index for easy scanning. The categories are subdivided under the headings "Creative Writing," "Non-fiction," and "Other," this last of which includes autobiography, cartoons, illustrations, and reference.

Although criteria for inclusion are unclear—for example, E. Annie Proulx is listed but Carol Shields, another contemporary Pulitzer Prize-winning novelist, is not—this directory is quite useful for locating writers who would not be listed in the Contemporary Authors series (see entries 949 and 950) nor in a faculty directory.

—**Susanna Van Sant**

Dictionaries and Encyclopedias

959.   **Cyclopedia of Literary Characters.** rev. ed. A. J. Sobczak and Janet Alice Long, eds. Pasadena, Calif., Salem Press, 1998. 5v. index. $350.00/set. ISBN 0-89356-438-0.

This comprehensive set contains all the titles from the original *Cyclopedia of Literary Characters* (1963) and the *Cyclopedia of Literary Characters II* (see ARBA 91, entry 1104), as well as titles included in *Masterplots* (2d ed.; see ARBA 97, entry 906) and the *Masterplots II* set (see ARBA 96, entry 949). However, only the *Masterplots II* volumes that survey novel-length fiction and drama are covered. This revision analyzes 3,300 titles, an increase of 574 titles. As with the previous editions, the volumes can be used alone or as a companion to *Masterplots*.

Entries are arranged alphabetically by the title of the work. Additional information includes the original foreign title (if appropriate), the author's name, birth and death dates, date of first publication or production (for drama), genre, locale, time of action, and plot type. Within each entry, characters are arranged in order of importance, with main characters receiving more detailed descriptions. Three indexes complete the set and enhance its usefulness. The 1st is a complete list of titles covered, including cross-references. The 2d provides access to the titles grouped by author. The final index is a comprehensive alphabetic list of the more than 20,000 characters described.

There is no other treatment of the subject that equals this set in scope and detail. It is helpful both for quick reference and more in-depth research and criticism. With all of the new and updated material included, even those libraries owning the previous editions should consider its purchase. This set is recommended for public, academic, and high school reference collections. [R: Choice, Sept 98, p. 86]—**Barbara E. Kemp**

960.   **A Dictionary of Literary Terms and Literary Theory.** 4th ed. By J. A. Cuddon. Revised by C. E. Preston. Malden, Mass., Blackwell, 1998. 991p. (Blackwell Reference). $89.95. ISBN 0-631-20271-4.

This 4th edition of Cuddon's classic dictionary was well underway when he died in 1996. Other scholars, including Preston of Cambridge University, carried the project through to revise and extensively update the entries. Included are many new categories, ranging from crime fiction to a four-page entry for pornography. Many terms provide titles and excerpts of actual works, mostly poetry, to illuminate and enhance the definitions of the listing. The entries are cross-indexed.

The alphabetic entries range from very brief (*facetiae* is defined as a "bookseller's term for humorous or obscene books") to 40 pages for *novel*, consisting largely of worldwide titles in that genre, the last of which is dated 1989. Many entries are imbued with the personality and biases of their writers; the entry for *senhal* notes that it is a "fanciful name used to address people in Old Provencal poems. Perhaps we should now call it a pet name."

Among its more exotic entries, *tawddgyrch cadwynog* is defined as a "Welsh syllabic verse form similar to the rhupunt" and *orismology* is defined as "the explanation of technical terms, which this dictionary is in aid of." As with previous editions, this 4th edition of *A Dictionary of Literary Terms and Literary Theory* will serve scholars well, but is also a surprisingly entertaining work.—**Kay O. Cornelius**

961.   **Encyclopedia of Feminist Literary Theory.** Elizabeth Kowaleski-Wallace, ed. New York, Garland, 1997. 449p. index. (Garland Reference Library of the Humanities, v.1582). $75.00. ISBN 0-8153-0824-8.

This dictionary features articles on keywords, topics, proper names, and terminology relevant to feminist literary theory. Although dictionaries already exist on both literary theory and feminist theory, which no doubt supply entries on each other, this dictionary is one of the first to bring the disciplines together in a reference format, and indeed feminist literary theory is a discipline in its own right. Feminist literary theory is not just the study of feminist writings since the 1970s but rather the interpretation of canonical or other works in a feminist light. Thus, this dictionary would be useful not just for people studying feminist literary theory, but for those studying general literary theory and literature as well.

Some entries are no surprise—"Children"; "Marxism"; "Beauty"; "Beauvoir, Simone de"; "Lacan, Jacques"; and "Hysteria." Others are pleasantly surprising; for example, "Comedy," "Cyborg Feminism," "Physical Disability," "Orientalism," and "Feminist Jurisprudence." The entries on keywords and large topics define terms and discuss the people who have influenced or been influenced by them. Entries on people treat their major works and their relationships to feminist literary theory. All entries provide a bibliography, and all are signed by one of an extensive list of contributors from around the country, with a few from Great Britain and Canada.

The content of the dictionary focuses primarily on British and American topics and people. There is only a limited amount of French feminist theory (only that which influenced Anglo-American theory), which is a shame and somewhat silly, especially in light of the following sentence found in the entry on French theory: "French feminism has been the single most important theoretical influence on contemporary feminist literary criticism" (pp. 168-69). If that is the case, should not this dictionary make more of an effort to embrace it? Also, other terms from the broader subject matter of feminism are included, which seems unnecessary, for other dictionaries cover this territory. However, such inclusion ensures that readers will not need to consult other references. Also of concern is the price of the dictionary, which seems a bit excessive for a volume of less than 500 pages.

—**Melissa Rae Root**

962.   **Encyclopedia of Folklore and Literature.** Mary Ellen Brown and Bruce A. Rosenberg, eds. Santa Barbara, Calif., ABC-CLIO, 1998. 766p. index. $99.50. ISBN 1-57607-003-4.

Instead of being as comprehensive as its title implies, *Encyclopedia of Folklore and Literature* contains a mere 350 signed entries and a handful of illustrations. These entries range alphabetically from "Aarne, Antti" to "Zhirmunskii, Vikto Maksimovich," and discuss authors whose works often contain elements of folklore, folkloric works, folkloric scholars and movements, folkloric concepts and terms, and folkloric themes and characters. These entries tend to be well written and conclude with brief bibliographies; cross-references are provided. The volume itself is well indexed.

Encyclopedia of Folklore and Literature can easily be compared with *American Folklore: An Encyclopedia,* edited by Jan Harold Brunvand (see ARBA 97, entry 1088), but such a comparison is not quite fair, for Brunvand's volume limited itself to American folklore. By discussing folklore from around the world, and by including entries on authors whose texts often include folklore, the encyclopedia at hand has a larger focus and attempts to do more. It is indeed unfortunate that the encyclopedia fails to accomplish as much as it could, but a comprehensive encyclopedia of folklore would probably be incomplete at 35,000 entries and 10 volumes. *Encyclopedia of Folklore and Literature* is thus an amiable introduction for novice researchers but a work that fails to live up to its name. [R: LJ, 15 Oct 98, p. 60; BL, 15 Dec 98, pp. 762-763]—**Richard Bleiler**

963.   **Encyclopedia of the Novel.** Paul Schellinger, Christopher Hudson, and Marijke Rijsberman, eds. Chicago, Fitzroy Dearborn, 1998. 2v. index. $270.00/set. ISBN 1-57958-015-7.

The *Encyclopedia of the Novel* is an international, in-depth study of the novel genre. It is an exploration by more than 350 experts from around the world to examine the novel as a genre. The encyclopedia contains entries on novelists and their works, on types of novels, and on technical and formal aspects of novels. There are also passages on critical approaches and theoretical frameworks that critics have developed for discussing the genre as well as entries relating to various material factors behind the rise, spread, and enormous popularity of the novel. The encyclopedia contains entries tracing the origins and development of the novel in countries and regions around the world.

Emphasis is placed on the historical significance specific authors and works have had on novels as a whole. Contributors assess the role these novelists and novels have played in the development of the genre rather than offer a general overview. Thus the larger purpose of the encyclopedia is to promote understanding of the novel over time rather than just factual information. Due to the enormity of the subject area, editors have selected entries that they feel have historical importance. On its own, the encyclopedia is an excellent reference to the history of the novel, but it is not a complete source of all novelists and novels that readers may be researching.

—**Cari Ringelheim**

964.   **Merriam-Webster's Reader's Handbook.** Springfield, Mass., Merriam-Webster, 1997. 597p. index. $14.95pa. ISBN 0-87779-620-3.

This reasonably priced paperback volume is a joint effort between Merriam-Webster and Encyclopaedia Britannica. It contains nearly 2,000 entries on literary terms, styles, genres, and movements. No people are given entries, but the proper name index at the end of the volume leads to entries where they are mentioned. Cross-references or references to *compare* to other entries are frequently given. Some entries acknowledge the importance of other terms by defining them as well, hence the similarity between the entries for *metonymy* and *synecdoche*. Terms are often explained through example; for instance, the striking clock in William Shakespeare's *Julius Caesar* is used to illustrate *anachronism*. Secondary definitions are given if applicable.

Entries are not always thorough. For example, the one on *sublime* mentions Longinus but not Edmund Burke, and it only briefly mentions the Romantic poets. Some terms or movements are missing entirely. There are no entries on either postcolonial literature or criticism or orientalism. In fact, Edward Said is only briefly mentioned in the article on *deconstruction*. For a book that claims to be "Your Complete Guide to Literary Terms" (front cover), such gaps are disturbing. However, no book with such ambitious scope can hope to cover everything.

There are a variety of books on literary terms, some more complete than others. This one not only covers numerous terms but attempts to do so in a comprehensive and intelligible fashion. Although not filling a pressing need for literary handbooks, *Merriam-Webster's Reader's Handbook* should not be eliminated from purchasing contention. At the price, libraries should definitely consider it. Individuals should consider it as well.

—**Melissa Rae Root**

Handbooks and Yearbooks

965.   **Contemporary Literary Criticism Yearbook 1996, Volume 99: The Year in Fiction, Poetry, Drama, and World Literature....** Deborah A. Stanley and others, eds. Detroit, Gale, 1997. 547p. illus. index. $134.00. ISBN 0-7876-1063-1.

966.   **Contemporary Literary Criticism, Volume 100: Excerpts from Criticism of the Works of Today's Novelists, Poets, Playwrights....** Deborah A. Stanley and others, eds. Farmington Hills, Mich., Gale, 1997. 459p. illus. index. $134.00. ISBN 0-7876-1066-6.

967.   **Contemporary Literary Criticism, Volume 101: Excerpts from Criticism of the Works of Today's Novelists, Poets, Playwrights....** Deborah A. Stanley and others, eds. Detroit, Gale, 1997. 517p. illus. index. $134.00. ISBN 0-7876-1191-3.

968.   **Contemporary Literary Criticism, Volume 102: Excerpts from Criticism of the Works of Today's Novelists, Poets, Playwrights....** Deborah A. Schmitt and others, eds. Detroit, Gale, 1998. 485p. illus. index. $134.00. ISBN 0-7876-1192-1.

969.   **Contemporary Literary Criticism, Volume 103: Excerpts from Criticism of the Works of Today's Novelists, Poets, Playwrights....** Deborah A. Schmitt and others, eds. Detroit, Gale, 1998. 525p. illus. index. $134.00. ISBN 0-7876-1193-X.

In 1990, Gale introduced the *Yearbook* as part of its Contemporary Literary Criticism series (CLC). The *Yearbook* became an integral component of the five or six volumes of criticism issued annually on creative writers currently living or deceased after 1959.

Like its companion volumes, the *Yearbook* excerpts criticism. But its scope adds further dimensions to the series. The purpose of the *Yearbook* is to survey trends and events in contemporary literature and its genres, to introduce new authors, to list literary prizewinners, and to review the work of writers who died during the year. Coverage is international, featuring in the 1996 volume writers such as Wislawa Szymborska, the Polish recipient of the Nobel Prize for Literature in 1996 among "Prizewinners," and the Japanese writer Shusaku Endo in the "In Memoriam" section.

Another significant feature of the *Yearbook* is its "Topic(s) in Literature" section, which in this volume is devoted to true-crime literature. This section of excerpts gives extensive coverage to one or more topics under current discussion. Topics in previous yearbooks included, among others, "Multiculturalism in Literature and Education" (1991, v.70); "Feminism in the 1990s" (1992, v.76); "Revising the Literary Canon" (1993, v.81); and "The Vietnam War in Literature and Film" (1995, v.91).

Like earlier volumes in the CLC series the volumes under review reproduce excerpts from about 500 sources of criticism on novelists, poets, essayists, dramatists, screenwriters, science fiction and mystery writers, writers of children's literature, literary and social critics, foreign authors, and authors representing ethnic groups in the United States. These volumes feature 8 to 11 entries per volume, following a trend toward fewer writers covered in greater depth.

CLC culls excerpts from both scholarly and popular sources of criticism and explication, from book reviews and other general magazines, scholarly journals, monographs, and other books, as well as interviews, feature articles, and other published writings. As has been past practice, excerpts appear in chronological sequence, tracking the critical response to an author's work.

Volumes 100 to 103 continue to reflect the diversity of creative writers characteristic of the series as a whole. A new entry on Salman Rushdie concentrating on *The Moor's Last Sigh* joins critical excerpts on Joseph Brodsky, Carson McCullers, Cormac McCarthy, Theodore Roethke, Harold Bloom, Maya Deren, and Fritz Lang. These volumes, together with the *Yearbook*, provide a lot of literary information. They maintain the high quality of the series, making it an indispensable source for both public and academic libraries.—**Bernice Bergup**

970. **Dictionary of Literary Biography Yearbook: 1996.** Samuel W. Bruce and L. Kay Webster, eds. Farmington Hills, Mich., Gale, 1997. 375p. illus. index. $140.00. ISBN 0-8103-9972-5.

971. **Dictionary of Literary Biography Yearbook: 1997.** Matthew J. Bruccoli and George Garrett, eds. Farmington Hills, Mich., Gale, 1998. 453p. illus. index. $140.00. ISBN 0-7876-2519-1.

Each volume of the *Dictionary of Literary Biography Yearbook* (DLB) presents an eclectic mix of information. Each contains survey articles on the year's literary works, interviews with literary personalities, updates on literary figures covered in previous volumes of the DLB series, and articles on more specific topics. Both volumes under review include survey articles on "The Year in" the genres of poetry, fiction, literary biography, drama, and children's literature. Both volumes also offer articles on authors whose centenaries were celebrated recently—F. Scott Fitzgerald, Ira Gershwin, and John Dos Passos in 1996; and William Faulkner, Stephen Vincent Benét, and Thornton Wilder in 1997. Other articles that appear in each volume include one on book reviewing, one on the current Nobel Prize winner in literature, and a conversation with a publisher. The interview in the 1996 volume is with James Laughlin. In the 1997 volume four publishers are profiled, including the editor/publisher of an online literary magazine. Each volume also includes a necrology; a list of literary awards and honors awarded during the year; and "Checklist: Contributions to Literary History and Biography," which is a selected list of new books on literary and cultural history.

The 1997 volume offers several articles on the Internet's connection with literature, including an article on John Updike's foray into cyberwriting; a bibliographic essay on author Internet sites; and the aforementioned interview with Katherine McNamara, editor/publisher of an online literary magazine.

As with the earlier volumes, these editions of the *Yearbook* try to give a flavor of important events and scholarship in literature. Libraries that subscribe to the series will want to acquire all volumes.

—**Terry Ann Mood**

972. Kehler, Dorothea. **Problems in Literary Research: A Guide to Selected Reference Works.** 4th ed. Lanham, Md., Scarecrow, 1997. 230p. index. $32.50; $20.00pa. ISBN 0-8108-3216-X; 0-8108-3217-8pa.

The 4th edition of this resource differs little from the 3d edition (see ARBA 88, entry 1119) in terms of format and content. The 5 chapters cover in detail 36 reference works deemed essential, focusing in particular on English and American literature. Titles such as *The Oxford English Dictionary*, *MLA International Bibliography*, the American Library Association's *Guide to Reference Books*, *Dissertation Abstracts International*, and *Essay and General Literature Index* are found here. The detailed descriptions of the reference sources are followed by research questions. A final section of the text deals more cursorily with 180 works, including new entries for the subjects of world literature, technical writing, and writing across the curriculum. Not all entries here feature annotations, although many do.

A couple of problems mar the text. Although the preface stresses the use of the most current edition of any reference work, the material in the back of the text does not always list the most current edition. For example, the 3d edition of *Benét's Reader's Encyclopedia* is the one listed here, even though the 4th edition appeared in 1996. Perhaps the preface serves as a warning, recommending that students not necessarily use the edition listed here but seek out the newest one. Kehler's caveat should be sufficient as long as readers are aware that newer editions may be available. Another difficulty occurs in the "General Review" sections, which list more general queries than the research questions without elucidating in which books the answers can be found. It is up to the diligent student to ascertain where to find the answer. However, instruction and comprehension of the material appear to be goals of the book, so this haziness can be forgiven.

Despite its reference focus, this guide does not really operate as a reference text. The main resources discussed herein will already be owned by a reference library, virtually nullifying its collection development utility. *Problems in Literary Research* will best serve teachers and students of bibliography, literature, or research classes. The research questions give opportunity for hands-on activity in the library, ensuring a student's understanding of the tools through direct interaction.—**Melissa Rae Root**

973. **Nineteenth-Century Literature Criticism, Volume 61: Criticism of the Works of Novelists, Poets, Playwrights....** Gerald R. Barterian, Denise Evans, and Mary L. Onorato, eds. Detroit, Gale, 1998. 491p. illus. index. $140.00. ISBN 0-7876-1127-1.

974. **Nineteenth-Century Literature Criticism, Volume 62: Criticism of the Works of Novelists, Poets, Playwrights....** Gerald R. Barterian and Denise Evans, eds. Detroit, Gale, 1998. 498p. illus. index. $145.00. ISBN 0-7876-1243-X.

This well-established set complements Gale's other series in literary criticism, surveying major authors—primarily American, British, and European—who died between 1800 and 1899. Each entry includes an introduction, a list of principal works, a "criticism" section in which excerpts are reprinted in a chronological arrangement, and a reading list. Some articles concentrate on a particular work or update previous entries with more recent criticism. In volumes 61 and 62, 6 of the 11 authors have been covered before by *Nineteenth-Century Literature Criticism* (NCLC). Every fourth volume is a "topics volume," concentrating on such subjects as U.S. slave narratives and the Gothic novel. There are cumulative author, nationality, and topic indexes to all the Gale literary criticism series. Title indexes are included for each volume.

In earlier years (NCLC began publication in 1981), excerpts were rather short—a few paragraphs taken from a 15-page essay, for example. Approximately 30 authors could be covered in a single volume. Over the years the amount of critical material excerpted has increased; in many cases a chapter, book introduction, or article is now reprinted in its entirety. Recently, the critics' original footnotes and bibliographies have been incorporated into the excerpts as well. Currently each volume covers only five or six authors, but the critical information is so much more complete that students using the set may no longer find it necessary to seek out the original source. This is one of the features that make the set popular in libraries serving undergraduates and high school students and those who do not have access to large collections.—**Emily L. Werrell**

975. **Representative American Speeches, 1937-1997.** Calvin McLeod Logue and others, eds. Bronx, N.Y., H. W. Wilson, 1997. 778p. index. $55.00. ISBN 0-8242-0931-1.

Representative American Speeches, 1937-1997 is a compilation of more than 150 speeches gleaned from some 1,250 speeches previously printed in H. W. Wilson's annual *Representative American Speeches* volumes (see ARBA 98, entry 1131 for a review). Each speech is preceded by a brief biography of the speaker and an introduction providing the context of the speech and highlights of the speaker's most important points. Back material includes an alphabetic index to speakers, ranging from Bella Abzug to Whitney Young, and a subject index that begins with *abortion* and ends with *zionism*.

As with other volumes in this series, the chosen speeches are arranged in 16 categories: political community; nature and function of government; civil liberties; international affairs; war; human rights; civil rights; media; education; the arts; religion; business, industry, and labor; science, technology, and space; environment; urban issues; and crime and terrorism. According to the editor, the speeches chosen for inclusion in this volume "address themes which are relevant to both today's citizenry and, potentially, to people of the twenty-first century."

No doubt some will question the inclusion of some speeches and the exclusion of others. Few would question the presence of Martin Luther King Jr.'s "I Have a Dream" speech; others might wish that Carl Sagan had been represented by something other than his "Thoughts on the 125th Anniversary of the Battle of Gettysburg." On the whole, however, *Representative American Speeches, 1937-1997* succeeds admirably in presenting a wide diversity of opinion as reflected by the public discourse of these important decades.—**Kay O. Cornelius**

976.   **St. James Guide to Horror, Ghost, & Gothic Writers.** David Pringle, ed. Detroit, St. James Press, 1998. 746p. index. $140.00. ISBN 1-55862-206-3.

Issued as a companion to the *St. James Guide to Fantasy Writers* (see ARBA 97, entry 950), this volume provides biographical data and critical assessments on the lives and fiction of 425 English-language and 25 foreign-language writers. Entries generally range from 1,000 to 1,500 words (excluding bibliographies), and have been contributed by such cognoscenti as S. T. Joshi, Brian Stableford, and Mike Ashley. It should be noted, however, that the factuality and critical objectivity of eight entries is suspect, having been partially composed by the contributors themselves.

As a 1-volume resource for this genre, the breadth of coverage is commendable. More than a dozen authors born in the eighteenth century are found in its pages (Horace Walpole, Ann Radcliffe, M. G. Lewis, Mary Shelley, Charles Brockden Brown). Also, Victorian writers, such as A. M. Burrage, J. Sheridan Le Fanu, and Richard Marsh, are well represented.

The preponderance of entries examine the oeuvres of twentieth-century authors, such as T. E. D. Klein, Lisa Tuttle, Steve Rasnic Tem, and Stephen King. (Approximately 100 of the entrants were born after 1949.) Absent, however, are such Gothic romance writers as Victoria Holt, Barbara Michaels, Phyllis Whitney, Catherine Cookson, and Norah Lofts.

Although this work primarily spotlights fiction dominated by menacing supernatural forces and entities, this guide also discusses a fair number of psychological thrillers, such as those typical of Mary Higgins Clark, Robin Cook, William Golding, and Peter Benchley. Moreover, the editor has allotted space for writers popular with youngsters and adolescents, such as R. L. Stine, Christopher Pike, and Gary Crew. Lois Duncan and Robert Cormier have been passed over, regrettably. Writers of macabre yarns who have plied their trade for both adult and juvenile audiences are occasionally included (e.g., Walter de la Mare). Even the accomplishments of some graphic novelists are scrutinized (e.g., Neil Gaiman, Alan Brennert, and Tim Lucas). Authors who are rarely associated with blood-chilling works crop up as well (e.g., A. E. Coppard, John Updike, Harlan Ellison, and Jerzy Kosinski).

The capsules of biographical data preceding the respective entry articles often contain unexpected nuggets— obscure horror writer J. W. Brodie-Innes was a friend of Bram Stoker, Robert Aickman was the grandson of Richard Marsh, short story writer Robert Arthur is distinguished from the movie producer of the same name. Besides standard data (such as pseudonyms, publisher addresses, date of death), less accessible information appears in many entries. This includes nonscholarly occupations, names of spouse(s) and children, professional affiliations, and military service.

The bibliographies for such writers as Arthur Conan Doyle, H. G. Wells, and John Buchan are particularly lengthy, rife with many titles outside the ostensible scope of this volume. As a result, valuable space has been squandered that otherwise could have accommodated entries for such overlooked masters as Washington Irving, Amelia B. Edwards, Clara Reeve, Davis Grubb, Edward D. Hoch, John Bellairs, Jack Dann, Marie Belloc Lowndes, and Amelie Nothomb.

The horrific works of the writers who have been featured in this guide, however, have been analyzed therein with confidence, insight, balance, and candor. In critiquing Nancy Baker's fiction, Pauline Morgan observes, "Baker's plots are internally consistent but her characters lack the edge of bizarreness that would make these vampire novels really stand out from the rest" (p. 29). Nor is scholar Jack Adrian timid with his pronouncement regarding D. K. Broster: "Viewed dispassionately, it is difficult not to come to the conclusion that Dorothy Broster was one of the great schizophrenics of literature" (p. 95).

In general, currency of data extends to late-1997. For example, the 1997 deaths of William S. Burroughs and Carl Jacobi are reported. Unfortunately, however, the 1997 novel *Son of Rosemary* is not mentioned in the Ira Levin entry, nor is the acclaimed 1997 novel of murderous suspense, *The Ax*, cited in the Donald E. Westlake entry. Also unaccountable is the absence of even so much as estimates for the birth years of about 20 authors.

Cross-referencing between articles is incomplete. Although Susan Hill's *Mrs. de Winter* is identified (p. 270) as the sequel to Daphne du Maurier's *Rebecca*, no such information appears in the du Maurier entry itself. The volume's title index, which lists series, fails to include Clive Barker's *Books of Blood*. Also, this resource's name index is but a duplicative expansion of the "List of Entrants" at the outset of the book. Furthermore, the addition of a subject or theme index would greatly enhance the value of this guide. Despite these shortcomings, this is a praiseworthy reference source that complements both the preceding volume, as well as Mike Ashley and William Contento's *Supernatural Index* (see ARBA 96, entry 1194). [R: SLJ, Nov 98, p. 158; Choice, July/Aug 98, p. 1832]—**Jeffrey E. Long**

977.   **Scribner Writers Series.** selected authors ed. [CD-ROM]. New York, Scribner's/Simon & Schuster Macmillan, 1997. $650.00. Minimum system requirements: IBM or compatible 486/66MHz. CD-ROM drive. 16MB RAM. 20MB hard disk space. SVGA monitor. ISBN 0-684-80502-2.

This compact disk contains full-text essays on 808 "frequently requested writers and works." The essays are derived from the print sets of the Scribner Writers Series and the complete content of the base sets of the American Writers (1974) and British Writers Series (1979). The system runs on a Web browser interface, although an Internet connection is not required to run the database. When loading the database for the first time, the system asks the user to create a personal profile to keep each user's settings, preferences, bookmarks, and stored messages separate from those of other users of the Netscape Navigator 4.0 that is required to run the system. The introductory screen presents two sets of access points into the database. The most prominent set of links provide four different ways to search the database. The in-depth searching link brings up a template that allows the user to search by name, literary genre, sex, keyword, language, time period, and ethnicity or nationality. The "Research Ideas" button leads to information by broadly defined genre, such as African American male writers; time period, such as Renaissance writers; or specialized categories, such as prize-winning books. The third selection lists writers and works alphabetically. An alphabet at the top allows the user to jump down the list. The final link brings up a separate text box that provides definitions of literary terms derived from the 7th edition of Prentice Hall's *A Handbook of Literature*. The second set of links on the opening screen provides searching, printing, and citing tips as well as information about the Writers series.

A typical search using the in-depth searching link presents a list of hits that are grouped in sets of 12 for large returns. Author profiles include an extensive descriptive essay, the citation to the print equivalent of the Writers Series, and a selected, but usually comprehensive, bibliography of works both by and about the writer. A link at the top of the entry allows the user to jump down to the bibliography. The literacy genre essays are formatted in the same way and are also accompanied by a comprehensive bibliography.

The content of this database is clearly presented and adheres to the "three click rule" (requires three or fewer clicks to move from any found information back to the main menu). Every essay screen includes a menu bar that links back to the opening screen options and a help button that opens a separate text box for screen-specific instructions. The icon to searching tips merely provides a link to the "In-Depth Searching Help" box. Printing information from the disk is completed using the "Clip Print" function in an easy, six-step process. The system also allows the user to save text in Microsoft Word "doc" format. Cross-reference links are imbedded in the text of each essay, and searched keyword terms are highlighted in bold. A technical reference guide with detailed installation and search instructions is included, listing appropriate language, time period, and ethnicity or nationality fields. The system requires an IBM compatible computer and 20MB of free hard drive space. A toll-free telephone number is available for free technical assistance. This is an outstanding resource and an excellent example of how a traditional print resource can be enhanced and made more accessible in an electronic format.

Suggestions for improvement are to alphabetize grouped results and utilize stronger colors in some cases (for example, the cross-reference links in texts) to make them more readable. [R: BL, 15 May 98, p. 1660, 1662; Choice, Nov 98, p. 494]—**Robert V. Labaree**

978.   **Scribner's Writer's Series on CD-ROM: Comprehensive Edition.** [CD-ROM]. New York, Macmillan Library Reference/Simon & Schuster Macmillan, 1997. $999.00. ISBN 0-684-80552-9.

The *Scribner's Writer's Series on CD-ROM: Comprehensive Edition* collects 1,545 critical, evaluative, biographical essays and their complete bibliographies from 13 Scribner sets previously published in paper on U.S., Continental, and international authors, including authors of genre fiction. Some of the essays are not entirely current, but by virtue of the many ways they can be searched using an interface (which launches a familiar Netscape front end), this CD-ROM would be an excellent tool for those researching a variety of literature. One may search for specific authors or browse alphabetically; use a short list of genre-related and time period-oriented research ideas; use the options under "In Depth Search," with drop-down menus for sex, nationality, genre, language, nationality, or time period; or combine searches in different fields with an implied "and." Keyword searching is supported, and keywords can be combined with Boolean terms in a text entry box. Most valuable are the extensive use of hyperlinks between and within articles and links from literary terms to their definitions in the "Handbook of Literary Terms." An easy-to-find help button and conventions such as the default "and" in a keyword string unless parentheses are used will make the CD-ROM easy for librarians to use and teach, though the clip print function may prove to be more trouble than it is worth.

The research ideas include lists of prize-winning authors as catalysts for research, including many who are not included in the database; however, it is remarkable that 11 Newbery winners are represented. Both Scribner and Twayne can be opened in multiple windows, making comparisons between authors or works easier to do. This resource offers a quick, powerful, and understandable interface to a multitude of good works and will be welcome in any college or university library.—**Jennie Ver Steeg**

979.   **Twayne's World Authors.** [CD-ROM]. New York, G. K. Hall/Simon & Schuster Macmillan, 1997. Minimum system requirements: IBM or compatible 486. CD-ROM drive. 16MB RAM. 16MB hard disk space. SVGA monitor. $1,243.75. ISBN 0-7838-1718-5.

Twayne's World Authors, using the Macmillan Library Reference interface, shares many of the same assets as *Scribner's Writer's Series on CD-ROM* (see entry 978), with real production value without sacrificing load time (though one might expect a bit more lag using Windows 3.1), contextual help a click away, and a variety of ways to search by taking advantage of hyperlinks to related chapters and books. Like *Scribner's*, it gives the option of accessing chapters and entire entries from an alphabetic author list or of doing an in-depth search by genre, sex, time period, or other options. This product, however, contains 200 articles, some nearly book length, which provide thorough introductory criticism and overviews of the lives and writings of writers from ancient Greece to the present. One may also search or browse the authors or search a short list of research ideas, the strength of which is in showing connections between authors. The researcher will likely make the most use of the options under "In Depth Search," where searches using drop-down menus in sex, genre, and other fields can be combined with an implied "and," or do a full-text keyword search. Keywords can be combined with Boolean terms in the keyword text box. Each author entry has a hyperlinked table of contents, timeline, and bibliography, including a link to how the entry can be cited in a research paper, which is a valuable feature. Keyword searches scan full text, and the results are displayed in full chapters, as opposed to pulling out individual paragraphs that include the keyword(s); *Twayne's* gives a bit of context and continuity. Also, if searching the keyword "African American" pulls up a given chapter of the monograph on Lorraine Hansberry, the searcher is given the option of seeing the chapters that precede and follow the chapter displayed.

The CD-ROM's box indicates that readers would feel compelled to read the original monographs from which the entries were derived, to bring to the reading a basic knowledge. That is precisely what the reader will gain from this collection. This product will be useful for upper-level high school students as well as liberal arts students needing cogent and well-presented introductory insights. [R: BL, 1 Sept 98, p. 165]—**Jennie Ver Steeg**

980.   **Twentieth-Century Literary Criticism Topics Volume, Volume 70: Excerpts from Criticism of Various Topics in Twentieth-Century Literature....** Scott Peacock, Jennifer Gariepy, and Thomas Ligotti, eds. Detroit, Gale, 1997. 483p. index. $134.00. ISBN 0-7876-1170-7.

981.   **Twentieth-Century Literary Criticism, Volume 71: Excerpts form Criticism of the Works of Novelists, Poets, Playwrights, Short Stories, and Other Creative Writers....** Jennifer Gariepy and Thomas Ligotti, eds. Detroit, Gale, 1997. 527p. illus. index. $134.00. ISBN 0-7876-1172-7.

982.   **Twentieth-Century Literary Criticism, Volume 72: Excerpts from Criticism of the Works of Novelists, Poets, Playwrights, Short Stories, and Other Creative Writers....** Jennifer Gariepy and Thomas Ligotti, eds. Detroit, Gale, 1997. 529p. index. $134.00. ISBN 0-7876-1174-3.

Every fourth volume of Gale's *Twentieth-Century Literary Criticism* (TCLC) contains three to six broad thematic surveys, rather than treatments of specific authors or titles. Although "author" volumes in the series are restricted to people who died in the 1900 to 1960 period, the "topic" volumes may have a wider time frame. Volume 70 covers four subjects: "Alcohol and Literature," "Buddhism and Literature," "Modernism," and "Popular Literature." Each topic shares certain standard features, such as a brief introduction defining the topic, a list of representative works, often an overview, and further readings. Within this common framework, further categories are established as appropriate (e.g., genre, geography, and others). The well-chosen critical essays (some excerpted and all previously published) are given in chronological order.

All four of the topics surveyed provide good introductions to their subjects, although this reviewer would argue that better choices are available for some of the representative works. The essays presented under "Modernism" and "Popular Literature" present extraordinarily diverse collections of materials, owing, in no small measure, to the hazy outlines of the topics themselves. Each critical essay is prefaced by a helpful two- to three-sentence description enabling the reader to decide if the essay is relevant to his or her particular interest.

Volumes 71 and 72 are "author" volumes, with the exception of the latter's 150-page *omnium gatherum* devoted to Thomas Hardy's *Jude the Obscure* (1895). The remaining 16 authors are most notable for their diversity and, in some cases, for the obscurity of their connection to literature or even to the printed word. The Japanese and German-American film directors Kenji Mizguchi and Erich von Stroheim are both worthy of inclusion in cinematic reference works, but they are not literary figures, nor is statesman John Foster Dulles. Equally marginal to literature are Mary Baker Eddy, founder of Christian Science, and psychiatrist Karen Horney in volume 72. The inclusion of Russian philosopher and mystic G. I. Gurdjieff (*Meetings with Remarkable Men*) and German philosopher Hans Vaihinger (*The Philosophy of "As If "*) is more plausible because they both wrote works that either were fictional or had far-reaching implications for literature.

The TCLC volumes are a valuable series of reference works. There is no other source where researchers can find both basic facts about a writer and a well-chosen array of diverse opinions about his or her work. The utility of the series is greatly enhanced by the inclusion in each volume of updated cumulative indexes arranged by author, topic, and nationality. The author and topic indexes also include cross-references to entries in others of the numerous Gale reference series. Each volume contains its own book title index, enabling the user to immediately locate all of the information on any given work without perusing an entire article. These durable volumes will withstand years of heavy use.—**D. Barton Johnson**

983.   **World Literature Criticism Supplement: A Selection of Major Authors from Gale's Literary Criticism Series.** Polly Vedder, ed. Detroit, Gale, 1997. 2v. illus. index. $125.00/set. ISBN 0-7876-1696-6.

This 2-volume set is a supplement to the 5-volume *World Literature Criticism: 1500 to the Present* (see ARBA 93, entry 1119). The set at hand stretches coverage further back than the original, including such authors as St. Augustine, the *Beowulf*-poet, Confucius, and Muhammad, as well as adding newer authors like Nikki Giovanni and Salman Rushdie. Nonfiction writers, such as Martin Luther King Jr., Benjamin Franklin, Niccolo Machiavelli, and Plato are also profiled. The authors treated were selected by an advisory committee formed of teachers and librarians. The information presented is culled from Gale's Literary Criticism Series. The author, nationality, and title indexes at the end of volume 2 reference the earlier set as well as this update.

Each entry is composed of a picture of the author, an introduction, biographical information, a rundown of major works, an introduction of the critical reception, and excerpts from critical assessments. The critical assessments are duplicates of those that have appeared in other Gale works, such as in volumes of the Contemporary Literary Criticism series. The other information is often elementary and not very satisfying. The biographies and critical reception introductions skim the surface, glossing over interesting facts or controversies. For example, in Alice Walker's entry, the biography discusses her marriage to Melvyn Leventhal and the fact that they were the first interracial couple to reside in Jackson, Mississippi, but it does not mention the effect of that marriage on

Walker's career or that by contemporary Mississippi law, the union was illegal. Later on, when the entry is discussing *The Color Purple*, the writer classifies the relationship between Celie and Shug as an "intimate friendship," ignoring the lesbian aspects of that relationship. The commentary on *Possessing the Secret of Joy* refers to the protagonist as "Toshi" rather than Tashi, one of many typographical errors in the text. Finally, the excerpt from *In Search of Our Mothers' Gardens* defining the term *womanist* is so reduced as to detract from Walker's ideas (and where that definition comes from is not cited).

Finally, each entry gives reference to where author profiles appear elsewhere in the Gale family of literary criticism works, suggesting that there is nothing new here. The shallowness of the introductory information implies that this set is meant for school libraries; academic libraries can certainly pass on its purchase, especially if they already own other Gale series. School libraries may consider purchase, or they may give younger students some credit and allow them to consult more thorough and in-depth sources—including the critical essays excerpted here. Aside from the criticisms previously laid out, one has to ask: If Gale went to the trouble of continuing this set and expanding coverage, why not make it broader than 50 people?—**Melissa Rae Root**

Indexes

984. **Scribner's Writers Series Master Index.** New York, Macmillan Library Reference/Simon & Schuster Macmillan, 1998. 323p. $85.00. ISBN 0-684-80557-X.

Any library owning more than two or three works in the Scribner Writers Series will want to own this master index. Essentially a listing of the writers and essays in the 17 Scribner sets published through December 1997, this single volume provides a relatively easy look-up of the articles. However, this is not a keyword index and the volume lacks a comprehensive index to all of the entries. The user must refer to the table of contents preceding the entries in order to select from the alphabetic lists of subjects (subdivided into writers and themes, genres, collectives, and works) and the lists of subjects by period, language, nationality, genre, and special categories (e.g., Women and African American writers). There are also volume-by-volume lists of the contents of each of the volumes in the collections.

Although the lists of subjects contain a few cross-references, a single alphabetic index to all of the entries would have been desirable. Presumably it would not have been a difficult task to supply such an index for this volume with today's advances in technology. The volume is recommended for libraries that own the series, as noted above.—**Ingrid Schierling Burnett**

985. Semmes, Clovis E., comp. **Roots of Afrocentric Thought: A Reference Guide to *Negro Digest/Black World*, 1961-1976.** Westport, Conn., Greenwood Press, 1998. 322p. index. (Bibliographies and Indexes in Afro-American and African Studies, no.35). $75.00. ISBN 0-313-29992-7.

This reference guide to *Negro Digest* is an important contribution to African American studies. *Negro Digest* is the small, monthly magazine that helped to launch John H. Johnson as one of this country's most successful African American entrepreneurs. Johnson, who is better known as the publisher of *Ebony* magazine, began publishing *Negro Digest* in 1942 in an effort to combat negative and often inaccurate information about black people. Clovis Semmes's introduction succinctly summarizes the impact the magazine, and its 1961 successor *Black World*, had on black intellectuals and political and social activists.

Many of the essays published in *Negro Digest* from 1942 until it was discontinued in 1951 were reprinted from newspapers and scholarly books and journals. It was revived in 1961 under the direction of Hoyt Fuller, who began including more original articles and reviews. In 1970 Fuller changed the magazine's name to *Black World*. This guide, which is divided into 2 parts, covers the period beginning in 1961 through 1976 when the magazine was once again discontinued. Part 1 provides annotations of original articles and speeches in 4 categories: literature and literary criticism, history, mass media and the arts, and social and political analysis. Part 2 lists creative works and reviews and interviews alphabetically by author under the topics of poetry, short stories and plans, reviews, and interviews. Together they include 3,525 entries of works by and about black people, some of which offer a pan-African perspective. Students and scholars working in African American studies will find that their task of researching this magazine has been lightened considerably by this well-documented book. It is particularly recommended for researchers and students interested in the black arts movement of the 1960s. [R: Choice, Sept 98, p. 84]—**Sandra Adell**

CHILDREN'S AND YOUNG
ADULT LITERATURE

General Works

986. **Something About the Author: Facts and Pictures About the Authors and Illustrators of Books for Young People. Volume 94.** Alan Hedblad, ed. Detroit, Gale, 1998. 244p. illus. $85.00. ISBN 0-7876-1147-6.

This series serves the many elementary schools that require basic information about the authors of books for children and young adults. The editors seek to include in each volume both the authors of books that have status as classics and currently popular writers, keeping abreast of whose books remain popular and whose are of increasing interest to young people. The volume includes updated entries for exceptionally productive authors, and obituaries recap the work of deceased authors. For each entry, bulleted items include personal information, addresses (including e-mail, where available), career, awards, honors, writings, works in progress, sidelights, and a section for more information. Sources include published materials as well as author questionnaires. Editor Alan Hedblad says that this series has not yet been made available on CD-ROM, as young readers continue to prefer to browse the entries and 150 or more illustrations in the hardcopy volumes. A version available on CD-ROM, *Junior Discovery Authors*, which focuses on major children's and young adult authors, is gaining in popularity. Where budgets allow and curriculum warrants, schools should get both.—**Edna M. Boardman**

987. **Something About the Author: Facts and Pictures About Authors and Illustrators of Books for Young People. Volume 95.** Alan Hedblad, ed. Detroit, Gale, 1998. 323p. illus. index. $85.00. ISBN 0-7876-1148-4.

Something About the Author is an ongoing reference series that examines the lives and works of authors and illustrators of books for children. Volume 95 features approximately 105 authors or illustrators and 5 obituary notices, including that of Elspeth Huxley.

A typical entry includes personal data; addresses for home, office, and e-mail; career data; awards and honors; bibliography of works; adaptations of works; works in progress; references for further reading; and photographs, book illustrations, movie stills, or any other interesting visual work that may supplement the text. A section titled "Sidelights" discusses themes of works, anecdotes, quotations, and thoughts from the biographee as well as other pertinent information.

A new policy for the series is that indexes no longer appear in every volume, but are included in alternate (odd-numbered) volumes of the series, beginning with Volume 57. Volume 95 includes both illustrator and author cumulative indexes.

Those familiar with this series will find no surprises; the mission is to provide often hard-to-find information on authors and illustrators, both well known and lesser known, of children's literature. School and public libraries will want the latest volumes in the series.—**Dana McDougald**

988. **Something About the Author Autobiography Series, Volume 25.** Linda R. Andres and Marilyn O'Connell Allen, eds. Detroit, Gale, 1998. 391p. illus. index. $96.00. ISBN 0-7876-0118-7.

Gale has such a good thing going with this series that it is hard to come up with improvements. The current volume presents 16 well-chosen subjects fully self-described. The front matter, consisting of a table of contents, preface, sampler, and acknowledgments, precedes compelling personal narratives. For example, Claire MacKay's energized comments on the impetus to her career: "It was time to put up or shut up. Did I want to write? If the answer was yes—and it was, a resounding yes!—then I had to get at it." These short, incisive takes include a variety of studio and action snapshots along with art; for example, a photograph of Karen Hesse in stage makeup (p. 128), Peter Catalonotto's painting (p. 48), an illustration from Ted Lewin's unpublished *Souk in Marrekesh* (p. 181), and a drawing from Betsy Lewin's *Hounds and Hunter* (p. 165). A sizable but well-organized cumulative author list ties the volume to the 417 autobiographical sketches in its 24 predecessors for a grand total of 433 candid self-introductions, followed by bibliographies divided into fiction, nonfiction, picture books, plays, illustrations, and contributions to periodicals. The book concludes with a three-column cumulative index containing authors (Richard Adams, Isak Dinesen, Cynthia Rylant), titles (*Little Women*, "Sword" trilogy), honors (*The New York Times* award, Child Study Children's Book Award), publishers (Parents Magazine Press, School Papers of Australia), experience (Vietnam war, China), institutions (U.S. Marine Corps, University of California at

Riverside), and subjects (suicide, actors). One of the best in standard reference works, Gale's Something About the Author series is recognized worldwide for quality and sensitivity to the vital links between the author, publishing market, librarian, teacher, researcher, and reader. Although small libraries must gulp at the high cost of investing in such sets, the value remains unquestionable. Unlike anything else in print or on the Internet, these overviews of careers hold the magic of the moment, the cause and ongoing purpose of creative lives.

—**Mary Ellen Snodgrass**

Children's Literature

Bibliography

989.   Allen, Ruth. **Children's Book Prizes: An Evaluation and History of Major Awards for Children's Books in the English-Speaking World.** Brookfield, Vt., Ashgate Publishing, 1998. 333p. index. $84.95. ISBN 1-85928-237-7.

Children's Book Prizes is acclaimed as one of the first comprehensive surveys of awards given to children's books in the English-speaking world. More than 40 different prizes are covered in this volume, including established ones, such as the Newbery Award and prizes awarded by the commercial sector, as well as awards sponsored nationally for illustrators, such as the Caldecott Award.

The author presents some interesting insight into the motivation behind the awards and how they are viewed by everyone concerned, including authors, illustrators, and publishers, as well as librarians, booksellers, and potential readers. One interesting aspect of the book is how the author compares awards, their history, and the readership of authors or illustrators who have won them. Winning titles are described in great detail and, where appropriate, the runners-up are noted in each year the awards were given. The books that did not win the awards but were nominated are mentioned, especially if they proved to be of a more lasting quality than those that did win. The criteria applied to the judging of the awards are examined by the author along with her assessment of whether the "right" results were achieved in their selection and whether the winners have stood up to the test of time.

This volume brings together in one source the most outstanding awards for children's books. Librarians will relish the idea of having the award winners at their fingertips in one volume. Researchers and book collectors interested in the history of the children's book industry will find this book invaluable. *Children's Book Prizes* is highly recommended.—**Betty J. Morris**

990.   Berman, Matt, and Marigny J. Dupuy. **Children's Book Awards Annual 1998.** Englewood, Colo., Libraries Unlimited, 1998. 117p. index. $18.50pa. ISBN 1-56308-649-2.

Even though current bibliographic guides to award-winning books and recommended reading lists for children are easy to locate, Berman and Dupuy's inaugural edition of *Children's Books Awards Annual* is a worthy endeavor. Book titles are entered alphabetically under 4 major sections: "Picture Books," "Chapter Books," "Young Adult Books," and "Personal Picks." Each book entry consists of side-by-side sections. On the left-hand side, along with the pertinent bibliographic citation, are age levels, type of book (fiction or nonfiction), genre/subject, and awards/lists citing the book. Titles were drawn from nine of the best known award lists, including the Newbery, Caldecott, Coretta Scott King, and Pura Belpre awards. Eight highly regarded "best books" lists were selected, including American Library Notable Children's Books, Booklist Editor's Choice, Bulletin of the Center for Children's Books, and School Library Journal Best Books. The annotations, both descriptive and evaluative, are written to reflect the essence of the book, highlighting special features as well as gently questioning other features. The reader must not neglect to check out the "Personal Picks" section as well. The 8 indexes provide multiple guides to the 150 titles. The nominal price, attractive and easy-to-follow format, the combining of best books with annual award-winning lists, and the currency of titles identify this bibliography as a "must have" for public and school libraries as well as a valuable guide for parents. [R: BL, 1 Dec 98, p. 687]

—**Margaret Denman-West**

991. **Children's Books from Other Countries.** Carl M. Tomlinson, ed. Lanham, Md., Scarecrow, 1998. 304p. index. $24.50pa. ISBN 0-8108-3447-2.

Tomlinson has compiled an important bibliography of international children's literature published in the United States. This information has not been readily available since 1978. The American Association of School Librarians, a division of the American Library Association, compiled this information for their publications entitled *Books from Other Countries, 1968-1971* and *1972-1976*. The series was discontinued after the 1978 publication, however, and nothing has been available to take its place until now. The publication is sponsored by the United States Board on Books for Young People and the national section of the International Board on Books for Young People. The board believes that if teachers, librarians, and other professionals working with children have access to quality international children's literature, they will promote the books to young people. Eventually, this culture sharing will lead to a greater understanding among children throughout the world as similarities in their life experiences become apparent in a global sense.

Tomlinson, a professor in language arts and children's literature at Northern Illinois University, has gathered together 724 titles, published between 1950 and 1996, from 29 different countries, for children ranging from infant to age 14. Many of the books are now out of print, but they are necessary for inclusion to present an accurate picture of the materials that were published during the time period and of the current availability of the books in public libraries because of their lasting merit.

Tomlinson states at the beginning of *Children's Books from Other Countries* that it is not an all-inclusive list of international literature published during the period. Rather, it is a manageable, straightforward presentation of quality titles that were either originally written in a non-English language and later translated to an English format or written in English but not originally published in the United States. The book then gives an overview of international children's literature that can be promoted to a young audience. Tomlinson also provides a thorough list of associations and publications dealing with international children's books and their addresses. The final third of the book is the bibliography, organized by genre and annotated by a group of professionals working in the field of children's literature.

Tomlinson's book is welcome coverage of international children's books that has been sorely missed during the past two decades. Teachers and public school librarians will find this book to be a worthwhile addition for broadening the scope of their collections. [R: Choice, Sept 98, p. 86]—**Bridget Volz**

992. **Children's Books in Print 1998: An Author, Title, and Illustrator Index to Books for Children and Young Adults.** New Providence, N.J., R. R. Bowker, 1997. 2v. $165.00/set. ISBN 0-8352-3952-7. ISSN 0069-3480.

Having the world of children's books reduced to two volumes is a handy tool for librarians, booksellers, teachers, parents, and researchers. Even better, the purchaser can choose print or CD-ROM for a reasonable price. The print version covers more than 126,000 titles and features a fair number of publisher-provided annotations in bold typeface. Volume 1, the authors and illustrators index, provides an explanation of organization and concludes with R. R. Bowker's telephone numbers and e-mail, Website, and hotline addresses. A 40-page compendium of book awards offers additional data to help librarians and educators beef up collections with the best works in print. Following a guide to abbreviations, the text begins in earnest, averaging 140 to 150 titles per page. Ample cross-referencing makes the link between authors and pseudonyms, as with "Bradbury, Pamela Z., jt. auth. *see* Smith, Kathie B." Volume 2 reprises the introductory material as a preface to the titles index. The final 136 pages list symbols and abbreviations of publishing houses (e.g., Gr Arts Ctr Pub for Graphic Arts Center Publishing Co.).

R. R. Bowker's annual Books in Print products have remained in production for more than 35 years and have maintained high standards of printed data that set the pace for lesser reference compendiums. One detriment to the dignity of so revered a company is the colored advertising inserts, which pop up in the opening pages of volume 2 as annoyingly as the intrusive advertisements so popular on videos. However, this is a minor complaint, considering the competition of Web book services to print reference works.—**Mary Ellen Snodgrass**

993. **From Biography to History: Best Books for Children's Entertainment and Education.** Catherine Barr, ed. New Providence, N.J., R. R. Bowker, 1998. 508p. illus. index. $59.95. ISBN 0-8352-4012-6.

Entries for nearly 300 prominent people, past and present, are alphabetically arranged in this bibliography of biographies and related books suitable for readers in grades 3 through 9. Although some entries are for world figures such as William Shakespeare and Michelangelo, about 90 percent are either American or closely related to U.S. history, like Christopher Columbus and Amerigo Vespucci. Choices reflect current curriculum and social concerns and emphases. For example, 75 entries are for women and 56 for African Americans. Most of the subjects are deceased, but such contemporaries as Bill Clinton and Oprah Winfrey are included. After a sentence or two identifying the subject and his or her importance, entries are frequently divided into 4 sections, each containing 1 to 3 recommended books: "Biographies for Younger Readers" (grades 3-5), "Biographies for Older Readers" (6-9), "Related Books for Younger Readers," and "Related Books for Older Readers" (one or more of these sections are often omitted depending on the availability of suitable books). "Related Books" explore topics associated with the individual subject (e.g., the entry under Charles Lindbergh contains general books on aviation). Each book entry supplies basic bibliographic information (prices are not given, but in-print status is indicated) and a short, six- to eight-line annotation that is both evaluative and descriptive. In selecting titles for inclusion, preliminary choices were made by consulting various reviewing sources, but final decisions were made by two distinguished children's librarians and reflect a high standard of quality. Most of the titles are current and in print. There are indexes by author, title, topics related to each person (e.g., abolitionists, Native Americans), and chronological periods in which the subjects lived. Although this work is not a priority purchase, this interesting title will be of use in elementary and middle schools as well as children's rooms in public libraries. [R: SLJ, Dec 98, p. 41]—**John T. Gillespie.**

994.   **A Guide to Children's Reference Works and Multimedia Material.** Susan Hancock, ed. Brookfield, Vt., Ashgate Publishing, 1998. 203p. index. $59.95. ISBN 1-85928-256-3.

    This guide to children's reference books provides information on more than 250 recently published reference titles for students pre-K to 14 years of age. Texts chosen for the volume are reviewed by four specialists in the areas of education, humanities, science, and multimedia. The books are also reviewed by another review panel, each consisting of students from elementary and middle schools.

    The book under review is composed of an introduction and six chapters. The introduction sets the stage for the book by defining reference books for children and providing a brief historical survey of alphabet books, dictionaries, atlases, and encyclopedias. Chapter 1 serves as a guide to the volume, describing content of the chapters and reviews. It also discusses the matching of children and texts and the National Curriculum England tests. Chapter 2 deals with alphabet and first word books for preschool children (four years of age and younger), other reference works for this age group, and the editor's personal selections. Based on the National Curriculum England guidelines, chapters 3 through 5 include books within each key stage (age groups 1, 2, and 3) and utilize the children's assessment panel where students review books they have used in their research. Chapter 3 provides a listing of publications for "key stage 1" children between 5 and 7 years. Chapter 4 provides publications for "key stage 2" children between 7 and 11 years. Chapter 5 offers reference works for "key stage 3" children (11 through 14). Chapter 6 deals with children's reference and multimedia resources in an electronic format, such as CD-ROMs, and other sources such as journals and the Internet. A glossary of technical jargon is included.

    There is not much consistency throughout the chapters in using the same features for each book reviewed, which would have improved the content. There were some obvious omissions in chapter 6, such as *World Book Encyclopedia*, which should have been added in the electronic reference works.

    Three features of the book helpful for making purchasing decisions are the editor's personal selections, the criteria for selection of CD-ROM, and the National Curriculum test scores, which indicate how useful a particular text is in covering curriculum subjects. The most outstanding feature of this book is the children's assessment of the books, which teachers will find most beneficial in book selection.—**Betty J. Morris.**

995.   **The Newbery and Caldecott Awards: A Guide to the Medal and Honor Books.** 1998 ed. By the Association for Library Service to Children. Chicago, American Library Association, 1998. 154p. index. $16.00pa. ISBN 0-8389-3484-6. ISSN 1070-4493.

    Indexed by title and author/illustrator, this inexpensive paperback reference book provides annotations for all winning titles and honor books since the inception of the Newbery and Caldecott Awards. Used for collection development and curriculum development and as a reader's advisory, it is an essential guide to children's literature for teachers as well as librarians.

The awards are listed in reverse chronological order, so one does not need to know the author/illustrator or title of a work in order to locate the winners for any given year. In fact, most of the questions this reviewer has been asked as a reference librarian about the awards are for the titles and authors/illustrators for the most recent year. This book is perfect for answering those and almost any other questions about the most prestigious awards given for children's literature. [R: BR, Nov/Dec 98, p. 85]—**Lois Gilmer**

996.   Riechel, Rosemarie. **Children's Nonfiction for Adult Information Needs: An Annotated Bibliography.** North Haven, Conn., Shoe String Press, 1998. 152p. index. $30.00. ISBN 0-208-02447-6.
    The information needs of adults who find reading English difficult can be met through this annotated bibliography of children's books. Recent immigrants, literacy students, high school equivalency students, and poor readers need books that are easy to read but not too childish for adult use. Riechel, with the help of librarians, teachers, and literacy association members, has selected 175 recently published nonfiction books to include in this bibliography.
    According to the introduction, titles were chosen according to the following criteria: (1) they cover popular but complex topics using clear language; (2) they are relatively easy to read; (3) they have accurate, well-researched texts; (4) they have appealing illustrations that enhance the text; (5) they have a minimum of "childish" features; (6) they are readily available in public library collections; and (7) they are recent. Organized into 15 subject areas, each entry includes full bibliographic information; pagination; series title (if applicable); and whether or not there is a glossary, a bibliography, or an index. The annotation describes the content of the book and notes any childish terms or illustrations that may detract from the work.
    An author/title index and a subject index make the information readily accessible to the reader or librarian. This volume is a valuable addition to public library collections. [R: BL, 15 Nov 98, pp. 606, 609]—**Sara R. Mack**

997.   Roberts, Patricia L. **Language Arts and Environmental Awareness: 100+ Integrated Books and Activities for Children.** North Haven, Conn., Linnet Professional Publications/Shoe String Press, 1998. 295p. index. $35.00. ISBN 0-208-02427-1.
    According to a Washington-based polling firm, it is children who are concerned about saving the environment and do more about it than their parents. If this is the case, then it is especially important that teachers, librarians, and parents make their children aware of environmental issues. This text combines books on environmental education with language arts activities.
    Grouping the activities according to the language arts focus for each book, children are involved in language (prose and poetry), listening, folk literature, reading, speaking, and writing. To make the books and activities more pertinent, they are subdivided in each category according to age groups 5 through 8 and 9 through 14. Full bibliographic information for each book is given, followed by the environmental context, a synopsis of the content, an activity with a language arts focus, and a home activity.
    Worthwhile and specific, the suggested learning tasks not only teach basic skills but also enrich the class-room experience. From doing interviews to writing an environmental journal and researching books and articles on ecology, there are hundreds of ideas for interrelating reading, writing, and speaking with making a child conscious of the need for recycling, reducing, and reusing materials.
    All suggestions are for the most part absolutely correct. Only one minor error was found in the chapter involving children in writing, ages 5 through 8. In the example of the personal letter the letter writer's name was written above the inside address. (Not just a typographical error, it was done in two different letters.)
    This book will be useful not only to classroom teachers and librarians, it will be of value to parents, especially those who are homeschooling their children. It is recommended for use with elementary school children whose concern for the future will hopefully save the environment.—**Sara R. Mack**

998.   Roberts, Patricia L. **Taking Humor Seriously in Children's Literature: Literature-Based Mini-Units and Humorous Books for Children Ages 5-12.** Lanham, Md., Scarecrow, 1997. 219p. index. (School Library Media Series, no.11). $45.00pa. ISBN 0-8108-3209-7.
    Humor does not seem like a serious topic of research, but Roberts presents a compelling argument on the benefits of teaching children about humor. A bibliography of research that is included in the book supports Roberts's ideas that children move through stages of humor just like they move through stages of reading. The author feels that humor needs to be taught and has provided a resource for parents, teachers, and librarians to teach these skills to children ages 5 to 12.

The book is broken into 2 sections, children ages 5 to 8 and children 9 to 12. Each age group contains a section of mini-units and an annotated bibliography. Categories of humor include animals as humans, family, humorous humans, holidays, jokes, nonsense, rhymes, and unusual characters. Each unit describes a book appropriate to the age group and why it is funny. Activities for the book include things such as topics for discussion, writing activities, artwork, and other related topics.

There is a glossary at the end of the book defining literary terms such as *absurdity, parody,* and *satire,* but it is not comprehensive. *Irony* was not in the glossary even though it was part of a mini-unit.

An index at the end of the book lists author, title, and subject. Entry numbers instead of page numbers are used to refer to information in the book. This became a serious flaw when exploring a subject. When this reviewer looked for *irony* in the index, the index referred to two titles in the annotated bibliography but those titles did not refer to the mini-units where irony is discussed. In other words, the mini-units section is not indexed. This makes it difficult for a teacher to find activities related to a particular subject without having to browse the whole mini-units section.

Although the activities and annotated bibliographies are excellent, there are some serious editing problems, including the index, glossary, and a missing illustration (figure 1). Despite these problems, teachers and librarians wanting to incorporate humorous literature into classrooms and libraries will find good information in this book.
—**Suzanne Julian**

999.   Spencer, Pam, and Janis Ansell. **What Do Children Read Next? A Reader's Guide to Fiction for Children, Volume 2.** Detroit, Gale, 1997. 929p. index. $55.00. ISBN 0-8103-6448-4.

The 1st edition of *What Do Children Read Next?* and its companion volume *What Do Young Adults Read Next?* both appeared in 1994 (see ARBA 95, entries 1128 and 1139), to enthusiastic reviews. The present edition of *What Do Children Read Next?* is not a revision of the 1994 book but an all new continuation. Like its predecessor, it is intended as a readers' advisory tool to bring together children and appropriate fiction titles. The book highlights 1,558 main titles all published between 1993 and 1996 (contrary to a statement in the preface that erroneously indicates a much wider time span) that are suitable for children in kindergarten through grade 6 (again, not as the preface states, grade 8).

The main titles are arranged alphabetically by author. For each, coverage includes age range; a list of subjects; major characters; locale and time period; a brief but thorough summary; review citations; other important books by the author; and an annotated bibliography of three or four additional titles that are related to the main title by similarity of theme, style, or subject. These suggestions often include older standard titles. The selection of books is excellent and shows not only knowledge of children's literature but also an understanding of children's reading tastes.

The last third of the book is devoted to indexes, including ones for period; subjects; character names; character descriptors (e.g., professions); age level; and the usual author, illustrator, and title indexes. This is a distinguished volume that will be useful in both elementary school libraries and children's rooms as an effective tool for giving reading guidance as well as in evaluating and building library collections.—**John T. Gillespie**

1000.   West, Mark I. **Everyone's Guide to Children's Literature.** Fort Atkinson, Wis., Highsmith Press, 1997. 101p. index. (Highsmith Press Handbook Series). $15.00pa. ISBN 0-917846-90-7.

According to author West, "this resource was written and designed to provide library staff, teachers, parents, and students of children's literature with a convenient, low-cost, up-to-date source of information about virtually every important aspect of literature for youth." This guide is suitable for use as a supplementary text for children's literature courses or as a reference guide for locating sources of information about children's literature. Each chapter analyzes some aspect related to the subject, such as key reference works, journals and periodicals, organizations, children's literature on the Internet, special collections and libraries, major awards, and books about children's literature. The author draws information from library and information science, education, and the humanities. The book includes a general index as well as title, author/illustrator, and organization indexes. The scope of the book is fairly comprehensive despite the author's seeming assumption that nonfiction is not a part of children's literature and that children do not read nonfiction (only information about fiction books is included). This reference should be suitable for someone needing general information or for use as a guide to places to seek further information about a wide variety of subjects dealing with children's literature.—**Janet Hilbun**

1001.   Wright, Cora M. **Hot Links: Literature Links for the Middle School Curriculum.** Englewood, Colo., Libraries Unlimited, 1998. 173p. illus. index. $30.00pa. ISBN 1-56308-587-9.

This book contains some 280 children's literature titles, which represents a small, selective mix of recent and older titles that the author indicates would be of use for integrating literature into a middle school curriculum. Titles are suggested for use within several content areas and genres, and for recreational reading. The book is intended primarily for the classroom teacher, but is of use to librarians and parents as an introductory source for identifying and discussing children's literature in the middle-level curriculum. Books were included based on "their quality of writing, how well the illustrations accompany the text, the interest to students, availability, and a strong curriculum connection" (p. ix). Entries are listed within the book for several content areas: English classics; books that contain English usage; poetry; fine arts; mathematics; multicultural aspects; science; social studies (U.S. and ancient cultures); and sports and games. Certain genres are also included: biographies; recently published titles; high interest-low reading level books; myths, folktales, and legends; read aloud books; and books with a "unique presentation." Entries are annotated and contain basic citation information, including the ISBN and price. *See* references are also provided to other subject areas.

There is a chart at the end of the book that lists the titles alphabetically and has indicators to show the content and genre areas covered by each title. There is an indicator that shows under which content area the annotation can be found. An alphabetically arranged author/title index provides page numbers for the titles and authors listed. The book is useful for those interested in literature for students at the middle grades. This book would be more useful in a school or public library setting.—**Jan S. Squire**

Biography

1002.   Wyatt, Flora R., Margaret Coggins, and Jane Hunter Imber. **Popular Nonfiction Authors for Children: A Biographical and Thematic Guide.** Englewood, Colo., Libraries Unlimited, 1998. 207p. illus. index. $37.50. ISBN 1-56308-408-2.

This new volume in the Popular Author series fills a reference gap for the often-neglected area of children's nonfiction. It contains biographies of 68 modern authors. Included with each biography is a photograph of the author, date of birth and current address if available, a short message to students personally written by the author, and an annotated bibliography. There are author/title and subject indexes.

The scope of the work is limited to living authors or those who died after furnishing the information necessary for completing the book. All except two reside in the United States. Featured are individual biographies of 26 men, 36 women, and 3 collaborators (2 husband and wife teams, and one team of 2 women).

The format is attractive, and the print is easy to read. Biographies are short (two pages or less), and written in a style suitable for either adults or older children. The authors' messages to students emphasize the process of becoming a writer. As stated in the introduction, current classroom instruction often involves a wide range of reading materials beyond texts. The bibliographies at the end of each chapter should be useful as a book selection tool, with some limitations. The annotations are brief but succinct. Some of the subject index categories listed are quite broad (e.g., biography, geography, government, history). There are also a few omissions. For example, Robert Gardener's *Forgotten Players: The Story of Black Baseball in America* is indexed under *African-Americans* but not under sports. All aspects considered, this work should be a useful addition to any children's literature collection or teachers' reference shelf. [R: SLJ, Nov 98, p. 159; BL, July 98, pp. 1907-1908]
—**Patricia A. Eskoz**

Dictionaries and Encyclopedias

1003.   Llewellyn, Claire. **Our Planet Earth.** New York, Scholastic, 1997. 77p. index. (Scholastic First Encyclopedia Series). $14.95. ISBN 0-590-87929-4.

One of five books in the Scholastic First Encyclopedia Series, the volume begins with directions for use and tells what the book is about. The book divides the planet Earth into four general topics—an introduction, the Earth's surface, the changing planet, and life on Earth. Each of these divisions is further divided into colorful, two-page spreads, which discuss more specific topics. Each section is cross-referenced to topics in this and the other volumes in the series. Despite an introductory explanation of how to use the cross-references, the format of these references is rather confusing and, therefore, may be difficult for children to use. The book gives brief tidbits of information about a wide variety of subjects relating to Earth. It has value as an overview, but any child who wants or needs detailed information will not find much substance in this volume. The book includes both a glossary and index. [R: SLJ, Feb 98, p. 138]—**Janet Hilbun**

1004.   **The Oxford Dictionary of Nursery Rhymes.** new ed. Iona Opie and Peter Opie, eds. New York, Oxford University Press, 1997. 559p. illus. index. $35.00. ISBN 0-19-860088-7.

The Opies, well known for their work in the field of literature for children, have presented a revised and updated edition of their highly acclaimed 1951 dictionary of nursery rhymes. It comprises nursery rhymes historically and traditionally enjoyed by preschool-age children. Thorough coverage is evidenced through the extent and quality of their research. Topics include nursery rhymes, songs, lullabies, counting tunes, puzzlers, riddles, and tongue twisters. Their goal includes locating the earliest recording of each rhyme, identifying its origin and historical variants when possible, and identifying and illustrating variations in wording. To facilitate locating a rhyme, most entries are arranged by the most prominent word—for instance, "See-saw, Margery Daw" is entered under "Margery Daw." A good example of the thoroughness of the editors' research is found in the entry for the ever-popular rhyme "Humpty Dumpty." The historical elements, including humor; possible interpretations of who or what "Humpty" personifies; title variants from France, Sweden, and other countries; and the *Oxford English Dictionary*'s explanation of the meaning of the word "humpty-dumpty" all make for interesting reading.

The editors state: "We believe that we have assembled here almost everything so far known about nursery rhymes together with a considerable amount of material hitherto unpublished." Not only have they achieved their goal, they have presented it so that the novice as well as the professional will find it an enjoyable read, as well as a learning experience.—**Margaret Denman-West**

1005.   **Scholastic Encyclopedia of the United States.** By Judy Bock and Rachel Kranz. New York, Scholastic, 1997. 139p. illus. maps. index. $17.95. ISBN 0-590-94747-8.

This encyclopedia is a slender, oversized, 1-volume work for middle-grade students needing a source for reports on individual U.S. states and territories. A two-page spread is allocated to each state or territory (e.g., Guam, Puerto Rico, American Samoa, and U.S. Virgin Islands). A blue-background sidebar on the left lists "basic" information—total population, area, and state bird. Another on the right gives "Fascinating Facts," which includes different information for each state or territory but usually lists famous people and some touch of humor. The large-print text endeavors to encapsulate the state's geography; history; industry; and cultural, racial, and ethnic makeup. It also often spots some controversial element, such as race, in each state's history or situation. In some entries, the authors note special tourist attractions. A small line map identifies the location of each state in relation to the whole.

Librarians and teachers should not depend on this work entirely to teach a unit on the states. The map work is extremely weak; there is not a single map showing physical features, or any place other than the state itself. Even the location of state capitals is not given. The map of the United States has Hawaii and a tiny Alaska as insets. The frequent reference to elements of controversy is unfortunate because the issues are never examined adequately. Black-and-white archival photographs do not always show places as they currently look. The appendixes include a limited bibliography for child readers and a state-by-state list of places to visit. There are no reference to or pictures of state flags.—**Edna M. Boardman**

Handbooks and Yearbooks

1006.   Fredericks, Anthony D. **The Integrated Curriculum: Books for Reluctant Readers, Grades 2-5.** 2d ed. Englewood, Colo., Teacher Ideas Press/Libraries Unlimited, 1998. 189p. illus. index. $22.50pa. ISBN 1-56308-604-2.

This easy-to-read teacher's handbook provides practical curriculum ideas for reaching students who are reluctant to read for a number of reasons. The author lists children's books that he and other classroom teachers across the United States have used. The books are the focus of an integrated curriculum classroom approach. The book is divided into 3 major portions. The 1st section deals with strategies aimed at the classroom teacher.

Fredericks provides writings on motivating students to read and how to go about building an integrated curriculum by providing a how-to guide and suggestions for programs and project activities. He then discusses several methodologies for assessing the comprehension of reluctant readers. Among the methodologies discussed are Student Motivated Active Reading Technique (SMART), Metacognitive Modeling and Monitoring (MM&M), and what I Know, what I Want to learn, what I Learned (KWL). In addition, he also talks about the use of prediction cards, anticipation guides, and other activities.

In the 2d section of the book, 35 specific children's book titles and how they can be used in an integrated curriculum classroom are discussed. Under each title entry there is a brief summary; a set of critical thinking questions; and suggestions for activities and experiments in reading and language arts, science and health, art, math, music, social studies, and physical education. Additional reading sources are also suggested under the different content areas, and details are provided for most of the activities.

The last section of the book contains resource lists. The first is a list of children's book titles that will be of interest to reluctant readers. It is alphabetically arranged by author and then by grade levels, 1 through 2, 3 through 4, and 5 through 6. This is followed by a short list of Websites that deal with children's literature, children's and teachers' reviews of books, and other features. A helpful index concludes the book. This book is highly recommended for school libraries and academic libraries, especially those that have a teacher education program at their institution.—**Jan S. Squire**

1007.   Greeson, Janet. **Name That Book! Questions and Answers on Outstanding Children's Books.** 2d ed. Lanham, Md., Scarecrow, 1998. 223p. index. $32.50pa. ISBN 0-8108-3151-1.

Name That Book! is intended as an aid for elementary and middle school teachers. The introduction describes how to stage a "Battle of the Books" trivia contest, and the body of the work provides questions and answers drawn from almost 800 books, most of those being works published after the 1986 1st edition (see ARBA 87, entry 1103). The questions are divided by grade level, and the works treated are indexed by author and by title. An appendix includes additional activities, such as crossword puzzles and bingo, which draw on the same works.

Unfortunately, Greeson's concept of involving children in literary activities and developing their love of books is restricted almost entirely to the recognition of authors' and characters' names. The trivia questions, regardless of grade level, consist of three descriptions of plot events or characters, each with an admonition to the contestants to name the book in which they appear. Although such activity may be entirely appropriate for some grade levels, this reviewer was left wondering why an entire book should be devoted to an activity any classroom teacher could easily design herself. *Name That Book!* is also hampered by some errors in both indexing and copyediting.—**Marcus P. Elmore**

Indexes

1008.   Lima, Carolyn W., and John A. Lima. **A to Zoo: Subject Access to Children's Picture Books.** 5th ed. New Providence, N.J., R. R. Bowker, 1998. 1398p. index. $65.00. ISBN 0-8352-3916-0.

This 5th edition is arranged in the same manner as the earlier editions (see ARBA 94, entry 1176 and ARBA 90, entry 1082 for reviews of the 3d and 4th editions). More than 18,000 titles (4,000 more than the previous edition) are cataloged and indexed under some 1,000 subject headings. The main purpose of the book is to assist teachers, librarians, and parents in selecting picture books by desired subjects.

Sources of information came from public and university library collections, review copies from publishers, published reviews, and the authors' personal searches. The authors state in the preface that most of the books were read by them to determine the appropriate subject heading. Out-of-print works have also been included in this list because many will be available through the public libraries; however, there is not designation given to out-of-print book in the entries.

The scope of the book covers both fiction and nonfiction picture books, defined as books in which the illustrations accommodate greater space than the text, and the vocabulary used in the text is suitable in vocabulary and conceptual understanding for children in preschool to grade 2. An updated essay on the history of children's books appears in the front matter, with a fairly extensive bibliography of resources for those interested in pursuing further study into the history and development of picture books.

Access is made through either the subject index, title index, or illustrator index. The main entries in the bibliographic section are arranged by author. Entries include author, title, illustrator, date of publication, publisher, ISBN number, and subject headings. No annotations are given. As a quick reference index to picture book titles, this is an excellent resource. The lack of annotations limits its usefulness as a selection tool; however, covering such a large number of books, it is far more comprehensive than comparable resources containing annotations. This work is highly recommended for children's public libraries and academic libraries with children's book sections. [R: BL, 1 Sept 98, p. 141]—**Susan Zernial**

1009.   **Master Index to More Summaries of Children's Books, 1980-1990.** Eloise S. Pettus and Daniel D. Pettus Jr., eds. Lanham, Md., Scarecrow, 1998. 2v. $198.00/set. ISBN 0-8108-3269-0.

This 2-volume set is a rather hefty supplement at 1,411 pages to the 1985 edition of *Master Index to Summaries of Children's Books* (see ARBA 87, entry 1105). Fiction, nonfiction, poetry, traditional literature, and biographies published in the United States and included in this index are aimed at preschool to grade 6 readers. Excluded materials include books for older readers, audiovisual materials, reference works, textbooks, and comic books. The summaries indexed are found in bibliographies, textbooks on children's literature, and activity books that are based on children's books. Reviews in periodicals are not included because they are already itemized in widely available resources.

The introduction to the set explains the codes for the individual entries as well as the type of information indexed. The main entries are numbered and arranged alphabetically by author or editor and infrequently by title when no author can be identified. The entries in the title index and subject index, housed in the 2d volume, identify only the item numbers of the books. Cross-references to pseudonyms and variant spellings of the authors' names are also included in the master index. The inclusion of entries was determined by asking the following question in the affirmative: "Would the user know what the children's book was about by reading this summary?" A caveat about using this index as a selection guide is also mentioned in the introduction due to the fact that the index is inclusive, not evaluative. The use of this index is straightforward. However, rather daunting and long entries in the subject index include several columns of book entry numbers under such subject headings as "Adventure and Adventurers," "Alphabet," "Animals," "Black Americans," "Family Life," "Fantasy," "Friendship," and "Indians of North America." Perhaps the subject index could be done more effectively. This set is recommended for large public libraries and research facilities. [R: BL, 1 Nov 98, p. 532]—**Gail de Vos**

Young Adult Literature

Bibliography

1010.   Anderson, Vicki. **Fiction Sequels for Readers 10 to 16: An Annotated Bibliography of Books in Succession.** 2d ed. Jefferson, N.C., McFarland, 1998. 176p. index. $29.95pa. ISBN 0-7864-0185-0.

Anderson's second volume of young adult fiction sequels and prequels is a useful addition to the public library, school library, or bookstore that serves young readers. The compendium of 3,008 titles is a slim volume neatly presented in readable format. The introduction notes that journals, catalog cards, and book jackets often omit the essential tie of one title to a group of works about a single character, as with Helen Boylston's 7 Sue Barton novels and the 11 Young Indiana Jones adventure novels by William McCay. The text focuses on readable popular litera-ture appropriate to the age and geared to ethnic tastes. A broad selection includes familiar writers—Lois Lowry, Laurence Yep, Laura Ingalls Wilder, Robert Lipsyte, Caroline Cooney, Theodore Taylor, Mary Stewart, Fred Gipson, and Ursula LeGuin. Subjects extend to family, sports, mystery, science fiction, fantasy, adventure, and humor.

Anderson arranges the 154-page listing alphabetically by author, with surname in bold typeface. Subsequent entries by the same author are preceded by a blank line for ease of grouping. Each numbered entry includes fiction titles in chronological order with publisher and date in parenthesis. Plot summaries average 4 to 6 lines in length except for 14 titles by 2 authors, Margot Benary-Isbert and Christopher Black, which appear without summary. Guide words flank page numbers at the top of the two-column page. A title index presents works and entry numbers in a tricolumn arrangement. Cross-referencing connects pen names to authors (e.g., Bland, Edith *see* Nesbit, Edith). Overall, the work is a straightforward, nonjudgmental presentation in brief, easy format at a reasonable price. Anderson's work is a handy source for professionals who counsel young readers. [R: BL, 15 Oct 98, p. 440]—**Mary Ellen Snodgrass**

1011.   **Outstanding Books for the College Bound: Choices for a Generation.** Marjorie Lewis, ed. Chicago, American Library Association/Young Adult Library Services Association, 1996. 217p. index. $25.00pa.; $22.50pa. (ALA members). ISBN 0-8389-3456-0.

Lewis's catalog of must-read books for young readers reflects a shift in education from standardized lists to increasing vitality and creativity in education. According to her preface, as a result of the Young Adult Library Services Association's role in the change, librarians, teachers, students, and parents have a fuller choice of titles and a greater range of learning. A precise introduction establishes the parameters of book selection by defining outstanding works and anthologies, college-bound readers, and genre listing. The section concludes with a chart of books that have been on the list from 6 to 10 times.

The text opens on a 110-page listing by genre. Beautifully spaced in readable typeface and a single-column arrangement, the entries vary from two to five lines in length. Each entry names title, author, publication date, and dates the title appeared on the list. Part 2 presents the unannotated lists by year, beginning with 1959 and continuing to 1994. A two-page appendix states the guidelines for book selection. A 27-page double index lists authors and titles.

The American Library Association provides a valuable service in performing this tedious task of collating lists of books suited for bright young readers. The usual questions surface from a hasty perusal, such as, Why is Elie Wiesel's *Night* not named? It would also aid the first-time user to have a model entry explaining the series of dates that follow the publication date. Quibbles aside, the cataloging of reading lists offers librarians, teachers, students, and parents a worthy place to start.—**Mary Ellen Snodgrass**

1012.   **Serious About Series: Evaluations and Annotations of Teen Fiction in Paperback Series.** By Silk Makowski. Dorothy M. Broderick, ed. Lanham, Md., Scarecrow, 1998. 289p. index. $26.50pa. ISBN 0-8108-3304-2.

Makowski has responded to the 1980s paperback series boom for young adults with a guide to the selection and evaluation of fiction series popular with teenage readers. She includes new series titles as well as those that seem to go on forever. While doing her research she often was met with raised eyebrows and distasteful looks from young adult librarians she was interviewing; however, it is her contention that it behooves the profession to accept and provide for even the less-than-quality reading interests of the population being served. In her introduction she discusses evaluation criteria, concluding with five provocative statements supporting the purchase of teen fiction series by public and school libraries.

The series titles will pique the interest of older readers as well teenagers. Some readers will want to turn first to the comments on the Hardy Boys Casefiles, the Nancy Drew Files, or perhaps Tom Swift, while others will turn at once to series titles such as Buffy the Vampire Slayer, R. L. Stine's Fear Streets, or the Sweet Valley High series. Titles of books in the series are provided, along with a single-sentence description.

Makowski's evaluative comments on each series are both witty and insightful. This book will serve as a useful reference guide as well as a timesaver for those who want to be responsive to their young readers' interests but are reluctant to spend the time becoming familiar with each title.—**Margaret Denman-West**

Handbooks and Yearbooks

1013.   **Novels for Students, Volume 3: Presenting Analysis, Context, and Criticism on Commonly Studied Novels.** Diane Telgen and Kevin Hile, eds. Detroit, Gale, 1998. 387p. illus. index. $55.00. ISBN 0-7876-2113-7.

The 3d volume of *Novels for Students* includes reading guides for *Animal Farm*; *Annie John*; *The Awakening*; *Crime and Punishment*; *Cry, the Beloved Country*; *Democracy*; *Ellen Foster*; *The Giver*; *Grendel*; *Obasan*; *A Passage to India*; *Slaughterhouse-Five*; *Tess of the d'Urbervilles*; *Their Eyes Were Watching God*; *Wise Blood*; and *A Yellow Raft in Blue Water*. For each novel there is an introduction to the work and author, a plot summary, descriptions of major characters and discussions of their relationship to other characters in the novel, analysis of themes, a discussion of literary style demonstrated in the novel, historical or cultural context, critical background, and critical analysis geared especially for its targeted student audience. Other useful features for each novel include media adaptations, topic suggestions for further study, bibliography of sources, and suggestions for further related readings. Entries may also include photographs, drawings, or maps. The volume concludes with a glossary of literary terms and cumulative author/title, nationality/ethnicity, and subject/theme indexes.

The clear writing style, thorough coverage of each novel, excellent organization of guides, and attractive, easy-to-read layouts all serve to make this a welcome source for students needing to do literary research. [R: SLJ, Aug 98, p. 195; VOYA, June 98, pp. 153-154]—**Dana McDougald**

1014.   **Novels for Students, Volume 4: Presenting Analysis, Context, and Criticism on Commonly Studied Novels.** Marie Rose Napierkowski, ed. Farmington Hills, Mich., Gale, 1998. 393p. illus. index. $55.00. ISBN 0-7876-2114-5. ISSN 1094-3552.

The Novels for Students series by Gale is designed to meet curricular needs of high school and under-graduate college students and their teachers, as well as the interests of general readers and researchers considering specific novels. Each volume contains entries on both classic and contemporary novels. Each entry focuses on one novel and begins with a boldfaced heading that lists the title of the novel, the author, and the date of publication. Included in an entry are an introduction that provides a brief overview of the novel; an author biography; a plot summary that describes the major events in the novel and interprets how those events help articulate the novel's themes; a list of the characters, with descriptions and discussions of their actions, relationships, and possible motiva-tions; an overview of major topics, themes, and issues; style elements, such as setting, point of view, narration, literary devices, and genres; discussions of historical and cultural contexts; a critical overview; a bibliography of sources used in the entry; a bibliography of sources for further study; and a critical essay written especially for a student audience. Additionally, each entry contains highlighted sections set apart from the main text as sidebars, including a bibliography of media adaptations, a "What Do I Read Next?" feature that suggests other works of both fiction and nonfiction that complement the work under study, and a list of study questions or research topics dealing with the novel. Photographs, illustrations, and maps included with each entry enhance the text. Each volume includes a literary chronology, a cumulative author/title index for the series, a cumulative nationality/ethnicity index, and a subject/theme index. The organization, writing style that is appropriate for students, and content that is geared to meet curricular needs are features that make *Novels for Students*, including the volume under review, a series that will be welcome in libraries serving youth.—**Dana McDougald**

1015.   **Short Stories for Students, Volume 3: Presenting Analysis, Context, and Criticism on Commonly Studied Short Stories.** Kathleen Wilson, ed. Detroit, Gale, 1998. 420p. illus. index. $55.00. ISBN 0-7876-2218-4.

Volume 3 of *Short Stories for Students* continues the high quality presentation and content of the first 2 volumes (see ARBA 98, entries 1120 and 1121 for a review of volumes 1 and 2). The book follows the same format as the previous volumes and continues to choose stories from a variety of time periods and authors. A particular strength of this series is the strong inclusion of female and multicultural authors frequently studied in high school and undergraduate English courses. Each entry includes an author biography, plot summary, character description, and theme explanation and interpretation. The authors also address elements of style and discuss the historical and cultural contexts of each story. A critical overview and three critical essays are included for each selection. The essays, commissioned by *Short Stories for Students*, deal specifically with the included stories and are written for a student audience. The book lists media adaptations available for each work and includes a comparison and contrast box that enumerates differences between the author's time and culture and the late twentieth-century Western culture. Additional features include a glossary of literary terms and cumulative, author/title, nationality/ethnicity, and subject/theme indexes. This high-quality, well-organized series makes an excellent research and teaching tool. [R: VOYA, June 98, p. 154]—**Janet Hilbun**

1016.   **Short Stories for Students, Volume 4: Presenting Analysis, Context, and Criticism on Commonly Studied Short Stories.** Kathleen Wilson and Marie Lazzari, eds. Farmington Hills, Mich., Gale, 1998. 420p. illus. index. $55.00. ISBN 0-7876-2219-2. ISSN 1092-7735.

Continuing the previous standard of quality in content and presentation, volume 4 of *Short Stories for Students* follows the same format as the other 3 volumes. The stories, chosen from a variety of time periods, authors, and styles, include contemporary, female, and multicultural authors as well as old standards. Fulfilling the stated purpose of the book, "to provide readers with a guide to understanding, enjoying, and studying short stories by giving them easy access to information about the works," the volume provides valuable information for both students and teachers. Organization of this book follows the structure of the other volumes, with an introduction to each story and its author; a plot summary; descriptions of important characters, including explanations of their role in the narrative and their relationships to other characters; analysis of important themes; and explanations of literary techniques and movements as they apply to the story. Essays commissioned for the series and a critical overview add to the value of the reference. Illustrations depicting the time period for each story enhance the book, and a "What Do I Read Next?" box leads students to further exploration. The actual stories are not included in the volume. Indexing is the same as in the previous volumes.—**Janet Hilbun**

CLASSICAL LITERATURE

1017.   Brumble, H. David. **Classical Myths and Legends in the Middle Ages and Renaissance: A Dictionary of Allegorical Meanings.** Westport, Conn., Greenwood Press, 1998. 421p. illus. index. $95.00. ISBN 0-313-29451-8.
        This dictionary amasses allegorical meanings from myths and legends, concentrating on materials from the early Middle Ages to Milton. However, most entries quote from classical sources to give the reader needed background. Because of the widespread geographical location of the allegorical traditions, the cited materials are from English, Latin, Greek, Italian, French, Dutch, German, and Spanish sources. All quotations are translated into English. In general, Brumble includes those mythic figures who are identified with at least one specific allegorical tradition. If there is more than one allegorical interpretation, he presents them in chronological order. The dates for each author appear in the bibliography, and the list of illustrations dates each work of art.
        The names used in the dictionary were most common during the Middle Ages and the Renaissance, which favors Roman over Greek naming. Medieval and Renaissance Christians interpreted allegories their own way, resulting in a tendency to focus on detail. Brumble suggests that to understand the text historically, one needs to focus on individual lines, passages, and detail.
        This skillfully organized work has appropriate cross-references and a bibliography for each chronological entry. Appendix A gives some interpretation of music in allegories and directs the reader to other sources, appendix B treats the allegory of bestialization and gives cross-references and bibliography, and appendix C briefly describes the traditional treatment of the subject regarding "envying the animals." Following appendix C is an impressive annotated bibliography of primary sources and the bibliography of secondary sources. The index is useful for accessing names not listed in the individual articles. Brumble's well-researched work is highly recommended for libraries, schools, and anyone with an interest in literature and mythology. [R: Choice, Sept 98, p. 86]—**Magda Želinská-Ferl**

1018.   **A Companion to the Greek Lyric Poets.** Douglas E. Gerber, ed. Boston, Brill Academic, 1997. 287p. $100.00. ISBN 90-04-09944-1. ISSN 0169-8958.
        This useful companion covers four types of lyric poetry: iambic, elegy, personal poetry, and public poetry. Each section is introduced by a different scholar, and the editor has furnished a comprehensive general introduction for the whole volume. Gerber stresses that the "primary aim of this book is not to break new ground," but rather to deal with the "problems and controversies" surrounding the Greek lyric poets. The authors covered by this companion include Archilochus, Sermonides, Hipponax, Callinus, Tyrtaeus, Mimnermus, Solon, Theognis, Xenophanes, Alcaeus, Sappho, Ibycus, Anacreon, Corinna, Alcman, Stesichorus, Simonides, Pindar, and Bacchylides. There are several well-known names here (e.g., Archilochus, Pindar, Sappho), but the fact that many of them are unknown even to advanced readers indicates the scholarly level of this book. Moreover, most of the quotations from the poets are presented in the original Greek and left untranslated—a disservice to the average teacher or scholar. The work is designed chiefly for specialists who are already well versed not only in the ancient Greek language but also in the complex histories surrounding this sort of literature. Thus, *A Companion to the Greek Lyric Poets* will be a tool useful to the advanced scholar but probably not to the average college teacher.
        However, even the layperson can profit by the interesting and highly informative introductions to each of the volume's 4 main sections. In the "Iambic" section, for example, the introduction to the verse of Archilochus tells us how this volatile writer composed a song for a Dionysian festival and taught it to a chorus. Apparently the song was rejected because it was "too iambic," and the angry god Dionysus, in retaliation, rendered the citizens impotent. Similarly, in the introduction to the "Sappho" section, there is a pertinent discussion of the poet's apparent bisexuality. However, there are occasional lame remarks, such as "a married woman with a daughter, a series of

male and female lovers and a poetic career is a busy woman." Comments such as these may be accurate, but they seem to suggest obliviousness toward the thinking of modern-day feminists and gay writers or intellectuals.

One of the most famous names among the poets covered in this volume is Solon, the renowned lawgiver of Athens who was born c.640 B.C.E. and died at the approximate age of 80. It is likely that few modern readers know that Solon was also an accomplished poet and that a sizable portion of his considerable energies went not toward legislative matters but toward writing poems. The introduction states that "we have more of Solon's poetry than we have for any other elegist of the archaic period," and Diogenes claimed the total of Solon's elegies to be 5,000, although this may be excessive. In any case, the lawgiver looms as a major figure in the surviving body of Greek lyric poetry. (One could wish, by the way, that the introduction to Pindar had more of the vitality that one finds in the Solon introduction.)

Solon chooses a variety of topics for his verse and is not afraid to wade into politics. In one poem he blames the populace for "foolishly supporting a tyrant," and in another he defends himself for trying to adopt a middle course between the demands of the rich and those of the poor. This manifestation of what was later to be called "the Golden Mean" by the Aristotelians and others places Solon near the fulcrum of Athenian poetical-political thought and looks far ahead, toward the philosophical poets of the eighteenth century (e.g., Voltaire and Alexander Pope). Unlike many of the ancient Greek lyrical traditions, Solon frequently reaches outside his time and place in order to consider timeless universals or what we have come to call "the human condition."

The thoroughness of the Solon section is typical of the depth of all the sections in this scholarly volume. Although modern readers may regret that few of the Greek passages are rendered into English, there is enough lively information in the introductory material to keep the attention of experts and lay readers alike. *A Companion to the Greek Lyrical Poets* will not look out of place on the shelves of any reader's library.—**Peter Thorpe**

DRAMA

1019.   **Drama Criticism, Volume 7: Criticism of the Most Significant....** Lawrence J. Trudeau, ed. Detroit, Gale, 1997. 463p. index. $87.00. ISBN 0-8103-5532-9.

Like the other published volumes in this series, this volume focuses on some of the world's most frequently studied playwrights, excluding William Shakespeare, for whom critical commentary can be found in *Shakespearean Criticism* (see entry 1082). Authors are arranged alphabetically without regard to chronology or nationality, creating a somewhat eclectic mix. For example, this volume includes playwrights as diverse as the American monologist Spalding Gray (1941-), the Elizabethan dramatist John Lyly (1554-1606), the Russian novelist and playwright Ivan Turgenev (1818-1883), the American playwright and director Emily Mann (1952-), and Derek Walcott (1930-), a St. Lucian playwright who won the 1992 Nobel Prize for literature.

The book is well organized. Each author entry includes a brief introductory paragraph establishing the playwright's contribution to theater and drama, followed by biographical information, succinct editorial comments on major works and critical reception, and a list of principal works and other major works. These introductory pages are well suited for "beginning students of literature and theater" and "the average playgoer," which, according to the preface, is this series' intended audience. However, many of the overviews and general studies reprinted here are scholarly essays and presume considerable knowledge about the playwrights and drama in general. The essays on the Roman playwright Terence (185 B.C.E.-159 B.C.E.) are particularly erudite; the one by Terry McGarrity (p. 221) includes quotes from Terence's *The Girl from Andros* in Latin only. Readers will have an easier time with the entries for contemporary playwrights, which include interviews and some of the more influential reviews of their productions. An important feature of this volume for students and researchers is the cumulative author index, which lists all of the authors who have appeared in *Drama Criticism* and the other books in Gale Research's Literary Criticism series. Also helpful is the list at the beginning of the volume of the playwrights covered in the other volumes of *Drama Criticism*, and a "Note to the Reader" regarding the general format for citing reprinted materials.

This handsomely bound book, although not exactly for beginners, is certainly an important reference for drama and literature students interested in gaining a more global perspective on playwrights, both past and present. This work is highly recommended.—**Sandra Adell**

1020.   **Drama Criticism, Volume 8: Criticism of the Most Significant and Widely Studied Dramatic Works from All the World's Literatures.** Lawrence J. Trudeau, ed. Farmington Hills, Mich., Gale, 1998. 530p. illus. index. $96.00. ISBN 0-7876-1791-1. ISSN 1056-4349.

Since introducing this series in 1991, Gale has published a new volume each year (see ARBA 94, entries 1201-1203 for a review of volumes 1-3). Like the preceding volumes, this work focuses on playwrights from a variety of nationalities and periods. Of the nine dramatists featured, four are from the United States, two from Ireland, and one each from England, France, and Greece. In addition to six twentieth-century figures (among them Jean Anouilh, Brian Friel, and Marsha Norman), the volume also includes Aeschylus, John Ford, and Oliver Goldsmith.

Volume 8 follows the now-familiar format of earlier Drama Criticism volumes. Each entry begins with an introductory essay covering the playwright's life and dramatic writings and a bibliography of his or her principal works. These are followed by selections of criticism reprinted from previously published sources. Although some essays are reproduced in their entirety, other commentary is excerpted from longer studies. General criticism appears first, followed by commentary on selected plays. Most of the entries for contemporary playwrights also reproduce reviews of productions as well as interviews in which they discuss their works. Annotated bibliographies of selected additional sources conclude each entry. A cumulative author index provides references to writers covered in all Gale Literary Criticism series and indicates when they appear in other Gale biographical or literary compilations. Also included are indexes to play titles and to the nationalities of playwrights covered in volumes 1 through 8 of Drama Criticism.

With the exception of Ford, all of these playwrights are represented in at least one of Gale's other literary criticism series. However, a comparison of the entries in Drama Criticism with those in other series revealed that the number of sources duplicated is not significant. Moreover, in the case of the six writers who also appear in Contemporary Literary Criticism, the Drama Criticism entries are much longer and the extracts are more complete. Providing a quick and convenient means of obtaining an overview of the critical response to a playwright, this series is perhaps most valuable for collections that lack many of the books and periodicals from which commentary is reproduced. Those libraries that have benefited from earlier volumes of Drama Criticism will probably want to add this one as well.—**Marie Ellis**

1021.   **Drama for Students. Volume 1.** David Galens and Lynn Spampinato, eds. Detroit, Gale, 1997. 350p. illus. index. $55.00. ISBN 0-7876-1683-4.

1022.   **Drama for Students. Volume 2.** David Galens and Lynn Spampinato, eds. Detroit, Gale, 1997. 356p. illus. index. $55.00. ISBN 0-7876-1684-2.

1023.   **Drama for Students. Volume 3.** David Galens, ed. Detroit, Gale, 1998. 427p. illus. index. $55.00. ISBN 0-7876-2752-6.

In *Drama for Students* conveniently arranged guides for the appreciation of commonly studied dramatic works are found. Designed chiefly for high school and undergraduate college students, each volume covers 12 to 20 plays. The works are selected mainly on the basis of their popularity as study texts in literature courses; thus, the selection is extremely eclectic, ranging from classics such as *Antigone* and *A Doll's House* to such contemporary works as *The Odd Couple* and *Twilight: Los Angeles, 1992*. Each entry consists of an author biography, plot summary, description of the main characters, overview of the themes and style, and a critical essay commissioned by the editors. The analyses are straightforward and conventional, not unlike those found in *Cliff's Notes*. The distinguishing feature here is the rather cloying attempt to be politically correct, both in the selection of titles and in the relentless effort to show each play's relevance to contemporary concerns. For example, most entries include a "Compare and Contrast" section in which parallels are drawn between the cultural milieu of the time the play was written and that of today. In *Rosencrantz and Guildenstern Are Dead*, the editors are reduced to comparing the prevalence of credit cards between 1966 and today. Unfortunately, this kind of "reaching" is not uncommon in an otherwise useful and engaging work.—**Jeffrey R. Luttrell**

1024.   Drama for Students, Volume 4: Presenting Analysis, Context, and Criticism on Commonly Studied Dramas. David Galens, ed. Farmington Hills, Mich., Gale, 1998. 392p. illus. index. $55.00. ISBN 0-7876-2753-4. ISSN 1094-9232.

The 4th volume of *Drama for Students* is an excellent text geared to give students a more in-depth understanding of drama and the plays studied in this volume. The plays are organized alphabetically by chapter with the following elements: a brief overview of the play and its history; an author biography; plot summary; characters; themes; style; historical and cultural context; critical overview; and other sources for further study, criticism, and sources. *Drama for Students* also provides a list of media adaptations for each play, a comparison of the author's culture and late twentieth-century culture, a list of works for further reading in the same subject area, and study questions. Plays range from classical, such as *Iphigenia in Taurus* by Euripides to contemporary works, such as T. S. Eliot's *Murder in the Cathedral*.

Teachers and students will find *Drama for Students* a well-designed, informative text. It will be a useful tool in the classroom or for private study, but it is limited to only 19 plays. Previous and future volumes will help supplement this limitation. Readers may want to seek other sources for the plays that are not covered in this series.

—**Cari Ringelheim**

1025.   Partnow, Elaine, with Lesley Anne Hyatt. The Female Dramatist: Profiles of Women Playwrights from the Middle Ages to Contemporary Times. New York, Facts on File, 1998. 271p. illus. index. $45.00. ISBN 0-8160-3015-4.

The literary and cultural contributions of more than 200 female dramatists who have written plays since 935 C.E. are briefly outlined in this biographical encyclopedia. Although international in scope, most entries cover women whose works were written and produced in English. Each entry includes a memorable quotation from one of the writer's plays, a brief critical essay, a list of dramatic works, a list of other literary contributions, and a brief list of books about the dramatist. An added feature, the timeline, is impossible to follow in its present form as playwrights are listed in order by year of birth. A graphical presentation would be both more useful and more visually appealing. The supplemental index itemizes the contributions of 140 other women who have not yet developed a large repertoire of drama, yet are known for other activities or about whom little has been written. This supplemental index expands the scope to 350 artists and offers an excellent starting point for additional research. Although a significant amount of tough research is still needed to fill in the blanks in this sketchy tool, it is marvelous to see so many creative and influential women gathered together in one spot. This volume fills an empty niche for biographical material on women dramatists and is recommended for both public and academic libraries. [R: Choice, Dec 98, p. 664]—**Anne C. Moore**

1026.   Spanish Dramatists of the Golden Age: A Bio-Bibliographical Sourcebook. Mary Parker, ed. Westport, Conn., Greenwood Press, 1998. 286p. index. $89.50. ISBN 0-313-28893-3.

An exceptional work that spans the classical period of Spanish drama (1500-1700), this reference tool is a welcome addition to the critical literature on this topic. A brief preface, along with an introduction, presents the rationale and format of the current volume—a compilation of essays focused on the life and works of 19 dramatists of the period. These range from Alarcón through Encina, Fernando de Rojas, and Zamora.

Each dramatist is treated by a specialist. Each entry opens with a biographical overview, followed by discussions of the dramatugy (major works and themes) of the author as well as a summary of critical response to the works. In some instances, individual works receive special treatment, and additional notes are provided as necessary. Supplementing each discussion are selected bibliographies that include pertinent information regarding dramatic and nondramatic works, editions and translations, and collected works and critical studies.

With each entry spanning 10 to 12 pages, the writing is often terse yet accessible. Students and researchers will certainly welcome the selected critical bibliographies, and all should find the biographies and critical discussions of interest. The volume ends with a general bibliography, a topical index, and brief information about the contributors. This sourcebook is recommended for academic and large public library reference collections.

—**Edmund F. SantaVicca**

ESSAYS

1027. Schrader, Richard J. **H. L. Mencken: A Descriptive Bibliography.** Pittsburgh, Pa., University of Pittsburgh Press; distr., Ithaca, N.Y., CUP Services, 1998. 628p. illus. index. (Pittsburgh Series in Bibliography). $100.00. ISBN 0-8229-4050-7.

H. L. Mencken's publications from 1899 to 1996 are described in this meticulous bibliography. Included are Mencken's separate publications (chiefly books); books edited or introduced by Mencken; periodical appearances by Mencken (when not appearing in Betty Adler's *H.L.M.: The Mencken Bibliography* [1961]); and more ephemeral items such as blurbs, pamphlets, juvenilia, translations, and Braille versions. The books are described in exhaustive physical and bibliographic detail. Each entry begins with a facsimile of the title page of the first printing of the first edition. Then the copyright page is transcribed, followed by the collation formula. The item is then described in terms of its contents (a nearly page-by-page enumeration of the book's makeup), typography and paper, binding, dust jackets, publishing and printing history, and the location of the item described. This impressive and amazingly detailed volume will thus be an invaluable resource not only for bibliophiles and booksellers but also for scholars interested in Mencken's lengthy and varied publishing career.

—**Jeffrey R. Luttrell**

FICTION

General Works

1028. Barton, Wayne. **What Western Do I Read Next? A Reader's Guide to Recent Western Fiction.** Detroit, Gale, 1998. 545p. index. $69.00. ISBN 0-7876-1865-9.

Culled from previous editions of *What Do I Read Next?*, this collection describes and indexes 1,550 titles in the Western fiction genre that were published between 1989 and 1996. Similar to other Gale publications in organization and format, the book lists titles alphabetically by author, along with publication information (except prices and ISBNs) and book descriptions. Each entry provides the series name (if any), story type (e.g., subgenre), major character names, major character types, time period, locale, a plot summary, and recommendations of up to five similar titles. To allow users multiple points of access and connection, eight indexes (author, title, series name, setting, and so on) are included. Information about awards and descriptions of the story types precede the listings.

It is unfortunate that this book gives no definition or description of the Western because the genre has undergone tremendous changes in recent years. Many have claimed the traditional Western to be dead, and bookstores and trade publishers rarely refer to the genre these days. Instead, readers may find themselves confronted by "frontier fiction" or "historical fiction" that meet some, but not all, criteria of the traditional Western. This is exactly the kind of information most readers' advisers seek in such a tool. In addition, the large size of the book and multiple indexes may prove unwieldy for many users.

It should also be noted that all of the information in this volume can be accessed through the CD-ROM version of *What Do I Read Next?*, which indexes some 55,000 books. Diana Herald's *Genreflecting* (4th ed.; see ARBA 96, entry 1186) offers some guidance on the genre and is far cheaper than this book. For that reason, librarians should carefully consider their needs before making a purchase. In spite of its limitations, this book can be recommended for public libraries where this genre is popular. [R: SLJ, Aug 98, p. 188]—**Barbara Ittner**

1029. Husband, Janet G., and Jonathan F. Husband. **Sequels: An Annotated Guide to Novels in Series.** 3d ed. Chicago, American Library Association, 1997. 688p. index. $75.00; $67.50 (ALA members). ISBN 0-8389-0696-6.

The 3d edition of a work whose 2d edition appeared in 1990 (see ARBA 92, entry 1138), *Sequels* lists and describes the fictional series likely to be found in the typical medium-sized public library; it includes new series created since 1989 and updates its contents through 1995. In its arrangement, *Sequels* is similar to the previous volumes; it is alphabetical by author's name, beneath which, listed in the order in which they should be read, are the titles that comprise the series. Brief publication data—publisher and publication year—are provided, as are a short description of the series and the contents of each title. Separate lists are provided for authors having written more than one series, and the volume concludes with separate title and subject indexes.

Because *Sequels* is selective rather than comprehensive, it can be an easy target, for there are numerous omissions, some of which are significant. In the field of science fiction, one looks in vain for the series by Edgar Rice Burroughs, David Drake, and David Gerrold, to name but three. In addition, there are occasional errors. Rod Whitaker ("Trevanian") was not an English professor; the title of Stephen King's first Dark Tower novel was not simply *The Gunslinger*, and the 3d volume in the series was not first published by the New American Library. There are inconsistencies in listing pseudonyms; some are provided, others—such as Piers Anthony's and Robert Jordan's—are not, although they are hardly unknown. More seriously, the volume contains a number of titles that simply are unlikely to be found in a typical public library: what typical public library will hold Frank Stockton's *The Casting Away of Mrs. Lecks and Mrs. Aleshine* (1886) and *The Dusantes* (1888)? What typical public library is likely to have more than a volume or 2 (at most) of the 17 volumes in the 3 series by H. Rider Haggard published between 1886 and 1927? Nevertheless, *Sequels* should not be dismissed. It is flawed, but still offers much that is not readily accessible elsewhere. Many public libraries may find it quite helpful.—**Richard Bleiler**

Crime and Mystery

1030.   Barnett, Colleen A. **Mystery Women, Volume 1, 1860-1979: An Encyclopedia of Leading Women Characters in Mystery Fiction.** Wautoma, Wis., Ravenstone Books/E.B. Houchin Company, 1997. 299p. $19.99pa. ISBN 0-938313-29-0.

In the first of three projected volumes, the author covers the roles of females sleuths who are on their own or are close companions to or collaborators with male investigators (e.g., Harriet Vane with Lord Peter Wimsey, or Della Street with Perry Mason). Later volumes will cover 1980 to 1989 and 1990 to the present. There are 3 main sections. The first, "Biographies of Leading Women Characters," is subdivided into 5 time periods: 1860-1899, 1900-1919, 1920-1939, 1940-1959, and 1960-1979. Each volume has a title, the second being "The Authors of Leading Women Characters," and the third is "The Books of Leading Women Characters." The final is titled "Out of Turbulence, Towards Equality." All are alphabetic by name, with brief biographies; physical descriptions and characteristics, including eccentricities; and references to particularly well-known titles; among other details. There is also a 4th section (not mentioned on the contents page of the review copy) titled "The Resources of Leading Women Characters"—a rather casual and personal 8-page bibliography of books related to feminism, mysteries, and publishing. Coverage seems somewhat uneven. For example, Agatha Christie's Jane Marple gets a page and a half and Dorothy Sayers's Harriet Vane gets only one-half page. Perhaps this is related to the number of titles by each author. This will be useful in public libraries and collections on the writings of fiction. [R: LJ, 1 May 98, p. 92]—**Walter C. Allen**

1031.   Heising, Willetta L. **Detecting Men: A Reader's Guide and Checklist for Mystery Series Written by Men.** Dearborn, Mich., Purple Moon, 1998. 448p. index. $29.95pa. ISBN 0-9644593-3-7.

Willetta Heising is author of *Detecting Women* (see ARBA 97, entry 947), an award-winning guide to detective series written by women. *Detecting Men* is the guide to 813 mystery series written by men. Only living authors (as of 1995) are included. Firmly established writers are here—Tony Hillerman, Ed McBain, Robert B. Parker, Janwillem van de Wetering—as well as those relatively new to the genre—Robert Greer, John Straley, and Michael McGarrity.

More than one-half of the book is the "Master List": an alphabetic listing of authors with a short biography and a list of their series titles and dates. Chapters 2 through 8 provide fun information—listings by general mystery type (police procedural, private investigator, or espionage); background type (protagonist's occupation and interests); series protagonist (with occupation); setting (city and state); chronology; alphabet; author pseudonym; and mystery book award (also by award category and by author's last name). Thus, the reader looking for a series with a black detective will find author Kenn Davis, whose series began in 1976 and now includes eight books, with a character named Carver Bascombe, who is a "suave black poet private eye" based in San Francisco. Or, the reader can look up a title such as "Eye of the Storm," and see that it was published in 1992 by Jack Higgins, with a number "1" indicating it is the first book in that series. A glossary of mystery book awards, a bibliography, and an author index complete this reference book.

Mystery authors tend to be a prolific lot, and the 2d edition of *Detecting Men* is already slated for October 1999. This is a must for public libraries and mystery buffs.—**Lori D. Kranz**

1032.   **Mystery and Suspense Writers: The Literature of Crime, Detection, and Espionage.** Robin W. Winks and Maureen Corrigan, eds. New York, Macmillan Library Reference/Simon & Schuster Macmillan, 1998. 2v. index. $225.00/set. ISBN 0-684-80492-1.

Mystery and Suspense Writers is an extensive, in-depth study of many suspense and mystery writers from past and present. Mystery, detective, spy, and suspense novels compose the top-selling body of literature in the world. The editors have taken an academic approach to compiling the volumes. Although some readers' favorite authors may not be featured, the editors have chosen to examine the more influential writers of the genre. Each author's entry includes biographical information about life and career as well as detailed examinations of their works.

The 2d volume of this 2-volume set continues the examination of individual writers and also explores certain themes and subgenres. The appendixes provide information on pseudonyms, series characters, subgenres, and major prizewinners. This set proves to be a useful tool for the casual reader interested in learning more about their favorite mystery or suspense writer as well as for serious scholars studying the popular culture phenomena. Although the editors address the issue of the lack of certain writers studied in the set, they would do well to expand and include many more authors. This would make the set more complete.—**Cari Ringelheim**

1033.   Nichols, Victoria, and Susan Thompson. **Silk Stalkings: More Women Write of Murder.** Lanham, Md., Scarecrow, 1998. 635p. $49.95. ISBN 0-8108-3393-X.

Nichols and Thompson, two women frustrated with the lack of reference sources identifying women writers of mystery series, decided to create their own reference—*Silk Stalkings*. First published in 1988 (see ARBA 89, entry 1107), this title maintains its original mission—to classify the recurrent main characters found in mystery fiction written by women since 1976. In this edition, five new chapters have been added to reflect the changes in the genre: historical mysteries, the supernatural and occult, mysteries involving sports, books with criminals as protagonist, and "Senior Sleuths." Classified profiles of 1,300 characters comprise the main body of the work. Each character is fully described, including the year it first appeared in print. Returning supportive characters are identified and the character's relationship to the main character is defined. A master list of authors, including pseudonyms, provides a summary of the titles that each main character appears in; copyright dates are included, but publishers are not named. An appendix chronicles series characters. The authors admit that their selection is subjective; however, this title will be useful for collection development and reader's advisory services.

—**Susan D. Strickland**

Historical Fiction

1034.   Burt, Daniel S. **What Historical Novel Do I Read Next?** Detroit, Gale, 1997. 2v. index. $128.00/set. ISBN 0-7876-0388-0. ISSN 1052-2212.

The 1st volume of this set contains bibliographical information and annotations alphabetically arranged by author and title on 6,966 historical novels for adults—novels whose primary action occurs at least 50 or 60 years before the time in which the author was writing. Each title entry includes title and date of publication, the novel's subject, major fictional and historical characters, time period(s) and locale(s), a short (generally 50 to 100 words) plot summary, and a one or two sentence commentary on the historical accuracy of the novel. Each author entry contains brief biographical information on the author.

The indexes that comprise volume 2 provide time period, geographic, subject, fictional character name, historical character name, character description, author, and title information. The indexes are quite detailed. The time period is arranged by century and decade, beginning with the eighteenth century on. The subject index, although containing general headings such as "Mystery," can be quite specific (e.g., Black Sox Scandal, Battle of Trenton). The geographical index is by country and then by region or town within each country (e.g., United States—Massachusetts—Amherst).

Burt, an associate dean of the College at Wesleyan University and former professor at New York University, has compiled a useful guide to historical fiction. Although Burt makes no claims for inclusiveness, no glaring omissions or inaccuracies were found. The historical annotations are temperate and reasonable. The indexes are extremely helpful for reference and reader's advisory work. This set supercedes works such as Ernest Baker's venerable *Guide to Historical Fiction* (Routledge, 1914) and Daniel McGarry's *World Historical Fiction Guide* (2d ed.; see ARBA 74, entry 1301). This set is recommended for any public, academic, or high school library that has access to a good fiction collection. [R: RUSQ, Summer 98, pp. 373-374; SLJ, Aug 98, p. 188]

—**Jonathan F. Husband**

Science Fiction, Fantasy, and Horror

1035.   Altner, Patricia. **Vampire Readings: An Annotated Bibliography.** Lanham, Md., Scarecrow, 1998. 163p. illus. index. $19.50pa. ISBN 0-8108-3504-5.

This bibliography is designed to enable readers to find titles and authors worth seeking out and to appreciate the many themes that may be developed around a vampire character. The author has focused on fiction published since 1987 but has included selected older works, and she specifically disclaims attempting to provide an exhaustive listing of the literature. The bibliography is separated into five categories: novels, anthologies and novellas, young adult, additional readings, and the unread undead. The work is supplemented by two indexes. In the introduction the author briefly discusses the history of vampires in literature from *Bram Stoker's Dracula*, published in 1897 and continuously in print since then, to the present.

The 1st section, "Novels," contains the most entries (280 of 779), including many multivolume series. The anthologies and novellas section includes both individual stories found in non-vampire-focused collections and vampire-specific collections. For the latter, there is an annotation for the whole work followed by a listing of all titles in the collection, of which a representative sampling is annotated. The annotations are well written and informative, without giving away essential details, and include appropriate cross-references. In the "Young Adult" section, the author urges adults not to bypass the titles on the basis of their intended readers' age group, as they often offer "compelling plots and well-drawn characters." "Additional Readings" contains books that discuss the vampire myth, the literature of the genre, or historical personages who inspired vampire stories. The final section of unread undead includes those titles that the author was unable to find, read, and annotate. It is broken out in the same categories as the main body of the bibliography, and many of the titles have a brief summary.

The author/editor and title indexes provide a quick introduction for the reader who wishes to start with a known author or title, but the work lends itself well to simple browsing. This is a highly readable introduction and guide to a genre of literature that may not be well known to many readers, and quite useful for those who may wish to expand their familiarity with the genre into areas of which they might not be aware. This would be an excellent reader advisory resource for any library with a sizable fiction-reading population, and is also suitable for academic libraries with a strong literature collection.—**Kristin Doty**

1036.   Barron, Neil. **What Fantastic Fiction Do I Read Next? A Reader's Guide to Recent Fantasy, Horror, and Science Fiction.** Detroit, Gale, 1998. 1679p. index. $89.00. ISBN 0-7876-1866-7.

Describing more than 4,800 titles published between 1989 and 1996, this hefty volume is designed to aid readers' advisers and readers in locating the type of reading material they seek. Barron, author of *Anatomy of Wonder* (see ARBA 95, entry 1191), and his associates have selected the fantasy, horror, and science fiction titles they deemed best. Books are listed alphabetically by author or editor, along with publication information (except prices and ISBNs). Awards received, series names, story types (e.g., genre and subgenre), major characters (names and types), time periods, locales, and plot summaries are noted as well as recommendations for similar works. Each of these elements is indexed separately. In addition, the authors give background information on awards and explanations of the story types.

Although the book is formatted clearly and reads well, the size makes it somewhat cumbersome and the organization (eight indexes) may cause confusion in users who are not familiar with the layout. Users must flip back and forth between indexes to find titles in the same genre or subgenre. There is little background information on the three genres represented here and no guidelines or tips for the readers' adviser. The appeal of this volume may be limited. Public libraries that can afford NoveList or the electronic versions of *What Do I Read Next?* will not need the book, but those that cannot afford the electronic guides may not be able to afford this book either, with its weighty price of nearly $90, especially when the book does not offer background information on the genres or readers' advisory guidelines. For smaller libraries other print sources, such as Barron's *Anatomy of*

Wonder and Diana Herald's *Genreflecting* (see ARBA 96, entry 1186), will suffice for now. [R: VOYA, Aug 98, p. 229; BL, 15 May 98, p. 1652]—**Barbara Ittner**

Short Stories

1037. **Short Story Criticism, Volume 26: Excerpts from Criticism of the Works of Short Fiction Writers.** Anna J. Sheets, ed. Detroit, Gale, 1997. 550p. index. $99.00. ISBN 0-7876-1486-6.

1038. **Short Story Criticism, Volume 27: Excerpts from Criticism of the Works of Short Fiction Writers.** Anna J. Sheets, ed. Detroit, Gale, 1998. 553p. illus. index. $99.00. ISBN 0-7876-1663-X.

    The latest volumes in the Short Story Criticism series (SSC) do the series justice. These works seek to give critical and biographical information on important short story authors. The arrangement is a bit scattered because it does not go alphabetically or chronologically; however, cumulative indexes of the series—author, title, and nationality—make up for this. SSC is selective, covering those authors whose work has generated a good deal of criticism.

    By focusing on writers and their stories, the series delivers great detail and overviews of careers simultaneously. Volume 26 has 45 pages on the work of Philip Roth, and volume 27 features 10 pages on John Updike. Excerpts from critical works are included, and lists of "Principal Works" make this a strong series for those doing research in short fiction. This series is recommended for school, public, and academic libraries.—**Bob Craigmile**

NATIONAL LITERATURE

American Literature

General Works

Bibliography

1039.   Canfield Reisman, Rosemary M., and Suzanne Booker-Canfield. **Contemporary Southern Men Fiction Writers: An Annotated Bibliography.** Pasadena, Calif., Salem Press and Lanham, Md., Scarecrow, 1998. 427p. index. (Magill Bibliographies). $55.00. ISBN 0-8108-3195-3.

    A thorough, comprehensive tool for students and teachers of southern writing, this reference work is also a worthy source for librarians, reviewers, and the media. The coverage of 39 southern male writers includes the revered Reynolds Price, William Styron, Pat Conroy, Ernest J. Gaines, Fred Chappell, and James Dickey. Other entries list critical works on popular authors such as Larry McMurty, Clyde Edgerton, John Grisham, Ferrol Sams, and Allan Gurganus and less familiar figures, including Madison Smartt Bell, Padgett Powell, and Philip Lee Williams. The work focuses on commentary from *The New York Times Book Review*, *Atlanta Journal-Constitution*, *Library Journal*, *The Washington Post*, *Boston Globe*, *Sewanee Review*, and *Commonweal* as well as the lesser known critical interpretations of important authors and their creative work from *The Black Scholar*, *Pembroke Magazine*, *Delta 23*, and *Chattahoochee Review*.

    A parallel to Magill's *Contemporary Southern Women Writers* (1994), the compendium opens on Booker-Canfield's thought-provoking introduction and appends a general studies section containing 70 entries ranging in age from John Bradbury's respected *Renaissance in the South* (1963) to Robert O. Stephens's *The Family Saga in the South* (1995) and Edward Ayers and Bradley Mittendorf's *The Oxford Book of the American South* (1997). Keen, even-handed commentary on each bibliographic entry offers insight into Allan Gurganus's energetic storytelling, William Styron's stridence, Andre Dubus's lyricism, and Pete Dexter's moral integrity. The selection of critical works comes from a broad spectrum to cite respected writers—Rita Mae Brown, Jonathan Yardley, Annie Dillard, Joyce Carol Oates, Dannye Romine Powell, T. Coraghessan Boyle, Jill McCorkle, Frye Gaillard, Polly Paddock, Henry Louis Gates Jr., and Barbara Kingsolver. The indexing is straightforward and comprehensive. Sorely lacking from the lineup of entries are playwrights Robert Harling, Horton Foote, and

Alfred Uhry, whose contributions to southern literature have rejuvenated theater with their regional and universal vision. [R: Choice, Oct 98, p. 293]—**Mary Ellen Snodgrass**

1040.   Glitsch, Catherine, comp. **American Novel Explication 1991-1995.** North Haven, Conn., Archon Books/Shoe String Press, 1998. 319p. index. $39.50. ISBN 0-208-02481-6.

In *The American Novel 1789-1959: A Checklist of Twentieth-Century Criticism* (Swallow, 1961) and *The American Novel, Volume II: Criticism Written 1960-1968* (Swallow, 1970), Donna Gerstenberger and George Hendrick provided extremely useful bibliographies of commentary on long fiction. Glitsch's volume is a much-needed continuation of those earlier works. By focusing sharply on explication (and excluding criticism that is largely historical, biographical, or bibliographic), Glitsch limits the scope of her bibliography. At the same time, she broadens the geographic range by including authors from Canada as well as the United States. With coverage of more than 700 novelists, she even includes a number of Canadians who normally write in French. Unlike Gerstenberger and Hendrick, Glitsch also provides entries for some authors of juvenile or adolescent fiction (e.g., Frank Baum and Laura Ingalls Wilder).

The book's overall plan is straightforward and convenient for users. Author entries are arranged alphabetically, and each main entry is further subdivided with relevant criticism listed under the titles of specific novels. The front matter lists 189 journals cited by Glitsch, along with their Modern Language Association abbreviations. The back matter contains a list of 369 critical books and an index of all novels and novelists included.

Glitsch's compilation is intended as a companion to two other series of bibliographies published by Shoe String Press—English Novel Explication (see ARBA 95, entry 1208) and Twentieth-Century Short Story Explication (see ARBA 98, entry 1118). To achieve this end, Shoe String plans to publish three additional volumes of *American Novel Explication* covering the years from 1969 through 1990. Subsequent volumes to keep the series up-to-date will then appear at five-year intervals.—**Albert Wilhelm**

1041.   Hillstrom, Kevin, and Laurie Collier Hillstrom. **The Vietnam Experience: A Concise Encyclopedia of American Literature, Songs, and Films.** Westport, Conn., Greenwood Press, 1998. 322p. index. $65.00. ISBN 0-313-30183-2.

The facts surrounding a traumatic historical event rarely give any clear evidence as to exactly why the event was devastating. How do you explain how shaken the U.S. population was by the Vietnam War? In order to understand the terror and horror of shared societal experiences, we can often learn more by looking at art and literature than we can by reading works of serious history. By watching *Born on the Fourth of July* and *Platoon* or reading Tim O'Brien's *The Things They Carried* (Houghton Mifflin, 1990), we receive little factual information; what we do receive is an opportunity to look through a clearer window into the emotional content of the Vietnam experience.

The authors of *The Vietnam Experience* have done an admirable job of collecting a representative and substantive list of films, narratives, literary works, and popular songs that in many ways represent the "suppressed scream" of the Vietnam era. This is not a reference book to use for historical or political detail; for that the reader is referred to *The Encyclopedia of the Vietnam War* (see ARBA 97, entry 433). Rather, this encyclopedia should be used to get a critical grasp of the cultural and societal effects of the Vietnam conflict.

This reviewer does question the title because this is a selected as well as concise encyclopedia. However, it should be noted that it is indeed a well-selected group of works. Each of the 44 entries is a clearly written critical essay that includes a description of how its subject fits into the "Vietnam Era," issues surrounding the creation of the work, plot summary (when appropriate), critical and popular reactions, and sources for further reading. In addition, there are also lists of their notable works, including songs, films, and literary works. It would be easy to critique the lists of works included in either the body of the work or in the lists, because anyone from that era would have personal favorites that were not included in either place. The authors present a serious and balanced selection of works.

This is an excellent reference work and should be included in every public library of significant size and any school or academic library addressing the needs of people studying modern U.S. history and society. [R: Choice, July/Aug 98, p. 1830]—**Caroline M. Kent**

1042.   Lawlor, William. **The Beat Generation: A Bibliographical Teaching Guide.** Pasadena, Calif., Salem Press and Lanham, Md., Scarecrow, 1998. 357p. index. (Magill Bibliographies). $42.00. ISBN 0-8108-3387-5.

This bibliography is designed as a teaching guide that caters to the present student interest in the Beat generation. It is a comprehensive guide, addressing such problems as the definition of *Beat*, the identification of the Beat writers, and the selection of primary sources. After providing annotated bibliographies of the Beats in general, Lawlor devotes separate chapters to the three leading figures—William Burroughs, Allen Ginsberg, and Jack Kerouac. Another 75 Beat writers are covered briefly, their writings more fully covered than their lives. Finally, there is an excellent chapter of suggestions for students research topics.

Lawlor is understandably defensive about the value of Beat literature (which critic Ned Polsky describes as mostly "poor when it is not godawful"). The literature has an appeal to some students as representing rebellion against middle-class values, but it is usually dismissed by academics as second rate; it is steadily undermined by the Beats' espousal of spontaneous writing. Writers like Kerouac were not disposed to edit their work, believing that their minds were God.

Lawlor gives a brief account of the literary origins of the Beat movement, seeing Walt Whitman as a forerunner, but does not connect it with European literary developments like the *nouveau roman* in France. Nor does he endeavor to indicate its later development into the discontented middle-class literature of writers like Ann Beattie and Rick Moody. This book essentially studies the Beats as an isolated phenomenon, with few predecessors and no successors. [R: Choice, Nov 98, p. 492]—**John B. Beston**

Bio-bibliography

1043.   **American Writers: Selected Authors.** Leonard Unger and A. Walton Litz, eds. New York, Macmillan Library Reference/Simon & Schuster Macmillan, 1998. 3v. index. $180.00/set. ISBN 0-684-80604-5.

This set comprises 64 unabridged essays that have been chosen from the 13-volume American Writers series (4 volumes plus supplements) published by Scribner. None of the articles or the bibliographies have been updated but rather extracted from the more costly series and rendered more affordable for libraries with limited budgets.

However, 18 of the 64 articles are from the recent *American Writers Retrospective Supplement* (see ARBA 97, entry 961) and so provide revisions of articles on Willa Cather, Emily Dickinson, T. S. Eliot, William Faulkner, F. Scott Fitzgerald, Robert Frost, Nathaniel Hawthorne, Ernest Hemingway, Herman Melville, Vladimir Nabokov, and John Updike. Entries for all authors are basic critical bio-bibliographies, averaging some 20 pages in length. Written by specialists, each critical review is followed by a selected bibliography of primary and secondary works, including critical and biographical studies. Full indexing is included in the final volume.

The articles are solid and readable, and should appeal to the average high school or college student. Libraries that already own the larger series might consider adding this set as a duplicate source for those authors studied most frequently. Libraries that could not afford the larger series should seriously consider this set for purchase.

—**Edmund F. SantaVicca**

Biography

1044.   **American Travel Writers, 1776-1864.** James Schramer and Donald Ross, eds. Detroit, Gale, 1997. 418p. illus. index. (Dictionary of Literary Biography, v.183). $146.00. ISBN 0-7876-1072-0.

Editors Schramer and Ross emphasize the great diversity of antebellum American travel writing in this new Dictionary of Literary Biography (DLB) volume. The 36 essays cover 40 native-born or naturalized Americans who wrote accounts of their travels at home and abroad while either actively pursuing occupations (and, just as often, preoccupations) or simply suffering fortunes that cast them into exotic captivity, like James Riley, or sent them around the world, like Amasa Delano. Here Josiah Gregg's single publication, *Commerce of the Prairies* (1844), is said to have influenced and guided western migration; the Ojibwa Kah-ge-ga-gah-bowh (later known as George Copway) describes western Europe in what is called the first travel book written by a Native American; and John Lloyd Stephens, dubbed "The American Traveler," is cited (per Van Wyck Brooks) as "the greatest of American travel writers." Other American travel writers include presidents John Adams (with Abigail Adams) and Thomas Jefferson; statesman Benjamin Franklin; diplomat's spouse Fanny Calderón de la Barca; frontier explorers and folk heroes Meriwether Lewis and William Clark, Davy Crockett, John Charles Frémont (with Jessie Benton Frémont), and Zebulon Pike; artists John Woodhouse Audubon, Rembrandt Peale, and John

Trumbull; historians Joel Tyler Headley and Francis Parkman; naval hero Matthew Perry (along with many naval officers like Horatio Bridge, George Jones, Alexander Slidell Mackenzie, David Porter, and Charles Wilkes); scientist Benjamin Silliman; and many literati, like William Wells Brown, James Fenimore Cooper, Richard Henry Dana Jr., Ralph Waldo Emerson, Margaret Fuller, Nathaniel Hawthorne (with Sophia Peabody Hawthorne), Washington Irving, Catharine Maria Sedgwick, Lydia Huntley Sigourney, Henry David Thoreau, and Nathaniel Parker Willis.

For the literati especially, the entries update and supplement others in some of the earliest DLB volumes, including *The American Renaissance in New England* (see ARBA 80, entry 1224) and *Antebellum Writers in New York and the South* (see ARBA 80, entry 1240). For most of the writers, however, the volume's entries discover new ground. Schramer and Ross's extensive introduction, amounting to a literature review of American travel writing and major research on it, accurately and usefully describes "the general perspectives and conditions that informed the views of nineteenth-century Americans," particularly the biases that centered fashion, culture, and democracy (as well as barbarousness, ignorance, and savagery) in certain parts of the world. At the same time, the editors neatly identify and classify American travelers' several main narrative and rhetorical modes of discourse. An apppendixed bibliography of supplemental primary sources, "American Travel Writing, 1776-1864," effectively dramatizes the range of narratives and points to opportunities for further research. The volume contains excellent selections of illustrations, including portraits, maps, and works' title pages and manuscripts, that have come to be expected of DLB volumes. Like others in the DLB series that has now burgeoned for 20 years, this volume affords the full range of readers excellent biographical, critical, and bibliographic starting points for research. The volume's availability should promote wider interest in early American travel writing. [R: LJ, 1 Nov 98, p. 70; Choice, Dec 98, p. 658]—**James K. Bracken**

1045.   **American Writers: A Collection of Literary Biographies. Retrospective Supplement 1.** A. Walton Litz and Molly Weigel, eds. New York, Macmillan Library Reference/Simon & Schuster Macmillan, 1998. 457p. index. $120.00. ISBN 0-684-80494-8.

Although the initial 4-volume set of *American Writers* was published in 1974 (see ARBA 75, entry 1350), the essays within that compilation were originally issued as pamphlets by the University of Minnesota Press from 1959 to 1972. Because Scribner's reprinted versions incorporated only minimal revisions, the critical perspective reflected in those essays is now somewhat dated. Therefore, Scribner commissioned this retrospective supplement, which contains new essays on 19 of the 97 authors covered by the base set. The editors note that these writers were selected in consultation with teachers and librarians. Thus, the inclusion of such frequently studied figures as Emily Dickinson, William Faulkner, Langston Hughes, Herman Melville, and Eudora Welty comes as no surprise. However, the omission of Flannery O'Connor, Mark Twain, and Tennessee Williams is difficult to understand, particularly in light of the significant amount of new scholarship that has been published on these major authors during the past 30 years and in view of some of the other writers featured, such as Vladimir Nabokov, Wallace Stevens, and John Updike.

Contributed by noted scholars and averaging 23 pages in length, the scholarly, well-written essays skillfully blend biographical information with descriptions of major works and critical commentary. Selected bibliographies of primary and secondary works conclude each essay. The useful index provides access to names and titles mentioned in the articles.

All of these authors are included in Gale's Dictionary of Literary Biography series (DLB), and most of them are accorded multiple articles (ranging from two to five) in that set. Because the DLB articles frequently focus on a specific aspect of an author's writing, such as a particular genre or literary period, an advantage of *American Writers* is that each of its essays offers a unified overview of the whole of a writer's life and career. Libraries that have found the base set of *American Writers* and its four 2-volume supplements valuable will certainly want to add this new volume because it provides solid, up-to-date introductions to the lives and works of some of the most preeminent American writers of the nineteenth and twentieth centuries.—**Marie Ellis**

Dictionaries and Encyclopedias

1046.   **The New England Transcendentalists.** [CD-ROM]. Princeton, N.J., Films for the Humanities & Sciences, 1997. Minimum system requirements: IBM or compatible 486. Double-speed CD-ROM drive. 8MB RAM. 256-color monitor set to 640x480 resolution. Quick Time 2.5. $149.00.

For those with an interest in nineteenth-century American literature or social and religious movements, this database should prove quite useful. The core of the database are the works of three prominent transcendentalists: Ralph Waldo Emerson, Margaret Fuller, and Henry David Thoreau. Included are 12 works by Emerson, 1 by Fuller, and 3 by Thoreau. In addition to the full text, audio selections from each work are included. Using an options menu, users can freely search for keywords within a particular work, within the body of work of a particular author, or search all of the works included. Basic access to the disc is provided via five buttons. The first, "Program Overview," presents a welcome and sample demonstration of the product, along with directions and credits. A second button provides access to the full body of works. The third, "Screening Room," provides access to 23 QuickTime videos (averaging one minute each) on a variety of related topics. A "Contexts" button takes the user to explanations and essays related to the central topic. Both individuals and concepts (e.g., philosophy, religion, and social issues) are treated. In some cases, annotated bibliographies complement the text. The producers also include an "Internet" button that provides access through one's browser to the producer's homepage, which includes advertisements for various products and samples of some of the contexts mentioned above.

This tool is an interesting and useful multimedia product most useful for the high school or college research paper. Public libraries with spirituality and literature collections might also consider the product for purchase. [R: LJ, Jan 98, p. 158]—**Edmund F. SantaVicca**

1047.   Snodgrass, Mary Ellen. **Encyclopedia of Southern Literature.** Santa Barbara, Calif., ABC-CLIO, 1997. 550p. illus. index. (ABC-CLIO Literary Companion). $65.00. ISBN 0-87436-952-5.

The southern literary tradition is a long one, having roots in the works produced by the first English settlers. The approximately 250 essay entries in the *Encyclopedia of Southern Literature* attempt to survey the major southern authors and their works and to discuss the southern literary movements and themes. The authors discussed include such chronologically diverse talents as James Agee, Maya Angelou, George Washington Cable, Truman Capote, Kate Chopin, Pat Conroy, Frederick Douglass, Beth Henley, and Edgar Allan Poe. The movements and themes discussed range from "The Civil War Era" and "The Colonial and Federalist Eras" to "Fugitive Agrarians," "Humor, Southern," "Regionalism," "Theater in the South," and "Young-Adult Literature." Following the essays, there are a list of the home states of southern authors and a chronology of southern literature from 1612 to 1997. Lists of major works of southern literature and of the major southern authors and their works are provided. There are also a chronology of films of major works of southern literature followed by additional bibliographies. There is an index.

The *Encyclopedia of Southern Literature* might occasionally be useful to undergraduates wanting brief explanations, but the volume is inadequate and deeply flawed. At the very least, additional definitions should have been provided; the works of Truman Capote and Flannery O'Connor are described as "Southern gothic," but what does that mean? Worse, there are errors. Poe's entry in particular is riddled with incorrect dates, incorrect titles, incorrect given names, and factual errors. Finally, the *Encyclopedia* is far from encyclopedic, and the lacunae are significant; not only is no mention made of numerous important historical writers, but many significant contemporary writers have been omitted. No point would be served by listing these, but their names are numerous, and it is they who have given the literature of the South its richness and depth.—**Richard Bleiler**

Handbooks and Yearbooks

1048.   **Modern American Literature. Volume 6.** 4th ed. Martin Tucker, ed. New York, Continuum Publishing, 1997. 577p. index. (Third Supplement to the Fourth Edition). $95.00. ISBN 0-8264-0902-4.

A supplement to 5 earlier volumes in *A Library of Literary Criticism*, this book retains the dual purpose of those previous works. In presenting criticism from the past decade, Tucker attempts to provide detailed explication of specific literary works as well as an overview of critical responses to individual writers. He includes excerpts (usually less than 500 words) from 157 scholarly or popular journals and from numerous books. With sections on 202 authors—61 of whom are new to this supplement—Tucker provides expanded coverage of ethnic and female writers. The literary merit of a writer's work remains the primary criterion for inclusion, but Tucker acknowledges the occasional influence of extraliterary factors. Within each section, excerpts are presented chronologically to reflect an author's changing critical reputation.

For the 61 new writers included in this volume, the back matter supplies complete bibliographies of primary works; bibliographies for other writers list publications only from the past decade. Along with an index of critics included, this supplement provides two new indexes—a subject index and an index of authors covered in the volume who have written commentaries on other included authors.

The excerpts here are carefully chosen and reflect the insights of influential critics like Harold Bloom, Sandra Gilbert, and Joseph Epstein. Excerpts on a specific author are typically shorter and less numerous than those in *Contemporary Literary Criticism* annuals (see entries 966-969), but Tucker's work covers more authors in a single volume.—**Albert Wilhelm**

1049.   **Twayne's United States Authors on CD-ROM.** [CD-ROM]. new ed. New York, G. K. Hall/Simon & Schuster Macmillan, 1997. Minimum system requirements: IBM or compatible 486. CD-ROM drive. 16 MB RAM. 16 MB hard disk space. SVGA monitor. $1,243.75. ISBN 0-7838-1715-0.

A revision of the DiscLit series, this new compilation of literary criticism and interpretation includes 59 additional authors or topics, bringing the total to 201 authors. New among these are topical treatments of Native American poetry, Jewish American fiction, late-nineteenth-century American diary literature, and Native American literature. The range of additional authors includes Nikki Giovanni, Rita Mae Brown, Dr. Seuss, Chaim Potok, Thomas Pynchon, Toni Morrison, Margaret Titchell, and Edgar Rice Burroughs, to name a few.

Users will appreciate the new browser interface, similar to Netscape. Of equal value is the ability to move among chapters, search for bibliographies or chronologies, ask for on-screen help, or choose from a variety of menu commands. An initial menu provides a choice of "In Depth Search," "Research Ideas," or "Authors A-Z," as well as options for searching tips and printing tips. Color-coded screens remind the user of the context of any given search.

Search capabilities are more powerful in this revision, allowing for wild cards, truncation, and Boolean operators. References can be retrieved across all works on the disk, and additional keywords are suggested to assist the user. Printing options are expanded to allow single page, chapter, or highlighted sections. Citation information is provided in pop-up windows and is printed automatically for each section.

Price aside, most libraries should strongly consider acquiring this disk for its ease of use, compact storage, and the scope and nature of the criticism included. [R: BR, Sept/Oct 98, p. 90; BL, 1 Sept 98, p. 165]

—**Edmund F. SantaVicca**

Drama

1050.   Williams, Dana A. **Contemporary African American Female Playwrights: An Annotated Bibliography.** Westport, Conn., Greenwood Press, 1998. 124p. index. (Bibliographies and Indexes in Afro-American and African Studies, no.37). $55.00. ISBN 0-313-30132-8.

Williams has put together a much-needed and useful research tool that brings attention to the works of contemporary African American playwrights who are often forgotten in literary criticism. This comprehensive, annotated bibliography includes playwrights who have had at least one work published since 1969, the year of Lorraine Hansberry's *A Raisin in the Sun.*

The bibliography is divided into three sections: anthologies, general criticism and reference works, and individual dramatists. Section 1 lists annotated entries of selected anthologies that are listed alphabetically by author's or editor's names. The anthologies include one or more plays written by an African American female playwright. Section 2 gives entries for reference works and scholarly and critical studies of the playwrights and their works. Section 3 lists individual playwrights. For those playwrights with multiple works, the plays are listed chronologically, followed by a summary. Secondary sources are also listed.

The appendix of the bibliography is in two parts, A and B. Appendix A includes a list of periodicals and magazines that frequently publish articles on contemporary playwrights and their works. Appendix B is an alphabetic listing of biographical information about each playwright. Unpublished works are listed when that information is available. Extensive indexes, by author, title, and subject, add to the usefulness of this bibliography, which is strongly recommended for school, college, and public libraries. [R: Choice, Nov 98, p. 495]

—**Mary L. Bowman**

Individual Authors

Anne Tyler

1051.   Bail, Paul. **Anne Tyler: A Critical Companion.** Westport, Conn., Greenwood Press, 1998. 212p. index. (Critical Companion to Popular Contemporary Writers). $29.95. ISBN 0-313-30249-9.

This volume of literary criticism is part of the series Critical Companions to Popular Contemporary Writers from Greenwood Press. A biographical chapter opens the book and includes published information, autobiographical material, and interviews. Primarily presented in a chronological narrative, experiences within Tyler's life are related to her novels and the characters she develops. The following chapter focuses on literary influences on the author and explains how the author's work fits into the broader literary field. The main body of the volume analyzes Tyler's most important and popular novels in detail. Arranged in chronological order by publication date, each chapter focuses on a single title. The chapters are organized around three central literary elements: plot, characterization, and theme. Other elements often included are comparison and contrast to other titles within the genre, symbolism, and historical and social context. Bail often includes a subsection viewing the novel from a different perspective, such as feminist, mythological, or psychological.

The bibliography of primary and secondary sources is well organized into categories that are either alphabetically or chronologically arranged. The writings of Tyler are followed by interviews, reviews and criticisms, articles and books about Tyler, and additional works that were cited. A thorough index completes the volume. Bail contradicted himself on the number of novels by Tyler: stating 13 in one paragraph, 14 in the next, and listing only 13 in the bibliography. Tyler has published 14.

High school and college English students will find the book and the series most useful. The arrangement and extensive bibliography make it easy to use and provide the researcher with additional resources. Authors for the series are chosen by an advisory board consisting of high school English teachers and public and high school librarians. Criterion for inclusion includes best-selling authors with a succession of successful novels, writers of wide critical acclaim, and writers not receiving academic literary analysis within the past 10 years. Other volumes in the series are to be similarly arranged and structured.—**Elaine Ezell**

Emily Dickinson

1052.   **An Emily Dickinson Encyclopedia.** Jane Donahue Eberwein, ed. Westport, Conn., Greenwood Press, 1998. 395p. index. $85.00. ISBN 0-313-29781-9.

As women's studies departments in colleges and universities grow and develop, reference books focusing on specific women writers and their work are in demand. Eberwein has taken on the challenge of providing one such book in this ambitious project. In the preface Eberwein states that this encyclopedia "provides succinctly informative entries on people important to Emily Dickinson: family members, friends, neighbors and persons who influenced her. Other entries report on places and institutions familiar to her and aspects of nineteenth-century New England culture." The entries are thorough, comprehensive, and above all, interesting and easy to read. The contributors comprise an eclectic group of 100 scholars, graduate students, teachers, and even the husband of one scholar who is a dentist by profession, thus lending a variety of insightful and even entertaining perspectives to Dickinson's life and work. Several pages are devoted to the key figures in her life: Thomas Wentworth Higginson (the poet to whom she sent many of her poems for critique), Susan Gilbert Dickinson (her friend and sister-in-law), and Lavinia Dickinson (her sister).

The book contains two appendixes; the first lists which poems were discovered in which fascicle, and the second lists major archival collections for Dickinson research. A chronology of Dickinson's life follows the preface and lists events in the poet's life that will illuminate not only her poetry, but her letters to friends as well. A bibliography, an index of poems cited, a general index, and an about the contributors section precedes the main text of the book, all of which will prove valuable to serious researchers. Overall, Eberwein's book will be an attractive and useful addition to the libraries of Dickinson aficionados as well as to the collections of American literature experts. [R: C&RL, Oct 98, p. 711; BL, July 98, p. 1904; Choice, Dec 98, p. 660]—**Beth St. Cyr**

Esther Forbes

1053.   Bales, Jack. **Esther Forbes: A Bio-Bibliography of the Author of** *Johnny Tremain.* Lanham, Md., Scarecrow, 1998. 173p. index. (Scarecrow Author Bibliographies Series, no.98). $45.00. ISBN 0-8108-3370-0.

This book is number 98 in Scarecrow Press's series of author bibliographies which feature American and international authors of interest. Its title reveals the way in which it differs from other books in the series: *Esther Forbes: A Bio-Bibliography of the Author of Johnny Tremain* not only delivers information about Forbes's body of work and attendant criticism, it also sheds light on the life of the woman whose best-known work, *Johnny Tremain*, has remained a popular introduction to historical fiction for nearly six decades.

The volume begins with a chronology of Forbes's life and work. Next, an 18-page bibliographic essay details her lesser-known role as the Houghton Mifflin editor who discovered Rafael Sabatini. Part 1 of the bibliography presents reviews of Forbes's 11 books. Part 2, titled "General Criticism," includes vitae from other reference books as well as obituaries and memorial tributes. Part 3, devoted to criticism of Forbes's children's literature, also lists theses and dissertations as well as study guides for *Johnny Tremain*. The 3 appendixes contain additional material, including Ester Forbes's Newbery Medal acceptance speech. An index is also included.

As the author points out, although scores of others have written more books, few have received as many literary awards or as much widespread recognition, both popular and literary, as Forbes. For that reason *Esther Forbes: A Bio-Bibliography of the Author of Johnny Tremain* is a valuable addition to the body of information about this deserving American writer.—**Kay O. Cornelius**

F. Scott Fitzgerald

1054.   Tate, Mary Jo. **F. Scott Fitzgerald A to Z: The Essential Reference to His Life and Work.** New York, Facts on File, 1998. 340p. illus. index. $45.00. ISBN 0-8160-3150-9.

Any serious reader of F. Scott Fitzgerald will object to the hyperbole of the advertising release about this new encyclopedia, which states: "Many books have been written about F. Scott Fitzgerald, but you need only one." Nevertheless, this book is a useful source of facts about the writings and life of the man perhaps best known as the literary chronicler of the "Jazz Age." After a foreword by the well-known Fitzgerald scholar Matthew J. Bruccoli, the book includes an alphabetically arranged collection of entries covering all of the author's publications (e.g., novels, short stories, plays, essays, poems, public letters, and motion picture projects). There are separate entries for each fictional character (with the exception of very minor characters) and people in Fitzgerald's life (e.g., relatives, friends, associates, writers, illustrators, and critics), as well as places he visited and wrote about (both real and fictional), organizations in which he was involved, and publications in which he appeared. Also included are a detailed chronology of his life and career and a bibliography not only of Fitzgerald's work but also of that of his wife, Zelda. Additional features that make this book especially useful for reference include a selected categorized bibliography of works about Fitzgerald; a list of movie, play, and television adaptations; and a detailed index. Numerous illustrations also enhance the text.

Some controversy exists about the most authoritative edition of Fitzgerald's works, a controversy that is reflected both in the foreword by Bruccoli and his entry in this book, "Editing Fitzgerald's Texts." Bruccoli states that he withdrew from the Cambridge University Press edition of Fitzgerald, intended as the critical, scholarly edition, because of "interference with his editorial judgment" (p. 65). That controversy centers on Fitzgerald's inconsistencies and factual errors, some of which were due to his carelessness and some to his publisher, Charles Scribner's Sons. Bruccoli and the author of this encyclopedia believe it is important for an editor to silently correct Fitzgerald when an error of intention was mistakenly published by Scribner's. Clarification of such errors is also an object of some of the entries in this encyclopedia.

This book will be quite useful to advanced students needing to check facts about Fitzgerald's life and work but also to beginning readers who may need nothing more than a synopsis of the major works. [R: BR, Sept/Oct 98, p. 70]—**David Isaacson**

Hamlin Garland

1055. Newlin, Keith. **Hamlin Garland: A Bibliography, with a Checklist of Unpublished Letters.** Troy, N.Y., Whitston Publishing, 1998. 231p. index. $35.00. ISBN 0-87875-497-0.

The primary purpose of this bibliography is to help scholars identify, date, and locate 4,370 letters (out of a total of 5,342) found in 89 different libraries—the University of Southern California, Huntington Library, Miami University (Oxford, Ohio), and the University of Virginia having major holdings. The author provides a helpful overview of a library's collection of letters (family correspondence and correspondence with publishers, friends, institutions, and the like) as well as a thumbnail description of individual letters selected for inclusion, including 13 helpful identifiers such as autographs, drafts, telegrams, letters typed, typed letters signed, and transcribed letters. Also, letters that are included in the "Selected Letters of Hamlin Garland," edited by the author of this bibliography and Joseph B. McCullough, are noted. Another important feature is a title index to help users identify short fiction that Garland republished under different titles in various collections.

The author provides a chronology and a complete bibliography of Garland's publications, including books, contributions to periodicals and books, and articles that quote Garland extensively. Production features complement Newlin's scholarship: quality paper, strong cloth binding, attractive topography, and dark typeface. This is an essential purchase for all large academic libraries and any library having Garland's selected letters in its collection. [R: Choice, Dec 98, p. 664]—**Milton H. Crouch**

Jessamyn West

1056. Farmer, Ann Dahlstrom, and Philip M. O'Brien. **Jessamyn West: A Descriptive and Annotated Bibliography.** Lanham, Md., Scarecrow, 1998. 383p. index. (Scarecrow Author Bibliographies, no.100). $62.00. ISBN 0-8108-3509-6.

This comprehensive, annotated bibliography discusses works by and about Jessamyn West (1902-1984). Between 1939 and her death, she published 19 full-length works, including novels, autobiographies, short stories, poetry collections, dramas, and a Quaker anthology as well as countless shorter pieces in newspapers and periodicals. Following the lists of characters and subject of each work is a detailed physical description of collation, contents, paper, and binding of the various editions, with notes pointing out changes in each printing. The extensive bibliographic information about her most popular work, *The Friendly Persuasion*, runs 23 pages. Material on her shorter works are brief, but well annotated. Holograph and typed papers including schoolwork, various drafts and different versions of published titles, film scripts, and audiotapes, which are part of the Whittier College Jessamyn West Special Collection, are described as well as her correspondence. The hundreds of letters to her that are also part of the collection are not included.

West's life is detailed in a five-page chronology. The text is well organized into 3 sections: works by West, works about West, and miscellaneous. Cross-references are identified by the section entry number in both the text and the index. All fully described materials have been seen by the authors aided by West's husband, Harry Maxwell McPherson, and daughter, Ann McCarthy Cash, who also wrote the foreword. The authors state in the preface that the bibliography is intended for "scholars, collectors, and book dealers." It should prove invaluable to all three.—**Charlotte Lindgren**

Tennessee Williams

1057. **Tennessee Williams: A Guide to Research and Performance.** Philip C. Kolin, ed. Westport, Conn., Greenwood Press, 1998. 282p. index. $75.00. ISBN 0-313-30306-1.

This volume should prove to be a worthy addition to collections of criticism of modern American drama as well as theater and performance. It presents 22 essays, which review individual and collective works of this major playwright, bringing together a lot of information.

Each of the essays follows the same format. For the work being examined, the editor first summarizes the relationship between the work and Williams's personal life. Following this is a review of the bibliographic history of the dramatic work. Next comes a review of critical approaches to the work, including summaries of research regarding themes, characters, symbols, and plot. Major problems that the work has posed for critics are also examined. Using theater reviews, stage histories, and biographical tools, each specialist then reviews the chief theatrical productions of the work in question. Film and television versions are also examined, followed by a concluding overview of research regarding the particular dramatic piece. Finally, each essay ends with a full bibliography of sources used throughout the chapter.

Chapters vary between 10 and 20 pages, with the final 3 focusing on the fiction, the poetry, and the films of Tennessee Williams. The volume is supplemented by a general bibliography, including biographies, interviews, bibliographies, and critical studies; a set of full indexes to actors, choreographers, composers, designers, directors, librettists, producers, commentators, critics, reviewers, and the elements of the dramatic works; and brief profiles of the contributors. For its scope, quality, and style, the work is noteworthy among the vast array of literary criticism published in a reference format.—**Edmund F. SantaVicca**

Toni Morrison

1058.   Kubitschek, Missy Dehn. **Toni Morrison: A Critical Companion.** Westport, Conn., Greenwood Press, 1998. 203p. index. (Critical Companions to Popular Contemporary Writers). $29.95. ISBN 0-313-30265-0.

The original Critical Companions to Popular Contemporary Writers series treated best-selling authors who had not received book-length literary analysis (e.g., Anne Rice, John Grisham, Tom Clancy). This volume on Toni Morrison is one of several that extend the original concept to authors who have received wider critical attention.

Aimed at a large audience, ranging from students to fans, each volume follows the same general format. There is a biographical chapter, followed by a chapter on the literary context of the author's work. The remaining chapters focus on one or more of the author's novels, analyzing the works in terms of plot and character development and thematic issues. Each of these chapters concludes with what is termed an "alternative reading." This section first defines one contemporary theory of literary criticism (e.g., deconstructionism or feminist criticism), then applies that theory to the work in question. There is a bibliography of primary and secondary sources as well as reviews.

This volume provides a clear, basic introduction to Morrison's work and analyses of her novels from *The Bluest Eye* (1970) to *Paradise* (1998). The writing is direct, without critical jargon or highly technical language, which makes it accessible to beginning students and general readers. Given Morrison's popularity, this will be a welcome addition to any public, school, or academic library collection. Although it might be considered for reference, its greatest usefulness would be as part of the circulating collection.—**Barbara E. Kemp**

Poetry

1059.   **Dictionary of Literary Biography, Volume 193: American Poets Since World War II. Sixth Series.** Joseph Conte, ed. Detroit, Gale, 1998. 451p. illus. index. $151.00. ISBN 0-7876-1848-9.

This sixth series of *American Poets Since World War II* includes 32 poets—those skilled in traditional forms and familiar genres alongside those whose strengths lie in an avant-garde approach. Of this number, almost half appeared in the first series (1980). They are listed here again because since that time they produced major new works or have been the subjects of extensive critical studies.

These timely, insightful, signed critical essays for each poet are arranged alphabetically. Preceding each essay is a list of all published works, and following the essay is assorted information: interviews with the poet, bibliographies, articles and book chapters, letters, and libraries and archives where the poets' papers are held. Illustrations (author, photographs, dust jackets, and title pages)—accompany each entry. An excellent introduction begins the volume, which concludes with a cumulative index that lists each author included in the entire 193 volumes of the Dictionary of Literary Biography. This latest volume is one that most academic and all research libraries will want to acquire. [R: BL, 15 Nov 98, p. 610]—**Charles R. Andrews**

British Literature

General Works

Bibliography

1060.   Nilsen, Don L. F. **Humor in Eighteenth- and Nineteenth-Century British Literature: A Reference Guide.** Westport, Conn., Greenwood Press, 1998. 294p. index. $75.00. ISBN 0-313-29705-3.

This discussion of humor in British literature is divided into four time frames—eighteenth century, early nineteenth century, middle nineteenth century, and late nineteenth century. Each section begins with a list of the monarchs and their dates and a brief survey of the humor of the times. The word "humor" and its divisions are used so broadly that they need definition, especially terms such as "pathos of comedy."

Authors are listed chronologically according to birth year. The index makes them easy to locate because birth and death dates are listed both in the text and the index. Cross-references are also given by type of humor (e.g., satire, irony). There is a bibliography for each major writer, although some authors are listed without annotation except for a cross-reference to another sourcebook.

The book contains sweeping generalizations and errors. Charles Dickens was not describing the whole eighteenth century as the "best" and the "worst" of times. Most authors' quotations are taken from secondary sources, sometimes questionably. Samuel Johnson could not have compared puns to "wanton boys that put coppers on the railroad tracks," long before the coming of the railroad. There are also serious misprints. The date for Thomas Hardy's posthumously published "The Poor Man and the Lady" is given as 1668, and "Winter Words" is printed as "Womter Words." Researchers will find much information, but also many details open to challenge.
                                                                                            —**Charlotte Lindgren**

1061.   Soule, George. **Four British Women Novelists: Anita Brookner, Margaret Drabble, Iris Murdoch, Barbara Pym: An Annotated and Critical Secondary Bibliography.** Pasadena, Calif., Salem Press and Lanham, Md., Scarecrow, 1998. 520p. index. (Magill Bibliographies). $62.00. ISBN 0-8108-3505-3.

Major criticism, biographical studies, interviews, and reviews since 1988 of the novels of Anita Brookner, Margaret Drabble, Iris Murdoch, and Barbara Pym are alphabetically listed under "General Studies" and separately under the title of each of the authors' individual novels, which are organized by date of first publication. In the case of Pym, where composition date and publication date often differ widely, the composition and revision dates appear in brackets after the title. When an American title differs from the British, the American title appears in parentheses; for example, "Anita Brookner: *A Start in Life* (in the U.S. *The Debut*)."

Annotations include both a description of the bibliographic item and a critical evaluation. Other bibliographic studies are listed for all except Brookner, whose major work was in the field of art until 1980. There is also a brief mention under "Other Works" for each author, including her plays, essays, nonfiction, short stories, and movie adaptations. An index simplifies research for particular information.

More than half of the volume is on Murdoch. It may have helped the general reader to understand one reason that more has been written about her than all the others combined: If dates had been placed after each novelist's name, they would have shown that Murdoch was born 20 years before Drabble, and the Pym died in 1980. This volume is an essential tool for researchers, students, teachers, or anyone who is interested in learning more about these four British novelists. [R: Choice, Dec 98, p. 666]—**Charlotte Lindgren**

Biography

1062.   **Dictionary of Literary Biography: British Reform Writers, 1832-1914.** Gary Kelly and Edd Applegate, eds. Detroit, Gale, 1998. 442p. illus. index. (Dictionary of Literary Biography, v.190). $140.00. ISBN 0-7876-1845-4.

Spanning the years from the passage of the Reform Act of 1832 to the beginning of World War I and encompassing the entire Victorian era, this volume continues the coverage of British reform writers begun by volume 158 of this series, *British Reform Writers, 1789-1832* (see ARBA 97, entry 977). As the excellent introduction indicates, this was a period marked by enormous change and by a proliferation of reform movements in a myriad of areas, ranging from the economic and social conditions of the lower classes to religion to women's rights. Therefore, the editors note that their intent is not to be comprehensive but rather to cover a representative selection of reformers from a wide variety of fields of interest. The resulting compilation of 40 articles on 41 writers (Beatrice and Sidney Webb are treated in a single entry) includes an interesting mix of well-known authors, such as John Stuart Mill, Bernard Shaw, and Oscar Wilde, and lesser-known figures, such as John Doherty, Hugh Miller, and Edith Simcox.

Following the standard format of the Dictionary of Literary Biography (DLB) series, the signed articles consist of a primary bibliography, a biographical and critical essay, and references to secondary sources and manuscript collections. Illustrations, which generally include a portrait of the author, accompany each entry. Also included are a list of books for supplemental reading about the period and a cumulative index to all volumes in this series.

Half of the writers in this volume have been treated in earlier DLB volumes; in fact, Havelock Ellis and the Webbs are the only major figures who have not been featured previously. Due to this degree of overlap and to the specialized focus of this volume, it will be most appropriate for larger academic and research libraries that support graduate programs in English history and literature. [R: LJ, 1 Nov 98, p. 70]—**Marie Ellis**

1063.   **Dictionary of Literary Biography, Volume 191: British Novelists Between the Wars.** George M. Johnson, ed. Detroit, Gale, 1998. 442p. illus. index. $151.00. ISBN 0-7876-1846-2.

Volume 191 of the Dictionary of Literary Biography (DLB) discusses 48 British novelists whose literary careers began between 1918 and 1939. They range from such well-known names as Daphne du Maurier, Robert Graves, Edwin Muir, Siegfried Sassoon, and Alec Waugh to lesser-known novelists like Ernest Raymond, Romer Wilson, and Esmé Wynne-Tyson. The introduction discusses various literary movements of the early twentieth century, pointing out that for the writers in this volume, the dominant theme is war, with its accompanying alienation, postwar malaise, and changes in social class, even though rural novels and spiritual quests were also popular.

The formula used is the same as in preceding DLB volumes. Following a bibliography of each author's writings, essays of from 4 pages to as many as 17 (Graves) or 18 pages (Henry Williamson) in length come next. The essays are illustrated with photographs, often including the title pages of major novels, and end with a list of biographies and references about the subject. Archives and libraries where original papers are collected are also given.

At the beginning of the volume is a list of the preceding 190 volumes as well as 16 volumes in the Documentary Series and DLB yearbooks from 1980 to 1996. At the end is a cumulative cross-index listing every writer written about to date, giving page reference and volume number. Although reference libraries will want to collect the entire series, each volume is complete in itself. [R: BL, 15 Nov 98, p. 610]—**Charlotte Lindgren**

1064.   **Dictionary of Literary Biography, Volume 194: British Novelists Since 1960. Second Series.** Merritt Moseley, ed. Detroit, Gale, 1998. 415p. illus. index. $151.00. ISBN 0-7876-1849-7.

Just when it seems that the English-speaking world cannot possibly produce noteworthy writers fast enough to meet the publishing schedule of this distinguished Dictionary of Literary Bibliography (DLB) series, the 194th volume covers none less than Salman Rushdie, Bruce Chatwin, and Martin Amis for the first time. This installment continues the high quality and standard format of the earlier volumes in profiling the careers of 32 British writers of long fiction. Volume 14 of the DLB was the first in this series to cover British novelists since 1960. Some of those writers are covered here again, including Anthony Burgess, Iris Murdoch, Ian McEwan, Fay Weldon, A. S. Byatt, David Lodge, A. N. Wilson, and Auberon Waugh. Others, such as Julian Barnes and Anita Brookner, have only appeared in the DLB yearbooks. All continue to undergo critical reevaluations as new works appear.

A few features set this volume apart from others. There is no overall style or genre featured. These authors write traditional narratives, experimental fiction, political and religious-based works, screenplays, detective stories, and both historical and futuristic fiction. Many of the writers were either born abroad or spent part of their adult years living outside Britain, lending diversity to the selection. Among these are Rushdie, Kazuo Ishiguro, Chatwin, Timothy Mo, and Barry Unsworth. The volume also includes the Booker Prize shortlist from 1969 to 1996, a useful tool for collection development.

Following the formula of prior volumes, each entry covers the writer's upbringing, formative influences, critical reception, and thematic development as it is traced out in succeeding works. The larger part of each essay is a summary and evaluation of the high points of the novels. Frequently the authors will comment on their own works. The contributors are not reluctant to offer their own critical remarks. Apart from a typographical error on the spine of the book, this volume reflects the high standards readers have come to expect from the DLB series.

—**John P. Schmitt**

Handbooks and Yearbooks

1065.   Cooper, Robert M. **The Literary Guide & Companion to Southern England.** rev. ed. Athens, Ohio, Ohio University Press, 1998. 389p. maps. index. $39.95; $19.95pa. ISBN 0-8214-1225-6; 0-8214-1226-4.

Actual and armchair travelers alike will delight in the revised edition of this classic guide to southern England's 11 counties and towns with literary significance. This is not a dry list of literary tourist sites with opening hours and admission costs. Standard travel guides will have to be used for that information. This is a travel narrative in which fictional and real literary associations are presented through interesting and often amusing anecdotes. It is the kind of book to have a travelling companion read aloud to you as you drive through the English countryside or to peruse while downing a pint in a pub frequented by Rudyard Kipling.

That is not to say that useful and practical information is not given. There are motorist's maps for each county and clear directions for getting from place to place. Maps for walking tours are included for towns with several significant sites.

First published in 1985, this edition retains the original text. Revisions cover sites that have been destroyed or are no longer open to the public. The new edition will be important for travelers planning a literary pilgrimage but less so for the armchair traveler.

There is an alphabetical index of authors and churches. Hotels, pubs, and restaurants are indexed if they are of literary interest or are still serving the public.

Libraries with comprehensive travel collections will want to own this guide. Readers who want to follow in the footsteps of a favorite author or soak up the atmosphere of a beloved fictional character will find it enchanting.
                                                                                    —**Marlene M. Kuhl**

1066.   Lacy, Norris J., Geoffrey Ashe, and Debra N. Mancoff. **The Arthurian Handbook.** 2d ed. New York, Garland, 1997. 409p. illus. index. (Garland Reference Library of The Humanities, v. 1920). $22.95pa. ISBN 0-8153-2081-7.

For those familiar with the names of scholars who tirelessly pursue the elusive King Arthur and all things Arthurian, the name Geoffrey Ashe should lend both credence and intrigue to this informative handbook. The front matter is structured in a concise fashion, covering chronology, genealogy, and even heraldry associated with the Arthurian stories. One is taken on an eclectic, yet comprehensive, journey into "Arthuriana," a term used by the authors themselves.

In the chronology portion, a grid-like section gives the reader a unique visual perspective of the development on the Arthurian legend from the early period to the modern period. Five different genealogical charts are provided to demonstrate the differing versions of the tale from its apparent inception via Geoffrey of Monmouth to its high drama stage of Sir Thomas Malory, including versions by the French (Vulgate Merlin and Vulgate) and even a German (Wolfram Von Echenbach).

The historical Arthur is discussed in the 1st chapter, entitled "Origins." The 2d and 3d chapters go on to illuminate both early and modern Arthurian literature. In chronological order, various authors are listed by name, from Middle Ages chroniclers such as Gildas and Nennius to popular twentieth-century authors like T. H. White, Mary Stewart, and Marion Zimmer Bradley, their related work given a brief synopsis. Lacey, Ashe, and Mancoff concede the impossibility of presenting a completely comprehensive annotated bibliography on such an increasingly popular subject, encouraging the reader to explore each and every perspective of the Arthurian legend.

Unique to this particular literary reference guide is its section on the depiction of Arthur and the development of the various versions of the legend in the arts and humanities. This is an addition to the 1st edition of the handbook and will be appreciated by students of pre-Raphaelite art and artists such as Dante Gabriel Rossetti and John William Waterhouse, as well as by students of film and photography.

A glossary attached to the final pages of the book is helpful and will serve the Arthurian aficionado well in providing numerous links to other sources of information on all things Arthurian in nature. This handbook is an excellent springboard for those attempting to know the matter of Britain better and a must for students of Arthurian literature and its overall impact on humanity and the humanities. [R: VOYA, Oct 98, pp. 305-306]
                                                                                    —**Beth St. Cyr**

1067. **Twayne's English Authors on CD-ROM.** [CD-ROM]. New York, G. K. Hall/Simon & Schuster Macmillan, 1997. Minimum system requirements: IBM or compatible 486. CD-ROM drive. 16 MB RAM. 16 MB hard disk space. SVGA monitor.$995.00. ISBN 0-7838-1717-7.

Nearly 200 books on British authors from the popular Twayne's Author Series have been reproduced on this CD-ROM and made searchable with Netscape software. Advanced searching allows one to search by period, genre, or keyword as well as by author's name. A search for tragic heroes (keyword) and Renaissance (period) yielded more than 50 chapters. One of the Shakespeare chapters had many hits, but it is not clear how to find them beyond reading the complete chapter. The most efficient way of finding them was to use "CTRL F" to bring up a "find" box and type in the phrase. However, in another chapter discussing the works of Robert Greene, the phrase "tragic hero" brought no results, yet searching each word separately leads one to information on tragedy or heroes. Common Windows conventions such as drop-down menus allow the user to see which periods and genres are available. Online help is available for those who want more explanations and examples for citing CD-ROM versions of the books.

Other offerings on the main menu include "Research Ideas" and "Authors, A-Z." The first is a selection of well-known authors arranged by literary period and by gender. More specific topics for research (for example, "the tragic hero in Shakespearean drama") are not offered. The second is a dictionary listing of the British authors included.

At the top of each search screen and at the beginning of each document is a navigational bar that takes the user to any of the main menu options and to the help menu. Only when one is deep into a book is there no program-specific navigation assistance. This, however, is when the Netscape software is useful. The "back" option on the top bar quickly takes you out of the text and back to the "table of contents" of the book. High school and college students for whom this is designed will have no trouble with the search software.

Loading the CD-ROM is easy following the instructions in the technical reference pamphlet that accompanies the product. However, due to some organization-specific network software on this reviewer's personal computer, the program would not work. Using the technical support telephone number, I was able to talk to a helpful technician who walked me through several procedures, and finally sent me some additional software to ensure that the program worked.

Users may not want to read long chapters directly from the computer screen, so printing is likely to be excessive. To help avoid this, at the top of each chapter are simple instructions for printing out sections of text. However, for popular authors whose criticism is frequently checked out of the library, this reference source will be much appreciated by librarians and users. [R: BL, 1 Sept 98, p. 165]—**Juleigh Muirhead Clark**

Fiction

1068. Booker, M. Keith. **The Modern British Novel of the Left: A Research Guide.** Westport, Conn., Greenwood Press, 1998. 413p. index. $89.50. ISBN 0-313-30343-6.

Rebellion, working class struggles, colonialism, fascism, and the evils of capitalism are the themes Booker seeks out in this survey of British left-wing fiction. The author is a professor of English with a publishing record on colonialism in fiction and social literary criticism. The object here is to highlight the most important novels of leftist thinking from the last century and to annotate some of the more important works of Marxist literary criticism. Although the 136 novels discussed are a representative collection of left and left-leaning works, Booker grudgingly acknowledges art rarely conforms to political ideology; that Western individualism, not collective action, is the hallmark of much modern fiction; and that literary modernism is characterized more by stream of consciousness or fragmented representations than Marxist literary realism.

The research guide follows the structure of others in the Greenwood series. The opening essay introduces the subject and a critical approach. An annotated guide of 50 "critical and historical studies" is presented as a definitive list of Marxist critical theory, although half the works are more than 20 years old. The lengthier descriptions of 116 selected British novels of the left constitute the largest part of the book and are followed by descriptions of 20 postcolonial novels of the left. The latter includes writers from Ireland, Africa, the Caribbean, and South Asia. The novels are classified according to a thematic (and overlapping) scheme; a name and subject index follows.

Despite being selective in what the author describes as a major cultural and political phenomenon, Booker fails to find the pure novel that conforms to the critical theory of Georg Lukács and Antonio Gramsci. Instead his bibliographic essays lament Richard Llewellyn's nostalgia for bygone days, H. G. Wells's Fabian socialism, Graham Green's Catholicism, Doris Lessing's elevation of the personal over the historical, D. H. Lawrence's fascination with the instinctive life force, and George Orwell, whom he pillories as a "former quasi-leftist" (p. 3). Orwell seems to be the apotheosis of all that Booker resents, even if he includes *Burmese Days* in his guide and somewhat incongruously includes *Homage to Catalonia* as one of the critical and historical studies. Orwell went to great lengths in *Catalonia* to portray the distorted anti-Bolshevik reporting of the Spanish civil war, but Booker focuses only on Orwell's mentioning ideological divisions among the leftist republicans. Perhaps it is only a coincidence that the author omits *Burmese Days* from his thematic index.

Several irrelevant and spurious opinions sprinkle the text, as in the claims that Charles Dickens's bourgeois fiction connects in a straight line with the rhetoric of the Cold War (p. 15), or that the Red Army defeated Adolf Hitler, although the West would like to claim credit (p. 176). As a survey of leftist and anti-colonial literature, this book is a reasonable if pricey overview; but readers will have to overlook the author's gratuitous editorial statements and his desire to rewrite the plots of many works with a call to action.—**John P. Schmitt**

1069.   Kloesel, Christian J. W., comp. **English Novel Explication Supplement VI.** North Haven, Conn., Shoe String Press, 1997. 478p. index. $59.50. ISBN 0-208-02418-2.

This 6th supplement extends the English Novel Explication series nearly four years, from mid-1993 through early 1997. The scope of this supplement is identical to the previous five, as it includes critical interpretive works about novels written by British authors, both living and deceased. Commonwealth authors who lived in Great Britain during some significant portion of their creative years are also included. The format of this volume is similar to that of its five predecessors: the book is organized alphabetically by novelists' names, with individual listings of novels' titles appearing after each name. Beneath each title are listed citations of books and articles (published mid-1993 through early 1997) interpreting it, including page numbers of material specific to the novel at hand. The precision of these citations facilitates locating the explications about a particular novel one is searching for, as do the two indexes at the end of the book. This book belongs in any library serving humanities scholars.—**G. Douglas Meyers**

Individual Authors

Jane Austen

1070.   Poplawski, Paul. **A Jane Austen Encyclopedia.** Westport, Conn., Greenwood Press, 1998. 411p. illus. maps. index. $75.00. ISBN 0-313-30017-8.

Given the amount of scholarship on Jane Austen already published, it would seem difficult to justify yet another book on Austen. However, Poplawski makes a credible case for the unique value of *A Jane Austen Encyclopedia* by pointing out that there are few reference books on Austen that provide separate entries for all of her writing, including her juvenilia.

The volume is organized into 3 separate but interrelated sections. The 1st section contains 3 chronologies. The 1st chronology, focused on the life, works, and family of Austen, is structured in narrative form. Conceivably, this chronology can be used as an index to articles appearing in the main body of the encyclopedia. It is supplemented by a map of places associated with Austen as well as a genealogical chart of the Austen family. The 2d chronology, placing Austen within a historical perspective, is supplemented by illustrations detailing fashion and modes of transport described in Austen's novels. The 3d chronology, situating Austen in literary context, is particularly interesting because Poplawski highlights books that Austen is known to have read as verified in her correspondence. The 2d section will appeal to students of the work of Austen. Extensive articles include the publishing history, a detailed plot summary, and a commentary on the critical reception of Austen's principal works. Each novel's main characters and most secondary characters have a separate entry to facilitate ready-reference or to allow readers to deepen their familiarity with the work. Of particular importance is the article entitled "Criticism," which offers an overview of the development of Austen's reputation as a literary artist. Of equal interest is the in-depth study of social preoccupations in Austen's novels to be found in the article "Themes and Concerns."

For scholars of Austen, section 3 may alone be worth the price of purchase. It is organized as 3 separate bibliographies. The 1st bibliography details the publication history, including first editions and translations, of each of Austen's works. The remaining 2 bibliographies provide book and article references to scholarly output on Austen, with particular emphasis on the past two decades. The index that concludes the volume is useful for keyword access to themes that appear as leitmotifs in Austen's works. Because *A Jane Austen Encyclopedia* functions successfully as a ready-reference tool, an introduction to the work of Austen, and as a scholarly bibliography, it deserves a place in academic libraries with either an undergraduate or graduate reference collection in English literature. [R: BL, 15 Oct 98, p. 442; SLJ, Nov 98, p. 158]—**David G. Nowak**

C. S. Lewis

1071.   **The C. S. Lewis Readers' Encyclopedia.** Jeffrey D. Schultz, John G. West Jr., and Mike Perry, eds. Grand Rapids, Mich., Zondervan Publishing/HarperCollins, 1998. 464p. illus. $22.99. ISBN 0-310-21538-2.

C. S. Lewis remains one of the most oft-quoted writers of the twentieth century, and one whose works are rarely out of print. *The C. S. Lewis Readers' Encyclopedia* is "designed chiefly to help the reader get more out of his reading of Lewis—to gain a deeper and richer understanding" of Lewis. In the brief biography (57 pages), a description of Lewis's family and education and an overview of his writings are given. He relates much useful and anecdotal information concerning Lewis, including a preference to be known as Jack during his youth and an intensity shown by his immersion into literature and music. Encyclopedia entries include groups in which Lewis participated, such as the Inklings, with links to all other people in the group.

Other articles are on influences and friends, including J. R. R. Tolkien, G. K. Chesterton, Charles Williams, and William Shakespeare; his books, *Screwtape Letters*, *Mere Christianity*, and individual stories in the *Chronicles of Narnia*; essays on the Inner Ring; and spiritual issues or concepts (e.g., faith, demons, Satan, angels, sin, heaven, and hell). There are even essays on those with whom he disagreed, such as Friedrich Nietzsche, Sigmund Freud, and H. G. Wells. Lewis also became a renowned critic of medieval and Renaissance literature. Appendix A lists Lewis's resources, organizations, and libraries, including information about sites on the Internet. Appendix B is a detailed chronology of the life of Lewis. The editors are aware of some overlap with earlier books. In *The C. S. Lewis Handbook* (Monarch, 1990), Colin Duriez presents thumbnail sketches of titles and characters. In *C. S. Lewis: A Companion and Guide* (Harper, 1996), Walter Hooper analyzes selected works in depth, and presents an extensive bibliography of writings of Lewis. *The C. S. Lewis Readers' Encyclopedia* far surpasses Duriez in comprehensiveness but does not delve as deep as Hooper's volume. *The C. S. Lewis Readers' Encyclopedia* should prove to be an essential tool for the study of this influential author. [R: SLJ, Nov 98, p. 158]—**Ralph Hartsock**

Charles Dickens

1072.   Davis, Paul. **Charles Dickens A to Z: The Essential Reference to His Life and Work.** New York, Facts on File, 1998. 432p. illus. index. $45.00. ISBN 0-8160-2905-9.

Ever since Tiny Tim blessed us everyone, there has been no end to the spate of materials on everything Dickensian. In many ways, Dickens is the Horatio Alger of England—a poor boy who made it. It is a pity, however, that such human interest stories often become public policy. The New Deal had no better voice echoing from the grave than *Bleak House* or *David Copperfield*.

Although Gilbert Pierce's *Dickens Dictionary* (Haskell House, 1972) may have touched off the flood in 1878, only recently have we become awash in such books. First we had Alexander Fyfe's *Who's Who in Dickens* (Haskell House, 1971), soon followed by Michael Harwick's *The Charles Dickens Encyclopedia* (Scribner's Sons, 1973), only to be bested by a reprint of Arthur Hayward's *The Dickens Encyclopedia* (Chartwell Books, 1995). Three years ago we received George Newlin's voluminous *Everyone in Dickens* (Greenwood Press, 1995), from which it appeared, yes, indeed, everyone had been in Dickens.

Now Paul Davis comes along with his *Charles Dickens A to Z*. In many ways the volume mimics wholly unrelated titles (mainly Congressional Quarterly's series, including *Congress A to Z* [1998] and *The Supreme Court A to Z* [1993]). Davis has produced the coffee-table version of the scholarly *Everyone in Dickens*. Libraries having the latter may think it unnecessary to have this latest release. But Davis adds considerable extra-Dickensiana to round out his repeat of characters, settings, plots, and intrigues.

The entries, more than 2,500 of them, contain detailed synopses of all the major and minor works, along with the critical reception of the stories in literary London and beyond. More than four dozen illustrations add to the coffee-table appearance of this book, as does its quarto size. But the work is a valuable addition to an author's prodigious life's work, work only eclipsed by the towering giant of the author himself. [R: LJ, 1 Nov 98, p. 70]

—**Mark Y. Herring**

George Orwell

1073.   Fenwick, Gillian. **George Orwell: A Bibliography.** New Castle, Del., Oak Knoll Press, 1998. index. $85.00. ISBN 1-884718-46-9.

Another Orwellian year, 1998 was probably the most significant year for Orwell scholars since 1984. First, the controversy about Orwell's list of "communist" friends surfaced, which tarnished his reputation a bit. Then, in August, the long-awaited *Complete Works of George Orwell* was published in 20 volumes by Secker & Warburg, and it generated a spate of lengthy reviews and reassessments. Finally, this comprehensive and descriptive bibliography of Orwell was published, incredibly the first of its kind. Compiled by veteran bibliographer Fenwick (Trinity College, University of Toronto), this is truly an impressive achievement and long overdue.

There are nine main sections in the bibliography, which covers all facets of Orwell's literary and broadcasting career. The richest and most interesting section is part A, which is devoted to Orwell's published books. Included are descriptions of the 1st editions, important later editions, reissues, translations, and even a few unauthorized editions. A detailed physical description is provided for each book: the title page and publication information; type of binding (e.g., "Green calico textured cloth on boards. Off white endpapers. Purple topped leaves."); front and back covers; the spine; dust jacket; notes (such as the number of copies printed and the publication date); and a list of contemporary reviews of the book. Each book is prefaced by an essay in which Fenwick describes the composition and prepublication history of the book, drawn largely from Orwell's letters. These essays offer remarkable insight into the precarious nature of Orwell's literary career. Some of Orwell's books are, of course, more famous than others, and this condition is readily apparent in the bibliography. For example, 30 different English-language editions of *Nineteen Eighty-Four* are described, as well as 38 translations and several miscellaneous versions (abridgments, facsimiles, and broadcasts).

The remainder of the bibliography is almost equally fascinating. Although Orwell died at age 47, his literary output was staggering. Part B lists the books that Orwell edited and those to which he contributed. Part C is a listing of 842 periodical articles written by Orwell. Part D describes Orwell's published collections of essays. Part E lists 269 radio broadcasts. Many of these have "no surviving script," whereas others had been published in the posthumous collections *The War Broadcasts* (1985) and *The War Commentaries* (1985). Part F is a list of 519 British Broadcasting Corporation programs (or "talks") that were organized by Orwell. Part G is a list of 456 published letters. Part H lists 28 poems written by Orwell, and part I contains 1,262 unpublished items, mostly letters (which are now included in the *Complete Works*). Additionally, Fenwick includes a concise biographical sketch, a brief chronology of Orwell's life and writings, a list of payments and royalties he received, locations of Orwell archives, and a selected bibliography of books and articles about Orwell (only those items that Fenwick found to be particularly useful or interesting).

This volume is a major bibliographic work, yet it is not without its minor flaws. There are no illustrations in the bibliography, with the exception of a single photograph of Orwell (ca.1930s) opposite the title page. Photographs of the original dust jackets of the books would have been an appropriate addition. Also, there is very spotty coverage of the foreign-language editions of Orwell's works, although Fenwick admits having difficulty in this area of bibliographic control. Finally, the typeface used in the book is too small. However, these deficiencies should not seriously detract from the great value of the bibliography. It belongs in all academic libraries.

—**Thomas A. Karel**

Lawrence Sterne

1074.   **Critical Essays on Laurence Sterne.** Melvyn New, ed. New York, Simon & Schuster Macmillan, 1998. 335p. index. $48.00. ISBN 0-7838-0040-1.

Like most other volumes in G. K. Hall's Critical Essays on British Literature series, this collection of essays possesses no significant value as a reference work. The 18 essays (13 of which date since 1981 and are reprinted from well-indexed and readily available journals like *ELH*, *MLN*, and *Studies in Philology*; a translation of one that previously appeared in *Études Anglaise*; and 4 original contributions) address specific aspects of Sterne's life and works in sections that the editor labels as "Intertextual," "Skeptical," "Erotical," and "Ethical" Sterne. The original essays include Anne Bandry's "Imitations of *Tristram Shandy*"; Tom Keymer's "Narratives of Loss: *Tristram Shandy* and *The Poems of Ossian*"; Elizabeth Kraft's "The Pentecostal Movement in *A Sentimental Journey*"; and Donald R. Wehrs's "Levinas and Sterne: From the Ethics of the Face to the Aesthetics of Unrepresentability." A perfunctory index of names, literary titles, and selected subjects offers access. Lacking any semblance of a Sterne bibliography; chronology; or biographical, lexical, or topical dictionary, handbook, or compendium; New's volume is inappropriate for reference collections. It should be purchased to supplement existing book and journal collections already supporting research on Sterne and eighteenth-century fiction.—**James K. Bracken**

Oscar Wilde

1075.   Beckson, Karl. **The Oscar Wilde Encyclopedia.** New York, AMS Press, 1998. 456p. index. (AMS Studies in the Nineteenth Century, no.18). $125.00. ISBN 0-404-61498-1.

A must for the Wilde reference shelf presently filled mostly with quotation books, Beckson's encyclopedia offers substantial bibliographic information that complements existing standard resources, including Stuart Mason's *Bibliography of Oscar Wilde* (1914; new ed., London, Bertram Rota, 1967) and Thomas A. Mikolyzk's *Oscar Wilde: An Annotated Bibliography* (see ARBA 94, entry 1262), and that simultaneously offers much that is new. The majority of the entries provide significant detail for Wilde's individual writings. Nearly six pages for the play *The Importance of Being Earnest* give composition, production, and publication histories; a thorough plot synopsis; analyses of contemporary stage and book reviews; locations and details for the manuscripts; and references. Entries for poems, like *The Ballad of Reading Gaol*, additionally identify forms, themes, and autobiographical allusions.

Detail related to composition, revision, and publication of specific works is superior to that offered in Norman Page's often superficial and selective *An Oscar Wilde Chronology* (G. K. Hall, 1991). Entries supplying information about Wilde's life (such as "Lectures in America, 1882"; "Prison Years, 1895-97"; and "The Trials, 1895") and for members of his circle and other acquaintances are next most frequent. Beckson includes 13 black-and-white illustrations of Alfred Douglas and Wilde, Aubrey Beardsley, William Morris, William Butler Yeats, and others. Entries for places (Magdalen College, Oxford, and Trinity College, Dublin); allusions ("C.3.3" for Wilde's Reading Prison number and "green carnation"); and broad topics, such as "Dandyism," "Decandence," "Fashion and Theater," and "Uranians" (used for homosexuality) are more limited, but these likewise cite extensive references. A brief chronology, a key to abbreviated references, and a cumulative index complete the volume.

It is worth noting that the recently published Cambridge Companions to Literature volume *The Cambridge Companion to Oscar Wilde* (Cambridge University Press, 1997), a collection of 15 contributed essays edited by Peter Raby, is of little value as a reference work and does not in any way serve the same purpose as Beckson's work. Indeed, Anne Varty's *A Preface to Oscar Wilde* (Longman, 1998) contains a more substantial reference section than Raby's text. Written with authority and balance in mind, Beckson's unique encyclopedia is now the most comprehensive starting point for research on Wilde. [R: BL, 15 Sept 98, pp. 266-268; Choice, Nov 98, p. 490-491]—**James K. Bracken**

William Shakespeare

1076.　Coye, Dale F. **Pronouncing Shakespeare's Words: A Guide from A to Zounds.** Westport, Conn., Greenwood Press, 1998. 724p. index. $99.50. ISBN 0-313-30655-9.

Unlike most scholarly discussions of Shakespearean pronunciation that attempt to explain how Shakespeare may have pronounced his words 400 years ago, this volume is directed toward a more general audience of actors and students wishing to know how the words are pronounced today. It succeeds excellently at this task, in addition to providing an accessible summary of the linguistic issues affecting the sound of the playwright's English. The 30-page introduction is detailed, well organized, and clearly written. Based on a summary of current pronunciation among American, Canadian, and British scholars and dramaturges, Coye's work presents a descriptive guide rather than prescriptive instructions, as in the entry for *ergo*: "/UR go/is older, /Er go/ is newer. The former is more common in the UK, the latter in the US, CN, but both forms appear in all countries" (p. 355). The additional apparatus is helpful; there are guides to common "hard" words and reduced forms, five appendixes on additional topics, indexes to words and subjects, and a list of references.

Coye's work does not entirely replace Spain's *Shakespeare Sounded Soundly* (1989) or Linklater's *Freeing Shakespeare's Voice* (1991) because his exhaustive, linguistic approach differs from their more instructive theatrical purpose. This volume will be an essential addition to theater libraries and a useful supplement for university students and teachers desiring a brief and accessible background in current Shakespearean pronunciation. [R: BL, 15 Sept 98, pp. 268-270; Choice, Nov 98, p. 491]—**Christopher Baker**

1077.　MacCary, W. Thomas. **Hamlet: A Guide to the Play.** Westport, Conn., Greenwood Press, 1998. 150p. index. (Greenwood Guides to Shakespeare). $49.95. ISBN 0-313-30082-8.

This short book combines aspects of an overall Shakespeare handbook with a series of essays on various aspects of *Hamlet*, with generous dollops of reference to Shakespeare's other plays and to Sigmund Freud and other critics. The opening chapter, on the textual history of *Hamlet*, is only nine pages in length, hardly enough to get beyond the basic fact of there being three main texts that differ in some important ways. This superficial approach is perhaps appropriate for the undergraduate who has not previously studied Shakespeare, but it certainly leaves the specialist where it found him or her. The chapter on contexts and sources is a grab-bag of observations on historical and religious influences on the play, featuring the interesting although unproven notion that various aspects of *Hamlet* were influenced by a Catholic distant cousin of Shakespeare who was imprisoned and executed for his faith.

The chapter on dramatic structure provides a close reading of the play that would probably be useful to undergraduates writing papers. The chapter on theme, only five pages in length, declares that *Hamlet* "is about nothing" in many different senses—an interesting observation that probably could have been integrated into the previous chapter. The chapter "Critical Approaches," a 21-page overview of the play as seen by critics from Samuel Johnson to Jacques Lacan, is superficial but instructive for the novice. The final chapter, "The Play in Performance," is a discussion of the new Globe Theatre (with pictures) plus a quick overview of the play as performed in theater, on film, and on television. The book concludes with a five-page list of works cited and a four-page index.

What this title is, then, is a 150-page book that costs $50 and could be useful to undergraduates who do not wish to navigate the deeper waters of Shakespearean criticism. For such students, however, *Shakespeare A-Z* (see ARBA 92, entry 1209) would be a much better choice.—**Bill Miller**

1078.　McQuain, Jeffrey, and Stanley Malless. **Coined by Shakespeare: Words and Meanings First Used by the Bard.** Springfield, Mass., Merriam-Webster, 1998. 273p. $14.95. ISBN 0-87779-353-0.

Some idea of Shakespeare's contribution to English vocabulary is gained from the fact that he coined, by one statement, close to 29,000 different words (this volume cites a more conservative "close to 20,000"), almost 5 times the number of different words contained in the King James version of the Bible. This volume does not list them all; typically a dozen or so examples are provided for each letter of the alphabet, with only two each for "K," "Q," and "Y." Despite its brevity, readers do gain a glimpse of the Bard's lexical creativity, and the book provides a category of information not duplicated by other Shakespearean reference works. The closest comparison would be C. T. Orion's *Shakespeare Glossary* (3d ed.; 1986—cited by the authors), which offers definitions of archaic, obsolete, or provincial words but not exclusively the poet's own creations.

Each set of words is grouped alphabetically, with a short quiz on Shakespeareana at the end of each group (with answers). Each entry lists the word and its location in the author's canon, followed by a brief discussion of its etymology and the word's subsequent use by other noted authors. Amusing line drawings in green increase the book's visual appeal; the brief introduction highlights many now-common words that owe their origin to Shakespeare. The authors have chosen not to make the volume exhaustive but rather to offer a selection of words that illustrate the various parts of speech to which Shakespeare contributed and the several methods of words formation he employed (e.g., functional shift, back-formation, compounding). Its small size and attractive layout make the book as appropriate for the bedside table as for the reference shelf. Despite its size and popular (rather than scholarly) orientation, it offers a sampling of accurate information that any public, high school, or undergraduate library would find useful.—**Christopher Baker**

1079. **Shakespeare.** Joseph Rosenblum, ed. Pasadena, Calif., Salem Press, 1998. 482p. index. (Magill's Choice). $68.75. ISBN 0-89356-966-6.

For the playgoer, the student, or the general reader, this handy volume fulfills a purpose: to provide a quick summary of Shakespeare's works with brief backgrounds and bibliographies. *Love's Labour's Lost*, for instance, provides a two-page plot summary and a two-page critical evaluation, followed by a one-page list of works for further study. Similar treatment is accorded the more famous sonnets and narrative poems. Also covered is *Edward the Third*, which is often ascribed to Shakespeare but is of doubtful authorship.

Although the sections are written by many different scholars, there is a remarkable consistency in style throughout the volume. The sections are generally easy to read, and there is a pleasant lack of scholarly jargon. At the back of the book there is an index for characters, one for quotations, and one for subjects. Overall, this concise volume is user-friendly, making Shakespeare accessible to a wide variety of readers. The seasoned academic scholar, already steeped in the Bard, will have little use for this handbook; it is aimed at the popular audience, and it does a fine job of making Shakespeare available to millions of readers who are unable—because of time constraints or lack of background—to wade through the masses of scholarship and critical commentary that have accreted around England's greatest author for the past five centuries.

Doesn't it make just as much sense in studying Shakespeare to refer to popular pamphlets such as Cliff's Notes, Monarch Notes, or similar study aids? Why bother to purchase the heavier volume under review here? The answer lies in the finesse of Joseph Rosenblum's approach. He is brief without being sketchy, and it can be added that he presents his material in an open and friendly manner, enticing the reader to read and study the plays themselves. The enticement is furthered by the inclusion of many photographs of famous films or productions of Shakespeare (e.g., Sir Laurence Olivier as Hamlet, Marlon Brando as Mark Antony in the 1953 movie *Julius Caesar*, and Stephanie Zimbalist as Miranda in the film version of *The Tempest*).

There are, of course, some things that can be argued, such as Rosenblum's statement that Falstaff is "the most potent symbol of the violence and anarchy that follow the murder of an anointed king" in the history of plays. Although there is some truth in this, it does strike one as an oversimplification. Generally, the background material and the critical comments are handled in a responsible and interesting manner. For what it tries to do, the work is very successful. [R: BR, Sept/Oct 98, p. 70; BL, July 98, p. 1908]—**Peter Thorpe**

1080. **Shakespeare Interactive: As You Like It, A Midsummer Night's Dream, The Taming of the Shrew, Twelfth Night.** [CD-ROM]. Thorndike, Maine, G. K. Hall/ Macmillan, 1997. Minimum system requirements: IMB or compatible. Window 3.1, 4MB RAM. VGA 256 color monitor. 16-bit sound card with speakers. Mouse. $350.00/set. ISBN 0-7838-1811-4.

1081. **Shakespeare Interactive: King Lear, Macbeth, The Merchant of Venice, Othello.** [CD-ROM]. Thorndike, Maine, G. K. Hall/ Macmillan, 1998. Minimum system requirements: IMB or compatible. Window 3.1, 4MB RAM. VGA 256 color monitor. 16-bit sound card with speakers. Mouse. $350.00/set. ISBN 0-7838-0064-9.

This is another release of the 12 most popular Shakespearean plays being produced on CD-ROM by the G. K. Hall publishing house. Each CD-ROM contains the full text of a play, along with a running commentary explaining each passage and pop-up definitions of words the reader may not be familiar with. Accompanying the text is a stereo recording of the play being performed by a professional acting cast. In addition, period music and some interesting sound effects go along with the radio-style production.

There are other features of note on these CD-ROMs, which include a full-text Boolean search capability, a list of all characters with short profiles, a themes page explaining the basic plots of the plays, a glossary of terminology, and an "image gallery" that allows for viewing of more than 100 engravings from the seventeenth, eighteenth, and nineteenth centuries. The editors maintain that some of these images have been published for the first time on these CD-ROMs, and all the images are printable.

Recordings of the Shakespearean plays have been available for many years, but this is the first tutorial approach on this scale. The CD-ROMs are easy to load and use, and all the features are more or less obvious with the exception of the sound. If the user is not used to the standard sound control bar with the various symbols, he or she may not be able to get the sound to play right away. More online instructions should be incorporated for this operation. Also, the lack of a dual platform allowing for use on both Windows and Macintosh is a drawback.

These CD-ROMs will probably be popular with junior high through college-level students but may not be suitable for younger children. They are recommended for purchase by all academic and public libraries, and highly recommended for Shakespeare instructors. Although they probably do not allow for complete self-instruction on the plays, they will go a long way toward introducing students to Shakespeare.—**Robert L. Wick**

1082.   **Shakespearean Criticism 1996, Volume 38: Excerpts from the Criticism of William Shakespeare's Plays and Poetry....** Dana Ramel Barnes and Michelle Lee, eds. Detroit, Gale, 1998. 406p. index. $140.00. ISBN 0-7876-1251-0.

The breadth of William Shakespeare's work has left in its wake enough interpretations, analyses, criticisms, and essays to fill many pages and volumes. The range of topics and themes is abundant enough to fill volumes as well. As part of the Shakespearean Criticism series, volume 38 concentrates only on one such theme: desire.

Indeed, the entire volume is devoted to the theme of desire in Shakespeare's works and offers commentary on that theme as it is found in the plays *All's Well That End's Well, Love's Labour's Lost, The Merry Wives of Windsor*, and the poem "The Phoenix and Turtle." The volume is divided into 5 sections—a section devoted to the topic of desire, one section for each of the three plays, and a section for the poem. Each section comprises an introduction to the play, overview of the play, discussion on desire, commentary about language, and suggestions for further reading. The focus, however, is always limited to desire.

Such a narrow focus is naturally both good and bad. If the topic of desire is to be studied in depth, and in regard to the plays discussed in this book, students and teachers will want to use it extensively. Or, this book will be valuable when studying the plays or poem discussed within, but only as a point of reference. However, for a more comprehensive introduction and overview of the works, students may want to look to other books. Other volumes, for instance, within the Shakespearean Criticism series provide better overviews.

On the whole, the essays and the points they raise are provocative and at least somewhat insightful as to the works of Shakespeare. Although the book provides an introduction and overview of the works, unless the theme of desire is to be the sole subject of a research paper or topic of a course, this volume may be left on the bookshelf.

—**Tom Sullivan**

1083.   **Shakespearean Criticism Yearbook 1996, Volume 37: A Selection of the Year's Most Noteworthy Studies of William Shakespeare's Plays and Poetry.** Dana Ramel Barnes, Michelle Lee, and Aarti Stephens, eds. Detroit, Gale, 1998. 403p. index. $139.00. ISBN 0-7876-1135-2.

Although William Shakespeare wrote in the early 1600s, criticisms and analyses about his work are still being written today. However, most textbooks contain essays written at least several years ago. Thus, the essays written in the past couple of years are often overlooked by students and teachers alike. The *Shakespearean Criticism Yearbook 1996, Volume 37: A Selection of the Year's Most Noteworthy Studies of William Shakespeare's Plays and Poetry* offers students and educators access to such essays written within the specific year from which it contains criticisms.

The 1996 edition is filled with essays on topics ranging from straightforward character analysis of Hamlet to King Lear's tragic relationship between wisdom and power to latent sexual meanings in *Othello*. The style of these essays ranges as well from classic, timeless, unsettled arguments to newer radical thoughts.

In the essay entitled "Hamlet," Peter B. Murray contends that Hamlet was sane, but cowardly rationalization delayed his revenge. The fact that he was aware of his own cowardice and the effect it had on his plot for revenge proves Hamlet's sanity. Hamlet's confusion about how to proceed with the revenge is caused by his "complex interiority that makes self-knowledge difficult." Although both sides of Hamlet's mental health have been argued, the theme is so central to the value of studying the play that no inspection of the Hamlet character is complete without reading an essay about whether or not he knew what he was doing. In the essay "Have You Not Read of Such a Thing? Sex and Sexual Stories in Othello," Edward Pechter tackles the relevancy and validity of sexual content in *Othello*. Although the concept of hidden sexuality in Shakespeare's works is not a new one, essays on the subject are not found in every textbook.

This *Yearbook* houses 32 essays, broken into 4 sections: comedies, histories, tragedies, and romances and poems. Aside from the two works on differing topics about Henry V, no two essays pertain to the same play or poem. Although subjects such as Hamlet's sanity are necessary staples in every collection of Shakespearean criticism, the real value of this volume rests in essays such as Pechter's. Given that the essays consider age-old tales, current criticisms are not exactly current events. But bringing a fresh analytical perspective to plays that many students find difficult to absorb is a good way to catch and keep students' attention.—**Tom Sullivan**

1084.   West, Gilian. **A Dictionary of Shakespeare's Semantic Wordplay.** Lewiston, N.Y., Edwin Mellen Press, 1998. 216p. (Studies in Renaissance Literature, v.17). $89.95. ISBN 0-7734-8495-7.

West's book documents Shakespeare's fondness for wordplay by offering examples of what she terms the "secondary pun," a sense that "comes to our minds only because there is, or is suggested, in the immediate verbal context, a word or sense synonymous with it or semantically related to it." Users of the volume need to note carefully her introductory qualifying statement: the dictionary "cannot be other than a collection of suggestion—some of them very tentative for puns that might have been apparent when the plays were written." This is, thus, a reference volume in a restricted sense: It is not a complete list of puns, but rather a list of interpretive readings of selected passages that might be construed as containing puns that "may have dramatic significance."

The book is useful as documentation for a well-known stylistic device in Shakespeare; however, for those coming to Shakespeare for the first time the entries might carry an unwarranted factual weight because the volume is categorized as a dictionary. In the line "Fast asleep behind the arras, and snorting like a horse," the pun on *arras* and *haras* ("an enclosure in which horses and mares are kept for breeding") is evident. However, it is conjectural to assert that *argument* suggests the dialectical *argh* ("cowardly"), especially when corroborating pronunciation data is lacking. West is accurate in observing that "balls of murdering basilisks" puns on "cannonballs" from an early cannon called the basilisk, but she fails to note that it may also pun the "eyeballs" of the mythical basilisk, a creature that could kill with its glance. The volume contains a brief introduction, a bibliography of primary and secondary sources, and a list of puns not appearing as headnotes. A listing by plays of the passages referenced would have been useful. Taken within the limitations set out in her introduction, West's book will be helpful to graduate students and scholars. [R: Choice, July/Aug 98, p. 1832]—**Christopher Baker**

Thomas Hardy

1085.   Sherrick, Julie. **Thomas Hardy's Major Novels: An Annotated Bibliography.** Pasadena, Calif., Salem Press and Lanham, Md., Scarecrow, 1998. 195p. (Magill Bibliographies). $36.00. ISBN 0-8108-3382-4.

After a brief thematic guide and suggested books on Victorian England and biographies of Thomas Hardy, the bibliography is divided into separate lists under each of Hardy's six major novels: *Far from the Madding Crowd*, *The Return of the Native*, *The Mayor of Casterbridge*, *The Woodlanders*, *Tess of the d'Urbervilles*, and *Jude the Obscure*. Each of these is subdivided under five topics: circumstances of composition, comparative studies, nature of the novel, salient features of the novel, and character analysis. Because of this rather complicated arrangement, the work needs an index, which has not been provided.

Appendix A mentions the Internet as a source of information, but wisely urges caution because the material on it has not been sanctioned by any group of scholars. A complete listing of works cited is alphabetically placed in appendix B. Although the bibliographer purports to reflect trends in criticism over the past 30 years, the list is misleading because some works are reprints of earlier editions without reference to the earlier publication date. For example, although dated 1964, Mary Ellen Chase actually originally published *Thomas Hardy from Serial to Novel* in 1927. Also, the 1974 bibliography by Helmut Gerber and W. Eugene Davis is cited, but not the second extensive volume (1983), which brought their bibliography up to 1978.

High school pupils, teachers, and general readers interested in a particular novel by Thomas Hardy may find this bibliography helpful, but serious Hardy scholars will find its usefulness limited. [R: Choice, Nov 98, p. 494]

—**Charlotte Lindgren**

Thomas More

1086.   Geritz, Albert J., comp. **Thomas More: An Annotated Bibliography of Criticism, 1935-1997.** Westport, Conn., Greenwood Press, 1998. 428p. index. (Bibliographies and Indexes in World Literature, no.54). $89.50. ISBN 0-313-29391-0.

The continuing influence of Thomas More, who was a friend of Erasmus as well as a politician, saint, martyr, and the author of polemics, devotional works, letters, and *Utopia*, is abundantly clear in this annotated bibliography that covers more than 1,600 items, virtually everything written about him since 1935. It includes biographies, editions, and critical studies from books, dissertations, and more than 150 journals, especially *Moreana*, the bulletin devoted to More. The annotations are excellent—compact but balanced and thorough. It supersedes earlier reference works and belongs on the shelves of any library with a collection of Renaissance, humanist, or utopian literature.

—**Lynn F. Williams**

Virginia Woolf

1087.   **Major Authors on CD-ROM: Virginia Woolf.** [CD-ROM]. Woodbridge, Conn., Primary Source Media, 1997. Minimum system requirements (Windows version): IBM or compatible 486. Double-speed CD-ROM drive. Windows 3.1. 8MB RAM. 10MB hard disk space. VGA color monitor. Mouse. 8-bit Sound Blaster compatible sound card. $1,995.00. ISBN 1-57803-049-8.

Major Authors on CD-ROM: Virginia Woolf is part of a series that focuses on celebrated authors, including the Brontës and Walt Whitman. Woolf's complete published works, including essays, fiction, letters, diaries, biographies, autobiographies, more than 12,000 manuscript images (from the Henry W. and Albert A. Berg Collection at the New York Public Library and the University of Sussex's Monks House Papers), literary criticism, biographical information, photographs, sketches, paintings, and an eight-minute recording of her BBC talk "Craftsmanship" are contained on this CD-ROM, as well as many holographs of her work and the complete text of *Virginia Woolf A-Z* (see ARBA 96, entry 1221) by Mark Hussey, the CD-ROM's general editor.

This CD-ROM can be an invaluable tool for researchers and students of Virginia Woolf's works as well as for the casual enthusiast with an interest in reading her writings. The disk is full-text searchable with extensive cross-references and hyperlinks. Therefore, the student can easily reference works, expand searches, discover further information, and obtain full bibliographic citations. Hyperlinks to associated materials are in each work, and a variety of independent search tools are offered. Navigation is straightforward and flexible, providing forward, back, revisit, and bookmark options.

This reviewer found this to be an excellent educational and research tool. It is a sound product both in content and technical presentation. Primary Source Media is a division of Thomas Information, which is also the parent of Gale Research. With this pedigree the user should expect, and does receive, a finely researched product. This product will be a useful addition to any high school, college, or public library. [R: LJ, 15 May 97, p. 112]

—**Sheryl Sessa**

Canadian Literature

1088.   **The Oxford Companion to Canadian Literature.** 2d ed. Eugene Benson and William Toye, eds. New York, Oxford University Press, 1997. 1199p. $65.00. ISBN 0-19-541167-6.

This is an excellent revision of a 30-year-old classic. It began as *The Oxford Companion to Canadian History and Literature* in 1967, edited by Norah Story. A supplement was later issued, and the 1st edition of the current edition was published in 1983. And *The Oxford Companion to Canadian Theatre* was published in 1989.

The 1983 edition had 770 entries by 193 contributors; this new revision has added 342 new entries from 132 new contributors. The older entries have been reworked where appropriate. The Oxford Companion series are well known in their arrangement, setup, and mission; they are reference books for both ordinary people and the specialist. In this case, there is a lot of supporting material that should make laypeople quite happy. Lots of entries and space are devoted to non-English literature in Canada (e.g., writing by native peoples, Acadians, Quebecois, multicultural groups). Scope has been widened to include material on science fiction and fantastic literature, crime writing, and children's books.

Newer subjects cover awards, Caribbean-Canadian literature, censorship, gay and lesbian literature, and sportswriting. As always, there is no index, but there are many internal cross-references. This is an invaluable acquisition for all Canadian studies programs as well as a useful purchase for literary research collections. [R: BL, 15 Oct 98, p. 443; LJ, Aug 98, p. 78; Choice, Nov 98, p. 492]—**Dean Tudor**

Caribbean Literature

1089.   Goslinga, Marian. **Caribbean Literature: A Bibliography.** Lanham, Md., Scarecrow, 1998. 469p. index. (Scarecrow Area Bibliographies, no.15). $95.00. ISBN 0-8108-3452-9.

Caribbean literature is multicultural, encompassing Spanish-, French-, Dutch-, and English-language works along with indigenous dialects. Goslinga, Latin American and Caribbean librarian at Florida International University and author of *A Bibliography of the Caribbean* (see ARBA 97, entry 128), herein provides researchers with approximately 3,500 bibliographic entries on Caribbean literature. Entries are grouped by language group and then are divided by country. Country sections are then subdivided topically, with segments on individual authors. It appears that only books are listed, not articles, dissertations, or chapters in books. The titles included here are primarily in the four languages mentioned earlier, although there are occasional German or Creole entries. Dates of publication go up until 1996.

As useful as this tool could have been, there are a few problems. Although publication information is listed for the nonfiction titles, works of individual authors only provide the year of publication. In fact, rather than making each title an individual entry, titles listed for individual authors are lumped together in a confusing array. Also, it is not clear if the titles are novels, collections of short stories, or poetry. Books about individual authors' works are listed separately in an indented list immediately following. There are occasional brief annotations, but they are not necessarily useful for the researcher. Most of the annotations consist of lists of names of authors who appear in anthologies or collections of works. Having no quality assessment is a serious detriment to this book's research potential. Even though it is useful to see the variety of resources available, not being able to distinguish between the quality of two items on the same topic is of little value. As stated previously, publication information is given for the nonfiction titles, but of particular use would have been a sampling of libraries holding the particular work.

This bibliography would be helpful for finding works on Dutch Caribbean literature, at this point a little-studied field. Other than that aspect, the value of the bibliography is questionable. The value of the book is the fact that someone has already done the research and found books on Caribbean literature, but diligent researchers could amass their own lists by searching the WorldCat, MLA Bibliography, and OCLC databases. Without useful annotations, this volume is just a list of books.—**Melissa Rae Root**

Chinese Literature

1090.   **The Indiana Companion to Traditional Chinese Literature, Volume 2.** William H. Nienhauser Jr., Charles Hartman, and Scott W. Galer, eds. Bloomington, Ind., Indiana University Press, 1998. 547p. index. $59.95. ISBN 0-253-33456-X.

The first volume of this book, which received a great deal of interest and good comments, was published in 1986. People considered it an excellent guide to Chinese literature before 1911. Twelve years later, this volume emerges as both a supplement to and an update of the original volume. The entries are written by 32 scholars from different countries. Each entry presents basic information followed by a tripartite bibliography that lists editions, translations, and studies. One major difference in this volume is that original works, along with the original texts, are presented in some entries to help illustrate a style or technique. The sections of bibliographic updates following the main entries include selected titles published through 1998. Two appendixes are attached to the end of the text: a table of contents for volume 1 and an errata and corrigenda to volume 1. A name index, title index, and subject index to new entries are also available.

This book is a great asset to academic libraries, large public libraries, East Asian libraries, and the East Asian Studies Institute. It will help researchers and students in their research and studies in Chinese culture and literature. There are two mistakes this reviewer noted. First, the misuse of Chinese characters, some of which look very similar but have different meanings. The editors made a great effort to correct the errors in volume 1, but errors still can be found in volume 2. Second, the Chinese romanization used in this guide is different from the Pinyin system, which is adopted by the United Nations and U.S. government and news agencies. The Library of Congress is going to convert to Pinyin system for Chinese romanization in the near future. Therefore, cross-references to the names are necessary to reduce confusion.—**Xiao (Shelley) Yan Zhang**

East European Literature

1091. **South Slavic Writers Since World War II.** Vasa D. Mihailovich, ed. Detroit, Gale, 1997. 474p. illus. index. (Dictionary of Literary Biography, v.181). $146.00. ISBN 0-7876-1070-4.

This volume in the Dictionary of Literary Biography Series (DLB) follows the conventions of previous volumes in that its purpose is to place major figures in the larger perspective of literary history and offer appraisals of these figures. After a brief introduction by Mihailovich that sets the context for the biographies that follow, each of the writer's entries, from Ivan Aralica to Vitomil Zupan, are arranged alphabetically and not separated by country of origin. Each national literature (based on language) is well represented. Included are writers from Serbia, Croatia, Macedonia, Slovenia, and Bulgaria. Each biography is written by a well-known critic in the field.

The entries are structured similarly. Each begins with a bibliography of book-length works and, when appropriate, selected periodical publications. Following this is the biography, often with illustrations in addition to the mandatory picture of the author. Each ends with a bibliography of secondary sources on the author in both English and other languages. At the end of the volume is a section titled "Checklist of Further Readings" in various languages, a list of contributors with their institutional affiliations, and a cumulative index to the authors contained in all the previous DLB volumes, including this one. This is a solid reference work and deserves to be on the shelves of every major research library.—**Robert H. Burger**

French Literature

1092. **Dictionary of Literary Biography, Volume 192: French Dramatists, 1789-1914.** Barbara T. Cooper, ed. Detroit, Gale, 1998. 481p. illus. index. $151.00. ISBN 0-7876-1847-0.

French Dramatists, 1789-1914 represents another excellent offering in the distinguished Dictionary of Literary Biography series published by Gale. Edited by Cooper of the University of New Hampshire, the volume contains essays on major French dramatists by first-rate scholars in the fields of French literature and criticism. The book is well presented and contains an abundance of useful information about each dramatist, including bibliographical data on the plays (e.g., title, place, and date of first production) and published collection as well as a representative sample of criticism about the author and his or her work. The volume concludes with a "Checklist of Further Readings" that will point the student or scholar toward books in English and French that treat the history, aesthetics, or analysis of French drama and theater in the nineteenth century. Although this checklist appears a bit cursory, the bibliographies concluding each article more than compensate.

The essays themselves are written with clarity and rigor and appear to target readers ranging from under-graduate students to theater scholars. According to the editor, the essays "mark only the beginning of a much needed reassessment and reexamination of the role of theater in nineteenth-century France." Interestingly, the time span covered is actually much longer than the nineteenth century in that it includes playwright Marie-Joseph Chénier (the younger brother of the famous poet, André Chénier), who wrote during the French Revolution, as well as Paul Claudel, whose major works were written just before the outbreak of World War I. The period is vast, but the editor contends that there is a logic in chronicling such an extensive era in that "the period between 1789 and 1914 was the last era in the history of French literature to be marked in a significant way by drama."

One of the more interesting features of this volume is the inclusion of reproductions of paintings and photographs of the dramatists; costumes designed for their plays; manuscripts; and, in the case of Victor Hugo, his mistress, Juliette Drouet. This iconography lends a more pleasing and less tedious appearance to the text. College and university libraries as well as students and scholars intrigued by the noble genre of theater as it manifested itself in nineteenth-century France will do well to add *French Dramatists, 1789-1914* to their collections. [R: BL, 15 Nov 98, p. 610]—**John B. Romeiser**

German Literature

1093.   Furness, Raymond, and Malcolm Humble. **A Companion to Twentieth-Century German Literature.** 2d ed. New York, Routledge, 1997. 316p. $74.95; $18.95pa. ISBN 0-415-15056-6; 0-415-15057-4pa.

Furness and Humble's 1st edition of *A Companion to Twentieth-Century German Literature* appeared in 1991 (see ARBA 93, entry 1223) and included 414 entries; the present edition increases that number to 441 entries. Arrangement is again alphabetic by author, and numerous existing entries have been updated with mention of recent works, editions, and collections. New entries include former German Democratic Republic writers, such as Monika Maron, Uwe Kolbe, and Helga Konigsdorf; Austrians such as Christoph Ransmayr and Franz Innerhofer; and even Syrian-born Rafik Schami, an indication of Germany's increasing diversity. A single topical entry covers Prenzlauer Berg, a Berlin district important to the East German literary scene. Unfortunately the authors, both scholars of German at the University of St. Andrews, have still not added an index, which greatly reduces access to names, titles, and other references embedded in the author entries.

Collections needing a one-volume English language introduction to German-speaking writers will find this work useful, especially where the multivolume *Dictionary of Literary Biography* (which offers much more detail) is beyond the library's budget. For those owning the 1st edition, however, only the paperback version of the 2d edition should be considered, as the information added is not worth the hardcover's inflated price. [R: C&RL, Sept 97, p. 479]—**Willa Schmidt**

1094.   Hall, Clifton. **Head-Word and Rhyme-Word Concordances to *Des Minnesangs Frühling*: A Complete Reference Work.** Niwot, Colo., University Press of Colorado, 1997. 509p. $125.00. ISBN 0-87081-447-8.

Des Minnesangs Frühling, a collection of lyric poetry by Middle High German poets first published in 1857, has undergone frequent reprint and revision over the years, but Moser and Tervooren's 36th edition in 1977 provided significant re-editing that resulted in a new edition worth noting. The latest edition, revised in 1988, is now recognized as the standard for scholarly investigation. Hall's concordance, based on the 1988 version, will be of interest to researchers in German philology.

The main part of the work is a concordance of "principal forms," which are listed alphabetically with occurrences shown in a context of about 45 characters. (*Word-Index to Des Minnesangs Frühling* [University of Wisconsin, 1942], based on F. Vogt's 1923 edition, is by contrast strictly a word index with only page and line references.) Other sections provide word frequency rankings, a reverse index of forms, and a rhyme-word concordance, all useful enhancements facilitated by computer technology. Price is a definite consideration; academic libraries considering its purchase might want to look into the computerized version of the 1988 edition, *EDV-Text von Des Minnesangs Frühling* by Jean L. C. Putnams, Kümmerle, 1993 (not seen by this reviewer), which could possibly be used with text manipulation software to achieve the effect of a concordance at less cost.

—**Willa Schmidt**

1095.   **Women Writers in German-Speaking Countries: A Bio-Bibliographical Critical Sourcebook.** Elke P. Frederiksen and Elizabeth G. Ametsbichler, eds. Westport, Conn., Greenwood Press, 1998. 561p. index. $95.00. ISBN 0-313-28201-3.

This book is an outgrowth of Frederiksen's 1989 bio-bibliographical guide, *Women Writers of Germany, Austria, and Switzerland* (see ARBA 90, entry 856). Like its predecessor, it aims to increase awareness of the breadth and diversity of significant literary writing by German-speaking women authors from the Middle Ages to the present while providing useful factual information about their lives and writings. However, unlike its predecessor, which covered 185 writers in brief compass, this volume focuses on a representative selection of 54, each of whom is treated in articles of greater length (8 to 15 pages) and scope (critical surveys of the literary work and of the criticism on it are now included). The bibliographies are selective and include matter in German as well as in English. Frederiksen provides a fine, historically oriented introduction. The volume ends with a chronological listing of the authors covered, a 13-page general bibliography on women in German literature, three indexes (name, subject, and title), and notes on the contributors.

The articles themselves are arranged alphabetically by their subjects' surnames. In a novel development, not seen in the previous volume or in scholarship generally, medieval authors lacking surnames are tacitly ennobled by the use as surnames of their now traditional toponymic identifiers. For example, Hildegard von Bingen and Hrotsvit von Gandersheim are to be found not under the letter "H" but rather under "B" and "G," respectively. In a book written by academics, aimed chiefly at novices, and destined for ready-reference use, this seemingly uninformed and heterodox practice is both misleading and counterproductive. Again, although the articles are well written and generally informative, their accompanying bibliographies are not always as current or as full as one might expect. Thus, the secondary bibliography for Sarah Kirsch shows nothing after 1992, whereas the primary bibliography for Luise Rinser, which runs through 1994, unaccountably omits the expanded 1992 edition of her well-known *Bruder Feuer*. However, the important material through 1995 usually is listed, with more recent contributions often noted as well.

This book is recommended for academic libraries supporting programs in German literature, women's studies, or coursework in general or world literature. Major and some medium-sized public libraries will also find it useful. [R: Choice, July/Aug 98, p. 1832]—**Willa Schmidt**

Japanese Literature

1096. **Japanese Fiction Writers Since World War II.** Van C. Gessel, ed. Detroit, Gale, 1997. 370p. illus. index. (Dictionary of Literary Biography, v.182). $146.00. ISBN 0-7876-1071-2.

This Dictionary of Literary Bibliography volume is number 182 in a massive project. The editorial policy of this series is to present the history of an author's writing, not life, in order to illuminate the context and background of the literary works. The volumes are organized in several ways, such as topic, period or genre, in order to provide an overview of a particular body of literature. This volume, presenting Japanese fiction writers since World War II, includes many living authors and attempts to collect and establish the oeuvre as a whole.

Providing both bibliography and biography, the reference is quite useful, especially to students. Japan's defeat in the war led to a rich and complicated literary outpouring of modern Japanese writing. The break in continuity provided by the occupation and the subsequent reemergence of Japan on the world stage as a "superpower" all lends itself to the interpretation in fiction of the country's character. Of significant note is the powerful appearance of women authors and of the female viewpoint in other works. The introduction provides a simple, yet concise, history of modern Japanese literature. It should prove useful to the specialist and nonspecialist alike.—**Linda L. Lam-Easton**

Russian Literature

1097. **Reference Guide to Russian Literature.** Neil Cornwell and Nicole Christian, eds. Chicago, Fitzroy Dearborn, 1998. 972p. index. $125.00. ISBN 1-884964-10-9.

This weighty tome is intended to be a comprehensive guide to the main writers of Russian literature and to their best-known works. The 273 writers and 293 works span the chronological limits of Russian literature, from the Kievan period to the present-day postcommunist writing of the Russian Federation. The editors acknowledge their bias toward nineteenth- and twentieth-century authors. In terms of coverage, the selection breaks down as approximately 10 percent for eighteenth century and earlier, 33 percent nineteenth and early twentieth century, and the remaining 57 percent twentieth century.

The entries, each of which was written by one of the 180 contributors, are arranged in alphabetic order. Each entry contains a short biographical sketch (no illustrations), a list of publications and related critical studies, and, where applicable, published bibliographies of the author's works and related criticism. In each author's section there is always a critical appraisal essay and in most cases an essay about a major work of the author.

These individual author entries are preceded by a rich introduction that contains a general reading list (most of which are in English), a chronology of main historical and literary events, and a glossary of 51 terms with brief definitions, followed by a series of a dozen essays covering topics such as old Russian literature, women's writing in Russia, Russian literary theory, and Russian literature in the post-Soviet period. The volume is well equipped with a title index and notes on contributors and advisers.

This impressive work is sure to be useful for anyone studying Russian literature, at whatever stage. The introductory essays serve as a solid overview of the subject, and the bibliographies and essays on each writer are well done and will whet the appetite of the beginner as well as consolidate the knowledge of the specialist. [R: BL, 1 Sept 98, pp. 162-163; LJ, Aug 98, p. 79; Choice, Oct 98, p. 293]—**Robert H. Burger**

Spanish Literature

1098.   **Spanish American Literature: A Collection of Essays.** David William Foster and Daniel Altamiranda, eds. New York, Garland, 1997. 5v. $415.00/set. ISBN 0-8153-2677-7.

This series contains 122 essays from a number of Spanish- and English-language periodicals that are intended to provide basic texts and literary criticisms for students of Latin American literature. The editors do not include Portuguese- or French-speaking authors from the Caribbean, even though technically they also come from Latin American countries. The essays are divided into 5 volumes: *Theoretical Debates in Spanish American Literature*; *Writers of the Spanish Colonial Period*; *From Romanticism to Modernism in Latin America*; *Twentieth-Century Spanish Literature to 1960*; and *Twentieth-Century Spanish Literature Since 1960*.

The essays selected for inclusion appear to be reprinted as they appeared in the original publication, with the exception of a page number at the bottom of the page. The essays are written either in Spanish or English, and they come in a variety of font sizes and styles. Some of the essays are easy to read, whereas others are extremely difficult due to the minute size of the single-spaced text. These inconveniences pale in comparison to the benefits of seeing the documents as they were published because they provide an insight into the author that would be lost by transcribing and translating the texts. The illustrations and cartoons that are part of some of the essays speak volumes about the culture and political climate of Latin America. The essays all conclude with notes and a bibliography.

The reference value of this series is greatly diminished by the lack of indexing. No tools were provided to access the data in the essays. Each volume has its own table of contents, and there is no continuous pagination. The volumes were designed independently of each other and are available for sales as individual titles. Libraries supporting Latin American studies programs should consider purchasing this set for the circulating collection, rather than the reference collection.—**John R. Burch Jr.**

POETRY

1099.   Feinstein, Sascha. **A Bibliographic Guide to Jazz Poetry.** Westport, Conn., Greenwood Press, 1998. 230p. index. (Music Reference Collection, no.69). $65.00. ISBN 0-313-29469-0.

Everyone knows about Jack Kerouac's prose, but do many people know he also wrote jazz poetry? Feinstein, author of *A Bibliographic Guide to Jazz Poetry*, cautions, however: "A better prose writer than poet, Kerouac wrote verse in the spirit of a jazz soloist—with no revision. This resulted in energetic but wildly uneven pieces. He also recorded with live jazz accompaniment, with similar results" (p. 51). This excerpt is just one example of the many lively, informative, and accurate annotations that await the reader of this useful reference tool. Volume 69 of the series from Greenwood Press, entitled Music Reference Collection, Feinstein has compiled more than 500 citations to poems relating to jazz, and sometimes blues and other related musical forms.

The organization of the contents is well thought out. There are 13 anthologies listed, all thoroughly anno-tated with detailed information on which poets are anthologized. In addition, there is an index by individual poet, also with annotations, and a very useful cross-reference guide by jazz musician name. In other words, if readers want to know what poems may have been written about Ella Fitzgerald, they can simply look up her name in the musician index: There are 17 poems listed. The final section is entitled "Chronological Index: Poems Published Before 1970."

More than one subject specialist will be interested in this title. Not only is this a survey of poetry based upon a specific subject, but it offers an overview of the history of jazz itself; the history of African American poetry (on jazz as well as some other topics like civil rights); and the history of other social and literary movements of the 1950s, 1960s, and 1970s. There is only one minor distraction, which can be blamed on the computerization of book edition. It mostly occurs in the cross-reference guide. A heading for someone will be printed at the bottom of the page, yet the bibliographic citations will appear at the top of the next page. It is not a major drawback, but it happens often, which could be somewhat confusing for users.

This volume is a welcome addition to the research materials in both poetry and jazz. It is highly recommended for most academic and larger public libraries. It should be an essential purchase for all music libraries and extensive poetry collections. [R: Choice, Oct 98, p. 290]—**Roland C. Hansen**

1100.   **Index of American Periodical Verse 1996.** By Rafael Catalá and James D. Anderson. Lanham, Md., Scarecrow, 1998. 665p. index. $75.00. ISBN 0-8108-3545-2. ISSN 0090-9130.

The 26th annual volume of this index has nearly 7,000 entries for individual poets and translators and more than 20,000 entries for individual poems. It indexes poems published in a broad cross-section of poetry, literary, scholarly, popular, general, and "little" magazines, journals, and reviews from the United States, Canada, and the Caribbean. Poets are arranged alphabetically. Under each poet's name, the poems are arranged alpha-numerically by title or, if there is no title, by the first line. Notes about dedications, joint authors, translators, and sources follow the titles. The periodical citations include title, volume, issue numbers, date, and page numbers. Included is a list of periodicals added since the previous issue and another list of ones deleted with a reason why. This is an invaluable resource for academic and public libraries.—**Cari Ringelheim**

1101.   **International Who's Who in Poetry and Poets' Encyclopaedia 1997.** 8th ed. David Cummings and Dennis K. McIntire, eds. Cambridge, England, International Biographical Centre; distr., Bristol, Pa., Taylor & Francis, 1997. 476p. $160.00. ISBN 0-948875-37-2.

The 8th edition of the well-established biographical dictionary of poets marks the 40th anniversary of its first appearance in 1957. It has been completely revised; every poet featured has personally reviewed his or her entry, and several hundred new entries have been added. Coverage extends to poets from the United Kingdom, the Commonwealth, the United States, and Canada and well as to poets whose work is known through English translations. Each entry provides standard biographical data, such as date and place of birth, marriage, education, and career. Also included are information on awards and honors; memberships; and a list of publications, both monographic and periodical. A helpful set of appendixes rounds out the volume, giving lists of poetry publishers and poetry prizewinners, among other honors. This is a useful and up-to-date reference work on current English-language poets.—**Jeffrey R. Luttrell**

1102.   **Masterplots II: Poetry Series Supplement, Volume 9.** John Wilson, Philip K. Jason, and McCrea Adams, eds. Englewood Cliffs, N.J., Salem Press, 1998. 1v. (various paging). index. $225.00. ISBN 0-89356-628-4.

Masterplots II: Poetry Series Supplement volumes 7 through 9 complement the series' original 6 volumes and continue its pagination and volumes number sequence. The series has expanded to include more popular poems, such as Lord Byron's *She Walks in Beauty*. It also has extended coverage of more twentieth-century works, allowing more discussions of African American, Hispanic, Asian American, and American Indian writers. Overall, the set is primarily English-language poetry, therefore lacking in poems from around the world.

The supplements do well to expand multicultural work, but they are still unbalanced in the type of poetry covered. Like the original set, the supplements feature a great number more lyric poems than any other type. Nevertheless, the supplements are an excellent reference source and will be useful for the middle school through beginning college-level libraries.—**Cari Ringelheim**

1103. **Notable Poets.** Englewood Cliffs, N.J., Salem Press, 1998. 3v. illus. index. (Magill's Choice). $175.00/set. ISBN 0-89356-967-4.

This 3-volume illustrated set of biographical sketches and critical essays of 110 of the world's greatest poets from antiquity to the present provides an excellent introduction to the study of poetry. Designed to meet the needs of high school students and undergraduates, *Notable Poets* includes new and previously published essays that serve as excellent examples of clear and concise literary commentary. Each of the alphabetically arranged entries begins with the poet's date and place of birth and death (where applicable) and a chronological list of his or her principal works. This is followed by an "Achievements" section, which gives readers a brief overview of the poet's literary contributions. The biographical sketches provide basic information about the poets and the people, places, and events that shaped them and their poetry. The section titled "Analysis" is somewhat of a misnomer. A few of the essays do offer a poetic analysis or explication, but for the most part, the contributors summarize the poet's major works. This is by no means a weakness, however. Poetry is a difficult genre even for specialists in literature. Therefore, the level of discourse in *Notable Poets* is appropriate for the audience its publishers hope to reach. Included at the end of volume 3 are a glossary of literary terms, a chronology of the poets' birth dates, and a geographic and subject index. Aside from what is cited in the essays, samples of the poets' work are not included. *Notable Poets* is a supplement to the works of these great poets.—**Sandra Adell**

1104. **Poetry Criticism, Volume 18: Excerpts from Criticism....** Carol T. Gaffke, ed. Detroit, Gale, 1997. 577p. illus. index. $98.00. ISBN 0-7876-0958-7.

1105. **Poetry Criticism, Volume 19: Excerpts from Criticism....** Carol T. Gaffke, ed. Detroit, Gale, 1997. 615p. illus. index. $98.00. ISBN 0-7876-1546-3.

Collections that already shelve the first 17 volumes of *Poetry Criticism* (PC) will, of course, want to obtain the two latest additions to a fine series that offers more focused attention on poets and their works than is possible in the broader, survey-oriented entries on writers in the Gale Literary Criticism Series. In keeping with the international scope of PC, volume 18 features substantial critical excerpts and biographical information on three Americans (Ralph Waldo Emerson, Gertrude Stein, Charles Bukowski), an Englishman (Lewis Carroll), a Frenchman (Theophile Gautier), a Japanese (Hagiwara Sakutaro), an Irishman (Seamus Heaney), a Russian (Mikhail Lermontov), and a poet from the T'ang Dynasty (Wang Wei). In keeping with the objective of spanning the centuries, volume 19 features one ancient Greek poet (Pindar), one medievalist (Chaucer), one figure from the seventeenth century (Milton), and five contemporaries (Wilfred Owen, Stanley Kunitz, Amy Clampitt, Charles Owen, and Nikki Giovanni). Appended to both volumes are detailed indexes to all the volumes published thus far in the PC series as well as cross-references to author entries in the Gale Literary Criticism series and Gale's Biographical and Literary Sources. Librarians, researchers, teachers, and students will find the brief biographies and bibliographies, plus the generous critical excerpts and supplementary materials, extremely helpful for papers, oral presentations, and discussion groups.—**G. A. Cevasco**

1106. **Poetry for Students, Volume 1: Presenting Analysis, Context, and Criticism on Commonly Studied Poetry.** Marie Rose Napierkowski and Mary K. Ruby, eds. Detroit, Gale, 1998. 349p. illus. index. $55.00. ISBN 0-7876-1688-5. [R: VOYA, Oct 98, p. 308]

1107. **Poetry for Students, Volume 2: Presenting Analysis, Context, and Criticism on Commonly Studied Poetry.** Marie Rose Napierkowski and Mary K. Ruby, eds. Detroit, Gale, 1998. 343p. illus. index. $55.00. ISBN 0-7876-1689-3. [R: VOYA, Oct 98, p. 308]

1108. **Poetry for Students, Volume 3: Presenting Analysis, Context and Criticism on Commonly Studied Poetry.** Marie Rose Napierkowski and Mary K. Ruby, eds. Detroit, Gale, 1998. 337p. illus. index. $55.00. ISBN 0-7876-2724-0.

Napierkowski and Ruby make it a point to declare their purpose right at the outset of these works: "to provide readers with a guide to understanding, enjoying, and studying poems by giving them easy access to information about the work. Part of Gale's 'For Students' literature line, [this work] is specifically designed to meet the curricular needs of high school and undergraduate college students," as well as those of the general reader. The keynote of this approach is thoroughness, as can be seen by the fact that each of the 20 poems in each volume is accompanied by an overview essay, an analysis of its structure and form, a thematic examination, a discussion of the poem's historical and cultural context, selected criticism, a brief author biography, sources for further study, and suggested research topics. Also furnished are indexes for subject matter, themes, and nationality as well as the usual author and title indexes.

The strategy of both volumes of *Poetry for Students* is to focus on relatively few poems and analyze each in depth, as opposed to the "shotgun" approach of most teaching anthologies, which may include literally hundreds of poems with a "once over lightly" kind of approach. The advantage of the in-depth approach is that it helps students adopt thoroughness in their thinking, along with the sort of methodical patience that one needs to develop in order to read on a sophisticated, mature level. The disadvantage is that the exposure to poetry becomes relatively narrow, with the danger that the student does not get enough of a cross-section of authors to make the studies worthwhile. There are plenty of good arguments for both the in-depth and the shotgun approach, and in the case of *Poetry for Students* it is clear the editors, once having made their choice, were determined to make it work.

A case in point is the treatment of "Do Not Go Gentle into That Good Night," the famous villanelle by Dylan Thomas. There are four long paragraphs offering an engaging thumbnail biography of the author, after which the poem is quoted in its entirety and then analytically summarized in detail. After that, we are presented with analyses of several main themes that were crucial in Thomas's poetic thinking: anger, the human condition, and identity. In the sections covering background and biography, the editors leave nothing out; students are told that the poet was an alcoholic "who stole from his friends and lied to them, was loud and offensive in public, and died of poisoning from drinking too much too fast one day." (Not mentioned is a recent theory that severe diabetes also contributed to Thomas's demise.) Concerning the poem's literary heritage, the editors discuss Welsh mystical and poetic traditions but also raise the possibility that this highly original author was not deeply indebted to his forerunners in Wales. Rounding out the Dylan Thomas section of the book are excerpts from several distinguished critics and a selected bibliography. Upon finishing the material surrounding "Do Not Go Gentle into That Good Night," one of the best-known poems in the language, students will feel as though they have been well-immersed in this renowned work of art—but perhaps a few readers will feel a sense of "overkill." In literary studies there is sometimes a perilous balance between too much and not enough.

Napierkowski and Ruby successfully apply their in-depth approach to a number of other important poems, including Langston Hughes's "Harlem," Robert Frost's "Stopping by Woods on a Snowy Evening," Robert Browning's "My Last Duchess," Rita Dove's "This Life," and T. S. Eliot's "Love Song of J. Alfred Prufrock." It would seem that all of these classics are well worth the "deep" approach that is the modus operandi and the strong backbone of *Poetry for Students.*—**Peter Thorpe**

1109.   **Poetry for Students, Volume 4: Presenting Analysis, Context, and Criticism on Commonly Studied Poetry.** Mary K. Ruby, ed. Farmington Hills, Mich., Gale, 1998. 305p. illus. index. $55.00. ISBN 0-7876-2725-9. ISSN 1094-7019.

This lavish 4th volume of *Poetry for Students* continues the traditions of the previous volumes: Each of the 20 famous poems is accompanied by an introduction, an author biography, the text of the poem itself, a detailed summary of the poem, the themes and style of the poem, the historical and cultural context, and a critical overview. Finally, there is some information on media adaptations, a compare and contrast box, and some useful suggestions for further reading. The aforementioned box is particularly interesting, with its comparisons and contrasts between cultural, political, and scientific events of the author's time and those of the present day. Also useful is the chronology at the front of the volume, covering major literary and historical events from the time of *Beowulf* to 1998, when Charles Wright was awarded the Pulitzer prize in poetry. The keynote of this volume of *Poetry for Students*, as in the earlier volumes, is a thoroughness that invites students to immerse themselves in some of the most important authors in the English language—such as Alfred Tennyson, Robert Frost, Gwendolyn Brooks, W. H. Auden, Simon Ortiz, A. E. Housman, and William Shakespeare.

How well does this elaborate system work? Is the large mass of interpretation and background information too overwhelming, causing the student to be intimidated or turned off before these masterpieces of literature can work their magic? Fortunately, the materials in this coffee-table-sized book are presented in a brisk and readable manner that keeps interest page after page. Readers come away with the feeling that with each poem they have had a full literary experience and not the "once-over-lightly" sort of thing that modern culture often leaves with people. For example, Brooks's brief lyric "Strong Men, Riding Horses" is examined and explained from a variety of standpoints so that readers understand that this piece is not just about riders but actually about the important theme of westward expansionism and the destructive, territorial mind-set that can accompany this theme. Moreover, the biographical material about Brooks's impoverished childhood helps to illuminate the strong feelings behind the social concern in the poem. Although it may be that the line-by-line summary of "Strong Men, Riding Horses" is too detailed, perhaps even a little windy at times, the ultimate effect of the summary is to make doubly sure that readers have really traveled through the lines, rather than merely nibbling along the edges. In short, the elaborate system used in *Poetry for Students* can work not just for the pupil but for the general readers as well.

Does the system function equally well with all 20 poems in the book? That would seem to be the case, except perhaps for the few longer poems. Samuel Taylor Coleridge's "Rime of the Ancient Mariner" is possibly too complex and too long for a textbook of this sort, even though the apparatus that accompanies it is clear and easy to read. Similarly, Frost's "The Death of the Hired Man," with its 175 lines, seems somewhat out of balance when it is included with short lyrics of only a dozen lines or so. At this point, the book's philosophy of equal treatment for all seems to begin to break down.

However, there is much to learn and enjoy in *Poetry for Students*, and the lines of such greats as Thomas Hardy, Ted Hughes, Anne Sexton, and Emily Dickinson are made greater for readers by the sensitive, intelligent handling they receive here. The book is carefully assembled, and although Dickinson is called "Dickson" in the table of contents, such slips are rare indeed in this handsome volume.—**Peter Thorpe**

1110.   **Poets: American and British.** Ian Scott-Kilvert, George Stade, Leonard Unger, and A. Walton Litz, eds. New York, Macmillan Library Reference/Simon & Schuster Macmillan, 1998. 3v. index. $180.00/set. ISBN 0-684-80605-3.

The 72 signed, unabridged essays in this set have previously appeared in other Scribner series: American Writers (and supplements), British Writers (and supplements), Modern American Women Writers, African American Writers, and European Writers: The Middle Ages and the Renaissance. Articles appear exactly as they did in the original set, with no revision or updating. The editors claim that inclusion in this set is based upon a survey of U.S. libraries, and encompasses those English-language poets that are studied most often in high school and college. Given this, the reason for issuing the set is to allow libraries that were unable to afford any of the original sets the opportunity to purchase this core of critical information on important poets.

Entries for individual authors average 20 pages, with the majority of information presented in critical bio-bibliographic style. Because each essay is written by a specialist, emphasis on individual poems (versus collected works) varies by poet. Selected bibliographies are included for each poet, indicating individual and collected works, and works other than poetry. Selected lists of biographical and critical studies, interviews, and other formats are included as appropriate. In addition to individual authors, the set also includes essays on various schools or movements in poetry—the Cavalier poets, the Metaphysical poets, poets of World Wars I and II, and Restoration Court poets. The 3d volume includes indexing for the entire set.

What the set lacks in revision must be balanced by affordability and by the reparation of the essays themselves—recognized as sound critical secondary sources for the study of literature. This set is highly recommended for libraries with limited budgets that do not have adequate critical materials in their literature collections.
—**Edmund F. SantaVicca**

1111.   Sonntag Blay, Iliana L. **Twentieth-Century Poetry from Spanish America: An Index to Spanish Language and Bilingual Anthologies.** Lanham, Md., Scarecrow, 1998. 698p. $90.00. ISBN 0-8108-3527-4.

During the past 50 years, the best of Latin American poetry has been anthologized in more than 70 volumes. This valuable reference tool to such an important cultural legacy provides access to almost 13,000 poems published in the anthologies that were written by more than 2,000 authors of Spanish Latin America—Mexico, Central America, and South America (Brazil is excepted because of its Portuguese heritage). The listings are divided into author, title, and first line indexes. The author section provides not only full names, but also countries or origin, dates of birth, and dates of deaths when required. When a title varies in different anthologies because of translations or other reasons, it is appropriately noted in the 2d section. The final section should prove of help because it allows one to locate a poem when only the first line is known. *Twentieth-Century Poetry from Spanish America* is highly recommended for all university reference collections.—**G. A. Cevasco**

25 Music

GENERAL WORKS

Bibliography

1112. Lewis, Mary S. **Antonio Gardano, Venetian Music Printer 1538-1569: A Descriptive Bibliography and Historical Study. Volume 2: 1550-1559.** New York, Garland, 1997. 556p. index. (Garland Reference Library of the Humanities, v.718). $132.00. ISBN 0-8240-8455-1.

This work is the 2d volume of Lewis's work on Antonio Gardano, the Venetian music printer. It covers his publications from 1550 through 1559, or the middle decade of his career. The author has provided a definitive listing of Gardano's published music divided into 3 sections: "The Repertory of the 1550s," "Notes on the Editions of the 1550s," and a "Catalogue of Gardano's Publications, 1550-1559." In addition, appendixes provide a list of primary sources cited, secondary works cited, a short title index to Gardano's publications, a composer index, a text incipit index, an index of instrumental works, and a general index.

Both this volume and the 1st volume are based on a search of such sources as RISM, printed library catalogs, early bibliographies, nineteenth-century resources, Vogel's *Bibliothek*, *Fétis's Biographie universelle*, and additional sources that are listed at the end of the work. For each edition of Gardano's publications, a complete description was compiled from these sources or other sources discovered by the author. In most cases actual copies were examined before being described, and in some cases numerous editions were compared. The author points out that she visited more than 69 libraries in order to complete the work.—**Robert L. Wick**

1113. McTyre, Ruthann Boles, comp. **Library Resources for Singers, Coaches, and Accompanists: An Annotated Bibliography, 1970-1997.** Westport, Conn., Greenwood Press, 1998. 151p. index. (Music Reference Collection, no.71). $65.00. ISBN 0-313-30266-9.

McTyre describes her book as "a doorway into the vast world of library resources for anyone who deals with study of voice." The work begins with a preface and a "General Music Reference" section, which introduces readers new to voice research not only to music materials but also to some general reference works. This section was actually written by Ida Reed, and the publishers should have given her credit more prominently (McTyre gives attribution in the preface). Following this section are chapters on dictionaries and encyclopedias; repertoire and research; synopses, translations, and diction; preparation, accompanying, and coaching; discographies and videographies; pedagogical resources; stage resources; travel and education; electronic resources; and periodicals. In the back of the book are author, title, and subject indexes. Some entries are for series rather than individual works; for example, Greenwood's Bio-bibliographies in Music series for individual composers is listed here. McTyre's annotations are concise and adequate explanations and will help beginning users to quickly ascertain whether an included work is suitable for their purposes. Users should note that the work is restricted to English-language publications within the given time period; however, some works included are republications of earlier editions. Opera is within the work's scope, but all titles beginning "The operas of . . ." and "The songs of . . . " are excluded, as are works about choral music. Rather than attempt exhaustive coverage, McTyre recommends the user to browse adjacent titles on the library shelf.

The tool will be of assistance at the reference desk, and will be of particular help in collection development for all libraries supporting programs in music education and performance. It can also serve as a stimulus for term papers as well as scholarly research. Students majoring in voice would be well served by perusing the entire volume. [R: BL, 1 Nov 98, pp. 538, 540]—**Ian Fairclough**

1114.   Perone, James E., comp. **Form and Analysis Theory: A Bibliography.** Westport, Conn., Greenwood Press, 1998. 248p. index. (Music Reference Collection, no.67). $65.00. ISBN 0-313-29594-8.

Book-length studies, including master's theses and dissertations, of musical form and analysis comprise Perone's most recent bibliography. The studies, or treatises, as the compiler calls them, are listed alphabetically by author and are limited to those written primarily in the twentieth century (or sometimes, the very late nineteenth century). There are no annotations. Each entry, however, offers complete bibliographic information as well as reviews and other sources that discuss the treatises. The author has excluded studies that deal chiefly with the analysis of specific compositions. A 2d section, the general bibliography, offers more than 900 periodical articles that address form and analysis. These are also arranged in alphabetic order by author, with no annotations.

The compiler has also added an index of personal names, including composers whose works may be discussed in the studies. The lack of subject access is a serious shortcoming when trying to identify books or articles that deal with particular areas, such as semiotics. If readers do not know the author, they are left to peruse the entire book. At $65, this book is not a good value. [R: Choice, Sept 98, p. 90]—**Allie Wise Goudy**

Biography

1115.   **Contemporary Musicians, Volume 19: Profiles of the People in Music.** Stacy A. McConnell, ed. Detroit, Gale, 1997. 312p. illus. index. $72.00. ISBN 0-7876-1064-X.

1116.   **Contemporary Musicians, Volume 20: Profiles of the People in Music.** Stacy A. McConnell, ed. Detroit, Gale, 1997. 310p. illus. index. $72.00. ISBN 0-7876-1177-8.

Volumes 19 and 20 of this Gale series comprise the latest additions to these valuable profiles. This reference series saves the information seeker hours of searching time. Entries, of which there are approximately 80 in each volume, represent a broad spectrum of musical industry artists who may be composers, musicians, or singers, plus selective nonperforming members of the music community. Contemporary music includes pop, rock, jazz, blues, country, New Age, folk, rhythm and blues, gospel, bluegrass, rap, reggae, and more—even a few classical artists, like Luciano Pavarotti and Placido Domingo. Also considered "contemporary" are a few whose contributions to music were so enduring that, although they may no longer be on the music scene, they rate an entry. Some examples are Irving Berlin, Sophie Tucker, Cole Porter, Al Jolson, and Judy Garland.

Entries may be for individuals or groups. A typical entry consists of several pages of highly readable information. Data sections provide personal statistics, career summaries, listings of major awards, and mailing addresses. An essay accompanies each entry and offers one or more examples of critical responses to the artist's work. Often there are entertaining personal highlights. Each entry provides a discography of the artist's major recorded works, usually a photograph, and sources of additional information from books, magazines, and newspapers.

Each volume in the series contains cumulative subject and musician indexes. The entire series contains such comprehensive coverage not readily available elsewhere that it is recommended for music libraries and as an addition to major reference collections.—**Louis G. Zelenka**

1117.   Harrison, Nigel. **Songwriters: A Biographical Dictionary with Discographies.** Jefferson, N.C., McFarland, 1998. 633p. index. $125.00. ISBN 0-7864-0542-2.

This tool is meant to be used primarily for identifying songwriters, assisting users who have a known song title or writer's name to search by. The scope extends back to the nineteenth century, selectively covering popular artists as diverse as Paul Simon, Fats Waller, Bruce Springsteen, and Dolly Parton. Although the song texts in many such works are not known apart from the music, the orientation of the book is toward the writers of song texts—a fact to bear in mind when searching for music writers. Each entry begins with a brief biographical sketch, naming highlights of the biographee's recorded career, and continues with a list of such information as hit versions (including chart positions reached), albums (listed with dates and in some cases publishers), and the names of singers. Writers who are featured as co-lyricists may have their biographical data in the entry for the principal; for example, Sir Paul McCartney's work as a member of the Beatles is presented in John Lennon's entry, whereas McCartney's post-Beatles activity is documented in a separate entry. The *see also under* references at the end of some articles are particularly useful. Harrison considers the changing relationship between songwriter and singer in the introduction, and provides a three-page bibliography.

What is most noticeably missing from this book is a user guide. Specifically, a sample entry should be provided, with labels for each data element (such as recording company, publisher's number, and Billboard chart entry). Some of this information is provided in the preface, but librarians and other users would be better served with an illustration placed directly in front of the dictionary. The user is inconvenienced by seeing a Roman numeral in brackets, and then having to peruse the preface extensively to determine the significance of this notation. Some users will wish that more space had been allowed within each entry, presenting each title on a separate line rather than as one continuous text. The indexing is particularly thorough, but in cases where numerous articles are listed (by entry number only) many users will not have the patience to consult each of them individually. Moreover, in order to discover the indexed data element, some articles have to be scrutinized assiduously, but the information may be trivial (for example, McCartney is indexed for a quoted tribute to Arthur Alexander). Users will welcome the handy, compact size of this tool. Librarians can use the tool for collection development to identify the titles and dates of albums on which particular individuals, performing groups, and song titles are featured, but for full discographical data another source must be consulted. The publishers would do well, for future editions, to consider an electronic version with Boolean keyword searching. [R: LJ, 1 Nov 98, p. 72]
—**Ian Fairclough**

1118.   Mustazza, Leonard. **Ol' Blue Eyes: A Frank Sinatra Encyclopedia.** Westport, Conn., Greenwood Press, 1998. 436p. illus. index. $59.95. ISBN 0-313-30486-6.

The death of Frank Sinatra has unleashed a torrent of tributes, and this particular book will lead the (rat) pack. No other singer in U.S. history has reached the level of success enjoyed for so many decades by Sinatra, and his musical legacy is destined for greatness. The author is an associate dean and professor of English and American studies at Penn State University and is the author of two other books about Sinatra. This title is exactly what it says; there are no insights into alleged mob affiliations, no titillating revelations about his marriages, no glimpses into the dark side of Frank Sinatra. Instead, readers are treated to information about Sinatra's contributions to music, movies, and television. Every single, album, and compact disc he made, every song he recorded, every movie he ever appeared in, every composer and musical conductor he ever worked with, and every Internet site devoted to Sinatra is listed in detail. This is an exhaustive concordance to the artistic works of one of the most influential entertainers of our time and will be an invaluable resource for any large public library or any collection specializing in popular entertainment. [R: Choice, Oct 98, p. 292]—**Joseph L. Carlson**

Dictionaries and Encyclopedias

1119.   Barber, David W., comp. **Better Than It Sounds: A Dictionary of Humorous Musical Quotations.** Toronto, Sound and Vision, 1998. 107p. illus. index. $11.95pa. ISBN 0-920151-22-1.

The compiler, who has previously written best-selling books of musical humor, has given readers a new volume of refreshing quotations. Although a few quips are his own creation, most of the witty observations are from the pens of others. Arranged alphabetically, from *accordions* to *woodwinds*, we find the comments of musicians and composers, singers, conductors, and writers in general. Some remarks were written by music critics, and other gibes were by the critics of the critics. One would anticipate some of the more popular or well-known entries ("What time is the next swan?" by Leo Slezak), but most are items we might wish we had heard before. Reading them now for the first time is also great fun, such as the definition of phonograph by Ambrose Bierce ("Phonograph: n. An irritating toy that restores life to dead noises"). The quotes cover a spectrum from the ancient past to the pop/rock/video age present. Giuseppe Verdi rates 1 entry, whereas Richard Wagner has more than 20, including the source of the book title, *Wagner's Music Is Better Than It Sounds*, which has been attributed to both Mark Twain and Bill Nye. It is a slim volume, and if one finds oneself taking musical things too seriously, one needs to lighten up a bit and read what to do in case of an emergency, musical or otherwise: "1. Grab your coat. 2. Take your hat. 3. Leave your worries on the doorstep. 4. Direct your feet to the sunny side of the street."—**Louis G. Zelenka**

1120.   **The Garland Encyclopedia of World Music. Volume 9: Australia and the Pacific Islands.** Adrienne L. Kaeppler and J. W. Love, eds. New York, Garland, 1998. 1088p. illus. index. $125.00. ISBN 0-8240-6038-5.

With each volume devoted to a single region instead of the traditional alphabetic approach from A to Z, and each volume written by the experts on specific music cultures, this 10-volume encyclopedia is the first of its kind to cover the music of all the world's peoples. Volume 9 is devoted to the music of Australia and the Pacific Islands, grouped as New Guinea, Micronesia, and Polynesia. This volume introduces Oceanic music from ancient traditions and their modern developments to music introduced from near and far. The entries illustrate musical diversity, ranging from the famous (e.g., Hawaiian hula) to the unfamiliar (e.g., water-plunged idiophones of New Guinea), and reaching from the widespread novelty of the macarena to the local Kaluli tradition of torching dancers' skin. The entries set contemporary developments into historical backgrounds. The volume has lyrics in more than 80 languages, with English texts translated from those.

The volume has 3 large sections that cover the major topics of the region from broad general issues to specific music practices. These include "Introduction to Oceania and Its Music," "Concepts in Oceania Music," and "Peoples of Oceania and Their Music." Each section consists of articles written by leading researchers. Complementing the texts of the articles are photographs, maps, charts, music notations, and examples. At the end of the volume is a useful set of study and research tools—a glossary of terms, lists of audio and visual resources, a bibliography, notes on the audio examples, and an index. An audio compact disc is inside the back cover that provides sound examples that are linked to discussions in the text. This volume is an excellent resource on Oceania music for artists, educators, or anyone interested in music and its place in different world cultures. [R: BL, 1 Nov 98, p. 532]—**Vera Gao**

1121.   Hillila, Ruth-Esther, and Barbara Blanchard Hong. **Historical Dictionary of the Music and Musicians of Finland.** Westport, Conn., Greenwood Press, 1997. 473p. illus. maps. index. $85.00. ISBN 0-313-27728-1.

Finland, as an officially recognized independent republic, has existed only since 1920. From the twelfth century until 1809 it was a part of Sweden; then it became a grand duchy of Russia. Following the Russian Revolution, the Finns declared their independence. A spirit of national culture in the arts, of course, predates these political events of the nineteenth and twentieth centuries. A notable milestone was reached when *The Kalevala*, Finland's national epic, was compiled during the nineteenth century by a country doctor, Elias Lonnrot. Lonnrot compiled the ballads, lyrics, and incantations sung by the bards in all regions of the country.

This alphabetically arranged historical dictionary unifies in one volume the background of the ancient folk poetry along with the continual evolution of Finnish music to the present time. With more than 500 entries, the reader has available a summary of historical and modern composers and the accomplishments of hundreds of regional and internationally acclaimed performing artists and musicians. General articles and entries discuss folk music; early liturgical manuscripts and publications; cantors and hymnals, notably of early Roman Catholic, Eastern Orthodox, and Lutheran music; leading orchestras and choral groups; festivals; and much more.

Readers who are not fluent in Finnish or Swedish now have the first comprehensive work in English. Supporting material includes a map of Finland, a key to Finnish pronunciation, and an index. In addition to the entries, appendixes provide chronologies of Finnish history and Finnish music. A selected bibliography offers further resources. Musicologists and other historians will find this work well organized and presented in an easy-to-read and usable format. [R: RUSQ, Summer 98, p. 362]—**Louis G. Zelenka**

1122.   **The Oxford Companion to Australian Music.** Warren Bebbington, ed. New York, Oxford University Press, 1997. 608p. $75.00. ISBN 0-19-553432-8.

The Oxford Companion to Australian Music is a comprehensive reference work that will be of use to academic and special libraries. The preface describes the organization and rationale behind the entries, the subject areas to be covered, and the definitions used to include or exclude potential entries. The work, organized in alphabetic order, covers the full range of music in Australia, from Aboriginal traditions to contemporary rock and experimental music, with an emphasis on biographical entries.

One-half of the entries are biographical notes on performers, composers, teachers, instrument makers, and others associated with music. Most entries are brief but contain a biography, description of work, and some critical evaluation or appreciation. The subject entries cover topics as diverse as Aboriginal music, musical traditions of immigrant groups, popular music, and opera. Most subject entries also include discographies, bibliographies, and suggestions for further reference. The entries are signed by the contributors, who come from universities, conservatories, or other institutions and are listed in a directory at the beginning of the work. Black-and-white photographs illustrate subject and biographical entries. The editor's aim was to create a single volume in which a full account of music in Australia can be found and to bring Australian music to a wider audience, and in this Bebbington has succeeded. [R: Choice, Oct 98, p. 292]—**Kerie L. Nickel**

1123.   Slominsky, Nicolas. Richard Kassel, ed. **Baker's Dictionary of Music.** New York, Schirmer Books/Simon & Schuster Macmillan, 1997. 1171p. illus. $90.00. ISBN 0-02-864791-2.
        At first glance, this dictionary seems to be the updated version of *Thompson's International Cyclopedia of Music and Musicians*, a widely used reference source whose last edition dates from 1958. The actual genesis of the volume is more complicated than that, however. First of all, it is the work of the remarkable lexicographer, Nicolas Slonimsky (1894-1995), who gave us (among other works) the *Lectionary of Music*, the *Lexicon of Musical Invective*, and his magnum opus, *Baker's Biographical Dictionary of Musicians*. The present volume was compiled from Slonimsky's writings and edited by Richard Kassel, in close cooperation with Slonimsky's daughter Electra Yourke. Once again, this is a remarkable publication, but one that should warn readers not to throw older reference sources away. It closely resembles the Thompson cyclopedia, combining explanations of musical terms, forms, and descriptions of instruments with biographical sketches of major performers. It also provides essays on major composers and musical forms, all of them authored by Slonimsky and eminently worth reading. While trying to sum up all of this in one volume as well as add a great number of biographical sketches from the contemporary musical scene, some items fell by the wayside. One wonders, for instance, by what reasoning the dictionary provides biographical sketches of Carole Farley and Maria Ewing but not those of Eleanor Steber, Bidú Sayão, or Licia Albanese. Even Francesca Cuzzoni (1700-1770) was omitted. However, there are welcome additions from formerly underrepresented areas: Eric Clapton, Bob Dylan, Lester Flatt, Aretha Franklin, and Bill Haley are all represented. Some of the brief descriptions appended to several performers cause the eyebrows to raise: Soprano Eva Marton and tenor Peter Hofmann are both hailed as outstanding, whereas Birgit Nilsson merely merits a "greatly renowned" label. These are just minor quibbles, however. Clearly, this is a reference source that should be on the desk of every music student, teacher, and music professional and in the libraries of all classical music radio stations.
        Lastly, a major quibble concerning the dictionary title. Because *Baker's Biographical Dictionary of Musicians* is the widely acknowledged and extensively used resource in music libraries, universities, and other well-appointed desks, why publish another dictionary dealing with the same subject matter with the word "Baker's" in the title? It is bound to cause some confusion. [R: BL, 1 June 98, p. 1800; Choice, July/Aug 98, p. 1832]
                                                                                                    —**Koraljka Lockhart**

Handbooks and Yearbooks

1124.   Gann, Kyle. **American Music in the Twentieth Century.** New York, Schirmer Books/Simon & Schuster Macmillan, 1997. 400p. illus. index. $39.00. ISBN 0-02-864655-X.
        After a brief look at music in the United States from 1492 to the end of the nineteenth century, in which the author discusses the European influences during that time period (especially as seen in the compositions of Louis Moreau Gottschalk, Edward MacDowell, and others), he establishes the rebellious sense that propelled the new country politically. This, in turn, gradually led to a sense of complete freedom in the arts—in this case, music. A multicultural population also encouraged diversity in musical expression. The spirit of political freedom and the idea of creating a new land with a new musical heritage were becoming fully realized by the beginning of the twentieth century. Describing Charles Ives as the first "American to step deliberately outside European musical conventions in major works," the author then rapidly moves, mostly by decades, into a highly readable exploration of innovations and trends in serious music in the United States.
        This reference is not a work for a detailed discussion of ragtime, jazz, popular music, folk, or rock; however, when appropriate it is noted how these various styles may have influenced the works of various composers. Actual musical scores are used to illustrate examples of compositions throughout the text. "Forefathers" is the title of chapter 1, followed by chapters on "Ultramodernism," "Populism," and "Experimentalism." Looking at the second half of the century, Gann explores additional new movements, beginning with the work of the minimalists and continuing into numerous new musical ideas as the century nears its end. Musical explanations are in terms

understandable to the lay reader, not just to professional musicians. Biographical entries are used as a means of identifying new philosophies in music, and the author takes care to mention who studied under whom and where, which helps in giving continuity as needed. The work includes chapter notes, a bibliography, and an index. This is a significant resource for library music collections. [R: C&RL, July/Aug 98, p. 530]—**Louis G. Zelenka**

1125.   Studwell, William E. **The Americana Song Reader.** Binghamton, N.Y., Haworth Press, 1997. 186p. index. $14.95pa. ISBN 1-56023-899-2.

There are a number of reference sources that have the texts of popular U.S. songs. Studwell has compiled brief histories of the most popular of these, aiming to present them in an offbeat and lively presentation. There are 130 essays that describe songs and excerpts from longer works. He divides this into nine functional sections, mostly by the emotions they evoke—dancing; marching; rural and western songs; songs that excite or amuse; songs that soothe; children's songs; and circus, drinking, and college songs. Studwell describes five other volumes with more specific sets of songs described, such as rock and roll, holidays, and religious collections. This volume fills a void by describing those not in the other volumes. Interesting bits of information include the fact that before composing "Take Me Out to the Ball Game," Albert von Tilzer and lyricist Jack Norworth had never seen a baseball game.

Other examples include excerpts of classics like Rossini's William Tell overture, and folksongs, like "My Old Kentucky Home" and "Carry Me Back to Old Virginny." This reference is an easy-to-use quick source for the historical context of 130 songs. [R: LJ, 15 Nov 97, p. S40]—**Ralph Hartsock**

Indexes

1126.   **The Song Index of the Enoch Pratt Free Library.** By Ellen Luchinsky. New York, Garland, 1998. 2v. (Garland Reference Library of Social Science, v.1394). $200.00/set. ISBN 0-8153-3918-0.

There are many song indexes available (see ARBA 90, entries 1276 and 1279; ARBA 96 entry, 1318; and ARBA 97, entry 1032), each with a specific purpose. The purpose of this set is to be a finding guide for Baltimore's Enoch Pratt Free Library's extensive collection of songbooks of all types, dating from the early twentieth century. The 2-volume index is divided into 4 alphabetically arranged sections; the bibliography is a numbered list of more than 2,000 song books with their publishing information; the main song index contains some 160,000 lists of song titles with their alternative titles, composer, and bibliography number to refer the reader to the songbook where the title can be found; a composer index; and a source index listing larger works from which some of the songs originated—operas, musicals, movies, and other sources.

This is a "bare bones" listing; if a researcher does not know the title there is no stated provision for finding a song by first line, chorus first line, key word, or subject. However, this reviewer found that some titles can be found by looking up the first line of the song, with cross-references to the official title. Although the editor claims to have tried to identify composers by first names, most are listed by last name only, and this can cause confusion. For example, titles obviously by the same composer are listed separately under "Foster" and "Stephen Foster." Songwriters of such renown as Franz Schubert and John Denver are not fully identified. Song-seekers will probably do well to begin their search with more user-friendly guides such as those mentioned above, and consult the present work only if their initial efforts are unsuccessful.—**Larry Lobel**

COMPOSERS

1127.   Adams, K. Gary. **William Schuman: A Bio-Bibliography.** Westport, Conn., Greenwood Press, 1998. 269p. index. (Bio-Bibliographies in Music, no.67). $65.00. ISBN 0-313-27359-6.

William Schuman is not only an important U.S. composer, but he is also known for being an innovator in academia and arts administration. Schuman (1910-1992) composed 10 symphonies, a great number of works for voice (including choral works), and compositions in all genres. He occupied important posts at Sarah Lawrence College (1935-1945), Juilliard School of Music (1945-1962), and the Lincoln Center for the Performing Arts (1962-1968). At Juilliard he instituted the innovative idea of making the teaching of theory more pertinent by emphasizing its relation to music literature. Schuman hired many of the best composers of the time to teach at Juilliard. As president of the Lincoln Center, he shaped the complex from its inception.

William Schuman: A Bio-bibliography is a handy reference and research tool and offers a great deal of information about the composer. The volume covers his life, examines his works and performances (along with pertinent data), and includes a discography and a selective annotated bibliography (about and by Schuman). The volume is well indexed and cross-referenced. It is interesting to read the many reviews of Schuman's works that were performed around the world and realize the recognition that the composer received throughout his lifetime.

Adams has compiled an invaluable volume that extensively traces the career of an important U.S. composer. The work is a must for anyone researching Schuman and should be included in reference divisions of college/university libraries. The volume also should be useful to anyone studying or teaching musical composition. The work is highly recommended. [R: Choice, Nov 98, p. 490]—**Robert Palmieri**

1128.   **The Arnold Schoenberg Companion.** Walter B. Bailey, ed. Westport, Conn., Greenwood Press, 1998. 335p. index. $89.50. ISBN 0-313-28779-1.

Arnold Schoenberg died in 1951 but has continued to cast a long shadow over the musical world. After years of bouncing back and forth between Vienna and Berlin, where he established himself as both composer and teacher, he fled to the United States in the 1930s when well into his middle years (he was born in 1874). He had first made his mark early in the century as a composer of fairly accessible tonal works and then moved on to atonal compositions with the kind of chromaticism familiar from the works of other post-Wagerian composers. Always the teacher and theorist, Schoenberg codified his evolving compositional style into his revolutionary twelve-tone system that colored the musical thinking and compositional style of more than a generation of composers but that often failed to woo audiences. However, audiences continue to try to understand and appreciate his works. His compositions of all periods, styles, and sizes continue to appear on concert programs.

This companion is designed to help the listener of limited musical training to come to grips with this complex and challenging man and his music. It has been written by a team of Schoenberg specialists who explore, in different chapters, his work from its tonal beginnings on through the mature twelve-tone works. There are also a generous biographical section and a section that considers his legacy as a teacher, a theorist, and an influence. A selected bibliography contains useful annotations, although the selective discography is merely a listing.

Everything about this book meets its stated aim of helping the novice to understand Schoenberg's own aims and accomplishments. If, as it seems, young composers are moving away from his theories of composition as it may affect them, audiences seem more and more open to listening to and trying to understand his complex music. This is not a bad fate for a theorist and creative spirit. This book is prepared to help those in need.
—**George Louis Mayer**

1129.   Clark, Walter A. **Isaac Albéniz: A Guide to Research.** New York, Garland, 1998. 256p. index. (Composer Research Manuals, v.45; Garland Reference Library of the Humanities, v.1932). $60.00. ISBN 0-8153-2095-7.

Composer and pianist Isaac Albéniz (1860-1909) left a legacy of fabulous, distinctive Spanish national music, and a trail of half-truths and outright lies about his life that researchers have spent years trying to unravel with only partial success. This guide to research only briefly summarizes the biographical material in a 33-page essay. For a more in-depth biography, interested readers can consult the author's extensively researched *Isaac Albéniz: Portrait of a Romantic* (Clarendon Press, 1998). The focus of the work at hand is on the continuing popularity of Albéniz's music and the increasing interest in him by both scholars and the general public. These are documented through an annotated bibliography of archival sources, books, reviews, articles and dissertations; an exhaustive catalog of the composer's more than 100 works; and a 272-item discography, which certainly proves the author's contention of the long-standing appeal of Albeniz's music. In addition to these 4 main sections, there is a chronology of Albéniz's life, and separate indexes by proper names, works, and performers. Arrangement and presentation of the material is excellent. The guide is a welcome and important addition to the literature on Isaac Albéniz, one of the most important composers in the history of Spanish music.—**Larry Lobel**

1130.   Craggs, Stewart R. **Malcolm Arnold: A Bio-Bibliography.** Westport, Conn., Greenwood Press, 1998. 216p. index. (Bio-Bibliographies in Music, no.69). $65.00. ISBN 0-313-29254-X.

According to the preface, the brief biography that begins this work is intended only to provide a broad outline of the composer's life. The sections that follow the biography are the ones that researchers will find most useful.

The "Works and Performances" section lists titles alphabetically within genre. All entries list information about the work, which may include a listing of movements, instrumentation, dedications, setting of first performance, description of the work, the piece's duration, or other details. There are 91 recent works listed in the "Discography," which is a selective list that is arranged alphabetically by title. The "Biography" is the final section of this work. It contains writings by and about Arnold. Each entry is accompanied by a brief explanation of its origin (e.g., "A Birthday tribute to Arnold which contains interviews, a survey of his music and a complete 1996 concerts listing"). The *see* references used throughout this work are helpful to researchers. They make the connections from one section to another within this work.

Two appendixes are also included. The 1st one gives an alphabetic listing of all compositions. The 2d appendix lists compositions chronologically by year of publication. Finally, an index is included to ease searching various works. Fans of Malcolm Arnold will appreciate this comprehensive listing of his works. Libraries collecting heavily in music will want to add this to their collection.—**Laura K. Blessing**

1131.   Craggs, Stewart R. **Soundtracks: An International Dictionary of Composers of Music for Film.** Brookfield, Vt., Ashgate Publishing, 1998. 345p. index. $76.95. ISBN 1-85928-189-3.

Film music has only recently received the critical attention that it merits. This dictionary lists more than 500 composers for film, with brief biographical data where possible, including dates, nationality, and some anecdotal information. Films are listed alphabetically, disregarding articles. Information equals or exceeds that found in *Baker's Biographical Dictionary of Twentieth Century Classical Musicians* (see ARBA 98, entry 1197). Some composers, such as Irving Berlin and John Carpenter, have sound recordings listed. Others, such as Carlos Chavez, Simon Jurovsky, Karen Khachaturian, and Tilo Medek, have no films listed. This may be due to the poor documentation for films produced outside London and the United States, as evidenced by this reviewer's research in film music. The index, comprising 36 percent of the volume, is filed regarding articles. Thus, the sequence becomes *A Funny Thing Happened on the Way to the Forum*, *Abbott and Costello*, *American Ninja*, *An American in Paris*, *Star Wars*, and *The Red Pony*. There is a useful appendix titled the "Selected List of Feature and Documentary Films with Music Wholly or Partly by Classical Composers." Using this, one can cite Mozart's works heard in *Amadeus*, music featured in Disney's *Fantasia*, or that *Platoon* used Samuel Barber's *Adagio for Strings*. Foreign films are indexed only by their original titles, so Enrico Morricone's *The Good, The Bad and the Ugly* is indexed as *Il Buono, Il Brutto, Il Cattivo*. This book should serve as a quick reference source for major film composers. It is hoped that at some future date, experimental film festivals will also be documented as well as the feature films produced in the United States. [R: Choice, July/Aug 98, p. 1828]—**Ralph Hartsock**

1132.   Cramer, Eugene Casjen. **Tomás Luis de Victoria: A Guide to Research.** New York, Garland, 1998. 403p. index. (Composer Resource Manuals, v.43; Garland Reference Library of the Humanities, v.1931). $76.00. ISBN 0-8153-2096-5.

This new addition to Garland's series of Composer Resource Manuals feature Tomás Luis de Victoria, an important Spanish Renaissance composer. Unlike many books in this series, this volume omits biographical information except for a brief chronology and instead offers considerable detail about the early publications and manuscript sources for Victoria's works. The contents of early printed editions are itemized, and the RISM number is given for each collection. Manuscript sources are arranged by location.

An annotated bibliography of secondary sources comprises the next largest portion of the book. This section is extensive; Cramer has included even reference and general music history books that discuss Victoria. Critical and detailed annotations thoroughly assess each entry's coverage of the composer. A discography and a compilation of modern editions of Victoria's works are also included. The author has included a valuable title index to entries that discuss individual works and a name/subject index.

Cramer is a Victoria scholar, and he is well qualified to compile this bibliography. It is highly recommended to all academic libraries. [R: Choice, Dec 98, p. 660]—**Allie Wise Goudy**

1133.   Faucett, Bill F. **George Whitefield Chadwick: A Bio-Bibliography.** Westport, Conn., Greenwood Press, 1998. 304p. index. (Bio-Bibliographies in Music, no.66). $75.00. ISBN 0-313-30067-4.

During his career George Whitefield Chadwick (1854-1931) was considered the "Dean of American Composers," exerting great influence upon the New England Conservatory of Music. Faucett presents a biography that sufficiently illustrates Chadwick's interactions with such musicians as Dudley Buck, John Knowles Paine, Arthur Foote, John Philip Sousa, and Edward Burlingame Hill. His students included William Grant Still and Horatio Parker. The section on his style brings forth many anecdotes about his music and compositional style. The format of the volume is somewhat similar to others in the series, with a few variations. Faucett lists 272 original works, first by genre and then alphabetically, followed by 16 band arrangements of his music and 4 arrangements by Chadwick. Interfiled into the list of works and performances are 404 annotated bibliographic citations that refer to specific works. Faucett lists 75 recordings, followed by 81 bibliography entries describing the discography. A general bibliography of 267 items and Chadwick's writings are each arranged chronologically. Faucett includes two useful appendixes—a song title index provides access to each separate song, as does the choral music index. The general index is of authors, subjects, and performers but not titles. Because there is no general alphabetical list of compositions, to find *Symphony no. 2* one must thumb through the orchestral works. Thus, one may need to use this bibliography in conjunction with the *New Grove Dictionary of American Music* (see ARBA 88, entry 1277). Nevertheless, it is a welcome addition to the history of U.S. music and is recommended for academic libraries. [R: Choice, Oct 98, p. 290]—**Ralph Hartsock**

1134.   Furia, Philip, with Graham Wood. **Irving Berlin: A Life in Song.** New York, Schirmer Books/Simon & Schuster Macmillan, 1998. 321p. illus. index. $25.00. ISBN 0-02-864815-3.

After reading this admiring biography of Irving Berlin, one finds oneself agreeing with a critic who wrote as early as 1911 that his list of compositions "sounded like all the hits in the world." So many of his creations have become standards of U.S. musical culture that it requires a book such as this to remind us they were all the products of one fertile mind.

This chronological narrative of Berlin's life is written in an intimate and accessible style suited to its popular musical material. There is not a single bar of music reproduced for analysis or dissection. Instead, the author indulges in his fascination with Berlin's lyrics, a witty and impressive body of work, all the more amazing in that Berlin spoke only Yiddish when he arrived as an immigrant in New York. His secret of success was his ability to constantly evolve and adapt to the musical tastes of the twentieth century, from ragtime to wartime, from suggestiveness to sentimentality, and yet write themes and lyrics that seem to transcend any period.

Irving Berlin was a sensitive and retiring man throughout his 101-year life, and was always protective of his privacy. Although Furia had access to the Berlin estate while writing this biography, there are no great revelations here, nor much discussion of Berlin's personality other than his dedication to his craft. Rather, this book revels in the creativity of an individual who must be considered one of the most successful songwriters who ever lived. It brings together a collection of old friends—entertainers, composers, and most of all songs—that readers will be surprised they have neglected, and all due to the life of one awesomely creative man. Most readers will discover themselves singing by the 3d chapter.—**James Moffet**

1135.   Goss, Glenda D. **Jean Sibelius: A Guide to Research.** New York, Garland, 1998. 298p. index. (Composer Resource Manuals, v.41). $54.00. ISBN 0-8153-1171-0.

This book is a comprehensive annotated bibliography of writings on the life, times, and music of Finnish composer Jean Sibelius (1865-1957). The listings are culled from more than 1,000 sources in 11 languages from the 1890s through 1994. Also supplied is historical and background information, summarizing the article's or book's content, value, and credibility.

The volume is divided into 7 categorical chapters of references: reference works; background; the life; rezeptionsgeshichte; special categories; the music; and indexes of compositions and authors, editors and translators, and subjects. One of the subsections is devoted to published discographies of Sibelius's music. It is difficult to find fault with what the book does. However, it should have added some general historical and musical data, such as a musicography, perhaps coupled with a biographical outline of concurrent events. But this book is just what it claims to be, and for the serious student of works on the life and music of Jean Sibelius, it is an excellent reference.—**Kenneth I. Saichek**

1136.   Harper, Nancy Lee. **Manuel de Falla: A Bio-Bibliography.** Westport, Conn., Greenwood Press, 1998. 280p. index. (Bio-Bibliographies in Music, no.68). $65.00. ISBN 0-313-30292-8.

The Manuel de Falla Archive opened in Granada in 1991 with the aid of the great Spanish composer's niece and the Spanish government. Previous research guides to his life and works pre-date the assembling of this rich collection of primary and secondary source material, thus making this new work especially valuable. Harper, a pianist and harpsichordist teaching in Portugal, aims to have this work orient the English-speaking researcher to the archive.

The composer is certainly one of Spain's greatest and an important figure in twentieth-century music. His output was relatively small, but a handful of his works gained immediate popularity, which has never waned. These continue to be performed and recorded throughout the world.

The major parts of this guide are a short but substantial biography and an annotated bibliography divided into 11 sections by materials of different types ranging from de Falla's own writings to letters, iconography, and upcoming publications. Other sections contain a list of works and performances, a discography (too selective and too incomplete in the information about performers in its entries to suit this reviewer), three important articles about the de Falla archives, a genealogy, a chronology, a table of works, a list of lost works and manuscripts, and useful information and abbreviations. "Useful Information" is a section providing a list of addresses of archives and publishers. An index of names concludes the work.

This is an important guide to de Falla's life—troubled by religious and moral concerns, illnesses, and politics, which led him to spend the final years of his life during the period of the Spanish civil war in Argentina—and his compositions. The documentation of both benefits from the helpful and practical guiding hand of the author.
—**George Louis Mayer**

1137.   Harwood, Gregory. **Giuseppe Verdi: A Guide to Research.** New York, Garland, 1998. 396p. index. (Composer Resource Manuals, v.42; Garland Reference Library of the Humanities, v.1004). $75.00. ISBN 0-8240-4117-8.

This book is for music researchers and Verdi students and scholars, and it is a most valuable resource. Part of a remarkable ongoing series of Garland research guides that has already yielded nearly 50 volumes, it provides not just a customary bibliographic collection but well-annotated help for researchers. For instance, there are 48 entries on *Don Carlos*, and that is only in the section devoted to individual Verdi operas. This example brings up a caveat. The author divided the book into sections: "Correspondence and Other Documents" is one of them (general and listed by correspondent); "Studies of People Associated with Verdi" is another. In any of these and other chapters may be additional material on, say, *Don Carlos*, but if one is to search for all the material on that opera, the only way to arrive at it is by going through the general index.

All annotations are excellent and leave no doubt as to what is featured in which publication and what is not. The book also includes other valuable material, such as a list of discographies and videographies, libretto collections, editions and editing practices, a complete catalog of Verdi compositions, locations of Verdi's opera premieres, an extensive chronology of his life, and short thumbnail biographical sketches of people associated with Verdi during his life. Although some of the material is in foreign languages, all annotations are given in English.
—**Koraljka Lockhart**

1138.   Houlahan, Mícheál, and Philip Tacka. **Zoltán Kodály: A Guide to Research.** New York, Garland, 1998. 611p. index. (Composer Research Manuals, v.44). $97.00. ISBN 0-8153-2853-2.

Although Zoltán Kodály will undoubtedly remain an important figure in twentieth-century music and his compositions performed for centuries to come, there is scant literature in English on this diverse and inquisitive man. Those few titles in print in English are several decades old. This research guide, number 44 of the Garland Composer Resource Manuals, helps fill this void with quite a crescendo.

Solidly packed with information for the researcher, these closely printed pages present to U.S. collections the most detailed bibliography on Kodály currently available. Although the biographical outline is little more than a chronology, the remainder of the book organizes primary and secondary publications and studies into convenient sections: published composition, Kodály's writings, biographical studies, studies of his music, discussions of his theories of music education, and dissertations on the composer. The remaining 154 pages are indexes. Every entry is the bibliographic sections contain a translation of the citation if in a foreign language and a useful annotation ranging in length from one sentence to a full page. This broad guide is as comprehensive in its coverage of Kodály's ethnomusical and educational interests as it is with his compositions, further increasing its value in any musical research collection.

It is to be hoped that the current trend in investigating Kodály's music, theories, and educational concepts will continue to grow. If so, this guide to research will be an essential tool for anyone delving into the work and mind of this master.—**James Moffet**

1139.   Iger, Arthur L. **Music of the Golden Age, 1900-1950 and Beyond: A Guide to Popular Composers and Lyricists.** Westport, Conn., Greenwood Press, 1998. 269p. index. $69.50. ISBN 0-313-30691-5.

Designed for the enlightenment of fans and students of early twentieth-century popular music, *Music of the Golden Age* describes a wide range of musicians, including jazz and blues (e.g., Count Basie, Rube Bloom), composers of musicals and lyricists (e.g., Richard Rodgers, Frederick Loewe, Sammy Cahn), classical cross-overs (e.g., Duke Ellington, Victor Herbert), and tin pan alley (e.g., Johnny Mercer). Most chronologies cover through 1960, with a few extending to 1978. The author arranges each chapter according to a general chronological period or style, with biographies subarranged alphabetically. Early chapters have the most information and anecdotes. Iger provides much detail with separate Hollywood or Broadway chronologies for several entries (e.g., Frank Loesser, Irving Berlin), and a classical section for George Gershwin. The author shares some anecdotes or opinions that may not be in other sources.

Subsequent chapters list "Contemporaries: Songwriters of the 1960s to Today," "Significant Collaborators and Writers of Hit Songs," and "Celebrities and Women of Song," each with briefer biographies and chronologies. Two additional chronological lists are Oscar and Grammy winners.

This source is best used to identify individual songs from musicals and other popular venues, such as "Kansas City" from a Rodgers' musical, but not the big band version. Musicals' titles are not indexed unless a song is based on that title, such as that of *Oklahoma.*

For some names, like Carrie Jacobs-Bond, one needs to look in both places for the name; cross-references are not comprehensive. Although Peter Gammond's *The Oxford Companion to Popular Music* (see ARBA 92, entry 1297) serves as a primary source for popular music, *Music of the Golden Age* is a fine source for anecdotes.
—**Ralph Hartsock**

1140.   Marill, Alvin H. **Keeping Score: Film and Television Music, 1988-1997.** Lanham, Md., Scarecrow, 1998. 358p. index. $45.00. ISBN 0-8108-3416-2.

Although the author calls this book an "update," it is actually the fourth in a series that began in 1974, this one covering the years from 1988 to 1997. Like the earlier volumes, it is a compilation of theatrical film, television film, and miniseries scores, with access provided chronologically by year, alphabetically by film title, and alphabetically by composer. The author has included some foreign films, primarily in French, Italian, and Spanish, that are on the international market, as well as other foreign films with scores by composers with an international reputation, although exactly what constitutes the "international market" and an "international reputation" is not explained. The book also has a list of television and film music awards by year and a selected discography of soundtracks.—**Lori D. Kranz**

1141.   Parker, Robert. **Carlos Chávez: A Guide to Research.** New York, Garland, 1998. 180p. index. (Composer Research Manuals, v.46; Garland Reference Library of the Humanities, v.1925). $45.00. ISBN 0-8153-2087-6.

The Composer Resource Manuals of the Garland Reference Library of the Humanities keep coming, and it is a boon to musicologists, biographers, and serious music lovers alike. Volume 46 is a guide to the life, music, and writings of a little known Mexican composer and conductor, Carlos Chávez. Written by Parker, it should doubly serve as a model for the remaining series. Not only does it present the usual bibliographical sources of the composer's works, but it also gives a brief biography, a musicography, a bibliography of the composer's writings, general biographies and monographs, and further research aids.

Carlos Chávez (1899-1978) was more popular earlier in this century (1930s through the 1960s), but has suffered a decline since. Chávez began as a pianist, continuing to write for the instrument throughout his career, and composed his first symphony at age 16. He began conducting in the 1920s. Although his compositions, based upon native Mexican elements, were truly *sui generis*, it is also his advocacy of modern Mexican composers for which he is fondly remembered. Moreover, he brought much modern European music into Mexico, giving the first Mexican performances of works by Arnold Schoenberg, Igor Stravinsky, Darius Milhaud, and Erik Satie.

He served as a Charles Eliot Norton Lecturer at Harvard University. This guide should fill the need of even the most critical researcher, which is both necessary and ironic because little of Chávez' music remains available on CD-ROM. [R: Choice, Dec 98, p. 664]—**Kenneth I. Saichek**

1142.   Ping-Robbins, Nancy R. **Scott Joplin: A Guide to Research.** New York, Garland, 1998. 419p. index. (Composer Resource Manuals, v.47; Garland Reference Library of the Humanities, v.1139). $76.00. ISBN 0-8240-8399-7.
      This admirable publication begins with an important introduction in which the author specifies discrepancies within the literature. Considering that Joplin became the object of scholarly concern (following the Atlanta première of his only extant opera), and also a popular composer (especially after the music was appropriated by the media), there is still much to uncover and to verify. These problem areas are keyed to more than 1,200 entries that make up the core of the book, not all of which are bibliographic—a respectable number chronologically treat his output, clubs and societies, festivals, and special concerts. The bibliographic entries are gathered by such topics as collections, discographies, iconography, and reviews of performances, each of which is annotated. This obligates the researcher to fall back on one of the three indexes to secure a focus for the topical search, a slightly unusual responsibility. Some may be frustrated if they expect the general index to make reference to the critical matter of additive rhythm (versus syncopation) or even just rhythm, or if they assume that all proper names (e.g., authors, arrangers, artists, and others) are equitably indexed. One other reservation is that the annotations are not abstracts. How immediately helpful is it, for example, to read this annotation on Lottie Joplin: "Gives her birth and death dates as found on the death certificate. Also notes her burial site and parents' names." Nevertheless, this is a handsomely produced handbook that lacks competition and regards a key figure in American music.
                                                                           —**Dominique-René de Lerma**

1143.   Quigley, Thomas, and Mary I. Ingraham. **Johannes Brahms: An Annotated Bibliography of the Literature from 1982 to 1996 with an Appendix on Brahms and the Internet.** Lanham, Md., Scarecrow, 1998. 697p. index. $85.00. ISBN 0-8108-3439-1.
      The publication of *Johannes Brahms: An Annotated Bibliography of the Literature from 1982 to 1996* continues the excellent coverage of Brahms literature begun in the author's earlier bibliography (see ARBA 92, entry 1273). Quigley's previous effort included literature about Brahms published to 1982. The present work, which follows the same format, reflects research published since then as well as earlier research that the author has since discovered, mostly from the World Project Administration Music Periodical Index at Northwestern University and the Library of Congress Music Division's Periodical Index. The content of this bibliography meets the standard set by its predecessor; the expansion of the literature about Brahms is certainly welcome. One of the most notable features of this book is the extensive cross-referencing. Although the bibliography is classified and has no subject index, the cross-references allow access from all relevant topics.
      Quigley's bibliographies are important in providing access to the vast research on Brahms's life and works. This book is highly recommended for all academic libraries.—**Allie Wise Goudy**

1144.   Sitsky, Larry. **Anton Rubinstein: An Annotated Catalog of Piano Works and Biography.** Westport, Conn., Greenwood Press, 1998. 221p. index. (Music Reference Collection, no.72). $59.95. ISBN 0-313-25497-4.
      Sitsky's annotated thematic catalog of the piano works of Anton Rubinstein provides a useful list of the composer's piano repertoire along with information on his conducting technique. In addition, a short biography is included that will provide the reader with an introduction to the life and work of this seminal Russian composer. The thematic catalog is arranged by genre in alphabetic order. Each entry begins with the title; a brief annotation providing general information (e.g., where the work was first published or performed, dedications, and the like); and several measures of the major theme. In addition to the thematic section, the work provides a list of the piano repertoire, information on historic concerts, a list of lectures provided by Rubinstein, information on the "Farewell" concerts given in the United States, a list of works Rubinstein is known to have conducted, and an account of the 11 orchestral "Historic" concerts the composer conducted. Also, Sitsky has given a complete catalog of Rubinstein's work, including youthful composition, mature works, and works without opus numbers. The book is concluded with six bibliographies: Rubinstein's writings, items in Russian, a general bibliography, a bibliography less specific to Rubinstein, journal and newspaper references lacking the author's name, and manuscript sources. Finally, the work is complete with an index of names found in the bibliographies.

This catalog includes bibliographic information on Rubinstein not previously available in other lists. Some of the Russian sources had not been identified until Sitsky provided them in this work. Only two full-length biographical sources on Anton Rubinstein are in print at this time: *Autobiography of Anton Rubinstein, 1829-1889* (Reprint Services, 1988) and *Rubinstein, Anton Gregor, 1829-1894* by A. MacArthur (Gordon Press, 1971). The latter work provides an incomplete bibliography of Rubinstein's works but does not provide a thematic catalog.

The catalog at hand is highly recommended for all academic and public libraries with extensive music collections. Also, it will be an extremely valuable source for individual pianists who wish to have a handy reference to the piano works of Rubinstein.—**Robert L. Wick**

1145. **Women Composers: Music Through the Ages, Volume 3. Composers Born 1700-1799.** Sylvia Glickman and Martha Furman Schleifer, eds. New York, G. K. Hall/Simon & Schuster Macmillan, 1998. 405p. index. $100.00. ISBN 0-7838-1612-X.

"Little is known of the life of this composer" could be the initial sentence of a majority of the introductions to the musical selections in this book. Nevertheless, this volume—the 3d in a projected 12-volume set devoted to music by women from the Middle Ages through the twentieth century—contains musical treasures in keyboard music by women born during the eighteenth century. (Two future volumes will contain vocal music and music for instrumental ensembles from the same period.) In this volume one finds 43 keyboard works by 22 composers from 9 countries. As before, each composer is introduced by an intelligently written commentary that also contains a list of the composer's works and a helpful bibliography. The music editions adhere to the best scholarly principles: They are clean (with editorial additions and performance suggestions clearly set off from the original text) and easily used by performers, teachers, and scholars alike.

The composers represented here have some things in common aside from the century of their births. Many came from musical families, the Dussek clan being the most noteworthy. Most were both composers and performers, many of them musical prodigies who performed and published their music at early ages. Most of them married, perhaps curtailing their public careers afterward, whereas others had lifelong musical careers and even remained single. Some composed "ladies' music" for private performance and amusement, and others produced works that seem intended for the concert stage. Some had formal training in composition, whereas more were trained solely as performers. Sonatas, variations of well-known tunes, fantasias, etudes, stylized dances, even a battle piece appear in this volume, a cross-section of keyboard music from the mid-eighteenth century through the first decades of the nineteenth.

Unlike volumes 1 and 2 (see ARBA 97, entries 1047 and 1048), this volume seems to have been guided by a firm editorial hand. There are fewer inconsistencies in technical matters and fewer proofreading errors. One annoying flaw concerns the lists of works, which are too often incomplete or confusing. Also, readers should not have to put up with references to "feminine endings" (p. 182) in a publication devoted to women. Nevertheless, this volume is admirable and should not be missed by anyone interested in keyboard music of this period. [R: BL, July 98, p. 1909]—**Karin Pendle**

1146. Young, Ben, comp. **Dixonia: A Bio-Discography of Bill Dixon.** Westport, Conn., Greenwood Press, 1998. 418p. index. (Discographies, no.77). $69.50. ISBN 0-313-30275-8.

This reference tool may strike most users as overdone given the relative obscurity of its subject matter. Bill Dixon, a composer, educator, and theoretician who was instrumental in the development of a unique pan-tonal language of trumpet playing, is credited with having politically and musically influenced the evolution of many phases of African American music in the latter half of the twentieth century. However, many more widely known jazz artists have yet to receive the comprehensive bio-discographical coverage accorded Dixon in this work. The genesis of *Dixonia* appears related to the fact that the compiler had complete access to both Dixon and his body of work. As noted in the preface, Dixon evolved a policy of recording everything he did regarding music, including concerts, lecture demonstrations, workshops, rehearsals, classes, closed sessions, and a wide range of informal playing situations. Young had direct access to Dixon's insights via on-air and prerecorded discussions undertaken for the *Bill Dixon Radio* series on WKCR-FM radio, Dixon's written corrections to various drafts of the text, and recorded or printed lectures and concert introductions since 1971. Young was also able to consult Dixon's archive—consisting of letters, concerts, programs, scores, schedules, posters, periodical advertisements and articles, reviews, contracts, receipts, payrolls, and informal notes—as well as outside source materials. The result is a model bio-discography, seemingly accurate, thorough, and well organized; the work includes everything likely to shed light on Dixon's life and art. Furthermore, Young painstakingly outlines his mode of arrangement for both the individual entries and the work as a whole. A chronological approach is used, merging textual commentary (largely comprised of quoted material from Dixon) and disographical material.

The only flaws are the skeletal character of the biographical sections as well as a reliance on straightforward description to the complete exclusion of evaluative analysis in all portions of the work. Nevertheless, *Dixonia* remains a first-rate reference source, guaranteed to gain converts to Dixon's work and contemporary avant-garde jazz in general.—**Frank Hoffmann**

INSTRUMENTS

Guitar

1147.   **Orion Blue Book: Guitars & Musical Instruments.** 1998 ed. Scottsdale, Ariz., Orion Research, 1998. 908p. $179.00. ISBN 0-932089-87-9. ISSN 1046-3880.

As a well-established publication in its 25th year, the *Orion Blue Book* provides standardized pricing of used instruments, principally for music stores, vintage instrument dealers, and pawnshops. As its size indicates, it is a comprehensive guide covering all types of orchestral, band, and folk instruments in addition to guitars and amps, for a total of 49,118 products from 450 manufacturers. Special collectible models are excluded, appearing instead in the quarterly *Vintage Guitars and Collectibles* (see entry 182).

Introduced by a listing of manufacturer's names, addresses, and telephone numbers, the directory itself is arranged by manufacturer names, instrument type, and model and features. Pricing data includes four key figures: the list price when new, retail price used, and wholesale prices for pieces in average and mint condition. Used prices are based on national dealer surveys and are calculated to reflect the sales figure an average dealer could achieve in 30 days or less. Convenient, well-organized, and reliable, the *Orion Blue Book* meet the needs of a diverse range of users, from consumers to attorneys, insurers, and law enforcement personnel.—**Megan S. Farrell**

Piano

1148.   Axford, Elizabeth C. **Traditional World Music Influences in Contemporary Solo Piano Literature: A Selected Bibliographic Survey and Review.** Lanham, Md., Scarecrow, 1997. 441p. index. $55.00. ISBN 0-8108-3380-8.

The author sums up her work in the introduction: "This reference book for piano solo literature is Everything but Bach, Beethoven and Brahms." Axford has gone where few researchers have ventured by accepting the huge task of identifying and analyzing published solo piano music from around the world without duplicating the more standard work (European and American for the most part) done vis-à-vis the solo piano repertoire.

First written as a 300-page master's thesis for San Diego State University in 1995, this work has been expanded to 441 pages. Axford's stated goal was to gather, organize into a logical international framework, and briefly annotate solo piano music from around the world. Chapters are organized by geographic region and by varieties of folk, ethnic, and indigenous music, including chapters on such U.S. genres as jazz, blues, and boogie-woogie. Each chapter begins with a fine scholarly overview, followed by the entries arranged geographically, then alphabetically by composer. Playing level and scope notes are included when possible. The author was unable to analyze each work individually, so some entries are sketchy. Each chapter ends with a book and periodicals bibliography. The concluding chapter suggests areas for further research. A lengthy bibliography follows, as do two valuable indexes—countries and regions index and an index of composers, arrangers, publishers, and distributors.

This ambitious reference work has no real parallel. Rather it is the author's hope that future researchers will augment and expand upon her pioneering efforts. She has begun this process by gathering, organizing, and briefly describing numerous published piano solos. This is the first time such information of international scope has been collected under the confines of one easy-to-use reference work.

Target audiences for this work include musical researchers, pianists, piano teachers, composers, and scholars. All libraries supporting general music programs or piano pedagogy should consider purchase of this valuable reference work.—**Linda D. Tietjen**

Violin

1149.   Klugherz, Laura. **A Bibliographical Guide to Spanish Music for the Violin and Viola, 1900-1997.** Westport, Conn., Greenwood Press, 1998. 102p. index. (Music Reference Collection, no.70). $49.95. ISBN 0-313-30590-0.

Klugherz's guide grew out of her search for violin and viola music for her own use. She points out in the introduction "that there was no shortage of compositions. A lack of editions, diffusion, and systematic organization of works, as well as a general isolation of Spanish musicians, however, have contributed to the obscurity of this repertoire." The guide begins with a brief overview of Spanish music in this century and a history of the violin and viola in Spain. It then goes on to list more than 300 works for violin and viola with piano or orchestra. Each entry includes composer's name, title of the work, year of completion, instrumentation, duration, date of premiere if known, publisher or score location, recording location, level of difficulty, and information concerning the composer. Also in many cases, a reference to the work being available from the composer is included. Klugherz mentions that updated addresses may be obtained from *Recursos Musicales* published by the Spanish Instituto Nacional de las Artes Escénicas y de la Música (INAEM). In addition to the annotated list of violin and viola music, several useful appendixes are included: works arranged by instrumentation, a chronological list of composers, a list of festivals and seminars of contemporary music in Spain, a list of publishers that are referred to in the book and their addresses, a list of foundations and associations, a selected bibliography (26 items), and an index. This work provides a much-needed list of Spanish music for the violin and viola. Although some sources do include Spanish music listings, there has never been a list this complete published.

The work is highly recommended for larger public and academic libraries with specialized music collections and for individual violin and viola players who wish to explore Spanish compositions. It will probably not be that useful for smaller public libraries.—**Robert L. Wick**

MUSICAL FORMS

Blues

1150.   Herzhaft, Gerard. **Encyclopedia of the Blues.** 2d ed. Fayetteville, Ark., University of Arkansas Press, 1997. 300p. illus. index. $28.00pa. ISBN 1-55728-452-0.

Blues, largely a U.S. phenomenon, lives in its performers and creators. This encyclopedia describes terms, styles, and hundreds of musicians. Names are entered in the manner by which the musician was known, many of these being in direct order (e.g., Muddy Waters). The author uses an asterisk to refer to other entries from within the articles. The cross-references are well done and useful. In each of the several hundred biographies, Herzhaft gives the years of their lives, not exact dates. For certain blues musicians, such as B. B. King, he recommends specific recordings. Herzhaft approaches several of the minor blues artists by grouping them by their styles (e.g., East Coast blues, blues shouters, boogie woogie, zydeco). This work also includes more than 75 photographs. At the end of the volume Herzhaft includes a basic bibliography, select discography of individual musicians, and a list of recorded anthologies. Another appendix, "Blues Artists and Their Instruments," a listing by the instrument, is a useful addition. Headings include fingerpicking guitar, lead guitar, harmonica, and piano. The index is quite useful for gauging the influence of some blues artists, while aiding in the location of other, more obscure musicians.

In *The Big Book of Blues* (Penguin, 1993), Robert Santelli covers a broader group, with several biographies not found in Herzhaft's volume. Santelli also lists exact dates, when known, and recommends recordings for most of the entries. There are some conflicts—Big Bill Broonzy's birth is listed as 1897 by Herzhaft, whereas Santelli lists June 26, 1893, a date also used in the *New Grove Dictionary of American Music* (see ARBA 88, entry 1277). Both blues sources add the birth name in entries; for example, Muddy Waters was born McKinley Morganfield. Those who desire precise birthdates, places, and a historical approach should consult Santelli's work. Those who seek photographs and an alternative perspective with anecdotal information will find *Encyclopedia of the Blues* a useful source.—**Ralph Hartsock**

Choral

1151.   Green, Jonathan D. **A Conductor's Guide to Choral-Orchestral Works, Twentieth Century, Part II: The Music of Rachmaninov Through Penderecki.** Lanham, Md., Scarecrow, 1998. 300p. $40.00. ISBN 0-8108-3376-X.

The 1st volume of this handbook (see ARBA 96, entry 1297) was limited to works with texts in English and a duration of at least 15 minutes. This new volume covers the same time period (1900-1972, with a few earlier works by composers active after 1900), but most of the 89 works treated have texts in languages other than English (including a few for wordless choir, such as *Daphnis et Chloé*), and there is no minimum length, although most do exceed 15 minutes.

The arrangement is again alphabetic by composer, subarranged by date of composition. The basic information on the compositions is also the same, listing title; date of composition; duration; source of text; detailed list of performing forces required; date, place, and principal performers of the premiere; editions currently available; location of the autograph score; historical notes; an extensive analysis of performance issues; a discography; and a selective bibliography of reviews and criticism. Performance difficulty is rated separately for choir and orchestra. Short composer biographies (including brief bibliographies) are provided. An annotated list of text sources, a directory of publishers, and a general bibliography are appended.

This is a useful guide for choral conductors and advanced music students. Libraries where the 1st volume is being used will want to add this volume as well. [R: Choice, Oct 98, p. 290]—**Paul B. Cors**

1152.   Trice, Patricia Johnson. **Choral Arrangements of the African-American Spirituals: Historical Overview and Annotated Listings.** Westport, Conn., Greenwood Press, 1998. 235p. index. (Music Reference Collection, no.66). $69.50. ISBN 0-313-30211-1.

This manual will guide choral directors in their choice of spiritual settings. Each of the alphabetically ordered titles is provided along with the composer's name (ethnicity and life dates are not considered); the publisher (with year of imprint and order number); the range of each part; topical subjects of the text; designation of key, meter, and tempo; an indication of musical form; and texture or style, to which are added terse comments. Each composer has a biographical sketch, and there are indexes of titles (including cross-references), composers, and subjects. Giving consideration to the originality of these settings, one could regard them as more than "arrangements," thus not minimizing the composer's creativity. These are not just harmonizations of a cantus.

The front material has a fine introduction for the novice to the spiritual, but a second reservation could be use of the term "syncopation," valid in some instances but not in others ("Ev'ry time I feel the spirit," for example, exemplifies the additive rhythm of 3+2+3+3+2+3). This is not a small matter if spiritual (and ragtime) rhythms are to be related to African linguistics. Professional choral ensembles are cited, but here is minimal reference to the black college choruses, where this repertoire is most ardently and sacredly preserved. There is no mention of the most active of these or its conductor-composer—Baltimore's Morgan State University Choir and Nathan Carter. Possibly a select discography could have been included to illustrate performance practice for conductors new to the literature. These cautions may diminish the help this publication can provide such figures, but they will be well served in other respects.—**Dominique-René de Lerma**

Classical

1153.   Cohn, Arthur. **The Literature of Chamber Music.** Chapel Hill, N.C., Hinshaw Music, 1997. 4v. $275.00. ISBN 0-937276-16-2.

During his career, Cohn played a key role in many aspects of musical life, from curator to administrator, from conductor to composer, from author to critic. The richness of these experiences ideally qualifies him for this monumental cumulation of splendid essays on musical works for two to nine performers. Perhaps the methodology for gathering information is a bit abbreviated, and it is true this is not an exhaustive register of appropriate works by those composers cited, but it is a treasury of data. Emphasis is on international composers of this century, without any disregard for those of the past, seeming thus because so many lesser figures are joined with those whose contributions have made the canon.

This is not a biographical dictionary but a musical discussion of individually entered works—each given a totally comprehensible discussion (rather than a dry academic analysis)—running more than 3,000 pages. It is quite remarkable that Cohn writes so lucidly about many hundreds of compositions. A few subject essays, *hors-de-série* and mostly on contemporary matters, are included within the composer entries when deemed significant. No indexes are offered, but this will be the primary reference guide for its subject. Its value should be immediately evident to those working with repertoire selection, evaluation, and discussion—not only to those affiliated with universities and performance societies but also to critics, annotators, and radio stations. Coverage appears to have ceased by 1995, when the introduction was signed. [R: Choice, Dec 98, p. 660]—**Dominique-René de Lerma**

1154.   McLoskey, Lansing D. **Twentieth Century Danish Music: An Annotated Bibliography and Research Directory.** Westport, Conn., Greenwood Press, 1998. 149p. index. (Music Reference Collection, no.65). $69.50. ISBN 0-313-30293-6.

This annotated bibliography is an *omnium gatherium* of all things musically Danish. Not only does it contain music, music theories, and developments in Danish music, including discographies, journals, and articles covering in-print and out-of-print materials, but it also offers users a directory to all Danish musical facilities, institutions, and organizations that relate to twentieth-century Danish music. Reference tools also abound herein, as do catalogs.

Although some may scratch their heads over so specialized a source, it may be worth pointing out that Denmark has more musical composers per square kilometer than almost any other country. As McLoskey points out, where else in the world does one find, in a country of only 5 million people, 10 orchestras, 4 opera companies, 7 music conservatories, 15 classical music recording labels, and more than 12 classical musical festivals, not counting all the composers? Compare that with the United States (with 250 million citizens), where there are less than 3 dozen radio stations devoted to playing classical music exclusively.

This slender volume packs a punch, and any library interested in music will want to have it. Scandinavian music scholars will delight in this tool for courses in musicology and ethnomusicology. Professional musicians will find much to recommend in this tool because many sources named are hard to find. [R: Choice, Sept 98, p. 90]
—**Mark Y. Herring**

Operatic

1155.   Jackson, Paul. **Sign-Off for the Old Met: The Metropolitan Opera Broadcasts 1950-1966.** Portland, Oreg., Amadeus Press, 1997. 644p. illus. index. $49.95. ISBN 1-57467-030-1.

Opera lovers' knowledge of an opera company's accomplishments is enriched by reading about its history from old reviews, histories, and memories and by listening to recordings made by the artists associated most closely with it, and, until recently, by memories of broadcasts of live performances. Jackson is the first to undertake a systematic study of the Met's weekly broadcasts. He began in *Saturday Afternoons at the Old Met: The Metropolitan Opera Broadcasts, 1931-1950* (Amadeus Press, 1992) with the fragmentary transcriptions from the early 1930s. Within a few years, recordings of complete broadcasts had been tracked down and released on "private" long-playing discs and now on less private but elusive compact discs (due to the Met's desire to keep these out of the record stores in the United States). However, they exist in library archives for study and in the collections of avid collectors who have found ways of acquiring them from abroad.

The present volume picks up the history at the beginning of Rudolf Bing's tenure as manager and continues through the closing night in the old house, which was torn down and replaced by the company's new Lincoln Center home. A strong-minded and controversial figure, Bing gave the company a new profile by bringing in new artists, getting rid of others (not always justifiably or kindly), and giving new importance to production values. This part of his period with the company is generally considered the strongest, and among the new singers Jackson considers are Leontyne Price, Maria Callas, Renata Tebaldi, and Birgit Nilsson.

Jackson is too skillful and graceful a writer to bombard readers with a deadly chronological study broadcast-by-broadcast. He makes no attempt to cover everyone, and he lumps them together by period under such chapter headings as "Wagner in Limbo" and later "New Lease for Wagner." By considering such thematically related performance standards and practices, Jackson gives readers a vivid portrait of an institution that goes far beyond the mere pros and cons of its individual singer's performances. Jackson has proven himself to be an astute observer as well as listener. He is, however, also an expert on assessing individual singers. He knows how to listen to the difference between a singer's voice and the skill and imagination of the singing. He rightly prizes the flawed performance in which magical music-making outweighs tonal allure.

With these two books, Jackson has already established himself as a reliable authority. For the opera lover, no books of the past decade are of such compelling interest and such consistent virtue. Amadeus Press's index and format are as good as these books deserve. Opera lovers will look forward to new installments.

—**George Louis Mayer**

1156.   **Opera Premiere Reviews and Re-Assessments: A Listing.** Charles H. Parsons, comp. Lewiston, N.Y., Edwin Mellen Press, 1997. 139p. (Mellen Opera Reference Index, v.19). $199.95. ISBN 0-88946-172-4.

Representing volume 19 of the exhaustive Mellen Opera Reference Index series, this publication will be of enormous help to music scholars and students because it covers a previously uncharted area. The compiler provides lists of English-language reviews of all major opera premieres and revivals between the years of 1990 and 1997. This endeavor sprang from the compiler's wish to read what was really said, for instance, after the disastrous premiere of Puccini's *Madame Butterfly*. He soon realized how daunting a task it would be to chronicle all the important premieres, a fact that necessitated restricting the period of research to the years listed above. (In the preface, Parsons indicates he plans to keep working backward in time in order to cover more of the world's important opera premieres.) Entries are offered in alphabetic order by composers, under which their operas are covered. Reviews are arranged by their writers' names, followed by the review headline, name of the newspaper or magazine, and the date on which the review was published. Some entries include the page number the review appeared on. However, some do not, and actual reviews are not included, leaving it to the student or researcher to seek out the review through the archives of each individual newspaper or magazine.—**Koraljka Lockhart**

1157.   **Opera: The Rough Guide.** By Matthew Boyden. Jonathan Buckley, ed. London, Rough Guides; distr., New York, Penguin Books, 1997. 672p. illus. index. $24.95pa. ISBN 1-85828-138-5.

Opera: The Rough Guide is published by the same publisher that does the popular travel guides and looks much the same as those handbooks. The work is an attempt to provide, in a single volume, a complete guide to world opera. The book is structured chronologically, with each chapter beginning with a broad overview of the opera of the period, and then continuing on to the major opera composers, singers, and companies. Each entry begins with information on the composer, then continues with major works, compact disc recommendations, and a recording overview. In addition, there are frequent sidebars that provide information on various aspects of opera (e.g., opera trends, periods, specific opera companies, and audience reactions to specific operas). Also, the work is sprinkled with black-and-white photographs of composers, musicians, and recording jackets. The average entry contains about 1,500 words. In addition, there are several appendixes, including a directory of singers, a directory of conductors, a directory of opera houses, a glossary of opera terminology, and an index.

Opera: The Rough Guide is, of course, no replacement for such in-depth works as *The Metropolitan Opera Encyclopedia: A Comprehensive Guide to the World of Opera* (Simon & Schuster, 1987), or even the more recent *The St. James Opera Encyclopedia: A Guide to People and Works* (Visible Ink Press, 1997), but it does provide a handy volume to look up quick facts about a specific opera. The appendixes offer quick information concerning conductors, singers, and opera houses, which is useful. A problem for libraries will be the extremely flimsy binding, which barely survived this reviewer's perusal.

This guide is highly recommended for individual use in home collections, but may not provide the in-depth information needed in library collections. Having said that, it may have a place in very small public library branches where only one or two reference books on opera are available. But even then it must be rebound if it is expected to last for more than a few uses.—**Robert L. Wick**

Orchestral

1158.   Musiker, Reuben, and Naomi Musiker. **Conductors and Composers of Popular Orchestral Music: A Biographical and Discographical Sourcebook.** Westport, Conn., Greenwood Press, 1998. 335p. illus. index. $75.00. ISBN 0-313-30260-X.

Popular or light orchestral music as written and recorded primarily in the 1940s to the 1960s is the subject of this book. The authors have attempted to fill a gap by compiling a single resource that provides biographical and discographical information on approximately 500 conductors and composers who have promoted or composed middle-of-the-road music, which includes original compositions as well as folk songs, jazz, musicals, show tunes, film music, and other pieces arranged for popular orchestra.

The book's emphasis is on the biographical sketches of such conductors as Percy Faith, George Melachrino, and Nelson Riddle and on the selective discographies of their recordings of popular orchestral music. Composers, primarily British and American, who composed light orchestral music (including film music) also receive an entry, often with a discography of recordings of these works. A bibliography of readings about the person are occasionally included for some entries. Many of the people represented here have been successful in several areas of music; the biographies and discographies emphasize the musician's association with popular orchestral music.

This is a well-executed compendium on the topic, and libraries with a clientele who are interested in symphonic popular music or film music may find this compilation useful. At $75, the cost is prohibitive for many libraries that do not have specialized users. [R: Choice, July/Aug 98, p. 1832]—**Allie Wise Goudy**

Popular

General Works

1159.   Blumenthal, Howard J. **The World Music CD Listener's Guide.** New York, Billboard Books/Watson-Guptill, 1998. 204p. illus. index. (The Best on CD). $14.95pa. ISBN 0-8230-7663-6.

World music choices seem to be growing at an exponential rate. This guide is not a comprehensive listing, but rather an introduction to 150 world music artists whose compact discs are readily available for a core collection. The list of acknowledgments suggests a great deal of research by Blumenthal, who has been writing about music for 20 years. The guide is arranged alphabetically by musician, with each entry including a paragraph-length biography of the artist, country of origin, list of recommend compact discs, and a link to another compact disc that influenced the music. The index provides the names of the linked artists.

The selections provide full coverage of the world, including artists from Asia, Africa, and Europe as well as the Americas. What is missing is an indexing of country or music styles to make finding all the musical styles, for example, reggae artists or Latin jazz, easier. The work is valuable and recommended for libraries attempting to build a solid world music collection or as a tool for patrons wishing to do the same.—**Joshua Cohen**

1160.   Dixon, Robert M. W., John Godrich, and Howard Rye, comps. **Blues & Gospel Records 1890-1943.** 4th ed. New York, Oxford University Press, 1997. 1370p. index. $95.00. ISBN 0-19-816239-1.

Thirty-four years after its 1st edition, this monument has almost doubled in size. It is a highly disciplined discography of two African American idioms of international influence. The definition of gospel is broadened to include earlier sacred works (e.g., spirituals, jubilees), rather than those more specifically now termed "gospel blues" that originated largely in Chicago by the late 1920s. Many cross-over performances, stylistically inseminating sacred and secular characteristics, justify the alliance of the two, supposedly antithetic, idioms. The cut-off date (1943 was added with the 3d edition) coincides with the recording ban and the evolution of new styles during the war years. Entries are by principal performers, with their various sidemen acknowledged. Titles are allied with matrix numbers, label issues, and date of recording. Supplementary notes are provided when needed to provide clear documentation. This by itself is an extraordinary accomplishment, offered with an organization that is exemplary for other discographies. The front material includes a 20-page essay on the "race labels," followed by its own index and a bibliographic register of consulted sources. Many reference applications will be made possible by the concluding indexes: song title (251 pages), broadcast and films, vocalist, and accompanists. The volume is handsomely produced and sturdily bound, ready to accept the heavy use it merits. [R: Choice, Sept 98, pp. 86-88]—**Dominique-René de Lerma**

1161.   **International Who's Who in Music 1998/99, Volume Two: Popular Music.** 2d ed. Sean Tyler, ed. Cambridge, England, International Biographical Centre; distr., Bristol, Pa., Taylor & Francis, 1998. 526p. $175.00. ISBN 0-948875-97-6.
        Similar in style and scope to the 1st edition (see ARBA 97, entry 1063), this volume provides basic biographical and career information for approximately 5,000 popular musicians worldwide, with the largest number of biographees being from North America and Europe. "Popular music," for the purposes of this work, includes pop, rock, folk, jazz, blues, country and dance, world, film, and show music. In most cases the information is taken from questionnaires returned by the entrants. Profiles were researched and written for some individuals deemed to be of high reference interest who did not respond to the questionnaire. As might be expected with such a volume, it is relatively easy to find omissions of personal favorites. However, the inclusion of international performers who would otherwise be difficult to research will benefit many. Although it is not the primary purpose of the work, it can also be used to answer many "whatever became of . . . ?" questions. The geographically arranged appendixes that serve as mini-directories of the music and entertainment industries in many countries are an added benefit. This work will be helpful in performing arts and large general reference collections where demand warrants.—**Barbara E. Kemp**

1162.   Lowe, Allen. **American Pop from Minstrel to Mojo: On Record, 1893-1956.** Redwood, N.Y., Cadence Jazz Books, 1997. 278p. index. $18.00pa. ISBN 1-881993-33-7.
        The author of this work appears to know the subject matter. The approach is basically chronological, and is organized in year-by-year entries. Indexing is by "names" (mostly recording artists) and by a "song index." There are also an adequate bibliography and discography. The work is "an examination of the history of recordings," and it may be thought of as a survey. But, the reader should be aware that it consists of 243 pages of the author's subjective opinions, or, sometimes, citations of the opinions of others. For example, Al Jolson "was an obnoxious egotist . . . but also a great and important entertainer." The author can be generous in his praise, as in describing the playing of Bix Biederbecke as a "paradoxical blend of devil-may-care sensibility and martial discipline and precision." His comments on Fats Waller are too lengthy to quote here, but essentially say that Waller expresses his feelings about the "condition of the Black performer in a White controlled world . . . in largely self destructive ways." Virtually every page is riddled with numerous "black" and "white" references.
        This reviewer has been listening to recordings of the era in question (1893-1956) for nearly 60 years. And Vernon Dalhart's recording of "The Prisoner's Song" was one of the records played over and over during my childhood in the South. Lowe describes that recording and the song as sentimental and silly. Maybe he has a grasp of the recordings, but lacks a grasp of the social times they cover.
        In all fairness to the author, and to potential purchasers, especially librarians, the book needs to be read from beginning to end as a series of essays. With this approach, there is much merit. If one were new to American pop, how could one not seek out some Duke Ellington records or compact discs after reading that Ellington is one "with whom no one else can be compared?"—**Louis G. Zelenka**

1163.   **Popular Music Studies: A Select International Bibliography.** John Shepherd and others, comps. and eds. Herndon, Va., Mansell/Cassell, 1997. 450p. index. $150.00. ISBN 0-7201-2344-5.
        This work covers popular music of the world. Indeed, one of the main aims of the editors is to "rectify the Anglo-American bias of most other reference works in the field of popular music studies" (p. xxvii). They do this in two ways: (1) by using contributors who come from various regions of the world and (2) by including a broad range of geographic areas. These make this volume unique and important, given the explosive growth of interest in world popular music over the last 10 years.
        Popular Music Studies is organized conceptually into seven major categories. They include general works, genres, the industry, social and cultural contexts, musical practices, locations, and theory and method. Each main category is further subdivided, sometimes into more than one level. There are two useful indexes organized by subject and author.

Aimed primarily at popular music scholars and university or college students, all of the citations are of a scholarly nature. However, the editors do not limit themselves to academic sources only. This is a wise decision because some important writing in this field can be found in magazines and newspapers that are included here. Curiously, for no apparent reason dissertations and liner notes are not listed. References to biographical material are also omitted. The editors reason that because much of the literature of popular music is devoted to biography, this bibliography should focus predominantly on nonbiographical material. Aside from this omission, one look at the table of contents confirms that this book is very thorough. Although no definition is given as to what popular music is, certain categories are unexpected. One would be hard pressed to include bebop and avant-garde jazz as popular in any sense. Yet under the subdivisions of bebop, modern, and contemporary jazz there are more than 40 citations. This work is highly recommended for its breadth of scope and ease of use.—**Howard Spring**

1164.   **Popular Music. Volume 21, 1996: An Annotated Guide to American Popular Songs....** Bruce Pollock, ed. Detroit, Gale, 1997. 174p. index. $75.00. ISBN 0-7876-0069-5. ISSN 0886-442X.

Pollock pens an informed and lively discussion of the current music scene in his introduction to this annual list of notable popular tunes. He challenges both the Top 40 and the Oscars for their apparent oversight of rock and roll and black music. The blurring of lines between country music and rock and roll and the recognition of black tunes by Broadway are duly noted.

With cumulative volumes covering 1900-1919, 1920-1979, and 1980-1989 and annual volumes since 1989 (some earlier annual volumes are still available), the aim of the series is to record a selected, annotated list of the significant popular songs of the years covered. To do so, Pollock digs deeply into musical resources: American Society of Composers, Authors, and Publishers (ASCAP); Broadcast Music, Inc. (BMI); Society of Composers, Authors, and Music Publishers of Canada (SOCAN); and the Society of European Songwriters and Composers (SESAC). Research in the Copyright Office of the Library of Congress validates the precise date for the declaration of ownership of a piece. He gleans information on recordings from musical trade journals such as *Billboard*, *Radio and Records*, and *Cash Box*.

The alphabetic directory arranged by song title lists alternate title(s), country of origin (if not the United States), author(s) and composers, current publishers, copyright date, and annotations of the song's origins and performance history. Three indexes add value to the list. Lyricist and composer indexes place the song under credited individuals. Media—album, movie, musical, performer (individual or group), revue, or television—comprise the important performances index. The awards index includes nominees as well as winners of Academy and Grammy awards. A list of publishers with addresses (where available) follows.

It is difficult to imagine any comprehensive music library not holding this title, as well as every disk jockey in the nation. The average popular music lover turns here to settle debates on songs and circumstances. The history teacher could devise interesting units with information herein, and an event coordinator planning observances of memorable years or periods could add musical authenticity to the event.—**Eleanor Ferrall**

Jazz

1165.   Blumenthal, Howard J. **The Jazz CD Listener's Guide.** New York, Billboard Books/Watson-Guptill, 1998. 204p. illus. index. (The Best on CD). $14.95pa. ISBN 0-8230-7662-8.

Part of Billboard Books The Best on CD series, this is one of many such guides to recorded jazz currently available. It briefly discusses the work of more than 100 performers and includes short reviews of 900 recordings. Ratings are not used, but the author's admittedly subjective choices were influenced by the artist's overall importance, current interest in his other work, and the availability and quality of the listed recordings. References to other recordings by the same musician or to other relevant musicians are included in the reviews. Thus, although bandleader Stan Kenton, for example, does not have an entry of his own, one of his recordings is discussed as a "link" from the saxophonist Art Pepper, who was a star soloist in Kenton's orchestra. No claim to comprehensiveness is made, and knowledgeable readers may note the exclusion of some of their personal favorites. Nonetheless, despite a few factual errors—for example, that Louis Armstrong played with the Fletcher Henderson Orchestra in Chicago when that actually happened in New York—the biographical and critical commentary is straightforward, simple, and useful. The author, who has been a successful television producer and a nationally syndicated columnist, has written widely on musical subjects. He has published 16 books on home entertainment.
—**A. David Franklin**

1166.   Komara, Edward M., comp. **The Dial Recordings of Charlie Parker: A Discography.** Westport, Conn., Greenwood Press, 1998. 215p. index. (Discographies, no.76). $69.50. ISBN 0-313-29168-3.

Alto saxophonist Charlie Parker (1920-1955) is universally regarded as one of the towering figures in the history of jazz. In the 1940s, Parker, along with trumpeter Dizzy Gillespie, pianist and composer Thelonious Monk, and others, created bebop, the first modern jazz style and the language of most jazz improvisation even today. The influence of Parker's personal style on the alto saxophone is highly evident even among contemporary performers. Although Parker died at the relatively young age of 34, he left a considerable recorded legacy. Most of his studio recording was done for Savoy Records, Dial Records, and Norman Granz's Mercury/Clef/Verve labels. Because of Parker's stature, his recordings have been the subject of numerous traditional discographies. The present work, however, while focussing exclusively on the Dial sessions, provides extensive additional information about the music. Sections include a historical narrative (a history of the record company, Parker's contractual relationship with the company, studio conditions, reissues, and other related material), a basic catalog of the recordings (date, location, repertory, personnel, record issues, and reissues), and expanded commentary on the music and conditions under which it was recorded. Five appendixes provide nonessential but often interesting information, including the origin of titles for original compositions. There are also a four-page bibliography; indexes of names, titles, and transcriptions; and tables providing information on such items as the harmonic sources for Parker's recordings.

The book began as a master's thesis in music history at the State University of New York (SUNY) at Buffalo. By the time it reached its final form, numerous specialists, including Dial Records owner Ross Russell, had been involved in its development. This volume is an excellent addition to Parker scholarship.—**A. David Franklin**

1167.   Lord, Tom. **The Jazz Discography, Volume 17.** Redwood, N.Y., Cadence Jazz Books, 1997. 646p. $70.00pa. ISBN 1-881993-16-7.

The latest volume in a series that was previously reviewed in ARBA 96 (see entry 1326), ARBA 94 (see entries 1373 and 1374), and ARBA 93 (see entries 1287-1289) covers the Paradise Club Band through Roy Powell. As previously noted, the purpose of the discography is to provide pertinent information on every known jazz recording, regardless of style, made between the late 1800s and the publication of the latest volume (volumes 17 covers from 1896 to 1997). This is a departure from previous discographies, which have normally dealt with a single jazz style over a limited time period. Despite the inevitable occasional omissions, this work in progress has garnered high acclaim from jazz scholars. The completed set is now expected to contain approximately 25 volumes.—**A. David Franklin**

1168.   **MusicHound Jazz: The Essential Album Guide.** Steve Holtje and Nancy Ann Lee, eds. Detroit, Visible Ink Press/Gale, 1998. 1390p. illus. index. $26.95pa. ISBN 1-57859-031-0.

The close of the twentieth century marks the 100th anniversary of the uniquely American form of music known as jazz. Editors Holtje and Lee have collected some 1,300 jazz artists and their works to discuss the best and worst of their recordings. Just about every facet of jazz has been covered thoroughly—from New Orleans style (e.g., Bunk Johnson) to swing (e.g., Benny Goodman, Count Basie) to bebop (e.g., Charlie Parker, Thelonious Monk) to the soulful songstresses of the day (e.g., Billie Holiday, Sarah Vaughn). Artists are listed alphabetically and their recordings are listed according to what is essential to buy, what to "buy next," what is worth searching for, and what recordings can be avoided. The artists birth and death dates (when appropriate) are provided, along with a selection of artists that influenced their music and the artists that they have influenced. For example, under Ella Fitzgerald's entry it is noted that Maxine Sullivan, Connee Boswell, and Billie Holiday influenced her work and Fitzgerald has left her impression on the works of Sarah Vaughn, Lena Horne, Diana Ross, and Whitney Houston. Because this work is a buyer's guide only compact discs that are in print and available in the United States are discussed.

As with most music guides this work is subject to the opinions of the editors. Both are well researched in the area of jazz music—Holtje is a former senior editor of *Creem* magazine and music journalist and Lee is a freelance journalist/photographer and frequent contributor to *JazzTimes*. This guide will be a welcome addition to the music reference collection of public and university libraries. [R: LJ, Dec 98, p. 84]—**Shannon M. Graff**

1169.   Vladimir, Simosko. **Serge Chaloff: A Musical Biography and Discography.** New Brunswick, N.J., Institute of Jazz Studies and Lanham, Md., Scarecrow, 1998. 187p. illus. index. (Studies in Jazz, no.27). $45.00. ISBN 0-8108-3396-4.

Serge Chaloff was one of the greatest saxophone players of his time, a time cut short just before his 34th birthday, after many years of drug addictions and resultant diseases. All but forgotten now, except by the most ardent jazz fans, Scarecrow Press has issued the 27th volume in the series Studies in Jazz in tribute to an extraordinary talent and a major figure in the bop movement of the 1940s and 1950s.

The book is organized chronologically beginning with an extensive biography of Chaloff from birth to his final recordings and premature death. The biographical sections are thorough and contain innumerable details about his personal life, the recordings, and performances. These may weigh a little heavy for most readers. However, there are many personal reminiscences by family, friends, and fellow musicians that make the biographical sections readable. Chaloff's own first person accounts and interview excerpts enhance the readability of the text. A complete list of sources and a list of additional readings, as well as a few photographs, round out the biographical section. The discography is extensive, enumerating all known recordings, live performances, and radio performances. A discography for Leo Parker is also included "for convenience" because, as the author states, Parker "was the only serious challenge to the claim that Chaloff was the first prominent bop soloist to emerge on baritone sax" (p. 165). This work is highly recommended for all jazz collections and most academic and special music libraries.

                                                                         —**Roland C. Hansen**

Musicals

1170.   DeVenney, David P. **The Broadway Song Companion: An Annotated Guide to Musical Theatre Literature by Voice Type and Song Style.** Lanham, Md., Scarecrow, 1998. 210p. index. $35.00. ISBN 0-8108-3373-5.

This carefully researched guide, written by an author who has years of experience in teaching college students in musical theater, provides a quick means of identifying songs for solo voices, duets, trios, quartets, small ensembles, choruses, and company numbers. Solo selections are further identified as being suited for soprano, mezzo-soprano, tenor, or bass. Compositions in the *Companion* are primarily accessed through the "Catalog of Musicals," an alphabetic listing by the musical's title. The year the musical opened on Broadway, along with the names of the composer and lyricist, head the entries. This catalog further provides the vocal range of each selection in the show and a brief notation on the style of the song. Styles are usually described clearly in a few words. These brief descriptions fall into such categories as ballad, blues ballad, narrative ballad, rock ballad, waltz, uptempo, jazzy, and march. Each song is also identified by the character who sings the number. The catalog is followed by separate indexes for the various voice ranges. A final index provides an alphabetic identification to composers and lyricists. An appendix lists addresses for the publishers and agents of the shows.

This guide is intended as a resource for teachers and students of musical theater. More than 2,000 song titles from more than 210 musicals are categorized. The reference will also assist directors, producers, and others who need a quick reference to identify the selections. With coverage of musicals from the 1890s to 1990s, this work will not be quickly outdated. It is a well-organized and concise guide to the music literature of Broadway. [R: BL, July 98, p. 1909; Choice, Oct 98, p. 290]—**Louis G. Zelenka**

Reggae

1171.   Barrow, Steve, and Peter Dalton. **Reggae: The Rough Guide.** London, Rough Guides; distr., New York, Penguin Books, 1997. 395p. illus. index. $19.95pa. ISBN 1-85828-247-0.

To the many music fans who think Jamaican reggae begins and ends with Bob Marley and his son Ziggy, this spirited compilation will come as a revelation. Only a very small percentage of the more than 100,000 reggae records produced in Jamaica in the past four decades have crossed over and become popular with U.S. listeners. The rich musical history of reggae is chronological by chapter, from the beginnings in the 1950s with the style of music called "Mento," up through "Dub," "Dancehall," and "Ragga," to the latest development in African reggae. Each section includes biographical essays on notable performers, producers, and relevant topics for each period, together with excellent capsule reviews of specific recordings. Brimming with entertaining black-and-white photographs and informative sidebars, this sourcebook authoritatively fills what had been a void in reference works focusing on reggae exclusively.

The Rough Guides series, published in England, first made a name for itself with its hundred or so travel guides, and now is branching out into music; *Jazz: The Rough Guide* has been well received (see ARBA 97, entry 1076). But there are some difficulties with being "rough." Inexcusably, there is no table of contents in this reggae guide, impeding access to the material and making it difficult to get a simple overview of the subject. The index is minimal, only including people and omitting titles of songs and other potentially important access points. Good features include a serviceable bibliography and listing of reggae-related Websites. The authors are both reggae industry insiders with an incredible amount of savvy information and insight to share, but librarians will wish there were more attention to the technical details necessary to make this a well-crafted reference book. Nevertheless, there is much here to recommend, and this will likely become the definitive source on reggae in public as well as academic libraries. [R: RBB, 15 Nov 97, p. 580]—**Richard W. Grefrath**

Rock

1172.   **The Billboard Illustrated Encyclopedia of Rock.** Colin Larkin, ed. New York, Billboard Books/Watson-Guptill, 1998. 384p. illus. $45.00. ISBN 0-8230-7697-0.

As rock music attracts second- and third-generation fans, more library patrons will want to read about rock stars of the past. The *Billboard Illustrated Encyclopedia of Rock* presents current information in a serviceable, but often flawed way.

The book's 384 pages are bound in a hardcover format, which distinguishes it from other entries in the category. The binding features no special reinforcement. The main resource for the work's 1,800 entries is the previously published *Virgin Concise Encyclopedia of Popular Music*. Aside from a shared imprint, this book seems to have no affiliation with the popular and respected *Billboard* magazine.

As with most similar works, *The Billboard Encyclopedia of Rock* is not an encyclopedia at all. "Who's Who in Rock" would be a more descriptive title. Musical styles, musical instruments, trends, terminology, and festivals almost never appear. Terms like *acid rock, techno-pop*, and *heavy metal* are used frequently, but they have no entries of their own. The book has no index, making further reading on a topic difficult.

As with any encyclopedia, the editor must carefully budget page space. The concept is understandable; the practice herein often defies logic. Les Paul, the inventor of the solid-body electric guitar on which the genre is based, is given one paragraph. Historical supergroups The Moody Blues and U2 each receive two paragraphs, whereas short-lived Bananarama rates a longer write-up. And seminal rockers Led Zeppelin get four paragraphs—the same as fast-fading Oasis. And why omit so many rhythm and blues artists, and instead include such little-knowns as Gaye Bykers on Acid, and Men They Couldn't Hang? The selection process gives readers the impression that they are using a disc jockey's cheat sheet, not a well-planned reference book.

A brighter note seems to appear in the plentiful and colorful photographs that are included. However, with no captions to guide the way, the reader must use the process of elimination or just guess. Just who is that smiling man in the green shirt, and why does his photograph take an entire half-page? Notably absent are photographs of rock icons the Eagles and the Doobie Brothers, and pioneers Buddy Holly and Jerry Lee Lewis.

Each page features a sidebar listing each artist's top albums, collaborators, and associates. Recommendations for further reading are often mentioned. A 34-page artist discography appears at the end of the work. However, because the print in this section is so tiny, be prepared to offer a magnifying glass to your patrons.

The Billboard Illustrated Encyclopedia of Rock tries to be both a coffee-table book and a reference book, finding little success in either arena. This is especially disappointing, as some librarians, patrons, and purchasers will be drawn to the esteemed Billboard name. The prosaic *New Rolling Stone Encyclopedia of Rock and Roll* or the more accessible *DK Encyclopedia of Rock Stars* would better serve most readers. [R: LJ, Dec 98, p. 84]

—**Keith Kyker**

1173.　Cooper, B. Lee, and Wayne S. Haney. **Rock Music in American Popular Culture II: More Rock 'n' Roll Resources.** Binghamton, N.Y., Haworth Press, 1997. 404p. $39.95. ISBN 1-56023-877-1.

Envision an encyclopedia of rock music published in occasional volumes crossed with a collection of essays, and one has volumes 1 and 2 of *Rock Music in American Popular Culture*, with volume 1 having been published in 1995. Each volume begins with prepublication reviews and brief "Notes for Professional Librarians" and "Conservation and Preservation Notes." After the introductory material comes the essays, with main topics in alphabetic order (e.g., in this volume, "Answer Songs," "Cars," "Cigarettes," "City Life") and composed of short essays (generally around two pages in length, although some are longer). The essays are followed by a bibliography and an index; the essays themselves frequently have bibliographies or discographies. The focus of the works is on the influence of rock music on popular culture and vice versa. There is a first—at least for this reviewer— in that the introduction of the volume includes "Challenges for Librarians" and "Suggested Reading for Librarians." These volumes are for collections of rock music in public and academic libraries. [R: LJ, 15 Nov 97, p. S40]

—**Mary Larsgaard**

1174.　Talevski, Nick. **The Unofficial Encyclopedia of the Rock and Roll Hall of Fame.** Westport, Conn., Greenwood Press, 1998. 402p. illus. index. $45.00. ISBN 0-313-30032-1.

This 1-volume encyclopedia recognizes rock and roll as a large part of twentieth-century American culture by celebrating the Rock and Roll Hall of Fame, which opened in September 1995 in Cleveland, Ohio. This book is a welcome addition to any music lover's library.

The 1st section of the work summarizes the rock movement, from its roots in rhythm and blues and the life and career of Cleveland deejay Alan Freed, who gave rock and roll its name and popularized "black" music in the 1950s. Chapter 2 reveals the 12 years of effort and political battles involved in the decision of where to locate the hall of fame, and chapter 3 details each annual induction ceremony, from 1986 to 1997. Part 2 provides an alphabetic listing of inductees, from The Four Tops to Jimi Hendrix to Frank Zappa. Entries provide birth names and dates of the group members or individual artists and the year and category in which they were inducted, followed by biographical information describing the artists' careers and influence on the musical genre. The 1st appendix lists the inductees and nominees of each year, and the information in chapter 2 is summarized in a timeline in appendix 2. Occasional photographs illustrate the pages, and a bibliography and index are included. [R: LJ, 15 Sept 98, p. 67; Choice, Dec 98, p. 666]—**Felicity Tucker**

1175.　Trager, Oliver. **The American Book of the Dead: The Definitive Grateful Dead Encyclopedia.** New York, Simon & Schuster Trade Paperbacks, 1997. 434p. illus. index. $16.00pa. ISBN 0-684-81402-1.

It is unfortunate that Trager put the word "definitive" in the title of this interesting compilation of information about the Grateful Dead. For it is *not* definitive, if definitive means that it should set the standard for what a Grateful Dead encyclopedia should be. Rather, this is an idiosyncratic work that belongs on the shelf of every "Deadhead" and self-respecting radio station as well as in the circulating collections of public libraries everywhere. It is probably not necessary on the reference shelves of public or academic libraries. For such a work, even on a topic as seemingly ephemeral as a rock group, the approach would need to be more deliberate, and it would certainly not be a one-author work; rather, an editorial board would be appropriate.

Trager seems to have been rushed to get this book into print. There are a tellingly large number of plain old typographical errors—there are undocumented facts, and facts that are just omitted for lack of substantiation (see his entries on such early, unrecorded songs as "Cardboard Cowboy" and "Confusion's Prince," which note only that they are of unknown authorship).

Most of Trager's sources for the work seem to be the audiotape record, assembled lovingly and painstakingly documented over the years by thousands of Deadheads. From this he assembles what is the strongest and the weakest point of the entire book—a song-by-song listing of each song performed or recorded by the band. Unfortunately, much of this becomes dead weight because so many tunes were only performed once or twice, and Trager gives them as much weight in terms of entry length as many songs that deserve much fuller entries. This tendency leads to some inexplicable and inexcusable discrepancies; for instance, a large entry is devoted to the Carter family, on the basis of the song "Wabash Cannonball," which Bob Weir (not even the full band) performed once, but the entire album *Wake of the Flood* merits only part of a column.

Indexing is also spotty. There is no entry, for example, for Jerry Garcia's side band Reconstruction, although it is mentioned in the text under the entry for the Jerry Garcia Band. Some entries that would have been useful, such as "Mars Hotel" for "Grateful Dead from the Mars Hotel," are not included at all in the index. These kinds of missing cross-references diminish the book's overall usefulness. Similarly, the cross-referencing convention within the text, indicated by all-capital lettered names within entries (a common convention in reference books, and an admirable one) is inconsistent. For example, under the entry for the band Dose Hermanos, Bob Bralove's name is in caps, indicating the presence of a full entry on him, but Tom Constanten's name is not, although he also is given a full entry.

On the positive side, the entries are well-written. This is an entertaining book, but not truly a reference book. Nor should it be taken as the "definitive" Grateful Dead encyclopedia. [R: BL, 15 Oct 97, p. 377]—**David Dodd**

Sacred

1176.   **The Christian Music Directories: Recorded Music 1998.** San Jose, Calif., Resource Publications, 1998. 1472p. index. $175.00pa. ISSN 1048-6844.

This directory is useful for identifying song titles of Christian music recordings, album titles and contents, artists and their recordings, available formats of recordings, accompaniment tracks, video recordings, and publisher's names and addresses. The coverage appears to be comprehensive for contemporary Christian artists. Information is provided for materials that are both in print and out of print. Artists who are not typically identified as Christian are also included if the albums they recorded contain Christian music (e.g., Elvis Presley and Willie Nelson). Because it is the publisher's responsibility to supply the information, there may be some gaps. The guide warns that because publishers name their songs different ways, the searcher may need to check variant listings.

The directory consists of several different indexes, with the song and artist indexes making up the largest part. The largest index is the song index, which consists of an alphabetic list of song titles. Entries also include the composer or arranger, artist, album title, and publisher code and catalog number. For song titles that are the same, the entry becomes alphabetic by album title or by publisher name if the album title is the same. The "Artist Index" follows and is alphabetically arranged by the artist's last name or the group's name. Included in the index are a list of album titles and their contents in alphabetic order, along with the publisher code, catalog number, and format availability. The format availability indicates whether material is available on formats ranging from compact disc, audiocassette, LP, 8-track, single 45, reel-to-reel, or out-of-print. It was noticed that there are song title duplications under an album's contents in this section. Listings apparently repeat themselves (e.g., Acappella's *Conquerors* album and others' album listings under "Acappella.") This may be due to the fact that the same album may have different publishers and catalog numbers. This is not explained in the print version, but is evident in the CD-ROM version by looking at the "Song Detail Screen." There are also some duplications due to misspellings of names and cross-listings.

The additional indexes provided are the album index, accompaniment track index, and the music video index. There is a list titled "Publishers by Code," which includes cross-references, so that one can identify a publisher of a particular song or album and its address and telephone number. This is followed by an alphabetic list titled "Publishers by Name." This directory is a useful tool and should be included in any music library or large public or academic library with an extensive music collection.—**Lynne M. Fox**

1177.   **The Christian Music Finder: Spring 1998.** [CD-ROM]. San Jose, Calif., Resource Publications, 1998. Minimum system requirements: IBM or compatible 486. CD-ROM drive. Windows 3.1. Windows 95. 4MB hard disk space. $100.00.

The *Christian Music Finder* contains listings for more than 335,000 printed and recorded music from several hundred publishers. Installation is fairly simple. The disc opens and defaults to a basic "Search or Locate Screen." There are four primary and secondary index search choices—song title, artist, composer, and collection. As one selects the index to search, it positions itself as the first column. As one types in the search box, the indicator jumps to the corresponding alphabetic point in the index being searched. The screen display defaults to showing three of the index columns. By scrolling, the last index column can be viewed. By selecting "Options," columns can be narrowed so that all index listings are visible at one time. One can also adjust the columns' width to satisfy preferences.

Searching is done in a straightforward alphabetic way. There are tabs on the screen that allow one to switch from the search screen to a screen that displays "Song Details" or to a "Publisher" screen. The "Song Details" screen is useful because it allows one to distinguish publishers of different songs, who to contact, different collection titles, different availability formats, and catalog codes. The publisher screen provides addresses, telephone numbers, and corresponding code abbreviations. There is a match count feature that is useful mainly if simple matches are checked (e.g., total match count on an artist's name or song titles that are the same).

The CD-ROM can be useful in identifying an artist or a song title as a primary search and then doing a secondary search on a song title, a collection title, or an artist. There are some searches in which using the secondary feature does not work well. The user has to be conscious of a logical order when using the primary and secondary search feature. There is a great deal of information contained on the CD-ROM version because it is a combination of the *Christian Music Directories: Recorded Music* and the *Christian Music Directories: Printed Music*.

—**Lynne M. Fox**

1178.   **Hymntune Index and Related Hymn Materials.** D. DeWitt Wasson, comp. Lanham, Md., Scarecrow, 1998. 3v. (Studies in Liturgical Musicology, no.6). $325.00/set. ISBN 0-8108-3436-7.

Unlike some other indexes and reference works on hymns, this one limits its scope to hymntunes and does not approach or index the material by hymn text. It is more up-to-date and extensive than other key reference works in this field and, therefore, becomes an indispensable tool for church musicians and scholars working with hymn materials.

One of the work's primary aims is the identification of a hymntune by knowing nothing more than its melody, and then finding out a lot more about the hymn and identifying sources of the printed music. More than 33,000 tunes used internationally by a wide variety of U.S. and European churches are indexed and are to be identified by means of the Tonic Sol-fa system. Thus, knowing a tune but not remembering the words is enough to track down its name (perhaps with the help of a musician who can turn the tune into its do-re-mi components) and then also discover something about the hymn, find a list of hymnals that contain it, and also find a list of alternate (including origin) titles under which it is known and a list of musical compositions that use the tune.

The indexed hymnals and other musical publications are listed alphabetically as well as in "key" order (relating to the indexed tunes), and lists of publishers, composers, and editors of collections are provided. There are also an index of hymntune sources and other listings by alphabet and denominations. These lists offer their own usefulness to those seeking good lists of hymn books of such wide-ranging denominations as Tanzanian Lutheran, Canadian Baptist, Swedenborgian, and Spanish Evangelical.

The compiler has kept the scope broad. He has, therefore, indexed tunes by all their slight melodic variants as well as the most commonly known one. He has also given lists of all known title variants (including foreign-language ones) in the source material in each entry. Better to reward the user with a bit too much information than to frustrate him or her with too little. Wasson has been well served by his publisher, who has printed these volumes in a spacious format, making their use a joy to eye and mind.—**George Louis Mayer**

26 Mythology, Folklore, and Popular Culture

FOLKLORE

1179.   de Ley, Gerd. **Dictionary of 1000 Dutch Proverbs.** New York, Hippocrene Books, 1998. 142p. index. $11.95pa. ISBN 0-7818-0616-X.

Do the following proverbs sound familiar? "The apple never falls far from the tree." "Let sleeping dogs lie." These and 997 other proverbs are included in the latest Hippocrene book of proverbs. Proverbs are sequentially numbered and arranged alphabetically by Dutch keyword. There is an English keyword index. Each entry gives the proverb in Dutch and English. There are no source notes and no attempt to place the proverbs in their historical use context.

It is unclear whether the proverbs are simply familiar sayings translated into Dutch or if the compiler is purporting that they originated in the Netherlands. The latter seems unlikely because many are found with documentation in comprehensive proverb collections, and they are not Dutch in origin. Libraries needing Dutch-language proverbs might want to consider this collection, but it is not an authoritative proverb collection.
—**Marlene M. Kuhl**

1180.   **Folklore: An Encyclopedia of History, Methods, and Theory.** Thomas A. Green, ed. Santa Barbara, Calif., ABC-CLIO, 1997. 2v. illus. index. $150.00/set. ISBN 0-87436-986-X.

With more than 200 signed essays on the forms (e.g., folk dance, ballad) and methods (e.g., fieldwork, anthropological approach) of folklore study, this 2-volume set covers topics ranging from the classic to the contemporary, from animism to trickster and vampire folklore. The articles, written by a host of subject specialists, are consistently well written, and each concludes with a list of references for further research. Emphasis throughout the book is on North American and European scholarship. The entries are cross-referenced, and standard folklore indexes and classifications (e.g., type and motif indexes) are cited when appropriate. A general index concludes the work.

A unique feature of this book is that it describes the history and development of North American and international educational programs in folklore. This is of special interest to students of folklore, who are sure to be among the users. Designed as a general reference for students, scholars, and general readers, the book is recommended for academic libraries, particularly those that support folklore studies, and to large public libraries. [R: VOYA, Oct 98, p. 307; LJ, 15 Feb 98, p. 133]—**Barbara Ittner**

1181.   Mack, Carol K., and Dinah Mack. **A Field Guide to Demons, Fairies, Fallen Angels, and Other Subversive Spirits.** New York, Arcade, 1998. 282p. illus. $26.95. ISBN 1-55970-477-0.

The authors—mother and daughter writers with masters in religious studies and cultural anthropology—write as if demons could be found lurking outside our back door. Their field guide helps identify, understand, dispel, and disarm 95 of these creatures. The book is a clever and readable way to present demon mythology and folklore from around the world. Some mythological creatures on the Macks' subversive spirit list came as a surprise. If one assumed that fairies and mermaids were gentle beings, discovering their true characteristics is like seeing a hummingbird transform into a vulture.

The book is organized by where one might find demons—the water, forest, mountains, desert, domicile, even outside our own head in the realm of the psyche. Each spirit gets two to four pages of description and, in most cases, a pen and ink portrait. Descriptions are a combination of lore (a story of the demon's contact with humans), information (the demon's characteristics, traits, and physical appearance), and dispelling techniques (how to trick, accommodate, elude, and escape from them). Students may be surprised that none of the dispelling techniques involve killing the demon.

The book's best writing comes in its first 33 pages and in the material that introduces each of the 6 sections. When the demons are described, the writing loses some of its well-crafted quality and intensity. The beginning and introductory material is more mysterious and personal. This book is highly recommended for high schools and colleges and would be especially useful for social science and business departments where mythology provides a rich source for theories and models.—**Pete Prunkl**

1182.   Miller, Corki, and Mary Ellen Snodgrass. **Storytellers: A Biographical Directory of 120 English-Speaking Performers Worldwide.** Jefferson, N.C., McFarland, 1998. 324p. illus. index. $55.00. ISBN 0-7864-0470-1.

Storytellers and those who work with them will welcome this volume. Profiling 120 English-speaking performers from around the world, the engaging biographical sketches present pertinent personal and professional information about each storyteller. Black-and-white photographs accompany many of the biographies, as well as lists of publications (e.g., articles, books, stories, audiocassettes, videotapes) and awards.

The sketches, arranged alphabetically, are followed by a list of storytellers by state or country (where they were born, not where they now reside), a glossary, and a bibliography. A brief subject index covering, for example, the topics or specialties of the tellers would have been helpful, but there is none. Also, as with all works of this type, readers may question the inclusion or exclusion of specific individuals, and the book contains no statement of purpose, scope, or selection criteria to clarify its coverage. Finally, some of the profiles seem skewed, as with Norma Livo, whose contribution to the preservation of Hmong culture is stressed at the expense of her leadership role in the storytelling community. Or Diane Wolkstein, whose important work with Haitian and Caribbean cultures is barely mentioned.

However, these weaknesses are minor and should not detract from the book's overall appeal. Celebrating the renaissance of the oral tradition, it is a delightful and informative work for storytellers and those who employ them, particularly public and school librarians. [R: SLJ, Nov 98, p. 45; BL, 1 Sept 98, pp. 163-165]—**Barbara Ittner**

1183.   Varty, Kenneth. **The *Roman de Renart*: A Guide to Scholarly Work.** Lanham, Md., Scarecrow, 1998. 179p. index. $39.50. ISBN 0-8108-3435-9.

The title at hand is a bibliography of manuscripts, editions, translations, adaptations, iconography, and critical studies of the *Roman de Renart*, the majority of which have been examined by Varty. Japanese and other works that he did not personally study are marked by an asterisk and followed by the sources for the information. Most entries employ the system established by Ernest Martin in the 1880s, which divides the stories into 27 branches, each identified by a Roman numeral. Except for peripheral references, other medieval beast epics and influenced works—such as Geoffrey Chaucer's "Nonnes Preestes Tale"—have been omitted because they merit separate studies. There is a list of abbreviations at the beginning of the volume.

Each of the 719 items has a brief description of the book or article following the bibliographic information and sometimes a list of reviews of the work. Especially useful are the three indexes: an alphabetic list of scholars cross-referenced to the numbers assigned to their works, an index of the branches showing articles examining each, and a subject matter index. The latter is extremely informative, allowing the user to trace the influence of Renart the Fox on Babylonian, Sumerian, Indian, and Jewish fables; to locate images of Renart in Gloucester and Bristol cathedrals, Strasbourg, and Lescar; to check cassettes, films, and even comic strips; or to look up related material to Chaucer, Chrétien de Troyes, and the bestiaries. The volume is a useful, highly scholarly work created for a specialized readership. [R: Choice, Sept 98, p. 92]—**Charlotte Lindgren**

MYTHOLOGY

1184.   Andrews, Tamra. **Legends of the Earth, Sea, and Sky: An Encyclopedia of Nature Myths.** Santa Barbara, Calif., ABC-CLIO, 1998. 322p. illus. index. $65.00. ISBN 0-87436-963-0.

Focusing on the natural, nonliving, or spirit phenomena of the cosmos (e.g., wind, meteors), this book describes general beliefs, concepts, doctrines, and divinities of ancient cultures around the world. Entries explain such names and terms as Marduk, sirens, and the cosmic sea, or discuss the mythological significance of such objects and phenomena as constellations, ships, Persia, and waterfalls. Both primary and secondary sources have been consulted for this work, and these are listed in an appendix and in the extensive bibliography. To facilitate user access, the book also contains a culture index (arranged geographically) and a detailed subject index. The information provided in these essays is of a general nature, but it is well researched and the text is clearly written. Even middle and high school students could use such a source. An attractive layout and the limited number of black-and-white photographs and line drawings that illustrate the work add to its appeal.

Academic library collections that support study of folklore and mythology will want to consider this book, as will some public and high school libraries. Storytellers and other individuals interested in folklore may find it helpful as well.—**Barbara Ittner**

1185.   Dixon-Kennedy, Mike. **European Myth and Legend: An A-Z of People and Places.** London, Blandford/ Cassell; distr., New York, Sterling Publishing, 1997. 272p. $29.95. ISBN 0-7137-2676-8.

Whether one believes that the world's myths are similar because of contacts between populations or because humans' myth-making powers are universal, these Eastern European and Northwest Asian male and female gods, devils, heroes, enemies, places, architecture, swords, and gems name our days; give us words like cold, tuberculosis, and envy; and focus Wagner's music. Although most are unfamiliar, they include some old favorites, such as Robin Hood, King Arthur, Beowulf, and the Pied Piper. Dixon-Kennedy has digested countless sources. The most often mentioned are Iceland's Snorri Sturluson's *The Prose Edda*; the *Finno-Ugric Kalevala*, a compilation of earlier material about the first farmer; and the Teutonic (German) epic *Nibelungenlied* that inspired Wagner's Siegfried, Brunhilde, Woden, a dragon, and Attila the Hun. Dwarfs, giants, enchanted swords, curses, marriages, and weather color the fates of olden people in a way that can enrich the reader.

This book presents an alphabetic list of full elucidations of 50 Iron Age stories and extensive coverage of common and proper nouns with shorter related subjects. Sometimes the author notes parallels with other mythologies—such as Hiuki and Bil who carry water like Jack and Jill. [R: RBB, 15 Jan 98, p. 858]

—**Robert T. Anderson**

1186.   Wilkinson, Philip. **Illustrated Dictionary of Mythology: Heroes, Heroines, Gods, and Goddesses from Around the World.** New York, DK Publishing, 1998. 128p. illus. index. $24.95. ISBN 0-7894-3413-X.

This richly illustrated volume attempts to present the major and some of the minor deities and related myths from around the world. More than one-half of the material relates to the ancient Near East, including ancient Egypt and the classical world, with the rest providing information about India, China, Japan, the Native peoples of the Americas, Africa, Australasia, and Oceania. The volume seeks to present its material through major themes common to different peoples, including narratives and deities related to the creation of the universe, battles of the gods, destruction of the cosmos (especially through floods), trickster gods, and moving to the demi-gods/super humans.

This dictionary presents little more than the basics for any topic. Although it is supposed to appeal to readers of all ages, the print is rather small for younger readers and the content is rather shallow for the young adult. Given its specific content, the volume would have benefited greatly from a basic bibliography, something to which the interested reader could turn to for further reading. Unfortunately, not everything presented is accurate (e.g., an illustration on the opening page is the Egyptian god Thoth (later so identified) but titled here Seshat). In addition, the promise of the book jacket to reveal why Kronos ate his children is never answered in the text. The volume is thus not for every library, but it can be recommended for its lavish illustrations, many not commonly seen.

—**Susan Tower Hollis**

POPULAR CULTURE

1187.   Gaslin, Glenn, and Rick Porter. **The Complete Cross-Referenced Guide to the Baby Buster Generation's Collective Unconscious.** New York, Berkley, 1998. 248p. illus. $14.00pa. ISBN 1-57297-335-8.

This book of whimsical blurbs was written for people who grew up in the United States in the 1980s. It is an A through Z listing of definitions for anything that was popular during this period, from television personalities to political figures to lingo that is associated exclusively with this era. The "What Is Going to Have to Pass as an Introduction" warns readers that there really is no serious point to the book. It is, however, an entertaining source of memories and laughs.

The entries are humorous, with a somewhat one-sided view (which is sure to match the views of readers) and clever cross-references designed to be reminiscent of "channel surfing." Items include people and things most have forgotten since that time, such as erasable ink pens, gremlins, and Oliver North. The book is illustrated with occasional photographs, and "great moments" and classic movie lines enrich the pages. At the end of the guide is an unnecessary but amusing recipe for a typical 1980s high school movie.—**Felicity Tucker**

1188.   Hart-Davis, Adam. **Thunder, Flush, and Thomas Crapper: An Encycloopedia.** North Pomfret, Vt., Trafalgar Square, 1997. 162p. illus. index. $11.95. ISBN 1-57076-081-0.

There is a well-known story about a young girl whose school librarian once gave her a book to read on the subject of penguins. When the girl returned the book, the librarian asked what she had thought of it. "Well," she said, "It told me rather more about penguins than I really wanted to know." The analogy to the present situation is striking. Put simply, this is an encyclopedic treatment of all facets of the universal process of elimination, with special emphases on the receptacles used for such purposes throughout history, and the subsequent treatment of products created (or at least eliminated) in the act.

The "encycloopedia" is arranged alphabetically, listing as many toilet-related factoids and vignettes as seem to the author to pertain to his treatment. Along the way are anecdotes, trivia, and interesting facts about . . . well, you know. And pictures, yet! A generous helping of photographs, woodcuts, and line drawings accompany the entries, amounting to a bowlful of visual renderings of things one would probably prefer not to read about at all.

At no further charge, you get a wealth of what the author calls, charmingly, "lavatorial language!" There are, for example, over a dozen alternative terms for the "pot," as many more for the act of visiting the "smallest room," and plenty of euphemisms for what happens therein. Sure, everybody does it, but a whole book about it?

Still, for those consumed with curiosity about how people did their business in castles like Camelot, or how such things are managed in space, have we got a book for you! To be fair, author Hart-Davis writes cleverly and well, attacking his subject with ferocious British wit. By the way, there really was a Thomas Crapper (1836-1910), who is credited with being the inventor of the modern flush toilet. One is tempted to call this book a "solid waste," but let's be charitable and say that, although an inessential purchase, it may still amuse and instruct readerships in libraries (those flush with discretionary funds).—**Bruce A. Shuman**

1189.   **Holiday Symbols 1998.** Sue Ellen Thompson, ed. Detroit, Omnigraphics, 1998. 558p. index. $55.00. ISBN 0-7808-0072-9.

This useful and timeless reference book explains the origins and exact meanings of more than 750 holiday symbols associated with 174 holidays. The coverage is broad and includes religious, calendar, national, and ancient holidays with a good proportion of foreign holidays. Each entry begins with a brief essay on the origins of the holiday, then continues with a discussion of the symbols and folklore associated with the holiday. For example, the entry on the Fourth of July begins with a two-page history describing when it was first celebrated (Philadelphia, 1777) and when it became an official holiday (1941). Also described is the African American July 4th called Juneteenth and Thomas Jefferson's death on July 4th. The American flag, eagle, fireworks, Liberty Bell, parades, picnics, Uncle Sam, and "Yankee Doodle" are symbols that are analyzed with the holiday. The entry ends with a short bibliography of books with more information on the Fourth of July.

The two indexes make the book especially easy to use. The general index lists all religions, countries, names, and other significant terms found in the text. Symbols are found through the symbol list. Sturdily bound on high-quality paper, *Holiday Symbols 1998* will be a working reference source for years. [R: RUSQ, Summer 98, p. 363; C&RL, Jan 98, p. 37]—**Carol D. Henry**

1190.   **NTC's Dictionary of the USA.** By George Kurian. Lincolnwood, Ill., National Textbook, 1998. 237p. illus. $16.95. ISBN 0-8442-5862-8.

Guides to popular culture are not common, probably because it is so difficult to define and encompass the field. Recent efforts have included *The Dictionary of Cultural Literacy* (see ARBA 94, entry 305) and *The New York Public Library Book of Popular Americana* (see ARBA 95, entry 1334). This newest foray into the field by NTC, a publisher of educational textbooks and foreign-language dictionaries, does not succeed too well. Aimed at tourists, immigrants, and students of American English and culture, it purports to give "a good sampling of significant people, places, things, and ideas that signify the USA," with alphabetically arranged entries describing "musical forms, holidays, national parks, food, political and social movements, and historical events." In the limited space available, this is too tall an order to fill. Definitions may leave the reader more confused than enlightened; for example, *sourdough* is defined as "a prospector during the gold rush," without explaining that the word originated from the type of bread typically used by these prospectors. Omissions are inevitable in all dictionaries, but some are unacceptable; the entry for *Thomas Edison* states he was a prolific inventor and lists his major inventions, except for the one considered most notable by both himself and historians—the phonograph. Although this work's appearance, ease of use, cross-referencing, and black-and-white photographs are all good, the overall usefulness of this volume is not high because the information is already available in other common reference books.—**Larry Lobel**

1191.   Schwartz, Richard A. **Cold War Culture: Media and the Arts, 1945-1990.** New York, Facts on File, 1998. 376p. illus. index. (Cold War America). $55.00. ISBN 0-8160-3104-5.

This dictionary-format volume describes the people, art, literature, movies, and television programs that influenced U.S. culture during the Cold War years. Several hundred alphabetic entries are included on a wide range of popular culture topics, such as James Bond, J. Edgar Hoover, *Catch-22*, Ayn Rand, G. I. Joe, and *Star Wars*. The author relates each entry to its Cold War context, explaining how the subject reflects or responds to the culture. The length of entries varies from fewer than 50 words to nearly 1,500 words, with a typical entry being about 250 words. Entries are primarily descriptive. Although some analysis is offered, such brief entries limit the depth to which any single topic can be evaluated. However, topics have been carefully selected, and entries are well written. A strength of this volume is to cite obscure novels and films that underscore the attitudes and tensions of the age. These are successfully cross-referenced through such entries as "television westerns," "spy films," and "apocalyptic novels" through which the reader is directed to the more specific entries. Throughout the volume, emphasis is placed on film and literature subjects rather than music and the visual arts. This publication is a good summary of the popular culture of the period and will be appropriate for larger research collections. [R: Choice, July/Aug 98, p. 1838]—**Scott Seaman**

1192.   Somers, Paul P., Jr. **Editorial Cartooning and Caricature: A Reference Guide.** Westport, Conn., Greenwood Press, 1998. 205p. index. (American Popular Culture). $69.50. ISBN 0-313-22150-2.

As is appropriate for a volume of a series on American popular culture, the scope of this work is restricted to the United States. Somers gives the year 1747 as the beginning date for the editorial cartoon as an intellectual form. The cartoons under consideration focus on politicians and issues; thus, the work represents to some degree the "politically incorrect" historiography of the nation as seen through the caricaturist's pen. The text consists of a set of 5 bibliographic essays, plus 5 appendixes and an index. Each chapter has its own endnotes and an extensive list of works cited.

Chapters 1 through 4 give a historical background, review the work of other historians and critics (with 2 pages devoted to works of international scope featuring Americans), present anthologies and reprints of cartoons, and consider reference works and periodicals. Chapter 5, the only chapter organized with entries rather than continuous text, discusses research collections in the Library of Congress, the Cartoon Research Library at Ohio State University, the Archives of American Art, and other collections arranged by state. The appendixes (all of them selective) contain a chronology (which from 1922 on consists principally of a list of Pulitzer Prize winners) and bibliographies of relevant "how-to" books, theses and dissertations, historical periodicals, and single-artist anthologies. The index has a few topical entries, but contains mostly names. Within each chapter, subheadings are provided; the referencing capability of the work would be enhanced greatly if these were listed in the contents page. The first four chapters require the user to peruse the text more than is customary for finding information in a reference work. However, Somers's narrative style is engaging and entertaining, and for this reason library selectors may wish to consider placing the book in a circulating collection. Some users might wish the word "American" had been included in the title. Prospective acquirers should note that, with the exception of the frontispiece (a reproduction of Benjamin Franklin's snake urging the states to "Join or die"), this work contains no illustrations. [R: Choice, Sept 98, p. 102]—**Ian Fairclough**

1193. Thody, Philip. **Don't Do It: A Dictionary of the Forbidden.** New York, St. Martin's Press, 1997. 339p. $24.95. ISBN 0-312-17373-3.

Every society has established taboos that regulate what members cannot or should not say, do, wear, eat, act like, or be. The fascinating thing is that each society's list of forbidden practices differs from those of all others, such prohibitions being variously ascribed to God, a shared and common decency, or political correctness. Thody, a British professor of languages, originally planned to call this book *Taboos: A Dictionary Guide to the Forbidden* but changed his mind when he found out that not everyone understood the meaning of "taboo." The author then labors toward a working definition and launches into his list, divided (somewhat arbitrarily) into 5 sections as follows: "Actions," "Nourishment," "Words and Themes," "Ideas, Books, and Pictures," and "Signs." Even though the divisions do impose structure on the material presented, the lines between them are often blurred: Some terms are found in two or more segments, but only because they belong in both places. The work concludes with a thematic list of topics, an index, a select list of names, and a select bibliography.

What seems most staggering is the sheer number of present-day prohibitions and taboos on this planet and the spectrum of legal and social penalties for ignoring such societal imperatives. Thody has an obvious axe to grind. He seeks a world where taboos no longer exist, but he will settle, for now, for a great reduction in their number. His treatment is a delightful mix of historical research, contemporary observations, and witty (sometimes salacious) anecdotes. The historical perspective of many things unsaid or "not done" in polite society is interesting because most people quickly learned as children what not to do in public, but few really understand why not to do it or how ancestors came to feel that way about such practices. Incest aside, there are no universal taboos. Belching after meals, for example, engenders reactions that vary significantly with place and circumstances.

This work is not intended for anthropologists or sociologists. It presents material intelligible to the layperson in witty and often loving detail (even if it lacks pictorial accompaniment) and thus may be enjoyed either as a good read or consulted for specific nuggets of reference information. Yet be advised: Thody never shrinks from locker-room language or from delving into subjects that may make some readers uncomfortable due to frank and forthright treatment. *Don't Do It* is enthusiastically recommended, all the same, for reference collections serving adult and broad-minded audiences. [R: BL, 15 May 98, pp. 1656, 1658]—**Bruce A. Shuman**

1194. **World Holiday, Festival, and Calendar Books: An Annotated Bibliography of More Than 1,000 Books....** Tanya Gulevich, ed. Detroit, Omnigraphics, 1997. 477p. index. $55.00. ISBN 0-7808-0073-7.

This neat, orderly compendium catalogs accessible English-language sources on the subjects of calendars and a wide variety of festivals and holidays. Coverage is ambitious—four inclusive chapters on world, regional, ethnic, and religious holidays, calendars, and time-reckoning systems. The book opens with an adequate table of contents and an informative introduction, which is divided into succinct statements of purpose, scope, coverage, organization, content, format, spellings and forms, and special features. Numbered entries, composed in clear typefaces, present title, author or editor, illustrator, publisher, date, and textual features. Following a brief description of contents are Dewey Decimal, Library of Congress, and ISBN data. Brief appendixes list 39 periodicals, 18 associations, and 12 Websites. Comprehensive indexing by author, title, and subject includes subindexing by country. The editor offers excellent access to topics; for example, works on folk art, home life and rituals, neopaganism, Women's Equality Day, and the Yanggona Ceremony of Fiji.

Among the 1,000 works cited are 175 children's books, 100 scholarly titles, 50 general reference works, and 40 religious works. Coverage suggests a careful examination of holidays and festivals coupled with sensitivity to issues of gender, religion, and ethnic background. The editor appears to overreach by offering associations and Websites, which are too few to be comprehensive. Overall, the price is a reasonable exchange for timely, useful data. This work belongs on the shelves of school, college, and community libraries as well as those of newspapers and other media, civic planning boards, researchers, and scholars. [R: LJ, Aug 98, p. 80; Choice, Oct 98, p. 286]—**Mary Ellen Snodgrass**

27 Performing Arts

GENERAL WORKS

Biography

1195. **Contemporary Theatre, Film, and Television, Volume 17: A Biographical Guide....** Kathleen J. Edgar, Joshua Kondek, and Pam Zuber, eds. Detroit, Gale, 1998. 539p. index. $146.00. ISBN 0-7876-1153-0. ISSN 0749-064X.

Executed in Gale's typical format, this work provides basic biographical information as well as performing credits and awards for performers, directors, writers, composers, and others involved in theater, film, and television. Although this volume covers 400 people, the entire series (17 editions of *Who's Who in the Theatre* [Gale, 1981], 17 volumes of *Contemporary Theatre, Film, and Television*, and *Who Was Who in the Theatre* [Gale, 1978]) treats more than 8,000 names, going back to 1912. Gale provides a cumulative index to all 35 books in this volume. *Contemporary Theatre, Film, and Television* covers both the living and the dead, but emphasis is on those whose careers are currently active. Some entries revise and update information found in previous volumes. Entries follow a standard format and focus on careers. Credits are divided by type of medium and type of work. They list the part played (for actors), the name of the piece, and the date. Entries also provide a list of honors won, birth, marriage, and education details, alternative names as appropriate, and memberships in professional organizations. A bibliography includes both works by and works about the individual. Most of the biographical sources are articles taken from popular periodicals. The entries vary greatly in length. Readers should note that entries that end with an asterisk are taken from secondary sources only and have not been checked by the subject of the biography. The majority of entries appear to be of this type. A few obituaries are included. They present a short narrative summary of the deceased's career as well as a list of published obituaries. This volume will be most helpful to reference librarians and their patrons for its extensive list of credits. It should be used in conjunction with the other volumes in the series and with other sources such as *Who's Who in America* (52d ed.; Marquis Who's Who, 1997) and *Current Biography* (H. W. Wilson, 1997) for the most comprehensive information.—**Linda Keir Simons**

1196. Smith, Ronald L. **Comedy Stars at 78 RPM: Biographies and Discographies of 89 American and British Recording Artists, 1896-1946.** Jefferson, N.C., McFarland, 1998. 225p. illus. index. $45.00. ISBN 0-7864-0462-0.

From the end of the nineteenth century to the middle of the twentieth century, home entertainment often consisted of listening to a cylinder or disk recording, and for purposes of this reference, either format is considered a 78 rpm. Aside from Enrico Caruso and other classical artists, people may think of countless dance bands of the era, but there was also available much humor performed by individuals or comedy teams. Many of these humorous recordings were simply a three-minute, or less, abbreviation of a vaudeville routine.

Nearly 90 of the British and American artists who recorded from 1906 to 1946 are included in this collection of short biographies and discographies. The arrangement is alphabetic, beginning with Abbott and Costello and ending with Nat C. Wills. Some of these artists eventually became regulars on radio, and a few even survived into the television era. Their legacy extends from rare and scratchy records that were recorded acoustically to the more advanced electrical recordings that became available on Victor, Decca, Columbia, and other labels from the late 1920s on. Some of these artists are known to collectors yet are not generally recognizable to modern scholars. Billy Murray, for instance, recorded more than 1,000 singles, but he remains a more or less forgotten comedian. Others, although less prolific on records, remain better known: Fanny Brice, Burns and Allen, Spike Jones, and Mae West are examples.

Reading the bio-discography entries provides extensive insight into the type of humor then popular, particularly ethnic humor. Smith is knowledgeably adept at giving a fair evaluation of what superficially may seem to be self-depreciating humor that often targeted recent immigrant groups, southerners, and other ethnic groups. The earlier artists created much of their own material, which if it was good, was often repeated and revised by later comics. So alive is the author's handling of the material that even if the reader has never actually heard any of these recordings, the sense of the original material is there, and some social insight is gained into otherwise dated performances. Each biographical entry is followed by a list of at least some of the audio material—definitely not every recording made by each artist—including LP compilations. When CD releases are available, the author has listed those sources also. Broadway, film, and television appearances are listed separately, followed by books about the artists. This work should be in the collection of major libraries and in the home libraries of many record collectors. [R: LJ, 1 Oct 98, p. 78]—**Louis G. Zelenka**

Directories

1197.   **Peterson's Professional Degree Programs in the Visual & Performing Arts.** 4th ed. Princeton, N.J., Peterson's Guides, 1998. 587p. index. $24.95pa. ISBN 1-56079-854-8. ISSN 1073-2020.

Designed for high school students, their parents, and counselors, this guide briefly describes professional degree programs in art, dance, music, and theater in the United States and Canada. Readers should realize that although the book's appendix lists colleges that offer liberal arts degree programs in the arts, the main body of the book describes only professional programs. These programs are designed to prepare students for performance, composing, or studio art occupations. The book is arranged by discipline (art, dance, music, and theater) and then alphabetically by college. As with most books of this type, the information given in each profile is brief—types of degrees awarded, information about the faculty, details of expenses and financial aid, application procedures, and names and addresses of contacts. Some entries have an additional section labeled "More About the College," which expands on the brief description and provides a much more detailed view of the school. Unfortunately, only a few programs are described. Although Peterson's provides a clear explanation of the features in each profile, the editors do not explain why some entries are expanded, and the reader is left with the suspicion that schools may have paid for the additional information. A table at the beginning of the volume lists schools by state with a summary of professional degrees granted, enrollment figures, costs, and page numbers of their profiles. This feature enables one to locate programs geographically. This book should be of use as a starting point for students looking for a college, university, or conservatory program leading to a career in the fine or performing arts. It should certainly be followed up by study of school catalogs and campus visits.

—**Linda Keir Simons**

1198.   Sheward, David. **The Big Book of Show Business Awards.** New York, Billboard Books/Watson-Guptill, 1997. 619p. illus. index. $21.95pa. ISBN 0-8230-7630-X.

Sheward has compiled an entertaining, timely, and useful list of major (mostly national) awards in the fields of cinema, music, television, and theater. Although much of the information in this work is by no means unique to either print—see, for example, Don Franks's *Entertainment Awards: A Music, Cinema, Theatre and Broadcasting Reference, 1928 Through 1993* (see ARBA 97, entry 1099)—or to the online domain, Sheward's work does provide a convenient one-stop source that is fairly broad in its coverage. A complete listing of 22 major awards from their beginning to the present are given here. Inclusion of various, lesser-known critic's awards—those of the National Society of Film Critics and the New York Drama Critics Circle, for instance—is particularly useful. Organization of the work is chronological by entertainment type. In addition to a basic list of award winners, Sheward also provides informative and entertaining tidbits of behind-the-scenes information and insights concerning each year's award presentations and award winners. There is a short appendix of "additional facts," such as the winners of the most awards, winners of multiple awards in a single year, and winners of awards in multiple categories, that seems like an authorial afterthought. An adequate index of major award recipients is provided. This work will be a useful addition to general reference collections or the home libraries of devoted entertainment enthusiasts. [R: RBB, 1 May 98, pp. 1534-1536]—**Gary Handman**

Handbooks and Yearbooks

1199.　**Recording Industry Sourcebook.** 8th ed. Emeryville, Calif., Cardinal Business Media, Inc., 1997. 504p. index. $79.95 spiralbound. ISBN 0-918371-12-0.

As an all-purpose single-volume compendium, the *Sourcebook* has much to recommend it. Covering the gamut of needs of contemporary and pop musicians, it provides nationwide directory listings (and a few international listings) in a dozen key areas. Of course most of the book is given over to recording studios and engineering, whereas the rest is taken up by contacts for the business side of the music industry (labels, artist management, public relations, attorneys, and others), equipment and sound sales and rentals, compact disc and cassette manufacturing, and merchandising. Rounding things out is a brief, highly selective section of travel and support services. Because it is a directory, it is enumerative rather than evaluative, providing listings only, with no judgment of quality. A unique aspect is the "artist directory," an alphabetic list of artists followed by the names of their label and management.

Produced for the market of industry professionals (and not libraries), it carries the detestable spiral binding. It also carries a lot of advertising. Analogous (but not comparable) to the classically oriented *Musical America*, the *Sourcebook* features a useful arrangement complemented by a clear table of contents. As a trade annual for a fast-moving industry, this is a title libraries will want to keep up-to-date.—**Megan S. Farrell**

DANCE

1200.　**Dance on Camera: A Guide to Dance Films and Videos.** Louise Spain, ed. Lanham, Md., Scarecrow, 1998. 238p. illus. index. $65.00. ISBN 0-8108-3303-4.

A pricey reference guide to films and videos that feature dance, this volume compiles a source list from catalogs, flyers, two encyclopedias of film, and two reference works on musicals and dance. Opening with a brief foreword by dancer Jacques D'Amboise, the introductory matter sets a professional tone and establishes parameters. Following acknowledgments are an introduction and five thoughtful essays on the alliance of dance and film. The editor provides an alphabetized listing of films and videos by title, followed by date, length, color or black-and-white, format, distribution, producer, director, choreographer, composer, category, awards, and a brief description. Categories range from ballet and modern to documentary portrait, butoh, religious/ritual, martial arts, experimental, dance therapy, notation, women, social, anthropological, hula, festival, cinedance, Native American, dance history, folk, animation, African American, modern, ballroom, instructional, comedy, choreography, musical, feature, collaboration, children, Europe, United States, flamenco, Africa, break dance, gesture, belly dance, and dance drama. A series of 21 grainy black-and-white photographs precedes extensive indexing of awards, categories, choreographers, composers, dancers, dance companies, directors, excerpts, and series. The work concludes with a directory of distributors and two lists of domestic and international resources. The last list covers Europe, North America, and Australia with two entries for Israel and one for Argentina, but none from Central America or Asia.

Overall, the work is tastefully done and makes a serious effort to examine the subject. The cover is engaging; typefaces are clear, and the layout uncluttered. As a ready source of information, the compendium does what it sets out to do with a minimum of fuss. [R: BL, July 98, p. 1909; Choice, Oct 98, pp. 288-289]

—**Mary Ellen Snodgrass**

1201.   **International Dictionary of Modern Dance.** Taryn Benbow-Pfalzgraf and Glynis Benbow-Niemier, eds. Detroit, St. James Press, 1998. 891p. illus. index. $160.00. ISBN 1-55862-359-0.

Writing in the preface to this volume, Don McDonagh traces the development of modern dance from the term's first usage in the 1920s to its present position as a "liberated form of serious dance expression in each country that has been exposed to it." Following this is a chronological listing or timeline of significant people and events in the development of the genre. The body of the volume comprises 425 lengthy signed entries that focus on artists, works, companies, periods, dance production areas, and performances and schools of modern dance. A typical entry for an artist will include biographical information; roles and works listed chronologically; publications, films, and videotapes; and a descriptive and critical summary of the subject's contributions and impact. Other entries are covered with equally comprehensive appropriate data. More than 200 black-and-white photographs augment the text. A bibliography, nationality index, and subject index complete the reference. Noteworthy about this volume are its considerable scope, comprehensiveness of information, and currency in supplying useful information for students in dance and theater programs of all levels. This reference work will be a vital addition to any library of the performing arts. [R: BL, 15 Oct 98, pp. 441-442; LJ, 1 Nov 98, p. 72]

—**Jackson Kesler**

1202.   **International Encyclopedia of Dance.** Selma Jeanne Cohen and others, eds. New York, Oxford University Press, 1998. 6v. illus. index. $1250.00/set. ISBN 0-19-509462-X.

This work is both encyclopedic and international because it includes contributors from many countries writing articles on all aspects of world dance. Many articles detail aspects of Western European and American dance traditions, reflecting the interest by scholars and critics in these topics. The *International Encyclopedia of Dance* (IED) contains numerous articles on dance traditions of individual countries worldwide, usually broken down into individual articles on such topics as folk or indigenous traditions, theater dance, and the ballet and modern dance tradition of the country. It is noteworthy that the encyclopedia includes articles on the dance of nations in the former Soviet Union.

The editors have also included articles of theoretical or methodological interest, including dance methodology, Orientalism, and research and publication. Other articles discuss individual choreographers, producers, dancers, specific dance techniques, notation systems, musical forms, and historical and regional dances. The scope permits inclusion of dance forms, such as ice dancing, dance in sports (e.g., cheerleading, aerobic dance), and some of the individual proponents of these activities. Information and assessments of individuals are often included in articles on the dance form in which they made their greatest contributions. The roster of contributors is a list of dance scholars and critics active from the 1970s to the mid-1990s.

Because articles are written by many subject specialists, it is a pleasure to recognize individual styles coming through in the many readable, yet scholarly voices. Often a topic is treated in several articles written by different people; thus, one receives different emphases and more information overall than if a topic were restricted to only one article. The work makes use of recent scholarship; bibliographic entries with publication dates of 1996 are not rare. To fully take advantage of main and peripheral treatment of dancers, choreographers, and dance forms, it is a necessity to consult the thorough index. The IED is profusely illustrated with both familiar and rarely seen photographs and drawings. Like the *New Grove Dictionary of Music and Musicians* (Grove Dictionaries, 1995), the *International Encyclopedia of Dance* will serve as a resource for many years to come. This long-awaited work is highly recommended for academic libraries and larger public libraries with a clientele interested in all aspects of dance. It is well worth the price. [R: Choice, July/Aug 98, p. 1830]—**Lizbeth Langston**

1203.   Knowles, Mark. **The Tap Dance Dictionary.** Jefferson, N.C., McFarland, 1998. 254p. $45.00. ISBN 0-7864-0352-7.

The rich and varied language of tap dancing is documented here, including a record of steps and variations in terminology used. Because of the many variations in terms used by different performers, teachers, and choreographers, numerous cross-references lead to the name used for a single step. Rhythmic variations are noted.

A section describing the notation used for steps prefaces the dictionary. Each step entry contains the movements, direction, and rhythm (how it is counted, involved). Others offer explanations for frequently used terms in tap. Entries vary in length from one line to several pages, and a bibliography lists sources for further study.

Although historical references are included, this dictionary basically delineates the language of a particular art form. As such, it is a useful tool and a valuable source of information about a segment of U.S. history. [R: BL, 15 Oct 98, p. 445]—**Anita Zutis**

1204.   Ryman, Rhonda. **Dictionary of Classical Ballet Terminology.** 2d ed. London, Royal Academy of Dancing; distr., Hightstown, N.J., Princeton Book, 1997. 92p. $16.95pa. ISBN 0-9524848-0-3.

A modest, reasonably priced, and pleasantly scaled dictionary of dance terminology, this volume records current usage of the world's largest examining and teaching body, whose method dominates dance in more than 60 countries. The book opens with a foreword, two prefaces, a positioning model, and acknowledgments. A detailed introduction explains each segment of an entry and appends a workable list of 20 abbreviations and phonetic models. Entries contain either single-word or composite terms along with international and simplified pronunciations, part of speech, number, gender, meaning, and definition or description of position or action. Ryman, a student of the Royal Academy of Dancing and associate professor of dance, includes variations and equivalent terms from the Cecchetti and Vaganova systems.

Although the typeface is small and indentations are omitted, each entry is succinct and well ordered. The user's comprehension demands experience in the world of dance; for example, explanation of *grande pirouette* requires understanding of *en dehors, working leg, en l'air, 2d position,* and *petit sauté.* Coverage of 958 moves and poses is ample for basic needs and excludes the less common movements, such as *pas de poisson* and *en boité.* Frequent cross-referencing allies alternate phrasing with single conceptions. In addition to the basic turns, leaps, attitudes, partnering, and combinations are given simple practice and staging terms, including *barre, stage right, turn-out, position of the foot,* and *downstage.* The complexity of diction reduces the applicability of this work for simple reference libraries but assures the skilled dancer, teacher, choreographer, and media critic a handy reference for almost any occasion.—**Mary Ellen Snodgrass**

FILM, TELEVISION, AND VIDEO

Bibliography

1205.   McCallum, Lawrence. **Italian Horror Films of the 1960s: A Critical Catalog of 62 Chillers.** Jefferson, N.C., McFarland, 1998. 280p. illus. index. $45.00. ISBN 0-7864-0435-3.

This volume introduces 62 Italian horror films in the era when big screen spectacles and fantasy films were on the decline. During the 1960s the filmmakers developed their unique style of horror employing a wide variety of subject matter. Mario Bava enticed viewers by exploring the fear of the unknown, rooted in dark fantasies that came alive on lonely nights in such films as *The Evil Eye* (1964) and *Blood and Black Lace* (1965). Director Antonio Margheriti became known for his tales of vengeance that reached from beyond the grave in *Castle of Blood* (1964) and *The Long Hair of Death* (1964). The juxtaposition of horror and humor in Italian chillers of the 1960s appealed to viewers. The subjects ranged from the comic strip flavor of *The Wild, Wild Planet* (1966) to the surrealistic mixture of horror and social commentary of *Spirits of the Dead* (1969). Such endeavors gained international popularity among horror fans most notably because over the span of several decades this genre practically ceased to exist in Italy.

This work encompasses the entire spectrum of Italian horror productions of the 1960s, including the all-time classic of U.S. audiences *Black Sunday* (1961) with Barbara Steele. Each entry provides plot synopses and information on the film's personnel. The works are arranged alphabetically by title—English first then Italian. An appendix lists them chronologically. A list of abbreviations explains the credits and distributors. Each entry indicates studio, running time, year of release, and most of the works on which the film is based. These standard data are followed by a lengthy essay that includes plot synopsis, with critical commentary and behind the scenes information. Complementing the text are black-and-white stills, window and lobby cards, and press book art. Following the appendix is a short bibliography that includes a separate list of a few magazines and an index. *Italian Horror Films of the 1960s* is recommended for those interested in cinema and horror film.

—**Magda Želinská-Ferl**

1206.   Reis, Brian. **Australian Film: A Bibliography.** Herndon, Va., Mansell/Cassell, 1997. 622p. index. $125.00. ISBN 0-7021-2315-1.

With a history of involvement in motion pictures that extends back to the 1890s, Australia first established a significant place in motion picture history when a short film was made of the running of the 1896 Melbourne Cup. In 1906, the story of the Kelly Gang won acclaim as the world's first feature-length narrative film. A thriving business enterprise during the early part of the twentieth century, the Australian film industry virtually ceased in the 1950s and 1960s as the result of foreign dominance of distribution as well as competition from wealthy Hollywood studios. Thanks to the rise of governmental support in the 1970s, a vital film industry now exists in the Australia of the 1990s.

Reis's *Australian Film: A Bibliography* provides easy access to at least a substantial part of the published writing about Australia's involvement with motion pictures. A successful attempt is made to present all aspects of Australian film considered as art, industry, and sociological phenomenon. Part 1 of this easy-to-use reference book focuses on subjects—reference works, film periodicals, and book reviews; film archives and libraries; film societies, film festivals, and exhibitions; film awards, polls, and surveys; avant-garde, experimental, underground, and amateur film; super-8 mm film; literature and film; aborigines and film; multiculturalism and film; history and film; and women and film. Part 2 lists biographies and criticisms of "Film People," and part 3 provides information on film criticism and reviews. Of great help are numerous descriptive annotations throughout as well as the concluding author, book, and title indexes. An encyclopedic volume containing massive information about Australia's writing on the film industry, this bibliography is a must for scholars as well as enthusiasts who are interested in any aspect of Australian film culture.—**Colby H. Kullman**

Bio-bibliography

1207.   Cohen, Allen, and Harry Lawton. **John Huston: A Guide to References and Resources.** New York, G. K. Hall/Simon & Schuster Macmillan, 1997. 827p. index. (A Reference Publication in Film). $85.00. ISBN 0-8161-1619-9.

Although John Huston has long been considered one of the American film masters, it is only now that G. K. Hall's series on film references and resources has featured his works. However, the long wait has been worth it, and we can only hope that future volumes in this series are as well done as this. The authors depart from the standard series format by covering their subject's life and works in total, rather than just his directorial career. Cohen and Lawton open with a critical life and work survey of Huston, followed by an excellent filmography (including plot synopses) of Huston's entire film career, an annotated bibliography, an unannotated collection of articles and reviews of all of Huston's films (more than 200 pages of single-spaced citations), obituaries, studio histories, awards and honors, screenplays in collections, theatrical history, archival sources, Internet and CD-ROM resources, and more. Reviews and citations are garnered from the world press, including newspapers, magazines, and film journals, and the authors appear to be as comprehensive as humanly possible. The only minor complaints one might have are with the film availability chapter, which will possibly date too quickly to be useful; the index, which could be more thorough; and no reference to the Internet Movie Database (www.imdb.com), one of the most popular film guides on the World Wide Web.

No other bio-bibliography of Huston comes close to the quality and comprehensiveness of Cohen and Lawton's, which more than complements *Perspectives on John Huston* (G. K. Hall, 1994) and *Reflections in a Male Eye: John Huston and the American Experience* (Smithsonian Institution Press, 1993). This work is essential for all film collections. [R: Choice, July/Aug 98, p. 1828]—**Anthony J. Adam**

1208.   Malloy, Mike. **Lee Van Cleef: A Bibliographical, Film, and Television Reference.** Jefferson, N.C., McFarland, 1998. 196p. illus. index. $35.00. ISBN 0-7864-0437-X.

This is the work of a fan. Actor Lee Van Cleef is not a household name, although one might recognize his face. More often cast as a villain in westerns thanks to his menacing looks, he made his debut in *High Noon*. He went on to be featured in *Gunfight at the O.K. Corral*, *The Man Who Shot Liberty Valance*, and *How the West Was Won*. When the western died out in the United States, "Spaghetti western" director Sergio Leone brought Van Cleef to Europe to co-star with Clint Eastwood in *For a Few Dollars More*, and later in *The Good, the Bad and the Ugly*. Spaghetti westerns revived his career, and he succeeded Eastwood, who had returned to Hollywood, as the most popular star of that genre.

The book is presented in 3 parts: "The Life of Lee Van Cleef," "The Films," and "Television Work." The filmography makes up the major portion and is alphabetic by most common English title—a good choice considering his oeuvre. Full credits include release date, genre, financing, running time, cast, plot synopsis, and Van Cleef's role. The television section includes full episode information on his short-lived 1984 martial arts series called *The Master*, and all of his television credits, from *Adventures of Rin Tin Tin* to *Zorro*.

An appendix provides a chronological list of the films. The book is illustrated with film stills. This is a very thorough work, but too specialized for general collections. It will be of primary value to film and performing arts collections.—**Ruth A. Carr**

Biography

1209.   Liebman, Roy. **From Silents to Sound: A Biographical Encyclopedia of Performers Who Made the Transition to Talking Pictures.** Jefferson, N.C., McFarland, 1998. 309p. index. $65.00. ISBN 0-7864-0382-9.

The 1929 release of *The Jazz Singer* marked an epochal time in the motion picture industry. Virtually overnight, actors and actresses who had thrilled audiences were faced with a new threat. It was often hidden in a vase, suspended from a ceiling, or carefully camouflaged in a plant. It was a microphone, and it killed more careers in Hollywood than any bad review, lurid scandal, or messy divorce ever could. A relative handful of silent picture stars successfully made the transition to sound, but this carefully researched book serves as a final salute to such actors as Edmund Cobb, Phyllis Haver, and Lucien Littlefield. For every Charlie Chaplin, Reginald Denny, and W. C. Fields, there was a Juanita Hansen, Alice Joyce, and Olive Carey. Many of those who failed to make the transition had depended on their looks or their physical abilities to carry them through a film; when it came time to talk, they just didn't have the talent to express what they had been able to convey in a glance or a pratfall.

Liebman has combed the archival materials to produce this highly entertaining—and yet, often melancholy look—at those stars who were present at the birth of motion pictures and who helped to make them the entertainment choice of the world. By 1929, many of the silent movie stars were approaching middle age, and as is the case today, "youth" was prized over talent. Liebman limited his inclusions to those stars who had made three or more silent films and at least three "talkies." He includes vital statistics as well as reviews of films when available. This is a valuable addition to any film library because it includes biographical information not found in other resources. Large public libraries will want to consider it as well because of its well-written, educational, and eminently readable look at the turbulent history of an industry that affects us all. [R: Choice, July/Aug 98, p. 1831]

—**Joseph L. Carlson**

1210.   Stephens, Michael L. **Art Directors in Cinema: A Worldwide Biographical Dictionary.** Jefferson, N.C., McFarland, 1998. 350p. illus. index. $65.00. ISBN 0-7864-0312-8.

Stephens's book focuses on "the most neglected of cinema's important crafts," the art director. Short biographies of more than 300 of these students of architecture and set design, some of whom by the mid-1930s earned the broader title of production designer, are included here. Clearly a devotee of movies and an engaging writer, Stephens intermixes film and art history into the biographies, often to the exclusion of the personality, education, and defining moments of the subjects. Stories such as the one about Robert Usher attracting attention to himself by climbing a tree outside United Artists and launching a drawing folded into a paper airplane at a working director are rare.

Stephens is at his best showing readers how, when, and why an art director influenced the dominant visual style of a studio, of an era, and of a series of films. As the author of books on gangster films and film noir, he seems to favor art directors who worked in the 1930s and 1940s. Not covered as extensively are those from the silent era (no mention of Frank Wortman's work on *Birth of a Nation* or *Intolerance*); the 1980ss and 1990s (missing are Phillip Rosenberg II, Kristi Zea, Bruno Rubeo, Gene Rudolf, Peter S. Larkin, and Paul Sylbert), and almost anything or anyone connected with Stephen Spielberg's films. Filmographies are clearly labeled as "selected," but the basis for inclusion is not explained. Why, for instance, was *Rebel Without a Cause* left out of the listing of Malcolm Bert's work, and *Unforgiven* for Henry Burnstead?

Film titles, actors, actresses, directors, producers, and authors are included in the 28-page index. However, nearly 25 of the top 100 greatest U.S. movies listed recently in *Newsweek* and selected by the American Film Institute are not included. This title is recommended with reservations. [R: Choice, Nov 98, p. 494]

—**Pete Prunkl**

Dictionaries and Encyclopedias

1211.   Curran, Daniel. **Guide to American Cinema, 1965-1995.** Westport, Conn., Greenwood Press, 1998. 511p. index. (Reference Guides to the World's Cinema). $79.50. ISBN 0-313-29666-9.

Compact, authoritative, and fun to browse, this guide provides brief encyclopedic entries for films, actors, and directors active in the years 1965 to 1995. Curran sees this period as a transitional one between the studio system that dominated earlier American filmmaking and the technology-driven blockbusters of the late 1990s.

The evaluative entries provide plot summaries for films and biographical and career data for actors and directors. Filmographies, awards, and selective bibliographies follow each entry. Appendixes include material ranging form notable producers to titles on the National Film Registry. An index and selective bibliography complete the volume.

Although the coverage is clearly restricted to the years 1965 to 1995, these parameters appear without cultural context and seem a bit broad on the 1990s end. Certainly well written and edited, the guide reads much like a small encyclopedia, lacking a distinctive, individual voice. Likewise, the criteria for inclusion, defined as "purely subjective," lack quirkiness. Instead the guide sticks with the well-known names.

Overall, the brief discussions of individual films may warrant a purchase by collections supporting film history programs. Much of the material (especially biographical) can be found in such standard reference titles as the *International Dictionary of Films and Filmmakers* (2d ed.; see ARBA 95, entry 1370), *Magill's Cinema Annual* (14th ed.; see ARBA 97, entry 1131), *Contemporary Theatre, Film, and Television* (see entry 1195), and the Internet Movie Database at http://us.imdb.com. [R: BL, 15 Oct 98, pp. 440-441; Choice, Nov 98, p. 491]

—**Megan S. Farrell**

1212.   Hyatt, Wesley. **The Encyclopedia of Daytime Television.** New York, Billboard Books/Watson-Guptill, 1997. 516p. illus. index. $24.95pa. ISBN 0-8230-8315-2.

The Encyclopedia of Daytime Television is a staggering collection of information about the most trivial of things—major network daytime television shows from 1940 to the present. Each entry contains information on the dates the show aired, the network that broadcast it, and the cast, as well as a brief, informative description of the show. The volume includes three appendixes—"Daytime Reruns of Nighttime TV Series," "Longest Running Daytime Network TV Series," and a bibliography of other reference works on the subject. It also includes an index of titles and names. The coverage is extensive and the detail apparently painstaking.

The truly staggering amount of information one might collect on a daytime television show becomes apparent in those entries for long-running soap operas such as *As the World Turns* (which has run continuously since April 1956). The cast listing extends more than three and a half pages, and the plot synopsis is more than five pages. At the same time, such entries also make clear (albeit inadvertently) the utter banality of such shows, charting in great detail utterly predictable and often-repeated narrative trajectories. *The Encyclopedia of Daytime Television* will prove useful to those seeking specific, factual information on the who, what, and when of daytime television. However, it may prove disappointing to those seeking any critical perspective on or context for such shows.—**Marcus P. Elmore**

1213.   Lucanio, Patrick, and Gary Coville. **American Science Fiction Television Series of the 1950s: Episode Guides and Casts and Credits for Twenty Shows.** Jefferson, N.C., McFarland, 1998. 252p. index. $48.50. ISBN 0-7864-0434-5.

This volume is an exhaustive guide to the 20 science fiction television series broadcast nationally in the United States during the 1950s. Arranged alphabetically by series title, this volume covers such familiar standbys as *Adventures of Superman*, *Buck Rogers*, *Captain Midnight*, and *Flash Gordon* as well as lesser-known titles, such as the short-lived *Out There* and *World of Giants*. Various sources were used to collect the data. Episodes were viewed whenever possible, but unfortunately many have been lost or destroyed. A variety of secondary sources were also consulted, such as television logs, newspaper and magazine reviews and articles, television histories, and other reference books.

Following an introduction that gives a general history of science fiction on television during the 1950s, each series is introduced by three to six pages of text that give a description of the program, its history, technical innovations, character development, a directory of the production staff, and a critical summation. An analysis of each episode of the series follows, giving, whenever possible, a list of cast members, the original airing date, and a plot summary. The amount of detail supplied for each series varies according to the availability of data. The text ends with a bibliography of works consulted and two indexes, the first of episode names and the second a general name index, primarily of the cast and production crew members. This guide is a carefully prepared, encyclopedic treatment of a fascinating, if somewhat esoteric, facet of television history. [R: BL, 1 Oct 98, p. 354]
—**John T. Gillespie**

1214.   Melton, J. Gordon. **The Vampire Gallery: A Who's Who of the Undead.** Detroit, Visible Ink Press/Gale, 1998. 500p. index. $19.95pa. ISBN 1-57859-053-1.

Melton wrote this book to serve as a companion to *The Vampire Book* (see ARBA 95, entry 1328). Unlike the first title, which examined all aspects of vampirism, this book serves as a "who's who" of vampires in literature, film, and television.

The first entry in the book is a fascinating 17-page essay about Dracula. It includes information on the items one would expect, such as Bram Stoker's book and the various movie adaptations, although also including information on such novelties as a song entitled "Dinner with Drac" (Cameo, 1957). The essay is followed by approximately 350 alphabetically arranged entries, some of which contain bibliographic information, focusing on such vampires as Graf Orlock from *Nosferatu*. The book contains approximately 150 black-and-white pictures, ranging from movie stills to comic book covers, that greatly supplement the text.

The author claims the work is not meant to be comprehensive but rather representative of the genre, yet it manages to include entries for most of the vampires in Anne Rice's Vampire Chronicles. There should be entries for her major characters such as Lestat de Lioncourt and Akasha, but minor characters such as Baby Jenks and Killer should have been omitted. Two additional, alphabetically arranged sections supplement the main portion of the book. The first, "Vampire Groups and Clans," includes organizations such as the Camarilla from the role-playing game entitled Vampire: The Masquerade. "Vampire Hunters and Vampire Associates" includes entries on such characters as Abraham Van Helsing, who are not vampires but are major figures in vampire lore. Access to information throughout the book is provided by an excellent index that highlights main entries with bold typeface.

This entertaining volume is a good acquisition for libraries needing books about vampires. Plus, it is not every day that a reference title can also double as a flipbook.—**John R. Burch Jr.**

1215.   Slide, Anthony. **The New Historical Dictionary of the American Film Industry.** Lanham, Md., Scarecrow, 1998. 266p. index. $55.00. ISBN 0-8108-3426-X.

This work is a completely revised and updated edition of *The American Film Industry: A Historical Dictionary* (see ARBA 87, entry 1290), with more than 800 entries, 200 of which are new. This is not a "who's who" but a "what's what." Instead of the usual actors and directors, there are companies and chains (Buster Keaton Productions, Pussycat Theatre), studios (Inceville, Lucasfilm LTD), genres (film noir, gangster film, screwball comedy), film series (Passing Parade), place-names associated with motion pictures (Monument Valley; Fort Lee, New Jersey), technical innovations (smell-o-vision, vitaphone), and general subjects (blacks in film).

Entries vary in length from a sentence to more than a page. Words marked with an asterisk indicate a separate entry. If an organization is still active, an address is provided. Useful bibliographies follow many entries, and a section titled "Resources" indicates the whereabouts of institutional archives. Liberal cross-references lead the user through the volume. Although there is no entry or cross-reference for *Blacklist*, there are entries for *Communism* and *Dies Committee Investigation*. Individuals cited in the text have birth and death dates when available, and are indexed.

Like the most successful subject dictionaries, this one inspires the user to browse. The text is ripe with anecdotes and very amusing. This unique volume is highly recommended for even general reference collections. It deserves a place on the shelf next to the many biographical film dictionaries. [R: RBB, 15 Jan 98, p. 838]
—**Ruth A. Carr**

1216.   Tibbetts, John C., and James M. Welsh. **Encyclopedia of Novels into Film.** New York, Facts on File, 1998. 522p. illus. index. $60.00. ISBN 0-8160-3317-X.

Literature and film are, in this reviewer's opinion, natural affinities. Although everyone knows that the books are always better than the movies, there can be beautiful and thoughtful adaptations and films that are only loosely based on their literary counterparts. This intriguing resource discusses, as the title suggests, novels that have been turned into films. The encyclopedia contains approximately 300 entries that give synopses of both the novels and the film adaptations, examining how the films are similar or different from the novels from whence they originated. Many of the greatest, and worst, movies have been based on literary works. It is disappointing that this reference source should appear in the year when so many literary adaptations came to the big screen—*Les Misérables, Beloved, Mrs. Dalloway, Fear and Loathing in Las Vegas, Great Expectations,* and *Lolita,* for example. However, the book does not claim to be exhaustive but rather "ambitious and eclectic" (preface), so there is no guarantee that these newer films would have appeared even if it was published a year from now.

The encyclopedia begins with an introductory essay, written by Tibbetts and Welsh, entitled "Why Study Film Adaptations of Novels?" There is also a fascinating concluding essay—"Scenes from a Hollywood Life: The Novelist as Screenwriter"—that recounts the role of novelists as screenwriters in the history of Hollywood and how the "Hollywood Experience" spawned classic novels as well, such as Nathanael West's *The Day of the Locust.* In between these two instructive essays is the meat of this reference source. As the title stresses, the focus of the encyclopedia is novels, not short stories or plays. Not a single Shakespearean film adaptation appears here, nor does Stephen King's short story "The Body," the basis for the film *Stand by Me.* Novellas, such as *Billy Budd* by Herman Melville and *Heart of Darkness* by Joseph Conrad (the basis for *Apocalypse Now*), do appear, as does at least one short story, "It Had to Be Murder" by Cornell Woolrich—the basis for Alfred Hitchcock's *Rear Window.* Entries are listed under the title of the novel rather than the movie; if the title of the film differs, a cross-reference appears under the film title to lead users to the novel title. Made-for-TV movies are rarely cited, but the entries run the gamut from literary classics to the James Bond series of thrillers. Each entry gives the publication date of the novel, the date(s) of film production(s) with directors and studios, and references at the end (including reviews of both the novels and the films). Each entry is signed by the initials of the contributor. The encyclopedia is richly illustrated with movie stills and portraits of selected authors, although one has to wonder why the authors chose to use pen-and-ink pictures rather than actual photographs.

Although this book is immensely interesting and compulsively readable, its value as a research tool is open to debate. The two aforementioned essays would be of value to the researcher, but the entries themselves would have to be more in-depth to be of true assistance. For instance, it would be nice to have such statistics as length of novels (in page numbers), sales figures of novels and movies, film running times, MPAA ratings, and complete casting notes. Failure to provide such information impedes serious research. Of course, providing so much more information would make this encyclopedia unwieldy in size. The bibliography at the end of the volume could also prove as an aid to serious research. In any case, anyone looking for brief information on films based on literary works would surely benefit from reading any of these well-written essays. Perhaps the volume would be more suited to the circulating collection rather than the reference section. The encyclopedia is interesting and fun, and anyone who picks it up will want to spend considerable time with it. [R: BR, Sept/Oct 98, p. 67; LJ, 15 Feb 98, p. 134]—**Melissa Rae Root**

1217.   Whissen, Thomas. **Guide to American Cinema, 1930-1965.** Westport, Conn., Greenwood Press, 1998. 389p. index. (Reference Guides to the World's Cinema). $79.50. ISBN 0-313-29487-9.

The title of this modest handbook is deceptive in promising much more than is delivered. Libraries that order it expecting a scholarly history of the first decades of sound or an in-depth survey of significant films and personalities will be disappointed. It is actually a collection of short articles that list and describe, in alphabetical order, several hundred of the best known films, actors, and directors from this period. Typical of the personalities included are Doris Day, Greer Garson, Cary Grant, Alfred Hitchcock, Ernst Lubitsch, and Charlton Heston. Among those excluded are Irving Thalberg, L. B. Mayer, Norma Sherer, James Whale, Lewis Milestone, Betty Hutton, Boris Karloff, Marie Dressler, Wallace Beery, Esther Williams, Howard Keel, Linda Darnell, and Ann Sheridan.

This is obviously the work of someone who likes movies but is not a film scholar. Similarly, the book will appeal to the unsophisticated reader. Serious researchers will find most of the information easily available in more comprehensive and authoritative reference works. Biographical entries contain career sketches, filmographies, awards, and selected bibliography. Film entries provide credits, commentary, awards, and a selected bibliography. Readers who have a casual interest in film should find this book informative and fun to browse. Public libraries and junior colleges may find it useful for their collections. [R: BL, 15 Oct 98, pp. 440-441; Choice, Dec 98, p. 666]

—**Joseph W. Palmer**

1218.   Wlaschin, Ken. **Opera on Screen: A Guide to 100 Years of Films and Videos Featuring Operas, Opera Singers, and Operettas.** Los Angeles, Calif., Beachwood Press, 1997. 628p. $75.00. ISBN 1-888327-00-6.

This work delivers just what the title promises. The book's avowed goal, to show what it is possible to view, organized as an encyclopedia with minimal critical comment (because "it is apparent that opera lovers rarely agree"), is achieved in an attractive, entertaining volume and is also available on a CD-ROM.

Wlaschin is right about opera lovers' inability to agree. Of his list of the best operas on film and video, this reviewer agreed with several of his choices, such as the 1984 *Carmen*, with Placido Domingo (this great tenor has by far the most films and videos) and Ingmar Bergman's 1974 *The Magic Flute,* but found some of his other favorites, including the Met's 1984 *Francesca Da Rimini* and Losey's 1978 *Don Giovanni* almost too dull too watch. Wlaschin also presents some entertaining lists from which we learn that the most popular operas on film and tape are *Carmen, La Traviata, The Barber of Seville, Tosca, Pagliacci,* and *Don Giovanni*. The most popular singers, after Domingo, include Luciano Pavarotti, José Carreras, Joan Sutherland, and Kiri Te Kanawa.

A particularly helpful feature of *Opera on Screen* is the listing of a film's or video's distributor, although Wlaschin warns us that this area is in considerable flux. This is a delightful book, fun to browse, yet full of useful information for the serious researcher. [R: RBB, Aug. 97, p. 1929]—**Anthony Gottlieb**

Directories

1219.   Avallone, Susan, comp. **Film Writers Guide.** 7th ed. Los Angeles, Calif., Lone Eagle, 1998. 708p. index. $70.00pa. ISBN 0-943728-98-3. ISSN 0894-864X.

Many more films are written than produced, and this resource is a quick source to learn if a writer has had a successfully completed picture. The purpose of this guide is to provide researchers with information on how to contact a writer of films (including cable features, miniseries, stage plays, and short films). Each writer's entry gives the agent or manager, contact information, a list of screenplays written (not produced), and a list of produced screenplays. Other useful features include an index of the complete address, telephone number, and e-mail information on agents and managers. One index that will be used more by the layperson is the film title index. With this index, researchers can find out who wrote their favorite film.

The *Guide* is most useful for libraries whose clientele need current contact information for screenwriters. For most public and academic libraries, a more comprehensive source that provides a compilation of film credits, such as *The Motion Picture Guide* (see ARBA 98, entry 1311), would be more practical. For those researchers and libraries needing absolutely current information on film writers, perhaps a better investment would be to join the Lone Eagle Publishing Company's World Wide Web site at http://www.loneeagle.com/eaglei. For $199 a year, one gains access to not only the *Film Writers Guide*, but also to Lone Eagle's other noteworthy entertainment reference sources (such as their guides to cinematographers, actors, costume designers, producers, and others).

—**Elizabeth A. Ginno**

1220.   **Footage: The Worldwide Moving Image Sourcebook.** New York, Second Line Search, 1997. 1098p. index. $195.00pa. ISBN 1-890979-24-4.

The argument can be made that images—moving images in particular—have become among the most sought-after cultural commodities of the twentieth century. Film and video have evolved into the most significant primary "texts" of this century, the central focus of scholarly research in an increasingly wide number of disciplines. Moving images, in the form of both original and recycled footage, are also the basis for the wildly spinning commercial image producers' mills—from Web masters, to documentary producers, to advertisers and other corporate types. The problem for these sundry moving image seekers has always been how to track down the desired content—that just right shot of a honeybee in action, the collapse of the Tacoma Narrows Bridge, or a Berkeley protest march. That is the job of *Footage: The Worldwide Moving Image Sourcebook. Footage* is an updated and considerably expanded and improved continuation of film "archaeologist" extraordinaire Rick

Prelinger's landmark reference work *Footage 89: North American Film & Video Sources* (see ARBA 91, entry 966). The core of this work is an alphabetic listing by country of more than 3,000 international archives and libraries, commercial stock footage houses, film and video distributors, broadcasters, private collectors, and corporate collections. Along with standard address and contact information, each entry provides information about the agency or institution (solicited via a comprehensive survey), including information about access and cataloging of holdings or wares, licensing availability, and an often highly detailed description of collection or holdings.

As might be expected in a work this ambitious, subject indexing poses some difficulties. Although it does not claim to be absolutely comprehensive, the subject index does, nonetheless, list an impressive 10,000 loosely controlled headings (including personal names). Heading cross-referencing is minimal. Along with the subject index, there are a complete alphabetic listing of all the agencies and institutions and major collections listed in the body of *Footage* and a separate index listing entries by country. This work also offers information on intellectual property attorneys and archival management services. Finally, there is a handful of interesting introductory essays on moving image scholarship, preservation, and use that probably do not need to be in this particular book. Despite its few small quirks, *Footage* is an excellent and indispensable working tool that belongs in the collection of any library concerned with film and video production, history, or use. [R: C&RL News, Feb 98, p. 119]

—**Gary Handman**

1221.   **The Hollywood Reporter Blu-Book Directory 1997: Film & TV Production Directory.** Robert J. Dowling, ed. Gardena, Calif., SCB Distributors, 1997. 658p. illus. index. $64.95 spiralbound. ISBN 0-941140-21-0. ISSN 0278-419X.

The Hollywood Reporter Blu-Book Directory is a "Schwarzenegger-esque," 658-page, spiralbound blockbuster containing copious information about all things Hollywood, including names and addresses of key production and postproduction companies, facilities, and services; movie business financial and legal services; location, transportation, and travel services; movie hardware vendors; special effects houses; and distribution and marketing resources. There is an extensive directory of both above the line and below the line crew and talent and a roster of today's most popular film, television, and radio executives. Useful category and company name indexes are provided. Scattered among this thicket of data, there are slick advertisements—a lot of them, which is not surprising, given the trade audience for this work.

Most of the information included in the body of the *Blu-Book* has apparently been submitted by the individuals, organizations, and enterprises listed. Inclusion requires two verifiable industry references. Although this data-gathering mechanism has probably resulted in a certain number of omissions and gaps, there is still enough information in this resource to satisfy most avid film watchers (or film studies librarians). This is a useful specialized addition for collections with a strong focus on film production or the film industry.—**Gary Handman**

1222.   Kilmer, David. **The Animated Film Collector's Guide: Worldwide Sources for Cartoons on Video and Laserdisc.** Sydney, Australia, John Libbey; distr., Bloomington, Ind., Indiana University Press, 1997. 212p. $32.50. ISBN 1-86462-002-1.

As the title suggests, this painstakingly compiled guide will be quite valuable for collectors but otherwise will have limited appeal. Nearly 3,000 animated films (otherwise known as cartoons) are listed by title and producer, together with sources for videos and laser discs, with address, telephone and fax numbers, e-mail address, and Website address provided. The guide works best when one knows the title of the cartoon sought and uses the title index because the second index, by author, character, or studio, is put together haphazardly, with some Bugs Bunny films being listed under the studio and director, whereas others are listed under the character "Bugs Bunny." This sort of inconsistency is true for several popular characters, including Tweety Bird and Sylvester, and some characters appear to be listed only under the producer, whereas others are only under the character name. Unfortunately, this severely complicates a major potential use of the guide for the average cartoon viewer, who might just want to find sources for Road Runner films, for instance (they are listed under WB-Warner Brothers).

Japanese animated films (known as anime), which have become internationally renowned in recent years, are not included here, because the author, a lifelong cartoon fan, judges there to be sufficient material already on the subject. Indeed, the World Wide Web is brimming with anime Websites. Although dated, the best in-depth research guide to animated films is still *Animation: A Reference Guide* (see ARBA 83, entry 997).

—**Richard W. Grefrath**

1223. Langer, Adam. **The Film Festival Guide: For Filmmakers, Film Buffs, and Industry Professionals.** Chicago, Chicago Review Press; distr., Independent Publishers Group, 1998. 269p. index. $16.95pa. ISBN 1-55652-285-1.

Anyone needing information on international film festivals will welcome this comprehensive publication that delivers the facts on more than 500 events. This compact festival guide is useful for filmmakers, film buffs, industry professionals, and researchers. Arrangement of the entries is geographic. Chapter 1 covers the 16 best worldwide festivals. Festivals are arranged alphabetically according to name. All entries contain the essentials— where, when, background, major award winners, approximate number of entries, price of tickets, information on how to enter, and the entry deadline. In addition, some entries include noteworthy celebrity sightings that add to the legitimacy of the festival.

Entries are succinctly packed with valuable tips ranging from the organizer's viewpoint as seen in the Art Film Festival in Trenciansk Teplice, the Slovak Republic, that unquestionably sees cinema as an art form to movies showcased in the Sheffield International Documentary Festival in Sheffield, England, notable for choosing bluntly political films.

Chapter 2 lists 153 North American festival sites, plus 53 additional incomplete listings with the contact information. Interspersed are six insightful interviews with festival directors, including a discussion with Davon Johnson, a one-man operation from the Davon Johnson Annual Fall Film Festival.

The next five chapters cover festivals in Europe, Asia, Africa and the Middle East, Australia, and South America employing the same organizational principle as chapter 1. Chapter 8 is a guide to the best film houses in more than 100 cities around the world. There is a complete index organized according to chapters. [R: BL, 15 Sept 98, p. 262]—**Magda Želinská-Ferl**

1224. Morton, Alan. **The Complete Directory to Science Fiction, Fantasy, and Horror Television Series: A Comprehensive Guide to the First 50 Years 1946 to 1996.** Peoria, Ill., Other Worlds Books, 1997. 982p. $29.95pa.; $24.00pa (libraries). ISBN 0-9657358-0-X.

Often die-hard film and television fans and cultists spin out the best reference information available concerning a particular genre obsession. Such is the case with Morton's invaluable guide to television science fiction and fantasy series. Morton, a cinema studies grad and self-confessed science fiction film and video hobbyist, has compiled what is by far the most comprehensive listing of its type. The only reference resource in the same ballpark appears to be Harris Lenz's excellent multivolume *Science Fiction, Horror and Fantasy Film and Television Credits* (see ARBA 84, entry 967), which approaches television science fiction from the talent end of things, rather than indexing and describing individual series. Morton has set about providing credits, brief production data, background information, and plot synopses for more than 360 English-language series titles, from the 1949 *Lights Out* (the first science fiction/fantasy genre series) to currently running broadcast offerings, such as *The X-Files*. Series installments with credits and brief synopses are listed chronologically under each alphabetically arranged entry. Useful ancillary information for individual titles is also provided. Not included in this work are animated works, serials, and mini-series. Morton has made an effort to obtain information about the series directly from the episodes themselves. If there is a fault in this work, it is the annoying incidence of typographical errors and the occasional grammatical lapse—fairly minor prices to pay for the abundance and quality of information provided. This work is highly recommended for both public and academic library reference collections. [R: BL, 15 May 98, p. 1652]—**Gary Handman**

Filmography

1225. Gifford, Denis. **Entertainers in British Films: A Century of Showbiz in the Cinema.** Westport, Conn., Greenwood Press, 1998. 340p. illus. $65.00. ISBN 0-313-30720-2.

This filmography lists approximately 2,000 entertainers and the British motion pictures in which they appeared. Comedians, singers, musicians, musical groups, acrobats, and even poets are included, but persons who merely worked as actors are not. Thus, cabaret comedienne Elsa Lancaster is in the book, but her actor husband, Charles Laughton, is not. Information provided is limited to the entertainer's name and specialty and followed by a chronological list of his or her British films. Production or distributing company is identified, and often musical numbers or sketches performed are named. A song, sketch, and music index appears at the end of the volume. The fact that coverage extends all the way back to the nineteenth century will enhance the value of this reference tool for serious researchers. Although most North American libraries will find this book too esoteric for their needs, large cinema and theater collections will find it a source of highly specialized, but potentially useful, information.—**Joseph W. Palmer**

1226.   **A Guide to Latin American, Caribbean, and U.S. Latino-Made Film and Video.** Karen Ranucci and Julie Feldman, eds. Lanham, Md., Scarecrow, 1998. 361p. index. $74.50. ISBN 0-8108-3285-2.

The directors and producers whose works are featured in this book need only be agreed upon as "Latino" in ethnicity to qualify for inclusion. However, the scope of the coverage in this work goes far beyond Spanish-language films. In addition to titles from such nations as Argentina, Bolivia, Chile, Colombia, Cuba, and Mexico are films from Brazil (Portuguese), Guyana (English), the Netherlands Antilles (one film, in Dutch), and even the United States (referring to U.S. Latino directors whose films are in English). There is even a listing of films from "Latin America," which covers entries where no particular country of origin is evident.

This directory lists more than 400 films and videos available in the United States, and provides descriptions of these works from a U.S. user's point of view. Evaluation of each film, with helpful suggestions on how it might be profitably used in study, is provided by professors from varied disciplines, including anthropology, political science, language and literature, and film studies. Each listing is provided with original title; English translation (where necessary); directory; producer; running time; year; subtitles, where present; and distributor. There follows a fairly detailed description, a paragraph or two of strengths and weaknesses, advice on how to introduce the film, and the level of sophistication suggested for a suitable audience. In many cases, suggested readings are listed for those wishing background or more information. A distributor's index provides contact information for purchase or rental.

What is apparent to the reader, especially one from the United States, is that film-makers in Latin American countries overwhelmingly tend to focus on the thorny and complicated social issues of their time and place, rather than to emphasize the aesthetic or entertainment value of film as a medium of communication, as is typical of many films made in the United States. A great number of these films are documentaries, portraying social wrongs, problems, or grievances, and are designed to arouse shock, outrage, anger, and the desire for political action, rather than just to tell a story. For this reason, this title is recommended, especially for teachers of Spanish or Portuguese who want to place a new language in a larger social context for their students.—**Bruce A. Shuman**

1227.   Kinnard, Roy. **Science Fiction Serials: A Critical Filmography of the 31 Hard SF Cliffhangers; With an Appendix of the 37 Serials with Slight SF Content.** Jefferson, N.C., McFarland, 1998. 217p. illus. index. $39.95. ISBN 0-7864-0545-7.

Fond are the memories of the 10-cent Saturday matinees with two shows, a newsreel, and a cliff-hanging serial. Not so fond are the memories of the large amounts of gum on the floors, the candy consumed, and the popcorn tossed while waiting for these wonderful afternoons of escape to start. When they started there seemed to be always the serial, either the cowboy or the science fiction serial. This work describes 31 of the science fiction serials in detail along with an appendix describing others that had science fiction content. These are generally quickly shot works, most of which were ignored by the critics and usually 15 to 20 minutes in length. They nearly always ended with a cliff-hanging ending and a message saying "to be continued next week." These were, for the most part, low budget productions without famous cast or writers or directors, usually designed for children. However, they were financially important for the studios and allowed them to explore themes that the more mainstream movies ignored or considered too risky. Most of the themes found in science fiction movies of later years were first tried in these serials.

Each of the 31 serials described in this work has information on the production staff and crew; the cast with the name of the person that each actor played; the chapter titles; a detailed summary of the story; a section on comments, including background information on what was happening in the industry at the time; and how and why some decisions were made. If the serial is available on video that fact is also noted along with the name of the distributor of the video. The video information will be out of date almost immediately. There are labeled pictures from the serial and a picture of the posters, if available. The indexing is good. This is a fascinating look at these serials and will be useful in most film collections.—**Robert L. Turner Jr.**

1228.   Langman, Larry. **The Media in the Movies: A Catalog of American Journalism Films, 1900-1996.** Jefferson, N.C., McFarland, 1998. 333p. illus. index. $65.00. ISBN 0-7864-0433-7.

This is a first-rate listing and guide to 1,025 films that deal with Hollywood's version of media reality—both fiction (e.g., *Deadline, USA*) and docudrama (e.g., *All the President's Men*). It is alphabetically arranged, from *Abandoned* (1949) through *Zudora* (1914), covering the years 1900 to 1996. Each entry begins with the title, date, and studio, and moves through the main credits before giving a descriptive annotation (100 to 250 words) and cross-references to other films and remakes. Films deal with life in and around the newspaper, magazine, radio, or television world.

Langman, a teacher of film history, provides some context and meaning in his introductory essay. He presents stereotypes (much as is done in journalism), such as the news hound, the sob sister, and the crusader, plus a portrayal of society by the news machines of the past. There are also a handful of stills. At the end a bibliography along with a list of peripheral films and a name index (no subjects) is given.

Unfortunately, there is the whole rest of the world missing; no foreign-language films (some German beauties are missing), no British films (nothing about the remarkable 1938 *This Man Is News*, with Alastair Sim as an editor), and no Canadian films are listed. The annotations appear to be accurate for the most part, except for the glaring error in *The Front Page* (1931) where Langman identifies the name Mary Brian as both Hildy's and the condemned's girlfriend. A better book to get the sense of American journalism in the early part of this century was Alex Barris's *Stop the Presses! The Newspaperman in American Films* (A. S. Barnes, 1976), with a profusion of stills and narrative, contextual prose. [R: Choice, July/Aug 98, p. 1831]—**Dean Tudor**

1229.   Langman, Larry. **Return to Paradise: A Guide to South Sea Island Films.** Lanham, Md., Scarecrow, 1998. 373p. index. $48.00. ISBN 0-8108-3268-2.

Geography, rather than genre, is the guiding principle behind this filmography of 600 U.S. motion pictures released between 1908 and 1994. All are set in that part of the Pacific roughly bounded by Hawaii, New Zealand, and Easter Island. Included are escapist fantasies, lavish and low-budget musicals, silent serials, horror films, melodramas, historical epics, ethnographic and scientific documentaries, and lots of World War II battle films and comedies.

Each entry identifies the film's releasing or distributing company, director, screenwriter, and featured players. Annotations provide a plot summary and, frequently, a few lines of background information or critical commentary. Entries are arranged chronologically in 9 chapters, each representing a different decade, and each chapter is prefaced by an essay summarizing themes and titles prominent in that period. The volume concludes with indexes to film titles and personal names. Film buffs will enjoy examining this well-written book that could prove useful to students and researchers in the fields of cinema and pop culture.—**Joseph W. Palmer**

1230.   Martin, Len D. **The Republic Pictures Checklist: Features, Serials, Cartoons, Short Subjects, and Training Films of Republic Pictures Corporation, 1935-1959.** Jefferson, N.C., McFarland, 1998. 383p. illus. index. $65.00. ISBN 0-7864-0438-8.

Dubbed "The Thrill Factory" because of its reliable production of adventure serials and "B" Westerns, Republic Pictures began in 1915 as a motion picture laboratory and evolved into a studio by 1935. Nonetheless, despite its reputation, an "A" feature, such as *The Quiet Man*, would occasionally appear. All of Republic's output, including short subjects, cartoons, and training films, is documented, as are Academy Award nominations and winners. The volume is intended as a comprehensive handbook rather than a critical or historical work. It was compiled using several periodicals, such as *The New York Times*.

A brief historical overview of the corporation precedes the alphabetically arranged sections. Each entry contains release date, production credits, cast, plot synopsis, and supplementary notes, when needed. Serials also list chapter titles. Continuous entry numbering enables access by release date (appendix A) and by chapter title and name indexes. Black-and-white poster illustrations are included, as is a bibliography.

The checklist records and familiarizes the reader with a piece of U.S. entertainment history. Although Republic Pictures does not exist anymore, many of its titles are being re-released through television or home video, thereby "thrilling" viewers again.—**Anita Zutis**

1231. McCall, Douglas L. **Film Cartoons: A Guide to 20th Century American Animated Features and Shorts.** Jefferson, N.C., McFarland, 1998. 261p. index. $39.95. ISBN 0-7864-0584-8.

In 1928, Walt Disney released the black-and-white animated film *Steamboat Willie*. The first sound cartoon, this landmark film introduced Mickey Mouse and launched the Disney empire. Contrary to popular belief, however, U.S animation did not begin with Disney. As McCall notes in his useful catalog of animated features and shorts, U.S. animation probably began in 1906 with the James Stuart Blackton short, *Humorous Phases and Funny Faces*. In his guide McCall covers 90 years of animated films from this earliest effort to the ambitious 1997 feature, *Anastasia*. McCall arranges the 1,614 entries in this book into 3 sections. Part 1 provides credit and production information, ratings, and synopses for 180 (mainly) U.S.-produced features. Part 2 lists 57 live-action features that contain animation sequences. Part 3 lists more than 1,300 animated shorts and provides credits, notes awards, and gives some brief synopses. This section includes all the Warner Bros., Disney, MGM, and Walter Lantz products. A brief but highly informative appendix identifies the top animation studios. Although a general index provides access to various production personnel, a "character" index would have been useful to identify shorts featuring Bugs Bunny and Woody Woodpecker, among others. This work is recommended for academic libraries supporting film studies programs. [R: LJ, Dec 98, p. 84, 86; BL, 15 Nov 98, p. 606]
—**David K. Frasier**

1232. Presnell, Don, and Marty McGee. **A Critical History of Television's** *The Twilight Zone*, **1959-1964.** Jefferson, N.C., McFarland, 1998. 282p. index. $39.95. ISBN 0-7864-0448-5.

The classic television series *The Twilight Zone*, created and hosted by Rod Serling, is still viewed by countless numbers of people via cable and network television and videos. The episodes' stars included Robert Redford, William Shatner, Burgess Meredith, Mickey Rooney, Martin Landau, Ida Lupino, and Cliff Robertson. A guide for those interested in television history, science fiction, and *The Twilight Zone* itself, *A Critical History of Television's The Twilight Zone, 1959-1964* is arranged in several sections: preface, introduction, part 1: History, and part 2: The Episodes. The appendixes include a chronological list of episodes; writer biographies; principal writers and their *Twilight Zone* credits; principal actors and their *Twilight Zone* credits; "Close . . . But No Zone: Stories Never Filmed"; Serling's lost episodes; and genres, themes, and plot devices. The preface is primarily a bibliographic essay about books and one journal—Serling's *The Twilight Zone Magazine*. The introduction is an essay about the significance of the series itself. Part 1 discusses how Serling developed the series and a history of each season. Part 2, which comprises most of the book, is an episode guide featuring original airdate, cast, director, writer, synopsis, and notes and commentary. In addition to appendixes, the authors include bibliographic notes and an index.

This well-researched book provides a fascinating history of the series and a thorough guide to episodes. It is recommended to television history collections in college and public libraries. Fans of the series will certainly wish to purchase a copy or borrow one from their library.—**Lucy Heckman**

1233. Rabkin, Leslie Y. **The Celluloid Couch: An Annotated International Filmography of the Mental Health Professional in the Movies and Television, from the Beginning to 1990.** Lanham, Md., Scarecrow, 1998. 627p. index. $85.00. ISBN 0-8108-3462-6.

A clinical psychologist's perspective of his or her profession and colleagues, as portrayed on the silver screen, is contained in this selective filmography, which ranges from the early silent era through the 1980s. The broad audience sought includes cultural historians and those interested in twentieth-century public images of mental illness as well as film buffs of all types.

Entries are arranged by decade, except for "The Early Silent Era." Each period is prefaced by an introduction highlighting key films and subjects and discussing the interaction among movies, psychology, and history. The author's humorous remarks are well aimed. A coda summarizes the popular images of mental health and its practitioners, and is followed by an extensive bibliography and an index that lists included films with their year of origin. Entries contain the main title and alternatives, year, country of origin, cast, production notes, synopsis of plot, and genre. Comments on the professional and the type of therapy involved are included, if appropriate.

The self-proclaimed "celluloid safari" casts a new perspective on film and its "unconscious," producing a unique reference tool with which to view this form of mass media. Updates of this useful reference would be appreciated.—**Anita Zutis**

1234.   Richards, Larry. **African American Films Through 1959: A Comprehensive, Illustrated Filmography.** Jefferson, N.C., McFarland, 1998. 312p. illus. index. $65.00. ISBN 0-7864-0307-1.

Richards is a librarian at the Philadelphia Free Library and a collector of African American film memorabilia. For more than a decade, he has been organizing and hosting African American film festivals in theaters and on television. Using source materials, reference books, and historical African American newspapers, he has compiled a filmography of 1,324 short and feature-length films produced between 1895 and 1959 that have a predominantly African American cast or that have an African American as the lead star.

Arranged alphabetically by title, entries vary greatly in the amount of information provided, but they have production information, cast, songs, and similar details. Many include annotations, and some cite newspaper reviews. The text is illustrated with dozens of small black-and-white reproductions of contemporary movie posters. Excellent appendixes arrange the films chronologically and list credits for more than 1,800 actors, more than 200 film companies, and for producers and directors. Richards indicates that about one-fifth of the films are available on video, but he does not indicate which ones or where they might be obtained. Similarly, he speaks of the growing research and literature related to African American film, but, although several resources and two books are mentioned, there is no bibliography. A formal bibliography and some guidance concerning how to identify and obtain films on video would enhance this otherwise excellent reference book. [R: Choice, Sept 98, p. 90]
—**Joseph W. Palmer**

1235.   Sampson, Henry T. **That's Enough, Folks: Black Images in Animated Cartoons, 1900-1960.** Lanham, Md., Scarecrow, 1998. 249p. illus. index. $60.00. ISBN 0-8108-3250-X.

Sampson has given us many excellent black performing arts books, such as *Blacks in Black and White* (2d ed.; see ARBA 96, entry 1410) and *Blacks in Blackface* (see ARBA 81, entry 1059), and it is no surprise that his current volume is a must acquisition. Most cartoon and movie buffs have seen black stereotypes from the pens of Tex Avery, Chuck Jones, and Walt Disney (chapters are devoted to "the animated safari," "the plantation," and "the minstrel show"), but memories of series stars Sammy Johnsin, Bosko, and Buzzy the Crow are fading. More than 700 cartoons featuring black characters were produced in the United States before 1960, and Sampson provides production data, characters, and plot synopses for hundreds of them. His brief introductions to the series stars alone are worth the price of the book.

Although Sampson includes 59 black-and-white illustrations in the middle of the volume, such a work cries out for color. The author also makes no attempt to critique these works, but does include contemporaneous reviews from trade publications. The plot synopses are uniformly well written and informative. Overall, this is an essential work, to be shelved beside Donald Bogle's *Toms, Coons, Mulattoes, Mammies, and Bucks* (repr. ed.; Continuum, 1994) in all cultural collections.—**Anthony J. Adam**

1236.   Waldman, Harry. **Paramount in Paris: 300 Films Produced at the Joinville Studios, 1930-1933, with Credits and Biographies.** Lanham, Md., Scarecrow, 1998. 237p. $47.50. ISBN 0-8108-3431-6.

The years 1930 to 1933 were a time of experimentation and change in the motion picture industry. With the advent of talkies, audiences everywhere were no longer content watching silent films. The addition of sound to visual imagery in all major studios also created a demand by European audiences for films in their own mother tongues.

Then, as now, people did not care for subtitles, so Paramount—one of the United States' major studios—opened a branch in Europe, where films in other languages could be produced more cheaply (frequently one-tenth the cost of Hollywood productions) and closer to their intended audiences. To this end, Paramount dispatched one of its premier directors, Robert T. Kane, who set up a $10 million complex in Joinville, France, a half hour's train ride from downtown Paris, and began producing vernacular films from its six state-of-the-art sound studios. When word got around, talented actors and directors from all over Europe descended on Kane's studio, and the films—comedies, mostly—came rolling off the assembly line.

In its three years of operation (after which the studio folded, due mainly to resentment by increasingly nationalistic European studios), Kane released an astonishing 300 films, many of which he produced himself. The studio during that time operated 24 hours a day, and in some cases, the same story and set were actually used for several different casts to take turns making films in their respective languages, one after the other.

Waldman, using hundreds of available research sources and published reviews in assembling this information, has chosen to form his chapters by nationality and language (French, Spanish, Portuguese, Italian, Romanian, Swedish, Dutch, German, Polish, Czech, and Hungarian) of the film. Provided in the narrative are an interesting variety of narrative descriptions and personal tidbits concerning the various films and those who made them. This book is a useful source of European cinematic history, but due to the arcane nature of the subject and the films under discussion, this work is recommended only for larger and more serious collections of cinematic literature.

—**Bruce A. Shuman**

Handbooks and Yearbooks

1237.   D'Lugo, Marvin. **Guide to the Cinema of Spain.** Westport, Conn., Greenwood Press, 1997. 282p. index. (Reference Guides to the World's Cinema). $75.00. ISBN 0-313-29474-7.

The foreword to Greenwood's Reference Guides to the World's Cinema series, of which this is the 1st volume, puts it succinctly: "Because each volume seeks to present a balance between the interests of the general public and those of students and scholars of the medium, the choices are of necessity selective . . . and often reflect the author's own idiosyncrasies." The current volume lives up to this statement. The book starts with an extensive, 27-page introduction to Spanish cinema, after which it offers a section devoted to individual films, then directors, producers, cinematographers, actors, and actresses. The appendix contains a list of international awards won by Spanish films between 1941 and 1994, a selected bibliography, and a general index.

In the main body of the book, each entry is viewed and interpreted through the author's views. Pedro Almodóvar's biography, for instance, is brief and to the point and does not suggest the extreme recent popularity of his films. Luis Buñel, as a true classic of Spanish cinema, gets a more thorough description, but neither man's sketch includes a complete list of the works they created. Carlos Saura, along with Buñel and Almodóvar, the most internationally celebrated of Spanish filmmakers, is also represented with a concise and informative sketch. Short profiles of actors and actresses include major performers from the past, such as Imperio Argentina, Manuel Luna, and José Nieto; celebrated international stars, such as Fernando Rey; and current favorites Antonio Banderas, Victoria Abril, and Carmen Maura. Students and scholars in need of more facts regarding this fascinating subject will find an extensive bibliography offered throughout the book. Some of these follow individual entries: four books follow Luis Buñel's biography; there are two on Almodóvar; and the general bibliography at the end of the book includes these and many other books on the subject. Although this book is not as extensive as its title would lead one to believe, it is an excellent starting point from which to explore this fascinating subject. [R: BL, 1 June 98, pp. 1804-1806]—**Koraljka Lockhart**

1238.   Monsell, Thomas. **Nixon on Stage and Screen: The Thirty-Seventh President as Depicted in Films, Television, Plays, and Opera.** Jefferson, N.C., McFarland, 1998. 239p. illus. index. $42.50. ISBN 0-7864-0163-X.

Although written as a reference source, Monsell sees this work as providing a greater understanding of this century. Annotating, in chronological order, the variety of media events in which Nixon appears, is referred to, or is parodied, the list demonstrates the unique role Nixon played in our country's culture. The early appearances, beginning with the 1952 Checkers speech, are essentially news or campaign spots; during the 1970s parodies were produced; and the 1980s' material includes reflections and interviews with the elder statesman.

Monsell's annotations are inconsistent. All include heading data, such as title, date, length, distributor, type of show, and cast, but the text can either be one sentence or several pages with plot synopses and critical reviews. This is partially due to the disparate nature of the material. Some of the films, like *Shampoo*, only have Nixon on the television in the background; others are complete biographies or parodies, such as *Hail to the Chief*. Monsell allows his opinion to color the annotations, especially in the works of Oliver Stone.

This work is, as Monsell states, a reflection of the times and culture and Nixon's impact both as a leader and a personality. Reading through the work, one is struck by the effect Nixon had on the performance industry as well as the country. As a reference source, it is useful for libraries with film and television collections.

—**Joshua Cohen**

239.   van Heerden, Bill. **Film and Television In-Jokes: Nearly 2,000 Intentional References, Parodies, Allusions, Personal Touches, Cameos, Spoofs, and Homages.** Jefferson, N.C., McFarland, 1998. 306p. index. $39.95. ISBN 0-7864-0456-6.

This is one book that should not be judged by its cover. Packed with wonderful anecdotes and insider information from everyone's favorite movies and television shows, it's just a shame the publisher felt compelled to wrap it in an unattractive and uninspired cover. However, once inside readers will find nearly 2,000 different parodies, allusions, cameos, and references from both television and films that were undoubtedly missed by the less-detailed eye of the everyday viewer. All entries are alphabetized by either the name of the movie or show, or by the actor's name. The text is broken into 3 sections. One section is devoted to films, with entries ranging from early films such *Abbott and Costello Meet Frankenstein* from 1948 to more recent films such as the Star Trek series. The 2d section covers both old and new television shows with references, such as this one from a 1995 *Melrose Place* episode in which characters Michael and Kimberly are reprimanded by the chief of staff. His name, prominently shown on his door, is "Calvin Hobbs," after the comic strip *Calvin & Hobbs*. Another example comes from the popular hit series *The X-Files* The number "1013" has appeared in many episodes, and was used in many different ways ranging from agent Mulder's birthday to an autopsy case number performed on John Doe to an e-mail sent to agent Scully. What is the significance of the number 1013? It's the birthday of producer Chris Carter, October 13th. If these 2 sections are not enough, the reader can move on to the 3d section that is devoted to music videos. This section may shed some light and insider information onto some of the imagery found in many of the most popular music videos of our time. Great as a conversation piece or just fun to learn all you can about your favorite television show or movie, this book offers a treasure chest of inside information and interesting references.—**Michael Florman**

Indexes

240.   **Film Index International 1996.** [CD-ROM]. London, British Film Institute and Alexandria, Va., Chadwyck-Healey, 1993-1996. Minimum system requirements: IBM or compatible 286. CD-ROM drive and controller card with Microsoft CD-ROM Extensions 2.1. MS-DOS 3.1. 640K RAM. 5MB hard disk space. EGA or VGA monitor and card (preferably color). $1,895.00. ISSN 1355-4506.

Anyone doubting the long-term revolutionary potential of the Web to alter existing conventions and methods of publishing, bibliography, and information dissemination should carefully study the relationship of the Chadwyck-Healey *Film Index International* (FII) to the Internet Movie Database (IMDB). Weighing in at a lefty $1,895, the (FII) CD-ROM database purports to provide filmographic information—credits and brief plot synopses—for more than 90,000 international films from the silent era to the present, including links to a related biographical database (38,000 personalities), and to 400,000 journal articles for selected films and filmmakers. The IMD, however, is free (at least for the present), offering entries for more than 150,000 international films from all eras, with a total of more than 2,000,000 filmographic links (including links to biographical information, reviews, trivia, and awards). Although comparisons of database size are interesting, a side-by-side comparison of content offers the revelation. This reviewer searched for Giovanni Pastrone's landmark 1914 epic in both databases: The FII had no entry; the IMDB had full credit information. In a search for Cecil Hepworth's 1904 *Rescued by Rover* (a staple of introductory film studies courses), FII struck out, whereas the IMDB scored again. As a final shot, a search was done on "Alan Smitee" (a pseudonym used by directors and writers who ultimately wish to disavow responsibility for their work on a cinematic dog). The FII lists dozens of entries, with not a single indication of the name behind the name; the IMDB fastidiously lists the real name for each Smitee, along with an explanation of when the name is used.

Admittedly, the FII's connection with the British Film Institute does give it somewhat more of an academically correct cachet than the populist IMDB. The inclusion of a journal citation database is also a plus. For the money, however, this reviewer would rather look toward the IMDB for gratis filmographic information, and apply the savings toward a subscription to the *Film Literature Index*, which does a much better job than the FII of indexing international film journals.—**Gary Handman**

Videography

1241.   **Blockbuster Entertainment Guide to Movies and Videos 1999.** New York, Dell Publishing/Bantam Doubleday Dell, 1998. 1589p. $7.99pa. ISBN 0-440-22598-1.

Blockbuster Entertainment Guide to Movies and Videos 1999 serves as an exhaustive reference on the best, the mediocre, and the worst that the movie industry offers—from its earliest days through the present. The good, the bad, and the ugly are all mixed together in more than 23,000 review capsules listed in alphabetic order by movie title. Each entry gives the movie's year of release, origin of production when other than American, code for movie genre, a one- to five-star rating, and a list of the director and key cast members. Running times, alternate titles, and an indicator of video availability (a "V" symbol) are also given. Three other helpful lists follow the book's mammoth guide to movies and videos: a list of directors (a select group with six or more movies to their credit), a list of actors (a select group who appear in five or more films), and a list of family/children films. A succinct "How to Use This Book" preface explains all of the guide's abbreviations/codes.

The writing is as concise as is necessary for such an all-encompassing reference tool. Each review capsule gives a superficial treatment of plot and the movie's place in the larger cinematic context, and not much else. One helpful formatting feature in the lists of actors and directors is a checkmark-box system convenient for tracking which movies a person has already viewed. What is lacking from this guide is a category to help users avoid the murkiest of the movie muck, should they so choose. A section featuring just Academy Award winners/nominees would do the trick.

Overall, the guide serves as an outstanding jumping-off point for any research on popular movies, directors, and actors as well as a quick way to locate the basics on obscure and older cinematic works. The guide is a must-have for any library reference desk as well as an asset in the classroom for movie-related researching, but for in-depth information on individual films or biographical information on actors or directors, look elsewhere. [R: RBB, 1 Jan 98, p. 838]—**Deborah Cottin**

1242.   Everitt, David, and Harold Schechter. **The Manly Movie Guide.** New York, Boulevard Books/Berkley, 1997. 287p. illus. index. $11.00pa. ISBN 1-57297-308-0.

Manly movies are full of gunfights, fistfights, car chases, and other assorted action-packed events. What they do not include is romance, character development, or plot development. This volume is a guide to movies that fit the manly definition designed to prevent the ordinary guy from accidentally renting an inappropriate video. The films are placed in 12 categories of manly movies: westerns, war, action/adventure, crime, martial arts, mystery/suspense, horror, science fiction, comedy, drama, musicals, romance, and foreign films. For each category headings, such as "Stirring Sagas of Man Despoiling the Virgin Wilderness" or "Two Cops with Big Guns," assist the user in decision making. Included also are the "Manly Movie Hall of Fame" and the "Best Manly Movies."

The narrative offers insightful annotations of films selected with helpful explanations of how movies meet the manly criteria. Manly quotes from films, such as Arnold Schwarzenegger's in *Commando*, "I eat Green Berets for breakfast," provide valuable insights into the manly genre. Text boxes scattered throughout further assist the reader in techniques of manly movie watching, like how to convince one's girlfriend to watch a manly movie.

Although the book offers a unique examination of a film genre, the selection seems based on the author's preferences. Not a book for a reference collection, but film sections of libraries would find this a popular choice.
—**Joshua Cohen**

1243.   **Leonard Maltin's Movie & Video Guide.** 1999 ed. Leonard Maltin and others, eds. New York, Signet/Penguin Books, 1998. 1632p. $7.99pa. ISBN 0-451-19582-5.

Leonard Maltin is an articulate and witty movie critic who has issued his annual compilation of movies available on video, laserdisc, and DVD. He has included some nice sections, which tell a star's and director's film history. His writing ranges from acerbic to adulatory and his reviews of films are to the point and very complete. His book, however, is not for libraries, in this reviewer's opinion. For one thing, it is a paperback (as would be expected of an annual) and any attempts to bind or reinforce the cover would last as long as a June frost. Its size is also a problem for libraries; one might have to squeeze to place this book in a back pocket, but it would get lost on the shelves with other video guides such as *Roger Ebert's Video Companion* (see ARBA 98, entry 1319), *VideoHound's Golden Movie Retriever* (1994 ed.; see ARBA 95, entry 1399), or *Halliwell's Film & Video Guide* (1998 ed.; HarperCollins, 1997). Each of these books are of quality paperback size and lend themselves to a library's reference collection. Maltin's book is recommended, but for the La-Z-Boy, not the library.—**Joseph L. Carlson**

1244. **Musical Theater Synopses: An Index.** By Jeanette Marie Drone. Lanham, Md., Scarecrow, 1998. 441p. $75.00. ISBN 0-8108-3489-8.

This index is an update and supplement to the author's 1978 publication *Index to Opera, Operetta, and Musical Comedy Synopses in Collections and Periodicals* (see ARBA 79, entry 979). Included in the new edition are ballets, oratorios, dramatic cantatas, minstrel shows, plays, films and television productions with music, and some non-Western forms, including Kabuki, Beijing opera, and Chinese plays. All works listed in the 1978 compilation are included in this supplement with appropriate notations for consulting the 1978 index when necessary.

Arrangement of the index is in 3 parts. Part 1 contains the sources, which include collections of synopses, periodicals and journals, biographies, academic dissertations, scores, monumental sets, and Internet resources with Website addresses. This range is an expansion from the earlier edition, reflecting an inclusion of more sources and more types of musical works. Part 2 consists of an alphabetic list by title and variant title. Each title is followed by a code identifying location. Part 3 is a list by composers. The work includes a bibliography.

This index is a significant reference for academic and music libraries. The author has many years' experience in the music field as a librarian, educator, and consultant. [R: LJ, 1 Sept 98, p. 170]—**Louis G. Zelenka**

1245. Spencer, James R. **Spencer's Complete Guide to Special Interest Videos.** 4th ed. Scottsdale, Ariz., James-Robert; distr., Chicago, Independent Publishers Group, 1998. 746p. illus. index. $29.95pa. ISBN 1-888540-25-7.

This revision of the 1995 edition now includes 12,973 educational, self-help, and how-to videos from more than 1,000 video producers and distributors in 42 subject categories, including business, exercise, and travel, with a wide variety of specialized subjects. Most of these titles are hard to find, and although the author notes that one can order them through a local video outlet, patrons can also search Spencer's Website at www.videomarketplace.com and order any of these videos directly. Each entry includes the video title, a brief description, journal review citation, order number, price, length, and approval stamp from Kids First! (as applicable). A title and series index concludes the volume, but there is no subject listing beyond the broad table of contents.

Although the number of titles in any subject category is not overwhelming, the patron must have patience locating specific topics. For example, if one wants a how-to video on Quicken 5.0, one must scan through the pages on "Computers & Electronics—Software" for that product. A keyword index would be a major help for both the book and Web versions of this guide. However, the low price makes this guide a useful alternative to larger and costlier guides such as *Video Source Book* (21st ed.; Gale, 1998). This work is a recommended purchase for all public libraries.—**Anthony J. Adam**

THEATER

1246. **The Best Plays of 1996-1997.** Otis L. Guernsey Jr., ed. New York, Limelight Editions, 1997. 533p. illus. index. $47.50. ISBN 0-87910-097-4. ISSN 1071-6971.

This 78th edition has expanded coverage "to mirror our theater's volatile history." Plays are now selected by consensus. Chronological coverage is from June 1, 1996, to May 31, 1997, and include cast, credits, and a list of songs from the musicals. An article outlines the performances of top plays, with delightful caricatures. Articles include biographies of the writers and composers. There are analyses and excerpts of the Broadway plays *Skylight* and *The Last Night of Ballyhoo*, the musical *Titanic*, and the off-Broadway productions of *Old Wicked Songs*, *How I Learned to Drive*, and *Violet*. An extensive index lists almost all important data in the book. The volume has numerous photographs, which are not indexed. There are fine performance histories and tours, such as that in *Joseph and the Amazing Technicolor Dreamcoat*. Following this are analyses, biographies, and excerpts of American Theater Critics Association (ACTA) plays, including *Jack and Jill* and *The Ride Down Mount Morgan*, and an analysis of the off-Broadway production of *The Last Night of Ballyhoo*. A list of plays in specific theaters across the nation is arranged by city. A most useful recurring section, "Facts and Figures," includes the longest runs on and off-Broadway as well as Pulitzer, Tony, and other awards, the theater hall of fame, musical theater hall of fame, a necrology, and the best plays from 1894 to 1996. Guernsey has edited a source essential for the history and current events of the theatrical world.—**Ralph Hartsock**

1247.   **The Cambridge History of American Theatre, Volume 1: Beginnings to 1870.** Don B. Wilmeth and Christopher Bigsby, eds. New York, Cambridge University Press, 1998. 525p. illus. index. $69.95. ISBN 0-521-47204-0.

In this, the first of three volumes, the essays of nine contributors undertake historical and critical coverage of the subject in an authoritative and thorough manner. Because each contributor has a varied background in fields such as drama, theater, history, and English, and in view of the fact that each has been assigned a different aspect of the theater experience, the resulting volume is far-reaching. The editors note that for the purposes of this text, theater includes all aspects of the dramatic experience. A short introduction includes a discussion of the obstacle created by the puritanical background of colonial times, when cultural philosophies were not encouraging to theatrical performances. The introduction is followed with nearly 100 pages devoted to a skillfully prepared and detailed timeline that combines the theater events in the United States alongside selected historical/cultural events in both the United States and the world on a year-by-year basis from 1492 through 1870. Because each contributor draws upon his or her varied professional knowledge, the reader gains insight through historical context to performances, plays, playwrights, actors, acting, directing, stagecraft, state design, and theater architecture. Considerable biographical information is included in the text. Each essay, or chapter, is summarized with a conclusion and a bibliography.

The tenacity of actors and producers to triumph over the troubles of frontier life, performances under sometimes very primitive circumstances, financial difficulties, and frequent fires to the theater buildings themselves is impressed on the reader by nearly all of the essayists. From the days of travel by wagons to the emergence of trains, with shows seen in structures from small one-room buildings to great theaters, and from flatboats to showboats, the first volume in this history of U.S. theater addresses with great depth and insight the emerging nation with its diverse population seeking its own identity in dramatic art forms.—**Louis G. Zelenka**

1248.   Horn, Barbara Lee. **Lillian Hellman: A Research and Production Sourcebook.** Westport, Conn., Greenwood Press, 1998. 170p. index. (Modern Dramatists Research and Production Sourcebooks, no.15). $59.95. ISBN 0-313-30264-2.

Horn is an associate professor and chair of the Department of Speech, Communication Sciences, and Theatre at St. John's University in New York. Her treatment of Hellman is part of a Greenwood Press series on dramatists. This guide to references to Hellman's plays includes a lengthy biography and chronology of Hellman's life and career. Plot summaries of her plays, credits for their various productions, and a critical overview section that lists contemporary reviews fill the volume. Citations to reviews referenced in the critical overview section includes cogent lines from the cited review. An author and general index complete this work. This comprehensive listing of the considerable scholarship available on Hellman will update collections that own Mary Riordan's *Lillian Hellman: A Bibliography, 1926-1978* (see ARBA 81, entry 1284). This work is appropriate for graduate level theater collections.—**Glynys R. Thomas**

1249.   Shafer, Yvonne. **August Wilson: A Research and Production Sourcebook.** Westport, Conn., Greenwood Press, 1998. 142p. index. (Modern Dramatists Research and Production Sourcebooks, no.14). $65.00. ISBN 0-313-29270-1.

This most recent addition to the Modern Dramatists Research and Production Sourcebooks series of Greenwood Press continues the excellence of the series and provides valuable data on this prominent playwright of the American black experience. The note on codes and numbering is most vital in the use of this source; otherwise the organization is confusing. Two of the sections, "Chronology" and "Life and Career," provide biographical background and a justification of Wilson's position as a major playwright. The declaration is made that more work is in progress from Wilson. The next section of the study contains summaries and critical overviews of his six major plays thus far: *Fences* (1985); *Joe Turner's Come and Gone* (1986); *Ma Rainey's Black Bottom* (1984); *The Piano Lesson* (1990); *Seven Guitars* (1996); and *Two Trains Running* (1992). The primary bibliography is divided into annotations of nondramatic works and a listing of publications of texts of his plays. The main section of the study, the secondary bibliography, contains a chronologically arranged listing of reviews, articles and book length studies with brief annotations. The study concludes with both a primary and secondary bibliography, productions and credits, and both an author and general index. The study to date is complete. The annotations are concise and helpful; however, Wilson is still a productive playwright of whom many more plays are expected. The production of his next plays will obviously limit the scope of this study. [R: Choice, July/Aug 98, p. 1866]

—**Jackson Kesler**

28 Philosophy and Religion

PHILOSOPHY

Bibliography

1250. Radice, Roberto, and Richard Davies. **Aristotle's** *Metaphysics*: **Annotated Bibliography of the Twentieth-Century Literature.** Boston, Brill Academic, 1997. 904p. index. (Brill's Annotated Bibliographies, v.1). $305.50. ISBN 90-04-10895-5. ISSN 1386-8063.

This bibliography is first-rate. Before libraries and others rush to purchase this work, however, some caveats are in order. Those who intensely study Aristotle's *Metaphysics* are already familiar with a variety of sources. Radice's 1996 bibliography was a classic and lead to the production of a 2d edition in 1997. It is Radice's 2d edition that is translated here by Davies. Translation is entirely too narrow a term. Davies undertook the task of regularizing some of the language in the 1997 edition. The result is a better and cleaner bibliography. However, some libraries that are owners of the Radice 1997 Italian edition may not see that the regularization of the terminology is worth the price. Scholars interested in Aristotle's *Metaphysics* generally have some facility with foreign languages. The translation from Italian to English, especially when there is a great deal of foreign-language (non-English) material in the bibliography, may or may not make the material more accessible to scholars.

The overall premise of the bibliography is to gather, in as comprehensive a manner as possible, the literature on Aristotle from a variety of perspectives. Radice (and by extension, Davies) attempts to present material that will be of use in classics, philosophy, theology, or history of science. The material is as indifferent as possible to the well-worn and well-argued traditions of scholarship on Aristotle.

The inclusion of materials for this bibliography is done especially well, especially in this age of computer-assisted searching. A great amount of material on Aristotle is "hidden" material: That is, because of the central place *Metaphysics* occupies in western thought, much literature relies on *Metaphysics* without explicitly referencing the work. The materials cited here cover the time span from 1900 to 1996. In the opinion of the authors, to cover earlier works, such as ancient, medieval, or Renaissance literature, would have made the bibliography unwieldy and would have duplicated excellent work done by others.

The work is composed of five sections, followed by an extensive index. The first section is a list of the editions of *Metaphysics*. This list is followed by a list of translations into modern languages. Commentaries follow the section on translations. Bibliographic works complete the 4th section. The 5th and largest section (approximately 750 pages) is a chronological listing of secondary literature. Annotations in this section range from minimal ones to half a page or more in length. In general, the annotations are descriptive in nature. An excellent index is included in the volume. The typeface used in the index is of a readable size, and it is well laid out.

The larger question is not whether the work is good; it is. The real question is: Does a translation from Italian to English offer significant value for the relatively small audience for this work? This is a local question, driven by the depth of interest in *Metaphysics*. This work is highly recommended for collections with some existing specialty materials in Aristotelian philosophy and that do not have the Italian edition.—**C. D. Hurt**

Dictionaries and Encyclopedias

1251.   **The Encyclopedia of Applied Ethics.** Ruth Chadwick, ed. San Diego, Calif., Academic Press, 1997. 4v. index. $625.00. ISBN 0-12-227065-7.

As a field, applied ethics has become prominent during the past 25 to 30 years. This encyclopedia attests to the importance of developing ethical theories and their application to practical problems. The purpose of the encyclopedia is not to provide answers, but to lay out the ethical implications of an issue in its broadest perspective. Written for scholars and an educated audience, the encyclopedia explores the ethics of major contemporary issues—everything from the environment, law, science and engineering, the family and personal relationships, minority rights, and medicine to zoos and zoological parks.

Each of the 281 articles lays out an issue and the factors pertinent to ethical analysis. Each article begins with an outline followed by a glossary of terms, defining the sense in which particular words are used. For instance, the entry on brain death has definitions not only for "brain death," but also for "brain life," "brain stem death," and "persistent vegetative state." A glossary term may appear in more than one article depending on the context in which it is used.

For each entry the introduction states in clear concise terms the nature of an issue, the ethical factors involved, and the theories addressing it. The substantive discussion that follows objectively reviews the issue, often citing historical evidence and contemporary advancements affecting the debate, the philosophical and ethical approaches, and its secular and religious aspects. Related articles are cross-referenced. Short bibliographies do not list sources consulted but rather suggest materials for further study.

The *Encyclopedia of Bioethics*, now in its revised edition (see ARBA 96, entry 1429), covers some of the same issues. For example, both discuss "whistle-blowing." However, the *Encyclopedia of Bioethics* concentrates on the issue as it relates to health care, whereas this encyclopedia focuses on "whistle-blowing" in a wider context. This highlights the more general difference between the two encyclopedias—*Bioethics* is devoted more to the biological approach and *Applied Ethics* concentrates on the philosophical. These differences suggest that both of these landmark encyclopedias merit a place in academic and large public libraries serving an educated population.—**Bernice Bergup**

1252.   **Encyclopedia of Empiricism.** Don Garrett and Edward Barbanell, eds. Westport, Conn., Greenwood Press, 1997. 455p. index. $99.50. ISBN 0-313-28932-8.

Spelled with a lowercase "e," "empiricism" designates a philosophical emphasis on the relative importance of experience as a source of knowledge. Capitalized, "Empiricism" names a philosophical movement of the seventeenth and eighteenth centuries, centered in although not confined to Great Britain, which, at least as articulated by its leading lights, allowed experience exclusive claim to grounding anything qualifying as knowledge.

This concise encyclopedia embraces empiricism in its wider meaning, at the same time placing Empiricism—the particular historical movement—at center stage. The longest article of this work, not surprisingly, is on David Hume, the quintessential Empiricist. Prominently featured as well are other Empiricist household names such as John Locke and George Berkeley, and key Empiricist preoccupations such as causation, ideas, induction, and our knowledge of space. But concern with the historical antecedents of Empiricism, its wider intellectual context and especially the subsequent development of its themes, as well as with empiricism as a broader tendency of thought, yields substantial coverage of topics beyond the usual Empiricist focus. There are, for example, an 8-page article on Aristotle and a 12-page article on Bertrand Russell. A 13-page discussion of Isaac Newton explores the latter's complex relationship to empiricist convictions. Less prominent philosophical lights, such as Pierre Gassendi, Thomas Reid, and Ernst Mach receive proportionately more attention here than in general philosophical histories or reference works. Also coming in for substantial attention are related movements or schools of thought, including skepticism, behaviorism, logical positivism, operationism, and pragmatism.

Few if any entries here are unique or peculiar; most are duplicated in almost any general philosophical dictionary or encyclopedia. However, its treatment of topics in relation to a single common (if broad) theme, and at times with uncommon scope, should make this work a useful supplement to other sources wherever philosophy is studied in depth. Articles are signed (there are about 75 contributors), and a competent index is provided.
—**Hans E. Bynagle**

1253.   Hollis, Daniel Webster, III. **The ABC-CLIO World History Companion to Utopian Movements.** Santa Barbara, Calif., ABC-CLIO, 1998. 303p. illus. index. (ABC-CLIO World History Companions). $60.00. ISBN 0-87436-882-0.

Political creatures have long thought that they could make this world better than it is. From Plato's *Republic* to Thomas More's *Utopia* to Polybius's *Ultima Thule* to Henry David Thoreau's *Walden*, nearly every thinker, writer, poet, or muser has come up with his or her own utopia. No standard reference tool has been produced on utopias until now. The present volume really skims the surface of both political and literary utopias, citing texts, authors, places, and events. Noticeably missing are some obvious "perfect cities" such as Camelot or the Thule (mentioned in Virgil) referred to above. Yet included are unexpected delights, such as G. K. Chesterton's *Notting Hill* novel. Suffice it to say that the book has both a wide and a narrow grasp. As with any work, notable exceptions abound. The book's insistence on being politically correct by being multiculturally right more than likely tilted space toward inclusion of China's *Pingshu* and away from other places or events. As an *isagogic* on the topic, *Utopian Movements* more than satisfies.—**Mark Y. Herring**

Handbooks and Yearbooks

1254.   **Companion Encyclopedia of Asian Philosophy.** Brian Carr and Indira Mahalingam, eds. New York, Routledge, 1997. 1136p. index. $180.00. ISBN 0-415-03535-X.

This can be classified as a survey book, one of those massive attempts to present in a single volume the origins, tenets, development, and sociological conditions of the philosophy of an entire continent. Included are Persian, Indian, Chinese, Japanese, Buddhist, and Islamic philosophies. Glossaries of each philosophy's main terms are appended. Each chapter has copious footnotes. The work is a product of an international team of scholars under the guidance of Brian Carr of the University of Nottingham and Indira Mahalingam of the University of Exeter.

The single-volume work progresses as expected, with introductions of each area, main tenets and origins, development, social influences, and even contemporary trends. Sometimes the reader is even treated to analyses of the type of analysis being applied. The volume does not concentrate only on introductory concepts; some of the more esoteric issues are also covered. However, do not expect a treatise on the Discussions in the White Tiger Hall (Po Hu T'ung) or a chronology of events. The volume traces the evolution of concepts and often categorizes dialectically rather than historically. Although this is certainly traditional, a more comparative approach might have yielded fresh insights. This work should not be thought of as an introductory text. Readers would do well to have at least a nodding acquaintance with philosophy, and, more than that, Eastern philosophy. Students of René Descartes, David Hume, and Bertrand Russell, though more comfortable with Indian philosophy, would find themselves ill at ease in the Confucian shrines and Shingon temples. Also, this is not the accessible kind of survey book intended for the mass market, but rather is meant for the scholar of related disciplines needing a firmer hold on Asian philosophy. Finally, this is not a sourcebook whose primary aim is to quote main works while providing annotated explications. Quotations are made, but more parenthetically, because the main purpose of this work is explication.

Whether these are flaws must depend upon the reader's purpose. Some prefer the sourcebook format, whereas others may benefit from extensive works on individual philosophies. Still others may desire the more comparative approach. However, for the serious investigator beginning his work in Eastern thought, or for the scholar of Asian studies wanting to explore differing viewpoints offered globally, this is a fine work. [R: RUSQ, Fall 97, p. 86]—**Kenneth I. Saichek**

1255.   **From the Beginning to Plato.** C. C. W. Taylor, ed. New York, Routledge, 1997. 494p. index. (Routledge History of Philosophy, v.1). $85.00. ISBN 0-415-06272-1.

It is easy to count on one hand those histories or compendiums of philosophy that are both fact-packed and readable. *A History of Western Philosophy* (Routledge, 1994) comes to mind. For sheer amount of information, no one has yet improved upon *The Encyclopedia of Philosophy* (Macmillan and the Free Press, 1967). Given this lineage, the present volume could have gone in either direction, either inspiring or disappointing. It does neither, beginning well while never fully satisfying.

The articles are good and cover each subject thoroughly, but the writing is stilted at times. Thus, the article "The Polis and Its Culture" is informative but rudimentary. The article on Heraclitus is solid but plodding, and that on the Sophists is full but not full-bodied. Many will like this academic approach, but others will long to consort with the aforementioned *The Encyclopedia of Philosophy*. The contributors are a veritable "who's who" in philosophy. It is a pity that not many of them are ever far removed from the rigors of academic journal writing.

Librarians will be hard pressed trying to decide if this set fits the reference category exclusively or if it is better tailored for the general collection. Internal evidence makes it lean more toward the latter than the former, but a good case can be made for both. *Encyclopedia of Classical Philosophy* (see ARBA 98, entry 1334) is clearly more reference fodder. The Routledge set will be valuable for its updated bibliographies following each section and for newer interpretations. Yet even smaller libraries will want to stand for the previously mentioned titles.

—**Mark Y. Herring**

1256.   Magee, Bryan. **The Story of Philosophy.** New York, DK Publishing, 1998. 240p. illus. index. $29.95. ISBN 0-7894-3511-X.

Purists, such as this reviewer, are inclined to see such a book and turn up their noses. Coffee-table claptrap, they might say. But this purist breaks ranks, seeing a book like this and heaving a sigh of relief. In a discipline of arch-feminist studies, where people say things like "linguistify [my] positionality," and "Queer Studies," wherein places like Duke University are seriously considering serious study of transsexuals, philosophy needs all the help it can get. When that help comes in the form of a luscious and enticing book filled with ruminations both great and small, this reviewer exults.

This book, exorbitantly filled with pictures, drawings, etchings, and more, covers nearly all of western thought. From the Greeks and their world to the rationalists to the empiricists past Henri-Louis Bergson and Karl Popper to Jostein Gaarder's 1991 novelization of this subject in *Sophie's World*, Magee's book is water to a dry and thirsty land. Even the glossary is valuable. Yes, there are pitfalls in such an undertaking: Greek philosophy (all 500-plus years of it) is covered in less than 50 pages, pages covered with as many illustrations as text. The inscrutable medievals, wherein we get nearly all modern philosophy in some rechauffed form, is covered in eight pages, and so it goes.

But adversity's sweet milk, philosophy, finds its finest hour. Since sound bites have taken over the world, one cannot hope to hold the attention of modern minds much longer than 15 seconds. In an age so ripe for introspection beyond the "e" of me, this book comes as a must, not only for all libraries, but surely for all homes as well.

—**Mark Y. Herring**

1257.   **Sourcebook for Modern Japanese Philosophy: Selected Documents.** David A. Dilworth, Valdo H. Viglielmo, and Agustin Jacinto Zavala, eds. Westport, Conn., Greenwood Press, 1998. 420p. index. (Resources in Asian Philosophy and Religion). $95.00. ISBN 0-313-27433-9.

This sourcebook is an excellent addition to many libraries because it brings hard-to-find materials into a readable and useful form. Translations from the Japanese of the seven "Kyoto school" philosophers of this century provide scholars and students the readily accessible texts in order to begin work in this direction. The commentaries are useful to the casual reader and intriguing to the researcher. Especially valuable is their presentation of entire works, essays, and full chapters of books. The "golden years" of modern Japanese philosophy during World War II, and indeed the entire early Showa period, 1926 to 1949, is represented. The real struggle is between western and Asian influences on philosophy, and for this reason the book serves as a fascinating comparative source as well. The editors have provided a sourcebook that can be used by students and general readers in order to understand a particularly interesting period of Japanese philosophy and its interaction with the West.—**Linda L. Lam-Easton**

1258.   **A Young Person's Guide to Philosophy: "I Think, Therefore I Am."** Jeremy Weate, ed. New York, DK Publishing, 1998. 64p. illus. index. $16.95. ISBN 0-7894-3074-6.

A Young Persons Guide to Philosophy: "I Think, Therefore I Am" is a fascinating way of introducing the great philosophers to young readers. Why am I here? Am I dreaming? Is there a God? These are all questions that have perplexed young minds throughout the ages. The editor of this book presents to the reader philosophers who have grappled with these questions for centuries.

The 1st section of the book is a chronological journey through the history of Western philosophy, looking at the lives and the times of some of philosophy's greatest thinkers. The pronunciation guide after each philosopher's name is helpful. The 2d section looks at the philosophers in the context of their ideas and groups them into different schools of thought: early Greeks, cynics, stoics, idealists, materialists, scholastics, rationalists, empiricists, pragmatists, phenomenologists, existentialists, post-modernists, and a separate list of feminist philosophers. Socrates, the father of Western philosophy, receives special attention. An index, a glossary, and beautiful illustrations add to the usefulness of this book, which is recommended for public, elementary, and high school libraries.

—**Mary L. Bowman**

Indexes

1259.   **A Cumulative Index to Volumes I-VI of Paul Oskar Kristeller's Iter Italicum.** Kinderhook, N.Y., E. J. Brill, 1997. 581p. $182.50. ISBN 90-04-10592-1.

This book is a cumulative index to the finding aid to uncataloged and partly cataloged Renaissance humanist manuscripts. The main work emphasizes works in Italian collections, but is not confined to them.

The 6-volume original work has indexes, some of which are bound with the volume and some that are separate. The current cumulation aims at making access less cumbersome by reducing the number of volumes to be consulted. In compiling the index automatically, it was discovered that various Latin and vulgar versions of the same name were used over the course of the 30 years taken to produce the original volumes. Names that undoubtedly refer to the same individual have been grouped together under one of them, although the need to check variants has not been eliminated. The index is mainly one of proper names, although anonymous works have been entered under titles, subjects, or literary genres. Authors, translators, and commentators are all treated alike. The index entries give volume and page numbers in the main work and indicate with an asterisk if the name appears more than once on the page indicated.

There is also a CD-ROM version of the entire work, which was published in 1995. The digital version does not take into account pseudonyms and tacit attributions. The indexes do have these features, making the print volumes still valuable.

This is a highly specialized work that research collections owning the main work will want to acquire, funds permitting. [R: C&RL, Sept 97, p. 477]—**Nigel Tappin**

RELIGION

General Works

Bibliography

1260.   **Critical Review of Books in Religion 1997, Volume 10.** Charles Prebish and others, eds. Atlanta, Ga., Scholars Press, 1998. 307p. index. $35.00. ISSN 0894-8860.

As noted in its editor's foreword, this 1997 edition of the *Critical Review of Books in Religion* (CRBR) is the last to combine both brief reviews and longer review articles. Hereafter, the *Journal of Biblical Literature* and the *Journal of the American Academy of Religion* will publish short reviews electronically on the Scholars Press TELA Website, and further editions of CRBR will contain only review articles. This volume combines 7 review essays with 70 short reviews in 13 categories ranging from "Arts, Literature, and Religion" to "Women and Religion." Of the religions represented in these groups, three are devoted to biblical studies, with others on Buddhism and Hinduism but none on Islam, which is addressed in B. Wheeler's essay on four recent studies of religion and Islamic law by A. Reinhart, B. Weiss, M. Chamberlain, and N. Calder; inexplicably, the titles of their books are never mentioned in the review. M. Baumann's survey of recent studies and sources in Buddhism compactly discusses a variety of works dating from 1968. E. Epp reviews the state of early Christian literacy in commenting on Harry Gamble's *Books and Readers in the Early Church* (Yale University Press, 1997), and R. Gundy meticulously examines Hans Betz's massive commentary on the Sermon on the Mount. B. Holdrege reviews six books by F. Staal, J. Heesterman, and B. Smith on aspects of Vedic studies, and B. Stephens traces the links among several analyses of the U.S. churches in the eighteenth and nineteenth centuries by M. Valerie, D. Kling, J. Rohrer, S. Graham, and R. Wentz. New Testament scholars will find C. Newman's balanced review of N. Thomas Wright's *Jesus and the Victory of God* (Augsburg Fortress, 1996) of interest.

This volume of CRBR will be of most use to advanced students, especially those in schools of religion. One hopes that the next issue will reduce the number of distracting typographical errors; for example, Newman probably meant to say that in Jesus Yahweh acted "climactically," not "climatically."—**Christopher Baker**

Biography

1261. **Our Sunday Visitor's Encyclopedia of Saints.** By Matthew Bunson, Margaret Bunson, and Stephen Bunson. Huntington, Ind., Our Sunday Visitor, 1998. 797p. illus. index. $39.95. ISBN 0-87973-588-0.

When examining a copy of the *Encyclopedia of Saints* for the first time, readers might turn to the list of names to see if their name is also that of a saint. Should that fail, they might then look for feast days to see what saint is listed on their birthday.

The scope of the encyclopedia includes more than 10,000 alphabetic entries, making this the most comprehensive guide ever published on the saints. Entries, which range from *Aaron* to *Zoticus*, include names, dates, feast days, and biographical details on both saints and beati (candidates who have been declared blessed by the church). Many entries are just four or five lines, although a long one may be 14 to 20 lines. The writing style is simple, with succinct short stories. At 71 pages, the index is particularly exhaustive. Appendixes include "Emblems of the Saints," "Father of the Church," two pages of "Martyrs of the United States of America," "Mystics," and "Patron Saints."

The hagiography is assembled from biographies, legends, martyrologies, calendars, and liturgical texts. The earliest known collection is from 260 to 340 C.E. After official canonization the saint is forever a part of the church's official list of those venerated. The history of the process of canonization is of interest to everyone, familiar with it or not.

From a student needing help on a research project to a pastor refreshing himself on church history, a reader can enjoy studying or browsing about the saints. Many drawings suggestive of woodcuts are scattered throughout the text, giving a more authoritative tone than would any photographs. The slick, attractive hardcover is appropriately decorated with blue sky, white clouds, and, of course, a halo.—**Jerri Spoehel**

1262. **The Oxford Dictionary of Saints.** 4th ed. By David Hugh Farmer. New York, Oxford University Press, 1997. 547p. $15.95pa. ISBN 0-19-280058-2.

The Oxford Dictionary of Saints has been well covered by *American Reference Books Annual* in previous years (see ARBA 88, entry 1424, for a review of the 2d edition). By now this source is well known as a respected source of information, particularly on English saints. The author, knowing full well that there are other, more comprehensive reference works updated frequently, such as *Bibliotheca Sanctorum, Les Vies des Saints et des Bienheureux, L'Histoire des Saints de la Sainteté Chrètienne,* and *Butler's Lives of the Saints,* makes no claim to be comprehensive. Included are all English saints, including those dying abroad and those of foreign birth dying in Britain; all saints with notable cult followings as evidenced by churches dedicated to them or inclusion of their names in notable liturgical calendars for celebration, such as the *Book of Common Prayer* and the Roman Calendar of 1969; the most important and representative saints of Ireland, Scotland, and Wales; other saints important in the Christian church; saints of European countries and the United States; and recently canonized saints in whom there is public interest. In the case of this 4th edition, the latter category includes saints of Vietnam and Korea, founders/foundresses of religious congregations, and 40 martyrs of England and Wales (treated in 1 entry). This book excludes current candidates for sainthood and individuals who were candidates but failed to become canonized by the Roman Catholic Church.

Intended for personal collection, special religious libraries, and public and academic libraries, this book can be used by all adult readers. Entries all have bibliographic references and vary in length from one-half column to two pages. This edition is 17 pages longer than the 3d edition, is paperback, and is printed on paper typical of inexpensive paperbacks. All the appendixes of the 3d edition are present—principal patronages of saints and the principal iconographic emblems of saints. There is an index of places venerating particular saints and a calendar of principal feasts. New in this edition is a three-page list of Patron Saints of countries and towns (exclusive of

Great Britain and Ireland). Why this has not been merged with the regular index of places, which accomplishes the same purpose, is unclear. Persons seeking biographical information on recently canonized Roman Catholic saints may find their names listed in the annual *Catholic Almanac* (see ARBA 95, entry 1471), although there is no information there about most of them. Inclusion of more biographical entries of recently canonized saints would make this book more useful and worth purchasing as often as new editions of it are currently appearing. It is not useful as a source of Eastern Christian saints, nor does the author indicate that it will be.—**Agnes H. Widder**

1263.   Whiteside, Lesley. **The Book of Saints.** New York, Quadrillion, 1998. 142p. illus. $17.99. ISBN 1-85833-396-2.

Aesthetically alert church visitors appreciate stained-glass windows for their numinous value, although the creation of such devotional windows has not been a widely esteemed art. This beautifully illustrated volume indicates that it should be. *The Book of Saints* provides a fresh view of more than 60 of the best-loved saints rendered in stained glass. By and large, they are biblical figures and those from the days of the early church, among them Peter and Paul, Mark and Luke, Joseph of Arimathea, and Stephen. Additionally, there are such individuals as Ambrose and Augustine, Benedict and Patrick, Dunstan and Thomas Beckett, and representatives of the medieval period.

The sharp, bright photographs are the work of Sonia Halliday and Laura Lushington, who have photographed most of Europe's famous windows, and David Lawrence, historian and stained glass conservator. For each photograph, Whiteside has provided a corresponding page of text that details briefly its narrative, deciphers complex signs and symbols, and interprets other matters when necessary. The result is an artistic volume that enriches our knowledge of men and women whose lives still serve as inspiration. If a negative judgment be offered, this volume is too short. Possibly the author is planning several sequels or a much larger book.—**G. A. Cevasco**

Dictionaries and Encyclopedias

1264.   Beit-Hallahmi, Benjamin. **The Illustrated Encyclopedia of Active New Religions, Sects, and Cults.** rev. ed. New York, Rosen Publishing, 1998. 488p. illus. index. $59.95. ISBN 0-8239-2586-2.

Beit-Hallahmi provides a way for researchers to find their way through the thicket of active sects and cults that have blossomed worldwide within the past 200 years. Sources include direct contact with the groups. The longest articles are one-half page; most are a short paragraph, and many quote the group's distinguishing beliefs from its own literature. Most note roots in a parent group, name of founder, date of founding, a cross-reference to related groups, and geographic location. A comparison between the 1993 and 1998 editions shows that the strongest new feature is extensive indexing. Sorting out the more than 1,800 entries is an "Alternate Group Names Index"; a "Geographical Index"; a "Categorical Names Index," which clusters groups by parent group; and a "Personal Names Index." The new edition boasts 147 additional pages, and the author claims 700 changes. Black-and-white photographs, some full page, are also featured. Students, general readers, journalists, educators, and others who may need to research a group quickly should have access to this encyclopedia.
—**Edna M. Boardman**

1265.   Benowitz, June Melby. **Encyclopedia of American Women and Religion.** Santa Barbara, Calif., ABC-CLIO, 1998. 466p. illus. index. $75.00. ISBN 0-87436-887-1.

Throughout U.S. religious history, women have been a minority in many denominations and sects. The Pope spoke out against the ordination of women in the Anglican Church. The Promisekeepers have excluded women from their modern day revival meetings. Yet, other denominations, such as Episcopalians, Presbyterians, and Jews have begun to accept women as leaders. Others, such as the Christian Scientists, Shakers, and some Native Americans, have followed the spiritual teachings of women for centuries. The topics surveyed in this book include abortion, birth control, cults, divorce, equal rights amendment, feminist theology, Jews, and transcendentalism. There are more than 305 alphabetic entries, with many portraits and photographs of women who framed U.S. religious life. A sampling of the biographies covered include Tammy Faye Baker, Evangeline Booth, Coretta Scott King, Shirley MacLaine, Sojourner Truth, and Harriet Tubman.

Each entry has cross-references to related material and a list of supporting references. A comprehensive bibliography and chronology and an index are included. Public and academic libraries with large religious or women's studies collections will find this to be an invaluable reference tool.—**Kay M. Stebbins**

1266.   **The Encyclopedia of Apocalypticism.** John J. Collins, Bernard McGinn, and Stephen J. Stein, eds. New York, Continuum Publishing, 1998. 3v. illus. index. $285.00/set. ISBN 0-8264-1087-1.

Much will likely be said in the next year or so about "the Apocalypse," "apocalyptic," and "apocalypticism" due to the approach of and transition into the next millennium. However, the subject is nothing new. The relationship between good and evil on the stage of world history and the intervention of God to end that struggle has been a feature of Judaism, Christianity, and Islam for centuries. This work traces the history of apocalypticism from its roots in Near Eastern and Mediterranean mythologies to its flowering in the ancient Hebrew religion to its appearance in late twentieth-century political rhetoric. Volume 1, "The Origins of Apocalypticism in Judaism and Christianity," presents the mythological thought in which Jewish apocalyptic thought arose, the development of Jewish apocalyptic thought through the end of the first century C.E., and the development of Christian apocalyptic thought from Jesus through the end of the apostolic period. Volume 2, "Apocalypticism in Western History and Culture," continues the story of the development of apocalyptic traditions—primarily Christian—in Europe and the Near East through 1800 C.E. It includes chapters on apocalyptic themes in medieval art and literature. Volume 3, "Apocalypticism in the Modern Period and the Contemporary Age," picks up at the colonial period and continues the survey to current times, focusing at the end on the secularization of apocalyptic in popular culture, science, and politics.

This set is an encyclopedia in the classic sense rather than an expanded dictionary. It contains 43 comprehensive articles; each accompanied by a brief, sometimes annotated, bibliography. There is no comprehensive index for the set, but each volume has indexes of biblical references (volume 1 includes other ancient sources) and names. The articles are well written and the subject is fascinating. The *Encyclopedia of Apocalypticism* is highly recommended.—**Craig W. Beard**

1267.   **The Modern Encyclopedia of Religions in Russia and Eurasia. Volume 7.** Paul D. Steeves, ed. Gulf Breeze, Fla., Academic International Press, 1997. 244p. illus. maps. $40.00. ISBN 0-87569-106-4.

The 7th volume of this concise encyclopedia covers topics beginning with "Deeses" and ending with "Eastern Siberia." The articles range from one-half-page to lengthy signed articles. For example, the article on "Dmitry of Rostov's Catechism" is 25 pages. The signed articles have bibliographies for further reading. There is a list of helpful abbreviations used in the encyclopedia, and the table of contents is at the end of the volume.

This resource can be recommended to those libraries that have *The Modern Encyclopedia of Religions in Russia and Eurasia*, volumes 1-6, as well as to libraries with special collection on Eastern religions and large academic libraries.—**Kay M. Stebbins**

1268.   **Our Sunday Visitor's Catholic Encyclopedia.** rev. ed. Peter M. J. Stravinskas, ed. Huntington, Ind., Our Sunday Visitor, 1998. 1040p. illus. $39.95. ISBN 0-87973-669-0.

With more than 3,000 entries, this 1-volume encyclopedia covers the spectrum of topics in Catholic history, doctrine, and practice. Entries range from a sentence or two to a few pages in length and are clearly written. The economy used in writing the articles applies to details as well. They are used to guide, not to bury the reader with minutiae.

Many articles have illustrations and also suggestions for further reading (new to the revised edition). Articles have been rewritten, such as "Capital Punishment," which now refers to the *Catechism* and to *Evangelium Vitae*. The entry on "Catechism of the Catholic Church" has been redone to accommodate the 1992 document. Editorial changes have led to the dropping of some articles (e.g., "Aaron") and adding others (e.g., "Abel").

Our Sunday Visitor also publishes a weekly Catholic newspaper of the same name with a conservative editorial policy. This encyclopedia follows that viewpoint, and so the articles generally do not depart from Catholic Church doctrinal teachings. With that observation in mind, *Our Sunday Visitor's Catholic Encyclopedia* is an adequate basic reference for the Catholic faith. Fuller doctrinal coverage, which addresses the current debates in the church, can be found in *The Modern Catholic Encyclopedia* (see ARBA 95, entry 1469) or *The Harper-Collins Encyclopedia of Catholicism* (see ARBA 96, entry 1469). Libraries that can afford it should purchase all three encyclopedias for the best overall coverage.—**Gerald L. Gill**

Directories

1269. Durusau, Patrick. **High Places in Cyberspace: A Guide to Biblical and Religious Studies, Classics, and Archaeological Resources on the Internet.** 2d ed. Atlanta, Ga., Scholars Press, 1998. 302p. index. (Scholars Press Handbook Series). $29.95pa. ISBN 0-7885-0488-6.

This well-researched, extensive volume is useful for the novice Internet user as well as the skilled searcher, for the person needing information for personal reasons and the serious scholar. This 2d edition of the book, first published in 1996, expands on the listings and includes a URL where updates of the volume can be accessed. Durusau's inclusive introduction explains the Internet, with both its usefulness and problems. Instructions are given for accessing Internet resources and using them effectively. These sources include electronic mailing lists, FTP, online libraries, search engines, and the World Wide Web. More than 1,000 annotated topical lists are provided and organized by type of resource. These wide-ranging topics provide links to classical literature, archaeological resources, maps, denominational sites, and biblical and theological resources from a wide variety of sources. An extensive subject index aids in locating sites, which are listed alphabetically. The book also provides instructions for creating personal Websites. The amount of information presented in this volume is most impressive.—**Janet Hilbun**

Handbooks and Yearbooks

1270. Matsunami, Kodo. **International Handbook of Funeral Customs.** Westport, Conn., Greenwood Press, 1998. 204p. index. $75.00. ISBN 0-313-30443-2.

Funeral rites vary greatly according to location, culture, and religion. In this book, Matsunami examines the process of death, burial, and mourning for approximately 200 countries throughout the world, organizing the material by geographic region. The contents cover Asia, Oceania, Africa, the Middle East, Europe, the Commonwealth of Independent States, North and Central America, and South America. The author, who is a professor of international cultural studies in Japan, provides a brief overview of the history and theory of the subject in the introduction, explaining significant differences among the major religions. The geographic entries vary from one paragraph in length to five pages or more for such large areas as China and others such as Great Britain that have a complex array of religions. Occasionally, Matsunami treats the reader to interesting trivia, such as the cremation rate in Great Britain and the number of mortuaries in the United States at various times, but most of the data are general in nature, supplying a quick and easy reference to the different funeral practices around the world. The index is basic, listing only country and territory names, so it will not help the student looking for other points of access. Still, this handbook is a useful and needed resource for students who are not seeking great depth on the subject.—**Jean Engler**

1271. **Religious Holidays and Calendars: An Encyclopedic Handbook.** 2d ed. Karen Bellenir, ed. Detroit, Omnigraphics, 1998. 316p. illus. index. $70.00. ISBN 0-7808-0258-6.

From early days, religion has been closely linked with the division of time and the origin of the calendar. Early civilizations had crude means of keeping track of time, but they soon realized that if groups were to meet together for religious purposes at regular intervals, a system had to be developed that would give them a common understanding of keeping track of the passing of time. This handbook records the early efforts and describes the holidays and calendars that have developed throughout the ages.

The book begins with four essays on the history of lunar, lunisolar, and solar calendars. The uses of these calendars and calendar reform since the mid-eighteenth century are also discussed. Part 3 contains an appendix, bibliography, and indexes. The appendix lists Internet sources for more information. The indexes include an alphabetic list of holidays, a chronological list of holidays, a calendar index, and a master index.

This 2d edition includes 450 religious holidays, 200 of which are new to this edition. The primary holy days and festivals of minority religions are here as well as the Christian and Jewish holidays.

Questions concerning the celebration of Tiragan in Zoroastrianism, the number of days and months in the Bahai calendar, the name of the first day in the Jain calendar, or the purpose of the Chinese Kitchen God Festival can all be readily answered in this encyclopedia through its well-organized arrangement and indexes. This work contains a lot of information on time-keeping and holiday traditions in world religions that will be useful for years to come.—**Sara R. Mack**

Bahá'í Faith

1272.   Adamson, Hugh C., and Philip Hainsworth. **Historical Dictionary of the Bahá'í Faith.** Lanham, Md., Scarecrow, 1998. 504p. illus. (Historical Dictionaries of Religions, Philosophies, and Movements, no.17). $65.00. ISBN 0-8108-3353-0.

This historical dictionary of the Bahá'í religion was compiled by the General Secretary of the Bahá'ís of the United Kingdom and a member of the administrative board. This volume is the 17th in a series of historical dictionaries of religious movements. The authors state that in addition to clarifying the foundation of this tradition to outsiders, they hope to deepen the understanding of members within the faith. Bahá'í traditions are an amalgam of Judaism, Christianity, Islam, and Buddhism that was formulated a century and a half ago. The dictionary excludes living members and limits the details of the founders to simple explanations. A timeline and overview of historical events contextualizes the entries. The bibliography is among the best of its kind, and the many appendixes help the reader with detailed information. The dictionary is readable and comprehensive to the general reader. As an introduction to the religion, it serves as a gathering place for the data but lacks a critical explanation of the data assembled. [R: Choice, Oct 98, p. 286]—**Linda L. Lam-Easton**

Bible Studies

Bibliography

1273.   Hupper, William G., comp. **An Index to English Periodical Literature on the Old Testament and Ancient Near Eastern Studies, Volume VII.** Lanham, Md., Scarecrow, 1998. 378p. (ATLA Bibliography Series, no.21). $55.00. ISBN 0-8108-3493-6.

The 7th volume of *An Index to English Periodical Literature on the Old Testament and Ancient Near Eastern Studies* provides more than 5,700 English references for the Near Eastern literary context for the Old Testament (see ARBA 95, entry 1451, for a review of the 6th volume). After opening with sections on the development of literature and papyrology, the compiler continues with sections on numerous classifications of Egyptian texts, including demotic materials and followed by an extensive section of nonbiblical Semitic texts. In this grouping, in addition to including the expected cuneiform textual references, he includes Sumerian materials due to their geographic location, while noting that their "linguistic family has not been determined" (p. viii). The volume concludes with sections on Caucasian (Aryan) texts: Elamite, Hurrian, Hittite, Greek, Cypriote, Mycenaean/Minoan, Latin, and Persian texts.

Although again neglecting to remind its users that this volume includes no works postdating 1969-1970, like its predecessors, the index provides a useful tool for researchers and students alike. Although researchers may wish for references to articles in other languages, references within the English-language articles will provide some access. This book, along with its predecessors, belongs in every university and theological library.

—**Susan Tower Hollis**

Dictionaries and Encyclopedias

1274.   **Dictionary of the Later New Testament and Its Developments.** Ralph P. Martin and Peter H. Davids, eds. Downers Grove, Ill., InterVarsity Press, 1997. 1289p. index. $39.99. ISBN 0-8308-1779-4.

With this volume, InterVarsity Press expands its series of dictionaries on the New Testament, which currently includes *Dictionary of Jesus and the Gospels* (DJG) (see ARBA 93, entry 1428) and *Dictionary of Paul and His Letters* (DPL) (see ARBA 95, entry 1450). This latest volume covers Acts, Hebrews, the general epistles, Revelation, and developments in early Christianity through C.E. 150. The contributors include 120 evangelical scholars, the majority of whom are from the United States (82) as well as the United Kingdom (16), Canada (10), and Australia (7). Among the most recognizable names are George Beasl-Murray, James Dunn, Howard Marshall, and Graham Stanton. As with the first two dictionaries, the evangelical respect for the authority of scripture (which should by no means be equated with fundamentalism) is combined with critical rigor.

Included among the more than 230 articles are entries on topics previously covered in DJG and DPL—Christology, the death of Christ, the kingdom of God, the resurrection, and synagogue—although here they are dealt with as they pertain to the later New Testament writings and early noncanonical Christian works (particularly the Apostolic Fathers). In addition to the entries on the New Testament documents, there are several other chapters that appear only in this volume: "Christianity and Judaism: Parting of the Ways," "Centers of Christianity," and "Social Setting of Early Non-Pauline Christianity." Each article is accompanied by an up-to-date and often extensive bibliography. The volume is thoroughly cross-referenced and includes scripture and subject indexes. This is a timely and authoritative reference work that should be in every biblical and theological library.—**Craig W. Beard**

1275. **Illustrated Dictionary of Bible Life & Times.** New York, Reader's Digest/Random House, 1997. 416p. illus. maps. index. $30.00. ISBN 0-89577-987-0.

From such everyday things as tools, food, and clothing to common practices to special customs, Reader's Digest has assembled more than 1,500 entries pertinent to the Bible. Each of the alphabetically arranged entries contains well-researched information that is presented in an easy-to-read style, common to books by this publisher. A verse that shows how the word is used in the Bible accompanies each one. Following the dictionary is a glossary of additional terms (also accompanied by Bible verses) that do not require lengthy explanations as do the entries in the dictionary.

The book is well illustrated with more than 500 photographs, maps, charts, and boxed features. The latter shows such processes as brick-making and spinning and weaving. These add substantially to the interest in browsing of the book and, in many cases, to the understanding of the definitions. A pronunciation guide would have added to the value of this reference tool, which will surely be appreciated by churches, religious schools, and the layperson studying the Bible. This work is recommended for public libraries. [R: BL, 1 Apr 98, p. 1348]
—**Jo Anne H. Ricca**

1276. **Theological Dictionary of the Old Testament, Volume IX.** G. Johannes Botterweck, Helmer Ringgren, and Heinz-Josef Fabry, eds. Translated by David E. Green. Grand Rapids, Mich., William B. Eerdmans, 1998. 563p. $48.00. ISBN 0-8028-2333-5.

In this volume, Green (who was the translator for volumes 4 through 7 and part of volume 3) provides a translation of Band V, Lieferungen 1 through 5 covering the Hebrew words from *marad* to *naqa*. The editors have put together a strong team of international scholars who can speak authoritatively on the meaning and use of these biblical terms in light of the cognates in the other Semitic languages and have maintained the format and high standards of the earlier volumes. The translator, by regularly transliterating the ancient scripts, has made the work accessible to readers without strong linguistic backgrounds, but because each word treated is introduced in transliterated Hebrew and the discussion presupposes some acquaintance with the grammar of biblical Hebrew, the reader must have at least some knowledge of Hebrew to make effective use of this dictionary. Libraries in institutions with strong programs in the area of biblical studies, and which have accessioned the earlier volumes in the series, will want to add this volume to their collections while eagerly awaiting the publication of the remaining translations. Green deserves great gratitude for his role in the translation of this critical reference work into English.—**Harold O. Forshey**

Handbooks and Yearbooks

1277. **The Expositor's Bible Commentary.** [CD-ROM]. Grand Rapids, Mich., Zondervan Publishing/ HarperCollins, 1997. Minimum system requirements: Windows 95 or Windows 3.1. 3MB hard disk space. $79.95.

The Expositor's Bible Commentary (EBC) is an established standard among evangelical Bible students. Now the 12-volume set, published between 1976 and 1992, is available on CD-ROM. The CD-ROM includes the New International Version of the Bible (NIV), so it can stand alone or be added to the *NIV Complete Bible Library* (see ARBA 98, entry 1380). The program can be run from the CD-ROM or loaded onto the computer's hard drive. The EBC data are divided into 5 files: volume 1 (introductory articles), Old Testament, Old Testament footnotes, New Testament, and New Testament footnotes. The commentary can be used in conjunction with the NIV text module. Multiple windows may be linked and tiled. Thus, as the user scrolls through the Bible, the corresponding commentary is displayed alongside. If both Old Testament and New Testament commentaries are opened and linked to the NIV, the user can move back and forth between the testaments and the commentary windows will react accordingly. In addition, the scripture references in the EBC are tagged so that clicking on them causes the referenced passage to be displayed in the NIV window.

Although this is a useful program, it needs some refining. First, the internal cross-references—from one article or commentary to another—are not tagged. Therefore, the reference "for further discussion, see EBC 1:13-20" in the note on Matthew 3:7 is not very helpful because there are no volume and page numbers in the CD-ROM version. Also the footnote numbers in the Old Testament and New Testament commentaries are not tagged, linking them to the footnotes themselves (although those in the introductory articles are), nor do the footnotes scroll in unison with the commentary text even when the windows are linked. Second, numerous scripture references are mistagged, primarily those that appear as chapter and verse numbers without the name of the book. For example, when the tagged reference in "This Jerusalem appearance also figures in John's account (20:19, 24)" (from Howard Marshall's article, "Jesus in the Gospels") is clicked, Matthew 20:19 is displayed in the NIV window. Furthermore, because the NIV does not contain the Apocrypha, unless the optional New Revised Standard Version module is installed, clicking on an Apocrypha reference is answered by an error message. Finally, authors are noted for the introductory articles but not for the commentaries. This program is good, but with attention to the shortcomings it could be very good.—**Craig W. Beard**

1278.   Finegan, Jack. **Handbook of Biblical Chronology: Principles of Time Reckoning in the Ancient World and Problems of Chronology in the Bible.** rev. ed. Peabody, Mass., Hendrickson, 1998. 426p. index. $34.95. ISBN 1-56563-143-9.

This text is a thorough resource for the chronological problems and questions associated with Biblical study. The author's detailed analysis of the vocabulary of time as presented in the Bible sets the tone for the parts that follow.

Part 1, section 2, "The Reckoning of Time in the Ancient World," carefully describes the chronological systems at work in the ancient world. The interspersed tables illustrate concepts discussed in the numbered sections. These divisions, however, do not hinder the reading of the text or the flow of the conceptual development. The section numbers also serve the index, facilitating topic location by the paragraph numbers.

Part 2, "Problems of Chronology in the Bible," is built on the understanding of the cultures, systems, chroniclers, and chronographers. The author admits it is not his intent to "deal with all the data or solve all the problems," rather to apply the approaches of the first part to the written references to time in the scripture. For example, the discussion at the end of the Old Testament section discussing the dates in Ezekiel begins with a brief citing of literature relevant to the topic. The following 4 numbered sections encompass references to one of the tables, discussion of specified dates, reckoned dates, and the methodologies used to reach the chronological conclusion.

The *Handbook of Biblical Chronology* is not for the casual reader seeking succinct and easily digested answers to questions of time, flow, and events in the Bible. This reference is distinctly focused and crafted for the student interested in exploring the framework of time in which the Biblical events are set. Further, any student of ancient chronological systems and their relevance to chronicled history or historiography can find ample foundational information in this work.—**Deborah K. Scott**

1279.   **The New Interpreter's Bible.** [CD-ROM]. Nashville, Tenn., Abingdon Press, 1997. Minimum system requirements (Windows version): IBM or compatible 386. CD-ROM drive. Windows 3.1 or higher. 4MB RAM. 6MB hard disk space. Minimum system requirements (Macintosh version): System 7.1 or greater. CD-ROM drive. 4MB RAM. 8MB hard disk space. $264.95.

The electronic edition of *The New Interpreter's Bible* (NIB) offers the New International Version (1978) and the New Revised Standard Version (NRSV, 1989) of the Bible in a full-text online database. The Apocryphal and Deuterocanonical books are represented by texts of the NRSV and the New American Bible (1970). In addition to the verse-by-verse English translation, NIB provides, besides exegetical commentary and interpretation mainly composed by Christian scholars, numerous visual arts (e.g., maps, charts, timelines, illustrations); footnotes;

word and phrase research; cross-references; ability to make marginal notes, insert bookmarks, and highlight portions of text; and other search engines for an informed academic and ecclesiastical read. For example, under the section "General Articles," the user will find relevant discussion on Hebrew literary genres, and in "Reflections" there are helpful thoughts for pulpit hermeneutics and Bible study classes. Overall, NIB is well designed, easy to navigate (if one has basic computer skills), and a worthwhile expository tool for students of the Bible. Regrettably, a number of Hebrew typographical errors were detected, such as a capital *K* in *zkr*, *tsdq* ("righteous") not *tsqd* (nonword), and *'l* ("God") not *l'* ("no").—**Zev Garber**

1280.   Richards, Larry. **The Bible: God's Word for the Biblically-Inept.** Lancaster, Pa., Starburst, 1998. 338p. illus. index. $16.95pa. ISBN 0-914984-55-1.

Written in the same style as the various "computer for dummies" books, this 352-page book discusses both the Old Testament and the New Testament. It includes margin notes, definitions of unfamiliar terms, cross-references, and identification of key points; commentary from seven other authors (although the credentials of these authors are not provided); and maps and other illustrations. Each chapter ends with a "Chapter Wrap-Up" summarizing the information in that chapter and "Study Questions," with an answer key in the back of the book.

The book follows the Bible itself, starting with Genesis in the Old Testament and ending with Revelation from the New Testament. There is a table of contents and an index, but neither is particularly helpful in finding information. Although most of Richards's explanations of the meaning of various Bible passages are good and would be helpful to someone just beginning to learn about the Bible and God's word, the number of factual errors is bothersome. Some of the errors are peripheral—such as attributing the authorship of the Pentateuch to Moses, when both Jewish and Christian authorities believe it was written by several authors. Others errors may confuse and misinform a newcomer to the Bible, such as placing Mary the Mother of Jesus among the women at the tomb the morning of the resurrection. Therefore, this book can only be recommended for someone who is truly biblically inept.—**Kay Mariea**

Christianity

Biography

1281.   **Biographical Dictionary of Christian Missions.** Gerald H. Anderson, ed. New York, Macmillan Library Reference/Simon & Schuster Macmillan, 1998. 845p. index. $100.00. ISBN 0-02-864604-5.

This is a biographical dictionary of deceased Christian missionaries arranged by surname. Entries are provided by a team of about 50 professors of missiology and those who promote mission work, recruit missionaries, administer, write, pray about, or fund mission work. There are no entries for missions. Included are articles of a paragraph or more on 2,400 persons from Roman Catholic, Orthodox, Anglican, Protestant, Pentecostal, and Independent traditions, as well as persons who worked in indigenous churches. All of the missionaries have served since post-New Testament times. There are no other biographical dictionaries of missionaries of the past. Bibliographies follow practically all the entries. A list of standard religious biographical works is included—the text is not referenced to these entries, but they will certainly contain information on prominent missionaries included in this work.

The editor has edited or coedited at least eight other works on various mission-related topics. He is editor of the journal *International Bulletin of Missionary Research*, which is indexed by *Religion Index One*. He is also director of the Overseas Ministries Study Center in New Haven, Connecticut, a 75-year-old interdenominational, cross-cultural residential center for continuing education in Christian missions. Various appendixes enhance the usefulness of the work. These allow one to look up areas of the world and find those who have been missionaries there. There is a list of missionaries by broad denomination or religious order (e.g., Lutherans, Baptists, Dominicans). There are lists of martyrs; missionaries who worked with women, children, and youth; missionaries by period (e.g., pre-800, 1851-1900); medical missionaries; and Bible translators.

The objective of the book is to provide a "who's who" in the history of the expansion of Christianity throughout the world since the New Testament times. This work will be used by ministers, missionaries, seminary and Bible college students and teachers, church libraries, and large academic libraries on campuses with active religious studies or religious history programs. Persons with expert knowledge of mission works by particular denominations may well find errors of omission and commission. Among those missing are James and Amanda Ferry, American Board missionaries to Indians on Mackinac Island in the 1820s and 1830s; James Cantine, Jay Capinga, and Sharon and Marion (Wells) Thoms, who worked in the Middle East; and Thomas Valpy French, who is indexed under India but not under the Middle East. It would seem that there should be more Orthodox missionaries, such as Armenians, Copts, Ethiopians, Greeks, Russians, and Syrians, than the Presbyterian and reformed category, but there is not. All in all, however, this is a good, although specialized work, with no competitors. [R: Choice, July/Aug 98, p. 1828]—**Agnes H. Widder**

1282.   Carpenter, Ronald H. **Father Charles E. Coughlin: Surrogate Spokesman for the Disaffected.** Westport, Conn., Greenwood Press, 1998. 204p. index. (Great American Orators, no.28). $69.50. ISBN 0-313-29040-7.

Although the title may indicate that this book is a biography, it is instead one volume of a series on great U.S. orators focused primarily on the nature of their persuasive discourse. Not a reference book in the real sense of the term, it is intended to meet the needs of scholars and students of the history and criticism of U.S. public address.

Charles E. Coughlin, pastor of a Catholic church in a suburb of Detroit during the Depression era, is surely one of the great orators of his time. In 1926 he began broadcasting his sermons on a weekly radio program. The popularity of the radio and his exceptional talent as a speaker combined to make the programs immediately successful, first on the local level and later on the national level. Many of the people who were struggling to survive through the desolate days of the Great Depression were looking for someone to voice their dissatisfaction and alleviate their pain. Coughlin became in reality "the surrogate spokesman for the disaffected," the phrase aptly used as the subtitle of the book. In time, as his programs became more involved in social, political, and economic issues, and especially as he railed ever more vehemently against the financial community and the policies of the Roosevelt administration, many politicians and his religious superiors became alarmed. In the end, when it became evident that he was espousing anti-Semitic and even Nazi ideology, the church ordered him to cease all nonreligious activities.

The present volume is devoted to a critical analysis of different aspects of Coughlin's life and work, with focus on the rhetorical criticism. It also includes copies of six of his most significant speeches. Extensive notes are appended to each of the five critical chapters, and a lengthy bibliography and index are included. The material is well written and thoroughly researched, drawing on primary sources and scholarly secondary sources, but again with the emphasis on the impact of Coughlin's rhetorical abilities. Although it is a worthwhile contribution to the literature of oratory, because the arrangement of the analyses is somewhat difficult to follow and the work presupposes some knowledge of the subject, it is recommended only for academic libraries serving primarily upper division and graduate students.—**Lucille Whalen**

1283.   Cohn-Sherbok, Lavinia. **Who's Who in Christianity.** New York, Routledge, 1998. 361p. $75.00; $19.99. ISBN 0-415-13582-6; 0-415-13583-4pa.

This volume is a desk reference-sized guide to 1,200 prominent persons in the history of Christianity. The primary criterion for inclusion was whether the individual has had a continuing impact on the life of the Christian church. Curiously, secular composers, artists, and writers such as Johann Wolfgang von Goethe and Wolfgang Amadeus Mozart are included, as well as saints, theologians, and missionaries, from Jesus to Billy Graham, Wolfhart Pannenberg, Sun-Myung Moon, and Gustavo Gutierrez. The entries are listed alphabetically, are brief (150 words on average, with some more than 500 words), and include the source or sources from which the information was compiled. Each entry contains a short biographical sketch, with the significance of the individual's contribution and a history of his or her work. There are no illustrations.

At the end of the volume, following a glossary of Christian religious terms, the categories (e.g., popes, apostles, missionaries, and more) assigned to each of the entries are listed. In place of an index of entries, the 1,200 persons are listed under these categories. Apparently each person in this handbook has been assigned to only one of the categories. For example, Martin Luther is listed as a theologian but not a denomination founder. In addition, within the volume there are few cross-references. Menno Simons is found before Thomas Merton, with no reference from Simons to see under Menno. In that this person, who gave his name to the Mennonites, is commonly known by his given name, the position is correct; but the uninitiated user could be confused. In an otherwise useful resource these are small flaws.

The volume contains a chronology of the chief historical events in the Christian church and concludes with a short bibliography of encyclopedias and reference works for additional information. The author has been involved in the authorship of several reference works on Christianity and Judaism and declares that a serious attempt has been made to provide global coverage. Although not as detailed as the 1,824-page *Oxford Dictionary of the Christian Church* (3d ed.; see ARBA 98, entry 1389), this is nonetheless recommended for libraries wanting a single-source biographical dictionary of Christianity, and is a particularly good value at the paperback price for those with limited funds. [R: BL, 1 Feb 98, p. 942]—**Ingrid Schierling Burnett**

Catalogs and Collections

1284. **Vatican Archives: An Inventory and Guide to Historical Documents of the Holy See.** Francis X. Blouin Jr., ed. New York, Oxford University Press, 1997. 588p. index. $150.00. ISBN 0-19-509552-9.

The Holy See remains both the best known and the least penetrable institution in worldwide Christianity. To make the private archives (Archivio Segreto Vaticano) more public requires adeptness in archival research and computer-based technology. This volume is parsed into 7 parts and 3 appendixes. Each part contains a mini-introduction, annotated entries, bibliographic references, lists of official indexes and inventories, notes, and the location where the records are physically located (mainly in archives within the Apostolic See but also in holdings at Trinity College, Dublin; at the Archives Nationales, Paris; and at the Bibliothèque Nationale, Paris).

The historical documents and other official materials that Blouin and his editorial staff have assembled provide an important resource for the scholarly community. Readers will encounter the role played by the Roman Catholic Church in the history of Christianity, the history of western culture and institutions (a notable lacuna is the many records of the Holy Office pertaining to the Inquisition), the history of the evolution of the modern state, the history of exploration and colonization, world affairs, and much more. Above all, data from the sixteenth century to the present on the papacy—especially in reference to the authority, jurisdiction, and function of government that derive from it—are now accessible in a properly designed and readable format. A comprehensive multilingual bibliography, sweeping in its content, adds to this magisterial work. All in all, this volume is an indispensable research tool and guide for a study of the Vatican and its multiple activities and agencies. [R: Choice, July/Aug 98, p. 1826]—**Zev Garber**

Dictionaries and Encyclopedias

1285. **A Dictionary of Early Christian Beliefs: A Reference Guide to More Than 700 Topics Discussed by the Early Church Fathers.** David W. Bercot, ed. Peabody, Mass., Hendrickson, 1998. 704p. $34.95. ISBN 1-56563-357-1.

In this day when so many diverse opinions exist concerning the tenets of the Christian religion, a book such as this dictionary can help bring us back to the thinking of the early fathers of the Christian faith. This book contains quotations from the writings of more than 40 early Christian writers of the pre-Nicene era. Bercot has included material mainly from orthodox sources, although Manes, Marcion, Valentinus, and other early Christian writers who were later declared heretical are discussed, at least from the point of view of their orthodox peers. The quotations have been translated into contemporary English, making them more understandable to the general reader. More than 700 theological, moral, and historical topics are included. These include both topics of modern concern, such as abortion and evolution; long-standing Christian topics, such as free will versus predestination; and topics more typical to early Christianity, such as the question of salvation for Jewish people, eschatology, or the nature of Christ. Although this book is meant mainly to be used as an index to the more extensive 10-volume set edited by Alexander Roberts and James Donaldson, *Ante-Nicene Fathers* (Hendrickson, 1994), it is also useful by itself as a condensed guide to the writings of the early orthodox church fathers on various topics of concern to Christian thinkers. [R: Choice, Dec 98, p. 660]—**Kay Mariea**

1286.   **The Encyclopedia of American Catholic History.** Michael Glazier and Thomas J. Shelley, eds. Collegeville, Minn., Liturgical Press, 1997. 1567p. illus. index. $79.95. ISBN 0-8146-5919-5.

More than 1,200 articles cover the 500-year history of American Catholicism in this single-volume encyclopedia. Hundreds of historians were enlisted to write and research the signed articles. In addition to covering the major events and various groups involved in exploration, missions, revolutions, and immigration, there are biographical articles on the men and women from all walks of life who shaped American Catholicism. The growth of Catholicism in each of the 50 states is also traced. Additionally, representative selections are included on universities and colleges as well as religious orders and congregations. Articles vary in length from a quarter page to multiple pages, and many of them end with brief bibliographies. Black-and-white photographs and illustrations enhance the text. Although many more topics have been amply covered in other sources probably already found in most library collections, the articles in this encyclopedia offer valuable, fresh perspectives on both historical and current events. The articles on Hispanics and African American Catholics are examples of this. Lastly, it is worth mentioning that this authoritative work is especially well written. With estimates of more than 60 million Catholics in the United States today, this work belongs in every library. [R: Choice, July/Aug 98, pp. 1828-1830]
—**Edward Erazo**

1287.   Parrinder, Geoffrey. **A Concise Encyclopedia of Christianity.** Boston, Oneworld Publications; distr., Rockport, Mass., Element Books, 1998. 278p. illus. maps. index. $16.95pa. ISBN 1-85168-174-4.

A Concise Encyclopedia of Christianity provides information about people, churches, movements, beliefs, doctrines, rituals, devotions, and practices from times past to the present. Included is an informative introduction with several statistical charts, maps, a brief history, and a short description of the encyclopedia. The entries are brief but well researched and are arranged alphabetically. There is a liberal sprinkling of illustrations throughout the book. Four indexes, which contain chronology, a thematic bibliography, themes, and proper names, complete the encyclopedia. An excellent and affordable resource for all libraries and those seeking information about Christianity, this encyclopedia is aimed for a middle school through adult audience.—**Mary L. Trenerry**

Handbooks and Yearbooks

1288.   **Destination: Vatican II: An Interactive Exploration of the Second Vatican Council.** [CD-ROM]. Allen, Tex., Resources for Christian Living, 1997. Minimum system requirements (Windows): IBM or compatible 486. Double-speed CD-ROM drive. Windows 3.1 or Pentium processor with Windows 95. 8MB RAM. Color monitor with 256 colors. Minimum system requirements (Macintosh): 7.1 or higher. Double-speed CD-ROM drive. 16 MB RAM. Color monitor with 256 colors. $54.95.

This CD-ROM provides an opportunity to study not only the documents of Vatican II but, perhaps more important, to discover the impact this Council has had on the attendees, Catholics in general, and even those of other Christian denominations. From the elegantly designed opening screen, which is accompanied with appropriate music, the user can choose from five areas of exploration: "Destinations," "Text," "People," "Timeline," and "Themes." To set the stage, "Destinations" allows one to view, through photographs and video, the various locations related to the Council—the Vatican archives, for example—and to link from there to an interview with the Vatican archivist who explains, in Italian but with English text, how the thousands of documents are organized. Although there is no particular order, chronologically, one would go from here to the "Timeline" section, which presents in timeline format all of the councils from 325 C.E. By clicking on any of the dates in red, one is presented with a brief history of that council.

The "Documents" section contains more than 4,000 pages of documents. The opening screen presents four main choices: a list of documents by topic in official English translation; the same documents "in plain English"; the Council Daybooks, including events by each day; and letters from Vatican City by Xavier Rynne, who provided detailed commentary on Council activities in articles that appeared in *The New Yorker* at the time of the Council and formed the basis of a four-volume book on Vatican II. In all of these choices, it is possible to search for a word or phrase and find the appropriate documents. It is also possible to bookmark any sections and to print the desired texts. The "People" section presents three choices for information: biographies of council attendees, a who's who of anyone mentioned on the CD-ROM (both include photographs), and lists of attendees by country.

For those somewhat familiar with the Council and its documents, the "Themes" path is perhaps the most interesting. The 18 themes include such topics as ecumenism, religious freedom, women religious, and liberation theology. For each of these a screen presents four choices: interviews, text, photographs, and video. Many of the interviews are with people fairly prominent today who comment on how the Vatican Council has affected the church or what it meant to their personal lives. One, for example, shown as a young nun in a traditional religious community at the time of the Council, is now an Episcopalian priest working in the skid row area of Los Angeles. She tells how the Council made possible the freedom for herself and other religious women to explore areas of service that had not been open to them before.

This CD-ROM is exceptionally well choreographed. Although the transitional screens are somewhat slow, and the links are not quite clear in the "Destinations" section, there is a flow from one screen to the next that makes for ease of use. Although not produced by church authorities, which may be evident from the selection of people interviewed, it was produced by a team of dedicated and talented people rooted in the Christian, mostly Catholic, faith. They have provided a tool that should be extremely useful not only for reference and research but also for teaching younger generations the influence of Vatican II. [R: LJ, 15 Mar 98, p. 103]—**Lucille Whalen**

1289. **Dictionary of Heresy Trials in American Christianity.** George H. Shriver, ed. Westport, Conn., Greenwood Press, 1997. 511p. index. $99.50. ISBN 0-313-29660-X.

This *Dictionary of Heresy Trials in American Christianity* is a mature, scholarly anthology of articles by 41 academics of history, religion, theology, church history, and philosophy, with each telling the story of the 50 most noted formal or informal heresy trials in American history from early colonial times through the past decade. Shriver, the editor and a professor of western religious history, has been publishing on heresy in the United States since the 1960s. He is also a biographer of Philip Schaff, of whom he writes in this volume. *American Religious Heretics* (1966) covers five heresy trials, all of which are written up here again, by the same individuals. There are several other books with which the dictionary invites comparison. One is *Encyclopedia of Religious Controversies in the U.S.* (see ARBA 98, entry 1345) by Shriver and Bill Leonard, which is also recently published by Greenwood Press. The primary difference between the two appears to be that the title under review is primarily a biographical approach. Also to be considered are Leonard George's *Crimes of Perception, an Encyclopedia of Heresies and Heretics* (see ARBA 96, entry 1468), which is much larger in scope, covering heresies in Judeo-Christian culture from the time of Christ to the twentieth century, and *Encyclopedia of Heresies and Heretics* (see ARBA 94, entry 1530), by a freelance writer, which covers "128 controversial people, sects, movements, and other historical events . . . to the 16th century."

A far more accurate title for this work would be "Biographical Dictionary of Heresy Trials in American Christianity," as all but five of the entries are for individuals. Four entries cover heresies at particular seminaries: Andover Theological, Concordia Theological, Lane Theological, and Southeastern Baptist Theological. Another covers the Salem witchcraft trials of 1692. Each article, of about 4,000 words, is by a different contributor and includes a bibliography at its conclusion. There is also a selected bibliography at the end of the work, containing references but no annotations to some nineteenth-century and many twentieth-century books and articles. There is an index by denomination, allowing the reader to see that these trials, either formal or informal, have arisen chiefly in Protestant denominations, among Baptists, Congregationalists, Episcopalians, German Reformeds, Lutherans, Methodists, Presbyterians, Mormons, and Quakers. Two Roman Catholics are profiled. Heresy is defined in the introduction.

One can find fault with all the works mentioned in this review, and all the reviews mentioned do point out sins of omission and commission. No doubt, the larger, multivolume encyclopedias of religion will have articles on the individuals and on the heresies, so a work like this is not essential. But, supposing that a whole class is set upon the task of writing papers all at once on major heretics in the United States, a volume like this could be very useful in college, university, seminary, and large public libraries. [R: RUSQ, Summer 98, p. 350]
                                                                                    —**Agnes H. Widder**

Hinduism

1290.   Klostermaier, Klaus K. **A Concise Encyclopedia of Hinduism.** Boston, Oneworld Publications; distr., Rockport, Mass., Element Books, 1998. 243p. illus. maps. index. $16.95pa. ISBN 1-85168-175-2.

Researched and written for students of religious studies, this dictionary describes Hinduism as "a way of life," rather than just a religion. The entries, listed alphabetically, are mostly brief descriptions of words and terms from the Hindu languages that relate to the politics, personalities, rituals, and deities. Some lengthier entries detail concepts as they relate to this way of life, such as afterlife, sin, and time. The introduction summarizes the history of this more than 5,000-year-old faith, and provides a map of present-day India where Hinduism is predominant, and a map of the ancient land with temple sites. It also discusses sacred books, languages, beliefs, and politics.

A chronology follows the entries, listing important time periods and events from about 4,000 B.C.E., when the earliest Vedic hymns are thought to have existed, up to the present. The appendixes provide "The Philosophical Schools of Hinduism," "Hindu Scriptures," "The Ten Principal Schools of Vedanta," and "The Eightfold Practice of Yoga: Astanga Yoga." The bibliography is divided into subjects, and the index breaks up mythology, history, and concepts. Black-and-white photographs and drawings illustrate the pages.

—**Felicity Tucker**

Judaism

1291.   Cohn-Sherbok, Dan. **A Concise Encyclopedia of Judaism.** Boston, Oneworld Publications; distr., Rockport, Mass., Element Books, 1998. 237p. illus. maps. index. $16.95pa. ISBN 1-85168-176-0.

With more than 1,000 entries, *A Concise Encyclopedia of Judaism* contains information commonly needed by students of the Jewish tradition. The entries have been cross-referenced and direct the reader to similar or related content. An excellent historical introduction is provided that briefly covers Jews in the Ancient World, Rabbinic Judaism, Judaism in the Middle Ages, Jewry in the Early Modern Period, Judaism in the Modern World, and Jews in the twentieth century.

The main body of the encyclopedia is arranged alphabetically and has many illustrations. Each entry is brief but has been well researched. The content covers people, places, rituals, texts, and art. Three indexes containing a chronology, a thematic bibliography, and a thematic index complete the volume. A wonderful and extremely affordable resource for the researcher or for someone wanting more information about Judaism, the encyclopedia is geared for a middle school through adult audience.—**Mary L. Trenerry**

1292.   Isaacs, Robert H. **Messengers of God: A Jewish Prophets Who's Who.** Northvale, N.J., Jason Aronson, 1998. 273p. index. $35.00. ISBN 0-7657-9998-7.

Rabbi Isaacs, who has written more than a dozen books on Judaism, discusses here the prophets of the Old Testament. Although the "who's who" of the title suggests a biographical dictionary, this is not the case. Prophets are grouped by chapter as literary prophets, women prophets, false prophets, and prophets according to Rashi. Following this are individual chapters on each of the 15 major and 12 minor prophets. Chapters cover the life and character of the prophet, major concepts of their writing, notable quotations, and a summary of the book. Aside from these 27, the remaining men and women prophets are discussed only briefly, most in a few paragraphs, some in only a sentence. Because the book is not arranged alphabetically it is difficult to use and the heavy reliance on biblical quotations and citations to chapter and verse require a more than cursory familiarity with the Bible. Biblical scholars would use monographs on the prophets they need to study; beginners would do better consulting a standard biblical dictionary or who's who for basic information. It is difficult to understand the audience for this book; it could be useful in some large public libraries that can afford to have a broad religion collection. [R: LJ, 1 April 98, p. 82]—**Deborah Hammer**

1293.   Nulman, Macy. **The Encyclopedia of the Sayings of the Jewish People.** Northvale, N.J., Jason Aronson, 1997. 358p. index. $40.00. ISBN 0-7657-5980-2.

Written in English, this one-volume reference work presents nearly 2,000 Hebrew, Aramaic, and Yiddish expressions arranged in 4 sections—Bible, Talmud, liturgy, and rabbinic and folk sayings. A precise definition of each expression is followed by notes on its origin, history, and usage.

This book seems to be aimed at a very specific audience, namely traditional Jews who are religiously observant, conversant with Hebrew and Yiddish, and close to the European and immigrant experience. Although others may find this a helpful source on occasion, there is not the wit and sparkle that characterizes books like Leo Rosten's, which could be read and enjoyed by anyone. Each saying is stated in transliteration, followed by unpointed (no vowel markings) Hebrew, Yiddish, or Aramaic, and then translated into lucid English.

This reviewer tried finding several expressions and hit on only 25 percent. That one hit was on *davenen*, "a term meaning to pray, utilized by Eastern European Jews." The discussion was quite thorough and interesting, with several possible etymologies suggested, including words of Aramaic, Arabic, and English (from dawn, referring especially to the early morning prayers) origin. A helpful glossary, Bible citations, and an index in several languages complete this attractive, well-made book.—**Anthony Gottlieb**

Taoism

1294.   Pas, Julian F. **Historical Dictionary of Taoism.** Lanham, Md., Scarecrow, 1998. 414p. illus. (Historical Dictionaries of Religions, Philosophies, and Movements, no.18). $64.00. ISBN 0-8108-3369-7.

In this series of historical dictionaries by Scarecrow Press, most volumes deal with a religion, a philosophy, or a movement. Taoism can be said to be all three. It is a very complex cultural tradition that had a deep influence on Chinese ways of thinking and spiritual practice. In the West, Taoism is best known through translations of the *Tao Te Ching* and *Chuang-tsu* and through some of its offshoots, which include martial arts and Chinese medicine.

Pas, professor emeritus of religious studies and distinguished instructor of Far Eastern studies at the University of Saskatchewan, believes that Taoism must be understood the way it really was or is, not as it is imagined to be. Despite his personal preference for Taoist philosophy, Pas presents an objective and historically correct view of Taoism as both religion and philosophy, indicating that the distinction between two Taoisms is not just a western device; it is also found in Chinese tradition.

This volume attempts to fill a gap in current studies of Taoism. It provides a helpful chronology and a lengthy introduction to Taoist history and tradition, including its current influence in philosophical and religious studies. Entries are well developed, outlining basic teachings, concepts, and writings with details of their historical significance. The dictionary section provides many details of Taoist history and current practice in a readable and easily understood form. Written by an accomplished scholar who has obviously found personal enrichment in his subject, this book will be of significant value to students of religious studies and to anyone interested in learning more about this fascinating ancient tradition. [R: BL, 15 Oct 98, p. 441]—**Cheryl Eckl**

Part IV
SCIENCE
AND
TECHNOLOGY

29 Science and Technology in General

ATLASES

1295. **Facts on File Wildlife Atlas.** rev. ed. By Robin Kerrod and John Stidworthy. New York, Facts on File, 1997. 80p. illus. maps. index. $18.95. ISBN 0-8160-3714-0.

A comprehensive study of animals, plants, habitats, evolution, and threats to nature, this Facts on File compendium undertakes a grand study for only 80 pages. In full color and at a modest price, this work begins instruction on the front cover and continues all the way to the back cover. A small box on page 2 explains how to access data. A locator map of the world indicates the pages on which readers can find maps and data. A 10-part introduction to terms and themes on pages 4 through 23 covers the world's habitats and biota. The authors present seven continent-by-continent studies, including maps and scale charts, sketches of habitats, and appealing color photographs of animals in the wild with each caption marked by an arrow to connect to the appropriate illustration. The volume concludes with a 3-part index of place-names, plants and animals, and wildlife locator maps by continent.

Overall, the book is well written for young readers and features straightforward composition, suitable diction and models, and tasteful commentary. Inclusion of such examples as the capercaillie, guillemot, and surf scoter augments more familiar reptiles, insects, and mammals. Two hindrances weaken the effect and may prove troublesome for disadvantaged or ESL readers—small typeface, particularly in the index, maps, and sidebars, and text overwhelmed by sidebars. The layout makes it difficult to follow the commentary among a dizzying array of captions and illustrations. There is one unacceptable illustration, the drawing of Charles Darwin (p. 19). Despite flaws, the work is a worthy addition to school and public libraries, classrooms, and home reference collections.

—**Mary Ellen Snodgrass**

BIBLIOGRAPHY

1296. **Resources for Teaching Middle School Science.** Washington, D.C., National Academy Press, 1998. 479p. illus. index. $24.95pa. ISBN 0-309-05781-7.

The publisher of this book is operated by the National Academy of Sciences, the Smithsonian Institution, the National Academy of Engineering, and the Institute of Medicine to gather and disseminate information to improve science teaching. The resources listed represent the consensus of a panel of 67 educators and include curriculum materials, reference materials, and ancillary resources (e.g., museums, government organizations) that address national science teaching standards. Appendixes supply additional information, such as publishers and suppliers, evaluation criteria of materials, and national science content standards. A broad variety of indexes allow easy access to information by author, title, subject, standard, and grade level.

This volume lists more than 400 books and units and information about 700 facilities and organizations that can provide resources helpful to delivering inquiry-based science programs in grades six through eight. Written materials were primarily published between 1987 and 1998. Entries are grouped by subject area (e.g., physical, life environmental, earth and space, multidisciplinary, and applied science), and by type (e.g., core materials, supplementary units, and science activity books). A typical entry includes a short overview, a summary of the student edition and teacher guide, keys to applicable science standards, prices, information about materials needed, and recommended grade levels.

At a time when science education is under close scrutiny, when programs across the country are being modified to more closely align with national or local contents standards, and when many teaching staffs are being increased by those new to the profession, this volume should be in every school, department, or district library. Whether designing a new curriculum, planning a new unit, or preparing a lesson, the teaching professional can be helped by the information in this book. At $24.95, a middle school science program cannot afford to be without it.

—**Craig A. Munsart**

BIO-BIBLIOGRAPHY

1297. Howsam, Leslie. **Scientists Since 1660: A Bibliography of Biographies.** Brookfield, Vt., Ashgate Publishing, 1997. 150p. $76.95. ISBN 1-85928-035-8.

The author of this bibliography has gathered biographical material on 565 men and women scientists from the natural sciences, excluding the medical sciences, whose careers began after the 1660s. Scientists from several nationalities are included, although the majority are English, European, or American. More than 1,100 English-language biographies are listed, including substantial texts from rare works and other works still accessible on the shelves at research or public libraries. Not included are brief articles, reference works, or children's literature. With this work, Howsam also tries to demonstrate the relationship between bibliography and the history of books, in this case the history of biography, as a literary and scholarly genre.

Entries are listed alphabetically by scientists' names, including birth and death dates, with a brief statement of their specialization. All biographies under the entries are listed in chronological order of first publication, not by author. Full author, title, place of publication, and publisher information is given. Most entries include a brief annotation of each work listed. Also included are three appendixes that list information by specialization, publisher, and book series titles.

This work will be useful to those needing biographical information beyond that found in the usual sources. However, reference selectors should keep in mind what sources have been included and excluded and decide if the level of information found here warrants its purchase. This book is most appropriate for research collections.

—**Julia Perez**

1298. Smith, Roger. **Biographies of Scientists: An Annotated Bibliography.** Pasadena, Calif., Salem Press and Lanham, Md., Scarecrow, 1998. 293p. index. (Magill Bibliographies). $36.00. ISBN 0-8108-3384-0.

Scientific biographies are increasingly of interest to professional historians. They are now published in profusion and used in teaching at the elementary school level through college. This bibliography serves the latter audience and includes only English-language titles. It does not claim to be comprehensive and will be of little use for the professional.

The 736 books represented include biographies, dictionaries and encyclopedias, and collections of profiles. The topics range from titles identified as "for readers 12 years and older" to titles presupposing technical knowledge; some are as recent as 1996. Although selection is a matter of taste, there are surprising omissions (e.g., *Louis Agassiz: A Life in Science* [University of Chicago Press, 1960] and *Sir William Rowan Hamilton* [Johns Hopkins University Press, 1980]) and inclusions (e.g., the famously unreliable *Men of Mathematics* [Simon and Schuster, 1937]). Single-paragraph descriptions inform about the nature and level of the books, and give capsule accounts of the biographees. There is little comparison of titles on the same subject (e.g., the many biographies of Albert Einstein). The introduction includes a useful list of Websites of scientific biographies, although some of the URLs are outdated or have typographical errors. The indexing is good. Overall, this is a useful compilation for instructors to consult in designing course reading lists, with possible value as a librarian's selection tool. [R: Choice, Nov 98, p. 498]—**Robert Michaelson**

BIOGRAPHY

1299. Bailey, Martha J. **American Women in Science, 1950 to the Present: A Biographical Dictionary.** Santa Barbara, Calif., ABC-CLIO, 1998. 455p. illus. index. $60.00. ISBN 0-87436-921-5.

A supplement to the author's *American Women in Science: A Biographical Dictionary* (see ARBA 96, entry 1486), this volume concentrates on women born from 1920 on but also includes earlier women omitted from the previous volume (which also includes some women born from 1920 on). Fields covered have been expanded, using as a guideline professions included by the National Academy of Sciences and the National Academy of Engineering, to include sociologists and others who might not ordinarily be considered scientists. This inclusiveness extends to pop psychologists such as Shere Hite and the occasional practitioner of "pseudo-science" (e.g., Ida Rolf of "rolfing"), but most of the entries are on important scholars or writers.

The introduction surveys pertinent issues. Entries are in alphabetic order, and there is a convenient listing by profession. The entries have been compiled from books and professional and popular magazine articles, and from information obtained from the biographees themselves. The entries tend to be much less impersonal than those found in many scientific biographies. Book and index sources are listed in the entries; there is a thorough, up-to-date bibliography of sources. Unfortunately, the indexing is erratic. This is a worthwhile addition to any science reference or general reference collection.—**Robert Michaelson**

1300. **Biographical Encyclopedia of Scientists.** Richard Olson, ed. Tarrytown, N.Y., Marshall Cavendish, 1998. 5v. illus. index. $299.95/set. ISBN 0-7614-7064-6.

This 5-volume set profiles some 472 figures in the history of science that have been gathered from across disciplines and throughout history, with the focus being on the hard sciences at the exclusion of the social sciences. Included is a mixture of scientists from the famous to the little known, from ancient Greeks to today's working scientists.

Each volume includes an index and pronunciation key. Entries are arranged alphabetically, ranging in length from 750 to 1,250 words, although some longer essays are included that cover individuals who made significant contributions to the field of science. Each entry begins with the scientist's name along with their area of achievement and contribution to the sciences, followed by a biography. Photographs, drawings, and diagrams are included along with separate boxed-off areas within the articles that further explain theories and research related to the scientist's work. Bibliographies are also listed along with the author of each biography. The 5th volume of this work also includes a glossary, country list, achievement list, and timeline. Of these, the most useful is the country list—a listing of each scientist under the primary country or countries where he or she lived and conducted scientific work. Also useful is the separate listing for members of minority groups and women (and the achievement list) and a listing of scientists under categories such as astronomy, biology, chemistry, and others.

This work compares favorably to other biographical encyclopedias already available. High school and undergraduate college students will find the biographies accompanied by their illustrations informative. The separate listing for locating biographies on minority groups and women is also useful. This biographical set is recommended for purchase. [R: SLJ, Aug 98, p. 194; BL, 1 Dec 98, p. 694; BL, 15 May 98, p. 1651]—**Julia Perez**

1301. Creese, Mary R. S. **Ladies in the Laboratory? American and British Women in Science, 1800-1900: A Survey of Their Contributions to Research.** Lanham, Md., Scarecrow, 1998. 452p. index. $98.50. ISBN 0-8108-3287-9.

Women in science, generally ignored by historians before the 1970s, have been the subjects of many publications in the past few years. Creese's work is unique in its attempt to explore systematically the output of women scientists in the United States and Great Britain during the nineteenth century. Sifting through a major catalog of scientific papers from this time period, Creese identified 680 women from these 2 nations who published serious research in their disciplines. The title of the book may be misleading; these women scientists included those who also specialized in field research, such as botany and geology, as well as some social scientists doing anthropological and psychological research.

Creese includes biographical sketches of her subjects in a continuous narrative about women researchers in each discipline, which makes the names somewhat more difficult to browse. Sketches range from less than one page to several pages, depending on the magnitude of the scientists' publication records. The entries concentrate on the professional lives of the women, although some personal data and anecdotes enliven the narratives.

Creese summarizes the presence of women within each discipline, looking at trends and regional differences. The text is supported by extensive citations and a name index. The bibliography of all 680 authors and their publications completes the work.

This volume provides much more information about the scientific work performed by these women and includes more women from that time period than many other biographical sources. Greenwood Press's recent series, including *Notable Women in the Life Sciences* (see ARBA 97, entry 1231), is aimed at a general audience, covers only major names, and focuses more on the current century. Greenwood's more detailed "bio-bibliographic" series, including titles such as *Women in the Biological Sciences* (Greenwood Press, 1997), has lengthier biographies as well as secondary bibliographies that this work lacks, but the series is more selective in its choices. Overall, this work offers a substantial addition to more comprehensive reference collections.—**Christopher W. Nolan**

1302. **Scientists: Their Lives and Works, Volume 4.** Marie C. Ellavich, ed. Detroit, U*X*L/Gale, 1997. 262p. illus. index. $34.00. ISBN 0-7876-1874-8. [R: BL, 1 Dec 98, p. 694]

1303. **Scientists: Their Lives and Works, Volume 5.** Marie C. Ellavich, ed. Detroit, U*X*L/Gale, 1998. 224p. illus. index. $39.00. ISBN 0-7876-2797-6.

Younger students frequently use biographical reference sources for their assignments and as a tool for learning about various careers. Gale aims at these elementary school/middle school student needs with this ongoing series on famous scientists. The current volume adds 34 additional biographies of current and earlier scientists, including figures as ancient as Hippocrates and as current as Marc Andreessen, founder of Netscape. The editor avoids the narrow focus of some scientific biographical works by incorporating women and men, Americans and other nationalities, and persons of various races. Science is interpreted broadly to include social scientific disciplines, such as anthropology and psychology.

The entries themselves are clearly written articles averaging four pages in length, focusing on early life events that led to the scientists' interest in their subjects and the major contributions of their careers. Most entries include a photograph, a summary of awards and distinctions, and a brief list of further reading sources. Many entries also include inset boxes with summaries of the scientists' principal impact or brief biographies of other scientists whose careers are related to the main subject. The articles use some technical jargon, but parenthetical definitions of these terms immediately following their first use are common, and a good glossary supplements these explanations. Indexes to this volume and the 5 volumes published to date are included, as is a timeline and chronology of major scientific events. This work, although fairly basic in content, should be useful and appealing to its intended audience. [R: BL, 1 Dec 98, p. 694]—**Christopher W. Nolan**

1304. **Scientists and Inventors.** Judy Culligan, ed. New York, Macmillan Library Reference/Simon & Schuster Macmillan, 1998. 389p. illus. index. (Macmillan Profiles, v.1). $75.00. ISBN 0-02-864983-4.

Scientists and Inventors is the inaugural volume in a proposed series of volumes devoted to biographies entitled Macmillan Profiles. The volume contains more than 100 biographies of individuals selected with input from a team of high school teachers and librarians. Among the selection criteria used were students name recognition, historical significance, relevance to curriculum, and respect for cultural diversity. Each of the biographical sketches is generally two to three pages in length and has its origin in earlier Macmillan sources, although all entires have been modified for a younger audience. Some of the text, however, remains difficult for younger (and probably most older) readers. For example, the entry for Richard Phillips Feynman reads: "His doctoral dissertation . . . which presented his path integral formulation of nonrelativistic quantum mechanics, helped clarify in a striking manner the assumptions that underlay the usual quantum mechanical description of the dynamics of microscopic entities" (p. 112).

Inventors and scientists are listed alphabetically, from Jean Louis Agassiz to the Wright brothers. Most entries contain a photograph or reproduction of a painting of the subject, and some contain a sidebar elaborating some aspect of the subject's work (e.g., Benjamin Franklin's lightning rod or the development of the rocket-powered airplane fewer than 50 years after the Wright brother's first flight). The format is user friendly with technical terms in bold typeface defined in the adjacent margin, quotations from the subject (such as Thomas Edison's "Genius is one percent inspiration and ninety-nine percent perspiration"), and a short timeline placing the subject's life and claim to fame in a historical frame of reference.

More than 60 pages of end matter include a suggested reading list for more information about each biographical subject, a chronological list of Nobel Prize winners by subject, a glossary (listing all the words printed in bold typeface in each entry), and an index including both names and subjects.

With any such volume there is always potential for discussion about why one individual was included and another (e.g., Henri Becquerel, Karl Benz, Chester Carlson, Robert Goddard, Nikola Tesla) was omitted. One might also question some of the page apportionments; Michael Faraday is discussed for 9½ pages, whereas Charles Darwin and Alexander Graham Bell have fewer than 3 each. The entries are a step beyond the typical, brief encyclopedic entry. They provide a comprehensive introduction to each biographical subject, or they can serve as a strong step in a student's research.—**Craig A. Munsart**

1305. **Who's Who in Science and Engineering 1998-1999.** 4th ed. New Providence, N.J., Marquis Who's Who/Reed Reference Publishing, 1997. 1638p. index. $259.95. ISBN 0-8379-5756-7. ISSN 1063-5599.

This book is from the same publisher of myriad other "who's who" references since 1899, many broken down by profession and some by country of fame and fortune. The list of referenced specialties in this 4th edition of *Who's Who in Science and Engineering* includes architecture and design, communications, computers, education, engineering (with 21 specialties given), executives and specialists (16 specialties), associations, government and military, health care, law, life sciences (20 specialties), mathematics, medical education and research, medical support, medicine (33 specialties), physical sciences (15 specialties), and social sciences (4 specialties).

The publisher's intent is to provide a reference tool to promote communication among those in the fields of science and engineering, to identify achievers in the scientific community, and to allow others to become aware of and understand some of the significant work in progress. Of necessity, scientists are often involved with only a narrow specialty; this volume may provide the means to broaden that focus and encourage wider lines of communication with related specialties. The volume includes biographies of nearly 31,000 scientists from more than 125 countries whose careers include 110-plus specialties.

Most of the work (1,327 pages) contains detailed biographical sketches of scientists, in alphabetic order, including information about family, education, occupation, professional certifications, military service, religion, political affiliation, awards and achievements, and present address. Other listings within the volume include recipients of major honors and awards (through August 1997), a geographic index, and a professional index (by specialty). This volume could be useful in technical libraries or in libraries of secondary schools and institutions of higher education whose students may want to communicate with practicing scientists and engineers while investigating career choices.—**Craig A. Munsart**

CHRONOLOGY

1306. Francis, Raymond L. **The Illustrated Almanac of Science, Technology and Inventions: Day by Day Facts, Figures and the Fanciful.** New York, Plenum, 1997. 1v. (unpaged). illus. index. $28.95. ISBN 0-306-45633-8.

April 15th carries a deserved notoriety as "Income Tax Day," but here are other distinctions: the (illegitimate) birth of Leonardo Da Vinci and of the great mathematician Leonhard Euler, the opening of the first modern McDonald's, the sinking of the *Titanic*, and the publication of a paper by the Swiss high school teacher Johann Balmer concerning the light frequencies emitted by the hydrogen atom. Balmer's paper was the catalyst in Niels Bohr's development of a model for the atom. The above are only a part of the events chronicled for this day in Francis's almanac, surely the ultimate coffee-table book. One page is devoted to the events that happened on each day of the year, followed by a name index. Illustrations range from factual to fanciful.—**Robert B. McKee**

1307. **The Wilson Chronology of Science and Technology.** By George Ochoa and Melinda Corey. Bronx, N.Y., H. W. Wilson, 1997. 440p. index. (Wilson Chronology Series). $55.00. ISBN 0-8242-0933-8.

This new, broad chronology of science, technology, and occasionally social sciences joins other titles in the Wilson Chronology Series. This volume runs about 400 pages and spans more than 2 million years, covering significant developments with a sentence or paragraph description (but no illustrations or photographs). To give a sense of the time emphasis, the B.C.E. era is covered in 70 pages, and the twentieth century is given 150 pages.

About 50 sidebars address interesting topics and anecdotes (e.g., ancient surgery, important scientific books, women in science) not necessarily linked to a single year. These add to the appeal of this work as a browsing book.

The authors have clearly looked at earlier scientific chronologies such as Alexander Hellemans's and Bryan Bunch's *Timetables of Science* (see ARBA 90, entry 1422). What *The Wilson Chronology of Science and Technology* does differently than earlier chronologies is to give fuller entries, attempt to include developments in geographic areas outside Europe and the United States, and include women and lesser known scientists. A detailed index helps the user in search of a specific topic or person. This work will be useful in high school, public, and college libraries as a quick reference, but perhaps even more for browsing, to pique interest in the remarkable developments in science and technology over time.—**Jean C. McManus**

DICTIONARIES AND ENCYCLOPEDIAS

1308.   Bruno, Leonard C. **Science and Technology Breakthroughs: From the Wheel to the World Wide Web.** Detroit, U*X*L/Gale, 1998. 2v. illus. $55.00/set. ISBN 0-7876-1927-2.

The 1,300 entries in this work cover major scientific and technological achievements and vary in length from two sentences to eight or nine. The paragraphs provide the date or approximate period in which the milestone occurred, location, person responsible, and the individual's nationality.

Each volume comprises six subject areas, which are arranged chronologically, allowing the reader to follow the development of a discovery or invention through its stages and understand the progression and influences. Cross-references to related entries in that section are provided. The indexes found in each volume are comprehensive for the set and provide quick access to specific topics with illustrations noted. Each volume is prefaced with a 362-word glossary, a table of contents to the set, and a bibliography with suggested titles for each of the 12 categories. The earliest milestone was the introduction of the bow and arrow in 50,000 B.C.E.; the most recent entry was the birth of Dolly, a genetically engineered lamb on June 25, 1997.

The boldfaced headings and the visually pleasing page format make it easy for the student to focus on the date and the milestone. Approximately 150 black-and-white photographs and drawings illustrate the set. Twenty-one sidelines provide further interesting and fascinating facts on topics, such as measuring earthquakes. Three of the sidelines are biographical, providing information on George Washington Carver, Charles Darwin, and Rosalind Franklin. Grades four through eight will find this set useful, especially for following the influences of early milestones on later discoveries.—**Elaine Ezell**

1309.   **DK Nature Encyclopedia.** New York, DK Publishing, 1998. 304p. illus. index. $29.95. ISBN 0-7894-3411-3.

Lovely to look at and a delight to browse, this reference guide to the world of plants and animals covers a wide range of life on Earth. Although it may not provide enough information for many reports, it can serve to provide ideas for topics and provide adjunct information. To get the most out of it students will need to read the double-page spread titled "How to Use This Book."

In traditional DK style, each page is a montage of text and illustrations that include photographs, drawings, cutaways, paintings, maps, and charts. Organized into 2-page spreads, the first third covers topics concerning the beginning of life and how living things work—ranging from a spread on cells through respiration; reproduction; movement; communication; defenses; homes; and ecology, including nutrient cycles and the food chain as well as several different habitats and the relationships between people and nature. The major portion of the book examines living things arranged by classification, starting with spreads on bacteria and viruses, single-celled organisms, and fungi. Plants, with topics ranging from algae and lichens to carnivorous plants, are covered in a dozen 2-page spreads. Animals from invertebrates to mammals are covered in increasing depth. Sometimes the divisions seem somewhat arbitrary; owls merit a 2-page spread of their own, but all other birds of prey are given only one 2-page spread. The classification charts in the reference section at the end of the book are rather confusing in that monerans, protists, fungi, and plants are on one 2-page spread and animals on another. Credentials for the authors and consultants are listed on the back flap of the cover. [R: BL, 1 Dec 98, p. 690]—**Diana Tixier Herald**

1310.   **The DK Science Encyclopedia.** rev. ed. New York, DK Publishing, 1998. 448p. illus. index. $39.95. ISBN 0-7894-2190-9.

The DK Science Encyclopedia is an outstanding, comprehensive reference work. That so much can be packed into one volume and still maintain clarity, organization, and scope is a tribute to the efforts of the exceptional team of science writers and specialists. The encyclopedia is divided into 12 topical sections covering matter, reactions, materials, forces and energy, electricity and magnetism, sound and light, Earth, weather, space, living things, how living things work, and ecology. Within the topical sections are more than 280 main entries describing such topics as the chemistry of foods, elements, friction, robots, lasers, fossils, forecasting, Mars, viruses, blood, conservation, and more. More than 1,900 subentries include biographies of great scientists and inventors, time charts, and fact boxes on information highlighting specific aspects of a main entry. In addition to the concise table of contents, a detailed index assists the user. The illustrations are colorful, clear, and accurate.

Even though the encyclopedia was planned to support elementary and middle school science curricula, it is so well written that even the most nonscientific person would benefit and understand the concepts presented. DK Publishing has provided an excellent resource for all. [R: BL, 1 Dec 98, p. 690]—**Mary L. Trenerry**

1311.   **DK Ultimate Visual Dictionary of Science.** New York, DK Publishing, 1998. 448p. illus. index. $29.95. ISBN 0-7894-3512-8.

DK Publishing has established a tradition of excellent visual works of reference; this work continues that tradition. Following the precept of "a picture is worth a thousand words," the publishers have produced a volume that seems to be worthy of its title.

The book is user friendly. Contents are divided among nine chapters: physics, chemistry, life sciences and ecology, human anatomy, medical science, earth sciences, astronomy and astrophysics, electronics and computer science and mathematics. Each chapter begins with a guide to the topics within that chapter, a historical overview of the subject matter, and a timeline of discoveries. Important names within the historical overview are shown in bold typeface and are detailed in the biography section at the back of the book. Each topic is shown on a facing, two-page spread and contains a short introductory text supported by many illustrations and explanatory notes. Words in bold typeface are defined in the glossary. Color photographs are supplemented by detailed artwork in color.

The "Useful Data" appendix contains such reference material as conversions; formulas; geometric figures; star charts; and a diverse group of facts, among which are the energy requirements of animal species, lengths of cave systems, and binary codes of various numbers. In addition to appendixes containing biographies and a glossary, the back matter also includes an excellent index that also references the appendixes. If there is a shortcoming to this work, it is a minor one. Some pages in the volume were reproduced from the Visual Dictionary Series, published earlier by DK Publishing.

This is a well-designed and well-executed dictionary that would be an excellent addition to any library, classroom, or home. At a time when some books seem to offer little for the price, it is an excellent value and quite affordable. [R: SLJ, Nov 98, p. 151; BL, 1 Dec 98, p. 690]—**Craig A. Munsart**

1312.   **Instruments of Science: An Historical Encyclopedia.** Robert Bud, Deborah Jean Warner, and Stephen Johnston, eds. New York, Garland, 1998. 709p. illus. index. (Garland Encyclopedias in the History of Science, v.2 and Garland Reference Library of the Social Sciences, v.936). $138.00. ISBN 0-8153-1561-9.

This handsome volume, published in association with the Science Museum of London and the National Museum of American History, Smithsonian Institution, is unlike other histories of scientific instruments in that it covers instruments from antiquity to the present day, both those used in routine measurements and those used for cutting-edge research. It even has entries on organisms in biological research, such as *E. coli*, neurospora, drosophila, and the mouse. It is impossible to cover scientific instruments comprehensively, and different choices might have been made, but the editors tried to encompass most well-known devices and those important in creating new scientific fields.

Individual entries are written by well-known scholars and give references for further reading. On the whole they are splendidly written and well illustrated, though discussing modern instruments can be hindered by sensitive issues—entries for "Magnetic Resonance Imaging" and "Computer, Digital" do not hint at acrimonious priority and patent disputes. This work is cross-referenced and contains an extensive index, but some information can be hard to locate: a search for "glass electrodes" is not redirected by cross-reference or index to the entry on "Ion-Sensitive Microelectrode," nor does the index indicate mentions of this device in entries for "Blood Gas Analyzer" and "pH Meter."

Entries are written for a wide audience. Any collection in the history of science will want to add this volume, and its coverage of modern instruments makes it useful for scientists and engineers. It will also be of significant interest in general reference collections. [R: BL, 1 June 98, p. 1812; Choice, July/Aug 98, pp. 1833-1834]

—**Robert Michaelson**

1313.   **Interactive Science Encyclopedia.** [CD-ROM]. Austin, Tex., Raintree/Steck-Vaughn, 1997. Minimum system requirements (Windows version): IBM or compatible 486DX/33MHz. Double-speed CD-ROM drive. Windows 95. 8MB RAM. 10MB hard disk space. 256-color monitor. SVGA video card. Mouse. Sound card. Speakers or headphones. Printer (optional). Minimum system requirements (Macintosh version): 68040 microprocessor. Double-speed CD-ROM drive. OS system 7.1. 8MB RAM (16MB with PowerMac). 10MB hard disk space. 13-inch, 256-color monitor. Mouse. Speakers or headphones. Printer (optional). $99.95. ISBN 0-8712-3914-6 (Windows version); 0-8172-3913-8 (Macintosh version).

This electronic encyclopedia is a collection of nearly 3,000 articles covering numerous aspects of science, with more than 3,000 graphics, 50 video clips, 50 animations, 75 sound effects, and 8 narrated slide shows. In addition, it contains more than 150 experiments called "ProActivities" in 3 levels of difficulty. Twenty of these activities can be performed onscreen, whereas the rest are offline activities. Learners can also study the history of science through eight timeline capsules that show key historical events and important scientists in context. Overall, entries are current and appear to be well written.

The disk was easy to load. The contents are easily navigated either by searching the topical subcategories or by clicking on an alphabetic index. Hypertext entries link various topics. Keyword searching is also available, with advanced features such as proximity searching. The sound bites did not work even though two different personal computers were tried. This may have been the fault of the review disk. Animations worked well, and the speed could be regulated. Overall, the technical characteristics are generally user-friendly and reliable, and the quality of graphics is excellent.

The level of interactivity is generally better than with many other similar encyclopedias that act principally as reference sources. Instructional characteristics include the ability to make notes about the projects or entries. One could easily envision collaborative team projects or group viewing for demonstration. The multimedia support for text makes the product more appealing for visual learners; children in the earlier grades will especially benefit. [R: LJ, Jan 98, pp. 157-158]—**Andrew G. Torok**

1314.   **The Kingfisher First Science Encyclopedia.** By Anita Ganeri and Chris Oxlade. New York, Larousse Kingfisher Chambers, 1997. 112p. illus. index. $14.95. ISBN 0-7534-5089-5.

This colorful science encyclopedia is a great introduction to science for young children as they begin to do simple research. Each entry includes a definition, step-by-step instructions for experiments, fact boxes that contain extra information, facts and figures, pictures to illustrate the word(s), and a section that helps the students find out more about each topic. Some pictures show the different parts of an object and label each part for clarification.

An alphabetic table of contents provides a fast way to find information on the main topics in the book. The alphabetic index gives a more detailed listing of topics and helps the student to find additional subjects not found in the table of contents. Main entries are in bold typeface in the index. A glossary is included, which lists words and their definitions that the science students may encounter for the first time. The illustrations and pictures are appropriate for a young child. Most children would find this encyclopedia interesting and entertaining as they learn basic science facts. The experiments can be easily performed with common household products, making the book a fun resource to learn about scientific experiments. The "find-out-more" feature of the encyclopedia allows further research into related topics. The design of the book and the illustrations add to the book's appeal for young children. This book is highly recommended. Every elementary school should own several copies of this creatively designed science encyclopedia.—**Betty J. Morris**

1315. Magill's Survey of Science: Applied Science Series Supplement. Volume 7 Index. Donald R. Franceschetti, ed. Englewood Cliffs, N.J., Salem Press, 1998. 1v. (various paging). $90.00. ISBN 0-89356-934-8.

This is a 7th volume to extend and update the original 6-volume series published in 1993. The tome at hand adds 52 articles to the 382 previously published. Each article follows a standard format, starting with the type of science, specific field of study, abstract, and principal terms. A substantial overview leads to discussion of uses of the technology, and concludes with a historical and technological context. An annotated bibliography provides a few sentences describing each reference, and there are cross-references to other articles in the set.

Topics included in this volume are adaptive optics, amorphous materials, biological and chemical weapons, computer viruses, electronic music, graphical user interfaces, thermography, and ultrasound, among others. This reviewer found some items to be very interesting, even more so when next to nothing was known of the technology under discussion. In general the quality of the articles can be roughly compared with an essay in *Scientific American*, although they are definitely less comprehensive. This reviewer was also disappointed that there was almost no indication of current or recent work on any topic in the context discussion.

This collection might provide a starting point for an introduction into a field in which the reader has no background. Certainly a number of the topics would not be included in general encyclopedias, even given the limited information provided. However, any decently stocked public library should have material that goes beyond this, and any determined search on the Internet could, probably within an hour, turn up resources that went significantly further. [R: BL, 1 Dec 98, p. 698]—**Robert M. Slade**

1316. McGraw-Hill Multimedia Encyclopedia of Science & Technology. [CD-ROM]. New York, McGraw-Hill, 1998. Minimum system requirements: IBM or compatible 386. Double-speed CD-ROM drive. Windows 3.1. 4MB RAM. 10MB hard disk space. VGA or SVGA color monitor. $995.00 (single user); $1,295.00 (LANs); $1,595.00 (WANs). ISBN 0-07-853074-1 (single user); 0-07-853083-0 (LANs); 0-07-853085-7 (WANs).

The *McGraw-Hill Multimedia Encyclopedia of Science & Technology* comes with an excellent instruction booklet that provides the user with step-by-step loading and usage directions as well as technical support telephone numbers. Navigating the encyclopedia is relatively easy after one has read the booklet. The "Filter" button on the program toolbar is a nice feature that enables users to select text-only articles or multimedia articles. Graphics and illustrations are nice but lack depth, quantity, and pizzazz. This reviewer was unable to experience any animations, and technology support was unable to resolve the problem. There is not much "multi" in multimedia.

An interesting and somewhat useful characteristic is the individual windows that are opened each time the user selects another option. The stacked windows make it easy to see where the user has been. The study guides are helpful for those wanting to do independent studies. Article coverage seems to be a general overview of the knowledge on a given topic. This CD-ROM is an extremely pricey resource for a somewhat general science encyclopedia that lacks depth and vigor. [R: BL, 15 Dec 98, pp. 765-766]—**Mary L. Trenerry**

1317. The New Book of Popular Science. 1998 ed. Joseph M. Castagno, ed. Danbury, Conn., Grolier, 1998. 6v. illus. maps. index. $259.00/set. ISBN 0-7172-1221-1.

This set covers subjects from basic science and mathematics to engineering and medicine. Volumes are topically arranged, with many illustrations. There is an index in volume 6, which is also a paperback supplement. There are no cross-references within the volumes, but suggestions for further reading are located at the end of each volume. This work has been revised every few years since 1978; earlier it appeared as *The Book of Popular Science* from 1924 to 1977.

This is popular science in the best sense—the articles are clearly written, with minimal mathematics that generally avoid oversimplifications and do not patronize the reader. Contributors listed in volume 1 include prominent scientists (some long since deceased). Older articles have been revised to keep them current, and topics of recent interest, such as ceramic superconductors, virtual reality, and cloning are discussed—even the 1996 cloning of a sheep (announced in 1997) can be found here—although some topics such as prions are not present. There are some dated illustrations are in the article "Data Processing," such as old computer terminals, tape drives, and personal computers; however, most illustrations are up-to-date. Interesting features in some articles include discussions of areas for future research and career discussions on what it is like to work in a number of life science fields (e.g., agronomy, botany, and entomology, to name a few). This is clearly a useful reference for audiences at junior high school and high school levels, and should be made available in public libraries. [R: SLJ, Oct 98, p. 36; BL, 1 Dec 98, p. 695]—**Robert Michaelson**

1318.   Turner, Gerard L'E. **Scientific Instruments 1500-1900: An Introduction.** Berkeley, Calif., University of California Press, 1998. 144p. illus. index. $40.00. ISBN 0-520-21728-4.

Well-crafted scientific instruments have a unique beauty that touches the heart of any scientist. As the author of this book writes, they are "ideas made into brass, ivory, and wood." The oldest devices featured in this book, splendid astrolabes from the fourteenth century, show in their detail and workmanship the intense human desire to know nature and the heavens. The polished (and superfluous) decorations indicate the joy and honor their users felt as they explored the world around them. This book is a short but comprehensive guide to scientific instruments made prior to 1900, almost all from western Europe. From the careful descriptions and numerous illustrations (including many color plates), it is clear that the author knew he was not just cataloging disciplinary tools—he was also charting the rise of modern science as both a vocation and a philosophy.

This book is designed to be a resource for collectors of scientific instruments. There are many instrument categories, including those used for astronomy, chronology, navigation, surveying, optics, medicine, and several other fields. The primary instruments in each field are briefly described, with an emphasis on their histories and most prominent manufacturers. The range of devices is extraordinary, and it increases geometrically toward the beginning of the twentieth century. The coverage is thorough for the earliest instruments, primarily astronomical and navigational, and inevitably is thinner with the nineteenth-century revolution in scientific instrumentation. The broad title may lead us to expect some devices from Asia, particularly China and Japan, or even from the United States, but most of the material is British, French, or German.

The author ends the book with practical advice for collectors, and an extensive bibliography of primary sources on scientific instruments. Anyone who collects such instruments, or simply enjoys their elegance and what they tell us about scientific progress, will want to read this book.—**Mark A. Wilson**

1319.   **U*X*L's Science Fact Finder.** Phillis Engelbert, ed. Detroit, U*X*L/Gale, 1997. 3v. illus. index. $79.95/set. ISBN 0-7876-1727-X.

The volumes are organized around the natural world, the physical world, and the technological world. Within each volume, information is further separated into chapters and smaller subject listings. For instance, volume 1 (The Natural World) contains a chapter entitled "The Human Body," with subject headings of "Characteristics and Functions," "Parts of the Body," and "Senses and Sleep." Although touted as a middle-school reference containing answers to 750 commonly asked student questions, those about Batesian mimicry, the Great Boston Molasses Disaster, or Ralph Nader and the Corvair may be obscure for many students.

Each book in the 3-volume set contains an 18-page listing of recommendations for further reading, online sources, and CD-ROMs. Although helpful, they might have been more student-friendly if arranged by subject. Each volume also contains a comprehensive index of entries in all 3 volumes; cross-referencing of entries could have helped students find additional information about subjects more easily.

Answers to many specific questions provide a springboard to a more in-depth discussion of a general subject. ("Are there any mammals that fly?" evolves into a detailed discussion of bats.) Certain questions of general interest are highlighted throughout the text. Each entry provides a reference citation for additional information, which is a useful feature. Although well-illustrated with black-and-white photographs and diagrams, some entries on such subjects as the recycling symbol, universal product code, or types of bridges might be more helpful to students with an illustration.

Although organized within the framework of specific questions, this 3-volume set functions like an informal encyclopedia of science and, as such, could be useful to middle-school libraries or a home setting. [R: BL, 1 June 98, pp. 1818-1820]—**Craig A. Munsart**

DIRECTORIES

1320.   **ASTM Directory of Scientific & Technical Consultants & Expert Witnesses.** 1997-98 ed. West Conshohocken, Pa., ASTM, 1997. 165p. index. $40.00. ISBN 0-8131-1845-7.

This reference work provides information about expert witnesses, and lists both organizations and individuals acting either as consultants or as actual expert witnesses. Those listed have paid a fee and completed a questionnaire that provides the basis for the information supplied here. A quick reference index is offered identifying experts by their fields of scientific or technological expertise—ranging from chemicals and computers and construction materials (e.g., asbestos, wood trusses) to consumer matters, such as amusement rides, aquatic safety and sports equipment, engineering, forensic science, medical issues (including medical and scientific instruments), occupational health and safety, products liability, quality control, and thermal and fire protection. Each listing gives the name of a contact person, a detailed description of what the individual's or firm's areas of expertise is, and whether or not expert witness services are provided or not. There are 182 categories listed, with key words and an alphabetic index to help locate a particular topic or subject of interest. This directory is also available on the ASTM Website at http://www.astm.org/consultants.—**Joseph W. Dauben**

1321.   **ASTM International Directory of Testing Laboratories.** 1998 ed. West Conshohocken, Pa., ASTM, 1997. 381p. index. $69.00pa.; $62.00pa. (members). ISBN 0-8031-1849-X. ISSN 0895-7886.

This directory lists professional laboratories that provide testing services in the areas of biology, chemistry, environmental studies, construction, water, textiles, and similar subjects. More than 1,000 laboratories are described, the vast majority located in the United States. Entries provide contact information, including Website and e-mail addresses, if available; a description of each laboratory's special areas of testing and materials analyzed; a list of specific tests identified by issuing agency (such as the Environmental Protection Agency); accreditation credentials; and the numbers of staff Ph.D.'s, engineers, and other employees.

The entries are arranged geographically, although normal access will probably be through the sufficiently detailed subject and test indexes. Both of these indexes are further subdivided by geographical region, making it easy to determine whether the major office of a testing lab exists in one's local area. Although branch locations are noted in the entries, many of these branches are not listed in the indexes. Consequently, users may not be aware of some branch laboratories that could perform suitable testing. Although the labs are not endorsed by the ASTM, the desirability of appearing in an ASTM publication allows the publisher to charge labs for inclusion, which may have eliminated some companies from being represented. However, this annual directory offers an extensive list of prospective contacts for government agencies, companies, or individuals who seek tests of their products or environment.—**Christopher W. Nolan**

1322.   **Directory of Physics, Astronomy, & Geophysics Staff.** 1997 biennial ed. Woodbury, N.Y., American Institute of Physics, 1997. 524p. $65.00pa. ISBN 1-56396-665-4.

Although directories become inaccurate when the first person listed changes jobs, the American Institute of Physics (AIP) deserves praise for a well-organized, highly informative, and useful catalog of names, academic departments, corporations, agencies, and laboratories. The directory will be useful for students, recruiters, and colleagues.

AIP sifts 31,000 individuals and 2,000 institutions and organizations into 10 alphabetic parts with names, addresses (mailing and e-mail), and telephone and fax numbers. The undergraduate and graduate faculty in every academic department in the United States teaching one or more courses in physics, astronomy, geophysics, or related fields are listed. Laboratories with one physicist are included along with those whose staffs take up two, three-column, single-spaced pages (e.g., Argonne National Laboratories).

New to the 1997-1999 biennial edition is expanded information on the scientific societies in the United States and around the world. Although AIP has published a directory since 1959, there are a few organizational annoyances. Readers locate each of the directory's 10 parts by using staggered markings on the forward edge of the book. To locate a part, you must find its number on the introduction page and count the edge marks. Edge marks are solid black and do not include the part number or title. Within the geographical listings of academic institutions, it is confusing to have an upper case "A" stand for "Associate" degree and "Astronomy." The *Directory of Physics, Astronomy, & Geophysics Staff* is an important addition to technical libraries and, with few exceptions, a model of useful detail and organization.—**Pete Prunkl**

1323.   **World Guide to Scientific Associations and Learned Societies.** 7th ed. Michael Zils, ed. New Providence, N.J., R. R. Bowker/Reed Reference Publishing, 1998. 529p. index. $300.00. ISBN 3-598-20581-3. ISSN 0939-1959.

Although by their very nature most catalogs are dull, one should not underestimate the interesting information that can be recovered from this one. Where else can one see listed, complete with addresses (although no telephone numbers), the learned societies in North Korea? Where else can one calculate the number of citizens per association for, say the United Kingdom (26,810) and the United States (59,325)? There is even some fun in seeing juxtapositions of groups such as the "Quaker Esperanto Society" and the "Queen's English Society," which immediately follows.

Of course, this volume is designed for practical utility, not arcane entertainment. It is comprehensive and well organized, listing more than 17,100 associations, first by country, then by name, subject, and publications. Each citation is numbered, making it easy to find from the indexes. The typical information on a society includes its address, telephone and fax numbers, an officer's name, founding date, membership numbers, and sponsored periodicals. (Somehow, however, this reviewer's treasured Palaeontological Association in the United Kingdom slipped through the net.) International organizations are listed by the country in which they maintain their headquarters. The price for this book is high, but it will be an important reference in major libraries for students and professionals.—**Mark A. Wilson**

HANDBOOKS AND YEARBOOKS

1324.   **Magill's Survey of Science CD-ROM.** 1998 ed. [CD-ROM]. Pasadena, Calif., Salem Press, 1998. Minimum systems requirements (Windows): IBM or compatible 386/20MHz. CD-ROM drive. Windows 3.1 or Windows 95. 4MB RAM. 4MB hard disk space. VGA monitor. Minimum system requirements (Macintosh): 68020. CD-ROM drive. System 7.0. 5MB RAM. 4MB hard disk space. 12-inch color monitor. $750.00. ISBN 0-89356-271-8.

The 1,509 previously issued essays in 4 of Magill's science publications—Applied Science Series, 1993 (see ARBA 94, entry 1583); Earch Science Series, 1990 (see ARBA 91, entry 1778); Life Science Series, 1991 (see ARBA 92, entry 1522), and Physical Science Series, 1992 (see ARBA 93, entry 1699)—have been combined into a single CD-ROM product that uses AND Complex 3, a sophisticated browser and search engine. The AND Complex 3 software allows other compressed books, such as *Magill's Masterplots*, to be added to the bookshelf and searched through a single screen. Although the textual information is not new, more than 1,000 color and black-and-white images, including photographs, have been added to the essays and integrated via links to enhance and supplement the text. A list of the images available for a given essay is provided at the end of the text, and sometimes reference is made to them within the article. The basic bibliographies from the original publications are outdated, with copyright dates from the 1970s and 1980s; however, each essay has been updated with an additional current bibliography that includes recent material. The essays follow a set format: scientific field, definition of the topic, principal terms defined, overview or summary, application, context, basic and current bibliographies, related essays that are linked, and images.

A List Selector Box offers the user eight searchable indexes for locating information. These indexes are categorized as either word or text, which searches all words in the field or term/phrase and delimits the search to terms and phrases. The extensiveness of the indexes includes searching the essay categories alphabetically or hierarchically, as well as searching image captions and bibliographies. Once a list is chosen, the user inputs the word or phrase into a text box. A listing then appears beneath the list and input boxes showing the words or phrases for that index. The user can scroll and highlight the desired topic; double-clicking will open the essay in the adjoining window to the right. Multiple results are displayed in a separate window that automatically opens. The software uses many of the features of a Windows environment: frames, toolbars, scroll bars, picture and graphic icons, pull-down menus, links, and clicking to open a window. The user can also easily copy and paste, set preferences, and change the page setup. This familiar display assists in making the product user-friendly for researchers. Advanced searches are possible using Boolean operators, parentheses, proximity operators, and wildcards. The History Window maintains a list of all the essays that were displayed during a current session and allows the user to readily go back to previous topics. The spike, a similar feature, allows users to save their own list of essays for later retrieval.

Magill's Survey of Science CD-ROM is an excellent product for high schools, public libraries, and university libraries looking for basic materials in the science fields. The AND Complex 3 browser and search engine allows the information of 23 volumes of scientific information to be easily searched in a basic manner or in great depth.
—**Elaine Ezell**

1325.   **McGraw-Hill Yearbook of Science & Technology 1999.** New York, McGraw-Hill, 1998. 447p. illus. index. $125.00. ISBN 0-07-052625-7. ISSN 0076-2016.

This new update supplements the 8th edition of the *McGraw-Hill Encyclopedia of Science & Technology* (see ARBA 98, entry 1407). As is common with the other yearbooks in this series, a wide overview of the most significant recent developments in science, technology, and engineering is delivered here. Current topics such as

Comet Hale-Bopp, HDTV, prion diseases, and others are covered. Because ongoing and important trends in science and technology are tracked, the yearbook's editors tap one or more specialists in their field to author an article. To track these specialists, an alphabetic list of contributors along with their affiliation and title of their article can be found in the appendix. A bibliography is also included at the end of each article. Numerous illustrations and graphics are also included, as well as an index.

This yearbook will complement the encyclopedia set mentioned above, but it can also stand on its own if purchased separately. This yearbook is recommended for public or academic libraries.—**Julia Perez**

1326. **Science Projects for All Students.** New York, Facts on File, 1998. 1v. (various paging). illus. index. $165.00 looseleaf w/binder. ISBN 0-8160-3569-5.

This recent volume from Facts on File follows its familiar three-ring-binder format and is divided into numbered sections and printed on heavy stock. Users are given permission for photocopying. Larger text and bold typeface headings make for easy reading. The goal of the resource is to provide traditional science experiments that are modified for students with learning problems or physical challenges in such a way that the modifications are not evident to other students. The experiments are designed so that all students can experience hands-on science together.

The opening pages on safety guidelines provide instruction and precautions applicable to all the experiments. The 6 skills and 47 experiments follow the same format. Each begins with a question followed by an informational paragraph, safety procedures, supplies needed, directions, observations, and findings. The ample white space, illustrations, and verbs in bold typeface make the experiments easy to follow. The experiments are divided into the three science areas: life, earth, and physical science. These sections are arranged in the same numerical order as the skills and experiment sections. Several appendixes for teachers follow the experiments. A section titled "Our Findings" answers questions found in the observation section of each activity. The "Related Literature" section provides a bibliography of four to six nonfiction and fiction titles for each experiment to assist the teacher in developing interdisciplinary lessons. Most recommended titles were copyrighted in 1993 or earlier; those with more recent dates are other Facts on File editions. "Additional Activities," "Hints," "Adaptations," and "Guidelines for Dealing with Students with Disabilities" sections all provide suggestions, modifications, and methods to assist teachers in using the activities in the classroom. A glossary of terms highlighted in the text provides the number of the experiment to which it applies. The index assists the teacher in locating all experiments featuring that topic.

With most special needs students now being served in the regular classroom, teachers will find this volume useful in adapting the science curriculum. Advanced students may view the large and boldface directions as elementary. This guide is most useful for grades four through eight. [R: SLJ, Aug 98, p. 188]—**Elaine Ezell**

1327. Thomas, Brian J. **The World Wide Web for Scientists & Engineers: A Complete Reference for Navigating, Researching, & Publishing Online.** Warrendale, Pa., Society of Automotive Engineers, 1998. 357p. index. $35.00pa. ISBN 0-8194-2775-6.

This book, written for the research community, is essentially two books in one, each having roughly the same number of pages. The 1st is an introduction to Web technology and applications, and the 2d is a listing of research resources listed under 22 broad subject categories, such as "Agricultural Sciences," "Computer Science," "Medicine," and "Physics." The first 5 chapters cover online access issues, e-mail and discussion lists, and Web browsers and their associated applications. Chapters 6 through 8 introduce Web authoring and publishing, focusing on HTML and file formats. This treatment of HTML tagging is cursory at best, and only serves as an introduction. The last chapter is an introduction to search engines and their operation, including Boolean operators, rankings, and sample searches. Most chapters contain references and resource links for further exploration of a particular topic. The research resource listings are next. Like any such listing, outdated links abound, with some 15 percent of the listed links broken at the time of this review. Under the broad categories, the individual links are listed alphabetically, with no annotations. Sites listed include online journals, professional organizations, research centers, government resources, publishers, indexes, and databases. Unless one knows the name of a resource, locating specific subject sites is difficult. A valuable appendix compares five search engines—Alta Vista, Excite, HotBot, InfoSeek, and Lycos—using 28 features, from size, freshness, and pages-crawled-per-day to meta tag support, display options, and relevancy boosters. The book ends with a useful glossary, a bibliography, and a subject index. The bibliography suffers from being outdated by the fast-changing nature of the Web.—**Michael R. Leach**

QUOTATION BOOKS

1328.   **Mathematically Speaking: A Dictionary of Quotations.** Carl C. Gaither and Alma E. Cavazos-Gaither, eds. Philadelphia, Institute of Physics Publishing, 1998. 484p. illus. index. $40.00pa. ISBN 0-7503-0503-7.

This witty, quite straightforward compendium of quotations in the area of mathematics may be just the right solution for speakers trying to find a quotation to flavor a speech. It is a useful source for students, professors, and public speakers who love to quote—and to quote correctly.

This dictionary includes sayings by famous people ranging from Pythagoras to Ice-T (rapper). One can easily identify the author of a quotation. The book lists familiar and less well-known quotations. Bill Gates is quoted in the section entitled "Subtraction."

Sources such as *The Complete Essays & Other Writing of Ralph Waldo Emerson* and the *Complete Works of Lewis Carroll: Through the Looking Glass* are quoted prolifically. For the most part, the sources are named. Subjects are arranged alphabetically. A quotation for a given subject may be found by looking for that subject in the alphabetic arrangement of the book itself. For example, there are nine quotations listed under the heading "PI." There is a subject by author index and an author by subject index.

The cartoon illustrations by Andrew Slocombe add delightful dimension of humor. They would be a wonderful source of inspirations for T-shirt designers. The book is a companion volume to *Statistically Speaking* (see ARBA 98, entry 82) and *Physically Speaking* (Institute of Physics Publishing, 1997), both collections of quotation in related fields of science. *Mathematically Speaking* will have infinite appeal for the wider public interested in mathematics.—**Marilynn Green Hopman**

30 Agricultural Sciences

GENERAL WORKS

1329. **Dictionary of Agriculture.** 2d ed. Alan Stephens, ed. Middlesex, Great Britain, Peter Collin, 1996; repr., Chicago, Fitzroy Dearborn, 1998. 277p. $45.00. ISBN 1-57958-076-9.

This is the 2d edition of a dictionary of agricultural terms written from a British perspective. Approximately 5,000 terms are defined, with some topics supplemented with quotes from farming publications. Phonetic pronunciation is included for the main entry words.

Agriculture covers a broad territory, and this book does remarkably well, covering aspects ranging from breeds of livestock, crop varieties, agricultural economics, agrarian terminology, farming equipment and buildings, and agricultural organizations. It covers not only agriculture of temperate regions, but also attempts to cover topics related to the agriculture of the tropics. With the British focus, there are naturally some topics of interest to Americans that are omitted. For example, the organizations Future Farmers of America (FAA) and National Farmer's Organization (NFO) are not present.

There are several other agricultural dictionaries that can be compared to this one. *The Dictionary of Agriculture: From Abaca to Zoonoisis* (see ARBA 96, entry 1517) provides definitions for 3,400 terms with a focus on U.S. agricultural policy and economics. *The Agriculture Dictionary* (see ARBA 93, entry 1468) defines 10,000 terms, with a slant toward scientific terminology. Any of these dictionaries, solely or in combination, would be useful for public libraries serving a rural population, or academic libraries with an agriculture curriculum.

—**Elaine F. Jurries**

FOOD SCIENCES AND TECHNOLOGY

Dictionaries and Encyclopedias

1330. **The Brooks and Olmo Register of Fruit & Nut Varieties.** 3d ed. Alexandria, Va., American Society for Horticultural Science, 1997. 743p. $139.95. ISBN 0-9615027-3-8.

The 3d edition of the *Register of Fruit & Nut Varieties* represents the first update for this work in nearly 25 years. The register is the definitive list of varieties for fruits and nuts that are suitable for commercial or home use in the United States and Canada. More than 35 specialists from around the world collaborated in reviewing and adding the thousands of new varieties to this edition. In addition to updating the older material, the editors have chosen to include many European and Asian varieties, broadening the work's coverage.

The 3d edition also boasts a new format. Entries are arranged alphabetically by commodity, from "Almonds" to "White Sapote." Within each section there is an alphabetic list by variety that details the discovery, description, and physical characteristics of each variety in 100 words or less. Plant patent numbers are included when appropriate. Generally, this format is easy to use; however, the sections are not clearly identified. It is very easy to lose track of the section in which one is looking.

Register of Fruit & Nut Varieties is the most up-to-date and complete reference text available today. It is a necessity for growers, researchers, packers, distributors, students, or anyone interested in the technical side of fruits and nuts. [R: Choice, Oct 97, p. 275]—**Steven J. Schmidt**

1331.   Fant, Maureen B., and Howard M. Isaacs. **Dictionary of Italian Cuisine.** Hopewell, N.J., Ecco Press, 1998. 296p. index. $27.50. ISBN 0-88001-612-4.

Dictionary of Italian Cuisine offers 6,000 terms. The introduction explains the regional differences in Italian food, how shopping for meat and fish differs from U.S. shopping, and that herbs are given by their botanical taxonomy whenever possible to eliminate confusing a cook. The "Instructions for Use" section not only describes how the book is arranged for easier use but also gives a pronunciation guide for the Italian language. All cross-referenced items are in bold capital letters. The main text is arranged alphabetically, followed by a chapter on weight, measure, and temperature conversion; a bibliography; and English-Italian index. The definitions range in length from 3 to 4 word explanations to more than 50 words when necessary. The book is not overly wordy and is a good reference for Italian cuisine. It is not a cookbook. This work is recommended for public and academic libraries with an interest in food collections, especially Italian cuisine. [R: LJ, Dec 98, p. 90]—**Betsy J. Kraus**

1332.   Forget, Carl. **The Dictionary of Beer and Brewing.** 2d ed. Dan Rabin, comp. Chicago, Fitzroy Dearborn, 1998. 306p. $45.00. ISBN 1-57958-078-5.

This dictionary, published jointly in the United States and the United Kingdom, contains some 2,400 entries on terms related to beer. The preface was written by Gregg Smith, and consists of a brief essay on the historical significance of beer during the past 6,000 years, including the history of the word "beer." Most definitions include a brief but accurate phrase or sentence, but several longer entries contain a paragraph (e.g., for terms such as "bock," "lager," and "steam beer.") The book has a pronunciation key, and the pronunciation is marked in parentheses after most terms. Four appendixes in the back of the volume provide thermometer scales, temperature conversion table, conversion factors for United Kingdom and United State measurements, and conversion tables for alcohol percentages by volume to alcohol percentages by weight.

Few similar dictionaries can be found in print. In 1995, however, Christine P. Rhodes and others edited a more scholarly publication entitled *The Encyclopedia of Beer* (see ARBA 96, entry 1525) with 900 more comprehensive entries. Robert A. Lipinski and Kathleen A. Lipinski authored a broader title in 1992 titled *The Complete Beverage Dictionary* (see ARBA 94, entry 1601). After checking 46 entries in the "B" section of *The Dictionary of Beer and Brewing* against the Lipinskis' beverage dictionary, only 13 entries could be found. Libraries with clients studying or practicing in the food, beverage, or hospitality areas will find this dictionary helpful, even though it has a slight British and European emphasis, especially if they lack the Rhodes or Lipinski titles.
—**O. Gene Norman**

1333.   Jackson, Michael. **Ultimate Beer.** New York, DK Publishing, 1998. 192p. illus. index. $29.95. ISBN 0-7894-3527-6.

Great wine has been appreciated for centuries, and it is not difficult to find books rating everything from their character and spirit to their appropriateness for specific occasions. The popularity of beer, however, is a more recent phenomenon that begs for similar attention that has been granted its grape-based counterpart. This is exactly what Jackson has set out to do in *Ultimate Beer.*

The book begins by explaining what makes a great beer—how the barley, hops, and specific conditions can alter both its texture and flavor. Through the use of maps and vivid photographs the reader learns the historical roots of beer. The book then goes on to list suggested beers for special occasions. Beers are listed under such topics as "Seasonal Beers," "Sociable Beers," "Thirst Quenchers," "Winter Warmers," "Nightcap Beers," and "Aperitifs." Each of the more than 450 beers are pictured in full color and explains where the beer originated, its style (e.g., ale, stout, lager), alcohol content, and ideal serving temperature.

The final 2 sections are titled "Beer and Food" and "Cooking with Beer." Here, beers are suggested for almost every type of meal imaginable. Several suggestions are provided to suit the tastes of even the pickiest diners. Suggestions for using beer in marinades, stews, and batters are presented here as well. The book concludes with a glossary, a list of addresses of beer-lovers clubs and liquor stores, and an index.

This book is obviously not a choice for all libraries, but public libraries with a section of wine and beer tasting will do well to purchase this informative, well-written book.—**Shannon M. Graff**

1334.   Luce, Bernard. Dictionary of Gastronomic Terms, French/English. Dictionnaire Gastronomique. Paris, La Maison du Dictionnaire; distr., New York, Hippocrene Books, 1997. 500p. $24.95. ISBN 0-7818-0555-4.

This book originated in France, where it was intended to help organize menus for smaller restaurants and cafés as well as serve as a useful tool to butchers, bakers, patissiers, and others involved with the food industry. In theory, it should work equally well when translated into English. Too many restaurants in English-speaking countries insist on printing menus in French, and many of them are filled with mistakes. This book will help in getting the spellings right, but it will not be of much assistance in understanding what some names are about. For instance, *Crespet des Landes* translates simply as "a sweet," and one is left wondering what it really is. *Agneau de Paulliac* is translated as "Paulliac lamb," but no explanation is given as to whether it refers to lamb from the Paulliac region or a particular way of preparing it. Entries range from basic terms to more complicated items, such as *Filets de maquereau à la lyonnaise*, meaning mackerel filets baked with onions and white wine; or *Crépinettes de lapin*—rabbit stuffed with a hash of bacon, mushrooms, shallots, wrapped in a pork caul, sprinkled with melted butter, and baked in the oven. There are also some that will pose further questions, such as *Baguette triérarche*, which comes out as "cow's milk cheese shaped in parallelepiped," a translation that might pose a challenge to the vocabulary of a small restaurant owner.

The book is arranged in several parts. After the preface (given in French and English), there is a basic section on arranging the menus. A thesaurus devoted to main culinary terms is next, followed by the main section—an extensive dictionary of French gastronomic terms. The French entries are impeccably spelled, but there are a few odd omissions on the English side, such as *Wiskies* or *Fishes*. Still, the usefulness of the volume by far outweighs its flaws.—**Koraljka Lockhart**

Directories

1335.   Bradney, Gail. Best Wines! 1999: The Gold Medal Winners. 3d ed. Bearsville, N.Y., Print Project; distr., Chicago, Independent Publishers Group, 1998. 369p. index. $14.95pa. ISBN 0-9651750-2-2. ISSN 1088-8608.

Most wine consumed in the United States is "jug wine" (pro rated as under $3.99 a 750-ml bottle). Most of it is domestic, but some comes from Italy and Chile. This book, first published in 1996, is Bradney's attempt to get Americans to drink good wine for only a few dollars more a bottle.

The concept is easy: Take all the gold medal winners from 21 wine competitions (ranging from InterVin to VinItaly to the Beverage Testing Institute to the Orange County Fair to the *Dallas Morning News* Wine Competition), and extract only the New World winners from the United States, Canada, Chile, Argentina, Australia, New Zealand, and South Africa. Then sort these winners by style or grape variety and provide brief overall notes on taste and food pairings.

Each entry has noted the producer, year, name, national retail price, where the medal came from, and a score, if applicable. There are a number of appendixes; dealing with multiple award winners; an extensive glossary; an Internet shopping guide; and a wine index organized alphabetically by producer, with page references and indication of whether it is from the United States or imported.

The core section is the appendix of wine bargains—winners under $15 national retail, which usually sell for $9.99 or less. This is excellent for the novice or the jug wine drinker. Just take the list into a discount liquor store and start buying, noting what is likable and what is not. The book as a whole is extremely useful for determining upscale purchases based on numerical scores in wine magazines or as medal winners. Consumers can start at the top, with the obvious winners, until they can get their bearings. Even the wine connoisseurs will appreciate this book. The only drawback is that some wineries just do not enter competitions, especially foreign ones, and consequently they are not represented here.—**Dean Tudor**

1336.   Culinary Schools: Where the Art of Cooking Becomes a Career. Princeton, N.J., Peterson's Guides, 1998. 299p. illus. index. $21.95pa. ISBN 1-56079-943-9.

At long last Peterson's has issued a much-needed guide to culinary education. *Culinary Schools* looks to be the definitive guide on the subject. It is well organized, written at a level for most readers, and full of practical advice from many people working in food service industries as well as the authors of the essays.

Three essays make up the first section of the book. The content centers on the three most crucial topics facing prospective students: "Choosing a Cooking School," "Paying for Your Culinary Education," and "Charting a Successful Culinary Career." Each essay is written by notable people in the food service industry. Each provides solid advice as well as accurate information about the state of affairs both in the culinary education world and the outside food service world. In the first essay dealing with choosing the school, the following excerpt appears: "Some chefs found that the most important lessons they learned came outside the classroom. 'I spent a lot of time in the library,' says [chef] Gary Danko." There are many references to the hard work involved in being a chef or running a restaurant. This is a good approach because it does not glamorize the profession. Not everyone will be as successful as Wolfgang Puck.

The directory of programs and schools follows. It is the standard Peterson's format—alphabetic order by state and then by city. Each entry contains information in the following categories: general information, program information, areas of study, facilities, student profile, faculty, expenses, financial aid, application information, and contact department or person. International entries follow the U.S. entries and have the same format. Examination of the entries of schools familiar to this reviewer indicates a high level of accuracy of information. One oddity noted, although it does not detract from the overall value of the book, is the presence of advertisements scattered throughout this section; some of them are full-color, full-page advertisements.

Other worthwhile features include a list of scholarships, a quick reference chart, and a list of professional organizations and resources. There are two indexes, one by institution name and one organized by type of degree or program offered. This reviewer found the inclusion of quotes from working professionals dispersed throughout the essays in the first section to be insightful. The candor and honesty of what was said adds a great deal to this guidebook. This title is highly recommended for most public, high school, and community college libraries and academic libraries with strong vocational guidance collections.—**Roland C. Hansen**

1337. Regan, Gary, and Mardee Haidin Regan. **The Bourbon Companion: A Connoisseur's Guide.** Philadelphia, Running Press, 1998. 191p. illus. $19.95. ISBN 0-7624-0013-7.

The Regans, both professional food and wine writers, present extremely useful data about the resurgence in straight bourbon's popularity, similar to single-malt scotch. Most of the book contains descriptions of about 100 different bourbons, with full tasting notes and ratings for each. This reviewer dusted off old notes going back 15 years, and in general, would have to agree with the Regan's assessment for the 35 or so actually tasted and noted. The Regans also include "export bottlings," meant for sale in duty-free shops. Each entry is accompanied by a label picture (for the two Makers Mark export bottlings, these are reversed) and a cross-reference to a distiller's directory, which has names and addresses, telephone numbers, and a short history as well as material on production methods (water source, mash percentages, yeast strains, barrel char levels, and warehousing).

Wild Turkey brands get the highest overall ratings, with a 98 for "Wild Turkey Single Barrel Bourbon 50.5 percent ABV Bottled on 11/9/96 From Barrel No. 3 Stored in Warehouse B on Rick No. 13" (label name). It also has a char level of 4, which is the highest and the darkest in color. Woodford Reserve is the only one still using copper pot stills throughout.

The remainder of the book has histories of techniques, some interesting photographs, a list of whiskey societies and newsletters (no Websites), a bibliography, a glossary of terms, and a name index. Missing, unfortunately, are actual production figures (by volume and by sales) and national retail prices.—**Dean Tudor**

1338. **Wine Spectator Magazine's Guide to Great Wine Values: $10 and Under.** New York, Wine Spectator Press/M. Shanken Communications; distr., Philadelphia, Running Press, 1997. 270p. maps. index. $9.95pa. ISBN 1-881659-41-0.

The above titles have been published by the respected *Wine Spectator* magazine that has been around for more than two decades. *Ultimate Guide to Buying Wine* evaluates more than 40,000 foreign and domestic wines, provides tasting notes for 20,000, and advises whether the wine should be drunk now or later. In this edition, each section has been revised, and a new section has been added of 850 better wines that scored toward the top of the 100-point scale at a cost of $12 or less per bottle. This book also expands the listing of wines for South Africa and Austria. In addition, a small pullout vintage chart is provided to use for trips to favorite wine stores. The volume reviews a broad range of wines in an attempt to evaluate the best wines and the best-selling wines from various countries and districts, and it provides many recent and older wine evaluations not easily found elsewhere. For example, *Buyer's Guide to American Wines* (see ARBA 94, entry 1605) covers only 5,000 domestic wines.

The smaller *Guide to Great Wine Values* describes and recommends more than 1,200 current wines with vintages of 1993, 1994, 1995, and 1996 that fall into the $10 and less price range. The main part of the book consists of tasting notes, evaluations of each wine using a 100-point scale, and the retail price. The book is divided by country, and the beginning of each country section provides a selection of the "Most Reliable Values" in wines that consistently have good quality, an illustrated wine label, and a small map of the country showing where grapes are produced. An index of winery names gives quick access. This pocket book will be particularly helpful in assisting the consumer in locating an inexpensive wine of quality.—**O. Gene Norman**

Handbooks and Yearbooks

1339.   **Food and Beverage Market Place, 1997/98.** 2d ed. Lakeville, Conn., Grey House Publishing, 1997. 994p. index. $195.00pa. ISBN 0-939300-77-X.

The 2d edition of this resource profiles more than 7,500 public and private companies providing their name, address, telephone and fax numbers, and in most instances officers, brands, product category, number of employees, and divisions and plants. Somewhat unique to this type of directory are the sections on mail-order catalog companies and the "Information Resources" section. Nearly 750 mail-order companies are noted by product category; the "Resources" section lists magazines, newsletters, trade associations, directories, and databases focusing on the food and beverage field. When known, e-mail and Web addresses are given. The brand name, catalog and information, and product category indexes are useful and provide additional access to the information.

Some inaccuracies were found, such as in the names and job titles and less than complete information with regards to brand names and divisions and plants. These are not major faults given that all directories share this common trait due to timeliness and accuracy of information supplied. As noted in the introduction, all these data can be found elsewhere and in many instances more comprehensively—*Brands and Their Companies* (see ARBA 93, entry 188) or *The Directory of the Canning, Freezing, Preserving Industries* (deluxe ed.; see ARBA 92, entry 1492) to name just two. Except for the Gale publication, which is very expensive, all the others are comparable in price. If one already has any or all of these publications, this volume will not be needed because it does not replace them. However, if only one or two directories of this type can be purchased, this would be a wise choice because it does an excellent job of pulling together diverse information in one place and the price is right. Food libraries could use this to complement the *Thomas Food Industry Register* (a portion of which is available on the Internet), and public libraries could use this as a stand-alone reference.—**Joy Hastings**

1340.   Joseph, Robert. **Good Wine Guide 1999.** New York, DK Publishing, 1998. 287p. maps. index. $12.95. ISBN 0-7894-3528-4.

Published in Great Britain and the United States, Joseph's guide provides the promised general background on wine and consists of 3 parts: an A to Z encyclopedia of 2,700 wines, wine terms and regions, and a selected list of wine retailers in North America. The basic section covers such topics as types of wine; tasting and buying wine; the wine label; countries that make wine; types of grapes; storing, serving, and investing in wine; wine vintages; and the use of wine with food. In the A to Z encyclopedia section the author recommends wines using a five star system, and he provides pronunciation for most terms. The North American retailers listing by state gives the name of business, telephone and fax numbers, type of services and products offered, a brief statement about each establishment, and a list of wine specialists by type. The book also has its own Website at www.goodwineguide.com, which presents an electronic wine atlas and links to some 200 wineries and shops worldwide.

This title complements and expands *Wine Spectator Magazine's Guide to Great Wine Values: $10 and Under* (see entry 1338) that describes more than 1,200 wines of current vintages. Joseph's guide lists and evaluates more than twice that number of wines, even though some of them probably are not as widely available. In Joseph's book, prices also range from under $7.50 to more than $30, with vintages going back more than 25 years. This is a small, attractive, informative, and inexpensive hardback volume that will be a good buy for libraries and individuals.—**O. Gene Norman**

1341.   Roby, Norman S., and Charles E. Olken. **The Connoisseurs' Handbook of the Wines of California and the Pacific Northwest.** 4th ed. New York, Alfred A. Knopf/Random House, 1998. 413p. maps. $19.95pa. ISBN 0-375-70329-2.

Compared with many of the other wine producing regions of the world, California has a relatively short history that is measured in decades as opposed to centuries. The 4th edition of this guide to the wines of California demonstrates the growth in the industry and the changes in the buying habits of wine drinkers.

The book begins with a chapter titled "Basics of Winemaking" that discusses the technical side of creating great wines and provides comprehensive definitions of many of the procedures. Following this are chapters on the different wine types, the geographic regions of California well known for producing great wines, and a short commentary explaining the importance of vintages in choosing wine. The main chapter of the book, entitled "Wineries and Wines," alphabetically lists the wineries of first California and then of the northwestern United States. Each entry lists the owner, acreage owned, variety of wine produced, and the quality of wine. The authors have a rating system for the quality of wines that includes such standards as "below average quality," "wine of average quality," "a very fine wine likely to be memorable," and "an exceptional wine likely to be worth a special search." The peak time a wine should be used within is also noted with such ratings as "a wine now past its peak," "ready to drink now," "drinkable now but will improve with further aging," and "needs further aging before drinking." The final sections include a list of wineries rated and a glossary.

This book will be appreciated by the wine connoisseur looking to California and the Pacific Northwest in search of the perfect wine. Although there are many similar guides to wine on the market, this work is original in its focus and will be a useful reference for public libraries.—**Shannon M. Graff**

1342.   Stevenson, Tom. **The Millennium Champagne & Sparkling Wine Guide.** New York, DK Publishing, 1998. 192p. illus. index. $19.95 flexibinding. ISBN 0-7894-3561-6.

This award-winning author has produced an impressive work, one that is physically a little larger than pocket-sized. But then, Stevenson has been writing about champagne for some time. Here he presents brief material about history, techniques, styles, storing, and service. Stevenson's textual coverage deals with the "best producers," mainly champagne, but there are also sections on other French sparklers, Spanish cava, German sekt, Italian spumante, plus the new world equivalents in America, Australia, New Zealand, and South Africa. There is one page for all the other countries. Copious but small color photographs and maps, along with addresses of all American producers and a glossary, complete the book. For tasting notes, the user needs to consult the directory.

This A to Z listing of some 900 recommended wines, along with notes from blind tastings, price ranges, and some numeric ratings, also contains newly written reviews about recent vintages. Not all wines are available in all markets. None of the "best" wines here are cross-referenced to the "best producers" section nor vice versa—a definite weakness in the book's structure because there is also no index. This reviewer also wishes that the comments were more sharply focused. The author's scoring system, out of 100 points, is not quite the same as other wine writers. (A score of 70 here is not particularly inferior, whereas in most cases, nobody would even go near the stuff.) Still, this is a book with high reference value as society heads into a new millennium and desperately needs sparklers to celebrate.—**Dean Tudor**

FORESTRY

1343.   **Directory of the Wood Products Industry, 1998.** San Francisco, Calif., Miller Freeman, 1997. 945p. index. $297.00. ISSN 1064-749X.

Molding or matchsticks, kitchen utensils or laminated beams, if a wood product is what you seek, this is a great place to start the search. It is also an excellent resource for vendors wanting to know their suppliers, competitors, or potential collaborators better. Profiles include all the usual contact information along with Website addresses, when available. Published since 1919, this directory shows the decades of expertise behind it. The subcategories and cross-indexes make it as easy to use as it is visually appealing. Secondary manufacturers and lumber mills are treated with equal depth. A section on highlights in the wood industry launches the text. One can use those preliminary pages to review the relation between southern timber production and federal restrictions in the western United States. Or to review the housing starts and financing paths of recent years. Besides providing a fast and simple way to locate wood products vendors and equipment manufacturers, the volume also makes quick work of zeroing in on Bureau of Land Management directors, forest industry agencies, state and United States Department of Agriculture foresters, industry associations, and more.—**Diane M. Calabrese**

HORTICULTURE

Dictionaries and Encyclopedias

1344.   Riffle, Robert Lee. **The Tropical Look: An Encyclopedia of Dramatic Landscape Plants.** Portland, Oreg., Timber Press, 1998. 428p. illus. maps. index. $49.95. ISBN 0-88192-422-9.

This book is an anthology of nearly 2,000 plants that are not strictly tropical but are instead "tropical-looking." These are plants such as palms and those with large, showy foliage and flowers and colored or variegated leaves. The author defines tropical plants as those that cannot withstand a freeze; however, tropical-looking plants need not be strictly tropical in the geographic or horticultural sense. Additionally, not all tropical plants look tropical in the aforementioned sense, so those lacking this appearance are excluded.

The encyclopedia is for gardeners and landscapers intending to develop the tropical look in Europe or North America either outdoors or in greenhouses, conservatories, atria, and so forth. Hardiness zone maps for both continents are included to afford some estimate of the probability of survival if these plants are established outdoors. The plants are arranged by genus scientific name, with a narrative of essential details included for each. All individual plants sections contain a tabular listing of such pertinent information as family name and examples of members, common name(s), general plant description, hardiness zones, light and moisture requirements, soil type preferences, special considerations, and propagation techniques. Plants are also grouped according to common-alities in useful landscape lists, such as those that are drought-tolerant, erosion-controlling, succulents, poisonous, and so on. A glossary, a bibliography, and an index are included, making the book user-friendly. The 400 or so color photographs and large format make this an attractive coffee-table book, but there is also enough technical detail to make it an indispensable reference for growers interested in the tropical look.—**Michael G. Messina**

1345.   Tenenbaum, Frances. **Taylor's Dictionary for Gardeners: The Definitive Guide to the Language of Horticulture.** New York, Houghton Mifflin, 1997. 351p. illus. $25.00. ISBN 0-395-87606-0.

Gardening is one of the fastest-growing hobbies. As a resource for this popular pastime, *Taylor's Dictionary for Gardeners* can provide the novice or intermediate gardener with answers to many questions. Arranged in a pleasing format, each entry is titled in bold typeface with a short but thorough paragraph describing the word or phrase, or, in the case of a famous gardener, a brief biography is given. Entries vary from gardening terms to botanical names for most common garden plants to how-to explanations to interesting discoveries about phrases as they relate to gardening and more. Complementing the entries are many excellent illustrations that serve to clarify definitions where words are not enough. This is a wonderful gardening tool that never has to be weeded.
—**Mary L. Trenerry**

Handbooks and Yearbooks

1346.   **Ball RedBook.** 16th ed. Vic Ball, ed. Batavia, Ill., Ball Publishing, 1997. 802p. illus. index. $71.95. ISBN 1-883052-15-7.

Although intended for growers and students of floriculture, this 4-part work also contains information of value to home gardeners. The 1st section details greenhouse construction, equipment, and the changes in both in the last 6 years. This is followed by sections on growing basics and the business aspects of floriculture. The 4th section, which deals with crop culture in general and 136 species in particular, will appeal to home gardeners. Two appendixes include information on flower buying holidays through the year 2004 and plant hardiness zones.

Chapters within each section are written by various specialists. Information includes, but is not limited to, environmental laws, employment opportunities in floriculture, resources, the relative life span of various seeds, tissue culture, trends in species popularity, and marketing techniques. The text is thorough, clearly written, and well organized. It is complemented by an abundance of tables and black-and-white photographs.

Plant horticulture information notwithstanding, home gardeners will do better with *The American Horticultural Society A-Z Encyclopedia of Garden Plants* (see ARBA 98, entry 1432), or *America's Garden Book* (Macmillan, 1996). Funds permitting, however, libraries serving professional growers and students should purchase two copies—one for reference and one to circulate.—**January Adams**

1347.   Bloom, Adrian. **Adrian Bloom's Year-Round Garden: Colour in Your Garden from January to December.** Portland, Oreg., Timber Press, 1998. 287p. illus. index. $39.95. ISBN 0-88192-457-1.

For many, a garden is a seasonal thing, to be enjoyed in the warmer months and ignored in the colder. But for a few, the creation of a garden becomes an exercise in the micromanagement of year-round perfection; the pursuit of a never-ending visual treat of color and form through all seasons. Normally such treasures go unrecorded, but in this book the author documents 33 years worth of plantings that have led to a garden of unprecedented seasonal depth. The well-written text is accompanied by wonderful photographs. The setting is Norfolk, England, a temperate and seasonal climate with adequate rain; thus the book will interest residents in similar settings.

The book is broken into 2 sections, one concerning the "quiet" seasons of autumn, winter, and spring, the other the "busy" season of summer. Each section is further bisected. The first half involves a series of illustrated essays on color in the garden, container plants, matters of maintenance, planting associations, and garden design, to name a few. The second half is broken into several directories to trees, shrubs, and herbs that the author has used in his garden. Plants are presented alphabetically by genus within each directory. A summary presents the horticultural data for each species within the genus, with a particular attention to culture in eastern England. The work concludes with a brief bibliography and index.

The book is a republication of the author's *Winter Garden Glory* (HarperCollins, 1993) and *Summer Garden Glory* (HarperCollins, 1996), and unites these two volumes in one. This reviewer would hesitate to call it a true reference book, but it is a useful and imaginative planning tool for gardeners of temperate, moist environs.
—**Bruce H. Tiffney**

1348.   **Bulbs.** New York, DK Publishing, 1997. 200p. illus. maps. index. (Eyewitness Garden Handbooks). $17.95 flexibinding. ISBN 0-7894-1454-6.

DK's bulb manual is a virtual flower feast. A meticulous handbook to choosing, planting, and enjoying more than 500 varieties, the work is surprisingly compact. Its neat, accessible arrangement is a DK specialty. Color arrangements in the same hue create a subtle control of the subject. Every part of the book invites, from the tulip on the cover to the daffodil on the back flap.

Organization, which is the test of a gardening manual, meets the needs and demands of professional and hobby gardeners, librarians, and bulb dealers. The endpapers contain the rare DK errors—a muddy attempt at the North American hardiness zones, the last four of which form a purplish ink blotch. The table of contents divides the subject by size—large, medium, and small. Within the divisions are subsets by season. Two pages explain the arrangement, symbols, hardiness, and catalog use. Sidebars point out headings, plant portraits, and entries; feature pages on special interest genera; and feature plant descriptions, symbols, and sizes. There are five pages that encapsulate the rationale of using bulbs in mixed borders, formal plantings, naturalized settings, containers, and under cover. A planting guide summarizes the best choices for distinct purposes; for example, dry shade, cutting garden, rock garden, and moist shade.

The text is vivid. Each entry offers the focal plant in a natural setting. Most of the photography is stunningly beautiful, particularly the dahlia section. A few shy flowers disdain to be photographed, as with the nepalense. Others, like the iris, are clearly out of focus. A puzzler is the arums (pp. 141 and 155), which appear only in leaf. The book concludes with tips on selection, soil preparation, potting, staking, dividing, and storage. The writing is crisp and even. A glossary clarifies such specific terms as *tepal, rosette, cultivar,* and *offset.* Indexing is set in three columns and uses italic and roman typefaces to good advantage. Tucked into the acknowledgments page is a listing of abbreviations that would be effective in the front matter. Overall, the book is well paced, suitably priced, and cheery—a worthy addition to a crowded garden book market.—**Mary Ellen Snodgrass**

1349.   Cooke, Ian. **The Plantfinder's Guide to Tender Perennials.** Newton Abbot, Devon, David & Charles Publishers and Portland, Oreg., Timber Press, 1998. 192p. illus. maps. index. $34.95. ISBN 0-88192-450-4.

A challenge for gardeners who live in areas where various degrees of frost make the difference between grand displays of color and large expanses of dirt in springtime, the plants discussed in this book tempt even the most rational enthusiasts at some stage in their passion. This collection is truly the "feast of unusual genera" as reported on the book cover, with more than 250 species described in the plant directory, which makes up the second section of this book. The first section describes tender perennials and discusses their general history, habitat, and hardiness.

The author has included plants from all over the world. An overall description with general and anecdotal information on each entry is followed by sections on its botany, history, and cultivation. A plant list describes individual members of the genus, giving the common name and a description of their variations and color. As with the main entries, the lists of individual varieties are selective.

A wonderful selection of planting schemes, many with brilliantly colored photographs is found in part 3, and a discussion of propagation and cultivation of tender perennials is covered in part 4. Photographs and illustrations accompany the text throughout these sections. The book concludes with an interesting appendix of various gardens where displays of this genera can be seen and a second one that lists places from which plants of this type can be obtained. This is a great volume to add to the reference collection of libraries serving gardeners, who will certainly find it valuable for selection before hitting the garden shops.—**Jo Anne H. Ricca**

1350.   **Gardener's Supply Company Passport to Gardening: A Sourcebook for the 21st-Century Gardener.** By Katherine LaLiberte and Ben Watson. White River Junction, Vt., Chelsea Green, 1997. 312p. illus. index. $24.95pa. ISBN 1-890132-00-4.

The objective of this gardening sourcebook is twofold: to provide an overview of gardening topics of perennial interest and of those "new" areas that have achieved recent popularity, and to provide lists of the most unique, original, and useful resources. Part 1 begins with building a healthy soil, composting, starting plants from seed, extending the season, and pest and disease control. Part 2 describes edible gardening (herbs, vegetables, fruits), and part 3 covers ornamental or flower gardening. Selected specialty topics, such as container, water, and hydroponic gardening, are outlined in part 4. Using native plants and wildflowers in the garden is covered in part 5, "Gardening in Harmony with Nature." The book concludes with information on community gardens, guides to garden tours, and regional gardening in the United States.

There are a prodigious number of gardening books available, ranging from works on a single species to general gardening books. This work can be compared to *Gardening by Mail: A Sourcebook* (see ARBA 95, entry 1525) and *The Home Gardener's Source* (Random House, 1997). These directories are more comprehensive in their listings but do not include an overview of gardening topics as does the book under review.

This work is recommended for the beginning gardener who wants to have a gardening resource to consult that is general in scope. It would also be a useful purchase for public libraries that collect gardening books for their users.—**Elaine F. Jurries**

1351.   Grounds, Roger. **The Plantfinder's Guide to Ornamental Grasses.** Newton Abbot, Devon, David & Charles Publishers and Portland, Oreg., Timber Press, 1998. 192p. illus. maps. index. $34.95. ISBN 0-88192-451-2.

Environmental concerns and ease of care have led to an increase in the popularity of ornamental grasses in the United States. This book, written from an Englishman's perspective, dwells mainly on the beauty and interest these plants lend to a garden. As this book shows, they have become more popular throughout the world for this reason and for their tolerance for various soils and weather conditions.

The 5 parts in this book cover a basic introduction to grasses that covers their history and biology, colored-leaf grasses, flowering grasses, planting plans for uses of grasses, and plant care. Perhaps of most interest to the reader are the inspiring planting plans. The author has filled this section with information on using grasses in all sorts of areas (e.g., formal gardens, wetlands, meadows, dry gardens) as well as in the greenhouse and in containers. There are also chapters on bamboos, subtropical effects, grasses in the winter garden, and grass-lime plants. Colorful photographs and plates that show the distinct differences of plants are interspersed throughout the book.

The book concludes with 7 appendixes that concern special uses for grasses, common names, an A to Z chart that gives information on plants at a glance, where particular grasses can be seen, outlets for purchasing grasses, a reference list of pertinent books, and a hardiness zone map. An index of Latin names completes the volume.

After perusing this book, the reader will find it hard to believe that there could be more information on this subject, or that gardeners who pick it up will not be inspired to add at least one ornamental grass to their collections. Informative, accurate, and seemingly comprehensive, this volume should be included in any library's collection on gardening.—**Jo Anne H. Ricca**

1352.   Page, Martin. **The Gardener's Guide to Growing Peonies.** Portland, Oreg., Timber Press, 1997. 160p. illus. maps. index. $29.95. ISBN 0-88192-408-3.

A professional botanist and photographer, Page has selected more than 600 species for inclusion in this book. Chapter topics include history, cultivation, and the use of peonies in the garden. The peony species are presented alphabetically by their botanical names. Each entry includes geographic origin (most include the year introduced), physical description, season of bloom, and growing height. Chapter on tree peonies and hybrids are similarly arranged. The final chapter on where to see peonies lists gardens in the United Kingdom, China, France, and North America as well as peony societies from around the world. Appendixes include a glossary and a thorough list of where to buy the plants.

This is a lovely book, interspersed with beautiful color photographs of peonies in actual garden settings. As a reference it is thoughtfully arranged and easy to use and should answer any patron's questions. It should be a part of any gardening collection.—**Rachael Green**

1353.   **Rock Garden Plants.** New York, DK Publishing, 1997. 192p. illus. maps. index. (Eyewitness Garden Handbooks). $17.95 flexibinding. ISBN 0-7894-1455-4.

Part of the Eyewitness Garden Handbooks series, this book provides a quick reference guide to more than 450 rock garden plants by type, size, season of interest, and color. The opening chapter is a helpful introduction, giving advice on choosing suitable plants for a particular site or purpose, such as for a border, container, or simply as a specimen. Following chapters are subdivided into sections according to the average size of the plants and their main season of interest. Family name, common name(s), and botanical name are provided. Photographs show each plant's main features and color. A brief description gives details of growing habits, flowers, fruits, and leaves, followed by information on nature habitat, tips on cultivation, and propagation. Symbols indicate the sun, soil, and hardiness requirements.

At the end of the work is a useful two-page glossary that explains key terms. An index of every rock plant, its synonyms, and common names, with a brief genus description allows quick and easy access to the book by plant name.

Rock Garden Plants is cleverly arranged and a joy to page through, with more than 500 beautiful photographs. It would make a fine addition to any reference collection; however, with its affordable price, one would be tempted to purchase an additional copy to circulate.—**Rachael Green**

VETERINARY SCIENCE

1354.   Giffin, James M., and Tom Gore. **Horse Owner's Veterinary Handbook.** 2d ed. New York, Macmillan General Reference/Simon & Schuster Macmillan, 1998. 538p. illus. index. $39.95. ISBN 0-87605-606-0.

Revised and updated, this edition of *Horse Owner's Veterinary Handbook* is an excellent resource for horse owners. Basic health care; medicines; immunizations; and treatment of wounds, illnesses, and emergencies are dealt with in easy to understand terms. The latest breakthroughs in equine medicine are included in updates of the original chapters, along with two additional chapters on pediatrics and geriatrics. An index of signs and symptoms on the inside front cover gives the user quick access to the text for immediate problems, and the detailed table of contents and general index makes specific information easily attainable. Certainly, this handbook is not meant to take the place of professional veterinary care; however, it does answer the most vital care and emergency questions, and would provide the owner or caregiver an excellent understanding of symptoms and problems, enabling better communication with the veterinarian. The advice may well give the owner the necessary information and suggest steps to take that could save the life of the horse until professional help arrives.

Although many horse owners will purchase this excellent resource for their home libraries, many public libraries in areas where horse ownership is prevalent will also want to include a copy in their reference section, and possibly have a circulating copy as well.—**Susan Zernial**

31 Biological Sciences

BIOLOGY

Dictionaries and Encyclopedias

1355. **Encyclopedia of Human Biology.** 2d ed. Renato Dulbecco, ed. San Diego, Calif., Academic Press, 1997. 9v. illus. index. $1799.00/set. ISBN 0-12-226970-5.

The 1st edition of the *Encyclopedia of Human Biology* appeared in 1991 (see ARBA 92, entry 1516 for a review). With the rapid changes occurring in the biomedical sciences, there have been many discoveries in the past six years. The 2d edition of this work contains 670 articles, ranging in length from 5 to 20 pages, that cover topics in 35 broad subject areas, such as behavior (addiction, mating behavior, problem solving), biochemistry (adenosine triphosphate, ion pumps), biotechnology (artificial heart, biomechanics), organs and systems (heart, digestive system, color vision), evolution (comparative anatomy, population genetics), public health (emerging and reemerging infectious diseases, drug testing), and sociobiology (bioethics, aggression). One-third of the articles are new, and the rest have been revised in varying degrees.

The signed articles are written by eminent scientists with academic appointments. Ten of the contributors are Nobel laureates. All of the articles contain bibliographies, and the entries are arranged alphabetically. Each one begins with an outline, a glossary, and a definition statement. Cross-references appear in brackets within the text. Because the same typeface is used, they are sometimes difficult to find. Photographs, charts, tables, and line drawings illustrate the text. A center section of color plates, mostly anatomical, appears in each volume. Every volume has its own table of contents and general instructions for using the encyclopedia. Volume 9 serves as a research guide, containing the complete table of contents, a list of articles by subject, an index, and a list of contributors with their affiliations.

The articles are written at a technical level, but educated readers will be able to understand them. By providing comprehensive overviews of biomedical subjects for a broad range of users—general public, students, and professionals—the *Encyclopedia of Human Biology* serves as an introductory reference source that will be useful for academic and large public libraries with sufficient funds. It brings together a diverse group of subjects of interest to everyone.—**Barbara M. Bibel**

1356. **Magill's Survey of Science: Life Science Series Supplement. Volume 7 Cumulative Index.** Laura L. Mays Hoopes, ed. Englewood Cliffs, N.J., Salem Press, 1998. 1v. (various paging). $90.00. ISBN 0-89356-936-4.

This volume, a supplement to the original 6 volumes of the series published in 1991, contains 52 additional topics, including updated research on AIDS/HIV, apoptosis, environmental estrogens, the Human Genome Project, prions, schizophrenia genes, and telomerase. Geared toward the layperson, most of the topics are well written and concise and reflect current research in the broad field of life sciences. A few topics are too broad and would have been better served using more specific subject headings. For instance, instead of "immunology," specific topics on "lymphocytes" or the "Major Histocompatibility Complex" would better serve the reader. Each article follows a similar format, beginning with a placement of the topic in the broader field of research, related fields of study, a short description of the topic's relevance and importance, and terms with their corresponding meaning.

The summary section detailing the major features of the topic with appropriate background materials forms the heart of each article. This is either a "Summary of the Phenomenon" or a "Summary of the Methodology," depending on the topic. "Apoptosis" is an example of the former, and "chemotherapy" an example of the latter. Following each phenomenon summary is a section describing the techniques or instruments used in studying the phenomenon. Following each methodology summary is a section describing how researchers or physicians apply the method in their work. A "context" section examines the implications of each topic with regard to historical, social, or scientific perspectives. Each article ends with an annotated bibliography and a listing of cross-references to other related articles in the series. A majority of the bibliographic references are current and accessible to the average reader. The volume ends with an alphabetic and subject listing of each topic, followed by a cumulative index of all 7 volumes. These three tools integrate this supplement with the previous volumes. [R: BL, 1 Dec 98, p. 698]

—**Michael R. Leach**

Handbooks and Yearbooks

1357.   **Genetics and Cell Biology on File.** By the Diagram Group. New York, Facts on File, 1997. 1v. (various paging). illus. index. $165.00 looseleaf w/binder. ISBN 0-8160-3572-5.

Compiled within a three-ring looseleaf binder are a series of sheets (plates) depicting various aspects of cell biology and genetics. Each sheet considers a specific topic using textural and illustrative material. The illustrative material, which is handsomely displayed, is extremely well done and easy to follow. The textural information enhances the illustrations. The work begins by depicting the various types of tools and techniques used in cell biology, such as transmission electron microscopy, centrifugation, cell fractionation, mass spectroscopy, isotope labeling, and autoradiography, just to name a few. A total of 28 sheets are devoted to this aspect. Cell types and their evolution and cell biology follow, taking into account both the anatomical and physiological aspects of the subject. A separate sheet is devoted to each of the cell organelles.

An additional section on cell division is also portrayed that considers mitotic and meiotic splitting. The rest of this work is devoted to genetics and is divided into 3 parts. The 1st of the 3, entitled "Classical Genetics," begins with Gregor Mendel and ends with genetic counseling. The 2d considers the various aspects of molecular genetics. The 3d and final portion of genetics delves into a variety of aspects of population genetics.

The "Molecular Genetics" section provides, among a large number of other topics, the various experiments by influential biologists that pioneered genetics in the molecular realm. A subject index at the end of the work provides easy access to the one-page monographs. This is an excellent work not only for its reference value but for its teaching value as well. Teachers at the high school, community college, and the undergraduate level of a university are well advised to be aware of this work. It presents great supplementary material to whatever text is being used. In addition, this work is highly recommended for high school, community college, university, and public libraries.—**George H. Bell**

BOTANY

General Works

Dictionaries and Encyclopedias

1358.   Miglani, Gurbachan S. **Dictionary of Plant Genetics and Molecular Biology.** Binghamton, N.Y., Food Products Press/Haworth Press, 1998. 348p. $49.95. ISBN 1-56022-871-7.

Miglani combed standard college and high school texts as well as scholarly primary and secondary sources to identify terms associated with plant genetics. The dictionary includes definitions and descriptions of more than 3,500 terms and concepts used in various specializations of plant genetics: molecular genetics, cytogenetics, biochemical genetics, population genetics, mutagenesis, evolutionary genetics, and plant biotechnology. Definitions are written to promote understanding among a large group of users, including scientists, farmers, high school teachers, and students. Laypersons will appreciate the many cross-references that help to clarify definitions. A highly useful feature is keying many definitions of seminal works and important review articles.

Here, Miglani promotes understanding and helps serious users review and locate published sources. The dictionary has an extensive subject bibliography, and users will find complete citations to those sources selected for inclusion.

Arrangement is alphabetic and the typeface used is pleasing and dark. Quality paper is used, and the binding should withstand ordinary use. Public and regional libraries located in agricultural areas will wish to make this book available to their users. Schools and colleges supporting agricultural programs should consider this an essential purchase. [R: Choice, Oct 98, p. 294]—**Milton H. Crouch**

Handbooks and Yearbooks

1359.   Dallman, Peter R. **Plant Life in the World's Mediterranean Climates: California, Chile, South Africa, Australia, and the Mediterranean Basin.** Berkeley, Calif., University of California Press, 1998. 257p. illus. maps. index. $29.95pa. ISBN 0-520-20809-9.

This richly illustrated and engaging work fills an important and unique niche in botanical literature. As western coastal geographic areas between 30 and 45 degrees latitude, the five Mediterranean climatic areas of the world occur on only 2 percent of the world's total land area, yet these temperate areas garner as much attention as population and cultural centers. Their plant life is especially interesting as examples of convergent evolution.

Dallman does an excellent job of explaining the "diverse adaptations that enable plants to survive the prolonged summer droughts typical of these regions, the plant communities found there, and human influences that have shaped the physical and botanical landscapes." Robert Ornduff, a highly respected botanist from the University of California at Berkeley, makes this claim as the scientist who assisted the author, a retired pediatrics professor who chairs the docent council of the Strybin Arboretum in San Francisco.

The book is well organized. Chapter 1 describes the unusual Mediterranean climate, comparing it to other climates. Chapters 2 through 4 examine the ancient origins of the vegetation, describe plant adaptations, and introduce the major plant communities. Chapters 5 through 9 detail each community in landscape, climate, and vegetation. It is clear that California and central Chile form a pair, as do the western cape of South Africa and Australia. The Mediterranean stands alone. Finally, chapter 10 offers suggestions for travelers to these areas. For the growing number of traveling nature lovers, "wildflowers are at their best in Mediterranean climate regions during off-peak travel seasons when planes are less crowded and accommodations are readily available."

This book will be of interest to plant scientists as well as general natural history readers and travelers. It can be used as a textbook or as a reference tool. The bibliography is extensive and the book is indexed. Both color and black-and-white photographs, maps, line drawings, charts, and graphs make this book a delight.

—Georgia Briscoe

1360.   Powell, Charles C., and Richard K. Lindquist. **Ball Pest & Disease Manual.** 2d ed. Batavia, Ill., Ball Publishing, 1997. 426p. illus. index. $65.00. ISBN 1-883052-13-0.

Commercial growers looking for a thorough assessment of common diseases and health management for flower and foliage crops should have an accessible copy of this book in the greenhouse. Whether the plant is wilting or dying from an exotic stem-bug from overseas, bad soil from bad habits, or general blight caused by foliar nematodes, the solution is in these pages. Replete with both color and black-and-white close-up photographs of powdery mildews, rust disease, bacteria, and viral and fungal maladies, the book walks us through each step from diagnosis to remedy.

Ball Pest & Disease Manual covers major insect pest identification, how to recognize and eradicate plant pathogens, and the economic impact of allowing spider mites or bacterial canker to go unchecked. Early detection and diagnosis of botanical trauma followed by vigorous therapy are central to bringing in the harvest, and these horticultural and entomological experts guide us through mystifying microorganism afflictions, effective treatments, and safety procedures designed to ensure the well-being of the plant and the planter. Brand-name pesticides, herbicides, and fungicides are discussed along with definite instructions regarding their application. Charts comparing chemicals with each other and with well-known carcinogens put benefits and dangers in perspective. This book is specifically for those whose greenhouses are in an emergency situation, yet familiarity with the book beforehand is what will save the grower precious time.

Numerous addresses for diagnostic labs, soil testing labs, and poison control centers, plus conversion tables, a glossary, and an adequate index make this book user-friendly and necessary for commercial floral pursuits.

—Mary Pat Boian

Indexes

1361. **IUCN Red List of Threatened Plants, 1997.** Kerry S. Walter and Harriet J. Gillett, eds. Cambridge, U.K., IUCN; distr., Bronx, N.Y., Scientific Publications, 1998. 862p. index. $45.00pa. ISBN 2-8317-0328-X.

This book is the latest in Red Data Books and Red Lists, a series published by the International Union for Conservation of Nature and Natural Resources beginning in 1963. This Red List includes 33,798 threatened or extinct plants, or approximately 12.5 percent of the world's total vascular plants.

The list is arranged by major taxa, principally fern allies, true ferns, gymnosperms, and angiosperms. Within each of these major taxa, families and their respective genera and species are listed alphabetically. Each entry includes data sources by numeric code, which are then included numerically in a separate list at the end of the book, thereby allowing interested readers to pursue further information about any species. Countries and states/regions are listed for each entry indicating geographic origin of data. Entries are also given a global and local threat status, if local data are available. Each entry's threat status is listed as either extinct, extinct/endangered, endangered, vulnerable, rare, or indeterminate. Users of the list are strongly encouraged to read the introduction, which includes valuable information on how to use the book and explains such items as the criteria used for classifying plants among the threat statuses listed above.

This book is highly recommended as an excellent reference for those working on ecosystem restoration, botany of rare and endangered plants, and related areas. However, the editors state that the list is incomplete, as one may guess considering the scope of the book. Data for North America, Australia, South Africa, and Europe should be reasonably accurate, as well as data for certain taxonomic groups like ferns, conifers, cycads, palms, and cacti that received particular attention. Alternatively, data for many parts of Africa, Asia, the Caribbean, and South America are either patchy or lacking.—**Michael G. Messina**

Flowering Plants

1362. Horn, Elizabeth L., comp. **Sierra Nevada Wildflowers.** Missoula, Mont., Mountain Press, 1998. 215p. illus. index. $16.00pa. ISBN 0-87842-388-5.

Flower identification guides are written typically as field guides or as reference library volumes. Horn's guide to the flowers of this California mountain range is one of the former: a small, heavily illustrated paperback designed for the general reader. More than 300 species of wildflowers are described in this guide, and some 200 of them are illustrated with color photographs. Descriptions of each species include data on the size of the plant and its flowers, color, blooming season, and leaf type. Most entries include considerable information about habitats and sometimes mention popular roads and hiking trails where the flowers are commonly seen. Both popular and scientific names are provided, and Horn occasionally explains the meaning of the Latin names when they shed light on flower characteristics. The compiler also provides a brief but useful glossary of botanical terms, charts of flower parts and how to identify common California conifers, a list of other popular and academic books on this subject, and an index that includes common and Latin names.

This guide is attractive and easily readable by those without any botanical training. The photographs are generally good for comparing with specimens in the field. The only questionable decision is the arrangement of the flowers by families, then alphabetically within the families. Most casual flower observers are not familiar with the various botanical families and prefer to look up unknown flowers by color and arrangement of flowers or petals; see, for example, the *National Audubon Society Field Guide to North American Wildflowers, Western Region* (Knopf, 1998). This guide's arrangement does not encourage rapid identification for novices.

—**Christopher W. Nolan**

1363. Keenan, Philip E. **Wild Orchids Across North America: A Botanical Travelogue.** Portland, Oreg., Timber Press, 1998. 321p. illus. index. $39.95. ISBN 0-88192-452-0.

This is a beautifully presented book with gorgeous photographs, all taken in the field. The text is a set of rich habitat portraits, with natural features lovingly characterized. The chapters are organized geographically and cover Alaska, Canada, New England, midatlantic/midwestern states, southeastern states, and western states as a botanist's notebook might. An introduction covers general topics, such as the numbers of orchid species; provides labeled anatomical drawings; culture information; environmental descriptions; and biogeographic patterns. Within each area, Keenan selects particular places and orchid types on which to focus. His topical discussions includes history, ecology, conservation biology, wildlife, geography, and geology. There are no directions to the exact sites to ensure plants remain relatively undisturbed. Sprinkled throughout the text are quotes from naturalists and poets as well as some of the hazards of orchid hunting.

Not surprisingly, as it is Keenan's home ground, New England is the most expansively covered area and these descriptions of orchids are particularly evocative. Appendixes are useful and interesting. They include a glossary, an orchid checklist, photography notes, descriptions of Keenan's favorite orchids, and an identification synopsis. There is an index to plant names.

The accounts can be somewhat disappointingly disjointed because this is not a comprehensive account. The book will whet the appetites of amateur botanists but cannot be considered an academic offering. It is recommended for personal or amateur naturalist collections.—**Constance Rinaldo**

1364.   Macoboy, Stirling. **The Illustrated Encyclopedia of Camellias.** Portland, Oreg., Timber Press, 1998. 304p. illus. index. $39.95. ISBN 0-88192-421-0.

Whether one is a committed camellia enthusiast or an enthusiastic camellia neophyte, this book has the photographs, drawings, details, and descriptions to satisfy. The camellia, "Queen of the Winter Flowers," is written about carefully and completely with definitions of color and size, cultivar names and synonyms, original Oriental names, date of registration, parentage, flowering season, and flower form. More than 1,000 entries are divided into sections of wild camellias, sasanquas, japonicas, higos, reticulatas, and hybrids. Each chapter has a chronicle of the species or cultivar liberally scattered with anecdotes and lore, such as how *c. sinensis* (tea) is said to have grown from the severed eyelids of a Buddhist ascetic who vowed never to fall asleep during his meditation.

Camellias are shown adorning palaces, temples, royal botanic gardens, and ancient cemeteries. Macoboy exposes the reader to the history, variety, and endurance of these shrubs. A section on soil balance, climate, transplanting, pruning, watering, and propagating takes much of the mystery out of growing camellias, but should one prefer to garden in one's mind, there is a seasonful of gorgeous photographs.

A glossary, bibliography, and index ensure a productive browse, and the perceptive writing and rich images captivate any level of horticulturist. [R: LJ, Aug 98, p. 77]—**Mary Pat Boian**

1365.   Taylor, Ronald J. **Desert Wildflowers of North America.** Missoula, Mont., Mountain Press Publishing, 1998. 349p. illus. maps. index. $24.00pa. ISBN 0-87842-376-1.

Every spring the deserts of North America transform themselves into vast carpets of colorful flowers. *Desert Wildflowers* documents this change with explanatory text and more than 500 color photographs of the flowers that bloom in the Great Basin Desert, the Painted Desert, the Mojave Desert, the Sonoran Desert, and the Chihuahuan Desert. Aimed at the amateur botanist, the book includes basic information on desert ecosystems and a geologic history of North American deserts. The flower entries are arranged alphabetically by family. Each includes descriptions of the plant, its common and botanical names, and a color photograph. Some also have small location maps. These are followed by an identification key (which is hopefully easier to use than it appears), plant anatomy illustrations, a glossary, and a bibliography.

Desert Wildflowers is unusual because it encompasses the wildflowers of all the deserts of North America, rather than only those found within states or regions. The work is not comprehensive, however, as it does not cover the Mexican components of the Chihuahuan and Sonoran Deserts or plants that grow along waterways unless they are exclusive to deserts. With its reasonable cost, libraries in the western United States should consider purchasing one copy for reference and one for circulation. This book is meant to be taken out into the field where it will be most useful.—**January Adams**

1366.   **Wild Flowers of the Pacific Northwest.** By Lewis J. Clark. John G. Trelawny, ed. Madeira Park, Harbour, 1998. 604p. illus. index. $49.95. ISBN 1-55017-195-X.

The Pacific Northwest is a region rich in native wildflowers that are sought after by gardeners the world over. This work, which is a further rendition of the original edition entitled *Wild Flowers of British Columbia*, written in 1973 and then expanded as *Wild Flowers of the Pacific Northwest* in 1976 (see ARBA 78, entry 1287), is a treasure for gardeners, botanists, and plant lovers of all persuasions. The photography is absolutely exquisite. Unlike many present-day field guides with their postage-size plant images, the photographs in this work are large, at minimum a quarter of a page in size. The photographs are clear and sharp with true colors. Aside from its obvious botanical value, this is also a beautiful book.

This work is not a primary identification tool or meant to be used as a field guide. The gardener must already know either the common or Latin name in order to locate a particular species in the book. The sheer size and heft of the book would also discourage the botanist from packing it on a plant identification field trip. The work is arranged by families, with each species within the group described in a very poetic, descriptive style that captures the charm and beauty of the plant. Each entry includes interesting historical references, clear description of the species, and a vignette of the plant in its habitat. The text of the work is completely unchanged from the original edition, which testifies to the writing skills of Clark, who died in 1974. During the intervening years since the 1st edition appeared, plant taxonomists working with the nomenclature of North American flora have produced many changes in the names of genera, species, and authors, among others. Rather than integrate these changes into the original text, the taxonomic changes that have occurred are listed at the end of the book. The original bibliography has also been updated to a small degree. Aside from these two additions and the inclusion of a few more panoramic photographs at the front of the book, the work remains fundamentally the same as the 1976 version. Every library that serves botanists and gardeners must have this classic work in its collection.—**Elaine F. Jurries**

Trees and Shrubs

1367. Leopold, Donald J., William C. McComb, and Robert N. Muller. **Trees of the Central Hardwood Forests of North America: An Identification and Cultivation Guide.** Portland, Oreg., Timber Press, 1998. 469p. illus. maps. index. $49.95. ISBN 0-88192-406-7.

There were not many pages turned in this book when it became obvious that the authors were following the footsteps of the great Alexander von Humboldt in concentrating on the geographic distribution of plants. Spread out like a giant inkblot covering a large portion of a map of eastern North America was an outline of the Central Hardwood Forest Region. This region embraces whole, or parts of, five physiographic provinces where these broad-leaved deciduous species thrive. In turn, this large area was subdivided into forest communities where groups of plants growing together are identified. These are called by plant names such as oak-hickory forests, beech-maple forests, and others.

With this basic outline provided, the reader is quickly brought up to speed with discussion of seed propagation techniques, some basic dendrology augmented by very clean and clear line drawings of plant parts, and then on to a detailed discussion of more than 200 species of trees, including how they fit into the great central hardwood forests. Many clear photographs with an understandable and clear supporting text accompany each tree description. A unique final sentence for each species is "Best Recognizable Features" that provides a clue for those attempting field identification of the tree. The great assembly of acorn photographs for those interested in the oaks will prove invaluable when trying to separate the various species in the genus *Quercus*. This is a usable book with a lot of environmental, propagation, distribution, and dendrological data on some of the more important forest trees in North America.—**James H. Flynn Jr.**

Weeds

1368. Holm, LeRoy, and others. **World Weeds: Natural Histories and Distribution.** New York, John Wiley, 1997. 1129p. illus. index. $195.00. ISBN 0-471-04701-5.

The authors have incorporated more than four decades of research into a comprehensive and up-to-date resource on plants that are identified as a weed in one or more areas of the world. Scientists, farmers, and botanists around the world were consulted; weed specialists in each country provided rankings of the most common, serious weeds in their respective country. There are 104 species of plants that cause 90 percent of the world's food losses due to their presence in agriculture. These are arranged alphabetically by scientific name as given in the International Rules of Botanical Nomenclature. Entries range in length from 5 to 18 pages and provide in-depth information on each species. Each entry begins with identifying the family and genus and noting where the species is common in the world. World distribution maps follow and show where the plant is reported to be a weed. Subsections giving a complete description as well as the habitat and distribution are included for each species. Further subsections vary from biology and ecology to agricultural importance, propagation, morphology and physiology, economic importance, resistance to herbicides, importance to humans, and bracken toxicity. Besides scientific information, the reader also is given interesting background details. In the section on Queen's Anne Lace a history of the carrot, its color, and the origin of the common name are discussed. Detailed black-and-white line drawings with plant parts labeled assist the user in plant identification.

The authors point out the volume does not include details and photographs of careful anatomical and cytological studies, chemical procedures for isolation of secondary metabolites, or clinical studies on weed toxicity to human and animals. The extensive 3,300 references provided in the bibliography provide researchers with the sources of this information. Other supplemental sections include a 236-word glossary; a list of crops; herbicide, growth regulator, and metabolite nomenclature; a list of common weed names that refers the user to the scientific name and the country using the common name; and a thorough index. This comprehensive, well-organized reference will be valuable to scientists, botanists, and anyone working in an area of agriculture.—**Elaine Ezell**

NATURAL HISTORY

1369. Achor, Amy Blount. **Animal Rights: A Beginner's Guide: A Handbook of Issues, Organizations, Actions, and Resources.** 2d ed. Yellow Springs, Ohio, WriteWare, 1996. 452p. illus. index. $19.95pa. ISBN 0-9631865-1-5.

The 1st edition of this work was the winner of the 1993 Animal Rights Writing Award from the International Society for Animal Rights. It is a guide for committed action, not a dispassionate reference work.

This work is divided into 4 parts. Part 1, "Introduction to Animal Rights," covers the philosophy and history of the animal rights movement. Part 2, "The Issues," discusses particular topics, such as companion animals, vegetarianism, factory farms, and animals in entertainment, and emphasizes why one should be committed to furthering animal rights. This part includes explicit pictures of "the disturbing realities of animal experimentation." Part 3, "Personal Action," urges readers to "live their convictions" and offers suggestions for participating in animal rights and a short list of resources for activists.

Part 4, "Resources for Animals," is a categorized directory of organizations, products, services, and a list of further readings. It comprises about one-half of the work. There are directories of animal advocacy and vegetarian organizations, arranged into lists of international and national and local groups. There is a third directory, covering products and services, which is arranged into categories (e.g., companion animal products and services) and subcategories (e.g., boarding and sitting services, cat fences and enclosures, cat litter, doors, foods, supplements and supplies, gates, holistic health practitioners, interspecies communicators, poison control, ramps and carts, spay/neuter referrals, tattoo, and registry services). The introduction to part 4 lists the main categories, but not the subcategories. Some services and products are listed under more than one category. The final chapter is a 30-page categorized list of further reading, and the work ends with a list of dates to remember, endnotes, a short glossary, and an index.

This is a committed and comprehensive work. Two recent works, *Animal Rights Movement in the United States, 1975-1990: An Annotated Bibliography* (see ARBA 96, entry 1424) and *Animal Rights: A Reference Handbook* (see ARBA 96, entry 1435) are bibliographies of the animal rights movement and do not contain the directory information included in the present work.

This guide should prove useful in public and academic libraries and can be recommended as long as librarians are aware of its straightforward commitment to the cause of animal rights. Unfortunately, its usefulness as a reference work is limited by incomplete indexing. Subjects and organizations are included in the index, but services and products are not.—**Richard H. Swain**

1370. Sherry, Clifford J. **Endangered Species: A Reference Handbook.** Santa Barbara, Calif., ABC-CLIO, 1998. 269p. index. (Contemporary World Issues). $39.50. ISBN 0-87436-810-3.

Sherry, a senior scientist and principal investigator with Veridian, has written a convenient introduction for eager youth working on merit badges, undergraduates, scholars, activists, and general readers confronting this complex problem. After explaining how species becomes endangered, major protection measures and controversies surrounding organisms, such as the darter and the northern spotted owl, are presented in a chronology of 21 biographical sketches of conservationists, illustrators, legislators, and researchers. Researcher Jean Goddall discusses U.S. legislation and international treaties and summarizes complex issues such as the Endangered Species Reauthorization Act of 1997. The author provides print resources such as books on endangered species, extinction, biodiversity, conservation, ecology, federal publications, and law school reviews. The constantly evolving Internet is often unable to locate the Internet addresses Sherry's provides for researchers. Those persevering will reach the excellent Amazing Environmental Organization Web Directory at http://www.webdirectory.com, or Institute for Global Communications Discussion Groups Page at http://www.igc.org/igc/issuees/habitats to find a cornucopia of fascinating hyperlinks. Unfortunately, this reviewer was unable to examine the authors CD-ROMs and computer simulation programs or virtual reality examples. Finally, a glossary, geological timeline, and index conclude this brief overview that is recommended for high school, public, and undergraduate collections. [R: SLJ, Nov 98, pp. 134, 136; BL, 1 Dec 98, p. 698]—**Helen M. Barber**

1371. **Wildlife Conservation.** Hilary D. Claggett, ed. Bronx, N.Y., H. W. Wilson, 1997. 192p. index. (The Reference Shelf, v.69, no.2). $20.00pa. ISBN 0-8242-0915-X.
    This is a researched and documented volume of wildlife conservation in the United States and other countries. The editor sets out to challenge the reader on the reasons to conserve wildlife—ecologically biologists have determined that lions, bears, and wolves are essential to entire systems. The 4 sections of this book include endangered species and their enemies (which are in the bibliography and 3 appendixes offered to the reader), the legislation and politics of wildlife, managing ecosystems, and new directions in the field. Lists of individuals and organizations (e.g., National Wildlife Federation, Wildlife Conservation Society) involved in conservation are provided.
    No photographs are included in this volume except for the cover. It would have been helpful had illustrations of the endangered wildlife been inserted. This volume is a good starting point for researchers of endangered species and is recommended for special, public, and academic libraries.—**Lisé Rasmussen**

ZOOLOGY

Birds

1372. Attenborough, David. **The Life of Birds.** Princeton, N.J., Princeton University Press, 1998. 320p. illus. index. $29.95. ISBN 0-691-01633-X.
    The Life of Birds is designed to accompany Attenborough's latest television production, a 10-part series of the same name that will air on PBS sometime in 1999. More than 200 color photographs accompany the readable narrative text that covers bird life broadly, but with many specific examples taken from all over the world, in chapters covering locomotion, breeding, and care of the young, among others.
    Although *The Life of Birds* is an attractive, well-written, accurate, and up-to-date book that would grace the circulating collection of any library, its reference value is limited. The only index is to the scientific and colloquial names of the birds mentioned in the text. There is no subject index and no bibliography or any other reference help. Libraries wishing to have a general purpose ornithological reference work should acquire either *The Cambridge Encyclopedia of Ornithology* (see ARBA 93, entry 1540) or *Encyclopedia of Birds* (see ARBA 86, entry 1519) or *A Dictionary of Birds* (see ARBA 86, entry 1513).—**Jonathan F. Husband**

1373. Barlow, Clive, and Tim Wacher. **A Field Guide to Birds of The Gambia and Senegal.** Robertsbridge, East Sussex, Pica Press and New Haven, Conn., Yale University Press, 1997. 400p. illus. maps. index. $40.00. ISBN 0-300-07454-9.
    The region of western Africa included in this field guide extends from the arid Sahel/Sahara in the north to the humid tropics in the south. The region's ecological diversity ranges from marine habitats and freshwater wetlands to acacia-dominated savanna. The bird life of these two nations is rich, with more than 650 species—almost all of which are illustrated in the book's 48 color plates. The high-quality artwork shows seasonal and sexual differences in plumage, when appropriate. The text presents individual species accounts with identification features and includes behavioral and ecological notes. Status and distribution are describe with some detail, whereas calls and songs are briefly noted. The authors' field experiences emphasize Gambia, where Barlow is a resident leader for bird-watching tours. (Gambia is a popular tourist destination, and this volume is its first field guide to

birds.) In several sections of the book, information is given about current nature preservation efforts and conservation groups in the region.—**Charles Leck**

1374.   Beaman, Mark, and Steve Madge. **The Handbook of Bird Identification for Europe and the Western Palearctic.** Princeton, N.J., Princeton University Press, 1998. 868p. illus. maps. index. $85.00. ISBN 0-691-02726-9.

Nearly 900 species of birds of the Western Palearctic are included in this handbook, more than two-thirds of which are native and introduced species that breed in the region, the rest being primarily vagrants. The Western Palearctic, as described and mapped here, encompasses all of Europe; the British Isles; North Africa to the central Sahara; the Middle East to the Iranian border; and the Azores, Madeira, Canary, Banc d'Arguin, and Cape Verde islands.

Information on each species (grouped by family) includes taxonomy, size (in metric units), appearance, voice, sex and age difference, status, habitat, and color-coded distribution map. Page numbers refer to plates of artist renderings in color for each bird (considered more accurate than photographs by most birders), including summer and winter, juvenile and adult, male and female, and other forms. A brief appendix includes recent additions and omitted species. There are two indexes: one for English and one for scientific names, with page numbers for illustrations in bold typeface. For avid birders—beginner or expert—and especially for those traveling in the region, this attractive and authoritative guide cannot be beat. It is recommended for all public libraries.—**Lori D. Kranz**

1375.   **Bull's Birds of New York State.** Emanuel Levine, Berna B. Lincoln, and Stanley R. Lincoln, eds. Ithaca, N.Y., Cornell University Press, 1998. 622p. illus. maps. index. $39.95. ISBN 0-8014-3404-1.

This work is a completely revised edition of John Bull's *Birds of New York State* (Doubleday, 1974; reissued with supplements and corrections by Cornell University Press, 1985). The basic format remains the same: taxonomically arranged species accounts of the 451 bird species recorded on the official New York state checklist. Each account contains a succinct statement concerning range, state, breeding, and nonbreeding (or occurrence if the bird does not breed within the state). Some accounts have a remarks section that discusses subspecies occurring within New York state or other information of interest to the reader, such as a summary of records from neighboring states. In addition to the species accounts, which constitute nearly 80 percent of the volume, there are several maps, 30 line drawings by bird artist Dale Dyer, several background articles on such matters as ecozones and bird habitats in New York state, a lengthy bibliography, a list of the more than 60 authors of species accounts, and indexes of English and scientific bird names.

Although *Birds of New York State* has been the standard authority for bird occurrences and ranges since its 1974 publication, the book has been in need of serious updating for a number of years, particularly since the publication of the *Atlas of Breeding Birds in New York State* (Cornell University Press, 1988). This completely rewritten revision is essentially a new book using Bull's basic format and incorporating information from the aforementioned *Atlas of Breeding Birds* and *The Kingbird* (the journal of the Federation of New York State Bird Clubs) through the end of 1996.

The new version of *Bull's Birds* is a necessary purchase for public and academic libraries in New York and adjacent states. It would be a useful purchase for birding libraries everywhere.—**Jonathan F. Husband**

1376.   Cleere, Nigel. **Nightjars: A Guide to the Nightjars, Nighthawks, and Their Relatives.** New Haven, Conn., Yale University Press, 1998. 317p. illus. maps. index. $40.00. ISBN 0-300-07457-3.

The author has spent five years researching this book, which is the first to describe in detail every species of the *Caprimulgiformes* order. Most of the birds in this order are secretive birds of the night (nocturnal), becoming active at twilight or before sunrise. As the author notes in the introduction, these birds have long been the subject of local folklore. For instance, there is a widespread belief going back thousands of years that the European nightjar visits livestock during the night and suckles milk from goats and other animals. Hence the common name "goatsucker" that to this day is still used to refer to many nightjars.

The order comprises 119 species in 5 families—the nightjars, oilbirds, frogmouths, owlet-nightjars, and potoos. Members of the order are distributed throughout the world on every continent except Antarctica, with the largest proportion in the warmer regions of the world, including South America, Africa, and Australia. The most familiar North American species is the whippoorwill (*Caprimulgus vociferus*) distributed widely on the continent.

The 1st section of the book is an overview of the *Caprimulgiformes* order covering taxonomic relationships, distribution, topography and morphology, physical structure and mechanics, plumage and molt, behavior, and fossil origins. This is followed by 36 color plates with beautiful and precise illustrations of each species in the order. The rest of the book is a detailed description of each species. Each entry includes an abbreviated list of references for all known subspecies and information on identification, voice, habitat, habits, food, breeding, description, measurement, molt, geographic variations, status, distribution and movements, and references. A map of the species range is included with each description. A complete bibliography follows at the end of the book. Libraries that have a clientele of serious ornithologists will want to purchase this complete and authoritative guide.—**Elaine F. Jurries**

1377. **Encyclopedia of Birds.** 2d ed. Joseph Forshaw, ed. San Diego, Calif., Academic Press, 1998. 240p. illus. maps. index. $34.95. ISBN 0-12-262340-1.
This oversized reference work covers the world of birds. The 1st part notes commonalities of all birds, then goes on to explain the method of classification, chronology and development, habitats and adaptation, behavior, and endangered species. The 2d part identifies the different kinds of birds and the species/family/order they fall into. At the beginning of each section is a "Key Facts" panel that defines the order, a size chart (smallest to largest) in relation to humans, and a "Conservation Watch" section listing the endangered species within that order. A map of the world highlights the regions where the species can be found, and a one- to two-paragraph review of the family precedes articles on specific birds. A section listing further reading sources and an index are also provided.
Unlike its companion pieces *Encyclopedia of Mammals* (see entry 1391) and *Encyclopedia of Reptiles & Amphibians* (see entry 1395), the *Encyclopedia of Birds* (like the *Encyclopedia of Fish*) is not as in-depth. This is not the fault of anyone but is because there are simply more kinds of birds (and fish) to recognize. Because of this, instead of giving a one- or two-page review of a species, only one or two paragraphs are offered. If the Academic Press had been as in-depth with birds as it was with mammals or reptiles and amphibians, this reference source would have easily ended up being three or four volumes. However, as it is an overview of sorts, what is there is perfectly acceptable, well thought out, and educational.
The photographs are a tad disappointing. But for a few exceptions (i.e., a kingfisher coming out of the water with a fish, a barn owl swooping down from the sky preparing for a landing, and two Australian owls looking down from their knarred tree branch perch), the pictures here are standard. One can find more dramatic photographs of birds from amateur photographers in *Wildbird* magazine, but the addition of colorful illustrations increases the quality of the book, and the captions accompanying each photograph and illustration are always informative.
As this reviewer is more familiar with birds than, say, amphibians, I found the text here a little stale. Still, students will more than likely find the data most helpful. In reading and viewing the pictures, I did reaffirm a few things about birds I had already noted: It is still difficult to think of baby birds as being "cute"; parrots always look friendly; ducks are cool; it is a shame, but aesthetically speaking, it is probably just as well dodo birds are extinct; and a buzzard is a buzzard is a buzzard. . . .
Encyclopedia of Birds is an excellent reference resource for any library shelf. Its colorful photographs and drawings and well-presented text will surely assist any student in preparing a report on birds. Get this book; it is well worth the price.—**Joan Garner**

1378. Juniper, Tony, and Mike Parr. **Parrots: A Guide to Parrots of the World.** New Haven, Conn., Yale University Press, 1998. 584p. illus. maps. index. $55.00. ISBN 0-300-07453-0.
The parrot family is remarkably diverse, with more than 350 species worldwide. All of these are illustrated within this guide's 88 superb color plates. The spectacular array includes avian giants such as the macaws and cockatoos, down to diminutive pygmy parrots and parrotlets. As a group, parrots have long received the attention of humans, and sadly, we have entered an age when man-related environmental pressures threaten almost one-third of the family (90 species) with extinction. The introductory portions of the book deal with conservation concerns (e.g., habitat loss, pet trade, hunting) and achievements, such as captive breeding programs. The book also provides good reviews of the evolution of parrots, their ecology, and social behavior. The majority of the text is given to species accounts, which summarize the key identification features, voice, distribution (with map), ecology, and plumages (including geographic variations). References, mostly recent, conclude each species account. Both authors have been notably active in international bird conservation, especially with endangered parrots. As an authoritative reference this book will be used by aviculturists, conservation biologists, birders, avian custom agents, and others of a wide audience.—**Charles Leck**

1379.   Kightley, Chris, and Steve Madge. **Pocket Guide to the Birds of Britain and North-West Europe.** Robertsbridge, Great Britain, Pica Press and New Haven, Conn., Yale University Press, 1998. 299p. illus. maps. index. $20.00pa. ISBN 0-300-07455-7.

This truly pocket-sized field guide describes 385 species of bird that regularly appear throughout Britain and northwestern Europe. Collectively and individually, the authors have many years of experience in the field, and it shows. For example, the introductory pages present brief sections on topography (complete with excellent line drawings), a glossary, notes on fieldcraft (tips on improving your bird-watching skills), and useful addresses. Throughout the guide, the written text is highlighted with many anecdotal scraps of information, giving a friendly aspect to the work, which is a nice touch.

Most of the book comprises the well laid out species accounts. Each species merits at least two illustrations and in some cases (such as the yellow wagtail) as many as eight in order to illustrate geographic variation. The quality of the artwork is high, with lifelike poses and generally good color reproduction. A wide range of plumages is depicted. The text is concise and accurate, with many useful field marks noted that tend to be missing from similar guides.

A nice feature of this guide is the extensive captioning of the illustrations and highlighting of relevant field marks. This is especially useful for shorebirds and gulls. The range maps are well done, with bold colors depicting resident, summer, and winter ranges. It is useful to see the political borders drawn for each country.

One drawback is that an index is provided but only depicts the English name of the species. To be thorough and more accessible to the European community, the authors should have provided an index to the scientific name. This book delivers all that it claims and more and is highly recommended for both the beginner and more experienced bird-watcher. This work is a must for general and specialized collections. [R: Choice, July/Aug 98, p. 1879]—**Katherine Margaret Thomas**

1380.   Lefranc, Norbert. **Shrikes: A Guide to the Shrikes of the World.** New Haven, Conn., Yale University Press, 1997. 192p. illus. maps. index. $35.00. ISBN 0-300-07336-4.

Lefranc has written a comprehensive bird guide to shrikes, showcasing this bird species that is currently experiencing a population decline. Shrikes are small- to medium-size passerine birds known to have similarities to raptors and are found throughout the world except Australia and South America. The 31 bird species in 3 genera of this family are examined here.

The guide includes chapters on taxonomy and an overview of several genera, which also gives information on names, morphology, plumages and molt, origins, and distribution. Following this, the author goes into further detail on each of the 31 species. Each species account has up to 13 sections that include a description; information on movement, habitats, and food; and references. An extensive bibliography and an index of scientific and common names are also included. Color plates and illustrations also highlight this guide.

The author has skillfully put together information that cannot be easily found in other sources. The overviews and species accounts are full of information. This work is definitely recommended for bird collections because it includes more than what a typical bird guide does.—**Julia Perez**

1381.   **National Audubon Society First Field Guide: Birds.** By Scott Weidensaul. New York, Scholastic, 1998. 159p. illus. index. $10.95pa. ISBN 0-590-05482-1.

This beginner's guide to North American birds is designed to be of great appeal to children, with large typeface and full-page color illustrations of 50 widely found species. Brief notes on the biology, voice, and distribution (with range map) are given for these common birds. Throughout the text there are also small photographic inserts of related or "look-alike" species to assist in the identification of an additional 125 birds. The 30-page introductory section of the guide is similarly rich in illustrations—it concisely explores such topics as avian flight, feathers, nesting, bird song, and habitats. A short reference section includes a brief glossary, further readings for juniors, birding organizations, and Websites. The book's scholastic design includes a water-resistant cover and a bird identification card. [R: SLJ, Oct 98, p. 160]—**Charles Leck**

Domestic Animals

1382.   **Barron's Encyclopedia of Cat Breeds: A Complete Guide to the Domestic Cats of North America.** By J. Anne Helgren. Hauppauge, N.Y., Barron's Educational Series, 1997. 312p. illus. index. $25.00. ISBN 0-7641-5067-7.

The domestic version of the mysterious cat, in its many different shapes, colors, and sizes, is showcased in this informative encyclopedia. The book is the result of six years of research. A brief history of cats is followed by a basic discussion of genetics and cat breeding; of conformation, color, and coat; and of Cat Fancy (the name for people who breed and show cats).

The 1st section of the book profiles 40 currently recognized North American breeds of cats in alphabetic order, from Abyssinian to Turkish Van. Each profile includes a history of the breed, a discussion of personality, and a description of the unique characteristics for the breed. In addition, two charts are provided for each breed. The first chart rates characteristics such as activity level, playfulness, need for attention, affection toward owners, vocality, docility, intelligence, independence, healthiness and hardiness, need for grooming, compatibility with children, and compatibility with other pets. These traits vary from one bloodline to the next, but the chart gives the reader a general idea of what to expect from each breed. The second chart describes conformation standards that define an ideal specimen of the breed—general shape, body, head, ears, eyes, legs and paws, tail, coat, color, disqualifying marks, and allowable outcrosses. A boxed notation indicates which associations recognize the breed and gives a Cat Fanciers Association rank for popularity of the breed in 1996.

The next section of the book profiles seven new or experimental breeds currently seeking association acceptance. This section also explains the process for having a new breed recognized. The subsequent section discusses the American domestic cat—a randomly bred cat that makes up about 95 percent of the cat population in the United States. These two sections do not include the chart rating the various characteristics. In experimental breeds there is not enough information available, and in randomly bred cats, characteristics are unpredictable. The final chapters give advice in choosing a breed, choosing a purebred cat, and showing a cat. A brief glossary, additional reading list, and an index complete the volume.

Overall, this is an entertaining and informative volume, accessible to most age groups. The pictures are excellent, capturing each breed's outstanding physical characteristics. The charts make identifying and comparing breeds easy. The histories and other accompanying materials make fascinating reading. This would be an excellent tool for choosing a breed of cat to own. This encyclopedia is recommended for all public and school libraries and general reference collections.—**Joanna M. Burkhardt**

1383.   Holderness-Roddam, Jane. **The Horse Companion: A Comprehensive Guide to the World of Horses....** Hauppauge, N.Y., Barron's Educational Series, 1997. 224p. illus. index. $35.00. ISBN 0-7641-5047-2.

This colorful book is a readable and appealing introduction to many aspects of horses and riding. Descriptions are to the point and will be useful to more than just beginners. Although the style is informal, the information is precise, accurate, and easily understandable.

The emphasis is on English riding, which mirrors the author's experience. Besides her career as an Olympic performer and an instructor and trainer, Holderness-Roddam has written a number of pamphlets, articles, and books. *The New Complete Book of the Horse*, published in 1992, is clearly the source for much of this new volume. The earlier volume is written in more depth and detail.

The Horse Companion, however, has a fresh approach. It contains briefer articles with more profuse illustration. The more than 400 drawings and photographs are clear and striking, and the style is brisk and informal. The material is presented in detailed sections with many subtopics: history of the horse; description of breeds; and a lengthy section on owning, riding, and caring for a horse. Equipment for riding is described in detail, as are a number of styles of competition.

It includes a useful glossary and a competent index with a few minor misspellings. In the sections on special breeds, brevity may be a fault. The section on warmbloods is confusing to those who are familiar with the various breeds that compose this group.

Despite the minor flaws, this is an excellent general book. It is highly recommended for all public and academic libraries with equine interests, as a circulating book as well as for reference.—**Joann H. Lee**

1384.   Puotinen, C. J. **The Encyclopedia of Natural Pet Care.** New Canaan, Conn., Keats Publishing, 1998. 522p. index. $19.95. ISBN 0-87983-797-7.

With Americans' growing interest in homeopathy and natural medicine, it is no surprise that they would want to explore holistic health care for their pets as well. This new encyclopedia is an excellent guide to everything from choosing a pet to first aid for injuries. The author discusses dogs, cats, rabbits, and birds. Included are natural foods, herbal supplements and immunizations, and homeopathic treatments (including recipes); hands-on therapy (such as acupuncture and massage); training and dealing with behavior problems; and an A to Z section on specific ailments.

Puotinen bases her book on interviews with veterinary experts as well as her own research, the latter is reflected in the lengthy recommended reading and resource list at the end of the book. A thorough index makes information easy to find. Although this is a do-it-yourself guide, it is not intended to be a diagnostic manual. As she states in her introduction: "An informed owner is a pet's best medical insurance." *The Encyclopedia of Natural Pet Care* is highly recommended for public libraries.—**Lori D. Kranz**

1385.   Rice, Dan. **Dogs from A to Z: A Dictionary of Canine Terms.** Hauppauge, N.Y., Barron's Educational Series, 1998. 412p. illus. $14.95pa. ISBN 0-7641-0158-7.

The answers to 6,000 questions about dogs are gathered in this attractive, readable, A to Z glossary of terms. The author sets out to collect all the words and phrases pertaining to dogs and their long-standing partnership with humans. All librarians and many general readers will find this a useful and enjoyable tool. The author covers breeds around the world, canine illnesses and medicines, training, reproduction, showing, hunting, and grooming, as well as literary references to dogs. Anyone who has ever wondered where the phrase "Mad dogs and Englishmen go out in the noon-day sun" came from will find the answer here. There are numerous cross-references, as on page 260: "Madame de Pompadour Dog *see* Phalene." Some breed definitions refer the reader to 1 of 66 full-color photographs of popular American Kennel Club (AKC) and many non-AKC recognized breeds. Some of the definitions tend to be obscure, such as the one for the ugliest mutt contest, which takes place in Fredericksburg, Virginia. The definitions of more general terms, such as *overbreeding*, are done in a concise, readable style. *Dogs from A to Z* also provides a useful bibliography; for example, an English glossary of dog terms appeared three years ago and is cited here.

The American reader will find the format of Rice's book more attractive and the writing style much more geared to the general reading public on this side of the Atlantic. Moreover, its perspective addresses dogs in the context of an American rather than British lifestyle. Finally, although the author urges readers to contact him about mistakes or omissions, it is hard to imagine there are any.—**Ellen R. Strong**

1386.   Viner, Bradley. **A-Z of Cat Diseases & Health Problems: Signs, Diagnoses, Causes, Treatment.** New York, Howell Book House/Simon & Schuster Macmillan, 1998. 255p. illus. index. $24.95. ISBN 0-87605-043-7.

Being a lifelong cat owner, this reviewer can confidently say cat owners everywhere will adore this book as much as they adore their cats. Written by a veterinarian who has obviously had many whiskered patients and owners, the compact text gives a wonderful introduction to cats, discusses the various signs of disease, and prescribes common treatments.

"Health and Husbandry" is a brief but thorough how-to section for bringing up kitty. On the social side, two chapters explain the history of cats and the reasons for their behavior and give brief profiles and beautiful photographs of pedigrees. For a medical slant, three chapters cover the responsibilities of pet owners and veterinarians, discuss the physical characteristics and nervous system of a healthy cat, and write extensively about caring for a cat from birth to death.

Viner organized the section titled "Signs of Diseases and Health Problems" by common recognizable symptoms, such as fever, coughing, scratching, or bad breath. Each entry has a brief description of the symptom, cross-references to topics in the treatment section, and a degree of urgency (e.g., immediate veterinary attention, make an appointment, or visit the vet when convenient).

The most substantial portion in the book, "Treatment of Diseases and Health Problems," is organized alphabetically by treatment name. Examples are abortion, feline leukemia virus, and ticks. Most topics include signs of the illness, causes, and diagnosis or treatment. The only criticism of this book is the emphasis on a veterinarian's intervention. For example, the treatment section does not include any home remedies. A good companion book to this clinical text is Anita Frazier's holistic work *The New Natural Cat: A Complete Guide for Finicky Owners* (Dutton, 1990).—**Susan D. Baird-Joshi**

1387.   Viner, Bradley. **The Cat Owner's Question and Answer Book.** Hauppauge, N.Y., Barron's Educational Series, 1998. 160p. illus. index. $19.95pa. ISBN 0-7641-0648-1.

The Cat Owner's Question and Answer Book presents 300 questions that are of concern to cat owners and offers advice on the most common problems of cat ownership. This book attempts to be comprehensive in subject matter, including everything from choosing a cat or kitten to addressing the needs of an elderly cat.

The book begins with a short introduction explaining the origin of cats as pets. It then goes on to a very thorough table of contents in which specific questions are presented. For those who want to get to the bottom of a specific problem or question, the book offers a section titled "Solution Finder." This section takes a general concern, such as eating habits, and breaks it down into very specific questions and then directs the reader to the page where the problem is addressed.

The most valuable feature of this work is its tips on how to keep one's pet healthy. It stresses the importance of finding a good veterinarian and giving pets regular checkups and shots. It also discusses the reason behind common problems, such as vomiting and hairballs, and offers everyday solutions.

This book is easy to use and addresses almost any problem or question that cat owners might have. It will be a source that will be used often for quick reference, and with its vivid photographs and interesting information, will be in the hands of browsers as well.—**Shannon M. Graff**

Fishes

1388.   McEachran, John D., and Janice D. Fechhelm. **Fishes of the Gulf of Mexico, Volume 1: Myxiniformes to Gasterosteiformes.** Austin, Tex., University of Texas Press, 1998. 1112p. illus. maps. index. $125.00. ISBN 0-292-75206-7.

Seeking to provide a single reference source to the identification and description of the fishes living in the Gulf of Mexico, the authors have compiled a thorough resource directed toward scientists, students, and fishers. Volume 1 of the proposed 2-volume set covers 40 of the 44 orders of fish in the Gulf of Mexico. Scorpaeniformes, Perciformes, Pleuronectiformes, and Tetraodontiformes will be treated in a forthcoming volume 2. The 20-page introduction provides extensive background information on the Gulf of Mexico and the fish there. The physical and biological description of the gulf includes geological history, currents and tides, freshwater input and sediment patterns, and biological assemblage. Detailed information on how to identify fish explains the grouping and naming of fish as well as their structural anatomy and measurements. Line drawings provide identification to body parts.

Orders and families are arranged phylogenetically with keys provided for all families and species within a family. The completeness of the descriptions includes the scientific name and the accepted common name if it is available, physical details, where the species occurs, food sources, development patterns, known size ranges, and references for further study. Detailed black-and-white line drawings supplement the extensive text.

A glossary of 212 terms, abbreviation key, index to scientific names, and reference section provide the user with tools to better use this reference source. Although the authors narrowed their identification to the Gulf of Mexico, they do note worldwide locations of the fishes, which gives this reference volume wider appeal. Serious researchers will find the book most useful.—**Elaine Ezell**

Insects

1389.   **National Audubon Society First Field Guide: Insects.** By Christina Wilsdon. New York, Scholastic, 1998. 159p. illus. index. $10.95pa. ISBN 0-590-05483-X.

This book is one of the selections in the First Field Guide series from the National Audubon Society aimed at children age eight and older. The guide covers 12 insect orders, containing information on 50 of the most widely found insects of North America plus 125 additional species. Introductory pages in the guide define what insects are, how to tell them apart, and explain and give examples of what the 12 insect orders are. In the field guide portion, brief descriptions of the insect or related species include information on the common and scientific name, habitat and range, identification cues, and examples of similar insects or arthropods. The appendix includes a reference section, which offers a glossary; additional books and tapes, organizations, and Website resources, and an index of species listing the common and scientific name. Lots of large and small colorful pictures and illustrations are used effectively throughout the work.

This book offers a lot of information for children interested in the topic. The pictures alone will keep any reader entertained. This resource is recommended for purchase by school, public, and personal libraries. [R: SLJ, Oct 98, p. 160]—**Julia Perez**

1390.   Sbordoni, Valerio, and Saverio Forestiero. **Butterflies of the World.** Willowdale, Ont., Firefly Books, 1998. 312p. illus. index. $45.00. ISBN 1-55209-210-0.

This impressive book provides a broad overview of lepidoptera (butterflies and moths) of the world. It has been written in an authoritative, yet understandable, manner by renowned experts in the field. Visually the book is pleasing. The 125 full-color plates are both attractive and accurate. Everything from geographical variation to migration is wonderfully captured using known examples. The plates include sidebars that cross-reference to the scientific name, average size, and anecdotal information such as geographical range. In addition, the text is complemented by black-and-white figures and diagrams.

One of the more important sections in the book is the systematic survey of butterfly and moth families. Although not exhaustive, it gives the reader a broad overview of each family and its taxonomic placing. The section is nicely illustrated with representative examples from the larger families. Glaringly missing from the book are scholarly references. Although a bibliography is provided at the end, it lists only 26 general works, and no scientific papers are cited.

Physically, the book is well bound and stays open easily at any given page. An index is included that lists the scientific name and gives page numbers in italics for illustrations. *Butterflies of the World* is highly recommended.

—**Katherine Margaret Thomas**

Mammals

1391.   **Encyclopedia of Mammals.** 2d ed. Edwin Gould and George McKay, eds. San Diego, Calif., Academic Press, 1998. 240p. illus. maps. index. $34.95. ISBN 0-12-293670-1.

This oversized reference work covers a vast amount of information concerning mammals. The 1st part notes commonalities of all mammals and then goes on to explain the method of classification, chronology and development, habitats and adaptation, behavior, and endangered species. The 2d part identifies the different kinds of mammals and the animals that fall into the species, family, or orders. At the beginning of each section is a "Key Facts" panel that defines the order; a size chart (smallest to largest) in relation to humans; and a "Conservation Watch" section listing the endangered species within that order. A map of the world highlights the regions where the mammals can be found, and a one- to two-page review of the family precedes articles on specific animals. A section listing further reading sources and an index are also provided.

Packed full of data and generously sprinkled with color photographs and illustrations, this book offers a well-thought-out overview of the animal (mammal) kingdom. Although rather dry in description and peppered with long scientific names—names no one can pronounce except the experts (e.g., *Lophiomys imhausii* for rat)—the *Encyclopedia of Mammals* gives us an excellent source in which to learn more about our "brethren" mammals. The photographs are of a higher standard than clip art fare, and the illustrations provide a more complete look at the animal, although the illustrations are so detailed they often take on a kind of surreal, creepy appearance. What is nice about the captions accompanying the pictures is that they give new information relating specifically to the visual as opposed to repeating sentences drawn from the text.

The 232 oversized pages of information and pictures make this a wonderfully rich resource for elementary, middle, and high school students (although the higher grades may find the data somewhat sparse). It is an ideal book for both public and school libraries that will be found and used often. [R: SLJ, Oct 98, p. 36]—**Joan Garner**

1392.   Grassy, John, and Chuck Keene. **National Audubon Society First Field Guide: Mammals.** New York, Scholastic, 1998. 159p. illus. index. $10.95pa. ISBN 0-590-05489-9.

More than 450 color photographs make this slim volume a gold mine for budding ecologists and children. Published under the auspices of the reputable and long-standing children's press, Scholastic, and in conjunction with the National Audubon Society, this guide makes an ideal starting place for children with an interest in mammals and their place in nature.

This book is part of the National Audubon Society's First Field Guide series, which includes companion guides on wildflowers, birds, insects, weather, and rocks and minerals. It is intended, as its name implies, to be used not only for reference, but as an outdoor tool. At only 5¼-by7¼-inches and 159 pages, it will fit into a big pocket or daypack for easy portability. A removable water-resistant spotter's card, about the size of a sheet of microfiche, is tucked into a convenient flap inside the back cover and features postage-stamp size photographs of 50 North American mammals.

Although this book is aimed at children, it makes an ideal learning tool for people of all ages, as it does not talk down to its audience. The guide is divided into 4 sections: "The World of Mammals," which defines the term and describes such characteristics of mammals as social life, eating habits, and mating behavior; "How to Look at Mammals," an analysis of habitat and a "detective work" section that teaches the reader to track and identify various mammals; "Field Guide," the heart of the book, which consists of two-page summaries for each profiled animal that include a large color photograph, habitat map, Latin nomenclature, and "look-alikes," which are subspecies or near relatives; and "The Reference Section," which includes a glossary and a bibliography of related videos, CD-ROMs, books, and Websites. Pages 154-157 index the work.

Because any book endorsed by the National Audubon Society will enjoy almost instant credibility and name recognition with most patrons, *First Field Guide: Mammals* should be considered for purchase by all public libraries, no matter how small. The adult version of nearly the same title by John O. Whitaker Jr., *The Audubon Society Field Guide to North American Mammals*, which expands coverage to more than 700 pages, may be considered a companion volume. In addition, parents may want to purchase a personal copy for their adventurous offspring.—**Linda D. Tietjen**

1393.   Linzey, Donald W. **The Mammals of Virginia.** Granville, Ohio, McDonald & Woodward, 1998. 459p. illus. maps. index. $59.95. ISBN 0-939923-36-X.

This book is a comprehensive work on the mammals of Virginia and its surrounding areas, ranging from the time period of the mid-1580s to the present. Linzey has done a thorough study of the topic, including information on the history of mammals in Virginia, species accounts, shaded drawings of skulls, color photographs, and informational appendixes. The main body of the work is the species accounts in which 114 mammal species currently or previously inhabiting Virginia are examined. These accounts include descriptions on 11 parameters, such as description, distribution, habitat, food, reproduction, and location of specimens, among others. References are included for each species. Also of use are the appendixes that include a glossary, a variety of checklists and tables, a history of the fauna of Virginia from the last Ice Age, and a lengthy bibliography that provides more than 2,800 citations that also range over a period from the mid-1580s to the present.

Users of this book will find it similar in format to Joseph Chapman's *Wild Mammals of North America* (Johns Hopkins, 1982). The extensive information provided will be useful to any student, zoologist, or researcher interested in the natural history of Virginia. This volume is recommended for college, university, or special libraries.—**Julia Perez**

Marine Animals

1394.   Pollock, Leland W. **A Practical Guide to the Marine Animals of Northeastern North America.** New Brunswick, N.J., Rutgers University Press, 1998. 367p. illus. index. $70.00pa. ISBN 0-8135-2399-0.

This work is an identification guide to the marine animals, from sponges to whales, in the ocean off the coasts from Cape Hatteras in North Carolina to the maritime provinces of Canada. Marine birds, not considered truly aquatic, are not included. The coverage of species is selective, concentrating on the larger and more common ones. There is a detailed introduction covering geographic range, how identification keys work and are constructed, notations used, and information on fieldwork and habitats. A beginning chapter is based on the assumption the reader is not familiar with marine organisms, and it has keys designed to allow the reader to determine to which major phylum or other group an organism belongs. The next chapters identify gelatinous organisms, worm-shaped organisms, zooplankton, and egg masses. After these chapters, each chapter covers a major phylum or group of phyla.

Each chapter begins with descriptive information and an illustrated list of morphological characteristics coded in two-letter codes. These codes are then used in charts to identify species. Then the species are listed, with description of each and illustrated with black-and-white drawings. In the species descriptions are biogeographic and habitat codes (which are defined back in the introductory chapter). A tiny happy face is used to indicate the most common species. Handling and preserving specimens are dealt with in an appendix.

This guide fills a niche between the more superficial, popular field guides and works primarily for zoologists and marine biologists that require a strong technical vocabulary. It is thus of greatest use to undergraduate students. It will serve their needs well because it is not too technical for their use, yet they will learn much from it. [R: LJ, 15 April 98, p. 70]—**John Laurence Kelland**

Reptiles and Amphibians

1395.   **Encyclopedia of Reptiles & Amphibians.** 2d ed. Harold G. Cogger and Richard G. Zweifel, eds. San Diego, Calif., Academic Press, 1998. 240p. illus. maps. index. $34.95. ISBN 0-12-178560-2.

This oversized reference work covers a vast amount of information concerning reptiles and amphibians. The first part notes commonalities of all reptiles and amphibians and then goes on to explain the method of classification, chronology and development, habitats and adaptation, behavior, and endangered species. The second part identifies the different kinds of reptiles and amphibians and the species/family/order they fall into. At the beginning of each section is a "Key Facts" panel that defines the order; a size chart (smallest to largest) in relation to humans; and a "Conservation Watch" section listing the endangered species within that order. A map of the world highlights the regions where the species can be found, and a one- to two-page review of the family precedes articles on specific reptiles and amphibians. A section listing further reading sources and an index are also provided.

This book could easily be retitled *More Than I Ever Wanted to Know About Reptiles and Amphibians, but Find Fascinating Anyway*. The beautiful photographs entice one to read all the captions that accompany them. An appreciation of how unique and different this world is from our own is easily established within the text. It is an alien world of snakes, lizards, frogs, toads, turtles, tortoises, crocodiles and alligators, and—stranger yet—salamanders, newts, amphisbaenians, and caecilians. So extraordinary are their habits, and so remarkable is their ability to adapt to the environment, it is difficult to realize that these creatures live alongside us. This resource helps identify this land of weird and bizarre and can also help students gain a new perspective on reptiles and amphibians (e.g., the gastric-brooding frog incubates her young in her stomach and "gives birth" to them through her mouth).

Besides providing the standard information, *Encyclopedia of Reptiles & Amphibians* is also full of interesting tidbits (i.e., crocodiles are generally regarded as slow and clumsy out of water, but the Johnston's Crocodile of Australia is capable of a full gallop if startled into it). Also, it seems that the most brightly colored and beautiful (yes, beautiful) reptiles and amphibians secrete through their skin the most toxic poisons known. Another interesting observation about this book is that nearly a dozen photographs show species mating.

This work is highly recommended reference work for school and public libraries. It is a good resource for students because it provides more information than what a standard encyclopedia generally gives, yet is not as involved or complicated as an in-depth, scientifically structured book would be.—**Joan Garner**

1396.   Petranka, James W. **Salamanders of the United States and Canada.** Washington, D.C., Smithsonian Institution Press, 1998. 587p. illus. maps. index. $60.00. ISBN 1-56098-828-2.

Petranka is well qualified to produce a major work on North American salamanders because he is a biology professor with many publications on salamanders. The primary reference on North American salamanders, until now, was Sherman Bishop's classic published in 1943 and reissued in 1994, *Handbook of Salamanders* (see ARBA 96, entry 1635). Petranka has incorporated into his new book information from the 1,500 papers published since 1943, on the systematics, ecology, and natural history of North American salamanders.

There is a substantial introduction that describes salamander biodiversity, ecology, value to humans, and general natural history. The 2d section is a description of how to identify salamanders, including illustrations and a discussion of terminology and salamander morphology, and a description of the layout of the species descriptions. Next is an extensive, well-documented discussion of the conservation biology of amphibians.

Keys to adult and larval salamanders introduce the 127 species accounts. The accounts are arranged by family and include extensive reviews of identification, systematics, distribution, adult habitat, breeding and courtship, aquatic and terrestrial ecology, predators, community ecology, and conservation biology. These accounts are well written, thoroughly researched (the book cites more than 2,100 references), and accessible to laypeople as well as useful for scientists. Each account includes range maps and black-and-white photographs. Additionally, there are 172 beautiful and clear color plates. The glossary at the end of the book adds to the accessibility of the book, which is highly recommended for library reference collections serving zoologists and users with an interest in salamanders. [R: LJ, 1 Nov 98, p. 72]—**Constance Rinaldo**

32 Engineering

GENERAL WORKS

1397. Berlow, Lawrence H. **The Reference Guide to Famous Engineering Landmarks of the World.** Phoenix, Ariz., Oryx Press, 1998. 250p. illus. index. $59.95. ISBN 0-89774-966-9.

This extraordinary single-volume reference work contains more than 125 illustrations and photographs of some of the world's greatest engineering landmarks. Providing concise, factual entries about human engineering achievements around the world, this source will pique the interest of anyone who uses it. The book covers mausoleums, skyscrapers, roads, dams, tunnels, castles, temples, cathedrals, churches, and a variety of other structures. The information was collected from periodicals, books, encyclopedias, Websites, and other reference sources. Because Websites are subject to change, some of those listed can no longer be located. This phenomenon happens on a daily basis with Web addresses, so it is not a real drawback and can lead to further research.

Significant events in civil engineering from 3000 B.C.E. to the present are included as well as some brief biographies of important builders and designers. Useful appendixes are provided. Appendix C, for example, lists the 10 highest dams, the 20 longest suspension bridges, and the 20 tallest buildings in 1997. A subject index makes it easy to find everything from *Acropolis* to the *Zola Dam*. A glossary of important terms and a useful bibliography for further research enhance this straightforward reference. This source will be useful in any public or academic library to help librarians and library users find the answers to basic landmark questions and to encourage further research into specific landmarks. [R: RUSQ, Summer 98, pp. 370-371]—**Diane J. Turner**

1398. Heisler, Sanford I. **The Wiley Engineer's Desk Reference: A Concise Guide for the Professional Engineer.** 2d ed. New York, John Wiley, 1998. 690p. index. $75.00. ISBN 0-471-16827-0.

This 2d edition is an update of the 1st edition, written 10 years earlier. It includes new chapters on structures and the design process; information on new materials, lasers, and computer data; a greater emphasis on application data; and revised information on preferred practice reflecting state-of-the-art operations. Because of the importance of the computer in the industry, the data presented conform to current computer programs. Conversely, many computer programs now include fundamental data that used to be found in reference tables; such data have been deleted from this edition. An expanded and updated list of references has also been added.

Chapters cover mathematics, mechanics/materials, structures, fluid mechanics, thermodynamics/heat transfer, electricity and electronics, controls, economics/statistics, energy sources, the design process, engineering operations, and reference tables. In some respects, the book may be trying to include too much information and almost appears like a high-level textbook or a review text for the Fundamentals of Engineering (FE) examination. Chapters about economics (explaining, among other things, simple interest); the design process (including sizes and scales of engineering drawings); or engineering operations (explaining calculation of fees) seem too basic to be of much use to most practicing engineers. By trying to be all things to all engineers, much of the book may be too general. For instance, a structural engineer may use the chapters on mathematics, materials, and structures but would probably have little to do with chapters on fluid dynamics, heat transfer, electronics, controls, or energy sources. Although useful, the small number of tables provided may not be comprehensive enough for a specific field. Most engineers in a specific field have large, comprehensive volumes dealing with the specific aspects of their field alone.

The book may be more useful to a specific type of engineer who must deal with those engineers in other disciplines and who needs to have a general knowledge of that work and jargon. It could also serve as a general, upper-level review text for many types of engineering.—**Craig A. Munsart**

CHEMICAL ENGINEERING

1399. **International Petroleum Encyclopedia 1998.** Tulsa, Okla., PennWell Publishing, 1998. 335p. illus. maps. index. $140.00. ISBN 0-87814-744-6.

International Petroleum Encyclopedia 1998 is a valuable reference tool and one that is convenient to use. The first half consists of eight major geographic divisions subdivided by country. Approximately 80 countries are listed. For each nation, the reader will find the capital city, the monetary unit, refining capacity, oil production, oil reserves, and gas reserves. Under each country entry is an essay summarizing the status of the nation's petroleum industry. For countries with marginal petroleum interests, the essays are approximately 200 to 300 words in length. The most significant countries merit several thousand words. There is an abundant use of color maps and photographs. The last half of the book contains 39 topical essays on such things as deepwater frontiers, global warming, the European gas deregulation, prices, product consumption, and world fiscal terms. These essays are also enhanced by an abundant use of color. A subject index is appended to the main text. For libraries serving users with a serious interest in the petroleum industry, this volume will be a valued title, the contents of which cannot be as comprehensively and conveniently found in other titles or on the Internet.—**John M. Robson**

1400. **Rules of Thumb for Chemical Engineers: A Manual of Quick, Accurate Solutions to Everyday Process Engineering Problems.** 2d ed. Carl R. Branan, ed. Houston, Tex., Gulf Publishing, 1998. 418p. index. $79.00pa. ISBN 0-88415-788-1.

Gulf Publishing has issued several "rules of thumb" books, starting with *Rules of Thumb for Engineers and Scientists* by David J. Fisher (1991). The subtitle sums up the goal of this work—they are sources of quick, accurate solutions to common problems. Its contents are organized into 25 chapters within 4 sections leading from equipment design through process and plant design to operations; there are 8 appendixes. This logical arrangement makes it fairly easy to locate information on a specific topic. The brief index is less useful.

Information is clearly presented and includes diagrams, charts, equations, tables, and source references. This book will be frequently consulted for its sound, practical advice based on the editor's broad experience. This edition is expanded and in places updated from the 1st edition (see ARBA 96, entry 1650). It is highly recommended for libraries serving students and researchers in chemical engineering.—**Robert Michaelson**

CIVIL ENGINEERING

1401. **ASTM Standards in Building Codes.** 34th ed. West Conshohocken, Pa., ASTM, 1997. 4v. illus. index. $495.00/set. ISBN 0-8031-1842-2. ISSN 0192-2998.

Annually, the American Society for Testing and Materials (ASTM) produces a comprehensive reference set of the various approved national standards. By accessing the index, a user can search out the standards relevant to a particular topic. However, to facilitate the task in the area of building and construction codes, ASTM has gathered together all commonly applicable standards. This will assist libraries, which might not be able to justify buying the entire set. Standards contained are (1) Building Officials and Code Administrators (BOCA); (2) Southern Building Code Congress International (SBCCI); (3) International Conference of Building Officials (ICBO); (4) United States Housing and Urban Development (HUD); (5) Council of American Building Officials (CABO); (6) National Research Council of Canada, Building Systems Design (BSD); and (7) International Association of Plumbing and Mechanical Officials (IAPMO). Also included are any ASTM standards referenced by the American Institute of Architects (AIA), National Institute of Building Sciences, Army Corps of Engineers, and Naval Facilities Engineering Command (NAVFAC). Users will commonly bring a standard number reference from one of the above entities and seek to see the full text. The standards themselves are technical in nature and sufficiently explanatory to experienced people. The diagrams are excellent, and the work contains an essential index. Despite the cost, this is a convenient tool for users and librarians concerned with building practices.—**John M. Robson**

1402.   **CD Estimator, 1998.** [CD-ROM]. Carlsbad, Calif., Craftsman Book, 1998. Minimum system requirements: IBM or compatible. Double-speed CD-ROM drive. 4MB RAM. 4MB hard disk space. VGA monitor.
$68.50. ISBN 1-57218-054-4.

The *CD Estimator, 1998* is a great program. It will be a breeze for Windows buffs, and thanks to the excellent
90-minute multimedia instruction video, by far the best this reviewer has ever seen, virtually anyone can become
an expert in a short time. No matter what level of expertise a user brings to the program, it is recommended that
the video be watched. There is likely something for everyone, such as directions for adding one's own information to any of the six cost books, how to create additional cost books, and much more. The program behaves like
a database as well as a spreadsheet. After entering costs into any one of the 40 different estimating forms, costs
are extended and columns are totaled automatically. It is fast and easily adaptable to the exact needs of any type
of construction business. Accurate, superbly formatted estimates can literally be compiled in minutes.

Six current costbooks are provided on the CD-ROM: National Construction Estimator, the National Repair
and Remodeling Estimator, National Electrical Estimator, National Plumbing and HVAC Estimator, National
Painting Cost Estimator, and National Renovation and Insurance Repair Estimator. Quarterly updates to these
costbooks can be downloaded from the Internet at no cost. This is a must-have time and money saver for practitioners, and a great resource for those involved in training for all types of construction estimating. The *CD
Estimator, 1998* is highly recommended.—**Barbara Delzell**

1403.   Hutchings, Jonathan F. **National Building Codes Handbook.** New York, McGraw-Hill, 1998. 545p.
illus. index. $64.95. ISBN 0-07-031819-0.

This handbook is a compilation of national codes required for use in the construction industry. These are
the Standard Building Code, the Uniform Building Code, and the National Building Code. Hutchings's purpose
is to provide a "reference handbook of a specific topic section with discussion, commentary and analysis of the
most commonly encountered sections and regulations." The Standard Building Code (used mostly in the southern
United States) is used as the base document, with related section numbers in the others noted. This book provides
an excellent treatment of seismic construction details and a thorough discussion of new construction materials
and techniques.

For those who need to be familiar with all three codes, this handbook is quite useful. For many professional engineers and construction managers, however, only one code is accepted in their state or municipality.
All codes are now available in electronic format, and most professional libraries will want to make these available
to their patrons.—**Connie Williams**

1404.   Hutchings, Jonathan F. **OSHA Quick Guide for Residential Builders and Contractors.** New York,
McGraw-Hill, 1998. 323p. index. $54.95; $34.95pa. ISBN 0-07-031836-0; 0-07-031837-9pa.

This easy-to-understand, 10-step solution kit answers a variety of questions about Occupational Safety
and Health Administration (OSHA) compliance and will be welcomed by residential builders, contractors, renova-
tors, and remodelers. Including a disk with a full set of downloadable and customizable forms, this guide is a
hassle-free way to deal with OSHA. Written by a residential builder, the book offers real-life solutions to OSHA
concerns and other uncertainties in complying with government safety rules and regulations.

The 10 chapters highlight information about OSHA, construction regulations, meeting requirements,
inspections, risk management, safety orders, confined space entry, fall protection, preparing for inspections, and
defending against citations. An appendix lists local and regional OSHA offices, and the alphabetic index makes
it easy to find topics of interest. The files on the enclosed disk can read and write to Rich Text Format (RTF) and
Microsoft Excel file formats on Windows 3.1 or higher. One must also have a hard drive with 1.5MB available
disk space.

Residential builders should invest in this valuable source and keep it handy to prevent or to handle potential
problems. The guide is also recommended for public libraries and academic libraries supporting architecture
curricula.—**Diane J. Turner**

ELECTRIC ENGINEERING
AND ELECTRONICS

1405.   **The Electrical Engineering Handbook.** 2d ed. Richard C. Dorf, ed. Boca Raton, Fla., CRC Press and Piscataway, N.J., IEEE Press, 1997. 2719p. index. $110.00. ISBN 0-8493-8574-1.

CRC Press has an ambitious task in producing a variety of titles for its Electrical Engineering Handbook series. The nine volumes as a set thoroughly cover the constituent topics that make up electrical engineering. Engineering libraries will want to own all of the titles. But for most general libraries, whether academic or public, the new 2d edition of *The Electrical Engineering Handbook* is the one to purchase. The 2,719 pages are divided into 12 sections: biomedical systems; circuits; communications; computer engineering; digital devices; electrical effects and devices; electromagnetics; electronics; energy; mathematics, symbols, and physical constants; signal processing; and systems. As is the pattern with all CRC handbooks, each section is broken down into subsections and further divisions that are individually compiled and authored. Users—whether scholars, seasoned practitioners, or students—will find the key terminology, discussion of the basic concepts, referral to related topics, references cited in the presentation, and listing of texts to check out if a more thorough understanding is needed. The entire work is heavy on math and includes excellent illustrations. In addition to the usual author and subject indexes, the reader will find indexes to the tables, figures, and equations, the latter being particularly useful. Because areas like communications and biomedical engineering are far from static, this new edition is a worthwhile addition as a technical reference. *The Electrical Engineering Handbook* is an essential tool that has been admirably laid out for efficient access.—**John M. Robson**

1406.   **International Electric Power Encyclopedia 1998.** James A. Ferrier and others, eds. Tulsa, Okla., PennWell Publishing, 1998. 398p. illus. maps. index. $150.00. ISBN 0-87814-735-7.

This annual covering the global power industry is a new version of the *Electric Power Industry Outlook and Atlas*. The current work is illustrated in full color and covers power resources on both a regional (by continent) and a country-by-country basis. Each section has a regional overview of trends and provides graphs and charts of various data (e.g., carbon emissions, residential/industrial energy consumption), and maps. The maps show power cooperation regions and include sites of power plants and what fuel is used to generate electricity. The maps are colorful, but are not always particularly easy to read and use.

The second half of the book has 13 encyclopedia articles on aspects of finance for energization, deregulation, privatization, marketing, fuels, renewable energy, and the environment. Each chapter has a variety of statistical data and an overview and executive summary. The final chapter is a worldwide statistical compendium, including generation per capita, general economic information (i.e., gross national product), energy reserves, and fuel mix percentage of each country. There is an index, but it is not as extensive as it should be to pinpoint the many fine sources of data within the book.

The subject of this reference book is very specialized, and it will serve special situations well, such as corporate libraries and larger public and academic libraries that support interest in power resources, utility deregulation, and global economic forecasting. The majority of the information here would be extremely difficult to gather from standard reference sources and through research in periodicals, which makes an encyclopedia such as this timely and welcome.—**Gary R. Cocozzoli**

ENVIRONMENTAL ENGINEERING

1407.   Lee, C. C., comp. **Environmental Engineering Dictionary.** 3d ed. Rockville, Md., Government Institutes, 1998. 682p. $89.00. ISBN 0-86587-620-7.

Acronyms accumulate rapidly in government regulations and manuals. Anyone who needs help separating the likes of VOM (volatile organic materials) and VOS (vehicle operating survey) or hundreds of other abridgments for environmental terms can start with the appendix to this dictionary. Approximately 15,000 entries and their definitions fill out the body of the lexicon. The diligent effort to exact terms from environmental publications means somewhat mundane words—for example, abandoned well, levee, rural area—are included among the less well known ones. Multiple meanings (e.g., five for fly ash, and three for flux) are listed and cross-listed to the reference from which they were taken. Pulled from context, a few terms, such as freeze area (a defined intrastate region in the Boston, Massachusetts, area), do not make much sense. The bottom line: This is an economical desk reference of great utility. However, the compiler's disclaimer advises the reader to beware regarding errors and omissions.—**Diane M. Calabrese**

MATERIALS SCIENCE

1408. **ASM Ready Reference: Properties and Units for Engineering Alloys.** Materials Park, Ohio, ASM International, 1997. 168p. index. (Materials Data Series). $68.00. ISBN 0-87170-585-0.

This is a fast and easy reference for finding summarized material property data associated with engineering alloys. Each page is devoted to a single material property, indicating category or property and outlining common uses for property name, common abbreviation, preferred unit, alternate unit, example test method, material or text parameters, conversion factors, synonyms-symbols-abbreviations-related terms, example values, and concise definition. ASM standard definitions are incorporated where applicable into mechanical property definitions. Complex concepts are not defined, but the book is quite usable for a dictionary, and handy "refresher," and certainly for what the publishers intended, supporting consistency and equivalency when integrating material property data from multiple sources into reference print, databases, or electronic publications. Because of its organization, it would also be useful to neophytes for quickly distinguishing between mechanical and physical data. There is a suggested list of standard in-depth material property data sources contained in the introduction, and a thorough, cross-referenced index. This volume is highly recommended for engineers' and technical writers' desktops as well as engineering reference collections.—**Barbara Delzell**

1409. **Concise Metals Engineering Data Book.** Joseph R. Davis, ed. Materials Park, Ohio, ASM International, 1997. 245p. $75.00 spiralbound. ISBN 0-87170-606-7.

Designed as a quick-look-up tool for students, salespeople, and purchasing agents, the *Concise Metals Engineering Data Book* provides practical information about a wide range of metals-related subjects. Topics specifically covered include chemical composition, physical properties, and mechanical properties of common commercial metals and alloys.

Surprisingly, there is no index. As a result, access by subject is possible only through the table of contents. This means that a user desiring a specific phase diagram must page through chapter 6, "Phase Diagrams," to see if it is included. The final chapter consists of a bibliography of selected references for each general area, such as heat-treating ferrous alloys or steel making. Many of the references are to other ASM International books—*ASM Materials Handbook*, *ASM Handbook of Corrosion Data*—whereas others are to publications from related societies, such as the Society of Automotive Engineers (SAE) and the Iron and Steel Society. Some of the individual chapters also include specific references.

Because of its tabular format, this is an easy book to leaf through. One oddity stands out, however—the chemical composition tables are arranged by the UNS number followed by SAE-AISI number, but tables covering the mechanical properties of metals and alloys are arranged by AISI number. Users with an American Society for Testing and Materials number would be out of luck. All in all, this is a fine book, but it is not inexpensive. Large materials science collections with access to ASM handbooks could probably pass—this is really aimed at people in the field because of its small compact size and spiral binding.—**Susan B. Ardis**

1410. Morena, John J. **Advanced Composites World Reference Dictionary.** Malabar, Fla., Krieger Publishing, 1997. 87p. $16.50. ISBN 0-89464-991-4.

The steady growth in the number of titles in the area of advanced composites is indicative of the importance of this area of materials engineering. Morena has created a slim volume "of domestic and international words, terms and definitions collected form advanced composites education and industry leaders." Entries are in a straight alphabetical order and average a carefully chosen 10 to 20 words in length. The definitions are in clear, technical prose. With only about two dozen illustrations, the reader may need to search elsewhere for fuller explanations and diagrams. The six-page section of abbreviations and acronyms is very useful. The dictionary is easy to use with an abundance of space, unlike most specialty dictionaries that try to cram text from margin to margin. This is an economical purchase for those needing reference sources on this subject.—**John M. Robson**

1411.   Mouser, Jeffrey D. **Welding Codes, Standards, and Specifications.** New York, McGraw-Hill, 1998. 398p. illus. index. $69.95. ISBN 0-07-043550-2.

Originally intended for inspectors and quality assurance personnel, the work was seen by the author as having added value to engineers, architects, contractors, instructors, students, and, of course, welders needing a single comprehensive volume on codes, standards, and specifications. Other welding handbooks and manuals reference the codes, standards, and specifications but not in such a nicely integrated and straightforward manner. For each topic the author cites relevant texts from the American Institute of Steel Construction, American Welding Society, Building Official & Code Administrators International, Code of Standard Practice, Southern Building Code Congress International, and Uniform Building Code. The work is divided into 6 sections: general information, structural steel, tables, high-strength bolts, reinforcing steel, and sheet steel (decking). Within each section there is an alphabetic arrangement of several hundred topics and subtopics. For each topic the reader will find a summation of the relevant code and citations to all applicable materials, speeding up the reference process for those needing to see the larger context. There is a good usage of figures and tables and an appended subject index. The work will be a convenient, easy-to-use reference for those who need it.—**John M. Robson**

MECHANICAL ENGINEERING

1412.   Fegan, Sean. **North American Furniture Standards.** High Point, N.C., AKTRIN Furniture Research, 1997. 99p. index. $350.00 spiralbound. ISBN 0-921577-73-7.

This collection of standards is a spiralbound, separately published reprint from volume 5, chapter 3 of *Handbook of Furniture Manufacturing and Marketing*, published by AKTRIN Furniture Research. "North American" refers to the United States and Canada, with standards collected from 10 organizations and 7 state and local agencies. The 144 standards covered here are summarized in a table, noting the issuing agency, which of the categories (household furniture, office/institutions, mattresses, kitchen cabinets, furniture, paints, and so on) it serves, and whether the standard is regulated (defined in law) or voluntary (not subject to legal force).

The full entries describe each standard, giving its purpose, dates of introduction and revisions, an informative description, and general comments. Each entry is classified within 1 of the 9 sections, and it appears only once, even if related to more than a single category. Users will need to consult both the table and the index to be assured of finding all applicable standards. A directory of the standards issuers with addresses and telephone numbers is furnished.

Even though some of this information could be found in other sources with great effort, having it combined in one place will be welcomed by specialized reference collections serving manufacturing interests. The volume would also be useful in some law and governmental collections.—**Gary R. Cocozzoli**

1413.   Walsh, Ronald A. **McGraw-Hill Machining and Metalworking Handbook.** 2d ed. New York, McGraw-Hill, 1998. 1683p. illus. index. $79.95. ISBN 0-07-068059-0.

At the core of many if not all manufacturing processes is working with metal to create a product. Engineers and managers are constantly searching for ways to make the metal products more efficiently, ideally with higher production quality and lower cost. With so much being invested in machining and metalworking, the technology is constantly changing. New standards are issued by trade and professional associations and new materials introduced into the marketplace. Thus, this new edition of the handbook will be a worthwhile addition to the reference library of many groups, including design engineers, tool designers, die-makers, machinists, and metal workers. The book is divided into 25 chapters ranging from the traditional topics of materials (steels, aluminum, alloys, and plastics), gears, and springs, to such newly important ones as CAD/CAM, CAE, and CNC software systems. Underpinning most chapters are the applicable standards from ASTM, SAE, SMI, AGMA, and others.

As with all handbooks, the explication is terse but quite readable both for the serious student and the practitioner. There are an abundance of useful illustrations and tables. If users want to know current practice, need a mathematical formula, want the properties of a particular material, or need to know where to seek a more complete explanation of a topic, this handbook will be a good beginning point. Users will also want to own the *Machinery's Handbook* (25th ed.; Indus Press, 1997), which has a different but complementary focus.—**John M. Robson**

33 Health Sciences

GENERAL WORKS

Atlases

1414. **The Dartmouth Atlas of Health Care 1998.** Chicago, American Hospital Association, 1996. 305p. maps. $350.00. ISBN 1-55648-217-5.

The chief author of this reference work, Dartmouth Medical School professor John E. Wennberg, has published previously in *Science, Scientific American*, the *Journal of the American Medical Association*, the *New England Journal of Medicine*, and the *Lancet*. The information in his book is authoritative; there is no question about that. The question is, will readers use it?

Librarians should note that the reference questions they would use this book to answer would tend to be highly specialized. Take, for example, the section on the U.S. physician workforce. It could not be used to answer any hypothetical reference questions about who U.S. physicians are (e.g., "What percentage of U.S. physicians are women, African American, or over the age of 65?") or the specialties they practice (e.g., "What medical specialty pays the most?"). Rather it goes into detail about the physician workforce in different areas of the United States, specifically the various hospital referral regions into which the nation is divided. Over and over again in this book, a map of the United States showing the division into its 306 hospital referral regions is shown, and information for those regions is given that varies according to the title of the map. At the end of each chapter there is a multipage table that gives statistics, again for the 306 U.S. hospital referral regions. This kind of detail is the strength of the book. If reference questions dealing with U.S. health care statistics at the substate level are rare, the library may want to consider another work, such as the *Statistical Record of Health & Medicine* (see entry 1436), whose statistics are primarily at the national level. However, if the library supports degree programs in health care administration, is a hospital library, or is a special library in a managed care corporation, there may be plenty of reasons to purchase the *Dartmouth Atlas of Health Care*.—**Penny Papangelis**

1415. **The Johns Hopkins Atlas of Human Functional Anatomy.** 4th ed. George D. Zuidema, ed. Baltimore, Md., Johns Hopkins University Press, 1997. 166p. illus. index. $39.95; $22.95pa. ISBN 0-8018-5651-5; 0-8018-5652-3pa.

The study of human anatomy is basic to medical and premedical education as well as the fields of dentistry, nursing, and many of the allied health sciences. This reasonably priced, attractively presented volume serves as a worthwhile introduction to this subject.

This reference work combines the clear illustrations drawn by the noted medical illustrator Leon Schlossberg, with the anatomical knowledge provided by a number of the Johns Hopkins University School of Medicine faculty. The text is comprised of 29 chapters, each covering a specific part of the body. There are 79 plates, mostly in color, which present sharp, detailed images of human anatomy and are the main strength of this volume. This 4th edition of the reference tool includes 16 new plates with accompanying text that, like the rest of the textual material in this book, is concisely and clearly written.

Although there are a number of excellent, lengthy texts available on human anatomy, including several outstanding atlases, this new edition of the Johns Hopkins University human anatomy atlas is a useful addition as an introductory work on this subject for health care, science, and public libraries.—**Jonathon Erlen**

Bibliography

1416. **Consumer Health Information Source Book.** 5th ed. Alan M. Rees, ed. Phoenix, Ariz., Oryx Press, 1998. 226p. index. $59.50. ISBN 1-57356-047-2.

Readers familiar with *Consumer Health Information Source Book* will find in this 5th edition the same insightful and comprehensive guide to popular health information that characterized earlier editions. Both the volume and the means of communicating consumer health information (CHI) have burgeoned in recent years. Approximately 1,400 health-related books are published annually. There are more than 150 magazines and newsletters devoted to CHI issues. Thousands of Websites promote consumer health products and information. Tens of thousands of brochures, pamphlets, fliers, posters, and information cards provide CHI.

Clearly, no single volume can hope to capture the entire panoply of CHI sources. Yet Rees comes as close as any. His 5th edition reviews more than 600 books published between 1994 and 1997, 130 serials, 1,400 pamphlets, 200 toll-free hot lines, 278 resources and referral organizations, 139 select Websites, and more. These materials are organized into 9 chapters by type of media and subject matter (55 topic areas for books and 62 for pamphlets). Except for health-related organizations and telephone numbers, all entries are annotated with brief, well-written descriptions and evaluative comment. Rees has selected a small number of his favorite entries for inclusion as "best sources" in chapter 2.

This guidebook contains a well-researched introduction and excellent indexing by author, subject, and title. It is highly recommended for public libraries, reference collections, and health sciences libraries. [R: Choice, July/Aug 98, p. 1834]—**Bruce Stuart**

1417. Palmegiano, E. M. **Health and British Magazines in the Nineteenth Century.** Lanham, Md., Scarecrow, 1998. 282p. index. $59.50. ISBN 0-8108-3486-3.

Throughout the nineteenth century, the British public was both interested in and concerned about a diverse group of health-related topics, ranging from epidemics to personal hygiene to government involvement promoting public health. Many of the major popular and medical journals of that era reflect these concerns over wellness issues, as demonstrated by the article titles relating to medical/health matters found in these publications. Using the *Wellesley Index* and *Poole's Index*, Palmegiano has selected article titles found in 48 leading British journals published between 1824 and 1900 that pertain to the public's chief health interests.

Regrettably, this novel approach to social history of medicine is seriously flawed in its implementation. The 2,604 entries in this mostly unannotated bibliography are organized chronologically under each of the 48 journal titles rather than by subject headings. This fact forces the reader to rely on the limited subject index to find articles on any given topic. This organization is the major weakness of this reference tool and greatly decreases its potential value. There is no explanation for the selection of these subject headings, and one has to question how thoroughly they have been used in compiling this index. The author, who is not a medical historian, fails to explain the inclusion/exclusion of articles from these journals: Were all health-related titles included, or were there some limiting factors applied for selection? Even the author index is of limited usefulness unless one is interested in finding articles by such public health leaders as Edwin Chadwick. There are simply too many unanswered questions about the purpose and organization of this book to justify its inclusion as a history of medicine reference work.

The approach of examining popular journal article titles to determine the public's health interests is a worthwhile venture. Unfortunately, this initial attempt does not live up to this challenge and will be of little, if any, value to history of medicine scholars. Future bibliographic surveys of a similar nature should construct their studies based on a subject approach to this important topic.—**Jonathon Erlen**

Dictionaries and Encyclopedias

1418. **Encyclopedia of Biostatistics.** Peter Armitage and Theodore Colton, eds. New York, John Wiley, 1998. 6v. illus. index. $2,400.00/set. ISBN 0-471-97576-1.

Considerable understanding of statistical methods and theory and some knowledge of biomedical sciences is needed for best utilization of this major reference work. "Biostatistics" means application of statistical methods in medical and health sciences; however, social sciences are well represented here as well.

The application of statistical methods to medical research has expanded rapidly in recent years, as has the reporting of such in many technical journals and books. The number of individuals and institutions involved with some aspect of health care has also increased dramatically. Although there have been older statistical encyclopedias, such as the *Cambridge Dictionary of Statistics in the Medical Sciences* (see ARBA 96, entry 1699), the editors decided that a new and more comprehensive work was overdue: hence, this monumental product, in which they have eminently succeeded.

A panel of international experts is responsible for subject areas, but the entries of varying length are alphabetized by title. The final volume contains long subject and author indexes for the full set. Most of the illustrations are formulas, requiring skill to decipher. Others are tables and charts, with occasional portraits of famous persons who made significant contributions to statistics as a science. Both cross-references and bibliographies are extensive.

A selected list of review articles in the encyclopedia, such as "Disease Modeling," indicates the extensive coverage of the work, and serves as a rapid index to the main components of biostatistics. A long list of acronyms, many specific to the subject, is also provided in the index volume.

Subjects include the design of studies and experiments, collection of data and analysis, descriptions and application of statistical theories, definition of terms, listings of research and scientific organizations, and historical notes. Authors and researchers can find material on many specific questions. For example, the reader can look up BMI (body mass index) being discussed in the popular press because of new standards on obesity, and discover that Quetelet's index was developed in the 1830s by a scientist working on the statistically "average man." Or one can look up the biostatistical requirements in the design of health and morbidity surveys. This set is a significant addition to the literature of biostatistics. Many of the review articles are of general interest, such as the overview on vital statistics, but this is primarily a research tool.—**Harriette M. Cluxton**

1419. **Encyclopedia of Immunology.** 2d ed. Peter J. Delves and Ivan M. Roitt, eds. San Diego, Calif., Academic Press, 1998. 4v. illus. index. $750.00/set. ISBN 0-12-226765-6.

Immunology has emerged as a science that is vital for understanding physiology and disease. The rapid advances in this field during the past few years have made a new edition of *The Encyclopedia of Immunology* a necessity. First published in 1992, this 2d edition contains 64 new articles. The majority of the other entries have been completely rewritten.

An international group of distinguished academic scientists make up the editorial board and the group of 1,200 contributors who have created this 4-volume encyclopedia. The 630 alphabetic entries provide the most pertinent information on the subjects that are covered. All articles are signed and all have brief bibliographies of review articles and key papers in the field. The articles range in length from one to four pages. Many have charts, diagrams, black-and-white photographs, or color plates. They cover a broad range of subjects that are of interest to biomedical researchers: the behavioral regulation of immunity; ABO blood group system; spleen; nutrition and the immune system; reptile immune system; gel electrophoresis; and Candida, infection and immunity are examples. Although the articles are written at the professional level, educated lay readers will be able to understand them. Each volume has the complete table of contents and index for the set as well as a glossary.

The Encyclopedia of Immunology is a fine addition to academic science and health sciences reference collections. Purchase of the print set includes a trial subscription to the online version available on the World Wide Web.
—**Barbara M. Bibel**

1420. **Handbook of Health Behavior Research.** David S. Gochman, ed. New York, Plenum, 1997. 4v. index. $85.00/vol.; $275.00/set. ISBN 0-306-45443-2 (v.1); 0-306-45444-0 (v.2); 0-306-45445-9 (v.3); 0-306-45446-7 (v.4).

This is not a handbook in the traditional sense; rather, it is a state-of-the-art review presenting "a broad and representative selection of mid-1990s health behavior findings and concepts in a single work." The 4 volumes cover broad interdisciplinary fields, focusing on the health behavior of individuals, society, and providers; the demography, development, and diversity of health behavior; the professional relevance of health behavior research, and future issues. Each volume begins with an introductory chapter and ends with a chapter integrating the topics covered. There are 117 authors, many of whom are acknowledged experts in their fields, who contributed 75 chapters to this work. Each chapter ends with a list of bibliographic references.

The index is extensive, but not comprehensive, and this fact is acknowledged in the book. Most terms in the 16-page glossary cite the handbook volume and chapter in which they are defined—a useful feature, particularly because some words, such as *healmeme*, are unique to this area of study, and other words, such as *prevention*, have specific meanings in this field of research. The use of figures, tables, graphs, and other illustrations is minimal.

This is clearly an academic work, not intended for the average layperson. The style of writing is concise and pedagogic, as found in a research article. The stated objectives are fulfilled, and no other single work in the field comes close to it in terms of coverage, comprehensiveness, scholarship, and currency. It is recommended for libraries supporting medical, behavioral, and social science collections.—**Michael R. Leach**

1421. Lee, Kelley. **Historical Dictionary of the World Health Organization.** Lanham, Md., Scarecrow, 1998. 333p. (Historical Dictionaries of International Organizations, no.15). $62.00. ISBN 0-8108-3371-9.

Publishers have been marking the World Health Organization's (WHO) 1998 golden anniversary with a number of publications. Scarecrow Press offers the *Historical Dictionary of the World Health Organization*, the 15th entry in the Historical Dictionaries of International Organizations series. During its 50 years, WHO has evolved to become an important force in the health care of citizens worldwide. This required numerous committees, commissions, forums, and task forces. These groups are incorporated into a complex set of bureaus, agencies, and offices. The groups' efforts include a variety of declarations, symposiums, reports, programs, guidelines, and recommendations. Any government documents librarian can attest to the challenge of acquiring, organizing, and then locating a WHO document for a patron. This dictionary helps with those tasks by offering thoroughly researched entries; a chronology; list of acronyms; and information on units, key figures, events, and major publications. A bibliography includes major publications of WHO. The work features eight appendixes. Appendix A presents the Constitution; appendix B lists member countries and the year they joined; appendix C includes contact information; appendix D reprints organizational charts (some are poorly reproduced); appendix E lists personnel; and appendixes F through H include other documents, financial information, and cooperating organizations. International documents collections and medical libraries where international health and health policy are important will want to add this resource to their collections. [R: Choice, Dec 98, p. 667]—**Lynne M. Fox**

1422. **Physicians' Desk Reference Companion Guide 1998.** 52d ed. Mukesh Mehta, ed. Montvale, N.J., Medical Economics Data, 1998. 1769p. index. $56.95. ISBN 1-56363-255-1.

The *Physicians' Desk Reference* (PDR) has long been the accepted standard reference tool concerning appropriate usages and potential dangers of available prescription drugs, both for health providers and the general public (1993 ed.; see ARBA 94, entry 1880). Besides the basic annual publication, the publisher also produces separate PDRs for nonprescription drugs, herbal medicines, and ophthalmology, along with a number of other supplementary publications.

Most of the text is product information concerning individual drugs arranged alphabetically under the names of the pharmaceutical firms that produce these products. This information is provided solely by these pharmaceutical firms in compliance with Food and Drug Administration (FDA) regulations and the PDR editors make no effort to confirm or contradict the accuracy of this material. The following information, when available, is provided for each drug: a biochemical description of the substances found in the drug, the clinical pharmacology of the product, and the therapeutic uses and potential hazards of the drug. This information is provided in advanced scientific language, which may be too technical for the public to understand, and the potential dangers listed might scare a patient into not taking a recommended therapy. This volume is well indexed by manufactures' names as well as by brand and generic drug name. A separate product identification guide provides useful color pictures of more than 2,400 of the drugs described in the PDR's text.

The *Physicians' Desk Reference Companion Guide* first appeared in 1998 and replaced the *PDR Guide to Drug Interactions, Side Effects, Indications, Contraindications*. The 1999 edition of this reference work will be published in February 1999. The text of this useful volume presents a number of separate sections that greatly enhance the PDR's usefulness, particularly for health providers. These color-coded guides provide such diverse information about the drugs listed in the PDR as contraindications, generic availability, international drug names, off-label treatments, drug and food interactions, side effects, and daily costs of drug therapy guidelines. As with the PDR, some of the materials in this volume may confuse rather than enlighten the general public.
—**Jonathon Erlen**

1423.   **Quick Reference Dictionary for Occupational Therapy.** Karen Jacobs, ed. Thorofare, N.J., Slack, 1997. 340p. illus. $24.00pa. ISBN 1-55642-297-0.

This pocket-sized dictionary has been developed to assist students of occupational therapy in their coursework. Terminology is drawn from the major textbooks in beginning occupational therapy courses, as well as that used in American Occupational Therapy Association (AOTA) documents, which includes many terms from the health care field in general. Some basic medical, psychological and sociological terms, and references to historical figures and federal legislation are included in the main dictionary of terms.

The rest of the book contains a remarkable collection of 19 appendixes. The first, "Suggested Reading," amounts to little more than advertisements of the author and publisher. The acronym lists that follow should be useful. The AOTA's uniform terminology for occupational therapy, code of ethics for practice, and core values serve as guides for students in understanding the field they have chosen. Whether excerpts from other classification schemes, such as *Diagnostic and Statistical Manual of Mental Disorders*, are of much value at this level seems unlikely, and items such as the metric system are readily available elsewhere or else are likely to be included in the textbooks being studied. As a learning tool and review source, this book is significant.—**Harriette M. Cluxton**

Directories

1424.   **Health & Medicine on the Internet.** James B. Davis, ed. Los Angeles, Calif., Health Information Press, 1997. 610p. illus. index. $19.95pa. ISBN 1-885987-03-X.

One of the benefits of the Internet is supposed to be the decrease in the need for bulky, inflexible printed sources. Now we are seeing a new wave of books on how to use the Internet. However, given the limitations of Web browsers, there may be a need, at least temporarily, for such guidebooks. This is a particularly nice one; it is both comprehensive and easy for the layperson to use. It lists Websites in the areas of health and medicine that are of interest to health consumers. There are 69 sections, which cover broad topics such as "Fitness," "Diabetes," and "Infectious Diseases." Within each topic are subtopics, including "Organizations," "Treatment," or specific conditions or aspects of conditions. Under each of these subtopics are several Websites, many with annotations giving a description of their contents and who maintains the Website. For instance, for the subtopic "Sports Medicine," eight sites are listed. Putting these terms into AOL Netfind and Netscape yielded hits in the millions. Both browsers had ways to narrow down the focus, but it took quite a while, and none of the Websites listed in this book were easily pulled up. Five of the sites listed under "Sports Medicine" were excellent sources on the topic, giving self-diagnosis help, advice on treatment, and help in finding sports medicine professionals. However, three of the sources could not be found, either because they were temporarily down or are no longer available. That, of course, is the problem with Internet directories—any printed source is instantly out of date. Still, as a starting point this book is a great help in providing access to one of the most useful areas of cyberspace, particularly because the publishers plan on putting out yearly editions. Now if only they would put it online.—**Carol L. Noll**

1425.   **Health Professions Education Directory, 1998-1999.** 26th ed. Chicago, American Medical Association, 1998. 485p. $54.95pa.; $44.95pa. (AMA members). ISBN 0-89970-922-2.

People often do not realize the vast opportunities available for education and subsequent employment in the health care field. This informative and well-organized directory provides data regarding 47 diverse health care careers. The overall majority of the careers listed would be considered allied health (e.g., dental technician, medical assistant) rather than professional. The major health professions—medicine, dentistry, nursing, pharmacy, and others—are not included in this book. Criteria for inclusion of the careers chosen are a formal, postsecondary educational program and a national accreditation or approval process for the program. In addition, the graduate of the program must primarily participate in the delivery of health care.

The directory has 4 major sections. The 1st lists general information about the accrediting agencies. The 2d section alphabetically lists each career with a brief description of the job responsibilities and the educational preparation required. This narrative is followed by an alphabetic list, by state, of the institutions offering the program. More than 5,000 programs are included. Besides the usual directory information, many institutions list length of the program, costs, and degree awarded. The 3d major section gives a cross-referenced directory list, by state, of each institution and its programs. The final section provides data from recent surveys regarding the various occupations—number of graduates, attrition rates, and employment. This easy-to-use guide is an essential for libraries serving career counselors and is highly recommended for public libraries.—**Mary Ann Thompson**

1426.   **Medical and Health Information Directory 1998: A Guide to Organizations....** 9th ed. Bridget Travers, ed. Detroit, Gale, 1998. 3v. index. $569.00/set. ISBN 0-7876-1556-0.

Since the 1st edition in 1977, Gale's *Medical and Health Information Directory* has established a track record as a convenient compilation of information appropriate for all types of libraries dealing with requests for medical information. Although this 3-volume set is priced beyond the means of many libraries, it provides access to information not easily or quickly found in other reference works. Listings include professional organizations; funding sources; health management and insurance-related businesses; and educational, libraries, research, and governmental institutions. One volume lists specialty care facilities and hospitals for services such as burn care, hospice, or sleep disorders. A detailed index provides access by name and keywords for each volume. This resource assists busy medical librarians who need contact information at their fingertips. It is a recommended purchase for most large medical libraries and many hospital libraries where cost is not a consideration.—**Lynne M. Fox**

1427.   **National Guide to Funding in Health.** 5th ed. Elizabeth H. Rich, ed. New York, Foundation Center, 1997. 1195p. index. $150.00pa. ISBN 0-87954-710-3.

More than 4,000 foundation, corporate, or charitable entities fill the directory section of this subject-specific guide to grants. Interest, stated or demonstrated, in health programs or activities qualified international, national, or regional grant-makers for inclusion. Some may consider a narrow field of health considerations, whereas others cover a broader spectrum. Users will benefit from the delineation of interests in the entries.

Entries are arranged alphabetically by grant-maker name under geographic location. In addition to personnel and contact information, grant-maker notations include purpose and activities, fields of interest, type of support, and limitations on giving. In some entries, specific grants are noted. A new category cites any international interests of the grant-maker.

Of special interest is the refining and expansion of the grants classification system (GCS) used by the foundation. The resulting greater level of specificity produces more entry terms for identifying grant possibilities. This access expansion is reflected in the indexes to types of support, to foundation and corporate giving programs by subject, and to grants by subject.

The Foundation Center wisely provides basic information in each of its guides: how to use the volume, a glossary of terms, information about the Foundation Center, and a bibliography of pertinent journal articles and books. Users will welcome not having to search other locations for these helpful tips. Editing errors, uncharacteristic of Foundation Center publications, appear in this edition. An introductory page heading indicates that the volume covers library and information services rather than health. In addition, the heading for the state of Maryland is missing, so Maryland entries tail the Maine entries, and the running heads on Maryland pages continue to say Maine. No Maryland information, however, is omitted or incorrect. The center quickly distributed corrected pages. The errors detract little from this health funding guide's usefulness to hospital personnel, students, researchers, social workers, doctors, and care center staffs.—**Eleanor Ferrall**

1428.   Smallwood, Carol, comp. **Free or Low Cost Health Information: Sources for Printed Materials on 512 Topics.** Jefferson, N.C., McFarland, 1998. 332p. index. $39.50pa. ISBN 0-7864-0309-8.

Pamphlets are a free or inexpensive source of basic health information. Librarians in need of items for vertical files and teachers or community organizations who need to distribute educational material rely on them. Finding an appropriate source of current, accurate information is sometimes difficult. *Free or Low Cost Health Information*, compiled by a librarian, provides a list of sources for printed material on 512 health and safety topics.

The book is organized alphabetically by subject. Within each subject, the organizations are listed alphabetically by name. Each entry includes the name, address, and telephone and fax number. A description of the organization and the types of publications that it produces and their prices follows. Information is available on a wide range of topics—adolescent health, ethics, health careers, school safety, and Tourette's syndrome are examples. The sources include government agencies (National Health Information Center), independent agencies (National Safety Council), trade and professional organizations (American Dental Association), and nonprofit organizations (National Organization for Rare Disorders). A few commercial publishers who provide low-cost materials or quantity discounts are also included. There is a fair amount of repetition among the source listings because organizations publish material on many topics. A detailed table of contents and a subject and source index make it easy to locate specific material. *Free or Low Cost Health Information* is a source that public and school librarians, teachers, and health educators will appreciate. [R: LJ, 1 Sept 98, p. 170; BL, 1 Oct 98, pp. 362-363; Choice, Dec 98, p. 668]—**Barbara M. Bibel**

Handbooks and Yearbooks

1429. Exploring Health Care Careers: Real People Tell You What You Need to Know. David Hayes, ed. Chicago, Ferguson, 1998. 893p. index. $89.95. ISBN 0-89434-217-7.

This 2-volume set from the publisher of *Encyclopedia of Careers and Vocational Guidance* (see ARBA 98, entry 215) provides information about careers in the health care field. About 110 careers are covered and include professional, technical, and some nontraditional jobs, such as acupuncture and hypnotherapy. Each chapter is devoted to a job title and includes job descriptions, important personal traits and skills needed, education and licensing requirements, job market and outlook, salary ranges, and advancement opportunities. Each chapter also includes a profile of a health care worker, who describes what his or her job is like. A list of professional organizations and a bibliography of books and periodical articles provides additional information sources for each career.

There are 3 indexes. The first index lists health care careers by their *Dictionary of Occupational Titles* (DOT) groups. Although this reviewer is not sure why a high school student would care about DOT group numbers, it does provide a bit of subject indexing. The second index lists careers by broad interest areas, such as artistic or mechanical, and may help a student to narrow the choices. Finally, there is a job title index that lists all major jobs discussed and offers appropriate cross-references. There is little duplication between this work and the *Encyclopedia of Careers and Vocational Guidance* (10th ed.; see ARBA 98, entry 215), but the arrangement is very similar. It would have been nice if the editor had included an overview section of the health care industry as well as a list of related articles for each chapter. The introductory scenes at the beginning of each chapter are sometimes overly dramatic, but the first-person accounts of a typical workday are useful. A combination of interesting, well-written text and effective layout makes this work a useful resource for academic, school, and public libraries.—**Teresa U. Berry**

1430. Health: United States, 1996-97 and Injury Chartbook. By the Department of Health and Human Services. Washington, D.C., Government Printing Office; distr., Lanham, Md., Bernan Associates, 1997. 341p. index. $38.00. ISBN 0-16-049096-0.

This compendium of national health statistics is published annually as a report to the president and congress from the Department of Health and Human Services. The 150 tables give data over multiple year periods on health status measures, utilization of ambulatory and inpatient facilities, availability of medical professionals by job category, and national expenditures for health care. A representative sampling of table headings are low-weight births by age and race of mother, ambulatory care visits, active physicians in the United States by specialty and state, hospital occupancy rates, and national health costs by category of expense and more.

Health: United States includes a chartbook, which focuses on a different topic with each edition. Injury is featured in the 1996-97 volume. There are 33 figures presented, and accompanying text provides data on injury mortality, hospitalization, emergency room usage, and other statistics. This subject was selected for the current chartbook because injuries account for 12 percent of all U.S. medical spending. In 1991 the cost for medical treatment and work time lost associated with injuries was $325 billion. The chartbook concludes with suggestions for using this information to design injury prevention programs.

The report is indexed by subject, and appendixes describe the agencies reporting data as well as definitions of the terms used in the tables. The material in this book is also available electronically on disk and on the National Center for Health Statistics Web page. This reference provides useful trend data on a wide variety of health care statistics.—**Adrienne Antink Bendel**

1431. Health Care Almanac: Every Person's Guide to the Thoughtful and Practical Sides of Medicine. 2d ed. Chicago, American Medical Association, 1998. 546p. index. $27.95pa. ISBN 0-89970-900-1.

The American Medical Association's *Health Care Almanac*, now in its 2d edition, contains a plethora of disparate but useful listings for both health consumers and professionals. One will find it a useful guide for finding an association address, checking the credential process for an allied health profession, locating a copy of the Hippocratic oath, finding a definition for a condition, checking a description for a treatment or therapy, or determining whether the *Journal of the American Medical Association* (JAMA) published a theme issue on a topic. All of these questions can be answered by this reasonably priced, informative resource. Articles reprinted from JAMA often form the basis of entries, providing advice for health professionals, especially physicians.

Most of this almanac is arranged alphabetically by topic and features a thorough index. Articles are brief, but typically include references to additional resources. When appropriate, Website addresses are included. Appendixes include history and organizational information about the American Medical Association. This valuable resource will be an asset in any library. It provides an essential starting point for general health reference questions.
—**Lynne M. Fox**

1432.   **Issue Briefs: 1997 Annual Edition.** Washington, D.C., Health Policy Tracking Service, 1997. 1v. (unpaged). $450.00 spiralbound.

This reference documents major health legislation considered by various U.S. state legislative bodies during calendar year 1997. More than 30 issues are covered, ranging from access to various types of health care providers to physician-assisted suicide and uninsured children. Many of the policies deal with managed care. Each issue is addressed in a separate section that begins with background information, including a brief definition and legislative history. Key issues surrounding the topic and activity current to 1997 are included. Some of the listings include a section on the pros and cons of the particular issue. Each section then concludes with a table of each state's legislative activity on that policy, including bill numbers and status.

Considering the high cost of this reference, it is not overly user-friendly. It has no index, no page numbers, and no running heads, making it difficult to locate particular sections. The sections are compiled in alphabetic order by title of the issue and are separated by colored paper. A table of contents lists the alphabetized sections. Although the reference provides an interesting account of the history of health legislation in one fairly active year (due to managed care), the book would be of true interest to a fairly specialist audience. *Issue Briefs* is recommended for state libraries, libraries serving state legislatures, and for professional health organizations that have lobbyists.—**Mary Ann Thompson**

1433.   **Major State Health Care Policies: Fifty State Profiles, 1997.** 6th ed. Washington, D.C., Health Policy Tracking Service, 1998. 294p. $147.00pa. ISBN 1-55516-819-1.

Health Policy Tracking Service (HPTS) correspondents in each state watch state legislatures, executive speeches, studies, press reports, and other subjects related to health policy efforts, and contribute this information to HPTS's on-line service. This volume summarizes what occurred in 1997 and matters expected to be considered in 1998.

Tables in the front check off topics such as various insurance reforms in all states, and maps show current interests in such activities as genetic testing. But most of the book is a series of 50 state profiles, each providing a narrative followed by brief statements on the current status of health related bills, in categories such as finance (managed care and insurance), Medicaid, providers, behavioral health, and pharmaceuticals. Because HPTS followed 13,085 bills in 1997, with all their variations, the number of concise factual statements here is tremendous. The overall view of any state's health care policy situation is clearly evident and may readily be compared with other states. Staffs involved in developing major health care policies and getting them adopted, those who must work under these directives, and researchers on health care trends in general or in specific subjects (such as parity—equal insurance coverage of mental illnesses) will appreciate this easily accessible collection of very current data.—**Harriette M. Cluxton**

1434.   **Physician Marketplace Statistics 1997-98: Profiles for Detailed Specialties, Selected States and Practice Arrangements.** Martin L. Gonzalez and Puling Zhang, eds. Chicago, American Medical Association, 1998. 157p. $399.00pa. ISBN 0-89970-911-7.

This annual survey provides statistics on practice time (by weeks/year and hours/week), patient encounters, office visit fees, professional expenses, physician net income, and percentage of revenue by source (Medicare, Medicaid, private insurers, and managed care). The report's 125 tables and 37 figures are divided by category, with an introduction that includes definitions and a summary of the questions used to elicit the responses. Variables are divided into 26 medical specialties, 6 geographic regions, and the number of physicians in the practice.

This reference provides a useful yearly overview of physician practice patterns, but there are two areas that are missing. It would be helpful to add a section comparing the current year's key indicators with past data to more readily identify trends. The survey provides the total number of administrative, secretarial, and clerical employees but does not include clinical support staff such as nurses, physician assistants, and others. With managed care changing how medicine is practiced, data on the use of physician extenders are of key interest.
—**Adrienne Antink Bendel**

1435. **Plunkett's Health Care Industry Almanac 1997-98.** Jack W. Plunkett and others, eds. Galveston, Tex., Plunkett Research, 1997. 733p. index. $149.99pa. ISBN 0-9638268-7-5.

This guide has two major focuses. The 1st part of the volume provides an overview of U.S. medical practice with statistics on the cost of delivering care, utilization data, and trends in Medicare and Medicaid expenditures. Also helpful are the updates on technological advances; the listing of related government agencies and professional associations with addresses and telephone numbers; and information on the health care professions to include training requirements, current salary ranges, and future employment trends.

The 2d part of this reference features profiles with economic indicators of 500 high performing for-profit health care corporations. These cover the gamut from Health Maintenance Organizations (HMOs) to pharmaceutical companies, bioengineering firms, and waste management. The tables in this section are indexed by alphabet; industry; state and region; size of annual research budget; opportunities for women and minorities; and by subsidiaries, brand names, and affiliations. This volume is a good starting point for research on the costs of delivering medical care and the financial performance of health care companies.—**Adrienne Antink Bendel**

1436. **Statistical Record of Health and Medicine.** 2d ed. Arsen J. Darnay, ed. Detroit, Gale, 1998. 1029p. index. $115.00. ISBN 0-7876-0093-8. ISSN 1078-6961.

With 11 chapters, more than 1,000 pages, 950 tables, and topics ranging from hospital truck driver salaries to the risk of blood clots from sitting in cramped airline seats, this compendium is fascinating, frustrating, and highly idiosyncratic. For example, chapter 2, entitled "Health Status of Americans," contains 274 tables organized under 35 headings. The first heading, "Aging," contains a single 3-line quotation from *Time* magazine indicating that 1 in 5 Americans over the age of 60 regularly take pain pills, and many have side effects. There are just two entries in the one-page section devoted to cerebrovascular disease—both quotations from *Time* magazine. By contrast, there are 45 tables and 64 pages devoted to sexually transmitted diseases (STDs). In chapter 8, which is on medical professions, 82 pages are devoted to occupational compensation in health services facilities, including wages for accountants, janitors, key entry operators, warehouse specialists, and 25 other occupations.

Huge chunks of the book are lifted directly from government sources: 218 pages of data on health care establishments from a 1992 economic census report, 70 pages on hospital procedures from a single National Center for Health Statistics publication, and the 64 pages on STDs from a September 1996 U.S. Public Health Service report. Outside of governmental publications, there is a heavy reliance on newspaper and magazine articles. No indication is given that the information taken from these secondary sources has been checked or verified. Yet the most frustrating feature of this volume is its uneven content. Obviously, with a title like *Statistical Record of Health and Medicine*, the editor needed to be selective in the choice of topics and depth of coverage. However, the reader is given no clue as to what those editorial guidelines may be. The book contains an excellent keyword index, but this addition cannot save an otherwise flawed effort.—**Bruce Stuart**

1437. Wellner, Alison. **Best of Health: Demographics of Health Care Consumers.** Ithaca, N.Y., New Strategist, 1998. 455p. index. (American Consumer Series). $89.95. ISBN 1-885070-18-7.

There are many sources of statistics about health care consumers, such as the National Center for Health Care Statistics, the National Opinion Research Center, and medical associations, but there has not been a comprehensive book about consumer demand for health care. This book attempts to provide such a research tool. Although much of the data used are from government sources, it has been compiled, analyzed, and arranged in tables and graphs, with commentary, to reveal trends behind those statistics. Sources are always identified.

Each chapter covers a particular aspect of the health care industry and the consumers of health care related to it. Subjects include the changing relationships between health care providers and patients; growth in out-patient as opposed to in-patient care; growing use of alternative medicine; and changing attitudes toward specific areas, such as fitness, disability, and mental health. The author provides insightful discussion of important trends, with current bibliographies. The following tables show the demographic characteristics of the consumers behind the trends—race, sex, age, place, and type of care. Percent of change over a given time period (such as hospital bed occupancy) has been calculated by New Strategist and backs up the author's points about current trends and future expectations. Growth of the "self-care" industry is astounding. This excellent study will be useful to those involved in any aspect of the large health care industry and its future course.—**Harriette M. Cluxton**

1438. **Women's Health Concerns Sourcebook.** Heather E. Aldred, ed. Detroit, Omnigraphics, 1997. 567p. illus. index. (Health Reference Series, v.27). $78.00. ISBN 0-7808-0219-5.

This book is an example of an increasingly popular type of publication—a reprint collection of health information articles by government and nonprofit agencies. The advantage is that useful articles from a variety of sources are conveniently gathered together, arranged by topic, and indexed for maximum accessibility. The disadvantage, of course, is that what was once free now costs $78. This volume covers conditions and disorders either exclusive to or more common in women, from everyday issues of female health, such as menstruation, birth control, and menopause, to more unusual diseases, such as lupus, breast cancer, and anorexia. (Pregnancy, certainly one of the central health events in most women's lives, is not covered in this book, but will be the subject of a future volume.) The articles are arranged by topic in 24 chapters. Most are from patient-information publications by the National Institutes of Health, the Federal Drug Administration, or the Department of Health and Human Services. A few of the articles are as old as from 1983, although most are two to six years old. Most are written in an easy-to-read, simple manner, with diagrams and charts to aid in understanding. The information in most of these articles tends to be fairly general and basic. For some patients the articles will be just enough information, but for those determined to research a topic in depth, this will be just an introduction and starting point. [R: BR, Jan/Feb 98, p. 51]—**Carol L. Noll**

MEDICINE

General Works

Dictionaries and Encyclopedias

1439. **The Cambridge Encyclopedia of Human Paleopathology.** By Arthur C. Aufderheide, Conrado Rodríquez-Martín, and Odin Langsjoen. New York, Cambridge University Press, 1998. 478p. illus. index. $100.00. ISBN 0-521-55203-6.

Nowhere other than in the study of human diseases is it so obvious that humans are only one of a vast array of life forms on this planet. This encyclopedia is a major reference work for all those interested in the identification of disease in human remains. The scope of the encyclopedia encompasses almost every disease that produces in human tissues an anatomic pathological change large enough to be detected by the unaided eye.

The most active research areas are explored, including the following: circulatory disorders, joint diseases, infectious diseases, diseases of the viscera, metabolic diseases, endocrine disorders, hematological disorders, skeletal dysplasia, and neoplastic conditions. In addition, a dental chapter by Langsjoen is included. Each chapter consists of several sections. The chapter on infectious disease, for example, contains various articles about bacterial, viral, and fungal infections. All articles are designed as self-contained treatments of important topics in human paleopathology and are presented on a first-principle basis, including appropriate charts, detailed figures, photographs, tables, and drawings. "Natural History" sections are employed to present the disease as a succession of tissue events that gradually cause and shape the final form of the lesions. "Antiquity, History and Epidemiology" sections are included to help maximize the integration of identified pathological conditions with information about archaeological, anthropological, cultural, and other aspects of a studied ancient population. The authors intentionally omitted a glossary of basic terms in order to prevent themselves from minimizing medical vocabulary. A subject index is included.

This major reference work will meet the needs of investigators and consultants. It will aid them in identifying the nature of the disease and in its diagnosis. The suggested reading audience will be mostly physicians and anthropologists.—**Marilynn Green Hopman**

1440. **Dictionary of Medicine.** 2d ed. P. H. Collin, ed. Middlesex, Great Britain, Peter Collin, 1993; repr., Chicago, Fitzroy Dearborn, 1998. 393p. illus. $55.00. ISBN 1-57958-074-2.

First published in the United Kingdom, this plain medical dictionary defines fairly simple terms that most individuals understand or believe they understand. Using a limited vocabulary of 500 words to define each of the 12,000 main terms, this dictionary gives clear explanations of the various terminology used in the medical profession. In-depth discussion, symptomatology, and causation are rarely indicated. Each entry provides the parts of speech and multiple definitions when appropriate; some include sentences demonstrating proper usage, while others include "comments" or "quotes." The comment on emphysema states that the disease can be caused by smoking, among other causes. Quotes are obtained from reputable sources—*Lancet, Nursing Times*, and the *Journal of the American Medical Association*. Common acronyms and abbreviations used by doctors and in hospitals are identified with accurate reference to a definition—OP stands for Outpatient and GDC stands for General Dental Council. Common names for diseases refer to the formal medical terminology. Lou Gehrig's Disease refers to Amyotrophic Lateral Sclerosis. Few entries, such as the eye, include a detailed illustration of the organ.

Not to replace more popular medical reference books, this dictionary provides clear and simple definitions to help young adults and adults understand common medical terminology. Originating in the United Kingdom, this title does have a bias towards British spelling and usage.—**Susan D. Strickland**

1441. **Encyclopedia of Family Health.** Tarrytown, N.Y., Marshall Cavendish, 1998. 17v. illus. index. $499.95/set. ISBN 0-7614-0625-5.

First published in 1971 in England, Marshall Cavendish's *Encyclopedia of Family Health* is a source of basic medical and health information. The current edition, prepared with David B. Jacoby of the Johns Hopkins University School of Medicine, is aimed at U.S. readers. British spelling, usage, and vocabulary have been eliminated.

This edition continues to present simple, profusely illustrated articles on anatomy, physiology, health care, diseases, and conditions. The alphabetic entries range in length from one to three pages. Each entry has a sidebar with questions and answers that serve as an introduction to the topic. The text is written in language that is accessible to readers from middle school to adult levels. Many new illustrations and articles have been added, and older articles have been revised in varying degrees. *AIDS* has been extensively updated with the latest information on the HIV viruses and treatment options. *Cancer*, however, needs further revision. Treatments are covered superficially, and the book states that hormonal therapy has no unpleasant side effects. The first aid guide in volume 17 contains obsolete information and errors in the protocols for treating choking and performing cardiopulmonary resuscitation. New articles include "Acid Rain," "Carpal Tunnel Syndrome," "Mind-Body Therapy," and "Sick Building Syndrome." The entries dealing with alternative therapies, such as aromatherapy, are objective.

Volume 1 has a table of contents for the entire set. The other volumes have tables of contents for their own entries. The addition of cross-references to this edition makes finding related material easy. A glossary and a short list of U.S. and Canadian associations for referral complement the text. A bibliography of recent books provides further information. Most of the works are current, but the 1993 edition of *The Mayo Clinic Family Health Book* is listed instead of the 1996 edition. Alphabetic subject indexes complete the work.

Encyclopedia of Family Health serves as a starting point for students doing reports and patrons in need of basic information. Those who need greater depth can consult the *Merck Manual of Medical Information, Home Edition* (see ARBA 98, entry 1540). *Everything You Need to Know About Medical Emergencies* (Springhouse, 1997) provides current, accurate information on first aid. The encyclopedia's ease of use, accessibility, and illustrations make it a good, but rather expensive, addition to school and public library collections. [R: RUSQ, Summer 98, p. 376]—**Barbara M. Bibel**

1442. Isler, Charlotte. **The Patient's Guide to Medical Terminology.** 3d ed. Los Angeles, Calif., Health Information Press, 1997. 258p. $12.95pa. ISBN 1-885987-08-0.

Few fields are filled with as much specialized and obfuscatory terminology as medicine. Yet, in no other area is it so important that laypeople understand what specialists are telling them. This reference guide is just the tool for the patient who walks out of the doctor's office confused as to the meaning of a diagnosis, test, or treatment. It also could be invaluable in translating the medical language in billing statements or correspondence with insurance companies. The guide is divided into 3 parts. The 1st is a list of abbreviations with one-word definitions. There are more than 30 pages in this section, which contains most acronyms commonly used by medical professionals, an indication of the enormity of the problem facing the uninformed patient. Section 2 is an alphabetic list of terms, with clear, understandable definitions. A valuable feature is the inclusion of normal ranges of values for the results of diagnostic tests. The coverage is comprehensive, including pediatric to geriatric conditions, both common and obscure. The contents are particularly valuable for the myriad of tests involved in the modern management of pregnancy. Finally, at the end of the guide is a short section explaining some of the measurement units used in diagnostic results and prescriptions.

A guide such as this should be in every doctor's waiting room. More and more, patients must be the managers in managed care, and the first step is being able to speak, or at least understand, the language.—**Carol L. Noll**

1443. **Magill's Medical Guide.** 1998 rev. ed. Dawn P. Dawson and Tracy Irons-Georges, eds. Englewood Cliffs, N.J., Salem Press, 1998. 3v. illus. index. $310.00/set. ISBN 0-89356-937-2.

This encyclopedic set aims to provide a survey of the current state of medical science. It contains articles on the anatomy and physiology of the human body, major diseases and disorders, common medical and surgical procedures, and medical specialties and training. Articles range in length from brief definitions to 3,500-word essays and cover such things as particular diseases, afflictions affecting a particular part of the body, and broad topics such as alternative medicine and bionics and biotechnology. This revised edition updates the 1995 version (see ARBA 96, entry 1700) and its 3 supplements. Existing articles were updated and 22 additional ones added. Medical drawings and other illustrations are adequate and clear, if not lavish; a general glossary and a variety of indexes are included. Articles make an attempt to cover both the history and recent research and trends in knowledge of a condition. The longer articles include definitions and key terms, information on system affected, causes, symptoms, treatment, and future perspectives as well as a brief annotated bibliography. Articles are signed by the authors, who are generally academicians in the life sciences and medicine; all entries were reviewed by a panel of five medical experts. They are generally written in a clear, minimally technical style reasonably intelligible to the layperson. This would be a useful guide for any library, providing considerably more information than one-volume medical guides for the consumer, although less than medical professionals would need in their practice.
—**Marit S. MacArthur**

1444. **Routledge German Dictionary of Medicine, Volume 1: German-English/Deutsche-Englisch. Worterbuch Medizin Englisch.** 2d ed. By Fritz-Jurgen Nohring. New York, Routledge, 1997. 1117p. $150.00. ISBN 0-415-17130-X.

The 2d edition of this attractive, easy-to-use dictionary was necessitated by the recent plethora of new words appearing in fast-breaking fields, such as genetic engineering, molecular biology, immunology, and transplantation. In fact, 16,000 of the 92,000 entries are new. To test the dictionary's practical usefulness, this reviewer attempted to translate an article from a German cardiology journal. Looking up the words in this article, for a guy who uses his college German only occasionally, was quick and painless (the hardest part was finding umlauts on my font list). This is an excellent resource for someone needing to translate a article only available in German, a situation that this reviewer rarely runs across, but that must be much commoner in some areas of medicine.—**Anthony Gottlieb**

1445. Turkington, Carol, and Bonnie Ashby. **Encyclopedia of Infectious Diseases.** New York, Facts on File, 1998. 370p. index. $50.00. ISBN 0-8160-3512-1.

Finally, this broad-based encyclopedia of infectious diseases from Facts on File has arrived on the book-shelves. This is a concise guide and easy-to-read resource for the layperson. There are roughly 600 entries discussing the cause, diagnosis, symptoms, treatment, and prevention of the known infectious diseases. For other infectious disease terms, readers need to go for a medical textbook for more information. However, this book would be more interesting if there were color illustrations of cases inserted. This work claims to have the "curriculum-oriented information" that includes biology, health, anatomy, and premed courses. The glossary at the end of the book is a plus, and the bibliography, sorted by authors, would be more helpful if each citation was cross-referenced to the disease in the content. Six useful appendixes are provided—"Drugs Used to Treat Infectious Disease," "Home Disinfection," "Health Organizations," "Disease Hot Lines," "Health Publications," and "Infectious Disease-Related Websites." The Websites and drugs sections give readers a new perspective on how to use the information in a more meaningful way. Usually an encyclopedic item does not need an index, but the index in this book collects the keywords in the content to give more access points for the readers. This book is recommended for public or school libraries. Because there are not many publications of this type in the market, this reviewer thinks *Encyclopedia of Infectious Diseases* is a timely resource to supply consumers the much-needed information on infectious diseases. [R: LJ, 1 Oct 98, p. 78; BL, 15 Dec 98, p. 763]—**Polin P. Lei**

1446.   Wiseman, Nigel, and Feng Ye, comps. **A Practical Dictionary of Chinese Medicine.** 2d ed. Brookline, Mass., Redwing Book Company, 1998. 945p. index. $125.00. ISBN 0-912111-54-2.

     Wiseman and Ye have created an exemplary reference work characterized by its erudition, completeness, and accessibility. The compilers' preface details every aspect of the work's purpose, genesis, and scope. The stated objective was to create a dictionary that would be "useful to practitioners, students, and teachers of Chinese medicine in the English-speaking world, whether or not they have knowledge of Chinese and whether or not they are familiar with the terminology presented." The arrangement is alphabetic in order (as opposed to a thematic ordering) of English terms, with each entry followed by the original Chinese term and Pinyin transliteration. The definitions are often followed by extensive clinical information that may include specification of western medical correspondences, medication, acupuncture, and treatment. Entries are extensively cross-referenced, which is a key feature to accessing the content of this work given the unfamiliarity of many of the concepts. The entries conclude with references to sources, the vast majority of which are in Chinese. Also included are four appendixes and an index that allows access to the English entries by their Pinyin transcriptions as well as an index to medicinals and acupuncture-point names appearing in the text.

     With its approximately 6,000 entries, this encyclopedic dictionary may serve as a clinical manual and would make an invaluable tool for those learning about Chinese medical concepts. It will also be of interest to translators as the compilers have extensive experience with terminological work in this area. This is a dictionary designed for specialists and can be expected to appeal to a specific audience; nevertheless, current interest in acupuncture and other forms of alternative medicine may indicate a wider audience for this title.—**Michael Weinberg**

Directories

1447.   **The Complete Directory for People with Rare Disorders, 1998/99: A Comprehensive Guide to Over 1,000 Rare Disorders....** Joy E. Bartnett, Debra L. Madden, and Robert P. Tomaino, eds. Lakeville, Conn., Grey House Publishing, 1998. 726p. index. $190.00. ISBN 1-891482-03-3.

     A rare disorder is defined as one that affects fewer than 200,000 people in the United States at any given time. Patients afflicted with such disorders, their families, and their caregivers often find that information about their condition may be as rare as the condition itself. *The Complete Directory for People with Rare Disorders* provides access to organizations with information about these diseases.

     The directory has 4 sections. The 1st offers alphabetically arranged entries that describe 1,102 rare diseases. The entry has a brief explanation of the disorder, followed by a list of organizations that are concerned with it. These organizations have their own entries in the 3 sections that follow; the section on disease-specific organizations lists 445 groups, that on umbrella organizations covers 444 general groups, and that on government agencies contains entries for 74 federal agencies. A name and keyword index is the main access point. The organization entries are alphabetic within their sections. Each contains the name, address, telephone and fax numbers, e-mail address, and Website address if available. A description of the organization, list of officers, number of members and chapters, year established, and a list of publications are also provided.

     The book has a number of quirks. Entries are numbered consecutively throughout rather than section by section. The index is the only cross-reference, and there are no user instructions. The only introductory material is the mission statement of the National Organization for Rare Disorders and a brief guide on how to lobby members of Congress. Some of the disorders listed here are far from rare: Chlamydia is the most common sexually transmitted infection, and the incidence of tuberculosis has risen sharply in recent years.

     The 2d edition of *The Physicians Guide to Rare Diseases* (Dowden, 1995) has more information, costs less, is hardbound, and includes information on orphan drugs. *The Encyclopedia of Associations* and the directory links on MEDLINE provide listings for organizations. This directory is not a necessary purchase. [R: LJ, Dec 98, p. 86; BL, 1 Dec 98, pp. 687, 690]—**Barbara M. Bibel**

1448.   **Directory of Schools for Alternative and Complementary Health Care.** Karen Rappaport, ed. Phoenix, Ariz., Oryx Press, 1998. 250p. index. $49.50pa. ISBN 1-57356-110-X.

     Although interest in alternative and complementary health care has been increasing for some time, the establishment of the Office of Alternative Medicine within the National Institutes of Health in 1992 has, probably more than any other factor, increased the interest of not only young people, but also those making a career change, in seeking careers in alternative medicine. This directory provides information on some 675 schools and colleges in the United States and Canada that offer training for careers in many areas of alternative health care, including acupuncture, biofeedback, herbal medicine, and homeopathy. Essays on some of the better-known fields, written by experienced practitioners, and a subject index precede the directory part of the book.

Directory information is arranged by state in the United States and by province in Canada and includes such typical items as name and address of the institution, administrative staff, average enrollment, accreditation and approval or licensing board, admission requirements, and cost, although not all institutions provided the complete information requested. Particularly important for this type of directory is the list of national organizations and accrediting agencies that follows the directory information. It does not, however, include state agencies, which usually set the standards for state licensing in these areas. Both the editor's introduction and the essays on particular fields, however, caution prospective students to investigate the qualifications for practitioners in the locale where they intend to practice. Other sections of the directory that enhance its usefulness are a brief bibliography, the indexes by name of school and by specialization, a list of abbreviations used, and a glossary.

Although the editor states that the directory information was taken mainly from questionnaires sent to schools, with a smaller portion coming from professional organizations, there is no indication of the criteria used for selecting the schools except that medical schools and schools offering programs in the expressive arts, transpersonal psychology, and psychospiritual fields were excluded. Because not all schools were included, it would be helpful to know if a particular school was omitted because it did not respond to the questionnaire or for reasons that had to do with the quality of the school. Nevertheless, because of the uniqueness of the subject field, the ease of access to directory information, and the added material included, this directory should be valuable to public and academic libraries, particularly on the community college level where many students are seeking career information that might lead them from an AA degree into an area of health care that is becoming increasingly popular. [R: BL, July 98, p. 1904; Choice, Oct 98, p. 294]—**Lucille Whalen**

1449. Janoulis, Brenda H., and Jason F. Janoulis. **State Medical Licensure Guidelines 1998: Information Manual for MD and DO Physicians in the United States of America.** Atlanta, Ga., St. Barthelemy Press, 1998. 78p. $175.00 spiralbound. ISBN 1-887617-59-0.

This directory, compiled from individual states' applications, rules, and instructions, is intended to provide a single source for finding how states' regulations for licensure differ and what requirements must be met for each. A single-page summary is provided for each state, with a list of criteria and a column for that state's requirements in that area. Examples include years of postgraduate training required, acceptable exams, documentation required, and fees. Some criteria are not included for all states. No explanation is provided for what the various criteria mean (e.g., "Copy of CV required?"). Perhaps it is assumed correctly that most applicants would know the meaning of these terms, but there might be exceptions, especially among foreign medical graduates. Assorted tables at the book's beginning may help, such as a list of abbreviations and their meanings, lists of relevant accrediting and testing organizations with their addresses, and an explanation of some examinations. A tentative test schedule for 1998 and 1999 is provided, although without locations; there is also a table of licensure processing time guidelines by state. Because licensing procedures are subject to change, a prospective applicant should verify current regulations when he or she writes for applications. This book should be most useful to those considering where to apply and what requirements will be needed. This work provides information not available elsewhere in one place and is therefore recommended for libraries serving health services professions and large public libraries.
—**Marit S. MacArthur**

1450. Nagy, Andrea, and Paula Bilstein. **The Best Medical Schools.** 1998 ed. New York, Random House, 1997. 332p. index. $20.00pa. ISBN 0-679-77782-2. ISSN 1067-2176.

Guides to medical schools are popular in many libraries, and many are available with different emphases. This one is unique in that it involves input from more than 6,000 students, who rate their schools on such areas as curriculum, teaching, and student life. Two pages are included for each school, including information on admissions selection factors and financial aid. A sidebar for each school provides Gourman report ratings, application information, tuition and fees, average grade point average and Medical College Admission Test (MCAT) scores, statistical figures on the makeup of the student body, and other practical information. Both medical and osteopathic colleges are included.

Introductory chapters discuss general application guidelines, studying for the MCAT, and how to write an admissions essay. There is also relatively brief information on opportunities for women and minorities and a listing of schools with postbaccalaureate programs for adult students changing careers. Other chapters discuss financing medical school and successful interviewing skills. Another medical school guide, *Barron's Guide to Medical and Dental Schools* (Barron's Educational Series, 1997), includes dental schools, a sample MCAT test, and more supplementary information. *The Association of American Medical Colleges' Medical School Admission Requirements* (49th ed.; AAMC, 1998) contains official information supplied by the colleges. Because of its unique student input, *The Best Medical Schools* is a worthwhile purchase for public, academic, and medical libraries, even if they have other such guides.—**Marit S. MacArthur**

Electronic Resources

1451. **Mosby's Primary Care Medicine Rapid Reference.** [CD-ROM]. St. Louis, Mo., Mosby, 1997. Minimum system requirements (Windows version): IBM or compatible 386. CD-ROM drive (double-speed recommended). Windows 3.1. 4MB RAM. VGA or compatible video graphics card (256 colors). Mouse. Minimum system requirements (Macintosh version): 68030 or higher processor. CD-ROM drive (double-speed recommended). System 7.1. 4MB RAM. Color monitor with display resolution of 640x480 with 256 colors. Mouse. $129.95.

This CD-ROM product from Mosby is the combination of the 2d edition of *Textbook of General Medicine and Primary Care Medicine* by John Noble (Mosby, 1995), more than 50,000 Primary Care Medline abstracts, plus the 1997 edition of *Physicians GenRx*. Considering the 1996 *Textbook of Primary Care Medicine* was selling at around $90, comparatively speaking, the cost of this software sounds like a bargain. And the use of this product is quite transparent for the general public.

Rapid Access Medical Information (RAMI) software is used for the three databases. RAMI provides two button bars. One button bar is to provide access to the most commonly used features, such as Save, Print, Back, History, Picture/Table, Notes, Bookmark, Hide/Show, Split, Search, Results, Match, and Word buttons, and the other button bar is specific to the database being viewed. There is a Mega Index button for searching the index in the *Textbook* and *GenRx* at the same time. The Search button is a powerful engine that does rapid Boolean searching with the search results displaying instantaneously. Extra features include the use of the notepad, preferences, hyperlinks, three-dimensional structures, and more.

For the textbook, an additional 29 chapters are added exclusively for this CD-ROM version from "common eye examination" to "cultural issues." This database intends to offer comprehensive primary care practice for modern physicians. A Lab Values button opens the appendix document on this topic. A Chapter Heading button allows access to other chapters. Physicians GenRx shows buttons on interaction tools, drug names, keyword index, pharmacological class, therapeutic class, indications for use, imprint index, and drug topic. The content is arranged slightly different from the printed version.

The Primary Care Medline abstracts are pulled from 31 commonly read medical journals, such as *American Journal of Medicine*, *Chest*, *JAMA*, and *Science*. However, the dates of the articles range from 1988 to 1995 only. A handy user's guide comes with this product, explaining "how to" on various buttons except on how to install. For the practitioners who prefer CD-ROM products, this might be a good resource to enhance their practice. The Web version of these databases would be even more convenient for keeping the state-of-the-art information more up-to-date.—**Polin P. Lei**

Handbooks and Yearbooks

1452. **Ear, Nose, and Throat Disorders Sourcebook.** Linda M. Shin and Karen Bellenir, eds. Detroit, Omnigraphics, 1998. 576p. index. (Health Reference Series, v.37). $78.00. ISBN 0-7808-0206-3.

The introduction to this reference notes that ear, nose, and throat (ENT) problems are one of the most common reasons for people to seek medical care. The editors thus establish the importance of this book, an addition to an extensive series of texts for the layperson on health care and medical problems. The book begins with a glossary of terms, descriptions of the various ENT specialists, and a directory of associated organizations. The nearly 70 chapters provide comprehensive coverage of ENT problems, from minor to serious. As appropriate, each chapter provides definitions of terms, explanations of the problems, and a discussion of the treatments available, from home care to radical surgery. The information in each chapter is reprinted from reputable sources, including government agencies and ENT specialty organizations. The chapters are referenced, and directory or Internet addresses are included for further information.

Only a few negatives deter from the overall good quality of the reference. A few chapters are more appropriate for physicians than the general public. Second, more comprehensive coverage of hearing loss should have been included. The editors note that this problem is covered in another volume in the series. Finally, explanations and illustrations of the anatomy and physiology of the system are scattered throughout the text. One introductory chapter on this topic would have been more helpful for the reader. Overall, this sourcebook is helpful for the consumer seeking information on ENT issues. It is recommended for public libraries. [R: BL, 1 Dec 98, p. 698]

—**Mary Ann Thompson**

1453.   **Making Wise Medical Decisions: How to Get the Information You Need.** Lexington, Mass., Resources for Rehabilitation, 1998. 224p. index. $39.95pa. ISBN 0-929718-21-6.

This volume provides an overly generalized guide for health care consumers. The book has 11 chapters and 2 appendixes. Each chapter follows a standard format—questions to ask the health care providers, publications relevant to the topic, and organizations providing additional information or assistance. Chapter 1 directs health care consumers to appropriate information sources, including the library as a resource. Chapter 2 helps individuals locate suitable health care, listing questions to ask a potential health care provider and organizations to verify credentials. Additional chapters address understanding medical tests, how to work with a hospital, resources for comprehending pharmaceutical issues, and sections on health care for special populations (e.g., children, elderly, chronic conditions). Chapter 10 discusses somewhat controversial issues in health care—mammograms, prostate care, hysterectomies—defining the controversy and supplying resources to help individuals make the best personal decision. The appendixes provide an additional list of organizations and a list of publications from the publisher of this work titled "Resources for Rehabilitation."

Although not comprehensive for all diseases and illnesses, this handbook provides a general starting point for conscientious health care consumers. It cannot, however, replace a good reference on individual diseases and health concerns.—**Susan D. Strickland**

1454.   **The Patient's Guide to Medical Tests.** By the Faculty Members of The Yale University School of Medicine. New York, Houghton Mifflin, 1997. 620p. illus. index. $40.00. ISBN 0-395-76536-6.

It is refreshing to note that Barrett Zaret, a prolific writer and editor of many books and journal articles on cardiology, edited a timely collaborative reference text on diagnostic tests for patients. There are many books published in this category, but this guide is a good source for patients. There are 29 chapters, and each chapter is on a special subject that is written by a Yale faculty member who is an expert in the area. Medical testing is important and is a part of the diagnostic procedure. Required medical tests assist in the decision-making process. However, many medical tests are costly and unknown to patients, who are hesitant to ask for explanations. Thus, this book is useful and necessary to provide relevant answers to patients and other health professionals on screening guidelines, blood tests, cancer screening, fasting for the glucose tolerance test, and many other medical tests.

There are 2 parts in this book. The 1st part is the general overview that includes patients' rights and informed consent, tests for people without symptoms, diagnostic imaging, and an overview of diagnostic laboratory testing. Part 2 contains 25 chapters on specific tests relating to various anatomical parts and systems such as, the heart, vascular, respiratory, digestive, endocrine, reproductive, renal, musculoskeletal, immune, blood, skin, nervous, genetic, vision, and others. Uncommon medical tests that are not included in this source are searchable in other laboratory tests and handbooks. An added bonus of this tool is the appendix that covers tests that patients can do at home. There are essential illustrations to further explain the medical terminology. Each test is presented in a standard format that includes general information, where it is done, when is the result ready, other names, purpose, how it works, preparation, test procedure, after the test, and factors affecting the test. Each chapter in part 2 begins with a clinical case study that leads to the tests and the outcome. The index is well done and easy to use.

This reference tool was presented to several medical students and practicing physicians for locating tests of their choice. They have also found this book invaluable. Every library that provides consumers' or patient care information should acquire this copy to provide practical and reliable answers on medical tests. [R: RUSQ, Summer 98, pp. 375-376; LJ, Aug 97, p. 80]—**Polin P. Lei**

1455.   Segen, Joseph C., and Joseph Stauffer. **The Patient's Guide to Medical Tests: Everything You Need to Know About the Tests Your Doctor Prescribes.** New York, Facts on File, 1998. 419p. index. $29.95; $17.95pa. ISBN 0-8160-3471-0; 0-8160-3530-Xpa.

The Patient's Guide to Medical Tests by Facts of File is similar to another publication titled *Everything You Need to Know About Medical Tests* by Springhouse Publishers (see ARBA 97, entry 1337). However, the newer publication contains newer tests that were not available a few years earlier. The introduction informs the patient about specimen collection, what affects the results, where tests are performed, and costs. It alphabetically lists the tests, including a description, patient preparation, procedure, specimen, reference range, abnormal values, cost, and comments. Also, it contains a glossary of unfamiliar medical terms as well as an index. Many doctors today do not have the time or inclination to inform consumers why medical tests are needed. This publication gives the consumer the opportunity to make informed medical decisions. The book is highly recommended for all consumer health collections in public libraries.—**Theresa Maggio**

Alternative Medicine

1456.   **The Complete Book of Symptoms and Treatments: Your Comprehensive Guide to the Safety and Effectiveness of Alternative and Complementary Medicine for Common Ailments.** By Roland Bettschart and others. Edzard Ernst, ed. Rockport, Mass., Element Books, 1998. 953p. index. $24.95pa. ISBN 1-86204-424-4.

This book neither promotes nor condemns alternative and complementary medicine. Instead, it attempts, through description and a rating system, to provide persons considering the use of remedies or techniques from this burgeoning field of health care with information about orthodox and complementary treatment for common complaints, enabling the consumer to make responsible and objective assessments.

A panel of experts based its ratings on "available published data" about what the therapies are supposed to do, how well they work, and potential risks. The problem is that remedies and systems of medicine, such as traditional Chinese medicine (often called alternative), are backed by centuries of tradition, but not much clinical research, so there are a lot of "cautions" and "unknowns." For example, Asians and Europeans are far more experienced with phytotherapeutics (herbal remedies) than Americans, who are now spending millions on herbs, perhaps with only "biased" information on the label.

This book is basically a translation of a popular 1995 German text. The 1st part of the book describes common ailments, by type of complaint or organs affected, and summarizes the orthodox approach and alternative or complementary therapies. Each chapter concludes with tables listing specific herbal remedies, including the benefits and risks. Often the caveat is to get professional advice from one's regular physician before turning to other "experts" or trying self-treatment. In this sense "complementary" means "collaborative" or "supportive" rather than entirely different, as the older term "alternative" may suggest.

The 2d part of the book is a fascinating compendium of the many kinds of therapies used in complementary medicine, such as acupuncture and reflexology, with history, rationale, risks, and potential benefits. The total body of scientific knowledge available today is the measure for rating each therapy. Suggestions are given for choosing a reputable therapist who should offer a treatment plan and limited trial as well as personal assistance.

A 3d section discusses the diagnostic techniques used in complementary medicine, with effectiveness claims by its practitioners. This is followed by a list of professional organizations in the United Kingdom, Australia, and the United States.

As an overview of complementary medicine in its many forms and a comprehensive guide for choosing therapies, this book ranks far above other available paperbacks. It is well indexed and cross-referenced, rather scholarly in approach, and well suited for its intended users.—**Harriette M. Cluxton**

1457.   Marti, James, with Andrea Hine. **The Alternative Health & Medicine Encyclopedia.** 2d ed. Detroit, Gale, 1998. 462p. index. $47.00. ISBN 0-7876-0073-3.

The author's stated objective in this 2d edition of *The Alternative Health & Medicine Encyclopedia* is to present fully the different specialized therapies that fall under the umbrella of alternative medicine. The format of the 1st edition has not changed. Chapter 1 presents a brief overview of 15 medical systems in alternative medicine, such as acupuncture, chiropractic medicine, hypnosis, and yoga. Also discussed are other specialized alternative therapies, such as music therapy and massage; unique to the 2d edition are entries for aromatherapy, flower essences, hypothermia, and ozone therapy.

Chapters 2 through 8 describe the treatment components of alternative medicine, such as diet and botanical medicines. The remaining 11 chapters discuss treatments for specific disorders. Here, for example, the reader can identify a botanical therapy for the treatment of prostate enlargement in the chapter on common male health problems.

As in the 1st edition (see ARBA 96, entry 1716) much of the emphasis is on generally accepted principles of good health practices. Curiously, the index to the 2d edition is briefer and less detailed than that of the 1st edition. Despite the author's claim that the primary source materials for this book are available in most medical libraries, there are a number of citations to various newsletters and other forms of gray literature. Although this is a useful resource for general reference collections, there is not enough additional content in the 2d edition to warrant its purchase for most libraries already owning the 1st edition.—**Michael Weinberg**

1458.   **Nerys Purchon's Handbook of Natural Healing.** By Nerys Purchon. St. Leonards, Australia, Sue Hines Books; distr., Chicago, Independent Publishers Group, 1998. 412p. $19.95pa. ISBN 1-86448-645-7.

With people in the United States spending more than $1.5 billion a year on herbal products alone, it is no wonder that books on natural healing have become so popular. Many of these books contain much of the same information. The present work, however, brings a somewhat different perspective to the subject because its author grew up in Wales, which has a long tradition of herbal knowledge, and where she and her family found all the remedies needed for health and healing readily available near their home. After migrating to Australia, she started an herb-growing business and has written several books on various types of natural healing.

The handbook focuses mainly on herbal therapies but also includes information on other forms of natural healing, such as massage and meditation. It is arranged alphabetically but not by just herbs and therapies. Interspersed throughout the texts are various conditions for which these natural therapies are recommended, such as emphysema, hepatitis, and shingles. Furthermore, there are entries for the maintenance of good health, including sections on skin care and liver care. Although there are variations in the entries, for the herbal therapies there is generally a brief section on the part of the herb used, how it works, and conditions for which it is used. For most ailments, there is a description of the condition followed by sections on internal treatment, daily supplements, essential oil treatment, and homeopathic treatment.

Although there is a bibliography at the end of the volume, there is no index. The alphabetic arrangement makes an index less necessary, but it would probably simplify the finding of specific information. The work has a great deal of useful material that is made more easily accessible by its attractive page layout and use of different typefaces for headings. Because of the handbook's somewhat different viewpoint, its easily readable information, and its convenient arrangement, it should be a welcome addition to both public libraries and those academic libraries having alternative health collections.—**Lucille Whalen**

1459.   Null, Gary. **The Complete Encyclopedia of Natural Healing.** New York, Kensington Publishing, 1998. 612p. index. $35.00. ISBN 1-57566-258-2.

This hardbound encyclopedia consists of 2 alphabetically arranged sections. The 1st section is a list of medical conditions with a short essay discussing causes, symptoms, and treatments. The 2d section addresses various modalities popular among alternative medicine practitioners. The index is comprehensive and easy to use. There are no appendixes, no bibliography, no additional reading lists, and no footnotes or endnotes. Readers wanting more information must fend for themselves. The content is extremely broad and superficial. There is an abundance of anecdotal patient stories, some with questionable connections to the topic at hand. The author addresses his newest book to confused health care consumers to give them a second opinion. The introduction claims that "every natural alternative will be here for you to refer to." Not only is his stated scope impossible to achieve, but his authority to make this claim is suspect. Neither the book jacket nor the Websites give any clue to the author's educational history except to display "Ph.D." prominently on the cover. After extensive searching, this reviewer found that the author's educational credentials appear to be sadly lacking. It will be wiser to spend limited library funds for reference books in this area on works that have better documentation and authority.

—**Deborah D. Nelson**

1460.   Shealy, C. Norman. **The Illustrated Encyclopedia of Healing Remedies.** Rockport, Mass., Element Books, 1998. 496p. illus. index. $49.95. ISBN 1-86204-187-3.

Ancient humans practiced healing methods on each other until they got well or died, then made a note of the recipe and passed it down through the generations. Now, due to tedious research and careful thought, we can apply natural healing therapies thousands of years old to modern circumstances. Shealy has compiled spirited historical information on eight healing methods: ayurveda, herbalism, homeopathy, aromatherapy, traditional Chinese medicine, folk remedies, flower remedies, and vitamins and minerals and how and why they work.

Part 1, "Therapies and Healing Remedy Sources," explains how the body is physically connected from the big toe to the crown, and how influences such as attitude, pollution, planetary alignment, posture, diet, occupations, and surroundings affect our health. The five elements of the universe—space (respiration), air (movement), fire (intelligence), water (blood), and earth (bones)—are present in each of us, and when these elements are in balance we are healthy. These concepts could be complicated and intense, yet Shealy's text, illustrations, scope, resources, and sidebars make this reference work easy to absorb and understand.

Part 2, "Treating Common Ailments," deals with more than 200 disorders such as addictions, obsessions, compulsions, and phobias; troublesome lungs, teeth, and livers; and problems with circulatory, digestive, musculaskeletal, immune, endocrine, and reproductive systems. *The Illustrated Encyclopedia of Healing Remedies* contains ordinary and obscure treatments and herbal recipes and instructions on how to make salves, ointments, tinctures, and decoctions. It also includes a section of common ailments in children and the elderly. What Shealy has shared with us is more than health information, it is a healthy attitude.—**Mary Pat Boian**

1461.   Wardwell, Joyce A. **The Herbal Home Remedy Book: Simple Recipes for Tinctures, Teas, Salves, Tonics, and Syrups.** Pownal, Vt., Storey Communications, 1998. 169p. illus. index. $14.95pa. ISBN 1-58017-016-1.

Wardell is a self-taught herbalist and director of a nonprofit sustainable lifestyle organization. The 1st chapter offers practical advice on plant identification, even for the botanically challenged; gathering plants (with an eye toward conservation); and storage. Other chapters address selection of ingredients and equipment; making teas, tinctures, salves, vinegars, and syrups; drawings and descriptions of 25 useful herbs and their uses; stocking the home medicine cabinet; blending herbs; an alphabetic arrangement of symptoms and remedies; and finally, a discussion of the spirit of herbalism. Wardell cautions readers that information in the book is not to be construed as medical advice and that anyone should discuss health concerns with their primary health care practitioner. The book is folksy and warm, with careful directions and recipes for making teas, salves, syrups, and tonics, which are interspersed with Native American folktales. Sidebars warn about potential problems, cite proverbs, and provide common sense advice. There is a helpful list of suggested books for a home remedy library, which is organized by topic, a list of suppliers of materials, and educational organizations. There are also a table of metric conversions and a useful index. *The Herbal Home Remedy Book* is recommended for personal or consumer health collections.—**Constance Rinaldo**

Ophthalmology

1462.   **Physicians' Desk Reference for Ophthalmology 1998.** Montvale, N.J., Medical Economics Data, 1997. 320p. illus. $49.95. ISBN 1-56363-254-3.

The 26th edition of *PDR for Ophthalmology* joins a family of nine Physicians' Desk References in book format, many of which are also available through www.medecinteractive.com. It is important to remember that all information—retained, updated, or new—is furnished by the manufacturers; the publishers collect, organize, and distribute this to interested professionals.

There are 4 indexes: manufacturers, product name, product category, and active ingredients. The initial sections cover pharmaceuticals used in ophthalmology arranged in tabular form by type (e.g., ocular decongestants), suture materials, and lenses, among others. Only a few photographs appear in the identification guide. This edition combines pharmaceutical and equipment product information into the main portion of the book where they are listed alphabetically by manufacturer, now including Storz Opthalmics replacing Wyeth-Ayerst. Intraocular products are in a separate section. A list of poison control has been added.

Although some over-the-counter preparations such as "Hypotears" are included, and laypersons may be interested in some of the background material on lenses or vision standards, this is an indispensable reference designed for eye specialists.—**Harriette M. Cluxton**

1463.   **Quick Reference Glossary of Eye Care Terminology.** 2d ed. Hoffman, Joseph, ed. Thorofare, N.J., Slack, 1998. 224p. (The Basic Bookshelf for Eyecare Professionals). $22.00pa. ISBN 1-55642-370-5.

Designed for the eye care clinician and student, the goal of this small book is to define the ophthalmic terms most often used in eye care clinics and the literature of ophthalmology. As such, this eye care terminology book is directed to the same audience as *Dictionary of Eye Terminology* (see ARBA 98, entry 1553), now in its 3d edition.

With a similar audience and goal in common, a comparison of the two titles is in order. Both books are in paperback format to give easy portability for the busy student or clinician. The spiral binding of *Dictionary of Eye Terminology* makes it a bit more convenient to handle because the selected page will easily stay open. Pricing is similar, with both books in the $20 to $25 range. *Quick Reference Glossary of Eye Care Terminology* has a separate section of abbreviations, which is useful.

The most dramatic difference between the two works lies in the number of entries in each book, with *Quick Reference Glossary of Eye Care Terminology* containing less that one-half the entries found in *Dictionary of Eye Terminology*. This more comprehensive coverage clearly makes the latter title the better choice for medical schools, clinics, and other institutions offering ophthalmic programs.—**Elaine F. Jurries**

Pediatrics

1464.   **American Academy of Pediatrics Guide to Your Child's Symptoms: The Official, Complete Home Reference, Birth Through Adolescence.** Donald Schiff and Steven P. Shelov, eds. New York, Villard/ Random House, 1997. 256p. index. $18.95pa. ISBN 0-375-75257-9.

As we approach the millennium, the American Academy of Pediatrics is now giving parents a reference guide to a child's symptoms. This is a no-nonsense book written and reviewed by members of the American Academy of Pediatrics. This guide is one of a series of guides for parents developed by this Academy. The included information is derived from the consensus of accepted pediatric practice. However, this book does not provide the ultimate solution to caring for children in need of medical care. It is a means to provide the needed and ever-changing information. This reference guide is divided into 2 sections. One section is a list of more than 100 most common childhood symptoms, and the other section is an illustrated first aid manual and safety guide.

The 1st section is presented in 3 parts according to age: early infancy (first three months), later infancy and childhood, and adolescence. In each area, the symptoms are listed alphabetically according to their common names. If the user looks up fever, a general and clear description is given. It even mentions normal temperature variations according to time of day. The chart following is easy to follow. Each symptom is described in general, then proceeds with advice on when to call your pediatrician, questions to consider, possible causes, action to take, or illustrated boxes.

The 2d section is an illustrated first aid manual and safety guide, which is a reference tool for parents dealing with unexpected emergencies or minor mishaps. This information is valuable for parents to administer first aid before seeing the pediatrician in case of emergency. Again, there are 2 sections with this segment and the 1st section is divided into 2 parts: how to administer first aid and frequently used first aid measures. The 2d section is a guide to safety and prevention and a guide to food safety.

The index at the end is well put together and thorough. Every parent with small children should keep one of these guides by the Academy at home. Public or school libraries might consider adding this item for reference.
—**Polin P. Lei**

1465.   **The Cambridge Encyclopedia of Human Growth and Development.** Stanley J. Ulijaszek, Francis E. Johnston, and Michael A. Preece, eds. New York, Cambridge University Press, 1998. 497p. illus. index. $95.00. ISBN 0-521-56046-2.

This book has an introduction and a history of human growth and development. The contents of this publication include information on measurement and assessment, patterns of human growth, genetics of growth, fetal growth, postnatal growth and maturation, behavioral and cognitive development, clinical growth abnormalities, the human life span, and the future. A favorite feature is the excellent biographies of people important in the field of human development. There are many excellent charts and graphs for help in understanding the complex subject matter. Although the encyclopedia includes many technical terms, there is a glossary in the back as well as a good index and bibliographies. *The Cambridge Encyclopedia of Human Growth and Development* is best suited for reference collections in larger public libraries and in academic libraries. [R: BL, 15 Oct 98, p. 437]

—**Theresa Maggio**

Psychiatry

1466.   **Handbook of Child and Adolescent Psychology. Volumes 5-7.** Joseph D. Noshpitz, ed. New York, John Wiley, 1998. 3v. $125.00/set. ISBN 0-471-19329-1.

This set expands the old *Basic Handbook of Child Psychiatry* by two new volumes, plus a revision of the outdated volume 5. The new title reflects the growth within child psychiatry and the shifting concern from medical issues of development and syndromes of actual illness toward how children and adolescents can be enabled through early intervention and treatment, improvement in parenting, and cooperative efforts of other health care workers to achieve a better life and adjustment to our changing world.

The lists of contributors reads like a "who's who" of psychiatric clinicians and instructors, plus some other specialists in related fields, such as psychology, education, and pediatrics. Chapters are arranged under sections in each volume and are easily located through the detailed table of contents. Volume 5 deals with studies on assessment and evaluation of children, adolescents, and their families. Volume 6 considers basic science issues in the field and the current status of various treatment techniques. The concluding book, intriguingly called "Advances and New Directions," discusses the impact of sociocultural events, topics such as prevention and the process of consultation with other professionals, forensic issues, and handling emergency assessment and intervention, as well as professional issues in child and adolescent psychiatry.

This scholarly trio of books was carefully compiled and subjected to much revision and review, even by editors of the other volumes and the late editor Noshpitz. Bibliographies are extensive. It is a major contribution to the literature of child and adolescent psychiatry, containing much practical material useful to its practitioners, students, various mental health workers, and those who represent other cooperating professions. There are some articles in the final volume, such as those involving young persons who have witnessed violence (as in the current school shootings), that may be of interest to general readers, but some knowledge of mental health activities is really needed for understanding the vocabulary and discussions in these impressive volumes.—**Harriette M. Cluxton**

Specific Diseases and Conditions

General Works

1467.   **The Complete Directory for People with Chronic Illness.** 3d ed. Leslie Mackenzie, ed. Lakeville, Conn., Grey House Publishing, 1998. 1009p. index. $180.00pa. ISBN 0-939300-93-1.

Millions of Americans suffer from a wide variety of chronic diseases and need access to the thousands of agencies, societies, organizations, and educational groups that have been created to meet the informational needs of those suffering from these ailments. This 3d edition of Grey House Publishing's major reference tool seeks to meet the needs of patients and their families by providing "a comprehensive overview of the support services and information resources available for people diagnosed with a chronic illness."

This important reference guide is arranged into 77 chapters, each covering a unique chronic disease or disease grouping. These chapters vary from specific diseases (e.g., tuberculosis, hepatitis, ulcerative colitis) to broad disease categories (e.g., allergies, birth defects, substance abuse). The following types of information are included in each chapter: a very brief description of the chronic illness; available literature (books, journals, newsletters, videos); national and state associations and agencies; support groups; libraries; and research centers. Descriptions of organizations include address, contact person, telephone number, and e-mail and homepage addresses. All this information is provided by the listed groups, and the publisher has not checked its accuracy. This new edition added more than 5,000 entries but deleted some 3,000 former citations, added e-mail and homepage addresses

whenever possible, and included coverage of 2 more chronic illnesses—aging and fibromyalgia. Any library that wants to provide reference services concerning assistance to patients and their families confronting life with a chronic disease, from public libraries to medical research centers, must include this volume in its collection.
—**Jonathon Erlen**

AIDS

1468.   **The AIDS Crisis: A Documentary History.** Douglas A. Feldman and Julia Wang Miller, eds. Westport, Conn., Greenwood Press, 1998. 266p. index. (Primary Documents in American History and Contemporary Issues Series). $49.95. ISBN 0-313-28715-5.

This text, geared toward high school and college students, is the latest in a series on controversial contemporary issues from Greenwood Press. The focus is not on medicine and science, but rather the "social, political, psychological, public health and cultural" aspects of the history of AIDS. The book provides short excerpts from accepted professional or governmental publications and is organized under 9 comprehensive topical chapters ranging from the history of the epidemic to ethics, developing countries, special populations, and the future. A full range of viewpoints are represented. The editors provide an introductory chapter, an additional introduction to each topical chapter, and a brief comment on each entry. The full citation for each excerpt is given, and each chapter ends with a suggested reference list, which allows the user to pursue the topic in more depth. The book is well indexed for ease of use, and is written at a level appropriate to the target audience. A glossary of terms is included for those unfamiliar with the complex language of AIDS.

One concern about his work is that some students might see this reference as an ending point. This reviewer would hope that students are encouraged by this text to read the entire primary source rather than relying on the excerpts. The book then becomes much like an encyclopedia, a starting point for their learning. *The AIDS Crisis* is highly recommended for college and high school libraries.—**Mary Ann Thompson**

1469.   **HIV/AIDS Internet Information Sources and Resources.** Jeffrey T. Huber, ed. Binghamton, N.Y., Harrington Park Press/Haworth Press, 1998. 165p. index. $34.95; $19.95pa. ISBN 0-7890-0544-1; 1-56023-117-3pa.

This volume is both a collection of essays dealing with the state of information regarding HIV and AIDS as well as a valuable reference tool that analyzes and profiles information that is accessible via the Internet and World Wide Web. It was also simultaneously published under the same title as a special issue of *Health Care on the Internet* (1998). Among the topics and perspectives covered are strategies for creation of Websites by AIDS community-based organizations, a profile of AIDS service organizations on the Internet, strategies for networking of organizations, the use of Websites as educational tools aimed at at-risk populations, resources available for HIV-positive children and adolescents, Websites that provide information relevant to HIV and women, HIV-related news and discussion groups and their use as support tools, resources and services available through the National Institutes of Health, relevant resources from the Centers for Disease Control, Internet resources pertaining to complementary and alternative medicine and HIV/AIDS, Internet resources that can be used for clinical management of HIV disease, and Internet resources regarding the development of antiretroviral drugs. A full index complements the essays.

Each of the essays is written by an individual with expertise in the area presented. As appropriate, full bibliographic references and URLs are given. All essays are well organized and quite readable. All in all, the work is a valuable addition to any reference collection, given the abundance of information presented—to be updated in time.—**Edmund F. SantaVicca**

1470.   Watstein, Sarah Barbara, with Karen Chandler. **The AIDS Dictionary.** New York, Facts on File, 1998. 340p. index. $45.00; $24.95pa. ISBN 0-8160-3149-5; 0-8160-3754-Xpa.

This work will find its greatest audience among students, social service and health care organizations, and health care workers and administrators. With more than 3,000 entries, this dictionary includes terms pertinent not only to the basic biological and medical aspects of the disease but also to the financial, legal, psychological, emotional, political, and social aspects of HIV and AIDS. Most of the entries are short (5 to 10 lines), whereas others are quite lengthy. Cross-references to related entries are given throughout. A valuable quality is the inclusion of terms that may not be currently used but that are found in the early literature of the disease.

Appendixes include a list of frequently used abbreviations; a statistical profile of the epidemic through 1996; and a select list of resources that includes associations and organizations, education and training centers, journals and newsletters, and a comprehensive list of Internet and World Wide Web sites available on a variety of topics. A separate three-page bibliography completes the volume.

The authors are careful to indicate that this work is not exhaustive and that the fields of HIV and AIDS are constantly changing. Keeping this in mind, it is still hard to imagine an academic, public, or high school library that would not benefit from adding this tool to its reference collection. [R: BL, 15 Sept 98, p. 256; Choice, Nov 98, pp. 498-499]—**Edmund F. SantaVicca**

Diabetes

1471.   **Diabetes A to Z: What You Need to Know About Diabetes—Simply Put.** 3d ed. Peter Banks and Sherrye Landrum, eds. Alexandria, Va., American Diabetes Association, 1997. 195p. illus. index. $11.95pa. ISBN 0-945448-96-1.

Diabetes A to Z is described in the preface as an encyclopedia of diabetes. This book is supposed to tell one everything one needs to know about diabetes in clear and simple terms. It is interesting to note the disclaimer of the American Diabetes Association on the verso of the title page about the accuracy of the information in this book. According to the preface, "the information in each entry will help you understand how to balance your diabetes care with a full and active lifestyle." Helpful tips for coping with the social and emotional challenges are presented for the person with diabetes. Much of the information in this book is not supported by the newest writings and research on diabetes care. Some of the newer writings suggest high protein, low fat, low carbohydrate diets for treating diabetes patients. There is no mention in the book that diet can reverse its damaging effects. After reading all the possibilities of complications from the disease, a newly diagnosed diabetic could find the information in this book terrifying.

The encyclopedic style of the book makes it easy to use. The charts and tables are easy to read and serve as a helpful guide through the topics. The alphabetic listings provide quick, easy access to the subjects. The fact that the American Diabetes Association does not support the content in this book, although it is their own publication, is reason enough not to purchase it.—**Betty J. Morris**

Leprosy

1472.   Wood, Corinne Shear. **An Annotated Bibliography on Leprosy.** Lewiston, N.Y., Edwin Mellen Press, 1997. 176p. (Studies in Health and Human Services, v.30). $89.95. ISBN 0-7734-8441-8.

A carefully prepared work published by Edwin Mellen Press, this reference source presents an up-to-date bibliography and a "panoramic view" on Hansen's disease. It appears that each reference is reviewed and selected for medical professionals, social scientists, and for those who wish to know more about this disease. The author admits that this book is not intended to be comprehensive in scope, but includes collective contributions on international publications and journal articles from different global sites such as India, Australia, Germany, Switzerland, and Africa.

The work features 14 chapters. The first few chapters are on leprosy related to historical, social, and biblical concerns. A few references in these chapters were published in the eighteenth century and are worth exploring. For the clinical aspects, there are chapters on research and fieldwork, treatment, diagnosis and rehabilitation, epidemiology, compliance studies, control and prevention, and immunology. Women and children with leprosy are separately listed. In addition, publications on biographies, literature, and texts on leprosy are listed to enlighten the curious mind. However, the health education chapter could be enriched a little. Overall, the concise annotations help to define the scope of the items and to identify the source country of work performed. The author clarifies whether the annotations are the original author's summary or an abstract. The index of authors is alphabetic and thorough. However, it would have been useful if a list of keywords had been included. In general, this is a great resource and a good compilation of publications on this disease. Academic libraries should consider acquiring this title to add to the reference collection. [R: Choice, July/Aug 98, p. 1834]—**Polin P. Lei**

Pain

1473. **Pain Sourcebook.** Allan R. Cook, ed. Detroit, Omnigraphics, 1998. 667p. illus. index. (Health Reference Series, v.32). $75.00. ISBN 0-7808-0213-6.

As pain is a virtually universal experience, this book will be a valuable addition to Omnigraphics' Health Reference Series. Addressed to the layperson, it is not intended to replace professional advice and treatment. Pain is too often ignored or undertreated by physicians, although this attitude is slowly changing. The book aims to help the reader understand the types of chronic and acute pain and conventional and alternative methods for its control. There are many practical suggestions for managing pain, especially in part 7.

The text is composed of brief discussions and recent reprints and excerpts, used by permission, from such publications as the *Mayo Clinic Newsletter*, *FDA Consumer*, and government and association reports. These are skillfully arranged under sections with general designations, such as "Headache," with subchapters covering more specific topics, such as "Tension-type Headache." Sources of material are clearly cited. Further references are frequently included, as well as brief glossaries of medical terms.

Although some items are moderately technical (e.g., pain assessment), the text is readable, easily understood, and well indexed. This excellent volume belongs in all patient education libraries, consumer health sections of public libraries, and many personal collections.—**Harriette M. Cluxton**

NURSING

1474. **Annual Guide to Graduate Nursing Education 1997.** Delroy Louden and Dawnette Jones, eds. New York, NLN Press, 1997. 132p. $27.95pa. ISBN 0-88737-749-1.

This guide has been a useful annual general reference tool for nursing students who seek higher education opportunities in the United States since 1995. The information collected is based on data collected by NLN Press from more than 300 master's and doctoral programs across the nation. Any data changes after November 1996 will not be reflected in this source. The publication is divided into 5 sections. Section 1 is the executive summary and contains tables of emerging infections. Sections 2 and 3 are the "Master's Degree Programs" and the "Doctoral Degree Programs." The programs are arranged alphabetically by state. The information about each program includes the name of school, address, director, telephone number, NLN accreditation, number of graduates in 1996, enrollments in 1996, length of study, program options, master of science in nursing (MSN) for nonregistered nurses with a degree in another field, tuition, and areas of study with specialization. Section 4 is on research projects funded by the National Institute of Nursing Research, with topics varying from wound healing to cancer. This is a good stop to locate institutions and contact persons for funding. Section 5 covers states that recognize clinical nurse specialists in advanced practice. This section lists the statute or regulation citation, requirements for recognition, and prescriptive authority. For the next update, perhaps it would be helpful if the Website of each institution offering programs is included so that readers can perform Net navigating as well. This publication is a must in academic nursing libraries.—**Polin P. Lei**

1475. Bua, Robert N. **The Inside Guide to American Nursing Homes.** New York, Warner Books, 1997. 1282p. $24.99. ISBN 0-446-67308-0.

This is an excellent yet affordable reference book to nursing homes in the United States. Its key features include rankings and ratings based on quality of care, insider tips on how to pay for nursing home care, comparison charts organized by state and county, and a 10-step program to help readers pick the best nursing home for their family. The publication is divided into 2 parts. The 1st section introduces the history of the rankings and ratings system as well as various aspects of the nursing home environment and health care decision-making and advance directives. The 2d section is devoted to the rankings and ratings for every certified nursing home in the United States. It is composed of the comparison charts, "best" nursing homes, most frequently violated nursing home standards, and state-by-state rankings and ratings. This publication is unique in its coverage and so inexpensive that almost any library could afford to purchase it.—**Theresa Maggio**

1476.   Janoulis, Brenda H., and Jason F. Janoulis. **Nursing Licensure Guidelines, 1998: State Information Manual for Nursing in the United States of America.** Atlanta, Ga., St. Barthelemy Press, 1998. 145p. $150.00 spiralbound. ISBN 1-887617-57-4.

Compiled from each state's nursing practices act, rules and regulations, and licensure applications and from Canadian provincial and territorial registration and licensing guidelines, this reference provides answers to the pertinent questions of licensure by examination or by endorsement. Licensure criteria and requirements for both registered nurses (RNs) and licensed practical nurses (LPNs) are listed alphabetically in a two-column question-and-answer format by state or province. Directory information for the specific licensing board is printed at the top of the page. Current fees, instructions to foreign nursing graduates, and special notes are included in the criteria.

A list of abbreviations, a statement on the issuance of licenses, information about the National Council Licensure Examination (NCLEX), a directory of the various boards of nursing, and a listing of nursing agencies and associations are also available. The authors have pulled into one source current information that will benefit the new nurse graduate and facilitate career moves for the practicing RN or LPN. Libraries supporting schools of nursing or large medical centers will find this resource useful.—**Vicki J. Killion**

1477.   **NLN Guide to Undergraduate RN Education.** 5th ed. Delroy Louden and Dawnette Jones, eds. New York, NLN Press, 1997. 295p. $19.95pa. ISBN 0-88737-737-8.

This guidebook provides pertinent information about nursing and nursing educational programs that lead to registered nurse (RN) licenses. The book is divided into 3 parts. The 1st part describes the profession of nursing, educational requirements, and various professional roles of the nurse. The 2d part is a directory of schools of nursing in the United States. The 3d part includes a brief glossary of terms commonly used in nursing. Unlike the earlier editions, this revised edition for the first time includes the information about the National League for Nursing (NLN) accredited nursing programs as well as the schools that offer nursing programs for nonregistered nurse students.

For those who are not familiar with, or are interested in the nursing profession, the first part of this book is of great relevance. It addresses the different educational requirements and responsibilities for a RN and a licensed practical nurse (LPN). Also included are information about the various career choices and benefits in the nursing field. The section on the 1,508 degree programs is divided into 4 areas: Associate Degree Program, Baccalaureate Degree Programs, Diploma Programs, and Baccalaureate Degree Programs Designed Exclusively for RNs. Under each program, the school information is then organized by state. The information provided in the entries is succinct and pertinent, such as the number of enrollment; affiliation; degrees offered; and availability of weekend, evening, and distance education programs. Those who are interested in further information are referred to the name of the contact person, school address, and telephone number. For anyone considering nursing as a profession, this guidebook is a valuable source of information. This directory is recommended for reference collections in public and academic libraries.—**Eveline L. Yang**

1478.   **Peterson's Guide to Nursing Programs.** 4th ed. Princeton, N.J., Peterson's Guides, 1998. 662p. index. $26.95pa. ISBN 1-56079-998-6. ISSN 1073-7820.

The American Association of Colleges of Nursing has again collaborated in producing this authoritative guide to approximately 700 United States and Canadian colleges with accredited nursing programs, from baccalaureate degrees through master's, doctoral, and beyond. Because health care delivery is changing so rapidly, nurses must be prepared educationally to serve in many sites outside the hospital and to assume a much greater role in primary and preventive care throughout the community, into which managed care and insurance companies are pushing the way health care will increasingly be provided.

In "The Nursing School Advisor," leaders of the profession describe the requirements for entering each program level and anticipated results, with some discussion of continuing education and distance learning opportunities. The main portion of the book contains self-submitted profiles of the colleges, organized by states. Information includes contact person, enrollment figures, expenses, entrance requirements, and degree requirements for each program offered. A separate section gives in-depth descriptions of some of these schools.

This guide goes far beyond providing help for young students considering nursing as a profession. It is also for practicing nurses desiring to upgrade their qualifications, to acquire another degree, or to study for specialties. Persons seeking to transfer to nursing as a second career will also find it useful. Many tailored programs, both full- and part-time, are available. This excellent educational directory belongs in school, public, and health science libraries, as well as in career counselors' and nursing department offices.—**Harriette M. Cluxton**

1479.   **Scholarships and Loans for Nursing Education 1997-1998.** New York, NLN Press, 1997. index. $16.95pa. ISBN 0-88737-730-0.

The previous title for this annual was *Scholarships and Loans for Beginning Education in Nursing* (1972-1983). Updated yearly, this reference tool attempts to identify as many funding sources as possible and to be comprehensive. The present edition has been increased from 124 pages to 141 pages, with the "Special Awards, Postdoctoral Study, and Research Grants" section expanded.

This book includes "all types of scholarships, awards, grants, fellowships, and loans for nursing education and nursing and health science research." Public, private, Canadian, governmental, academic, and profit or non-profit funding agencies are listed for those wishing to apply for financial assistance in pursing a nursing career. The programs are listed alphabetically. Each agency entry is annotated, with contact information listed. There are numeric codes that categorize the funding level, with "1" being "Beginning RN Study" to "7" being "Special Grants, Research, Traineeships, or Postdoctoral Work" to a special category for minority students. Codes are placed next to each heading to determine the level of appropriateness for the financial seekers.

The appendix is a listing of addresses of the State Boards of Nursing. The index is grouped by the numeric codes mentioned above, the NLN Constituent Leagues for Nursing, and nursing specialties. The readers can consult the index for a quick rundown of all the programs listed in the chapters. This book is a great reference source for those who seeking funding for their nursing education. To catch up with the recent advances in information technology, it would be ideal if NLN inserted e-mail addresses for contact and Website addresses for each funding organization. This little paperback, with solid information, can be easily carried around and is highly recommended for inclusion in any nursing library or health science library.—**Polin P. Lei**

PHARMACY AND
PHARMACEUTICAL SCIENCES

1480.   Friedman, J. M., and Janine E. Polifka. **The Effects of Neurologic and Psychiatric Drugs on the Fetus and Nursing Infant: A Handbook for Health Care Professionals.** Baltimore, Md., Johns Hopkins University Press, 1998. 369p. index. $49.50pa. ISBN 0-8018-5962-X.

Health care professionals face a number of challenges when a woman receiving medication for a mental health condition or abusing substances becomes pregnant. *Effects of Neurologic and Psychiatric Drugs on the Fetus and Nursing Infant* is an indispensable resource for health professionals in maternal and fetal or infant care. Experts in teratology and toxicology prepared the entries based on a thorough review of existing medical literature. Controlled and common illicit substances are included. Herbal preparations or alternative treatments with possible teratogenic effects are not included. Arrangement is alphabetic by drug or substance name. Cross-references are given from product names to main entries by agent. Entries include risk ratings and an evaluation of the amount and quality of existing research on effects. Short reviews cite relevant studies and include references lists of significant research. Special attention is given to the impact of maternal drug use on nursing infants. This title is recommended for libraries with an interest in maternal and fetal or infant care, due to the convenience and authority of information provided.—**Lynne M. Fox**

1481.   McLaughlin Jr., Arthur J., and Stuart R. Levine. **Respiratory Care Drug Reference.** Gaithersville, Md., Aspen, 1997. 383p. index. $45.00 pa. ISBN 0-8342-0788-5.

This guide is intended to provide health care professionals treating patients for respiratory or cardiovascular problems with a convenient, concise, easy-to-read, and portable guide to the information needed to treat patients. Drugs covered include not only those intended to alleviate respiratory symptoms, but other drugs the patients may have been prescribed or which they have bought over the counter.

Part 1 is a useful guide to various categories of drugs. Information in this section includes an overview of their pharmacology, uses, precautions, and possible adverse reactions, as well as advice to give patients and a list of individual drugs in that category included in the book. Part 2 is an alphabetic listing of generic drugs. Under each is a prominent box giving respiratory care considerations for that drug, as well as information on the drug's uses, dosages, administration routes, and availability. The index includes both generic and trade names. Appendixes include lists of drugs on the Drug Enforcement Agency Schedule of Controlled Substances, U.S. Food and Drug Administration pregnancy risk categories, and frequently used drugs in the treatment of pulmonary and cardiovascular conditions as well as a resource bibliography. Because the book's language is less technical and information on respiratory considerations easier to find than in standard sources such as the *Physicians' Desk Reference* (see ARBA 95, entry 1684), it will be a useful resource for those suffering from respiratory diseases as well as health care professionals, although, of course, it is not a substitute for consulting a physician.

—**Marit S. MacArthur**

1482.   **Mosby's GenRx: The Complete Reference for Generic and Brand Drugs.** 8th ed. [CD-ROM]. St. Louis, Mo., Mosby's GenRx, 1998. Minimum system requirements: IBM or compatible 486. CD-ROM drive. Windows 3.1. $69.95.

Mosby's GenRx is a CD-ROM database of drug prescribing information. Its scope encompasses prescription drugs only. Both generic and brand-name drugs are included. The database aims to be comprehensive, and indeed, with its drug name index, supplier profiles, keyword index, listings by pharmacological and therapeutic class, indications for use, imprint index (photographic images of pill markings), and drug interaction tool, is capable of replacing a number of print reference works. These might include *Mosby's Medical Drug Reference* (1999 ed.; Mosby, 1998) and *Mosby's Nursing Drug Reference and Review Cards* (1999 ed.; Mosby, 1998). This reviewer does not recommend canceling one's standing order for *Physicians' Desk Reference* (52d ed.; Medical Economics Data, 1998) yet, however, as the articles in PDR are long and full of desirable detail.

The database represents a beautiful marriage of reliable drug information and modern computer searching. However, a user who is not a professional searcher, such as a physician or pharmacist, would not get the full benefit of this CD-ROM. But for libraries, this resource can be thoroughly recommended.

This CD-ROM comes in a cardboard sleeve with no instructions as to how to install it on one's computer. But if not including a pamphlet helps keep the price down, this reviewer is in favor of it, because drug information needs to be updated frequently and one will want to get the new edition every year. The product does come with a postage-paid card to send back to the publisher to be eligible to receive technical support.—**Penny Papangelis**

1483.   **The PDR Family Guide to Prescription Drugs.** 5th ed. New York, Crown, 1997. 797p. illus. index. $23.00pa. ISBN 0-609-80153-8.

The Physicians' Desk Reference (PDR) is a standard reference source that has been providing information about prescription drugs for 50 years. It is written in technical language for health professionals. *The PDR Family Guide to Prescription Drugs* (see ARBA 94, entry 1879) is an abridged version of the PDR written in lay language. It provides information on more than 1,000 commonly prescribed medications.

The book has 2 sections. The main part consists of drug profiles. The drugs are listed alphabetically by both generic and brand name, with the profile appearing under the most familiar term. Thus, information about nitroglycerin appears under *nitroglycerine*, whereas the profile of diphenhydramine appears under *Benadryl*. Drugs with several brand names appear under the one with the highest sales figures. *See* references direct users to the information. Each entry explains indications for use, a key point about the drug, how to take the medication properly, side effects, contraindications and special warnings, possible interactions with foods or other drugs, safety during pregnancy and breast-feeding, recommended dosage, and signs of overdose. A color drug identification guide helps users identify stray pills.

The 2d section contains disease overviews. These are brief explanations of common ailments and their treatments. Heart disease, arthritis, allergies, and common childhood infections are among the conditions covered. These articles are superficial, but they do contain some useful information, such as warnings about the effects of drugs on the elderly. Two appendixes offer guidelines for safe medication use and a list of poison control centers.

The PDR Family Guide to Prescription Drugs is a source that belongs in circulating and home collections rather than reference collections because it contains a limited amount of simplified information. The PDR (52d ed.; Medical Economics Data, 1998) itself, *Mosby's GenRx* (see entry 1482), or the *Complete Drug Reference* (Consumer Reports, annual) are better choices for the reference desk.—**Barbara M. Bibel**

34 High Technology

GENERAL WORKS

1484. Cone, Robert J., and Patricia Barnes-Svarney. **How the New Technology Works: A Guide to High-Tech Concepts.** 2d ed. Phoenix, Ariz., Oryx Press, 1998. 133p. index. $28.50pa. ISBN 1-57356-136-X.

This is a reference book that works for the most part. The authors do an admirable job of explaining a combination of technological areas and specific devices. The ordinary nontechnical reader will find the text easy to follow without any trace of talking down to the reader. There are 3 sections: the 1st covers 17 major topics of interest, such as cryogenics, networking, and superconductivity; the 2d section examines 5 general areas, such as the electromagnetic spectrum and digital signals; and the final section covers 20 specific devices, including bar coding, global positioning system, and optical character recognition. Enough background in each case is supplied to provide some historical context without losing sight of the ultimate goal—to provide "concise, lucid explanations." Each entry is followed by an excellent small bibliography of books and articles. Finally, the index is comprehensive and easy to use. Many authors overlook the importance of detailed indexing, but not the authors of this work. There are line drawings to illustrate the text. In some cases these drawings are adequate, but some are not satisfactory. This is a good source as long as one ignores the illustrations. Most public librarians will find this a helpful reference work in spite of itself.—**George M. Cumming Jr.**

1485. **Orion Blue Book: Car Stereo 1998.** 1998 ed. Scottsdale, Ariz., Orion Research, 1998. 644p. $144.00. ISBN 0-932089-90-9. ISSN 1046-3853.

This is 1 of 12 Orion reference sources on electronic audio and related products, designed for the benefit of dealers in those products, in particular for those in the used equipment market. Included are guidelines for dealers (the aspect of profit regional pricing, testing of equipment before allowing trade-ins, cosmetic or external condition, and advertising), explanation of the need for a source like the Orion books, definitions of terms and abbreviations, and a directory of manufacturers (from which at least one producer, Asahi, is missing). Some 640 pages of close print provide information on products (type; year, including discontinuation if applicable; manufacturer; mounting type of the equipment; power; and model identification by number or name) and their prices (new retail or suggested price, retail price of used items, wholesale price of used equipment in mint condition, and wholesale average price paid to customers). The guide is useful to retail dealers and to insurance companies as well as to manufacturers, libraries, pawnbrokers, and other parties concerned with valuation of car audio equipment.—**Bogdan Mieczkowski**

COMPUTING

1486.   Henderson, Chuck. **Xtravaganza! The Essential Sourcebook for Macromedia Xtras.** Berkeley, Calif., Macromedia Press/Peachpit Press, 1998. 1257p. index. $44.95pa. ISBN 0-201-68893-X.

   Xtravaganza! The Essential Sourcebook of Macromedia Xtras is a useful quick reference tool for those in the field of graphic arts or anyone interested in high-end graphics development. The book allows developers to add features to their work (called Xtras). These range from sound and special effects graphics to network connectivity and database solutions. The book gives a good introduction to Xtras and techniques for using them. It also comes with a CD-ROM of countless examples. Billed as a "one stop shopping center" timesaver of lists of Xtras, *Xtravaganza!* is a quick solution for those working on projects and looking to spruce up their work. [R: LJ, Dec 98, p. 147]—**Kelly M. Jordan**

1487.   McComb, Gordon. **Web Programming Languages Sourcebook.** New York, John Wiley, 1997. 609p. index. $49.95pa. (with disk). ISBN 0-471-17576-5.

   This book promises to be a collection of timesaving tips on how to use programming languages such as Java, JavaScript, Perl, UNIX, and C to produce better designed and more appealing Web pages. Aimed at "webmasters," the author begins with a basic introduction to Web servers and the World Wide Web. Next they discuss server side issues, followed by chapters devoted to UNIX shell, Perl, Java, JavaScript, VBScript, and C. Other issues discussed include "swiping other HTML designs and programs"; locations of web script "repositories"; and a HTML "Primer."

   The accompanying CD-ROM contains sample programming scripts that are useful in exploring the printed text. For example, one of the files contains a small graphic of the planet Mars. The computer used must have the required software already loaded for the script to be viewed. For example, to view the C scripts, UNIX, Windows, and DOS must be loaded and operating. Perl, C, and "Shell" (as the author calls it), both require operating system UNIX. (Perl and C require DOS [or OS/2] and Windows as well as UNIX.) Java, JavaScript, and VBScript require Microsoft Internet Explorer 3.0 or greater or Netscape Navigator 3.0 or greater to view the scripts. The CD-ROM installed and ran easily and will help some readers better understand the text.

   This book has a variety of uses. For example, if one wants a better understanding of how the Web works, this is a good place to start. Basic information and exercises on Web design can be found in the text and accompanying CD-ROM and will get readers started on the road to their first homepage. Reader's interested in a refresher on Web design will also find lots of tips here. The book is now unfortunately somewhat dated (1997), and more automated methods of Web page design have emerged. The work is better used as a basic text rather than a reference "sourcebook," although some questions can be answered using it. The sample scripts on the CD-ROM, although illustrative of the text, were for the most part dated and simplistic. Most libraries will find patrons who can benefit from this book.—**Ralph Lee Scott**

1488.   **Microsoft Press Computer Dictionary.** 3d ed. Redmond, Wash., Microsoft Press, 1997. 539p. illus. $34.99. ISBN 1-57231-743-4.

   This is an excellent dictionary of computer terms for most nontechnical users of microcomputers. It is comprehensive and the definitions are clear. The book's explanations of acronyms and abbreviations are particularly useful. The illustrations and photographs serve the text well. However, there is a disturbing quality to this dictionary. This is a Microsoft publication, and, thus, product placement is important. Perhaps it is old-fashioned to expect a reference work to stay above the commercial fray, but librarians distrust the marketplace and its goals (profits first, facts second). There are no outright distortions of facts in this book, and it is a good dictionary for its intended audience, but any reader must surely wonder. When ideology or salesmanship invade science, the results are questionable. Windows 95 is, of course, the dominant operating system for microcomputers, but does every screen shot have to be from a Microsoft product? This reviewer has no problem with using this dictionary, but users should realize there are more microcomputer products available and take this knowledge into account. This will be a useful addition to any collection.—**George M. Cumming Jr.**

1489.   **Official Internet Dictionary: A Comprehensive Reference for Professionals.** Russ Bahorsky, Jeffrey Graber, and Steve Mason, eds. Rockville, Md., Government Institutes, 1998. 227p. $49.00pa. ISBN 0-86587-606-1.

In the preface of the *Official Internet Directory* Bahorsky recognized that a wide variety of professionals are involved with the Internet and have a differing degree of knowledge about it. Therefore, terms are included from such differing fields as computer networking and electronic commerce.

The dictionary lists numerous acronyms that are cross-listed under the full terms. The definitions are duplicated so one does not have to waste time looking from one entry to another. Numerous organizations are defined. A suggestion for improving future editions is to include the URL of the organization's Website.

One nice touch, given the exploding number of software applications, is that file extensions are included, labeled as file name extensions, and defined. The first of the outstanding appendixes to the book is a list of all these extensions, the file type, the platform it runs on, and any special application requirement.

Appendix B lists top-level domains, including the commonly used codes and the country codes. Appendix C will enlighten the Usenet and chat user whose messages are full of inexplicable acronyms such as "rotfl" (roll on the floor laughing) and "imho" (in my humble opinion). Internet error messages are defined in appendix D.

Search engine operations are covered well in appendix F. For the top search engines (Yahoo!, AltaVista, Webcrawler, Excite, Lycos, HotBot, and Infoseek) charts list the availability of features such as Boolean operators, proximity operators, phrase searching, wildcards, relevance ranking, and more. Finally, appendix F lists basic mailing list commands for Listserv, Mailserv, and Mailbase. The inside front cover lists standard measurements and rates for the Internet. The Association of Internet Professionals and the Webmasters' Guild helped create the book and endorse it. Overall, the *Official Internet Dictionary* is a quality book and recommended for anyone who uses the Internet.—**Mary A. Axford**

1490.   Taylor, Ed. **Encyclopedia of Network Blueprints.** New York, McGraw-Hill, 1998. 1123p. index. $59.95pa. ISBN 0-07-063406-8.

Taylor has written numerous communications technology and computer network books. This work is the latest on a list that includes *Network Architecture: Considerations for Design* (McGraw-Hill, 1997) and *Integrating TCP/IP into SNA* (Wordware, 1993). This encyclopedia is part of the McGraw-Hill series on computer communications, and is a guide for network administrators and engineers. Taylor also aims, however, to explain the basic principles of computer networks. His work thus enables computer network design, construction, implementation, and later troubleshooting. It provides blueprints for how a variety of networks (e.g., TCP/IP, Windows NT, SNA, ATM, APPN, and Frame Relay) can be built to integrate data, voice, video, and multimedia. Diagrams are numerous and clear, and the choice of fonts and page layout is quite good. The work concludes with an alphabetic list of acronyms used, a glossary, a bibliography (with the works in no particular order), a list of product names and their makers, and a lengthy index. Although the typographical errors are distracting, Taylor's work will be of use to an organization's systems office and computer science and information technology curricula.

—**Susanna Van Sant**

TELECOMMUNICATIONS

Dictionaries and Encyclopedias

1491.   Clayton, Jade. **McGraw-Hill Illustrated Telecom Dictionary.** New York, McGraw-Hill, 1998. 501p. illus. index. $29.95pa. ISBN 0-07-012063-3.

This dictionary contains more than 2,000 state-of-the-art and standard terms. There are 300-plus illustrated definitions. The dictionaries covers all facets of telecommunications; however, there are so many errors that it will be confusing for the layperson. Telecommunications terminology and technology defined in the dictionary include network traffic switching, private branch exchange services, SONET network engineering, PBX configuration and administration, LAN/WAN installation, fiber optics, and public telephone network services. This reviewer noted the following errors: A T1 is also known as a DS0; an OC-3 has 225.520 megabytes of bandwidth, and an OC-192 is capable of transporting three DS-3 signals.

A much better acquisition for college and university libraries would be *The Essential Guide to Telecommunications* by Annabel Z. Dodd (Prentice Hall, 1998), which offers overviews and broad summaries of limited depth. *Newton's Telecom Dictionary* by Harry Newton (Miller Freeman Books, 1998) is written for the layperson and is easy to understand and use. [R: BL, 1 Dec 98, p. 700]—**Marilynn Green Hopman**

1492. Held, Gilbert. **Dictionary of Communications Technology: Terms, Definitions, and Abbreviations.** 3d ed. New York, John Wiley, 1998. 692p. $160.00; $69.95pa. ISBN 0-471-97516-8; 0-471-97517-6pa.

In its 3d edition, this work continues to be a comprehensive and current source of communications terminology. The book is arranged alphabetically with acronyms and abbreviations included with terms. Major standards and key companies in the communications field are also defined. Numeric entries follow separately. A complete list of current Internet requests for comments (RFCs) is included in an appendix.

The layout of the book is designed for easy reading. Each term is in bold typeface and followed by its definition. Some entries even include tables or illustrations. Held is an internationally known authority who has once again provided the field of communications with a practical and useful reference work. Many academic, public, and corporate libraries could use this excellent tool.—**Deborah Sharp**

1493. Muller, Nathan. **Desktop Encyclopedia of Telecommunications.** New York, McGraw-Hill, 1998. 602p. index. $49.95pa. ISBN 0-07-044457-9.

Desktop Encyclopedia of Telecommunications is a collection of about 200 articles on topics of current or historical interest in telecommunications. The range of topics is broad, covering switching and transmission systems, protocols, computer software, regulatory institutions, and much more.

The more technical articles are the book's strength. Although written in a daunting style that requires constant reference to an included list of acronyms, it is clear that the author knows his stuff when writing about traditional telecommunications technologies. Articles on ISDN, frame relay, and other new transmission and switching technologies cover the needed ground well. Similarly, articles on older technologies, such as key systems and PBXs, are thorough and accurate.

As the topics move further from traditional telecommunications, the quality gets lower. An article on the computer programming language Java might have been written by Sun Microsystems' public relations department. It repeats the "Java jive" hype shallowly and uncritically, telling the reader nothing about the mixed acceptance the language has had in the marketplace and the reasons for uncertainty about its future. An article on help desks describes how an ideal help system might be imagined to work but offers no insights into the practical problems of running and staffing a help desk.

Although the book calls itself an encyclopedia, its scope and organization do not deserve the name. It lacks the comprehensiveness of an encyclopedia. Java, for example, is the only computer language covered. Company listings are too selective. There are index references to America Online, AT&T (but not American Telephone and Telegraph!), and Microsoft Network, but none for Intel, RBOCs, GTE, Sprint, MCI, or Bellcore. Selectivity is not a bad thing, but it should not claim to be encyclopedic.

Cross-referencing is weak, relying too much on use of the index. Given that the book's articles are organized alphabetically, it would have been easy to integrate cross-referencing into the body of the text. But there is no integrated cross-referencing at all, and the index fails to distinguish main entries on a topic from secondary references. For example, the X.25 protocol is described in the article on "Packet-Switched Networks," not an intuitive choice and hard to track down through the indexing.

This book offers a useful introduction to traditional telecommunications technologies in both their historical and modern forms. It tries to branch out into related areas but is weaker there. It is not nearly as comprehensive in its coverage as its name implies.—**Ray Olszewski**

1494. **Routledge French Dictionary of Telecommunications: French-English/English-French. Dictionnaire anglais des telecommunications.** New York, Routledge, 1997. 437p. $130.00. ISBN 0-415-13348-3.

This is a standard bilingual dictionary. An expert team of subject specialists compiled more than 30,000 entries in both French and English, resulting in the present volume. The dictionary covers the major areas of telecommunications. In only 472 pages, however, any monolingual dictionary would be hard-pressed to cover the breadth of telecommunications, especially when the compilers add terms related to the Internet to the mixture.

There are elements with which one can quibble, and this dictionary is no different. It is rare, for instance, to see the acronym *TCP* alone. Normally it is joined with *IP* to form a single term, *TCP/IP*. This dictionary separates the two, and no indication is given that they are normally joined. This is a danger of incorporating Internet terms into a telecommunications dictionary. On the one hand, the compilers would be castigated if they did not include them, but on the other hand, they will be castigated for including terms for such a fast-moving field.

Nonetheless, this is a solid dictionary. Because the work was originally published in England, British spelling is preferred. There is a notation when an American/English spelling variant is listed. The work is very good at listing both British and American usage.

The arrangement of the work is standard. The 1st section of the dictionary is the French and the later section is the English. Each entry generally consists of a translation of the entry together with gender indications for the French. Also included are subjects for the term, such as *ELEC* or *IMFORMAT*, to list two. Where there are compound terms such as *Avalanche*, one finds terms such as *~diode* and *~effect*.

This dictionary is part of a series of bilingual dictionaries produced by Routledge. The major objection to the title is the cost. Although some may find the dictionary indispensable, the majority of libraries and information centers do not require this dictionary. It will find good use in a specialized or large library where there is a need for quick and clear translation of French, British English, and American English telecommunications terms.

—**C. D. Hurt**

Directories

1495.   **Gale Directory of Databases March 1998.** Erin E. Braun and Lisa Kumar, eds. Farmington Hills, Mich., Gale, 1998. 2v. index. $249.00. ISBN 0-8103-5756-9. ISSN 1066-8934.

This 2-volume set is a comprehensive guide to some 5,600 databases and database products in all formats, covering online databases (volume 1) as well as CD-ROM, diskette, magnetic tape, handheld, and batch access database products (volume 2). It results from the merger of Gale's *Computer-Readable Databases* and Cuadra/Gale's *Directory of Online Databases* and *Directory of Portable Databases*.

Each volume is approximately 1,000 pages and provides a brief introduction, an overview of the current status of databases, a guide to using the volume, a list of databases, a list of database producers and their products, a geographic index, a subject index, and a master index that includes all product and organization names. In addition, volume 1 includes a listing of online services and their products, and volume 2 provides a list of vendors and distributors and the products they sell.

The majority of each volume features an alphabetic listing of databases, with a typical entry averaging 20 to 40 lines in a columnar format. Each entry is keyed with an indexing number and includes the name of the database and acronym; a symbol indicating whether this is a new entry or product; producer's name, address, and telephone number; contact person or department; co-producer, former producer, alternate database name, or former database name; type of database (bibliographic, bulletin board, dictionary, directory, full-text, image, numeric, properties, software, statistical, time series, or transactional); description of content scope and coverage; subject coverage; language; geographic coverage; year first available; time span; updating; online availability (and whether it is part of another product); and the available alternate electronic formats. If appropriate, indication is also made regarding audio formats, video formats, vendor, system requirements, and price.

For the wealth of information presented, most large libraries and library systems will want to have a copy of this guide to meet the needs of reference and collection development. This directory is also useful to the consumer who might be seeking new products and is available in various formats—print, diskette/magnetic tape (field format), online, through GaleNet, and on CD-ROM.—**Edmund F. SantaVicca**

1496.   Hahn, Harley. **Harley Hahn's Internet & Web Yellow Pages 1998.** 5th anniversary ed. New York, McGraw-Hill, 1998. 914p. illus. index. $34.99pa. (with disk). ISBN 0-07-882387-0.

An interesting guide aimed at the general reader and user of the Internet and World Wide Web, this work is an anecdotal selection of sites and other resources with potential reference value. It is also highly idiosyncratic in its introduction and general annotation of sites. Hahn includes all four of the introductions to previous editions as well as a few frequently asked questions and a guide to subscribing and unsubscribing to mailing lists. Also included are a detailed and classed table of contents—arranged alphabetically by broad subject category—and a detailed index.

The majority of the text is given over to identification and annotation of Internet, Web, and Usenet resources regarding a given topic. Hahn accepts no commercial advertising, and emphasizes that all resources included are free to the user. This seems to hold true. Comprehensive in nature, sites included are those that would be of value primarily in the public library setting or for use by individuals. Many of the sites have academic value, but some do not. Most are clearly adult in nature, although others are geared for a younger audience.

A CD-ROM version for Macintosh, Windows 3.1, and Windows 95 accompanies the print volume. It is easily accessed and provides adequate structure and help for most users. All in all, this guide is recommended as a general and useful guide to selected electronic information resources.—**Edmund F. SantaVicca**

1497. **International Satellite Directory 1998: The Complete Guide to the Satellite Communications Industry.** 13th ed. Sonoma, Calif., Design Publishers, 1998. 2v. index. $260.00/set. ISBN 0-936361-13-1. ISSN 1041-4541.

International Satellite Directory 1998 is a reference work for participants in the satellite communications industry, including its customers. Most of the set is devoted to listings of the facilities in place as of the beginning of 1998. Basic reference information is provided for each geosynchronous satellite, including its owner and operator, its location, its physical characteristics, transponder details, and a map of its footprint. This information occupies most of the 2d volume, along with a directory of uplink facilities, a listing of what services are currently on each satellite, and a schedule of planned satellite launches for 1998, 1999, and the twenty-first century.

The 1st volume is principally a directory of industry participants, providing contact information for manufacturers (of satellites and of ground equipment); for providers of network services (systems integrators, corporate and business networks, VSAT systems, and conferencing services); for users of satellite systems (oriented to television, not other satellite services such as paging); for providers of satellite services (hardware, transmission, and transponder brokers); and for companies offering support services (consulting, legal, and others). These listings appear to be simple compilations of material provided by the companies listed; the information available varies widely from entry to entry in completeness.

This is a reference work designed for use by knowledgeable people, specifically the actual participants in the industry. As such, it includes no background information on how the industry is organized and it assumes considerable mastery of a detailed technical vocabulary. In a library setting its value will be that of a specialized reference work with a limited audience, most likely individuals and companies seeking to find opportunities to enter the satellite industry in some capacity. For industry insiders, however, it appears to be the sort of indispensable basic reference that every industry has. The work is published annually, so by the time this review appears the 1999 edition may be either available or soon to be released.—**Ray Olszewski**

1498. Kyker, Keith. **Wading the World Wide Web: Internet Activities for Beginners.** Englewood, Colo., Libraries Unlimited, 1998. 170p. index. $18.00. ISBN 1-56308-605-0.

The subtitle, "Internet Activities for Beginners," sums this book up well. Kyker's goal is to provide entry-level experiences, in scavenger hunt form, that highlight the information value of the Internet. Showcasing well-designed Websites is a secondary goal. Kyker first discusses Internet basics, such as its history, required hardware and software, providers, Website characteristics, online searching, and evaluating Websites. He then examines the Internet in a school setting, including acceptable use policies and myths about students and the World Wide Web. A bibliography is provided at the end of each of these sections.

Teacher plans and master activity sheets make up most of the book. The teacher plans cover before-and-after Internet exercise activities. The activity sheets help students in various grade levels "wade" into the Internet. Kyker carries the metaphor into more advanced searches—Super Surfer and Kowabunga Dude! These plans and activities delve into literature, health, the arts, and government and emphasize science. The book has its own Website with a page of hyperlinks to the Websites highlighted in the book. An answer key, index, and index to the Websites complete the book.

Although this is more a professional work rather than a reference book, it provides a basis for both school and public libraries seeking to offer beginning Internet programs. *Wading the World Wide Web* can be used to integrate the Internet into basic reference skills.—**Esther R. Sinofsky**

1499. Wendland, Michael. **The Complete "No Geek-Speak" Guide to the Internet.** Grand Rapids, Mich., Zondervan Publishing/HarperCollins, 1998. 265p. illus. $19.99pa. ISBN 0-310-22000-9.

This book is a starting point for the Christian who has decided to join the Internet revolution. Wendland assumes that the reader knows nothing about the Internet, beginning with a chapter that gives examples of some of the material available in cyberspace. He follows with information on how to get on the information highway, explaining the difference between a commercial online service and a local Internet service provider. Wendland describes several interesting sites throughout the book, such as www.monster.com, a Website for serious job seekers. This writer has the gift of writing in such a way that it seems as if he is talking to the reader, explaining unfamiliar concepts without patronizing. He describes material on the Internet by use of scenarios, which show individuals using the Internet for various projects in a narrative form. The book boasts several appendixes, the most useful of which is the 44-page listing of useful Internet sites. This reviewer found only one instance where the author presented his personal opinion rather than allowing the reader to form his or her own. The position that removing life support from a terminally ill patient is a non-Christian decision was jarring in a book about the Internet (pp. 16-17). This book is an optional purchase for a circulating collection that offers material for the Christian community.—**Nancy P. Reed**

1500. Wilson, William H., Jr. **Telecommunications: Key Contacts and Information Sources.** Rockville, Md., Government Institutes, 1998. 353p. index. $59.00pa. ISBN 0-86587-583-9.

On the verso of the title page of this book is the following disclaimer: "The reader should not rely on this publication to address specific questions that apply to a particular set of facts." This sums up in one statement a basic review of this book. Although in theory it would be nice to have an up-to-date list of key contacts and information sources in the telecommunications industry, this book falls short of its mark. For example, in its entry for the North Carolina Utilities Commission, this book has the wrong chairperson, mailing address, telephone number, and Website address listed. Basic entries in this book are overly simplistic in their construct. For example, in the RBOC section of this guide, BellSouth is described as "headquartered in Atlanta . . . provides . . . service with the southern region . . . [with] over 20 million access lines utilizing one of the most modern telecommunications networks in the world." Although this statement is not inaccurate, it is perhaps more self-serving than one would normally expect to find in an impartial resource guide. Similarly, the "Education and Training Programs" section appears to be a listing of colleges and universities taken from Peterson's Guides that offer M.S., M.A., M.B.A., or Ph.D. programs in telecommunications along with their address and Web links. Notably missing are the engineering schools of most major universities, all of which have extensive programs in telecommunications engineering. Another section features telecommunications specialist "Law Firms and Practices," along with the address for Martindale-Hubbell. This volume also features a four-page "TimeLine of Telecommunications Events," preceded by the Santayana quote: "Those who cannot remember the past are condemned to repeat it." Other sections cover international, federal, and state contacts; associations and organizations; publications and media; major telecommunications companies; a list of authorization contacts (people who certify that equipment meets FCC regulations); and an interesting list of radio frequency coordination contacts. There are a small personal name index (not all names cited are listed), a short listing of Internet addresses, and a subject index.

Portions of this book appear to have been written by someone who has very little experience. For example, the subject heading "gateway" has two references. One is to page 51 where a brief mention is made of the fact that HawTel (GTE Hawaiian Telephone Company) is a gateway for international telecommunications traffic (hardly much information there as to what a "gateway" is or perhaps not even unusual considering the location of Hawaii). The other reference is to page 23 where the New Jersey Board of Public Utilities is listed as having an address of "Two Gateway Plaza."

Although this volume claims to be a handy one-volume compendium of reference information on the telecommunications industry, much of the information is out of date and more easily found on the Internet. The layout and typography of the volume is best described as poor. Some of the pages appear to be poorly constructed line tables. The content is rapidly changing and now outdated (the preface is dated November 1997). Some will no doubt find this compilation handy, especially if they have need for a quick reference to the industry and are unfamiliar with the lay of the land. Most libraries can find this information more quickly on the Internet.—**Ralph Lee Scott**

35 Physical Sciences and Mathematics

PHYSICAL SCIENCES

General Works

1501.   Armantrout, Neil B., comp. **Glossary of Aquatic Habitat Inventory Terminology.** Sewickley, Pa., American Fisheries Society, 1998. 136p. illus. $33.00 spiralbound. ISBN 1-888569-11-5.

This book is as straightforward as its title. It is a comprehensive, cross-referenced, accessible glossary of terms used in aquatic habitat research. The terminology is gleaned from the disciplines of hydrology, geology, ecology, and meteorology, with other definitions from environmental engineering, fisheries research, and hydraulics. Because such an interdisciplinary effort inevitably leads to different and sometimes conflicting uses for some words, the compiler has been careful to include all appropriate definitions. Many dimensions and equations are covered, making this book a handy resource for simple statistical work. There are also several helpful drawings scattered through the text. The spiral binding, although often an irritation to librarians, keeps the open book lying flat on the laboratory bench or car seat, which is important to the harried investigator needing quick definitions as he or she details notes or writes a report. There is no other modern, single source for the scientific terminology of aquatic research. This book will thus be an important tool in most libraries and science departments.

—**Mark A. Wilson**

1502.   **Magill's Survey of Science: Physical Science Series Supplement. Volume 7 Cumulative Index.** Thomas A. Tombrello Jr., ed. Englewood Cliffs, N.J., Salem Press, 1998. 1v. (various paging). $90.00. ISBN 0-89356-935-6.

The first 6 volumes of Magill's Survey of Science: Physical Science Series were published in 1992 (see ARBA 93, entry 1699). This volume comprises 52 additional articles along with an alphabetic list, a list by category of articles in the whole series, and a cumulative index. The format and subject range of the articles—astronomy and astrophysics, physics, physical chemistry, computation, and mathematical methods—are uniform with the earlier volumes. Each article contains a definition of the topic, a list of terms with definitions, an overview of the topic, applications, a statement of context that situates the topic in relation to other physical science disciplines or in the history of science, a bibliography of books and articles chosen to be understandable to nonscientist readers, and cross-references.

The 36-page index consistently includes the topics and the lists of terms. Beyond this level, indexing seems erratic. Sometimes the persons named as chiefly concerned with the discovery or development of a topic are indexed, but often they are not. More indexing of persons would improve access. This is a useful addition to a valuable work. [R: BL, 1 Dec 98, p. 698]—**Frederic F. Burchsted**

Chemistry

Dictionaries and Encyclopedias

1503.   Encyclopedia of Chemical Technology Supplement Volume. 4th ed. Jacqueline I. Kroschwitz and Mary Howe-Grant, eds. New York, John Wiley, 1998. 901p. illus. $325.00. ISBN 0471-52696-7.

These are among the final volumes of the 4th edition of the *Encyclopedia of Chemical Technology*, known to chemists, chemical engineers, and librarians as "Kirk-Othmer" after its first editors, Raymond E. Kirk and Donald F. Othmer. Because the original work dates from 1947, the present edition has a long and distinguished tradition to live up to, and this reviewer is glad to report that these volumes maintain the very high standards of their predecessors.

Articles include the broad overviews needed by general readers as well as detailed technical data and up-to-date literature references needed by advanced students and researchers. The work also continues the tradition of construing chemical technology in the broadest sense, so one can find here information on topics that would not ordinarily be thought of as chemical—for example, articles on "Wheat and Other Cereal Grains" and "Sterilization Techniques." This encyclopedia is the first source to turn to for a wide range of reference questions, and is indispensable for any serious reference collection. It is important to note, however, that earlier editions of this work include information that is omitted from the later editions, so research libraries will want to retain all editions, although in most cases only the most recent edition will be kept in the reference collection.—**Robert Michaelson**

1504.   Encyclopedia of Toxicology. Philip Wexler, ed. San Diego, Calif., Academic Press, 1998. 3v. illus. index. $425.00/set. ISBN 0-12-227220-X.

Whether it is hazardous materials in the workplace, toxic substances at home, or pollution at a recreational site, poison can appear anywhere. Information is vital for understanding the danger and dealing with it effectively. The *Encyclopedia of Toxicology* is a comprehensive, up-to-date reference source that provides information about the adverse effects of chemicals on biological systems. Research professionals, physicians, students, and the general public will be able to use this source easily.

The 3-volume set contains more than 750 alphabetically arranged, signed articles with bibliographies. The editors and contributors are professionals or academics whose credentials are listed in the 3d volume. The entries range in length from a few paragraphs to 25 pages. They cover a broad range of topics: substances (carbaryl, hemlock, aerosols); processes and mechanisms (absorption, distribution, excretion); organs and systems (liver, reproductive system, kidney); toxic organisms (E. coli, mushrooms, spiders); environmental issues (diesel exhaust, red tide, indoor air pollution); concepts (maximum tolerated dose, toxicity); legislation (Safe Drinking Water Act, Clean Air Act); and agencies and organizations (American Board of Toxicology, Environmental Protection Agency). Articles on substances include name, synonyms, CAS numbers if applicable, formula, chemical or pharmaceutical class, chemical structure, exposure pathways, toxicity, and clinical management. Cross-references note related entries. Technical terms are defined within the entry when used. There is also a glossary in volume 3. A detailed table of contents and a subject index facilitate access to the material.

The *Encyclopedia of Toxicology* is an excellent source for students doing research and professionals dealing with industrial safety or the clinical management of patients. With information on emergency response and behavioral toxicology as well as specific substances, it is a fine addition to health sciences and academic libraries. Large public libraries with funding will want it as well.—**Barbara M. Bibel**

1505.   Hawley's Condensed Chemical Dictionary. 13th ed. Revised by Richard J. Lewis. New York, Van Nostrand Reinhold, 1997. 1229p. illus. $99.95. ISBN 0-442-02324-3.

The publication of a new *Hawley's Condensed Chemical Dictionary* calls for "automatic purchase" in chemical special libraries and referral to the subject departments for replacement of their bench copies with the new edition. A long-term objective for the text has been to have enough information in the most logical place to respond to the urgent need in emergencies—a common sense approach that has been largely realized. As quoted from the back cover "the thirteenth edition brings that legacy forward to again serve as the world's foremost dictionary of industrial chemicals, nomenclature, processes, reactions, products, and related terminology." One necessary feature is the clear indication of trademarked entities—invariably shown by quote marks and the name of the holder in brackets. Alphabetic arrangement is letter-by-letter and numerical order.

There are one-paragraph entries on each outstanding chemist in its alphabetic place, including all chemical Nobel Prize winners through 1996. One needs to recall there is some ambiguity in the listings when physicists have been recipients in chemistry and the reverse. An important fact is that chemical abstract numbers for all compounds have been fully verified. Short histories of the American Chemical Society, *Chemical Abstracts*, and Center for the History of Chemistry follow. Finally there are short histories of the following industries: drug and pharmaceutical, paper, plastics, petroleum, and rubber. This work is recommended for any library where chemistry reference works are vital.—**Eugene B. Jackson**

1506.   Kaplan, Steven M. **Wiley's English-Spanish, Spanish-English Chemistry Dictionary: Diccionario de Quimica Ingles-Espanol Espanol-Ingles Wiley.** New York, John Wiley, 1998. 530p. $79.95. ISBN 0-471-19288-0.

In a world where English has become the dominant medium of communication in science, any technical dictionary of English terms into another language would be useful for those who translate scientific works from English into their own languages. A technical dictionary from another language into English would serve people of another native tongue who wish to publish the results of their research in international journals. The book under review will serve these needs for the Spanish-speaking world.

Like all bilingual dictionaries, this is simply an alphabetically arranged list of English-Spanish and Spanish-English equivalents of chemistry-related technical terms. There is explanation but no etymology, no formula, and no meaning attached to any of the other 20,000 terms in each language. The book will thus be useful only to those who are technically trained and engaged in deciphering or translating into/from a language not their own. A few words not unique to chemistry, such as *dome, ice, butter, lard, refraction, semi, sensitive*, and *seniority* have also found a place here.

This is the sort of book that not many may buy but that all libraries should have. It will be a useful addition for the service and propagation of science.—**Varadaraja V. Raman**

1507.   Knapp, Brian. **ChemLab Series.** Danbury, Conn., Grolier, 1998. 12v. illus. index. $299.00/set. ISBN 0-7172-9146-4.

Colorful, informative, detailed, and practical are all good descriptors for Grolier's 12-volume set, *ChemLab*. Aimed at middle school and high school students, each of the 12 volumes covers one aspect of chemistry: gases, liquids, and solids; elements, compounds, and mixtures; the Periodic Table; metals; acid, bases, and salts; heat and combustion; oxidation and reduction; air and water chemistry; carbon chemistry; reaction rates and electro-chemistry; preparations; and standard laboratory tests.

The 12 clearly written volumes feature vivid, close-up photography detailing step-by-step chemical reactions and changes, including the exact color a substance will become when another substance is added or the form an element may be expected to take when heat is applied. In volume 8, "Air and Water," it is possible to read text material about the reaction of water with metals and to see, at the same time, a series of illustrations revealing just what happens when sodium metal is added to water or when calcium metal is introduced. The standard apparatus shown in the experiments is helpfully defined in the master glossary for those who might need to find alternative equipment. Each volume's index serves the entire set, which is an asset when browsing through all 12 volumes. Biographies of "Great Experimental Scientists" are scattered throughout in inset boxes at appropriate places, serving to make the work and processes being explained with such care more relevant. In many cases, chemical formulas are provided along with their atomic diagrams so the reader can visualize the written formulas for elements and their combinations. *ChemLab* is a hands-on, useful reference tool and an excellent purchase for middle school, high school, and public libraries.—**Marcia Blevins**

1508.   **Routledge German Dictionary of Chemistry and Chemical Technology, Volume 2: English-German/Englisch-Deutsche. Worterbuch Chemie und Chemische Technik Englisch.** 6th ed. Technische Universitat Dresden, eds. New York, Routledge, 1997. 807p. $115.00. ISBN 0-415-17336-1.

The English-to-German volume of this chemistry dictionary remains consistent with the quality of the previous five editions. Of approximately 63,000 terms, 3,000 are new and are drawn primarily from organic, physical, and biochemical as well as chemical engineering. In addition to new entries, considerable effort has been made by the publisher to revise existing entries and correct existing errors.

Definitions are concise, covering a broad range of subjects—organic, inorganic, physical, analytical and industrial chemistry, and laboratory techniques as well as primary categories of chemical process engineering, including chemistry and technology of petroleum and coal, plastics, building materials, food, biotechnology, hydrochemistry and waste-water technology, metallurgy, and mineral technology. Subject area labels are included where appropriate. This volume in the Routledge set of technical dictionaries is a fine product and highly recommended for practitioners and research libraries.—**Barbara Delzell**

Handbooks and Yearbooks

1509. **Elements Explorer: A Multimedia Guide to the Periodic Table.** [CD-ROM]. New York, McGraw-Hill, 1998. Minimum system requirements (Windows): IBM or compatible 486. Double-speed CD-ROM drive. Windows 3.1. Windows 95. 8MB RAM. 10MB hard disk space. 256-color VGA monitor. Sound card. Minimum system requirements (Macintosh): Macintosh 68040. Double-speed CD-ROM drive. System 7.1. 8MB RAM. 10MB hard disk space. 256-color VGA monitor. $150.00 (single user); $295.00 (network version). ISBN 0-07-853099-7 (single user); 0-07-853092-X (network version).

This CD-ROM organizes information about the chemical elements in two different ways. The main interface is the periodic table; clicking on a symbol brings up a screen that displays basic elemental information, such as atomic mass and number, melting and boiling points, size, and ionization energies. The second option is a text menu, which leads to more than 300 articles on the individual elements or on common chemical concepts. Many of these articles are from the *McGraw-Hill Encyclopedia of Science and Technology* (8th ed.; see ARBA 98, entry 1407) and are written by well-known authorities. The articles are connected by an assortment of hyperlinks.

Technically, the package seems quite good. The CD-ROM is intended for use with either IBM PC compatible or Macintosh computers. Installation works smoothly and fairly quickly on both a PowerMac and a Pentium machine. The interface was intuitive and easy to use.

The disk did have some surprising shortcomings, including the relative lack of images, which is often a strength of CD-ROM reference works, and the failure to cite the sources for the elemental values. The latter oversight is unfortunate because the values given did not always agree with those for other sources.

This CD-ROM invites browsing and general exploration but is also well organized enough to support searches on specific topics. It should be an enjoyable reference work for general audiences as well as professional chemists.

—**Harry E. Pence**

1510. Krebs, Robert E. **The History and Use of Our Earth's Chemical Elements: A Reference Guide.** Westport, Conn., Greenwood Press, 1998. 346p. index. $39.95. ISBN 0-313-30123-9.

Although it was created more than 100 years ago, the periodic table still represents the major organizing principle for the study of chemistry and is probably one of the most significant unifying ideals in science. The author of this book uses the periodic table to arrange the information about each known chemical element through atomic number 118. Each listing includes basic chemical data (e.g., symbol, atomic number, atomic mass), characteristics (chemical reactivity), abundance and source, history of the discovery, common uses, most important compounds, hazards, and a diagram of the electron shell structure of the element. The utility of this book is limited by the fact that it does not include any chemical equations, nor does it show diagrams of important apparatus used to obtain and purify the elements.

The author uses bold typeface to designate technical terms that are defined in the glossary at the back of the book. There is an alphabetic index that provides a good alternative for those who are not familiar with the periodic table. The author gives a brief history of chemistry, but the bibliography does not include modern histories of chemistry, such as *Norton History of Chemistry* by William Brock (Norton, 1993) or *Creation of Fire* by Cathy Cobb and Harold Goldwhite (Plenum, 1995).

The back cover of the book suggests that the intended audience is high school and college students. The book may be valuable for those in high school, but the usefulness for college students will be limited because it lacks the depth usually expected at this level. [R: Choice, July/Aug 98, p. 1880; LJ, 15 Feb 98, p. 134]

—**Harry E. Pence**

1511.   Maizell, Robert E. **How to Find Chemical Information: A Guide for Practicing Chemists, Educators, and Students.** 3d ed. New York, John Wiley, 1998. 515p. index. $64.95. ISBN 0-471-12579-2.

The chemical literature is a rich and varied source that can, when used well, save considerable time and money for the practicing chemist. Thus, mastering these resources is a fundamental skill for anyone who is seriously interested in chemistry. The latest version of this standard textbook is a welcome addition to the relatively limited number of books in this area. The reviewer of the 2d edition (see ARBA 89, entry 1647) said it was excellent, and the current edition is equally splendid.

Maizell goes beyond just discussing how to use the various information sources. Reading this book is like doing a literature search while an experienced mentor looks over one's shoulder, offering wise advice based on long experience. For example, chapter 3, on search strategies, and chapter 4, on developing a personal program for current awareness, should be required reading for every young chemist (as well as many who are experienced). Equally valuable is the way Maizell critically evaluates possible reference resources. To cite only one example, his weighing of the advantages and disadvantages of Internet sources offers clear guidance for those who wish to use this new technology intelligently. In addition to treating more traditional sources, some of the especially notable sections include environment and safety, business information sources, and analytical chemistry.

This guide is a thorough and clear treatment of the chemical literature that is a delight to read. It should be an invaluable resource for information specialists as well as practicing chemists. [R: LJ, 1 Sept 98, p. 172; Choice, Nov 98, p. 549]—**Harry E. Pence**

1512.   Pohanish, Richard P. **Rapid Guide to Trade Names and Synonyms of Environmentally Regulated Chemicals.** New York, Van Nostrand Reinhold, 1998. 850p. index. $29.95pa. ISBN 0-442-02594-7.

Our society is increasingly concerned about the hazards of industrial chemicals, but looking for information about these hazards is complicated by the bewildering variety of chemical names in use. Not only do chemists use several different types of "official nomenclature," but there are also a wide variety of trade names, common names, and other means of identification. Finding a correct name can be the most difficult step when looking for information.

To help with the problem, this book lists approximately 30,000 names used for the substances included on the major U.S. lists of commonly encountered hazardous chemicals. Although it does not attempt the impossible job of covering every known compound, it does cover those most likely to be of concern. This guide is well organized to simplify the search process. It lists the names in three ways: (1) based on the Environmental Protection Agency's consolidated list; (2) by a cross-index that alphabetically gives all the synonyms for the included chemicals; and (3) according to the chemical abstracts number, generally recognized as a unique chemical identifier.

The back jacket of the book suggests that it is "a must for domestic and foreign regulatory managers, safety officers, and chemical importers and exporters." This is probably an accurate identification of the most likely audience. Listings of information on hazardous chemicals normally provide alternate names, and although this guide is somewhat more complete, many libraries will probably find that this reference is not essential. The possible exception could be libraries that support extensive environmental programs.—**Harry E. Pence**

Earth and Planetary Sciences

General Works

1513.   **Earthscape: Exploring Endangered Ecosystems.** [CD-ROM]. New York, McGraw-Hill, 1997. Minimum system requirements: IBM or compatible 386/33 MHz. Double-speed CD-ROM drive. Windows 3.1. 8MB hard disk space. 256-color VGA monitor. Minimum system requirements (Macintosh version): 68040 or higher. Double-speed CD-ROM drive. System 7.1. 8MB hard disk space. 3MHz or faster. Color monitor. Mouse. $89.95 (single users); $199.95 (network). ISBN 0-07-852951-4 (single user); 0-07-852956-5 (network).

This easy-to-use program has much information about ecosystems and endangered species. A beginning menu offers 4 section choices: the "Environmental Basics" section, which allows the user to get acquainted with environmental definitions and concepts and to discover how conservationists and management can work to make a difference; the "Ecosystem" section, which allows the user to explore 13 different ecosystems from around the world and the diversity of life that inhabits them; the "Endangered Species" section, which includes the legislation that protects endangered plants and animals in seven U.S. ecosystems and provides information about endangered species in six more ecosystems worldwide; and the "Conservation Directory" section, which allows users to browse through a list of international agencies and organizations concerned with the management of natural resources.

Each of the 4 main sections have subsections; the contents of each main section are displayed in a directory at the beginning of the section. The user can click on a topic name to go to the corresponding article. A search screen allows the user to type in a search term if preferred.

Articles may be printed or copied to a clipboard if these features have been allowed in the preferences. (The system has the option of selecting or deselecting various features in the preferences file, including printing text or images, copying, or using the built-in Netscape Internet connection.) Special menus appear in the bottom left-hand corner of section menus and article screens to allow easy movement to other sections, to use special tools, to print or copy, or to exit. There is a dictionary to look up terms pertaining to the subject matter.

This program is easy to install and navigate. A back button returns the user to the previous screen, and a menu button allows quick access to desired sections; the Macintosh version includes a menu bar that displays standard options by pointing to the top of the screen. It is primarily a text-based program, with some maps and images. There is no sound, but the Internet connection will, when selected as an option in the preferences, provide a link to ecology-related sites on the Internet.—**Dana McDougald**

1514. **Encyclopedia of Earth and Physical Sciences.** Tarrytown, N.Y., Marshall Cavendish, 1998. 11v. illus. maps. index. $459.95/set. ISBN 0-7614-0551-8.

Consisting of 11 volumes and 1,440 pages, this important reference work by Marshall Cavendish offers well-written summaries of 400 topics in the earth and physical sciences. These subjects were deemed the most important today by an editorial board of scholars and scientists active in these fields. The articles are profusely illustrated with colorful and informative photographs, maps, and diagrams.

Subjects are organized alphabetically from A to Z. Entries range in length from about two to four pages—almost half of each entry consists of colorful graphics or sidebars. The text is readable and well-edited in that it flows easily from entry to entry. It is also effectively cross-referenced; when a subject is mentioned that needs further explanation, there is a reference to another entry in the encyclopedia. Sidebars present basic facts, more detailed information, and profiles of important scientists. At the end of each article is a list for further reading that includes the most up-to-date books on the subject.

Even the index volume contains a lot of information, such as conversion charts, the periodic table, geologic time scale, lists of Nobel Prize winners, a bibliography by scientific field (almost all are books published since 1990), a master index, and eight subject indexes. Perhaps the most telling fact about the usefulness of this encyclopedia is how fun it is to browse through—every page presents interesting facts and details that leave the reader thinking. This is a great resource for anyone interested in the earth and physical sciences. [R: SLJ, Nov 98, p. 151; BL, 15 May 98, p. 1658; LJ, 15 Feb 98, p. 133]—**Mark J. Crawford**

1515. **Magill's Survey of Science: Earth Science Series Supplement. Volume 6 Cumulative Index.** Roger Smith, ed. Englewood Cliffs, N.J., Salem Press, 1998. 1v. (various paging). $90.00. ISBN 0-89356-933-X.

This book is a supplement to the original 5-volume series surveying the earth sciences in an encyclopedic form. An additional 55 topics are included in this volume, from the "African Rift Valley System" to "Xenoliths." Each topic starts with a brief abstract, followed by definitions of pertinent terms, a "summary of the phenomenon" (or methodology), methods of study (or applications), "context," and a brief annotated bibliography. A comprehensive index to terms used in the entire series is appended at the end of the volume. The volume is designed for use by nonspecialists and students. Its spotty coverage of topics will decrease its value for earth scientists themselves.

The individual articles are well written, showing the work of a good editor. Some of the topics are quirky, including "waterfalls" and "land bridges," but they may prove useful to someone. A major shortcoming of the volume, however, is the almost complete lack of illustration. There is, in fact, only one, and that is a simple set of concentric circles explaining "discontinuities" in the earth. Most of the topics, especially those concerning plate tectonics, atmospheric and ocean circulation patterns, seismicity and the like, need at least line drawings for comprehensibility. The articles are also sometimes out of date, which is most effectively demonstrated by the use of old sources in the bibliographies. This may be the result of having so many contributors who are not "experts" on the topics they covered.

A survey series such as this one is beset by an important question: Why use it instead of a good encyclopedia? Indeed, a modern encyclopedia includes as much scientific information as well as full-color illustrations and articles consistently written by real experts. It seems a reasonable conclusion for a librarian to purchase this supplemental volume only to complete the original set. For libraries without the series, it would be more effective to simply keep the encyclopedias updated and skip this purchase. [R: BL, 1 Dec 98, p. 698]—**Mark A. Wilson**

1516.   Ritter, Michael E. **Earth Online: An Internet Guide for Earth Science.** Belmont, Calif., Wadsworth Publishing, 1997. 264p. illus. index. $12.00pa. ISBN 0-534-51707-2.

Earth Online represents a curious dilemma in modern publishing. It is essentially a manual for using the Internet as an earth scientist or student, but as the author acknowledges at the start, a book about such a "fluid medium" is quickly outdated. Indeed, the most immediately valuable part of this printed book is its reference to its cousin version on the Web (http://ritter.wadsworth.com). All the exercises in the book are posted at this site, along with chapter abstracts and Internet resource addresses that are updated at least every month. Once a reader visits this Web page, interest in the printed book immediately declines. The book contains the very seed of its obsolescence. This is a pity because *Earth Online* is well written, and the goals of the author are too improve not only our access to Internet resources, but the ways in which we find and use them.

So why buy the book? Librarians and teachers will buy it because it appears useful, and then will likely find that the book sits little-used on library and classroom shelves. The Web is so attractive and so intuitively easy to navigate that students will dash into cyberspace and never look back. But here is the pedagogical danger of the Web. Although the Internet is astonishingly easy to use, it is also easy to be misled into thinking one knows all the tricks. *Earth Online* reviews the basics of the Internet, showing that there is much more to it than just pointing and clicking. The author explores the variety of available electronic resources, including TELNET and Gopher as well as the Web. He explains file transfer protocol, Archie and Veronica searches, and e-mail dynamics. There is even a section on professional activities, such as grant writing and publishing on the Web. *Earth Online* is a worthwhile purchase for librarians and teachers—and is worth reading all the way through.

—**Mark A. Wilson**

1517.   **Sciences of the Earth: An Encyclopedia of Events, People, and Phenomena.** Gregory A. Good, ed. New York, Garland, 1998. 2v. illus. maps. index. (Garland Encyclopedias in the History of Science, v.3 and Garland Reference Library of Social Sciences, v.745). $150.00/set. ISBN 0-8153-0062-X.

Earth sciences have an increasing impact on our lives. Most people are aware of the role that fossil fuels play in international economies and recognize growing concerns about human-induced changes in the world climate. But the effects of geological processes (flooding) and the impacts of new discoveries (fossils) also garner more and more public attention. This growing interest in earth (and some space-related processes) is reflected in these first volumes on what amounts to the history of geology.

Approximately 500 subjects are covered in about 225 articles by 125 authors. This is not an encyclopaedia of geologic terms, processes, and history. There are other sources for such details (e.g., publications of the American Geological Institute). The authors come from several countries and include faculty members in science departments and social science departments as well as independent scholars. Articles trace the development of concepts, observations in nature (with an overall emphasis on specific technical advances), and origins of important earth science organizations. Each article has a short bibliography, and the 2d volume closes with a name and subject index. Some articles are quite brief, only a few paragraphs in length, whereas others are 10 or more pages with photographs and drawings. Articles vary in coverage of title material and readability. Some are useful only if the reader has some background in the subject. These volumes make a good beginning source for someone seeking to learn how and when critical ideas in earth science emerged. [R: LJ, Aug 98, p. 79; VOYA, Oct 98, p. 308; BL, 1 Dec 98, p. 702; Choice, Nov 98, p. 498]—**David Bardack**

Astronomy and Space Sciences

1518.   **A Dictionary of Astronomy.** Ian Ridpath, ed. New York, Oxford University Press, 1997. 536p. (Oxford Paperback Reference). $14.95pa. ISBN 0-19-211596-0.

This book is the ideal specialized science dictionary. It is edited by an authority with strong credentials in the profession—Ridpath is a fellow of the Royal Astronomical Society—who also happens to be a successful popular writer and astronomical journalist. There are almost 4,000 entries on astronomy and related topics written by 21 experts. The scope and timeliness of the dictionary is extraordinary, with historical figures ranging from Hipparchus to Stephen Hawking, and topics including cosmology, instrumentation, space missions, deep space, the solar system, stellar dynamics, and much more. The entries are well written and seamlessly edited so that they flow easily from one to another through extensive cross-referencing. The numerous tables and line drawings are clearly labeled and simple to interpret. The book works so well as a reference that the editor, contributors, and format are virtually transparent to the reader as he or she collects information and new ideas.

Teachers of physics, astronomy, and the earth sciences will find this book particularly useful. Because it is up-to-date, they can look up large topics (such as the Big Bang theory) and follow the numerous internal references as an efficient way to revise their concepts and class notes. This dictionary will also be an excellent resource for high school, college, and graduate students assembling reports or trying to make sense of new findings described in the literature. Every working astronomer will also want this book easily at hand.

Many modern specialized dictionaries have either become so loaded with poorly connected jargon that they are too cumbersome to use, or they have tried to be so integrative that they have lost the primary defining concepts of the field. This dictionary avoids both problems by combining professional definitions with an efficient, friendly format. It is highly recommended for all libraries.—**Mark A. Wilson**

1519.   Kope, Spencer. **Kope's Outer Space Directory: The Products, Places, and People Directory.** 1998 ed. Silverdale, Wash., Willow Creek Press, 1997. 305p. illus. index. $19.95pa. ISBN 0-9647183-2-4.

This directory greatly expands upon the type of information found in the annual astronomy-related directories published by *Sky and Telescope* and *Astronomy* magazines. Kope claims that only companies and organizations that replied to his inquiries have full entries. Each entry is one to two paragraphs long and often contains an illustration. He provides addresses and telephone and fax numbers as well as Internet and e-mail addresses when available. All listings in the "Products & Services" section have full entries and include a wide variety of equipment, software, publishing, and other commercial services one would expect to advertise in the magazines above. The "Places of Interest" section emphasizes observatories and planetariums and includes brief, unverified entries for locations that did not reply to the author's inquiries. The "Organizations" section consists primarily of amateur astronomy clubs. The directory limits itself to the United States, and includes geographic indexes as well as a master index.

Although the coverage of this work is quite broad, it is not exhaustive. For example, organizations and locations not listed for the "Inland Empire" area of Southern California include the Riverside Astronomical Society, the Pomona Valley Amateur Astronomers, the Riverside Community College Planetarium, and San Bernardino Valley College's G. F. Beattie Planetarium and N. A. Richardson Astronomical Observatory, although smaller clubs and comparable sites for other areas have listings. For the next edition, the author might consider including major annual events, such as the Stellafane Convention in Springfield, Vermont; the Texas Star Party at the Prude Ranch; and Universe '98, held in various locations and cosponsored by *Astronomy* and the Astronomical Society of the Pacific. Though not all-inclusive, this directory is useful, compact, reasonably current, and visually appealing.—**Richard S. Watts**

1520.   Launius, Roger D. **Frontiers of Space Exploration.** Westport, Conn., Greenwood Press, 1998. 204p. illus. index. (Greenwood Press Guides to Historic Events of the Twentieth Century). $39.95. ISBN 0-313-29968-4.

Launius's *Frontiers of Space Exploration* is a convenient one-volume compilation of information on the history of space exploration. It comprises a chronology of major events in space flight from 1923 to 1997, four essays on space exploration, biographical sketches of major figures in space exploration, a collection of primary documents, a list of U.S.-manned space flights, an annotated bibliography (including video and film), and an index. There are 14 black-and-white photographs. Launius is chief historian at the National Aeronautics and Space Association (NASA).

The historical essays are mainly a history of the U.S. space program. The primary documents section includes presidential and congressional documents as well as NASA documents and statements and transmissions of the astronauts. The annotated bibliography highlights publications that include primary documents. Of the 18 biographees, three are Russians, two are Germans (including Wernher von Braun), and the rest are Americans. No sources for further reading are given with the biographies, although some material can be found in the book's bibliography. Persons interested in a worldwide list of space flights must go elsewhere for information. Mrinal Bali's *Space Exploration: A Reference Handbook* (see ARBA 92, entry 1590) is a good resource for this type of information. The juxtaposition of the chronology, biographies, and flight list as well as primary documents and interpretative essays make this book a useful one-stop source on U.S. space exploration.—**Frederic F. Burchsted**

1521.   Long, Kim. **The Moon Book: Fascinating Facts About the Magnificent, Mysterious Moon.** rev. ed. Boulder, Colo., Johnson Books, 1998. 149p. illus. maps. index. $12.50pa. ISBN 1-55566-230-7.

The Moon is a perpetual source of interest, passing nightly like a reflection to remind humans of our isolated place in space. Not surprisingly, it looms large in mythology—and, because it is so close, in our scientific knowledge of extraterrestrial bodies. Such information turns up in a variety of sources, from weighty technical tomes to more historical and speculative summaries of ethnography and religion. *The Moon Book* is a compilation of facts about the moon assembled from a wide range of sources.

The first one-third of the book provides data on orbit, reflectivity, eclipses, and other features involving the Moon as viewed from Earth. The next one-third covers aspects of lunar geography, origin, and exploration. This feeds into a listing of various lunar calendars and Moon-inspired names for the months as conceived of by different cultures. The text ends with a summary of "vital statistics," including comparisons with other bodies in the solar systems and tables of time and weight conversions. The work is rounded out by a list of published and electronic sources and references for further data, a bibliography, a glossary, and an index.

The text is generally straightforward and is often accompanied by clear graphics. The work is well suited to public collections and high school libraries.—**Bruce H. Tiffney**

1522.   **Outer Space.** Danbury, Conn., Grolier, 1998. 12v. illus. $269.00/set. ISBN 0-7172-9179-0.

Each of the 12 volumes in this set contains a table of contents, a short introduction and conclusion, a glossary unique to that volume, and an index to the entire set. The first 4 volumes examine objects in our solar system; the next 3 examine the sky, stars, and astronomy in general; and the final 5 examine human presence in space, such as space flight and satellites. The text is printed in two columns, and items printed in bold typeface are explained in the glossary. Explanations of more complex concepts, such as parallax or the Apollo Lunar Launch System are given in large sidebars. Cross-references are also shown in bold print. The text is well-supplemented with color and black-and-white photographs, drawings, and data tables.

It is difficult to avoid the impression that the volumes are written independently with only minimal effort to coordinate among them. More stringent editing could have reduced many of the problems with improved indexing and cross-referencing and elimination of repetition. The same photograph of Mercury appears in two places (vol. 1, 16 and vol. 3, 14), as does discussion of the Barrington Meteor Crater in Arizona (vol. 1, 43 and vol. 3, 19; not indexed or cross-referenced). The captioned photograph of Venus de Milo is missing from the sidebar (vol. 3, 9).

Some index entries could be more helpful. On the pages given for "Jupiter, comet collision with" one might expect to find photographs of the dramatic Shoemaker-Levy impact sequence. Those photographs are merely cited in the Jupiter index citation but are shown in other discussions in different volumes and indexed under "Comet, Shoemaker-Levy." Although a short discussion of "Life in the Universe" can be found in volume 6, *Stars and Galaxies*, it cannot be found in the index.

An introduction explaining details of the format would have been helpful. For instance, the student must discover that bold text is explained in the glossary, or that all colored boxes with a solid line above are figure-captions and boxes surrounded by a dashed line (called sidebars) provide detailed explanations of items in the text. Although indicated by the publisher to be useful for students "in elementary school and up," the set may be of limited use to students in primary grades. The work is indicated to be "an engaging alternative to standard science textbooks," but most teachers might consider it a research supplement to other materials. Although there is much useful information here, students may have a difficult time finding and forming a comprehensive picture of what is available about a given subject. [R: SLJ, Nov 98, p. 158; BL, 1 Dec 98, pp. 700, 702]—**Craig A. Munsart**

1523.   Ridpath, Ian. **Stars and Planets.** New York, DK Publishing, 1998. 224p. illus. maps. index. (Eyewitness Handbooks). $18.95 flexibinding. ISBN 0-7894-3521-7.

Stars and Planets may well be the star of the Eyewitness Handbooks series by DK Publishing. Crystal clear describes this handbook in terms of superb charts, illustrations, and graphics as well as excellent, readable content. Compact and yet comprehensive, the handbook is organized in 4 parts, beginning with a general introduction to astronomy. Next there is a detailed guide to the solar system containing descriptions of the nine planets, the Sun, the Earth's Moon, and significant smaller bodies, along with advice on how and where to find them. The 3d part is an alphabetic catalog of the constellations. The charts in this section, taken together, form a complete sky atlas. The 4th part is a month-by-month companion to the night sky. There is a detailed sky chart for every month of the year, with separate charts for each hemisphere. Interesting celestial phenomena are described and accompanied by charts for location and identification. This handbook is highly recommended for all types of libraries, and for anyone interested in astronomy, both beginners and the advanced.—**Barbara Delzell**

1524.   **The Solar System.** Roger Smith, ed. Pasadena, Calif., Salem Press, 1998. 3v. illus. index. $175.00/set. ISBN 0-89356-961-5.

The knowledge of our solar system has expanded exponentially in the 1990s. Therefore, it is appropriate to develop an encyclopedic resource based on our solar system. This 3-volume set of 140 essays gives extensive coverage on just about anything conceivably associated with our solar system. Each essay begins with a concise definition, followed by an overview of the topic and then a discussion of the topic in context or application. The average essay is about 3,000 words. A bibliography of both basic and current resources, plus cross-references to other articles within the set, conclude each essay. Nearly every essay is illustrated with either a photograph or line drawing.

The essays were written by 90 recognized authorities. It should be pointed out, however, that 131 of the essays were collected from 3 previously published Magill's Survey of Science series: the Space Exploration Series (1989), the Earth Science Series (1990), and the Physical Science Series (1992). The remaining nine essays were specifically commissioned for this set. Some editing was performed on the earlier essays to bring them up-to-date.

The essays are directed to the interested layperson; no math or equations appear. Where appropriate, human interest elements add flavor to the topics. Although most of the essays came from previously published series, this set holds together well. It can be questioned whether the repackaging of old material, even if it is reviewed and edited for updating, is worth the price for the set. This set is recommended for public libraries or general academic collections that may not have the previous series. [R: Choice, Sept 98, p. 96; LJ, Aug 98, p. 80]
—**Margaret F. Dominy**

Climatology and Meteorology

1525.   Allaby, Michael. **Blizzards.** New York, Facts on File, 1997. 138p. illus. maps. index. (Dangerous Weather). $24.95/vol.; $149.00/set. ISBN 0-8160-3518-0.

1526.   Allaby, Michael. **A Chronology of Weather.** New York, Facts on File, 1998. 154p. illus. index. (Dangerous Weather). $24.95/vol.; $149.00/set. ISBN 0-8160-3521-0.

1527.   Allaby, Michael. **Droughts.** New York, Facts on File, 1998. 135p. illus. maps. index. (Dangerous Weather). $24.95/vol.; $149.00/set. ISBN 0-8160-3519-9.

1528.   Allaby, Michael. **Floods.** New York, Facts on File, 1998. 135p. illus. maps. index. (Dangerous Weather). $24.95/vol.; $149.00/set. ISBN 0-8160-3520-2.

1529.   Allaby, Michael. **Hurricanes.** New York, Facts on File, 1997. 136p. illus. maps. index. (Dangerous Weather). $24.95/vol.; $149.00/set. ISBN 0-8160-3516-4.

1530.   Allaby, Michael. **Tornadoes.** New York, Facts on File, 1997. 131p. illus. maps. index. (Dangerous Weather). $24.95/vol.; $149.00/set. ISBN 0-8160-3517-2.

Extreme and dangerous weather phenomena are presented in this 6-volume series. *A Chronology of Weather* differs from the other volumes by taking an inclusive view of all dangerous weather conditions. It discusses how climates have changed and outlines how our understanding of the weather and our ability to forecast it have developed over time. Most of this volume is devoted to two chronological accounts: major weather disasters arranged by the year they occurred and important developments and improvements in the understanding and forecasting of weather. Chronological coverage goes back 10,000 years and includes the discovery of basic instruments, such as the barometer, hygrometer, and thermometer. The chronology of destruction not only lists major disasters beginning with the year 3200 B.C.E. but also explains how we know these events occurred so many years ago. The number of included events dramatically increases in the late 1800s because of better record keeping. There are 30 easy-to-perform experiments with step-by-step directions using basic household equipment that provide students and teachers with activities that will expand their understanding of weather principles. A glossary of 129 definitions of weather-related terms, a bibliography that also includes Websites, and an index complete the volume.

The remaining 5 volumes are each devoted to a single destructive natural weather occurrence. The science behind these dangerous weather occurrences is explained, including how, why, and where they are likely to take place. Information is included on how our lives are affected and what can be done to prepare for, cope with, and survive these destructive forces. Biographical information is provided on significant inventors, discoverers, and climatologists. Sidebars provide additional background information on meteorological concepts including adiabatic warming and cooling, cloud formation, and latent heat and dew point. When these sidebars pertain to more than one type of weather development, they are repeated in subsequent volumes. Extensive use of black-and-white maps, diagrams, charts, and photographs provide further information and enhance the text. Although each of these 5 volumes includes a section on the history of these occurrences, the topic is not sensationalized. Rather, the reader will gain a lot of information regarding the topic in an understandable presentation. Each volume is indexed individually, and there is no comprehensive index to the set. An excellent resource for grades 6 through 12.
—**Elaine Ezell**

1531.   Barnes, Jay. **Florida's Hurricane History.** Chapel Hill, N.C., University of North Carolina Press, 1998. 330p. illus. maps. index. $19.95pa. ISBN 0-8078-4748-8.

Barnes has written a companion to his book *North Carolina's Hurricane History* (University of North Carolina, 1995) that documents the larger hurricanes that have struck Florida, beginning in 1546 to Hurricane Opal in 1996. The opening chapters of the book provide an overview of hurricane meteorology. Chronological narratives follow this on more than 100 storms that have struck the state. There are 121 sobering photographs presented that bear witness to the destructive power of hurricanes throughout the text. There is also a limited tracking map for each hurricane that shows the parts of Florida that were affected by the various storms. It would have been useful to have a complete tracking map that begins where they formed and conclude when the storm dissipates. A concluding chapter entitled "The Next Great Storm" follows the reference portion of the book. It contains information on hurricane survival and warnings about Florida's lack of preparation for a major hurricane. The author specifically mentions the vulnerability of people living in the Florida Keys because there is only one road for evacuation. This warning proved prophetic as Hurricane Georges hit that very region in 1998. The appendixes are as follows: "The Deadliest Mainland United States Hurricanes, 1900-1997"; "The Costliest Mainland United States Hurricanes, 1900-1997"; "The Most Intense Mainland United States Hurricanes at Time of Landfall, 1900-1997"; "Selected Notorious Hurricanes in Florida, 1900-1997"; and "Hurricane Tracking Map."

This book is an excellent read and is targeted at a general audience. It provides information on more hurricanes than *Florida Hurricanes & Tropical Storms* (University Press of Florida, 1997), which is an excellent title but focuses on storms from 1871 to 1995. Both books are worthwhile additions to meteorology collections in academic and public libraries and should be purchased by all libraries in Florida.—**John R. Burch Jr.**

1532.   Longshore, David. **Encyclopedia of Hurricanes, Typhoons, and Cyclones.** New York, Facts on File, 1998. 372p. illus. maps. index. $40.00. ISBN 0-8160-3398-6.

This work is a complete listing and discussion of worldwide tropical storms from 1281 through 1995, with related subject matter. The book purports to cover history, culture, and science. Both history and culture are covered excellently. Unfortunately, some of the science is incorrect; it is wrongly stated that near the equator is a belt of high pressure (p. 76); sea level pressure is given as 29.53 inches, when it is actually 29.92; and the chamber of aneroid barometer is not a vacuum, it contains air. These are a few of the many incorrect facts found in this volume. A scientific reviewer should have corrected these errors. In spite of these problems, the volume is great. There is an appendix listing tropical storms in chronological order and a second that lists storms by name. Hurricane safety procedures are included as well as a good index and a bibliography. Other selling points include the history of instruments, satellites, and weather service in general. This book provides good information for the general public. [R: LJ, 15 Sept 98, p. 63; BL, 1 Sept 98, p. 156; Choice, Dec 98, pp. 667-668]—**Allen E. Staver**

1533.   **National Audubon Society First Field Guide: Weather.** By Jonathan D. W. Kahl. New York, Scholastic, 1998. 159p. illus. index. $10.95pa. ISBN 0-590-05488-0.

Field guides are written for any number of subjects found in nature; many include the night sky and the weather along with companion volumes on mammals, birds, insects, rocks, flowers, and the like. This small book is thorough, with any number of color photographs illustrating the types and classifications of clouds, fog, rainbows, and even examples of air pollution and smog. This is not the book for those with an interest in climate and its changes. Such issues as global warming, acid rain, and ozone depletion are treated only briefly here, if at all. The book is intended for the observer of weather phenomena, who wishes to understand what can be seen in the sky. For this purpose, the book is as good as any and is up-to-date. This is an excellent addition to any school or public library.—**Arthur R. Upgren**

1534.   **The Weather Almanac: A Reference Guide to Weather, Climate, and Related Issues in the United States and Its Key Cities.** 8th ed. Richard A. Wood, ed. Detroit, Gale, 1998. 741p. illus. maps. index. $135.00. ISBN 0-8103-5522-1. ISSN 0731-5627.

This updated edition contains climatic data for more than 100 U.S. cities and includes weather details from 1966 through 1995. The data for 550 worldwide locations has not been updated. Many of the maps are also based on old data and should have been updated or withdrawn. This is a worthwhile book because it explains virtually every type of weather phenomena: severe storms, floods, drought, and heat and cold waves; environmental concerns such as acid rain, ozone depletion, global warming; and related subjects such as earthquakes, volcanic activity, and tsunamis. A selling point is not only the inclusion of data from 1990 through 1995 but a discussion of the severe weather of the 1990s in the United States—Hurricane Andrew, 1992; Midwest floods, 1993; winter superstorm, 1993; Northridge earthquake, 1994; hurricanes, 1996; and floods, December 1996 through January 1997. The chapter on "Retirement and Health Weather" has been expanded, and safety rules are included regarding each hazard. Seasonal affective disorder and El Niño are discussed. A glossary of weather terms and a good general index are included. This reference book should be in all libraries; this update is worthwhile.
—**Allen E. Staver**

Geology

1535.   **National Audubon Society First Field Guide: Rocks and Minerals.** By Edward Ricciuti and Margaret W. Carruthers. New York, Scholastic, 1998. 159p. illus. index. $10.95pa. ISBN 0-590-05484-8.

The beginning rock hound needs a field guide that gives some basic information on geology, provides information on types of rocks and minerals, and helps the beginner identify common rocks and minerals. A useful field guide has good quality photographs against which one can compare finds. It should also fit into a pocket or backpack.

This field guide meets the above criteria. For each of the 50 highlighted rocks or minerals there are photographs that covers three-fourths of the double-page spread; its name, whether it is a mineral or an igneous, metamorphic, or sedimentary rock; its properties, such as color, texture, and hardness; and information on where it is found and how it is used. Brief descriptions and small photographs of an additional 120 rocks and minerals occupy the remaining one-quarter of the double-page spreads. These appear near rocks and minerals of a similar type.

This first book, intended for the budding scientist, is clearly and simply written without talking down to the reader. With a few exceptions—galena, rhodochrosite, muscovite mica, and talc—the photographs are an accurate depiction of the mineral and can be easily used to identify a specimen. The photographs of rocks are of particularly good quality.

Additional information includes a glossary of commonly used terms, a short list of common minerals and their chemical formulas, a bibliography of items for further study by the young rockhound, some noted organizations in the field, and a selection of Websites. It lives up to its title as a "First Field Guide" and is the appropriate first guide to give today's hobbyists and tomorrow's geologists. Because this guide is limited in scope, it will not satisfy the serious rockhound for very long, so be prepared to provide a higher-level field guide.—**Ann E. Prentice**

Hydrology

1536. Patrick, Ruth. **Rivers of the United States, Volume IV, Parts A and B.** New York, John Wiley, 1998. 2v. index. $140.00/set. ISBN 0-471-30347-X.

The preface succinctly states the purpose of this work: to describe the organisms that compose the structure and function in the ecosystems in each river that make possible the conversion of waste into energy and food. The ecosystems of natural streams are complex and diverse.

This work is the 4th in the series. It is a treasure trove of information about rivers, marine resources, and fisheries. Its scope is to show how ecosystems function in every different types of rivers. Did you know, for example, that headwater streams in the Appalachian Mountains are found to be very low in conductivity and contain small amounts of alkaline metals? This work emphasizes that biodiversity is essential for the functioning of the ecosystem of our planet in the same way that many previous books have done. It updates and expands a systematic work of great value entitled, *An Introduction to the Aquatic Insects of North America* by R. W. Merritt and K. W. Cummins (Kendall Hunt, 1978).

Contents include the physical elements of the rivers and their tributaries that are a part of the Mississippi drainage, with facts and figures about microorganisms, megafauna, meiofauna, and fish. Compilation of the data of many of the rivers in this book are a result of the findings of a team of scientists that study rivers at the Academy of Natural Sciences.

This 2-volume set in the series should be useful to students of rivers and to people of all ages who are interested in conservation and preserving the naturalness of streams. It will be of particular interest to industrialists as well as land planners. *Rivers of the United States* is recommended for special libraries.—**Marilynn Green Hopman**

Mineralogy

1537. Gaines, Richard V. and others. **Dana's New Mineralogy: The System of Mineralogy of James Dwight Dana and Edward Salisbury Dana.** 8th ed. New York, John Wiley, 1997. 1819. index.$295.00. ISBN 0-471-19310-0.

What could be new about a catalog of minerals, barring new minerals? *Dana's New Mineralogy*, which is "entirely rewritten and greatly enlarged," follows its previous edition, which began being published more than 50 years ago. This text represents a clear but monumental task—to describe and classify all known and recognized minerals reported in the scientific literature up to the end of 1995. Since the first volume of the last edition appeared, several important developments have taken place that have influenced the format and authority of this edition. The International Mineralogical Association, founded in 1958, sponsors the Commission on New Minerals and Mineral Names, which officially "recognizes" minerals reported after 1959 by application of accepted criteria and affirmation of a new species of mineral by its international members. The new edition includes naturally occurring minerals as well as those found only in minute quantities (and reported in *Chemical Abstracts*, rather than standard mineralogical sources), but also some anthropogenic (human-made) and synthetic equivalents of minerals.

For compiling and selecting the data for the 8th edition, the compilers consulted extensive bibliographic and mineral databases that have come into being since the last edition. The hierarchical numbering system that covered only some of the minerals in the 7th edition has been expanded by several scientists, allowing all entries to be classified and accorded Dana classification numbers, which group minerals by composition or structure.

Entries include Dana number, chemical composition, information on naming, physical properties, occurrence in the earth, locations of deposits, initials of the author of the mineral description, and bibliographic references. Excellent illustrations accompany some of the mineral descriptions.

James Dwight Dana, the American geologist and mineralogist, devised the system of mineral classification while completely revising his text *A System of Mineralogy*. He would no doubt be impressed with this revision.

—**Jean C. McManus**

Oceanography

1538.   **Library of the Oceans.** Ellen Dupont and others, eds. Danbury, Conn., Grolier, 1998. 12v. illus. maps. index. $289.00/set. ISBN 0-7172-9180-4.

From the deepest trenches to the shallowest lagoons, a world as complex and compelling as life on land exists. Now students have the perfect resource to discover the secrets of the deep with Grolier's outstanding new set, *Library of the Oceans*. This 12-volume, comprehensive set presents oceanography, sea exploration, and the development of the oceans as factors in human life. Organized topically to cover all of the science and other aspects of the seas, each volume in *Library of the Oceans* includes a clear introduction that sets the stage for the information to follow. The set offers many pictures and photographs to intrigue elementary students, while at the same time providing solid information to be useful for high school students.

Each volume is 64 pages in length. There are easy-to-use features, such as lists of subjects covered and box features in each volume. A thorough glossary, bibliography, and full set index are found in every volume. There are informational boxes with related topics in every chapter and many illustrations and photographs to bring the topics to life. This 12-volume set is divided into 12 specific topics: the shape of the ocean (sea floor, ocean floor, rocks, fossil evidence); the restless waters (water in motion, tides, undersea avalanches, global warming); the prehistoric ocean (geological time, fossil record, evolution of life, Darwin's travels); life in the ocean (food webs, gray whales, migration); hunters and monsters (sharks, man-eaters, monsters of the deep, poisonous animals); the cold seas (kingdom of ice, the Arctic, the Antarctic, penguins); the warm seas (coral reefs, the giant clam, ospreys in danger, green turtles); the shallow seas (rocky shores, tide pools, algae on the shore, estuaries); exploring the oceans (the Bermuda triangle, great voyages, measuring longitude, sounding the depths); the world's oceans (the Atlantic, the Pacific, El Niño, the polar oceans); coasts and islands (islands, coasts, deltas, destruction by erosion); and the future of the ocean (the sea's riches, fish and fuel, sea salt, the dirty sea).

Library of the Oceans is one of those rare sets of books that students hope for and teachers dream of owning. From the deepest trenches to the shallowest lagoons, the world below provides substantial material to be incorporated into both science and geography lessons. Grolier Educational produces books aimed at helping students of all ages expand their understanding of the world and its history. This latest offering will have students on the edge of their seats in anticipation of what will come next. [R: BR, Nov/Dec 98, p. 76]—**Barbara B. Goldstein**

Paleontology

1539.   **Encyclopedia of Dinosaurs.** Philip J. Currie and Kevin Padian, eds. San Diego, Calif., Academic Press, 1997. 869p. illus. index. $99.95. ISBN 0-12-226810-5.

If you do not have an eight-year-old child handy, this is the next best source of information on dinosaurs. Although other books, such as David Norman's *The Illustrated Encyclopedia of Dinosaurs* (Salamander Books, 1985), possess a similar title, they often fall short of this goal. (Norman's is an excellent and well-illustrated introduction to the group, but is not encyclopedic in scope or organization.)

The present volume is a true encyclopedia, with several hundred alphabetically arranged entries, each authored by a professional specialist in the field. Entries vary in length and complexity, depending upon their subject. Most are one to several paragraphs, and all assume a working biological and geological vocabulary. Many entries are accompanied by technical illustrations, and several color plates depict reconstructions and classic dinosaur collection localities, among other things. Virtually every entry terminates with a list of references for further reading in the primary literature. Topics covered include the major groups of dinosaurs, the places of their occurrence, aspects of their biology (e.g., reproduction, behavior), and major public collections. A nice aspect of the volume is several entries that explain how dinosaurs are collected, prepared, and studied. The book is an excellent and up-to-date summary of the group, and deserves a place in any collection catering to existing or would-be paleontologists. [R: RBB, 1 Nov 97, p. 508]—**Bruce H. Tiffney**

MATHEMATICS

1540. Assistantships and Graduate Fellowships in the Mathematical Sciences, 1997-1998. Providence, R.I., American Mathematical Society, 1998. 130p. $20.00. ISBN 0-8218-1070-7. ISSN 1040-7650.

This directory, the 11th from the American Mathematical Society (AMS), is intended to guide undergraduate students to select the graduate program in mathematics that suits their need. The directory is arranged alphabetically by state and by institution within the state. Besides the standard entry, some institutions opted to include an additional larger advertisement (some are full page).

The standard entry includes Website address, department chair, faculty and graduate student breakdown, and application deadline(s). What makes this directory unusual is the additional information provided about the department. AMS has provided for each department the number of tenured faculty that have published within the last three years and a breakdown of the financial support available to graduate students as well as the kind of work required to obtain support. From a student's point of view, these additional data are vital in the selection process.

The American Mathematical Society has provided a valuable aid to students in the mathematical sciences. Providing honest data and information to enable students to make the best decision for their graduate careers is probably the smartest investment in the profession. This guide is highly recommended for any academic institution with an undergraduate mathematics major.—**Margaret F. Dominy**

1541. Notable Mathematicians: From Ancient Times to the Present. Robyn V. Young and Zoran Minderovic, eds. Detroit, Gale, 1997. 612p. illus. index. $85.00. ISBN 0-7876-1930-2.

One can ascertain from some of the earliest known human artifacts that humans had already developed the desire and ability to count. During the millennia that followed, individuals stepped up to further the understanding of numbers and then mathematics. This work brings together the stories of 303 of these people who, according to an advisory board of university and high school mathematics educators, including a librarian, are renowned for their insight, discovery, inventions, influence, or impact in the mathematical arena. Of the 303 individuals, 50 are women. Considerable effort was made toward ethnic and cultural diversity among the selections, although the selections still favor Western European and North American mathematicians. To highlight the diversity, the editors have included indexes arranged by gender and ethnicity.

Because mathematics is the foundation of the sciences, it is commendable that the advisory board included astronomers, physicists, and other scientists not normally associated with mathematics. Truly, these scientists had to master mathematics in order to master their science. The biographies, labeled as "sketches" and ranging from about 600 to 3,000 words, are signed, and most are accompanied by an illustration. A bibliography that may include a list of selected writings by the individual, with further readings about the individual from books and periodicals, completes each sketch.

Other appendixes include a list of the recipients of honors and awards in mathematics, a field of specialization index, and a subject index. A selected bibliography lists Internet sites that have a mathematics focus. Although by no means exhaustive in selection or biographical details, the stories provide an insight, albeit brief, into a sampling of individuals whose accumulated mathematical abilities have brought humanity to where it is today. This volume is a great read, and it is highly recommended for any reference collection. [R: SLJ, Aug 98, p. 194; LJ, 1 April 98, p. 82; BL, 1 Dec 98, p. 694; Choice, Nov 98, p. 498]—**Margaret F. Dominy**

1542. Notable Women in Mathematics: A Biographical Dictionary. Charlene Morrow and Teri Perl, eds. Westport, Conn., Greenwood Press, 1998. 302p. illus. index. $49.95. ISBN 0-313-29131-4.

This work presents articles on the lives of 59 women, recognized as leaders and innovators in mathematics and related fields. Nearly all of the women are from the nineteenth and twentieth centuries. Although more than three-fourths of the women exercised their professional work in the United States, one-half were born in other countries. Considerable effort was made to include women from diverse ethnic backgrounds. It should be noted that most of the women selected are still alive with long professionally active lives, but a few are under 50, with one in her thirties. At a time when female role models are desperately needed in mathematics and the sciences, this collection is a great mentoring tool for mathematics.

The signed articles run from about 1,400 to about 2,000 words. Each is accompanied by a photograph or sketch of the subject. Each article concludes with a selected bibliography that includes titles by or about the subject. Much of the information is gathered from published material, but some information was collected through interviews with the subjects. The 36 contributors hold doctorate or advanced degrees in the mathematical sciences or education. Each of the contributors, along with his or her credentials, is listed at the end of the book. There are two appendixes, a listing by date of birth, and a list of countries of employment and origin.

The biographies are well written and interesting, especially about the way the individuals became involved in mathematics, and inspirational in the way some had to overcome obstacles in their career paths. This resources should be in every school library and general reference collection. [R: SLJ, Nov 98, p. 156; BL, 1 Dec 98, p. 694; Choice, Nov 98, p. 498]—**Margaret F. Dominy**

1543.   **Standard Math Interactive.** [CD-ROM] Boca Raton, Fla., CRC Press, 1997. Minimum system requirements: IBM or compatible 486. CD-ROM drive. Windows 95 or Windows 3.51. 16MB RAM. 32MB hard disk space. $249.95.

Standard Math Interactive is a computer version of the familiar *CRC Standard Mathematical Tables* (30th ed.; CRC Press, 1996). It contains the complete text of the book version, augmented by a search engine; an application that can be used to evaluate, graph, and otherwise manipulate equations and tables; and an animated program demo. This reviewer tested this program on a Pentium 200 with a 17-inch display and generous (by the program's standards) memory and hard disk space.

The book portion of the package presents the materials usually found in the print edition completely and clearly. The specialized symbols needed in a math text are well rendered, although the smallest equation font was difficult to read. The search capabilities work as promised, providing an effective way to locate material. The search capability is likely to be of most use to the inexperienced user, as the book version is a well-organized reference and designed to make finding things easy for regular users.

The major superiority of the CD-ROM version over the print version is its inclusion of the evaluation module MathDoc. Based on the Maple math engine, this program allows you take preselected equations and expressions from the reference book component, edit them, and evaluate the result. One can also transfer a table into a mini-spreadsheet. Although this component does allow the user to manipulate the form's individual terms of equations, MathDoc does not appear to provide a simple way to assign values to some of the unknowns in an equation, then solve for a remaining unknown. This limitation seriously limits its usefulness in comparison to full-blown symbolic mathematics packages (such as *MathCAD* and *Mathematica*).

The package has small defects as well, including a wide variety of default volume settings (during the review the speaker volume control needed to be readjusted), poor indexing of the online manual, and an introductory demo that combined visual flash with too little content.

This package is, however, quite useful to anyone who uses the print version regularly. In a library setting and for occasional users its advantages over the print version are less clear. Beginners will find that the search capabilities speed up the process of getting familiar with the material, but the improvements will not, in many cases, be enough to justify using the CD-ROM version. [R: LJ, 1 Feb 98, p. 124]—**Ray Olszewski**

1544.   Tuma, Jan J., and Ronald A. Walsh. **Engineering Mathematics Handbook.** 4th ed. New York, McGraw-Hill, 1998. 566p. illus. index. $79.95. ISBN 0-07-065529-4.

This is a 4th edition of a well-known and well-used handbook. The handbook is predominantly used in general engineering as a bench handbook or for its many tables, equations, and solutions. This edition continues the solid work of the first 3 editions, despite the death of Jan J. Tuma, one of the authors.

The preface suggests a number of changes and developments in science and mathematics. Unfortunately, the authors do not address the nature of these changes except for a curious two paragraphs dealing with Texas Instruments and Hewlett Packard handheld calculators. It seems unusual to discuss handheld calculators in a handbook directed at engineers and more curious to name models. The TI-85 and the HP-48G are both good models, but more advanced models have already taken their place. The inclusion of specific models of handheld calculators was a mistake on the part of the authors.

The preface aside, most of this handbook is a compendium of tables, equations, and general information related in some way to engineering. In this respect, this is and continues to be a solid handbook. However, there is nothing to distinguish this particular handbook from others on the market. The ultimate purchase decision will be made more on the basis of factors other than the contents. This is not a second-place handbook, but neither has it gone out of its way to distinguish itself. Personal preference will dictate the use and purchase decision for this title. It is recommended for community college and university libraries and special information center collections.
—**C. D. Hurt**

1545.   **World Directory of Mathematicians 1998.** 11th ed. Rio de Janeiro, Brazil, International Mathematical Union; distr., Providence, R.I., American Mathematical Society, 1998. 1093p. $60.00pa.

The 11th edition of the *World Directory of Mathematicians* contains 4 major sections. It lists 62 country members of the International Mathematical Union, 177 mathematical organizations, and the names of 53,849 individual mathematicians from countries around the world. Although the criteria for inclusion have been circulated to the National Committees for Mathematics in all countries and academies adhering to the International Mathematics Union, preparation, printing, and distribution of this directory are handled by the American Mathematical Society (AMS). This new edition contains lists of names submitted to the AMS by electronic mail, hard copy, and disk.

After an explanatory note on the ordering of entries and a list of abbreviations, the body of the directory begins with an alphabetic list of countries with organizations and committees reporting to the secretariat of the International Mathematics Union. Under each country the entries are listed alphabetically. The 2d section is composed of mathematical organizations from 4 of the following broad geographic areas: Africa, the Americas, Asia and Oceania, and Europe. It is in this section of the directory where many entries without recent verification first appear. According to the preface, the AMS has tried to contact all the math societies in the world for the preparation of this directory but has been unable to get updated lists in many cases. In such cases, data have been reprinted from the 10th edition and marked with an asterisk. The preface also states that data from editions prior to the 10th have been omitted, except in the case of Bulgaria. Africa lists 4 of 12 total entries with asterisks, the Americas list 2 of 52, Asia and Oceania list 6 of 39, and Europe lists 17 of 74 total entries with asterisks. Hence, a total of 16 percent of all the entries in this section are based solely on information from previous editions.

The 3d major section is an alphabetic list of individual mathematicians. It is the core of the directory. Each entry lists an address for the affiliate institution of each individual. Many entries include e-mail addresses as well. The 4th and last section of the directory is a geographic list of individual mathematicians. The order is alphabetic first by country, then by individual. This section also totals the number of individual mathematicians by country. Like the 2d section of the directory, the last section uses asterisks to indicate information from the 10th edition. The last section uncovers another weakness of this tool. Because most readers will use section 3, the alphabetic list of individual mathematicians, it would have been more informative for the asterisks in section 4 to have been placed by the corresponding entry of each individual in section 3 to indicate dated information. However, from the information provided by section 4 of the directory, only 1,192 of the 53,849 individuals in section 3 are listed with information from previous editions. This represents less than 3 percent of the total.

What is most impressive about this directory is its scope and size. It includes worldwide organizations of every type in the mathematical sciences. This title will be especially useful to academic libraries that support graduate programs in mathematics.—**C. Michael Phillips**

36 Resource Sciences

ENERGY RESOURCES

1546. Beaty, Wayne. **U.S. Electric Utility Industry Directory 1998.** 7th ed. Tulsa, Okla., PennWell Publishing, 1997. 785p. index. $195.00pa. ISSN 1058-2479.

The purpose of this directory is to provide information about investor-owned, municipal, and publicly owned electric utilities as well as rural electric membership corporations, federal power agencies, systems or projects, and power pools. A section listing Canadian utilities is also featured. Addresses and telephone numbers for various regulatory agencies have been provided for convenient reference. The 1st part of the directory contains 2 industry reports on Electric Light and Power's top 100 electric utilities, 1996 financial performances, and 1996 operating performances. General information on investor-owned electric utilities holding companies that are indeed a special grouping of companies is provided. These are companies that have taken hold of their new place in a competitive electric utility industry market in part using innovative operating strategies and strategic investments in both domestic and international energy markets.

The major part of this directory contains the following sections: holding companies; investor-owned electric utilities; municipal and other publicly owned utilities; rural electric membership corporations; federal, state, and district systems; councils and power pools; Canadian utilities; regulatory agencies; and indexes by company, geographic locale, and personnel. This directory is highly recommended for everybody involved in the electric utility industry.—**Ludmila N. Ilyina**

1547. **Energy Statistics Yearbook, 1995. Annuaire des Statistiques de l'Energie.** By the Department for Economic and Social Information and Policy Analysis, Statistics Division. New York, United Nations, 1997. 486p. $100.00. ISBN 92-1-061170-5. ISSN 0256-6400. S/N E/F.97.XVII.8.

This yearbook is a major contribution to energy statistics on both global and regional levels. The work contains data in original and common units (coal equivalent, oil equivalent, joules) for the years 1992 to 1995. By referring to previous volumes of the publication, a time series can be established from 1950 to the present. It should be noted that in addition to the basic tables showing production, trade, stock changes, bunkers, and consumption, information is included on various other topics such as (1) the ratio of crude petroleum reserves to petroleum production; (2) principal importers and exporters of coal, crude petroleum, and natural gas for the years 1994 to 1995; (3) the capacity of petroleum refineries, natural gas liquids plants, and electric generating plants by type; (4) the new and renewable sources of energy—fuelwood, charcoal, bagasse, peat, and electricity generated from hydro, solar, wind, tide, wave, or geothermal sources; and (5) heat obtained from combined heat and power plants generating electricity and useful heat in a single installment, district heating plants, and nuclear power plants and geothermal sources. The book will be used as the most reliable source of compatible information for everyone who is working in fields of energy, geography, economy, environment, and other branches.
—**Ludmila N. Ilyina**

1548.   **Pricing Statistics Sourcebook.** 4th ed. Sandra Meyer and others, eds. Tulsa, Okla., PennWell Publishing, 1998. 709p. $245.00 w/disk. ISSN 1078-4489.

This volume, produced by the editors of the *Oil & Gas Journal* as part of their Database Publications, reports prices on energy, U.S. crude oil, international crude oil, refiner (U.S.), natural gas, gasoline, and fuel oil. This is an amazing array of data, well deserving of the "sourcebook" designation for its 4th edition. For example, the data on gasoline prices in the United States include the following: average, leaded regular, premium, unleaded regular, unleaded midgrade; by state; by month; and from 1985 to July 1997. In addition, the sourcebook gives prices on aviation gasoline, jet fuel, kerosene, propane, fuel oil, diesel oil, residual fuel oil, and others, with different tables for product for resale or product for end users. Also given are the posted price for U.S. crude for 14 varieties (grades) and the average export prices (also spot price) for 36 grades of international crude. The appendixes include a chronology of major events in the industry, a glossary, Organization of Petroleum Exporting Countries and Organization for Economic Cooperation and Development members; and conversion factors (e.g., tonnes to long tons to short tons, gallons to barrels). Fortunately, these data are available on nonreturnable diskettes or CD-ROM.
—**Richard A. Miller**

1549.   **Worldwide Petroleum Industry Outlook: 1998-2002 Projection to 2007.** 14th ed. Robert J. Beck, ed. Tulsa, Okla., PennWell Publishing, 1997. 301p. $195.00pa. ISBN 0-87814-730-6.

Beck (economics editor, *Oil and Gas Journal*) reviews the recent history (since 1970 or 1975) and offers projections (generally to 2007) in each of a variety of categories: worldwide outlook; U.S. outlook; capital expenditures (drilling, refining, petrochemicals, pipelines, transportation, and other areas); exploration, drilling, and production; refining and petrochemicals; transportation; natural gas; other energy sources; the Organization of Petroleum Exporting Countries (OPEC); and other forecasts (a miscellaneous category). Within each chapter Beck presents a historical (25-year) overview with considerable detail; the outlook (10 years); and especially "Keys to the Future," well-written points of considerable importance in each section for consideration of the development of the industry segments during the next decade. Tables (approximately 150 throughout the book) cover enormous amounts of data—for example, the table on OPEC shows gas production, liquids production, crude reserves, gas reserves, crude production and capacity, refining production and capacity, exports, prices, demand, production/ reserves, quotas, and value, each by country and by year where appropriate.

This annually published sourcebook is useful. This volume appeared in August 1997. Fifteen-day inspection volumes are available from PennWell Publishing by calling 1-800-742-9764.—**Richard A. Miller**

ENVIRONMENTAL SCIENCE

Atlases

1550.   **The Atlas of Global Change.** Lothar Beckel, ed. New York, Macmillan Library Reference/Simon & Schuster Macmillan, 1998. 164p. illus. maps. index. $90.00. ISBN 0-02-864956-7.

This book is concerned with environmental change on a planetary scale. A wide range of topics is covered through text, photographs, and maps. However, the real attraction of this book are the more than 130 satellite images of the Earth's surface, illustrating everything from geographical features to recently popularized phenomena like El Niño and the ozone holes.

The book will not serve as an information or data source for the serious researcher, but rather is intended to "foster growth of consciousness and sharpen our understanding of natural processes and of the consequences of human interventions in the natural environment." The book is successful in this regard as even the most disinterested browser will marvel at the beauty of geographic features as photographed from satellites. The book is not just an atlas that contains pictures and maps of the various continents and countries, but also an attempt to illustrate global change and humankind's imprint on the planet. It starts with some general satellite images of the Earth, illustrating changes through the day and the seasons, contours of the Earth and the ocean floors, plate tectonics, atmospheric circulation, and so forth. Coverage then moves to key environmental topics like ozone holes and the silting of Lake Chad, as well as natural phenomena like Mount Saint Helens and a sandstorm over the Persian Gulf. Each topic is generally covered by some descriptive text, an on-the-ground photograph, and a large-scale satellite image. A map of the photographed area is included to orient the reader.

The book was poorly edited, containing problems such as improper grammar and inconsistent use of parentheses. In one location, the text for a particular topic simply ends in mid-sentence, leaving the reader searching for more. Also, it is unfortunate that, due to binding, much of western Europe is lost in the two-page maps of the entire planet. Despite these problems, the atlas belongs in libraries as an important illustration of global-scale environmental events and characteristics. [R: BL, 15 Dec 98, p. 762]—**Michael G. Messina**

1551.   **Facts on File Environment Atlas.** rev. ed. By David Wright. New York, Facts on File, 1997. 96p. illus. maps. index. $18.95. ISBN 0-8160-3715-9.

This book offers a broad, global overview of environmental problems, with interesting facts and challenging quizzes (answers are at the end of the book). Information ranges from map reading to rice growing. Each section of the world is covered with an overview and then a discussion of environmental issues on various countries in that region. For example, the section on North America includes a two-page introduction with maps, pictures, and a discussion of the continent. The rest of the section covers Canada, the United States, Central America, and the Caribbean.

The book is written at a junior high or high school level. The information will not become quickly outdated because it is more of a generic presentation than a statistical outline of the problems. The original copyright date is 1992. The writing style has a European flavor. Because it was first published in Great Britain, measurements are given in metric units, and it has a European viewpoint. The tone of the book is extremely pro-environment. This is not a balanced look at both sides of an issue, and sometimes the author's editorializing is carried to an extreme, such as when commenting on cars and stating that "adults STILL 'worship' them!" (p. 21).

The book's uniqueness stems from its global perspective on problems that affect everyone. It also provides a valuable overview of environmental issues. The book will be a useful resource for raising students' consciousness of environmental issues or generating a classroom discussion on these issues.—**Suzanne Julian**

Biography

1552.   **Biographical Dictionary of American and Canadian Naturalists and Environmentalists.** Keir B. Sterling, Richard P. Harmond, George A. Cevasco, and Lorne F. Hammond, eds. Westport, Conn., Greenwood Press, 1997. 937p. index. $175.00. ISBN 0-313-23047-1.

The *Biographical Dictionary of American and Canadian Naturalists and Environmentalists* provides biographical information on more than 400 U.S. and Canadian naturalists, ecologists, environmentalists, scientists, writers, conservationists, and artists from the late fifteenth century to the present. Each entry contains basic biographical information including name, place and date of birth and death, titles, a brief paragraph on family history and education, positions held, a general essay on the individual's career, and a list of major contributions and a bibliography. The entries are succinct and carefully edited to provide only vital information. Little extraneous material is found.

There are no comparable reference works that cover the same areas found in this volume. Many of the same individuals do appear in other biographical sources, but this collection is unique. It is possible to find the pioneers of many of the basic environmental sciences in this work, including the early geographers, botanists, and a few individuals not usually associated with the environmental movement, such as Peter the Great of Russia, who initiated what would be called a "sustained yield" basis for logging; Meriwether Lewis, who described both the land and fauna and flora of much of North America; and even George Catlin and Henry David Thoreau, who wrote on the values of the wilderness.

This book is highly recommended for all larger public and academic libraries and for smaller collections that are attempting to be comprehensive in the areas of environmentalism and naturalism. It is bound to become a basic reference source for these areas. [R: RUSQ, Summer 98, p. 343; LJ, 15 Feb 97, p. 127; RBB, 1 April 97, p. 1352]—**Robert L. Wick**

Dictionaries and Encyclopedias

1553.   Dictionary of Ecology and the Environment. 3d ed. P. H. Collin, ed. Middlesex, Great Britain, Peter Collin, 1995; repr., Chicago, Fitzroy Dearborn, 1998. 253p. $35.00. ISBN 1-57958-075-0.

This dictionary, originally published in 1995, provides simple definitions for terms that comprise the basic vocabulary of ecology and environmental studies. The primary audience is the layperson for whom scientific or technical terms are made accessible. All entries include phonetic pronunciation, part of speech, and a brief definition. Selected entries include an additional "comment," which amplifies the definition; this portion of the entry is graphically highlighted to distinguish it from the definition proper. For example, the definition of *acid-proof* is accompanied by a comment that references the measurement of acidity via the pH scale. Other selected entries are accompanied by a quotation, which employs the term in question. The source of these quotations is indicated, and they range from the journal *Nature* to *Farmers Weekly*. The dictionary concludes with several appendixes, including an outline of the classification of living organisms, a selective list of endangered species (based on the 1994 IUCN Red List of Threatened Animals), and a list of recent major man-made disasters.

A criticism of this work may center on the brevity of some of the definitions. The choice to include certain terms may be questioned as well. And not all of the comments or quotations are instructive. Despite these concerns, this dictionary should prove useful to individuals requiring basic, nontechnical definitions. It is recommended for undergraduate science collections and public libraries.—**Michael Weinberg**

1554.   Papadakis, Elim, comp. Historical Dictionary of the Green Movement. Lanham, Md., Scarecrow, 1998. 223p. (Historical Dictionaries of Religions, Philosophies, and Movements, no.20). $62.00. ISBN 0-8108-3502-9.

This is one of those problematic "historical dictionaries" that attempts to delineate a history while also defining terms and identifying groups, characters, and events, all in an alphabetic format. The "Green Movement" refers to a diverse mixture of environmental groups that developed primarily in the West in the 1960s. One purpose of this book is to connect the "Greens" to their forebears in the nineteenth and early twentieth centuries. Another is to attempt to summarize the many philosophical underpinnings of modern environmentalism. The compiler's 30-page introduction does indeed begin to meet these goals, but this history can be read in much more detail elsewhere. Most of the book consists of dictionary entries that are sometimes several pages long, making them more like encyclopedia articles (for example, see "Green Parties, Australia"). The compiler includes in most of the entries an analysis of the event, phenomenon, or group, obscuring the actual defining information. One result is that the reader can quickly infer that most "Green" movements are on the political far left, with lots of crypto-Marxist rhetoric about "wealth redistribution," "socialization," and "postmaterialism." Furthermore, the choice of topics in the book is eclectic, including "Think globally, act locally" (under "T"), "Small Is Beautiful," and "Spirituality." Some places, such as Australia, Germany, the United Kingdom, Czechoslovakia, and even Tasmania have entries detailing the history and status of their local Greens, but other big players are missing, such as China, Russia, France, and the United States. Conventional conservationists (e.g., Theodore Roosevelt) are not mentioned, but David Foreman of "Earth First!" is. Animal rights are covered in detail, but abortion is not. In short, there are three reasons why this book is not necessary for library collections: it has a poor format for the transmission of information and ideas, the entries it does have are not complete, and the whole package is not worth $62.—**Mark A. Wilson**

1555.   Routledge German Dictionary of Environmental Technology: Deutsch-Englisch/Englisch-Deutsch. Worterbuch Umwelttechnologie. New York, Routledge, 1997. 271p. $140.00. ISBN 0-415-11243-5.

This translation dictionary follows the Routledge tradition of thorough, professional preparation. Considerable effort appears to have been put into covering all core areas of environmental technology without overlapping into general technology, for a total of 25,000 entries. Subject areas include air quality control; analysis, sampling, and testing; environmental policy and legal instruments; environmentally related safety engineering; general environmental management; noise pollution and control; soil contamination and remediation; water pollution and wastewater treatment; water supply and drinking water; and waste treatment and management. Content was prepared by German and English terminologists with current experience in environmental technology. Their work was subsequently edited for coverage and spelling variants. The final product was edited by another team of expert English and German lexicographers to ensure consistency and overall focus. This dictionary is recommended for practitioners and all types of libraries, particularly libraries supporting environmental engineering programs.
—**Barbara Delzell**

Handbooks and Yearbooks

1556.   Becher, Anne. **Biodiversity: A Reference Handbook.** Santa Barbara, Calif., ABC-CLIO, 1998. 275p. index. (Contemporary World Issues). $39.50. ISBN 0-87436-923-1.

This work is part of the Contemporary World Issues series. It provides a good starting point for research by businesspeople who use environmental data. Chapter 1 contains an overview of the subject. Chapter 2 is a detailed chronology of events relating to biodiversity. The subsequent four chapters provide biographical sketches, facts and data or documents and other primary-source material, a directory of organizations and agencies, and an annotated list of print and nonprint resources. The entries for organizations include the name, address, telephone number, fax number, e-mail address, Website URL, description of the organization, and a list of its publications. The directory is limited to organizations in the United States. The glossary at the end of the book defines the technical terms and abbreviations used throughout the text. The alphabetically arranged subject index will help to locate information.

This book, carefully organized and easy to use, will help readers find the environmental information they need relating to biodiversity. It is recommended for public, academic, and special libraries. [R: LJ, 1 Sept 98, p. 168; Choice, Nov 98, p. 542]—**Marilynn Green Hopman**

1557.   **Book of Lists for Regulated Hazardous Substances.** 8th ed. By the Editorial Staff of Government Institutes. Rockville, Md., Government Institutes, 1997. 604p. $79.00pa. ISBN 0-86587-585-5.

This latest edition of the *Book of Lists for Regulated Hazardous Substances* follows the format of the previous edition published in 1993 (see ARBA 94, entry 2010). The editors have compiled more than 100 lists of substances, standards, or related information (compared to 72 lists in the 7th edition) that are frequently referenced in regulatory compliance and implementation literature. The vast majority of the lists are found in the Code of Federal Regulations dated July 1, 1996. They were selected for inclusion by environmental attorneys, engineers, and consultants who are named in the acknowledgments. The goal of the publisher, who specializes in government regulatory topics, is simply to provide the regulated community with convenient access to these lists pulled from 21 environment, health, and safety *Code of Federal Regulations* (CFR). There is no editorial comment provided; the lists are literally copied from pages of the CFR, with proper citations included. The table of contents, which is the only access point, consists of chapters corresponding to the major environmental, health, and safety acts (e.g., Occupational Health and Safety Act). Under each act are the name of pertinent lists and their sources in the CFR or other government literature.

With the understanding that this book does not presume to be a comprehensive compilation of every environmental, health, and safety CFR list, it continues to serve as a useful reference for its targeted audience.
—**Michael Weinberg**

1558.   Brownell, F. William and others. **Clean Air Handbook.** 3d ed. Rockville, Md., Government Institutes, 1998. 280p. $95.00pa. ISBN 0-86587-616-9.

This handbook will help the user begin to understand the Clean Air Act (CAA), which is continuously described as the most complicated piece of environmental legislation ever established. Brownell, the principal author, is well versed in environmental law and heads the Hunton & Williams Environmental Team. Several members of this team contributed their expertise to help make this a more user-friendly reference source.

A researcher can find a variety of publications, both government and private, to look at the ever-changing issues involving clean air. For a person acquainted with the basic information, the *Clean Air Handbook* provides an enlightening overview of the Clean Air Act, giving the reader more insight into the enormous legal, health, and financial considerations related to this act and its amendments. Thankfully, the handbook helps to make these important issues more understandable; it also provides citations for those hardy souls who wish to delve deeper into the federal regulations, cases, and so forth. Four appendixes aid the user with a list of acronyms, source categories subject to CAA programs, pollutants subject to CAA programs, and the Clean Air Act Implementation: the Environmental Protection Agency's regulatory agenda into the year 2000.

Another practical guide, edited by Robert J. Martineau Jr. and David P. Novello, *The Clean Air Act Handbook* (American Bar Association, 1997), gives a more in-depth and legalistic view of the Clean Air Act. This 3d edition of the *Clean Air Handbook* is recommended for academic libraries with environmental science programs and large public libraries.—**Diane J. Turner**

1559. **Cooper's Comprehensive Environmental Desk Reference.** [CD-ROM]. New York, Van Nostrand Reinhold, 1997. Minimum system requirements (Windows version): IBM or compatible. CD-ROM drive. Windows 3.1. 4MB RAM. 8MB hard disk space. Minimum system requirements (Macintosh version): 68202 processor. CD-ROM drive. System 7. 4MB RAM. 8MB hard disk space. $99.95. ISBN 0-442-02161-5.

This desk reference was designed as a specialized reference tool for the standard environmental jargon used by environmentalists, planners, compliance officers, bureaucrats, professionals, and others working in this field. It is an expanded version of the author's previously self-published publication, *Cooper's Pocket Environmental Reference*.

The disk is easy to install, and the use of the standard Windows-based format makes the product easy to navigate. An added feature is the use of the Folio Bound Views software to make available more sophisticated features for searching and creating personal files. A searching guide is available on the CD-ROM, which is helpful for explaining the toolbar functions, and extensive help screens are also provided. Off the main screen, users can search by keyword or use one of the eight categories provided. Of note are the sections that include environmental terms and terminology with entries ranging from a sentence to a paragraph; a listing of environmental acronyms and abbreviations; a sample environmental site assessment; and a listing of Environmental Protection Agency offices, programs, and regional contacts. Tool bar functions allow the user to save, print, highlight, and create personal files or shadow files for searching or annotating.

Although this product is not encyclopedic in nature, it does have some useful information that should appeal to a more specialized audience. This reference is recommended for research collections and special libraries.

—**Julia Perez**

1560. Crawford, Mark. **Toxic Waste Sites: An Encyclopedia of Endangered America.** Santa Barbara, Calif., ABC-CLIO, 1997. 324p. illus. maps. $65.00. ISBN 0-87436-934-7.

This book summarizes the United States' effort to clean up some 1,300 Superfund sites—the hazardous waste (or toxic) sites that the U.S. Environmental Protection Agency has determined to be especially hazardous to human health and the environment. It provides basic information on each site. Many sites were landfills or waste dumps in operation before 1970 and are now in conditions known to be inadequate. Older sites include deserted mining operations or sites of coal-gasification plants once used by many cities to provide town lighting gas. All involve contamination of land and often of local surface water, groundwater, and air. The book's introduction describes how the sites came into being, how they are evaluated for hazards, and what potential emergency cleanup action will be taken. The long-term (sometimes many years) actions that are then necessary to evaluate, find, and determine who will pay and clean up these sites are summarized. This book does not describe the many sites that the government itself contaminated; these would need a separate book to describe. The book will be useful to environmental professionals, to environmental studies students, and to citizens concerned about a local site. [R: RUSQ, Summer 98, pp. 372-373]—**Marquita Hill**

1561. **The Environment Encyclopedia and Directory 1998.** London, Europa; distr., Detroit, Gale, 1998. 560p. index. $385.00. ISBN 1-85743-028-X.

Environmental concern has become commonplace, both locally and at a world scale. Indeed, political as well as scientific identification with ecological issues has become the stuff of daily headlines and countless international conferences. Controversial topics such a global warming, atmospheric ozone depletion, species extinction, and the general quality of human life in an increasingly crowded and industrialized world draw universal attention from all points of the ideological and philosophical spectrum. As debate focused on environmental issues reaches increasingly emotional levels, what is needed is a relatively dispassionate source of basic information, which this volume abundantly provides.

The book contains a brief introductory essay by the editors, a series of pertinent, well-drafted maps, and a dictionary of environmental terms that comprises roughly one-quarter of the text. Most of the volume consists of a comprehensive listing of organizations and agencies (arranged by country) concerned with environmental issues. Addresses, fax numbers, e-mail addresses, contact persons, and general focus of concern are included in each case. A biographical index of prominent environmental scientists and activists and a cross-referenced index of environmental organizations by specific field of activity complete the volume. This is a detailed, refined reference work that should prove indispensable for any agency or individual with an environmental agenda.

—**James R. McDonald**

1562.   Guttentag, Roger M. **Recycling and Waste Management Guide to the Internet.** Rockville, Md., Government Institutes, 1997. 267p. index. (Government Institutes Internet Series). $49.00pa. ISBN 0-86587-582-0.

Guttentag is well qualified to review issues of recycling and waste management with years of experience consulting on these issues. He has pulled together a useful guide to Internet sites in recycling and waste management. The general introduction describes the organization of the guide and provides useful tips for its use and Internet problem resolution. The guide is organized by subject and site name. It also lists discussion groups and newsgroups and contains an index.

Site descriptions include key site pages, e-mail address, descriptive overview of the site, and site resources—for instance, whether the site has an index, fees, or links and if it has search engine and downloading capability. Of course, due to the nature of the Internet and Websites, this printed volume will be outdated quickly. Nonetheless, as is pointed out in the introduction, it can be frustrating to search the Internet for relevant sites, and human judgment and experience are still necessary to identify good sites. This guide succeeds in its stated purposes of identifying relevant sites and saving a user time and effort by summarizing site content. This guide is recommended for personal or library reference collection.—**Constance Rinaldo**

1563.   **Human Choice and Climate Change.** Steve Rayner and Elizabeth L. Malone, eds. Columbus, Ohio, Battelle Press, 1998. 4v. index. $100.00/set. ISBN 1-57477-040-3.

The editors introduce each volume of this 4-volume set with a general explanation of the set and a specific description of each work's focus. Raynor and Malone so completely define academic concepts and terms that a lay reader can understand the topics. Insets highlighted major points that the editors felt were most important. Articles for each volume were contributed and peer reviewed by contributors associated with the Pacific Northwest National Laboratory. As part of its Global Studies Program, the Pacific Northwest National Laboratory initiated programs to correlate the relationships between human and natural systems. Climate changes around the world and their affects on mankind were a natural topic. Of course, human actions and creations can conversely influence the world's weather. All of the articles in the 4 volumes are well written and thoroughly documented. Charts and graphs are appropriately placed within the text. Each article concludes with numerous references.

Academic libraries will find this set informative. Students in a variety of disciplines from sociology to meteorology will use articles from *Human Choice and Climate Change* for research and reviews.
—**Marjorie H. Jones**

564.   **The International Handbook of Environmental Sociology.** Michael Redclift and Graham Woodgate, eds. Northhampton, Mass., Edward Elgar, 1997. 485p. index. $120.00. ISBN 1-85898-405-X.

Redclift and Woodgate, two U.K. professors of environmental sociology, have collaborated again, with their new work, *The International Handbook of Environmental Sociology.* Redclift and Woodgate commissioned essays from more than 30 scholars representing more than 10 countries around the world. Each author writes with a distinctive style, yet the work flows well because the editors selected recognized scholars with outstanding credentials. Adding to the cohesiveness of the material is the fact that the editors grouped the essays in related sections. Part 1, "Concepts and Theories in Environmental Sociology," contains writings that explain the status and emphasis of environmental sociology. Part 2, "Substantive Issues for Environmental Sociology," covers current concerns and questions for further research. Part 3, "International Perspectives on Environment and Society," describes specific global movements and problems. Readers will be hindered because the work lacks a detailed glossary. The introduction indicates that the work is meant to provide background on this new field, so the addition of a glossary would be prudent. It is unfortunate that the essayists' credentials are listed collectively at the front of the book; it is inconvenient to continually flip to the front. A one-sentence biography would be better placed at the beginning of each essay. Academic libraries, especially those serving a strong social science community, will find this work a worthwhile addition. Professors of sociology and environmental studies could use the essays for additional readings and reviews.—**Marjorie H. Jones**

565.   Miller, E. Willard, and Ruby M. Miller. **Indoor Pollution: A Reference Handbook.** Santa Barbara, Calif., ABC-CLIO, 1998. 330p. index. (Contemporary World Issues). $39.50. ISBN 0-87436-985-2.

The challenges of dealing with indoor air quality have been with us since the beginning of time. This book, one of the Contemporary World Issues series from ABC-CLIO, provides readers an overview and general understanding of "sick building syndrome." Although there are many laws regulating outdoor pollutants, there are few governmental regulations to regulate home and work environments. This easy-to-use source is divided into 5 sections covering topics from asbestos to formaldehyde to radon. It provides the average consumer with information about the air we breathe indoors that is both educational and frightening. The compact volume covers laws and regulations, organizations and associations, and audiovisual aids, and provides a bibliography of books, journal articles, and governmental documents. Also included are listings of acronyms, measurements, testing information, and sources of volatile organic compounds in indoor air; a glossary of key terms; and an alphabetic index. The topic of indoor air pollution applies to everyone, and yet is has not been taken nearly as seriously as outdoor pollution. Civil litigation will continue to increase as consumers become more aware of how the air in the workplace affects health. Indoor pollution will be getting increasing attention, and a volume like this will be invaluable to consumers looking for answers. High school, public, and academic libraries will find this book and excellent addition to their collection. [R: BL, 1 Dec 98, p. 698]—**Diane J. Turner**

1566.   **Patty's Industrial Hygiene and Toxicology.** [CD-ROM]. New York, John Wiley, 1998. Minimum system requirements: IBM or compatible. Single-speed CD-ROM drive. Windows 3.0. 4MB RAM (16MB preferred). 4MB hard disk space. VGA monitor. $2,495.00. ISBN 0-471-18192-7.

Patty's Industrial Hygiene and Toxicology has long been a standard reference source for information on industrial health and toxicology. It is especially strong in information on toxic chemicals and their effects in the workplace. Now in its 4th edition, this heavyweight is published in 10 volumes containing more than 10,000 printed pages. The CD-ROM version of this set allows for searching through all 10,000 pages with a single search, an advantage over the printed version. However, there are problems with its searching capabilities and in getting around in the database.

There are several ways to use the CD-ROM. From the opening screen, one can click on any of the volume and read through it just like the print version. The main reason for buying the CD-ROM is to use the search capabilities, yet searching in this program is different from searching in most databases and requires the use of the accompanying manual to figure it out. Online help is not readily apparent. One must either press control-L or click on the title area (which is not at all noticeable) and from there select Help from the File menu. A "Help" button would be useful.

From the search screen, one can search by a single term or combine them. Searching by a specific compound such as "vinylcyclohexene dioxide," is excellent. The software finds the term anywhere in the text. The problem comes when the search is for a more common term, "lead," for instance. The program finds this word and the word "led" and "lead" (as in "lead and I shall follow") anywhere in the database, making this an impossible search. Users can select the category Topic Names, then do the search, and this narrows the search to lead in category. To search by a category *only*, one must click off the check mark by body text. This is not apparent to one just sitting down to the computer to do a search, as most patrons would do in a library. This software needs to be redesigned to make searching easier for library patrons who will not take the time to read through the 32-page user's guide before they do a search.

Once the search is done, a user can view the text but *only one* section or topic at a time. The Next arrow must be hit to get to the next screen for more information. The text should scroll down, not be limited to one section at a time. The software allows printing and downloading, but the same problem of printing just the single topic or section will occur. It is possible to print or download an entire topic section only if the user had read the manual to "pull down the file menu by clicking on title bar and select Print Topics" (p. 26 of manual). This system is not user friendly. However, system requirements for the software are standard, and the installation is easy.

The current price for the print version of *Patty's* is $1,790, and the price for the version 2.0 CD-ROM is $2,495, plus an update for current users for $395. Although searching capabilities for specific compounds is a plus, this software is not worth the extra price until some of the problems listed above are solved.—**Diane B. Rhodes**

1567.   Pohanish, Richard P., and Stanley A. Greene. **Electronic and Computer Industry Guide to Chemical Safety and Environmental Compliance.** New York, John Wiley, 1998. 624p. index. $79.95pa. ISBN 0-471-29285-0.

This is the first of a projected new series of handbooks on hazardous materials in specific major industrial sectors. It is conveniently arranged, with entries in alphabetic order and indexed by synonyms and trade names and by Chemical Abstracts Service Registry Number. Entries are complete, giving trade names and synonyms, various identification numbers; health and safety information (including recommendations for respirator selection chemical reactivity hazards; fire information; and environmental information. This self-contained handbook also includes an appendix of sources of information, including government hotlines and Websites as well as reference books; a directory of Poison Control Centers in the United States; and a thorough well-written glossary of terms used in the text. Coverage is extensive for materials found in the electronics/computer industry, but the authors caution that "absence of data does not necessarily mean that a substance is neither hazardous, nor unregulated under a specific law or statute."

There are now many guides to hazardous properties of materials, from the encyclopedic *Sax's Dangerous Properties of Industrial Materials* (9th ed., Van Nostrand Reinhold, 1996) to many more specialized titles. The authors of this guide have been co-authors of several other guides. It is likely that many large science and technology libraries are adequately served by the works that are already in their collections. However, this book would be an excellent acquisition for any collection serving the electronics and computer science industry or students and researchers in electronics and computer science.—**Robert Michaelson**

1568.   **Rapid Guide to Hazardous Air Pollutants.** By Howard J. Beim, Jennifer Spero, and Louis Theodore. New York, Van Nostrand Reinhold, 1998. 582p. $29.95pa. ISBN 0-442-02515-7.

1569.   **Rapid Guide to Hazardous Chemicals in the Environment.** By Richard P. Pohanish. New York, Van Nostrand Reinhold, 1997. 519p. index. $29.95pa. ISBN 0-442-02527-0.

This work will be useful for researchers with the name of a chemical who want to know the federal laws applying to it. The *Rapid Guide to Hazardous Chemicals in the Environment* provides information on chemicals covered by the following laws: Clean Air Act, Clean Water Act, Resource Conservation and Recovery Act, Safe Drinking Water Act, Superfund or CERCLA (including Emergency Preparedness and Community Right to Know), California's Proposition 65, and Marine Pollutants from the Hazardous Materials Transportation Act. Its 1st chapter, "Using the Book and Summary of Federal Statutes and Regulations," will guide the reader through the information found in each entry. Cross-reference indexes are provided. If the chemical being researched is among the 189 defined as a hazardous air pollutant under the 1990 Clean Air Act Amendments, then the *Rapid Guide to Hazardous Air Pollutants* has pages of information on that chemical. Its 1st chapter provides guidance on understanding that information. Each entry includes the chemical's formula, synonyms, physical properties, chemical properties, and toxic exposure guidelines (which provide ACGIH's threshold limit value, OSHA's permissible exposure limits, the LD50, and the chemical's acute and chronic health risks). These books are useful additions to individual or organizational reference libraries.—**Marquita Hill**

1570.   Strong, Debra L. **Recycling in America: A Reference Handbook.** 2d ed. Santa Barbara, Calif., ABC-CLIO, 1997. 330p. illus. index. (Contemporary World Issues). $39.50. ISBN 0-87436-889-8.

The 2d edition of *Recycling in America* updates and expands Strong's 1992 book of the same title (see ARBA 94, entry 2013 for a review). An introductory chapter and chronology present a concise but informative overview of the current state and the history of recycling. Student researchers in pursuit of often-elusive statistics are sure to appreciate the "Facts and Data" chapter. Directories provide information on dozens of organizations and agencies involved with recycling, and annotated bibliographies point researchers to books, journals, and other useful information sources.

This volume's brief section covering online rescues raises an important question: How useful are books such as *Recycling in America* when so much of the information they contain could be found via the World Wide Web? The answer is that selective, well-organized, and methodical reference books such as this one will remain useful so long as the Web remains in its present unselective, disorganized, and random state. Indeed, even the most expert Web searcher would need days to round up, evaluate, organize, and index all the information contained in this volume. This 2d edition is recommended for libraries supporting undergraduate studies. [R: Choice, July/Aug 98, p. 1834]—**Donald A. Barclay**

NATURAL RESOURCES

1571.   **Natural Resources.** Mark S. Coyne and Craig W. Allin, eds. Pasadena, Calif., Salem Press, 1998. 3v. illus. maps. index. $290.00/set. ISBN 0-89356-912-7.

This 3-volume set provides information about natural resources, such as coal and oil. Eighty-four of the articles focus on specific elements ranging from actinium to zirconium. Other articles focus on topics as diverse as soil, fisheries, and timber. The 483 entries are alphabetically arranged. Entries vary from short summaries of 250 words to articles nearly 4,000 words in length.

"Geologic Processes" covers such resource categories as coal and provides statistics, prices, and supply and demand information. "Health, Resource Exploitation, and Pollution" is about the syntheses of available data on exposure of workers to toxic chemicals and the effects of pollutants on public health. "Environmental Law" includes 13 articles covering particularly significant pieces of legislation. Next come articles on the environmental movement and the Environmental Protection Agency (EPA). Other articles delineate the issues and choices surrounding resource management, recycling, conservation, hazardous waste treatment, and pollution prevention. The article on recycling contains a further reading section. This set of books also includes biographies of such people as Jimmy Carter.

This work is well organized, and the cross-references are helpful for finding additional information. Statistics are collected from such reliable sources as *Statistical Abstracts of the United States* and the *Yearbook of Forest Products*. All of the articles are signed by leading experts and reflect a smooth continuity unusual in reference works of this kind. A wide variety of useful resources are provided at the end of volume 3: a timeline, the periodic table of the elements, and a list of major resources by country and by states in the United States. A glossary is also furnished. The bibliographic section is divided by such subject areas as conservation and energy resources. *Natural Resources* will be a treasure trove of information for resource managers, planners, attorneys specializing in environmental issues, students, and anyone involved in any aspect of managing the planet's natural resources. [R: BL, 1 Sept 98, pp. 160-162; LJ, Aug 98, pp. 77-78; Choice, Oct 98, pp. 294-295]—**Marilynn Green Hopman**

37 Transportation

GENERAL WORKS

1572. **Transportation & Public Utilities USA.** Arsen J. Darnay, ed. Detroit, Gale, 1998. 1007p. index. $199.00. ISBN 0-7876-1665-6.

Transportation & Public Utilities USA (TRUSA) covers all transportation and public utilities, the range of industries in the Standard Industrial Code's (SIC) 4000-4970. There are 124 industries covered at the 2-, 3-, and 4-digit level of the SIC.

Drawing on federal government and private sources for its information, including the *U.S. Economic Census, National Occupational Matrix and County Business Patterns*, TRUSA presents the most recently available national statistical data. The years analyzed include 1987, 1992, and beyond, with data extrapolated or projected when there is no federal reporting. Detailed state-level statistics are provided for each industry for 1992, with ratios. In addition, there is coverage of 736 metropolitan statistical areas or counties. Nearly 5,000 public and private companies that participate in these industries, along with 100 occupational groups employed by the services sector on or before 1994, are included.

Data are presented in 3 distinct parts. Part 1 presents national and state data organized by SIC. Part 2 shows metropolitan area data. Part 3 shows county data. Metro and county sections are organized alphabetically. There are tables to illustrate the data. Six indexes cover SIC codes, subject, companies, counties and metropolitan areas, and occupations. The appendix provides textual descriptions of each industry.

This work is similar to other titles that provide transportation statistics: *Motor Vehicle Facts and Figures* (Detroit: Motor Vehicle Manufacturers Association); *Highway Statistics/Public Roads Administration, Federal Works Agency* (Washington, D.C., GPO, 1947-); and *National Transportation Statistics* (Cambridge, Mass.: GPO, 1977-).

TRUSA is a must for government depository libraries. This work is recommended for all academic, special, and public libraries with gaps in this subject area in their collections.—**Marilynn Green Hopman**

AIR

1573. **Airlines Worldwide.** Stillwater, Minn., Voyageur Press, 1998. 320p. illus. $29.95pa.. ISBN 1-85780-067-2.

Originally published in Germany as *Gluggesellschaften Weltweit*, this directory includes 301 "leading or more interesting airlines." Each of the alphabetically arranged entries (one per page) gives name; mailing address, telephone, and fax numbers of the corporate headquarters; three-letter code; IATA number; ICAO call sign; a short historical and descriptive narrative; a summary of routes; a listing of aircraft owned or on order; and a color photograph showing the line's paint scheme. Coverage is primarily of companies operating scheduled passenger services, but a few large charter and freight/express carriers are included. Most local lines, air taxi companies, and similar small companies are omitted.

The information is current as of August 1997, and appears to be accurate. A few spelling errors are not significant. The layout and typography are attractive, and the reproduction of the photographs is good. A selective, but quite extensive, listing of airport codes and an index of three-letter airline codes are useful additions.

Although specialized transportation collections will require more comprehensive information sources, this is a useful tool for general libraries at a reasonable price.—**Paul B. Cors**

1574.   Guttery, Ben R. **Encyclopedia of African Airlines.** Jefferson, N.C., McFarland, 1998. 291p. illus. index. $75.00. ISBN 0-7864-0495-7.

The slow development of the infrastructure, the varied terrain, the changing weather, and the politics of the various countries are some of the factors in the aviation history of Africa. The author wrote this African aviation history to initiate this historical study of the African airlines and their evolving story.

This book is arranged alphabetically by the airline's home country. Each country section begins with a history of the airline industry within that country. The airlines are arranged alphabetically by name in each of the country chapters. The companies were analyzed on the basis of their origin, growth, route structure, and airline usage. Aircraft data such as registration numbers and nicknames are included if the information was available. All airlines within the continent of Africa were examined. Black-and-white photographs of the planes are included in the entries if available. The information is current as of December 31, 1996. The sole exception is the incorporation of Zaire's 1997 name change to the Democratic Republic of the Congo.

A thorough bibliography and a comprehensive index are located at the back of the book. The appendix lists the major airports by country and city. Annual reports, airline-supplied information, flight schedules, and interviews were used to support this volume. Hundreds of periodicals providing pieces of information were reviewed to provide a comprehensive story. Due to African countries changing their names, the author has a section listing the former name and the new name. Accompanying this list is a current map of the African continent, with a name of the dominant European power, followed by the year of independence. This book is recommended for libraries supporting international business, with interests in African collections and aviation collections.

—**Kay M. Stebbins**

1575.   **Jane's All the World's Aircraft 1998-99.** 89th ed. Paul Jackson, Kenneth Munson, Lindsay Peacock, and John W. R. Taylor, eds. Alexandria, Va., Jane's Information Group, 1998. 848p. illus. index. $410.00. ISBN 0-7106-1788-7.

The introductory matter states that the intent of this work is to provide descriptions of "all known powered aircraft, of which details have been received currently in, or anticipating, commercial production in all countries of the world, apart from rapidly dismantled, ultralight recreational machines" (p. 6). Once again Jane's has clearly met that goal successfully. The arrangement continues to be alphabetic by country, firm name, and aircraft name/model number, respectively, and although the entries do vary in length, most contain detailed technical data, liberally illustrated with photographs (mostly black-and-white), line drawings, and plans. Lighter-than-air craft appear in a separate section; there are brief tabular listings of air-launched missiles and aero-engines. There are extensive indexes, covering not only this edition but also referencing aircraft listed in the previous 10 editions that no longer appear (including gliders and sailplanes, which were last covered in 1992-1993).

This is not an inexpensive work, but it has no rivals for comprehensiveness of coverage and depth of detail. It remains an essential purchase for serious aviation collections in all types of libraries.—**Paul B. Cors**

1576.   Merry, John A. **200 Best Aviation Web Sites: And 100 More Worth Bookmarking.** New York, McGraw-Hill, 1998. 237p. index. $16.95pa. ISBN 0-07-001646-1.

Although "best" is inevitably a subjective decision, pilot/consultant Merry spent more than 3,200 hours online compiling this directory, and every site he has selected is worth the attention of anyone seriously interested in aviation. The entries are grouped in 9 broad subject categories—directories, organizations and associations, weather, pilot resources, museums/education/flight schools, online magazines and news, aviation parts/supplies/aircraft, entertainment, and aviation employment—and the subarrangement appears to be arbitrary. The entries for the "200 best" sites include site name, Website address, a usefulness rating on a scale of 1 to 5, a brief comment on how the site can be used, a more detailed description of content, and an indication of whether the site is free or fee-based. For the 100 sites "worth bookmarking," only name, address, and one or two lines of description are provided. The writing style is informal, but still conveys a good deal of information. There is an index of subjects, but not of Website names. Because Websites are constantly changing, updates are available online at http://www.200bestaviation.com/updates. Almost every aircraft owner or pilot will want to keep a copy of this handy guide at the computer terminal. It will also be useful in any library where there is a demand for aviation information.—**Paul B. Cors**

GROUND

1577. Standard Guide to Cars & Prices: Prices for Collector Vehicles 1901-1990. 10th ed. James T. Lenzke and Ken Buttolph, eds. Iola, Wis., Krause Publications, 1997. 672p. illus. $15.95pa. ISBN 0-87341-532-9.

This is a straightforward guide to prices for thousands of collector vehicles built in the first nine decades of this century. Produced under the editorial guidance of two experts in the field and drawing upon a wealth of data sources, the volume provides a quick overview of the amount one should pay for a particular old vehicle.

Apart from a quick-and-easy introduction on how to use the book and some notes about the advantages and pitfalls of collecting cars, the guide consists of vehicle designations and six columns of prices for conditions ranging from "parts only" to "as good as new." The prices given establish a range rather than an absolute value, as the editors note how specific transaction conditions can modify general market values. About 180 monochrome photographs depict selected models, albeit with no clear reason for choosing one type over another.

Inspection of selected data revealed no errors. Both domestic and imported vehicles (including light trucks and jeeps) are listed, although coverage is not comprehensive. In the domestic section, a photograph of a Dusenberg notes the car sold for $1 million and asks whether it would be worth that much today, but Dusenberg prices are not listed (even though the related Auburn and Cord prices are). Similarly, in the foreign section, Ferrari is conspicuous by its absence.

Overall, however, this is a useful ready-reference guide to its subject, crisply printed on quality paper in a sturdy binding and worth consideration for any library serving patrons who are interested in car collecting.

—**John Howard Oxley**

WATER

1578. Jane's Merchant Ships 1998-99. 3d ed. David Greenman, ed. Alexandria, Va., Jane's Information Group, 1998. 742p. illus. index. $410.00. ISBN 0-7106-1800-X.

This highly technical, fully illustrated recognition guide will be welcomed by maritime academies, shipping lines, and other facilities with maritime interests. How often an institution library acquires such a costly updated edition has to be balanced with its current identification needs and its budget. Consideration must be given to the fact that there is a large fleet of merchant ships—perhaps as many as 25,000 vessels—which will grow by approximately 1,200 ships each year, and that older ships in service will be converted and rebuilt.

The recognition system here describes a merchant vessel using features that should be visible at a distance where the ship's name cannot be read. The three elements in this system are ship type, sequence, and hull form. There are 21 ship types, among them tankers and combination carriers, refrigerated cargo ships, vehicle carriers, and passenger ships and ferries. The sequence element lists features on the ship in the order in which they occur, working forward to aft (e.g., ramps, cranes, funnels, and masts). The final element, hull form, is the arrangement of islands (e.g., superstructures attached to the upper deck). A typical ship entry will include a photograph or diagram, the sequence of features, and the hull form. This is followed by the ship's name, the flag under which it is registered or the country where built, the shipbuilder, the year built, the tonnage, the dimensions, design of main machinery or builder, and the service speed. Each entry uses abbreviations throughout, which must then be checked in a separate section. An alphabetic master index lists the ship's name, type, page number, and the reference number on the page. Readers turning to this excellent guide for the first time will find that its ease of use comes eventually. Their patience, however, will be rewarded.—**Charles R. Andrews**

Author/Title Index

Reference is to entry number.

A. Samarsinghe, S. W. R. de, 484
A-Z of cat diseases & health problems, 1386
A-Z of creative photography, 860
A to Z of Native American women, 386
A to zoo: subject access to children's picture bks, 1008
ABA official American Bar Assn gd to approved law schools, 1999 ed, 558
Abate, Frank R., 900
ABC of bookbinding, 855
ABC-CLIO world hist companion to capitalism, 158
ABC-CLIO world hist companion to utopian movements, 1253
AbuKhalil, As'ad, 507
Accredited insts of postsecondary educ, 1997-98, 316
Acevedo, Margaret, 192, 195, 213, 214
Achor, Amy Blount, 1369
Adams electronic job search almanac 1998, 264
Adams jobs almanac 1998, 265
Adams, K. Gary, 1127
Adams, McCrea, 1102
Adamson, Hugh C., 1272
Adamson, Lynda G., 449, 450, 512, 513, 797
Adkins, Lesley, 500
Adkins, Roy A., 500
Adoption, 755
Adrian Bloom's yr-round garden, 1347
Advanced composites world ref dict, 1410
AFB dir of servs for blind & visually impaired persons in the US & Canada, 748
AFB dir of servs for blind & visually impaired persons in the US & Canada [CD-ROM], 749
Africa: Africa world press gd to educ resources from & about Africa, 94
African-American baby name bk, 407
African American criminologists, 1970-96, 575
African American films through 1959, 1234
African American quotations, 80
African biog, 373
Aging sourcebk, 744
Agriculture, mining, & construction USA, 187
AIDS crisis, 1468
AIDS dict, 1470
Airlines worldwide, 1573
Alabama hist, 451
Alampi, Mary, 602
Albania, rev ed, 118
Albanian etymological dict, 921
Aldighieri, Ann Marie, 2
Aldred, Heather E., 1438
Aldrich, Richard, 289
Ali, Javed, 644
Allaby, Michael, 1525, 1526, 1527, 1528, 1529, 1530
Allen, Larry, 158
Allen, Marilyn O'Connell, 953, 988

Allen, Ruth, 989
Allin, Craig W., 1571
Allison, Robert J., 467, 469
Almanac of American employers 1998-99, 266
Almanac of famous people, 6th ed, 17
Altamiranda, Daniel, 1098
Alternative health & medicine ency, 2d ed, 1457
Alternative travel dir 1998, 4th ed, 439
Altherr, Thomas L., 711
Altner, Patricia, 1035
America votes 22, 677
American Academy of Pediatrics gd to your child's symptoms, 1464
American art dir 1997-98, 56th ed, 871
American attitudes, 2d ed, 90
American bk & mag illustrators to 1920, v.188, 884
American bk collectors & bibliographers, 2d series, 591
American bk of the dead: the definitive Grateful Dead ency, 1175
American bk publishing record, cum 1997, 9
American decades on CD [CD-ROM], 457
American dream: the 50s, 466
American eras: dvlpmt of a nation 1783-1815, 467
American eras: the reform era & eastern US dvlpmt, 468
American eras: the revolutionary era 1754-83, 469
American Heritage dict of American quotations, 75
American Heritage ency of American hist, 458
American immigrant cultures, 365
American Indian law deskbk, 2d ed, 561
American music in the 20th century, 1124
American naturalization records 1790-1990, 2d ed, 402
American novel explication 1991-95, 1040
American paintings in the Detroit Institute of Arts, v.2, 887
American pop from minstrel to mojo: on record, 1893-1956, 1162
American prisons, 574
American proverbs about women, 807
American Revolutionary War sites, memorials, museums, & lib collections, 472
American sci fiction TV series of the 1950s, 1213
American sign lang, unabridged ed, 910
American travel writers, 1776-1864, 1044
American univs & colleges, 15th ed, 348
American women in sci, 1950 to the present, 1299
American writers, 1043
American writers, retrospective suppl 1, 1045
Americana song reader, 1125
Americans & their homes, 783
Americans 55 & older, 279
America's best genealogy resource centers, 399
America's new fndns 1998, 12th ed, 760
America's Standard Gauge electric trains, 852
Ametsbichler, Elizabeth G., 1095
Amey, Lawrence, 607

Amico, Eleanor B., 796
Amsterdam, 135
Anaya, Alison, 316
Ancestrial trails: the complete gd to British genealogy & family hist, 401
Ancient civilizations of the Mediterranean [CD-ROM], 490
Ancient Greece & Rome, 491
Ancient Romans, 518
Ancient Rome chronology, 264-27 BC, 523
Andersen, Charles J., 349
Anderson, Gerald H., 1281
Anderson, Gordon T., 201
Anderson, James D., 1100
Anderson, Vicki, 1010
Andres, Linda R., 953, 988
Andrews, Tamra, 1184
Animal rights, 2d ed, 1369
Annimated film collector's gd, 1222
Anne Tyler: a critical companion, 1051
Annotated bibliog of N America doctoral dissertations on old Norse-Icelandic, 892
Annotated bibliog on leprosy, 1472
Annotated gd to adoption research 1986-97, 754
Annual gd to graduate nursing educ 1997, 1474
Annual register 1997, 657
Annual report of the USA 1998, 673
Ansell, Janis, 999
Anthropology bibliog on disc [CD-ROM], 362
Antique Trader Books antiques & collectibles price gd, 1999 ed, 840
Anton Rubinstein, 1144
Antonio Gardano, Venetian Music Printer 1538-69, 1112
Anzovin, Steven, 46
Appel, Marsha C., 876
Applegate, Edd, 1062
Arceneaux, Elizabeth, 213
Archaeology of prehistoric Native America, 443
Architecture & ornament, 879
Arden, Andrea, 424
Area bibliog of Japan, 111
Aristotle's Metaphysics: annot bibliog of the 20th-century lit, 1250
Armantrout, Neil B., 1501
Armitage, Peter, 1418
Arnest, Lauren Krohn, 551
Arnold Schoenberg companion, 1128
Art: a world hist, 874
Art directors in cinema, 1210
Art marketing sourcebk for the fine artist, 3d ed, 872
Art nouveau, 862
Arthurian hndbk, 2d ed, 1066
Artist's & graphic designers market, 1998, 875
Artz, John C., 566
Ash, Russell, 63
Ashby, Bonnie, 1445
Ashe, Geoffrey, 1066
Ashment, Catherine, 650, 651
Asia, 2d ed, 240
Asia-Pacific petroleum dir 1998, 14th ed, 195
Asian American woman, 795

ASIS thesaurus of info sci & librarianship, 2d ed, 598
ASM ready ref properties & units for engineering alloys, 1408
Assistantships & graduate fellowships in the mathematical scis, 1997-98, 1540
Associated Press lib of disasters, 64
Association for Library Services, 995
ASTM dir of scientific & tech consultants & expert witnesses, 1997-98 ed, 1320
ASTM intl dir of testing laboratories, 1998 ed, 1321
ASTM standards in bldg codes, 34th ed, 1401
Aston, Mick, 444
Atlas of ...
    American migration, 780
    archaeology, 444
    global change, 1550
    histl county boundaries: Iowa, 447
    histl county boundaries: N.C., 448
    the langs & ethnic communities of S Asia, 101
Attenborough, David, 1372
Atwood, Thomas C., 701
Auchter, Dorothy, 40
Auchterlonie, Paul, 139
Aufderheide, Arthur C., 1439
August Wilson: a research & production sourcebk, 1249
Australia, 436
Australian film, 1206
Authentic Jane Williams' home school market gd, 305
Avallone, Susan, 1219
Axelrod, Alan, 538
Axford, Elizabeth C., 1148
Axsom, Richard H., 867

B* student's (or lower) complete scholarship bk, 338
Bacon's business media dir 1998, 821
Baer, Beverly, 68
Bagby, Meredith, 673
Bahamonde, Ramon, 697
Bahjat, Andrew, 643
Bahorsky, Russ, 1489
Bail, Paul, 1051
Bailey, Joseph A., 552
Bailey, Martha J., 1299
Bailey, Walter B., 1128
Baker, Charles F., III, 518
Baker, Daniel B., 418
Baker, Mark Allen, 851
Baker, Mona, 896
Baker, Rosalie F., 518
Baker, William, 592
Baker's dict of music, 1123
Bald, Margaret, 604
Bales, Jack, 1053
Ball pest & disease manual, 1360
Ball redbook, 1346
Ball, Robert W. D., 848
Ball, Vic, 1346
Banks, Peter, 1471
Banned bks: lit suppressed on pol grounds, 603

Banned bks: lit suppressed on rel grounds, 604
Banned bks: lit suppressed on sexual grounds, 605
Banned bks: lit suppressed on social grounds, 606
Banned in the media, 825
Barbanell, Edward, 1252
Barber, David W., 1119
Barber, Katherine, 41
Barile, Michele A., 142
Barlow, Clive, 1373
Barnes, Dana Ramel, 1082, 1083
Barnes, Jay, 1531
Barnes, Judy, 427
Barnes-Svarney, Patricia, 1484
Barnett, Colleen A., 1030
Barnhart, Richard M., 888
Baron, Scott, 623
Barone, Michael, 674
Barr, Catherine, 993
Barron, Neil, 1036
Barron's best buys in college educ, 5th ed, 317
Barron's ency of cat breeds, 1382
Barron's gd to graduate business schools, 318
Barrow, Steve, 1171
Barterian, Gerald R., 973, 974
Bartnett, Joy E., 1447
Barton, Wayne, 1028
Baseball: a comprehensive bibliog, suppl 2, 717
Basic Newbury House dict of American English, 898
Bastian, Dawn E., 98
Batten, Donna, 670
Baum, Harald, 546
BBI dict of English word combinations, rev ed, 913
Beaman, Mark, 1374
Beanie family album & collectors gd, 853
Bear, John, 302
Bear, Mariah, 302
Beat generation, 1042
Beaty, Wayne, 1546
Bebbington, Warren, 1122
Becher, Anne, 1556
Beck, Robert J., 1549
Beckel, Lothar, 1550
Beckson, Karl, 1075
Beeley, Brian W., 134
Beim, Howard J., 1568
Beit-Hallahmi, Benjamin, 1264
Bellenir, Karen, 1271, 1452
Benally, AnCita, 387
Benamati, Dennis C., 547
Benbow-Niemier, Glynis, 1201
Benbow-Pfalzgraf, Taryn, 1201
Benewick, Robert, 655
Benjamin Franklin: a biogl companion, 455
Bennett, John M., 573
Benowitz, June Melby, 1265
Benson, Eugene, 1088
Benson, Evelyn, 913
Benson, Morton, 913
Bentley, Michael, 829
Bercot, David W., 1285

Berger, James L., 357
Berlow, Lawrence H., 1397
Berman, Matt, 990
Bermuda, 137
Berner, Brad K., 626
Bertram, Anne, 902, 914, 915
Bessette, Joseph M., 667
Best distance learning graduate schools, 304
Best graduate programs: humanities & social scis, 2d ed, 335
Best graduate programs: physical & biological scis, 2d ed, 336
Best law schools, 560
Best medical schools, 1450
Best of health, 1437
Best plays of 1996-97, 1246
Best private high schools & how to get in, 2d ed, 313
Best 75 business schools, 1999 ed, 320
Best Web sites for teachers, 2d ed, 308
Best wines! 1999, 3d ed, 1335
Bestseller index, 12
Better than it sounds: a dict of humorous musical quotations, 1119
Bettschart, Roland, 1456
Bianco, David, 275
Bible: God's word for the biblically-inept, 1280
Bibliographic gd to ...
    conference pubs 1996, 7
    jazz poetry, 1099
    Spanish music for the violin & viola, 1900-97, 1149
Bibliographies on SE Asia, 103
Bibliography of ...
    the Indians of San Diego county, 383
    the Indonesian Revolution, 481
    the myth of Don Juan in literary hist, 944
    Va. legal hist before 1900, 2d ed, 548
    works on Canadian foreign relations 1991-95, 689
Bidwell, Robin, 508
Big bk of minority opportunities, 7th ed, 339
Big bk of show business awards, 1198
Bignaud, Marie-Claude, 185
Bigsby, Christopher, 1247
Bill James presents: STATS all-time major league hndbk, 715
Billboard illus ency of rock, 1172
Bilstein, Paula, 1450
Biodiversity, 1556
Biographical dict of ...
    American & Canadian naturalists & environmentalists, 1552
    Chinese women, 798
    Christian missions, 1281
    N American & European educationists, 289
Biographical ency of scientists, 1300
Biographies of scientists, 1298
Biographies of Western photographers, 861
Biography & genealogy master index 1999, 404
Bjorling, Joel, 708
Black hndbk, 375
Black/White relations in American hist, 454
Blanchard, Margaret A., 820

Blizzards, 1525
Blockbuster Entertainment gd to movies & videos 1998, 1241
Bloom, Adrian, 1347
Blouin, Francis X., Jr., 1284
Blues & gospel records 1890-1943, 1160
Blum, George P., 694
Blumberg, Arnold, 509
Blumenthal, Howard J., 1159, 1165
Blunden, Caroline, 106
Bock, Judy, 1005
Bollard, John K., 900
Book of ...
    lists for regulated hazardous substances, 8th ed, 1557
    mosts, 65
    rules, 713
    saints, 1263
Book review index: 1997 cum, 68
Booker, M. Keith, 1068
Booker-Canfield, Suzanne, 1039
Bor, Victoria L., 566
Borck, Jim Springer, 515, 516
Boswell, David M., 134
Botterweck, G. Johannes, 1276
Bouloukos, Adam C., 547
Boultbee, Paul G., 137
Bourbon companion, 1337
Bowker's dir of videocassettes for children 1998, 10
Bowman, John S., 471
Boyden, Matthew, 1157
Boylan, Henry, 132
Bradford, John, 750
Bradley, David, 588
Bradley, J., 258
Bradney, Gail, 1335
Branan, Carl R., 1400
Branch, Robert Maribe, 356
Brands & their cos suppl, 17th ed, 148
Braun, Erin E., 1495
Braun, Marina, 553
Brawarsky, Sandee, 396
Bray, Dorothy, 936
Breakup of Yugoslavia & the war in Bosnia, 116
Brecka, Shawn, 853
Breitsprecher, Roland, 928
Bremer, Ronald A., 399
Breton, Roland J.-L., 101
Bricker's intl dir 1998, 358
Brier, Bob, 445
Bright, William, 420
Broadway song companion, 1170
Brobeck, Stephen, 176
Broderick, Dorothy M., 1012
Brodersen, Martha, 617
Bronoel, Stacey, 142
Brookesmith, Peter, 709
Brooks & Olmo register of fruit & nut varieties, 1330
Brown, Chris W., III, 430
Brown, David S., 660
Brown, Jean E., 453
Brown, Kyle D., 883

Brown, Lynda W., 451
Brown, Mary Ellen, 962
Brownell, F. William, 1558
Brownstone, David M., 802
Bruccoli, Matthew J., 971
Bruce, Anthony, 639
Bruce, Colin R., II, 844
Bruce, Samuel W., 970
Bruijn, Ria Koopmans-de, 111
Brumble, H. David, 1017
Bruno, Leonard C., 1308
Bruntjen, Scott, 13
Bryson, William Hamilton, 548
Bua, Robert N., 1475
Buckley, John F., 559
Buckley, Jonathan, 1157
Bud, Robert, 1312
Buening, Alice P., 828
Bulbs, 1348
Bull's birds of N.Y. state, 1375
Bunson, Margaret, 1261
Bunson, Matthew, 1261
Bunson, Stephen, 1261
Burack, Sylvia K., 832
Burden, Ernest, 880
Burels, Ned, 55
Burg, David F., 653
Burgess, Guy M., 554
Burgess, Heidi, 554
Burke, David, 924
Burrelle's media dir, 1998 ed, 837
Burt, Daniel S., 1034
Burwell, Helen P., 595
Burwell world dir of info brokers, 13th ed, 595
Buse, Dieter K., 129
Business & legal forms for crafts, 854
Business & legal forms for photographers, rev ed, 859
Business stats of the US, 159
Business traveler's world gd, 441
Bute, E. L., 375
Butler, Robert Brown, 881
Butt, John, 938
Butterflies of the world, 1390
Buttolph, Ken, 1577
By the numbers: emerging industries, 188
By the numbers: nonprofit orgs, 48
By the numbers: publishing, 620

C. S. Lewis readers' ency, 1071
Callendar, John Hancock, 882
Cambodia, 105
Cambridge biogl ency, 2d ed, 18
Cambridge ency of human growth & dvlpmt, 1465
Cambridge ency of human paleopathology, 1439
Cambridge French-English thesaurus, 925
Cambridge hist of American theatre, v.1, 1247
Cambridge hist of the native peoples of the Americas, v.1:
    N America, pt.1, 392
Canadian almanac & dir 1999, 152d ed, 2

Canadian bk review annual 1997, 16
Canadian insurance claims dir 1997, 246
Canadian Oxford dict, 41
Canadian sourcebk 1998, 33d ed, 3
Canadian who's who 1997, v.32, 38
Canfield Reisman, Rosemary M., 1039
Cannon, John, 503
Cantor, Nathan L., 57, 157
Career Xroads, 3d ed, 267
Caribbean lit, 1089
Carlos Chavez: a gd to research, 1141
Carpenter, Allan, 89
Carpenter, Ronald H., 1282
Carr, Brian, 1254
Carruthers, Margaret W., 1535
Carter, Craig, 718
Cartographic satellite atlas of the world, 410
Caruso, Luisa, 919
Carvajal, Carol Styles, 941
Cashmore, Ellis, 366
Cassell companion to quotations, 76
Castagno, Joseph M., 1317
Castro, Emilio G. Muniz, 146
Castronova, Frank V., 17
Cat owner's question & answer bk, 1387
Catala, Rafael, 1100
Catalogue of the 15th century printed bks in the Harvard
    Univ Lib, v.5, 614
Catanese, Lynn Ann, 801
Cavazos-Gaither, Alma E., 1328
CD estimator, 1998 [CD-ROM], 1402
CD-ROMs in print, 12th ed, 8
Celluloid couch, 1233
Censorship, 607, 608
Century of design, 878
Cerutti, Steve, 732
Cevasco, George A., 1552
Chadwick, Ruth, 1251
Chambers 21st century dict, 42
Chambers, Frances, 127
Champion, Dean J., 576
Chan, Karen Y., 142
Chandler, Karen, 1470
Chandler, Ralph C., 555
Channel Isalnds, 130
Charles Burchfield, 889
Charles Dickens A to Z, 1072
Charlton standard catalogue of Canadian govt paper
    money, 11th ed, 843
Chase's calendar of events 1998, 4
Checklist of American imprints for 1846, 13
ChemLab series, 1507
Chenes, Betz Des, 522
Chicago Bulls ency, 726
Childhood & children, 779
Children in foster care & adoption, 756
Children, YAs, & the law, 551
Children's bk awards annual 1998, 990
Children's bk prizes, 989
Children's bks from other countries, 991
Children's bks in print 1998, 992
Children's museums, 71
Children's nonfiction for adult info needs, 996
Children's writer's & illustrator's market, 1998, 828
China, 7th ed, 110
China: a dir & sourcebk, 2d ed, 107
China: facts & figures annual hndbk, v.23, 108
China hndbk, 241
China mktg data & stats, 242
China State Statl Bureau, 242
China-Burma-India campaign, 1931-45, 517
Chinese-English-French Kuaisu dict, 920
Choral arrangements of the African-American spirituals,
    1152
Christian music dirs, 1998, 1176
Christian music finder [CD-ROM], 1177
Christian, Nicole, 1097
Chronicle of the Olympics, 1896-2000, 738
Chronology of the Cold War at sea 1945-91, 643
Chronology of weather, 1526
Chumash & their predecessors, 381
Cibbarelli, Pamela R., 609
Cibbarelli, Shawn E., 609
Cindric, Susan J., 56
Citizen's companion to US Supreme Court opinions,
    1996-97 term, 562
Civil law lexicon for lib classification, 599
Civil rights movement, 473
Civil serv career starter, 272
Civil War 100, 625
Claggett, Hilary D., 1371
Clark, Lewis J., 1366
Clark, Paul C., Jr., 462
Clark, Suzanne M., 452
Clark, Walter A., 1129
Clarkson, Christopher, 600
Classical myths & legends in the Middle Ages & Renais-
    sance, 1017
Clayton, Jade, 1491
Clean air hndbk, 3d ed, 1558
Cleere, Nigel, 1376
Cline, Camille N., 67
Clothier, Galina, 553
Clotworthy, William G., 428
Coasting: an expanded gd to the N gulf coast, 3d ed, 427
Cochrane, John, 636
Coffman, Steve, 596
Cogar, William, 639
Cogger, Harold G., 1395
Coggins, Margaret, 1002
Cohen, Allen, 1207
Cohen, Elliot D., 826
Cohen, Selma Jeanne, 1202
Cohl, H. Aaron, 65
Cohn, Arthur, 1153
Cohn-Sherbok, Dan, 1291
Cohn-Sherbok, Lavinia, 1283
Coined by Shakespeare, 1078
Cold War, 544
Cold War culture media & the arts 1945-90, 1191

Coll, Susan, 873
Collapse of communism in the Soviet Union, 693
Collecting world coins, 7th ed, 844
College costs & financial aid hndbk 1998, 340
College degrees by mail & modem 1998, 302
College financial aid, 341
College hndbk 1998, 350
College students research companion, 610
Collin, P. H., 145, 654, 1440, 1553
Collins German-English, English-German dict, unabridged
     3d ed, 928
Collins Spanish-English, English-Spanish dict, unabridged
     5th ed, 939
Collins, John J., 1266
Collinwood, Dean W., 102
Colombo, John Robert, 77
Colombo's concise Canadian quotations, 77
Colton, Theodore, 1418
Columbia gd to the Cold War, 543
Comedy stars at 78 RMP, 1196
Companion ency of Asian philosophy, 1254
Companion to …
     historiography, 829
     the Greek lyric poets, 1018
     the US Constitution & its amendments, 2d ed, 685
     20th-century German lit, 2d ed, 1093
Comparative gd to American elem & secondary schools, 311
Compendium of social stats & indicators, 4th issue, 787
Complete bk of symptoms & treatments, 1456
Complete college financing gd, 4th ed, 342
Complete cross-ref gd to the baby buster generations
     collective unconscious, 1187
Complete dir for people with chronic illness, 1467
Complete dir for people with rare disorders, 1998/99, 1447
Complete dir of large print bks & serials 1998, 11
Complete dir to sci fiction, fantasy, & horror TV series, 1224
Complete ency of natural healing, 1459
Complete gd to America's natl parks, 10th ed, 429
Complete learning disabilities dir, 1998, 303
Complete Marquis who's who on CD-ROM [CD-ROM], 19
Complete "no geek-speak" gd to the Internet, 1499
Completely queer: the gay & lesbian ency, 757
Concise dict of medical-legal terms, 552
Concise ency of
     Christianity, 1287
     Hinduism, 1290
     Judaism, 1291
Concise histl atlas of Canada, 409
Concise metals engineering data bk, 1409
Concise Oxford dict of linguistics, 893
Concise Oxford dict of quotations, 78
Conductors & composers of popular orchestral music, 1158
Conductor's gd to choral-orchestral works, 20th century,
     pt.2, 1151
Cone, Robert J., 1484
Congress & the nation, 1993-96, 675
Congressional dir: 105th congress, 669
Congressional elections 1946-96, 676
Connoisseurs' hndbk of the wines of Calif. & the Pacific
     Northwest, 4th ed, 1341

Conservation & the law, 584
Constitutional law dict, v.2, suppl 1, 555
Consulting spirits, 708
Consumer Asia 1998, 215
Consumer China 1998, 216
Consumer E Europe 1998/9, 248
Consumer Europe 1998/9, 14th ed, 249
Consumer health info source bk, 5th ed, 1416
Consumer intl 1997/98, 218
Consumer Middle East 1998, 217
Conte, Joseph, 1059
Contemporary African-American female playwrights, 1050
Contemporary authors, v.158, 949
Contemporary authors, v.159, 950
Contemporary authors autobiog series, v.28, 953
Contemporary authors new revision series, v.59, 947
Contemporary authors new revision series, v.60, 948
Contemporary Barbie dolls, 847
Contemporary black biog, v.16, 376
Contemporary designers, 857
Contemporary heroes & heroines, bk 3, 20
Contemporary literary criticism, v.100, 966
Contemporary literary criticism, v.101, 967
Contemporary literary criticism, v.102, 968
Contemporary literary criticism, v.103, 969
Contemporary literary criticism yrbk 1996, v.99, 965
Contemporary men fiction writers, 1039
Contemporary musicians, v.19, 1115
Contemporary musicians, v.20, 1116
Contemporary theatre, film, & TV, v.17, 1195
Cook, Allan R., 1473
Cook, Chris, 690
Cook, Rhodes, 677
Cooke, Ian, 1349
Cooke, Jacob Ernest, 464
Cooper, B. Lee, 1173
Cooper, Barbara T., 1092
Cooper, Robert M., 1065
Cooper's comprehensive environmental desk ref
     [CD-ROM], 1559
Corey, Melinda, 525, 818, 1307
Cornett, Lloyd H., Jr., 451
Cornwell, Neil, 1097
Corporate dir US public cos, 149
Corporate giving dir 1999, 20th ed, 761
Corporate giving yellow pages 1998, 13th ed, 762
Corriente, F., 922
Corrigan, Maureen, 1032
Costello, Elaine, 909
Cotterell, Arthur, 526
Countries of the world & their leaders yrbk 1999, 658
Courtroom drama: 120 of the world's most notable trials, 556
Coville, Gary, 1213
Cowlard, Keith A., 504
Cox, Mary, 875
Coye, Dale F., 1076
Coyne, Mark S., 1571
Craft, Donna, 271
Craggs, Stewart R., 1130, 1131

Craig, Robert D., 459
Cramer, Eugene Casjen, 1132
Crawford, Mark, 1560
Crawford, Tad, 854, 859
Creese, Mary R. S., 1301
Creeth, Terry, 92
Cremeans, John E., 220
Crime in America's top-rated cities, 579
Criminal justice info, 547
Criminal justice research in libs & on the Internet, 581
Crispin, Gerry, 267
Critical essays on Laurence Sterne, 1074
Critical hist of TVs The Twilight Zone, 1959-64, 1232
Critical review of bks in religion 1997, v.10, 1260
Crosbie, Michael J., 882
Crossley, Heather, 906
Cruising gd to N.Y. waterways & Lake Champlain, 430
Crutchfield, Roger S., 901
Crystal, David, 18
Cuban Americans, 397
Cuddon, J. A., 960
Cueto, Gail, 93
Culinary schools, 1336
Cullen, Tony, 646
Culligan, Judy, 24, 143, 582, 1304
Cultural atlas of ...
    Africa, rev ed, 95
    China, rev ed, 106
    Russia & the Former Soviet Union, rev ed, 125
Cultures of color in America, 367
Cultures of the World, 84
Cummings, David, 956, 1101
Cummings, Robert, 863
Cummins, Alex G., 123
Cumulative index to vols. 1-6 of Paul Oskar Kristeller's
        Iter Italicum, 1259
Curran, Daniel, 1211
Currie, Philip J., 1539
Cutshaw, Charles C., 645
Cuvalo, Ante, 120
Cyclopedia of literary characters, rev ed, 959
Czech republic, 121

Dabbagh, Maureen, 752
Dahl, Anne, 931
Daily life in ancient Mesopotamia, 511
Daily life of the ancient Greeks, 501
Dalby, Andrew, 890
Dale, Leigh, 946
Dallman, Peter R., 1359
Dalton, Peter, 1171
Dalzell, Tom, 43
Damon, William, 707
Dana's new mineralogy, 1537
Dance on camera, 1200
Danilov, Victor J., 69
Darnay, Arsen J., 187, 1436, 1572
Dartmouth atlas of health care, 1414
David, Rosalie, 510

Davids, Peter H., 1274
Davidson, George, 42
Davies, Richard, 1250
Davis, James B., 1424
Davis, John B., 161
Davis, Joseph R., 1409
Davis, Lloyd, 776
Davis, Paul, 1072
Davis, Todd M., 352
Dawson, Dawn P., 1443
Day, Alan, 83
Day, Alan J., 649, 657
de Ley, Gerd, 1179
De Mente, Boye Lafayette, 193
Dead countries of the 19th & 20th centuries, 530
Dean, William G., 409
DeFranco, Laurence J., 674
Dejevsky, Nikolai, 125
Delaney, John, 954, 955
Delgado, James P., 446
Delves, Peter J., 1419
DenBoer, Gordon, 447, 448
Dennis, Marguerite J., 342
Department of Economic & Social Affairs Population
        Division, 784, 790, 794
Department of Health & Human Services, 1430
Dervaes, Claudine, 425
Desert wildflowers of N America, 1365
Desk ref on the fed budget, 687
Desktop ency of telecommunications, 1493
Destination: Vatican II [CD-ROM], 1288
Detecting men: a reader's gd & checklist for mystery
        series written by men, 1031
Detrez, Raymond, 494
DeVenney, David P., 1170
Devereux, Paul, 709
Devine, Mary Elizabeth, 315
Dewan, John, 715
Diabetes A to Z, 3d ed, 1471
Dial recordings of Charlie Parker, 1166
Dickinson, Donald C., 616
Dictionary of ...
    agriculture, 2d ed, 1329
    American antiquarian bkdealers, 616
    American biog [CD-ROM], 33
    American criminal justice, 576
    Andalusi Arabic, 922
    astronomy, 1518
    banking terms, 186
    beer & brewing, 2d ed, 1332
    business, 2d ed, 145
    business, English-Spanish, Spanish-English, repr ed, 147
    Canadian place names, 423
    classical ballet terminology, 1204
    communications tech, 3d ed, 1492
    contemporary Spain, 943
    early Christian beliefs, 1285
    ecology & the environment, 3d ed, 1553
    English place-names, 2d ed, 422
    gastronomic terms, French/English, 1334

Dictionary of ... (*continued*)
  govt & politics, 2d ed, 654
  heresy trials in American Christianity, 1289
  histl allusions & eponyms, 40
  intl biog 1998, 26th ed, 21
  intl business terms, 194
  Irish biog, 3d ed, 132
  Italian cuisine, 1331
  literary biog, v.191, 1063
  literary biog, v.192, 1092
  literary biog, v.193, 1059
  literary biog, v.194, 1064
  literary biog: British reform writers, 1832-1914, 1062
  literary biog documentary series, v.16, 954
  literary biog documentary series, v.17, 955
  literary biog yrbk: 1996, 970
  literary biog yrbk: 1997, 971
  literary terms & literary theory, 4th ed, 960
  La Creole, 935
  medicine, 2d ed, 1440
  modern Arab hist, 508
  1000 Dutch proverbs, 1179
  plant genetics & molecular biology, 1358
  pseudonyms, 408
  race & ethnic relations, 366
  Shakespeare's semantic wordplay, 1084
  symbols, 886
  TV & audiovisual terminology, 838
  the Holocaust, 528
  the later new testament & its dvlpmts, 1274
  world biog, v.1: the ancient world, 519
  world biog, v.2: the middle ages, 520
Digby, Joan, 331
Dikel, Margaret Riley, 268
Dilworth, David A., 1257
Dinan, Desmond, 691
Dines, Nicholas T., 883
Directory of ...
  American youth orgs 1998-99, 7th ed, 52
  cos offering dividend reinvestment plans, 163
  cos required to file annual reports with the securities & exchange commission, 1997, 164
  consumer brands & their owners 1998: E Europe, 250
  consumer brands & their owners 1998: Europe, 251
  consumer brands & their owners 1998: Latin America, 260
  corporate affiliations 1998, 150
  corporate & fndn givers, 1998, 763
  financial aids for women 1997-99, 773
  grants in the humanities 1998/99, 12th ed, 812
  intl corporate giving in America & abroad 1998, 764
  lib automation software, systems, & servs, 609
  mail order catalogs 98, 175
  medical health care libs in the UK & Republic of Ireland 1997-98, 10th ed, 611
  multinationals, 197
  natl helplines, 1998 ed, 49
  physics, astronomy, & geophysics staff, 1997 biennial ed, 1322
  population ageing research in Europe, 745
  publishers in religion, 619
  pub 1999, 24th ed, 618
  schools for alternative & complementary health care, 1448
  social service grants, 2d ed, 765
  the wood products industry, 1998, 1343
  US military bases worldwide, 3d ed, 631
DISCovering nations, states, & cultures [CD-ROM], 85
Divorce yourself, 4th ed, 567
Dixon, Robert M. W., 1160
Dixon, Ted, 165
Dixon-Kennedy, Mike, 1185
Dixonia: a bio-discography of Bill Dixon, 1146
DK illus Oxford dict, 44
DK nature ency, 1309
DK sci ency, rev ed, 1310
DK student atlas, 411
DK ultimate visual dict of sci, 1311
D'Lugo, Marvin, 1237
Docherty, James C., 695
Doctoral dissertations on China & on inner Asia, 1976-90, 15
Documents of Soviet-American relations, v.3, 122
Documents of Soviet hist, v.4, 123
Dodd, Donald B., 451
Dodge, Richard W., 782
Dodgers ency, 716
Doerr, Juergen C., 129
Dogs from A to Z, 1385
Doig, Melissa Walsh, 389
Dollarhide, William, 399
Donahue, Debra L., 584
Don't do it: a dict of the forbidden, 1193
Dorf, Richard C., 1405
Dori, John T., 219
Dow, Sheila, 56
Dowling, Robert J., 1221
Downs, Buck, 57, 157
Drama criticism, v.7, 1019
Drama criticism, v.8, 1020
Drama for students. v.1, 1021
Drama for students. v.2, 1022
Drama for students, v.3, 1023
Drama for students, v.4, 1024
Drescher, Seymour, 542
Drone, Jeanette Marie, 1244
Droughts, 1527
Dudenredaktion & the German Section of the Oxford Univ Press Dict Dept, 930
Duffy, Paul, 502
Duiker, William J., 488
Dulbecco, Renato, 1355
Dunnigan, James F., 627
Dupont, Ellen, 1538
Dupuy, Marigny J., 990
Durham, Jennifer L., 455
Durusau, Patrick, 1269
Dyal, Donald H., 884

Ear, nose, & throat disorders sourcebk, 1452
Earl Mountbatten of Burma, 1900-79, 505

Earth online, 1516
Earthscape: exploring endangered ecosystems [CD-ROM], 1513
East, Roger, 650, 651
Eastern Europe, 2d ed, 252
Eberwein, Jane Donahue, 1052
Echeruo, Michael J. C., 932
Eckl, Corina, 678
Eckstein, Richard M., 765
Economic & Social Commission for Asia and the Pacific, 746, 808
Economic & Social Commission for Western Asia, 787
Edgar, Kathleen J., 1195
Editorial cartooning & caricature, 1192
Editorial Staff of Government Institutes, 1557
Education sourcebk, 296
Educational media & tech yrbk, 356
Educational opportunity gd, 1998, 312
Educational rankings annual 1998, 297
Educational software preview gd, 1998, 306
Educator's gd to free multicultural materials 1998, 285
Educator's gd to free sci materials 1998-99, 39th ed, 286
Educator's gd to free social studies materials 1998-99, 38th ed, 287
Educator's gd to free videotapes 1998, 45th ed, 357
Edwards, Jolane, 427
Edwards, Paul M., 514
Effects of neurologic & psychiatric drugs on the fetus & nursing infant, 1480
Eighteenth century, 515, 516
Eisaguirre, Lynne, 563
Eisenberg, Harry K., 167
Eisenmann, Linda, 803
Electrical engineering hndbk, 1405
Electronic & computer industry gd to chemical safety & environmental compliance, 1567
Elements explorer [CD-ROM], 1509
Elfstrom, Gerard, 698
Elgar companion to classical economics, 160
Ellavich, Marie C., 1302, 1303
Elliott, Deni, 826
Elliott, Stuart, 636
Elsevier's dict of acronyms, initialisms, abbreviations, & symbols, 1
Elsevier's dict of financial terms, rev ed, 185
Elvin, Mark, 106
Elwood, Ann, 27
Ember, Melvin, 365
Emily Dickinson ency, 1052
Employment opportunities, USA, 269
Encyclopaedia of occupational health & safety, 4th ed [CD-ROM], 280
Encyclopaedic dict in the 18th century, v.1, 813
Encyclopaedic dict in the 18th century, v.2, 814
Encyclopaedic dict in the 18th century, v.3, 815
Encyclopaedic dict in the 18th century, v.4, 816
Encyclopaedic dict in the 18th century, v.5, 817
Encyclopedia Americana, 45
Encyclopedia of ...
    Africa S of the Sahara, 100

African airlines, 1574
American Catholic hist, 1286
American communes, 1663-1963, 747
American govt, 667
American Indian wars, 1492-1890, 460
American women & religion, 1265
apocalypticism, 1266
applied ethics, 1251
assns: an assns unlimited ref, 32d ed, 50
assns: regional, state, & local orgs, 7th ed, 51
biog, 22
biostats, 1418
birds, 2d ed, 1377
capital punishment, 577
chemical tech suppl vol, 1503
civil rights in America, 588
conflict resolution, 554
contemporary French culture, 128
daytime TV, 1212
dinosaurs, 1539
earth & physical scis, 1514
empiricism, 1252
family health, 1441
feminist literary theory, 961
figure skating, 739
folklore & lit, 962
govtl advisory orgs 1997, 11th ed, 670
housing, 792
human biology, 1355
hurricanes, typhoons, & cyclones, 1532
immunology, 2d ed, 1419
infectious diseases, 1445
Japanese pop culture, 112
lib & info sci, v.60, suppl 23, 593
lib & info sci, v.61, suppl 24, 594
mammals, 2d ed, 1391
mental health, 704
modern American social issues, 742
mummies, 445
Native American legal tradition, 388
natural pet care, 1384
Naval hist, 639
network blueprints, 1490
novels into film, 1216
reptiles & amphibians, 2d ed, 1395
small business, 277
Southern lit, 1047
student & youth movements, 653
the blues, 2d ed, 1150
the consumer movement, 176
the EU, 691
the novel, 963
the sayings of the Jewish people, 1293
the Vietnam War, 527
toxicology, 1504
underwater & maritime archaeology, 446
urban America, 793
women artists of the American west, 869
world biog, 2d ed, 23
Encyclopedia USA, v.25, 461

Encyclopedic dict of conflict & conflict resolution,
    1945-96, 628
Endangered species, 1370
Energy stats yrbk, 1995, 1547
Engel, Peter H., 283
Engelbert, Phillis, 1319
Engerman, Stanley L., 542
Engineering mathematics hndbk, 1544
English-Norwegian, Norwegian-English dict, 937
English novel explication suppl 6, 1069
English-Russian dict of American criminal law, 553
English usage & style for editors, 836
English vocabulary quick ref, 901
Enslen, Richard A., 555
Entertainers in British films, 1225
Environment ency & dir 1998, 1561
Environment property & the law, 585
Environmental engineering dict, 3d ed, 1407
Epstein, Eric Joseph, 528
Erickson, Judith B., 52
Ernst, Carl R., 597
Ernst, Edzard, 1456
Estell, Kenneth, 391, 774
Esther Forbes, 1053
Ethnic groups worldwide, 368
Ethnohistorical dict of China, 370
EU Insts' register, 3d ed, 692
Europa world yrbk 1998, 39th ed, 66
European dir of retailers & wholesalers, 2d ed, 253
European dir of SE Asian studies, 319
European mktg data & stats 1998, 33d ed, 254
European myth & legend, 1185
European pol facts, 1900-96, 690
Europe's major cos dir 1997, 2d ed, 255
Europe's medium-sized cos dir, 2d ed, 256
Evans, Denise, 973, 974
Events that changed America in the 18th century, 456
Everitt, David, 1242
Everyone's gd to children's lit, 1000
Evinger, William R., 631
Executive order 9066 [CD-ROM], 470
Explorers, 417
Explorers & discoverers, v.5, 418
Exploring health care careers, 1429
Expositor's bible commentary [CD-ROM], 1277
Eyston, Felice, 740

F. Scott Fitzgerald A to Z, 1054
Fabry, Heinz-Josef, 1276
Fact bk on higher educ, 1997 ed, 349
Facts about the American wars, 471
Facts on File children's atlas, rev ed, 412
Facts on File environment atlas, rev ed, 1551
Facts on File wildlife atlas, rev ed, 1295
Falk, Peter Hastings, 868
Famous 1st facts, 46
Fant, Maureen B., 1331
FAQ's of life, 67
Faragher, John Mack, 458
Farmer, Ann Dahlstrom, 1056

Farmer, David Hugh, 1262
Farry, Mike, 619
Father Charles E. Coughlin, 1282
Faucett, Bill F., 1133
FaxUSA, 1998, 151
Fechhelm, Janice D., 1388
Feczko, Margaret Mary, 768
Federal chemical regulation, 586
Federal grants & funding locator [CD-ROM], 766
Federal wildlife laws hndbk with related laws, 587
Fee, Margery, 907
Fegan, Sean, 1412
Feinstein, Sascha, 1099
Feldman, Douglas A., 1468
Feldman, George, 539
Feldman, Julie, 1226
Female dramatist, 1025
Fenwick, Gillian, 1073
Ferguson's gd to apprenticeship programs, 2d ed, 359
Fernandez, Ronald, 93
Ferrara, Miranda H., 958
Ferrier, James A., 1406
Fiction sequels for readers 10 to 16, 2d ed, 1010
Field guide to ...
    America's historic neighborhoods & museum houses, 433
    birds of the Gambia & Senegal, 1373
    demons, fairies, fallen angels, & other subversive spirits,
        1181
Fierro, Alfred, 497
Film & TV in-jokes, 1239
Film cartoons: a gd to 20th century American animated
    features & shorts, 1231
Film festival gd, 1223
Film index intl 1996 [CD-ROM], 1240
Film writers gd, 7th ed, 1219
Financial aid for African Americans 1997-99, 292
Financial aid for Asian Americans 1997-99, 293
Financial aid for Native Americans 1997-99, 772
Financial aid for the disabled & their families 1998-2000, 294
Findlay, Michael Shaw, 894
Findling, John E., 456
Finegan, Jack, 1278
Finkelman, Paul, 535
Fischel, Jack R., 540
Fischer, Carolyn A., 822
Fisher, Richard D., Jr., 219
Fisher, Helen S., 48
Fishes of the Gulf of Mexico, v.1, 1388
Fishing tackle source dir, 729
Fishkin, Shelley Fisher, 588
Fitch, Thomas P., 186
Fitt, Stephen D., 383
Fitzgerald, Mary Ann, 356
Fitzpatrick, Kathleen A., 298
Fitzroy Dearborn intl dir of venture capital funds 1998-99, 198
Flags of the world, 406
Flanders, Stephen A., 780
Floods, 1528
Florida's hurricane hist, 1531
Fodor's upclose Europe, 437

Foerstel, Herbert N., 825
Folcarelli, Ralph J., 601
Folklore: an ency of hist, methods, & theory, 1180
Food & beverage market place, 1997/98, 1339
Fools & jesters in lit, art, & hist, 951
Footage, 1220
Ford, A., 257
Forestiero, Saverio, 1390
Forget, Carl, 1332
Form & analysis theory, 1114
Forrester, William H., 611
Forshaw, Joseph, 1377
Foss, Christopher F., 646
Foster, David William, 1098
Foundation reporter 1999, 30th ed, 767
Foundations of the 1990s, 768
Four British women novelists, 1061
Franceschetti, Donald R., 1315
Francillon, Rene J., 637
Francis, Raymond L., 1306
Franck, Irene M., 802
Fredericks, Anthony D., 1006
Frederiksen, Elke P., 1095
Free or low cost health info, 1428
Friedl, Friedrich, 885
Friedman, Howard S., 704
Friedman, J. M., 1480
Friedman, John B., 810
From Aristotle to Zoroaster: an A to Z companion to the
          classical world, 526
From biog to hist, 993
From silents to sound, 1209
From the beginning to Plato, 1255
Frontiers of space exploration, 1520
Frost, Lee, 860
Frost-Knappman, Elizabeth, 556, 572
Fund raiser's gd to human serv funding 1997, 774
Funding sources for community & economic dvlpmt 1998,
          770
Funding sources for K-12 schools & adult basic educ, 290
Fundukian, Laurie, 59
Furia, Philip, 1134
Furness, Raymond, 1093

Gabrielsen, Egill Daae, 937
Gaffke, Carol T., 1104, 1105
Gailey, Harry A., 638
Gaines, Richard V., 1537
Gaither, Carl C., 1328
Galante, Steven P., 199
Galante's venture capital & private equity dir, 1998 ed, 199
Galante's venture capital & private equity dir, 1997 ed
          [CD-ROM], 200
Gale dir of databases, 1495
Gale dir of pubns & broadcast media, 131st ed, 822
Gale ency of childhood & adolescence, 778
Gale ency of Native American tribes, 389
Gale, Robert L., 957
Galens, David, 1021, 1022, 1023, 1024

Galer, Scott W., 1090
Gall, Susan, 806
Gall, Tim, 806
Gall, Timothy L., 364
Gallant, Frank K., 421
Gander, Terry J., 645
Ganeri, Anita, 1314
Gann, Kyle, 1124
Gaquin, Deirdre A., 782
Garcia, Maria J., 943
Gardener's gd to growing peonies, 1352
Gardener's Supply Co passport to gardening, 1350
Gardiner, Vince, 130
Gariepy, Jennifer, 980, 981, 982
Garland ency of world music, v.9, 1120
Garland, Robert, 501
Garoogian, Andrew, 579
Garoogian, Rhoda, 579
Garrett, Don, 1252
Garrett, George, 971
Gaslin, Glenn, 1187
Geddes, Joan Bel, 779
Gelbert, Doug, 472
Geller, Kenneth S., 569
Gemmette, Elizabeth Villiers, 945
Genetics & cell biology on file, 1357
George Orwell: a bibliog, 1073
George Whitefield Chadwick, 1133
Georgieva, Valentina, 495
Gerald, Debra E., 299
Gerber, Douglas E., 1018
Geritz, Albert J., 1086
Gessel, Van C., 1096
Gibbon, Guy, 443
Giffin, James M., 1354
Gifford, Denis, 1225
Gilbert, Nedda, 320
Gill, Kay, 151
Gillespie, John T., 601
Gillett, Harriet J., 1361
Giuseppe Verdi: a gd to research, 1137
Glazier, Michael, 1286
Glenn, Leigh, 590
Glickman, Sylvia, 1145
Glitsch, Catherine, 1040
Global ency of histl writing, 529
Global links: a gd to key people & insts worldwide, 54
Glossary of aquatic habitat inventory terminology, 1501
Gobbett, Brian, 489
Gochman, David S., 1420
Godrich, John, 1160
Gold, David L., 942
Goldberg, Harold J., 122
Goldmine price gd to rock 'n' roll memorabilia, 851
Gonen, Amiram, 371
Gonzalez, Martin L., 1434
Gonzalez-Pando, Miguel, 397
Good, Gregory A., 1517
Good skiing & snowboarding gd 1998, 740
Good wine gd 1999, 1340

Goodloe, Carolyn Lee, 427
Gordon, Bertram M., 498
Gordon, Peter, 289
Gore, Tom, 1354
Goslinga, Marian, 1089
Goss, Glenda D., 1135
Gottlieb, Richard, 141, 175
Gough, Jeanne, 296
Gould, Edwin, 1391
Gourman, Jack, 321
Gourman report of undergraduate programs, 321
Government info on the Internet, 61
Government on file, 684
Graber, Jeffrey, 1489
Graber, Steven, 264, 265
Grace, Betsy, 173
Grading student writing, 310
Graduate Group's new internships for 1997-98, 322
Graduate student's complete scholarship bk, 343
Graham, Robert J., 843
Grant, Tina, 203, 204, 206, 208
Grants & awards available to American writers, 30th ed, 830
Grassy, John, 1392
Great admirals, 624
Great artists, 863
Great misadventures, 522
Great war: a gd to the serv records of all the worlds fighting
        men & volunteers, 635
Green, David E., 1276
Green, Jonathan D., 1151
Green, Philip, 655
Green, Thomas A., 1180
Greene, Stanley A., 1567
Greenfield, Jane, 855
Greenman, David, 1578
Greeson, Janet, 1007
Gressman, Eugene, 569
Greve, Bent, 777
Grolier lib of women's biogs, 799
Grolier student lib of explorers & exploration, 419
Grossman, Mark, 577
Grotpeter, John J., 477
Grounds, Roger, 1351
Guernsey, Otis L., Jr., 1246
Guide to ...
    American cinema, 1930-65, 1217
    American cinema, 1965-95, 1211
    bk publishers' archives, 617
    Canadian English usage, 907
    children's ref works & multimedia material, 994
    free computer materials 1998-99, 16th ed, 288
    Internet job searching, 1998-99 ed, 268
    Latin American, Caribbean, & US Latino-made films
        & video, 1226
    popular US govt pubns 1995/96, 5th ed, 60
    public policy experts, 1997-98, 701
    the cinema of Spain, 1237
    the Indian wars of the West, 474
    the most competitive colleges, 325

the sources of US military hist, suppl 4, 622
    world lang dicts, 890
Guides to collection dvlpmt for children & YA lit, 601
Guillermo, Artemio R., 487
Gulevich, Tanya, 1194
Guttentag, Roger M., 1562
Guttery, Ben R., 1574

H. L. Mencken: a descriptive bibliog, 1027
Haeberle, Erwin J., 775
Hahn, Harley, 1496
Haig, John H., 933
Haines, Miranda, 426
Hainsworth, Philip, 1272
Hall, Amy, 51
Hall, Carolyn M., 593, 594
Hall, Clifton, 1094
Hall of fame museums, 69
Halper, Evan, 431
Halperin, Michael, 228
Hamadeh, Samer, 270
Hamlet: a gd to the play, 1077
Hamlin Garland, 1055
Hammond atlas of the world, 413
Hammond, Lorne F., 1552
Hancock, Susan, 994
Handbook of ...
    biblical chronology, rev ed, 1278
    bird identification for Europe & the W Palearctic, 1374
    child & adolescent psychology, v.5-7, 1466
    child psychology, 5th ed, 707
    economic methodology, 161
    health behavior research, 1420
    Latin American studies: social scis, no.55, 398
    N American industry, 220
    N American stock exchanges, 168
    pol sci research on the Middle East & N Africa, 648
    the American frontier, 393
    world stock indices, 221
Handbook to life in ancient Egypt, 510
Handbook to life in ancient Greece, 500
Hands, D. Wade, 161
Haney, Wayne S., 1173
Harding, Les, 530
Hardy, Peter, 740
Hardy, R. Willson, 57, 157
Harlem renaissance, 378
Harley Hahn's Internet & Web yellow pages 1998, 5th
        anniversary ed, 1496
Harmer, H. J. P., 375
Harmond, Richard P., 1552
Harper, David C., 845
Harper, Judith E., 800
Harper, Nancy Lee, 1136
Harris, Brian, 897
Harris, Charles W., 883
Harris, Dan R., 744
Harris, David, 642

Harrison, Nigel, 1117
Hart-Davis, Adam, 1188
Hartman, Charles, 1090
Harvard Business School core collection, 1998, 140
Harwood, Gregory, 1137
Hastedt, Catherine A., 884
Hastings, Elizabeth Hann, 81
Hastings, Philip K., 81
Hattendorf, Lynn C., 297
Having children: the best resources to help you prepare, 753
Hawley's condensed chemical dict, 13th ed, 1505
Hayes, David, 1429
Hayes, James L., 837
Head-Word & rhyme-word concordances to Des Minne-
    sangs Fruhling, 1094
Health: US, 1996-97 & injury chartbk, 1430
Health & British mags in the 19th century, 1417
Health & medicine on the Internet, 1424
Health care almanac, 1431
Health professions educ dir, 1998-99, 1425
Heard, J. Norman, 393
Hedblad, Alan, 986, 987
Heenan, Patrick, 198
Heidenreich, Conrad E., 409
Heising, Willetta L., 1031
Heisler, Sanford I., 1398
Held, Gilbert, 1492
Helgren, J. Anne, 1382
Heller, Mark A., 634
Helmer, William, 580
Henderson, Chuck, 1486
Hendrickson, Robert, 904
Herbal home remedy bk, 1461
Herber, Mark D., 401
Heritage Fndn Congressional dir, 671
Heroes & pioneers, 24
Herrmann, Robert O., 176
Herzhaft, Gerard, 1150
Hewett, Janet B., 475
Heyman, Neil M., 541
Heyn, Udo, 492
High places in cyberspace, 2d ed, 1269
Higham, Robin, 622
Hile, Kevin, 1013
Hill, Raymond, 131
Hillila, Ruth-Esther, 1121
Hillstrom, Kevin, 277, 1041
Hillstrom, Laurie Collier, 277, 1041
Hine, Andrea, 1457
Hippocrene standard dict Dutch-English, English-Dutch,
    923
Hirsch, Peter, 438
Historic docs of 1997, 679
Historical abstracts on disc [CD-ROM], 545
Historical dict of ...
    Bosnia & Herzegovina, 120
    Brunei Darussalam, 482
    Bulgaria, 494
    Burkina Faso, 2d ed, 96
    Denmark, 493

    Eritrea, 479
    Honolulu & Hawaii, 459
    Lebanon, 507
    Libya, 3d ed, 480
    Paris, 497
    Russia, 502
    school segregation & desegregation, 301
    socialism, 695
    Sri Lanka, 484
    Taoism, 1294
    the Baha'i faith, 1272
    the Czech state, 496
    the green movement, 1554
    the gypsies (Romanies), 380
    the music & musicians of Finland, 1121
    the People's Republic of China: 1949-97, 483
    the Persian Gulf war 1990-91, 630
    the Philippines, 487
    the Republic of Macedonia, 495
    the United Kingdom, v.2, 504
    the US Marine Corps, 638
    the US-Mexican war, 462
    the US Navy, 641
    the wars of the French Revolution, 499
    the welfare state, 777
    the World Health Org, 1421
    Vietnam, 488
    women's educ in the US, 803
    world slavery, 531
    WW I, 532
    WW II France, 498
    Zambia, 2d ed, 477
Historical ency of world slavery, 531
Historical gd to the US govt, 668
Historical gd to world slavery, 542
History & use of our Earth's chemical elements, 1510
History of ...
    black business in America, 144
    Israel, 509
    the mass media in the US, 820
HIV/AIDS Internet info sources & resources, 1469
Hochman, Jiri, 496
Hochman, Neil E., 665
Hoehner, Jane, 578
Hoffman, Joseph, 1463
Hoffmann, Frank W., 60
Hogan, Steve, 757
Hogg, Ian V., 532
Holderness-Roddam, Jane, 1383
Holiday symbols 1998, 1189
Hollander, David Adam, 560
Hollander, Jolanda Leemburg-Den, 319
Hollis, Daniel Webster, III, 1253
Hollywood blu-book dir 1997, 1221
Holm, LeRoy, 1368
Holmes, Marie S., 381
Holocaust, 540
Holocaust series, 533
Holtje, Steve, 1168
Hong, Barbara Blanchard, 1121

Hoopes, Laura L. Mays, 1356
Hoover's hndbk of ...
    American business 1998, 169
    emerging cos 1998, 170
    private cos 1998, 171
    of world business 1998, 222
Hoover's hndbks index 1998, 172
Hoover's masterlist of major intl cos 1998-99, 201
Horn, Barbara Lee, 1248
Horn, Elizabeth L., 1362
Horse companion, 1383
Horse owner's veterinary hndbk, 2d ed, 1354
Horwood, Jane, 941
Hostels USA, 431
Hot links: lit links for the middle school curriculum, 1001
Houlahan, Micheal, 1138
How products are made, v.3, 189
How the new tech works, 1484
How to find chemical info, 3d ed, 1511
Howe-Grant, Mary, 1503
Howsam, Leslie, 1297
Hubbs, Clayton A., 439
Huber, Jeffrey T., 1469
Hudson's Washington news media contacts dir 1998, 823
Hudson, Christopher, 241, 963
Hudson, Lee, 757
Huffman, James L., 486
Hughes, Alex, 128
Human choice & climate change, 1563
Humble, Malcolm, 1093
Humor in 18th- & 19th-century British lit, 1060
Hungary, 131
Hunt, Kimberly N., 210
Hupper, William G., 1273
Hurh, Won Moo, 374
Hurricanes, 1529
Husband, Janet G., 1029
Husband, Jonathan F., 1029
Husfloen, Kyle, 840
Hussar, William J., 299
Hutchings, Jonathan F., 1403, 1404
Hutchinson dict of ancient & medieval warfare, 534
Hutchinson gd to the world, 3d ed, 86
Hyatt, Lesley Anne, 1025
Hyatt, Wesley, 1212
Hyman, Paula E., 394
Hymntune index & related hymn materials, 1178

Icons of architecture, 877
Igbo-English dict, 932
Iger, Arthur L., 1139
Illustrated almanac of sci, tech, & inventions, 1306
Illustrated dict of ...
    architecture, 880
    Bible life & times, 1275
    mythology, 1186
Illustrated ency of ...
    active new religions sects & cults, rev ed, 1264
    camellias, 1364

healing remedies, 1460
Illustration index 8, 1992-96, 876
Ilson, Robert, 913
Imber, Jane Hunter, 1002
Index of American per verse 1996, 1100
Index of majors & graduate degrees 1998, 326
Index to ...
    black pers 1997, 377
    English per lit on the Old Testament & ancient Near
        Eastern studies, v.7, 1273
    intl public opinion, 1996-97, 81
    Marquis who's who pubs 1998, 25
    the House of Commons parliamentary papers on
        CD-ROM [CD-ROM], 571
    US marriage record, 1691-1850 [CD-ROM], 405
India & S Asia, 3d ed, 104
India hndbk, 243
Indian slavery, labor, evangelization, & captivity in the
    Americas, 382
Indiana companion to traditional Chinese lit, v.2, 1090
Indiana factbk 1998-99, 5th ed, 92
Indians of N & S America, 2d suppl, 385
Indicators of school quality, 298
Indoor pollution, 1565
Industrial commodity stats yrbk 1995, 29th ed, 223
Information industry dir 1998, 18th ed, 602
Information sources 98, 202
Ingraham, Mary I., 1143
Inhaber, Herbert, 363
Inside gd to American nursing homes, 1988-99 ed, 1475
Instruments of sci, 1312
Integrated curriculum: bks for reluctant readers, grades
    2-5, 2d ed, 1006
Interactive sci ency [CD-ROM], 1313
Interior design sourcebk, 858
International authors & writers who's who, 15th ed, 956
International business & trade dir, 2d ed, 141
International business info, 228
International dict of modern dance, 1201
International dict of univ hists, 315
International dir of ...
    arts, 811
    co hists, v.16, 203
    co hists, v.17, 204
    co hists, v.18, 205
    co hists, v.19, 206
    co hists, v.20, 207
    co hists, v.21, 208
International electric power ency 1998, 1406
International ency of dance, 1202
International ency of public policy & admin, 702
International ethics, 698
International fndn dir 1998, 8th ed, 769
International hndbk of environmental sociology, 1564
International hndbk of funeral customs, 1270
International instruments of the UN, 696
International labor & employment laws, v.1, 564
International league, 724
International mktg data & stats 1998, 224
International mktg forecasts, 225

International petroleum ency 1998, 1399
International policy insts around the Pacific Rim, 697
International satellite dir 1998, 1497
International student hndbk of US colleges 1998, 327
International tax summaries, 1998, 226
International who's who in music 1998/99, v.2, 2d ed, 1161
International who's who in poetry & poets' ency 1997, 8th ed, 1101
International who's who of women, 26
Internet resource dir for K-12 teachers & librarians, 98/99 ed, 307
Internet resources & servs for intl business, 209
Internet-Plus dir of express lib servs, 596
Internship bible, 1998 ed, 270
Interstate exit authority, 432
Introducing Canada, 489
Iowa state constitution, 568
Ireland: a dir 1998, 32d ed, 133
Irons-Georges, Tracy, 1443
Irving Berlin, 1134
Irwin, Robert, 489
Isaac Albeniz, 1129
Isaacs, Howard M., 1331
Isaacs, Katherine M., 900
Isaacs, Robert H., 1292
Isler, Charlotte, 1442
Israel, Elaine, 6
Issue briefs: 1997 annual ed, 1432
Italian horror films of the 1960s, 1205

Jackson, Kenneth T., 35
Jackson, Michael, 1333
Jackson, Paul, 1155, 1575
Jacobs, Karen, 1423
James, Bill, 715
James, Elizabeth, 70
James, Ewart, 908
Jane Austen ency, 1070
Jane's all the world's aircraft 1998-99, 89th ed, 1575
Jane's infantry weapons 1998-99, 24th ed, 645
Jane's land-based air defense 1998-99, 11th ed, 646
Jane's major warships 1997, 640
Jane's merchant ships 1998-99, 3d ed, 1578
Janik, Vicki K., 951
Jankowski, Katherine E., 760, 763, 764
Janoulis, Brenda H., 1449, 1476
Janoulis, Jason F., 1449, 1476
Japan & the Pacific Rim, 4th ed, 102
Japan trade dir 1997-98, 244
Japanese business law in W languages, 546
Japanese fiction writers since WW II, 1096
Jarvis, Helen, 105
Jason, Philip K., 1102
Jaszczak, Sandra, 50
Jazz CD listener's gd, 1165
Jazz discography, 1167
Jean Sibelius: a gd to research, 1135
Jenkins, Everett, Jr., 478
Jessamyn West: a descriptive & annot bibliog, 1056

Jessup, John E., 628
Jewish roots in Poland, 400
Jewish women in America, 394
Johannes Brahms: an annot bibliog of the lit from 1982 to 1996, 1143
Johansen, Bruce Elliott, 388
John Huston: a gd to refs & resources, 1207
Johns Hopkins atlas of human functional anatomy, 1415
Johnson, George M., 1063
Johnson, John R., 381
Johnston, Francis E., 1465
Johnston, Stephen, 1312
Jones, Daniel, 947, 948
Jones, Dawnette, 1474, 1477
Jones, Peter, 919
Jones, Tiffany M., 665
Jorgenson, John D., 947, 948
Joseph, Robert, 1340
Journalism ethics, 826
Juniper, Tony, 1378
Jurinski, James John, 300
Justice, Keith L., 12

Kaeppler, Adrienne L., 1120
Kagan, Jerome, 778
Kahl, Jonathan D. W., 1533
Kahn, Ada P., 705
Kane, Joseph Nathan, 46
Kanner, Barbara Penny, 39
Kaplan, Steven M., 1506
Karolides, Nicholas J., 603
Karr, Nicholas P., 57, 157
Karr, Paul, 431
Kassel, Richard, 1123
Katz, Bill, 72
Katz, Linda Sternberg, 72
Kaufeld, Jennifer, 53
Kaufeld, John, 53
Kearns, Patricia M., 641
Keenan, Jerry, 460
Keenan, Philip E., 1363
Keene, Chuck, 1392
Keeping score: film & TV music, 1988-97, 1140
Kehler, Dorothea, 972
Kehoe, Cynthia A., 596
Keller, William L., 564
Kelly, Gary, 1062
Kelly, W. A., 612
Kemp, Herman C., 103
Kennedy, Mary Lynch, 831
Kenrick, Donald, 380
Kent, Allen, 593, 594
Kerrod, Robin, 1295
Kerschen, Lois, 807
Kerwin, Christine, 150
Kesler, Christine A., 148
Ke-wen, Wang, 109
Kightley, Chris, 1379
Killion, Tom, 479

Kilmer, David, 1222
Kingfisher 1st sci ency, 1314
Kingfisher illus jr dict, 906
Kinnard, Roy, 1227
Kinoshita, Sumie, 163
Kittrie, Nicholas N., 476
Klein, Milton M., 464
Klett's modern German & English dict, 929
Klingler, Thomas A., 935
Kloesel, Christian J. W., 1069
Klooster, H. A. J., 481
Klostermaier, Klaus K., 1290
Klugherz, Laura, 1149
Knapp, Brian, 1507
Knappman, Edward W., 556
Knight, Virginia Curtin, 373
Kniskern, Nancy V., 781
Knives: military edged tools & weapons, 647
Knowles, Mark, 1203
Kolin, Philip C., 1057
Komara, Edward M., 1166
Kondek, Joshua, 1195
Konechni, Sasha, 495
Kope, Spencer, 1519
Kope's outer space dir, 1519
Korean Americans, 374
Korean war: an annot bibliog, 514
Kort, Michael, 124, 543
Kovinick, Phil, 869
Kowaleski-Wallace, Elizabeth, 961
Kranz, Rachel, 1005
Krapp, Kristine M., 189
Krause, Chester L., 846
Krebs, Robert E., 1510
Krippes, Karl A., 934
Kronenwetter, Michael, 742
Kroschwitz, Jacqueline I., 1503
Kubitschek, Missy Dehn, 1058
Kumar, Lisa, 1495
Kurian, George, 656, 1190
Kurian, George Thomas, 668
Kurz, Heinz D., 160
Kyker, Keith, 1498
Kyrgyz-English/English-Kyrgyz glossary of terms, 934

Lacy, Norris J., 1066
Ladies in the laboratory? American & British women in sci, 1800-1900, 1301
Lahti, N. E., 870
LaLiberte, Katherine, 1350
Lamar, Howard R., 463
Lamontagne, Monique, 198
Lamy, Marie-Noelle, 925
Landrum, Sherrye, 1471
Lane, Megan, 875
Langer, Adam, 1223
Langman, Larry, 1228, 1229
Langsjoen, Odin, 1439
Language & communication, 894

Language arts & environmental awareness, 997
Language of art from A to Z, rev ed, 870
Larkin, Colin, 1172
Larousse concise French/English, English/French dict, rev ed, 926
Larousse concise Spanish-English, English-Spanish dict, rev ed, 940
Larousse English dict, 899
LaRue, C. Steven, 243
Lassiter, Sybil M., 367
Last word: The New York Times bk of obituaries & farewells, 34
Latin America: a dir & sourcebk, 2d ed, 261
Latin America petroleum dir 1998, 17th ed, 196
Lauber, Daniel, 273
Launius, Roger D., 1520
Law, Barbara, 3
Law in lit, 945
Law, Nicholas S., 28
Lawlor, William, 1042
Lawson, Alan, 946
Lawton, Harry, 1207
Lawyer's research companion, 549
Lazich, Robert S., 188, 190, 620
Lazzari, Marie, 1016
Leana, Frank C., 313
Learning about...the Civil War, 453
Lee, C. C., 1407
Lee, Kelley, 1421
Lee, Lily Xiao Hong, 798
Lee, Michelle, 1082, 1083
Lee, Nancy Ann, 1168
Lee Van Cleef: a bibliog, film, & TV ref, 1208
Lefranc, Norbert, 1380
Legal info buyer's gd & ref manual 1997-98, 570
Legalized gambling, 714
Legends of the Earth, sea, & sky, 1184
Lehman, Jeffrey, 389
Leiter, Richard A., 565
Lemerand, Karen E., 20
Lemke, Robert F., 846
Lenzke, James T., 1577
Leonard Maltin's movie & video gd, 1999 ed, 1243
Leopold, Donald J., 1367
Lesch, Ann M., 699
Leslie, Rodrigues, 644
Levine, Emanuel, 1375
Levine, Jeffrey P., 152
Levine, Marc H., 194
Levine, Martin G., 308
Levine, Stuart R., 1481
Levinson, David, 365, 368
Levy, Cynthia J., 54
Levy, Patricia, 84
Levy, Peter B., 473
Lewis, Cynthia A., 586
Lewis, Marjorie, 1011
Lewis, Mary S., 1112
Lewis, Richard J., 1505
Lewis, Susan A., 858

Lewon, Paul, 202
Library of Lord George Douglas, 612
Library of the oceans, 1538
Library resources for singers, coaches, & accompanists, 1113
Liebman, Roy, 1209
Life is just a bowl of cherries & other delicious sayings, 914
Life of birds, 1372
Ligotti, Thomas, 980, 981, 982
Lilley, William, 674
Lillian Hellman: a research & production sourcebk, 1248
Lima, Carolyn W., 1008
Lima, John A., 1008
Lincoln, Berna B., 1375
Lincoln, Stanley R., 1375
Lindquist, Richard K., 1360
Linzey, Donald W., 1393
Literary gd & companion to S England, rev ed, 1065
Literary lifelines, 952
Literature connections to American hist, K-6, 449
Literature connections to American hist, 7-12, 450
Literature connections to world hist, K-6, 512
Literature connections to world hist, 7-12, 513
Literature of chamber music, 1153
Littman, Mark S., 791
Litz, A. Walton, 1043, 1045, 1110
Liu, Lewis-Guodo, 209
Llewellyn, Claire, 1003
Logue, Calvin McLeod, 975
Long, Janet Alice, 959
Long, John H., 447, 448
Long, Kim, 1521
Long, Robert Emmet, 369
Longe, Jacqueline L., 189
Longshore, David, 1532
Lopez, Billie Ann, 438
Lord, Tom, 1167
Los Angeles A to Z, 91
Losada, Jose Manuel, 944
Louden, Delroy, 1474, 1477
LoVaglio, Frank, 174
Love, Catherine E., 940
Love, J. W., 1120
Lovejoy's college gd, 24th ed, 351
Lowe, Allen, 1162
Lucanio, Patrick, 1213
Luce, Bernard, 1334
Luchinsky, Ellen, 1126
Luey, Beth, 617
Lumley, Elizabeth, 38

MacCary, W. Thomas, 1077
MacGregor, Alexander P., 891
MacHale, Des, 79
Mack, Carol K., 1181
Mack, Dinah, 1181
Mackenzie, Leslie, 1467
Macmillan ency of world slavery, 535
MacNee, Marie J., 578
Macoboy, Stirling, 1364

Madden, Debra L., 1447
Madge, Steve, 1374, 1379
Madigan, Carol Orsag, 27
Magazines for libs, 9th ed, 72
Magee, Bryan, 1256
Maggio, Rosalie, 895
Maghreb, 97
Magill, Frank N., 519, 520, 663, 706
Magill's medical gd, 1998 rev ed, 1443
Magill's survey of sci: earth sci series, 1515
Magill's survey of sci: life sci series suppl, 1356
Magill's survey of sci: physical sci series suppl, 1502
Magill's survey of sci CD-ROM [CD-ROM], 1324
Magill's survey of sci, v.7, 1315
Magnaghi, Russell M., 382
Mahalingam, Indira, 1254
Maizell, Robert E., 1511
Major authors on CD-ROM: Virgina Woolf [CD-ROM], 1087
Major cos of Central & E Europe & the Commonwealth of
　　Independent States 1998, 257
Major cos of Europe 1998, 258
Major cos of Latin America & the Caribbean 1998, 262
Major cos of the Arab world 1998, 239
Major cos of the Far East & Australasia 1998, 245
Major state health care policies, 1433
Maki, Kathleen E., 263, 361
Maki, Uskali, 161
Making wise medical decisions, 1453
Makowski, Colleen Lahan, 889
Makowski, Silk, 1012
Malcolm Arnold, 1130
Mali, 98
Malinowski, Sharon, 389
Maliszewski-Pickart, Margaret, 879
Malless, Stanley, 1078
Malloy, Mike, 1208
Malmkjer, Kirsten, 896
Malone, Elizabeth L., 1563
Malone, John, 739
Maloney, David J., Jr., 841
Maloney's antiques & collectibles resource dir, 841
Malta, rev ed, 134
Maltin, Leonard, 1243
Mammels of Va., 1393
Man, John, 440
Mancoff, Debra N., 1066
Mandler, Crystal, 771
Mankiller, Wilma, 804
Manly movie gd, 1242
Manuel de Falla, 1136
Maps on file, 414
Marchington, James, 647
Marill, Alvin H., 1140
Mark, Claudia, 600
Mark, Deborah, 396
Market share reporter 1998, 8th ed, 190
Markoe, Arnold, 35
Markoe, Karen, 35
Marley, David F., 629
Marsh, Lori, 165

Marsh, Sue, 140
Marshall, Margaret M., 935
Marti, James, 1457
Martin, Deborah L., 754
Martin, Dolores Moyano, 398
Martin, Len D., 1230
Martin, Ralph P., 1274
Masks from antiquity to the modern era, 363
Mason, Jane, 919
Mason, Steve, 1489
Master index to more summaries of children's bks, 1980-90, 1009
Masterplots II: poetry series suppl, v.9, 1102
Mathematically speaking, 1328
Matsunami, Kodo, 1270
Matthews, P. H., 893
Mattia, Fioretta Benedetto, 1
Mattix, Rick, 580
Matuz, Roger, 865
Matz, David, 523
Mautz, Carl, 861
May, James F., 562
Mayer, Robert N., 176
Mazurek, Joseph P., 561
McAlester, Lee, 433
McAlester, Virginia, 433
McAlpine, Janice, 907
McCall, Douglas L., 1231
McCallum, Lawrence, 1205
McCann, Gary, 549
McComb, Gordon, 1487
McComb, William C., 1367
McConnell, Elizabeth Huffmaster, 574
McConnell, Stacy A., 1115, 1116
McCracken, Penny, 864
McCutcheon, Mark, 916
McDermott, John D., 474
McEachran, John D., 1388
McElroy, Lorie Jenkins, 536
McFarland, Daniel Miles, 96
McFarland, Ruth, 821
McGee, Marty, 1232
McGillivray, Alice V., 677
McGinn, Bernard, 1266
McGraw-Hill illus telecom dict, 1491
McGraw-Hill machining & metalworking hndbk, 2d ed, 1413
McGraw-Hill multimedia ency of sci & tech [CD-ROM], 1316
McGraw-Hill yrbk of sci & tech 1999, 1325
McGregor, Andrew, 689
McGuckin, Frank, 583
McIlwraith, Thomas F., 409
McIntire, Dennis K., 956, 1101
McKay, George, 1391
McKenzie, Carol A., 637
McKinzey, Rima, 900
McLaughlin, Arthur J., Jr., 1481
McLelland, Y., 239
McLoskey, Lansing D., 1154
McNeil, William F., 716

McNenly, Jennifer, 689
McQuain, Jeffrey, 1078
McTyre, Ruthann Boles, 1113
Mead, Thomas, 701
Media French, 927
Media in the movies, 1228
Medical & health info dir 1998, 9th ed, 1426
Medieval & Renaissance mss in the Walters Art Gallery, 600
Medieval iconography, 810
Mehler, Mark, 267
Mehta, Mukesh, 1422
Melton, J. Gordon, 1214
Men of achievement 1997, 17th ed, 28
Mendez, Serafin Mendez, 93
Menon, Elizabeth K., 862
Merriam-Webster's concise hndbk for writers, 833
Merriam-Webster's manual for writers & editors, 834
Merriam-Webster's reader's hndbk, 964
Merry, John A., 1576
Messengers of God: a Jewish prophets who's who, 1292
Meyer, Sandra, 1548
Meyerink, Kory L., 403
Microsoft press computer dict, 1488
Middle East & N Africa 1998, 87
Middle East military balance, 1996, 634
Middle innings: a documentary hist of baseball, 1900-48, 722
Middleton, John, 100
Miglani, Gurbachan S., 1358
Mihailovich, Vasa D., 1091
Miniature empires, 537
Military aircraft insignia of the world, 636
Military contracts/procurement locator [CD-ROM], 632
Military personnel installations locator CD-ROM [CD-ROM], 633
Millennium champagne & sparkling wine gd, 1342
Miller, Allan W., 852
Miller, Corki, 1182
Miller, David, 640
Miller, E. Willard, 1565
Miller, Elizabeth B., 307
Miller, Eugene, 318
Miller, Joseph C., 535
Miller, Julia Wang, 1468
Miller, Ruby M., 1565
Miller's intl antiques price gd 1999, 842
Mills, A. D., 422
Milner-Gulland, Robin, 125
Milstead, Jessica L., 598
Minahan, James, 537
Minderovic, Zoran, 1541
Miner, Jeremy T., 770, 812
Miner, Lynn E., 770, 812
Miner, Margaret, 75
Minority & women's complete scholarship bk, 344
Mitchell, Susan, 90
Modern American lit, v.6, 4th ed, 1048
Modern British novel of the left, 1068
Modern China: an ency of hist, culture, & nationalism, 109
Modern ency of religions in Russia & Eurasia, v.7, 1267
Modern Germany, 129

Modern Japan, 486
Moe, Barbara, 755
Monkman, Karen, 805
Monsell, Thomas, 1238
Moodie, Michael, 644
Moon bk, rev ed, 1521
Moore, Chris, 281
Moore, Deborah Dash, 394
Morad, Deborah, 761
Morad, Deborah J., 59
Morena, John J., 1410
Morgan, Rick L., 558
Moriarty, J. Laura, 574
Morningstar mutual fund 500, 1997-98 ed, 173
Morris, Audrey Brichetto, 617
Morris, James M., 641
Morris, Wendy V. A., 928
Morrone, John, 830
Morrow, Charlene, 1542
Morton, Alan, 1224
Mosby's GenRx, 8th ed [CD-ROM], 1482
Mosby's primary care medicine rapid ref [CD-ROM], 1451
Moseley, Edward H., 462
Moseley, Merritt, 1064
Moshkovitz, Moshe, 838
Moulton, Carroll, 491
Mouser, Jeffrey D., 1411
Moving & relocation sourcebk 1998, 2d ed, 781
Mrozek, Donald J., 622
Muller, Nathan, 1493
Muller, Robert N., 1367
Multicultural projects index, 856
Multiculturalism, 369
Multistate gd to benefits law, 559
Mulvenon, James, 108
Mundell, P. Sue, 398
Municipal yr bk 1998, v.65, 680
Munro, Neil, 715
Munson, Kenneth, 1575
Murphy, J. L., 245
Murray, Jocelyn, 95
Musgrave, Ruth S., 587
Music of the golden age, 1900-50 & beyond, 1139
Musical theater synopses, 1244
MusicHound jazz, 1168
Musiker, Naomi, 1158
Musiker, Reuben, 1158
Mussen, William A., Jr., 729
Mustazza, Leonard, 1118
Myers, Robert A., 98
Mystery & suspense writers, 1032
Mystery women, v.1 1860-1979, 1030

Nagy, Andrea, 1450
Name that bk! questions & answers on outstanding
     children's bks, 2d ed, 1007
Namibia, rev ed, 99
Napierkowski, Marie Rose, 1014, 1106, 1107, 1108
National Audubon Society 1st field gd: birds, 1381

National Audubon Society 1st field gd: insects, 1389
National Audubon Society 1st field gd: mammals, 1392
National Audubon Society 1st field gd: rocks & minerals,
     1535
National Audubon Society 1st field gd: weather, 1533
National building codes hndbk, 1403
National consumer phone bk USA 1998, 153
National dir of ...
     corporate public affairs 1998, 154
     minority-owned business firms, 9th ed, 155
     nonprofit orgs 1998, 55
     woman-owned business firm, 9th ed, 156
National e-mail & fax dir 1999, 56
National faculty dir 1999, 29th ed, 328
National gd to funding in health, 5th ed, 1427
National Hockey League official gd & record bk 1997-98,
     733
National Hockey League Stanley Cup playoffs fact gd
     1998, 734
National party conventions 1831-1996, 681
National survey of state laws, 2d ed, 565
National trade & professional assns of the US 1998, 157
Native American info dir, 2d ed, 391
Native American sun dance religion & ceremony, 384
Native Americans, 390
Native North American firsts, 387
Natural resources, 1571
Naval Institute gd to world military aviation 1997-98, 637
NCAA football, 730
Nehmer, Kathleen Suttles, 285, 288
Nelson almanac, 642
Nelson, Bonnie R., 581
Nemet-Nejat, Karen Rhea, 511
Nerys Purchon's hndbk of natural healing, 1458
New bk of popular sci, 1998 ed, 1317
New ency of the American west, 463
New England in US govt pubs, 1789-1849, 452
New England transcendentalists [CD-ROM], 1046
New histl dict of the American film industry, 1215
New Interpreter's Bible [CD-ROM], 1279
New, Melvyn, 1074
New members of Congress almanac, 661
New Nelson Japanese-English character dict, rev ed, 933
New Yawk tawk: a dict of New York City expressions, 904
New York Public Lib business desk ref, 282
New Zealand, rev ed, 114
Newbery & Caldecott awards, 1998 ed, 995
Newell, Clayton R., 630
Newlin, Keith, 1055
Newman, Graeme R., 547
Newman, John J., 402
Newman, Richard, 80
Ng, Man Lun, 775
Nicholls, C. S., 22
Nichols, Victoria, 1033
Niemi, Richard G., 683
Nienhauser, William H., Jr., 1090
Nightjars: a gd to the nightjars, nighthawks, & their
     relatives, 1376
Nilsen, Don L. F., 1060

1998 franchise annual, 165
1997-98 hockey annual, 737
Nineteenth-century American western writers, 957
Nineteenth-century British bk-collectors & bibliographers, 592
Nineteenth-century lit criticism, v.61, 973
Nineteenth-century lit criticism, v.62, 974
Nixon on stage & screen, 1238
NLN gd to undergraduate RD educ, 5th ed, 1477
Nofi, Albert A., 627
Nohria, Nitin, 278
Nohring, Fritz-Jurgen, 1444
Nonprofit sector yellow bk, winter 1999 ed, 142
Nordquist, Joan, 758, 795
Norfolk, Elizabeth, 842
Norman, Teresa, 407
Norris, Joann, 71
North America in colonial times, 464
North American coins & prices, 845
North American furniture standards, 1412
North American industry classification system, 1997, 162
North American labor markets, 227
Norton, James H. K., 104
Noshpitz, Joseph D., 1466
Notable mathematicians, 1541
Notable poets, 1103
Notable women in math, 1542
Notable women in world hist, 797
Notess, Greg R., 61
Nottage, Luke R., 546
Novels for students, v.3, 1013
Novels for students, v.4, 1014
NTC's thematic dict of American idioms, 905
NTC's dict of ...
    British slang & colloquial expressions, 908
    commonplace words in real-life contexts, 915
    euphemisms, 902
    Japan's business code words, 193
    the USA, 1190
NTC's thematic dict of American slang, 911
Null, Gary, 1459
Nulman, Macy, 1293
Nursing licensure gdlines, 1998, 1476

Oakes, Elizabeth, 339
Oakes, Elizabeth H., 359, 750
Oakley, Stewart P., 493
O'Brien, Philip M., 1056
Occupational safety & health law 1997, 566
Ochoa, George, 525, 818, 1307
Official America online yellow pages, 53
Official fantasy hockey gd, 732
Official Internet dict, 1489
Official rules of ...
    golf, 731
    ice hockey, 735
    softball, 741
    the Natl Basketball Assoc 1997-98, 725
Ogden, Suzanne, 110

Ol' blue eyes: a Frank Sinatra ency, 1118
Oldenburg, Philip, 243
Oldman, Mark, 270
Oliver, Judith H., 600
Olken, Charles E., 1341
Olson, James S., 370
Olson, Richard, 1300
OMRI annual survey of E Europe & the former Soviet Union 1996, 115
On the road with your pet, 424
100 best stocks to own in America, 166
1500 Calif. place names, 420
Onorato, Mary L., 973
Open doors 1996/97: report on intl educl exchange, 352
Opera: the rough gd, 1157
Opera on screen, 1218
Opera premiere reviews & re-assessments, 1156
Opie, Iona, 1004
Opie, Peter, 1004
Orel, Vladimir, 921
Origins & dvlpmt of the Arab-Israeli conflict, 699
Orion blue bk: audio 1997, 177
Orion blue bk: camera, 178
Orion blue bk: car stereo 1998, 1485
Orion blue bk: copier, 179
Orion blue bk: guitars & musical instruments 1998, 1147
Orion blue bk: gun 1998, 849
Orion blue bk: professional sound 1998, 180
Orion blue bk: video & TV 1998, 181
Orion blue bk: vintage guitars & collectibles 1998, summer ed, 182
Oscar Wilde ency, 1075
Oserman, Steve, 268
OSHA quick gd for residential builders & contractors, 1404
Otfinoski, Steven, 121
Ott, Nicolaus, 885
Our planet Earth, 1003
Our Sunday Visitor's Catholic ency, rev ed, 1268
Our Sunday Visitor's ency of saints, 1261
Outer space, 1522
Outlaws, mobsters, & crooks, 578
Outstanding bks for the college bound, 1011
Outstanding women athletes, 2d ed, 710
Oxford atlas of exploration, 415
Oxford companion to ...
    Australian music, 1122
    British hist, 503
    Canadian lit, 1088
Oxford dict of ...
    foreign words & phrases, 903
    nursery rhymes, 1004
    saints, 1262
Oxford Spanish desk dict, 941
Oxlade, Chris, 1314

Pacific war ency, 627
Paddock, Lisa, 556
Padian, Kevin, 1539
Page, Martin, 1352

Pagell, Ruth A., 228
Pain sourcebk, 1473
Palac, Pete R., 871
Palmegiano, E. M., 1417
Pan-African chronology 2, 478
Panton, Kenneth J., 504
Papadakis, Elim, 1554
Paramount in Paris, 1236
Pardeck, Jean A., 756
Pardeck, John T., 756
Paris, 127
Parker, Mary, 1026
Parker, Robert, 1141
Parr, Mike, 1378
Parrinder, Geoffrey, 1287
Parrots, 1378
Parsons, Charles H., 1156
Partington, Angela, 78
Partnow, Elaine, 1025
Pas, Julian F., 1294
Patient's gd to medical terminology, 1442
Patient's gd to medical tests, 1454
Patient's gd to medical tests: everything you need to know
      about the tests your doctor prescribes, 1455
Patrick, Ruth, 1536
Patterson, Brad, 114
Patterson, Kathryn, 114
Patty's industrial hygiene & toxicology CD-ROM
      [CD-ROM], 1566
Paxton, John, 690
Pazzanita, Anthony G., 97
PDR family gd to prescription drugs, 1483
Peacemaking in medieval Europe, 492
Peacock, Lindsay, 1575
Peacock, Scot, 949, 950, 980
Pear, Nancy, 418
Pearson, Joyce A. McCray, 62
Peck, Terrance W., 271
Pederson, Jay P., 205, 207, 208
Pedowitz, Arnold H., 589
Pellam, John L., 113
Peltzman, Barbara Ruth, 309
Pendergast, Sara, 857
Peniston-Bird, C. M., 119
People of the Holocaust, 521
Peoples of the world, 371
Perez, Arturo, 678
Perl, Teri, 1542
Perle, E. Gabriel, 621
Perone, James E., 1114
Peroni, Gwen, 246
Perry, Mike, 1071
Pessl, Molly, 753
Peterson's professional degree programs in the visual &
      performing arts, 4th ed, 1197
Peterson's colleges with programs for students with learn-
      ing disabilities or attention deficit disorders, 329
Peterson's gd to 4-year colleges 1999, 29th ed, 330
Peterson's gd to nursing programs, 4th ed, 1478
Peterson's honors programs, 331

Peterson's internships 1998, 18th ed, 291
Peterson's private secondary schools 1998-99, 19th ed, 314
Peterson's scholarships for study in the USA & Canada
      1999, 2d ed, 345
Peterson's sports scholarships & college athletic programs,
      3d ed, 346
Peterson's study abroad 1998, 353
Peterson's vocational & technical schools & programs, 360
Petranka, James W., 1396
Pettenati, Jeanne, 661
Pettus, Daniel D., Jr., 1009
Pettus, Eloise S., 1009
Pfalzgraf, Jennifer J., 265
Phelps, Shirelle, 376, 379
Phillips, Charles, 538
Phillips, Diana, 185
Phillips, Vicky, 304
Physician marketplace stats 1997-98, 1434
Physicians' desk ref companion gd 1998, 52d ed, 1422
Physicians' desk ref for ophthalmology 1998, 26th ed, 1462
Pilger, Mary Anne, 856
Ping-Robbins, Nancy R., 1142
Pioneers of early childhood educ, 309
Pitt, Dale, 91
Pitt, Leonard, 91
Pittsburgh business dir, 152
Place called Peculiar, 421
Places, towns, & townships 1998, 782
Plant life in the world's Mediterranean climates, 1359
Plantfinder's gd to ornamental grasses, 1351
Plantfinder's gd to tender perennials, 1349
Platzker, David, 867
Pletcher, James R., 477
Plunkett, Jack W., 266, 827, 1435
Plunkett's entertainment & media industry almanac, 827
Plunkett's health care industry almanac 1997-98, 1435
Pocket gd to the birds of Britain & NW Europe, 1379
Pocket Oxford-Duden German dict, rev ed, 930
Podell, Janet, 46
Poetry criticism, v.18, 1104
Poetry criticism, v.19, 1105
Poetry for students, v.1, 1106
Poetry for students, v.2, 1107
Poetry for students, v.3, 1108
Poetry for students, v.4, 1109
Poets: American & British, 1110
Pohanish, Richard P., 1512, 1567, 1569
Polifka, Janine E., 1480
Pollock, Bruce, 1164
Pollock, Leland W., 1394
Polmar, Norman, 643
Poplawski, Paul, 1070
Popular music studies, 1163
Popular music, v.21, 1996, 1164
Popular nonfiction authors for children: a biogl & thematic
      gd, 1002
Population Division of the United Nations Secretariat, 809
Portable MBA desk ref, 2d ed, 278
Porter, Rick, 1187
Post-colonial lit in English, 946

Powell, Charles C., 1360
Practical dict of Chinese medicine, 1446
Practical gd to the marine animals of northeastern N America, 1394
Prebish, Charles, 1260
Preece, Michael A., 1465
Presidential also-rans & running mates, 1788-1996, 662
Presidential elections 1789-1996, 682
Presidential sites, 428
Presnell, Don, 1232
Preston, C. E., 960
PRI index, 771
Pricing stats sourcebk, 1548
Pringle, David, 976
Printed sources, 403
Printed stuff: prints, posters, & ephemera by Claes Oldenburg, 867
Pritzker, Barry M., 390
Problems in literary research, 4th ed, 972
Professional & technical careers, 274
Professional careers sourcebk, 5th ed, 361
Professionals job finder 1997-2000, 273
Profiles of American colleges, 332
Profiles of American labor unions, 271
Profiles of worldwide govt leaders 1998, 4th ed, 649
Projections of educ stats to 2008, 299
Prokopowicz, Gerald J., 468
Pronouncing dict of proper names, 2d ed, 900
Pronouncing Shakespeare's words, 1076
Provorse, Carl, 89
Psychology basics, 706
Public enemies, 580
Publishing law hndbk, 2d ed, 621
Puerto Rico past & present, 93
Puotinen, C. J., 1384
Purcell, L. Edward, 664
Purchon, Nerys, 1458

Qualitative inquiry: a dict of terms, 743
Quaratiello, Arlene Rodda, 610
Queer theory, 758
Quick ref dict for occupational therapy, 1423
Quick ref glossary of eye care terminology, 1463
Quigley, Thomas, 1143
Quotable lawyer, rev ed, 572

Rabin, Dan, 1332
Rabkin, Leslie Y., 1233
Racial & ethnic diversity, 2d ed, 372
Radice, Roberto, 1250
Raffel, Jeffrey A., 301
Raine, David F., 137
Rajewski, Brian, 658
Randall, Lilian M. C., 600
Random House German-English, English-German dict, 931
Random House Latin-American Spanish dict, 942

Random House Webster's American sign lang dict, rev ed, 909
Random House Webster's concise thesaurus, 917
Random House Webster's large print thesaurus, 918
Ranking of world stock markets, 229
Ranucci, Karen, 1226
Rapid gd to ...
    hazardous air pollutants, 1568
    hazardous chemicals in the environment, 1569
    trade names & synonyms of environmentally regulated chemicals, 1512
Rapkin, Lenore, 599
Rappaport, Karen, 1448
Rappaport, Susan S., 873
Rasmussen, R. Kent, 667
Rasor, Eugene L., 505, 517
Rawson, Hugh, 75
Rayburn, Alan, 423
Rayhawk, Peggie, 661
Raymond, Boris, 502
Rayner, Steve, 1563
Reader, Keith, 128
Reader's companion to US women's hist, 804
Reader's Digest illus great world atlas, 416
Reader's gd to women's studies, 796
Record of the Carnegie Institutes intl exhibitions 1896-1996, 868
Recording industry sourcebk, 1199
Recovery of internationally abducted children, 752
Recycling & waste mgmt gd to the Internet, 1562
Recycling in America, 1570
Red list of threatened plants, 1997, 1361
Redclift, Michael, 1564
Rees, Alan M., 1416
Rees, Nigel, 76
Reference gd to famous engineering landmarks of the world, 1397
Reference gd to Russian lit, 1097
Regan, Gary, 1337
Regan, Mardee Haidin, 1337
Reggae: the rough gd, 1171
Reich, Bernard, 648
Reis, Brian, 1206
Religion in the schools, 300
Religious holidays & calendars, 1271
Renstrom, Peter G., 555
Renz, Loren, 771
Representative American speeches, 1937-97, 975
Republic pictures checklist, 1230
Research centers dir 1999, 24th ed, 333
Researching Canadian markets, industries, & business opportunities, 247
Resources for people with disabilities, 750
Resources for teaching middle school scis, 1296
Respiratory care drug ref, 1481
Retail trade intl, 1998 ed, 230
Return to paradise: a gd to S Sea Island films, 1229
Rhodes, Anne K., 214
Ricciuti, Edward, 1535
Rice, Dan, 1385

Rich, Elizabeth H., 1427
Richards, Larry, 1234, 1280
Richardson, Andy, 264
Riddick, John F., 485
Riddle, Gay, 852
Riddle, Peter H., 852
Rideout, Philip M., 898
Ridpath, Ian, 1518, 1523
Riechel, Rosemarie, 996
Riffle, Robert Lee, 1344
Rijckaert, Arseen, 923
Rijsberman, Marijke, 963
Riley, Gail Blasser, 608
Rinderknecht, Carol, 13
Ringgren, Helmer, 1276
Rise of fascism in Europe, 694
Ritchie, Adrian C., 927
Ritchie, Roy, 850
Rittenhouse, Jo-Anne, 165
Ritter, Michael E., 1516
Rivers of the US, 1536
Roberts, Patricia L., 997, 998
Robertson, Lawrence R., 126
Robinson, Mairi, 42
Roby, Norman S., 1341
Rock garden plants, 1353
Rock music in American popular culture 2, 1173
Rodgers, Marie E., 378
Rodgers, Nigel, 440
Rodriguez, Junius P., 531
Rodriquez-Martin, Conrado, 1439
Roehm, Frances, 268
Rogel, Carole, 116
Roget's superthesaurus, 2d ed, 916
Rohrs, Roger, 180
Roitt, Ivan M., 1419
Roman de Renart: a gd to scholarly work, 1183
Romania, rev ed, 136
Room, Adrian, 408
Rooney, Terrie M., 20
Roots of Afrocentric thought, 985
Rosen, Philip, 528
Rosenberg, Bruce A., 962
Rosenberg, Ronald H., 585
Rosenblum, Joseph, 591, 1079
Ross, Donald, 1044
Ross, Lee E., 575
Ross, Steven T., 499
Rosteck, Mary Kay, 521
Rottet, Kevin J., 935
Routledge dict of 20th-century pol thinkers, 2d ed, 655
Routledge ency of translation studies, 896
Routledge French dict of telecommunications, 1494
Routledge German dict of chemistry & chemical tech, v.2, 1508
Routledge German dict of environmental tech, 1555
Routledge German dict of medicine, v.1, 1444
Routledge Spanish dict of business, commerce, & finance, 146
Rowan, Davina, 843

Rowlands, Shane, 946
Roy, Geoffrey, 440
Ruby, Mary K., 1106, 1107, 1108, 1109
Rudman, Theo, 183, 184
Rudman's cigar buying gd, 183
Rudman's complete gd to cigars, 184
Rudolph, Lloyd I., 243
Rudolph, Susanne Hoeber, 243
Rugg, Frederick E., 334
Rugg's recommendation on the colleges, 334
Rules of thumb for chemical engineers, 2d ed, 1400
Rupley, Lawrence A., 96
Russell, Cheryl, 372, 783
Russell, Terence M., 813, 814, 815, 816, 817
Russia, rev ed, 124
Russia & Eurasia facts & figures, v.24, 126
Rye, Howard, 1160
Ryman, Rhonda, 1204

Saari, Peggy, 522, 806
Sachare, Alex, 726
Safety & health on the Internet, 2d ed, 281
St. James gd to horror, ghost, & gothic writers, 976
St. James Press gay & lesbian almanac, 759
Salamanders of the US & Canada, 1396
Salkeld, Audrey, 442
Salvadori, Neri, 160
Samarsinghe, Vidyamali, 484
Sampson, Henry T., 1235
Sankey, Michael L., 597
Sansfacon, Roland, 920
Sarasohn-Kahn, Jane, 847
Sarnoff, Irving, 696
Savage, Kathleen M., 263, 361
Sbordoni, Valerio, 1390
Scammon, Richard M., 677
Schaefer, Christina K., 635
Schechter, Harold, 1242
Scheindlin, Raymond P., 395
Schellinger, Jennifer, 198
Schellinger, Paul, 963
Schiff, Donald, 1464
Schilling, Mark, 112
Schlachter, Gail Ann, 292, 293, 294, 772, 773
Schlager, Neil, 759
Schleifer, Martha Furman, 1145
Schmitt, Deborah A., 968, 969
Schmittroth, Linda, 521
Schnorr, Veronika, 928
Schoeman, Elna, 99
Schoeman, Stanley, 99
Schoenenberger, Lori, 761
Scholarships & loans for nursing educ 1997-98, 1479
Scholastic dict of spelling, 912
Scholastic ency of the US, 1005
Schrader, Richard J., 1027
Schramer, James, 1044
Schroy, Ellen T., 839
Schuler, Chris, 440

Schultz, Jeffrey D., 54, 1071
Schultze, Phyllis A., 547
Schwandt, Thomas A., 743
Schwartz, Richard A., 1191
Science & tech breakthroughs, 1308
Science fiction serials, 1227
Science projects for all students, 1326
Sciences of the earth, 1517
Scientific instruments 1500-1900, 1318
Scientists: their lives & works, v.4, 1302
Scientists: their lives & works, v.5, 1303
Scientists & inventors, 1304
Scientists since 1660, 1297
Scott Joplin: a gd to research, 1142
Scott-Kilvert, Ian, 1110
Scribner ency of American lives, v.1, 35
Scribner's American hist & culture [CD-ROM], 465
Scribner's writers series master index, 984
Scribner's writers series on CD-ROM: comprehensive ed
     [CD-ROM], 978
Scribner's writers series, selected authors ed [CD-ROM], 977
Segen, Joseph C., 1455
Seldon, Philip, 441
Semmes, Clovis E., 985
Sendero Luminoso in context, 573
Sequels: an annot gd to novels in series, 1029
Serge Chaloff, 1169
Serious about series, 1012
7th annual Graduate Group's internships in fed govt, 323
Sex & age distribution of the world populations, 784
Sexual behavior in modern China, English-lang ed, 775
Sexual harassment, 2d ed, 563
Sexuality & gender in the English Renaissance, 776
Sgroi, Renee, 3
Shafer, Yvonne, 1249
Shafritz, Jay M., 702
Shakespeare, 1079
Shakespeare interactive [CD-ROM], 1080, 1081
Shakespearean criticism 1996, v.38, 1082
Shakespearean criticism yrbk 1996, v.37, 1083
Shapir, Yiftah, 634
Shapiro, Stephen M., 569
Sharp, Richard M., 308
Sharp, Vicki F., 308
Shave, David, 262
Shealy, C. Norman, 1460
Sheets, Anna, 389
Sheets, Anna J., 1037, 1038
Sheets, Tara E., 50
Shelley, Thomas J., 1286
Shelov, Steven P., 1464
Shepherd, John, 1163
Sherrick, Julie, 1085
Sherry, Clifford J., 1370
Sheward, David, 1198
Shields, Nancy E., 835
Shim, Jae K., 194
Shin, Linda M., 1452
Short hist of the Jewish people, 395
Short stories for students, v.3, 1015

Short stories for students, v.4, 1016
Short story criticism, v.26, 1037
Short story criticism, v.27, 1038
Shrager, David S., 572
Shrikes: a gd to the shrikes of the world, 1380
Shriver, George H., 1289
Shulman, Frank Joseph, 15
Shulman, William L., 533
Shumsky, Neil Larry, 793
Siani-Davies, Mary, 136
Siani-Davies, Peter, 136
Sibley, Katherine A. S., 544
Sidhu, Jatswan S., 482
Siegel, Brian V., 477
Siegel, Joel G., 194
Siegel, Marvin, 34
Sierra Nev. Wildflowers, 1362
Sign-off for the old Met, 1155
Sikkel, Robert W., 589
Silk stalkings: more women write of murder, 1033
Singh, D. Ranjit, 482
Sitarz, Daniel, 567
Sitsky, Larry, 1144
6th annual Graduate Group's internships in state govt, 324
Slang of sin, 43
Slater, Courtenay M., 159
Slide, Anthony, 1215
Slominsky, Nicolas, 1123
Smallwood, Carol, 1428
Smith, Clay, 561
Smith, Colin, 939
Smith, Constance, 872
Smith, Dan, 700
Smith, Darren L., 151, 712
Smith, Jennifer A., 873
Smith, Myron J., Jr., 717
Smith, Roger, 1298, 1515, 1524
Smith, Ron, 719
Smith, Ronald L., 1196
Smith, Shanea L., 665
Smith, Steven E., 884
Smithsonian on disc, 4th ed [CD-ROM], 613
Snodgrass, Mary Ellen, 1047, 1182
Snyder, Kurt, 558
Sobczak, A. J., 959
SOHO desk ref, 283
Solar system, 1524
Solorzano, Lucia, 317
Somers, Paul P., Jr., 1192
Something about the author, v.94, 986
Something about the author, v.95, 987
Something about the author autobiog series, v.25, 988
Song index of the Enoch Pratt Free Lib, 1126
Songwriters: a biogl dict with discographies, 1117
Sonneborn, Liz, 386
Sonntag Blay, Iliana L., 1111
Soule, George, 1061
Soundtracks: an intl dict of composers of music for film, 1131
Source bk on ageing, 746
Sourcebk for modern Japanese philosophy, 1257

Sourcebook of ...
  county demographics, 11th ed, 785
  local court & county record retrievers 1998, 597
  ZIP code demographics, 13th ed, 786
South America, Central America, & the Caribbean 1999, 7th ed, 138
South Slavic writers since WW II, 1091
Southwick, Leslie H., 662
Sova, Dawn B., 605, 606
Spaihts, Jonathan, 335, 336
Spain, Louise, 1200
Spampinato, Lynn, 1021, 1022
Spanish American lit, 1098
Spanish-American war, 626
Spanish dramatists of the golden age, 1026
Spanish verbs, 938
Sparke, Penny, 878
Speace, Geri, 404
Speake, Jennifer, 903
Spears, Richard A., 905, 911
Special-needs reading list, 751
Speck, Bruce W., 310
Spencer, James R., 1245
Spencer, Pam, 999
Spencer's complete gd to special interest videos, 4th ed, 1245
Spero, Jennifer, 1568
Sponholz, Joseph, 347
Sporting News complete baseball record bk, 1997 ed, 718
Sporting News selects baseball's greatest players, 719
Sports in N America, v.1, 711
Sports phone bk USA , 1998, 712
Springfield armory: shoulder weapons 1795-1968, 848
St. James gd to native N American artists, 865
St. John, Ronald Bruce, 480
Stade, George, 1110
Staff dirs on CD-ROM [CD-ROM], 672
Stalker, Geoffrey, 919
Stamm, Andrea L., 98
Standard & Poor's stock & bond gd, 1998 ed, 174
Standard catalog of basketball cards, 1998 ed, 727
Standard catalog of US paper money, 846
Standard gd to cars & prices, 1577
Standard hndbk of architectural engineering, 881
Standard knife collector's gd, 3d ed, 850
Standard math interactive [CD-ROM], 1543
Standard per dir 1998, 73
Stanley, Deborah A., 965, 966, 967
Stanley, Harold W., 683
Stark, Jack, 568
Stars & planets, 1523
State & regional assns of the US 1998, 57
State budget actions 1997, 678
State legislative elections: voting patterns & demographics, 674
State medical licensure gdlines 1998, 1449
State occupational outlook hndbk, 275
State of war and peace atlas, 700
State tax actions 1997, 284
Statesman's yrbk 1998-99, 135th ed, 82

Statistical indicators for Asia & the Pacific, v.27, no.2, June 1997, 788
Statistical portrait of the US, 791
Statistical record of health & medicine, 1436
Statistics on occupational wages & hours of work & on food prices 1997, 231
STATS hockey hndbk 1997-98, 736
STATS minor league hndbk 1998, 720
STATS player profiles 1998, 721
STATS pro basketball hndbk 1997-98, 728
Stauffer, Joseph, 1455
Steading, Alma D., 451
Steele, J. Valerie, 665
Steele, Valerie J., 154
Steen, Sara J., 355
Steeves, Paul D., 1267
Stefanowska, A. D., 798
Stein, Bernard, 885
Stein, Stephen J., 1266
Stellman, Jeanne Mager, 280
Stephens, Aarti, 1083
Stephens, Alan, 1329
Stephens, Elaine C., 453
Stephens, Michael L., 1210
Sterling, Keir B., 1552
Stern, Robert L., 569
Sternberg, Martin L. A., 910
Stevens, Kenneth R., 659
Stevenson, Tom, 1342
Stewart, Ron, 850
Stidworthy, John, 1295
Stockwell, Foster, 747
Story of philosophy, 1256
Storytellers: a biogl dir of 120 English-speaking performers worldwide, 1182
Straughn, Barbarasue Lovejoy, 351
Straughn, Charles T., II, 351
Stravinskas, Peter M. J., 1268
Street French slang dict & thesaurus, 924
Stress A-Z, 705
Stromquist, Nelly P., 805
Strong, Debra L., 1570
Structural & ownership changes in the chemical industry of countries in transition, 232
Stuart, Ralph B., III, 281
Student Services, L. L. C., 338, 343, 344
Studwell, William E., 1125
Study abroad 1998-99, 30th ed, 354
Suchowski, Amy R., 8
Suderow, Bryce A., 475
Sullivan, Dean A., 722
Sullivan, Lawrence R., 483
Summerfield, Carol, 315
Supplement to the official records of the Union & Confederate armies, 475
Supreme Court rules: the 1997 revisions, 569
Susan B. Anthony: a biogl companion, 800
Sutnick, Barbara P., 371
Svengalis, Kendall F., 570
Sweeney, Wilma K., 751

Sweetman, Jack, 624
Swisher, Karen Gayton, 387

Tacka, Philip, 1138
Taking humor seriously in children's lit, 998
Talevski, Nick, 1174
Talking about people: a gd to fair & accurate lang, 895
Tallia, Rob, 560
Tap dance dict, 1203
Tapster, C., 257
Tardiff, Joseph C., 602
Tate, Mary Jo, 1054
Taylor, C. C. W., 1255
Taylor, Ed, 1490
Taylor, John W. R., 1575
Taylor, Ronald J., 1365
Taylor, Tim, 444
Taylor's dict for gardeners, 1345
Telecommunications: key contacts & info sources, 1500
Telgen, Diane, 1013
Ten yrs of classicists: dissertations & outcomes 1988-97, 891
Tenenbaum, Frances, 1345
Tennessee Williams, 1057
Terban, Marvin, 912
Terrell, Peter, 928
Thackeray, Frank W., 456
Thailand, 435
Thatcher, Virginia S., 836
That's enough folks: black images in animated cartoons, 1235
Theodore, Louis, 1568
Theological dict of the Old Testament, 1276
Theorizing composition, 831
They also served: military bios of uncommon Americans, 623
Thiel-Siling, Sabine, 877
Thody, Philip, 1193
Thomas, Alastair H., 493
Thomas, Brian J., 1327
Thomas Hardy's major novels, 1085
Thomas Jefferson: a biogl companion, 660
Thomas More: an annot bibliog of criticism, 1935-97, 1086
Thompson, Sue Ellen, 1189
Thompson, Susan, 1033
Thompson, William N., 714
Thorowgood, Sarah, 426
3,000 yrs of Chinese painting, 888
Thunder, flush, & Thomas Cooper, 1188
Thunder, James M., 586
Tibbetts, John C., 1216
Tiffin, Helen, 946
Timbrell, Martin C., 197
Time-saver standards for architectural design data, 7th ed, 882
Time-saver standards for landscape architecture design & construction data, 883
Timelines of world hist, 524
Tischauser, Leslie V., 454
Tomaino, Robert P., 1447
Tomas Luis de Victoria: a gd to research, 1132
Tomaselli-Moschovitis, Valerie, 684

Tombrello, Thomas A., Jr., 1502
Tomlinson, Carl M., 991
Toni Morrison, 1058
Top 100: the fastest growing careers for the 21st century, rev ed, 276
Top 10 of everything 1999, 63
Tornadoes, 1530
Townsend, Murray, 737
Toxic waste sites, 1560
Toye, William, 1088
Trade secrets: a state-by-state survey, 589
Trade shows worldwide 1998, 12th ed, 210
Traditional world music influences in contemporary solo piano lit, 1148
Trager, Oliver, 1175
Translation & interpreting schools, 897
Transportation & public utilities USA, 1572
Travel dict, new ed, 425
Traveler's atlas, 440
Traveler's gd to art museum exhibitions, 10th ed, 873
Traveler's gd to Jewish Germany, 438
Traveler's hndbk, 7th ed, 426
Travers, Bridget, 1426
Treasure, Geoffrey, 506
Tree of liberty: a documentary hist of rebellion & pol crime in America, rev ed, 476
Trees of the central hardwood forests of N America, 1367
Treiber, Rikard, 771
Trelawny, John G., 1366
Tressider, Jack, 886
Trice, Patricia Johnson, 1152
Trigger, Bruce G., 392
Tropical look: an ency of dramatic landscape plants, 1344
Trudeau, Lawrence J., 1019, 1020
Trudeau, Noah Andre, 475
Trujillo, Rosanne, 617
Truscott, Sandra, 943
Tschirgi, Dan, 699
Tucker, Spencer C., 527
Tull, Pamela M., 62
Tuma, Jan J., 1544
Turkington, Carol, 1445
Turner, Barry, 82
Turner, Gerard L'E, 1318
Twayne's English authors on CD-ROM [CD-ROM], 1067
Twayne's US authors on CD-ROM [CD-ROM], 1049
Twayne's world authors [CD-ROM], 979
Tweedie, Diana L., 197
Twentieth century Danish music, 1154
Twentieth-century literary criticism topics volume, v.70, 980
Twnetieth-century literary criticism, v.71, 981
Twentieth-century literary criticism, v.72, 982
Twentieth-century poetry from Spanish America, 1111
200 best aviation Web sites, 1576
Two Jews, 3 opinions: a collection of 20th-century American Jewish quotations, 396
Tycoons & entrepreneurs, 143
Tyler, Sean, 1161
Typography, 885

UFOs & ufology, 709
Uhle, Mary E., 835
Ulijaszek, Stanley J., 1465
Ulrich's intl pers dir 1998, 36th ed, 74
Ultimate beer, 1333
Ultimate visual dict, 919
Understanding the Holocaust, 539
Unger, Leonard, 1043, 1110
United Nations dir of agencies & insts in public admin &
       finance, 703
US & Asia statl hndbk, 1997-98 ed, 219
US chemical-biological defense guidebk, 644
United States Constitution, 686
US electric utility industry dir 1998, 7th ed, 1546
US govt dirs, 1982-95, 62
US govt leaders, 663
US industry & trade outlook '98, 191
USA & Canada 1998, 88
USA oil industry dir 1998, 37th ed, 192
USA Today baseball weekly almanac, 1997, 723
Unofficial ency of the rock & roll hall of fame, 1174
Untener, Deborah J., 210
Urrutia, Manuel R., 147
Utah state constitution, 688
U*X*L sci fact finder, 1319

Vacation study abroad, 355
Valdman, Albert, 935
Vampire gallery: a who's who of the undead, 1214
Vampire readings, 1035
Van Dijk, Kees, 319
Van Heerden, Bill, 1239
van Os, Andre, 135
van Vliet, Willem, 792
Varty, Kenneth, 1183
Vatican archives: an inventory & gd to histl docs of the
       Holy See, 1284
Vedder, Polly, 983
Vegetarian Journal's gd to natural foods restaurants in the
       US & Canada, 3d ed, 434
Vice presidents, 664
Victims rights, 590
Victoria & Albert Museum, 70
Vienna, 119
Vietnam experience, 1041
Viglielmo, Valdo H., 1257
Vile, John R., 685, 686
Villains & outlaws, 582
Viner, Bradley, 1386, 1387
Violence in American society, 583
Vital stats on American politics 1997-98, 6th ed, 683
Vladimir, Simosko, 1169
Vocational careers sourcebk, 263
Voices of the Holocaust, 536

Wacher, Tim, 1373
Wading the World Wide Web, 1498

Walden, Gene, 166
Waldman, Harry, 1236
Walford's gd to ref material, v.2, 83
Walker, Juliet E. K., 144
Walker's manual of penny stocks, 167
Walsh, D., 245
Walsh, James E., 614
Walsh, Michael, 83
Walsh, Ronald A., 1413, 1544
Walter, Kerry S., 1361
Wardwell, Joyce A., 1461
Warkentin, John, 409
Warman's Americana & collectibles, 839
Warmenhoven, Henri J., 117
Warner, Deborah Jean, 1312
Wars of the Americas, 629
Washburn, Wilcomb E., 392
Washington representatives 1998, 22d ed, 665
Wassall, J., 239
Wasson, D. DeWitt, 1178
Watson, Ben, 1350
Watson, Bruce, 643
Watson, Donald, 882
Watson, William E., 693
Watstein, Sarah Barbara, 1470
Weate, Jeremy, 1258
Weather almanac, 1534
Web programming lang sourcebk, 1487
Web site source bk 1998, 58
Weber, R. David, 293, 294, 772
Webster, L. Kay, 970
Wedlock, Eldon D., Jr., 476
Wegmann, Jessica M., 810
Weidensaul, Scott, 1381
Weigel, Molly, 1045
Weiner, Miriam, 400
Weis, Erich, 929
Weisberg, Gabriel P., 862
Welding codes standards & specifications, 1411
Wellner, Alison, 1437
Welsh, James M., 1216
Wemhoff, Rich, 753
Wendland, Michael, 1499
Wertheim, Eric, 643
West, John G., Jr., 1071
West, Gilian, 1084
West, Mark I., 1000
Western Apache-English dict, 936
Western Europe, 5th ed, 117
West's ency of American law, 557
Wetterau, Bruce, 687
Wexler, Philip, 1504
What do children read next? v.2, 999
What everyone should know about the 20th century, 538
What fantastic fiction do I read next? 1036
What histl novel do I read next? 1034
What Western do I read next? 1028
When they were kids: over 400 sketches of famous
       childhoods, 27

Where credit is due: a gd to proper citing of sources—print & nonprint, 2d ed, 835
Whisenhunt, Donald W., 461
Whissen, Thomas, 1217
Whitaker's almanack 1999, 131st ed, 5
Whitaker's almanack world heads of govt 1998, 650
Whitaker's almanack world heads of state 1998, 651
White, Jean Bickmore, 688
White, Paul, 723
White, Phillip M., 383, 384
Whiteside, Lesley, 1263
Who was who in British India, 485
Who's wealthy in America, 1998, 59
Who's who among African Americans, 1998/99, 379
Who's who in ...
    American art 1997-98, 866
    American law 1998-99, 10th ed, 550
    American pols 1997-98, 666
    Australasia & the Pacific nations, 3d ed, 29
    British hist, 506
    Christianity, 1283
    intl affairs 1998, 2d ed, 652
    sci & engineering 1998-99, 1305
    the media & communications 1998-99, 819
    the Midwest 1998-99, 26th ed, 36
    the S & SW 1999-2000, 26th ed, 37
    the world 1998, 30
    Vietnam, 113
Who's who 1998, 31
Wiedensohler, Pat, 596
Wild flowers of the Pacific NW, 1366
Wild orchids across N America, 1363
Wildlife conservation, 1371
Wiley engineer's desk ref, 2d ed, 1398
Wiley's English-Spanish, Spanish-English dict, 1506
Wilhite, Robert E., 846
Wilkinson, Philip, 1186
William Henry Harrison: a bibliog, 659
William Schuman: a bio-bibliog, 1127
Williams, Bob, 196
Williams, Dana A., 1050
Williams, Jane, 305
Williams, John Taylor, 621
Willings press gd 1998, 124th ed, 824
Wilmeth, Don B., 1247
Wilsdon, Christina, 1389
Wilson chronology of ideas, 525
Wilson chronology of sci & tech, 1307
Wilson chronology of the arts, 818
Wilson chronology of women's achievements, 802
Wilson, John, 1102
Wilson, Joyce M., 16
Wilson, Kathleen, 1015, 1016
Wilson, Laurel, 427
Wilson, William H., Jr., 1500
Win, May Kyi, 487
Wine Spectator Mag's gd to great wine values, 1338
Wingard, Helene F., 823
Winks, Robin W., 1032
Winning athletic scholarships, 1998 ed, 347

Wiseman, Nigel, 1446
Wisner-Broyles, Laura A., 762, 767, 774
Wit: humorous quotations from Woody Allen to Oscar Wilde, 79
Wlaschin, Ken, 1218
Wolf, Carolyn, 385
Wolf, Kirsten, 892
Womack, Kenneth, 592
Women artists & designers in Europe since 1800, 864
Women composers, v.3, 1145
Women in China, 808
Women in context, 39
Women in the Third World, 805
Women writers in German-speaking countries, 1095
Women's firsts, 806
Women's health concerns sourcebk, 1438
Women's hist, 801
Wood, Corinne Shear, 1472
Wood, Donna, 333
Wood, Richard A., 1534
Wood, Richard J., 60
Woodgate, Graham, 1564
Woolf, D. R., 529
Woolum, Janet, 710
Wooster, Robert, 625
Words on cassette 1998, 14
World almanac for kids 1999, 6
World almanac of the USA, rev ed, 89
World biogl index, 3d ed, 32
World Bk multimedia ency, 1998 [CD-ROM], 47
World database of consumer brands & their owners 1998 [CD-ROM], 259
World dir of ...
    business info libs, 3d ed, 615
    mktg info sources, 211
    mathematicians 1998, 11th ed, 1545
    non-official statl sources, 2d ed, 789
World econ factbk 1997/98, 5th ed, 233
World ency of parliaments & legislatures, 656
World gd to scientific assns & learned societies, 7th ed, 1323
World holiday festival & calendar bks, 1194
World investment report 1998, 234
World labour report 1997-98, 235
World list of univs & other insts of higher educ, 21st ed, 337
World lit criticism suppl, 983
World mktg data & stats on CD-ROM [CD-ROM], 236
World mountaineering, 442
World music CD listener's gd, 1159
World of learning 1999, 49th ed, 295
World population monitoring 1996, 809
World population prospects, 790
World retail dir 1997-98, 212
World Trade Org dispute settlement decisions, v.1, 237
World urbanization prospects, 794
World War I, 541
World weeds, 1368
World Wide Web for scientists & engineers, 1327
Worldmark ency of cultures & daily life, 364
Worldwide offshore petroleum dir 1998, 30th ed, 213
Worldwide petrochemical dir 1998, 36th ed, 214

Worldwide petroleum industry outlook, 1549
Wrend, Julie, 561
Wright, Cora M., 1001
Wright, David, 412, 1551
Wright, Jill, 412
Wright, Marshall D., 724
Writer's dir 1998-2000, 13th ed, 958
Writer's hndbk, 832
Wyatt, Flora R., 1002

Xtravaganza! the essential sourcebk for Macromedia
     Xtras, 1486

Yager, Cindy, 304
Ye, Feng, 1446
Yearbk of labor stats, 1997, 238
Yemen, rev ed, 139

Yntema, Sharon, 279
Yoshinki-Kovinick, Marian, 869
Young person's gd to philosophy, 1258
Young, Antonia, 118
Young, Ben, 1146
Young, Claiborne S., 430
Young, Robyn V., 1541

Zavala, Agustin Jacinto, 1257
Zelio, Judy, 284
Zhang, Puling, 1434
Zich, Joanne, 549
Zils, Michael, 1323
Zminda, Don, 715
Zoltan Kodaly: a gd to research, 1138
Zuber, Pam, 1195
Zuidema, George D., 1415
Zweifel, Richard G., 1395

Subject Index

Reference is to entry number.

ABBREVIATIONS
Elsevier's dict of acronyms, initialisms, abbreviations, & symbols, 1

ABORTION
World population monitoring 1996, 809

ACRONYMS
Elsevier's dict of acronyms, initialisms, abbreviations, & symbols, 1

ACTORS. *See also* **MOTION PICTURES**
Entertainers in British films, 1225
Guide to American cinema, 1930-65, 1217
Guide to American cinema, 1965-95, 1211
Lee Van Cleef: a bibliog, film, & TV ref, 1208

ADMINISTRATIVE AGENCIES
Encyclopedia of govtl advisory orgs 1997, 11th ed, 670
Global links: a gd to key people & insts worldwide, 54
United Nations dir of agencies & insts in public admin & finance, 703
US govt dirs, 1982-95, 62

ADOLESCENCE
Gale ency of childhood & adolescence, 778

ADOPTION
Adoption, 755
Annotated gd to adoption research 1986-97, 754
Children in foster care & adoption, 756

AERONAUTICS
Airlines Worldwide, 1573
Encyclopedia of African airlines, 1574
Jane's all the world's aircraft, 1575
200 best aviation Web sites, 1576

AERONAUTICS, MILITARY
Military aircraft insignia of the world, 636
Naval Institute gd to world military aviation 1997-98, 637

AFFLUENT CONSUMERS
Who's wealthy in America, 1998, 59

AFRICA
Black hndbk, 375
Cultural atlas of Africa, rev ed, 95
Encyclopedia of African airlines, 1574
Roots of Afrocentric thought, 985

AFRICA—BIBLIOGRAPHY
Africa: Africa world press gd to educ resources from & about Africa, 94
Mali, 98

AFRICAN HISTORY
Historical dict of Eritrea, 479
Historical dict of Libya, 3d ed, 480
Historical dict of Zambia, 2d ed, 477
Pan-African chronology 2, 478

AFRICA, NORTH
Middle East & N Africa 1998, 87

AFRICANS
African biog, 373
Black hndbk, 375

AFRICA, SUB-SAHARAN
Encyclopedia of Africa S of the Sahara, 100

AFRICA, WEST
Historical dict of Burkina Faso, 2d ed, 96

AFRO-AMERICAN ARTS
Harlem renaissance, 378

AFRO-AMERICAN AUTHORS
Roots of Afrocentric thought, 985
Toni Morrison, 1058

AFRO-AMERICAN—DRAMATISTS
Contemporary African-American female playwrights, 1050

AFRO-AMERICAN—HISTORY
Civil rights movement, 473
Roots of Afrocentric thought, 985

AFRO-AMERICAN—QUOTATIONS
African American quotations, 80

AFRO-AMERICANS
African-American baby name bk, 407
African American criminologists, 1970-96, 575
Contemporary black biog, v.16, 376
Financial aid for African Americans 1997-99, 292
History of black business in America, 144
Index to black pers 1997, 377
Pan-African chronology 2, 478
Who's who among African Americans, 1998/99, 379

AFRO-AMERICANS IN MOTION PICTURES
African American films through 1959, 1234
That's enough folks: black images in animated cartoons, 1235

AGED
Aging sourcebk, 744
Directory of population ageing research in Europe, 745
Source bk on ageing, 746

AGRICULTURE
Agriculture, mining, & construction USA, 187
Dictionary of agriculture, 2d ed, 1329

AIDS (DISEASE)
AIDS crisis, 1468
AIDS dict, 1470
HIV/AIDS Internet info sources & resources, 1469

AIR—POLLUTION
Clean air hndbk, 3d ed, 1558
Indoor pollution, 1565
Rapid gd to hazardous air pollutants, 1568

ALABAMA—HISTORY
Alabama hist, 451

ALBANIA
Albania, rev ed, 118

ALBANIAN LANGUAGE
Albanian etymological dict, 921

ALBENIZ, ISAAC
Isaac Albeniz, 1129

ALLOYS
ASM ready ref properties & units for engineering alloys,
1408

ALLUSIONS
Dictionary of histl allusions & eponyms, 40

ALMANACS
Canadian almanac & dir 1999, 152d ed, 2
Canadian sourcebk 1998, 33d ed, 3
Chase's calendar of events 1998, 4
Whitaker's almanack 1999, 131st ed, 5
Whitaker's almanack world heads of govt 1998, 650
Whitaker's almanack world heads of state 1998, 651
World almanac for kids 1999, 6
World almanac of the USA, rev ed, 89

ALTERNATIVE MEDICINE
Alternative health & medicine ency, 2d ed, 1457
Complete bk of symptoms & treatments, 1456
Complete ency of natural healing, 1459
Directory of schools for alternative & complementary
health care, 1448
Herbal home remedy bk, 1461
Illustrated ency of healing remedies, 1460
Nerys Purchon's hndbk of natural healing, 1458

AMERICANA
Warman's Americana & collectibles, 839

AMERICANISMS
NTC's dict of commonplace words in real-life contexts,
915
NTC's dict of the USA, 1190
NTC's thematic dict of American idioms, 905

AMERICAN SIGN LANGUAGE
American sign lang, unabridged ed, 910
Random House Webster's American sign lang dict, rev ed,
909

AMERICAN WEST
New ency of the American west, 463

AMERICA ONLINE
Official America online yellow pages, 53

AMPHIBIANS
Encyclopedia of reptiles & amphibians, 2d ed, 1395

AMSTERDAM (NETHERLANDS)
Amsterdam, 135

ANDALUSI ARABIC LANGUAGE—
    DICTIONARIES—ENGLISH
Dictionary of Andalusi Arabic, 922

ANIMAL RIGHTS
Animal rights, 2d ed, 1369
Endangered species, 1370
Federal wildlife laws hndbk with related laws, 587

ANIMALS. *See also* **MAMMALS; MARINE ANIMALS**
Facts on File wildlife atlas, rev ed, 1295

ANIMATED FILMS
Annimated film collector's gd, 1222
Film cartoons: a gd to 20th century American animated
features & shorts, 1231
That's enough folks: black images in animated cartoons,
1235

ANONYMS & PSEUDONYMS
Dictionary of pseudonyms, 408

ANTHONY, SUSAN B.
Susan B. Anthony: a biogl companion, 800

ANTHROPOLOGY
Anthropology bibliog on disc [CD-ROM], 362

ANTIQUE & CLASSIC CARS
Standard gd to cars & prices, 1577

ANTIQUES
Antique Trader Books antiques & collectibles price gd,
1999 ed, 840
Maloney's antiques & collectibles resource dir, 841
Miller's intl antiques price gd 1999, 842

APOCALYPTICISM
Encyclopedia of apocalypticism, 1266

APPLIED SCIENCE
Magill's survey of sci, v.7, 1315

ARAB COUNTRIES
Dictionary of modern Arab hist, 508

ARABIC LANGUAGE—DICTIONARIES—ENGLISH
Dictionary of Andalusi Arabic, 922

ARAB-ISRAELI CONFLICT
Origins & dvlpmt of the Arab-Israeli conflict, 699

ARCHAEOLOGY
Archaeology of prehistoric Native America, 443
Atlas of archaeology, 444
Encyclopedia of underwater & maritime archaeology, 446
High places in cyberspace, 2d ed, 1269

ARCHITECTURE
Architecture & ornament, 879
Encyclopaedic dict in the 18th century, v.1, 813
Encyclopaedic dict in the 18th century, v.2, 814
Encyclopaedic dict in the 18th century, v.3, 815
Encyclopaedic dict in the 18th century, v.4, 816
Encyclopaedic dict in the 18th century, v.5, 817
Icons of architecture, 877
Illustrated dict of architecture, 880
Standard hndbk of architectural engineering, 881
Time-saver standards for architectural design data, 7th ed, 882

ARCHIVES
Smithsonian on disc, 4th ed [CD-ROM], 613
Vatican archives: an inventory & gd to histl docs of the Holy See, 1284
World of learning 1999, 49th ed, 295

ARISTOTLE
Aristotle's Metaphysics: annot bibliog of the 20th-century lit, 1250

ARNOLD, MALCOLM
Malcolm Arnold, 1130

ART
Art marketing sourcebk for the fine artist, 3d ed, 872
Art: a world hist, 874
Artist's & graphic designers market, 1998, 875
Fools & jesters in lit, art, & hist, 951
Medieval iconography, 810

ART—CHRONOLOGY
Wilson chronology of the arts, 818

ART—DICTIONARIES
Language of art from A to Z, rev ed, 870

ART—DIRECTORIES
American art dir 1997-98, 56th ed, 871
International dir of arts, 811

ART—MODERN
Art nouveau, 862

ART DIRECTORS
Art directors in cinema, 1210

ART MUSEUMS
American art dir 1997-98, 56th ed, 871
International dir of arts, 811
Record of the Carnegie Institutes intl exhibitions 1896-1996, 868
Traveler's gd to art museum exhibitions, 10th ed, 873

ARTHURIAN ROMANCES
Arthurian hndbk, 2d ed, 1066

ARTIFICIAL SATELLITES
International satellite dir 1998, 1497

ARTISTS
American bk & mag illustrators to 1920, v.188, 884
Encyclopedia of women artists of the American west, 869
Great artists, 863
Printed stuff: prints, posters, & ephemera by Claes Oldenburg, 867
Who's who in American art 1997-98, 866

ASIA
Asia, 2d ed, 240
China, 7th ed, 110
Compendium of social stats & indicators, 4th issue, 787
Cultural atlas of China, rev ed, 106
India & S Asia, 3d ed, 104
Japan & the Pacific Rim, 4th ed, 102
Source bk on ageing, 746
Statistical indicators for Asia & the Pacific, v.27, no.2, June 1997, 788

ASIA—BIBLIOGRAPHY
Bibliographies on SE Asia, 103
Doctoral dissertations on China & on inner Asia, 1976-90, 15

ASIA—BUSINESS
Asia-Pacific petroleum dir 1998, 14th ed, 195
Consumer Asia 1998, 215
US & Asia statl hndbk, 1997-98 ed, 219

ASIAN AMERICANS. See also JAPANESE AMERICANS
Asian American woman, 795
Financial aid for Asian Americans 1997-99, 293
Korean Americans, 374

ASIAN STUDIES
European dir of SE Asian studies, 319

ASSOCIATIONS
Directory of American youth orgs 1998-99, 7th ed, 52
Encyclopedia of assns, 50
Encyclopedia of assns: regional, state, & local orgs, 7th ed, 51
National trade & professional assns of the US 1998, 157
State & regional assns of the US 1998, 57
World gd to scientific assns & learned societies, 7th ed, 1323
World of learning 1999, 49th ed, 295

ASTRONAUTICS
Frontiers of space exploration, 1520

ASTRONOMERS
Directory of physics, astronomy, & geophysics staff, 1997
    biennial ed, 1322

ASTRONOMY
Dictionary of astronomy, 1518
Kope's outer space dir, 1519
Moon bk, rev ed, 1521
Outer space, 1522
Solar system, 1524
Stars & planets, 1523

ATHLETES
Outstanding women athletes, 2d ed, 710
Sporting News selects baseball's greatest players, 719

ATHLETICS
Winning athletic scholarships, 1998 ed, 347

ATLASES
Atlas of archaeology, 444
Cartographic satellite atlas of the world, 410
Concise histl atlas of Canada, 409
DK student atlas, 411
Hammond atlas of the world, 413
Reader's digest illus great world atlas, 416
State of war & peace atlas, 700
Traveler's atlas, 440

ATTORNEYS
Who's who in American law 1998-99, 10th ed, 550

AUDIO EQUIPMENT
Orion blue bk: car stereo 1998, 1485
Orion blue bk: professional sound 1998, 180

AUDIOCASSETTES
Words on cassette 1998, 14

AUSTEN, JANE
Jane Austen ency, 1070

AUSTRALASIA
Who's who in Australasia & the Pacific nations, 3d ed, 29

AUSTRALIA
Australia, 436
Garland ency of world music, v.9, 1120
Oxford companion to Australian music, 1122

AUSTRIAN LITERATURE
Companion to 20th-century German lit, 2d ed, 1093

AUTHORS
Contemporary author autobiog series, v.28, 953
Contemporary authors new revision series, v.59, 947

Contemporary authors new revision series, v.60, 948
Contemporary authors, v.158, 949
Contemporary authors, v.159, 950
Contemporary literary criticism yrbk 1996, v.99, 965
Contemporary literary criticism, v.100, 966
Contemporary literary criticism, v.101, 967
Contemporary literary criticism, v.102, 968
Contemporary literary criticism, v.103, 969
Dictionary of literary biog documentary series, v.16, 954
Dictionary of literary biog documentary series, v.17, 955
Dictionary of literary biog yrbk: 1996, 970
Encyclopedia of the novel, 963
International authors & writers who's who, 15th ed, 956
Mystery & suspense writers, 1032
St. James gd to horror, ghost, & gothic writers, 976
Scribner's writers series, selected authors ed [CD-ROM], 977
Scribner's writers series on CD-ROM: comprehensive ed
    [CD-ROM], 978
Scribner's writers series master index, 984
Twayne's world authors [CD-ROM], 979
Twentieth-century literary criticism topics volume, v.70, 980
Twnetieth-century literary criticism, v.71, 981
Twentieth-century literary criticism, v.72, 982
Writer's dir 1998-2000, 13th ed, 958

AUTHORS, AMERICAN
American travel writers, 1776-1864, 1044
American writers, 1043
American writers, retrospective suppl 1, 1045
Contemporary men fiction writers, 1039
Dictionary of literary biog, v.193, 1059
Hamlin Garland, 1055
Jessamyn West: a descriptive & annot bibliog, 1056
Modern American lit, v.6, 4th ed, 1048
Nineteenth-century American western writers, 957
Twayne's US authors on CD-ROM [CD-ROM], 1049

AUTHORS—BIOGRAPHY—JUVENILE
    LITERATURE
Literary lifelines, 952
Popular nonfiction authors for children: a biogl & thematic
    gd, 1002

AUTHORS, EAST EUROPEAN
South Slavic writers since WW II, 1091

AUTHORS, ENGLISH
Dictionary of literary biog: British reform writers,
    1832-1914, 1062
Dictionary of literary biog, v.191, 1063
Dictionary of literary biog, v.194, 1064
Twayne's English authors on CD-ROM [CD-ROM], 1067

AUTHORS, FRENCH
Dictionary of literary biog, v.192, 1092

AUTHORS—HOMES & HAUNTS
Literary gd & companion to S England, rev ed, 1065

AUTHORS, IRISH
Oscar Wilde ency, 1075

AUTHORSHIP. *See also* **PUBLISHERS &**
    PUBLISHING
Children's writer's & illustrator's market, 1998, 828
Companion to Historiography, 829
English usage & style for editors, 836
Merriam-Webster's concise hndbk for writers, 833
Merriam-Webster's manual for writers & editors, 834
Where credit is due: a gd to proper citing of
      sources—print & nonprint, 2d ed, 835
Writer's hndbk, 832

AUTOMOBILES
Orion blue bk: car stereo 1998, 1485
Standard gd to cars & prices, 1577

BAHA'I FAITH
Historical dict of the Baha'i faith, 1272

BALLET
Dictionary of classical ballet terminology, 1204
International ency of dance, 1202

BANKS & BANKING. *See also* **ECONOMICS;**
    FINANCE
Dictionary of banking terms, 186

BARBIE DOLLS
Contemporary Barbie dolls, 847

BASEBALL
Baseball: a comprehensive bibliog, suppl 2, 717
Bill James presents: STATS all-time major league hndbk,
    715
Dodgers ency, 716
International league, 724
Middle innings: a documentary hist of baseball, 1900-48, 722
Sporting News complete baseball record bk, 1997 ed, 718
Sporting News selects baseball's greatest players, 719
STATS player profiles 1998, 721
USA Today baseball weekly almanac, 1997, 723

BASKETBALL
Chicago Bulls ency, 726
Official rules of the Natl Basketball Assoc 1997-98, 725
STATS pro basketball hndbk 1997-98, 728

BASKETBALL CARDS
Standard catalog of basketball cards, 1998 ed, 727

BEANIE BABIES (TOYS)
Beanie family album & collectors gd, 853

BEAT GENERATION
Beat generation, 1042

BEER
Dictionary of beer & brewing, 2d ed, 1332
Ultimate beer, 1333

BELARUS
Cultures of the World, 84

BERLIN, IRVING
Irving Berlin, 1134

BERMUDA
Bermuda, 137

BEST BOOKS
Children's bk awards annual 1998, 990
Children's bk prizes, 989
From biog to hist, 993
Newbery & Caldecott awards, 1998 ed, 995
Special-needs reading list, 751

BEST-SELLERS—BIBLIOGRAPHY
Bestseller index, 12

BEVERAGE INDUSTRY
Food & beverage market place, 1997/98, 1339

BIBLE
Bible: God's word for the biblically-inept, 1280
Expositor's bible commentary [CD-ROM], 1277
High places in cyberspace, 2d ed, 1269
New Interpreter's Bible [CD-ROM], 1279

BIBLE—CHRONOLOGY
Handbook of Biblical chronology, [rev ed], 1278

BIBLE—DICTIONARIES
Illustrated dict of Bible life & times, 1275
Theological dict of the Old Testament, 1276

BIBLE—N.T.
Dictionary of the later new testament & its developments,
    1274

BIBLE—O.T.
Index to English per lit on the Old Testament & ancient
    Near Eastern studies, v.7, 1273
Messengers of God: a Jewish prophets who's who, 1292
Theological dict of the Old Testament, 1276

BIBLIOGRAPHERS
American bk collectors & bibliographers, 2d series, 591
Nineteenth-century British bk-collectors & bibliographers,
    592

BIBLIOGRAPHICAL CITATIONS
Where credit is due: a gd to proper citing of
      sources—print & nonprint, 2d ed, 835

BIBLIOGRAPHY
American bk publishing record, cum 1997, 9
Checklist of American imprints for 1846, 13
Complete dir of large print bks & serials 1998, 11
Library of Lord George Douglas, 612
Nineteenth-century British bk-collectors & bibliographers, 592
Vampire readings, 1035

BIBLIOGRAPHY—BIOGRAPHY—SCIENTISTS
Scientists since 1660, 1297

BIBLIOGRAPHY—CHILDREN'S LITERATURE
Guides to collection dvlpmt for children & YA lit, 601

BIBLIOGRAPHY—YOUNG ADULT LITERATURE
Guides to collection dvlpmt for children & YA lit, 601

BIBLIOTHERAPY
Children in foster care & adoption, 756

BIODIVERSITY
Biodiversity, 1556

BIOGRAPHY
Almanac of famous people, 6th ed, 17
Ancient Romans, 518
Biographical dict of Chinese women, 798
Biographical ency of scientists, 1300
Biography & genealogy master index 1999, 404
Cambridge biogl ency, 2d ed, 18
Canadian who's who 1997, v.32, 38
Complete Marquis who's who on CD-ROM [CD-ROM], 19
Contemporary author autobiog series, v.28, 953
Contemporary authors new revision series, v.59, 947
Contemporary authors new revision series, v.60, 948
Contemporary authors, v.158, 949
Contemporary authors, v.159, 950
Contemporary heroes & heroines, bk 3, 20
Dictionary of American biog [CD-ROM], 33
Dictionary of intl biog 1998, 26th ed, 21
Dictionary of Irish biog, 3d ed, 132
Dictionary of literary biog documentary series, v.17, 955
Dictionary of literary biog, v.191, 1063
Dictionary of literary biog, v.192, 1092
Dictionary of literary biog, v.193, 1059
Dictionary of literary biog, v.194, 1064
Dictionary of world biog, v.1, 519
Dictionary of world biog, v.2: the middle ages, 520
Encyclopedia of biog, 22
Encyclopedia of world biog, 2d ed, 23
Heroes & pioneers, 24
Index to Marquis who's who pubs 1998, 25
International authors & writers who's who, 15th ed, 956
International who's who of women, 26
Last word: The New York Times bk of obituaries & farewells, 34
Men of achievement 1997, 17th ed, 28
People of the Holocaust, 521
Profiles of worldwide govt leaders 1998, 4th ed, 649
Scientists & inventors, 1304
Scribner ency of American lives, v.1, 35
Tycoons & entrepreneurs, 143
US govt leaders, 663
Villains & outlaws, 582
When they were kids: over 400 sketches of famous childhoods, 27
Who's who 1998, 31

Who's who among African Americans, 1998/99, 379
Who's who in American law 1998-99, 10th ed, 550
Who's who in Australasia & the Pacific nations, 3d ed, 29
Who's who in Christianity, 1283
Who's who in intl affairs 1998, 2d ed, 652
Who's who in sci and engineering 1998-99, 1305
Who's who in the media & communications 1998-99, 819
Who's who in the midwest 1998-99, 26th ed, 36
Who's who in the South & Southwest 1999-2000, 26th ed, 37
Who's who in the world 1998, 30
Who's who in Vietnam, 113
Women in context, 39
World biogl index, 3d ed, 32

BIOLOGICAL SCIENCES
Best graduate programs: physical & biological scis, 2d ed, 336

BIOLOGICAL WEAPONS
US chemical-biological defense gdbk, 644

BIOLOGY
Biodiversity, 1556
Encyclopedia of human biology, 1355
Genetics & cell biology on file, 1357
Magill's survey of sci: life sci series suppl, 1356

BIRDS
Encyclopedia of birds, 2d ed, 1377
Life of birds, 1372
National Audubon Society 1st field gd: birds, 1381
Nightjars: a gd to the nightjars, nighthawks, & their relatives, 1376
Pocket gd to the birds of Britain & NW Europe, 1379
Shrikes: a gd to the shrikes of the world, 1380

BIRDS—AFRICAN
Field gd to birds of the Gambia & Senegal, 1373
Handbook of bird identification for Europe & the W Palearctic, 1374

BIRDS—EUROPE
Handbook of bird identification for Europe & the W Palearctic, 1374

BIRDS—MIDDLE EAST
Handbook of bird identification for Europe & the W Palearctic, 1374

BIRDS—NEW YORK STATE
Bull's birds of N.Y. state, 1375

BISEXUALS
Queer theory, 758

BLIND—DEAF
AFB dir of servs for blind & visually impaired persons in the US & Canada, 748
AFB dir of servs for blind & visually impaired persons in the US & Canada [CD-ROM], 749

BLUES (MUSIC)
Blues & gospel records 1890-1943, 1160
Encyclopedia of the blues, 2d ed, 1150

BOOK COLLECTORS
American bk collectors & bibliographers, 2d series, 591
Nineteenth-century British bk-collectors & bibliographers, 592

BOOK REVIEWS
Book review index: 1997 cumulation, 68
Canadian bk review annual 1997, 16
Critical review of bks in religion 1997, v.10, 1260

BOOKBINDING
ABC of bookbinding, 855

BOOKSELLERS & BOOKSELLING
Dictionary of American antiquarian bkdealers, 616

BOSNIA & HERZEGOVINA
Breakup of Yugoslavia & the war in Bosnia, 116
Historical dict of Bosnia & Herzegovina, 120

BOURBON
Bourbon companion, 1337

BRAHMS, JOHANNES
Johannes Brahms: an annot bibliog of the lit from 1982 to 1996, 1143

BRAND NAME PRODUCTS
Brands & their cos suppl, 17th ed, 148

BROADCASTING
Burrelle's media dir, 1998 ed, 837
Dictionary of TV & audiovisual terminology, 838
Plunkett's entertainment & media industry almanac, 827

BROOKNER, ANITA
Four British women novelists, 1061

BRUNEI
Historical dict of Brunei Darussalam, 482

BUDGET—UNITED STATES
Desk ref on the fed budget, 687

BUILDING
ASTM standards in bldg codes, 34th ed, 1401
CD estimator, 1998 [CD-ROM], 1402
Encyclopaedic dict in the 18th century, v.1, 813
Encyclopaedic dict in the 18th century, v.2, 814
Encyclopaedic dict in the 18th century, v.3, 815
Encyclopaedic dict in the 18th century, v.4, 816
Encyclopaedic dict in the 18th century, v.5, 817
OSHA quick gd for residential builders & contractors, 1404
Time-saver standards for architectural design data, 7th ed, 882

Time-saver standards for landscape architecture design & construction data, 883

BUILDING LAWS
National building codes hndbk, 1403

BULBS (FLOWERS)
Bulbs, 1348

BULGARIA
Historical dict of Bulgaria, 494

BURKINA FASO
Historical dict of Burkina Faso, 2d ed, 96

BUSINESS. *See also* **BANKS & BANKING; CORPORATIONS; FINANCE; INTERNATIONAL BUSINESS**
Business stats of the US, 159
Handbook of world stock indices, 221
Major cos of Central & E Europe & the Commonwealth of Independent States 1998, 257
Major cos of Europe 1998, 258
North American industry classification system, 1997, 162
World investment report 1998, 234

BUSINESS—BIBLIOGRAPHY
Harvard Business School core collection, 1998, 140
International business info, 228

BUSINESS—BIOGRAPHY
Nonprofit sector yellow bk, winter 1999 ed, 142
Tycoons & entrepreneurs, 143

BUSINESS—DICTIONARIES & ENCYCLOPEDIAS
Dictionary of business, 2d ed, 145
Dictionary of business, English-Spanish, Spanish-English, repr ed, 147
Dictionary of intl business terms, 194
Encyclopedia of small business, 277
NTC's dict of Japan's business code words, 193
Portable MBA desk ref, 2d ed, 278

BUSINESS—DIRECTORIES
Almanac of American employers 1998-99, 266
Bacon's business media dir 1998, 821
Corporate dir US public cos, 149
Directory of corporate affiliations 1998, 150
Eastern Europe, 2d ed, 252
Europe's major cos dir 1997, 2d ed, 255
Europe's medium-sized cos dir, 2d ed, 256
Hoover's masterlist of major intl cos 1998-99, 201
National consumer phone bk USA 1998, 153
Pittsburgh business dir, 152

BUSINESS ENTERPRISES
Hoover's hndbk of American business 1998, 169
Hoover's hndbk of emerging cos 1998, 170
Hoover's hndbk of private cos 1998, 171

Hoover's hndbk of world business 1998, 222
Hoover's hndbks index 1998, 172
National dir of minority-owned business firms, 9th ed, 155
National dir of woman-owned business firm, 9th ed, 156
Researching Canadian markets, industries, & business
    opportunities, 247
World retail dir 1997-98, 212

BUSINESS—HISTORY
History of black business in America, 144
International dir of co hists, v.16, 203
International dir of co hists, v.17, 204
International dir of co hists, v.18, 205
International dir of co hists, v.19, 206
International dir of co hists, v.20, 207
International dir of co hists, v.21, 208

BUSINESS LIBRARIES
World dir of business info libs, 3d ed, 615

BUSINESS METHODS
Business & legal forms for crafts, 854
Business & legal forms for photographers, rev ed, 859
Portable MBA desk ref, 2d ed, 278

BUSINESS SCHOOLS
Barron's gd to graduate business schools, 318
Best 75 business schools, 1999 ed, 320

BUTTERFLIES
Butterflies of the world, 1390

CALDECOTT AWARD
Newbery & Caldecott awards, 1998 ed, 995

CALENDAR
Chase's calendar of events 1998, 4
Religious holidays & calendars, 1271
World holiday festival & calendar bks, 1194

CALIFORNIA
Los Angeles A to Z, 91
1500 Calif place names, 420

CALIFORNIA—BIBLIOGRAPHY
Chumash & their predecessors, 381

CAMBODIA
Cambodia, 105

CAMELLIA
Illustrated ency of camellias, 1364

CAMERA
Orion blue bk: camera, 178

CANADA
Bibliography of works on Canadian foreign relations
    1991-95, 689
Canadian almanac & dir 1999, 152d ed, 2
Canadian Oxford dict, 41

Canadian sourcebk 1998, 33d ed, 3
Charlton standard catalogue of Canadian govt paper
    money, 11th ed, 843
Colombo's concise Canadian quotations, 77
Concise histl atlas of Canada, 409
USA and Canada 1998, 88

CANADA—HISTORY
Introducing Canada, 489

CANADIAN LITERATURE
Oxford companion to Canadian lit, 1088

CANADIANISMS
Guide to Canadian English usage, 907

CANADIANS
Canadian who's who 1997, v.32, 38

CAPITAL PUNISHMENT
Encyclopedia of capital punishment, 577

CAPITALISM
ABC-CLIO world hist companion to capitalism, 158

CAREERS
Almanac of American employers 1998-99, 266
Career Xroads, 3d ed, 267
Exploring health care careers, 1429
Ferguson's gd to apprenticeship programs, 2d ed, 359
Professional & technical careers, 274
Professional careers sourcebk, 5th ed, 361
Professionals job finder 1997-2000, 273
State occupational outlook hndbk, 275
Top 100: the fastest growing careers for the 21st century,
    rev ed, 276
Vocational careers sourcebk, 263

CARIBBEAN AREA
Bermuda, 137
Caribbean lit, 1089
South America, Central America, & the Caribbean 1999,
    7th ed, 138

CARIBBEAN AREA—MOTION PICTURES
Guide to Latin American, Caribbean, & US Latino-made
    films & video, 1226

CARTOONING
Editorial cartooning & caricature, 1192

CATALOGS, COMMERCIAL
Directory of mail order catalogs 98, 175

CATHOLIC CHURCH
Destination: Vatican II [CD-ROM], 1288
Encyclopedia of American Catholic hist, 1286
Father Charles E. Coughlin, 1282
Our Sunday Visitor's Catholic ency, rev ed, 1268
Vatican archives: an inventory & gd to histl docs of the
    Holy See, 1284

CATS
A-Z of cat diseases & health problems, 1386
Barron's ency of cat breeds, 1382
Cat owner's question & answer bk, 1387

CD-ROM BOOKS
CD-ROMs in print, 12th ed, 8
Gale dir of databases, 1495

CD-ROMs
Ancient civilizations of the Mediterranean [CD-ROM], 490
Anthropology bibliog on disc [CD-ROM], 362
CD estimator, 1998 [CD-ROM], 1402
Christian music finder [CD-ROM], 1177
Complete Marquis who's who on CD-ROM [CD-ROM], 19
Cooper's comprehensive environmental desk ref
    [CD-ROM], 1559
Destination: Vatican II [CD-ROM], 1288
Dictionary of American biog [CD-ROM], 33
DISCovering nations, states, & cultures [CD-ROM], 85
Earthscape: exploring endangered ecosystems [CD-ROM],
    1513
Elements explorer [CD-ROM], 1509
Encyclopaedia of occupational health & safety, 4th ed
    [CD-ROM], 280
Executive order 9066 [CD-ROM], 470
Expositor's bible commentary [CD-ROM], 1277
Federal grants & funding locator [CD-ROM], 766
Film index intl 1996 [CD-ROM], 1240
Galante's venture capital & private equity dir, 1997 ed
    [CD-ROM], 200
Historical abstracts on disc [CD-ROM], 545
Index to US marriage record, 1691-1850 [CD-ROM], 405
Interactive sci ency [CD-ROM], 1313
Magill's survey of sci CD-ROM [CD-ROM], 1324
Major authors on CD-ROM: Virgina Woolf [CD-ROM], 1087
McGraw-Hill multimedia ency of sci & tech [CD-ROM], 1316
Military personnel installations locator CD-ROM
    [CD-ROM], 633
Mosby's GenRx, 8th ed [CD-ROM], 1482
Mosby's primary care medicine rapid ref [CD-ROM], 1451
New England transcendentalists [CD-ROM], 1046
New Interpreter's Bible [CD-ROM], 1279
Patty's industrial hygiene & toxicology CD-ROM
    [CD-ROM], 1566
Scribner's American hist & culture [CD-ROM], 465
Scribner's writers series, selected authors ed [CD-ROM], 977
Scribner's writers series on CD-ROM: comprehensive ed
    [CD-ROM], 978
Shakespeare interactive [CD-ROM], 1080
Shakespeare interactive [CD-ROM], 1081
Smithsonian on disc, 4th ed [CD-ROM], 613
Staff dirs on CD-ROM [CD-ROM], 672
Standard math interactive [CD-ROM], 1543
Twayne's English authors on CD-ROM [CD-ROM], 1067
Twayne's US authors on CD-ROM [CD-ROM], 1049
Twayne's world authors [CD-ROM], 979
World Bk multimedia ency, 1998 [CD-ROM], 47
World mktg data & stats on CD-ROM [CD-ROM], 236

CELEBRITIES
Almanac of famous people, 6th ed, 17
They also served: military bios of uncommon Americans,
    623
When they were kids: over 400 sketches of famous
    childhoods, 27

CENSORSHIP
Banned bks: lit suppressed on pol grounds, 603
Banned bks: lit suppressed on rel grounds, 604
Banned bks: lit suppressed on sexual grounds, 605
Banned bks: lit suppressed on social grounds, 606
Censorship, 607
Censorship, 608

CENTRAL AMERICA
Handbook of Latin American Studies: social scis, no.55, 398
South America, Central America, & the Caribbean 1999,
    7th ed, 138
Wars of the Americas, 629

CENTRAL AMERICA—BUSINESS
Directory of consumer brands & their owners 1998: Latin
    America, 260
Latin America: a dir & sourcebk, 2d ed, 261

CHADWICK, G. W. (GEORGE WHITEFIELD)
George Whitefield Chadwick, 1133

CHALOFF, SERGE
Serge Chaloff, 1169

CHAMPAGNE (WINE)
Millennium champagne & sparkling wine gd, 1342

CHAMPLAIN, LAKE
Cruising gd to N.Y. waterways & Lake Champlain, 430

CHANNEL ISLANDS (GREAT BRITAIN)
Channel Islands, 130

CHARACTERS & CHARACTERISTICS IN
    LITERATURE
Cyclopedia of literary characters, rev ed, 959

CHARITABLE USES, TRUSTS, & FOUNDATIONS.
    See also **GRANTS-IN-AID**
America's new fndns 1998, 12th ed, 760
Corporate giving dir 1999, 20th ed, 761
Corporate giving yellow pages 1998, 13th ed, 762
Directory of corporate and fndn givers, 1998, 763
Foundation reporter 1999, 30th ed, 767
International fndn dir 1998, 8th ed, 769
PRI index, 771

CHAVEZ, CARLOS
Carlos Chavez: a gd to research, 1141

CHEMICAL ELEMENTS
Elements explorer [CD-ROM], 1509
History & use of our earth's chemical elements, 1510

CHEMICAL ENGINEERING
Rules of thumb for chemical engineers, 2d ed, 1400

CHEMICAL INDUSTRY
Structural & ownership changes in the chemical industry
    of countries in transition, 232

CHEMICAL WEAPONS
US chemical-biological defense gdbk, 644

CHEMICALS
Federal chemical regulation, 586
Rapid gd to hazardous chemicals in the environment, 1569
Rapid gd to trade names & synonyms of environmentally
    regulated chemicals, 1512

CHEMISTRY
ChemLab series, 1507
Encyclopedia of chemical tech suppl vol, 1503
Hawley's condensed chemical dict, 13th ed, 1505
How to find chemical info, 3d ed, 1511
Routledge German dict of chemistry & chemical tech, v.2,
    1508
Wiley's English-Spanish, Spanish-English dict, 1506

CHICAGO BULLS (BASKETBALL TEAM)
Chicago Bulls ency, 726

CHILD DEVELOPMENT
Childhood & children, 779
Gale ency of childhood & adolescence, 778

CHILD PSYCHOLOGY
Handbook of child psychology, 5th ed, 707

CHILDBIRTH
Having children: the best resources to help you prepare,
    753

CHILDREN—LAW
Children, YAs, & the law, 551
Recovery of internationally abducted children, 752

CHILDREN'S ATLASES
DK student atlas, 411
Facts on File children's atlas, rev ed, 412
Facts on File environment atlas, rev ed, 1551
Facts on File wildlife atlas, rev ed, 1295

CHILDREN'S ENCYCLOPEDIAS &
    DICTIONARIES
Associated Press lib of disasters, 64
Blizzards, 1525
Chronology of weather, 1526
Courtroom drama: 120 of the world's most notable trials,
    556
Cultures of the World, 84
DK illus Oxford dict, 44
DK nature ency, 1309
DK sci ency, rev ed, 1310
Droughts, 1527

Encyclopedia of earth & physical scis, 1514
Explorers & discoverers, v.5, 418
Flags of the world, 406
Floods, 1528
Grolier lib of women's biogs, 799
Grolier student lib of explorers & exploration, 419
Hurricanes, 1529
Kingfisher 1st sci ency, 1314
Kingfisher illus jr dict, 906
Library of the oceans, 1538
Literary lifelines, 952
Outer space, 1522
Peoples of the world, 371
Scholastic ency of the US, 1005
Science & tech breakthroughs, 1308
Tornadoes, 1530
Women's firsts, 806
Young person's gd to philosophy, 1258

CHILDREN'S LITERATURE
A to zoo: subject access to children's picture bks, 1008
Children's bk awards annual 1998, 990
Children's bk prizes, 989
Children's bks from other countries, 991
Children's bks in print 1998, 992
Children's nonfiction for adult info needs, 996
Everyone's gd to children's lit, 1000
Hot links: lit links for the middle school curriculum, 1001
Learning about...the Civil War, 453
Newbery & Caldecott awards, 1998 ed, 995
Popular nonfiction authors for children: a biogl & thematic
    gd, 1002
Taking humor seriously in children's lit, 998
What do children read next? v.2, 999

CHILDREN'S LITERATURE—BIOGRAPHY
From biog to hist, 993
Something about the author, v.94, 986
Something about the author, v.95, 987
Something about the author autobiog series, v.25, 988

CHILDREN'S LITERATURE—INDEXES
Master index to more summaries of children's bks,
    1980-90, 1009

CHILDREN'S LITERATURE—RELATED
    ACTIVITIES
Integrated curriculum: bks for reluctant readers, grades
    2-5, 2d ed, 1006
Language arts & environmental awareness, 997
Name that bk! questions & answers on outstanding
    children's bks, 2d ed, 1007

CHILDREN'S LITERATURE—TECHNIQUE
Children's writer's & illustrator's market, 1998, 828

CHILDREN'S MUSEUMS
Children's museums, 71

CHILDREN'S NONFICTION
Children's nonfiction for adult info needs, 996

From biog to hist, 993
Guide to children's ref works & multimedia material, 994
Our planet Earth, 1003
World almanac for kids 1999, 6

CHILDREN'S VIDEOCASSETTES
Bowker's dir of videocassettes for children 1998, 10

CHINA
China, 7th ed, 110
China: a dir & sourcebk, 2d ed, 107
China: facts & figures annual hndbk, v.23, 108
China mktg data & stats, 242
Consumer China 1998, 216
Cultural atlas of China, rev ed, 106
Modern China: an ency of hist, culture, & nationalism, 109
Sexual behavior in modern China, English-lang ed, 775
Women in China, 808

CHINA—BIBLIOGRAPHY
Doctoral dissertations on China & on inner Asia, 1976-90, 15

CHINA—BIOGRAPHY
Biographical dict of Chinese women, 798

CHINA—ECONOMIC CONDITIONS
China hndbk, 241

CHINA—HISTORY
Historical dict of the People's Republic of China: 1949-97, 483

CHINESE LANGUAGE DICTIONARIES—ENGLISH
Chinese-English-French Kuaisu dict, 920

CHINESE LITERATURE
Indiana companion to traditional Chinese lit, v.2, 1090

CHORAL MUSIC
Choral arrangements of the African-American spirituals, 1152
Conductor's gd to choral-orchestral works, 20th century, pt.2, 1151

CHRISTIAN BIOGRAPHY
Who's who in Christianity, 1283

CHRISTIAN MUSIC
Christian music finder [CD-ROM], 1177

CHRISTIAN SAINTS
Book of saints, 1263
Our Sunday Visitor's ency of saints, 1261
Oxford dict of saints, 1262

CHRISTIANITY
Bible: God's word for the biblically-inept, 1280
Concise ency of Christianity, 1287
Dictionary of early Christian beliefs, 1285
Encyclopedia of apocalypticism, 1266

CHRONIC DISEASES
Complete dir for people with chronic illness, 1467

CHRONOLOGY, HISTORICAL
Illustrated almanac of sci, tech, & inventions, 1306
Timelines of world hist, 524
Wilson chronology of ideas, 525

CHUMASH INDIANS
Chumash & their predecessors, 381

CIGARS
Rudman's cigar buying gd, 183
Rudman's complete gd to cigars, 184

CIVIL ENGINEERING
ASTM standards in bldg codes, 34th ed, 1401

CIVIL RIGHTS MOVEMENTS
Civil rights movement, 473
Encyclopedia of civil rights in America, 588
Historical dict of school segregation & desegregation, 301

CIVIL SERVICE
Civil serv career starter, 272

CIVILIZATION—HISTORY
High places in cyberspace, 2d ed, 1269

CLIMATE
Human choice & climate change, 1563
Weather almanac, 1534

COINS
Collecting world coins, 7th ed, 844
North American coins & prices, 845

COLD WAR
Chronology of the Cold War at sea 1945-91, 643
Cold War, 544
Columbia gd to the Cold War, 543

COLLECTIBLES
America's Standard Gauge electric trains, 852
Antique Trader Books antiques & collectibles price gd, 1999 ed, 840
Maloney's antiques & collectibles resource dir, 841
Miller's intl antiques price gd 1999, 842
Warman's Americana & collectibles, 839

COLLECTION DEVELOPMENT (LIBRARIES)
Guides to collection dvlpmt for children & YA lit, 601

COLLEGE CHOICE
Barron's best buys in college educ, 5th ed, 317
Best graduate programs: humanities & social scis, 2d ed, 335
Best graduate programs: physical & biological scis, 2d ed, 336
College hndbk 1998, 350
Gourman report of undergraduate programs, 321
Guide to the most competitive colleges, 325

International student hndbk of US colleges 1998, 327
Lovejoy's college gd, 24th ed, 351
Peterson's colleges with programs for students with learning
        disabilities or attention deficit disorders, 329
Peterson's gd to 4-year colleges 1999, 29th ed, 330
Profiles of American colleges, 332
Rugg's recommendation on the colleges, 334

COLLEGE COSTS
Big bk of minority opportunities, 7th ed, 339
College costs & financial aid hndbk 1998, 340
College financial aid, 341
Complete college financing gd, 4th ed, 342
Peterson's sports scholarships & college athletic programs,
        3d ed, 346

COLLEGE MAJORS
Index of majors & graduate degrees 1998, 326

COLLEGE SPORTS
Peterson's sports scholarships & college athletic programs,
        3d ed, 346
Sports phone bk USA, 1998, 712

COMEDIANS
Comedy stars at 78 RMP, 1196

COMMONWEALTH LITERATURE (ENGLISH)
Post-colonial lit in English, 946

COMMUNAL LIVING
Encyclopedia of American communes, 1663-1963, 747

COMMUNICABLE DISEASES
Encyclopedia of infectious diseases, 1445

COMMUNICATION
Dictionary of communications tech, 3d ed, 1492
Language & communication, 894
Who's who in the media & communications 1998-99, 819

COMPOSERS
American music in the 20th century, 1124
Anton Rubinstein, 1144
Arnold Schoenberg companion, 1128
Baker's dictionary of music, 1123
Carlos Chavez: a gd to research, 1141
Conductors & composers of popular orchestral music, 1158
Contemporary musicians, v.19, 1115
Contemporary musicians, v.20, 1116
George Whitefield Chadwick, 1133
Giuseppe Verdi: a gd to research, 1137
Irving Berlin, 1134
Isaac Albeniz, 1129
Jean Sibelius: a gd to research, 1135
Johannes Brahms: an annot bibliog of the lit from 1982 to
        1996, 1143
Keeping score: film & TV music, 1988-97, 1140
Malcolm Arnold, 1130
Manuel de Falla, 1136

Music of the golden age, 1900-50 & beyond, 1139
Scott Joplin: a gd to research, 1142
Songwriters: a biogl dict with discographies, 1117
Soundtracks: an intl dict of composers of music for film,
        1131
Tomas Luis de Victoria: a gd to research, 1132
Zoltan Kodaly: a gd to research, 1138

COMPOSITE MATERIALS
Advanced composites world ref dict, 1410

COMPUTER—EDUCATION
Guide to free computer materials 1998-99, 16th ed, 288

COMPUTER INDUSTRY
Electronic & computer industry gd to chemical safety &
        environmental compliance, 1567

COMPUTER NETWORKS
Encyclopedia of network blueprints, 1490

COMPUTER SOFTWARE
Educational software preview gd, 1998, 306

COMPUTERS
Microsoft press computer dict, 1488
Xtravaganza! the essential sourcebk for Macromedia
        Xtras, 1486

CONDUCTORS (MUSIC)
Conductors & composers of popular orchestral music, 1158

CONFEDERATE STATES OF AMERICA
Supplement to the official records of the Union & Confed-
        erate armies, 475

CONFERENCE PROCEEDINGS
Bibliographic gd to conference pubs 1996, 7

CONFLICT MANAGEMENT
Encyclopedia of conflict resolution, 554

CONSTITUTIONS—IOWA
Iowa state constitution, 568

CONSTITUTIONS—UTAH
Utah state constitution, 688

CONSULTANTS
ASTM dir of scientific & tech consultants & expert
        witnesses, 1997-98 ed, 1320

CONSUMER BEHAVIOR
Americans 55 & older, 279
Consumer intl 1997/98, 218

CONSUMER GUIDES
Orion blue bk: professional sound 1998, 180
Orion blue bk: video & TV, 1998 ed, 181
Orion blue bk: vintage guitars & collectibles 1998,
        summer ed, 182

CONSUMER PROTECTION
Encyclopedia of the consumer movement, 176
Inside guide to American nursing homes, 1988-99 ed, 1475

CONTEMPORARY CHRISTIAN MUSIC
Christian music dirs, 1998, 1176
Christian music finder [CD-ROM], 1177

CONTINUING EDUCATION
Bricker's intl dir 1998, 358

CONVENTION FACILITIES
Trade shows worldwide 1998, 12th ed, 210

COOKERY
Dictionary of gastronomic terms, French/English, 1334

COOKING SCHOOLS
Culinary schools, 1336

COPYING MACHINES
Orion blue bk: copier, 179

CORPORATIONS. *See also* **BUSINESS;**
    INTERNATIONAL BUSINESS
Brands & their cos suppl, 17th ed, 148
By the numbers: emerging industries, 188
Corporate dir US public cos, 149
Directory of cos required to file annual reports with the
       securities & exchange commission, 1997, 164
Hoover's hndbk of American business 1998, 169
Hoover's hndbk of emerging cos 1998, 170
Hoover's hndbk of private cos 1998, 171
Hoover's hndbk of world business 1998, 222
Hoover's hndbks index 1998, 172
International dir of co hists, v.16, 203
International dir of co hists, v.17, 204
International dir of co hists, v.18, 205
International dir of co hists, v.19, 206
International dir of co hists, v.20, 207
International dir of co hists, v.21, 208
International tax summaries, 1998, 226
Market share reporter 1998, 8th ed, 190
National dir of corporate public affairs 1998, 154

CORPORATIONS—ARAB COUNTRIES
Major cos of the Arab world 1998, 239

CORPORATIONS—AUSTRALASIA
Major cos of the Far East & Australasia 1998, 245

CORPORATIONS—CARIBBEAN
Major cos of Latin America & the Caribbean 1998, 262

CORPORATIONS—CHARITABLE FOUNDATIONS
Corporate giving dir 1999, 20th ed, 761
Corporate giving yellow pages 1998, 13th ed, 762

CORPORATIONS—EAST ASIA
Major cos of the Far East & Australasia 1998, 245

CORPORATIONS—EUROPE
Major cos of Central & E Europe & the Commonwealth of
    Independent States 1998, 257

CORPORATIONS—LATIN AMERICA
Major cos of Latin America & the Caribbean 1998, 262

CORRESPONDENCE SCHOOLS & COURSES
College degrees by mail & modem 1998, 302

COUGHLIN, CHARLES E.
Father Charles E. Coughlin, 1282

COUNSELING
Directory of natl helplines, 1998 ed, 49

CRIME
Crime in America's top-rated cities, 579
Violence in American society, 583

CRIMINAL JUSTICE
African American criminologists, 1970-96, 575
American prisons, 574
Criminal justice info, 547
Criminal justice research in libs & on the Internet, 581
Dictionary of American criminal justice, 576
Encyclopedia of capital punishment, 577

CRIMINALS
Outlaws, mobsters, & crooks, 578
Public enemies, 580
Sendero Luminoso in context, 573
Villains & outlaws, 582

CUBAN AMERICANS
Cuban Americans, 397

CURIOSITIES & WONDERS
Book of mosts, 65
FAQ's of life, 67
Top 10 of everything 1999, 63

CURRICULUM PLANNING
Resources for teaching middle school scis, 1296

CYCLONES. *See also* **WEATHER**
Encyclopedia of hurricanes, typhoons, & cyclones, 1532

CZECH REPUBLIC
Czech republic, 121
Historical dict of the Czech state, 496

DANCE
Dance on camera, 1200
International dict of modern dance, 1201
International ency of dance, 1202
Tap dance dict, 1203

DATABASES
Gale dir of databases, 1495

DE FALLA, MANUEL
Manuel de Falla, 1136

DEMOGRAPHICS
Americans & their homes, 783
Atlas of American migration, 780
Moving & relocation sourcebk 1998, 2d ed, 781
Places, towns, & townships 1998, 782
Racial & ethnic diversity, 2d ed, 372
Sex & age distribution of the world populations, 784
Sourcebk of county demographics, 11th ed, 785
Sourcebk of ZIP code demographics, 13th ed, 786
Statistical portrait of the US, 791
World urbanization prospects, 794

DEMONOLOGY
Field gd to demons, fairies, fallen angels, & other subversive spirits, 1181

DENMARK
Historical dict of Denmark, 493

DESIGNERS
Contemporary designers, 857

DETECTIVE & MYSTERY STORIES
Detecting men: a reader's gd & checklist for mystery series written by men, 1031
Mystery & suspense writers, 1032
Mystery women, v.1 1860-1979, 1030
Silk stalkings: more women write of murder, 1033

DEVELOPMENTAL PSYCHOLOGY
Cambridge ency of human growth & dvlpmt, 1465

DIABETES
Diabetes A to Z, 3d ed, 1471

DIAGNOSIS
Making wise medical decisions, 1453
Patients gd to medical tests, 1455

DICKENS, CHARLES
Charles Dickens A to Z, 1072

DICKINSON, EMILY
Emily Dickinson ency, 1052

DICTIONARIES—ENGLISH LANGUAGE
American sign lang, unabridged ed, 910
Canadian Oxford dict, 41
Chambers 21st century dict, 42
DK illus Oxford dict, 44
DK ultimate visual dict of sci, 1311
New Yawk tawk: a dict of New York City expressions, 904
Random House Webster's American sign lang dict, rev ed, 909
Scholastic dict of spelling, 912
Slang of sin, 43

DICTIONARIES, POLYGLOT
Chinese-English-French Kuaisu dict, 920

Dictionary of business, English-Spanish, Spanish-English, repr ed, 147
Elsevier's dict of financial terms, rev ed, 185

DINOSAURS
Encyclopedia of dinosaurs, 1539

DISASTERS
Associated Press lib of disasters, 64
Great misadventures, 522

DISCOVERIES IN GEOGRAPHY
Explorers & discoverers, v.5, 418
Grolier student lib of explorers & exploration, 419
Oxford atlas of exploration, 415

DISCOVERIES IN SCIENCE
Famous 1st facts, 46

DISPUTE RESOLUTIONS (LAW)
Encyclopedia of conflict resolution, 554

DISSERTATIONS, ACADEMIC
Doctoral dissertations on China & on inner Asia, 1976-90, 15
Ten yrs of classicists: dissertations & outcomes 1988-97, 891

DISTANCE EDUCATION
Best distance learning graduate schools, 304
College degrees by mail & modem 1998, 302

DISTRIBUTORS (COMMERCE)
Trade shows worldwide 1998, 12th ed, 210

DIVORCE
Divorce yourself, 4th ed, 567

DIXON, BILL
Dixonia: a bio-discography of Bill Dixon, 1146

DOCUMENT DELIVERY SERVICES. *See*
INFORMATION SERVICES

DOGS
Dogs from A to Z, 1385

DOLLS
Contemporary Barbie dolls, 847

DON JUAN (LEGENDARY CHARACTER) IN LITERATURE
Bibliography of the myth of Don Juan in literary hist, 944

DRABBLE, MARGARET
Four British women novelists, 1061

DRAMA
August Wilson: a research & production sourcebk, 1249
Cambridge hist of American theatre, v.1, 1247
Drama for students, v.1, 1021
Drama for students, v.2, 1022
Drama for students, v.3, 1023
Drama for students, v.4, 1024

Fools & jesters in lit, art, & hist, 951
Hamlet: a gd to the play, 1077
Shakespeare interactive [CD-ROM], 1080
Shakespeare interactive [CD-ROM], 1081

DRAMATISTS
Contemporary African-American female playwrights, 1050
Dictionary of literary biog, v.192, 1092
Drama criticism, v.7, 1019
Drama criticism, v.8, 1020
Female dramatist, 1025
Shakespeare, 1079
Spanish dramatists of the golden age, 1026
Tennessee Williams, 1057

DRUGS
Effects of neurologic & psychiatric drugs on the fetus &
    nursing infant, 1480
Mosby's GenRx, 8th ed [CD-ROM], 1482
PDR family gd to prescription drugs, 1483
Physicians' desk ref companion gd 1998, 52d ed, 1422
Respiratory care drug ref, 1481

DUTCH LANGUAGE
Dictionary of 1000 Dutch proverbs, 1179
Hippocrene standard dict Dutch-English, English-Dutch, 923

EARLY CHILDHOOD EDUCATION
Pioneers of early childhood educ, 309

EARTH SCIENCES
Associated Press lib of disasters, 64
Earth online, 1516
Earthscape: exploring endangered ecosystems [CD-ROM],
    1513
Encyclopedia of earth & physical scis, 1514
Glossary of aquatic habitat inventory terminology, 1501
Magill's survey of sci: earth sci series, 1515
Our planet Earth, 1003
Sciences of the Earth, 1517

EASTERN EUROPE
Directory of consumer brands & their owners 1998:
    Eastern Europe, 250
Eastern Europe, 2d ed, 252
Historical dict of the Republic of Macedonia, 495
OMRI annual survey of E Europe & the former Soviet
    Union 1996, 115

ECOLOGY
Biodiversity, 1556
Dictionary of ecology & the environment, 3d ed, 1553
Earthscape: exploring endangered ecosystems [CD-ROM],
    1513
Facts on File environment atlas, rev ed, 1551

ECONOMICS
ABC-CLIO world hist companion to capitalism, 158
Elgar companion to classical economics, 160
Handbook of economic methodology, 161
Statesman's yrbk 1998-99, 135th ed, 82

EDITING—HANDBOOKS. *See also* **AUTHORSHIP**
English usage & style for editors, 836

EDITORIAL CARTOONS
Editorial cartooning & caricature, 1192

EDUCATION
Best Web sites for teachers, 2d ed, 308
Education sourcebk, 296
Educator's gd to free multicultural materials 1998, 285
Educator's gd to free sci materials 1998-99, 39th ed, 286
Educator's gd to free social studies materials 1998-99,
    38th ed, 287
Ferguson's gd to apprenticeship programs, 2d ed, 359
Guide to free computer materials 1998-99, 16th ed, 288
Historical dict of school segregation & desegregation, 301
Historical dict of women's educ in the US, 803
Indicators of school quality, 298
World of learning 1999, 49th ed, 295

EDUCATION, ELEMENTARY
Comparative gd to American elem & secondary schools, 311

EDUCATION—FINANCIAL AID. *See also*
    GRANTS-IN-AID
Assistantships & graduate fellowships in the mathematical
    scis, 1997-98, 1540
Financial aid for African Americans 1997-99, 292
Financial aid for Asian Americans 1997-99, 293
Financial aid for Native Americans 1997-99, 772
Financial aid for the disabled & their families 1998-2000, 294
Minority & women's complete scholarship bk, 344
Scholarships & loans for nursing educ 1997-98, 1479

EDUCATION, HIGHER
Accredited insts of postsecondary educ, 1997-98, 316
American art dir 1997-98, 56th ed, 871
Annual gd to graduate nursing educ 1997, 1474
Barron's best buys in college educ, 5th ed, 317
Best 75 business schools, 1999 ed, 320
Best distance learning graduate schools, 304
European dir of SE Asian studies, 319
Fact bk on higher educ, 1997 ed, 349
Guide to the most competitive colleges, 325
National faculty dir 1999, 29th ed, 328
NLN gd to undergraduate RN educ, 5th ed, 1477
Peterson's gd to 4-year colleges 1999, 29th ed, 330
Peterson's gd to nursing programs, 4th ed, 1478
Research centers dir 1999, 24th ed, 333
Translation & interpreting schools, 897
World list of univs & other insts of higher educ, 21st ed, 337

EDUCATION—POLITICAL ASPECTS
Encyclopedia of student & youth movements, 653
Religion in the schools, 300

EDUCATION, SECONDARY
Best private high schools & how to get in, 2d ed, 313
Comparative gd to American elem & secondary schools, 311
Educational opportunity gd, 1998, 312
Peterson's private secondary schools 1998-99, 19th ed, 314

EDUCATION—STATISTICS
Educational rankings annual 1998, 297
Projections of educ stats to 2008, 299

EDUCATIONAL FUND-RAISING
Funding sources for K-12 schools & adult basic educ, 290

EDUCATIONAL TECHNOLOGY
Educational media & tech yrbk, 356
Educational software preview gd, 1998, 306
Educator's gd to free videotapes 1998, 45th ed, 357

EDUCATORS
Biographical dict of N American & European educationists, 289

EGYPT
Handbook to life in ancient Egypt, 510

ELECTIONS—UNITED STATES
America votes 22, 677
Congressional elections 1946-96, 676
State legislative elections: voting patterns & demographics, 674

ELECTRIC ENGINEERING
Electrical engineering hndbk, 1405
Electronic & computer industry gd to chemical safety & environmental compliance, 1567
International electric power ency 1998, 1406

ELECTRICITY
US electric utility industry dir 1998, 7th ed, 1546

ELECTRONIC MAIL
National e-mail & fax dir 1999, 56

EMERSON, RALPH WALDO
New England transcendentalists [CD-ROM], 1046

EMPIRICISM
Encyclopedia of empiricism, 1252

ENCYCLOPEDIAS. *See also* **CHILDREN'S ENCYCLOPEDIAS & DICTIONARIES**
Encyclopedia Americana, 45
Famous 1st facts, 46
World Bk multimedia ency, 1998 [CD-ROM], 47

ENDANGERED PLANTS
Earthscape: exploring endangered ecosystems [CD-ROM], 1513
Red list of threatened plants, 1997, 1361

ENDANGERED SPECIES
Endangered species, 1370

ENDOWMENTS
Directory of intl corporate giving in America & abroad 1998, 764

ENERGY INDUSTRIES
Energy stats yrbk, 1995, 1547
US electric utility industry dir 1998, 7th ed, 1546

ENGINEERING
ASTM intl dir of testing laboratories, 1998 ed, 1321
Concise metals engineering data bk, 1409
Reference gd to famous engineering landmarks of the world, 1397
Standard hndbk of architectural engineering, 881
Who's who in sci and engineering 1998-99, 1305
Wiley engineer's desk ref, 2d ed, 1398
World Wide Web for scientists & engineers, 1327

ENGINEERING MATHEMATICS
Engineering mathematics hndbk, 1544

ENGLISH LANGUAGE—CANADA
Guide to Canadian English usage, 907

ENGLISH LANGUAGE—COMPOSITION & EXERCISES
Grading student writing, 310

ENGLISH LANGUAGE—DICTIONARIES
Basic Newbury House dict of American English, 898
Larousse English dict, 899

ENGLISH LANGUAGE—DICTIONARIES—DUTCH
Hippocrene standard dict Dutch-English, English-Dutch, 923

ENGLISH LANGUAGE—DICTIONARIES—FRENCH
Larousse concise French/English, English/French dict, rev ed, 926
Routledge French dict of telecommunications, 1494

ENGLISH LANGUAGE—DICTIONARIES—GERMAN
Collins German-English, English-German dict, unabridged 3d ed, 928
Klett's modern German & English dict, 929
Random House German-English, English-German dict, 931
Routledge German dict of chemistry & chemical tech, v.2, 1508
Routledge German dict of environmental tech, 1555

ENGLISH LANGUAGE—DICTIONARIES—IGBO
Igbo-English dict, 932

ENGLISH LANGUAGE—DICTIONARIES, JUVENILE
Kingfisher illus jr dict, 906

ENGLISH LANGUAGE—DICTIONARIES—KYRGYZ
Kyrgyz-English/English-Kyrgyz glossary of terms, 934

ENGLISH LANGUAGE—DICTIONARIES— NATIVE AMERICAN
Western Apache-English dict, 936

ENGLISH LANGUAGE—DICTIONARIES— NORWEGIAN
English-Norwegian, Norwegian-English dict, 937

ENGLISH LANGUAGE—DICTIONARIES—SLANG
NTC's dict of British slang & colloquial expressions, 908
NTC's thematic dict of American slang, 911

**ENGLISH LANGUAGE—DICTIONARIES—
SPANISH**
Collins Spanish-English, English-Spanish dict, unabridged
    5th ed, 939
Dictionary of business, English-Spanish, Spanish-English,
    repr ed, 147
Dictionary of contemporary Spain, 943
Larousse concise Spanish-English, English-Spanish dict,
    rev ed, 940
Oxford Spanish desk dict, 941
Random House Latin-American Spanish dict, 942
Routledge Spanish dict of business, commerce, & finance, 146
Wiley's English-Spanish, Spanish-English dict, 1506

ENGLISH LANGUAGE—EPONYMS
Dictionary of histl allusions & eponyms, 40

**ENGLISH LANGUAGE—ETYMOLOGY—
DICTIONARIES**
English vocabulary quick ref, 901

ENGLISH LANGUAGE—EUPHEMISM
NTC's dict of euphemisms, 902

**ENGLISH LANGUAGE—FOREIGN WORDS &
PHRASES**
Oxford dict of foreign words & phrases, 903

ENGLISH LANGUAGE—GRAMMAR
Merriam-Webster's concise hndbk for writers, 833

ENGLISH LANGUAGE—IDIOMS
NTC's thematic dict of American idioms, 905

ENGLISH LANGUAGE—LEXICOGRAPHY
Encyclopaedic dict in the 18th century, v.1, 813
Encyclopaedic dict in the 18th century, v.2, 814
Encyclopaedic dict in the 18th century, v.3, 815
Encyclopaedic dict in the 18th century, v.4, 816
Encyclopaedic dict in the 18th century, v.5, 817

**ENGLISH LANGUAGE—PRONUNCIATION—
DICTIONARIES**
Pronouncing dict of proper names, 2d ed, 900
Pronouncing Shakespeare's words, 1076

ENGLISH LANGUAGE—RHETORIC
Merriam-Webster's concise hndbk for writers, 833
Theorizing composition, 831

ENGLISH LANGUAGE—SYNONYMS & ANTONYMS
Cambridge French-English thesaurus, 925
Roget's superthesaurus, 2d ed, 916

ENGLISH LANGUAGE—TERMS & PHRASES
BBI dict of English word combinations, rev ed, 913
NTC's dict of commonplace words in real-life contexts, 915

ENGLISH PLACE-NAMES
Dictionary of English place-names, 2d ed, 422

ENOCH PRATT FREE LIBRARY
Song index of the Enoch Pratt Free Lib, 1126

ENTERTAINERS
Entertainers in British films, 1225

ENVIRONMENTAL ENGINEERING
Environmental engineering dict, 3d ed, 1407

ENVIRONMENTAL HEALTH
Electronic & computer industry gd to chemical safety &
    environmental compliance, 1567
Patty's industrial hygiene & toxicology CD-ROM
    [CD-ROM], 1566

ENVIRONMENTAL LAW
Conservation & the law, 584
Environment property & the law, 585
Federal wildlife laws hndbk with related laws, 587

ENVIRONMENTAL POLICY
Human choice & climate change, 1563

ENVIRONMENTAL SCIENCES
Atlas of global change, 1550
Clean air hndbk, 3d ed, 1558
Cooper's comprehensive environmental desk ref
    [CD-ROM], 1559
Dictionary of ecology & the environment, 3d ed, 1553
Environment ency & dir 1998, 1561
Facts on File environment atlas, rev ed, 1551
Historical dict of the green movement, 1554
Indoor pollution, 1565
Rapid gd to hazardous chemicals in the environment, 1569
Rapid gd to trade names & synonyms of environmentally
    regulated chemicals, 1512

ENVIRONMENTALISM
International hndbk of environmental sociology, 1564

ENVIRONMENTALISTS
Biographical dict of American & Canadian naturalists &
    environmentalists, 1552

ERITREA
Historical dict of Eritrea, 479

ETHICS
Encyclopedia of applied ethics, 1251
International ethics, 698

ETHNIC STUDIES. *See also* **MINORITIES**
American immigrant cultures, 365
Black hndbk, 375
Black/White relations in American hist, 454
DISCovering nations, states, & cultures [CD-ROM], 85
Ethnic groups worldwide, 368
Korean Americans, 374
Racial & ethnic diversity, 2d ed, 372

ETHNOLOGY
Cultures of color in America, 367
Peoples of the world, 371
Worldmark ency of cultures & daily life, 364

ETHNOLOGY—ASIA
Atlas of the langs & ethnic communities of S Asia, 101
Ethnohistorical dict of China, 370

EURASIA
Modern ency of religions in Russia & Eurasia, v.7, 1267
Russia & Eurasia facts & figures, v.24, 126

EUROPE
Directory of population ageing research in Europe, 745
Fodor's upclose Europe, 437
Western Europe, 5th ed, 117

EUROPE—BIBLIOGRAPHY
Malta, rev ed, 134
Paris, 127
Romania, rev ed, 136

EUROPE—BUSINESS
Consumer Europe 1998/9, 14th ed, 249
Directory of consumer brands & their owners 1998: Eastern
        Europe, 250
Directory of consumer brands & their owners 1998:
        Europe, 251
European mktg data & stats 1998, 33d ed, 254
Major cos of Europe 1998, 258
World database of consumer brands & their owners 1998
        [CD-ROM], 259

EUROPE, EDUCATION
European dir of SE Asian studies, 319

EUROPE—ENCYCLOPEDIAS
Encyclopedia of contemporary French culture, 128

EUROPE—HISTORY
Historical dict of the gypsies (Romanies), 380
Peacemaking in medieval Europe, 492
Rise of fascism in Europe, 694

EUROPE—POLITICS & GOVERNMENT
Encyclopedia of the EU, 691
European pol facts, 1900-96, 690
Rise of fascism in Europe, 694

EUROPEAN UNION
Encyclopedia of the EU, 691
EU Insts' register, 3d ed, 692

EXECUTIVE DEPARTMENTS. UNITED STATES
US govt dirs, 1982-95, 62

EXECUTIVES—TRAINING OF
Bricker's intl dir 1998, 358

EXPLORERS
Explorers, 417

Explorers & discoverers, v.5, 418
Oxford atlas of exploration, 415

EYE
Quick ref glossary of eye care terminology, 1463

FACSIMILE TRANSMISSION
FaxUSA, 1998, 151
National e-mail & fax dir 1999, 56

FAIRIES
Field gd to demons, fairies, fallen angels, & other subver-
        sive spirits, 1181

FANTASY HOCKEY (GAME)
Official fantasy hockey gd, 732

FASCISM
Rise of fascism in Europe, 694

FEDERAL GRANTS
Federal grants & funding locator [CD-ROM], 766

FEDERAL REPUBLIC OF YUGOSLAVIA
Breakup of Yugoslavia & the war in Bosnia, 116

FEMINISM
Encyclopedia of feminist literary theory, 961
Historical dict of women's educ in the US, 803
Reader's companion to US women's hist, 804
Susan B. Anthony: a biogl companion, 800

FESTIVALS
Holiday symbols 1998, 1189
Religious holidays & calendars, 1271
World holiday festival & calendar bks, 1194

FICTION
American novel explication 1991-95, 1040
Mystery & suspense writers, 1032
Mystery women, v.1 1860-1979, 1030
Novels for students, v.3, 1013
Novels for students, v.4, 1014
Sequels: an annot gd to novels in series, 1029
Short stories for students, v.3, 1015
Short stories for students, v.4, 1016
What fantastic fiction do I read next?, 1036
What Western do I read next?, 1028

FIGURES OF SPEECH
Life is just a bowl of cherries & other delicious sayings, 914
NTC's thematic dict of American idioms, 905

FILM ADAPTATIONS
Encyclopedia of novels into film, 1216

FILM FESTIVALS
Film festival gd, 1223

FINANCE
Elsevier's dict of financial terms, rev ed, 185

FINANCIAL AID. *See* **GRANTS-IN-AID**

FIREARMS
Orion blue bk: gun 1998, 849
Springfield armory: shoulder weapons 1795-1968, 848

FISHES
Fishes of the Gulf of Mexico, v.1, 1388
Practical gd to the marine animals of northeastern N
    America, 1394

FISHING EQUIPMENT
Fishing tackle source dir, 729

FITZGERALD, F. SCOTT
F. Scott Fitzgerald A to Z, 1054

FLAGS
Flags of the world, 406

FLOWERS
Adrian Bloom's yr-round garden, 1347
Ball redbook, 1346
Bulbs, 1348
Desert wildflowers of N America, 1365
Illustrated ency of camellias, 1364
Wild orchids across N America, 1363

FOLKLORE
Encyclopedia of folklore & lit, 962
Field gd to demons, fairies, fallen angels, & other subver-
    sive spirits, 1181
Folklore: an ency of hist, methods, & theory, 1180

FOOD—DICTIONARIES
Dictionary of gastronomic terms, French/English, 1334
Dictionary of Italian cuisine, 1331

FOOD INDUSTRY & TRADE
Bourbon companion, 1337
Brooks & Olmo register of fruit & nut varieties, 1330
Food & beverage market place, 1997/98, 1339
Statistics on occupational wages & hours of work & on
    food prices 1997, 231

FOOLS & JESTERS
Fools & jesters in lit, art, & hist, 951

FOOTBALL
NCAA football, 730

FORBES, ESTHER
Esther Forbes, 1053

FOREIGN STUDY
Alternative travel dir 1998, 4th ed, 439
Peterson's study abroad 1998, 353
Study abroad 1998-99, 30th ed, 354
Vacation study abroad, 355

FOREST PRODUCTS
Directory of the wood products industry, 1998, 1343

FORMER SOVIET REPUBLICS. *See also* **RUSSIA**
Cultural atlas of Russia & the Former Soviet Union, rev
    ed, 125
Documents of Soviet-American relations, v.3, 122
Documents of Soviet hist, v.4, 123
Miniature empires, 537
OMRI annual survey of E Europe & the former Soviet
    Union 1996, 115
Russia & Eurasia facts & figures, v.24, 126

FORMER YUGOSLAV REPUBLICS. *See also*
    YUGOSLAVIA
Historical dict of the Republic of Macedonia, 495

FOSTER CARE
Children in foster care & adoption, 756

FRANCE—BIBLIOGRAPHY
Paris, 127

FRANCE—ENCYCLOPEDIAS
Encyclopedia of contemporary French culture, 128

FRANCE—HISTORY
Historical dict of the wars of the French Revolution, 499
Historical dict of WW II France, 498

FRANCHISES (RETAIL TRADE)
1998 franchise annual, 165

FRANKLIN, BENJAMIN
Benjamin Franklin: a biogl companion, 455

FRENCH LANGUAGE—DICTIONARIES—ENGLISH
Chinese-English-French Kuaisu dict, 920
Dictionary of gastronomic terms, French/English, 1334
Dictionary of La Creole, 935
Larousse concise French/English, English/French dict, rev
    ed, 926
Routledge French dict of telecommunications, 1494
Street French slang dict & thesaurus, 924

FRENCH LANGUAGE—DICTIONARIES—IDIOMS
Media French, 927

FRENCH LANGUAGE—SYNONYMS & ANTONYMS
Cambridge French-English thesaurus, 925

FRUIT
Brooks & Olmo register of fruit & nut varieties, 1330

FULLER, MARGARET
New England transcendentalists [CD-ROM], 1046

FUNERAL RITES & CEREMONIES
International hndbk of funeral customs, 1270

FURNITURE
Century of design, 878
North American furniture standards, 1412

GAMBLING
Legalized gambling, 714

GAMES
Book of rules, 713
Multicultural projects index, 856

GARDANO, ANTONIO
Antonio Gardano, Venetian Music Printer 1538-69, 1112

GARDENING
Adrian Bloom's yr-round garden, 1347
Bulbs, 1348
Gardener's Supply Co passport to gardening, 1350
Plantfinder's gd to ornamental grasses, 1351
Plantfinder's gd to tender perennials, 1349
Rock garden plants, 1353
Taylor's dict for gardeners, 1345
World weeds, 1368

GARLAND, HAMLIN
Hamlin Garland, 1055

GASTRONOMY
Dictionary of gastronomic terms, French/English, 1334

GAYS
Completely queer: the gay and lesbian ency, 757
Queer theory, 758
St. James Press gay & lesbian almanac, 759

GENDER IDENTITY
Sexuality & gender in the English Renaissance, 776

GENEALOGY
American naturalization records 1790-1990, 2d ed, 402
America's best genealogy resource centers, 399
Ancestrial trails: the complete gd to British genealogy &
     family hist, 401
Biography & genealogy master index 1999, 404
Index to US marriage record, 1691-1850 [CD-ROM], 405
Jewish roots in Poland, 400
Printed sources, 403

GENERATION X
Complete cross-ref gd to the baby buster generations col-
     lective unconscious, 1187

GENETICS
Genetics & cell biology on file, 1357

GEOGRAPHY
Facts on File children's atlas, rev ed, 412
1500 Calif place names, 420
Hutchinson gd to the world, 3d ed, 86
Maps on file, 414

GEOLOGY
National Audubon Society 1st field gd: rocks & minerals,
     1535

GEOPHYSICISTS
Directory of physics, astronomy, & geophysics staff, 1997
     biennial ed, 1322

GERMAN LANGUAGE—DICTIONARIES—ENGLISH
Collins German-English, English-German dict, unabridged
     3d ed, 928
Klett's modern German & English dict, 929
Pocket Oxford-Duden German dict, rev ed, 930
Random House German-English, English-German dict, 931
Routledge German dict of environmental tech, 1555
Routledge German dict of medicine, v.1, 1444

GERMAN LITERATURE
Companion to 20th-century German lit, 2d ed, 1093
Head-Word & rhyme-word concordances to Des Minnesangs
     Fruhling, 1094
Women writers in German-speaking countries, 1095

GERMANY
Modern Germany, 129
Traveler's gd to Jewish Germany, 438

GHOST STORIES
St. James gd to horror, ghost, & gothic writers, 976

GIFTED & TALENTED
Educational opportunity gd, 1998, 312

GOLF
Official rules of golf, 731

GOSPEL MUSIC
Blues & gospel records 1890-1943, 1160

GOTHIC LITERATURE
St. James gd to horror, ghost, & gothic writers, 976

GOVERNMENT INFORMATION
US govt dirs, 1982-95, 62

GOVERNMENT LEADERS
Global links: a gd to key people & insts worldwide, 54
Profiles of worldwide govt leaders 1998, 4th ed, 649

GOVERNMENT PUBLICATIONS
Government info on the Internet, 61
Guide to popular US govt pubs 1995/96, 5th ed, 60
New England in US govt pubs, 1789-1849, 452

GOVERNMENT SPENDING POLICY
Desk ref on the fed budget, 687

GRADUATE WORK
Barron's gd to graduate business schools, 318
Graduate student's complete scholarship bk, 343
Index of majors & graduate degrees 1998, 326
Peterson's honors programs, 331

GRANTS-IN-AID. *See also* **ENDOWMENTS;**
    CHARITABLE USES, TRUSTS,
    & FOUNDATIONS
B* student's (or lower) complete scholarship bk, 338
Big bk of minority opportunities, 7th ed, 339
College financial aid, 341
Directory of financial aids for women 1997-99, 773
Directory of grants in the humanities 1998/99, 12th ed, 812
Directory of intl corporate giving in America & abroad
    1998, 764
Federal grants & funding locator [CD-ROM], 766
Financial aid for African Americans 1997-99, 292
Financial aid for Asian Americans 1997-99, 293
Financial aid for Native Americans 1997-99, 772
Foundation reporter 1999, 30th ed, 767
Foundations of the 1990s, 768
Funding sources for community & economic dvlpmt 1998,
    770
Funding sources for K-12 schools & adult basic educ, 290
Graduate student's complete scholarship bk, 343
International fndn dir 1998, 8th ed, 769
Minority & women's complete scholarship bk, 344
National gd to funding in health, 5th ed, 1427
Peterson's scholarships for study in the USA & Canada
    1999, 2d ed, 345
Peterson's sports scholarships & college athletic programs,
    3d ed, 346
Scholarships & loans for nursing educ 1997-98, 1479
Winning athletic scholarships, 1998 ed, 347

GRAPHIC ARTS
Artist's & graphic designers market, 1998, 875
Typography, 885

GRASSES
Plantfinder's gd to ornamental grasses, 1351

GRATEFUL DEAD
American bk of the dead: the definitive Grateful Dead
    ency, 1175

GREAT BRITAIN—BIOGRAPHY
Who's who in British hist, 506

GREAT BRITAIN—HISTORY
Earl Mountbatten of Burma, 1900-79, 505
Health & British mags in the 19th century, 1417
Oxford companion to British hist, 503
Who was who in British India, 485

GREECE—HISTORY
Ancient civilizations of the Mediterranean [CD-ROM], 490
Ancient Greece & Rome, 491
Daily life of the ancient Greeks, 501
Handbook to life in ancient Greece, 500

GREEK LITERATURE
Companion to the Greek lyric poets, 1018

GREEN MOVEMENT
Historical dict of the green movement, 1554

GREEN TECHNOLOGY
Routledge German dict of environmental tech, 1555

GUATEMALA
Cultures of the World, 84

GUITARS
Orion blue bk: guitars & musical instruments, 1998 ed, 1147
Orion blue bk: vintage guitars & collectibles 1998,
    summer ed, 182

GYPSIES
Historical dict of the gypsies (Romanies), 380

HALL OF FAME
Hall of fame museums, 69

HANDICAPPED
Financial aid for the disabled & their families 1998-2000,
    294
Resources for people with disabilities, 750

HANDICAPPED CHILDREN
Special-needs reading list, 751

HANDICRAFTS
Business & legal forms for crafts, 854
Multicultural projects index, 856

HARDWOODS
Trees of the central hardwood forests of N America, 1367

HARDY, THOMAS
Thomas Hardy's major novels, 1085

HARLEM RENAISSANCE
Harlem renaissance, 378

HARRISON, WILLIAM HENRY
William Henry Harrison: a bibliog, 659

HAWAI'I
Historical dict of Honolulu & Hawai'i, 459

HAZARDOUS SUBSTANCES
Book of lists for regulated hazardous substances, 8th ed,
    1557
Federal chemical regulation, 586
Toxic waste sites, 1560

HEALTH. *See also* **MEDICINE; NURSING**
Encyclopedia of biostats, 1418
Encyclopedia of family health, 1441
Health & British mags in the 19th century, 1417
Health: US, 1996-97 & injury chartbk, 1430
Historical dict of the World Health Org, 1421
Medical & health info dir 1998, 9th ed, 1426
Statistical record of health & medicine, 1436

HEALTH BEHAVIOR
Handbook of health behavior research, 1420

HEALTH—BIBLIOGRAPHY
Consumer health info source bk, 5th ed, 1416

HEALTH CARE POLICY
Major state health care policies, 1433
World population monitoring 1996, 809

HEALTH CARE REFORM
Issue briefs: 1997 annual ed, 1432

HEALTH CARE—VOCATIONAL GUIDANCE
Exploring health care careers, 1429

HEALTH CONSUMER EDUCATION
Free or low cost health info, 1428
Health & medicine on the Internet, 1424
Making wise medical decisions, 1453

HEALTH FACILITIES
Dartmouth atlas of health care, 1414

HEALTH OCCUPATIONS SCHOOLS
Health professions educ dir, 1998-99, 1425

HEALTH SERVICES
Health care almanac, 1431

HEALTH STATISTICS
Best of health, 1437

HELLMAN, LILLIAN
Lillian Hellman: a research & production sourcebk, 1248

HELPING BEHAVIOR
Directory of natl helplines, 1998 ed, 49

HERBS—THERAPEUTIC USE
Herbal home remedy bk, 1461

HERETICS, CHRISTIAN
Dictionary of heresy trials in American Christianity, 1289

HEROES
Heroes & pioneers, 24

HIGH TECHNOLOGY
How the new tech works, 1484

HINDUISM
Concise ency of Hinduism, 1290

HISPANIC AMERICANS
Cuban Americans, 397
Guide to Latin American, Caribbean, & US Latino-made
    films & video, 1226
Handbook of Latin American Studies: social scis, no.55, 398

HISTORIANS
Global ency of histl writing, 529

HISTORIC SITES
American Revolutionary War sites, memorials, museums,
    & lib collections, 472

Field gd to America's historic neighborhoods & museum
    houses, 433
Guide to the Indian wars of the West, 474
Presidential sites, 428

HISTORICAL FICTION
What histl novel do I read next?, 1034

HISTORIOGRAPHY
Companion to Historiography, 829
Global ency of histl writing, 529

HISTORY
Dictionary of world biog, v.2: the middle ages, 520
DISCovering nations, states, & cultures [CD-ROM], 85
Fools & jesters in lit, art, & hist, 951
Historical abstracts on disc [CD-ROM], 545
Hutchinson gd to the world, 3d ed, 86

HISTORY—AFRICA
Historical dict of Eritrea, 479
Historical dict of Libya, 3d ed, 480
Historical dict of Zambia, 2d ed, 477

HISTORY—AMERICAN
American decades on CD [CD-ROM], 457
American dream: the 50s, 466
American eras: the revolutionary era 1754-83, 469
American Heritage ency of American hist, 458
Guide to the Indian wars of the West, 474
Outlaws, mobsters, & crooks, 578
Scribner's American hist & culture [CD-ROM], 465
Supplement to the official records of the Union & Confed-
    erate armies, 475

HISTORY—ANCIENT
Ancient civilizations of the Mediterranean [CD-ROM],
    490
Ancient Greece & Rome, 491
Ancient Romans, 518
Daily life in ancient Mesopotamia, 511
Daily life of the ancient Greeks, 501
Dictionary of world biog, v.1, 519
From Aristotle to Zoroaster: an A to Z companion to the
    classical world, 526
Handbook to life in ancient Egypt, 510
Handbook to life in ancient Greece, 500
Hutchinson dict of ancient & medieval warfare, 534

HISTORY—BIBLIOGRAPHY
Eighteenth century, 515
Eighteenth century, 516
Walford's gd to ref material, v.2, 83

HISTORY—CZECH REPUBLIC
Historical dict of the Czech state, 496

HISTORY—EUROPEAN
Historical dict of Denmark, 493
Historical dict of the gypsies (Romanies), 380

HISTORY—FRANCE
Historical dict of the wars of the French Revolution, 499
Historical dict of WW II France, 498

HISTORY, MIDDLE EAST
Daily life in ancient Mesopotamia, 511
Origins & dvlpmt of the Arab-Israeli conflict, 699

HISTORY—MODERN
American dream: the 50s, 466
Annual register 1997, 657
Miniature empires, 537
What everyone should know about the 20th century, 538

HISTORY—RUSSIAN
Historical dict of Russia, 502

HISTORY—UNITED KINGDOM
Historical dict of the United Kingdom, v.2, 504
Nelson almanac, 642
Who's who in British hist, 506

HOCKEY
National Hockey League official gd & record bk 1997-98,
    733
National Hockey League Stanley Cup playoffs fact gd
    1998, 734
1997-98 hockey annual, 737
Official rules of ice hockey, 735
STATS hockey hndbk 1997-98, 736

HOLIDAYS
Chase's calendar of events 1998, 4
Holiday symbols 1998, 1189
World holiday festival & calendar bks, 1194

HOLOCAUST, JEWISH (1939-1945)
Dictionary of the Holocaust, 528
Holocaust, 540
Holocaust series, 533
People of the Holocaust, 521
Understanding the Holocaust, 539
Voices of the Holocaust, 536

HOME OFFICES
SOHO desk ref, 283

HOME OWNERSHIP
Americans & their homes, 783

HOME SCHOOLING
Authentic Jane Williams' home school market gd, 305

HOME VIDEO SYSTEMS
Orion blue bk: video & TV, 1998 ed, 181

HORROR TALES
St. James gd to horror, ghost, & gothic writers, 976

HORSES
Horse companion, 1383
Horse owner's veterinary hndbk, 2d ed, 1354

HORTICULTURE
Taylor's dict for gardeners, 1345

HOUSING
Encyclopedia of housing, 792

HUMAN ANATOMY
Johns Hopkins atlas of human functional anatomy, 1415

HUMAN ECOLOGY
Human choice & climate change, 1563

HUMAN GROWTH & DEVELOPMENT
Cambridge ency of human growth & dvlpmt, 1465

HUMANISM
Cumulative index to vols. 1-6 of Paul Oskar Kristeller's
    Iter Italicum, 1259

HUMANITIES
Best graduate programs: humanities & social scis, 2d ed, 335
Directory of grants in the humanities 1998/99, 12th ed, 812

HUMOR IN LITERATURE
Taking humor seriously in children's lit, 998

HUNGARY
Hungary, 131

HURRICANES. *See also* **WEATHER**
Encyclopedia of hurricanes, typhoons, & cyclones, 1532
Florida's hurricane hist, 1531
Hurricanes, 1529

HUSTON, JOHN
John Huston: a gd to refs & resources, 1207

HYDROLOGY
Rivers of the US, 1536

HYMNS
Hymntune index & related hymn materials, 1178

ICELANDIC PHILOLOGY
Annotated bibliog of N America doctoral dissertations on
    old Norse-Icelandic, 892

IGBO LANGUAGE—DICTIONARIES—ENGLISH
Igbo-English dict, 932

ILLUSTRATION OF BOOKS
Children's writer's & illustrator's market, 1998, 828
Newbery & Caldecott awards, 1998 ed, 995

ILLUSTRATORS
American bk & mag illustrators to 1920, v.188, 884

IMMIGRANTS
American immigrant cultures, 365
Atlas of American migration, 780

IMMUNOLOGY
Encyclopedia of immunology, 2d ed, 1419

INCUNABULA
Catalogue of the 15th-century printed bks in the Harvard
    Univ Lib, v.5, 614

INDEXES
Book review index, 68
Index to black pers 1997, 377
World biogl index, 3d ed, 32

INDIA
India & S Asia, 3d ed, 104
India hndbk, 243
Who was who in British India, 485

INDIANA
Indiana factbk 1998-99, 5th ed, 92

INDIANS OF NORTH AMERICA
A to Z of Native American women, 386
American Indian law deskbk, 2d ed, 561
Archaeology of prehistoric Native America, 443
Bibliography of the Indians of San Diego County, 383
Cambridge hist of the native peoples of the Americas, v.1:
    N America, pt.1, 392
Chumash & their predecessors, 381
Encyclopedia of Native American legal tradition, 388
Financial aid for Native Americans 1997-99, 772
Guide to the Indian wars of the West, 474
Handbook of the American frontier, 393
Indian slavery, labor, evangelization, & captivity in the
    Americas, 382
Indians of N & S America, 2d suppl, 385
Native American info dir, 2d ed, 391
Native American sun dance religion & ceremony, 384
Native Americans, 390
Native North American firsts, 387
St. James gd to native N American artists, 865
Western Apache-English dict, 936

INDIANS OF NORTH AMERICA—WARS
Encyclopedia of American Indian wars, 1492-1890, 460
Guide to the Indian wars of the West, 474

INDIANS OF SOUTH AMERICA
Indians of N & S America, 2d suppl, 385

INDONESIA
Bibliography of the Indonesian Revolution, 481

INDOOR AIR POLLUTION
Indoor pollution, 1565

INDUSTRIAL RELATIONS
World labour report 1997-98, 235

INDUSTRIAL SAFETY
Electronic & computer industry gd to chemical safety &
    environmental compliance, 1567
Encyclopaedia of occupational health & safety, 4th ed
    [CD-ROM], 280
Occupational safety & health law 1997, 566

OSHA quick gd for residential builders & contractors, 1404
Patty's industrial hygiene & toxicology CD-ROM
    [CD-ROM], 1566
Safety & health on the Internet, 2d ed, 281

INDUSTRY
Agriculture, mining, & construction USA, 187
Business stats of the US, 159
By the numbers: emerging industries, 188
Handbook of N American industry, 220
How products are made, v.3, 189
Industrial commodity stats yrbk 1995, 29th ed, 223
Market share reporter 1998, 8th ed, 190
North American industry classification system, 1997, 162
US industry & trade outlook '98, 191

INFORMATION NEEDS & USES
Children's nonfiction for adult info needs, 996

INFORMATION SERVICES
Burwell world dir of info brokers, 13th ed, 595
Information industry dir 1998, 18th ed, 602
Information sources 98, 202
Internet-plus dir of express lib servs, 596

INSECTS
National Audubon Society 1st field gd: insects, 1389

INSTRUCTIONAL MATERIALS CENTERS
Educational media & tech yrbk, 356

INSURANCE
Canadian insurance claims dir 1997, 246

INTERIOR DECORATION
Interior design sourcebk, 858

INTERNATIONAL AGENCIES
Encyclopedia of the EU, 691
Europa world yrbk 1998, 39th ed, 66
International instruments of the UN, 696
Statesman's yrbk 1998-99, 135th ed, 82

INTERNATIONAL BUSINESS
Asia, 2d ed, 240
Canadian insurance claims dir 1997, 246
China mktg data & stats, 242
Consumer Asia 1998, 215
Consumer China 1998, 216
Consumer E Europe 1998/9, 248
Consumer Europe 1998/9, 14th ed, 249
Consumer intl 1997/98, 218
Consumer Middle East 1998, 217
Dictionary of intl business terms, 194
Directory of consumer brands & their owners 1998:
    Eastern Europe, 250
Directory of consumer brands & their owners 1998:
    Europe, 251
Directory of consumer brands & their owners 1998: Latin
    America, 260
Directory of corporate affiliations 1998, 150

Directory of multinationals, 197
Eastern Europe, 2d ed, 252
European mktg data & stats 1998, 33d ed, 254
Europe's major cos dir 1997, 2d ed, 255
Europe's medium-sized cos dir, 2d ed, 256
Handbook of N American industry, 220
Handbook of world stock indices, 221
Hoover's hndbk of world business 1998, 222
Hoover's masterlist of major intl cos 1998-99, 201
Industrial commodity stats yrbk 1995, 29th ed, 223
International business & trade dir, 2d ed, 141
International mktg data & stats 1998, 224
International mktg forecasts, 225
International tax summaries, 1998, 226
Internet resources & servs for intl business, 209
Latin America: a dir & sourcebk, 2d ed, 261
North American labor markets, 227
Ranking of world stock markets, 229
Retail trade intl, 1998 ed, 230
Statistics on occupational wages & hours of work & on
    food prices 1997, 231
Structural & ownership changes in the chemical industry
    of countries in transition, 232
World database of consumer brands & their owners 1998
    [CD-ROM], 259
World econ factbk 1997/98, 5th ed, 233
World investment report 1998, 234
World labour report 1997-98, 235
World mktg data & stats on CD-ROM [CD-ROM], 236
World retail dir 1997-98, 212
Worldwide offshore petroleum dir 1998, 30th ed, 213
Worldwide petrochemical dir 1998, 36th ed, 214
Yearbook of labor stats, 1997, 238

INTERNATIONAL EDUCATION
Open doors 1996/97: report on intl educl exchange, 352

INTERNATIONAL LAW
Recovery of internationally abducted children, 752

INTERNATIONAL LEAGUE (BASEBALL)
International league, 724

INTERNATIONAL RELATIONS
Bibliography of works on Canadian foreign relations
    1991-95, 689
Encyclopedia of the EU, 691
Encyclopedic dict of conflict & conflict resolution,
    1945-96, 628
International ethics, 698
International instruments of the UN, 696
International policy insts around the Pacific Rim, 697
Whitaker's almanack world heads of govt 1998, 650
Whitaker's almanack world heads of state 1998, 651

INTERNATIONAL TRADE
Consumer E Europe 1998/9, 248
Japan trade dir 1997-98, 244
Retail trade intl, 1998 ed, 230
US & Asia statl hndbk, 1997-98 ed, 219
World dir of mktg info sources, 211

World mktg data & stats on CD-ROM [CD-ROM], 236
World Trade Org dispute settlement decisions, v.1, 237

INTERNET (COMPUTER NETWORK)
Official Internet dict, 1489
Web programming lang sourcebk, 1487
Xtravaganza! the essential sourcebk for Macromedia
    Xtras, 1486

**INTERNET (COMPUTER NETWORK)—
    DIRECTORIES**
Adams electronic job search almanac 1998, 264
Best Web sites for teachers, 2d ed, 308
Career Xroads, 3d ed, 267
Complete "no geek-speak" gd to the Internet, 1499
Earth online, 1516
Government info on the Internet, 61
Guide to Internet job searching, 1998-99 ed, 268
Harley Hahn's Internet & Web yellow pages 1998, 5th
    anniversary ed, 1496
Health & medicine on the Internet, 1424
High places in cyberspace, 2d ed, 1269
HIV/AIDS Internet info sources & resources, 1469
Internet resource dir for K-12 teachers & librarians, 98/99
    ed, 307
Internet resources & servs for intl business, 209
National e-mail & fax dir 1999, 56
Official America online yellow pages, 53
Safety & health on the Internet, 2d ed, 281
200 best aviation Web sites, 1576
Wading the World Wide Web, 1498
World Wide Web for scientists & engineers, 1327

INTERNSHIP PROGRAMS
Graduate Group's new internships for 1997-98, 322
Internship bible, 1998 ed, 270
Peterson's internships 1998, 18th ed, 291
7th annual Graduate Group's internships in fed govt, 323
6th annual Graduate Group's internships in state govt, 324

INTERSTATE HIGHWAY SYSTEM
Interstate exit authority, 432

INVENTIONS
Famous 1st facts, 46
Illustrated almanac of sci, tech, & inventions, 1306

INVENTORS
Scientists & inventors, 1304

INVESTMENTS
Directory of cos offering dividend reinvestment plans, 163
Directory of cos required to file annual reports with the
    securities & exchange commission, 1997, 164
Fitzroy Dearborn intl dir of venture capital funds 1998-99, 198
Galante's venture capital & private equity dir, 1998 ed, 199
Galante's venture capital & private equity dir, 1997 ed
    [CD-ROM], 200
Handbook of world stock indices, 221
Morningstar mutual fund 500, 1997-98 ed, 173
100 best stocks to own in America, 166

Standard & Poor's stock & bond gd, 1998 ed, 174
US industry & trade outlook '98, 191
Walker's manual of penny stocks, 167
World investment report 1998, 234

IOWA
Atlas of histl county boundaries: Iowa, 447

IRAQ—HISTORY
Daily life in ancient Mesopotamia, 511

IRELAND
Dictionary of Irish biog, 3d ed, 132
Ireland: a dir 1998, 32d ed, 133

ISLAM
Encyclopedia of apocalypticism, 1266

ISLANDS OF THE PACIFIC
Return to paradise: a gd to S Sea Island films, 1229

ISRAEL
History of Israel, 509

ITALY
Ancient Greece & Rome, 491
Dictionary of Italian cuisine, 1331
Italian horror films of the 1960s, 1205

JAPAN
Area bibliog of Japan, 111
Encyclopedia of Japanese pop culture, 112
Japan & the Pacific Rim, 4th ed, 102
Japan trade dir 1997-98, 244
Modern Japan, 486
NTC's dict of Japan's business code words, 193

JAPANESE AMERICANS
Executive order 9066 [CD-ROM], 470

**JAPANESE LANGUAGE—DICTIONARIES—
   ENGLISH**
New Nelson Japanese-English character dict, rev ed, 933

JAPANESE LITERATURE
Japanese fiction writers since WW II, 1096

JAZZ IN LITERATURE
Bibliographic gd to jazz poetry, 1099

JAZZ MUSIC
Jazz CD listener's gd, 1165
Jazz discography, 1167
MusicHound jazz, 1168

JAZZ MUSICIANS
Dial recordings of Charlie Parker, 1166
Serge Chaloff, 1169

JEFFERSON, THOMAS
Thomas Jefferson: a biogl companion, 660

JEWISH WOMEN
Jewish women in America, 394

JEWS
Jewish roots in Poland, 400
Short hist of the Jewish people, 395
Traveler's gd to Jewish Germany, 438
Two Jews, 3 opinions: a collection of 20th-century American
   Jewish quotations, 396
Understanding the Holocaust, 539

JOB HUNTING. *See also* **CAREERS**
Adams electronic job search almanac 1998, 264
Adams jobs almanac 1998, 265
Career Xroads, 3d ed, 267
Civil serv career starter, 272
Employment opportunities, USA, 269
Guide to Internet job searching, 1998-99 ed, 268
Professionals job finder 1997-2000, 273
State occupational outlook hndbk, 275
Top 100: the fastest growing careers for the 21st century,
   rev ed, 276

JOPLIN, SCOTT
Scott Joplin: a gd to research, 1142

JOURNALISTIC ETHICS
Journalism ethics, 826

JOURNALISTS IN MOTION PICTURES
Media in the movies, 1228

JUDAISM
Concise ency of Judaism, 1291
Encyclopedia of apocalypticism, 1266
Encyclopedia of the sayings of the Jewish people, 1293
Messengers of God: a Jewish prophets who's who, 1292

JUDAISM—HISTORY
History of Israel, 509

KIDNAPPING
Recovery of internationally abducted children, 752

KNIGHTS & KNIGHTHOOD IN LITERATURE
Arthurian hndbk, 2d ed, 1066

KNIVES
Knives: military edged tools & weapons, 647
Standard knife collector's gd, 3d ed, 850

KODALY, ZOLTAN
Zoltan Kodaly: a gd to research, 1138

KOREAN AMERICANS
Korean Americans, 374

KOREAN WAR, 1950-53
Korean war: an annot bibliog, 514

KRISTELLER, PAUL OSKAR
Cumulative index to vols. 1-6 of Paul Oskar Kristeller's
   Iter Italicum, 1259

KYRGYZ LANGUAGE—DICTIONARIES—ENGLISH
Kyrgyz-English/English-Kyrgyz glossary of terms, 934

LABOR
Almanac of American employers 1998-99, 266
North American labor markets, 227
Statistics on occupational wages & hours of work & on
        food prices 1997, 231
World labour report 1997-98, 235

LABOR LAWS & LEGISLATION
International labor & employment laws, v.1, 564
Multistate gd to benefits law, 559

LABOR—STATISTICS
Yearbook of labor stats, 1997, 238

LABOR UNIONS
Profiles of American labor unions, 271

LANDSCAPE GARDENING
Time-saver standards for landscape architecture design &
        construction data, 883
Tropical look: an ency of dramatic landscape plants, 1344

LANGUAGE & LANGUAGES
Guide to world lang dicts, 890
Language & communication, 894

LARGE PRINT BOOKS
Complete dir of large print bks & serials 1998, 11
Random House Webster's large print thesaurus, 918

LAW
American Indian law deskbk, 2d ed, 561
Divorce yourself, 4th ed, 567
Lawyer's research companion, 549
Multistate gd to benefits law, 559
National survey of state laws, 2d ed, 565
Publishing law hndbk, 2d ed, 621

LAW—BIBLIOGRAPHY
Bibliography of Va. legal hist before 1900, 2d ed, 548

LAW—DICTIONARIES & ENCYCLOPEDIAS
Children, YAs, & the law, 551
Concise dict of medical-legal terms, 552
Constitutional law dict, v.2, suppl 1, 555
Encyclopedia of civil rights in America, 588
Encyclopedia of Native American legal tradition, 388
English-Russian dict of American criminal law, 553
West's ency of American law, 557

LAW—DIRECTORIES
ASTM dir of scientific & tech consultants & expert
        witnesses, 1997-98 ed, 1320
Guide to public policy experts, 1997-98, 701
Who's who in American law 1998-99, 10th ed, 550

LAW IN LITERATURE
Law in lit, 945

LAW—INDEXES
Index to the House of Commons parliamentary papers on
        CD-ROM [CD-ROM], 571

LAW—JAPAN
Japanese business law in W languages, 546

LAW—QUOTATIONS
Quotable lawyer, rev ed, 572

LAW SCHOOLS
ABA official American Bar Assn gd to approved law
        schools, 1999 ed, 558
Best law schools, 560

LEARNING DISABLED YOUTH
Complete learning disabilities dir, 1998, 303
Peterson's colleges with programs for students with learning
        disabilities or attention deficit disorders, 329

LEBANON
Historical dict of Lebanon, 507

LEGAL HISTORY
Bibliography of Va. legal hist before 1900, 2d ed, 548

LEGAL RESEARCH
Criminal justice info, 547
Criminal justice research in libs & on the Internet, 58
Lawyer's research companion, 549
Legal info buyer's gd & ref manual 1997-98, 570

LEGENDS IN LITERATURE
Classical myths & legends in the Middle Ages & Renaissance,
        1017

LEGISLATIVE BODIES
State legislative elections: voting patterns & demographics,
        674
World ency of parliaments & legislatures, 656

LEPROSY
Annotated bibliog on leprosy, 1472

LESBIANS
Completely queer: the gay and lesbian ency, 757
Queer theory, 758
St. James Press gay & lesbian almanac, 759

LEWIS, C. S.
C. S. Lewis readers' ency, 1071

LIBERIA
Cultures of the World, 84

LIBRARIES
American art dir 1997-98, 56th ed, 871
College students research companion, 610
Directory of medical health care libs in the UK & Republic
        of Ireland 1997-8, 10th ed, 611
Encyclopedia of lib & info sci, v.60, suppl 23, 593
Encyclopedia of lib & info sci, v.61, suppl 24, 594
World of learning 1999, 49th ed, 295

LIBRARIES—AUTOMATION
Directory of lib automation software, systems, & servs, 609

LIBYA
Historical dict of Libya, 3d ed, 480

LICENSES
State medical licensure gdlines 1998, 1449

LIFE SCIENCES
Magill's survey of sci: life sci series suppl, 1356

LINGUISTICS
Atlas of the langs & ethnic communities of S Asia, 101
Concise Oxford dict of linguistics, 893

LITERARY AWARDS
Grants & awards available to American writers, 30th ed, 830

LITERARY LANDMARKS
Literary gd & companion to S England, rev ed, 1065

LITERATURE
Beat generation, 1042
Cyclopedia of literary characters, rev ed, 959
Dictionary of literary biog yrbk: 1996, 970
Fools & jesters in lit, art, & hist, 951
Novels for students, v.3, 1013
Novels for students, v.4, 1014
Problems in literary research, 4th ed, 972
Short stories for students, v.3, 1015
Short stories for students, v.4, 1016
Vampire readings, 1035

LITERATURE—AMERICAN
American novel explication 1991-95, 1040
Contemporary men fiction writers, 1039
Encyclopedia of S lit, 1047
Modern American lit, v.6, 4th ed, 1048

**LITERATURE—BIO-BIBLIOGRAPHY—JUVENILE
   LITERATURE**
Literary lifelines, 952

LITERATURE—CARIBBEAN
Caribbean lit, 1089

LITERATURE—CHINESE
Indiana companion to traditional Chinese lit, v.2, 1090

LITERATURE—DICTIONARIES
Dictionary of literary terms & literary theory, 4th ed, 960
Merriam-Webster's reader's hndbk, 964

LITERATURE—ENCYCLOPEDIAS
Encyclopedia of folklore & lit, 962
Encyclopedia of the novel, 963

LITERATURE—ENGLISH
C. S. Lewis readers' ency, 1071
Charles Dickens A to Z, 1072

Dictionary of literary biog: British reform writers, 1832-1914,
   1062
English novel explication suppl 6, 1069
Four British women novelists, 1061
George Orwell: a bibliog, 1073
Humor in 18th- & 19th-century British lit, 1060
Jane Austen ency, 1070
Literary gd & companion to S England, rev ed, 1065
Major authors on CD-ROM: Virgina Woolf [CD-ROM], 1087
Modern British novel of the left, 1068
Pronouncing Shakespeare's words, 1076
Shakespeare interactive [CD-ROM], 1080
Shakespeare interactive [CD-ROM], 1081
Thomas Hardy's major novels, 1085
Thomas More: an annot bibliog of criticism, 1935-97, 1086

LITERATURE HISTORY
H. L. Mencken: a descriptive bibliog, 1027
Literature connections to world hist, K-6, 512
Literature connections to world hist, 7-12, 513
World lit criticism suppl, 983

LITERATURE, MEDIEVAL
Classical myths & legends in the Middle Ages & Renaissance,
   1017

LITERATURE, MODERN
Contemporary literary criticism, v.100, 966
Contemporary literary criticism, v.101, 967
Contemporary literary criticism, v.102, 968
Contemporary literary criticism, v.103, 969
Contemporary literary criticism yrbk 1996, v.99, 965
Modern American lit, v.6, 4th ed, 1048
Modern British novel of the left, 1068
Nineteenth-century lit criticism, v.61, 973
Nineteenth-century lit criticism, v.62, 974
Twentieth-century literary criticism, v.71, 981
Twentieth-century literary criticism, v.72, 982
Twentieth-century literary criticism topics volume, v.70, 980

LITERATURE, SLAVIC
South Slavic writers since WW II, 1091

LITERATURE—SPANISH LANGUAGE
Twentieth-century poetry from Spanish America, 1111

LOCAL LAWS
National survey of state laws, 2d ed, 565

LOS ANGELES (CALIF.)
Los Angeles A to Z, 91

LOS ANGELES DODGERS (BASEBALL TEAM)
Dodgers ency, 716

LOUISIANA CREOLE LANGUAGE
Dictionary of La Creole, 935

LYRICISTS
Songwriters: a biogl dict with discographies, 1117

MACEDONIA
Historical dict of the Republic of Macedonia, 495

MACHINERY
McGraw-Hill machining & metalworking hndbk, 2d ed, 1413

MAGAZINES
Bacon's business media dir 1998, 821
By the numbers: publishing, 620

MAGHREB (AFRICA)
Maghreb, 97

MALI—BIBLIOGRAPHY
Mali, 98

MALTA—BIBLIOGRAPHY
Malta, rev ed, 134

MAMMALS
Encyclopedia of mammals, 2d ed, 1391
Mammels of Va., 1393
National Audubon Society 1st field gd: mammals, 1392

MANUFACTURERS
Brands & their cos suppl, 17th ed, 148
Handbook of N American industry, 220
How products are made, v.3, 189
Industrial commodity stats yrbk 1995, 29th ed, 223
Market share reporter 1998, 8th ed, 190

MANUSCRIPTS
Medieval & Renaissance mss in the Walters Art Gallery, 600

MARINE ANIMALS
Practical gd to the marine animals of northeastern N
    America, 1394

MARKETING
Americans 55 & older, 279
China mktg data & stats, 242
Consumer Asia 1998, 215
Consumer China 1998, 216
Consumer Europe 1998/9, 14th ed, 249
Consumer Middle East 1998, 217
European mktg data & stats 1998, 33d ed, 254
International mktg data & stats 1998, 224
International mktg forecasts, 225
World dir of mktg info sources, 211
World econ factbk 1997/98, 5th ed, 233
World mktg data & stats on CD-ROM [CD-ROM], 236

MARRIAGE RECORDS
Index to US marriage record, 1691-1850 [CD-ROM], 405

MASKS
Masks from antiquity to the modern era, 363

MASS MEDIA
Plunkett's entertainment & media industry almanac, 827
Who's who in the media & communications 1998-99, 819
Willings press gd 1998, 124th ed, 824

MASS MEDIA—CENSORSHIP
Banned in the media, 825

MASS MEDIA—HISTORY
History of the mass media in the US, 820

MATERIALS SCIENCE
Concise metals engineering data bk, 1409

MATHEMATICIANS
Notable mathematicians, 1541
World dir of mathematicians 1998, 11th ed, 1545

MATHEMATICS
Assistantships & graduate fellowships in the mathematical
    scis, 1997-98, 1540
Engineering mathematics hndbk, 1544
Mathematically speaking, 1328
Standard math interactive [CD-ROM], 1543

MEDICAL CARE. *See also* **HEALTH; NURSING**
Dartmouth atlas of health care, 1414
Major state health care policies, 1433
Plunketts health care industry almanac 1997-98, 1435
Women's health concerns sourcebk, 1438

MEDICAL EDUCATION
Best medical schools, 1450
Health professions educ dir, 1998-99, 1425
Peterson's gd to nursing programs, 4th ed, 1478

MEDICAL LAWS & LEGISLATION
Issue briefs: 1997 annual ed, 1432

MEDICAL LIBRARIES
Directory of medical health care libs in the UK & Repub-
    lic of Ireland 1997-8, 10th ed, 611

MEDICINE
Health care almanac, 1431
Mosby's primary care medicine rapid ref [CD-ROM], 1451
National gd to funding in health, 5th ed, 1427
Physicians' desk ref for ophthalmology 1998, 26th ed, 1462
Statistical record of health & medicine, 1436

MEDICINE, CHINESE
Practical dict of Chinese medicine, 1446

MEDICINE—DICTIONARIES & ENCYCLOPEDIAS
Concise dict of medical-legal terms, 552
Dictionary of medicine, 2d ed, 1440
Encyclopedia of biostats, 1418
Encyclopedia of immunology, 2d ed, 1419
Encyclopedia of infectious diseases, 1445
Historical dict of the World Health Org, 1421
Magill's medical gd, 1998 rev ed, 1443
Mosby's GenRx, 8th ed [CD-ROM], 1482
Patient's gd to medical terminology, 1442
Physicians' desk ref companion gd 1998, 52d ed, 1422
Respiratory care drug ref, 1481
Routledge German dict of medicine, v.1, 1444

MEDICINE—DIRECTORIES
Complete dir for people with rare disorders, 1998/99, 1447
Health & medicine on the Internet, 1424
Medical & health info dir 1998, 9th ed, 1426

MEDICINE—PEDIATRICS
American Academy of Pediatrics gd to your child's symptoms, 1464

MEDICINE—POPULAR
American Academy of Pediatrics gd to your child's symptoms, 1464
Complete bk of symptoms & treatments, 1456
Consumer health info source bk, 5th ed, 1416
Ear, nose, & throat disorders sourcebk, 1452
Encyclopedia of family health, 1441
Illustrated ency of healing remedies, 1460
Making wise medical decisions, 1453
Patients gd to medical tests, 1454
PDR family gd to prescription drugs, 1483

MEDICINE, STATE
Issue briefs: 1997 annual ed, 1432

MEDICINE—VOCATIONAL GUIDANCE
Exploring health care careers, 1429
Physician marketplace stats 1997-98, 1434

MEDITERRANEAN PLANTS
Plant life in the world's Mediterranean climates, 1359

MENCKEN, H. L.
H. L. Mencken: a descriptive bibliog, 1027

MENTAL ILLNESS IN MOTION PICTURES
Celluloid couch, 1233

MERCHANT SHIPS
Jane's merchant ships 1998-99, 3d ed, 1578

MESOPOTAMIA
Daily life in ancient Mesopotamia, 511

MEXICAN WAR, 1846-1848
Historical dict of the US-Mexican war, 462

MICROCOMPUTERS. *See* **COMPUTERS**

MIDDLE AGES—HISTORY
Peacemaking in medieval Europe, 492

MIDDLE EAST
Consumer Middle East 1998, 217
Dictionary of modern Arab hist, 508
Handbook of pol sci research on the Middle East & N Africa, 648
History of Israel, 509
Middle East & N Africa 1998, 87
Middle East military balance, 1996, 634
Origins & dvlpmt of the Arab-Israeli conflict, 699

MIDDLE EAST—BIBLIOGRAPHY
Index to English per lit on the Old Testament & ancient Near Eastern studies, v.7, 1273

MILITARY BASES
Directory of US military bases worldwide, 3d ed, 631
Military personnel installations locator CD-ROM [CD-ROM], 633

MILITARY BIOGRAPHY
They also served: military bios of uncommon Americans, 623

MILITARY CONTRACTS
Military contracts/procurement locator [CD-ROM], 632

MILITARY PERSONNEL
Military personnel installations locator CD-ROM [CD-ROM], 633

MILITARY STUDIES
Encyclopedic dict of conflict & conflict resolution, 1945-96, 628
Guide to the sources of US military hist, suppl 4, 622
Middle East military balance, 1996, 634
Military aircraft insignia of the world, 636
Spanish-American war, 626
Wars of the Americas, 629

MILITARY WEAPONS
Jane's land-based air defense 1998-99, 11th ed, 646
Knives: military edged tools & weapons, 647

MINERALOGY
Dana's new mineralogy, 1537
National Audubon Society 1st field gd: rocks & minerals, 1535

MINING
Agriculture, mining, & construction USA, 187

MINOR LEAGUE BASEBALL
STATS minor league hndbk 1998, 720

MINORITIES. *See also* **ETHNIC STUDIES**
American immigrant cultures, 365
Big bk of minority opportunities, 7th ed, 339
Cultures of color in America, 367
Dictionary of race & ethnic relations, 366

MINORITY BUSINESS ENTERPRISES
National dir of minority-owned business firms, 9th ed, 155

MISSIONARIES
Biographical dict of Christian missions, 1281

MODERN DANCE
International dict of modern dance, 1201

MOON
Moon bk, rev ed, 1521

MORE, THOMAS, SIR, SAINT
Thomas More: an annot bibliog of criticism, 1935-97, 1086

MORRISON, TONI
Toni Morrison, 1058

MOTION PICTURE AUTHORSHIP
Film writers gd, 7th ed, 1219

MOTION PICTURE INDUSTRY
Footage, 1220
New histl dict of the American film industry, 1215
Paramount in Paris, 1236
Republic pictures checklist, 1230

MOTION PICTURE MUSIC
Keeping score: film & TV music, 1988-97, 1140
Soundtracks: an intl dict of composers of music for film, 1131

MOTION PICTURES. *See also* ACTORS
Art directors in cinema, 1210
Big bk of show business awards, 1198
Contemporary theatre, film, & TV, v.17, 1195
Film & TV in-jokes, 1239
Film cartoons: a gd to 20th century American animated
        features & shorts, 1231
Film festival gd, 1223
Film index intl 1996 [CD-ROM], 1240
From silents to sound, 1209
Guide to American cinema, 1930-65, 1217
Guide to American cinema, 1965-95, 1211
Media in the movies, 1228
Opera on screen, 1218
Return to paradise: a gd to S Sea Island films, 1229

MOTION PICTURES & LITERATURE
Encyclopedia of novels into film, 1216

MOTION PICTURES—AUSTRALIAN
Australian film, 1206

MOTION PICTURES—FRANCE
Paramount in Paris, 1236

MOTION PICTURES—ITALY
Italian horror films of the 1960s, 1205

MOTION PICTURES—PRODUCTION & DIRECTION
Hollywood blu-book dir 1997, 1221

MOTION PICTURES—REVIEWS
Blockbuster Entertainment gd to movies & videos 1998,
        1241
Celluloid couch, 1233
Guide to Latin American, Caribbean, & US Latino-made
        films & video, 1226
Leonard Maltin's movie & video gd, 1999 ed, 1243
Manly movie gd, 1242
Science fiction serials, 1227

MOTION PICTURES—SPAIN
Guide to the cinema of Spain, 1237

MOTION PICTURES—UNITED STATES
African American films through 1959, 1234
New histl dict of the American film industry, 1215

MOUNTAINEERING
World mountaineering, 442

MOUNTBATTEN OF BURMA, EARL
Earl Mountbatten of Burma, 1900-79, 505

MOVING & RELOCATION
Moving & relocation sourcebk 1998, 2d ed, 781

MULTICULTURAL EDUCATION
Educator's gd to free multicultural materials 1998, 285
Multicultural projects index, 856

MULTICULTURALISM
Multiculturalism, 369

MULTIMEDIA SYSTEMS
Guide to children's ref works & multimedia material, 994

MUMMIES
Encyclopedia of mummies, 445

MUNICIPAL GOVERNMENT
Municipal yr bk 1998, v.65, 680

MURDOCH, IRIS
Four British women novelists, 1061

MUSEUMS
American art dir 1997-98, 56th ed, 871
American Revolutionary War sites, memorials, museums,
        & lib collections, 472
Field gd to America's historic neighborhoods & museum
        houses, 433
Hall of fame museums, 69
International dir of arts, 811
Medieval & Renaissance mss in the Walters Art Gallery, 600
Victoria & Albert Museum, 70

MUSIC
Baker's dictionary of music, 1123
Library resources for singers, coaches, & accompanists, 1113
Literature of chamber music, 1153
Music of the golden age, 1900-50 & beyond, 1139
Women composers, v.3, 1145

MUSIC—20TH CENTURY
American music in the 20th century, 1124
Conductor's gd to choral-orchestral works, 20th century,
        pt.2, 1151
Songwriters: a biogl dict with discographies, 1117

MUSIC—AUSTRALIA
Garland ency of world music, v.9, 1120
Oxford companion to Australian music, 1122

MUSIC—AWARDS
Big bk of show business awards, 1198

MUSIC—DENMARK
Twentieth century Danish music, 1154

MUSIC—FINLAND
Historical dict of the music & musicians of Finland, 1121

MUSIC—INDEXES
Keeping score: film & TV music, 1988-97, 1140
Song index of the Enoch Pratt Free Lib, 1126

MUSIC INDUSTRY
Recording industry sourcebk, 1199

MUSIC—QUOTATIONS
Better than it sounds: a dict of humorous musical quotations,
  1119

MUSIC—SPAIN
Bibliographical gd to Spanish music for the violin & viola,
  1900-97, 1149

MUSIC THEORY
Form & analysis theory, 1114

MUSICAL INSTRUMENTS
Orion blue bk: guitars & musical instruments, 1998 ed, 1147
Orion blue bk: vintage guitars & collectibles 1998,
  summer ed, 182

MUSICALS
Broadway song companion, 1170
Musical theater synopses, 1244

MUSICIANS
Arnold Schoenberg companion, 1128
Billboard illus ency of rock, 1172
Contemporary musicians, v.19, 1115
Contemporary musicians, v.20, 1116
Dixonia: a bio-discography of Bill Dixon, 1146
Encyclopedia of the blues, 2d ed, 1150
Entertainers in British films, 1225
International who's who in music 1998/99, v.2, 2d ed, 1161
Jazz CD listener's gd, 1165
MusicHound jazz, 1168
Serge Chaloff, 1169
William Schuman: a bio-bibliog, 1127

MUTUAL FUNDS
Morningstar mutual fund 500, 1997-98 ed, 173

MYSTERY & DETECTIVE STORIES. *See*
    DETECTIVE & MYSTERY STORIES

MYTHOLOGY
Classical myths & legends in the Middle Ages & Renaissance,
  1017
European myth & legend, 1185
Illustrated dict of mythology, 1186
Legends of the Earth, sea, & sky, 1184

NAMES, GEOGRAPHICAL
Dictionary of Canadian place names, 423
Place called Peculiar, 421

NAMES, PERSONAL
African-American baby name bk, 407
Pronouncing dict of proper names, 2d ed, 900

NAMIBIA
Namibia, rev ed, 99

NATIONAL LEAGUE FOR NURSING
Annual gd to graduate nursing educ 1997, 1474
NLN gd to undergraduate RD educ, 5th ed, 1477

NATIONAL LIBRARY OF SCOTLAND
Library of Lord George Douglas, 612

NATIONAL ORGANIZATION FOR RARE
    DISORDERS
Complete dir for people with rare disorders, 1998/99, 1447

NATIVE AMERICANS. *See* **INDIANS OF NORTH**
    AMERICA

NATURAL RESOURCES
Natural resources, 1571

NATURALISTS
Biographical dict of American & Canadian naturalists &
  environmentalists, 1552

NATURE—MYTHOLOGY
Legends of the Earth, sea, & sky, 1184

NAVAL HISTORY
Chronology of the Cold War at sea 1945-91, 643
Earl Mountbatten of Burma, 1900-79, 505
Encyclopedia of Naval hist, 639
Great admirals, 624
Historical dict of the US Navy, 641
Nelson almanac, 642

NAVY
Jane's major warships 1997, 640

NEGRO DIGEST
Roots of Afrocentric thought, 985

NELSON, HORATIO
Nelson almanac, 642

NEW ENGLAND STATES
New England in US govt pubs, 1789-1849, 452

NEW YORK
Bull's birds of N.Y. state, 1375
Cruising gd to N.Y. waterways & Lake Champlain, 430

NEW ZEALAND
Cultures of the World, 84
New Zealand, rev ed, 114

NEWBERY AWARD
Newbery & Caldecott awards, 1998 ed, 995

NEWS AGENCIES
Hudson's Washington news media contacts dir 1998, 823

NEWSPAPERS
Bacon's business media dir 1998, 821
By the numbers: publishing, 620
Gale dir of pubns & broadcast media, 131st ed, 822
Ulrich's intl pers dir 1998, 36th ed, 74

NIXON, RICHARD M.
Nixon on stage & screen, 1238

NONPROFIT ORGANIZATIONS
By the numbers: nonprofit orgs, 48
Encyclopedia of assns, 50
Encyclopedia of assns: regional, state, & local orgs, 7th
    ed, 51
National dir of nonprofit orgs 1998, 55
Nonprofit sector yellow bk, winter 1999 ed, 142

NONSEXIST LANGUAGE
Talking about people: a gd to fair & accurate lang, 895

NORTH AFRICA
Handbook of pol sci research on the Middle East & N
    Africa, 648

NORTH AMERICAN FREE TRADE AGREEMENT
Handbook of N American industry, 220
North American labor markets, 227

NORTH CAROLINA
Atlas of histl county boundaries: N.C., 448

**NORWEGIAN LANGUAGE—DICTIONARIES—
    ENGLISH**
English-Norwegian, Norwegian-English dict, 937

NURSERY RHYMES
Oxford dict of nursery rhymes, 1004

NURSING
Annual gd to graduate nursing educ 1997, 1474
NLN gd to undergraduate RN educ, 5th ed, 1477
Nursing licensure gdlines, 1998, 1476
Peterson's gd to nursing programs, 4th ed, 1478
Scholarships & loans for nursing educ 1997-98, 1479

NURSING HOMES
Inside guide to American nursing homes, 1988-99 ed, 1475

NUTS
Brooks & Olmo register of fruit & nut varieties, 1330

OBITUARIES
Last word: The New York Times bk of obituaries & farewells,
    34

OCCUPATIONAL HEALTH & SAFETY
Encyclopaedia of occupational health & safety, 4th ed
    [CD-ROM], 280
Occupational safety & health law 1997, 566
OSHA quick gd for residential builders & contractors, 1404
Safety & health on the Internet, 2d ed, 281

OCCUPATIONAL THERAPY
Quick ref dict for occupational therapy, 1423

OCCUPATIONS. *See* **CAREERS**

OCEANOGRAPHY
Glossary of aquatic habitat inventory terminology, 1501
Library of the oceans, 1538
Practical gd to the marine animals of northeastern N
    America, 1394

OFFICE PRACTICE
New York Public Lib business desk ref, 282
SOHO desk ref, 283

OLD NORSE PHILOLOGY
Annotated bibliog of N America doctoral dissertations on
    old Norse-Icelandic, 892

OLDENBURG, CLAES
Printed stuff: prints, posters, & ephemera by Claes Oldenburg,
    867

OLYMPIC GAMES
Chronicle of the Olympics, 1896-2000, 738

ONLINE DATABASES
Information industry dir 1998, 18th ed, 602

OPERA
Giuseppe Verdi: a gd to research, 1137
Opera: the rough gd, 1157
Opera on screen, 1218
Opera premiere reviews & re-assessments, 1156
Sign-off for the old Met, 1155

OPHTHALMOLOGY
Physicians' desk ref for ophthalmology 1998, 26th ed, 1462
Quick ref glossary of eye care terminology, 1463

ORCHESTRAL MUSIC
Conductors & composers of popular orchestral music, 1158
Conductor's gd to choral-orchestral works, 20th century,
    pt.2, 1151

ORCHIDS
Wild orchids across N America, 1363

ORWELL, GEORGE
George Orwell: a bibliog, 1073

OUTER SPACE
Frontiers of space exploration, 1520
Kope's outer space dir, 1519
Outer space, 1522

PACIFIC AREA
Asia-Pacific petroleum dir 1998, 14th ed, 195
Garland ency of world music, v.9, 1120
Japan & the Pacific Rim, 4th ed, 102
Source bk on ageing, 746
Statistical indicators for Asia & the Pacific, v.27, no.2,
        June 1997, 788
Who's who in Australasia & the Pacific nations, 3d ed, 29

PAIN
Pain sourcebk, 1473

PAINTING—AMERICAN—CATALOGS
American paintings in the Detroit Institute of Arts, v.2, 887

PAINTING—CHINESE
3,000 years of Chinese painting, 888

PALEOPATHOLOGY
Cambridge ency of human paleopathology, 1439

PAPER MONEY
Charlton standard catalogue of Canadian govt paper
        money, 11th ed, 843
Standard catalog of US paper money, 846

PAPUA NEW GUINEA
Cultures of the World, 84

PARAMOUNT PICTURES CORP.
Paramount in Paris, 1236

PARENTING
Having children: the best resources to help you prepare, 753

PARIS (FRANCE)
Historical dict of Paris, 497
Paris, 127

PARKER, CHARLIE
Dial recordings of Charlie Parker, 1166

PARLIAMENTARY PAPERS
Index to the House of Commons parliamentary papers on
        CD-ROM [CD-ROM], 571

PATIENT EDUCATION. See also **HEALTH CARE;
        MEDICINE**
Complete dir for people with rare disorders, 1998/99, 1447
Making wise medical decisions, 1453
Patients gd to medical tests, 1455

PEACE
Peacemaking in medieval Europe, 492

State of war & peace atlas, 700

PEDIATRICS. See **MEDICINE—PEDIATRICS**

PEONIES
Gardener's gd to growing peonies, 1352

PERENNIALS
Plantfinder's gd to tender perennials, 1349

PERFORMING ARTS
Big bk of show business awards, 1198
Peterson's professional degree programs in the visual &
        performing arts, 4th ed, 1197

PERINATAL PHARMACOLOGY
Effects of neurologic & psychiatric drugs on the fetus &
        nursing infant, 1480

PERIODICALS
Health & British mags in the 19th century, 1417
Index to black pers 1997, 377
Magazines for libs, 9th ed, 72
Standard per dir 1998, 73
Ulrich's intl pers dir 1998, 36th ed, 74

PERSIAN GULF WAR, 1991
Historical dict of the Persian Gulf war 1990-91, 630

PESTICIDES
Ball pest & disease manual, 1360

PETROLEUM INDUSTRY & TRADE
Asia-Pacific petroleum dir 1998, 14th ed, 195
International petroleum ency 1998, 1399
Latin America petroleum dir 1998, 17th ed, 196
Pricing stats sourcebk, 1548
USA oil industry dir 1998, 37th ed, 192
Worldwide offshore petroleum dir 1998, 30th ed, 213
Worldwide petrochemical dir 1998, 36th ed, 214
Worldwide petroleum industry outlook, 1549

PETS
Cat owner's question & answer bk, 1387
Encyclopedia of natural pet care, 1384
On the road with your pet, 424

PHILANTHROPY. See also **GRANTS-IN-AID**
America's new fndns 1998, 12th ed, 760
Directory of social serv grants, 2d ed, 765
Financial aid for the disabled & their families 1998-2000, 294
Foundation reporter 1999, 30th ed, 767
Foundations of the 1990s, 768
Fund raiser's gd to human serv funding 1997, 774
Funding sources for community & economic dvlpmt 1998,
        770
National gd to funding in health, 5th ed, 1427
PRI index, 771

PHILIPPINES
Historical dict of the Philippines, 487

PHILOSOPHERS
Routledge dict of 20th-century pol thinkers, 2d ed, 655

PHILOSOPHY
ABC-CLIO world hist companion to utopian movements, 1253
Cumulative index to vols. 1-6 of Paul Oskar Kristeller's Iter Italicum, 1259
Encyclopedia of applied ethics, 1251
From the beginning to Plato, 1255
Story of philosophy, 1256
Ten yrs of classicists: dissertations & outcomes 1988-97, 891
Young person's gd to philosophy, 1258

PHILOSOPHY, ASIAN
Companion ency of Asian philosophy, 1254

PHILOSOPHY—BIBLIOGRAPHY
Aristotle's Metaphysics: annot bibliog of the 20th-century lit, 1250

PHILOSOPHY, JAPANESE
Sourcebk for modern Japanese philosophy, 1257

PHOTOGRAPHERS
Biographies of Western photographers, 861

PHOTOGRAPHY
A-Z of creative photography, 860
Business & legal forms for photographers, rev ed, 859

PHYSICAL SCIENCES
Best graduate programs: physical & biological scis, 2d ed, 336
Encyclopedia of earth & physical scis, 1514
Magill's survey of sci: earth sci series, 1515
Magill's survey of sci: physical sci series suppl, 1502

PHYSICIANS
Physician marketplace stats 1997-98, 1434
State medical licensure gdlines 1998, 1449

PHYSICISTS
Directory of physics, astronomy, & geophysics staff, 1997 biennial ed, 1322

PIANO MUSIC
Traditional world music influences in contemporary solo piano lit, 1148

PICTURE BOOKS FOR CHILDREN
A to zoo: subject access to children's picture bks, 1008

PICTURE DICTIONARIES
DK illus Oxford dict, 44
Ultimate visual dict, 919

PICTURES—INDEXES
Illustration index 8, 1992-96, 876

PITTSBURGH (PENN.)
Pittsburgh business dir, 152

PLANT GENETICS
Dictionary of plant genetics & molecular biology, 1358

PLANTS. *See also* GARDENING
Adrian Bloom's yr-round garden, 1347
Ball pest & disease manual, 1360
Ball redbook, 1346
Bulbs, 1348
Plant life in the world's Mediterranean climates, 1359
Rock garden plants, 1353

POETRY
Dictionary of literary biog, v.193, 1059
Masterplots II: poetry series suppl, v.9, 1102
Poetry for students, v.1, 1106
Poetry for students, v.2, 1107
Poetry for students, v.3, 1108
Poetry for students, v.4, 1109
Poets: American & British, 1110

POETRY, AMERICAN
Bibliographic gd to jazz poetry, 1099

POETRY—INDEXES
Index of American per verse 1996, 1100
Twentieth-century poetry from Spanish America, 1111

POETS
Companion to the Greek lyric poets, 1018
International who's who in poetry & poets' ency 1997, 8th ed, 1101
Notable poets, 1103
Poetry criticism, v.18, 1104
Poetry criticism, v.19, 1105
Poets: American & British, 1110

POISONS
Encyclopedia of toxicology, 1504

POLAND
Jewish roots in Poland, 400

POLITICAL CONVENTIONS
National party conventions 1831-1996, 681

POLITICAL SCIENCE
Annual report of the USA 1998, 673
Countries of the world & their leaders yrbk 1999, 658
Dictionary of govt & politics, 2d ed, 654
DISCovering nations, states, & cultures [CD-ROM], 85
Encyclopedia of student & youth movements, 653
European pol facts, 1900-96, 690
Father Charles E. Coughlin, 1282
Government on file, 684
Handbook of pol sci research on the Middle East & N Africa, 648
International ency of public policy & admin, 702
Municipal yr bk 1998, v.65, 680
Routledge dict of 20th-century pol thinkers, 2d ed, 655

United Nations dir of agencies & insts in public admin & finance, 703
Who's who in intl affairs 1998, 2d ed, 652

POLITICAL SCIENCE—ETHICS
International ethics, 698

POLITICIANS
Congressional dir: 105th congress, 669
Global links: a gd to key people & insts worldwide, 54
New members of Congress almanac, 661
Profiles of worldwide govt leaders 1998, 4th ed, 649
US govt leaders, 663
Whitaker's almanack world heads of govt 1998, 650
Whitaker's almanack world heads of state 1998, 651
Who's who in American pols 1997-98, 666

POLITICS & LITERATURE
Modern British novel of the left, 1068

POLLUTANTS
Federal chemical regulation, 586
Rapid gd to hazardous air pollutants, 1568

POPULAR CULTURE
American dream: the 50s, 466
Cold War culture media & the arts 1945-90, 1191
Complete cross-ref gd to the baby buster generations collective unconscious, 1187
Encyclopedia of Japanese pop culture, 112
NTC's dict of the USA, 1190
Rock music in American popular culture 2, 1173

POPULAR MUSIC. *See also* **MUSIC**
American pop from minstrel to mojo: on record, 1893-1956, 1162
Broadway song companion, 1170
Christian music dirs, 1998, 1176
Christian music finder [CD-ROM], 1177
International who's who in music 1998/99, v.2, 2d ed, 1161
Music of the golden age, 1900-50 & beyond, 1139
Popular music, v.21, 1996, 1164
Popular music studies, 1163

POPULATION
Sex & age distribution of the world populations, 784
World population monitoring 1996, 809
World population prospects, 790
World urbanization prospects, 794

PRESIDENTIAL CANDIDATES
National party conventions 1831-1996, 681
Presidential also-rans & running mates, 1788-1996, 662

PRESIDENTS—UNITED STATES
Presidential sites, 428
Thomas Jefferson: a biogl companion, 660
William Henry Harrison: a bibliog, 659

PRESIDENTS—UNITED STATES—ELECTIONS
Presidential elections 1789-1996, 682

PRESS
Hudson's Washington news media contacts dir 1998, 823

PRISIONS
American prisons, 574

PRIVATE SCHOOLS
Best private high schools & how to get in, 2d ed, 313

PROFESSIONAL SPORTS
Sports phone bk USA, 1998, 712

PROFESSIONS. *See* **CAREERS**

PROGRAMMING LANGUAGES (ELECTRONIC COMPUTER)
Web programming lang sourcebk, 1487

PROGRAM-RELATED INVESTMENTS
PRI index, 771

PROPHECY
Messengers of God: a Jewish prophets who's who, 1292

PROVERBS
American proverbs about women, 807
Dictionary of 1000 Dutch proverbs, 1179
Encyclopedia of the sayings of the Jewish people, 1293

PSYCHOLOGY
Handbook of child & adolescent psychology, v.5-7, 1466
Handbook of child psychology, 5th ed, 707
Psychology basics, 706
Stress A-Z, 705

PSYCHOTROPIC DRUGS
Effects of neurologic & psychiatric drugs on the fetus & nursing infant, 1480

PUBLIC OPINION
Index to intl public opinion, 1996-97, 81

PUBLIC POLICY
Guide to public policy experts, 1997-98, 701
International ency of public policy & admin, 702

PUBLIC RECORDS
Printed sources, 403

PUBLIC RELATIONS
National dir of corporate public affairs 1998, 154

PUBLIC UTILITIES
Transportation & public utilities USA, 1572

PUBLISHERS & PUBLISHING. *See also* **BOOKSELLERS & BOOKSELLING**
American bk publishing record, cum 1997, 9
Antonio Gardano, Venetian Music Printer 1538-69, 1112
By the numbers: publishing, 620
Dictionary of literary biog documentary series, v.17, 955
Directory of publishers in religion, 619

Guide to bk publishers' archives, 617
Information industry dir 1998, 18th ed, 602
Information sources 98, 202
Publishing law hndbk, 2d ed, 621

PUBLISHERS & PUBLISHING—INTERNATIONAL
Directory of pub 1999, 24th ed, 618

PUERTO RICO
Puerto Rico past & present, 93

PYM, BARBARA
Four British women novelists, 1061

QUALITATIVE RESEARCH
Qualitative inquiry: a dict of terms, 743

QUESTIONS & ANSWERS
FAQ's of life, 67

QUOTATIONS
African American quotations, 80
American Heritage dict of American quotations, 75
Better than it sounds: a dict of humorous musical quotations, 1119
Cassell companion to quotations, 76
Colombo's concise Canadian quotations, 77
Concise Oxford dict of quotations, 78
Mathematically speaking, 1328
Quotable lawyer, rev ed, 572
Two Jews, 3 opinions: a collection of 20th-century American Jewish quotations, 396
Wit: humorous quotations from Woody Allen to Oscar Wilde, 79

RACE
Racial & ethnic diversity, 2d ed, 372

RACE RELATIONS
Cultures of color in America, 367
Dictionary of race & ethnic relations, 366

RADIO STATIONS
Bacon's business media dir 1998, 821
Burrelle's media dir, 1998 ed, 837
Gale dir of pubns & broadcast media, 131st ed, 822

READER GUIDANCE
What do children read next? v.2, 999
What Western do I read next?, 1028

READING INTERESTS
Integrated curriculum: bks for reluctant readers, grades 2-5, 2d ed, 1006

RECYCLING
Recycling & waste mgmt gd to the Internet, 1562
Recycling in America, 1570

REGGAE MUSIC. See also **MUSIC**
Reggae: the rough gd, 1171

RELIGION
Critical review of bks in religion 1997, v.10, 1260
Encyclopedia of American women & religion, 1265
Encyclopedia of apocalypticism, 1266
High places in cyberspace, 2d ed, 1269
Illustrated ency of active new religions sects & cults, rev ed, 1264
Modern ency of religions in Russia & Eurasia, v.7, 1267
Native American sun dance religion & ceremony, 384
Religion in the schools, 300

RELIGION—CHRISTIANITY
Book of saints, 1263
Dictionary of early Christian beliefs, 1285
Our Sunday Visitor's Catholic ency, rev ed, 1268

REPRODUCTION
World population monitoring 1996, 809

REPTILES
Encyclopedia of reptiles & amphibians, 2d ed, 1395

REPUBLIC PICTURES
Republic pictures checklist, 1230

RESEARCH. See also **QUALITATIVE RESEARCH**
College students research companion, 610
Problems in literary research, 4th ed, 972
Research centers dir 1999, 24th ed, 333

RESPIRATORY DRUGS
Respiratory care drug ref, 1481

RETAIL TRADE
European dir of retailers & wholesalers, 2d ed, 253
World retail dir 1997-98, 212

REYNARD THE FOX (LEGENDARY CHARACTER)
Roman de Renart: a gd to scholarly work, 1183

RHETORIC
Talking about people: a gd to fair & accurate lang, 895

RIGHT OF PROPERTY
Environment property & the law, 585

RIVERS
Rivers of the US, 1536

ROCK & ROLL HALL OF FAME & MUSEUM
Unofficial ency of the rock & roll hall of fame, 1174

ROCK MUSIC. See also **MUSIC; POPULAR MUSIC**
American bk of the dead: the definitive Grateful Dead ency, 1175
Billboard illus ency of rock, 1172
Rock music in American popular culture 2, 1173
Unofficial ency of the rock & roll hall of fame, 1174

ROCK MUSIC—COLLECTIBLES
Goldmine price gd to rock 'n' roll memborabilia, 851

ROCK PLANTS
Rock garden plants, 1353

ROCKS. *See also* **GEOLOGY**
National Audubon Society 1st field gd: rocks & minerals, 1535

ROMAN DE RENART
Roman de Renart: a gd to scholarly work, 1183

ROMANIA, BIBLIOGRAPHY
Romania, rev ed, 136

ROME—HISTORY. *See also* **HISTORY, ITALY**
Ancient civilizations of the Mediterranean [CD-ROM], 490
Ancient Rome chronology, 264-27 BC, 523

RUBINSTEIN, ANTON
Anton Rubinstein, 1144

RUSSIA. *See also* **FORMER SOVIET REPUBLICS**
Collapse of communism in the Soviet Union, 693
Cultural atlas of Russia & the Former Soviet Union, rev ed, 125
Historical dict of Russia, 502
Modern ency of religions in Russia & Eurasia, v.7, 1267
Russia, rev ed, 124
Russia & Eurasia facts & figures, v.24, 126

RUSSIAN LANGUAGE DICTIONARIES
English-Russian dict of American criminal law, 553

RUSSIAN LITERATURE
Reference gd to Russian lit, 1097

SACRED MUSIC
Hymntune index & related hymn materials, 1178
Tomas Luis de Victoria: a gd to research, 1132

SAINTS
Book of saints, 1263
Our Sunday Visitor's ency of saints, 1261
Oxford dict of saints, 1262

SALAMANDERS
Salamanders of the US & Canada, 1396

SCHOENBERG, ARNOLD
Arnold Schoenberg companion, 1128

SCHOLARSHIPS. *See* **GRANTS-IN-AID**

SCHOOL INTEGRATION
Historical dict of school segregation & desegregation, 301

SCHOOL LIBRARIES
Wading the World Wide Web, 1498

SCHOOLS
Indicators of school quality, 298

SCHUMAN, WILLIAM
William Schuman: a bio-bibliog, 1127

SCIENCE
New bk of popular sci, 1998 ed, 1317
Science & tech breakthroughs, 1308
U*X*L sci fact finder, 1319

SCIENCE—DICTIONARIES & ENCYCLOPEDIAS
DK nature ency, 1309
DK sci ency, rev ed, 1310
DK ultimate visual dict of sci, 1311
Interactive sci ency [CD-ROM], 1313
Kingfisher 1st sci ency, 1314
McGraw-Hill multimedia ency of sci & tech [CD-ROM], 1316

SCIENCE—DIRECTORIES
ASTM intl dir of testing laboratories, 1998 ed, 1321
World gd to scientific assns & learned societies, 7th ed, 1323

SCIENCE FICTION
American sci fiction TV series of the 1950s, 1213
Science fiction serials, 1227
What fantastic fiction do I read next?, 1036

SCIENCE—HANDBOOKS & YEARBOOKS
Illustrated almanac of sci, tech, & inventions, 1306
Magill's survey of sci, v.7, 1315
Magill's survey of sci CD-ROM [CD-ROM], 1324
McGraw-Hill yrbk of sci & tech 1999, 1325
Wilson chronology of sci & tech, 1307
World Wide Web for scientists & engineers, 1327

SCIENCE PROJECTS
Science projects for all students, 1326

SCIENCE—STUDY & TEACHING
Educator's gd to free sci materials 1998-99, 39th ed, 286
Resources for teaching middle school scis, 1296

SCIENTIFIC APPARATUS & INSTRUMENTS
Instruments of sci, 1312
Scientific instruments 1500-1900, 1318

SCIENTISTS
American women in sci, 1950 to the present, 1299
ASTM dir of scientific & tech consultants & expert witnesses, 1997-98 ed, 1320
Biographical ency of scientists, 1300
Biographies of scientists, 1298
Scientists & inventors, 1304
Scientists: their lives & works, v.4, 1302
Scientists: their lives & works, v.5, 1303
Scientists since 1660, 1297
Who's who in sci and engineering 1998-99, 1305

SCRIBNER (PUBLISHER)
Dictionary of literary biog documentary series, v.16, 954
Nineteenth-century American western writers, 957

SEGREGATION IN EDUCATION
Historical dict of school segregation & desegregation, 301

SENDERO LUMINOSO
Sendero Luminoso in context, 573

SERIES (PUBLICATIONS)
Sequels: an annot gd to novels in series, 1029
Serious about series, 1012

SEX
Sexual behavior in modern China, English-lang ed, 775
Sexuality & gender in the English Renaissance, 776

SEX DISCRIMINATION
Sexual harassment, 2d ed, 563

SEXUALLY TRANSMITTED DISEASES
World population monitoring 1996, 809

SHAKESPEARE, WILLIAM
Coined by Shakespeare, 1078
Dictionary of Shakespeare's semantic wordplay, 1084
Hamlet: a gd to the play, 1077
Pronouncing Shakespeare's words, 1076
Shakespeare, 1079
Shakespeare interactive [CD-ROM], 1080
Shakespeare interactive [CD-ROM], 1081
Shakespearean criticism 1996, v.38, 1082
Shakespearean criticism yrbk 1996, v.37, 1083

SHORT STORIES
Short stories for students, v.3, 1015
Short stories for students, v.4, 1016
Short story criticism, v.26, 1037
Short story criticism, v.27, 1038

SHRIKES
Shrikes: a gd to the shrikes of the world, 1380

SIBELIUS, JEAN
Jean Sibelius: a gd to research, 1135

SIGN LANGUAGE
American sign lang, unabridged ed, 910
Random House Webster's American sign lang dict, rev ed,
    909

SIGNS & SYMBOLS
Dictionary of symbols, 886
Elsevier's dict of acronyms, initialisms, abbreviations, &
    symbols, 1

SINATRA, FRANK
Ol' blue eyes: a Frank Sinatra ency, 1118

SINGERS. *See also* **MUSIC**
Contemporary musicians, v.19, 1115
Contemporary musicians, v.20, 1116

SKATING
Encyclopedia of figure skating, 739

SKIING
Good skiing & snowboarding gd 1998, 740

SLANG. *See also* **ENGLISH LANGUAGE**
        DICTIONARIES—SLANG
New Yawk tawk: a dict of New York City expressions, 904
Slang of sin, 43

SLAVERY
Historical gd to world slavery, 542
Indian slavery, labor, evangelization, & captivity in the
    Americas, 382
Macmillan ency of world slavery, 535

SMALL BUSINESS
Encyclopedia of small business, 277
SOHO desk ref, 283

SMITHSONIAN INSTITUTION
Smithsonian on disc, 4th ed [CD-ROM], 613

SNOWBOARDING
Good skiing & snowboarding gd 1998, 740

SOCIAL NORMS
Don't do it: a dict of the forbidden, 1193

SOCIAL SCIENCES
Best graduate programs: humanities & social scis, 2d ed, 335
Qualitative inquiry: a dict of terms, 743
Walford's gd to ref material, v.2, 83

SOCIAL STUDIES—TEACHING
Educator's gd to free social studies materials 1998-99,
    38th ed, 287

SOCIAL WELFARE
Directory of social serv grants, 2d ed, 765
Encyclopedia of modern American social issues, 742
Historical dict of the welfare state, 777

SOCIALISM
Historical dict of socialism, 695

SOFTBALL
Official rules of softball, 741

SOFTWARE MANUALS
Xtravaganza! the essential sourcebk for Macromedia
    Xtras, 1486

SOLAR SYSTEM
Solar system, 1524

SOLDIERS. *See also* **MILITARY STUDIES**
Great war: a gd to the serv records of all the worlds fight-
    ing men & volunteers, 635

SONGS—UNITED STATES. *See also* **MUSIC**
Americana song reader, 1125

SOUND—EQUIPMENT & SUPPLIES
Orion blue bk: audio 1997, 177

SOUND RECORDING INDUSTRY
Recording industry sourcebk, 1199

SOUTH AMERICA
Handbook of Latin American Studies: social scis, no.55, 398
South America, Central America, & the Caribbean 1999, 7th ed, 138
Wars of the Americas, 629

SOUTH AMERICA—BUSINESS
Directory of consumer brands & their owners 1998: Latin America, 260
Latin America: a dir & sourcebk, 2d ed, 261
Latin America petroleum dir 1998, 17th ed, 196

SOUTH AMERICA—MOTION PICTURES
Guide to Latin American, Caribbean, & US Latino-made films & video, 1226

SOUTH ASIA
India & S Asia, 3d ed, 104

SOUTH ASIA—LANGUAGE
Atlas of the langs & ethnic communities of S Asia, 101

SOVIET UNION. *See also* **FORMER SOVIET REPUBLICS**
Collapse of communism in the Soviet Union, 693

SPANISH AMERICAN LITERATURE
Spanish American lit, 1098

SPANISH DRAMA
Spanish dramatists of the golden age, 1026

SPANISH LANGUAGE—DICTIONARIES— ENGLISH
Collins Spanish-English, English-Spanish dict, unabridged 5th ed, 939
Dictionary of business, English-Spanish, Spanish-English, repr ed, 147
Dictionary of contemporary Spain, 943
Larousse concise Spanish-English, English-Spanish dict, rev ed, 940
Oxford Spanish desk dict, 941
Random House Latin-American Spanish dict, 942
Routledge Spanish dict of business, commerce, & finance, 146
Spanish verbs, 938
Wiley's English-Spanish, Spanish-English dict, 1506

SPARKLING WINES
Millennium champagne & sparkling wine gd, 1342

SPECIAL LIBRARIES
American Revolutionary War sites, memorials, museums, & lib collections, 472
World dir of business info libs, 3d ed, 615

SPEECHES, ADDRESSES, ETC.
Representative American speeches, 1937-97, 975

SPELLERS
Scholastic dict of spelling, 912

SPIRITUALISM
Consulting spirits, 708

SPIRITUALS. *See also* **MUSIC; SACRED MUSIC**
Choral arrangements of the African-American spirituals, 1152

SPORTS
Book of rules, 713
Chronicle of the Olympics, 1896-2000, 738
Sports in N America, v.1, 711
Sports phone bk USA, 1998, 712

SPORTS MUSEUMS
Hall of fame museums, 69

SPY STORIES
Mystery & suspense writers, 1032

SRI LANKA
Historical dict of Sri Lanka, 484

STATESMEN
US govt leaders, 663

STATISTICS
Agriculture, mining, & construction USA, 187
Compendium of social stats & indicators, 4th issue, 787
Projections of educ stats to 2008, 299
Statistical indicators for Asia & the Pacific, v.27, no.2, June 1997, 788
Statistics on occupational wages & hours of work & on food prices 1997, 231
Women in China, 808
World dir of non-official statl sources, 2d ed, 789
World population prospects, 790
World urbanization prospects, 794

STERNE, LAWRENCE
Critical essays on Laurence Sterne, 1074

STOCKS
Handbook of N American stock exchanges, 168
Handbook of world stock indices, 221
100 best stocks to own in America, 166
Ranking of world stock markets, 229
Standard & Poor's stock & bond gd, 1998 ed, 174
Walker's manual of penny stocks, 167

STORYTELLERS
Storytellers: a biogl dir of 120 English-speaking performer worldwide, 1182

STRESS—PHYSIOLOGICAL & PSYCHOLOGICAL *See also* **PSYCHOLOGY**
Stress A-Z, 705

STUDENT AID. *See also* **GRANTS-IN-AID**
Big bk of minority opportunities, 7th ed, 339

College financial aid, 341
Complete college financing gd, 4th ed, 342
Peterson's sports scholarships & college athletic programs,
        3d ed, 346

STUDENT MOVEMENTS
Encyclopedia of student & youth movements, 653

SUN DANCE—GREAT PLAINS. *See also* **DANCE**
Native American sun dance religion & ceremony, 384

SUSTAINABLE DEVELOPMENT
International hndbk of environmental sociology, 1564

TABOR—DICTIONARIES
Don't do it: a dict of the forbidden, 1193

TANZANIA
Cultures of the World, 84

TAOISM
Historical dict of Taoism, 1294

TAP DANCING
Tap dance dict, 1203

TAXATION
Desk ref on the fed budget, 687
International tax summaries, 1998, 226
State tax actions 1997, 284

TECHNICAL INSTITUTES. *See also* **CAREERS**
Peterson's vocational & technical schools & programs, 360

TECHNOLOGY
Dictionary of communications tech, 3d ed, 1492
Illustrated almanac of sci, tech, & inventions, 1306
McGraw-Hill multimedia ency of sci & tech [CD-ROM],
        1316
McGraw-Hill yrbk of sci & tech 1999, 1325
Science & tech breakthroughs, 1308
Wilson chronology of sci & tech, 1307

TELECOMMUNICATIONS
Desktop ency of telecommunications, 1493
Dictionary of communications tech, 3d ed, 1492
International satellite dir 1998, 1497
McGraw-Hill illus telecom dict, 1491
Plunkett's entertainment & media industry almanac, 827
Routledge French dict of telecommunications, 1494
Telecommunications: key contacts & info sources, 1500

TELECOMMUNICATIONS IN EDUCATION
College degrees by mail & modem 1998, 302

TELEPHONE DIRECTORIES
FaxUSA, 1998, 151
National consumer phone bk USA 1998, 153

TELEVISION
Contemporary theatre, film, & TV, v.17, 1195

Dictionary of TV & audiovisual terminology, 838
Film & TV in-jokes, 1239

TELEVISION EQUIPMENT
Orion blue bk: video & TV, 1998 ed, 181

TELEVISION—PRODUCTION & DIRECTION
Hollywood blu-book dir 1997, 1221

TELEVISION PROGRAMS
American sci fiction TV series of the 1950s, 1213
Big bk of show business awards, 1198
Complete dir to sci fiction, fantasy, & horror TV series, 1224
Critical hist of TVs The Twilight Zone, 1959-64, 1232
Encyclopedia of daytime TV, 1212

TELEVISION STATIONS
Bacon's business media dir 1998, 821
Gale dir of pubns & broadcast media, 131st ed, 822

TERRORISM
Sendero Luminoso in context, 573

THAILAND
Thailand, 435

THEATER
Best plays of 1996-97, 1246
Big bk of show business awards, 1198
Cambridge hist of American theatre, v.1, 1247
Contemporary theatre, film, & TV, v.17, 1195
Lillian Hellman: a research & production sourcebk, 1248
Musical theater synopses, 1244

THESAURI. *See also* **ENGLISH LANGUAGE—
        SYNONYMS & ANTONYMS**
ASIS thesaurus of info sci & librarianship, 2d ed, 598
Civil law lexicon for lib classification, 599
Random House Webster's concise thesaurus, 917
Random House Webster's large print thesaurus, 918
Roget's superthesaurus, 2d ed, 916

THOREAU, HENRY DAVID
New England transcendentalists [CD-ROM], 1046

THOUGHT & THINKING—HISTORY
Wilson chronology of ideas, 525

TOILETS
Thunder, flush, & Thomas Cooper, 1188

TOXICOLOGY
Effects of neurologic & psychiatric drugs on the fetus &
        nursing infant, 1480
Encyclopedia of toxicology, 1504

TOYS. *See also* **DOLLS**
America's Standard Gauge electric trains, 852
Beanie family album & collectors gd, 853

TRADE. *See also* **INTERNATIONAL BUSINESS**
International business & trade dir, 2d ed, 141
Japan trade dir 1997-98, 244
US industry & trade outlook '98, 191

TRADE & PROFESSIONAL ASSOCIATIONS
National trade & professional assns of the US 1998, 157
Trade shows worldwide 1998, 12th ed, 210

TRADE SECRETS
Trade secrets: a state-by-state survey, 589

TRAINS, ELECTRIC. *See also* **TOYS**
America's Standard Gauge electric trains, 852

TRANSLATING & INTERPRETING
Routledge ency of translation studies, 896
Translation & interpreting schools, 897

TRANSPORTATION
Jane's merchant ships 1998-99, 3d ed, 1578
Transportation & public utilities USA, 1572
Travel dict, new ed, 425
200 best aviation Web sites, 1576

TRANSSEXUALS. *See also* **GAYS; LESBIANS**
Queer theory, 758

TRAVEL
Alternative travel dir 1998, 4th ed, 439
Australia, 436
Business traveler's world gd, 441
Coasting: an expanded gd to the N gulf coast, 3d ed, 427
Complete gd to America's natl parks, 10th ed, 429
Cruising gd to N.Y. waterways & Lake Champlain, 430
Field gd to America's historic neighborhoods & museum
    houses, 433
Fodor's upclose Europe, 437
Hostels USA, 431
Interstate exit authority, 432
On the road with your pet, 424
Presidential sites, 428
Travel dict, new ed, 425
Traveler's atlas, 440
Traveler's hndbk, 7th ed, 426
World mountaineering, 442

TRAVELERS' WRITINGS
American travel writers, 1776-1864, 1044

TREES
Trees of the central hardwood forests of N America, 1367

TRIALS
Courtroom drama: 120 of the world's most notable trials, 556

TROPICAL PLANTS. *See also* **PLANTS; GARDEN**
Tropical look: an ency of dramatic landscape plants, 1344

TWILIGHT ZONE (TELEVISION PROGRAM)
Critical hist of TVs The Twilight Zone, 1959-64, 1232

TYLER, ANNE
Anne Tyler: a critical companion, 1051

TYPHOONS. *See also* **HURRICANES; WEATHER**
Encyclopedia of hurricanes, typhoons, & cyclones, 1532

TYPOGRAPHY
Typography, 885

UNDERWATER ARCHAEOLOGY. *See also*
    ARCHAEOLOGY
Encyclopedia of underwater & maritime archaeology, 446

UNIDENTIFIED FLYING OBJECTS
UFOs & ufology, 709

UNITED KINGDOM—HISTORY
Historical dict of the United Kingdom, v.2, 504

UNITED KINGDOM—MASS MEDIA
Willings press gd 1998, 124th ed, 824

UNITED NATIONS
International instruments of the UN, 696

UNITED STATES
Puerto Rico past & present, 93
USA and Canada 1998, 88

UNITED STATES—CIVIL WAR, 1861-1865
Civil War 100, 625
Learning about...the Civil War, 453
Supplement to the official records of the Union & Confed-
    erate armies, 475

UNITED STATES—CIVILIZATION
American eras: the reform era & E US dvlpmt, 468
Cold War culture media & the arts 1945-90, 1191

UNITED STATES—CONGRESS
Congress & the nation, 1993-96, 675
Congressional dir: 105th congress, 669
Heritage Foundation Congressional dir, 671
New members of Congress almanac, 661
Washington representatives 1998, 22d ed, 665

UNITED STATES—CONGRESS—ELECTIONS
Congressional elections 1946-96, 676

UNITED STATES—CONSTITUTION
Companion to the US Constitution & its amendments, 2d
    ed, 685
Constitutional law dict, v.2, suppl 1, 555
United States Constitution, 686

UNITED STATES—ECONOMIC CONDITIONS
Annual report of the USA 1998, 673
US & Asia statl hndbk, 1997-98 ed, 219

UNITED STATES—GOVERNMENT
Annual report of the USA 1998, 673
Encyclopedia of American govt, 667

Events that changed America in the 18th century, 456
Government on file, 684

UNITED STATES GOVERNMENT—DIRECTORIES
Staff dirs on CD-ROM [CD-ROM], 672
US govt dirs, 1982-95, 62

UNITED STATES—HISTORY
American decades on CD [CD-ROM], 457
American dream: the 50s, 466
American Heritage ency of American hist, 458
Atlas of histl county boundaries: Iowa, 447
Atlas of histl county boundaries: N.C., 448
Encyclopedia USA, v.25, 461
Historic docs of 1997, 679
Historical dict of Honolulu & Hawai'i, 459
Outlaws, mobsters, & crooks, 578
Scribner's American hist & culture [CD-ROM], 465
Tree of liberty: a documentary hist of rebellion & pol
     crime in America, rev ed, 476
Wars of the Americas, 629

UNITED STATES—HISTORY—BIBLIOGRAPHY
Black/White relations in American hist, 454
Literature connections to American hist, K-6, 449
Literature connections to American hist, 7-12, 450
New England in US govt pubs, 1789-1849, 452

UNITED STATES—HISTORY—COLONIAL ERA
American Revolutionary War sites, memorials, museums,
     & lib collections, 472
North America in colonial times, 464

UNITED STATES—HISTORY—18th CENTURY
American eras: dvlpmt of a nation 1783-1815, 467
Events that changed America in the 18th century, 456

**UNITED STATES—HISTORY—JUVENILE
LITERATURE**
Literature connections to American hist, K-6: resources to
     enhance & entice, 449

UNITED STATES—HISTORY, MILITARY
Facts about the American wars, 471
Historical dict of the US Marine Corps, 638
Historical dict of the US Navy, 641

UNITED STATES—HISTORY—19TH CENTURY
American eras: the reform era & E US dvlpmt, 468

**UNITED STATES—HISTORY—REVOLUTIONARY
ERA**
American eras: the revolutionary era 1754-83, 469

UNITED STATES—HISTORY—WEST
New ency of the American west, 463

UNITED STATES—IMPRINTS
Checklist of American imprints for 1846, 13

UNITED STATES—JUVENILE LITERATURE
Scholastic ency of the US, 1005

UNITED STATES MARINE CORPS
Historical dict of the US Marine Corps, 638

UNITED STATES—NATIONAL PARKS
Complete gd to America's natl parks, 10th ed, 429

UNITED STATES NAVY
Historical dict of the US Navy, 641

UNITED STATES—POLITICS & GOVERNMENT
Encyclopedia of modern American social issues, 742
Historic docs of 1997, 679
Historical gd to the US govt, 668
State budget actions 1997, 678
Vital stats on American politics 1997-98, 6th ed, 683

UNITED STATES—SOCIAL CONDITIONS
American attitudes, 2d ed, 90
Encyclopedia of modern American social issues, 742

UNITED STATES—SPANISH-AMERICAN WAR, 1898
Spanish-American war, 626

UNITED STATES—STATISTICS
American attitudes, 2d ed, 90
Health: US, 1996-97 & injury chartbk, 1430
Indiana factbk 1998-99, 5th ed, 92
Sourcebk of county demographics, 11th ed, 785
Sourcebk of ZIP code demographics, 13th ed, 786
Statistical portrait of the US, 791
World almanac of the USA, rev ed, 89

UNITED STATES, SUPREME COURT
Citizen's companion to US Supreme Court opinions,
     1996-97 term, 562
Supreme Court rules: the 1997 revisions, 569

UNIVERSITIES & COLLEGES
American univs & colleges, 15th ed, 348
Barron's gd to graduate business schools, 318
College costs & financial aid hndbk 1998, 340
College hndbk 1998, 350
Guide to the most competitive colleges, 325
Index of majors & graduate degrees 1998, 326
International dict of univ hists, 315
International student hndbk of US colleges 1998, 327
Lovejoy's college gd, 24th ed, 351
Peterson's honors programs, 331

URBAN STUDIES
Encyclopedia of urban America, 793
World urbanization prospects, 794

UTAH
Utah state constitution, 688

UTOPIAS
ABC-CLIO world hist companion to utopian movements,
     1253

VAMPIRES
Vampire gallery: a who's who of the undead, 1214
Vampire readings, 1035

VAN CLEEF, LEE
Lee Van Cleef: a bibliog, film, & TV ref, 1208

VATICAN ARCHIVES
Vatican archives: an inventory & gd to histl docs of the Holy See, 1284

VEGETARIAN RESTAURANTS
Vegetarian Journal's gd to natural foods restaurants in the US & Canada, 3d ed, 434

VENTURE CAPITAL
Fitzroy Dearborn intl dir of venture capital funds 1998-99, 198
Galante's venture capital & private equity dir, 1998 ed, 199
Galante's venture capital & private equity dir, 1997 ed [CD-ROM], 200

VERDI, GIUSEPPE
Giuseppe Verdi: a gd to research, 1137

VICE-PRESIDENTIAL CANDIDATES
Presidential also-rans & running mates, 1788-1996, 662

VICE-PRESIDENTS—UNITED STATES
Vice presidents, 664

VICTIMS OF CRIMES
Victims rights, 590

VICTORIA & ALBERT MUSEUM
Victoria & Albert Museum, 70

VICTORIA, TOMAS LUISDE
Tomas Luis de Victoria: a gd to research, 1132

VIDEO RECORDINGS. *See also* **MOTION PICTURES**
Blockbuster Entertainment gd to movies & videos 1998, 1241
Bowker's dir of videocassettes for children 1998, 10
Educator's gd to free videotapes 1998, 45th ed, 357
Leonard Maltin's movie & video gd, 1999 ed, 1243
Manly movie gd, 1242
Spencer's complete gd to special interest videos, 4th ed, 1245

VIDEO RECORDINGS—PRODUCTION & DIRECTION
Hollywood blu-book dir 1997, 1221

VIENNA (AUSTRIA)
Vienna, 119

VIETNAM
Historical dictionary of Vietnam, 488
Who's who in Vietnam, 113

VIETNAMESE CONFLICT, 1961-1975
Encyclopedia of the Vietnam War, 527
Vietnam experience, 1041

VIOLA MUSIC
Bibliographical gd to Spanish music for the violin & viola, 1900-97, 1149

VIOLENCE
Violence in American society, 583

VIOLIN MUSIC
Bibliographical gd to Spanish music for the violin & viola, 1900-97, 1149

VIRGINIA
Bibliography of Va. legal hist before 1900, 2d ed, 548

VISUAL, HANDICAPPED
AFB dir of servs for blind & visually impaired persons in the US & Canada, 748
AFB dir of servs for blind & visually impaired persons in the US & Canada [CD-ROM], 749

VOCABULARY—DICTIONARIES
English vocabulary quick ref, 901

VOCATIONAL GUIDANCE. *See* **CAREERS**

VOCATIONAL SCHOOL. *See also* **INTERNSHIPS**
Ferguson's gd to apprenticeship programs, 2d ed, 359
Peterson's vocational & technical schools & programs, 360

WAR. *See also* **MILITARY STUDIES, HISTORY**
Encyclopedia of the Vietnam War, 527
Hutchinson dict of ancient & medieval warfare, 534
State of war & peace atlas, 700

WARSHIPS. *See also* **NAVY**
Jane's major warships 1997, 640

WASHINGTON, D.C.
Hudson's Washington news media contacts dir 1998, 823

WEALTH
Who's wealthy in America, 1998, 59

WEAPONS. *See also* **MILITARY STUDIES**
Jane's infantry weapons 1998-99, 24th ed, 645
Jane's land-based air defense 1998-99, 11th ed, 646

WEATHER. *See also* **HURRICANES; TYPHOONS; CYCLONES**
Associated Press lib of disasters, 64
Blizzards, 1525
Chronology of weather, 1526
Droughts, 1527
Floods, 1528
National Audubon Society 1st field gd: weather, 1533
Tornadoes, 1530
Weather almanac, 1534

WEEDS
World weeds, 1368

WELDING
Welding codes standards & specifications, 1411

WESTERN EUROPE
Western Europe, 5th ed, 117

WESTERN STORIES
What Western do I read next?, 1028

WEST, JESSAMYN
Jessamyn West: a descriptive & annot bibliog, 1056

WHISKEY
Bourbon companion, 1337

WHOLESALE TRADE—EUROPE
European dir of retailers & wholesalers, 2d ed, 253

WILDE, OSCAR
Oscar Wilde ency, 1075

WILD FLOWERS
Desert wildflowers of N America, 1365
Sierra Nev. Wildflowers, 1362
Wild flowers of the Pacific NW, 1366

WILLIAMS, TENNESSEE
Tennessee Williams, 1057

WILSON, AUGUST
August Wilson: a research & production sourcebk, 1249

WINE
Best wines! 1999, 3d ed, 1335
Connoisseurs' hndbk of the wines of Calif. & the Pacific
    Northwest, 4th ed, 1341
Good wine gd 1999, 1340
Wine Spectator Mag's gd to great wine values, 1338

WIT & HUMOR
Film & TV in-jokes, 1239
Humor in 18th- & 19th-century British lit, 1060
Wit: humorous quotations from Woody Allen to Oscar
    Wilde, 79

WOMEN & LITERATURE
Emily Dickinson ency, 1052
Four British women novelists, 1061
Silk stalkings: more women write of murder, 1033
Women writers in German-speaking countries, 1095

WOMEN & RELIGION
Encyclopedia of American women & religion, 1265

WOMEN ARTISTS
Encyclopedia of women artists of the American west, 869
Women artists & designers in Europe since 1800, 864

WOMEN ATHLETES
Outstanding women athletes, 2d ed, 710

WOMEN AUTHORS
Anne Tyler: a critical companion, 1051
Encyclopedia of feminist literary theory, 961
Jessamyn West: a descriptive & annot bibliog, 1056
Toni Morrison, 1058

WOMEN—BIOGRAPHY
A to Z of Native American women, 386
Biographical dict of Chinese women, 798
Grolier lib of women's biogs, 799
International who's who of women, 26
Notable women in world hist, 797
Susan B. Anthony: a biogl companion, 800
Women in context, 39

WOMEN COMPOSERS
Women composers, v.3, 1145

WOMEN—DEVELOPING COUNTRIES
Women in the Third World, 805

WOMEN DRAMATISTS
Contemporary African-American female playwrights, 1050
Female dramatist, 1025

WOMEN—EDUCATION
Historical dict of women's educ in the US, 803

WOMEN—HISTORY
Grolier lib of women's biogs, 799
Wilson chronology of women's achievements, 802
Women's firsts, 806
Women's hist, 801

WOMEN IN BUSINESS
National dir of woman-owned business firm, 9th ed, 156

WOMEN IN SCIENCE
American women in sci, 1950 to the present, 1299
Ladies in the laboratory? American & British women in
    sci, 1800-1900, 1301

WOMEN MATHEMATICIANS
Notable women in math, 1542

WOMEN—QUOTATION, MAXIMS, ETC.
American proverbs about women, 807

WOMEN—SCHOLARSHIPS, FELLOWSHIPS, ETC.
Directory of financial aids for women 1997-99, 773

WOMEN—UNITED STATES
Asian American woman, 795
Reader's companion to US women's hist, 804

WOMEN'S HEALTH
Women's health concerns sourcebk, 1438

WOMEN'S RIGHTS
Women in the Third World, 805
World population monitoring 1996, 809

WOMEN'S STUDIES
Asian American woman, 795
Reader's gd to women's studies, 796
Women in China, 808

WOOD PRODUCTS
Directory of the wood products industry, 1998, 1343

WOOLF, VIRGINIA
Major authors on CD-ROM: Virgina Woolf [CD-ROM], 1087

WORLD GOVERNMENT
Dictionary of govt & politics, 2d ed, 654
Statesman's yrbk 1998-99, 135th ed, 82

WORLD HEALTH ORGANIZATION
Historical dict of the World Health Org, 1421

WORLD HISTORY
Columbia gd to the Cold War, 543
Dead countries of the 19th & 20th centuries, 530
Dictionary of world biog, v.1, 519
Dictionary of world biog, v.2: the middle ages, 520
Eighteenth century, 515
Eighteenth century, 516
Europa world yrbk 1998, 39th ed, 66
From Aristotle to Zoroaster: an A to Z companion to the classical world, 526
Great misadventures, 522
Historical gd to world slavery, 542
Hutchinson dict of ancient & medieval warfare, 534
Literature connections to world hist, K-6, 512
Literature connections to world hist, 7-12, 513
Macmillan ency of world slavery, 535
Miniature empires, 537
Timelines of world hist, 524

WORLD LEADERS. *See also* **POLITICIANS**
Countries of the world & their leaders yrbk 1999, 658
Whitaker's almanack world heads of govt 1998, 650
Whitaker's almanack world heads of state 1998, 651

WORLD MUSIC. *See also* **MUSIC**
Traditional world music influences in contemporary solo piano lit, 1148
World music CD listener's gd, 1159

WORLD POLITICS. *See also* **POLITICS;**
    POLITICIANS
Cold War, 544
Countries of the world & their leaders yrbk 1999, 658
Europa world yrbk 1998, 39th ed, 66
Profiles of worldwide govt leaders 1998, 4th ed, 649
Statesman's yrbk 1998-99, 135th ed, 82

WORLD RECORDS
Book of mosts, 65
Top 10 of everything 1999, 63

WORLD TRADE ORGANIZATION
World Trade Org dispute settlement decisions, v.1, 237

WORLD WAR, 1914-1918
Great war: a gd to the serv records of all the worlds fighting men & volunteers, 635
Historical dict of WW I, 532
World War I, 541

WORLD WAR, 1939-1945
China-Burma-India campaign, 1931-45, 517
Executive order 9066 [CD-ROM], 470
Holocaust, 540
Pacific war ency, 627
Understanding the Holocaust, 539

WORLD WIDE WEB. *See also* **INTERNET**
Web site source bk 1998, 58

WRITING COMPOSITION. *See also* **AUTHORSHIP**
Theorizing composition, 831

YEMEN
Yemen, rev ed, 139

YOUNG ADULT LITERATURE
Fiction sequels for readers 10 to 16, 2d ed, 1010
Learning about...the Civil War, 453
Novels for students, v.3, 1013
Novels for students, v.4, 1014
Outstanding bks for the college bound, 1011
Serious about series, 1012
Short stories for students, v.3, 1015
Short stories for students, v.4, 1016

YOUNG ADULT LITERATURE—BIOGRAPHY
Something about the author, v.94, 986
Something about the author, v.95, 987
Something about the author autobiog series, v.25, 988

YOUNG ADULTS—LAW
Children, YAs, & the law, 551

YOUTH HOSTELS
Hostels USA, 431

YOUTH MOVEMENTS
Encyclopedia of student & youth movements, 653

YOUTH ORGANIZATIONS
Directory of American youth orgs 1998-99, 7th ed, 52

YUGOSLAVIA
Breakup of Yugoslavia & the war in Bosnia, 116

YUGOSLAV WAR, 1991-
Breakup of Yugoslavia & the war in Bosnia, 116

ZAMBIA
Historical dict of Zambia, 2d ed, 477